1974 MLA ABSTRACTS
of Articles in
Scholarly Journals

ISBN 0-87352-237-0

Copyright © 1976 by the Modern Language Association of America

62 Fifth Ave., New York, N.Y. 10011

1974 MLA ABSTRACTS
of Articles in
Scholarly Journals

Compiled by

WALTER S. ACHTERT AND EILEEN M. MACKESY

*with the assistance of those whose
names appear in the staff list*

New York • Modern Language Association

1976

1974 MLA ABSTRACTS

LIBRARY EDITION

MLA Abstracts is a three volume annual following the arrangement of the *MLA International Bibliography*. Volume One contains sections on General, English, American, Medieval and Neo-Latin, and Celtic literatures, and Folklore. Volume Two includes sections on European, Asian, African, and Latin-American literatures, and Volume Three is devoted to Linguistics. All three volumes are available separately to MLA members or together in a bound "Library Edition."

The 1974 *MLA Abstracts* provides a classified collection of abstracts of journal articles on the modern languages and literatures to be used in conjunction with the 1974 *MLA International Bibliography*. All items for which abstracts appear in this volume are indicated by an asterisk preceding the item number in the appropriate volume of the 1974 *Bibliography*. Journals from which abstracts are included in this volume are preceded by an asterisk in the Master List of Journal Acronyms in the *Bibliography*.

The MLA Abstracts is intended to supplement the author, title listings in the annual *Bibliography* and thus provide for the scholar and student additional access to current scholarship. It is thought that a scholar beginning research on an author or topic will turn first to the appropriate sections of the *Bibliography* to obtain lists of all the items of possible relevance. Then the researcher may turn to the abstracts collections to learn more about the articles included there. The *MLA Abstracts* includes an index. Articles are indexed according to approach, themes, genres, and special techniques. The index is intended primarily as a means of manual access into the collections. These terms will later be used in automatic retrieval of the abstracts data.

The abstracts have been set from tapes and will eventually be available for indexing and automatic retrieval. Spellings have been regularized within the body of the abstracts, but not in the titles of the articles.

Entry format follows that used by the *MLA International Bibliography*. Arabic numbers have replaced roman to denote the volume number of a journal. Undated items are understood to have been published in 1974. When an issue number of a journal is required for a given entry, it appears in lower case roman immediately after the arabic volume number. An arabic number preceded by F in square brackets following an entry title refers to an item listed in the *Festschriften* and Other Analyzed Collections division which begins this volume.

In the main, these abstracts have been prepared by the authors of the original articles, whose initials appear at the end of the abstract. Where an abstract has been prepared by another person, the abstractor's initials appear at the end of the abstract. Through a special arrangement, the MLA exchanges abstracts with *Language and Language Behavior Abstracts*. Abstracts ending with the initials LLBA have been supplied by *LLBA*. These collections could not have appeared without the generous assistance of the editors of the journals listed in the Table of Journal Acronyms and the thousands of authors who have prepared abstracts of their articles.

1974 MLA ABSTRACTS
of Articles in
Scholarly Journals

Volume I

General, English, American, Medieval and Neo-Latin,
Celtic Literatures; and Folklore

Compiled by

WALTER S. ACHTERT AND EILEEN M. MACKESY

*with the assistance of those whose
names appear in the staff list*

Published by

THE MODERN LANGUAGE ASSOCIATION OF AMERICA

1976

This is Volume I of three volumes of the 1974 *MLA Abstracts*. The three volumes are collected in a cumulative edition for libraries.

The *MLA Abstracts* is partially supported by a grant from the National Endowment for the Humanities.

ISBN 0-87352-234-6

1974 MLA ABSTRACTS

MLA Abstracts is a three volume annual following the arrangement of the MLA *International Bibliography*. This is Volume One of the set, and includes sections on General, English, American, Medieval and Neo-Latin, Celtic literatures, and Folklore. Volume Two contains sections on European, Asian, African, and Latin-American literatures; and Volume Three is devoted to linguistics. All three volumes are available separately to MLA members, or together in a bound "Library Edition."

The 1974 *MLA Abstracts* provides a classified, indexed collection of abstracts of journal articles on the modern languages and literatures to be used in conjunction with the 1974 *MLA International Bibliography*. All items for which abstracts appear in this volume are indicated by an asterisk preceding the item number in the appropriate volume of the 1974 *Bibliography*. Journals from which abstracts appear in this volume are preceded by an asterisk in the Master List of Journal Acronyms in the *Bibliography*.

The *MLA Abstracts* is intended to supplement the author, title listings in the annual *Bibliography* and thus provide for the scholar and student additional access to current scholarship. It is thought that a scholar beginning research on an author or topic will turn first to the appropriate sections of the *Bibliography* to obtain lists of all the items of possible relevance. Then the researcher may turn to the abstracts collections to learn more about the articles included there. The *MLA Abstracts* includes a subject index in which articles are indexed according to approaches, themes, genres, and special techniques. The index is intended primarily as a means of manual access into the collections. These terms will later be used in automatic retrieval of the abstracts data.

The abstracts have been set from tapes and will eventually be available for indexing and automatic retrieval. Spellings have been regularized within the body of the abstracts, but not in the titles of the articles.

Entry form follows that used by the *MLA International Bibliography*. Arabic numbers have replaced roman to denote the volume number of a journal. Undated items are understood to have been published in 1974. When an issue number of a journal is required for a given entry, it appears in lower case roman immediately after the arabic volume number. An arabic number preceded by F in square brackets following an entry title refers to an item listed in the *Festschriften* and Other Analyzed Collections division which begins this volume.

In the main, these abstracts have been prepared by the authors of the original articles, whose initials appear at the end of the abstract. Where an abstract has been prepared by another person, the abstractor's initials appear at the end of the abstract. Through a special arrangement, the MLA exchanges abstracts with *Language and Language Behavior Abstracts*. Abstracts ending with the initials LLBA have been supplied by *LLBA*. These collections could not have appeared without the generous assistance of the editors of the journals listed in the Table of Journal Acronyms and the thousands of authors who have prepared abstracts of their articles.

Staff for the 1974 *MLA Abstracts*

WALTER S. ACHTERT, *Director of Research and Special Publications*
EILEEN M. MACKESY, *Coordinator, Research Data Bank*
WAYNE A. VARRICCHIO, *Assistant to the Coordinator*
MAUREEN E. FULLAM, *Research Assistant*
BRIAN L. HICKEY, *Research Assistant*
JANE R. MATSINGER, *Research Assistant*
TIMOTHY M. PERRIN, *Research Assistant*
KAREN MATEYAK, *Administrative Assistant*
RACHEL ARFA, *Journals Assistant*

HANS RÜTIMANN, *Director of Computer Services*
PAT BERNARD, *MT / ST Operator*

Staff of the *MLA International Bibliography*

HARRISON T. MESEROLE, *Bibliographer of the Association*
DAVID L. ANDERSON, *Assistant Bibliographer*
JAYNE K. KRIBBS, *Assistant Bibliographer*
JAMES ARIETI, *Assistant Bibliographer*
PRISCILLA J. LETTERMAN, *Administrative and Editorial Assistant*
PATRICIA CRAMBLITT, *Secretary*

TABLE OF CONTENTS
VOLUME I

TABLE OF JOURNAL ACRONYMS

ELT	English Literature in Transition (1880–1920)
ELWIU	Essays in Literature (Western Ill. U.)
Emily Dickinson Bulletin	
EngR	English Record
ESA	English Studies in Africa (Johannesburg)
ESQ	Emerson Society Quarterly
ETC: A Review of General Semantics (LLBA)	
ETJ	Educational Theatre Journal
EWN	Evelyn Waugh Newsletter
Expl	Explicator·
FaN	Le Français au Nigeria
FHA	Fitzgerald/Hemingway Annual
FI	Forum Italicum
FLang	Foundations of Language (Dordrecht, Neth.) (LLBA)
FM	Le Français Moderne (LLBA)
FMonde	Le Français dans le Monde (LLBA)
FN	Filologičeskie Nauki (LLBA)
Focus on Robert Graves	
FoLi	Folia Linguistica (LLBA)
FolkloreC	Folklore (Calcutta)
ForumH	Forum (Houston)
FR	French Review
FsD	Fonetică şi Dialectologie
FUF	Finnisch-ugrische Forschungen: Zeitschrift für Finnisch-ugrische Sprach- und Volkskunde
GaR	Georgia Review
GAS	German-American Studies
GL	General Linguistics
Glossa: The Journal of Linguistics	
GN	Germanic Notes
GQ	German Quarterly
GR	Germanic Review
GRM	Germanisch-romanische Monatsschrift, Neue Folge
GSlav	Germano-Slavica
GSLI	Giornale Storico della Letteratura Italíana
HAB	Humanities Association Bulletin (Canada)
Hasifrut: Quarterly for the Study of Literature	
HC	Hollins Critic (Hollins Coll., Va.)
HCompL	Hebrew Computational Linguistics
Hermathena: A Dublin University Review	
Hispania (U. of Mass.)	
Historiographia Linguistica	
HJAS	Harvard Journal of Asiatic Studies
HJb	Hebbel-Jahrbuch
HLQ	Huntington Library Quarterly
HR	Hispanic Review
HSE	Hungarian Studies in English (L. Kossuth U., Debrecen)
HSL	Hartford Studies in Literature
HUSL	Hebrew University Studies in Literature
IAN	Isvestija Akademii Nauk S.S.S.R., Serija Literatury i Jazyka (Moscow) (LLBA)
IBLA	Institut des Belles-Lettres Arabes Revue
IEY	Iowa English Bulletin: Yearbook
IF	Indogermanische Forschungen (LLBA)
IFR	International Fiction Review
IIJ	Indo-Iranian Journal (LLBA)
IJAL	International Journal of American Linguistics (LLBA)
IJAS	Indian Journal of American Studies
IncL	Incorporated Linguist (London) (LLBA)
Independent Shavian	
IR	Iliff Review (Denver)
ItalAm	Italian Americana
Italica	
ITL: Review of Applied Linguistics	
JAmS	Journal of American Studies
JAOS	Journal of the American Oriental Society
JArabL	Journal of Arabic Literature
JAS	Journal of the Acoustical Society (LLBA)
JBalS	Journal of Baltic Studies
JDSG	Jahrbuch der Deutschen Schiller-Gesellschaft
JEGP	Journal of English and Germanic Philology
JEngL	Journal of English Linguistics
JGa	Juanā Gaita (Hamilton, Ont.)
JGE	Journal of General Education
JHI	Journal of the History of Ideas
JIES	Journal of Indo-European Studies
JISHS	Journal of the Illinois State Historical Society
JML	Journal of Modern Literature
JNES	Journal of Near Eastern Studies (Chicago)
JNT	Journal of Narrative Technique
Journal of Ethnic Studies	
Journal of the International Phonetic Association	
JPS	Journal of the Polynesian Society (Auckland) (LLBA)
JQ	Journalism Quarterly
JRS	Journal of Russian Studies [Formerly *ATRJ*]
JSHD	Journal of Speech and Hearing Disorders (LLBA)
JSHR	Journal of Speech and Hearing Research (LLBA)
JSSTC	Journal of Spanish Studies: Twentieth Century
JWGV	Jahrbuch des Wiener Goethe-Vereins
KanQ	Kansas Quarterly [Formerly *KM*]
KFQ	Keystone Folklore Quarterly
Kivung: Journal of the Ling. Soc. of the U. of Papua and New Guinea (LLBA)	
KSJ	Keats-Shelley Journal
L&S	Language and Speech
Langages (Paris) (LLBA)	
Lang&S	Language and Style
LangS	Language Sciences
Language	
LanM	Les Langues Modernes
LATR	Latin American Theater Review
LB	Leuvense Bijdragen (LLBA)
LBib	Linguistica Biblica: Interdisziplinäre Zeitschrift für Theologie und Linguistik
LBR	Luso-Brazilian Review
LC	Library Chronicle (U. of Penn.)
LCUT	Library Chronicle of the University of Texas
LE&W	Literature East and West
LeS	Lingua e Stile (Bologna)
LHR	Lock Haven Review (Lock Haven State Coll., Pa.)
LimR	Limbă Română (Bucureşti) (LLBA)
Lingua (Amsterdam) (LLBA)	
Linguistics	
Linguistique (Paris) (LLBA)	
Lithanus: Lithuanian Quarterly (Chicago)	
LL	Language Learning
LLBA	Language and Language-Behavior Abstracts
LOS	Literary Onomastics Studies
LP	Lingua Posnaniensis (LLBA)
LSoc	Language in Society
LURev	Lakehead University Review
LY	Lessing Yearbook
LyC	Lenguaje y Ciencias (Univ. Nacional de Trujillo) (LLBA)
MagN	Magyar Nyelvör (LLBA)
MAL	Modern Austrian Literature: Journal of the Intl. Arthur Schnitzler Research Assn. [Supersedes *JIASRA*]
M&C	Memory & Cognition

M&H	Medievalia et Humanistica (North Texas State U.)
ManR	Manchester Review
Manuscripta	
MarkhamR	Markham Review
Mary Wollstonecraft Journal	
MDAC	Mystery and Detection Annual (Beverly Hills, Calif.)
MelbSS	Melbourne Slavonic Studies
Menckeniana	
MFS	Modern Fiction Studies
MichA	Michigan Academician [Supersedes *PMASAL*]
MiltonQ	Milton Quarterly [Formerly *MiltonN*]
MiltonS	Milton Studies
MinnR	Minnesota Review
MissQ	Mississippi Quarterly
ML	Modern Languages (London)
MLN	Modern Language Notes
MLQ	Modern Language Quarterly
MLR	Modern Language Review
MLS	Modern Language Studies
MNy	Magyar Nyelv (LLBA)
Monatschefte	
Moreana (Angers)	
Mosaic: A Journal for the Comparative Study of Literature and Ideas	
Mov	Movoznavstvo (Kiev) (LLBA)
MQ	Midwest Quarterly (Pittsburg, Kan.)
MQR	Michigan Quarterly Review
MS	Mediaeval Studies (Toronto)
MTJ	Mark Twain Journal
MW	Muslim World (Hartford, Conn.)
NALF	Negro American Literature Forum
Names	
NC	Nuova Corrente (LLBA)
NCarF	North Carolina Folklore
NCF	Nineteenth-Century Fiction
NCFS	Nineteenth-Century French Studies
NDQ	North Dakota Quarterly
NewL	New Letters [Formerly *University Review*]
NHJ	Nathaniel Hawthorne Journal
NK	Nyelvtudományi Közlemények (LLBA)
NLauR	New Laurel Review (The Pennington School, Pennington, N.J.)
NLH	New Literary History (U. of Va.)
NS	Die Neueren Sprachen (LLBA)
NsM	Neusprachliche Mitteilungen aus Wissenschaft und Praxis
NTLTL	Teaching Language Through Literature
NWZam	New Writing from Zambia
NYH	New York History
NZSJ	New Zealand Slavonic Journal
Oceania	
OcL	Oceanic Linguistics
OhR	Ohio Review
OL	Orbis Litterarum
OntarioR	Ontario Review: A North American Journal of the Arts
Orbis (Louvain) (LLBA)	
PAAS	Proceedings of the American Antiquarian Society
PADS	Publication of the American Dialect Society
PAPS	Proceedings of the American Philosophical Society
Paunch (Buffalo, N.Y.)	
PBML	Prague Bulletin of Mathematical Linguistics (Charles U., Praha) (LLBA)
PBSA	Papers of the Bibliographical Society of America
PCP	Pacific Coast Philology
PFr	Présence Francophone
PIL	Papers in Linguistics

PLL	Papers on Language and Literature
PMLA: Publications of the Modern Language Association of America	
PoeS	Poe Studies
PolP	Polish Perspectives
PPR	Philosophy and Phenomenological Research (LLBA)
PQ	Philological Quarterly (Iowa City)
Proceedings of the Comparative Literature Symposium	
Proceedings of the Pacific Northwest Conference on Foreign Languages	
Proof: Yearbook of American Bibliographical and Textual Studies	
QJLC	Quarterly Journal of the Library of Congress
QJS	Quarterly Journal of Speech
QQ	Queen's Quarterly
RAL	Research African Literatures
RALS	Resources for American Literary Studies
RdSO	Revista degli Studi Orientali (Roma)
RECTR	Restoration and 18th Century Theatre Research
REH	Revista de Estudios Hispánicos (U. of Ala.)
RELC	RELC Journal (Singapore)
Renascence	
RenD	Renaissance Drama (Northwestern U.)
RES	Review of English Studies
RevR	Revue Romane (LLBA)
RJŠ	Russkij Jazyk v Škole (LLBA)
RLC	Revue de Littérature Comparée
RLI	Rassegna della Letteratura Italiana
RLM	La Revue des Lettres Modernes
RLMC	Revista di Letterature Moderne e Comparate (Firenze)
RLV	Revue des Langues Vivantes (Bruxelles)
RNL	Review of National Literatures
RomN	Romance Notes (U. of N.C.)
RORD	Research Opportunities in Renaissance Drama
RPL	Revue Philosophique de Louvain (LLBA)
RQ	Riverside Quarterly (U. of Saskatchewan)
RS	Research Studies (Wash. State U.)
RUS	Rice University Studies
SAF	Studies in American Fiction
S&W	South & West
SAQ	South Atlantic Quarterly
SB	Studies in Bibliography: Papers of the Bibliographical Society of the University of Virginia
SBHT	Studies in Burke and His Time [Formerly *The Burke Newsletter*]
Scan	Scandinavica
SCB	South Central Bulletin
SCN	Seventeenth-Century News
Scottish Literary News	
SCR	South Carolina Review
SDR	South Dakota Review
SE	Slovenski Ethnograf (LLBA)
Sean O'Casey Review	
SeAQ	Southeast Asia Quarterly
SEEJ	Slavic and East European Journal
SEL	Studies in English Literature, 1500–1900
Séminar: A Journal of Germanic Studies (Victoria Coll., Toronto; and Newcastle U., New South Wales)	
Serif	The Serif (Kent, Ohio)
SFQ	Southern Folklore Quarterly
SFS	Science-Fiction Studies
SFUS	Sovetskoe Finno-Ugrovedenie/Soviet Fenno-Ugric Studies
SH	Studia Hibernica (Dublin)
ShakS	Shakespeare Studies (U. of Cincinnati)
ShawR	Shaw Review
SHR	Southern Humanities Review
ShS	Shakespeare Survey

SIL	Studies in Linguistics
SIR	Studies in Romanticism (Boston U.)
Skandinavistik	
SL	Studia Linguistica (Lund) (LLBA)
SlavR	Slavic Review (Seattle)
SLitI	Studies in the Literary Imagination (Ga. State Coll.)
SLJ	Southern Literary Journal
SlReč	Slovenská Reč (Bratislava) (LLBA)
SM	Speech Monographs
SML	Statistical Methods in Linguistics (Stockholm) (LLBA)
SNNTS	Studies in the Novel (North Texas State U.)
SoQ	Southern Quarterly (U. of So. Miss.)
SoR	Southern Review (Louisiana State U.)
Soundings: A Journal of Interdisciplinary Studies [Formerly *ChS*]	
SP	Studies in Philology
Speculum	
Spirit: A Magazine of Poetry	
SQ	Shakespeare Quarterly
SRC	Studies in Religion. A Canadian Journal
SRen	Studies in the Renaissance
SS	Scandinavian Studies
SSG	Schriften der Theodor-Storm-Gesellschaft
StCL	Studii si Cercetări Lingvistice (LLBA)
Studi Italiani di Linguistica Teorica Applicata	
Studies in 18th Century Culture	
STS	Scottish Text Society (LLBA)
Style (U. of Arkansas)	
Sub-stance: A Review of Theory and Literary Criticism	
SwAL	Southwestern American Literature
SWR	Southwest Review
Synthese (Dordrecht, Holland) (LLBA)	
TCL	Twentieth Century Literature
TD	Theatre Documentation
TDR	The Drama Review [Formerly *Tulane Drama Review*]
TESOLQ	Teachers of English to Speakers of Other Languages Quarterly
Theoria: A Journal of Studies in the Arts, Humanities, and Social Sciences	
Thesaurus: Boletín del Instituto Caro y Cuervo (LLBA)	
Thoth (Dept. of English, Syracuse U.)	
Thought	
ThR	Theatre Research/Recherche Theatrales
ThS	Theatre Survey (Amer. Soc. for Theatre Research)
Tlalocan (Mexico)	
TLL	Travaux de Linguistique et de Littérature Publiés par le Centre de Philologie et de Littératures Romanes de l'Université de Strasbourg (LLBA)

TN	Theatre Notebook
TNTL	Tijdschrift voor Nederlandse Taal- en Letterkunde (Leiden)
TPS	Transactions of the Philological Society (London)
Transactions of the Samuel Johnson Society of the Northwest	
Trivium (St. David's Coll., Lampeter, Cardiganshire, Wales)	
TSB	Thoreau Society Bulletin
TSE	Tulane Studies in English
T. S. Eliot Newsletter	
TSL	Tennessee Studies in Literature
TSLL	Texas Studies in Literature and Language
UCTSE	University of Cape Town Studies in English
UDQ	University of Denver Quarterly
UDR	University of Dayton Review
UES	Unisa English Studies
UP	Unterrichtspraxis
Vir	Virittäjä: Revue de Kotikielen Seura (Société pour l'Etude de la Langue Maternelle) (LLBA)
VJa	Voprosy Jazykoznanija (Moscow) (LLBA)
VLang	Visible Language
VMHB	Virginia Magazine of History and Biography
VMU	Vestnik Moskovskogo U. Ser VII. Filologija, Žurnalistika (LLBA)
VN	Victorian Newsletter
VP	Victorian Poetry (W. Va. U.)
VPN	Victorian Periodicals Newsletter
VR	Vox Romanica (LLBA)
VS	Victorian Studies (Indiana U.)
WascanaR	Wascana Review (Regina, Sask.)
WC	Wordsworth Circle
WF	Western Folklore
WHR	Western Humanities Review
WMQ	William and Mary Quarterly
WPL	Working Papers in Linguistics (Ohio State U.)
WPLUH	Working Papers in Linguistics (U. of Hawaii)
WVUPP	West Virginia University Philological Papers
WW	Wirkendes Wort (LLBA)
WWR	Walt Whitman Review
WZUG	Wissenschaftliche Zeitschrift der Ernst Moritz Arndt-Universität Griefswald (LLBA)
YCGL	Yearbook of Comparative and General Literature
YFS	Yale French Studies
Zambezia (Salisbury, Rhodesia)	
ZMF	Zeitschrift für Mundartforschung (LLBA)
ZPSK	Zeitschrift für Phonetik, Sprachwissenschaft und Kommunikationsforschung (LLBA)
ZRP	Zeitschrift für Romanische Philologie (Halle) (LLBA)

FESTSCHRIFTEN AND OTHER ANALYZED COLLECTIONS

General

General. 26. Kraft, Walter C.,ed. *Proceedings:Pacific Northwest Conference on Foreign Languages.* Twenty-fifth Annual Meeting, April 19-20, 1974, Eastern Washington State College. Vol. xxv, Part 1:*Literature and Linguistics.* Corvallis: Ore. State U. 296 pp.
Articles from this *Festschrift* are abstracted separately below.

English

English. 49. Benson, Larry D.,ed. *The Learned and the Lewed:Studies in Chaucer and Medieval Literature.* (Harvard Eng. Studies 5.) Cambridge: Harvard U.P. 405 pp. [In honor of Barlett Jere Whiting; David Staines, "Bartlett Jere Whiting," 1-9; McKay Sundwall, "The Writings of Bartlett Jere Whiting," 389-402.]

Articles from this *Festschrift* are abstracted separately below.
92. Ward, J.A.,ed. *Renaissance Studies in Honor of Carroll Camden. RUS* 60,ii. Houston, Texas: Rice U. 169 pp.
Articles from this *Festschrift* are abstracted separately below.

Medieval Latin

Medieval Latin. 114. Davidson, Clifford,ed. *Studies in Medieval Drama in Honor of William L. Smoldon on His 82nd Birthday. CompD* 8,i. Kalamazoo: Western Mich. U. 139 pp.
Articles from this *Festschrift* are abstracted separately below.
120. Miller, William E., and Thomas G. Waldman,eds., with Natalie D. Terrell. *Bibliographical Studies in Honor of Rudolf Hirsch. LC* 40,i. Philadelphia: U. of Pa. Lib., Friends of the Lib. 145 pp. ["Rudolf Hirsch Bibliography," 140-45.]
Articles from this *Festschrift* are abstracted separately below.

GENERAL LITERATURE AND RELATED TOPICS†

I. AESTHETICS

162. Basch, David. "Logic and Aesthetic Identity:A Defense." *ConnR* 6,i(1972):78-87.
A common definition derived for both logical and esthetic form is "forms whose elements relate through unity and coherence within completeness so as to yield to the percipient an experience of consummation." This thesis appeared implausible to some critics since logic and esthetics were thought to stand in an antithetical relationship of reason and emotion. But the fact of this antithesis is contradicted since, just as ideas unfolding through relationships of unity and coherence may lead to the experience of a conclusion, so may feelings correspondingly evolve through the same relationships of unity and coherence into the conclusion of deep emotion. (DB)
163. —— "The Aesthetic as a System." *ConnR* 8,i:72-83.
All systems are necessarily whole or complete having the invariant structural form of unity and coherence so as to manifest the capacity to yield an end. Through the variable material elements that comprise them, systems take on dimensions of qualitative and quantitative attributes, which contribute to system ends. An esthetic system shares in the definition and conditions true of all systems. Accordingly, an esthetic system is defined as an entity whose elements relate through unity and coherence within completeness so as to manifest the capacity to yield the esthetic end. After considering three traditionally proposed ends, the esthetic end is identified as the intrinsically valuable experience of consummation, which encompasses both the experiences of the flow of premises to conclusions (logic) and the flow of feelings to emotion. System concepts suggest three criteria for evaluating esthetic system experiences: system structural form (esthetic form), qualitative attribute and quantitative attribute (complexity)—each a contributor to the intrinsic value of such experiences. A barrier to the appreciation of the intrinsic value of undergoing the experience of consummation yielded by esthetic systems often resides in the perceptual incapacity of some men to enter into such system processes. (DB)
164. —— "Values:Aesthetic and Otherwise." *ConnR* 7, i(1973):73-83.
Three values commonly held to be esthetic values are experiential value, symbolic value, and the value of idea. The first is the authentic esthetic value while the others are found wanting. Experiential value is based upon the value of undergoing experiences, especially those scopeful "peak experiences" characterized by rich perceptual qualities which culminate in an

experience of consummation. Undergoing such experiences is of universal and intrinsic value, worthy of being called esthetic value. In contrast, the value of the experience of emotions derived from symbols is not intrinsic to the process of its experience and not universal since it is based upon unique and accidental factors personal to the experient. Similarly, the value of ideas is of instrumental and relative value dependent upon the varying circumstances of individuals. (DB)
170. Bolsterli, Margaret. "Aesthetic Revaluation:The Recognition of Modern Consciousness." *CentR* 18:307-18.
The Esthetic Movement was the recognition of a change in consciousness which produced the following characteristics of modernism: immediacy in poetry, abstraction in painting, and functionalism in architecture, decoration, and furniture design. The tendency to identify estheticism with decadence is misleading because it ignores the vitality implied. For example, in Pater's statement experience itself is the purpose of life. But the desire to live by this prescription made it possible to stop revering the past to the point of writing medieval poems or even poems which describe experience rather than provide it, of designing medieval buildings, and medieval furniture. T.S. Eliot's *Four Quartets* is the ultimate extension of the resultant immediacy in poetry as the pure functionalism in buildings by Mies van der Rohe and Corbusier are the height of this tendency in architecture. (MJB)
176. Calinescu, Matei. " 'Avant-Garde':Some Terminological Considerations." *YCGL* 23:67-78.
"Avant-garde," originally a French military term, was first used metaphorically as a political catchword during the French Revolution. Subsequently, it became an important concept in the language of political radicalism, from the early 19th-century French socialists to the anarchists (Kropotkin) to the followers of Marx and Lenin. The first use of avant-garde in a cultural context occurred in 1825 in a text written by Saint-Simon's disciple, Olinde Rodriguez. At the beginning of this century, the artistic avant-garde developed its extreme style (or anti-style) in independence from the political avant-garde. "Avant-garde" soon became an international label for esthetically revolutionary art. Contemporary American criticism tends to use avant-garde rather loosely as a synonym for modernism. However, the avant-garde in its extremist negativism and promotion of esthetic anarchy is both anti-traditional and anti-modern. As such it should be distinguished from modernism and regarded rather as an anticipator of what is currently called postmodernism. (MC)
180. Chalmers, F. Graeme. "Aesthetic Experience and Social Status." *ASoc* 11:302-06.
Art serves as an aid in identifying social position. Some historical, ethnological, and contemporary aspects of this phenomena are

---

† *Festschriften* and Other Analyzed Collections are listed in the first division of this volume. "F" numbers in brackets following a title refer to these items.

examined. The maintenance of a hierarchical social structure seems to directly encourage the development of certain art objects. The status of art as a commodity, or as an investment, the possession of which may increase the prestige and power of the owner influences the way we perceive art objects and the activity of artists. (FGC)

199. Ivaşiuc, Alexandru. "L'esthétique marxiste en tant qu'esthétique appliquée." *CREL* 1:85-88.
The Marxist critic must make a complex value judgment relating to the intrinsic quality of the work and also relating it to the practical action potential, bearing in mind that, besides the individual factors that concur to produce it, there is its historical necessity that must be taken into account. The Marxist critic approaches the work with the austerity of a scientist, standing at a distance from the object in his capacity as the knowing subject. Just as any other science, Marxism disenchants, it reveals a reality that tends to disguise itself. The absence of a prescriptive Marxist esthetic thought corresponds to the premises of Marx's thinking for he systematically avoided closed systems. (AI)

206. Kiralyfalvi, Bela. "Lukács:A Marxist Theory of Aesthetic Effect." *ETJ* 26:506-12.
Lukács finds the ultimate effect of art to be ethical in nature. He does not mean, however, that art is didactic, that it intends to interfere with the practical lives of men (artists are not "engineers of the soul" as Stalin put it). The ethical effect occurs only during the after-stage of the direct-emotional esthetic experience. Even at this stage, it is a possible consequence rather than a necessary result. The core of the esthetic experience proper is the catharsis, which consists not of empathic response or "intoxication," but of a sense of joy aroused by the perception of the beautiful portrayal of man's intensive totality, the perception of new and freshly seen contents. These perceptions overflow into ethical categories only in the after-stage of the direct artistic experience, bringing about a readiness for the morally good in the individual receiver. (BK)

252. Wayne, June. "The Male Artist as Stereotypical Female." *ASoc* 11:107-13.
The ancient demonic myth imposes stereotypes on artists that duplicate stereotyping of women by the feminine mystique. Artists as a group, and women as a sex, are assumed to be biologically determined, the first to create art and the second to create babies. Both artists and women are socially perceived as non-cerebral people who are functionally inadequate in the real world. These and many other subtly paralyzing givens in both mythologies explain why male artists have passively accepted disenfranchisement as though they were women. Female artists who fight sexism in the arts are obliged to fight the demonic myth as well. In so doing they are catalyzing male artists to a new acceptance of cerebral competence as integral both to creativity and to social self-determination. (JW)

255. Wilson, A.C. "Lenin's Ideas on Art and Discussion of Them." *NZSJ* 12(Sum 1973):130-41.
Although Lenin was not a systematic philosopher of art and wrote little on the subject, his ideas exert a great influence on Soviet esthetics. They have also been subject to different interpretations by critics. The hard-line approach insists that Lenin wanted to make all art subject to political control and had little respect for the integrity of the esthetic as such. The moderate line insists that Lenin was not a totalitarian in the artistic sphere and that he was sensitive toward "esthetic integrity." Wilson suggests that Lenin wanted neither to politicize all art nor to examine the necessary and sufficient conditions of great art. (ACW)

II. LITERARY CRITICISM AND LITERARY THOERY

Literary Criticism. 263. Antoine, Gérald. "La nouvelle critique:How Far Has It Got?" *Style* 8:18-33.
After a brief history of the French "Nouvelle Critique" school, the problematics of criticism are examined under four major questions: (1) critical method and objectivity; (2) criticism, the science of literature vs. a "literature about literature"; (3) thematic criticism vs. stylistic criticism; and (4) stylistic criticism vs. poetic criticism. Tentative classification of the movement is suggested and proposals are offered. (LLBA)

265. Bashford, Bruce. "Literary History in Northrop Frye's *Anatomy of Criticism*." *ConnR* 8,i:48-55.
Despite the widespread tendency to view Frye's *Anatomy* as a subjective vision, the book's first essay, "Historical Criticism," actually exhibits a logical structure. Frye states that the essays in the *Anatomy* are developed "deductively," and investigation of what he means reveals that a critic proceeding deductively begins his reasoning by distinguishing two formal aspects of literature, "narrative" and "meaning." These distinctions are the basic divisions of the historical essay, "fictional" and "thematic" modes. In each case, Frye first elaborates the logical possibilities of the mode and then looks at the history of literature to see how these possibilities have been fulfilled. Frye, therefore, gives a shape to literary history, rather than inferring one from it. Because Frye proceeds deductively, his literary history lacks the concern with sequence and development normally found in literary history, even in other formal histories like that given by Aristotle in the *Poetics*. (BWB)

286. Davenport, Guy. "The Symbol of the Archaic." *GaR* 28:642-57.
20th-century art and literature have been concerned with the archaic past which archeologists began discovering in the 19th century. Modern artists have longed for the vitality and clarity of earliest beginnings. Many artists have imitated archaic styles, and the subject of the archaic is pervasive in modern art and writing. The common symbolization of modern civilization as a waste land or hellish maze can be traced by noting the symbolic figure of an innocent girl, who represents the human soul. She enters American and European literature in the early 19th century and can be thought of as the archaic figure Persephone or Eurydice. (GD)

306. Freilich, Joan S. "An Introduction to New Techniques of Literary Analysis." *NTLTL* 14,i:12-22. [Examples from Prévert.]
Three new methods of literary analysis now being taught in advanced language classes are stylistics, structuralism, and psychoanalytic interpretation. The use of stylistics in elementary classes is first illustrated through analysis of a French magazine advertisement, then through an analysis of Jacques Prévert's poem, "Il ne faut. . . ." The application of structuralist analysis to works read by beginning and intermediate students will also involve poetry. The structure, "constraint-rebellion-breakthrough" is traced through several of Prévert's poems. Psychoanalytic interpretation involves an attempt to elucidate the most fundamental affective concepts conveyed through the text. Anouilh's *Antigone* is used to illustrate how a strong emotional current can underlie what is on the surface a philosophical work. (JSF)

319. Hamon, Philippe. "Narrative Semiotics in France." *Style* 8:34-45.
The situation of narrative semiotics in France is described and a bibliography as complete and as detailed as possible is set up. Narrative semiotics developed in the 1960s against the conceptual domination and the loose concepts of literary history and traditional critics, first under the influence of structural linguistics, then under the influence of semiotics liberated from the linguistic model. The main theoretical efforts in this field are those of Greimas, Barthes, Brémond, Todorov, Genette, Coquet, and Rastier. (LLBA)

322. Harari, Josué V. "The Maximum Narrative:An Introduction to Barthes' Recent Criticism." *Style* 8:56-77.
An attempt to present Barthes's recent literary production in view of his earlier attempts to establish himself as the leading French theoretician of literature. In the process of this presentation, the continuity of Barthes's critical theories is demonstrated, as well as the break that occurs in it from S/Z onward, and more abruptly in his most recent work *Le plaisir du texte*. By focusing on S/Z, an illustration of Barthes's textual analysis was made possible. The

richness and validity of the typology of narrative Barthes offers in his study of Balzac's short story "Sarrasine" is highlighted. (LLBA)

331. Hirsch, E.D.,Jr. " 'Intrinsic' Criticism." *CE* 36:446-57.
The programmatic idea behind the academic criticism of 1940-70, namely the literary study of literature, was illusory. Literature is no species-idea capable of sustaining the "literary study of literature"; the esthetic conception behind the formulation is neither priviliged nor desirable; literature professors should be oriented to ethical as well as esthetical categories; and the teaching of composition deserves high status and renewed emphasis. (EDR,JR)

335. Ingarden, Roman. "Psychologism and Psychology in Literary Scholarship." *NLH* 5:213-23. [Tr. John Fizer.]
A critique of the use of psychology and psychologism in literary scholarship is made. A distinction is made between the science of psychology and psychologism, where this science transcends its own field. Psychologism is a point of view where epistemological, critical, and esthetic investigations are psychologically oriented. In literary scholarship, the following can be investigated from a psychological point of view: (1) the relationship between literary creation process and psychology; (2) relations between the author's psychology and the literary work; (3) reader reactions; and (4) a work's content. A totally psychological approach is limiting and often misleading. (LLBA)

344. Juhl, Peter D. "Zur Interpretation eines literarischen Werkes und ihrer Begrenzung durch die Anschauungen seines Autors." *LiLi* 12(1973):37-52.
Although the fact that the speaker or narrator in a literary work holds certain beliefs does not imply that the author shares these, the fact that the *word* expresses or suggests certain beliefs does imply that the author holds the latter. The motivation for distinguishing between the speaker and the author of a literary work is discussed. An example is given to illustrate that in interpreting a literary work as expressing or suggesting a certain belief we are (implicitly, at least) committing ourselves to the view that the author does not regard the belief in question as immoral. Third, two examples of interpretive controversies concerning two poems by Wordsworth and Blake are introduced. A possible counterexample to this thesis is considered. (LLBA)

347. Kartiganer, Donald M. "The Criticism of Murray Krieger:The Expansions of Contextualism." *Boundary* 2:584-607.
Krieger's aim throughout his work is to define and employ contextualist criticism. Remaining consistent with New Critical principles, he insists that a poem be at once "closed" and "open." A poem must separate itself from the world and the common uses of language; it must comprise a complete, unique, and untranslatable system. In Krieger's first four books this meaning is invariably extreme—Manichean—since by definition it violates conventional thought. (DMK)

351. Kramer, L. "Zur Anwendung der Wortfeldlehre auf die Analyse literarische Komik." *RLV* 39(1973):238-47.
Through the use of word field theory it is possible to achieve a proper view of the function of esthetic phenomena in literature, especially the element of humor. The structure of a linguistic field makes possible conclusions about the function of its members. Insight into the relationship between kernel words and satellite words gives an idea of the various influences of a word field and its goals. (LLBA)

364. Levine, George. "Politics and the Form of Disenchantment." *CE* 36:422-35.
Recognition of the political implications of literature will move us away from an organicism which has radically inorganic effects. The discovery that, as critics, we have no effect on our culture is reflected in a central fictional tradition of disenchantment. The discovery of disenchantment in *Don Quixote* and in the tradition it generated leads to conservative and apolitical positions. Flaubert, Scott, and George Eliot all imagine political activity as naive, destructive, and secondary to private experience. Pynchon brings this tradition to culmination. Though literature thus teaches us to distrust politics, political criticism may be a step toward healing the breach between the study of literature and the life that surrounds that study—that is, beyond disenchantment. (GLL)

403. Payne, Michael. "Origins and Prospects of Myth Criticism." *JGE* 26:37-44.
Myth criticism springs from Jung's and Neumann's account of the psychological origins of myth and Cassirer's and Langer's studies of the implications of mythical modes of thought. Frye's literary theories avoid deriving a theory of literature from anything beyond literature itself by substituting the totality of literary experience for Jung's externalizations of the collective unconscious. The prospect of myth criticism is to achieve a unity of thought and the object of thought, a community of readers who share the perceptions of the monomyth of literature and the sense of the inseparability of the perception itself and the responsibility of working to achieve its harmonious vision in the world. (MDP)

423. Robinson, Lillian S. "Criticism—and Self-Criticism." *CE* 36:436-45.
Literary history is fundamentally ahistorical, remote from the actual forces that shape human consciousness and its expressions. Interpretation of art assumes the character of "commodity fetishism." The act of criticism is assumed to be a social relation between objects—the work of art and the work of criticism—we perceive ourselves, creators and interpreters, as subjective beings. This distortion is as irrational in the realm of esthetic production as it is in the commodity marketplace. We must put ourselves as historical beings back into the process, so that we can apprehend it as a social act. The operant term is "ourselves as historical beings"—not as ambulant subjectivities, but individuals with consciousness informed by sex, class, and race, where these categories are understood as forces in history, rather than personal attributes. (LSR)

465. Tatham, Campbell. "Critical Investigations:Language Games:(Post)Modern(Isms)." *Sub-stance* 10:67-80.
A significant characteristic of contemporary literature is a shifting vision of the function and limits of language. A sense of renewal potentially inherent in "language-games" replaces the obsession with linguistic uncertainty and "silence." The inevitable ambiguity of verbal activity emerges less as a threat than as an essential mystery, a fluid space which enhances free-play. Accordingly, a critical method which attempts to decipher a text runs against the grain of the literature it professes to encounter. Analysis and explication become insufficient, even inappropriate; the postmodern critic must learn to indulge in creative play, must join in the "language-games." (CT)

467. Thomas, Johannes. "G. Poulet und der Wahrheitsanspruch der Literaturkritik." *RLV* 39(1973):520-25.
One of Poulet's basic ideas is that the meanings of texts are produced by their readers, and that they represent the author's ideas. This assumption seems problematic to Poulet, because he postulates that any "subject" is defined by its ideas ("predicates") and cannot have "predicates" of other "subjects." As a solution, he proposes to imagine a second "subject" inside the reader-"subject," that produces the meanings of the text. The distinction between production and the content of the products destroys Poulet's "solution": The second "subject" is only a product of the reader-"subject," not a principle of production. Hence, Poulet's "phénoménologie" cannot justify any interpretation. (JT)

469. Tsur, Reuven. "Poem, Prayer and Meditation:An Exercise in Literary Semantics." *Style* 8:404-24.
The three possible uses of one message may be related to it via Jakobson's model of linguistic functions. In a poem, the poetic (message-oriented) function is dominant; in a prayer, the conative (addressee-oriented) function; in a meditation, the emotive (addresser-oriented) function (in each of them, several functions serve in a hierarchy). The three uses relate to one another like three deep structures of one surface structure. The different hierarchies have significant logical and psychological corollaries. (RT)

478. Wellek, René. "Poetics, Interpretation, and Criticism." *MLR* 69:xxi-xxxi. [Presidential Address of MHRA, Univ. College, London, 4 Jan 1974.]
There are continuities in the history of criticism. Two main trends, both descended from Aristotle, persist today: the search for laws of literature, for poetics, and the interpretation of individual works and minds. The history of modern poetics ends

with French structuralism and its allies. It aims "not at a better knowledge of the object but at perfecting scientific discourse" (Todorov). What remains is a disembodied methodology. The second trend, exegesis, led to subjective hermeneutics (Gadamer) and to "interpretation" as practiced by the critics of consciousness (Poulet) and their precursor (Wilson Knight), which resulted mostly in arbitrary fictions. (RW)

Literary Theory. 529. Chețan, Octavian. "L'humanisme et les difficultés de l'ambiguïté théorique." *CREL* 2:53-62. [Marxist humanism.]
The current controversy over the concept of humanism started with the advent of Marxist thought. The pre-Marxist humanism was founded upon a concept whose starting point is marked by the problems of human nature understood from an abstract-speculative and non-historical standpoint. By laying the foundations of new problems, new principles, and a new method, Marxism proposes a theory concerning society and its history and, implicitly, man. It is possible to elaborate from the Marxist perspective a systematic and rigorous theory of humanism, understood as an explanation and revelation of human nature. (OC)

530. Chumbley, Robert. "On Model Building On Model Building On Model Building." *Diacritics* 4,iii:15-19. [Rev. art.]
Anthony Wilden's *System and Structure* provides a point of departure for a discussion of model-building in the context of semiotics. In order to erect a proper model, there must be homology between structures, not just similarity between elements or relations of structures. Such a distinction is essential when the doors are opened to transdisciplinary work such as that of Wilden. If careful mapping by homology is not followed, the path of analogy can lead to confusion or even incongruity. In order to avoid these pitfalls, C.S. Peirce's semiotic model which affords the possibility of reference is preferred to Saussurian signification. The general problem of the nature and use of signs subtends an analysis of Wilden's efforts to integrate concepts from various disciplines. (REC)

612. Iosifescu, Silvian. "Littéraire et non littéraire." *CREL* 2:23-31.
The main difficulty in defining literature derives from the close mixture of literary communication with other types of verbal communication: daily, scientific, or philosophic. The specific character and interferences are sought out on the basis of some leading criteria: the presence of fiction, linguistic differences entailed by contact with various types of verbal communication, differences in composition, the relation between literary and conceptual. Another condition proper to literature only and existing in no other art is its capacity to be transmitted graphically or orally on a plane of equivalence. The latter evolution of the two means of communication is treated and connected with the new stream of orality due to "mass media." (SI)

617. Jacquart, Emmanuel C. "Can Literature Convey Knowledge?" *FR* 48:291-97.
Although the essay may reflect knowledge through conceptual information, its merit consists less in providing answers than in raising questions; *littérature à thèse* belongs to epistemology only insofar as the underlying theory is valid. As these two examples show, the strength of literature does not lie in the realm of systematized knowledge. Drama imparts only a specific type of information: qualitative information. This is also true for the novel. Although literature may lead to uncertainty, this does not mean that it is not an instrument of knowledge, for the uncertainty principle is part of today's epistemology. Literature is not so much a receptacle for conceptual knowledge as a medium which makes knowledge "come alive." (ECJ)

624. Johnsen, William A. "Toward a Redefinition of Modernism." *Boundary* 2:539-56.
Moderns such as Joyce, Lawrence, Yeats, and Eliot present a similar pattern of experience, in three movements. (1) Man, disgusted by the chaos of the modern world, retreats to a superior interior world of order; (2) recognizing his betrayal of "reality," he returns to immerse himself in disorder; (3) he recognizes the system underlying his opposition of order-disorder, and achieves the excluded middle, the third term unavailable to those who

totalize their perceptions of order and/or disorder. The middle term in Joyce was coincidence—the partial order with ragged edges, achieved through juxtaposition, whose spirit defies totalization. (WAJ)

630. Klinkenberg, Jean-Marie. "Vers un modèle théorique du langage poétique." *Degrés* 1(1973):d-d12.
The search for definitive criteria of poetic language gives rise to a host of misunderstandings, for it is often done in a literary perspective. In a scientific perspective, it is less important to describe an object than it is to formulate a theoretical construct of this object. Among the proposed criteria, one of the most usual is that of divergence. A typology of the different approaches to this concept, a typology of the critiques referring to it, and a test of the counter proposals which are derived from it show the dangers of this definition at the same time that they lead to theorizing about the naive dichotomy between prose and poetry. The most satisfying of the theories of poetic language is that of Solomon Marcus, who is opposed to scientific language and lyric language. In a series of rigorous theorems, scientific language is defined as a language without homonymy but with infinite synonymy. Lyric language has infinite homonymy but no synonymy. This model, being both economical and strong, mathematically accounts for several characteristics recognized in poetic language. (AH)

646. LeRoy, Gaylord, and Ursula Beitz. "The Marxist Approach to Modernism." *JML* 3:1158-74.
The Marxist scholar will trace the major features of Modernism to the heightened irrationalities and increasing alienation of the epoch of imperialism. The bourgeois scholar, in contrast, sees Modernism as representing the timeless condition of man. The contrast between the Marxist and bourgeois view of Modernism intensifies if we remember the differing attitudes toward the extremes of the literary spectrum, Modernism and socialist realism. It is also helpful to compare the Marxist view of the dialectic of form and content with that of establishment scholars. The approach to Modernism developed here suggests guidelines for a chapter in the much needed Marxist literary history. (GCL & UB)

665. Marino, Adrian. "The Future:A Modern 'Topos'." *CREL* 2:85-95.
Three essential objectives are discussed: a brief historical study of the idea of future as a topos from antiquity to the modern age; the successive recuperation of this topos by modern theories; the structural description of the topos through the identification of its recurrent invariants. The structure of the relationship between "future" and "modernity" is (1) A better world will necessarily come into being; (2) a perfect, complete, genuine, pure modernity will be achieved only in the future; (3) the future will confirm the "modern" aspirations of the present. The topos of the "future" reveals the following elements: progress, the kinetic aspect of the future; the sense of progress, always "forward"; the permanent target: "tomorrow" substituted for "today"; progress toward the farthest end of the future; being ahead of time. (AM)

676. Michiels, Archibald. "A propos du concept d'ambiguïté." *RLV* 40:633-49.
Calls attention to recent studies of "inference" and "isotopie," insofar as these attempt to account for essential mechanisms by which information is built up in texts, highlight the relevance of cultural assumptions in the semantic description of discourse, and thus help to bridge the gap between two ways of looking at ambiguity. The first is illustrated in the main trends of present-day linguistics in which ambiguity is made use of as an adequacy test in the recognition of different levels of grammatical analysis. The second is to be found in literary theory, which looks at ambiguity as a privileged device of fantastic literature and studies its mechanisms at text-level, but in a much looser frame than that of linguistics. (AM)

687. Morse, J. Mitchell. "Race, Class, and Metaphor." *CE* 35:545-54,563-65.
Sometimes literal terms are taken metaphorically, as in the cases of "petrified" (scared), "clothes horse" (well-dressed woman), and "bastard" (disagreeable person), because literal meanings are not known. This is a rather rare disorder of the vocabulary and does little harm. Much more frequently, and with much worse effects, metaphorical terms are taken literally. The social and political

effects of using metaphors as if they were statements of fact are extremely harmful. (LLBA)

690. Munteanu, Romul. "Réflexions sur les pouvoirs de la littérature." *CREL* 2:16-21.

A consideration of the role played by literature in contemporary civilizations; or, rather, whether literature can still justify its being in an age of technology. The influence of literature on society has varied from one epoch to another. Furthermore, the impact of writers on the public has been greater or less according to the conditions created by social and political forces whose major interests have required men of letters to commit themselves to great strategic actions in order to win the favor of the people. These reflections on the function of contemporary art and on its future are grouped around the opinions of such thinkers as Jean-Paul Sartre, Claude Roy, Walter Jens, Herbert Marcuse, etc. References are made to conditions of Romanian arts and letters. (RM)

694. Needler, Howard I. "On the Art of Pirandello:Theory and Praxis." *TSLL* 15:735-58.

Pirandello's theoretical statements in *L'umorismo* and in his preface to *Six Characters in Search of an Author* serve to define a unified critical approach to both his plays and his short stories. Pirandello made extensive metaphorical use of the relation of author and character, which provides the key to this approach. It allows a joint consideration of problems of characterization in the dramatic and fictional prose works. The theoretical argument makes use of a modified idea of Marxian praxis and gives rise to a suggestion for its redefinition in Pirandellian terms. (HIN)

695. Nevo, Ruth. " 'Esso Keeps Your World Happening':A Test Case for Metaphor." *HUSL* 2:1-29.

Theories of metaphor tend to stress either the object-comparison theories or the verbal-opposition theories and have encountered difficulties in their explanations of the difference between noun and verb metaphors, the relationship between metaphor and simile on the one hand, and between metaphor and metonymy on the other, and the puzzling co-presence of the concrete and the abstract in metaphor. Metaphor is a special process of analysis and synthesis requiring two coordinates—an axis of classification violation and an axis of cross-comparison—in order to forge the new identity we call a metaphor. Four elements whereby a metaphor is rendered intelligible are distinguished. (RN)

718. Prince, Gerald. "Narrative Signs and Tangents." *Diacritics* 4,iii:2-8. [Rev. art.]

The achievements of narratology—as exemplified in *Sémiotique narrative et textuelle*, edited by Claude Chabrol—are undeniable. Yet the problems it faces are also undeniable and many of its results are denounced as trivial and/or pseudo-scientific. Fortunately, narratologists are aware of the state of their art and a fundamental program for narratology, designed to solve its most vexing problems, can be abstracted from their work. The domain of narratology must include all possible narratives without discrimination on the basis of literariness or medium of expression. A model of narrative must account only for those elements and rules which characterize narrativity. A successful semantics of narrative must be developed as well as rigorous

procedures mediating between narrative structures and the symbolic systems in which they are realized. Finally, the place of pragmatics in narratology must be re-examined and, perhaps, redefined. (GP)

727. Ruthrof, H.G. "Aspects of a Phenomenological View of Narrative." *JNT* 4:87-99.

The relationship between narrative and reader concretizations is investigated. While the text is artistically determined, it also allows a wide range of concretizations. Gradual concretizations in the act of reading (*noesis*) always result in the retrospective view of the work as a whole (overall *noema*). Narrative here is language containing phenomena of both presented world and presentational process, each with its aspects of space, time, action, and personae. These features form a ladder of priorities according to degree of abstraction and the amount of extrinsic knowledge the reader requires to understand each aspect. Thus, our grasp of the spatial and temporal *locus* of point of view relies much less on our stock of knowledge at hand than does the inference of narrator tone or, more conspicuously, the drawing of interpretative abstraction at a high level. (HGR)

741. Shopen, Tim. "Some Contributions from Grammar to the Theory of Style." *CE* 35:775-98. [Incl. bibliog.]

Claims about the grammatical structure of language are significant for style because they say what grammmatical structures are available to speakers and writers for putting their ideas into linguistic form. Elliptical utterances such as "The airport!" and "Don't forget!" provide examples. The grammatical choices involved are typically just the ones for the words pronounced. The mind is free to move along parameters of structure other than language for the rest of the concept being transmitted. The choice to ellipse or not to ellipse is not just a matter of surface grammatical form, but also an important stylistic decision affecting the extent to which thought submits to being channeled into the conventional categories of language. (TAS)

746. Simonson, Harold P. "Literature as Knowledge." *MQ* 15:302-10.

To relate literature and knowledge, or to speak of one's knowing literature, presupposes at least three epistemological levels. The cognitive level includes objective facts pertaining, for example, to biographical, generic, sociocultural, and textual matters, and also to literary nomenclature. Another level is that of imagination, i.e., knowledge that embraces subjectivity and quickens feelings, enabling one to participate imaginatively in the artist's vision. Literary knowledge gained through imagination reaches beyond the cognitive, extending, according to Northrop Frye, to all time and all space. Still another level is existential knowledge: literature that heightens a sense of self. Literature read this way not only engages the reader's personality and in some way affects his existence but also demands that he penetrate the work of art in order to touch the consciousness of the artist. At this existential level of knowledge the consciousness of the reader unites with that of the artist. It is at this level that today's critics of consciousness are doing their critical work. The result is to authenticate a common existence shared by reader and artist alike. (HPS)

III. LITERATURE, GENERAL AND COMPARATIVE

Bibliography. 793. Doak, Robert. "Color and Light Imagery: An Annotated Bibliography." *Style* 8,supp.:208-59.

The recent burgeoning in the field of color and light criticism is a product of contemporary objectivist critical theories. But there are problems in philosophy and in methodology, and coordination and synthesis of the critical efforts are needed at this point. Accordingly, this bibliography emphasizes studies with important technical and theoretical approaches. It also includes a section on reference material dealing with color; and it points out, in the index, criticism which is related to color imagery. The bibliography surveys criticism of color from its beginnings in the 19th century through 1973. (RWD)

796. Etiemble, [René]. "Sur une bibliographie du *haiku* dans les langues européenes." *CLS* 11:1-20.

G.L. Brower and D.W. Foster have been courageous enough to try to fill a vacuum and to publish a critical bibliography of Japanese "Haiku in Western Languages." Unfortunately, their book does not fill the vacuum: first of all, because English, French, German, Portuguese, and Spanish are not the only "western languages" on which the impact of haiku is to be felt. Moreover, because, even in the few languages here taken into consideration, the items are selected at random, with many factual errors and without a critical approach. (RE)

806. Petig, William E. "A Bibliography of German Literary Texts Available in the U.S." *UP* 7,ii:154-62.

This bibliography presents all German literary texts available in the United States in three categories: individual authors, literary anthologies, and readers. (WEP)

Comparative Literature. 820. Booth, A. Peter. "Abraham and Agamemnon:A Comparative Study of Myth." *HAB* 25:290-97.
The impression of similarity between the myths of Agamemnon's sacrifice of Iphigeneia and Abraham's near-sacrifice of Isaac is strengthened by an examination of the primary features of the two narratives. Each reflects the propitiatory sacrifice of the first-born by a royal figure in a time of national crisis to a specific deity at a specified cult site. As psyche myth the narratives convey theological perceptions: Agamemnon becomes a type of the hero in Greek tragedy, and Isaac reflects the Suffering Servant of Israelite theology. (APB)

821. Brodsky, Patricia P. "Fertile Fields and Poisoned Gardens:Sologub's Debt to Hoffmann, Pushkin, and Hawthorne." *ELWIU* 1:96-108.
The Russian symbolists, including Fedor Sologub, are usually considered to have been influenced primarily by French Symbolism. Yet Sologub based his story "Otravlenny sad" ("The Poisoned Garden") on earlier, non-French traditions, represented by E.T.A. Hoffmann's story "Datura Fastuosa," Alexander Pushkin's poem "Ančar," and Nathaniel Hawthorne's tale "Rappaccini's Daughter." The four works share the basic image of poisonous flowers as a symbol of evil. In each of the three stories a conflict is set up, expressed in Hoffmann as good vs. evil, in Hawthorne as body vs. spirit, and in Sologub as real vs. ideal worlds. To Pushkin's plot Sologub adds motifs of revenge and class struggle. Hoffmann's influence is in the image of a garden of temptation and in symbolic language. From Hawthorne Sologub takes directly the general structure and certain descriptions. His characters are sympathetically portrayed. His concern is not, like Hoffmann's, with balance, or, like Hawthorne's, with salvation, but with liberation and transcendence. (PPB)

824. Clark, Priscilla P.,et al. "Symposium:The Comparative Method: Sociology and the Study of Literature." *YCGL* 23:5-28.
Four basic perspectives inform studies of literary phenomena from a sociological point of view: the place and function of literature in society, the effect of literature on society, the function of social phenomena in literary works, and the effect of social phenomena on literature. Literature can be conceived as a process which generates a system of relations. The stages of the literary process are creation (the writer), production (the publisher), diffusion (the advertiser but also the critic), and consumption or reception (the reader). (PPC)

861. Maşek, Victor E. "Art et la littérature des computers." *CREL* 2:32-39.
The advent of the computer in contemporary art theory and esthetics implies a reassessment of ideas on art and the beautiful, and on their social function. There are two relationships between the creator and the computer: when the computer becomes a helping tool (amplifying human intelligence); when the computer becomes an independent creator (a process which allows the machine to produce "free" esthetic structures which do not presuppose an absolutely free activity on the part of the computer; the machine is the "main author" while the esthetician assumes the responsibility of programming). (VEM)

872. Schulz, Max F. "The Perseverance of Romanticism: From Organism to Artifact." *ClioW* 3:165-86.
Both Romantic and Modern theories of art conceive of the art object as modeled on nature. Although this underlying assumption discloses the continuity of thought of the past 150 years, changes in definitions of nature have left the consanguinity of Romantic and Modern art often unrecognizable. This difference is characterized by the terms organism and artifact as applied to the respective art objects. Contrary to the Romantic view of nature as organically whole, the Modern view often as not posits a world fragmented and meaningless, or if whole, beyond the comprehension of the human mind. As a consequence, the roles of art and nature have been reversed: from nature providing an ideal for art to imitate to being a flawed component for art to order and beautify. For modern proponents of cosmic pluralism, art becomes indistinguishable from other forms of nature; and boundaries between art and life threaten to dissolve, art becoming an object equivalent to the other objects that comprise the natural world, but as artifact rather than as organism. Examples of this view of art are found in the works of Nabokov, Robbe-Grillet,

and Barth, and of contemporary Minimalist and Conceptualist artists. (MFS)

881. Woodman, R.G. "Satan in the 'Vale of Soul-Making':A Survey from Blake to Ginsberg." *HAB* 25:108-21. [Eng., Fr., Ger. esp.]
In aligning the poet with what Blake called "the Devils party," the Romantics endowed Satan with creative powers and virtues lacking in the Satan of *Paradise Lost*. The moral and spiritual fervor of Blake's and Shelley's Satanism distinguishes it from the more orthodox Satanism of Baudelaire, Rimbaud, Genet, Joyce, and Ginsberg. The first four of these writers invest Romantic Satanism with those characteristics which belong to Satan proper. Their art explores a far more ambiguous conception of the revolutionary artist and his role in society. At its worst, Romantic Satanism in our time becomes the hysterical rhetoric of a spent power that parodies the poet-legislators championed by Shelley in his *Defence*. (RGW)

General Literature. 916. Chambers, Ross. "Literature and Its Uses:Thoughts on Literary Education in the Seventies." *AUMLA* 42:207-17.
Literary education in the capitalist framework is caught between a traditional, elitist conception of literature as an accumulation of cultural wealth and a newer, popular culture which is non-exclusive but treats its objects as consumerist junk. We therefore need an education for a culture of productivity which will continue to respect the lasting value of texts as producers of meanings but will make their function as such accessible to the popular majority. To this end both teaching and research should be oriented toward understanding the social function of the phenomenon of literature and developing a theory-based pedagogy of literature which will substitute for the current ideology of "giftedness" a more methodical introduction to the procedures of reading which make texts "work." (RC)

936. Eskey, David E. "The Case for the Standard Language." *CE* 35:769-74.
The primary function of standard English is to provide the basic means by which the educated members of English-speaking society can communicate, as easily as possible, with each other. Standard English is essentially a complex set of rules and abandoning the rules or stretching them too far can result in a total breakdown. That the rules of standard English are an arbitrary set intrinsically no better than those of nonstandard dialects in no way detracts from their immeasurable value as the agreed upon rules. (DEE)

942. Frye, Northrop. "The Renaissance of Books." *VLang* 8:225-40.
Frye discusses the place of the book among the instruments of communication in modern society. The paperback revolution is characterized as a change in the conception of the book from cultural monument to intellectual tool. The cultural context of this change is discussed, and the effect of radio and more particularly television on 20th-century society is briefly considered. The book cannot only be read but reread, consulted at will as a stationary focus for the community. The book is the technological instrument that makes democracy possible, and public access to written documents the principle that keeps it functioning. (NF)

952. Haberly, David T. "The Search for a National Language:A Problem in the Comparative History of Postcolonial Literatures." *CLS* 11:85-97.
Considerable attention has been paid to European influence on post-colonial literatures; it is equally valid to look comparatively at various post-colonial literatures that developed during the 19th century in terms of the responses of these new literatures to common, non-European problems. One such problem was the widely felt need for a separate national language as the essential basis for a separate national literature. Of particular interest is the wide-spread longing of nationalistic intellectuals to replace the inherited European language with a native, non-Western tongue. The solutions to the problem of linguistic identity proposed in the United States, Brazil, Argentina, French Canada, and Australia reflect a deeper and quite sophisticated debate over the nature of language itself: does language irrevocably control the thoughts

and emotions it is used to express; or is language itself shaped by the ideas, perceptions, and feelings of those who use it. The debate was everywhere resolved in favor of the second view of language, but the search for linguistic identity did strongly influence both the form and the content of post-colonial literatures. (DTH)

966. Kostelanetz, Richard C. "The Rule of Ignorance & Philistinism." *MQR* 12(1973):27-41.
Although developments in many scientific and artistic fields in the U.S. represent the best, the most advanced, and most influential thinking in the world today, writing in supposedly literate publications blocks comprehension and appreciation. This essay scrutinizes remarks by noted commentators and periodicals for evidence of ignorance and philistinism—iCommentary, Benjamin DeMott, Hilton Kramer, Harold Rosenberg, Irving Howe, Herbert Marcuse, Louis Kampf, George Steiner, et al. It documents implicit double standards in dealing with the new art, cites typical fallacies, and identifies reasons for the dominance of such ignorance. (RCK)

977. Lotringer, Sylvère. "La politique des restes." *Semiotext(e)* 1,i:29-43.
Human sciences expel man as a substantial entity in order to replace him by a mere formula or structure. The "reduced model," while it claims to represent reality, in fact constitutes it as forever absent, beyond reach, an endless prey to desire. It can be so, however, only insofar as reality is defined as exterior to the chain of language where the "subject" is caught. Whether the barrier of language is deemed essential to the definition of reality gives rise to two distinct conceptions, or politics, that question the metaphysics of reality and the status of the "subject" in the name of heterogeneity. One position (Julia Kristeva) accepts, in order to destroy it, the pre-eminence of language, while the other (Félix Guattari), refusing any dialectical process, initiates a new logic of desire. (SL)

980. Macnamara, Michael R.H. "The Meaning of L—Return of Another Exile?" *UES* 11,iii(1973):36-43. [On the relationship between lit. and philosophy.]
The relationship between literature and philosophy within the crucial problem-field of "life and meaning" is shown by exemplification. An expansion of interest among modern philosophers in the subject of the meaning of life—a subject with which creative writers have always been concerned—is indicated. A short survey is made of a selection of literary and philosophical works in which some of the topics that cluster under the main subject of life and meaning are involved. These topics include the consideration of meaningfulness in terms of the following contrasts: theistic and non-theistic world views: the postulates of mortality and immortality; the doctrines of determinism and libertarianism; the attitudes of pessimism and optimism. The role of self-deception is also considered. (MRHM)

1010. Roudiez, Leon S. "In Dubious Battle:Literature vs. Ideology." *Semiotext(e)* 1,i:87-95.
Because of the narrative's role in conveying information and ideology within any given society, the novelist who wishes to challenge or subvert dominant ideology faces serious problems. No matter what his intentions are, his work is liable to become a carrier of that ideology. Sartre himself has recognized the failure of political *engagement* as an effective force; the writers of the so-called *nouveau roman* group have hardly been more successful. Today the practice of the *Tel Quel* group, and that of related writers, holds the promise of providing a more fundamental means of challenging the ideology. (LSR)

1012. Said, Edward. "An Ethics of Language." *Diacritics* 4,ii:28-37. [Rev. art.]
Foucault's *Archeology of Knowledge* clarifies as well as revises the conceptual framework of his earlier work. In defining "statement," "discourse," and "archive" he makes distinctions between his "archeological" method, the history of ideas, ideological description, chronicle history. The similarities between Foucault, Canguihelm, Kuhn, and Polanyi are examined, and Foucault's contribution is the definition of effectiveness which language in practice, and as an institution, possesses. The view that discursive practice has *ethical* meaning is compared with Walter Benjamin's *Sprachtheorie*. Foucault's epistemological renovation in scholarship and in the theory of criticism is part of a major attempt to redefine the unit of analysis and/or verbal production. Thus Foucault avoids concepts like work, author, and text. (EWS)

1028. Southall, Ivan. "Sources and Responses [on Children's Literature]." *QJLC* 31:81-91.
Writing creatively for children involves not rigid method but a disciplined seeking for awareness of the impact and intensity of childhood events. An author of a good children's book will reach the child as an equal, knowing that the same things that happen to an adult can happen to a child. Children's literature will reflect truth as its author sees it and appeal to the child who experiences that same truth. (EE)

1052. Weimann, Robert. "The Concept of Tradition Reconsidered." *YCGL* 23:29-41.
Intended as a critical survey and analysis of how certain major American, English, and continental critics of the late 19th and early 20th centuries have come to grips with tradition as a concept, Weimann discusses the principal reasons for the failure of modernist notions of the past and the corresponding dissociation of sensibility. Using the treatment of Milton's epic as a paradigm, literary theories of Arnold and T.S. Eliot are compared. Subsequently, he demonstrates how the methodological foundations of historical criticism are surrendered in favor of the spatial idea of an ideal order. (RW)

Medieval Literature. 1069. Davidson, Clifford. "Medieval Drama:Diversity and Theatricality." [F 114]:5-12.
Medieval drama has received increasing attention in recent years from scholars and directors. Extending from the *Christos Paschon*, written at the point in history when antiquity had only just merged into the Middle Ages, to the late vernacular plays of Western Europe, the drama of this period cannot be drawn together under a single set of esthetic principles applicable to all. Thus liturgical drama, for example, is an iconic art which stands in contrast with the realism which crept into certain of the later vernacular plays. The morality play, however, is in part a revival of iconic art—a revival that finds its last pure expression in the dramas of John Lyly. (CD)

1085a. Scheper, George L. "Reformation Attitudes Toward Allegory and the Song of Songs." *PMLA* 89:551-62.
Generalizations about Reformation attitudes toward allegory are based on polemical denunciations by reformers of medieval "dialectical" exegesis. But Reformation definitions of the senses of Scripture agree with the definitions of medieval theologians. The reformers' attempts to draw a radical distinction between typology and allegory never succeeded and Reformation commentaries continued to allegorize, as demonstrated in the numerous Protestant commentaries on the Song of Songs. The crucial difference between medieval and Protestant spirituality in the Song commentaries lies not in their attitude toward allegory but in their conception of the nuptial metaphor, wherein human love symbolizes the love between God and man. (GLS)

1087. Sticca, Sandro. "The *Christos Paschon* and the Byzantine Theater." [F 114]:13-44.
A critical reading of *Christos Paschon*, the only authentic dramatic expression of the Byzantine religious theater, is undertaken in terms of the play's imaginative range, intellectual and liturgical content, and against the background of the origins and development of the theater. After an analysis of its meager documentary evidence, the focus centers on the *Christos Paschon*, the redaction of the play attributed to Gregory Nazianzenus. The *Christos Paschon* constitutes an intermediate link between Classical Antiquity and the Byzantine Middle Ages. Structurally, the play is a dramatic trilogy comprising three successive episodes which abide by the norms of biblical and classical tradition. Theologically, the play propounds the anti-Apollinarian thesis by emphasizing Christ's Incarnation and Mary's role in it as the *theotokos*, Mother of God. (SS)

IV. THEMES AND TYPES

Biography and Autobiography. 1107. Goldberg, Jonathan. "Cellini's *Vita* and the Conventions of Early Autobiography." *MLN* 89:71-83.

An understanding of the conventions of early autobiography can make Cellini's *Vita* more accessible to modern readers. Crucial differences in earlier attitudes about the nature of the self which render self-examination in the Renaissance objective, impersonal, and public affect Cellini's self-scrutiny. Spiritual traditions shape the prophetic rhythms of the *Vita*, its emphasis on conversion, and its use of other plot motifs frequently found in saints' lives. By Cellini's time, these models for self-understanding and these narrative techniques had been secularized in picaresque fiction. (JSG)

1114. Rosenthal, Peggy. "Feminism and Life in Feminist Biography." *CE* 36:180-84.

A new series of books published in 1972 by The Feminist Press and called "feminist biography" indicates what directions current feminist thinking is moving in. The feminist biographers' emphasis is on education and achievements: what society has put into these women and what they have then put into society. The inner life of the subject is excluded or reduced to stock phrases. There is no awareness in these books that the women being written about had somehow to manage the transitions from their private feelings to their public achievements. The feminist biographers seem to have turned their eyes from what previous writers have showed us about the complex relations between individual uniqueness and individual achievement. Similarly, the familiar feminist claim that by examining themselves women come to a collective discovery of how much each is a product of society ignores the possibility that a woman might come, by examining herself, to a unique discovery. (PR)

1115. Taylor, Dennis. "Some Strategies of Religious Autobiography." *Renascence* 27:40-44. [Bunyan, Newman, Merton, esp.]

If man by nature is a liar (Augustine), how can he write religious autobiography, a highly "interested" form of expression which presumes to be divinely disinterested? This problem inspires the great autobiographies of Bunyan, Newman, and Merton. Each struggles with their demonic substitutions of will, mind, and heart respectively which are representative of the moral character of their historical periods. To defeat their substitutions and "raise" their age, they choose an artful strategy: "allegory," "argument," and "autobiography" respectively. Bunyan transforms his changes of will into the ritual paradigms of bible experience; Newman validates his changed mind by showing it as the result of an integration of mind and feeling, reflection and discussion. Merton creates a dialectic in which earlier spiritual stages are continually rejected in favor of newer ones. (DT)

Computer-Assisted Literary Research. 1116. Allen, John R. "Methods of Author Identification through Stylistic Analysis." *FR* 47:904-16.

Although principles of author identification through stylistic analysis have been known for more than a century, they have been little used in the study of French literature, perhaps because many critics feel unqualified to undertake such research. Yet often the critic is the most qualified to use these methods: the amount of further training is minimal, as the critic's background enables him to formulate questions which can be studied with computational stylistics. This method isolates traits of style which shed light on previously unsolved problems of author attribution and literary history. Some criteria which can be used toward that goal are: average word and/or sentence length, distribution of parts of speech, vocabulary choice, word length of parts of speech, vocabulary distribution, and relative entropy. Statistical tests already developed measure the significance of any traits observed. Given the proven effectiveness of computational stylistics in other fields, critics ought to examine the possibilities for applying these methods to the study of French literature. (JRA)

1127. Grundlehner, Philip E. "Computer-Based Education: PLATO in German." *UP* 7,ii:96-105.

The German department at the University of Illinois (Urbana-Champaign) has developed several computer-assisted German programs for both high school and college classes. PLATO, the computer teaching system based at Illinois, enables each student to advance through selected material at his own pace, while allowing teachers to write and program lessons themselves. There are currently four programs at Illinois: the German reading program, sentence construction through symbols, conversation with a caricatured face, and vocabulary drills. Unique PLATO accessories include a slide viewer, a random-access audio system and a touch panel which replaces the typing keyset. (PEG)

1134. Waltman, Franklin M. "A Literary Analysis by Computer." *Hispania* 57:893-98.

The application of a concordance program to a literary work, the *Cantar de Mío Cid*, in an attempt to resolve the polemic of authorship which has existed since 1929 is discussed. The concordance was used to ascertain if differences exist in the use of formulaic expressions, synonyms, syntax, or verb tenses. This program also gives statistical data such as sentence length, frequency of word occurrence, and alphabetical listing of words in descending or increasing frequency of occurrence. (FWW)

Drama and Theater. 1136. Addington, David W. "Varieties of Audience Research:Some Prospects for the Future." *ETJ* 26:482-87.

Although scientific research focusing on theater audiences was begun early in the 1950s, the continuous effects of plays on audiences have not received the concentrated attention of the modern researcher. While not exactly rich, product research —research focusing on the final effects of performances—has at least been steady and has led to some fairly sophisticated studies capable of taking into account the extreme complexity of both the audience response and the theatrical event. The technology for sophisticated process research is currently available. (DWA)

1142. Astalos, Georges. "Théâtre floral spatial:La pluri-dimensionalité ou la pulverisation de l'action dans l'espace." *Degrés* 4(1973):j-j8.

Euclidian geometry, which imposes a parallel development, does not correspond to the artistic, economic, poetic, or religious exigencies of the modern world. Theater, being a global art, gathers all the other arts, and offers a possible model of globality to the pedestrian, stroller, or pilgrim, corresponding metaphorically to the exchanges of merchandise, ideas, and men. The multidimensionality of the theater includes the stages: traditional (the auditorium), common (modern essays), and aerial (futurism). Spatial structuralizatio n creates for the text conditions of affirmation in all their interior-exterior dimensions. (GA)

1184. Hinden, Michael. "Ritual and Tragic Action:A Synthesis of Current Theory." *JAAC* 32:357-73.

The historical evidence for a ritual origin of tragedy is inconclusive, but a discussion of tragedy based on its resemblance to ritual can prove illuminating. Nietzsche's concept of tragedy as a Dionysian conflict rendered in Apollonian form remains useful when this conflict is viewed as a psychological tension of contrary impulses. In a number of tragedies the hero suffers an internal conflict of this kind. The impulses of the audience similarly are engaged, suggesting the relationship of audience response (catharsis) to the resolution of the hero's internal conflict. (MH)

1197. Koelb, Clayton. "'Tragedy' as an Evaluative Term." *CLS* 11:69-84.

Although the term "tragedy" is usually considered a descriptive term, an examination of the use of the word by influential critics suggests that it contains a large element of the evaluative. Most literary hierarchies place tragedy at the top, clearly suggesting that tragedies are more valuable than other poems. A particularly important example of such a hierarchy occurs in Hegel's *Aesthetik* (1835). The system of ranked genres set up in this work makes it very difficult for Hegel to call any play a tragedy without implying that it is also a masterpiece. The history of Shakespearean criticism from Voltaire to Bradley provides further evidence. While early critics such as Voltaire, Samuel Johnson, and A.W. Schlegel had admiring things to say about Shakespeare, they were firm in denying that any of his works could be called tragedies. But as the admiration increased, so did the pressure to call the admired plays tragedies. A.C. Bradley's *Shakespearean Tragedy* (1904) shows the result of that pressure. (CK)

1208. Lukács, György. "About the Principles of Dramatic Form." *ETJ* 26:512-20. [Tr. Bela Kiralyfalvi.]
Drama's aim, to affect the masses, necessitates sensuousness, while the limitations of its magnitude necessitate universality. That the masses respond better to symbols and pictures than to abstractions further justifies universality. Typical characters in typical actions make the dramatic universality concrete in substance. Manifested through struggle in a social context, the will symbolizes the whole man and his destiny. The drama is built from social struggle and a world view which is the chief element of its forming. The struggle arises in ages of class decline. Drama is born at times of sharp struggle between the old and the new. (BK)

1225. Olf, Julian. "The Man/Marionette Debate in Modern Theatre." *ETJ* 26:488-94.
Modern performance theory has shown ambivalence toward the living actor. Kleist, Craig, Appia, Meyerhold, Artaud, and some Dada, Futurist, and Bauhaus theorists have at various stages in their careers endorsed the mechanism as an ideal. Actually, this endorsement is less an esthetic platform than it is an inevitabe phase of a profound re-evaluation of the role of man in art. Whereas prior to the Industrial Revolution literary and theatrical conventions served to maintain a clear distance between man's ego and the art product, modern attitudes have eliminated that distance. The result has been a generation of artists attempting, vainly, to re-present reality in their art—while at the same time permitting reality to form a primary ingredient of art. (JMO)

1236. Schechner, Richard. "From Ritual to Theatre and Back:The Structure/Process of the Efficacy-Entertainment Dyad." *ETJ* 26:455-81.
Ritual celebrations and performances among communal peoples are holistic, ecological events which use performances as a means of effecting actual changes in economics, social hierarchy, individual and group relations. In all performances—no matter how ritualistic—there are strong qualities of entertainment; and in all entertainment there are strong qualities of ritual. The two exist in a "braided relationship" to each other in which, in any given social setting and performance, one is dominant. Each society's theater history, in fact, can be read as a dialectical relationship between efficacy and entertainment. (RS)

Emblem. 1260. Daly, Peter M. "The Semantics of the Emblem—Recent Developments in Emblem Theory." *WascanaR* 9:199-212.
A central aspect in the revaluation of the emblem that has been going on in German studies during the last decade is concern with the semantics of the emblem. It was common in the past to assume that the emblem was "arbitrary," "enigmatic," or "contrived" almost by definition. Modern emblem theory, however, has redirected attention to medieval typological and exegetical tradition as an essential intellectual root of the emblem. Meaning is seen to derive from one or more of the attributes, functions, forms or uses of the object depicted by the emblematic *pictura*. A visual motif, such as the snake, may connote several different, at times mutually exclusive meanings; and this may well be the reason for the modern reader's impatience with the emblem. (PMD)

Epic. 1270. Kurman, George. "Ecphrasis in Epic Poetry." *CL* 26:1-13.
Ecphrasis, or the description in verse of an object of art, is a common feature of epic style. It can be likened to the Homeric simile—both devices serve temporarily to remove the reader/listener from the course of the literal action and thereby retard the pace of the narrative. Prophecy and dreams can likewise be related to ecphrasis. Like the simile and the digression, ecphrasis can also be employed not only to reinforce the emotional mood of the scene in which it occurs, but to sustain central concern of the entire poem. Although Renaissance epic employed ecphrasis primarily to present quasi-historical chronicles, different effects

have been achieved by epic poets stressing the timeless striving and imminent quickening of the figures portrayed on the art object described. (GK)

1271. Palomo, Delores. "Homeric Epic, the Invention of Writing, and Literary Education." *CE* 36:413-21.
Both Lévi-Strauss and Roland Barthes link the appearance of writing in a culture to the proliferation of political authority: documentation, record keeping, and legal codification permit severe regulation of individual and social life, and endow the literate class with great power. An examination of the absence and presence of writing in the history of Homeric epic appears to uphold such contentions, yet Eric Havelock's investigation of pre-Socratic Greek education in his *Preface to Plato* indicates that cultural control does not depend upon written texts but rather upon a method of education intended to inculcate uncritical acceptance of the cultural image embodied in a revered text. (DJP)

Other Forms. 1305. Hume, Kathryn. "Romance:A Perdurable Pattern." *CE* 36:129-46.
The archetypal romance pattern gives its shape to works ranging from classical myth and folktales to medieval and renaissance romances, gothic narratives, and contemporary science fiction and fantasy. Because much of the literature lacks academic respectability, it is little understood. The first step to comprehending the form is recognizing its origin—the universal psychological process of centroversion or ego development. The persistence of generic characteristics like the polarization of good and evil, or the existence of the non-rational (supernatural) may be explained as imitations, however displaced, of the prototypal situation of the ego in the unconscious. The superficial diversity of the works can be simplified to the existence of eight basic hero configurations, two types of hero, and three systems of morality. Many romances are bad literature, but the causes are not attributable to the genre. (KH)

1311. Keenan, Edward L.,Jr. "The Trouble with Muscovy: Some Observations upon Problems of the Comparative Study of Form and Genre in Historical Writing." *M&H* 5:103-26.
Russian historians have had some difficulty deciding upon a periodization for what they call "Russian" history; no conceptually helpful definition of "the Russian Middle Ages" has been put forward. In view of the fact that Slavic cultural history is a part of the general development of Christian European culture, it might well be a matter of some consternation to the comparativist, as well as to the historian of Russia, that repeated attempts to "align" Muscovite institutions with those of the West or to bring her development into "phase" with Western cultural history have been at best brilliant and appealing hypotheses and more commonly hindrances to the progress of historical understanding. This article considers the historiography of Muscovy and the mentality of those who shaped the historical consciousness of Muscovy at a time when she began to play a prominent role in Eastern Europe. (ELK,Jr)

1339. Ranta, Jerrald. "Palindromes, Poems, and Geometric Form." *CE* 36:161-72.
Like palindromes, certain modern American poems possess forms that pivot in more or less intricate reversal patterns around their centers. While they are all cyclic in design, these forms vary considerably from poem to poem, differing in such important matters as length, complexity, and in the elements that make up the palindrome-like formal design. Detailed analyses of William Carlos Williams' "The Locust Tree in Flower" (the shorter version), E.E. Cummings' "[If you can't eat you got to]," and Marianne Moore's "The Chameleon" illustrate this and support the notion that such poems belong to a class of poetic form other than continuous form, fixed form, and stanzaic form described by Laurence Perrine in *Sound and Sense*. This other class of poetic form is geometric form, which has been around at least since Homer wrote the *Iliad*. Many 20th-century poets have used this kind of form but very little has been written about it. (JR)

Other Themes. 1353. Anzulovic, Branimir. "Mannerism in Literature:A Review of Research." *YCGL* 23:54-66.
The concept of Mannerism was first applied to literature around

1920, but literary scholars did not generally accept the term until 1948. This acceptance has resulted in a confusing variety of definitions. One type of definition views Mannerism as the expression of a period dominated by feelings of anxiety, uncertainty, and alienation. Another extremely influential definition defines literary Mannerism as an excess of rhetorical ornatus, the eternal counterpart to classicism which is present in any period. Shearman is the best known representative of the definition which regards refinement and sophistication as being the main traits of Mannerist style in the art and literature of the 16th and early 17th centuries. Other definitions of Mannerism frequently combine features from each of these three types. (BA)

1354. Austen, Roger. "But for Fate and Ban:Homosexual Villains and Victims in the Military." *CE* 36:352-59.

Although there are archetypal repetitions in five works dealing with the yearning of an officer for an enlisted man, of greater interest from a homosexual perspective are the differences that result from the implicit moral judgments made by the authors. In three of the works—Melville's *Billy Budd*, Lawrence's "The Prussian Officer," and Dennis Murphy's *The Sergeant* (1958) —the officers' homosexual desires are equated with evil, while chief among the many virtues of the beloved younger enlisted man is his shining heterosexuality. The equation in James Purdy's *Eustace Chisholm and the Works* (1967) and Carson McCullers' *Reflections in a Golden Eye* (1941) is not nearly so black and white. What is being condemned in Purdy's novel is not homosexuality but Daniel Haws's refusal to love when he had the chance, and there is no condemnation at all in McCullers' novel—only a sad brooding over the fact that love makes victims of many of us, heterosexual or homosexual. (RA)

1388. Crew, Louie, and Rictor Norton. "The Homophobic Imagination:An Editorial." *CE* 36:272-90. [Introd. to spec. issue on "The Homosexual Imagination."]

Homosexual literature is written, read, criticized, and taught within a homophobic culture that damages its expression and reception. Homosexual authors often engage in self-censorship and express internalized guilt. Reputable scholars overtly censor material, suppress biographical data, and conspire to maintain silence. Research into homosexual literary history is hindered by political threat, by limited library access, and by varieties of taboo and academic dishonesty. Homophobic critics have demonstrated widespread ignorance and prejudice, often employing rhetorical strategies to degrade the homosexual sensibility. Virtually all traditional criticism exhibits a subjective heterosexual bias that distorts homosexual literature. Teachers arrogantly assume that heterosexuality is a universal norm, create a heterosexual confraternity that excludes homosexuals, and have significantly contributed to the disenfranchisement of gay people from their rightful literary heritage. Reform can best be achieved by gay academics who are willing to actively challenge the homophobia in their profession. (RN)

1393. Dick, Bernard F. "The Origins of Homosexual Fiction." *ColQ* 22:509-15.

Much homosexual fiction promotes a romantic view of ancient Greece as a homoerotic paradise where reality is seen through the gauze of a bogus Hellenism that filters out the decay and leaves behind the shining eidolon. In Forster's *Maurice* and Renault's *The Charioteer*, young men seek models not in their contemporaries but in the circle immortalized in Plato's *Symposium* and *Phaedrus*. Allied to the Hellenic fallacy is the Arcadianism of Theocritus' *Idylls* and Virgil's *Eclogues* where ambisexual shepherds woo their loves without concern for the laws of gender. Yet the delicate homoeroticism of the pastoral world defies man's attempt to imitate it; hence Michel's confusion of Theocritan art and his own sensuality in *The Immoralist*. It is precisely the impermanence of Arcadia and the illusory nature of the Arcadian world that create the unresolved tension in homosexual fiction. (BFD)

1400. Foster, Leslie D. "Poetry Both Sacred and Profane:The History of the Conception of the Artist from Plato to Sidney's *Defence*." *MichA* 7:57-74.

Sidney was perhaps one of the last great spokesmen for medieval theology, and at the same time the first to formulate the essential thrust of modern Romantic critical theory. His special position is shown by tracing the conception of the artist in earlier theories, and by relating his ideas to what have been described as the essential qualities of modern poetic theory, with its emphasis upon the special gifts of the artist and its definition of poetry not as an artifact but as the expression of a power. (LDF)

1410. Helson, Ravenna. "Inner Reality of Women." *ASoc* 11:25-36.

The image of woman as mother is losing its central place. Women have moved into the labor force, but there they work at a low status level. Our social definitions and institutions make little place for an image of women as creative in work, and in various ways they reduce and dissolve it when it tries to appear. Among women authors of fantasy for children, one may see a variety of ways in which the inner urge to creative expression copes with social restrictions. Some authors use outer images of women for maximum effect, some turn to a woman within, some struggle with a small heroine against demonic forces in search of a sense of higher male authority, and some muster a peer group to confront the "establishment." The increase in heroic themes since the late 1950s suggests a renewed effort toward a less constricting identity. (RMH)

1419. Johnston, Walter E. "The Shepherdess in the City." *CL* 26:124-41.

Modern novelists often reflect the traditional ideals and conventions of pastoral poetry when they place an extremely simple, virtuous, "natural" character in the center of a sophisticated "city" novel or story: the praises of natural virtue are directly "sung" by the narrator or are implicit in the narration. Virgil's first Eclogue is used to establish a definition of pastoral as an exile's song which suggests the limitations of the idyll through praise of its virtues. This perspective is applied in detail to Lena Grove in Faulkner's *Light in August* (1932) and Tonka in Musil's "Tonka" (1924). Their significance as pastoral emblems, and allusions by Faulkner and Musil to Romantic writers, lead to a consideration of the special emphasis that Romantic writers brought to pastoral emblems and to a contrast of the use of the dominant conventions of pastoral by Wordsworth and the modern writers. The novelists are dramatizing the failure of the mind to arrive at any new understanding or harmony through contemplation of pastoral simplicity; even the potential of the pastoral as a symbol of human values is ironically undercut. (WEJ)

1426. Kantrowitz, Arnie. "Homosexuals and Literature." *CE* 36:324-30.

The course title "Homosexuals and Literature" was a political choice which frightened some potential students. The syllabus included works by Walt Whitman, Oscar Wilde, John Rechy, Radclyffe Hall, and a number of filmmakers, with stress on the contemporary, including both women and men. Much of the discussion was personal reaction to Dennis Altman's *Homosexual: Oppression and Liberation*, leading to more intimate discussion than is usual in the classroom. The result was a heightened gay consciousness, growing self-acceptance, and less concealment of homosexual identity on campus. Human contact became the focus and literature the catalyst. Not only did we abandon the posture of closeted homosexuals and lesbians, but we abandoned the traditionally formal roles of professor and students in favor of more egalitarian spontaneity, validating our learning with our real experience rather than validating our experience with our studies. (AK)

1460. Prosen, Rose Mary. " 'Ethnic Literature'—of Whom and for Whom; Digressions of a Neo-American Teacher." *CE* 35:659-69.

Chicanos, American Indians, and Orientals are emerging American groups whose literature is being incorporated into the schools, but white minority groups have not yet been adequately recognized or defined. Literature by and/or about Slavic-Americans, for instance, remains largely unknown. The American writer, Richard Bankowsky, whose novels about Polish-Americans remain little known, and Nelson Algren, whose novel *Never Come Morning* describes Polish-American struggles in Chicago's underworld, are writers who define a particular immigrant consciousness which is not currently a part of American literature. Blacks are not one people; neither are whites one people. Slavic-Americans, a "white" people, are a minority group whose literature is distinctive. Such literature, like Afro-American literature, should enter the mainstream of American literature. (RMP)

1499. Vogel, Dan. "A Lexicon Rhetoricae for 'Journey' Literature." *CE* 36:185-89.

The term "journey," or similar terms ("wandering," "pilgrimage"), used to interpret physical movement in plots, are too imprecise to aid readers. Used alone, "journey" implies no spiritual or symbolic possibilities in the plot; as a general term, "journey" requires modification by another term. "Wandering" describes an apparently purposeless movement—significance being hinted to the reader, never to the hero. "Quest" labels a plot that affords to the reader and the hero an original sense of mission in the journey. "Pilgrimage" is a "quest" with an early and clearly defined goal to the journey. An "odyssey" contains a pre-decided terminus as a purpose, but has no organic plot or sense of spiritual mission. A "going-forth" (new term) is a story of unintended discovery by the hero that he had been on a fated journey, a secret vouchsafed to the reader earlier. (DV)

Poetry. 1519. Beiman, Abbie W. "Concrete Poetry: A Study in Metaphor." *VLang* 8:197-223.

Various characteristics of concrete poetry have been examined, but little attention has been focused on this art form's contribution to literature. Indeed, the concrete poem exemplifies a dramatic variation in the most basic element of poetry: figurative language. Traditionally, figurative language has established a relationship between the tangible objects around man and the intangibles which he seeks to know. The most common form of such figurative yokings has been the metaphor, a trope that creates a tension between the similarities and dissimilarities of the juxtaposed elements. With concrete poetry the focus of that trope is no longer just the abstract and spiritual leg of the metaphor, but the sensory perception of the literal and concrete as well. (AWB)

1531. Cohn, Robert G. "Nodes." *Diacritics* 4,i:34-41; ii:44-47.

The ancient concept of tetrapolarity becomes increasingly important in the modern era. According to this concept the four poles of a "cross" pattern interpenetrate in the same way as the two poles of a bipolar paradox do. The vertical and horizontal axes of the "cross" are thus both same and different. The concepts of modern physics, sexual differentiation, number, musical tones based on the octave, biological generation, and language all derive from this system. Derrida's critique of Rousseau can be defended against the demurrer of Paul de Man on these grounds. Grave deficiencies in Northrop Frye's *Anatomy of Criticism* result from his lack of core vision (in these terms). Georges Poulet, in his essays on Proust, fares better but misses some important points. Camus's *The Rebel* comes to grief on this plane. (RGC)

1533. Cooper, Helen. "The Goat and the Eclogue." *PQ* 53:363-79. [On the form.]

The false derivation for the word "eclogue" that was generally accepted from the early Middle Ages until the Renaissance meaning "goatish speech," had some effect on the way the genre itself developed. Conrad of Hirschau (fl. 1100) combined the etymology with the current belief that the eclogue was essentially allegorical and concluded that the *egloga* was a genre that castigated the vices symbolized by the goat. The biblical imagery of sheep and goats and the traditional Christian use of the eclogue are combined by Theodulus and satirically in Petrarch's anti-ecclesiastical eclogues. The association of animal, etymology, and Christianity also applied to the bucolic and the ox (*bos*). Spenser's July eclogue in *The Shepheardes Calender* works within the "goat" tradition; and the idea was also used by Edward Fairfax in *Hermes and Lycaon* (1603), where the exponent of Catholicism is cast as a goatherd and the Protestant as a shepherd. (HC)

1535. Davies, Phillips G. "A Check List of Poems, 1595 to 1833, Entirely or Partly Written in the Spenserian Stanza." *BNYPL* 77:314-28.

A bibliography of over two hundred poems written in the Spenserian stanza from the date of publication of Spenser's *Faerie Queene* to 1833, the publication date of Tennyson's "The Lotos-Eaters." The poems are arranged alphabetically by author; the date of composition or publication (if known) and the number of stanzas in each poem are included. (PGD)

1548. Germain, Edward. "Four Surrealist Images." *VLang* 8:319-32.

Surrealism has consistently asserted its desire to comprehend the essence of thought—a statement usually read in esthetic terms by art and literary critics or in clinical terms by psychological critics. If this statement is taken more literally, certain overlooked insights arise, including the hypothesis that the surrealists' search for an ultimate synthesis may itself reflect as structure of the mind. (EG)

1564. Jones, Rhys S. "Symbolism and Zen: Two Views of Reality." *Trivium* 9:144-50.

Poetry is an attempt to describe "reality." East and West differ profoundly in this, but one finds a resemblance between the cosmogony of the *Upanishads* and Valéry's. Describing the origins of consciousness and language—and therefore of poetry—both reach the impasse of putting the ineffable into words. As Mallarmé realized, one can only "suggest." But how best to do so? The Symbolists used words as symbols of reality; whereas Zen-Buddhist poetry effectively suggests reality without being symbolic. Zenists concluded long ago that conceptual dichotomies like seer and seen, abstract and concrete, natural and supernatural, were profoundly misleading. (RSJ)

1583. Marcus, Aaron. "An Introduction to the Visual Syntax of Concrete Poetry." *VLang* 8:333-60.

Many different forms of concrete poetry have emerged in the past 20 years. One way to appreciate, describe, and compare these works is to examine them in terms of their visual syntax. This includes emphasis on figure-field relationships, implied depth, spatial structure, and movement. Examples are presented which illustrate basic types of visual organization and are analyzed to relate their visual syntax to their total meaning. This initial classification could be elaborated and supplemented to provide a basis for a semiotic of concrete poetry. (AM)

1592. Murdoch, Brian. "Transformations of the Holocaust: Auschwitz in Modern Lyric Poetry." *CLS* 11:123-50.

Images deriving from the horrors of the Nazi concentration camps have become commonplace in much modern lyric poetry, in a manner that does not hold true for other large-scale crimes against humanity. The use of such imagery is traced from the ghetto and the camps themselves, through the war and after it, and later with greater distancing, by *engagé* poets. Poets who use the imagery on a personal level thus stand at the end of a poetic development that has been well established in little more than a quarter of a century. (BM)

1601. Perrine, Laurence. "The Poet and the Pulpit." *SWR* 59:113-23. [A defense of poetry.]

Poetry can serve the function prescribed by Arnold, that of interpreting life, of consoling and sustaining humankind, heretofore performed by religion. Poetic truth, which lies in the deep feeling and experience communicated by poetry, can be found in the works of Wordsworth, Tennyson, Housman, Arnold, Shelley, Keats, and Whitman. (CTW)

1618. Turner, Alberta T. "A Second Bite of the Muskrat: Further Pursuit of Excellence in Contemporary Poetry." *MQ* 15:177-89.

A detailed analysis of William Stafford's poems "Carols Back Then," "Garden City," and "Demolition Project" demonstrates the usefulness of the criteria of wholeness and surprise in determining poetic excellence in contemporary poems. By these criteria "Garden City" is the best of the three poems because it is both whole and surprising; "Carols Back Then: 1935" is a close second because, though whole, it is less surprising; and "Demolition Project" is a distant third because it is neither. (AT)

1627. Wright, George T. "The Lyric Present: Simple Present Verbs in English Poems." *PMLA* 89:563-79.

Poets writing in English frequently use the simple present form of action verbs where the progressive form would be more natural in speech. They do so in order to take advantage of overtones resident in the simple form, overtones that permit a physical action to seem timeless yet permanent, pastlike yet edging toward the future, repeatable yet provisional, urgent yet distant, ceremonious and archaic. The action verb cast in the lyric present serves every epoch of English literary history differently but is always expressive of the poets' deepest perceptions and fears. (GTW)

1629. Yip, Wai-Lim. "Classical Chinese and Modern Anglo-American Poetry:Convergence of Languages and Poetry." *CLS* 11:21-47.

The sparseness of syntactical demands of the classical Chinese poetic medium promotes a unique mode of presentation. The Chinese poets are able to authenticate the fluctuation of concrete events with a most immediate cinematic visuality. The objects form an ambience in which the reader may move and directly take part in completing the esthetic experience. Using montage or mobile points of view in the perceiving act, the Chinese poets highlight the acting-out of these visual objects and events, letting the spatial tensions reflect conditions and situations rather than coercing them into some preconceived artificial orders by sheer human interpretive elaboration. This language, as a medium for poetry, is supported by an age-old esthetic horizon in which the self easily dissolves into the undifferentiated mode of existence. There is an inseparability between medium and poetics, between language and worldview. The rejection of abstract systems for concrete existence, and the attempt to negate or underplay the garrulous self in modern Anglo-American poetics have brought about an adjustment of the English language to the degree of violating the normal syntactical structures, achieving certain significant parallels to the esthetic ideal of the Chinese. (WY)

Prose Fiction. 1644. Beauchamp, Gorman. "Future Words: Language and the Dystopian Novel." *Style* 8:462-76. [Considers Orwell's *1984* and Zamiatin's *We*.]

Although dystopias are ideologically opposite utopias, writers of both face the same artistic problems. One concerns creating a "language" that reflects the political and technological realities of their fictive futures. Most utopian/dystopian writers fail to solve this problem successfully; exceptions are Orwell's *1984* and Zamiatin's *We*. Orwell demonstrates the stultification of language in a totalitarian regime where heretical ideas cease to exist because the words to express them are systematically eliminated. Zamiatin develops a technologese perfectly in accord with its mechanized anthill society. (GB)

1680. Fogel, Stanley. " 'And All the Little Typtopies':Notes on Language Theory in the Contemporary Experimental Novel." *MFS* 20:328-36.

The contemporary experimental novelist overthrows the easy passage from language to reality. Concomitant with the theories of structuralists, experimental writers who might be termed writers of metafiction, locate the reader in their language constructs, in the prison-house of language. *Omensetter's Luck* by William Gass provides the most graphic image of the inability to transcend or resolve language-games. Jethro Furber struggles to find an integrated, harmonious existence with the world through language. Unable to discover "Logos" in his incessant verbal constructs, Furber is driven mad. For Humbert Humbert the lack of an exit from the labyrinth of language is not as debilitating as it is for Furber. Rather, he finds a richness and a satisfaction in his play with language. (SHF)

1684. Glicksberg, Charles I. "Experimental Fiction:Innovation Versus Form." *CentR* 18:127-50.

When the experimental method in fiction is carried to extremes it produces results that are deplorably bad. The semantic range and variety of meanings, from the pejorative to the eulogistic, attached to such key terms as "experimental" and "avant garde" are examined. *Tristram Shandy* by Sterne emerges as the classic example of the open as contrasted with the closed form of fiction. The work of the New Novel in France is analyzed as is the development of the experimental vogue in the United States. *The Exaggerations of Peter Prince*, by Steve Katz, is pointed to as the typical bad experimental novel. (CIG)

1689. Greenman, Myron. "Understanding New Fiction." *MFS* 20:307-16.

New fiction attempts to imitate the creation of literature. To view fiction writing as itself the principal mimetic referent suggests that the fundamental reality represented by art is the act of mimesis itself. This idea is supported by the fact that the "realities"

believed by writers and critics to constitute life are various. But what has always remained constant is the necessity to attempt to achieve a mimesis of something. This effort by the artist is an act of self-preservation; and in the case of the new-fiction writers it has resulted in transferring critical focus from the esthetic object to its maker's attitudes. The new-fiction writers burlesque the writing of literature at the same time that, in a nonepiphanic, nonrealistic world, it remains the one mimetic referent which promises them value. (MG)

1709. Karl, Frederick R. "Enclosure, the Adversary Culture, and the Nature of the Novel." *Mosaic* 7,iii:1-15.

Kafka's presentation of burrow and castle keep in his short story "The Burrow" has profound reverberations in cultural terms, for such an enclosure represents those time considerations which have dominated our thought since the early 18th century. It represents the profane nature of our society, as apart from the sacred, which is space oriented, and the resistance to development, adventure, and exploration which are a concomitant of the need to move out and seek. Here, inward-turning becomes an adversary movement. Rejecting, turning back, burrowing in, building a castle keep—all of these indicate a culture that rejects a regularizing, moderating society which creates, establishes, "makes things possible." (FRK)

1735. McConnell, Frank D. "Toward a Syntax of Fiction." *CE* 36:147-60.

The last 20 years have seen a growing concentration in American criticism upon the history and theory of fiction. This movement, based in part upon the influence of European theoreticians, also reflects a larger change in the direction of the intellectual life of the United States. But writers on fiction have not yet taken sufficient account of the precise linguistic nature of the art of fiction. A syntax of fiction may be constructed along the lines of contemporary syntactic theory; this syntax should help us obtain a clearer and more usable insight into the peculiar functioning of the storyteller's imagination, and should also reveal important and hitherto unsuspected qualities of such novelists as Gide, Dickens, and Henry James. (FDM)

1737. Merivale, Patricia. "The Raven and the Bust of Pallas:Classical Artifacts and the Gothic Tale." *PMLA* 89:960-66.

Classical artifacts, particularly busts and statues, play an important part as image, symbol, plot element, or even character, in a large number of "Gothic" (i.e., romantic horror) contexts. 18th century neoclassicism provides "classically" serene artifacts to contrast with "Gothic" ones in, for instance, Poe and Hawthorne. But medieval tradition provides the Venus statue story, where the statue itself is the focus of Gothic horror, in Eichendorff, James, Mérimée, Gautier, and others. For the 20th century, statues become "Dionysian," classical yet fearful, as in Forster and Lagerkvist. More recently, statues represent a frivolous, melodramatic terror, or else mere emblematic pageantry. (PM)

1758. Plank, Robert. "Imaginary Voyages and Toy Novels." *HSL* 6:221-42. [On works by Austrian, Ital., Eng., and Danish writers.]

Some speculative fiction reveals its character best when conceptualized as both "imaginary voyage" and "toy novel." Four Austrian novels of the turn of the century (Th. Hertzka, *Eine Reise nach Freiland*; Th. Herzl, *Altneuland*; A. Kubin, *Die andere Seite*; F.V. Herzmanovsky-Orlando, *Maskenspiel der Genien*) give a realistic but perfunctory description of the real world and focus on the small imaginary country. Examples of the toy novel, notably some of Andersen's *Fairy Tales*, clarify the underlying longings and the derivation of political ideas from father figures. The imaginary voyage embodies the often unconscious fantasies, the toy novel makes them innocuous, hence acceptable. (RP)

1770. Ryf, Robert S. "Character and Imagination in the Experimental Novel." *MFS* 20:317-27.

Fundamental changes in the concept of character have taken place in much fiction since World War II. Such changes, however, have not negated the importance of character. Study of O'Brien's *At-Swim-Two-Birds*, Nabokov's *Pale Fire*, Fuentes' *A Change of Skin*, and Mailer's *The Armies of the Night* reveal that the center of interest and importance is the author-character relationship, which focuses light on the very process by which the novelist creates character. Thus, the nature and working of the novelist's imagination become matters of primary importance, and the underlying process by which we ourselves come to terms with our environment as the shaping imagination orders or "writes" it. (RSR)

1771. Sams, Henry W. "Malinowski and the Novel; or, Cultural Anthropology *versus* Mere Fiction." *JGE* 26:125-38. During Bronislaw Malinowski's years in New Guinea he read novels ranging in quality from Conrad downward to *Brewster's Millions* and recorded his response to his reading in his diary. For the most part, his response was personal, emotional, and unperceptive, in contrast to the sophisticated analysis which he succeeded in making of the primitive culture in which he was living. This contrast extends into his philosophy of "human science" and foreshadows a course of events in Western academies since World War I. Implicit in the argument is an assumption that literary and cultural criticism have a potential for mutual exchange which has been frustrated by accidents of academic organization and emphasis. (HWS)

1794. Wicks, Ulrich. "The Nature of Picaresque Narrative:A Modal Approach." *PMLA* 89:240-49. Contemporary usage of the term "picaresque" has blunted its usefulness as a literary concept. What once referred to the historically identifiable genre of *la novela picaresca* in 16th- and 17th-century literature is now applied whenever something "episodic" tied together by an "antihero" needs a label. One way to reconcile these extremes is to approach the problem from the wider perspective of narrative types in general: a modal approach, which can account both for a specific kind of narrative whose exclusive preoccupation is an exploration of the fictional world of the picaresque and for a primitive fictional possibility which may be part of much fiction outside that genre. The modal perspective leads next to generic awareness, which yields the strict attributes of the genre—the "total picaresque fictional situation"—some of which are: (1) dominance of the picaresque mode, (2) panoramic structure, (3) first-person point of view, (4) the picaro figure, (5) the picaro-landscape relationship, (6) a gallery of human types, (7) parody, and (8) certain basic themes and motifs. (UW)

Satire. 1798. Clark, John R. "Bowl Games:Satire in the Toilet." *MLS* 4,ii:43-58. Numerous major satirists deal overtly with the normally taboo subject, the latrine. Satirists strive to plump their readership into unmentionable and objectionable settings. The toilet is an obvious case in point. Recent satirists continue to assault us with varieties of bathroom hijinks and pot-boiling. Such satiric "chamberpottery" ranges from comic indecorum, through the bizarre and the fantastic, to the lunatic and hallucinating absurd. (JRC)

Translation. 1816. Elbaz, Shlomo. "Traduction littérale ou littéraire?" *CLS* 11:48-68. A comparative analysis of four different versions of a French poetic text (Canto i of *Anabase*, 1924, by Saint-John Perse) helps define and explore the problem of translation in a practical way. Special emphasis on T.S. Eliot's translation (1930) reveals faults on many counts: syntax, vocabulary, tonality, and rhythm. The liberties taken by Eliot with the original led either to gross errors, to amplification and interpretation destroying the necessary poetic ambiguity, or to the introduction of foreign and un-

desirable elements coming straight from Eliot's poetic world so opposed to Perse's specific vision and diction. This last point raises the question whether a poet is the most apt person to translate poetry from a foreign language into his own. In fact the first virtue required of a translator of poetry is humility toward the original, scrupulousness and rigor in the rendering of the minutest details. The most recent translation, by Roger Little (1970), best fulfills this fundamental requirement, a prerequisite for lessening the unavoidable losses in any translation of poetry. (SE)

1817. Furst, Lilian. "Stefan George's *Die Blumen des Bösen*:A Problem of Translation." *RLC* 48:203-17. Stefan George's rendering of Baudelaire's *Fleurs du mal* presents a striking example of the intrusion of the translator's personality. George has enobled and purified Baudelaire by his selective choice of poems, by his changes and omissions in the text, and by his tendency to greater abstraction. Linguistically, George's imprint is ever more evident. In part these changes are due to the need to transfer alexandrines into pentameters. In the main *Die Blumen des Bösen* were for George not so much a question of translation as an exercise of considerable importance in his training as a poet. (LRF)

1835. Rubenstein, Roberta. "Genius of Translation." *ColQ* 22:359-68. [On Constance Garnett.] Constance Garnett learned Russian in a casual manner from Russian friends in England and went on to become the primary translator of Russian literature into English. During her lifetime she translated over seventy volumes of works by Russian authors. Her enormous contribution to literature is even more remarkable in view of the fact that she was partially blind during more than half of her career. Her son, David Garnett, notes that she received little remuneration or recognition for her efforts, not even receiving royalties until late in her career. A Russian linguist, Augusta Tovey, undertook a comparative study of the Garnett and other translations from Russian into English, and concluded that Garnett's were superior in style, rhythm, and nuance to other translations, including more recent ones. Tovey attributed Garnett's excellence as a translator to her sense of rhythm and her musical ear. (RR)

1837. Savvas, Minas. "Translating Verse." *ColQ* 23:239-45. The translation of a poem is an act of recreation or imitation. In the majority of cases, most grammatical relationships, most sonic subtleties, most corresponding ambiguities, most localized ironies cannot be satisfactorily rendered into another language. The problem is similar to that of the original poet when he was turning his vision into a poem; there is disparity in both translation and original creation, between perception and utterance, between feeling and communication. The translator of verse—like the original poet—must have a constantly shifting coordination of priorities. (MS)

1844. Woolsey, Wallace. "The Art of Translation." *SCB* 34:166-68. Translation is an art and requires people, not machines. Ear is important in translation, for it lies at the base of all good writing. The translator must know two languages well; perhaps he needs to know the target language better. Language teachers should be aware of this phase of language use, but need not change the present approach to teaching elementary language. At higher levels courses may be developed in which the techniques and the art of translation are studied and put into practice. (WW)

V. BIBLIOGRAPHICAL

1854. Broderick, John C.,et al. "Recent Acquisitions of the Manuscript Division." *QJLC* 31:235-67. [Foll. by "Manuscript Division Acquisitions, 1973."] Recent additions to the Library of Congress Manuscript Division include archives of the Bollingen Foundation, including subject files on the controversial award of the Bollingen Prize to Ezra Pound; papers of Agnes E. (Mrs. Eugene) Meyer, with correspondence files pertaining to Paul Claudel and Thomas Mann; and additional papers of the Kermit Roosevelt-Joseph E. Willard

family, with correspondence of Rudyard Kipling, Hamlin Garland, and others. The Library has completed a 12-reel microfilm edition of its Benjamin Franklin papers. (JCB)

1860. Davis, Robert M. "On Editing Modern Texts:Who Should Do What, and To Whom?" *JML* 3:1012-20. A comparison of the English and American texts of Iris Murdoch's *Under the Net* shows that unauthorized editorial changes vary considerably in quality, some being necessary, some neutral, and some extremely questionable. Blanket condemnation of the publishing process or even of individual examples of editing is fruitless, since publishers have both the power and the inclination to do as they have always done. Textual scholars can only identify and evaluate the effect of changes in order to provide critics with information about reliable and complete texts and perhaps, by gradual and largely indirect suasion, persuade the publishers to edit with more intelligence and sensitivity. (RMD)

1869. Hancher, Michael. "The Text of 'The Fruits of the MLA'." *PBSA* 68:411-12. [By Edmund Wilson.]
Various printings of Wilson's article on the MLA editions exhibit a number of substantive textual variants themselves, thus posing various problems in determining the genealogy of his own text and the final state of his readings. (WBT)

1905. Tanselle, G. Thomas. "Addenda to Wyllie:Paste-over Cancels." *PBSA* 68:69-71.
To John Cook Wyllie's pioneer survey of "The Forms of Twentieth-Century Cancels" in *PBSA*, 47 1953, 95-112 may now be added two unrecorded examples of paste-over imprints, as well as two additional categories of paste-overs—those altering copyright notices and those effecting textual revision or correction. (GTT)

1906. —— "Bibliography and Science." *SB* 27:55-89.
Comparison of analytical bibliography with science has been common from the last third of the 19th century onwards. A survey of the way this analogy has been used over the years reveals the shifting meanings of the two terms, the repetitiveness of the discussions, and the growing tendency to be critical of the comparison itself. Recently four articles in particular have called renewed attention to the matter; although they continue the historical trend toward the criticism of the scientific analogy, they nevertheless offer extended discourses on the philosophic background, the methodology, and the logic of bibliographical demonstration by reference of one sort or another to science. (GTT)

1908. —— "Philip Gaskell's *A New Introduction to Bibliography*." *Costerus* N.S. 1:129-50. [Rev. art.]
Gaskell's new book takes a very different approach from its predecessor, R.B. McKerrow's *An Introducton to Bibliography for Literary Students* (1927): the earlier work stressed the application of the physical analysis of books to textual problems, whereas the new work concentrates on the history of the technical processes of book production. Gaskell's book has many excellences, but it also contains a number of errors and oversights, and it raises several larger questions. Why is textual study called "the heart of the matter" when the central focus of the book is on something else? Is it proper for an "introduction" to set forth new proposals as if they were established conventions? Is it fair for a book with this title to ignore the large body of work in the field of analytical bibliography? The concluding discussions of descriptive bibliography and textual study seem somewhat perfunctory, and the section on textual study is the least satisfactory in the book. (TGT)

VI. MISCELLANEOUS

Other Miscellaneous Items. 1964. Howe, Florence. "Literacy and Literature." *PMLA* 89:433-41.
Central to understanding the crisis of the teaching profession is the historical separation of the study of literature from the teaching of literacy. Literature has become a luxury and the teaching of skills empty of literary power. The profession must renew its responsibility for teaching meaningful literacy and work cooperatively as literature teachers within interdisciplinary programs. Literature and literacy can provide courage and skills necessary for survival and growth. (FH)

1982. McCartney, Jesse F. "The Humanities:A Traditional Defense for Modern Times." *SoQ* 12:107-12.
One might assume that the long standing of the humanities as well as the eloquent defenses of the humanities made in the past had assured their permanence, if not their pre-eminence, in the university curriculum. However, the modern university increasingly yields to social pressures to train students for careers, often to the neglect of the humanities. Despite these social pressures, teaching students how to be fully human remains a legitimate aim for American universities; for there is clear historical evidence that, unless we deliberately pursue this goal, we can lose both our knowledge and our understanding of the traditions, beliefs, and arts which unify the human race. (JFM)

ENGLISH LITERATURE†

I. GENERAL

Bibliography. 2027. Brockway, Duncan. "The Macdonald Collection of Arabian Nights." *MW* 63(1973):185-205; 64:16-32. [Pt. I appeared in *MW* 61(1971):256-66; see Bibliog. for 1971, Vol. I, Item 1489; Vol. II, Item 11729.]
A bibliography of the Arabic texts of the Arabian Nights, of the translations into languages other than English, and of works about the Arabian Nights held by Case Memorial Library, Hartford Seminary Foundation, in its Macdonald Collection. (DB)

General and Miscellaneous. 2042. Jago, David. "School and Theater:Polarities of Homosexual Writing in England." *CE* 36:360-68.
"School" and "Theater" symbolize divergent trends among English homosexual writers, which are reflected in homosexual political movements today. One trend, the School, is seen in the work of E.M. Forster; the other, the Theater, in that of Oscar Wilde. Wilde exploited his separateness from the normal patterns of life by depicting satirically the contradictions and shortcomings in those patterns and by claiming a greater freedom in his own lifestyle. His conviction and imprisonment, however, created a hypersensitivity toward any expression of emotion between males. A rare exception to this was the English public-school story, evoking the intense emotions and idealisms of adolescence. Forster developed from this tradition, and his writings breathe a firm commitment to traditional morality, recalling the teachings of Plato. Similarly today there are those who would extend existing conventions in homosexual terms, while others wish to sweep them away as the marks of a sick society. (DMJ)

2060. Warner, Alan. "How Irish Are the Irish Writers?" *Theoria* 42:1-17.
Anglo-Irish literature generally includes all writers who were born and bred in Ireland, but some are clearly more Irish than others. If the test of a truly Irish writer is "the condition of being involved in the Irish situation and usually of being mauled by it" (Conor Cruse O'Brien), then we would include Swift, but exclude Goldsmith. George Moore and Louis MacNeice are involved with, and troubled by, Ireland in a way that Oscar Wilde and Samuel Beckett are not. Many Irish writers, for example Yeats, John Hewitt, and Patrick Kavanagh, are deeply involved in a

† *Festschriften* and Other Analyzed Collections are listed in the first division of this volume. "F" numbers in brackets following a title refer to these items.

love-hate conflict with Ireland. Involvement with Ireland does not mean that a writer has only a local or regional appeal: the local becomes universal. (AJW)

II. AUSTRALIA, CANADA, ETC.

General and Miscellaneous. 2071. Robertson, R.T. "Interpreters All:The Commonwealth Context of African Literature in English." *RAL* 5:52-59.
Kerr's checklist of African literature courses indicates that African literature is taught in the context of Commonwealth literature courses; it is also taught in several other kinds of courses, e.g., World Literature; all these courses use texts prepared by Africanists. But both the cultural assumptions and the aims of these courses may differ from those in African literary studies: what may appear to be African concerns are universal matters. The theme of culture conflict and the different roles of male and female characters in this conflict are found in African and Commonwealth stories, forming a monomyth of the New World hero "no longer at ease" in his changing culture. This is found in Canadian literature as a search for personal and cultural identity, but the old African cultural identity lies in the past, the new Canadian in the future. Both African and Canadian writers are therefore "interpreters" of another identity to their own societies and themselves participants in the New World monomyth which incorporates the struggle for both personal and cultural identity. (RTR)

Australia. 2078. Bērziņa, Lūcija. "Nobeļa prēmijas laureāts Patriks Vaits." *JGa* 99:10-14.
Patrick White has won more renown abroad than in his native Australia. One reason may be his frequently negative portrayal of Australian life; also, White's novels are extremely complex, full of symbolism and Joycean experiments with language, permeated with mythological and religious overtones. *Voss* is an allegorical Dantean journey, its central theme the struggle between pride and humility. *The Solid Mandala* analyzes the problem of evil and is the most gloomy and perverse of White's novels. *The Vivisector* explores the nature of artistic creation and the dilemma of artist-creator and artist as man whose art vivisects and destroys others. (LB)
2079. Beston, John B. "The Influence of John Steinbeck's *The Pastures of Heaven* on Patrick White." *ALS* 6:317-19.
Traces of Steinbeck's *The Pastures of Heaven* are found in Patrick White's *Happy Valley* (1939) and *The Solid Mandala* (1966). Both *The Pastures of Heaven* and *Happy Valley* reject a utopia, showing the failure of life to fulfill one's dreams. However, Steinbeck's attitude to life is basically affirmative while White's is negative; Steinbeck's characters accept life while White's withdraw from personal relationships. Steinbeck's scene (in *The Pastures of Heaven*) in which a woman becomes a sort of life force, revitalizing a shattered man, appears at the end of *The Solid Mandala* as Mrs. Poulter revitalizes Arthur Brown. (JBB)
2081. Beston, John B. and Rose Marie. "The Theme of Spiritual Progression in *Voss*." *ArielE* 5,iii:99-114.
The theme of spiritual progression is the central theme of White's *Voss*. It is given emphatic utterance by Laura in her doctrine of the three stages of man's spiritual development. The three stages, God into man, man, and man returning into God, outline man's development from his childhood, through his assumption of Godlike powers unto himself, to his attainment of humility through suffering and thence his return to God. The doctrine takes its inspiration from the life of Christ, but is explored within the novel chiefly with respect to Voss. Laura's analysis of Voss in Mr. Bonner's garden, Voss's song as he rides into the hinterland, and Le Mesurier's poems lead to the articulation of the doctrine. (JBB & RMB)
2084. Boehm, Harold J. "The Date of Composition of *Ralph Rashleigh*." *ALS* 6:428-30.
The date of composition of James Tucker's *Ralph Rashleigh* is probably 1850 rather than the now accepted 1845. This is indicated by references in the novel to time spans between certain historical occurrences and the "present" at which the author was writing. In the first such reference, he states that malefactors were sent to the colony of New South Wales until "about ten years ago." As transportation of convicts to New South Wales ceased in 1840, Tucker's present must be 1850. He later states that convicts were treated badly at Newcastle about 20 years previously, when the novel's hero, Rashleigh, arrived there. Since Tucker earlier stated that Rashleigh was sent to Emu Plains during a great two year drought, and that drought could only have been the 1827-29 disaster in New South Wales, the present of the author could only be 1849 or 1850. As the drought is broken when Rashleigh is released, and some months pass before he is sent to Newcastle, the compositon date is probably 1850. Tucker may have been trying to further conceal his identity to avoid official recriminations by placing the 1845 date on the manuscript. (HJB)
2087. Brissenden, R.F. "A.D. Hope's 'The Double Looking Glass':A Reading." *ALS* 6:339-51.
Hope's "The Double Looking Glass" is concerned with the isolation of the individual, the sexual urge, and the paradox and illusions inherent in the notion of sexual communion. But instead of finding these matters a cause for despair, as he does in earlier poems, Hope here finds them a cause for joy and wonder. The poem is a celebration of the essential element of solitariness that is inevitably part not only of all sexual activity but also of all creativity. The poem explores the relationship between the solitary, inward-turning imagination and the external, multitudinous world which it recreates and transforms. As Susannah withdraws into the private world of her imagination she manifests an intensified sensitivity to the outer world. (RFB)
2089. Burns, D.R. "Vance Palmer and the Unguarded Awareness." *ALS* 6:259-68.
Vance Palmer's central area of interest is small communities of men who have a direct and effortful relationship to (Australian) Nature. Manhood, in Palmer's view, is best sustained and developed in such a relationship. Yet the language in the novels is less than resourceful. An air of complacency lies overall while along with the inherent male supremacy the novels endorse a rigid sexual puritanism. By contrast, there is that quite separate area of Palmer's fiction which explores states of uncertainty and apprehensiveness. In this unguarded state, the awareness of all that is occurring in and around one is full, sharp, painfully immediate. The language is alert, exploratory, freshly poetic in keeping with this immediacy while the narrative offers individuals winning, or attempting to win, confusedly, toward some sense of an order in things, as between the human and the natural. This order is not simply assumed to be existent, as in the fiction celebrating Australian manhood. (DRB)
2094. Core, George. "A Terrible Majesty:The Novels of Patrick White." *HC* 11,i:1-16. [Rev. art.]
The mode and subject of White's *The Eye of the Storm* are at once characteristic and unique, and this life history in the form of the satiric novel of manners reveals White at his best. The protagonist of *The Eye of the Storm* is one of his most believable and rewarding characters; and her story, which is presented from many points of view but chiefly through her own fragmentary memories, is finally comic in the highest sense—the redemptive —not perverse or pessimistic as some critics have charged. Once again White is dramatizing the lonely and agonizing search of human beings seeking definition in the bond of sympathy and love. (GC)
2107. Haberly, David T. "Edward E. Morris and Linguistic Nationalism:A Comparative View." *ALS* 6:352-63.
A number of puzzling features of Edward E. Morris' *Austral English* (1898) may better be understood against the backdrop of linguistic nationalism in other post-colonial nations. While a number of authors in the Americas defined language as an external phenomenon with the power to control both what is thought and what is expressed, Morris' theory and practice are the most extreme exposition of the contrary definition of language as an internal phenomenon moulded by the natural and social

environment. Thus, Morris believed, Australasia already possessed a new and unique language, similar to English but quite distinct from it. The consequences, in Australian literature, of Morris' ideas are briefly explored; the short-lived and futile reaction against Morris' pat consensus by the Jindyworobaks is also considered. (DTH)

2111. Heales, Robyn S. "Rosemary Dobson:The Influence of Art." *ALS* 6:249-58.
Many of Rosemary Dobson's poems contemplate human experience and have been inspired by paintings. A sensitive analysis of the so-called painting-poems reveals that Dobson uses paintings as a starting-point for exploring her concern with the nature of experience as it might appear to an artist, and despite detailed descriptions of paintings she never reiterates another artist's interpretation of human experience. Through themes of time and dreams she investigates the relative values of art. The most significant value lies in the nature of paintings to act, like dreams, against the destructive process of time. Dreams and pictures suspend the flux of time to preserve moments of experience for observation and understanding from a point of view which, being imposed by art, is esthetic and accordingly contemplative. Paintings represent the idea of Art with its abilities to transcend time and provoke a contemplative awareness which Dobson finds is the experience of an artist at work. (RSH)

2118. Klein, H.M. "The Structure of Frederic Manning's War Novel *Her Privates We*." *ALS* 6:404-17.
Manning's *Her Privates We* belongs to the most widely read novels about World War I. It has so far been considered only from the point of view of contents and attitude to the war. An analysis of its structural patterns reveals this is a carefully and effectively written work of fiction. The 18 chapters are organized into a central block (viii to xi) in which the actual fighting is remote, surrounded by two blocks of 7 chapters each, the first leading away from battle, the second leading up to the next. The middle of the book contains the culmination of the first movement and the beginning of the other. The personal fate of the central character, Bourne, is linked to this overall development. The entire book, while faithfully presenting the life of a whole military unit during a period of some months on the Western front, is constructed in such a way that the eventual death of the hero, a "Private" of "Fortune" (*Hamlet*) seems both cruelly fortuitous and inevitable. In addition to structural emphases this is achieved by a succession of parallel events and a tight web of human relationships, in which Clinton, Martlo, and "Weeper" Smart figure predominantly. (HMK)

2125. Martin, Ged. "'Bush':A Possible English Dialect Origin for an Australian Term." *ALS* 6:431-34.
By 1820 the term "bush" had supplanted "woods" in Australian English. Standard works derive it from the Dutch "bosch" and suggest a South African origin. It is however difficult to explain the mechanics of transfer. Since the term also existed in America, a common origin in Britain seems possible. The place-names of Essex provide examples with the element "bush," many of them consistent with subsequent Australian usage, and there are examples in adjoining countries. 18th-century Londoners, many of them country born, probably knew the term. Since one third of convicts transported before 1819 were Londoners, it is not surprising that "bush" should have established itself so quickly in Australian English. (GM)

2138. Pons, Xavier. "*The Battlers*:Kylie Tennant and the Australian Tradition." *ALS* 6:364-80.
In *The Battlers* Kylie Tennant, though outwardly faithful to the Australian tradition, rejects its optimistic spirit. There are many obvious resemblances between her novel and the works of the writers of the 90s, in themes as well as in style: she insists on the ethos of the outback dwellers, shows a great interest in her native land and in social problems, which she describes in a realistic, even journalistic manner. But, whereas the nationalists felt that society could be perfected and social justice was attainable, Tennant sees little hope in the future. Her characters are quite unable to improve their condition. Their life is absurd and meaningless; they drift from town to town without getting any closer to their goal of economic and emotional security. Their efforts are all in vain, and social action is of little avail. This pessimistic view of life reflects the general dejection which followed the Depression, and calls into question the complacency of the social prophets of the 90s. (XP)

2139. Poole, Joan E. "'Damne Scamp':Marcus Clarke or James Erskine Calder?" *ALS* 6:423-28.
Marcus Clarke (1846-81) is mentioned unfavorably in unpublished letters from James Erskine Calder to Sir George Grey during 1881 and 1882. Calder charges Clarke with "pirating . . . from articles first contributed . . . by me." Calder's accusation was noted by Bruce Nesbitt in "Marcus Clarke, 'Damned Scamp'" (*ALS*, 5 [1971], 93-98). Examination of Calder's letters and published articles and of details of Clarke's *Old Tales of a Young Country* (1871) and *His Natural Life* (1870-72), including dates of publication, indicates that Calder's charge of plagiarism is unfounded. Clarke almost always acknowledged printed sources which (unlike Calder) he used in a masterly fashion to interpret the significance of Australia's convict past to the young nation in the 1870s. (JEP)

2140. Poole, Joan E., and Michael Wilding. "Marcus Clarke's Contribution to *Notes & Queries*." *ALS* 6(1973):186-89.
The Australian novelist Marcus Clarke, author of *His Natural Life*, schoolboy friend of Gerard Manley Hopkins, joined the Melbourne Public Library in 1870 as clerk to the trustees and in 1873 became sub-librarian. From 1874 until his death in 1881 he contributed various items to the English antiquarian and academic journal *Notes & Queries* on miscellaneous topics, including the bibliography of Australian drama. This note details his contributions. (JEP & MW)

2147. Sellick, Robert. "Francis Webb's 'Sturt and the Vultures':A Note on Sources." *ALS* 6:310-14.
One of Francis Webb's last poems, "Sturt and the Vultures," demonstrates his long-standing interest in Australian exploration. The poem finds its inspiration in an incident from Charles Sturt's expedition to Central Australia in 1844-46. As the explorers were moving across the desert they were visited by a flock of several hundred birds. The experience is recounted in Sturt's published journal *Narrative of an Expedition into Central Australia* (London, 1849). Accounts of the same or similar experiences occur in the diaries of the surgeon John Harris Browne and the collector Daniel Brock. Of these, Sturt's is the relevant account. Sellick traces the correspondences between Sturt's prose and Webb's poem. (RS)

2148. Stewart, Annette. "The Design of *For the Term of His Natural Life*." *ALS* 6:394-403. [Marcus Clarke.]
The interest of the historical content of Marcus Clarke's novel *For the Term of His Natural Life* has led to a neglect of its artistic merits. The design is considered here against a background of the longer original novel *His Natural Life*. Although changes made in the novel were often imperfect, Clarke's skill in making a new design increased as the revision progressed. The gradual tightening of the structure is echoed in several ways, one of them being the use of dramatic devices creating the impression that the novel is a kind of "play" with acts, scenes, and a chorus to comment on events. The revision also allows the growth of a theme in the novel, which is concerned with questioning the ultimate value of human life. This is enacted in incidents, especially escapes and mutinies in the prison world, which are paralleled and counterpointed with dramatic irony and form a rich, complex pattern. But the most successful and convincing use of design is in the symbolism of the sea, which, though it also existed in *His Natural Life* is heightened by revision. Though much of this structure can only be seen in retrospect after we have read the whole work it makes the novel fit to compare with other Victorian novels of similar length, such as *Bleak House*. (AMS)

2150. Stuart, Lurline. "Marcus Clarke:*Long Odds* and the 1873 Melbourne Cup." *ALS* 6:422-23.
A note on Marcus Clarke's adaptation of a passage from *Long Odds*, as evidenced by textual comparison with his Cup report for the Melbourne *Herald*. (LLS)

2151. Sykes, Arlene. "Alan Seymour." *ALS* 6:277-87.
Alan Seymour's plays fall into two groups: compassionate observation of ordinary people, in such plays as *The One Day of the Year* and *A Break in the Music*, and grotesque, macabre drama, including *Swamp Creatures* and *The Shattering*. The plays

have sometimes shocked audiences who failed to recognize the grim humor beneath the grotesque. Repeated motifs include kidnapping, conflict of generations, and endings in which characters are either isolated or trapped in unhappy situations. (AMS)

2158. Wilding, Michael. "Marcus Clarke's *Chidiock Tichbourne*." *ALS* 6:381-93.
Australian novelist Marcus Clarke's *Chidiock Tichbourne* (serialized 1874-75, book 1893) is a historical romance about the English conspiracy to replace Elizabeth I by Mary Queen of Scots. Clarke's source was Isaac D'Israeli's essay on Tichbourne in *Curiosities of Literature*, parts of which he incorporates verbatim. The novel's protagonist Walter Gerrard is employed to spy on the conspirators by Walsingham, but falls in love with Tichbourne's sister. The novel's interest lies in Clarke's presentation of a shift in values from official Anglican establishment ideology, to the Catholic conspirators. A comparable conflict and shift occurs in Clarke's novel of the Australian convict system *His Natural Life* (1874). Both novels have significant episodes on Hampstead Heath, scene of Clarke's English schooldays; this directs us to Clarke's own ambivalence about his emigration to Australia. There are also sexual ambivalences in the novel, partly relating to Tichbourne's sister whom Gerrard first sees disguised as a boy; the novel's note is generally one of hostility to women and of latent homosexuality. (MW)

Canada. 2172. Beckmann, Susan. "A Note on Duncan Campbell Scott's 'The Forsaken'." *HAB* 25:32-37.
Scott's "The Forsaken" was probably influenced by Wordsworth's "The Complaint of a Forsaken Indian Woman." Wordsworth, following an account in Samuel Hearne's *Journey from Hudson's Bay to the Northern Ocean*, writes a poem emphasizing the pathos in the situation of an abandoned woman. Wordsworth allows his own feelings to obtrude onto his character's reaction to her predicament, so that she loses the dignity and stoicism Hearne had noted in his journal. Scott emphasizes this dignity, while drawing a more colorful and authoritative background. (SAB)

2189. Davies, Barrie. "The Makeshift Truce:Lampman and the Position of the Writer in Nineteenth-Century Canada." *DR* 53(1973):121-42.
Lampman's poems, essays, and letters, marked by struggle, despondency, and anguish, demonstrate clearly that the ethos of late 19th-century Canada was not the most favorable one for poets. Lampman's so-called "hypochondria" was a manifestation of a chronic sense of alienation. For him a life out of harmony with one's nature was a life in abeyance, and he feared compromise with the pressures of his society and the attitudes and tendencies of his age. What is examined is not the work which directly attacks what he feared and hated in society. Rather, it is that area of his work in which he is concerned with art, the artist, and his place in society. Such themes are the external expresson of an apprehension that contemporary life threatens with disintegration the core of being. In brief, art affirms the identity and is the means to self-hood and unity; society and the times demand self-deception, compromise, and eventual dehumanization. (BD)

2193. Djwa, Sandra. "Litterae ex Machina." *HAB* 25:22-31.
Because Darwinism coincided with the major romantic movement in Canada, Canadian romanticism was tinged from the first with overtones of Darwin's nature, an association which continued with the social Darwinist, "northern" vision of the 1920s. This hypothesis evolved through the use of computer thematic concordances to the complete texts of 7 representative Canadian poets (1875-1960). Examination of Pratt's diction revealed that terms descriptive of nature and human nature tended to cluster under distinctively Darwinian concepts. The "northern" vision of much modern Canadian poetry and art is more a complex of cultural reactions to the Darwinian hypothesis than it is an artistic reaction to the land per se. (SD)

2217. Jones, D.G. "David Helwig's New Timber:Notes on 'The Best Name of Silence'." *QQ* 81:202-14.
With his moral concern, his emphasis on clarity and reason, his journeyman interest in different genres, Helwig is closer in spirit to Jonson's classicism than to more recent metaphysical,

symbolist, surrealist, or even imagist poetics. Occasional treatment of myth in narrative and allegorical fashion furthers the parallel. Helwig may emphasize Thanatos over Eros, viewing common delights as superficial and the long-term constructions of desire (family, city, nation) as delusory. Rather, he writes of cities, "We name them often as a way of naming death." "Death is at the edge of all life. Death is the best name of silence." The poet risks doubting his own imagination's sense of liberation and participation in a larger life. In the title poem, a dramatic variation on the Bluebeard story, the lady rejects her rescuers, accepts her bloody marriage to the mortal world, and discovers that the visionary is reconciled with the realist. Paradox is expressed in plain language and in a renewed convention. (DGJ)

2221. Kertzer, Jon M. "*The Stone Angel*:Time and Responsibility." *DR* 54:499-509.
Laurence's heroine, Hagar, reviews her life in order to determine its temporal and moral logic, its causality and its responsibility. She must tie together the divergent aspects of her long life in order to find who is to blame for its painful changes. Her causal analysis breaks down when she finds so many factors contribute to each event in a causal chain stretching endlessly into the past. It is not through reason but through feeling that she discovers the essential continuity of her life. She feels guilty, despite her arguments to the contrary, and only by accepting this guilt can she discover the responsibility and hence the freedom and justice she demands for herself. Only by accepting her own weakness can she grant and request pardon, which proves the only way of transcending the confusion of time. But she remains too proud to beg for a higher pardon, that of divine mercy. (JMK)

2222. Killam, G.D. "African Literature and Canada:A Progress Report and One or Two Analogies." *DR* 53(1973-74):672-87.
The production of African literature in English is comparatively recent in origin, more recent and less abundant than Canadian literature. Yet African universities and schools have been much quicker and more forceful in making the study of African literature the center of their concern than have schools and universities in Canada in regard to the study of Canadian literature. A shift in the emphasis which currently exists in Canada is suggested. The intrinsic worth and the development of a Canadian tradition can be focused and enriched by adding to our syllabuses examples of the literature in English from countries other than those in which we dwell—from Africa, the Caribbean, India, Australia, and New Zealand—literatures with which we have more in common than might at first be supposed. (GDK)

2226. Lee, Dennis. "Cadence, Country, Silence:Writing in Colonial Space." *Boundary* 3:151-68.
Grant's *Technology and Empire* is relied upon in trying to understand a 4-year dry period experienced by Lee in the late 1960s. Grant explicates Canadian civilization as an unsuccessful refusal of liberal modernity—of the belief that man is essentially free, and is most himself when mastering what is. To be a Canadian in the colonial space of the American empire is to dissent from that belief and from the civilization it has engendered, and yet to have no access to other models of being human. To write in Canadian space is to experience the death of authentic language. It was only after living through that death of language that Lee was able to write in a cadence which mimed our being here. A person, thing, or situation becomes most real for us when we experience its life and its death simultaneously. To know the wordlessness of colonial space is the precondition to speaking its words. (DBL)

2230. MacDonald, R.D. "The Power of F.P. Grove's *The Master of the Mill*." *Mosaic* 7,ii:89-100.
Grove's novel is a nightmare prophecy set appropriately amid the vast, cold spaces of Canada. It is a naturalistic world in which man is dwarfed by a huge universe and his own huge machines, a world in which *homo faber* is captured by his means and is only partially aware of having lost his end, purpose, or will. Sam Clark, the "master" of the mill, then, like so many of Grove's "heroes," strives mightily but arrives nowhere. The unreality of his life is emphasized by a richly ironic imagery, shifting multiple perspectives, and a heavily theatrical style. The unreality becomes even more pronounced as Sam Clark and his survivors fail to

understand his failure. (RDM)

2240. Mitchell, Beverley,S.S.A. " 'How Silence Sings' in the Poetry of Dorothy Livesay." *DR* 54:510-28.
Because Livesay's *Collected Poems—The Two Seasons* is arranged chronologically, it creates a "psychic autobiography" of the poet and illustrates the various poetic techniques she has used over the past 46 years. An examination of her use of "silence" reveals three successive stages in the "psychic autobiography" into which the poems may be arranged. Those in the first group show a groping sense of self-awareness and concomitant sense of mystery; those in the second, a sense of the collective "other" and awareness of social ills; those in the third, a mature realization of the "separateness" of the self, an exultation in nature and sexuality, and a passionate desire for fulfillment. Although "silence" is used as a symbol almost consistently throughout, the psychological dimensions it reveals and the poetic techniques Livesay uses change. The absence of "silence" in the last poems is as significant in terms of the "psychic autobiography" as is its presence in the other works. (BJM)

2244. Morley, Patricia. "*Over Prairie Trails*:'a poem woven of impressions'." *HAB* 25:225-31.
Over Prairie Trails (1922) illustrates the artistic maturity which Grove had achieved by his early forties in his adopted language. The work is an account of seven journeys made in 1917-18 in the wilds of Manitoba. Grove describes his technique as one of allowing impressions to ripen into words. He calls his work a mood-poem with a symphonic structure. Each of the seven chapters has a distinctive mood: "Fog" is melancholy and weird; "Snow," macabre and sinister; "Dawn and Diamonds" is a Christmas pastoral of joy and innocence. Grove's poetic prose combines an imaginative approach with scientific accuracy. (PAM)

2256. Pacey, Desmond. "Areas of Research in Canadian Literature:A Reconsideration Twenty Years Later." *QQ* 81:62-69.
Noting that the study of Canadian literature in schools, colleges, and universities is growing rapidly, and that theses and critical monographs multiply, Pacey pleads for original research in such areas as bibliography, biographies of Canadian writers, the relationships between Canadian society and Canadian literature, the intellectual history of Canada, the study of internal and external critical reputations, and editions of letters and texts by Canadian writers. (DP)

2257. Pacey, Desmond, and J.C. Mahanti. "Frederick Philip Grove:An International Novelist." *IFR* 1,i:17-26.
It now appears that Frederick Philip Grove was the prolific German translator, novelist, poet, and playwright Felix Paul Greve. No definite proof of Grove being Greve has yet been found, but the cumulative weight of the circumstantial evidence in favor of identification is overwhelming. Thus we have the unique case of an author who had two quite distinct careers, one conducted in German in Europe, and the other conducted in English in Canada. (JCM)

2269. Schaeffer, Susan F. " 'It Is Time that Separates Us':Margaret Atwood's *Surfacing*." *CentR* 18:319-37.
Traces through the imagery and repeating patterns of events, which run parallel in the past and present, one woman's desperate attempts to reconcile herself to death and loss. Margaret Atwood's *Surfacing* has nothing to do with its ostensible subject, the contemporary problems of men and women swept up in the feminist tide, but with the universal fear of death. Events in the novel are ostensibly part of a contemporary drama, but have their true significance as re-enactments of past events. (SFS)

2270. Scobie, Stephen. "I Dreamed I Saw Hugo Ball: bpNichol, Dada, and Sound Poetry." *Boundary* 3:213-25.
The central figure in experimental poetry in Canada today is bpNichol. His work is divided between conventional poetry, visual concrete poetry, and sound poetry. In sound poetry, he works with a group of Toronto poets called The Four Horsemen, who acknowledge as one of their sources the sound experiments of the Dadaist Hugo Ball. Ball's sound poetry grew out of his interest in the theater and in Nietzsche. Ball's experiments were predated by a group in Russia who used an invented language called Zaum. The Four Horsemen, Dada, and Zaum all share basic esthetic presuppositions about sound poetry as the direct

language of the emotions, bypassing intellect. (SACS)

2275. Spettigue, Douglas O., and Anthony W. Riley. "Felix Paul Greve Redivivus:Zum früheren Leben des kanadischen Schriftstellers Frederick Philip Grove." *Seminar* 9(1973):148-55.
In all German reference books listing the life and works of the novelist, poet, and translator Felix Paul Greve, the date of his death is given as 1910. In fact, Greve did not die in that year, but emigrated to North America, where in Canada he began a totally new life as Frederick Philip Grove. It was under this name that Grove established himself as one of the major Canadian twentieth-century novelists, and his literary reputation has grown over the years since his death in 1948. It is only now that careful research has revealed the identity of Grove with Greve, thus making further investigation of Grove's early career as a German writer essential for scholars interested in Canadian literature in general and in German-Canadian literary relationships in particular. (DOS & AWR)

2281. Stouck, David. " 'Secrets of the Prison-House':Mrs. Moodie and the Canadian Imagination." *DR* 54:463-72.
As the classic account of pioneer life in Canada, Moodie's *Roughing It in the Bush* reveals a good deal about the Canadian imagination. *Roughing It* is a tale of hardship and misery which ends in withdrawal and defeat and denies the American myths of renaissance and power in a new land. Moodie's homesickness for England and her sense of failure and inadequacy as a pioneer woman extend to all aspects of her narrative. At the end of the book Moodie reminds us of the Ancient Mariner who has voyaged through guilt, despair, and death and warns those who might follow the same path. Her feelings of exile, her sense of failure, and her ascetic response to the wilderness are recurrent attitudes in Canadian writing and are apparently central to what is imaginative in the Canadian experience. (DS)

2282. —— "The Mirror and the Lamp in Sinclair Ross's *As for Me and My House*." *Mosaic* 7,ii:141-50.
Critical appreciation of Ross's *As For Me and My House* has been limited by the mistaken belief that Mrs. Bentley is the novel's central character. But in fact plot and characterization take their direction from the psychology of her husband Philip. as determined by the drama of his parents' lives. Philip's withdrawal from his wife is an extension of the aversion he once felt for his waitress-mother who bore him illegitimately, while his absorption in art reflects his desire to be like his father. Philip's quest for a self-image through art creates the world of failure and repression in which the Bentleys live; his shrinking from his motherly wife fuels a passion which cannot be filled. Ultimately Philip re-enacts his father's primal sin and unwittingly provides his sterile wife with the child she desires. (DS)

India. 2314. Garebian, Keith. "Strategy and Theme in the Art of R.K. Narayan." *ArielE* 5,iv:70-81.
The episodic structure of Narayan's *Swami and Friends* suits perfectly the Karmic theme, and the Nataraj leitmotif in *The Printer of Malgudi* forms a mythopoeic matrix for themes of equilibrium and wholeness. Although many of his novels are parables, Narayan subordinates metaphor to story as we see in the subtle form of *The Guide* (1958). Narayan's novels build comedy through architectonic coalescence and cumulative ironies, but sometimes they are weakened by overly insistent didacticism. Narayan's special strength is *comédie-humaine* realism and his most obvious fault is a collision between realism and fabulism as in the thesis novel, *The Man-Eater of Malgudi*. (KG)

2318. Parameswaran, Uma. "On the Theme of Paternal Love in the Novels of R.K. Narayan." *IFR* 1:146-48. [In *The Financial Expert* and *The Sweet-Vendor*.]
Narayan insinuates that a man who has no paternal love in himself is fit for treasons, stratagems, and spoils. Except for Vasu the Man-Eater of Malgudi, there is no character in Narayan's work who is so vile as not to respond warmly to children. This theme of paternal love is the central element in *The Financial Expert* and *The Sweet-Vendor*. Margayya and Jagan each have two overwhelming passions in life, one of these for each is his son. Whereas Margayya never finds himself as father, Jagan ascends to a higher level of perception through his discovery of the limits

of a father's responsibilities. (UP)

New Guinea. 2329. Boore, W.H. "Papua New Guinea Writers." *AWR* 24,liii:143-45. [On Okut Matak, Jack Lahui, Aloysius Aita, Peter Kilala.]
Words and antics respectively evoke the gods behind Wales and Papua New Guinea; eloquence and pageantry make gaudy faiths in both. Both peoples come new to the English language in which they write. The Welsh have a long literary tradition in their own ancient tongue. Papua New Guinea, however, was divided by a babel of languages without any written word. Both are initiating their own style in English—the Welsh discovering new emphases upon an age-old scene, the Papua New Guinean finding a new wholeness in what was utterly fragmented. (WHB)

New Zealand. 2334. Doyle, Charles. "James K. Baxter:In Quest of the Just City." *ArielE* 5,iii:81-98.
Baxter believed that children have an essential animism and sense of paradise, both soon lost, leaving the adult New Zealander lacking a religious sense, secular but inhibited by puritanism, loveless, materialisitic, and unhappy. This is bourgeois man, processed by a bad education system and kept in place by a bureaucratic state. His complement is natural man, freer, but still incomplete. Both are victims of acedia and imprisoned in a corrupt, chaotic society. Increasingly through his career Baxter came to admire the Maori, who retained some measure of freedom, animism, religious sense. He felt it the poet's job, as "a cell of good living," to help restore the soul's freedom and inward order. (CD)

South Africa. 2352. Beeton, D.R. "Pauline Smith and South African Literature in English." *UES* 11(Mar 1973):35-50.
Pauline Smith's contribution to South African English literature is considerable; she has strong affinities with other South African writers in English. She had a deep understanding of a specific setting and of a community, and brought considerable insight to her delineation of people. She, like Olive Schreiner, was given her impetus as an artist by the somewhat bleak Karoo area of South Africa: Olive Schreiner wrote of the desolate Great Karoo; Pauline Smith wrote of the Little Karoo with its simple Afrikaner communities. Pauline Smith was born in Oudtshoorn in the Karoo and spent her first twelve years there. She was then sent to a boarding school in England and was only to visit South Africa periodically for the remainder of her life. Yet the memory of her childhood, recalled principally during these visits, permitted the production of her most considerable work: the short stories entitled *The Little Karoo* and the novel *The Beadle*. She also owed much of her success as a writer to the encouragement of Arnold Bennett who became a life-long friend and a sympathetic literary adviser. (DRB)

West Indies. 2356. Baugh, Edward. "Questions and Imperatives for a Young Literature." *HAB* 24(1973):13-24.
During the last decade or so, there has been a growing ferment of discussion in the West Indies about the direction in which West Indian literature is developing and should develop. There has been a shift away from the general opinion that West Indian literature is necessarily rooted in English literature. This shift is an inevitable part of the compulsion toward self-asserti on. The dominant trend focuses on actual or desired black African connections. Individualism and introspection are suspect, and much is made of the ideas of "commitment" and "relevance" to "the society." Some of the major writers—V.S. Naipaul, Derek Walcott, Wilson Harris—are criticized because they do not seem to commit themselves sufficiently to the popular line. Their relevance is therefore questioned. However, they have made invaluable contributions to the debate. (EACB)

2357. Blodgett, Harriet. "Beyond Trinidad:Five Novels by V.S. Naipaul." *SAQ* 73:388-403.
V.S. Naipaul writes precisely phrased, deftly ironic universalized fiction. His concern is contemporary man, who survives, and sometimes even flourishes, despite psychic conflict, cultural fragmentation, and an indifferent universe. Naipaul admires man's indomitable spirit even while satirizing his weaknesses.

Essentially a moralist, he insists upon principled behavior. Not only the farcical *Suffrage of Elvira* reflects his moral concerns. Beneath its levity, *The Mystic Masseur* pursues a serious truth: men's failure to accept personal responsibility. The more sombre *A House for Mr. Biswas*, whose fumbling but plucky hero is apparently victimized by circumstances, actually develops the same theme. *Mr. Stone and the Knights Companion*, which has a symbolic structure, is a renewal myth in which an elderly hero belatedly gains his manhood by losing his illusions. The alienated hero of *The Mimic Men* also succeeds in learning to live with harsh reality. No illusionist himself, Naipaul believes that the novel should concern itself with the condition of men in the world today. (HB)

2358. Boxill, Anthony. "The Concept of Spring in V.S. Naipaul's *Mr. Stone and the Knights Companion*." *ArielE* 5,iv:21-29.
In *Mr. Stone and the Knights Companion* V.S. Naipaul, by associating and comparing Mr. Stone with natural creatures such as a cat and a tree, suggests the extent to which certain societies have become separated from the cycle of nature. Earlier Naipaul had written about the problem of trying to be creative in a society which is without order. In Mr. Stone, Naipaul suggests that creativity is as difficult in a society which is so highly ordered that natural responses have been replaced by stereotyped social ones. The problem with certain sophisticated societies, as Naipaul sees it, is that spring and the concept of natural renewal has ceased to have meaning. (AB)

2361. Davies, Barrie. "The Novels of Roger Mais." *IFR* 1:140-43. [*The Hills Were Joyful Together, Brother Man, Black Lightning*.]
Detailed analysis of Mais's three published novels, *The Hills Were Joyful Together, Brother Man*, and *Black Lightning*, reveals that they are not realistic novels of protest against the political, social, and economic conditions existing in the British West Indies during Mais's lifetime. Mais is concerned with a reality which must be distinguished from the merely factual. As a result his methods are closer to poetry than to realistic prose, and the inner experience of his characters is realized through rhythmic repetition, image patterns, and symbols, and not through external events, objective reporting, and logical narrative sequences. (BD)

2362. Fabre, Michel. " 'Adam's Task of Giving Things Their Name':The Poetry of Derek Walcott." *NewL* 41,i:91-107.
Examination of Walcott's work shows his development as poet, toward more perfect expression of his people's experience; as critic, toward understanding the tension between the separate critical responses to his writing. Walcott's *In a Green Night* and *The Castaway* present a "traumatic" and "visceral" concern with his origins. A public side of this concern merges racial themes with themes of exile and searches power and politics to discover the Caribbean identity; personally, a preoccupation with religion, love, and innocence helps define his mission as a writer. *Dream on Monkey Mountain*, four one-act plays and the particularly important introductory essay "What the Twilight Says," dramatizes Walcott's crisis and accomplishment from his boyhood schizophrenia (British vs. Creole traditions, Christianity vs. Paganism) to his unromanticized interpretation of the Caribbean folk experience. This collection foreshadows in mood and content the perfect balance of poetry and dialect of *Another Life*. With this volume, Walcott begins to solve the Third World artist's language dilemma: this poetry is tonally one with that of the Caribbean people and portrays honestly, his personal growth without sacrificing universality. (GMcC)

2363. Fido, Martin. "Mr. Biswas and Mr. Polly." *ArielE* 5,iv:30-37. [Naipaul's *A House for Mr. Biswas* compared to Wells's *The History of Mr. Polly*.]
Naipaul's *A House for Mr. Biswas* derives directly from Wells's *The History of Mr. Polly*. The eponymous heroes have similar social handicaps and ambitions. Close similarities in plotting, characterization, and language show that this is not accidental. Although the type of the "little man" represented by Biswas and Polly recurs in 20th-century literature, the detailed similarities between the two suggest that Naipaul consciously set out to recreate, in the West Indian setting, the essence of Wells's book. (MAF)

III. THEMES, TYPES, AND SPECIAL TOPICS

Themes. 2447. Humphreys, Arthur R. "'The Genius of the Place':Turkey in English Letters." *SAQ* 73:[306]-23.
Survey of the idea of Turkey as conveyed by English writing since the 16th century. Outlines the powerful imaginative hold, of melodramatic fascination, exerted over Elizabethan and 17th-century drama and over political and historical commentators. Indicates the various motives—commercial, diplomatic, archaeological, and adventurous—which impelled visitors, and traces the growth in the 18th century, from Lady Mary Wortley Montagu on, of a serious attention to Turkish culture and history. Develops the theme of Romantic and Victorian oriental interests, through varied individual temperaments from Byron's time to Thackeray's, as reflected in topographical writing and picturesque engraving. Glances at 20th-century archaeologists, travelers, and imaginative writers, from Gertrude Bell to Lawrence Durrell. (ARH)

IV. OLD ENGLISH

General and Miscellaneous. 2462. Campbell. Jackson J. "Some Aspects of Meaning in Anglo-Saxon Art and Literature." *AnM* 15:5-45. [Incl. plates.]
The Irish art of the 7th and 8th centuries and the English art developed from it used form and color to express an abstract or intellectual meaning, relying heavily on previously learned, standard figural types and symbols. When the style of art changed in England around the end of the 9th century toward the so-called "Winchester" manner, the principle of meaningful expression of idea still outweighed any attempt at naturalism, and the elements taken from actual life were nugatory compared with the ultimate aim, which remained in the area of symbolic meaning. Poets who used the conventions of Germanic verse form also used the traditional Christian typology and metaphors stirring audience reaction simultaneously with intellectual ideas and natural emotion to produce meaningful themes rather than *tranches de vie.* (JJC)

Poetry. 2493. Friedman, Albert B. "'When Adam Delved...':Contexts of an Historic Proverb." [F 49]:213-30.
"When Adam delved and Eve span, / Who was then a gentleman?" was an established proverb in England long before John Ball used it as a slogan in the Peasants' Revolt of 1381. Due to its association with Ball, it and related proverbs exude subversive connotations for modern historians. In their discussions of gentilesse, medieval moralists, preachers, and poets employed these egalitarian proverbs while asserting that the qualities of nobility and gentility were not matters of blood, position, or possessions, but stem from an inherent impulse, inspired by God's grace, to conduct oneself virtuously. (ABF)
2503. Rendall, Thomas N. "Bondage and Freeing from Bondage in Old English Religious Poetry." *JEGP* 73:497-512. [In *Advent, Exodus,* and *Andreas,* esp.]
In both biblical texts and the early medieval "ransom theory" of the Atonement, bondage is an image for the condition of fallen man, and freeing from bondage is a metaphor by which Christ's salvation of man is expressed. Alertness to these implications of the frequently encountered bondage theme in Old English religious poems considerably sharpens our appreciation of their artistic and doctrinal sophistication. (TNR)

Riddles. 2510. Barley, Nigel F. "Structural Aspects of the Anglo-Saxon Riddle." *Semiotica* 10:143-76.
Data were derived from the Old English *Exeter Book.* Broad aspects of riddle structure are examined so that conclusions are not confined to Anglo-Saxon culture. Basic analytical distinctions between riddles of generalization, riddles of negation, metaphoric riddles, and joke riddles are proposed. These are related according to transformational rules operating on a tree-structure of nesting categories, allowing sideways motion across branchings, or according to rewrite rules permitting motion up and down the branchings. In this way it becomes possible to specify the semiotic processes linking given image and hidden answer, the matching of which is the core of the riddling process. (LLBA)

Aelfric. 2513. Kuhn, Sherman M. "Was Aelfric a Poet?" *PQ* 52(1973):643-62.
The alleged late Latin prose features (rhyme, balance with antithesis, wordplay) of Aelfric's alliterative works are shared by Old English poems in the most conservative tradition. Their alleged non-poetic features (non-traditional alliteration, abundance of unstressed syllables, heavily loaded half-lines, lack of the older poetic diction) are shared by the later alliterative poems. If they lack the emotional power of *Beowulf,* they are far more inspired than several poems composed in the conservative manner. Aelfric's audience consisted of ordinary Christians, rather than the warrior aristocracy or the learned elite; his language was some centuries later than that of the best poems in the older style; his purpose was primarily to instruct. With his own audience, language, and purposes in mind, he helped to produce a new kind of alliterative poetry. (SMK)

Battle of Brunanburh. 2519. Berkhout, Carl T. "*Feld Dennade*—Again." *ELN* 11:161-62.
The most satisfactory reading of the troubled passage "feld dennade / secga swate" in *The Battle of Brunanburh* (12b-13a) remains "the field resounded with the blood of men." The verb *dennade* and its variants are plausible forms of WS *dynade*; and, although scholars have doubted the poet's use of such violent or bizarre synesthetic imagery, this figure of spilt blood sounding the deed of slaughter has notable precedents elsewhere, particularly in Gen. iv.10 ("Vox sanguinis fratris tui clamat ad me de terra"). (CTB)

Bede. 2523. Andersson, Theodore M. "The Caedmon Fiction in the *Heliand* Preface." *PMLA* 89:278-84.
The *Heliand* "Preface" comprises a "Praefatio" in prose and 34 hexameter "Versus." According to the "Praefatio" a Saxon poet was commissioned by Louis the Pious to execute a metrical paraphrase of the Bible. The "Versus" add the fiction, borrowed from Bede's Caedmon story, that the poet was inspired in a dream to carry out the undertaking. The "Praefatio et Versus" appear for the first time in a printed book from 1562 and were once thought to be a humanist counterfeit, but they are now considered to be medieval in origin. The prose "Praefatio" seems to justify our confidence, but the first 15 lines in the "Versus" make this composition suspect; they belong to the tradition of the country idyll, a genre unknown in the 9th century, but well documented in the 16th. The sentiments and wording are particularly close to Angelo Poliziano's popular poem "Rusticus" (1483). It is likely that the "Versus" were added to the "Praefatio" by an anitquarian familiar with Bede sometime in the middle of the 16th century. (TMA)

Beowulf. 2528. Anderson, Earl R. "*Beowulf* 2216b-2217:A Restoration." *ELN* 12:1-5.
There has been little agreement among editors and critics over a suitable restoration for the damaged passages in *Beowulf,* ll. 2216b-17, but a decision can be made for these verses by consulting diction elsewhere in the poem. The use of *sinc* in formulaic contexts suggests that line 2217a should read "since fahne," thereby disqualifying all restorations which begin 2217b with the particle *ne.* On the basis of diction and narrative progression in ll. 2270b-2327a, l. 2217b should read "He Þæt syððan [onfand]." Line 2216b may read "hond [maððum nam]." The restoration creates double alliteration for l. 2217, and the verb *onfand* suggests an ironic contrast between what the dragon discovered and what the Geats discovered, "Þæt sie ðiod onf[and]," l. 2219b. (EA)
2543. Hanning, Robert W. "*Beowulf* as Heroic History."

M&H 5:77-102.

In *Beowulf* the hero's courage becomes, for a brief moment, the instrument of providence aiding a nation; later, however, we see unredeemed, uncontrollable history overwhelm Beowulf. The poet represents and judges the Germanic past with an ambivalence about its worth that characterizes much Anglo-Saxon retrospection. Early in *Beowulf*, the hero brings with him to Denmark a power which God uses to carry on his feud with Cain's kin; Beowulf's triumph over Grendel and the resultant restoration of Danish unity in Heorot suggests that God sends heroes to direct history according to his will. Yet the negative and ironic uses of treasure objects make the claim that time and history in a non-Christian world are destructive; triumph turns to disaster, while human worth is transitory and futile. (RWH)

2550. McNamara, John. "*Beowulf*, 2490-2508a." *Expl* 32:Item 62.
Scholars generally take it for granted that Beowulf slew Daeghrefn to avenge Hygelac's death, but Beowulf's own account of the episode (2490-2508a) does not bear this out. He begins by boasting of his loyalty to Hygelac to show that he has always lived according to the heroic code. But when he shifts to his victory over Daeghrefn, it is not to claim that he fulfilled the code by avenging Hygelac's death; in fact, he does not even mention Hygelac's death. Beowulf is instead reminiscing about his former glory and observing that he must now fight his greatest adversary with a weapon that had been unnecessary when he was younger. (JM)

2566. Whitbread, L.G. "The *Liber Monstrorum* and *Beowulf*." *MS* 36:434-71.
The *Liber monstrorum* has attracted comment mainly for its allusion to the giant Hugilaicus, the Hygelac of *Beowulf*. The complete work is in three books, describing monsters of human shape, wild animals, and serpents, examples being collected from a variety of sources and retold in a generally mistrustful tone in keeping with the author's unobtrusive Christianity. Consensus of opinion favors the 7th or 8th centuries, perhaps before the 740's when controversy broke out over the existence of the Antipodes. Certain Celtic features suggest an Irish center, and the scholarly interests of Aldhelm and his circle overlap considerably. The compiler has for several centuries extracted not only Hygelac but some of the more prominent characteristics of the *Beowulf* monsters. The Old English poem may have been in circulation well before the mid-8th century. (LGW)

Cynewulf. 2573. Adams, R.W. "*Christ II*:Cynewulfian Heilsgeschichte." *ELN* 12:73-79.
Cynewulf's poem on the Ascension, *Christ II* of the *Exeter Book*, is neither primarily homiletic nor doctrinal; rather, it is a lyric celebration of the *Heilsgeschichte* and the poet's place as man in that history. The opening question concerning the Advent and the Ascension, though answered as the poem progresses, serves more importantly to introduce these two elements of the *Heilsgeschichte*, and the two are then fully supplemented by references to the Creation, Fall, Incarnation, Harrowing, and Judgment. (RWA)

2575. Brown, George H. "The Descent-Ascent Motif in *Christ II* of Cynewulf." *JEGP* 73:1-12.
The recurrent image of descent and ascent in Cynewulf's poem on the Ascension is a typical motif of the medieval theology of glory, based on New Testament, early Christian, and patristic patterns. Cynewulf exploits the juxtaposition, apt for Old English poetic techniques of contrast, repetition, and variation, more fully than does his immediate source, Gregory the Great in Homily 29. The elaborated descent/ascent motif unifies the poem artistically and explains elements within the poem which have puzzled critics, such as the section on the Harrowing of Hell. The last major section of the poem contrasts Christ's Ascension with his final descent at the Last Judgment. (GHB)

2577. Hieatt, Constance B. "*The Fates of the Apostles*: Imagery, Structure, and Meaning." *PLL* 10:115-25.
Cynewulf's *The Fates of the Apostles* interweaves several structural principles. One of these results in a complex of images and verbal motifs centering on "light" and "journey," key concepts which occur throughout and converge significantly in the ending. The

rhetorical patterns previously suggested by Boren occur 13 (not 12, as he thinks) times, creating a sequence: from apostles to poet to reader to all mankind. The structure may, however, incorporate "12" symbolism elsewhere; seen as a tripartite structure, the body of the poem occupies 144 verses, while the prologue and epilogue occupy 100. (CBH)

Deor. 2583. Kossick, Shirley G. "The Old English *Deor*." *UES* 10,i(1972):3-6.
Despite the strophic form and elegiac quality of *Deor*, the poem may more profitably be compared with *Widsith* than with *Wulf and Eadwacer* or the Old English elegies. Various possibilities for interpretatio n are offered, the most compelling of which is perhaps that of Morton W. Bloomfield who associates the poem with "sympathetic" magic. This idea is an attractive one, and can be related to Kemp Malone's reading of *Deor* as a poem of consolation, as the two interpretations are complementary rather than mutually exclusive. A brief comparison of *Deor* and "Fear No More the Heat o' the Sun" suggests the nature of the consolatory element in the Old English poem. (SGK)

Dream of the Rood. 2585. Berkhout, Carl I. "The Problem of OE *holmwudu*." *MS* 36:429-33.
Editors of *The Dream of the Rood* commonly favor the emendation *holtwudu* ("tree of the forest") over the MS *holmwudu* ("sea-wood, ship") in the passage comparing the Cross and Mary, ll. 90-94. The MS reading should be retained, however, for the poet is drawing upon an established figure of the Cross as the vessel, the *lignum maris*, by which earth-dwellers are transported across the "sea" of this present life to their eternal homeland. This theme is introduced in the *lifes weg* passage immediately preceding the *holmwudu* analogy and is developed throughout the entire latter half of the poem, making more vivid the eschatological meaning of the Crucifixion both for the dreamer and for the poet's audience. (CTB)

Exeter Book. 2589. Joyce, John J. "Natural Process in *Exeter Book* Riddle #29:'Sun and Moon'." *AnM* 14(1973):5-8.
Exeter Book Riddle 29, "Sun and Moon," offers an instance of the riddle form invested with impressive poetic values. A central metaphor of military struggle extends throughout and is reinforced by syntactical oppositions as well as verbal echoes. The use of the motif of conflict to emblemize the true riddle behind the observation of the persona about sun and moon's interaction has been overlooked. The struggles between dew and dust, light and darkness, sun and moon do not result in an evolutionary "survival of the fittest" world view. Rather, the contending of nature's forces results in a universe which is somehow self-propelled yet inextricably mysterious in its process. The poet's use of craft and artifice diction, "listun gegierwed" and "searwum asettan," suggests his consciousness of the necessity of the reader's probing the workings of this riddle to discover its analogy to the natural world around him. (JJJ)

2590. Nelson, Marie. "The Rhetoric of the Exeter Book Riddles." *Speculum* 49:421-40.
Exeter Book riddlers may have derived certain descriptive techniques from their knowledge of classical rhetoric. For the riddlers, metaphor became a way of seeing and prosopopoeia a means of working out patterns of poetic description; anaphoras of antithesis and time helped to structure details; particular sound repetition devices reinforced meanings; and classical rhetoric provided a way to frame riddle description with the "envelope" pattern. (MN)

2591. Pope, John C. "An Unsuspected Lacuna in the Exeter Book:Divorce Proceedings for an Ill-Matched Couple in the Old English Riddles." *Speculum* 49:615-22.
In the *Exeter Book*, a leaf has been lost between folios 125 and 126, thus bringing together two unrelated fragments that have previously been treated as a single riddle. It is likely that Quire XVI has lost a leaf at the end, following folio 125. If we assume this loss, we have two internally coherent fragments, 70a and 70b. The second, 70b, becomes the intelligible close of a first-person riddle. Fragment 70a starts as a third-person riddle. Problems of its text and some previous solutions are discussed in the light of the

separation, but no new solution is reached. (JCP)

Genesis. 2599. Brockman, Bennett A. "'Heroic' and 'Christian' in *Genesis A*:The Evidence of the Cain and Abel Episode." *MLQ* 35:115-28.
Comparison of the Cain and Abel episode with corresponding patristic commentary suggests that the 8th-century poet appealed less to the theological understanding of his audience than to the moral expectations which derived from their pre-Christian culture. The poet was impressed more by biblical history, by new legends intelligible within the Germanic social framework, than by exegesis. His interests differ at almost every point from those of the Fathers. For them the story had profound meaning as it contrasted the Cities of God and Man and adumbrated the Atonement. While he does interrupt his narrative to moralize on the consequences of Cain's deed, the poet alludes pointedly to the legendary descendants of Cain and roots the entire account in the "heroic" ethos—in the secular mores of the pre-Christian society. What elicits the poet's deepest feeling is the fate of Cain the man, damned for violating one of the most basic Germanic laws. The figure of Cain the honorless exile, the social at least as much as the spiritual outcast, makes this moment vital. (BAB)
2600. Clausen, Christopher. "A Suggested Emendation in *Genesis B*." *ELN* 11:249-50.
Line 381b of the Old English *Genesis* reads, in B.J. Timmer's standard edition of *The Later Genesis*, "hyra woruld waes gehwyrfed." This reading is accepted by Krapp and Klaeber in their editions; its difficulty is that besides being vague it leaves the verb in the following line, *fylde*, without an apparent subject. By emending *woruld* to *werod* we achieve a more vivid reading (the fallen angels as a band of warriors) and provide an appropriate subject for *fylde* at the same time. (CJC)

Judgment Day. 2607. Daniels, Richard J. "Bibliographical Notes on the Old English Poem 'Judgment Day'." *PBSA* 68:412-13.
Four errors have been discovered among the references to the Old English poem *Judgment Day I* (*Bi Domes Dæge*) from the *Exeter Book*. Three of these confuse the *Exeter Book* poem with the *Judgment Day II* (*Be Domes Dæge*), found in CCCC Ms. 201. The fourth error consists of a misleading reference to a scholarly article on the *Exeter Book Christ III*. (RJD)

Seafarer. 2613. Davenport, W.A. "The Modern Reader and the Old English *Seafarer*." *PLL* 10:227-40.
Recent interpretations of *The Seafarer* have emphasized the homiletic and penitential nature of the poem's themes, its debt to early Christian Latin writings, and the figural and didactic quality of its speaker. The poet's rhetorical methods, his use of physical images, his emphasis on experience and feeling, his use of antithesis, irony, ambiguity, and paradox, his composition of the poem as a balance of parts and as a balance of thoughts within each part, all contribute to a texture and structure which contain too great a complexity to be read as simply homiletic or allegorical. (WAD)

V. MIDDLE ENGLISH

Literature (Excluding Chaucer)

General and Miscellaneous. 2626. Alexander, J.J.G. "English Early Fourteenth-Century Illumination:Recent Acquisitions." *BLR* 9:72-80.
A series of fragments in the Bodleian Library, acquired at different dates, are from a Breviary for Chertsey Abbey, Surrey. The manuscript was broken up probably in the early 19th century. The decoration consists of historiated initials, borders, and bas-de-page scenes and can be attributed to the Master of the Queen Mary Psalter MS. Royal 2 B.vii. The calendar includes the obit of abbot Bartholomew, d. 1307, in the original hand. (JJGA)
2640. Dwyer, Richard A. "The Appreciation of Handmade Literature." *ChauR* 8:221-40. [Transmission of texts.]
Details of manuscript variation can answer questions of literary history and interpretation, because the manual transmission of texts often resulted in active scribal participation in their esthetic refinement. Individual MSS may be viewed as textual performances adapted to varying audiences. The research of J.M. Manly, George Kane, and Rosemary Woolf reveal that texts of the *Canterbury Tales*, *Piers Plowman*, and many Middle English lyrics were altered by their copyists with distinct literary consequences. In the case of the 13 medieval Franch translations of the *Consolatio philosophiae*, scribal processes are carried further into complex medievalizing performances of the Boethian text. The 150 extant MSS of these translations show successive translators, revisers, compilors, and editors assimilating one another's work into truly medieval reinterpretations of their late classical origin. (ARD)
2645. Hands, Rachel. "'Dancus Rex' in English." *MS* 35(1973):354-69.
The twelfth-century Latin treatises on hawking attributed to Dancus Rex and Guillelmus falconarius, and (less importantly) to Gerardus and Alexander, provide a source for several passages in late medieval English treatises, chiefly *Prince Edward's Book* (best known from British Museum MS. Harley 2340) and the printed *Boke of St. Albans* (1486). Comparison of parallel passages shows something more than the re-use of a common tradition, indicating a knowledge either of some form of the Dancus and other treatises, or the adoption of material already incorporated into other works, while the various nonce-usages and errors in the English text indicate that a French intermediary is probable. This recognition of source and intermediaries enables an explanation to be made of several of the more obscure words and phrases in the English texts. Finally, comparison with chapters xviii and xix of Albertus Magnus, *De falconibus, asturibus et accipitribus*, suggests that it may be this version of Dancus, translated into French, which is the chief source of the material in England. (RH)
2648. Jolliffe, P.S. "Middle English Translations of *De Exterioris et Interioris Hominis Compositione*." *MS* 36:259-77.
Two Middle English versions of the Latin treatise *Formula noviciorum*, in Queen's College Cambridge MS. 31 and University Library Cambridge MS. Dd.2.33, are identified as translations of *De Exterioris et Interioris Hominis Compositione*, widely attributed to David of Augsburg, for the Middle English texts and the Quaracchi edition of the Latin agree exactly in content and arrangement of teaching. The Queen's College text differs in translation from that in the University Library. B.M. Arundel MS. 197 contains an abbreviated Middle English form of Book I which is essentially the same translation as in Q.C.C. MS. 31. Two short Middle English extracts from *De Exterioris* are noted. (PSJ)
2657. Shields, Hugh. "A Text of Nicole Bozon's *Proverbes de bon enseignement* in Irish Transmission." *MLR* 69:274-78.
A hitherto unidentified text of Nicole Bozon's *Proverbes de bon enseignement* exists in the Red Book of Ossory, Kilkenny, Ireland. Through a misreading of the MS title, this text was previously known as *Les Proverbis del Sibil*; the last word correctly reads *Bibil*, so that the proper title is *Proverbs of the Bible*. The Kilkenny MS provides some new textual variants of a work already published from nine MSS. Its particular interest, however, lies in the evidence it provides concerning the use of French in medieval Ireland and the part apparently played by the Franciscan order in the promotion of the language there. (HS)

Arthurian Romances. 2660. Matthews, William. "Where Was Siesia-Sessoyne?" *Speculum* 49:680-86.
The high-point of King Arthur's military career was his victory over Lucius and the Roman army at "Siesia" (Geoffrey of Monmouth). The name also appears as "Suison" (Wace), "Ceroise" (prose-*Merlin*), "Swesy" (Manning), and "Sessoyne" (Malory, alliterative *Morte Arthure*). The routes described for Arthur's expedition agree in all these works, and it is certain that

the site of the battle was in Burgundy. Ten identifications have been proposed. Seven of these are unsuitable. The most likely candidate for "Siesia" is Val-Suzon. Midway between Langres and Auton, on the popular route, its topography, name forms, and historical associations make it suitable as the site for the battle that actually took place only in Geoffrey's mind. (WM)

2660a. Morgan, Alice B. " 'Honour & Right' in *Arthur of Little Britain*." [F 49]:371-84.

Lord Berners' translation *Arthur of Little Britain* shows that its French author was familiar with romance motifs, for this lengthy book is encyclopedic in its plot devices. The narrative, however, lacks conviction; the hero is only mildly challenged by his struggles to win the noble Florence, and the author's main concern seems to have been with issues of social decorum and moral choice. Examination of the romance's incidents, characterization, and dialogue shows how the elaborate plotting and fantastic events are combined with realistic issues of courtesy and morality. (ABM)

Drama and Theater. 2662. Brawer, Robert A. "The Middle English Resurrection Play and Its Dramatic Antecedents." [F 114]:77-100.

The medieval drama of the resurrection provides the grounds for a reconsideration of the dramatic relations between the Latin drama of the church and the so-called vernacular tradition in England. Though the dramatization of the resurrection in the Towneley cycle differs from that of its antecedents in its mode of representation, significant analogies to the earlier drama may be found in the overall principle of action behind the medieval resurrection play, in the selection and deployment of individual scenes within the play, in the conception and use of character, and in the use of rhetorical elements for the purpose of closer audience identification with the drama. (RB)

2665. Davidson, Clifford. "Thomas Aquinas, the Feast of Corpus Christi, and the English Cycle Plays." *MichA* 7:103-10.

The vernacular cycle plays which flourished in the 15th and 16th centuries in England have several points of contact with the thought and influence of Thomas Aquinas. Aquinas provided the doctrinal base for specific incidents in the plays, as in the instance of the York Realist's *Creation, and Fall of Lucifer* in the York cycle. In this case, the dramatist presents a Lucifer who desires to be God "by likeness" in a scene that is in harmony with Aquinas' position in the *Summa Theologica*. Second, the philosopher encouraged and assisted Pope Urban IV in the establishment of the Feast of Corpus Christi, which provided an occasion in England for a civic drama that grew out of the procession on this day. Finally, Thomas' opinions with regard to play and recreation (he even approved drama as long as it was not offensive to his moral sense) helped to clear the way for the enjoyment of such plays as those presented at York, Wakefield, Coventry, Chester, etc. (CD)

2666. Dutka, JoAnna. "Mysteries, Minstrels, and Music." [F 114]:112-24.

Instrumental music in the English Mystery plays is noteworthy in that its presence is a departure from the tradition of sung drama. The texts and the account books pertinent to the plays' production reveal the diversity of instruments played. The actual music played must, however, be inferred from the dramatic context since none exists in the texts nor does any extant music of the period appear to have a connection with the plays. Where indications are given for it, instrumental music is revealed to have been essential in achieving the purposes of realism, symbolism, dramatic effect, and in the facilitating of stage business. (JD)

2668. Edwards, Robert. "Techniques of Transcendence in Medieval Drama." *CompD* 8:157-71.

The aim of transcendence in medieval drama forces one to reassess the structure of Aristotle's dramatic categories. Classical drama deals with human actions which can be repeated, but the medieval playwright has as his subjects the unique events of the Crucifixion and Resurrection. His works tend to reverse the structure of the six categories and give prominence to the element of spectacle. The dramatist complements imitation with mnemonics and builds his plays along the lines of musical structures,

reverie, and dreams. In the mystery cycles, the transcendence of the plays implies the deconstruction of human kinship systems. The bonds which link man to man are shown to be secondary and often antithetical to the bond of man and God. (RRE)

2671. Kahrl, Stanley J. "Teaching Medieval Drama as Theater." [F 49]:305-18.

The N-Town play of *The Assumption of the Virgin* is analyzed as an example of effective use of the place-and-scaffold theater in use in eastern England during the 15th and 16th centuries. The staging recreated is placed in Lincoln cathedral. Using such elaborate theatrical devices as a doll figure on wires, an ascending and descending cloud, and full funeral procession, together with music drawn from offices for the Virgin, the playwright has constructed an exciting theatrical spectacle. Movement between acting areas is always motivated by the action of the play, an action constructed around the prayer "Lord save me from the assaults of mine enemies." Set within a world of shrines and pilgrimages, the play is an example of excellent theater. (SJK)

2682. Theiner, Paul. "The Medieval Terence." [F 49]:231-47.

For medieval readers Terence was not a dramatist, but pre-eminently a moral philosopher, a commentator on human nature and human actions. In this capacity he is quoted by a wide variety of medieval writers from Augustine to Walter Burley. These writers mine his plays for their richness in sententious remarks, ignoring everything about the music of his verse. By the 14th century Terence had become a mere repository of such sententious sayings, and thus his contributions cannot always be distinguished from those provided by other sources of proverbial lore. (PFT)

Poetry. 2685. Bessinger, J.B.,Jr. "*The Gest of Robin Hood* Revisited." [F 49]:355-69.

The Gest of Robin Hood is a heroic ballad with affinities in genre and theme to English non-cyclic romances and with a curious structural resemblance to certain of the French prose romances. It has been overlooked by folklore science, Christian exegesis, and comparative heroic studies, although its folklore elements have been demonstrated. Its story is firmly rooted in popular and Latin Christian motifs, and its episodes, characterization, and use of sub-genres like praise and lament mark it as heroic. Nevertheless, its sequence of episodes, considered structurally, shows a reasonably well-articulated interlocking or interlace form, in the manner of earlier French prose romance. (JBB,Jr)

2686. Beston, John B. "How Much Was Known of the Breton Lai in Fourteenth-Century England?" [F 49]:319-36.

Some English lays in couplets are translations of French lais. The English lays in tail-rhyme stanzas deal, however, with the same material as the longer romances in tail-rhyme stanzas. Their authors must have known the English couplet lays, but need not have known any French lais. Information in the prologue to *Le Freine* and *Sir Orfeo* and the prologue to the Franklin's Tale show scant knowledge of the French lai, explaining why the English lay-writers did not create a genre comparable to the French. (JBB)

2690. Elliott, Thomas J. "Middle English Complaints Against the Times:To Contemn the World or to Reform It?" *AnM* 14(1973):22-34.

Poems from the late Middle Ages which lament social injustice have come to be recognized as a distinct genre or mode, but their relationship to *de contemptu mundi* writings has been distorted. Many complaints against the times suggest that action here and now, rather than the anodyne of an afterlife, is the answer. Some, especially those that are chiliastic or based on the myth of a Golden Age, are ambiguous, but others clearly argue for reform. Most are monologues; they grew from simple "songs" into complex dreams or debates with a narrative base. Complaint can be defined as a genre separate from satire. While *de contemptu mundi* writings may be an antecedent of complaint, there are two stages in its development as an independent form. (TJE)

2692. Hallwas, John E. " 'I Am Iesu, That Cum to Fith'." *Expl* 32:Item 51.

One of the finest lyrics in MS. Advocates 18.7.21 is "I am iesu, Þat cum to fith," which is an identification speech delivered by Christ the lover-knight after the battle of the crucifixion in which he asks to undertake a spiritual battle against sin on behalf of his beloved (the soul). During the course of the poem Christ gives his name, states his purpose, predicts victory, and asks for permission to undertake the fight. Therefore, his identification of himself as a knight who has come to engage in battle is not mere didacticism but is the esthetic basis for the poem. Moreover, the letters which begin lines 1, 3, 5, and 7 are an acrostic which spells IESV (Jesu), and so the very poem itself is emblazoned with a device to identify the speaker, the chivalric champion of the soul. (JEH)

2693. —— "The Identity of the Speaker in 'I am a fol, i can no god'." *PLL* 10:415-17.

When Furnivall edited the religious lyrics from MS. Harley 7322 for his volume of *Political, Religious, and Love Poems* in 1866 he included an 8-line lyric which he labeled as "Foolish Love," a translation of the Latin title in the manuscript, "Amor fatuus." The title is misleading, for the poem which begins, "I am a fol, i can no god," is a monologue by Satan, and reading it as such avoids the problems that develop when one attempts to understand it as a speech by Foolish Love. The opening line also contains puns that reveal meaning of which he is unaware, meaning that undercuts his boastful posture. The compiler of MS. 7322 probably misread the untitled poem and then gave it a label of his own: "Amor fatuus." But since this title has caused more misunderstanding than clarification, it ought to be discarded. (JEH)

2695. Hill, John M. "Middle English Poets and the Word: Notes Toward an Appraisal of Linguistic Consciousness." *Criticism* 16:153-67.

Several Middle English poems exhibit linguistic issues heretofore largely ignored: concern for precision in word and meaning; elaboration of the ways in which language—or the word—can fail us; manipulation of semantic distinctions in relation to various, usually privileged subjects. These issues lead to matters of reference and cognition, to the worlds we use language to apprehend. In *Pearl, Sir Gawein and the Green Knight, Piers Plowman*, and *Everyman* the common vehicle for such issues is a dramatic confrontation between mismatched sensibilities. Essentially, the poets concerned explore the vagaries of language use, especially in relation to figurative, private, or doctrinal utterance. The poets work with significant linguistic themes and so reveal a language consciousness not much registered in the critical literature. (JMH)

2703. Nelson, Alan H. "'Of the seuen ages':An Unknown Analogue of *The Castle of Perseverance*." [F 114]:125-38.

"Of the seuen ages," a previously unedited and virtually unknown poem in middle English (British Museum MS.37049, fols. 28ᵛ-29), bears several correspondences to *The Castle of Perseverance* and to other English morality plays. The poem, like the play, combines two morality topics: the Ages of Man, and the Debate between the Good Angel and the Evil Angel for the Soul of Man. This essay contains an edition of the poem, photographs of the illustrated manuscript pages, and a discussion of the relationships between the poem and the play. (AHN)

2704. Ogilvie-Thomson, S. "Some Unpublished Verses in Lambeth Palace MS. 559." *RES* 25:385-95.

The 15th-century Lambeth Palace MS. 559 contains an unpublished verse text of 197 prose lines which the *IMEV* (no. 2451) lists as a single work. It is described as a composite text, and the *Supplement* gives the various poems and, in three instances, manuscripts from which it suggests it has been compiled. Closer investigation indicates that this description is incorrect. The text consists of six separate verse items, which are textually independent of the manuscripts cited in the *IMEV*. One of these items is a hitherto unnoted lyric. The entire text is printed and discussed. Also printed, for the purpose of collation, are two unpublished lyrics from MS. Longleat 29. (SJO-T)

2710. Ridley, Florence H. "A Plea for the Middle Scots." [F 49]:175-96. [Henryson, Douglas, Dunbar.]

Henryson, Douglas, and Dunbar are indiscriminately lumped together as "Scots Chaucerians," as completely dependent upon Chaucer. Their poetry is found to be good when it successfully imitates his and bad when it does not, although evidence of their indebtedness is relatively slight. Henryson's *Testament of Cresseid* is a case in point. Long seen as a mere appendage of *Troilus and Criseyde*, it actually achieves its effect by means of contrast with rather than resemblance to Chaucer's poem. A detailed comparison between the settings, narrators, and heroines of the two makes it clear that Henryson develops in an unexpected way the outline of a static character and idea latent in *Troilus and Criseyde* to show the inevitable downward progression of one who rebels against God's will and violates the natural order of the universe. (FHR)

2712. Shannon, Ann. "The Meaning of *grein* in 'Winter Wakeneþ al my care'." *PQ* 53:425-27.

Line 11 of the Harley Lyric "Wynter wakeneþ al my care" presents problems of interpretation centering on the word *gre(i)n*, which is usually glossed as "seed." In light of the planting image and the theme of the transitoriness of life, however, a rarer homonym meaning "a cutting of a tree" gives a better reading. (AS)

2714. Turville-Petre, Thorlac. "'Summer Sunday,' 'De Tribus Regibus Mortuis,' and 'The Awntyrs off Arthure':Three Poems in the Thirteen-Line Stanza." *RES* 25:1-14.

Between the late 14th and the late 16th centuries a "school" of alliterative poets used a stanza of 13 lines, typically rhyming $abababab_4c_1dddc_2$. The stanza perhaps evolved from complicated stanzaic patterns such as those of the Harley Lyrics. Before 1400, examples of the stanza are found in the Vernon manuscript; later the stanza was used by dramatists and by Scottish poets. Three poems in this stanza—*Summer Sunday, De Tribus Regibus Mortuis*, and *The Awntyrs off Arthure*—show strong similarities in theme, for they have in common a description of a hunting scene to introduce a sombre vision of death. *Summer Sunday* describes a vision of Fortune's Wheel, *De Tribus Regibus Mortuis* retells the popular exemplum of "the Three Living and the Three Dead," while *The Awntyrs off Arthure* recounts the meeting of Guenevere and Gawain with the ghost of Guenevere's mother. In each case the function of the hunting preface is to illustrate the pleasure-seeking that is condemned by the subsequent vision. Verbal, metrical, and thematic similarities indicate that the three poems form a group. A list of works in the 13-line stanza is appended. (TTP)

Romances. 2718. Donovan, Mortimer J. "Middle English *Emare* and the Cloth Worthily Wrought." [F 49]:337-42.

Emare is called a Breton lay, but is set in the Mediterranean world far from Britain. Surprising also is the magic cloth described from lines 82 to 180. In his presentation of varieties of love in *Emare*, the resourceful author draws on the figure of a cloth richly embroidered with references to four pairs of lovers who animate and render magical the narrative. The cloth inspires the Emperor and the King, inspires Emare on her two voyages into exile, and functions as a character in the action. (MJD)

2721. Lee, Anne T. "*Le Bone Florence of Rome*:A Middle English Adaptation of a French Romance." [F 49]:343-54.

Le Bone Florence of Rome is a late 14th-century romance in Middle English tail-rhyme stanza. The author seems to have consciously altered the original with certain artistic considerations in mind. He has reduced the narrative from 6,000 to 2,000 lines, but in return he has provided more suspenseful plot development and more coherent dramatic focus. He has also omitted almost all reference to the supernatural which heightens the realistic atmosphere of his tale and renders his heroine more sympathetic by dramatizing her struggles on a human plane. Finally, the poet leaves out a great deal of lengthy and tedious religious material without, however, sacrificing the emphasis on the heroine as an exemplary figure. (ATL)

2723. Oberembt, Kenneth J. "Lord Berners' Translation of *Artus de la Petite Bretagne*." *M&H* 5:191-99.

A comparison of *Arthur of Lytell Brytayne*—a translation completed sometime after 1496 by Sir John Bourchier, second Lord Berners—with its French source *Artus de la Petite Bretagne*. Berners' method of translation is a continuation of the typical 15th-century procedure—to keep very close to the sentence and to the language of the original. However, Berners translated into formal style the colloquial style of communing of his source and by so doing created a substantive difference between *Arthur* and *Artus*. The pose struck by the English characters is obviously more impersonal than that of their French counterparts. More important, the non-representational characterization produced by Berners' stylistic adjustment of direct discourse helps transfer the allegiance of the Little Arthur story from the mimesis of the French original to allegoresis. Berners' change of style was probably the result of his intent to write the kind of courtly English prose advocated by William Caxton. (KJO)

Assembly of Ladies. 2734. Stephens, John. "The Questioning of Love in the *Assembly of Ladies.*" *RES* 24(1973):129-40.
To read the *Assembly of Ladies* as a vehicle for specific love complaints, and as an unsuccessful attempt to write allegorically, does the poem an injustice. It is rather a single, multifoliate complaint about love's nature and instability, built up through a mingling of naturalistic and symbolic forms within the conventional structures of dream, journey, and assembly. The autumn setting (a conventional image for middle age) and the maze frame (moralized previously in the *Ovide Moralisé* and by Boccaccio) are interlocking metaphors for a state of mind, impelling the narrator on a quest for self-knowledge. This is embodied in the operation of remembrance and the journey to Loyalty's assembly. The latter becomes a *rite de passage*, heralded by the symbolic change of clothing at the physical destination. The individual complaints made in the poem suggest that the quest's solution lies beyond the sphere of mutable love in a state of mind which completely abandons love. (JS)

Beves of Hampton. 2741. Baugh, Albert C. "The Making of *Beves of Hampton.*" [F 120]:15-37.
The Middle English romance *Beves of Hampton* survives in six manuscripts, and several others must be assumed if we are to explain the manuscript tradition. The source is an Anglo-Norman version, and the first English romance on the subject was a fairly faithful adaptation of the Anglo-Norman poem. The adaptation is known only from its descendants, but all the existing versions are derived from it. They reveal thousands of variants which traditionally have been attributed to errors of a copyist or considered mere scribal alterations. A careful consideration of these variants makes such an explanation unlikely. They can only be accounted for plausibly on the theory that the different redactions represent in each case a version as recited by a minstrel or *disour*, one who was reciting from memory and, where his memory failed him, resorted to improvisation. (ACB)

Blind Harry. 2742. Balaban, John. "Blind Harry and *The Wallace.*" *ChauR* 8:241-51.
The author of the 15th-century Scottish epic poem *The Wallace* is Blind Harry the Minstrel who describes himself as a simple "burel" man. Study of the 11,000-line poem reveals that he was neither blind nor simple, but that he had read Chaucer and other literature thoroughly. His name is probably an alias for someone at the Scottish court who flourished between 1470 and 1500. His alias leads back to Celtic mythology and to the kind of fantastical hero whom we see in his own portrayal of William Wallace in the latter's struggle against the English. Blind Harry blended Chaucerian literary conventions and folk myth to make a deliberately preposterous history which would make William Wallace seem to be of far greater significance in the struggle against the English than Wallace actually was. (JB)

Chester Cycle. 2747. Brockman, Bennett A. "Cain and Abel in the Chester *Creation*:Narrative Tradition and Dramatic Potential." *M&H* 5:169-82.
In the *Creation* the Chester playwright searched for an effective dramatic vehicle for a familiar story. The dramatist discovers the tragic potential latent in the plot by uniting its basic human meaning with doctrinal implications and emotional overtones derived from ecclesiastical interpretations and popular retellings of the biblical story. Moments within the episode are treated in ways suggested by the inherited tradition—usually successfully, but once to the detriment of the play's impact. The playwright's election of options within the tradition suggests that he carefully shaped the play and gave particular attention to its pathetic appeal. Cain's suffering and the suffering he causes form the play's irreducible center. (BAB)

2754. Travis, Peter W. "The Dramatic Strategies of Chester's Passion Pagina." *CompD* 8:275-89.
The dramatic strategies of the Passion sequence of the Chester cycle are unusual because they are controlled by a dramatic vision of Christ's mission that is substantially different from the visions of the other cycles. Chester unifies all the events of the Passion into a single, and relatively brief, play. The dramatic spectacle of Christ's Passion is made bearable by Chester's benevolent, quasi-ritualistic, manipulation of emotion; it is made intelligible by Christ's definition of transcendent truth; it is made religiously edifying by its Johannine Christology and by its insistence that the audience re-confirm its own belief in Christ's divinity. (PT)

Gesta Romanorum. 2771. Marchalonis, Shirley. "Medieval Symbols and the *Gesta Romanorum.*" *ChauR* 8:311-19.
The general discussion of the critical theories of D.W. Robertson,Jr. should give way to application of his theories to specific works of medieval literature. Close examination of the *Gesta Romanorum*, and especially its use of symbols, indicates clearly a lack of consistency that casts doubts on the universality of Robertson's theory of symbols. Rather the work suggests that symbols are used arbitrarily and often illogically to provide a superimposed didactic interpretation. (SM)

Gower. 2773. Farnham, Anthony E. "The Art of High Prosaic Seriousness:John Gower as Didactic Raconteur." [F 49]:161-73.
Examining the Prologue and the first tale of Book I of the *Confessio Amantis*, this article defines John Gower's moral concern and the characteristic manner of its expression in his last major work. The quality of humor which pervades the narrative style gives perspective to Gower's earlier didactic poetry. (AEF)

Henryson. 2786. Patterson, Lee W. "Christian and Pagan in *The Testament of Cresseid.*" *PQ* 52(1973):696-714.
While the leprosy inflicted upon Cresseid in Henryson's *The Testament of Cresseid* seems disproportionate to the blasphemy of which she is guilty, the actions of the gods must be understood as symptomatic of the defective relationship between Cresseid and her divinities: their simplistic concern with vengeance is consistent with her failure to understand her leprosy. However Henryson allows her to move from the objective pagan world of crime and punishment to the subjective Christian world of sin and repentance. Speaking in a genre that is both public and private, she faces the self she has become but evades understanding by assuming the static postures of abandoned maiden and cautionary example. In the confrontation with Troilus and with her guilt Cresseid completes the pattern, and the interrupted eloquence of her testament justifies the punishment inflicted upon her. (LP)

Hoccleve. 2788. Reeves, Albert C. "Thomas Hoccleve, Bureaucrat." *M&H* 5:201-14.
Thomas Hoccleve is customarily thought of as a poet of much less literary significance than his older contemporary Chaucer, but such a categorization, while true, obscures Hoccleve's poetry as a historical source. The comments Hoccleve made in his poems about himself and his occupation as a clerk of the Privy Seal are particularly revealing. Hoccleve's poetry and other records are used to construct a portrait of a functioning bureaucrat, his way of life, and his interests. Considerable attention is given to Hoccleve's political thought which is shown to be entirely moralistic rather than philosophical or analytical. (ACR)

James I of Scotland. 2789. Ebin, Lois A. "Boethius, Chaucer, and *The Kingis Quair.*" *PQ* 53:321-41.
The Kingis Quair is a direct response to, rather than an imitation of, Boethius' *Consolation of Philosophy* and Chaucer's *Troilus* and Knight's Tale. The *Quair* takes up questions about the workings of Fortune raised by Boethius and Chaucer, but answers them in terms quite different from those of its predecessors. As critics have not recognized, James makes several important changes in his sources. The effect of these changes is to reverse the

relationship between love and fortune found in earlier works and define a means by which man, while still involved in the world, can overcome Fortune. James demonstrates that man's full recognition of Fortune's role comes from all of the kinds of experience accessible to him—in life, in books, in dreams, and in writing. (LAE)

Little Sir Hugh. 2792. Bebbington, Brian. *"Little Sir Hugh*:An Analysis." *UES* 9,iii(1971):30-36.
In analyzing the symbols contained in the legend and ballad of the alleged murder of Hugh of Lincoln by the Jews, c. 1250, the writer is primarily concerned with various British and American versions of the ballad, and draws parallels with the symbols of religion, mythology, ritual, folklore, and literature. The divergence of the ballad from the legend is noted, chiefly in that (1) Hugh was perhaps murdered by his mother as a result of an incestuous relationship or because of his illegitimate birth, and (2) the ballad shows more affinity with the charge of *alilat dam* (the use of Christian blood in the making of matzoh) than with the killing in contempt of Christ which is the theme of the legend—this may be a later, more obviously anti-Semitic addition intended to increase the ballad's didactic value. (BB)

Ludus Coventriae. 2793. Mills, David. "Concerning a Stage Direction in the *Ludus Coventriæ*." *ELN* 11:162-64.
The *Ludus Coventriae* stage-direction after line 292 of "The Salutation and Conception" seems most intelligible if *bemys* is understood as "trumpet-blasts" and the Persons of the Trinity move forward to enter Mary's *bosom* or "embrace." (ADM)
2794. Poteet, Daniel P.,II. "Time, Eternity, and Dramatic Form in *Ludus Conventriae* 'Passion Play I'." *CompD* 8:369-85.
To the extent that *Ludus Coventriae* "Passion Play I" interprets a Christian universe, its esthetic principles derive from its theological milieu. An important aspect of this milieu—the distinction between time and eternity, and illusion and reality—is fundamental to the structure of "Passion I." Medieval timelessness is implicit in the play's conflation of history, its extended explication of the Last Supper, and its de-emphasis on causal action. These indications of timelessness suggest that traditional methods of analysis are misleading, and that approaches to the mystery plays via symbolic character and disjunctive form, and non-causal plot sequence, are desirable. (DPP,II)

Lydgate. 2796. Lampe, David. "Lydgate's Laughter:'Horse, Goose, and Sheep' as Social Satire." *AnM* 15:150-58.
John Lydgate's "Horse, Goose, and Sheep" uses the beast fable convention of speaking animals. Each animal in the poem represents a social estate shown arguing for its own absolute importance in a *parlement* before the highest secular authority. Instead of considering the "common profit," the prescribed concern of such meetings, each animal-estate presents evidence that to its own blindly proud understanding proves its claim of pre-eminence. Lydgate, the most rhetorical of English poets, has, however, established a double ethos, an ironic counter-argument based on the same evidence which undercuts these extravagant claims. (DEL)
2797. Miller, James I.,Jr. "Lydgate the Hagiographer as Literary Artist." [F 49]:279-90.
John Lydgate shows skill in artistic design and control throughout a section on miracles in his epic legend *St Edmund and St Fremund.* Selecting only seven miracles, he combines modification in content or context with patterns of balance in arrangement of phrase and word, even of syllable and letter. These patterns include: (1) recurrence of theme and proper name between miracles; (2) parallels in syntax, wording, and position among successive miracles, stanzas, or lines; and (3) elaborate, often extended varieties of common and otherwise reinforced rhyme. While Lydgate clearly uses the technique for emphasis and continuity, his primary concern was to produce a kind of harmony like that of musical refrain. (JIM,Jr)
2800. Walsh, Elizabeth,R.S.C.J. "John Lydgate and the Proverbial Tiger." [F 49]:291-303.
Surveys the tiger proverbs in Lydgate's works and in works relevant to his. The traditional legend of the tiger and its cubs which usually accompanies the description of the tiger in the bestiaries, although sometimes the nucleus of Lydgate's simile, is more often not mentioned by him. Lydgate did, however, make some distinction in his use of the tiger image. In poems concerning secular or pagan heroes the hero's behavior is often likened to that of a tiger. In poems concerning religious heroes and/or saints only the enemies of God are described as tiger-like. It is not evident why Lydgate used this beast imagery nor is it possible to deduce the source which impressed his imagination. (EW)

Malory. 2802. Gaines, Barry. "The Editions of Malory in the Early Nineteenth Century." *PBSA* 68:1-17.
Malory's *Le Morte d'Arthur* was published by Caxton in 1485 and reprinted five times by 1634. Both Scott and Southey contemplated editions of Malory early in the 19th century, but their plans were abandoned by 1811. In 1815, however, Southey was called on to supervise a reprint of Caxton's Malory for Longman and Company which appeared two years later. Southey's introduction was the first modern consideration of Malory and his sources. Yet before Southey's edition, two popular reprints of Malory were published in 1816, both modernizing the 1634 edition. Since Malory was not again reprinted until 1858, the pocket-sized modernizations of 1816 introduced King Arthur to generations of readers and the Southey edition presented scholarly volumes which were also influential although the text contained interpolations which went undetected for 50 years. (BG)
2805. Snyder, Robert L. "Malory and 'Historial' Adaptation." *ELWIU* 1:135-48.
When compared to its two recognized prototypes, the French prose romance *La Mort le Roi Artu* and the English stanzaic *Le Morte Arthur,* Malory's concluding tale of Arthur's death reveals a critical and independent understanding of history's "meaning." In adapting his source materials Malory carefully avoids traditional historiographic models which tend to schematize and reduce the complexity of temporal reality. Instead, he realigns the Arthuriad "historially" so as to emphasize the interpretive freedom with which man construes his experience in the world or saeculum. His own method of narrational revision thus mirrors perfectly his thematic concern with the process by which a human collective succeeds or fails in achieving historical self-consciousness. The result is a uniquely "original" narrative that both demythologizes the past and yet preserves its essential features as an organon of self-knowledge. As practiced by Malory, therefore, literary adaptation typifies exegesis of a very special sort. (RLS)
2808. Whitteridge, Gweneth. "The Identity of Sir Thomas Malory." *RES* 24(1973):257-65.
The identification of Sir Thomas Malory of Newbold Revel with the felon Sir Thomas Malory of Fenny Newbold is based on invalid arguments. The assumption that in the fifteenth century Fenny Newbold and Newbold Revel were merely alternative names for the same place is incorrect. The territorial appellation of Newbold Revel is given only to Sir Thomas Malory and the Lady Elizabeth, his wife, whereas that of Fenny Newbold is commonly used for a number of different people. The distinction in the terms of the two pardons given to Sir Thomas Malory of Fenny Newbold and to Sir Thomas Malory of Newbold Revel suggests that there were two Sir Thomas Malorys. There is some evidence to show that Sir Thomas Malory of Fenny Newbold was a Yorkist adherent, and much evidence to prove that Sir Thomas Malory of Newbold Revel was a Lancastrian supporter. (GGW)

Mankind. 2812. Clopper, Lawrence M. "*Mankind* and Its Audience." *CompD* 8:347-55.
The attribution of *Mankind* to popular rather than private auspices has been made in the belief the play was performed by a professional troupe before a crowd of provincials gathered in an innyard. The text suggests the play was performed indoors, and this calls into question the play's auspices and the criteria used to establish the audience of early plays. The play may be in the humanistic tradition and was intended for a literate audience. Determination of the play's audience, however, is ultimately less important than ridding the play of its pejorative label. The play is not an inept intermingling of comic and serious matter nor one in

which the comedic figures overwhelm the more serious character, Mercy; instead, it is a witty social satire integrated with a moving moral statement. (LMC)

Pearl. 2834. Peterson, Clifford J. "*Pearl* and *St. Erkenwald*: Some Evidence for Authorship." *RES* 25:49-53.
An attempt to confirm the authorship of *Pearl* and *St. Erkenwald*. The manuscript containing *St. Erkenwald* includes marginal inscriptions referring to "Thomas Masse." Anagrams based on letters of alliteration from lines of both poems, sorted out, spell "I. Masse." The same lines produce the identical anagrammatic signature in *Pearl* and *St. Erkenwald*. Both poems were written by the same author, who appears to have been a member of the extensive Massey family of Cheshire and Southern Lancashire, England. (LLBA)
2835. Sklute, Larry M. "Expectation and Fulfillment in *Pearl*." *PQ* 52(1973):663-79.
In *Pearl* the dreamer is only partially helpful in leading us through his vision because of his frustration. He understands little of what he is experiencing, whereas we understand much. We feel superior to him, for we understand the meaning of the symbolic landscape, the standard medieval theology that the maiden preaches, the poet's use of the term "courtesy" for "grace," and the celebration of innocents in the New Jerusalem. Yet we sympathize with the dreamer because we recognize in him the willfulness of the human condition and its attendant confusions in the face of divine absolutes. The dreamer's point of view, his degree of understanding, and the attitudes he displays are analyzed and contrasted with our own. (LMS)

Pearl-Poet. 2836. Peterson, Clifford J. "The *Pearl*-Poet and John Massey of Cotton, Cheshire." *RES* 25:257-66.
Studies of the *Pearl* and *St. Erkenwald*, and of a minor poem by Thomas Hoccleve, have led toward the possibility that a man named "John Massey" may have been the poet of the *Pearl* (a "maister Massy" was known to Hoccleve as a poet of great talent). In order to qualify for identification as the *Pearl* -poet, any historical John Massey (and there were many) must fit certain criteria implied by the evidence presented so far. A study of documents in the Public Record Office shows that there was a man named John Massey who fit all the criteria. He is the only man discovered so far who does so. In addition, certain other factors support the hypothesis that John Massey of Cotton was the poet of the poems in question. There is, for example, striking support for the identification in an independent study of the dialect of *St. Erkenwald*. (CJP)

Perceval of Galles. 2836a. Eckhardt, Caroline D. "Arthurian Comedy: The Simpleton-Hero in *Sir Perceval of Galles*." *ChauR* 8:205-20.
This anonymous 14th-century English romance belongs to a group of medieval poems which begin with a young hero characterized as a simpleton and include common incidents. It differs from the analogues in perpetuating the hero's simpleton characterization throughout and in relieving this naiveté of any negative moral implication by showing that it is harmless and actually helps the boy subdue King Arthur's enemies. The poem presents the career of a comic country bumpkin who overwhelms all adversaries, marries a queen, and becomes a king, all without wholly surrendering his initial rusticity. Economy of characters and incidents in the poem reinforces the impression that the author was a capable writer who exploited the potential comedy of the traditional situation which set a simpleton-hero into a chivalric context. (CDE)

Piers Plowman. 2840. Demedis, Pandelis. "*Piers Plowman*, Prologue B. 196." *Expl* 33:Item 27.
Editors have had difficulty interpreting line 196 in Prologue B of *Piers Plowman* because of the traditional definitions assigned to *mase* and *schrewe*. By re-examining their derivations the line is readily interpreted, enhancing the political satire of the belling-of-the-cat episode. (PD)
2844. Harwood, Britton J. "*Liberum-Arbitrium* in the C-Text of *Piers Plowman*." *PQ* 52(1973):680-95.

Liberum-arbitrium—a separate mental faculty constituted by reason and will, the act of which is choice—is a universal power of the soul only because its act, choice, elicits from the other powers their own activity. In *Piers Plowman*, *Liberum-arbitrium* describes himself as the result of conversion, specifically recognizing and choosing Christ as the source of all value and making the various loving choices entailed by this. Although *Liberum-arbitrium* merely assumes the existence of the knowledge (*liberum-consilium*—the vision of God) which makes *liberum-arbitrium* free, Will responds to *Liberum-arbitrium*'s description of charitable acts by doubting whether a charitable man can be found. The three props of the Tree of Charity represent the mental powers—volition, knowledge, choice—which *Liberum-arbit rium* as a universal power presumably deploys in making a loving choice; but his uselessness to unregenerate man is shown when the fruit of charity cannot abide the test of death: *Nemo bonus*. The poem moves from the frustrated stewardship of *Liberum-arbitrium* to the suppositum for the liberty of *Liberum-arbitrium*—the knowledge of the suffering Christ. (BJH)
2847. Schweitzer, Edward C. " 'Half a Laumpe Lyne in Latyne' and Patience's Riddle in *Piers Plowman*." *JEGP* 73:313-27.
The final allusion to the paschal moon points to the perspective from which Langland's riddling definition of Dowel can be solved. The grammatical tag "ex vi transicionis" is another punning reference to Christ's passage from the world to the Father at Easter and to its sacramental re-enactment in baptism, for *transitio* is a cognate synonym for *transitus*, the regular gloss to *pascha* (Passover, Easter). "Half a lamp line in Latin" refers to the injunctions with which the priest presents to the newly baptized a lighted candle. "The Saturday that set first the calendar" is the Passover. Its sign is the sign of the cross marked on the forehead of the baptized at confirmation prefigured in the blood of the paschal lamb smeared on the doorposts of the Hebrews' houses and symbolizing the full gift of the Spirit which makes possible a life of active virtue in the world. "The wit of the Wednesday of the next week after" is the theme of the mass for Wednesday of Easter Week. Once understood, the riddle proclaims the obligation to love placed upon every Christian at baptism as the only means to salvation and the gift of the Spirit which makes that love possible. (ECS)
2849. Trower, Katherine B. "Elizabeth D. Kirk's *The Dream Thought of Piers Plowman*." *Costerus* N.S. 1:151-64. [Rev. art.]
Elizabeth D. Kirk's *The Dream Thought of Piers Plowman* is provocative, but suffers from fundamental flaws. Her thesis is that the poem's dramatic structure is an enactment of the supervening of man's autonomy by God's omnipotence, and that this conflict is resolved by man's submission to the divine will. Piers's actions thus exemplify the submissive role all Christians must play in salvation history, as Piers occupies the center of the poem. Lapses in Kirk's study occur in insufficient usage of medieval theological traditions and of critical materials, as well as in errors of documentation and textual citation. (KBT)

Purity. 2852. Foley, Michael M. "A Bibliography of *Purity* (*Cleanness*), 1864-1972." *ChauR* 8:324-34.
A brief introduction and partially annotated bibliography of both published and unpublished items. (MMF)

Reynard the Fox. 2853. Sands, Donald B. "Reynard the Fox and the Manipulation of the Popular Proverb." [F 49]:265-78.
The Middle Dutch poem *Reinaerts Historie* of circa 1375 is, from the point of view of narrative technique, inferior to its source, *Van den vos Reinaerde*, written some 100 years before. The later poem, however, in its satiric thrust is far more subtle than the earlier, chiefly through its utilization of popular proverbs. These are consistently in the mouths of scoundrels and hypocrites and their "truth" utilized to bolster dishonest argument. The internal audience is duped by proverbial "truth"; the external audience witnesses the technique and its effectiveness and may well come to assume certain unpopular attitudes toward popularly accepted proverbial "truth"—that a display of it is a cue that its user has dishonest motives. (DBS)

Romaunt of the Rose. 2853a. Caie, Graham D. "An Iconographic Detail in the *Roman de la Rose* and the Middle English *Romaunt*." *ChauR* 8:320-23.

The iconographic detail of Amant's sleeve-basting at the beginning of the *Roman de la Rose* signifies that Amant was deliberately in search of the God of Love and *fol amour* and that he did not come upon the Garden by chance. There is evidence both intrinsic to the poem and in patristic writings which explains the significance of sewing one's sleeves, a gesture which both author and medieval illustrators of the poem took great pains to describe in detail. Throughout the poem both Guillaume de Lorris and Jean de Meun describe well-sewn sleeves as a mark of those lecherous characters who have given themselves up to *fol amour* and are servants of the God of Love, who specifically demands that his servants have carefully stitched sleeves. In Scripture and in St. Jerome's writings there is evidence to show that the iconographic action of sewing one's sleeves signifies the deliberate preparation of a vain, worldly garment after the rejection of the seamless coat, symbol of purity and of the Passion. (GDC)

Seven Sages of Rome. 2855. Runte, Hans R. "A Forgotten Old French Version of the Old Man of the Mountain." *Speculum* 49:542-45.

The Florence MS. Medicea-Laurenziana, Ashburnham 52 of ca. 1300 contains, within the framework of the *Histoire de la male marastre*, an account of "The Old Man of the Mountain" in which the two heretofore separate constituting motifs of the legend, the paradisiacal garden and the underground education, are combined for the first time. While the motif of underground education goes back to antiquity, its combination with the garden motif in the *Histoire* most certainly precedes all other examples presently known. (HRR)

Sir Gawain and the Green Knight. 2863. Leighton, John M. "Christian and Pagan Symbolism and Ritual in *Sir Gawain and the Green Knight*." *Theoria* 43:49-62.

Sir Gawain and the Green Knight should be interpreted as a test of Arthurian Christian values. Green is the ecclesiastical color of Epiphany, and the Christmas revels end on this day of manifestation. Testing of God's servants is as common in the Bible as testing of champions in medieval folklore. The knight's color may be seen as symbolic of the reward for those who uphold Christian values. (JML)

2867. Wright, Thomas L. "Sir Gawain *in vayres*." *PQ* 53:427-28.

In *Sir Gawain and the Green Knight* the poet's term "in vayres" in the bob of his stanza at line 1015 is an allusion to the vair pattern in heraldry. The vair design is a field of interlocked, repeated figures, and it serves here as an emblem of Gawain's condition as both captive and guest in Bertilak's court. (TLW)

St. Erkenwald. 2872. Peck, Russell A. "Number Structure in *St. Erkenwald*." *AnM* 14(1973):9-21.

St. Erkenwald is composed in exact balances and antitheses (cf. McAlindon, *SP*, 1970), and the intricate measures of its structure support its themes through conventional number symbolism. The significance of the number 8 in the structure of the poem is discussed. (RAP)

Tale of Gamelyn. 2873. Ruthof, Horst G. "The Dialectic of Aggression and Reconciliation in the *Tale of Gamelyn*, Thomas Lodge's *Rosalynde*, and Shakespeare's *As You Like It*." *UCTSE* 4(1973):1-15.

A dialectic of situations is employed to compare structure and ideas of the *Tale of Gamelyn*, Thomas Lodge's *Rosalynde*, and Shakespeare's *As You Like It*. In the *Tale* the violent opposition between Gamelyn and Iohan is raised to a legal conflict when Iohan is made sheriff and Gamelyn an outlaw. But the violence is transcended by a conscious emphasis on social background, a sense of suppression, aggression, and hope. Lodge's attempt to combine the Gamelyn action with a romance forms discrepancies resulting in a recurrent bathos. Although the elements of the pastoral outweigh the source material, Lodge fails to create a tight

interrelationship between the two. In *AYL* violent event is replaced largely by a game of attitudes, a change supported by the extended pun on "fall" and "overthrown." *AYL* is the playful objectification of the reconciliation of antagonisms; its interplay of the dialectic of aggression and its mock equivalent, the love pattern, reveal the central idea. An Appendix charts the substitution of the dialectic of love for that of aggression. (HGR)

Thomas of Erceldoune. 2874. Goedhals, Barrie J. "The Romance and Prophecies of *Thomas of Erceldoune*." *UES* 10,ii(1972):1-10.

Certain historical aspects of Thomas of Erceldoune are examined briefly in order to place in perspective the legendary figure of "trewe Thomas" and the poet himself. The emphasis is on a critical examination of the medieval romance convention, as well as the elements of legend and folklore contained in the poem. As a result of this emphasis discussion of the poem is mainly concerned with the first fitt. The remaining two fitts, which contain the actual prophecies of Thomas' Elf-Queen lover, are referred to only when they throw light on literary issues. Examination of the ballad of *Thomas Rymer* shows how it is clearly derived from the older romance. At the same time the ballad contains evidence of the selectivity peculiar to the oral tradition of balladry and the popular idiom. (BJG)

Towneley Cycle. 2880. Tyson, Cynthia H. "Noah's Flood, the River Jordan, the Red Sea:Staging in the Towneley Cycle." [F 114]:101-11.

Four plays of the Towneley Cycle—*Processus Noe cum filiis*, *Iacob*, *Pharao*, and *Iohannes baptista*—make use of water as a staging property. Studies of parallel situations in other medieval plays show that the water may be actual water or stretches of cloth. After examination of the texts of the four Towneley plays and with attention to staging effects the playwright has written into those texts, Towneley production seems clearly to require the use of real water. Thus a further indication is provided that production of the entire cycle is stationary rather than processional since it seems likely that a playing area complete with water would be provided at no more than one site in medieval Wakefield. (CHT)

Wakefield Cycle. 2886. Brockman, Bennett A. "The Law of Man and the Peace of God:Judicial Process as Satiric Theme in the Wakefield *Mactacio Abel*." *Speculum* 49:699-707.

The artistic integrity of the rowdy humor in *Mactacio Abel* is suggested by its using allusions to familiar elements of law and judicial process to enhance both comic impact and serious statement. Legal and historical records show that the audience would perceive allusions to the king's peace, the royal letter patent of protection, the royal pardon, and the privilege of sanctuary, the latter two widely resented as abuses of due process. These allusions satirize the administration of justice and denounce that society for ignoring its proper foundation. (BAB)

Wisdom. 2892. Gatch, Milton McC. "Mysticism and Satire in the Morality of *Wisdom*." *PQ* 53:342-62.

Wisdom is not simply based in large part on mystical writings; it is also informed by late-medieval mysticism in its development of character and plot. It is directed to an audience of laymen to whom it commends the *vita mixta*. Finally, its gentle but conventional satire is directed to the legal profession in London. The play as a whole puts one in mind of the distinctive characteristics of early English humanism and may be regarded as a forerunner of the dramas performed in the Morton-More circle. (MMcCG)

York Cycle. 2893. Davidson, Clifford. "Civic Concern and Iconography in the York Passion." *AnM* 15:125-49.

Additions to the York cycle of mystery plays by the York Realist include several plays on the Passion. The work of the Realist in these plays is infused with the civic piety prevalent in early 15th-century York. The iconographic features of earlier medieval representations of the Passion story are not rejected in these plays by the York Realist, but some new elements are present. Like the other arts (e.g., glass painting), drama in York turned to a realism designed to produce an emotional response in those who look upon it. Thus when plays XXVIII-XXXIII in the York cycle are subjected to analysis, they are proven to be at once traditional in their use of the received elements of iconography while at the same time they underline Christ's suffering in such a way that members of the audience will feel what the Savior endured between his arrest and his death on the cross. (CD)

Chaucer

General and Miscellaneous. 2909. Brookhouse, Christopher. "In Search of Chaucer:The Needed Narrative." [F 49]:67-80. The article concentrates on Chaucer's development as an artist—beginning with the early Chaucer as outsider, as watcher, as listener and working toward a later Chaucer who finds in art a way to disclose, interpret, and discover as well as make moral judgments which deeply involve the artist. The article treats Chaucer as the first English writer to produce a corpus of "signed" work and attempts to understand Chaucer's encounter with art—his love of language and form, his suspicion of language and form, and the final, compulsive need of several Canterbury pilgrims, including Chaucer himself, to reveal and speak about their lives. (CB)

2910. David, Alfred. "How Marcia Lost Her Skin:A Note on Chaucer's Mythology." [F 49]:19-29.
The source for Chaucer's allusion to the contest between Marsyas and Apollo in the *House of Fame* (1229-32) and for his mistaken idea that Marsyas was female is an interpolation in Jean de Meun's portion of the *Roman de la Rose* which exists in many manuscripts. In one branch of manuscripts, a scribe, experiencing difficulty with the interpolator's word for "satyr," began a series of textual changes that led to the metamorphosis of Marsyas into a female. A manuscript belonging to this group best accounts for Chaucer's error although it may well have been confirmed by the form "Marsia" occurring in the *Paradiso* and *Teseida*. The mistake carried over from the French source makes it doubtful that Chaucer learned the story from Ovid or any of the mythographic treatises or commentaries that have been considered important glosses on Chaucer's use of mythology. (AD)

2917. Garbáty, Thomas J. "The Degradation of Chaucer's 'Geffrey'." *PMLA* 89:97-104.
The narrator in Chaucer's poetry develops stylistically as he declines intellectually from the dream vision poems to the *Canterbury Tales* (1369-87). In the early works he represents a type we know in legal terms as the "reasonable man" who personifies the social-moral norms of society in an unemotional, unintellectual, and unimaginative fashion. This character "Geffrey" seems dull-witted and absurd only in contrast to the unusual situations or irrational and autocratic individuals he confronts. His "reasonable" perception is on a lower, second level to their sophisticated first. In the *Canterbury Tales*, the pilgrim "Chaucer" drops to the lowest, or third, level; he is an uncomprehending caricature who "agrees" with the first-level ironist, but who misunderstands his irony. Herry Bailly usually acts the part of the prosaic "reasonable man," but the poet raises the reader-listener to his own highest (first) level of perception. Thus Chaucer's degradation of his own pose brings about a progressive and significant intensification of his humor. (TJG)

2921. Lenaghan, R.T. "The Clerk of Venus:Chaucer and Medieval Romance." [F 49]:31-43.
Romances gave Chaucer a narrative role as a clerk in which he could accept various literary and cultural offices. The narrative interest of The Squire's Tale is in grandeur and in the sense of ethical exaltation implied by Canacee's sympathy with the falcon's love-grief. The Franklin's response is to infer the Squire's ethical merit from the rhetorical evidence and to frame a dialectical question on the commonplace topics, gentilesse and clerks against knights. The history of the two topics suggests that the literary-cultural roles of student, moralist, love-poet combined in the clerk and made him as *gentil* as the knight. Internal difficulties and the consequent dramatic complexity make The Squire's Tale and The Franklin's Tale less effective than The Knight's Tale and *Troilus and Criseyde* as exemplary Chaucerian

romances. Yet the lapses and discrepancies in even these poems show stress in that double authority. This literary complexity corresponds with a social complexity in the clerk's role in the court or household society. (RTL)

2922. Leyerle, John. "The Heart and the Chain." [F 49]:113-45. [Imagery in C.]
Several of Chaucer's poems have as a poetic nucleus either the heart or the chain. As such, the heart represents both love and its mutability; the chain represents both order and its confinement. The term nucleus is taken to mean both seed, implying origin and growth, and center, implying a surrounding structure. Chaucer's poetic use of the heart and the chain belongs to a tradition long established before him, seen, for example, in two of his principal sources, *The Romance of the Rose* and *The Consolation of Philosophy*. (JL)

2930. Reinecke, George F. "Speculation, Intention, and the Teaching of Chaucer." [F 49]:81-93.
Speculation and intentional conjecture are more important to the Chaucer scholar as teacher than as publishing critic. Seven cruxes in the *The Canterbury Tales* are examined as to conjectural interpretation in lectures. (GFR)

2931. Reiss, Edmund. "Chaucer's Courtly Love." [F 49]:95-111.
Chaucer presents love in detail and with apparent seriousness only in the *Book of the Duchess, Troilus and Criseyde*, and the Knight's Tale. In these three poems he is concerned with what we have come to call courtly love. But although the love-longing felt by the main characters in these works cannot be immediately dismissed as foolish, the love itself is ultimately to be seen as having dubious value. Love is finally for Chaucer the main ingredient in the human comedy. It may seem for a while to be something worthy and noble, but finally its inadequacies will be discernible, and it will appear at best laughable and at worst destructive. Even these three poems, where love seems noble and good, reveal the ultimate folly and destructiveness of courtly love. (ER)

2936. Utley, Francis L. "Boccaccio, Chaucer and the International Popular Tale." *WF* 33:181-201.
Attempts to bring together some of the more solid results of medieval literary study and modern techniques of folktale investigation, with illustrations from Chaucer and Boccaccio. The application of rich modern oral material as a tentative springboard for the study of the creative process in medieval literature raises theoretical problems. For Chaucer, Irish versions of Tale Type 1423 in which the supernatural interveners are Christ and the Virgin instead of Chaucer's Pluto and Proserpine are studied. For the Friar's Tale (Type 11186), another Irish version, Chaucer's conversion of the tale into an exemplum of Christian repentance is shown. For Boccaccio, an ancient exemplum, The Boy Who Had Never Seen Women (Type 1678), in the poem to the 4th book of the *Decameron* has been transformed from an exemplum on the dangers of concupiscence into a mock-exemplum on the natural aspects of desire. (FLU)

Book of the Duchess. 2943. Brosnahan, Leger. "Now (This), Now (That) and *BD* 646." [F 49]:11-18.
Translators seem uncertain of both the meaning and reference of "Now by the fire, now at table," l. 646 of Chaucer's *Book of the Duchess*, and its apparently sole critic finds the line uninspired and seeming to serve only to complete the couplet. Translator and critic alike fail to recognize the line as a proverb, or doubt the grammatical reference or intended image of the line, or some combination of these. When l. 646 is read as a "drastic" literary extension of the common proverb "Now (This) Now (That)," it becomes perfectly appropriate in its context although its content remains unusual and the precise image it conjures remains arguable. (LB)

2947. Lackey, Allen D. "Chaucer's *Book of the Duchess*, 330." *Expl* 32:Item 74.
Chaucer's allusion to Jason and Medea in line 330 of *The Book of the Duchess* is no anomaly. Consideration of Chaucer's use of the Jason-Medea myth elsewhere reveals that here he is sacrificing factual accuracy to create an image of wronged love. This image functions as a part of the natural structural movement away from

reality into a dream world where Chaucer can deal with his patron's grief without offense. It calls to the mind a sublimal perception of a point later stated explicitly—that the knight whose wife has died is more fortunate in having had a love fulfilled than in having had one betrayed. By thus preparing the reader for the later cathartic revelation, it serves an artistic purpose that negates any charge of factual inaccuracy. (ADL)

2948. Palmer, John H. "The Historical Context of the *Book of the Duchess*: A Revision." *ChauR* 8:253-61.
New light is thrown upon the date and meaning of the *Book of the Duchess* by a letter from the count of Flanders (1346-84) to Queen Philippa of England (d. 1369). The letter is concerned with a second marriage for John of Gaunt, whose first wife, Blanche of Lancaster—the subject of the *Book of the Duchess*—is believed to have died on 12 September 1369. Since this letter was written nine months previously, the accepted date of Blanche's death must be wrong. Blanche died on 12 Sept. 1368, and the *Book of the Duchess* may have been begun a year earlier than hitherto believed possible. Since John of Gaunt was planning to remarry by November of that year, the poem was probably completed before that date, since it would otherwise have been interpreted as a satire on the constancy of Gaunt's love. This means that Chaucer's famous allusion to his eight year sickness can no longer be interpreted as either a reference to his hopeless love for the wife of the Black Prince, or as a reference to his prolonged mourning for the wife of John of Gaunt. (JHP)

Canterbury Tales. 2949. Amoils, E.R. "Fruitfulness and Sterility in the *Physician's* and *Pardoner's Tales*." *ESA* 17:17-37.
The Pardoner's and Physician's Tales are linked by the theme of spiritual fertility and sterility and the defeat of death. The Pardoner, a eunuch in both physical and spiritual senses, contrasts with Virginia, the chaste heroine of the Physician's Tale. Chaucer's source in the *Roman de la Rose* indicates that Virginia's virtue is the spiritual fertility through which death may be vanquished. The link passage between the Tales plays upon the ideas of physical and spiritual virility and defeat of death. Both Pardoner and Physician should preserve life, but their principal interest is the multiplying of their gold. (ERA)

2951. Axelrod, Steven. "The Wife of Bath and the Clerk." *AnM* 15:109-24.
Critics have generally believed that the Clerk and the Wife of Bath are engaged in a fiercely antagonistic debate in *The Canterbury Tales*. A close reading of the text, however, demonstrates that they are engaged in incipient courtship rather than hostile competition, and that the tone of their relationship is essentially comic rather than melodramatic. Such a courtship justifies the sexual and regenerative motifs introduced at the outset of the *Tales*. The Wife's taunting remarks about clerks are merely witty banter, aimed at amusing and attracting the Clerk. The Clerk's Tale and Envoy are his playful rejoinder. (SGA)

2952. Beichner, Paul E.,C.S.C. "Confrontation, Contempt of Court, and Chaucer's Cecilia." *ChauR* 8:198-204.
In the trial scene in the legend of St. Cecilia she confronts the establishment, argues with the judge, insults him, makes him "lose his cool," and wins for herself more than a symbolic victory—real martyrdom. Chaucer improved upon his source by omitting questions and answers which in the Latin prose are repetitious, weaken the intensity of the verbal contest and delay the climax. What remained he translated in such a way as to intensify the clash between Almachius and Cecilia, creating for each a personality more Chaucerian than traditional; Cecilia had never before been quite so contentious or belligerent, nor had Almachius been so obtuse or stupid. (PEB)

2954. Biggins, Dennis. "Chaucer's 'Wife of Bath's Prologue,' D.608." *Expl* 32:Item 44.
The Wife of Bath's puzzling use of the term *quoniam* in Chaucer's Wife of Bath's Prologue (D.608) as a euphemism for her pudendum may be explained, partly at least, on stylistic grounds. Her earlier use of the French phrase *bele chose* (D.447, 510) appears to be an elegant variation of *queynte* (D.332, 444). In her next mention of her pudendum, at D.608, she uses not *queynte* again, as we might expect, but the metrically equivalent *quoniam*. Here we must consider Chaucer's poetry as oral art. The

substitution of *quoniam* for the expected *queynte* produces a kind of "double-take" effect. The use of *quoniam* for *queynte* invites us to look for meaning beyond the area of mere euphemism. There may also be a learned pun on *quoniam/cunnum* (Latin *cunnus*, 'pudendum'). (DB)

2956. Bleeth, Kenneth A. "The Image of Paradise in the *Merchant's Tale*." [F 49]:45-60.
Though the source of the final scene in the Merchant's Tale is a popular folk narrative, Chaucer provides a framework for the fabliau plot which brings into relief its latent religious elements. January's view of marriage as an earthly paradise echoes a Christian commonplace, but his use of this image is discredited by his own self-gratifying motives, by the narrator's ironic allusions, and by Justinus' characterization of wedlock as "purgatory." The true nature of January's union is exposed most clearly when he builds a garden which becomes the scene for a burlesque re-enactment of the Fall. The garden's topography reveals it to be a carnal analogue of Eden, and the activities within the pleasance recall the tropological reading of Genesis. January's allusion to the *hortus conclusus* of Canticles provides a further dimension of reference for the garden. Traditionally associated with the inviolate chastity of the Blessed Virgin, the enclosed garden here embodies January's fantasy of May's spotless purity. The pattern of Edenic references, however, shows May's true connection to be with the figure of Eve. (KAB)

2958. Bowker, Alvin W. "Comic Illusion and Dark Reality in *The Miller's Tale*." *MLS* 4,ii:27-34.
Illusion and reality combine in The Miller's Tale to comment on the effects of human weaknesses and to reveal a dark spirit beneath action too often construed as solely comic. An initial ebullience changes to the dark action of life in Oxenford's streets where, with John's fall from the eaves, man's cruelty becomes unalterably clear. By examining illusion and reality in The Miller's Tale, we may conclude that Chaucer found the fabliau a convenient genre for commenting on the serious and the comic in life. (AWB)

2960. Bugge, John. "Damyan's Wanton *Clyket* and an Ironic New *Twiste* to the *Merchant's Tale*." *AnM* 14(1973):53-62.
The tone of Chaucer's Merchant's Tale is offensive in part because of the narrator's specious delicacy concerning sexual matters. The number of phallic allusions he makes through imagery and the use of double entendre suggests a prurient interest in the business of sexual potency, the core of the winter-spring marriage joke. Two more instances of wordplay prove to be similarly coarse. One of them, the "clyket-wiket" combination, derives additional ironic significance through the Merchant's irreverent parody of the Song of Songs. The two puns, taken together, make the tale both wittier and dirtier. (JMB)

2966. Cullen, Dolores L. "Chaucer's *The Tale of Sir Thopas*." *Expl* 32:Item 35.
Chaucer's Host objects to the Tale of Sir Thopas on the grounds that it is "drasty." To understand "drasty" as anything less than "filthy" seems to miss Harry's point. The "lewednesse" of the tale comes to the fore by demonstrating one relationship between Sir Thopas' name and a medieval charm, and another between Sir Olifaunt's name and an affliction of the genitalia. With these identities in focus, the many sexual references throughout the story are clearly seen and Harry's objection is better understood. (DLC)

2970. Delasanta, Rodney. "Sacrament and Sacrifice in the *Pardoner's Tale*." *AnM* 14(1973):43-52.
Recent interpretations of the Pardoner's Tale have stressed Chaucer's parody of the Mass as a thematic value: e.g., in drinking the poisoned wine the rioters find eternal death instead of eternal life. Such a view is obviously valid, but incomplete, because it overlooks the commonplace medieval notion of the Mass as Sacrifice as well as Sacrament. An examination of the language of the Mass according to the Sarum Rite reveals the recurrent use of the word "sacrificium" and prepares us for its ritualistic implications in the Pardoner's Tale. The conjunction of death and the meal, after all, is where the tale leads us, as the two older rioters first slay and then celebrate the death of their victim, who in a parodic offertory has brought them food and drink of their own eternal death. The trio is parodic of the Trinity, for after

swearing fellowship in the name of unity they send the youngest (the Son) as a sacrificial victim on an errand (parodic of the Divine Mission) to fetch the "eucharistic" food. His death occasions his fellows' deaths via a prandial sacrifice which parodies the Priest-Victim paradox of the Mass. (RKD)

2972. Engelhardt, George J. "The Lay Pilgrims of the *Canterbury Tales*:A Study in Ethology." *MS* 36:278-330.
The General Prologue of the *Canterbury Tales* is an ethologue that reflects the medieval mixed congregation of elect and reprobate, good and bad, homines spirituales and homines animales—those perfect in ethos and those defective in ethos. This ethologue, which implies the dual vision of this world expressed in the complementary medieval traditions of the dignity of man and the contemptus mundi, is in turn implemented by the individual tales of the Canterbury sequence. The Prologue, furthermore, introduces paramythically the ethos of the poet, which is in turn implemented by the tales ascribed to Chaucer the pilgrim: the Man of Law's Tale, the Manciple's Tale, and the Retraction. (GJE)

2976. Gaylord, Alan T. "The Role of Saturn in the *Knight's Tale*." *ChauR* 8:172-90.
The role of Saturn has usually been interpreted as a bar to the romantic idealism attributed to the Knight's Tale. Saturn, Chaucer's addition to his sources, can be explained in terms of Chaucer's humanism and good humor. Contrary to most established criticism, Saturn should not be taken as a centrally important force of disorder, or a disquieting illustration of arbitrary fate, but should be seen as a star and interpreted within the traditional scheme of moralized astrology that Chaucer knew. He is a metaphorical elaboration of the unfortunate aspects of Venus and Mars, brilliantly exposed in the "oratories" which Theseus designs to express the condition of the contentious and lovesick young knights. Saturn is neither the thematic key nor the structural pivot of the poem, but an astrological adjunct to Boethian themes of providence, destiny, free will, and love. (ATG)

2978. Gellrich, Jesse M. "The Parody of Medieval Music in the *Miller's Tale*." *JEGP* 73:176-88.
Musical images in Chaucer's Miller's Tale parallel the love action and also contrast it with several religious themes. Several of the Psalms and spiritual meanings of the Divine Office of Lauds incongruously parallel the bedroom "melodye" of the lovers. By counterpointing love with many other sacred melodies Chaucer ironically contrasts sacred and profane, spiritual and carnal love for the purpose of creating an incongruous "melodye" of love. Musical images become a pattern which parallels closely the development and conclusion of the love action in the tale. While musical images allude to sacred values, the ironic echoes increase the comedy of the plot by magnifying the fabric of incongruity in the poem. (JMG)

2982. Herzman, Ronald B. "The Paradox of Form:*The Knight's Tale* and Chaucerian Aesthetics." *PLL* 10:339-52.
Chaucer's Knight's Tale is a microcosm of *The Canterbury Tales* as a whole, suggesting that works of art are means to an end rather than ends in themselves. The tale concerns the chivalric life and its importance in ordering chaos. Moreover, the formal qualities in its construction are similar to qualities of the chivalric life which are its subject matter. In both one sees the importance of form as a bastion against chaos, but also its paradoxical inability to achieve perfection. Theseus' prime mover speech establishes the frame of reference within which to examine this paradox. It suggests that rules for chivalry and composition approximate divine harmony: human structures are an imperfect earthly analogue of divine perfection. This simultaneous celebration and criticism suggests a pattern embodied in the *Tales* as a whole. Works of art, not sufficient in themselves, force us to look upward and outward. (RBH)

2983. Hoffman, Richard L. "The Wife of Bath's Uncharitable Offerings." *ELN* 11:165-67.
In 1910, G.L. Kittredge pointed out the parallelism between Chaucer's description of the Wife of Bath's wrath at any other wife who preceded her to the offering in church (*General Prologue* 449-52) and a similar passage in Chapter xxxv of Eustace Deschamps' *Miroir de Mariage* (lines 3262-90). Later Chaucerians

have accepted Kittredge's argument, although some have cited other lines from the *Miroir*. There is at least an equal likelihood, however, that Chaucer had in mind Christ's words on the same subject in the Sermon on the Mount (Matthew v.23-24), where we are taught that if we remember, while offering at the altar, that anyone has anything against us, we must leave our gift and "go first to be reconciled." It is ironic, therefore, that the Wife of Bath is sometimes put out of charity while performing an act which Christ said we must always be in charity to perform; and the point of the irony becomes clearer when we recall St. Augustine's definition of charity as "the enjoyment of one's self and one's neighbor for the sake of God" and the standard medieval gloss on Matthew v.23-24 in the *Glossa Ordinaria*. (RLH)

2987. Johnson, William C.,Jr. "Miracles in *The Man of Law's Tale*." *BRMMLA* 28:57-65.
Chaucer's artistic purpose in adapting Trivet's *Life of Constance* in the Man of Law's Tale remains an open question. His literary use of Trivet's hagiographical material, specifically of the miracles, reveals another instance of Chaucerian originality, which constitutes an empirical outlook and a corresponding interest in human psychology and in the problem of human knowledge. Although he explicitly incorporates three miraculous events from Trivet's *Life*, Chaucer transforms Trivet's didactic certainty with esthetic ineffability. A comparative analysis shows that in Chaucer the miracle *qua miracle* moves into a mysterious background and is accompanied by a poetic emphasis on emotional intensity and intellectual uncertainty. Chaucer's concern is not theological but esthetic; he seeks not to prove the invisible or to stimulate religious behavior, but to question the visible itself and to dramatize the experience of doubt. The miracles of the Man of Law's Tale illuminate the widening chasm between experience and knowledge—between what we can feel and what we can understand. (WCJ)

2988. Kealy, J. Kieran. "Chaucer's *Nun's Priest's Tale*, VII.3160-71." *Expl* 33:Item 12.
In Chaucer's Nun's Priest's Tale, VII, 3160-71, Chauntecleer's mistranslation of the Latin phrase "In principio / Mulier est hominis confusio" is more than an attack on the ignorance of his beloved Pertelote. His decision to ignore the warning inherent in his dream in fact is influenced more by his ironic mistranslation than by the actual translation, for it is his desire for the "solas" which only Pertelote can provide which brings him down from his "narwe perche." (JKK)

2991. Kloss, Robert J. "Chaucer's *The Merchant's Tale*: Tender Youth and Stooping Age." *AI* 31:65-79.
Chaucer's Merchant's Tale differs from its genre and analogues in focusing on the cuckolding of an aged man instead of on the wiles of women. While most critics believe January repulsive and ridiculous for his "senile lechery," the opposite is true: his conception of, attitudes toward, and behavior with women is thoroughly infantile, based on lingering modes of interaction with the original mother. Following the pleasure principle solely, he rejects super-ego warnings, marries, and suffers for it. The sexual symbolism—predominantly oral and genital—reinforces these pre-oedipal and oedipal themes. The garden, pear tree, cuckolding, and January's acceptance of May's explanation all form part pf January's infantile delusions about the nature of women. Maintenance of infantile narcissism is one of January's prime motives and accounts, perhaps, for some of the repugnance the reader feels: in identifying with the old man, we discover the shame we feel at our own infantile, narcissistic demands upon our loved ones, despite all they do to please us. (RK)

2994. Longsworth, Robert. "Chaucer's Clerk as Teacher." [F 49]:61-66.
In telling the story of Griselda, the Clerk skillfully appropriates the narrative form for pedagogical purposes. He seeks to refute the Wife of Bath's lesson in assertiveness by arguing for and by displaying the moral superiority of discipline and obedience. His skill as a teacher, however, is more conspicuous than his humanity or imaginative capacity, and Chaucer's gentle satire plays upon that perception. (RL)

2998. Mathewson, Jeanne T. "For Love and Not for Hate:The Value of Virginity in Chaucer's *Physician's Tale*." *AnM* 14(1973):35-42.

Virginius, Apius, Harry Bailly, and the Physician reveal a lack of awareness of Virginia's humanity. Virginius regards his daughter as a possession rather than a person, a "gemme of chastitee." The dialogue between Virginius and Virginia exposes the attitudes which allow Virginius to believe he is killing Virginia "for love and not for hate." Virginia's inappropriate reference to Jephthah's daughter underlines the pathetic irony of her situation. Jephthah's daughter, reflecting the values of her society, had mourned that she had to die without producing children. Virginia, reflecting her father's values, is able, although reluctantly, to thank God that she will die a maid. Apius and Virginius struggle for possession of an embodiment of virginity, beauty, and youth, a struggle which must end in destruction of the object. Harry Bailly can rightly claim that Virginia's beauty was her death because he shares the Physician's unreflecting sentimentality regarding beautiful young virgins. (JTM)

2999. McKee, John. "Chaucer's *Canterbury Tales*, 'General Prologue'." *Expl* 32:Item 54.
Chaucer's portraits in the General Prologue of *The Canterbury Tales* are usually highly individualized. However, the Five Guildsmen are described collectively. Chaucer's sudden lack of interest in individualization arises from his habit of proportioning his portraits as though they were governed by the priorities of the characters portrayed. Chaucer has indicated the guildsmen's middle-class tendency to conformity by assigning no space in their description to the matter of their individuality. Only two lines are allotted to the topic of the knight's physical description, which suggests his slight interest in personal appearance, whereas the squire's intense interest in his own personal appearance is indicated by the fact that most of the lines allotted to him are devoted to his physical description. Again, the Franklin loves food, and almost half of his description consists of a menu. Chaucer's portraits indicate which characteristics are important to the character portrayed. (JBM)

3001. Millichap, Joseph R. "Transubstantiation in the *Pardoner's Tale*." *BRMMLA* 28:102-08.
The analysis of transubstantiation and transformation imagery reveals that, although Chaucer's Pardoner relates his tale to the sacrificial ritual of the Mass, he is incapable of that personal sacrifice requisite to self-realization, which is no less the objective of Jung's religious psychology than of the doctrine of transubstantiation. (JRM)

3008. Palomo, Dolores. "What Chaucer Really Did to *Le Livre de Mellibee*." *PQ* 53:304-20.
Because Chaucer's Tale of Melibee has always been regarded as a near word-for-word translation of *Le Livre de Melibee*, his intentions in including it in *The Canterbury Tales* have remained obscure. Chaucer has consistently introduced techniques cited in medieval rhetorics for achieving "high style"—characteristics absent from the plain style of his source. But the rhetorical elegance is inappropriate to the vacuous content, and the unaltered "sentence" is consequently devalued by stylistic treatment. Chaucer both criticizes the treatise's pretentiousness and disproves the assumption that words are mere chaff concealing doctrinal truth. Chaucer satirizes the ordinary reader's attitude toward literature. In this way, the Tale of Melibee contributes to Chaucer's continuing commentary on the arts of reading and writing. (DJP)

3009. Pearcy, Roy J. "Does the Manciple's Prologue Contain a Reference to Hell's Mouth?" *ELN* 11:167-75.
Chaucer's Manciple's Prologue contains a strain of apocalyptic imagery which suggests a thematic association with the Parson's Prologue. Remarks addressed to the drunk Cook evoke an image of Hell's Mouth as traditionally represented in the pictorial and plastic arts and in the stage setting for dramatic representation of the Last Judgment, and the Cook himself comes to personify the damned souls incapable of responding to the Parson's exhortations to penitence. (RJP)

3016. Robertson, D.W.,Jr. "Chaucer's Franklin and His Tale." *Costerus* N.S 1:1-26.
The significance of the relationship between the Franklin and the Sergeant of the Law is explored in terms of the Franklin's career and specific attributes to show that the portrait of the Franklin is humorous and satiric. The portrait and the tale together can be understood as a part of Chaucer's humorous criticism of the administration of royal justice in England when it was in the hands of greedy and literalminded men who abused words to conceal the truth. (DWR,Jr)

3017. Rogers, William E. "Individualization of Language in the Canterbury Frame Story." *AnM* 15:74-108. [Appendix: "Romance and Latinate Loan Words in the Speech of Chaucer's Pilgrims in the Frame Story."]
The modern critic must earn by means of close analysis his sensitivity to the effects of Chaucer's reproduction of colloquial English. Significant variables in such a study are diction, sentence structure, speech mannerisms, and use of figurative language. The speech of Chaucer's pilgrims differs with respect to these variables, and the context in which individual speech-traits occur enables us to argue plausibly toward a determination of the characterizing value of any given speech-trait. The relevant context of any speech-trait includes not only the speech-traits of the other pilgrims, but also Chaucer's description of the particular pilgrim and the pilgrim's description of himself. The technique of comparing one pilgrim's speech to another's is most helpful in the cases of the Host, the Pardoner, and the Wife. (WER)

3019. Ryan, Lawrence V. "The Canon's Yeoman's Desperate Confession." *ChauR* 8:297-310.
In The Canon's Yeoman's Prologue and Tale Chaucer constructs a literary *confessio* which is unusual in that it echoes and parodies the form and doctrine of sacramental confession as taught in several Middle English didactic treatises and poems. The imagery of the Tale suggests that for seven years its narrator has felt uncomfortably close to hellfire as an alchemical "puffer;" apparently he hopes through an emergency confession to clear his conscience and escape his entrapment in this vain and deceptive trade. Yet his revelations are never completely frank; though the Tale exposes more than he intends, he holds back in his confession out of fear of temporal and eternal reprisals for his own part in the alchemical confidence game. (LVR)

3021. Scheps, Walter. "Chaucer's Man of Law and the Tale of Constance." *PMLA* 89:285-95.
The suitability of Chaucer's Man of Law's Tale to its teller can be demonstrated by analyzing: (1) those elements in the Man of Law's character that are dramatically prominent in the tale of Constance, (2) the references to legal proceedings and the use of legalistic rhetoric, especially *exclamatio* and *interrogatio*, in the tale, and (3) the affinities between the Man of Law's Tale and the other tales in the rhyme-royal group. As an example, the manner of the Man of Law's defense is heavily dependent upon the advice and examples given to lawyers in the *Rhetorica ad Herennium*, a dependence not found in those tales, like that of the clerk, that at first might seem similar to the tale of Constance. Since all of the legal rhetoric and most of the references to the law are Chaucer's additions to Trivet, it is likely that Trivet's account was deliberately modified to suit the Man of Law. (WS)

3025. Szittya, Penn R. "The Friar as False Apostle:Antifraternal Exegesis and the *Summoner's Tale*." *SP* 71:19-46.
The satirical and scatological comedy of the Summoner's Tale is reinforced by several patterns of learned allusion. One of these is the recently discovered Pentecostal parody at the end of the tale, which is anticipated by allusions to common biblical and exegetical traditions relating to Pentecost. More important is the blatant series of biblical allusions which implicitly compare Friar John to the apostles. These apostolic allusions help to anticipate the final scene and hence to unify the tale. The connection of the friars with both Pentecost and the apostles is made in the friars' own lore and by their critics. (PRS)

3027. Turner, Frederick. "A Structuralist Analysis of the *Knight's Tale*." *ChauR* 8:279-96.
Chaucer's Knight's Tale is a myth, in that the structure of its plot and the arrangement of its details are a coherent coded description of the norms of its culture. Claude Lévi-Strauss provides the methods of its exegesis. It contains four types of structure: binary oppositions, triadic hierarchies, quadratic frames, and the circular form of the poem itself. These structures are composed of divine and human characters; elements, passions, colors; legal, scientific, and political abstractions. Through opposition, mediation, balance, and harmony the

medieval universe is exhaustively displayed. At the bottom of the poem is a statement of the elementary European structures of kinship, in particular the sexual laws pertaining to siblings and siblings-in-law, and their potential perversions. The Knight's Tale is, however, consciously parodied by The Miller's Tale in precisely mythic dimension; where the former is conservative, the latter is revolutionary. The Structuralist method is adequate to describe closed systems, but fails before the open system of The Miller's Tale and *The Canterbury Tales* as a whole. (FT)

3031. White, Gertrude M. "*The Franklin's Tale*:Chaucer or the Critics." *PMLA* 89:454-62.
The Franklin's Tale may best be understood in the light of Chaucer's own writings, particularly The Merchant's Tale and three short lyrics, "Truth," "Gentilesse," and "Lak of Sted-fastnesse." The relationship between the characters and events of the two Tales dramatizes a moral ideal that operates throughout *The Canterbury Tales* and is given explicit expression in the lyrics. It may be summed up as "gentilesse," which consists, in the Knight's words, of "Trouthe and honour, fredom and curteisie." In a variety of contexts, this standard operates throughout Chaucer's writings. An understanding of it puts The Franklin's Tale into clear perspective, identifies its true theme, answers its critics, accounts for its apparent absurdities, inconsistencies, and contradictions, and reveals its suitability to its teller. (GMW)

3033. Wright, Constance S. "On the Franklin's Prologue, 716-721, Persius, and the Continuity of the Mannerist Style." *PQ* 52(1973):739-46.
In Chaucer's Franklin's Prologue, the Franklin mentions that his speech is "rude" and that he never slept on Mt. Parnassus. Medieval and Renaissance poet rhetoricans frequently make these statements as a form of the affected modesty topos—a commonplace in which the author denies that he knows anything about rhetoric, while simultaneously demonstrating that he is very well acquainted with it. The Franklin's second statement—that he never slept on Mt. Parnassus—is a medieval misunderstanding of a line from Persius and becomes, in the 10th century, part of the affected modesty topos. Its use as well as the use of the term "rude" in the mouth of Chaucer's Franklin suggests the Franklin is attempting to imitate a mannerist rhetorican. Since this line is the only occurrence of a quotation from Persius in Chaucer, it may well be that Chaucer had never read that author. Finally, the occurrence of this quotation from Persius in English, French, and German Renaissance poets suggests that there is a continuity of the mannerist style from the middle ages through the Renaissance in the use of this particular topos. (CSW)

3034. Zacharias, Richard. "Chaucer's *Nun's Priest's Tale*, B[2]. 4552-63." *Expl* 32:Item 60.
In the Nun's Priest's tale Chaucer punctures gentle knights and their ladies, the complacent transfer of educated manners into domesticity, the marital comfort of ignorant mutual support, the near-fatal inseparability of man's pride and his education. Noteworthy is the fate of Pertelote if she were to follow the example the priest calls up, after Chauntecleer's capture of the wife of the Carthaginian Hasdrubal and jump into a fire after "her" man. She would be a roast hen, a fried chicken, and one of a number of reflections upon the pompous or excessive employment of "authority" in this tale and others. The second analogy in these lines, while repeating the fire image, compares screaming to screaming. This is a return, from grotesque exaggeration of the humanity of a hen, and implicitly, of all human beings, to less expansive descriptive exaggeration. Long before the decline of "authority," Chaucer and his priest smile at the Dame's burned offering in the temple of love and wit. (RKZ)

Complaint to His Lady. 3035. Clogan, Paul M. "The Textual Reliability of Chaucer's Lyrics:*A Complaint to His Lady*." *M&H* 5:183-89.
The textual editing of Chaucer's lyrics and in particular *A Complaint to His Lady* is discussed. The extensive emendations in the text of *Lady* are unjustified because the poem is a series of unfinished metrical innovations, showing Chaucer experimenting with his art, and any emendation to perfect or improve rhyme or meter when the sense remains unaltered is unwarranted. While it is true that the manuscripts could not conceivably represent the poet's final intention, the unrevised text of *Lady* in the two so-called "bad" manuscripts is more trustworthy than the emended copy in modern editions. (PMC)

House of Fame. 3038. Carr, John. "A Borrowing from Tibullus in Chaucer's *House of Fame*." *ChauR* 8:191-97.
Although secondary medieval sources did not transmit Tibullus III.iv.95, verbal, rhetorical, and contextual similarities suggest that *House of Fame* I was a borrowing. Chaucer certainly knew of Tibullus, chiefly through Ovid and the *Roman de la Rose*, and he could have seen related quotations from Tibullus' poems in contemporary florilegia. Opportunity to examine a complete text, the only possible source of a borrowing, occurred during Chaucer's Italian journey of 1372-73. Coluccio Salutati was then in likely possession of the *Codex Ambrosianus*, and though not yet chancellor, was in Florence during Chaucer's visit there. Due to Salutati's local literary reputation and the common interests of the two men, an introduction probably took place. Not surprisingly, neither ever after referred to such a meeting. During their lifetimes, they were not of sufficient reputation for a meeting to have seemed to the participants other than casual. (JWC)

3039. Giaccherini, Enrico. "Una 'crux' chauceriana:I sogni nella *House of Fame*." *RLMC* 27:165-76.
The classification of dreams in Chaucer's *House of Fame* has never received satisfactory interpretation. Critics point to Macrobius' *Somnium Scipionis* and the *Roman de la Rose* as major sources, but the term *revelacioun* baffled them until a decisive contribution by F.X. Newman suggesting St. Paul's II Corinthians. More important has been his suggestion that those six terms form a coherent schematization of three pairs. Accurate analysis shows that two form a contrast between a true and false dream. The same contrast can be traced for the remaining one, because Middle English *avisioun* and Old French *avision* indicate possible interpretation as "a false dream," whereas *revelacioun* can only be interpreted as "a truthful dream, sent by God." (EG)

Troilus and Criseyde. 3049. Baron, F. Xavier. "Chaucer's Troilus and Self-Renunciation in Love." *PLL* 10:5-14.
Troilus's love for Criseyde is characterized by his self-renunciation, the perfect model of which in the Christian Middle Ages was based on Christ's sacrifice of himself and the ideal of martyrdom and mortification which it inspired. The conduct in love of Heloïse, Lancelot, and Tristan closely resembles that of Chaucer's hero. His self-renunciation is closely related to his vanity and his fatalism and clearly distinguises him from the others in the poem. Troilus's self-abnegation can be variously evaluated but it cannot be ignored. (FXB)

3055. Helterman, Jeffrey. "Masks of Love in *Troilus and Criseyde*." *CL* 26:14-31.
In *Troylus and Cryseyde*, Chaucer revised the conception of love found in Boccaccio's *Filostrato*. In *Troylus* there is a stripping away of attitudes that are called love until Troylus finally understands his love for Cryseyde. This process is analogous to the ascent through the levels of love in the *Vita Nuova* in which Dante adores first a *simulacrum* (the "screen lady"), then the god Amor, and finally Beatrice herself. Corresponding to these levels are love as courtly convention, love as metaphysical ideal, and finally love for Cryseyde. Only Troylus is flexible enough to proceed through all three stages of love. As Troylus matures, the style of the poem changes from Petrarchist (the rhetoric of Petrarch without the feeling) to Petrarchan (the form expressing the feeling). Troylus shakes off the limits imposed by Pandarus and becomes a far more selfless lover than Boccaccio's Troilo. The growth of Troylus explains his ascent at the close of the poem and a comparison with the *Filostrato* shows that the conclusion is fully integrated with the rest of the poem. (JAH)

3057. Kossick, Shirley G. "*Troilus and Criseyde*:The Aubades." *UES* 9,i(1971):11-13.
Close textual analysis shows that while the two aubades in *Troylus and Cryseyde* (III.1422-42 and 1450-70) are successful poems in their own right, Read in their proper context they gather additional meaning, counter-balancing each other by contrast, and helping to delineate the characters of the lovers. The connecting stanza (1443-49) serves as a bridge and prepares one

for the change of tone. The aubades also catch up some of the central themes of the poem, notably those of transience and the conflict between inner, subjective experience and outer reality. These features of the aubades are highlighted by comparison with Yeats's poem, "Parting," where general similarities of feeling serve to distinguish differences in attitude. (SGK)

3058. Maguire, John B. "The Clandestine Marriage of Troilus and Criseyde." *ChauR* 8:262-78.
An assumption common to all previous critical considerations of *Troylus and Cryseyde* is that Chaucer and his audience would necessarily have considered the love affair celebrated as fornicatory and hence immoral. The consistent teaching of the Church was that the sole essential ingredient of a valid marriage was the free and mutual consent of the parties to be wed. Ecclesiastical ceremonies, witnesses, etc. were desirable but not necessary. Marriages contracted without the benefit of clergy or other witnesses were considered valid but undesirable in view of the numerous abuses and social instability they led to. Numerous church councils legislated against such marriages. So Chaucer's audience would have been fully aware of this practice. A close reading of Boccaccio's and Chaucer's texts reveals a distinctly different attitude toward the love they celebrate. Every departure that Chaucer makes from his Italian source, when viewed in light of the social and religious customs known to his audience, suggest that he is treating a "clandestine marriage" rather than an illicit love affair. (JBM)

VI. RENAISSANCE AND ELIZABETHAN

Bibliography

3066. Craven, Alan E. "Proofreading in the Shop of Valentine Simmes." *PBSA* 68:361-72.
The specific information gained from collations of the dramatic quartos printed by Valentine Simmes allows some tentative judgments to be made about the amount and the nature of proof-correction in Simmes's shop. In 9 quartos an unexpectedly large number of formes were proof-corrected. For the most part, however, the changes effected were inconsequential and can often more properly be called sophistications than corrections of errors. Much of the proofreading of dramatic texts may have been done by the same person. If so, it is surprising that the proof-correction varies so markedly in quality, appearing to be of several different kinds. There is also apparent variation in the number and kinds of corrections within a single quarto. Simmes's proof-correction is often surprisingly comprehensive, but proof-correction seldom contributed significantly to the accuracy of the text and the integrity of a Simmes text depends primarily on the performance of the compositors and not the proofreader. (AEC)

Literature (Excluding Shakespeare)

General and Miscellaneous. 3077. Adams, Robert P. "Transformations in the Late Elizabethan Tragic Sense of Life:New Critical Approaches." *MLQ* 35:353-63.
Radical concerns about abuses of great power in the state appear *ca.* 1596-1603. Popular concerns with state justice and limits of monarchic power show in England after the 1572 Massacre of St. Bartholomew's. Tudor theory saw history as tragedy ruled by Providence. Under harsh censorship playwrights developed mirrors of society. Their common aim was to discover what great princes actually do. Tragedy then became history ruled by power-to-destroy. The best tragedies stressed the succession problem and mirrored abuses of supreme state power for politicized audiences who sensed that their role in amoral princely power-games was to be eaten. (RPA)

3080. Beck, Leonard N. "Things Magical in the Collections of the Rare Book Division." *QJLC* 31:208-34.
Accepting the definition of the theater magician as an actor playing the part of a magician, this note points out the origins of the role in the Renaissance literature of the white magician who has mastered the occult forces of nature. The literary course of the stage magician's use of the new sciences for his repertoire is then traced from the late Renaissance until early modern times, that is, from Porta and Cardano until Decremps in France and Wiegenleb and Eckhartshausen in Germany. This exploitation of the technical advances of science for purposes of entertainment is described as a kind of "liberalization." It is concluded that the efflorescence of the stage magician into a theatrical personality like Pinetti or Houdini coincides with this "liberalization" of science. The discussion throughout is based on the holdings of the Library of Congress. (LNB)

3082. Black, L.G. "Some Renaissance Children's Verse." *RES* 24(1973):1-16.
Cambridge University Library MS. Dd 5.75 (F) contains a group of new year's gift verses written by children between the ages of nine and fourteen. The miscellany of Henry Stanford includes verses by Stanford himself, and by William Paget (1572-1629) and George Berkeley (1601-58). Educational theorists of the time encouraged the writing of Latin verses in imitation of the classics and the rhetorical elaboration of themes, and the boys' families had extensive literary connections. Four English poems by William Paget and five by George Berkeley are transcribed and discussed in relation to information about the families concerned. All are complimentary poems, built up through ornamenting a theme with lists of exempla; and in making these lists the two boys often drew on their own experience. The verses probably reflect Stanford's rather early Elizabethan poetic tastes and so bear little relation to the sort of poetry being written in England between 1580 and 1610. (LGB)

3086. Clifford, Paula M. "The Grammarians' View of French Word-Order in the Sixteenth Century." *PQ* 53:380-88.
The 16th-century grammars of French may be more informative and of greater general interest than is often supposed. Their treatment of word-order illustrates the diverse approaches to a theory of the vernacular language at this time. (PMC)

3097. Lewalski, Barbara K. "Recent Studies in the English Renaissance." *SEL* 14:139-75. [Rev. art.]
Discusses major books and collections of articles on the literature of the English Renaissance (excluding drama), most of which were published during 1972 and 1973. (BKL)

3121. Williams, William P. "Other Patterns of Stoicism:1530-1670." *MLR* 69:1-11. [Senecan style.]
Earl Miner has recently indicated that the usual view of the rise of a Senecan, or Stoic, style in the late 16th century in England might be mistaken. His evidence is a series of tables of editions of classical works taken from the *Short-Title Catalogues*. However, in the cases of only Cicero and Seneca, the failure of the English to produce a Latin edition of either author before 1571 indicates that one important factor is the importation of continental editions. In this Croll's judgment may be strengthened rather than overturned. Other important considerations are domestic regulation of the book-trade and the effect of an author's prominence in the schools. The impact of popular and unpopular translations also proves to be a factor in the number of editions produced. Patterns of publication for both authors—that is, the number of editions in a given period of time and the intervals between them—show that the old theories are generally accurate. (WPW)

Drama and Theater. 3131. Charney, Maurice. "Recent Studies in Elizabethan and Jacobean Drama." *SEL* 14:297-314. [Rev. art.]
This review article discusses most of the major critical and scholarly books on Shakespeare and the Elizabethan and Jacobean dramatists published between late 1972 and early 1974. (MC)

3138. Edmond, Mary. "Pembroke's Men." *RES* 25:129-36.
The main subject is a newly-discovered Elizabethan actor, Simon Jewell, who died in Shoreditch—site of the first two London theaters—in August 1592. It seems likely that he was a member of the company known as Pembroke's Men, which is believed to

have been formed in 1592 and reconstituted in 1597; and from his will it is possible to deduce the size and constitution of the company. One of Jewell's fellows, Thomas Vincent, probably later became a prompter at the Globe theater; another, Robert Nicholls, can with some confidence be identified with an actor named in Henslowe's *Diary*. Jewell also mentions a "Mr Iohnson" who seems to have been a professional colleague, and it is possible that this was Ben Jonson, who was about 20 when Jewell died. The reference in the will, if correctly interpreted, predates by five years the first reference to Jonson's stage career previously known. (ME)

3149. Kernan, A[lvin] B. "This Goodly Frame, the Stage:The Interior Theater of Imagination in English Renaissance Drama." *SQ* 25:1-5.
The Renaissance playhouse was always undisguisedly visible, and represented the "real world" of heaven, earth, and hell which constituted the late medieval cosmos. There was in the plays another theater of the imagination, a world of scenes and playing created by the characters, imitating their creators and telling us by their hopes and efforts what the histrionic arts meant to the Renaissance. The internal theater of the imagination, which manifests man's belief in his ability to change himself and his world into the image of his desire, shows why Renaissance England found the theater such a powerful art form. (ABK)

3162. Salomon, Brownell. "Visual and Aural Signs in the Performed English Renaissance Play." *RenD* 5(for 1972):143-69.
A play's meaning lies in its language and in nonverbal elements like vocal tone, gesture, movement, makeup, costume, hand properties, the decor, lighting, music, and sound effects. Semiology has important new applications in the art of interpretive criticism, for it enables each of the preceding elements to be considered comprehensively and individually as sign systems which embody the style, form, and content of a performed play. A critically useful expansion of the semiology of spectacle demonstrates how all visual and aural sense-data can be evaluated in terms of dramatic function or relevancy: specifically, as to whether a datum is denotative (sign), connotative (symbol), or lacking in critical consequence (signal). (BS)

Poetry. 3169. Bradford, Alan T. "Mirrors of Mutability: Winter Landscapes in Tudor Poetry." *ELR* 4:3-39. [Sackville, Douglas, Spenser, Shakespeare.]
The stylized description of an ideal landscape defaced by winter becomes a recurrent *topos* in Tudor poetry. A study of its treatment in such works as Sackville's *Induction*, Spenser's "January," and Shakespeare's *Sonnets* (*passim*, but especially Sonnet 73) reveals a parallel evolution of sensibility and poetics throughout the latter half of the 16th century. Elizabethan poets enriched the expressive character of the *topos* while developing metaphorical techniques that made the winter landscape an effective mirror of the individual speaker's state of mind as well as of the changing attitude of the Renaissance toward universal mobility. (ATB)

3170. Deming, Robert H. "Love and Knowledge in the Renaissance Lyric." *TSLL* 16:389-410.
The self-conscious lyricism of late 16th- and early 17th-century poetry provides a functional relationship to concepts of self-reference, self-knowledge, and created self through the subject matter of love poetry. The inquiry turns to notions of "love" in the love treatises and psychological discourses of Aristotelian-Thomistic and Neo-platonic writers. The role and function of poetry in providing the epistemological basis for self-discovery is explained. The poetry reveals models of the complete foolish-wise lover attempting within the poetry itself to discover self-knowledge, awareness of self as a "thinking consciousness," and the nature and knowledge of love. Further illustrations from the work of Petrarch, Wyatt, Shakespeare, and Spenser illuminate these concepts. (RHD)

3176. Levin, Richard. "A Second English *Enueg*." *PQ* 53:428-30.
There is an anonymous 16th-century sonnet in British Museum Add. MS 36529 which seems to derive from the *Enueg*, a continental verse form built around a catalog of complaints. In certain respects it resembles Shakespeare's Sonnet LXVI, hitherto

regarded as the only English example of this form. (RLL)

3177. Linden, Stanton J. "The Breaking of the Alembic: Patterns in Alchemical Imagery in English Renaissance Poetry." *WascanaR* 9:105-13.
Alchemical images and allusions that appear in Medieval, Renaissance, and 17th-century literature fall into two broad, historically consecutive patterns of usage. Beginning with the Canon's Yeoman's Tale and extending into the period of Donne and Jonson, such references are dominated by a satiric intent. The art becomes synonymous with charlatanism, futility, and poverty. A strikingly different pattern begins to emerge late in the 16th century; alchemy is employed metaphorically to suggest change, growth, purification, and spiritual regeneration. These associations inform the majority of alchemical references in Donne and Herbert and in middle- and late-17th-century literature. Reasons for the decline of alchemical satire and the rise of the "purified" tradition may include Jonson's unrivaled triumph in alchemical comedy; the awakening of interest in esoteric alchemy through the influence of English and Continental hermetic studies; erosion of the philosophical foundations of transmutation through the rise of the New Science; and the hospitable attitudes toward alchemy of such men as Bacon, Boyle, and Newton. (SJL)

Ascham. 3201. Salomon, Linda B. "*The Courtier* and *The Scholemaster*." *CL* 25(1973):17-36.
Despite obvious differences Ascham's *Scholemaster* and Castiglione's *Courtier* share elements of humanist educational and esthetic theory. Their writers variously prescribe the physical, intellectual, moral, and social preparation of the future servant of prince and country. Thus in each the monarchical politics of the *speculum principis* are updated by common Renaissance concepts like Ciceronian eloquence employed in civic humanism; *grazia* and "good wit" have a similar nature and function. More distinctively, Castiglione's *sprezzatura* and Ascham's "comeliness" both express a decorum based on appropriateness and absence of affectation. Careful judgment in manners, in vocation, and in literary style is the hallmark of both the courtier and the civil gentleman. The apparent simplicity that conceals high art is their standard. Cultivation of the abstract faculty to appreciate such art is the joint contribution of Castiglione and Ascham to Renaissance educational theory. (LBS)

Cavendish. 3212. Edwards, A.S.G. "The Dugdale Manuscript of George Cavendish's *Metrical Visions*." *PBSA* 68:167-70.
Discusses the hitherto unexamined text of Cavendish's *Metrical Visions* in Bodleian MS. Dugdale 28. Demonstrates that the Dugdale manuscript was copied from the autograph British Library MS. Egerton 2402. The variant readings in Dugdale are not likely to have any authority. (ASGE)

Davies. 3224. Sanderson, James L. "Recent Studies in Sir John Davies." *ELR* 4:411-17.
Lists some 90 items concerning the life and works of Sir John Davies which have appeared since approximately 1935. Includes brief descriptive comments on 50 of these scholarly pieces as they relate to the poet's biography, editions of his poems, and critical, textual, and bibliographical aspects of his work. (JLS)

Eliot, T. 3240. Barry, Patricia S. "The Four Elements and *The Governour*." *WascanaR* 9:221-30.
The *Nature of the Four Elements*, attributed to John Rastell, and Sir Thomas Eliot's *The Governour* treat the Earth, Water, Air, and Fire as creatural beings, suggesting that Tudor Englishmen sometimes regarded the Four Elements as symbols of social ranks elaborating upon the Three Estates. As a device to create and elevate a new "estate," Eliot arranges the Elements in a hierarchy paralleling the ranks of men in the body politic. Through the imagery and properties of Fire, he equates magistrates with angelic beings, giving them divine status as mediators between heavenly and earthly realms. Eliot's sanctified judges and sheriffs participate in an allegorical dance of politic virtue by reflecting in their gentlemanly conduct the motions of celestial bodies. He connects allegorical dancing with such political phenomena as the

deification of rulers and the creation of heroic myth. (PSB)

Florio. 3241a. O'Connor, D.J. "John Florio's Contribution in Italian-English Lexicography." *Italica* 49(1972):49-67.
The first Italian-English dictionary, compiled by William Thomas in 1550, contained only 8,000 words on the collections made by Francisco Alunno and Acarisio da Cento in 1543. John Florio for his *Worlde of Wordes*, however, went much further and ransacked the Italian literature of the period—both dialectal and Florentine —consulting 72 works for his first edition (1598) and no less than 253 for his second (1611). His dictionary thus became not only a valuable teaching aid but also a means for spreading among English students of Italian a knowledge of the colorful Italian literature of the 16th century. In 1659 Torriano used Florio's two editions to produce a slightly larger Italian-English, English-Italian dictionary. Altieri in 1726 and Baretti in 1760 preferred instead to use as a basis for their bilingual dictionaries the renowned Florentine *Vocabolario della Crusca*. Nonetheless, their works still contain some words and definitions which can be traced back to Florio's earlier mammoth efforts. (DJO'C)

Gascoigne. 3243. Mills, Jerry L. "Recent Studies in Gascoigne." *ELR* 3(1973):322-26. [Since 1941.]
A bibliography of critical writings on the Elizabethan poet and dramatist George Gascoigne including all known work since 1941. (JLM)
3245. Philmus, M.R. Rohr. "Gascoigne's Fable of the Artist as a Young Man." *JEGP* 73:13-31. [On *The Adventures of Master F.I.*]
Critical discussions of *The Adventures of Master F.I.* have generally neglected to probe the significance of the framework established by presenting the inset poems as the occasion for the narrative, by introducing the hero as a writer, and by casting the narrator in the role of a man of letters. An examination of F.I.'s utterances in conjunction with the comments on them provided by the interventions of the editor-narrator, indicates that Gascoigne develops a coherent literary theme. He outlines the course of F.I.'s gradual progress as a poet as he experiments with practically all the literary modes available to an early Elizabethan writer. The idea of rendering what coming of age meant for a poet of his time is essential to the conception of Gascoigne's work and distinguishes it from all contemporary works of prose fiction as the single version of the "novel of the artist" in the Elizabethan period. (MRRP)
3246. Salamon, Linda B. "A Face in *The Glasse*:Gascoigne's *Glasse of Government* Re-examined." *SP* 71:47-71.
Glasse of Government owes its statement about varieties of students to Ascham's *Scholemaster*, its implicit concept of government to Elyot's *Governour*. The *Glasse*'s schoolmaster is chosen by Ascham's standards, the students exhibit his Socratic qualities of determined character and natural intelligence, and the servant who misleads youth embodies his scorn. Also like the *Scholemaster* there is differentiation of slow and quick learners, who respectively succeed and become criminal; insistence on comprehension of lessons; and emphasis on moral danger to adolescents from travel and extensive freedom. Virtuous partic-ipation in public life as a goal for education comes from Ascham and from Elyot. Low-life characters, "courtly" by-play, and verse choruses enliven the play slightly. Gascoigne demonstrates transmission of Tudor humanist ideas into the Elizabethan literary *milieu*. (LBS)
3247. Voytovich, Edward R. "The Poems of 'Master F.J.':A Narrator's Windfall." *Thoth* 13,iii:17-25.
In "The Adventures of Master F.J." the poems and the prose are both essential parts of Gascoigne's narrative technique. While G.T. describes F.J.'s experiences, he uses F.J.'s own poems as documentary evidence of the way in which F.J. regards his affair with Dame Elinor. The juxtaposition of G.T.'s mature point of view with F.J.'s naivete contributes an added dimension to G.T.'s first-person minor-character narrative voice. F.J. matures poet-ically as well as romantically in the course of his adventure. (ERV)

Greene. 3252. Larson, Charles H. "Robert Greene's *Ciceronis Amor*:Fictional Biography in the Romance Genre." *SNNTS* 6:256-67.
Although Robert Greene's *Ciceronis Amor: Tullies Love* (1589) is rarely read today, it was one of Greene's most popular works. Professing to be a biographical account of a love affair in the life of Cicero, the grave dictator of Renaissance thought, *Ciceronis Amor* is one of Greene's most imaginative and engaging pieces of fiction. The work needs to be evaluated as an example of prose romance. Greene presents the reader with three stylized main characters who are representative types—Lentulus of the suc-cessful general turned unsuccessful wooer, Cicero of the bright young commoner who earns social position by his wit, and Terentia of the girl whose extraordinary beauty is accentuated by her chastity. Greene uses these three figures for the intellectual examination of the value of male friendship and the independence of daughters in affairs of the heart. (CL)
3254. Wertheim, Albert. "The Presentation of Sin in *Friar Bacon and Friar Bungay*." *Criticism* 16:273-86.
Greene's *Friar Bacon* includes deaths and tempers its comedy with moral seriousness. The scenes involving Friar Bacon are part of Greene's well-conceived scheme to show how the necromancy of Bacon leads him to reflect in himself or foster in others each of the traditional Seven Deadly Sins. It is only after the deaths of Lambert, Serlsby, and their sons that Bacon recognizes the destructive power of his magic, sees his own pride, and repents "That even Bacon meddled in this art." The Margaret-Lacy plot balances the presentation of sin and its destructiveness with a positive romantic magic. (AW)

Greville. 3255. Farmer, Norman K.,Jr. "Holograph Revisions in Two Poems by Fulke Greville." *ELR* 4:98-110.
Close investigation of Fulke Greville's holograph revisions of two poems in *Caelica* gives unique insight into his poetic creativity. Of the 109 pieces in *Caelica*, half were subjected to some kind of revision in what appears to be the fairly late recension of Warwick MS. vol. E. The poems which underwent the most intensive revision (Sonnets 68 and 78) occur toward the conclusion of the sequence, and on the basis of available biographical data there is every reason to suspect that in these poems above all, Greville was concerned to raise his creations "on lines of truth." The conclusions drawn from these revisions suggest that *Caelica* is not merely a collection of short poems that Greville wished to survive. Rather, they suggest that *Caelica* is a consciously organized sequence of poems that were intended to cohere thematically. (NKF, Jr)

Guilpin. 3261. Carroll, D. Allen. "James Roberts' Compos-itors in 1598." *PBSA* 68:52-53.
An analysis of the text of Everard Guilpin's *Skialetheia* indicates that the same two orthographic personalities (X and Y) were at work in 1598 which were later to produce *Merchant* 1600, *Titus* Q$_2$, and *Hamlet* Q$_2$. (DAC)

Kyd. 3266. Colley, John S. "*The Spanish Tragedy* and the Theatre of God's Judgments." *PLL* 10:241-53.
Kyd's *The Spanish Tragedy* is set in an amoral, mythological universe but Kyd insists that his play is a treatment of moral questions pertinent to his 16th-century audience. Kyd addresses questions about ultimate justice and the "outer mystery" through theatrical references and manipulations of the dramatic meta-phor. This encourages the audience to detach itself from the stage fiction and to ponder the moral implications of Hieronimo's actions. Kyd interprets Hieronimo's dilemma in theatrical terms in order to apprise his audience that the mad, grieving Marshal of Spain is a "mirror" of the despairing souls who might play such parts in the cosmic theater of God's judgments. (JSC)
3267. Hamilton, Donna B. "*The Spanish Tragedy*:A Speaking Picture." *ELR* 4:203-17.
In Thomas Kyd's *Spanish Tragedy*, chaos, revenge, and injustice are presented not as qualities prescribed by supernatural forces but as patterns in life created and maintained by human error. The Ghost-Revenge frame, the function of which is to clarify this truth of human existence, depicts a naive Andrea who assumes that Revenge is in control and a sleepy Revenge who only

represents the way things are and controls nothing. Throughout the play, man's dependence on ceremonies which appear to confirm his belief in a providential order is ironically juxtaposed to a variety of conspiracies and accidents intended to suggest the tragedies and injustices human beings suffer are of their own making. When Hieronimo grasps this truth, he stops depending upon institutions to provide order and begins to search for an alternative way of dealing with his woe, one that will ease its pain by telling him both what it is and what it means. In this search, he turns in succession to oratory, to painting, to metaphor, and finally to the most complete speaking picture of all, the play. (DBH)

3268. McMillin, Scott. "The Book of Seneca in *The Spanish Tragedy*." *SEL* 14:201-08.
The three quotations from Seneca in the *vindicta mihi* soliloquy of *The Spanish Tragedy* at first appear to be misunderstandings of the original. All three quotations concern "safety" or "preservation," and all belong to an ironic pattern typical of Seneca, in which "safety" and "preservation" turn into their opposites and issue in loss. For Hieronimo, the death of a son is figuratively the loss of himself, and when he "preserves" himself until the moment is ripe for revenge, he is finding a Senecan way in which the experience of self-loss can be formalized as action in time. Thus he misrepresents the text of Seneca, but grasps an essential Senecan situation and acts upon it in taking revenge. (SM)

Lee, H. 3269. Clayton, Thomas. "'Sir Henry Lee's Farewell to the Court':The Texts and Authorship of 'His Golden Locks Time Hath to Silver Turned'." *ELR* 4:268-75.
The poem had its premiere performance on 17 November 1590, when it was sung to Queen Elizabeth on the occasion of her Tilt Champion's resigning his office to the Earl of Cumberland. Because it was appended to *Polyhymnia* (1590), a work written in celebration of the same occasion, the poem has ordinarily been ascribed to George Peele, but the only evidence for Peele's authorship is this occasional and "bibliographical" association. The accumulated internal and external evidence of ten MSS and printed texts of this poem, dating 1590-c.1630, and of texts of two other poems certainly or probably by Sir Henry Lee, makes "his own" retirement poem almost certainly of his authorship, too, and provides the data for definitive old- and modern-spelling texts of the poem. The Folger MS text supplies the title given here: it has no special authority, but it aptly and succinctly identifies the author, the content, and the occasion of the poem. (TC)

Lodge. 3273. Whitworth, Charles W. "The Plays of Thomas Lodge." *CahiersE* 4(1973):3-14.
Although Lodge's reputation does not rest upon his dramatic writing, his plays are of interest to the literary historian. Written almost certainly before *Tamburlaine*, *The Wounds of Civil War*, though unsuccessful as drama, is noteworthy in several respects. With its fidelity to chronicle sources, it is an early example of the genuine history play. The blank verse, generally uninspired, gives way occasionally to a more lyrical strain where Lodge's natural talent is manifest. In the annals of Elizabethan drama before Marlowe, Kyd, and Greene, Lodge's Roman play is not insignificant. Written in the turbulant mid-1580s, with Mary Stuart a potential *causa belli*, the play was obviously meant to convey a timely warning. *A Looking Glass for London*, written with Greene, probably several years after *The Wounds of Civil War*, shows improvement in all aspects of dramatic composition. It is likely that Lodge was responsible for the major portion of the play, which again reflects a close familiarity with sources, the Old Testament and Josephus. The work abounds in the kind of spectacular device made popular by Kyd and others. Here again, as so often in his works, Lodge dresses his old-fashioned morality in the latest mode. (CWW)

Lyly. 3274. Bond, Sallie. "John Lyly's *Endimion*." *SEL* 14:189-99.
Endymion was meant to advance Lyly's career as a courtier by pleasing the Queen. While complimentary to Elizabeth, the play also reflected court tensions which might have offended her; Lyly avoided such a reaction by couching *Endymion* in a playful allegory, with Elizabeth as Cynthia, the pattern of regal beauty and divinity, arbitrix of the courtiers' intrigues, and by distancing the play-world from the court. Friendship and courtly love triumph over the forces of intrigue, self-interest, and lawless passion. (SB)

Marlowe. 3281. Adamson, Jane. "Marlowe, *Hero and Leander*, and the Art of Leaping in Poetry." *CR* 17:59-81.
Although Marlowe's *Hero and Leander* has extrinsic similarities with other Elizabethan "epyllia," it is most profitably seen in the wider context of Elizabethan dramatic verse. Marlowe's verse is characteristically energetic and volatile, reflecting the ceaseless, metamorphic movement of all natural—and especially sexual—energies. It displays the interest to be seen throughout Marlowe's work in strife, the instability of natural forms, and hence in destructive violence; and as with his other works, the main critical question with it is the way he responds to the fluidity and violence he projects. The poem's narrative mode and style allow (while superficially concealing) the same kind of moral confusions or evasions as have often been noted in his plays: in particular, about the human need, implicit in its subject-matter, for stability and hence self-commitment. (JA)

3288. Cope, Jackson I. "Marlowe's *Dido* and the Titillating Children." *ELR* 4:315-25.
Marlowe's *Dido* is a carefully constructed vehicle designed to display the compatibility of declamation and farce in drama. Its success is dependent upon a cast of child actors, but its implications probably were recognized and extended in *A Midsummer Night's Dream*. (JIC)

3291. Friedenreich, Kenneth. "'You Talks Brave and Bold': The Origins of an Elizabethan Stage Device." *CompD* 8:239-53.
A recent development in criticism of Elizabethan history plays is the identification of the "public-confrontation scene" as a theatrical device. We may trace the transformations and adaptations of a pre-combat challenge-counter-challenge sequence to Mummers' plays and tournaments. Writers of the craft cycles employ language and demand actions from the Christ-hero which are informed by the sequence. The sequence also appears in various moralities. In the hands of Marlowe, the basic sequence was elevated by his poetry, so that such confrontation scenes became both more complicated and more dependent on the words of antagonists. (KF)

3293. Gill, Roma. "Marlowe, Lucan, and Sulpitius." *RES* 96(1973):401-13.
Marlowe's translation of Lucan's *Pharsalia* Book i, although a very early work, shows some characteristics of the more accomplished dramatist; in the characterization of the two central figures and in the graphic portrayal of the rebellion it looks forward to *Tamburlaine*. It is even possible, in the description of the sacrifice and divination, to forget that one is reading a translation. In his interpretation of Lucan Marlowe was greatly helped by the commentator Sulpitius, and in many instances it is the commentator and not the poet that he translates. Sulpitius helps him over matters of general knowledge and of Roman history and religion. More subtle are the instances where the gloss offered by Sulpitius suggests Marlowe's English word. Marlowe shares his debt to Lucan with Jonson (in *Catiline*) and with Daniel (in the *Civil Warres*), but further comparison of these works, so different in aims and methods, is unfruitful. (RG)

3303. Summers, Claude J. "Tamburlaine's Opponents and Machiavelli's *Prince*." *ELN* 11:256-58.
In addition to being progressively ordered according to their abilities, Tamburlaine's opponents in Part One may also represent the different kinds of monarchs distinguished by Machiavelli in *The Prince*. Mycetes is a hereditary prince; Cosroe is an usurping "new prince;" Bajazeth is a conquering emperor; and the Soldan is unique in being an elected monarch. Thus, Tamburlaine can take his truce with the world after he defeats the Soldan because with that conquest he has triumphed over all conceivable kinds of princes. That Marlowe may have structured his play according to a principle based on kingship has obvious implications for further study of *I Tamburlaine*. In addition, this ordering of Tamburlaine's opponents may be evidence more concrete than any heretofore offered that Marlowe did in fact consult *The Prince*

while writing *I Tamburlaine*. (CJS)

3305. Tibi, Pierre. "*Dr. Faustus* et la cosmologie de Marlowe." *RLV* 40:212-27.
Marlowe's views on cosmology result from the interconnection of various elements. His intellectual beliefs find support in his empirical skepticism and in the requirements of his concrete imagination: hence the rejection of the sphere of fire and the crystalline heaven in *Doctor Faustus*. But the same features are also traceable to the influence of factors of decorum and dramatic relevance. The compromise between tradition and innovation owes much to the supposed expectations of Marlowe's public, as well as to the game played by Mephostophilis, who tries to dupe Faustus in the pseudo-initiation of scene vi. This astronomy, both mathematical and judiciary (with elements of magic), stands at the crossroads of speculation and action. (PT)

3307. West, Robert H. "The Impatient Magic of *Dr. Faustus*." *ELR* 4:218-40.
Since Marlowe's *The Tragical History of Dr. Faustus* is about a magician turned witch and the devils to whom he assigns himself, and since it adheres in detail to orthodox views of spirit magic. critics ought to honor Elizabethan understanding of magic more than many do. Their failure to honor it results in their making Faustus more the heroic rebel than they would if they were more heedful of demonology. Faustus sins largely for ignoble reasons and by ignoble means; he compounds the sins of his prayer to devils and his pact with them by the further sins of presumption of both damnation and mercy. His strenuous though hopeless struggles to repent and the dangers and enticements that frustrate them are, like his sins, closed to the patterns found in demonology. The play allows Faustus enough of the dignity that goes with extreme recklessness to entitle us to call the tragedy not only a moral one but also a heroic one. (RHW)

3308. Williams, Gordon I. "Acting and Suffering in *Hero and Leander*." *Trivium* 8(1973):11-26.
The poem is full of ambiguities and opposites, some of which it seeks to reconcile. Sexual ambiguity is to the fore in both Hero and Leander, whether in hermaphroditic terms or in the conflation of chastity and licentiousness. In this respect the poem fits into an extensive Renaissance tradition found also in the fine arts, stemming from Platonic thought and Orphic theology. The poem is impressive for the way in which both Marlowe and Chapman keep this aspect in simultaneous focus with psychological concerns. Characterization has its place alongside myth and emblem in revealing the nature of love. Contradictions and ambiguities have a fundamental role in the poem since love itself is a paradox. (GW)

Mason. 3310. Williams, Gordon I. "Image Patterns in Mason's *The Turke*." *Trivium* 9:54-69.
Although in some ways a throw-back to the old Seneca-Kyd tradition, Mason's *Turke* has its share of Jacobean sophistication. There is a profusion of imagery which interlocks in a remarkable way to help the play to its conclusion. For all his crudity, Mason is comparable with the major Jacobean dramatists as a poet of violence. (GIW)

More, T. 3311. Baker, Howard. "Thomas More at Oxford." *Moreana* 43-44:6-11.
A discussion of the relationship between the University tradition that More was a student at St. Mary's Hall, Oxford, and the biographical evidence that he was a member of Canterbury College. The two views are not mutually exclusive. More probably had connections with both establishments, as is demonstrated by partial implications of Oxford historians and a reference in a Canterbury MS to an example of such a dual relationship. The effect of Oxford on More is briefly mentioned. (HB)

3313. Butkie, Joseph, Sabita Sankaran, and Donald Vecchiolla. "Some Reflections on the 'Vision' Attributed to Thomas More." *Moreana* 42:33-38.
In the seven "Vision" sonnets erroneously ascribed to More in a 17th-century manuscript, the anonymous poet creates a distinct symbology to depict specific personages and events during the reign of Henry VIII. The author of this sonnet sequence manipulates historical occurrences within an allegorical frame-

work, sustains an air of mystery through the strategic adoption of a controversial persona, and most significantly, employs a semi-dramatic structure. His strict control over imagery suggests a technique not dissimilar to that of writers within the emblematic tradition. A close analysis of the poem's historical and symbolic dimensions helps to decipher authorial intent, indicates the impossibility of assigning authorship to More, and underscores the unique talent displayed in the intellectual maneuverings of a writer concerned with sensitive politico-religious matters. (JDB, SS, & DAV)

3314. Butler, Johanna M. "More in Sixteenth-Century France." *Moreana* 42:21-22.
An allusion to More's execution and the Anglican schism appears in Diz. 147 of Maurice Scève's *Délie*, a Petrarchan sequence of love poems published in Lyon in 1544. No definitive answer has been given to the question—to what extent was the cultured public of the 16th century aware of contemporary international events and figures. Studies of 16th-century French private libraries show a striking lack of contemporary material. Such a reference to More and his drama by Scève, a provincial poet in a city with neither a royal court nor a university to serve as distribution center for international news, may be a significant indication of the degree of familiarity with contemporary events in England which could be expected of educated French society. (JMB)

3315. Doyle, Charles C. "Moreana, 1604-1660." *Moreana* 41:11-18.
This article continues from *Moreana*, 34, 38, and 41 a collection of materials supplementary to Gibson, *St. Thomas More: A Preliminary Bibliography of His Works and of Moreana to the Year 1750*. The materials range in time from the English Restoration to mid-18th century. 34 items of Moreana are described. These include references and allusions to More and his works, as well as quotations, translations, and adaptations from More's writings. (CCD)

3321. Gury, Jacques. "*L'Utopie* Tous Azimuts" [and] "The Abolition of Rural World in *Utopia*." *Moreana* 43-44:65-66,67-69.
The second half of chapter i of *Utopia* Book II is devoted to rural problems. In a few pages More puts forward the principles of a radical revolution: he does away with the countryman and leaves the countryside deserted but for a few food-production units around the city. In the days when England was mostly a rural country, More suppresses traditional farming and the village—a revolution justified in Utopia not only for political and economical reasons but also for social and ethical reasons: man can live to the full and blossom out only in an urban environment and in a congenial and convivial community, freed from rural bondage and from the mirage of Arcadian bliss. (JG)

3323. —— "Sequentia Utopica. 1. About the Maps of Utopia. 2. Similitudo Concordiam Facit. 3. Une Utopie chrétienne au siècle des lumières." *Moreana* 42:99-103.
1: Both the Louvain edition of More's *Utopia* in 1516 and the Basle edition in 1518 are illustrated with maps. Though the first one is a rather crude woodcut and the second is an elaborate print, their striking similarity leads us to think that both could have been designed by Ambrosius Holbein.
2: Nowadays we long for diversity and criticize More's Utopian commonwealth as too uniform and orderly, but in the 16th century, Europe was a very untidy patchwork of warring states and More saw similarity as a unifying factor. (JG)

3325. Himelick, Raymond. "Walter Ralegh and Thomas More: The Uses of Decapitation." *Moreana* 42:59-64.
The last stanza of Raleigh's "Passionate Man's Pilgrimage," written, as tradition has it, on the eve of execution, employs a macabre appropriation of the Pauline metaphor of Christ as head of the body of all Christian believers which More had anticipated 70 years earlier in his *Dialogue of Comfort*. Facing the virtual certainty of decapitation, More sought to strengthen himself for the ordeal with scripturally supported meditation on the glories of heaven, and a grim quip that no man could go headless to that great glory. Although Raleigh's poem is more opulently imagistic and baroque than the *Dialogue*, the prose piece could have provided him with certain motifs: white apparel, saving blood, radiance, slaking of thirst. The analogous handling of decapi-

tation in each work, mingling doctrinal orthodoxy with grisly jest. makes pure coincidence seem unlikely. (RH)

3328. Lloyd-Jones, Kenneth. "Thomas More and Maurice Scève's *Délie*." *Moreana* 42:23-32.

Scève mentions More's death once in *Délie*. Many important contemporary personages and events are also referred to, but More's death is specifically related to Scève's spiritual and sensual rebirth through his love for Délie. Scève's special treatment of More—no other figure is so intimately or so intricately bound to the poet's situation—suggests a particular sympathy for aspects of the Utopian ideal. More's concepts for the necessary equilibrium of society and the nature and function of Virtue are echoed in *Délie*. One may conclude that *Utopia* played a seminal role in Scève's formation. (KL-J)

3332. McLean, Andrew M. "A Note on Thomas More and Thomas Starkey." *Moreana* 41:31-36.

Starkey and More demonstrate common concerns for English problems but More's ideal reform is part and parcel of his Utopian society, whereas Starkey's *Dialogue between Reginald Pole and Thomas Lupset* particularizes his idealizations of justice in concrete proposals for immediate adoption. This is reflected, in part, in how he employs the dialogue form; Starkey's frame device is left undeveloped and no substantial distinctions are made in the characterization of his interlocutors. The *Dialogue* offers practical guidelines to reconstitute the commonweal as Pole is urged into the "active life" of governmental service. The striking similarities between the *Utopia* and the *Dialogue* demonstrate the reality of the problems both works attack and suggests Starkey's familiarity with More's work. (AMcL)

3335. Schuster, Louis A. "Reformation Polemic and Renaissance Values." *Moreana* 43-44:47-54.

The Reformation debate between More and Tyndale was supported by two value systems that initially seem opposed and even mutually exclusive, but from the deeper level of today's perspective often prove complementary. One of the main reasons for this disjunction in creed and cult that characterized Reformation polemic lay in the very nature of the polemical process. Since the polemical mode is committed to a problematic of exclusiveness, it follows almost inevitably that each opponent would pre-empt a series of positions advocating only a partial view of his complete vision and the value system that nurtured it. Beneath the preoccupations with faith and works, the true church, authority, and conscience lay the fundamental critical issue of the Reformation debate between More and Tyndale: namely, the question of certitude in salvation. (LAS)

3337. Spikes, Judith D. "*The Book of Sir Thomas More*: Structure and Meaning." *Moreana* 43-44:25-39.

Sir Thomas More by Anthony Munday and others, presents, in a thematically unified series of real and fictitious episodes, an examination of the predicament of the virtuous man trapped by a conflict between secular and spiritual responsibilities. The playwrights' view of their subject and manner of universalizing More's crisis were largely determined by Roper's *Life of Sir Thomas More*. The opening acts of the play show the title character in private and political action in the world. The middle scenes are largely taken up with More's soliloquy and with the interpolated play, a statement of the problem in terms of allegorical moral drama. The remaining scenes show how the world and the virtuous man may fall "at a little odds." All of the play's so-called "unrelated" episodes are exemplifications of one of these aspects, and the play is a complex but perfectly unified examination of the issue of responsibility. (JDS)

3338. Stevens, Irma N. "Aesthetic Distance in *Utopia*." *Moreana* 43-44:13-24.

More's use of esthetic distance in *Utopia* is effective because his satiric observer is usually at least twice removed from the author. More switches satiric spokesmen frequently. Hythloday is usually the satiric observer, but occasionally the arguments of both Hythloday and More are equally convincing. More also detaches himself by using inappropriate or paradoxical names, like "Hythloday," the nonsense babbler who speaks truth, and "Utopia," no place or every place. More also juxtaposes European values with their Utopian counterparts in order to reveal European folly as opposed to Utopian reason. Denun-

ciation is expressed not by More but by the Utopians or Hythloday in a traditional satiric mask, the upright, angry citizen. Much of the effectiveness of the satire derives from these techniques through which More achieves esthetic distance. (INS)

Mulcaster. 3342. DeMolen, Richard L. "Richard Mulcaster and Elizabethan Pageantry." *SEL* 14:209-21.

Mulcaster devoted considerable energy to the instruction of boys at Merchant Taylors' School (1561-86) and St. Paul's School (1596-1608) and early established a reputation as an educationalist. Combining pedagogy and letters, Mulcaster also maintained an active interest in literature and developed a taste for pageantry. Pageantry became for him a means of conveying adulation or a device for persuasion. He contributed to the three types of civic pageantry during a 45 year period of productivity. He summarized his reactions to the 1559 entry pageant of Elizabeth I to the city of London and prepared a Latin oration for the entry pageant of James I in 1604; he wrote "speaches and devyses" for two Lord Mayor's pageants in 1561 and 1568; and he contributed to the royal progress by participating in the Kenilworth fetes of 1575. (RLD)

Munday. 3343. Margeson, J.M.R. "Dramatic Form:The Huntington Plays." *SEL* 14:223-38.

The Downfall and *The Death of Robert Earl of Huntington* (Anthony Munday, 1598), condemned as typical Elizabethan hackwork, should be regarded rather as flourishing examples of dramatic romance. They have the simplified, idealized characters of romance and a plot which is both moral and romantic. Control is exercised not by cause and effect but by the familiar structure of an old tale. As in romance, characters and plot are enlarged in meaning through legend and myth. The two plays are linked in theme and through their being different phases of a cycle of life. The framework of induction and frequently broken illusion shows the dramatist's skill in drawing the audience into the very shaping of the play. (JMRM)

Nashe. 3344. Friedenreich, Kenneth. "Nashe's *Strange Newes* and the Case for Professional Writers." *SP* 71:451-72.

While much has been written concerning the place of the Nashe-Harvey controversy in the history and development of English prose style, little has been said about actual issues debated in the quarrel. *Strange Newes* by Nashe is an ardent defense of the literary professional and of the commercial press. Throughout the work Nashe presents two views of his opponent. *Strange Newes* is a tour de force of invective, and much of its power comes from Nashe's reliance on the essential qualities of popular literature, and in particular, news pamphlets. (KF)

3345. Leggatt, Alexander. "Artistic Coherence in *The Unfortunate Traveller*." *SEL* 14:31-46.

There is, especially toward the end of Nashe's *The Unfortunate Traveller*, a dominant sense of physical and moral corruption. Set against this is the pleasure-garden of Rome, which represents the unfallen world of Eden, but whose innocence, order, and beauty are possible only through mechanical contrivance. We may contrast the mechanical birds of the garden with the vulnerability of the flesh in the outside world. Some artistic control is also discernible in the figure of Jack. He is not a fully developed character, but his attitudes change in response to the changed nature of his experiences. The structure of the book also becomes steadier in the Italian scenes, which show a consistency of purpose and a tightness of organization unlike the episodic quality of the rest of the book. (AL)

Raleigh. 3349. Johnson, Michael L. "Some Problems of Unity in Sir Walter Ralegh's *The Ocean's Love to Cynthia*." *SEL* 14:17-30.

Walter Raleigh's "The Ocean's Love to Cynthia" dramatizes the frustrations and disappointments of a man of the court who has fallen from Elizabeth's grace and is trying to comprehend and communicate the meaning of his heavy sense of desolation. The elaboration of the theme is problematic because the structure of the poem's imagery is inconsistent, its language varies unevenly between the aureate and the plain style, and it is apparently incomplete. The poem's unity is tenuous and grounded more in the poet's mood than in the structure of the poem. The character of that tenuousness and what it tells us about the distracted poet's mind are of intriguing significance to anyone concerned with the problems of interpreting a richly made but confusingly unfinished imaginative work. (MLJ)

Sidney. 3361. Jones, Dorothy. "Sidney's Erotic Pen:An Interpretation of One of the *Arcadia* Poems." *JEGP* 73:32-47. Close examination of Sidney's *Arcadia* poems reveals subtlety and imaginative power. "What toong can her perfections tell" follows the conventional pattern of the blason, a standard formula popular in the Renaissance for descriptions of feminine beauty. Sidney's poem is an accomplished example in which the description of the lady is dominated by two pairs of contrasting ideas; nature and art on the one hand, passion and chastity on the other. Many *Arcadia* poems are highly erotic, this one among them. Analysis reveals that Sidney uses the blason and its associated images to provide a fixed framework for the subtle and elusive play of sexual imagery, while at the same time insisting upon the lady's purity and virtue. The poem was deservedly praised in its own time, for it is a masterpiece which transforms a well-worn formula into a witty and exquisitely beautiful work of art. (DLMJ)

3368. Waller, G.F. "A 'Matching of Contraries':Ideological Ambiguity in the Sidney Psalms." *WascanaR* 9:124-33. The Sidney Psalms, especially those written by the Countess of Pembroke, incorporate complex drives derived from the intellectual extremes of Renaissance thought. Many predictably reflect Reformed doctrines, although the Countess frequently reinforces their rhetorical impact by striking imagery and fine control of tone, sometimes developing hints from commentaries or glosses or from her own meditations. In other psalms, she also brings in some of the sophisticated courtly neoplatonic philosophy, marrying Hebrew and Renaissance modes of thought and contradicting the Reformation emphases found elsewhere. (GFW)

3372. Weiner, Andrew D. "Structure and 'Fore Conceit' in *Astrophil and Stella*." *TSLL* 16:1-25. A definition of Sidney's conception of structure is implicit in his discussion of the relationship between the work itself and the "fore conceit" or "*Idea*" of the work in the *Defence*. If the work is the only means by which we may come to the "fore conceit" and if the work is (as Sidney suggests) the sum total of our imaginative and emotional responses to it, then the structure may be said to be the organized sequence of responses it produces in the reader. Using this concept of structure as a guide to *Astrophil and Stella*, a five-part structure emerges, consisting of sonnets 1-20, 21-45, 46-69, 70-song VIII, and song IX-conclusion. These five parts are organized to form a tragi-comedy, according to Sidney's definitions of comedy, tragedy, and mixed genres in the *Defence*. (ADW)

Skelton. 3374. Atchity, Kenneth J. "Skelton's *Collyn Clout*: Visions of Perfectibility." *PQ* 52(1973):715-27. The Latin epigraphs set before and after John Skelton's *Collyn Clout* indicate the various levels of human awareness in the poem. The epigraphs provide a crucial insight into Skelton's satire on the contemporary state of humanity. Skelton's observations operate on three levels of human experience: the individual, the generally human, and the cosmic. Since he can see the corruption in both clashing orders, Collyn is concerned about "the commonwealth decayde" (353) and the general effect on mankind. Awareness of the cosmic dimensions of the human situation allows Collyn to maintain a satirical detachment while condemning the corrupt clergy for their failure to observe God's rule. Human perfectibility progresses on the same three levels, as reflected in the concluding epigraph: man alone is incomplete and ineffective; man within the community shares responsibility for perfection; beyond human potential, man must follow his natural impulse in order to imitate the perfection of God. Paslm xciv, quoted at the beginning, likewise deals with imperfect man's search for perfection. (KJA)

Spenser. 3383. Combellack, C.R.B. "Spenser's *Shepheardes Calender* (November), 158-162." *Expl* 33:Item 5. Lines 158, 159, and 161 of the November Eclogue of Spenser's *Shepheardes Calender* mean: All that a fleshly form can possess of beauty, that did the now-buried body of Dido possess, and that did I see when her body was on the bier (that is, she was still beautiful even in death). The interpretation differs from that proposed by A.C. Partridge in *The Language of Renaissance Poetry* (London, 1971): "the body of Dido, being buried, contained all virtues earthly mould bestowed; I still could see her on the bier, when it was carried to the grave" (p. 79). The interpretation Combellack proposes requires line 158 ("That did her buried body hould") to be added to Partridge's list of lines in the poem that begin with initial trochees (p. 71). (CRBC)

3393. Entzminger, Robert L. "Courtesy:The Cultural Imperative." *PQ* 53:389-400. Courtesy, the virtue with which Spenser concerns himself in Book Six of *The Faerie Queene*, is a necessary complement to the sternness of the ideal of justice Artegall pursues in the preceding book. If society requires force to establish and to maintain it. it also requires courtesy to make it accommodating and desirable. Thus personal satisfaction and its relation to social responsibility is the problem central to the book, and it finds resolution in the pervasive though altering figure of the sovereign lady with her admirers. (RLE)

3404. Harris, Duncan S. "The Paradox of Allegory:Being and Becoming in Spenser and Prudentius." *WascanaR* 9:66-74. The Redcrosse Knight of the first book of Edmund Spenser's *Faerie Queene* is both the representative of, and the quester for, holiness. This paradox is rooted in Prudentius' *Psychomachia*. There, the fiction is located in the mind of its hero, Mansoul, who is both the creator of the fiction and the composite of the characters within it. The allegorical hero's world replicates his mind. The allegorical fiction re-enacts the domination of the hero-creator's mind by the idea which the fictive hero seeks. The formal characteristics of moral allegory derive from this relationship. The constriction of the characters, plot, landscape, and theme reflects the fiction's domination by the mind of the virtue-obsessed hero. (DSH)

3409. Johnson, William C. "Spenser's *Amoretti* and the Art of the Liturgy." *SEL* 14:47-61. Sequential structure has always been a major consideration in the criticism of Spenser's *Amoretti*, yet until quite recently most critics have failed to note the tightness of organization in the sequence. Not only do some of the sonnets refer to specific days of the year, but all of the poems parallel days before, during, and after Lent, 1594. Furthermore, the sonnets which appear in the position of the Sundays form an even more unusual pattern, for in them Spenser breaks his narrative lines to include special effects. Verbal, thematic, and sometimes stylistic echoes of the *Book of Common Prayer* weave in and out of the sequence, creating quite a different narrative. The analogies are drawn from specific Collects, Gospels, Epistles, etc. In the final reading, then, two sequences emerge. On one level the *Amoretti* presents the courtship of a man and a woman, and on the expanded metaphoric level the sequence becomes a narrative of the penitent Christian's search for Christ. (WCJ)

3412. Klein, Joan L. "The Anatomy of Fortune in Spenser's *Faerie Queene*." *AnM* 14(1973):74-95. As Spenser anatomizes the medieval figure of Fortune, he assigns her various attributes to separate locations in *The Faerie Queene*. Chance, one of Fortune's principal attributes, is abstracted, disembodied, and unlocalized. It thus becomes a condition of human existence in fairyland's "middest." But Spenser relegates the figure of Fortune and her other attributes to hell under the figures of Lucifera and Philotime and to a long past golden age under the figure of Mutabilitie. When Spenser describes Lucifera and Philotime, he stresses those attributes of Fortune which were traditionally linked with Satan's temptation to the world. Mutabilitie becomes seen as an extension of Dame Nature in the way that medieval Fortune was seen as an instrument of Providence. However, that Spenser makes chance part of fairyland's "middest," and explicitly assigns Fortune to locales resembling hell or heaven suggests that he perceives a fundamental separation between empirical experience and faith in received, Christian tradition, a separation indicative of the distance between the Renaissance and the Middle Ages. (JLK)

3416. Maynard, John. "Perspectives on Change:Narrative Technique in Spenser's Cantos of Mutabilitie." *JNT* 4:100-18.
In Spenser's Cantos of Mutabilitie Spenser employs different narrative forms to present a variety of perspectives on the problem of change. No one view is definitive; but together they provide an effective anatomy of Spenser's subject. In Canto vi, the myth of Mutabilitie's challenge to the gods shows change as it appears from an individual human point of view. By contrast, the Faun Faunus interlude, a parody of more serious myths, presents change in a comic perspective as the result of human folly. In the judgment of nature at Arlo Hill, Spenser looks at change from a sober, philosophical point of view. Finally, in the conclusion of Nature's judgment, and in the two stanzas remaining from Canto vi, Spenser looks at change in the largest, religious perspective. (JRM)

3418. McKim, William M.,Jr. "The Divine and Infernal Comedy of Spenser's Mammon." *ELWIU* 1:3-16.
In representing Guyon's journey through the cave of Mammon in Book Two of *The Faerie Queene*, Spenser minimizes the element of dramatic tension and heroic conflict and, consequently, achieves a comic vision on several levels. On one level Mammon and his vain attempt to represent excrement as a means of grace represent an absurdity easily enjoyed by the man of reason. But on a higher level of meaning Mammon and his cave disclose a mystery beyond reason to discern and will to control. Mammon's ironic parody of I Corinthians before he and Guyon enter the cave is the first of a series of allusions pointing to the Christian doctrines of original sin and grace. Guyon's fainting and awakening to life at the end of the episode represent the natural man's participation in a mystery he does not understand, a divine comedy of death and resurrection. (WMcK)

3421. O'Connell, Michael. "History and the Poet's Golden World:The Epic Catalogues in *The Faerie Queene*." *ELR* 4:241-67.
In the historical catalogs of *The Faerie Queene* Spenser shows his characters' search for the past as a context and incentive for action in the present. The catalogs encapsulate, in Virgilian fashion, the myth and history of Britain from the Troy story up to the reign of Elizabeth. In the reader this amalgam of myth and history evokes a consciousness of the turbulent amorality of history. To this consciousness Spenser juxtaposes the moral possibilities of the golden world of his poem; each of the passages modeled on historical chronicles ends with a fictional image which gestures toward the present. But in the second half of the poem, Spenser insists less on the distinction between history and the ideal world of poetry; on the one hand (Book v) the poem moves closer to actual history, but, in other moments, it moves back and asserts the self-sufficiency of the poet's vision. One such moment, the marriage of the Thames and the Medway, is a version of the historical catalogs, but one which emphasizes the mythopoeia of the poet. Insisting on the specificity of his vision, Spenser celebrates the geography of Britain by weaving its rivers into a poetic tapestry which includes the mythopoeia of classical poetry. (MO'C)

3427. Sims, Dwight J. "The Syncretic Myth of Venus in Spenser's Legend of Chastity." *SP* 71:427-50.
Analysis of the mythical structure of Book III of *The Faerie Queene* by reference to Pico della Mirandola's myth of the three Venuses makes it clear that Spenser unified his Legend of Chastity through the logic of its allegory. The three forms of love and chastity, *celeste*, *umano*, and *bestiale*, signified in Pico's myth by the three Venuses, are unfolded in Spenser's allegory as Diana, the Venus of the Garden of Adonis, and the Venus of Malecasta's and Busirane's tapestries. They are described further and interpreted by example through the actions of the human characters. By using Pico's triadic myth to form this allegorical matrix of key characters, Spenser organizes the moral philosophy as well as the literary structure of his Legend of Chastity. (DJS)

3433. Waters, D. Douglas. "Spenser and Symbolic Witchcraft In *The Shepheardes Calender*." *SEL* 14:3-15.
Spenser in *The Shepheardes Calender* used symbolic witchcraft to satirize the Roman Mass, the Mass-priests as conjuring magicians, and their "conjuring ceremonies." Artistically manipulating literal witchcraft as a symbol of spiritual seduction practiced by Romanists on the simple English laity, the poet effectively interrelated magicians, false shepherds, wolves, and foxes. On ceremonies and vestments there seems to be no evidence in *The Shepheardes Calender* that Spenser felt too many "reliques of Popery" had been officially retained in the Church of England. His conformity was not that of "moderate" Puritanism. If he had used symbolic witchcraft against "popish conjuring garments" he would still remain, as he does now, within conforming range of the Elizabethan Settlement, as enforced by Archbishop Parker's "Advertisements." (DDW)

3435. Williams, Kathleen. "Spenser and the Metaphor of Sight." [F 92]:153-69.
Examines Spenser's use of sight as a metaphor for moral, intellectual, spiritual, poetic insight. The metaphor is traditional and inescapable and extends from the classical ancients to our own time. Plato, and the Renaissance neoplatonists, were especially concerned with it, and recognized its power over our imaginations, its ambivalence, and hence its rich expressiveness. Spenser's use of it is pervasive, and particularly varied within an overall tendency to see his poetry as vision, a thing presented to his inner sight. Most of the minor poems both use the metaphor and examine its possible meanings in a variety of contexts. In *The Faerie Queene* it is used differently in each book, as it applies to the aspect of life the book explores, culminating in the poetic and cosmic visions of Book VI and the *Mutabilitie* cantos. (KMW)

3436. Wilson, Rawdon. "Images and 'Allegoremes' of Time in the Poetry of Spenser." *ELR* 4:56-82.
Spenser's use of time-imagery is both complex and pervasive. Separate concepts are reflected in Spenser's imagery. These concepts are fundamental to the understanding of Spenser's poetry since they create a substructure of ideas that determines narrative situation, theme, and imagery. Most of the traditional Renaissance concepts of time are to be found in the substructure of Spenser's poetry but the most important—uniting *The Faerie Queene* and *The Shepheardes Calender* in a single vision of human experience—is that of time as the condition of action, the unfolding of moral dimension in which people experience, learn, fulfill themselves, and, perhaps, win salvation. Spenser employs three distinct kinds of imagery to express his varied sense of time: configurational imagery, eidetic imagery, and "allegoremes." The last implies a brief but inseparable episode—a fabric woven of narrative and allegorical materials—in which through the combination of character, incident, and action one of the several concepts of time is made inescapably clear. It is argued that Spenser's use of time-imagery is most distinctive, and most satisfying, on the level of "allegoreme." (RW)

3437. Wilson, Robert R. "Spenser's Reputation in Italy and France." *HAB* 24(1973):105-09.
Despite Spenser's great indebtedness to writers of the Italian romance-epic tradition, the *Faerie Queene* has never been adequately translated into Italian. Early translations, such as that by Mathias, are both incomplete and insufficient. Furthermore, there has never been a discussion of Spenser's work by Italian critics. Comment upon Spenser began in European criticism only after French critics toward the middle of the nineteenth century began to take note of him. This critical response was dominated by the opinions of Hippolyte Taine. An examination of critical writing on Spenser in Italian and French since the time of Taine shows that his assessment continues to have the weight of orthodoxy. (RRW)

3438. Wright, Lloyd A. "Guyon's Heroism in the Bower of Bliss." *TSLL* 15:597-603.
The negative response evoked by Guyon's destruction of the Bower of Bliss in *The Faerie Queene* is an integral element in Spenser's portrayal of his exemplary temperance. It gives an accurate account of our natural reaction to the destruction of anything so alluring and clarifies the nature of Guyon's heroism by objectifying his attitude. Guyon is driven to destructiveness by the tension between his rational awareness of the evil of the Bower and his sensuous and emotional attraction to its beauty.

The negative reaction evokes a similar attitude in readers who self-consciously remain aware of the dangers of the Bower. That reaction elicits a unique sympathetic identification with Guyon and accords with Spenser's elevated didactic purpose by enhancing our understanding of, and appreciation for, Guyon's heroic temperance. (LAW)

Surrey. 3440. Davis, Walter R. "Contexts in Surrey's Poetry." *ELR* 4:40-55.
Surrey's strength as a poet consists in his relation of an individual experience to different contexts which give significance and resonance to it. Such is the quality that his attempt to create an English voice like a Roman voice in his translations from the *Aeneid* indicates. In his original verse we find a variety of contexts by means of which individual experience becomes large in its implications. In his nature poems, the relation between man and natural objects defines his identity; in his poems on classical subjects, events from the past not only modify but also change present feelings; in his social poems, the relation between the individual and those around him is what defines a situation. It is in the elegiac pieces that Surrey's use of other people and other times comes to bear most powerfully upon individual feeling. The image of Surrey that results from this examination is that of a "classical poet" concerned with setting events in as broad a context as possible, with the resultant poetry both broad in its effects and impressive in its fluidity. (WRD)

Wager. 3445. Kutrieh, Ahmad Ramez. "The Doubling of Parts in *Enough Is as Good as a Feast*." *ELN* 12:79-84.
Although a caption under the title of the interlude *Enough Is as Good as a Feast* (1564?) suggests that seven players are needed, only four players are required to play all the parts. The author, William Wager (fl. 1565-69), manifests his sense of action in the manner in which he skillfully alternates the scene between the camps of good and evil. The shifting of the scene occurs after each of the four instances when the stage is cleared. Throughout the interlude there are no more than four players on stage at any one time. (ARK)

Wyatt. 3450. Dembo, Pamela. "Wyatt's Multi-Faceted Presentation of Love." *UES* 9,iv(1971):5-10.
The variety of Wyatt's attitudes toward love are examined in his portrayal of both woman's constancy and fickleness, of lovers' quarrels and reconciliations, and of the hazards of wooing a reluctant mistress. In the role of lover, Wyatt vaccillates between forceful insistence and gentleness, impatience and tolerance, assurance and doubt. Wyatt's appeal lies in his integrity and mature assessment of the vicissitudes of his broad experience of love and the world. (PD)

3456. Ogle, Robert B. "Wyatt and Petrarch: A Puzzle in Prosody." *JEGP* 73:189-208.
Scholars have not yet satisfactorily explained the roughness of rhythm in Wyatt's translations of Petrarch's sonnets. Since Petrarch was well versed in Latin prosody and was a skillful composer of Latin verse, he probably experimented with the logaoedic measures of Horace and Catullus. If Wyatt was also aware of these meters, as his classical training would suggest he was, he may well have put them to test in his English adaptations. The frequent appearance, in Petrarch's sonnets and in Wyatt's translations, of one or another variation of the logaoedic rhythmical patterns leads to the conclusion that both poets were imitating these popular classical meters. (RBO)

Shakespeare

Bibliography. 3460. Alexander, Nigel. "The Year's Contribution to Shakespearian Study: 2. Shakespeare's Life, Times, and Stage." *ShS* 27:172-79.
A review of the year's work concerned with Shakespeare's life, times, and stage containing notices of books and articles. The most important items dealt with are: G. Bullough, *Narrative and Dramatic Sources of Shakespeare Vol. VII: The Major Tragedies*; Richard Southern, *The Staging of Plays before Shakespeare*; and the new series of scholarly monographs from the University of

Salzburg. (NA)

3469. Proudfoot, Richard. "The Year's Contribution to Shakespearian Study: 3. Textual Studies." *ShS* 27:179-92.
The review covers publications relating to the text of Shakespeare, including editions and concordances, which appeared between August 1972 and August 1973. (GRP)

3470. Reid, S.W. "Justification and Spelling in Jaggard's Compositor B." *SB* 27:91-111.
Justification of lines often affected a compositor's normal spelling habits, and this recognition has led to the practice of isolating spellings in long lines from those in short, which serve as evidence of a workman's habits. But all spellings influenced by justification do not appear in fully long lines, and all spellings in long lines are not affected by justification. Study of the plays set from known printed copy by Compositor B in the First Folio of Shakespeare suggests that he sometimes deliberately shortened his normal spellings in lengthy lines of verse as he set them, and thus produced lines which do not quite fill the measure but nevertheless contain justified spellings, and he usually changed spellings toward the ends of his lines of prose, so that some of the words at the beginnings of these lines could be legitimate evidence of his normal spelling preferences and tolerances. (SWR)

General and Miscellaneous. 3474. Barry, Jackson G. "Shakespeare with Words: The Script and the Medium of Drama." *SQ* 25:161-71.
In most English classes the book not the stage provides our experience of Shakepeare, a fact which frequently leads to confusions as to what the medium of drama is. At its simplest this medium consists of two or more persons in a particular space interacting through and with time. Locating the work of dramatic art on the stage implies that the actor is neither an interpreter nor a neutral communicator of a work which exists elsewhere, presumably in the script. It also focuses on the problem of how different productions of a single work may be said all to constitute the same play and on what basis any of these productions might be called incorrect. (JGB)

3479. Bean, John C. "Passion Versus Friendship in the Tudor Matrimonial Handbooks and Some Shakespearean Implications." *WascanaR* 9:231-40.
Romantic passion in Shakespeare's comedies leads to fertile marriage, but marriage is possible only because passion is tempered with friendship. The ambiguous attitude toward love is illuminated by the passion-friendship conflict in the humanistic matrimonial books of Vives, Bullinger, Cleaver, and others. The matrimonial writers denounce romantic love as a bond for marriage and endorse friendship instead, insisting that marriage was instituted for the assuaging of loneliness. The significance of friendship is its non-transcendent nature, which acknowledges the beloved's finite, non-idealized human personality. Shakespeare's heroines are spontaneous romantics who yield to passion and self-aware realists who mock it. (JCB)

3491. Chan, Mimi, and Helen Kwok. "Figuratively Speaking: A Study of the Cantonese-Speaking Undergraduate's Response to Figures of Speech in Shakespeare." *SQ* 25:209-27.
Discusses the problems of understanding figurative language which confront undergraduates reading English literature in the University of Hong Kong, with emphasis on Shakespeare's works. Undergraduates are mostly native speakers of Cantonese who come to the study of English literature with a set of associations from their own language, and yet it would appear that many figurative expressions in Shakespeare and other English writers are almost paralleled in Chinese. An investigation of figures of speech drawn from four different areas illustrates this. The degree of similarity suggests that perhaps human beings have so much in common that similarities do exist in the way they symbolize their experience. (MC & HK)

3510. Fields, Albert W. "The Shakespearean Self-Author." *SCB* 34:150-56.
Certain Shakespearean characters rejected moral order and attempted to recreate "self" in the image of their own desires. Such a character thus presumed that he was the "author of himself," and in his egocentric quest, he developed an ideology of "self," coming inevitably into conflict with accepted ontological

and ethical concepts. Such conflict reflected the dualities in his nature and the extension of these dualities in society where benevolent impulses not only formed moral custom but were considered "natural" law. As the self-author's damaging quest was destined to failure, so was the restoration of his damaged society inevitable. He provided a negative and self-destructive *exemplum*, whose purpose was, in Hamlet's terms, to show "the very age and body of the time his form and pressure." (AWF)

3512. Fisch, Harold. "Shakespeare and the Puritan Dynamic." *ShS* 27:81-92.

Three plays in which Puritan characters appear show that Shakespeare takes Puritanism seriously as a religion of power. In *The Merchant of Venice* he studies the use and abuse of economic power; in *Twelfth Night* he deals with social power and ambition; and in *Measure for Measure* the theme is the temptation of political power. Puritanism is also exhibited in the style and structure of these plays. (HF)

3520. Gajdusek, R.E. "Death, Incest, and the Triple Bond in the Later Plays of Shakespeare." *AI* 31:109-58.

Shakespeare's later plays show a frequent confrontation with three women, or a triadic feminine power, which presages the overthrow of masculine consciousness. This danger is variously linked to incest which becomes the major spectre that the plays seek to exorcize. Exorcism of the incest spell is accomplished as the victim-sufferer manages to confront the features of the original incest situation in an inverted mirror image. As this occurs therapeutic ritual redeems the sufferer: all losses are restored and all sorrows end. The patterns of Shakespeare's late plays and also of Sophocles' Theban trilogy recommend that the incest taboo basically exists to guard against the peril to the consciousness of man of uroboric reversion into the womb of the Great Mother Goddess. Shakespeare's achievement in the later plays is to ask for the art role of perpetuator of the civilized condition of man as through its abstract metaphoric means. Man wins back from entrapment in the incest spell the humanity he was in danger of losing. (REG)

3525. Gillett, Peter J. "Me, U, and Non-U:Class Connotations of Two Shakespearean Idioms." *SQ* 25:297-309.

The superfluous (or ethic) "me" in Shakespeare often accompanies a tone of amazement or affront, often connotes presumption, and becomes strongly associated with personal honor. The dative of interest in commands connotes more strongly, the more superfluous it becomes, the speaker's pretension to superior status; irony shifted this connotation onto the person addressed, and thence onto the third person in declarative utterances. Thus the ethic "me," used parodically, implies that the person parodied habitually imputes presumption to others. The early expletive "me" in vulgar-colloquial narrative contributed, besides, connotations of vulgarity. "U" (upper-class) Englishmen adopt vulgarisms as bulwarks against the pretensions of the non-U (genteel aspirants to upper-class status); hence Shakespeare often associates the ethic "me" with the least genteel U activities. (PJG)

3536. Hoy, Cyrus. "Shakespeare and the Revenge of Art." [F 92]:71-94.

Shakespeare's sonnets are the direct expression of his profoundest feelings concerning love, its exultation and its despair; his plays are the oblique expression of these feelings, wherein emotions are objectified in the context of a dramatic fiction. The reality of ambiguous loves and hates, frustrations and fears which the sonnets record is transformed in the romantic fictions of the comedies, where Shakespeare's art seeks to create a more emotionally satisfying shape of things than the world provides. (CH)

3552. Levin, Richard. "On Fluellen's Figures, Christ Figures, and James Figures." *PMLA* 89:302-11.

The method used by some recent critics to prove that certain Shakespearean characters are "figures" of Christ (or of other biblical or Renaissance personages) was parodied by Shakespeare himself in Fluellen's comparison of Henry v to Alexander the Great. Its success is guaranteed in advance, since it allows the critic to select only the similarities between the two persons being compared without considering whether these are unique or whether they are more significant than the differences between them. The evidence is thus subjected to a double screening: the

critic determines which events in the character's career can be compared to the historical personage, and then which aspects of those events are relevant to the comparison. Even the differences between them can be converted into positive evidence. (RL)

3556. MacFadden, Fred R.,Jr. "Report on Opportunities for Teaching and Researching the Literature of Shakespeare Using the Computer." *CSHVB* 4(1973):3-8.

This report lists 68 research projects in Shakespearean stylistics and pedagogy which would be adaptable to some type of computer processing. Five pedagogical and 63 subject matter projects are described. The pedagogical projects give students and teachers an opportunity to apply closer logic to Shakespeare criticism by working with computerized programs of Shakespearean texts while at the same time developing a firmer grasp of computer science. The subject matter projects, which offer quantitative analyses of Shakespeare's works as a whole, are divided as follows: graphic arts, computer science, audio-visual techniques, communications, literary criticism, foreign languages, mathematics, musicology, logic, psychology, reading, and speech. (FRM,Jr)

3568. Meyers, Jeffrey. "Shakespeare and Mann's *Doctor Faustus*." *MFS* 19(1973):541-45.

Shakespeare's *Love's Labour's Lost* plays a significant though minor role in Mann's *Doktor Faustus* for it is used as a comic parody of the Faustian themes of the book and is subtly related to the recurrent motifs and rich fabric of tradition which Adrian spins round himself like a cocoon. The seeds of Adrian's genius and the tragic pattern of his allegorical life are foreshadowed in his demonically inspired adaptation of Shakespeare's play, for as Zeitblom regretfully confesses, the very definition of Germanism is "implicit Satanism." (JM)

3570. Milward, Peter. "Teaching Shakespeare in Japan." *SQ* 25:228-33.

Japanese students are introduced to Shakespeare's plays, partly through Lamb's *Tales* and partly through the many Japanese translations, such as those of Shoyo Tsubouchi and Tsuneari Fukuda. For university undergraduates the traditional method of teaching Shakespeare is the laborious process of translating the plays afresh in the classroom. An English teacher should dispense with the translation and give a detailed commentary on a particular play, followed by the assignment of a report and a class discussion on the proposed subjects of the report. At the undergraduate level the spontaneous interest of the students often leads them to undertake productions. (PCM)

3590. Pinciss, G.M. "Shakespeare, Her Majesty's Players, and Pembroke's Men." *ShS* 27:129-36.

Shakespeare's theatrical associations in the 1580s until his emergence as a payee of the Lord Chamberlain's company in 1592 are unknown. The number of literary and dramatic connections between the repertory of the Queen's Men and Shakespeare's own work suggests his intimate knowledge of the plays this company performed and possible Shakespearean influence on it. The likelihood that one section of the company operated briefly under the patronage of the Earl of Pembroke explains further cross-influences. (GMP)

3616. Thomson, Peter. "Shakespeare Straight and Crooked:A Review of the 1973 Season at Stratford." *ShS* 27:143-54.

Of the Stratford productions in 1973, *Love's Labour's Lost* was the "straightest." *As You Like It* was less perverse as a whole than it was in certain details, and Richard Pasco's Jaques was a brilliant presentation of a seedy, dyspeptic scholar. *Romeo and Juliet* was ill-controlled, with an unobtrusive Romeo and a perverted Mercutio who was played as a rival gang-leader to Tybalt. *Richard II* was an unusually dangerous piece of John Barton's work. It made a feature of role-playing and explored the play's awareness of the world as a stage. (PWT)

3629. Whitaker, Virgil K. "Shakespeare the Elizabethan." [F 92]:141-51.

Shakespeare was often very much of his own times, even in his greatest plays. Major critical concerns about his tragedies result from our demanding of him what we have no right to demand of an Elizabethan playwright. An Elizabethan, or even a Shakespearean, tragedy may only tell a well-known story. If a tragedy has a unified plot, we dare not assume that such unity results from concentration upon a single tragic hero. Third, granted a single tragic hero, we still have no right to demand in this hero a definite tragic flaw or error. These propositions are first established for Elizabethan tragedy as a whole and then applied, respectively, to *Antony and Cleopatra, Julius Caesar,* and *Hamlet.* (VKW)

Comedies. 3645. Miola, Robert. "Early Shakespearean Comedy:*sub specie ludi.*" *Thoth* 14:23-36.
Shakespeare's comedy exhibits all the significant characteristics of formal play as defined by Johan Huizinga and Roger Caillois. The openings of the early comedies present a set of participants who are quickly divided around a central *agon.* The action of the comedies takes place in areas removed from the ordinary business of daily routine, enveloped in an air of mysterious illusion. The exits from the Shakespearean playgrounds of Navarre, Ephesus, and the Athenian forest all feature a movement toward the creation of a new and permanent play community. (RSM)
    3647. Semon, Kenneth J. "Fantasy and Wonder in Shakespeare's Last Plays." *SQ* 25:89-102.
Fantasy and wonder are central concepts in *Pericles, Cymbeline, The Winter's Tale,* and *The Tempest.* The world of each of these plays indirectly reflects reality in terms of fantasy, and wonder is, as in tragedy, a basic emotional response to that fantasy. By setting up a fantasy world, Shakespeare provides us with a unique perspective from which to view the world outside the play. (KJS)

All's Well That Ends Well. 3675. Carson, Neil. "Some Textual Implications of Tyrone Guthrie's 1953 Production of *All's Well That Ends Well.*" *SQ* 25:52-60.
Study of Tyrone Guthrie's production of *All's Well* shows that many emendations in modern texts are either wrong or inapplicable to performances on an open stage. Directorial changes in the prompt-book of Guthrie's 1953 production are discussed. His stage business throws light on several of the Folio stage directions; his staging of Act III.v suggests an explanation of the origin of the ghost character Violenta; and his rearrangement of some speech-headings challenges the belief that the letters E and G following speech-prefixes in the Folio text refer to the actors who originally played the roles. Although Guthrie's alterations are sometimes extreme, they provide insights which could profitably be considered by future editors of the play. (NRC)
    3676. Godshalk, W[illiam] L. "*All's Well That Ends Well* and the Morality Play." *SQ* 25:61-70.
All's Well That Ends Well is a far different artistic entity from the Morality Play of the previous century. Although Parolles appears to be the conventional Vice, Helena is hardly the conventional Virtue, and Bertram is not the typical Everyman. Helena does not completely preserve her virtue in an evil world, and indeed, Parolles, Helena, and Bertram are all deceivers. As a practitioner of deceit, Helena receives her proper Morality reward, a deceptive man for a mate. The play may be seen as an ironic or comic confirmation of Morality ethics. (WLG)
    3677. Pearce, Frances M. "In Quest of Unity:A Study of Failure and Redemption in *All's Well That Ends Well.*" *SQ* 25:71-88.
Through the simultaneous development of romantic and realistic viewpoints in *All's Well* we are made aware of a paradox about the power of love and the powerlessness of love. If we appreciate this paradox we are able to understand the full implications of the play's basic organizing and unifying pattern, that of failure redeemed by grace. For perception of this paradox, made possible by the simultaneous development of romantic and realistic viewpoints, helps us to draw together and resolve the apparently conflicting implications of that pattern and to grasp the principles on which a rich and inclusive comic harmony is based. (FMP)
    3678. Wheeler, Richard P. "The King and the Physician's Daughter:*All's Well That Ends Well* and the Late Romances." *CompD* 8:311-27.
The action of *All's Well* is similar to that of the festive comedies, but there are several indications of Shakespeare's movement toward the late romances. The strong emphasis on parental figures suggests the family centered actions of the later plays. The relation of the king to Helena anticipates the father/daughter

bonds of *Pericles, The Winter's Tale,* and *The Tempest;* like them, it is doubly tied to the theme of loss and recovery. *All's Well* also shares with the romances the need to balance a woman's power to create or regenerate against a man's power within family and social relations. The festive action of the play cannot express fully these altered comic concerns, and *All's Well* is caught in the confusion of a fundamental shift in comic form. (RPW)

Antony and Cleopatra. 3683. Erwin, John W. "Hero as Audience:*Antony and Cleopatra* and *Le soulier de satin.*" *MLS* 4,ii:65-77.
The way Shakespeare and Claudel reduce their heroes to passive witnesses convinces audiences to experience their own freely chosen passivity as a source of power. Shakespeare can rely upon the close collaboration of a public, but Claudel must more elaborately stage theatrical mediation to educate audiences to authorize this apotheosis of response. (JWE)
    3687. Smith, Gordon R. "The Melting of Authority in *Antony and Cleopatra.*" *CollL* 1:1-18.
Discussion of the nature of constituted authority as portrayed in *Antony and Cleopatra.* Antony, Cleopatra, and Octavius share major faults. The nature of Shakespeare's changes from Plutarch, the extent to which power is portrayed as based upon prestige, and the rulers' faults together imply no particular adherence on Shakespeare's part to ideas of the rightful eminence and rule by persons of high degree. The authority of power which melts from Antony is paralleled by the melting of moral authority from all the rulers. Shakespeare's characterization implies strong skepticism about any inherent merit in those who have arrived at the summits of power. (GRS)
    3689. Waterhouse, Ruth. "Shakespeare's *Antony and Cleopatra* i.iv.12-13 and 44-47." *Expl* 33:Item 17.
The paradoxical nature of Lepidus' simile about Antony in Shakespeare's *Antony and Cleopatra,* i.iv.12-13, reflects both his own stupidity, in equating faults with stars and darkness with goodness, and also Antony's transcendental quality.
    In Shakespeare's *Antony and Cleopatra,* i.iv.44-47, Caesar's use of the flag iris simile for the fickleness of the mob exemplifies his tendency to ignore potential beauty to emphasize unpleasantness. This is consistent with his inability to see anything of value in the relationship between Antony and Cleopatra. (RW)

As You Like It. 3696. Schleiner, Winifried. "'Tis Like the Howling of Irish Wolves Against the Moone':A Note on *As You Like It,* v.ii.109." *ELN* 12:5-8.
This line from *As You Like It* has confused editors of Shakespeare, who may have complicated its meaning unnecessarily: Furness observed that wolves in England presumably howled against the moon quite as monotonously as wolves in Ireland and speculated that Shakespeare intended some allusion to which we no longer have any clue. Shakespeare's contemporaries generally thought that wolves were extinct in England, but believed that Scotland and particularly Ireland were infested with them. That the absence of wolves in England was a topic of conversation is apparent in a long disquisition of Sir Philip Sidney's quoted by the German Philip Camerarius. Camden's *Britain* contains a similar discussion on the topic of wolves. (WS)

Comedy of Errors. 3699. Petronella, Vincent F. "Structure and Theme Through Separation and Union in Shakespeare's *The Comedy of Errors.*" *MLR* 69:481-88.
Shakespeare's *Comedy of Errors* is built upon four inter-related levels of reality: Family, Commerce, State, and Cosmos. These levels undergo sophisticated development by means of a pervasive binding-severing or separation-union pattern in the language and action of the play. Literal and figurative occurrences of tying, fastening, uniting, confining, and finding are balanced by those of untying, releasing, divorcing, freeing, and losing. Family, State, and Commerce are the most fully rendered levels of reality in the play; nevertheless, the level of Cosmos is also incorporated, especially through lines spoken by Luciana (ii.i.7-25). All four levels are unified artfully by the separation-union motif, which lies at the center of this comedy and which generates the overall

dramatic movement from states of division to those of unity; from the unhappiness of separation to the contentment and satisfaction of reunion. (VFP)

Coriolanus. 3702. Johnson, Vernon E. "Shakespeare's *Coriolanus* IV.vii.27-57." *Expl* 33:Item 21.
The controversial speech of Aufidius in *Coriolanus* (IV. vii.27-57) reflects the pattern of the entire play and reveals a man who is devoted first to power and second to the appearance of honor. From his first appearance in the play, as the Volscian tactician, to his last, as the engineer of Coriolanus' murder, he is shown to be a pragmatic man who uses any means for achieving victory. In the crucial speech itself, the last philosophical commentary before the conclusion, Aufidius notes Coriolanus' great successes, analyzes the nature of the trouble, comments on the merits of Coriolanus, and observes that our virtues have no ultimate reality at all. It concludes, as does the play, with a cynical praise of power. (VEJ)

Hamlet. 3717. Bizley, W.H. "The Stars Over Denmark —Some Metaphysical Considerations for a Reading of *Hamlet*." *Theoria* 41(1973):31-44.
In *Hamlet* the moral and psychological only derive from the ontological, the state of "being" in a Thomist sense, as it effects the state of Denmark in Shakespeare's play. In the light of this, T. S. Eliot's reading of the play in terms of the objective correlative is attacked, as is also the charge of Platonism in the play's chief character. It is also shown how the unity of state and the unity of stars have entirely different metaphysical presuppositions of major importance for the way metaphor is used in the play. (WHB)
3729. Halio, Jay L. "Essential *Hamlet*." *CollL* 1:83-99.
Productions of *Hamlet* and modern thematic criticism alike suffer from critical reductivism, the attempt to "discover" or impose a unity or coherence upon the play that it may lack. In performance, coherence is often accomplished by selective cutting of the text; in criticism and teaching, by ignoring evidence that makes argument untidy. Although *Hamlet* doubtless needs cutting, it does not lack an essential structure. By closely examining the overall structural, rhythmic, as well as thematic design and by looking at some stage and film productions where alterations have been made, students can see essential aspects of *Hamlet* emerge. (JLH)
3730. Hamill, Paul. "Death's Lively Image:The Emblematic Significance of the Closet Scene in *Hamlet*." *TSLL* 16:249-62.
In the Closet Scene, two pictures of the elder Hamlet and Claudius recall Christ the King on the Mountain of Judgment and the Vice, from the morality stage. The scene becomes a psychomachy, in which the figures war for Gertrude's soul. Hamlet acts as an emblematic artist, using the figures in Ignatian fashion to awaken Gertrude's imagination by attacking her senses. The same violent type of emblematic homily helps Hamlet in meditation to understand and accept his own fate. Hamlet embodies qualities of allegoric characters—Death, the Vice, Justice, and so on. He recognizes his own emblematic aspect. He is an experiment in Christian heroism: he lives among Montaignesque paradoxes and guides himself by emblematized truths, because in his world corruption has become normal. (PJH)
3734. Jenkins, Harold. "Fortinbras and Laertes and the Composition of *Hamlet*." [F 92]:95-108.
The role of Fortinbras in *Hamlet* changes as the play develops. The manner of their introduction shows that both Fortinbras and Laertes are designed to be avenging sons, whose situations will reflect the hero's own. But the role of the second revenger is better filled by Laertes, whose revenge, necessarily having the first revenger as its object, determines the complexity of Hamlet's role and hence also of his character. The changed role of Fortinbras entails a dramatic use of Poland different from what may at first have been in Shakespeare's mind; and the headstrong youth of the opening scene is replaced by the noble warrior prince, who may appropriately succeed to Hamlet's Denmark. (HJ)
3735. Jorgensen, Paul A. "Elizabethan Ideas of War in *Hamlet*." *ClioW* 3:111-28.
There are more images of war than of disease and corruption in *Hamlet*, but the two subject matters have not been related into a thematic unity. Writings on war and peace by military theorists, intellectuals, and divines emphasize that a diseased society is often the result of a long, decadent peace. These writings, moreover, invariably use disease images similar to those of the play. War is usually necessary as a purgation; but it can be avoided, as Elizabethan accounts of biblical cities show, if a minister of judgment—here Hamlet—scourges the sick society. Since, according to the influential divines, there is only one cause of war, sin, Hamlet's principal function as God's scourge and minister is to serve as a surrogate form of war and to purge Denmark of its "imposthumes" and sins, principally those mentioned in the Ghost's "dread command," centering upon the rankness and luxury of the royal bed. (PAJ)
3743. McCombie, Frank. "*Hamlet* and the *Moriae Encomium*." *ShS* 27:59-69.
The penetrating influence of Erasmus' *Moriae Encomium* on *Hamlet* has not been sufficiently indicated. The whole pattern of thought has been taken over and made characteristic of the hero. The world of the treatise becomes the world out of which Hamlet speaks. There are many points in the play in which shifts of direction in thought are traceable to similar shifts in the source and, frequently, the full poignancy of the hero's responses can be felt only in the recognition of the parallel context in Erasmus. (FMcC)
3744. McLauchlan, Juliet. "The Prince of Denmark and Claudius's Court." *ShS* 27:43-57.
Murderous usurpation, not Hamlet's behavior, initially violates the natural order. Underlying concepts of "the king's two bodies" and a created hierarchy wherein man's unique potential involved ascent through reason toward angelic and godlike qualities or descent toward the beast, conflict with the embodiment of Machiavellian statecraft and Montaigne's conceptions of man's baseness. Enforced awareness of evil and imprisonment in a situation which cannot be righted bring disintegration of the whole man; obsessional hatred of evil, real and imagined, destroys Hamlet's ideals and aspirations, prompting irrational, destructive behavior. Although finally purged, the state suffers destruction of the future (Ophelia) and the death of Hamlet. (JMcL)
3745. Mills, John A. "The Modesty of Nature:Charles Fechter's *Hamlet*." *ThS* 15:59-78.
In his portrayals of Hamlet at the Princess' in 1861 and the Lyceum in 1864 (repeated at Niblo's Garden in New York in 1870), French actor Charles Fechter employed a style of acting never before applied to that role. Fechter's performance was revolutionary in its steadfast adherence to verisimilitude. Shunning "points" and traditional stage business, Fechter sought to make the character a "living human being," whose vocal and physical deportment were such as could be observed in creatures of flesh and blood. Though excoriated by some critics as wholly antithetical to the poetic nature of the play, the style was warmly received by the majority. A few thought Fechter's natural Hamlet the most artistically satisfying they had ever seen. (JAM)
3747. Noland, Richard W. "Psychoanalysis and *Hamlet*." *HSL* 6:268-81. [Rev. art.]
Examines the major psychoanalytic interpretation of *Hamlet* from the time of the publication of Freud's *The Interpretation of Dreams* to the present and suggests the kind of psychological reorientation necessary for an extension of the classic Freud-Jones view of the play into a more adequate statement of its psychological themes and meanings. (RWN)
3749. Petronella, Vincent F. "Hamlet's 'To be or not to be' Soliloquy:Once More unto the Breach." *SP* 71:72-88.
Hamlet's "To be or not to be" soliloquy is about suicide, but this does not mean that Hamlet is suicidal. Moreover, the soliloquy is a fusion of the general and the particular since it analyzes simultaneously the overall human condition and the individual dilemma of Hamlet. Hamlet's world-view supports the suicide theme of the soliloquy, as do rhetorical structure and metaphor. When Hamlet speaks of taking arms against a "sea of troubles," he is referring to his own heart. His wish to leave this life leads to his enumerating general human ills. Details in the soliloquy resemble or parallel incidents in the play as a whole. The soliloquy is correctly placed near the beginning of III.i, which is

mid-point between the "O that this too too solid flesh" speech early in the play and Hamlet's remarks to Horatio about suicide at the play's close. (VFP)

3750. Rice, Julian C. "Hamlet and the Dream of Something after Death." *HSL* 6:109-16.

The life-as-dream metaphor in Hamlet's "to be or not to be" soliloquy is agnostic in its implications. This can be seen by comparing other uses of the life-as-dream topos. The most illuminating comparison, however, can be drawn from a careful examination of Hamlet's soliloquy as it appears in greatly altered form in the First Quarto. While the accepted version of the soliloquy speaks conditionally about "what dreams may come" after death, the First Quarto communicates an explicit picture of the hell awaiting those who want to commit suicide. The "undiscovered country" is described in the First Quarto as if it were discovered, and in this version Hamlet avoids suicide because of his Christian "hope of something after death rather than from a less religiously secure "dread of something after death." The First Quarto Hamlet knows what he fears and is confident and considers the possibility that death may be only a dreamless sleep. (JCR)

3755. Skulsky, Harold. "'I know My Course':Hamlet's Confidence." *PMLA* 89:477-86.

At the outset, Hamlet remarks on the futility of attempting to guess at his state of mind by appeal to the *notatio*, or standard behavioral model, favored by the science of physiognomy. Although the possibility of knowing other minds is provided for by Renaissance theory of natural law and by certain tenets of Neoplatonism, Hamlet's initial skepticism is in full accord with the weight of received opinion—e.g., with folk wisdom, orthodox theological authority, and traditional reservations about friendship and self-knowledge. The deceptiveness of *notatio*, moreover, is illustrated in the play by the hubris of Polonius' art of espionage and by the bitter testimony of Claudius to his success as a dissembler. In practice, however, both Claudius and Hamlet rely with no less confidence than Polonius on the possibility of reading the inner by the outer man. Though Hamlet is sustained in this confidence by a hopeful theory of histrionic performance, a scholar's habits of observation, a flair for satirical portraiture, and even a few trivial successes, the treachery of *notatio* is ominously revealed, along with the Polonian arrogance of relying on it, in his encounter with Gertrude, and especially in his conception of how the Mousetrap can be sprung. (HS)

3758. Stafford, Tony J. "Hamlet's House of Death." *PLL* 10:15-20.

Carpentry images and references to edifices appear throughout *Hamlet*. Most of the construction images appear in the observations that Hamlet and Claudius make about Danish society, in Hamlet's appraisals of other characters, and in his reflections on the self and its destiny. In the graveyard scene, after the gravedigger has established that the houses he builds last till doomsday, Hamlet realizes that even great men such as Caesar and Alexander may end up as building materials for a house and that the house he himself is building will be constructed not by him but of him. (TJS)

Henry IV. 3766. Gottschalk, Paul A. "Hal and the 'Play Extempore' in *1 Henry IV*." *TSLL* 15:605-14.

The climax of the great tavern scene (II.iv) in *1 Henry IV* is the "play extempore" of Hal and Falstaff. This has been treated as a typical play within a play and as the crisis in Hal's development toward kingly responsibility, but it is neither. Instead of crisis, Shakespeare provides us with a series of increasingly powerful manifestations of Hal's future greatness: the play extempore is one of these. The play extempore is an important challenge to Hal in that through it Falstaff seeks to transform the pending interview between Prince and King into play. Because it is genuinely extemporaneous, Falstaff can imbue the skit with his own irresponsibility. When Hal replies to Falstaff's plea against banishment first in his persona as king, then in his own person—"I do, I will"—we see that he has not been acting at all, that his role as prince merges with his future role as king, and that Falstaff's trap has failed. (PAG)

3770. Maclean, Hugh. "Ben Jonson's *Timber*, 1046-1115, and

Falstaff." *PLL* 10:202-06.

The topics dealt with in Ben Jonson's *Timber*, 1046-1115, and the language of that passage, strikingly recall the speeches, actions, and outlook of Shakespeare's Falstaff in *2 Henry IV*. The passage, in which the realistic and racy idiom of 17th-century England is interfused with relatively formal and sober expressions drawn from the ancients, illustrates Jonson's continuing search for a style that appropriately indicates the significant continuity between classical tradition and present experience. At the same time, Jonson enlivens his advocacy of morality and decorum by making play with their opposites, represented by Falstaff's raffish language and questionable stance. (HM)

Henry V. 3777. Battenhouse, Roy. "The Relation of Henry V to Tamburlaine." *ShS* 27:71-79.

Analogy to *Tamburlaine* reinforces the many echoes of Marlowe's hero which Shakespeare has incorporated in *Henry V*. Henry likens himself to the sun, engages in horseback exploits rather than a shepherding role, utters threats in high astounding terms, is ruthless toward prisoners, kills Falstaff's heart almost as mercilessly as Tamburlaine slew his son Calyphas, and employs religious rites in a way which Shakespeare's irony lets us know is sacrilegious. The comic aspects of Shakespeare's drama, however, give it a spice of humor which Marlowe's lacks. While both plays have audience appeal as "spectacle," Shakespeare additionally invokes the concept of spectacle to characterize a Henry concerned chiefly with putting on a show. (RWB)

3781. Tucker, E.F.J. "Legal Fiction and Human Reality: Hal's Role in *Henry V*." *ETJ* 26:308-14.

Canterbury's speech on Hal's moral regeneration (I.i.24-31) suggests that Shakespeare is alluding to the doctrine of the King's Two Bodies, according to which the king assumes the sacred body politic (*character angelicus*) upon succession to the Crown. The phrase "no sooner" underscores the immediacy of moral transformation, while the mortification of wildness and the references to angels and "celestial spirits" reflect the belief that legally the king can do no wrong. Many writers, like Spenser, Bacon, and John Davies, describe monarchs as angelic beings; and the problems of royal succession were a source of deep anxiety during the later Elizabethan period. Hal's "Twin-born with greatness" soliloquy (IV.i.236-43) examines the clash between private ambition and public duty, and it is the king's greatest achievement to accept the burdens of kingship and to attain a political realism which successfully integrates his public and private selves. (EFJT)

Henry VI. 3782. Bordinat, Philip. "Shakespeare's Suffolk:An Exercise in Tragic Method." *WVUPP* 21:9-16.

The character Suffolk in *Henry VI*, Part 1 and Part 2, possesses ingredients later revealed in a fully developed form in the great tragic heroes. The arranged marriage between Henry and Margaret, leading to a dukedom and a fortune for Suffolk, and the cruel plots against the Duchess and the Duke of York, leading to the exile of the first and the murder of the second, establish a Machiavellian character similar to many others in the Henry VI plays. However, the love affair between Suffolk and Margaret produces a shift in emphasis from the public world of Machiavellian policy to the private world of love. Additional tragic emphasis arises in Suffolk's final scene, his death at the hands of Walter Whitmore, when he demonstrates qualities of personal insight and individual worth, requisite to tragic recognition and recovery. (PB)

3783. Born, Hanspeter. "The Date of *2, 3 Henry VI*." *SQ* 25:323-34.

A reassessment of the facts points to summer 1592 as the date of composition of *2, 3 Henry VI*. Evidence indicating that *1 Henry VI* is identical with Henslowe's "harey the vj" and was a new play in March 1592 is compelling. At the same time, the progressive development of language, characterization, and construction, the equable division of source material, and the organic design of the plays suggest that they were written in the folio order. Consequently *2, 3 Henry VI* must have been written after March 1592. The journalist Greene, in *Groatsworth*, parodied *3 Henry VI*, because he expected it to be newly on stage at the time when his pamphlet was to be published. *2, 3 Henry VI* never got into Henslowe's records, because in the late summer 1592, as a result of the plague, Pembroke's men branched off from Strange's and were allotted the two plays, which they produced under new titles. (HB)

3785. McNeir, Waldo F. "Comedy in Shakespeare's Yorkist Tetralogy." *PCP* 9:48-55.

Comic elements in Shakespeare's *Henry VI*, Parts 1, 2, 3 include acrobatic tricks, an unsexed witch and an adulterous queen, commoners turned pirate on sea and land, a bathetically incompetent king, venality, double-dealing, and incongruous disparity between works and deeds in scenes illustrating a variety of man's follies. Shakespeare's portrayal of Richard III begins in *Henry VI*, Part 2, becomes clear with the emergence of "Roscius" in *Henry VI*, Part 3, and dominates his own play with his own scenario and casting. He is a witty villain amused by his own virtuosity, histrionic to the last in his farewell performance at Bosworth Field. The humor of the Lancastrian tetralogy, more easily appreciated because of Falstaff and his cohorts, is less sardonic but equally ironic. (WM)

3787. Williams, Gwyn. "Suffolk and Margaret: A Study of Some Sections of Shakespeare's *Henry VI*." *SQ* 25:310-22.

In *Henry VI* Parts I and 2 Shakespeare gave Queen Margaret and Suffolk an illicit love which is unhistorical, though hinted at in Hall's *Chronicle*. This play within a play, Shakespeare's first essay in tragic, destructive love, has been ruthlessly cut in modern production. There are indications that Drayton accepted Shakespeare's inventions as history and that Drayton and possibly Shakespeare had read Suffolk's poems to Queen Margaret. (GW)

Julius Caesar. 3789. Auffret, Jean M. "The Philosophical Background of *Julius Caesar*." *CahiersE* 5:66-92.

Plutarch's *Lives* are re-examined, references to Seneca, Epictetus, and Marcus Aurelius are made in an effort at appraising the stoicism of Brutus and Portia. Brutus' position on suicide is discussed and compared with those of Hamlet and Gloucester as are his views on friendship and providence. Casca is revealed as a cynic, or in Elizabethan terms a malcontent, the malcontents being conscious of the cynical tradition and imitating its biting and jocular address. Source criticism comes in as a by-product of philosophical study. (JMA)

3790. Dachslager, E.L. " 'The Most Unkindest Cut': A Note on *Julius Caesar* III.ii.187." *ELN* 11:258-59.

Antony's well-known comment on Brutus' stabbing of Julius Caesar, "This was the most unkindest cut of all," is taken as reference to Plutarch's statement in *The Life of Julius Caesar*, "And then Brutus himself gave him one wound about his privities." The fact that Brutus was thought to have been Caesar's illegitimate son adds, in light of Brutus' act, further irony to Brutus' tragic role in the play. (ELD)

3792. Fuzier, Jean A. "Rhetorio versus Rhetoric: A Study of Shakespeare's *Julius Caesar* III,2." *CahiersE* 5:25-65.

Julius Caesar III.ii is a striking illustration of Shakespeare's knowledge of the art of language, and of his expertise in handling rhetorical figures or devices made subservient to a dramatic purpose. Brutus and Antony use rhetoric in a widely contrasting way, as appears from the number and nature of the figures and devices found in their speeches. Brutus' Stoic rhetoric is more close-packed, and resorts mainly to "logos," while Antony's is more subtle, and aims at "pathos." The interchange of fates between the two statesmen is underscored and explained by an interchange of rhetorical means and fortunes enacted in this capital scene. (JAF)

3794. Gerenday, Lynn de. "Play, Ritualization, and Ambivalence in *Julius Caesar*." *L&P* 24:24-33.

The drama of Brutus and Caesar provides psychological insight into the structure and dynamics of ambivalence, which is the norm, meaning, and motivation in this "problem play." Brutus uses rhetoric, ceremony, and ritualized play-acting to bind and distance intense love and hostility from conscious recognition, as he composes and creates an individual and isolated reality to fit his resolution to annihilate Caesar. In order to act, Brutus prevents his bound emotions from breaking loose; his final denial of feeling is not in the service of practical action, but of death.

(LdG)

3797. Maguin, Jean-Marie. "Play Structure and Dramatic Technique in Shakespeare's *Julius Caesar*." *CahiersE* 5:93-106.

Shakespeare's *Julius Caesar* offers a symmetrical, pyramid-like structure. The division into acts underlines this symmetry, the nature and business of each act in the first half of the play being echoed in a corresponding act of the play's second half. This interpretation proves helpful to the study of the time factor and its impact on the intellects and actions of the characters and takes Knight's analysis of the flesh/spirit duality in Caesar one step further by showing how this feature of character relationship is also an ironic dramatic movement. Shakespeare's use of parallel situations and verbal play is important within the framework of the play's regular geometry while some elements of irregularity and unbalance are designed to introduce tension in the symmetry of the structure. (J-MM)

3798. ——— "Preface to a Critical Approach to *Julius Caesar*, with a Chronological Catalogue of Shakespeare's Borrowing from North's Plutarch." *CahiersE* 4(1973):15-49.

Discusses Plutarch's influence on Shakespeare's *Julius Caesar*. A catalog is appended, listing Shakespeare's borrowings and divergences from North's translation of Plutarch. (J-MM)

King Lear. 3806. Boring, Phyllis Z. "More on Parody in Valle-Inclán." *RomN* 15(1973):246-47.

It is well known that Valle-Inclán utilized parody in his works. Specific episodes in his works parody scenes from Shakespeare or from Spanish literature, notably the Quijote. Two more examples which may be added to the list are the parody of *King Lear* in *Romance de lobos* and of *La Celestina* in *Divinas palabras*. Like the Shakespearian hero, Montenegro of *Romance de lobos* has divided his estate among his children and is left homeless, but Valle-Inclán's protagonist is a burlesque version of a feudal king. The parody of *La Celestina* is presented in two scenes of *Divinas palabras*: the intervention of the go-between in Act III and Pedro Gailo's attempted suicide at the end of the play. (PZB)

3811. Dawson, Anthony B. "Paradoxical Dramaturgy in *King Lear*." *WascanaR* 9:29-38.

King Lear projects experience in a way which challenges belief and demands acceptance. Gloucester's leap from the cliff exemplifies the problem created by the many "incredible" events in the play. When he leaps, Gloucester must defy his senses and accept a symbolic event as real. We too must defy our disbelief in order to have truth revealed to us. Gloucester's belief hence becomes an image for our acceptance of the "unbelievable" in the play. The comfort we derive from our acceptance of deception encourages us to expect that the theatricality of the scene will lead to comic realignment—so that we are overwhelmed by the tragic implacability of events. (ABD)

3814. Fly, Richard D. "Beyond Extremity: A Reading of *King Lear*." *TSLL* 16:45-63.

Lear is organized and propelled forward by the desire to "top extremity." The plot moves us from one instance of extreme suffering to another in a manner calculated to deprive us of any hope for the characters. The language contributes to this effect by making us aware of the final inadequacy of words when confronted by certain extreme kinds of experience. Lear's prolonged torture and sustained anguish generate passion of such intensity that it actually seems to disintegrate his initial personality and to drive him through several transformations. Lear is capable of generating subcharacters—variations on his essential self—with whom he interacts to achieve greater self-knowledge. (RDF)

3818. Hamilton, Donna B. "Some Romance Sources for *King Lear*: Robert of Sicily and Robert the Devil." *SP* 71:173-91.

The Famous true and historicall life of Robert second Duke of Normandy, surnamed for his monstrous birth and behauiour, Robin the Diuell is a central source for themes and incidents in *King Lear*. Lodge's *Robert*, a lengthy and elaborate retelling of the folktale of Robert the Devil deals with the archetypal pattern of the humbling of the proud man and also considers the issue of parental guilt for wicked children. It contains incidents which parallel Shakespeare's use of the Fool, of Edgar at the hovel, of the incidents between Kent and Oswald, of the trial by combat, and of Cordelia, all of which are elements which cannot be satisfactorily accounted for in other sources. (DBH)

3829. Mroczkowski, P.J. "Comparative Reception of *King Lear*: An Experiment in International Education." *SQ* 25:234-47.
Undergraduate responses to *King Lear* by students of English literature in the Universities of London, Sorbonne, and Cracow were revealed by collating the replies to a series of identical questions in English on selected scenes of the play. The basis for the selection of these scenes was that they contained sufficiently clear and powerful stimuli for students to be capable of specifying their moral and esthetic impact. The polling confirms that young educated persons find certain moral qualities worthy of approval, such as courage, loyalty, charity, truth or honesty, and sincerity. Conversely, cruelty, selfishness, deceit, and hypocrisy were condemned. (PPM)

3837. Roti, Grant C. "Shakespeare's *King Lear* i.i.56." *Expl* 32:Item 67.
In the first scene of Shakespeare's *King Lear*, Goneril flatters her father, telling him that he is more valuable than "eye-sight, space and liberty." "Eye-sight" refers to the sense of sight; and sight and blindness imagery appear throughout the play, even with regard to Goneril. Cordelia refers to Goneril's greed in the phrase, "still-soliciting eye" (i.i.231); Cordelia's eyes are "wash'd" (i.268) as they see through Goneril's hollowness; and it is Goneril who commands Gloucester's eyes to be plucked out. "Space" refers to the portion of the kingdom which Goneril will inherit; Lear later (i.i.79-81) uses the word in the same sense. "Liberty" refers to either her new freedom from the feudal authority of her father or to her new "domain or property." The words have precise meanings and are not the mere abstract fustian of flattery. (GCR)

Love's Labour's Lost. 3846. Brown, Kevan. "Telltale Poetry: A Study of the Four Courtiers in *Love's Labour's Lost*." *SoQ* 13:83-92.
The King of Navarre and his fellow courtiers in *Love's Labour's Lost* are unrealistic characters who each possess few, if any, personal or human traits. Others, however, have observed characteristics of these men which classify them as individuals. A careful analysis of the poetry of the king and his three attendants supports, clarifies, and possibly expands traditional interpretations of these characters. As a prosodic analysis will show, Shakespeare undoubtedly intended these men to exist as round characters, separate from one another. The love poems of each character, at first glance, appear to be similar; but a closer look gives the reader more insight into the personalities of the characters who wrote them, as well as an additional explanation of the tasks imposed upon them by the four women from France whom they pursue. (KRB)

3848. Goldstein, Neal L. "*Love's Labour's Lost* and the Renaissance Vision of Love." *SQ* 25:335-50.
While it is true that in *Love's Labour's Lost* Shakespeare is playing with language, and while it is true that both he and his Berowne enjoy their display of verbal wit, it is important that the reader bear in mind the fact that this verbal wit is highly functional in the play. The main thrust of Shakespeare's wit is the satirizing of Petrarchanism and Florentine Neoplatonism, the two main components of the Renaissance vision of love. (NLG)

3853. Lewis, Anthony J. "Shakespeare's Via Media in *Love's Labour's Lost*." *TSLL* 16:243-48.
In *Love's Labour's Lost*, the search for truth and fame by the major male characters leads them to choose first a cold and austere life of study, symbolized by winter, and then a comfortable and "gaudy" one of romance, symbolized by spring. The Princess of France and her ladies, through their commands to the King of Navarre and his courtiers, neither accept one lifestyle and reject the other, nor reject both, but establish in Act v a synthesis incorporating the best elements of each mistaken approach to truth. This via media is best represented by the two end songs, Ver's and Hiems', which describe a realistic approach to life with an unpleasant note in the spring, and a merry one in winter. (AJL)

Macbeth. 3855. Allen, Michael J.B. "Macbeth's Genial

Porter." *ELR* 4:326-36.
The Porter scene in *Macbeth* has never been explained in light of the etymological connections in Latin between the word for porter (both as gatekeeper and bearer of burdens) and the concept of a personal demon or genius, even though Shakespeare and at least some of his audience were unquestionably aware of these connections. We should respond to the Porter's appearance in the same way as we do to Banquo's ghost, the air-drawn dagger, and the witches themselves; for, ultimately, he is an evil phenomenon and his ostensible bawdiness is another instance of the play's grim, ubiquitous irony. (MJBA)

3859. Fosse, Jean. "The Lord's Anointed Temple: A Study of Some Symbolic Patterns in *Macbeth*." *CahiersE* 6:15-22.
In Shakespeare's *Macbeth*, various images concerned with the human body form one coherent image-cluster. These images help define evil as a state of mental perturbation. Heart images and face images are often associated (the face mirrors the heart); so are eye images and hand images (the eye controls the hand). But Macbeth's face does not mirror his heart, while it is his heart which controls his hand. Thus these images point to the effects of evil on Macbeth, that is, to the war within his little kingdom of human faculties. This theme also finds expression in images which liken the human body or the self to a receptacle or temple. These images suggest the unity and wholeness of the self characteristic of the true king. (JF)

3868. Kolin, Philip C. "Macbeth, Malcolm, and the Curse of the Serpent." *SCB* 34:159-60.
Allusions to the Genesis prophecy can be found in three sparsely annotated lines in *Macbeth*: IV.iii.45 and V.viii.27-28. Testing Macduff's loyalty, Malcolm refers to the punishment he would reserve for Macbeth were he not like him in crime. He would "tread upon the tyrant's head." In echoing the exact manner of revenge promised the serpent, this line links Malcolm with Christ and Macbeth with the devil, associations reinforced by other Satanic allusions in IV.iii. Malcolm's birth, his Christ-like virtues, and his victory over Macbeth also contribute to this allusion. (PCK)

3869. Lyle, E.B. "Macduff's Reception of Macbeth's Messenger: A Suggestion That the Eipsode at *Macbeth* III.vi.37b-45a Has Been Displaced from Earlier in the Scene." *AUMLA* 41:75-78.
H.L. Rogers has proposed that lines 37b-39a of *Macbeth* III.vi should be read following 45a, but this change causes a lack of connection before 39b. Instead, a set of 8 lines in the order Rogers proposes (39b-45a plus 37b-39a) should be brought forward to follow 23a. These lines are displaced in the Folio and, since they are not essential to the narrative, they might have been cut and restored at the wrong point. In the Folio text, the reference to Macduff's reception of Macbeth's messenger in Scotland occurs as a flashback after the news of his departure to England has been given, but, with the proposed change, events are presented in chronological order. (EBL)

3871. Mullin, Michael. "Augures and Understood Relations: Theodore Komisarjevsky's *Macbeth*." *ETJ* 26:20-30.
In a strange, surrealistic setting of twisted aluminum scrolls and blood-red, cloud-streaked backdrops, Komisarjevsky created an expressionistic *Macbeth*. The settings, costumes, and staging followed the play's dominant imagery, making the audience see the world through Macbeth's eyes. The Witches were corpse-robbing ghouls; the warriors, destroyers armed with modern weapons and sharp steel; and, leading them, Macbeth, the mutant adapted to this grotesque world. To stress the play's locus in nightmare, in the cauldron scene Komisarjevsky made the Witches speak through an entranced Macbeth as the apparitions appeared as silhouettes behind a scrim upstage. (MM)

3872. Rosenberg, Marvin. "Lady Macbeth's Indispensible Child." *ETJ* 26:14-19.
Shakespeare stipulated that Lady Macbeth had a child: she has "given suck"; but he avoids any suggestion that the babe was from an earlier marriage. We assume that it is Macbeth's child. The matter of an "heir," of establishing a "line," is the main reason Macbeth gives for needing to kill Banquo and Fleance. Some actors and critics have seen it as a primary impulse in his characterization. Can an object of his passion for dynasty be

shown in the theater? Can the presence of his child be suggested in pivotal scenes to give more meaning to the play? Various possibilities are suggested. (MR)

Measure for Measure. 3879. Altieri, Joanne. "Style and Social Disorder in *Measure for Measure*." *SQ* 25:6-16.
Dull is integrated into *Love's Labour's Lost* without losing the characteristics of his type. Dull takes his place as the linguistic expression of unadulterated nature in the thematic development of a play depicting a harmonious society. Dogberry is a parallel case, complexified not in himself but in relationship to the play. In these plays thematic multiplicity is achieved through different but equivalent methods: in the former a system of contrasts and parallels, in the latter a pair of contrasted actions are supported by the same speech and scenic patterns, which tend to unify as they define the disparate social groups. But Elbow moves in a linguistic context where, though the basic syntax and rhetoric are unchanged, levels of style are discrete, their discontinuity imaging and intensifying the isolation and polarities of a fragmented world. (JSA)
3881. Fleissner, Robert F. "Shakespeare's *Measure for Measure*, II.iv.136." *Expl* 32:Item 42.
Angelo's attempt to win Isabella in Shakespeare's *Measure for Measure* II.iv.136 involves wordplay on her being a Votaress of St. Clare ("if you be more [than a woman], you'r none," i.e., you're [a] nun). When "none" was pronounced as homophonic with "known," further double entendre was evident. The counterpoint of religious and secular values weighed against each other in the wordplay supports the intrinsic meaning of the play's title. It is also possible that the lack of piety in the pun was one of the causes behind the play's being removed from the Valladolid Folio by a Catholic censor. (RFF)
3882. Geckle, George L. "Poetic Justice and *Measure for Measure*." *Costerus* N.S. 1:95-111.
A particularly obvious example of wrong readings of works of literature is afforded by the English 18th-century criticism of Shakespeare's *Measure for Measure*. The concept of poetic justice so dominated the thinking of the critics of that age that they were unable to interpret *Measure for Measure* in terms of anything other than strict punishment and justice. Samuel Johnson's criticism of the play seemed to influence Samuel Taylor Coleridge in the 19th century, but it was also in that century that critics first suggested the presently orthodox notion that *Measure for Measure* might be about the New Testament theme of mercy and forgiveness. (GLG)
3883. Hawkins, Harriett. "What Kind of Pre-contract Had Angelo? A Note on Some Non-problems in Elizabethan Drama." *CE* 36:173-79.
The differing conclusions reached by responsible scholars who have discussed the relevance of Elizabethan betrothal laws to *Measure for Measure* raise a series of embarrassing questions about a whole school of Shakespearean scholarship that appeals to "the Elizabethans" for answers to questions that Shakespeare himself may purposely have left unanswered or unasked. A critical examination of various appeals to "the Elizabethan audience" reveals that modern scholarship too frequently imposes dogmatic and conventional interpretations upon highly unorthodox characters and plays. Equally frequently, modern discussions of "the Elizabethan audience" imply that the Elizabethans lacked any sense about human relationships or lacked our modern capacities for mercy, pity, generosity, and wonder. Perhaps, then, the time has come for us to stop looking for exclusively "Elizabethan" solutions to the fundamentally human problems that Shakespeare and his contemporaries exhibit before us. (HH)
3884. Levin, Richard. "The King James Version of *Measure for Measure*." *ClioW* 3:129-63.
There is no external evidence to support the claims that plays of Shakespeare's age were written for performance at court or the Inns of Court or the houses of the aristocracy. All the available evidence clearly indicates that the normal practice was to select plays of such occasions from the regular public repertories. Any attempt to show that a particular play was an exception to this practice must produce a very compelling case. One of the most

widely accepted of these "occasionalist" cases, advanced in a number of recent studies, is that *Measure for Measure* was written to please and flatter King James; but an examination of the evidence presented in these studies reveals that it is much too weak (when it is not actually distorted) to outweigh the fundamental objection to such claims. And if the case for an "occasional" *Measure for Measure* cannot withstand scrutiny, we are even less likely to be convinced by the cases advanced for other plays on much less evidence. (RL)
3887. McBride, Tom. "*Measure for Measure* and the Unreconciled Virtues." *CompD* 8:264-74.
Measure for Measure consistently follows a popular Renaissance allegory of salvation, the "Parliament of Heaven." In this allegory Christ's death satisfies the irreconcilable demands of Justice and Mercy, daughters of God, about fallen man's punishment. In *Measure for Measure* there are similar dilemmas between justice and mercy; but here the intervener, the Duke, is an inadequate Christ. The allegory's dialectical ideal calls for the salvation of souls, but the Duke does nothing to redeem any character's soul. Justice and mercy remain irreconciled and for all the Duke's providential presumptions, Shakespeare treats him as an ironic figure. Thus the play's structure ironically mirrors that of the allegory. (TM)
3888. Owen, Lucy. "Mode and Character in *Measure for Measure*." *SQ* 25:17-32.
Measure for Measure deals with the relation between justice and mercy and the meaning of forgiveness. Angelo, Isabella, and Claudio are brought to the understanding of themselves which allows them to accept and/or offer forgiveness. The Duke's role is analogous to that of God, but the play is not strictly allegorical. In so far as the Duke represents Providence, death is an absolute and life after death has no meaning within the play. For Isabella life after death is meaningful. In the last scene Isabella's vision of the divine reflected in the human and the Duke's suggestion of the human representing the divine meet in an understanding of the true relevance of mercy in the human action. (LDeGO)

Merchant of Venice. 3894. Fortin, René E. "Launcelot and the Uses of Allegory in *The Merchant of Venice*." *SEL* 14:259-70.
Launcelot, especially in his encounter with his father, is intended to offer a new perspective into the meaning of Shakespeare's *The Merchant of Venice*. In this allegorical encounter, he highlights the theme of filial piety and the theme of blindness, which prevents this piety from being realized. Launcelot's allegorical action thus seems intended as a severe qualification, but not a repudiation, of the "naive" allegory which would suggest the absolute vindication of the New Law. He offers in its place a more sophisticated allegory which grants full recognition to both Dispensations. This important corrective to the naive allegory, which accounts for the obtrusive ironies of the play, finally reveals a concept of Jewish-Christian relations that is fully consistent with the "official" theology of Christianity, as it is expressed primarily in Matthew and in the Pauline Epistle to the Romans. (REF)
3896. Henze, Richard. " 'Which Is the Merchant Here? And Which the Jew?' " *Criticism* 16:287-300.
Antonio's resurrected ships in *The Merchant of Venice* surprise the play's audience as well as its characters, for we expect that ships once sunk do not reappear. The play's major image of the lottery of life should warn us, however, that fortune, including misfortune, is never certain. We ignore that warning because the action of the play is highly predictable. Only the ships surprise. This should lead to a re-examination of the theme of fortune and of Shylock. As we share Antonio's intolerance and then disapprove of it in the trial scene, Shakespeare shows that the foundation for prejudice is as broad as human nature. (RH)
3899. Knight, W. Nicholas. "Equity, *The Merchant of Venice*, and William Lambarde." *ShS* 27:93-104.
There is a relationship between William Lambard, Master of Chancery (1597-1601), mercy and the forfeiture of a bond in *Merchant of Venice* (c. 1596), and Shakespeare's attempt to recover a mortgaged estate in Chancery (1597-99). Through Shakespeare's play and case, there is also evidence for his attempting to effect a grace period for bonds that Lambard does not introduce at this time through "Equity of Redemption."

(WNK)

3901. Morris, Irene. "A Hapsburg Letter." *MLR* 69:12-22. Presents the first complete transcription and translation into English of a letter written at Graz in 1608 by the Archduchess Maria Magdalena of Austria, later Grand Duchess of Tuscany, to her brother, later Holy Roman Emperor Ferdinand II, who was representing the Emperor Rudolph II at the Diet of Regensburg. The letter describes a visit of English actors and names the ten plays they performed; it mentions the dances and festivities held at Court and ends with a lively account of a duel involving one of the actors. The transcription of the original manuscript (Wien, Haus-, Hof-, und Staatsarchiv, Familienkorrespondenz A. Karton 6. fol. 312-15) includes punctuation and a few linguistic notes. The notes to the translation explain and comment on the plays (one of which is possibly *The Merchant of Venice*), the dances, and the persons and events mentioned in the letter; the notes also provide data pertaining to the political and religious disputes which occasioned Archduke Ferdinand's presence at Regensburg. (IM)

3903. Sullivan, Patrick J. "Strumpet Wind:The National Theatre's *Merchant of Venice*." *ETJ* 26:31-44. In Olivier's hands the part of Shylock becomes both a grotesque exercise in self-imposed isolation and a frightening instance of social cruelty and cultural decadence. Act v has the rare achievement of organically developing from the previous crisis. The Olivier-Miller version forces the audience to rethink and appreciate anew the perennial wisdom of this play when suffused with a complicated and authoritative moral vision. The play as it is received by the theater-goer is described. (PJS)

Merry Wives of Windsor. 3904. Bryant, J.A.,Jr. "Falstaff and the Renewal of Windsor." *PMLA* 89:296-301. Critics' neglect of *The Merry Wives of Windsor* results from a failure to appreciate the special nature of the play. The play is built upon the succession of Falstaff episodes, which give meaning to the Fenton-Anne plot and provide a resolution for it. Falstaff is no lecher but a discredited old adventurer, down on his luck, who becomes the scapegoat for a community afflicted by the lust and greed that some of its members seek to make him solely responsible for. At the end of the play he has become the visible bearer of punishment and the means whereby innocent love may triumph in Windsor in spite of parental vanity and economic interests. With the punishment of Falstaff death is once more temporarily defeated, and the renewal is presented for the approval of sympathetic audiences. (JAB,Jr)

Midsummer Night's Dream. 3910. Doran, Madeleine. "Titania's Wood." [F 92]:55-70. In the woodland setting of Acts II-IV of *Midsummer Night's Dream* there is as much artfulness as imitation of nature, both fused in a harmonious poetic invention. The setting is partly what it is on account of Titania. The homeliest creatures, described with metaphoric elegance, are ceremonial. The flowers of her bower would not all grow in one place; each has a history, varying in richness of literary associations or emblematic meanings. The moon in the wood appears allusively in its three aspects as Phoebe, Diana, and Hecate (or Proserpina). The fructifying aspect of the moon is symbolized in the new crescent's appearing on the nuptial day, and in the fairies' blessing of the bride-beds with the moon's field-dew. (MD)

3913. Pearson, D'Orsay W. " 'Unkinde' Theseus:A Study in Renaissance Mythography." *ELR* 4:276-98. One of the most significant "myths" confronting the serious student of *A Midsummer Night's Dream* is that of the metamorphosed Theseus, whose medieval and Renaissance image as an unnatural, perfidious, and unfaithful lover and father overshadowed his military or political reputation. The classical, medieval, and Renaissance sources available to Shakespeare stress Theseus' extreme sensuality as well as his lack of paternal devotion. Shakespeare seems to have anticipated audience awareness of Theseus' reputation as a part of the response he expected for *MND*, beginning with Theseus' opening speech, which uses images of ingratitude to portray his eagerness for marriage, moves to his lack of compassion for the plight of

Hermia and Lysander, and on to his neglect of state affairs. Even his abrupt and unmotivated shift to compassion at the end of the play takes on a strong ironic dimension because of his previous actions and his legendary reputation as perfidious lover and cruel father. (DWP)

Much Ado About Nothing. 3920. Fleissner, Robert F. "*Love's Labour's Won* and the Occasion of *Much Ado*." *ShS* 27:105-10. New evidence points to *Much Ado* as the original subtitle for *Love's Labour's Won*. The registration of *Won* as *Much Ado* in 1600 can be accounted for in terms of the inherent word-play associating the spelling "a Doo" with "1600 *a*(nno) *D*(omini)." (RFF)

3921. Jackson, MacD. P. "Compositor C and the First Folio Text of *Much Ado About Nothing*." *PBSA* 68:414-18. Analysis of the apprentice Compositor E's work in setting Folio *Romeo and Juliet* and *Titus Andronicus* from Quarto copy shows that, like B, he introduced many non-obvious errors, being especially prone to add or omit final "-s." Less is known about Compositor C, who had a large share in setting the Folio Comedies. The Folio text of *Much Ado* was, however, a straight reprint of the 1600 Quarto, and when Dover Wilson's classification of Folio errors is related to the compositorial stints, as determined by Hinman and Howard-Hill, Compositor C, who set most of the play, is seen to have corrupted the text considerably, especially by omission and substitution. (MPJ)

Othello. 3924. Adler, Doris. "The Rhetoric of *Black* and *White* in *Othello*." *SQ* 25:248-57. The complex use of the multiple values of black and white reinforces the theme of man's tragic blindness in Shakespeare's *Othello*. The negative values of black as the color of charcoal and the devil, as a racial designation, as literally soiled, as morally foul, and the positive values of white or fair as the opposite of each of these are intensified and confounded by substitution, coalition, and equivocation. Tragically blind in both sight and reason, man is unable to distinguish the relationship of the emblem to reality; he cannot tell black from white. (DRA)

3927. Crews, Jonathan V. "Death in Venice:A Study of *Othello* and *Volpone*." *UCTSE* 4(1973):17-29. Jonson's *Volpone* and Shakespeare's *Othello*, near-contemporary plays, are mutually illuminating. Iago and Mosca are two developments from a single stereotype, both having a "psychological" resemblance to the New Comedy Slave. Both react as disinherited individuals, rationalizing egoism by projecting distorting-mirror images of the world of values and rewards from which they are disinherited. The "gulling" comedy of *Volpone* has its counterpart in *Othello*. Desdemona and Celia are possibly intended to perform a similar dramatic function. In *Volpone*, the ambiguity of the titanic hero is registered but not developed, while in *Othello*, the ambiguity is fundamental to the play. Tragic and comic development of related themes is evident in these two plays. (JVC)

3928. Faber, M.D. "*Othello*:Symbolic Action, Ritual and Myth." *AI* 31:159-205. Multilevel analysis of *Othello* leads to appreciation of the deeply regressive, indeed oral affects that lie behind Othello's marriage and the subsequent destruction of Desdemona. Othello is vulnerable to the power of women harboring maternal qualities. Winnicott and Greenacre regard "the handkerchief" as a kind of transitional object; it establishes a tie between the Moor and his bride which recalls the tie that existed between Othello's own parents; it is also to preserve Desdemona as the good maternal object. Following lines set down by Hubert and Mauss, one regards Othello's murder of Desdemona as another magical act of transformation. Through his pathological manipulation of the scapegoat, Othello communicates with the deep paternal introject of his mind in a way that diminishes his anxiety. At the deepest unconscious level Desdemona is a version of the parent, toward whom the sacrificer feels great ambivalence. The tension of the murder scene reaches its climax when Desdemona claims to be the kind of victim who bears away the sin rather than the kind who needs to be consecrated and purified. (MDF)

3932. Jones, Millard T. "Press-Variants and Proofreading in

the First Quarto of *Othello* (1622)." *SB* 27:177-84.
Collation of the 19 extant copies of Shakespeare's *Othello*, a quarto printed by Nicholas Okes for the stationer Thomas Walkley, has not only provided knowledge about the variant states in particular copies, but also has suggested that proofreading did little to safeguard the accuracy of the text. Of the 24 formes 9 are variant. As distributed among the 9 formes, the 31 press-variants, including both accidental dislocations of type and deliberate changes, seem to reflect casual sampling on the part of the proofreader. In sheets H and I, however, many conspicuous errors apparently caused him to work more carefully. But even there the proofreading was primarily to eliminate obvious errors rather than to insure an accurate text. (MTJ)

3933. Levitsky, Ruth M. "Prudence Versus Wisdom in *Othello*." *DR* 54:281-88.
The word "jealous" was commonly used by Elizabethans to mean "tending to be wary, cautious, suspicious." Thus "jealousy" was a basic ingredient in the Machiavellian species of prudence—a virtue-vice irreconcilable with faith and trust. By nature, Othello was not jealous; but because of his admiration for Iago's prudence, he could be persuaded to abandon faith in human goodness. Desdemona's trust, on the other hand, is part and parcel of her love. Othello, recognizing both Love and Prudence as goods, suffers acutely in his ambivalence but finally opts for the prudence of Iago rather than the higher wisdom of his wife. (RML)

3941. Stodder, Joseph H. "Influences of *Othello* on Büchner's *Woyzeck*." *MLR* 69:115-20.
Critical interest in Shakespearean influence on Georg Büchner's dramatic work has generally centered on two plays, *Leonce und Lena* and *Dantons Tod*. Most critics have either ignored or dismissed influence on *Woyzeck*. But the plot and central character relationship of *Woyzeck*, if not the overall tone, is often reminiscent of *Othello*, and a close parallel reading of these two plays suggests striking instances of specific borrowings. These examples reflect similarities in dramatic situation, character relationship, imagery, and in psychological development of the protagonist. Review of these specific examples affords a more rewarding appreciation of Büchner's play. (JHS)

Pericles. 3943. Knapp, Peggy Ann. "The Orphic Vision of *Pericles*." *TSLL* 15:615-26.
The principle of causality in Shakespeare's *Pericles* is justified neither by the logic of ordinary events nor by an unambiguous moral doctrine. The structure of *Pericles* is the structure of the legend of Orpheus cast in a romance form, just as the anonymous author of *Sir Orfeo* had earlier cast it. Resemblances between the two works do not suggest the influence of *Sir Orfeo* on Shakespeare so much as a similarity of vision between the two poets. (PAK)

3945. Semon, Kenneth J. "*Pericles*:An Order Beyond Reason." *ELWIU* 1:17-27.
The "world" of *Pericles* is morally inscrutable, and the audience, like the characters, can only respond with admiration at the fantastic reconciliations at the end of the play. Gower, who tells a story in which the virtuous triumph and the vicious are destroyed, tries and fails to impose a moral on his tale. Moreover, during the course of the play, many of the characters themselves seek to impose some kind of formulaic explanation upon the fantastic events in which they find themselves caught up. All such explanations fail. Marina and Pericles both express wonder at the nature of events and finally do not question how those events have come to pass. They can only note their own suffering and joy; they never come to any rational understanding of their experience. (KJS)

Rape of Lucrece. 3950. Majors, G.W. "Shakespeare's First Brutus:His Role in *Lucrece*." *MLQ* 35:339-51.
In *Lucrece* Brutus enlists our curiosity and our suspicions. We applaud the sudden emergence of a leader, but we remain uncertain as to his motives. Although Shakespeare draws on traditional sources, he goes far beyond them in emphasizing the moral ambiguousness of the Roman liberator. He invites the reader to ask unanswerable questions about Brutus's heart, and to recognize that such questions in a political context become moot. Dispassionate, pragmatic, self-contained, Brutus contrasts eloquently with the main characters, good and bad, who suffer for want of the very arts by which he thrives. (GWM)

Richard II. 3951. Battenhouse, Roy. "Tudor Doctrine and the Tragedy of *Richard II*." [F 92]:31-53.
Defective political doctrine is exposed as a basic cause of tragedy in *Richard II*. According to today's historians, Richard developed without any logical consistency claims for royal absolutism that were more extreme than in any of his predecessors. Shakespeare probably sensed an analogy between Richard's claims and those of the Tudor *Homilie Against Disobedience*. Richard II of Shakespeare's play falls into intellectual muddle and self-contradiction through a Narcissus-like obsession with a martyr's pose emptied of Christian substance. But empty pose is characteristic also of other chief persons in the play—Carlisle, York, and John of Gaunt. The variant stances of these several spokesmen are Shakespeare's outworking of the deceptions and dilemmas latent in Tudor political orthodoxy. (RWB)

3957. Potter, Lois. "The Antic Disposition of *Richard II*." *ShS* 27:33-41.
Language in Shakespeare's *Richard II* is a function of situation rather than character. Emotional rhetoric is a substitute for real power, a powerful weapon in its own right. Hence the apparent change in Richard's character halfway through the play, when he ceases to control events and learns to control the responses of his onstage and offstage audiences. What links his two styles of speech is the presence behind both of an ironic intelligence using them for its own ends. (LDP)

3958. Zitner, Sheldon P. "Aumerle's Conspiracy." *SEL* 14:239-57.
The scenes dealing with Aumerle's conspiracy are important to the construction and interpretation of Shakespeare's *Richard II*. They constitute one of a series of political transactions on which the action rests. They humanize, but do not exculpate, Bolingbroke, hence preparing for the last scene. By their travesty of heroic politics through the deflation of its themes and exponents, they prompt a complex view of the play's significance. Their geriatric comedy, burlesque of Senecan bombast, and political nihilism suggest the attitudes embodied in Falstaff in the later plays. (SPZ)

Richard III. 3964. Higdon, David L. "Shakespeare's *King Richard III* v.ii.7-11." *Expl* 33:Item 2.
In his "incitement speech" (*Richard III*, v.ii.7-11) Shakespeare's Richmond identifies Richard III with the mythical Calydonian boar, thus further stressing the "scourge of God" motif in the play. (DLH)

3966. Toole, William B.,III. "The Motif of Psychic Division in *Richard III*." *ShS* 27:21-32.
In Shakespeare's *Richard III* the movement from civil disorder to political unity is inversely paralleled by the protagonist's movement from psychological integrity to an interlude of psychic disintegration. Richard intensifies the disorder in the country under the false face of conscience; appropriately, his psychological civil war results from the mutiny of his real conscience. This conflict of "self against self" is foreshadowed structurally by the establishment of two polarized bases for the metaphor of appetite, by the division that takes place between the two murderers who spoke in the voice of their master, and by the separation of the newly crowned king from his "other self," Buckingham. (WBT,III)

Romeo and Juliet. 3975. Toor, David. "Shakespeare's *Romeo and Juliet* II.iv.38-40, 54-57." *Expl* 33:Item 29.
Understanding Mercutio's reference to "roe" in *Romeo and Juliet* (II.iv), is helped by regarding it in a sexual context. The citation in the *OED* reads, in part: *Hard roe*, the spawn of a female fish; *soft roe*, the milt or sperm of a male fish. Romeo had disappeared right after the ball, leaving Benvolio and Mercutio ignorant of his meeting with Juliet. They still seem to assume he is in love with Rosaline, which for Mercutio would, of course, be seen in a purely sexual sense. Romeo has been gone for a time, Rosaline

had been at the ball, and Mercutio's conclusion seems to be that Romeo has spent the night with her. (DST)

Sonnets. 3979. Bunselmeyer, J. "Appearances and Verbal Paradox:Sonnets 129 and 138." *SQ* 25:103-08.
Throughout the sonnets Shakespeare explores the gulf between appearance and reality. In the sonnets to the lady, even love becomes a "lie" (138). The falseness in this personal relationship is expressed through verbal paradox. Rhetorical devices destroy the absolute meaning of words and capture a world of shifting appearances. When verbal ambiguity and paradox are used, as in sonnets 129 and 138, they embody the perpetual confusion of life rather than neat resolutions of its conflicts. Shakespeare builds subtle paradox into his wordplay; often a word weaves between lines, yet its second use contradicts its first. (JEB)

3981. Gardner, C.O. "Some Reflections on Shakespeare's Sonnets Nos. 33, 34 and 35." *Theoria* 42:43-55.
Sonnets 33 and 34 treat the speaker's deception by his friend by using the image of the clouding-over of the sun, but this image is employed in strikingly different ways. In sonnet 33 the friend is seen almost as a part of amoral "nature," and his dark deed is accepted, at first regretfully but in the end almost joyfully. In sonnet 34 the relationship with the friend is pictured as more directly personal, and the deed is one that can be forgiven only when the friend's grief has equaled that of the speaker. Thus the two sonnets embody completely different attitudes to human life. (COG)

3992. Toor, David. "Shakespeare's 'Sonnet xx'." *Expl* 32: Item 38.
In glossing line 11 of Shakespeare's Sonnet xx, "And by addition me of thee defeated," modern editors generally explain "defeated" as meaning "defrauded" or "cheated." The clear sexual implication of "addition," referring to a phallus, has usually been quickly glossed, ignoring possible secondary levels of meaning. The most frequent use of "addition" in Shakespeare is as "title," a use much more common in Elizabethan English than the currently purely mathematical implication. The tension of the poem evolves from a confusion that is stated in the opening lines—the masculine-feminine mixture of the poet's friend's physical and spiritual nature. If we read line 11 with this confusion in mind it is then possible to gloss it, "and by a title, a name, I am cheated of you"; or, a bit expanded, "because you have been given the title of man, rather than woman, I have been defrauded." (DST)

3995. West, Michael. "The Internal Dialogue of Shakespeare's Sonnet 146." *SQ* 25:109-22.
Conflicting interpretations of Sonnet 146 can be synthesized by imagining that Shakespeare treats body and soul dialectically, with rhetoric and logic urging spiritual purity, while the moral and emotional connotations of the imagery betray more sympathy for the flesh. Thus the poem resembles the medieval debates between Body and Soul, and their 17th-century successors. 16th-century theology and psychology were ambiguous about the degree to which the body was responsible for sin, and poetic conventions exploited this ambiguity variously. The sonnet suggests a thoroughly Christian sensibility, but a complex one, anticipating the tragedies. Shakespeare may be troubled by lingering ambivalence about the Dark Lady. (MW)

3996. Widmann, R.L. "Upon Looking into Shakespeare's Sonnet 73." *LC* 39(1973):81-88.
Probes the effectiveness of creating visual images in the reader and their appeal to a reader's sense of sight in Shakespeare's Sonnet 73. The images point not only to the passing of chronological time and life but to a situation in which the physical size of the speaker is emphasized in relation to objects around him. The impact of physical size for both speaker and observer is analyzed in each quatrain and in the couplet. Shakespeare uses dramatic, grammatical, and rhetorical devices to develop and dramatize the relationship of the speaker and beholder. (RLW)

Taming of the Shrew. 3997. Ranald, Margaret Loftus. "The Manning of the Haggard; or, *The Taming of the Shrew*." *ELWIU* 1:149-65.
In *The Taming of the Shrew* Shakespeare equates the taming of

Kate with the methods used by a falconer in manning a haggard, a wild, adult, female hawk, teaching her how to live among men. The aim of hawk-taming is not cruelly to alter the bird's predatory nature, but to lead her patiently until she makes a voluntary commitment of herself and her skills to her master in a partnership that recognizes mutual interdependence and different areas of superiority. From the taming process Kate learns the realpolitik of marriage and human relationships from a man who respects her integrity of spirit and independence. Her last speech, therefore, is not one of submission, but a celebration of a partnership in mutuality: "Each has duties and both have rights." Thus Shakespeare celebrates a modern, civilized, and rational view of marriage, the result of love and patience, not blows. (MLR)

Timon of Athens. 4020. Bulman, James C.,Jr. "The Date and Production of *Timon* Reconsidered." *ShS* 27:111-27.
There has been no persuasive evidence to establish when *Timon* was written and where it was produced. Muriel Bradbrook recently cited internal evidence for its being a reveling play of the Inner Temple. Bulman substantiates Bradbrook's theory with new findings, but challenges her assumption that *Timon* was intended to burlesque Shakespeare's play. Allusions to Jonson's "comicall satyres," topically produced between 1599 and 1601, suggest that *Timon* was written not long thereafter and certainly prior to *Timon of Athens*. (JCB,Jr)

Titus Andronicus. 4022. Danson, Lawrence N. "The Device of Wonder:*Titus Andronicus* and Revenge Tragedies." *TSLL* 16:27-43.
In *Titus* the close connection between Elizabethan drama and rhetoric is evident; but evident too is the danger that rhetoric might stifle dramatic action. In *Titus* Shakespeare brings into the open the struggle to turn the language of words into a language of action, to convert rhetoric itself into dramatic form. Rhetoric, which can be the index of man's reason, can also, when it grows to a surfeit, become the token of madness. In the tragic world, the pressure to speak can lead to an overwrought language which finally becomes mad-speech. The final stage is the ritualization of death with which Elizabethan tragedy culminates. (LND)

4023. Huffman, Clifford C. "Bassianus and the British History in *Titus Andronicus*." *ELN* 11:175-81.
Titus Andronicus (1594) opens with a competition for the Roman Imperial throne between the evil older brother Saturnine and the good younger one Bassianus; the dilemma between primogeniture and merit as criteria for succession is not resolved until Act v. Historical criticism has been deterred from providing guidance because, according to classical historians, the historical Bassianus (the Emperor Caracalla) was an evil older brother. Several British chroniclers, following classical writers and Geoffrey of Monmouth, thought Bassianus was British, for his mother was a Briton; in 1593, Richard Hervey added the vied that he was also a younger, virtuous brother, and that consanguinity was preferable to primogeniture. Shakespeare's treatment combines and transforms historical and legendary materials to bind his audience into the play's setting and to insure its immediate favorable response to Bassianus. (CCH)

4024. Hunter, G.K. "Shakespeare's Earliest Tragedies:*Titus Andronicus* and *Romeo and Juliet*." *ShS* 27:1-9.
King Lear can be regarded as in some ways the reworking of themes from *Titus Andronicus*. Throughout Shakespeare's mature tragedies the ritual of *Titus* is complemented by the domesticity of *Romeo*. The two plays open in a similar way, the opening movement establishing discord against rule. Both plays are the story of rival families, though handled differently. In both plays the city walls measure the limit of the ordered world. In both plays the tomb is an expression of Shakespeare's sense of the tragic importance of family and social continuities. (KM)

4028. Tricomi, Albert H. "The Aesthetics of Mutilation in *Titus Andronicus*." *ShS* 27:11-19.
Metaphor in *Titus Andronicus* shackles itself to the play's ghoulish events. Wittily and obsessively, the figurative language of the tragedy imitates the horror of events to render them more real and excruciating. The embedded metaphor in Titus' anguished

question ("Speak, Lavinia, what accursed hand / Hath made thee handless?") strives to make metaphor recapitulate the literal events of the tragedy. So important are these literal metaphors that they often prophesy the play's shocking mutilations. Shakespeare undertakes here a unique dramatic experiment which seeks to identify the power of metaphor with the power inherent in dramatic action itself. (AHT)

Troilus and Cressida. 4029. Aggeler, Geoffrey. "Madness in Reason:A Paradoxical Kinship in *Troilus and Cressida*." *WascanaR* 9:39-57.
Shakespeare's satiric handling in *Troilus and Cressida* of Stoicism, Machiavellian pragmatism, and Platonic dualism is discussed. The treatment of Stoicism is consistent with that in *Hamlet* and *Julius Caesar*. Like Chapman and Marston, Shakespeare juxtaposes Stoicism and Machiavellian pragmatism, but unlike these contemporaries, he ridicules both systems. The treatment of reason uninformed by love is shown to be consistent with that in *King Lear*, and, as in *A Midsummer Night's Dream*, the kinship of the rational with the irrational is proclaimed in connection with love relationships. Troilus' retreat into Platonic dualism satirizes both Neo-Platonism and "Petrarchism." (GDA)

4031. Jones-Davies, M.T. "Discord in Shakespeare's *Troilus and Cressida*; or, The Conflict between 'Angry Mars and Venus Queen of Love'." *SQ* 25:33-41.
The gods presiding over the destinies of Greeks and Trojans are playing their parts in the ambiguous atmosphere of a futile and cruel war. Jupiter expects to "find persistive constancy in men." The pagan mystery of the unlawful union of Mars and Venus giving birth to Harmony helps to interpret the discordant elements in *Troilus and Cressida*. The fable of Mars and Venus stresses the consonance arising when proportion tempers contraries. In the play, friendship sometimes tempers war, but the consonance between war and love is linguistic. In iconology, Mars and Venus in conjunction beget Harmony. In *Troilus and Cressida*, Sol has not corrected the planets' malignant relationship: chaos follows. But the roles of Mars and Venus recur within man or woman individually. This agrees with the Renaissance code of chivalry: the perfect lover is the perfect warrior. Although Troilus describes the emblem of the perfect union of Mars and Venus, he is no true prince of chivalry. (MTJ-D)

4035. Slights, Camille. "The Parallel Structure of *Troilus and Cressida*." *SQ* 25:42-51.
The parallelism of scenes, characters, and ideas in *Troilus and Cressida* controls the tone and resolves the basic problem of the implied attitude and the appropriate audience response. Scenes similar in form but contrasting in style function to expose false men. The audience recognizes the self-deception, hypocrisy, and cynicism permeating the Greek and Trojan camps. Patterns of antithetically parallel scenes create sympathy for human suffering and illuminate the complexity and dignity of human motives and aspirations as well as their degradation. In the carefully balanced pattern of purpose and inevitable defeat in the war and love plots Shakespeare created a tragic satire that combines criticism with compassion. (CS)

Twelfth Night. 4040. Field, B.S.,Jr. "Fate, Fortune, and *Twelfth Night*." *MichA* 6(1973):193-99.
That Shakespeare's *Twelfth Night* has two central figures, in Viola as the figure to be emulated, and in Malvolio as the figure to be shunned, is supported by an analysis of the reaction of all the characters in the play to forces beyond their control. They are all given opportunities to respond to such forces and call them not only Fate and Fortune, but also give them such names as Time, Chance, Luck, Wit, and Jove. They respond with varying grace to the buffets and rewards of these forces, Malvolio showing the most imperfect grasp of what constitutes right behavior in the face of such buffets and rewards, and Viola the most perfect grasp of it. (BSF,Jr)

4041. Forrest, James F. "Malvolio and Puritan 'Singularity'." *ELN* 11:259-64.
Our appreciation of Malvolio's gulling in the letter-scene of *Twelfth Night* (II.iv) is enhanced by a proper understanding of "singularity" as a pejorative term, commonly applied to Puritans of Shakespeare's day and later. The word not only expresses the fact of dissenting, but also conveys a sense of apprehensiveness about innovation or novelty. An awareness of this connotation enriches the comedy, for it discloses the full irony of a situation in which the seemingly enlightened Malvolio is actually benighted, the modish steward outmoded. The topical reference also strengthens Malvolio's motivation, because Shakespeare appears to hold out hope for his success by exploiting the attractiveness of Puritan "singularity" to women, which was a phenomenon discussed in the *Laws of Ecclesiastical Polity* by Hooker, who may therefore be one of the "politic authors" Malvolio so excitedly vows to read. (JFF)

4042. Hartwig, Joan. "Feste's 'Whirligig' and the Comic Providence of *Twelfth Night*." *ELH* 40(1973):501-13.
The characters in *Twelfth Night* finally realize that their individual wills are secondary to a design that benevolently accords with what each truly desires. Malvolio is an exception because he fails to receive a benevolent fulfillment of his desires and fails to accept the controlled malevolence of Feste and Maria and the subplotters' design against him. Feste's summary statement of the play's action (v.i.360-66) attributes the subplot's revengeful resolution to the "whirligig of time"; whereas, he and Maria have been the chief instigators and manipulators of these revenges. The subplot's action of revenge parodies the higher providence that directs the play's main plot. (JH)

4047. Tromly, F[rederic] B. "*Twelfth Night*:Folly's Talents and the Ethics of Shakespearean Comedy." *Mosaic* 7,iii:53-68.
In *Twelfth Night* the lovers and roisterers play out their games in a world pervaded by mutability, hazard, and delusion. The central ethical question of the play concerns the values that mediate between the frailty of the characters and the happiness most of them reach at the end. The dominant value is the notion of spending folly's talents in the world. The idea of folly and its talents shapes the action, individuates the characters, and supplies some of the dominant symbols of the play. *Twelfth Night* suggests that all mortals are fools and that happiness resides in the generous commitment to life which allows people to escape from themselves. *Twelfth Night* denies the efficacy of self-knowledge but escapes cynical fatalism by suggesting that nature's bias can draw man to his happiness. (FBT)

Two Noble Kinsmen. 4050. Petronella, Vincent F. "Stylistic Logic in Shakespeare's Part of *The Two Noble Kinsmen*." *HAB* 25:38-40.
Dramatic plots in Shakespeare often reveal logical structures. The plots of *Othello*, *Hamlet*, and *Troilus and Cressida*, for example, hinge upon the pattern of the formal syllogism. Similar logical structuring is found in those sections of *The Two Noble Kinsmen* usually attributed to Shakespeare. Logical patterns in I.i, v.i, and v.iv constitute a frame for the Shakespeare-John Fletcher play and assist in lending rational, analytic stability to an otherwise strictly romantic flow of events. (VP)

Venus and Adonis. 4051. Gent, Lucy. "*Venus and Adonis:*The Triumph of Rhetoric." *MLR* 69:721-29.
Rhetoric in *Venus and Adonis* is a guide to Shakespeare's intentions in the poem, particularly when considered with the poem's relation to Marlowe's *Hero and Leander* and the original Inns of Court audience. The poem distinguishes itself both from ordinary life and other contemporary Ovidian poems by its quantity and use of rhetoric. Shakespeare casts Venus as a brilliant orator; her sex combined with her role as wooer amplify her eloquence. She attempts to impose on Adonis and life her own vision, which Adonis rejects with oratorical art which, ironically, he learns from Venus. The origin-myth which the poem delivers is both a placing and justification of poetic eloquence and truth. (LG)

4053. Sheidley, William E. " 'Unless it be a boar':Love and Wisdom in Shakespeare's *Venus and Adonis*." *MLQ* 35:3-15.
Shakespeare's *Venus and Adonis* has a unity of structure that reconciles its farcical beginnings with its violent end. By parodying courtly love poetry, by causing Adonis to voice familiar anti-amorist doctrines, and by allowing Venus to

philosophize cogently on love as the sustaining force of the universe, Shakespeare proclaims his intention to seek a resolution for the moral perplexities of conventional poetic love. Viewing the poem from the perspectives both of the male, Adonis, and of the suitor, Venus, the reader cannot escape noticing that a phallic deficiency predicates frustration and disaster. The Boar strikes as an embodiment of the dislocated phallic impulse, a destructive resurgence of what Adonis has spurned—love in its necessarily ungentle, bestial aspect. The Boar's onslaught replaces the missing sexual consummation, but paradoxically the tone of the poem is joyful. Instructed on the need to integrate his lower nature, the reader discovers and welcomes his capacity to do what Adonis will not. (WES)

Winter's Tale. 4057. Ludwig, Jay B. "Shakespearean Decorum:An Essay on *The Winter's Tale*." *Style* 8:365-404.
Behind the rich variety of moral, structural, generic, dramatic, and stylistic particulars in *The Winter's Tale* lies a highly abstract, but precise constructive principle which gives the play a pervasive and special unity. The principle consists of a continuing emphasis on a pattern of merging or merged opposites. Structurally the pattern is most obviously present in the tragicomic rhythm of the play, but it also appears in more particular arrangements of characters and action. In the thematics of the play the pattern figures as an insistence on presenting as coexisting or identical such opposites as court and country, art and nature, youth and age, faith and mistrust, and life and death. (JBL)
4060. Schwartz, Murray M. "Leontes' Jealousy in *The Winter's Tale*." *AI* 30:250-73.
A close examination of *The Winter's Tale* and of relations between characters reveals a complex fabric of motives for Leontes' paranoid response to the fear of separation from idealized others. Leontes' madness can be explained as an attempt simultaneously to act out and repudiate fears of sexual and social violence. In the first acts of the play he expresses and denies the violations of sexual decorum that are dialectically opposed to the sacred over-evaluation of women in Renaissance imaginations. Unlike his double, Polixenes, who avoids his ambivalence by idealization, and unlike the other courtly men, who reflect this over-evaluation, Leontes follows a regressive path toward the object of his ambivalent desires, Hermione, and he would destroy her to reunite himself with a fantasized, ideal maternal figure. At the root of his paranoid jealousy is a fear of maternal engulfment, symbolized by the spider. In the court scene of Act III, Leontes acts out his fear and prepares for his "recreation" by vowing to mourn the lost mother-son bond the rest of the play is designed magically to restore. (MMS)
4061. Siemon, James E. " 'But It Appears She Lives':Iteration in *The Winter's Tale*." *PMLA* 89:10-16.
Structural parallels between Acts I-III and Acts IV-V of *The Winter's Tale* are reinforced by repeated statements of motifs common to both parts of the play and by the variation in the second half of motifs important to the first. The dramatic evidence of Hermione's death is substantial, particularly in III.ii and III.iii, and later details (those in v.ii and v.iii) come too late to qualify the dramatic as well as thematic import of Hermione's loss. These later details must, therefore, stand as alternatives rather than as explanations. The second half of the play thus forms an alternative to the first, with Hermione's fate of central importance in pointing up their contrasting natures. Each part of the play makes a statement of the possibilities for gain and for loss within society, and the statement of neither is complete without the other. Together, they suggest limits as well as possibilities. (JES)

VII. SEVENTEENTH CENTURY

General and Miscellaneous. 4069. Brown, Mark N. "Trimmers and Moderates in the Reign of Charles II." *HLQ* 37:311-36.
Between 1682 and 1685 L'Estrange's Tory journal *The Observator* gave currency to the notion of a third party of "Trimmers" in England, described by him as neutrals or secret Whigs. Macaulay assumed the existence of a party of neutrals; others have spoken of a faction of moderate Tories; more recently, with the literal acceptance of L'Estrange's secret-Whig definition, the existence of such a party has been dismissed as a fiction of controversy and any connection with moderates has been denied. Yet individuals who were actually called Trimmers can be identified. These men, for the most part, were moderate Tories accused of sympathy toward the Whigs and moderate Anglicans similarly accused with respect to Protestant Dissenters. There was no self-proclaimed party or faction of "Trimmers"; the term was an insulting epithet for traitors in a partisan cause, and as such it was usually applied to moderates. (MNB)
4076. Foster, Elizabeth R. "Printing the Petition of Right." *HLQ* 38:81-83. [Note.]
Henry Elsyng, clerk of the parliaments 1621-35, compiled an account of parliament's proceedings in 1628 concerning the Petition of Right. This account, now among the Carte manuscripts at the Bodleian Library, Oxford, indicates that King Charles himself recalled the first printing of the Petition with his answer of June 7, which had been ordered by parliament. Elsyng was summoned to the royal court and ordered to bring with him copies of Charles' answer of June 2, Charles' and the Lord Keeper's speeches of June 7, and Charles' speech delivered on June 26, the last day of the session. These materials the King ordered to be printed with the text of the Petition and the public acts of the session. The King thus vitiated the effect of the publication of the Petition by attaching to it his own interpretation of its meaning. (ERF)
4077. Franklin, Wayne. "John Norton the Printer:An Attribution (1642)." *SB* 27:185-87.
John Norton (1606-63), the New England minister, is listed in Wing's *Short-Title Catalogue* as the author of *An Answer to a Late Scurrilous and Scandalous Pamphlet* (London, 1642). It seems likely that this attribution is the result of confusion—that, in fact, the John Norton connected with *An Answer* was a London printer who issued the work from his press. For one thing, certain border ornaments used in *An Answer* correspond in size and style to those used in other Norton issues, while an initial "T" in the pamphlet is identical with one which appears in a book printed by Norton in 1638. Finally, the "rebus of Norton" which *An Answer* bears on its title-page is essentially derived from ones used earlier by William and Bonham Norton, two illustrious relatives of John Norton the printer. The New England namesake of that London tradesman, at any rate, clearly was not the author of the work in question. (WSF)
4087. Osmond, Rosalie. "Body and Soul Dialogues in the Seventeenth Century." *ELR* 4:364-403.
The reappearance of English body and soul dialogues in the first half of the 17th century is explicable in relation both to the thought and to the literary convention of the period. The medieval prototypes of these debates dealing with the relative responsibility of body and soul for sin depend on confusion, both conceptual and linguistic, between body and flesh, soul and spirit, as well as on the ambivalent attitude toward body brought about by the conflicting implications of Platonism, the Fall, and the Incarnation. A naive imagination that sees body and soul as concrete entities is also essential. Most of these elements not only survive into the early 17th century but are encouraged and exaggerated by the dualistic and Puritanical characteristics of the age. Some of the dialogues, such as William Crashaw's, are almost identical with medieval prototypes; others, such as Marvell's, are more philosophical than moral. Still others, such as James Howell's, develop as discussion dialogues, and in these latter we see the gradual divorce of form and content and the dissolution of the genre. By mid-century certain general trends in thought made the subject matter itself untenable as well. (REO)
4091. Sampson, H. Grant. "Mimetic Relationships Between Music and Literature in England." *HAB* 25:197-210. [17th-18th cent., esp.]
Writers in England have frequently stressed the close relationship which exists between music and literature. However, the grounds

upon which this relationship is supposed to rest have not been firmly established. Although various critics have proposed certain terms and approaches for the discussion of this problem, the writers themselves have frequently referred to the doctrine of imitation. This concept seems to have undergone changes of implication and context which are important to note for the understanding of both literary and musical history. (HJG)

4096. Summers, Joseph H. "Stanley Fish's Reading of Seventeenth-Century Literature." *MLQ* 35:403-17. [Rev. art.] The chief virtues of *Self-Consuming Artifacts: The Experience of Seventeenth-Century Literature* derive from Fish's recognition that the basic data of literary criticism are the experiences of an alert, intelligent, and sensitive reader as he reads the texts within time. Its weaknesses stem from his concentration on the single perspective of a "fictional" first reading and his assumption that admirable literary designs on the reader should always be antagonistic, tricky, or evangelical, since major works undermine "reason" and "consume" the "self." Best on Bunyan and Donne and poorest on Sir Thomas Browne, the book presents the Bacon of the *Essays* as unconcerned with power, Herbert as a master of dialectic unconcerned with beauty, Milton as unalterably opposed to "reason," and Burton as an anguished nihilist unconcerned with comedy. (JHS)

Criticism. 4101. Berry, Herbert. "Italian Definitions of Tragedy and Comedy Arrive in England." *SEL* 14:179-87. [On Samuel Harsnett.]
In his *Declaration of Egregious Popish Impostures* (1603), Harsnett pursued an analogy throughout likening the operations of the Jesuit William Weston to events of the playhouse. He began the peroration of his book with a rational definition of comedy and tragedy in which he did what was unheard of in his time and place. He tied current Italian critical theory to current English stage practice. By using current critical language, like "invention" for comedy and "moving of affection" for tragedy, he bowed to Italian criticism, but he left out that Hydra which occupied much of it, Horace's profit. Instead, he dwelt on what Horace forbade and Aristotle disliked, lively acting. His definition of tragedy is a significant step toward definitions common at the end of the 17th century, which comprise the "affective" theory of tragedy. (HB)

4102. Dillon, George L. "Complexity and Change of Character in Neo-Classical Criticism." *JHI* 35:51-61.
The immediate background for Neoclassical discussions of character is not Humours psychology but the new historiography. Bacon's and Montaigne's calls for psychological analysis in historical writing provided some of the terminology and outlook of Dryden, Shadwell, Rymer, and Dennis. St. Evremond's discussions of character-drawing in Tacitus and Sallust (particularly of Tiberius and Catiline) focus on complexity and change of character, and these discussions clearly influenced Dennis. This developing interest mitigated the earlier Neoclassical insistence on consistency and simplicity of characterization: Dryden employed change of character in his last plays, defying the critics and Aristotle. The psychological criticism of the 18th century thus appears a more direct outgrowth of Neoclassical criticism when this criticism is understood as embracing historical as well as literary criticism. (GLD)

4103. Jensen, H. James. "A Note on Restoration Aesthetics." *SEL* 14:317-26.
The strength of a Restoration esthetics of delight is apparent from connotations of words such as "lively" and "motion," the role of the passions in art, and the kind of art the Restoration thought most excellent. Neo-Platonic philosophy of art rather than a materialistically oriented rules-criticism is behind the justification of a Restoration esthetic of delight. Dryden's definitions of "just" and "lively" are important: "just" clearly comes from the French; but "lively" is associated with aliveness, imaginative energy, and passion, besides French connotations associated with an intellectual appearance of verisimilitude. The argument between Lisideius and Neander in "The Essay of Dramatic Poesy" indicates Dryden's awareness of the two meanings. He connects "lively" with great Elizabethan drama, especially Shakespeare, using a vocabulary drawn from Neo-Platonism, because French rules-criticism is an inadequate vehicle for describing the great dramatic art of England. Dryden's usage and criticism set the tone for English criticism and attitudes. (HJJ)

Drama and Theater. 4109. Boni, John. "Analogous Form: Black Comedy and Some Jacobean Plays." *WHR* 28:201-15.
Formal similarities between contemporary black comic novels and several Jacobean plays suggest a similar vision, reflecting the flexibility of art and its adaptability to analogous visions in widely separated chronological periods. Novels by Pynchon, Heller, Vonnegut, and Donleavy reflect a form and tone similar to that in plays by Shakespeare, Webster, Marston, and Tourneur. Both share a skeptical, almost cynical, worldview, one which emphasizes survival of the self and the error of reliance upon externally proclaimed value systems. As the Jacobean plays gradually modified in tone, so black comedy will change as the worldview of our age is transformed. (JB)

4116. Forrest, James F. "Clarendon on the Stage." *MLR* 69:250-53.
Chroniclers of the theater have overlooked some significant observations on the 17th-century stage, which are contained in Clarendon's *Dialogue concerning Education*, published only in 1727, but written probably about 1668. After one participant in the discussion argues experience of the theater as a major cultural advantage of a stay at the Inns-of-Court, the claim is challenged and the playhouse attacked as one of the great corruptions of the age, a scandalous waste of time and money. There follows a lively defense, in which several, including a bishop, testify to the value of plays in delightfully conveying instruction and spiritual refreshment. Clarendon's *Dialogue* demonstrates that even after the advent of the English actress, difficulties associated with "disguising the Sexes" on the stage did not disappear, but rather became more acute; and in addition, it corroborates the opinion of Evelyn and others on the demoralizing effect of actresses on the Restoration stage. (JFF)

4125. Lancashire, Anne. "*The Second Maiden's Tragedy*:A Jacobean Saint's Life." *RES* 25:267-79.
The sub-plot of the anonymous *Second Maiden's Tragedy* (1611) is known to come from the Curious Impertinent story in Cervantes' *Don Quixote*; the main plot has been thought to come from the story of Ines de Castro and Pedro of Portugal, from the anonymous *Revenger's Tragedy*, and from two other tales of corpse-infatuation, one being the Talmudic story of Herod and Mariamne. The main plot comes, however, in large part from the story of the early Christian heroine Sophronia, who killed herself with a sword to preserve her honor, and has apparently also been influenced by the stories of King John and Matilda and of Appius and Virginia, as well as by the Herod and Mariamne legend. The play is in part a "saint's life," with several of the characteristics of the genre. (AL)

4126. Leech, Clifford. "The Incredible in Jacobean Tragedy." [F 92]:109-22.
The incredible in Jacobean tragedy occurs in the representation of man's capacity for evil and his capacity for anguish or suffering when witnessing or experiencing the progress of evil. The situations and language of Shakespeare, Webster, Ford, and Middleton are deliberately heightened and distorted in their attempts to comprehend and present the reality of evil and its effects; the incredible arises when dramatic fiction is pushed beyond its formal limits, and a play ceases to reflect a flux of good and evil, but is made in the course of a scene or speech an emblem of evil and suffering. (PDS)

4131. Oliver, H.J. "Literary Allusions in Jacobean Drama." [F 92]:131-40.
The use by Jacobean dramatists of plots, incidents, character-types from earlier drama is easily illustrated; and actual quotation from a predecessor is not uncommon. The purpose of such "borrowings," however, is far from certain. Does it expect recognition by the audience, in every instance, that another work is being alluded to? And if it does, how does such recognition add to the meaning of the later play? The right comparison may be with the sophistication of the use of literary allusion by modern artists such as Eliot or Joyce or with the deliberate artifice of a dramatist like Brecht. Perhaps also the device of allusion to Shakespeare was learned by the other Jacobean dramatists from

Shakespeare himself. (HJO)

4134. Reibetanz, John. "Hieronimo in Decimosexto:A Private-Theater Burlesque." *RenD* 5(for 1972):89-121.
When viewed as the production of an all-child company, and a deliberate parody of *The Spanish Tragedy* and other such plays, *1 Hieronimo* emerges as artful and successful. Much evidence, external and internal, supports this interpretation. Like Marston in the *Antonio* plays, the author both stresses the innate comedy arising when child actors attempt heroic drama and burlesques such common features of popular drama as disguises, stage battles, Machiavellian villains, and the practice of giving female roles to boy actors. *The First Part of Hieronimo* was most likely performed initially by the Queen's Revels between 1602 and 1604. Except for Beaumont's *Knight of the Burning Pestle*, it is the fullest Elizabethan theatrical burlesque that has survived; when recognized as such, its power to amuse its initial audience becomes evident, as does its value as a document relating to the contemporary dramatic milieu. (JR)

4139. Winton, Calhoun. "The London Stage Embattled: 1695-1710." *TSL* 19:9-19.
Social pressures on the London stage in the period 1695 to 1710 have been ascribed by literary historians to an increasingly bourgeois or "Puritan" audience, under the leadership of the Reverend Jeremy Collier. It seems clear, however, that the stage was the object of a concerted attack originating with the Anglican establishment, led by the evangelistic societies with the support of members of the Anglican hierarchy and having at least the sympathetic acquiescence of both King William and Queen Anne. The hypothesis of a bourgeois audience is not necessary. (CW)

Poetry. 4141. Brown, Gillian F. " 'The Session of the Poets to the Tune of Cook Lawrel':Playhouse Evidence for Composition Date of 1664." *RECTR* 13,i:19-26,62.
The anonymous "Session" poem originally published in *Poems on Affairs of State* (1697) concerns itself neither with literary criticism nor with questions of poetic decorum. Its genre is topical satire that relies on gossip about plays, people, and affairs of the Restoration theater. Although modern editors date the poem well after 1666 when the London theaters were reopened following the plague, all the evidence clusters around the theater world of the early 1660s. References, both specific and veiled, to particular plays, playwrights, and other members of a theatrical coterie strongly suggest that the poem was written in 1664. (GFB)

4146. Edwards, Philip. "Who Wrote 'The Passionate Man's Pilgrimage'?" *ELR* 4:83-97.
Although "The Passionate Man's Pilgrimage" ("Give me my scallop shell of quiet") is a poem which anthologists and others continue to refer to as Sir Walter Raleigh's, the attribution is no longer tenable. Doubts expressed over 150 years have been upheld by recent re-examinations of the early manuscripts. The association of the poem with Raleigh has hindered a proper examination of its qualities. Two fundamental questions are (1) whether the poem reflects a real experience of waiting for execution or whether it is a spiritual exercise, and (2) whether the lack of sophistication (in prosody, for example) is intended or artless. The poem, which includes a remarkable shift of the traditional use of the pilgrimage motif, falls into four separate sections, each a distinct meditation on the entry into blessedness. Though its imagery is ambiguous, its allusion to extreme unction argues that it is a Catholic poem. It belongs to a tradition of English recusant meditations on a martyr's death. The possibility that the poem deliberately creates the persona of a naive spiritual martyr is tempting but must be rejected. The unknown Catholic author is not necessarily a recognized poet. (PWE)

4156. McGuire, Philip C. "Private Prayer and English Poetry in the Early Seventeenth Century." *SEL* 14:63-77.
Analysis of six poems according to principles and models for praying formulated by Renaissance devotional writers demonstrates the important influence of private prayer (a devotional exercise distinct from meditation) upon English poetry in the early 17th century. (PCM)

Bacon. 4171. Linden, Stanton J. "Francis Bacon and Alchemy:The Reformation of Vulcan." *JHI* 35:547-60.

Bacon reveals interest in and an informed awareness of alchemical theory and practice. He is generally sympathetic toward its expressed aims and acknowledges that positive benefits have occasionally resulted from it. Bacon shares with his age the assumptions essential to serious belief in alchemy and other varieties of occult thought: the doctrine of sympathies, antipathies, and correspondences; the Four Elements theory; the importance of "spirits" in explaining the operations of nature; and the view of art as an "improver" of nature. Bacon attributes the decline of alchemy's reputation to the infiltration of Belief and Imagination into the methods of its practitioners, but he expresses confidence that success in transmutation can be attained if a course of reasoned investigation and careful experiment is followed. (SJL)

4174. Reiss, Timothy J. "Structure and Mind in Two Seventeenth-Century Utopias:Campanella and Bacon." *YFS* 49(1973):82-95.
The utopia is generally considered as a stasis, putting a halt to history, of which it is the conclusion and upon which it is a commentary. Campanella's *City of the Sun* (1602-23) would be the exemplary model for such a view: with its geographically circular form, and its concentric organization, it is represented as the union of individual and city, of society and God. The process of its own signification is included in this microcosmic-macrocosmic entity, since it claims to arrive at the union of perfect knowledge and absolute being by a direct, unmediated reading of things. Opposed to it is Bacon's *New Atlantis* (1627), whose ideal is praxis, and which can only be viewed as the installation of a history. It is a discourse whose main elements, the journey, the human viewing of things, the casting of intellectual "Light" (true knowledge) upon phenomena, present the dynamism of scientific experimentalism and possessive individualism. These two utopias thus reflect, at the level of discourse, the change in epistémè which is occurring at this time. They also suggest that the utopia should not be seen as a thinking about an object, but rather as the objectivization of a mode of thought. (TJR)

4175. Stephens, James. "Bacon's Fable-making:A Strategy of Style." *SEL* 14:111-27.
The new induction, as outlined in the Preface to Bacon's *New Organon*, is a process which gradually produces "a certain path for the mind to proceed in, starting directly from the simple sensuous perception." In leading his reader down the paths he is to follow, Bacon attempts to reduce the complexities of doctrines, ideas, and other abstractions to simple sensuous impressions, which then serve as bits of evidence for future, more general impressions. This procedure is philosophical induction, but it also works rhetorically to provide the imaginative appeal vital even to a scientist's argument. Bacon's major works, taken together are carefully-integrated, mutually-dependent arguments for the new science, arguments which often hinge on the author's ability to construct from the material of old fables and parables a new myth for the modern age. (JS)

Beaumont & Fletcher. 4178. Bowers, Fredson. "*Beggars Bush*:A Reconstructed Prompt-Book and Its Copy." *SB* 27:113-36.
The Lambarde MS (Folger Library) is a scribal favor copy transcribed c. 1637/8 from a prompt-book made up by Ralph Crane. The 1647 Folio text was set directly from the authorial papers that had been used as the basis for Crane's copy. Each, therefore, has independent authority. The MS contains purer readings for numerous Folio compositorial corruptions and retains text censored by alteration or deletion in the Folio. (FB)

4181. Gossett, Suzanne. "The Term 'Masque' in Shakespeare and Fletcher, and *The Coxcomb*." *SEL* 14:285-95.
Though confused critical tradition holds that a masque is missing from Fletcher's *The Coxcomb*, the evidence is insufficient. Act I requires only a dance to be coherent, and none of the presentational or surprise aspects of a masque are present. The question which stimulated speculation about revision, "Come, where's this masque," is one of many figurative usages of "masque" in Beaumont and Fletcher's work. "Masque" designates any kind of spectacle or presentationally constructed moment. In contrast Shakespeare always uses "masque" to refer

to an Elizabethan-type masque consisting of an entrance and dance. The change in usage from Shakespeare to Beaumont and Fletcher reflects the masque's dominance over other forms of Jacobean revelry, so that the collaborators could play with figurative and metaphorical meanings and depend upon audience comprehension. (SG)

4183. Turner, Robert K.,Jr. "The Printers and the Beaumont and Fletcher Folio of 1647:Section 1 (Thomas Warren's)." *SB* 27:137-56.

On evidence relating to presswork, composition, and distribution, the printing of Section 1 is reconstructed. Quires B-E, containing *The Mad Lover* are examined in detail, and a summary of the analysis of the rest of the quires, containing *The Spanish Curate* and *The Little French Lawyer*, is given. The section was set by formes by four compositors. (RKT,Jr)

Behn. 4184. Batten, Charles L.,Jr. "The Source of Aphra Behn's *The Widow Ranter*." *RECTR* 13,i:12-18.

Aphra Behn did not employ *Strange News from Virginia* (1677) as the source for the tragic plot in her *Widow Ranter* (performed 1689, pub. 1690). Rather, a report made by the king's commission sent to investigate Bacon's Rebellion must have served as the basis for her story about Nathaniel Bacon's unauthorized attack on the Pamunkey Indians. This official report contains all of the historically accurate details in Behn's play. Moreover, the report includes one passage which Behn quotes verbatim, and it suggests why she fabricated Bacon's heroic love for the Indian Queen. Thus, discovery of its correct source confirms more than ever *The Widow Ranter*'s reputation as "the earliest extant English play to be based on a historical event in British America." (CLB,Jr)

Betterton. 4185. Milhous, Judith. "Thomas Betterton's Playwriting." *BNYPL* 77:375-92.

Of the 12 plays attributed to Thomas Betterton by various scholars and bibliographers, only two are genuine adaptations. Six of the others (*The Bondman, The Counterfeit Bridegroom, The Revenge, The Roman Actor*, the 1703 *Hamlet*, and the *Sequel to Henry IV*) became associated with his name in dubious ways; the remaining four (*The Roman Virgin*, the 1674 *Tempest, The Prophetess*, and *King Henry IV*) are no more than production adaptations of previously existing scripts. One of the two plays he wrote, *The Woman Made a Justice*, was apparently never printed, but was probably a translation of Montfleury. His one extant work, *The Amorous Widow* (ca. 1670; published 1706), a pastiche of two French plays, shows a keen awareness of current trends in English comedy. The amount Betterton wrote, however, has been vastly overestimated, and the hallmark of his work is the actor-manager's economical modernization. (JM)

Birkenhead. 4186. Doyle, Charles, C. "An Unhonored English Anacreon:John Birkenhead." *SP* 71:192-205.

John Birkenhead tried his hand at translating lyrics from the popular *Anacreontea*. A comparison of versions of the same Greek poems by these four writers shows Birkenhead to possess a kind of wit not found in the other translators. By taking small liberties he heightened the humor in the situations which the lyrics present, rendering the informal Greek into lively colloquial English. Birkenhead himself wrote lyrics in a distinctive Anacreontic manner which were eventually set to music. (CCD)

Bunyan. 4192. Adeney, Elizabeth. "Bunyan:A Unified Vision?" *CR* 17:97-109.

In *The Pilgrim's Progress* Part 1 Bunyan's didacticism is at odds with his generously honest response to earthly life and the split caused in his argument concerning how man should react to his world is never truly resolved. It is primarily through comedy that his response to life is evident, and though this comedy is at times in harmony with the didactic purpose, many comic passages show a vivid delight in forces inimical to Bunyan's religion. Christian, a figure primarily of dry and narrow Puritanism, is his didactic vehicle and is incapable of Bunyan's appreciation of worldly existence. The two figures should not be confused; the book is not a spiritual autobiography. Christian reacts well to real threat, but with jarring severity to the least offensive and most generously

imagined characters—increasingly so as he nears Heaven. (EA)

4193. Howell, Elmo. "Bunyan's Two Valleys:A Note on the Ecumenic Element in *Pilgrim's Progress*." *TSL* 19:1-7.

Although *Pilgrim's Progress* is the most eloquent statement of Puritanism, its implications are not limited to the English 17th century. The valleys of Humiliation and the Shadow of Death, for example, represent difficult periods in Bunyan's religious experience, but they also conform to the pattern of spiritual development outlined a century earlier by St. John of the Cross in *The Dark Night of the Soul*. Bunyan wrote to a partisan audience and sparked his message with the strong idiom of the Midland English peasant, but what he achieved in *Pilgrim's Progress* is a parabolic representation not only of Puritan experience but that of any man who looks on life in terms of battle between matter and spirit. (EH)

Campion. 4203. Bryan, Margaret B. "Recent Studies in Campion." *ELR* 4:404-11.

Campion's secure though minor status among Renaissance poets is revealed by his inevitable inclusion in any serious study of Renaissance poetry and, at the same time, by the paucity of full-length studies of his work. Recent critics of Campion have considered the question of whether or not to separate his words and music, the quality of his remarks on prosody in *Observations*, the relationship of his own poetry to the theories in the essay, and his Neoclassical traits. Still lacking are a full-scale study of the poetry (including the Latin verse), a study of his metrics—both theory and practice—in the light of recent linguistic theory, and further reassessment of the masques, which, until recently, have been denigrated or ignored. Neither edition available today is entirely adequate. (MBB)

Clarendon. 4216. Watson, George. "The Reader in Clarendon's *History of the Rebellion*." *RES* 25:396-409.

Clarendon's diversity of purpose in his *History of the Rebellion* seems baffling, but the internal evidence of style and the external evidence of his first readers after the book appeared in 1702-04 suggest that his principal purpose cannot have been to criticize the policy of his royal master Charles I. It is more likely to have been the creation of a myth of kingship for posterity. The appeal to the authority of Hooker's *Laws*, which is echoed by the syntax of Clarendon's opening sentence, is unconvincing, and was seen to be so by his first readers in the 18th century; Clarendon was no master of Ciceronian English, and his incoherence of style suggests a passionate rather than a consistent temper of mind. (GW)

Cowley. 4222. Larson, Charles. "The Somerset House Poems of Cowley and Waller." *PLL* 10:126-35.

In 1664 Edmund Waller and Abraham Cowley wrote companion poems on Queen Mother Henrietta Maria's recently-completed remodeling of Somerset House in London. More than merely descriptions of a royal residence, the two poems indicate important Restoration attitudes both toward the glory of the nation and toward the subject matter of poetry. Traditionally seen as "Cavalier" poets, Cowley and Waller here help lead English poetry into the more public stance of the "Augustan" mode. The poems contrast the present harmonies of England and its Queen Mother with the chaos of the Interregnum and sound the encomiastic note that was to recur with such frequency during the next half century. (CHL)

Crashaw. 4228. Levitt, Paul. "Crashaw's 'The Weeper,' 113-114." *Expl* 32:Item 56.

Called by Edmund Gosse the worst lines in English poetry, Crashaw's lines 113-14 from "Sainte Mary Magdalene or The Weeper" must be read in the light of 17th-century word usage. In particular, the words "baths," "motions," "portable," "compendious," and "oceans" appear extravagant in emotion and imagery, but in fact are words two- and three-deep in allusions that give the lines in question a richness of imagery and enlarge the religious meaning of the poem. (PML)

Donne. 4235. Almasy, Rudolph. "John Donne's 'Air and

Angels' Again." *WVUPP* 21:17-22.

Various readings of "Aire and Angels" reveal two opposing views of the poem: either it concludes with perfect love or it does not solve the speaker's dilemmas. By explicating the poem with Renaissance commonplaces, critics overlook the emphasis in the last three lines. Studying the conclusion carefully within the context of the poem and comparing it with conclusions from a few "perfect love" poems of Donne, one sees that the speaker has not reached an affirmative understanding of his relationship with the woman because no union or oneness has resulted. Rather, the speaker finds himself unable to escape the regrettable and unsatisfying disparity he finds between his love and the woman's. (RPA)

4242. Collmer, Robert G. "Another Look at 'The Apparition'." *CP* 7,i:34-40.

Critics, describing the Petrarchan affinities of John Donne's "The Apparition" have noted a divergence from that tradition. The uniqueness of Donne's treatment of the theme of death-for-love is related to the meaning Donne and his contemporaries placed on the word "apparition," which, in the poem as well as in much religious interpretation, describes an epiphany. The poem is structured on the process of an ironic epiphany possessing elements of eschatological theories found in Christian theology but adapted in an audacious manner by an embittered lover against his scornful mistress. (RGC)

4246. Dietz, Jonathan E. "Donne's 'To His Mistress Going to Bed,' 33-38." *Expl* 32:Item 36.

Both Helen Gardner and Clay Hunt falsely note John Donne's apparent misuse of "Atlanta's balls" in Elegy xix, "To His Mistress Going to Bed." The word "balls" implies neither a confusion about the classical myth nor a sexual misidentification: it is a pun. Both William Warner in his popular *Albion's England* and Thomas Nashe in *The Unfortunate Traveller* use the word to mean "breasts." Thus, in Donne's poem, the reader should directly equate "Atlanta's balls" with the lady's "gems" and realize that the author is advising him to beware of any distraction which may inhibit his tasting "whole joyes." (JED)

4249. Flynn, Dennis. "The Originals of Donne's Overburian Characters." *BNYPL* 77(1973):63-69.

Among the most crabbed but yet least explicated of Donne's writings are his contributions to that spate of essays, characters, and poems connected with the publication of Sir Thomas Overbury's "A Wife" in 1614. Donne's Overburian characters appear to have been inspired by his observations of the Jacobean Court, and they caricature particular persons. There are certainly several points of relation between the "Dunce" of Donne's "The True Character of a Dunce" and what we know of Thomas Coryate, Prince Henry's court jester, a friend of Donne, and author of *Coryat's Crudities*. The point of Donne's character is aimed, if not personally at Coryate, then at the kind of person he exemplified at the Court of James I. We have better evidence for an identification of the Scot in Donne's "The Character of a Scot at the First Sight." This piece apparently recalls Donne's first sight of the new king on 11 May 1603 at the Charterhouse in London, where well over a hundred Englishmen able to muster the fee were knighted by James. If this is the occasion of the piece, it is a satirical character of the king himself, ridiculing his mass dubbings and his provincial dress and manners. (DF)

4250. Grant, Patrick. "Donne, Pico, and *Holy Sonnet* xii." *HAB* 24(1973):39-42.

Donne read the works of Pico della Mirandola during the period when the Holy Sonnets were composed. It is probable that a passage from *Heptaplus*, v.6-7, which closely resembles "Holy Sonnet 12," is a direct source. Significant verbal parallels confirm the suggestion. A point of detail in the poem is illuminated by the comparison, and some light is thrown on the appeal, pessimistic as well as optimistic, that Pico offers to his Renaissance readers. (PJG)

4253. Gregory, Michael. "A Theory for Stylistics—Exemplified:Donne's 'Holy Sonnet xiv'." *Lang&S* 7:108-18.

Stylistics can be seen as an activity we pursue when we focus attention on the language of a text in terms of its internal and external patterns. This needs a model of linguistics which not only accounts for patterning at the levels of grammar, lexis, phonol-

ogy/graphology, but also has a contextual level to handle the situational aspect of language events. With such a model, stylistics becomes fully interpretative. Donne's "Holy Sonnet 14" is analyzed by means of this model. (MJG)

4254. Harrison, James. "Syntax in Donne's 'The Dreame'." *HAB* 25:141-45.

"The Dreame" is unique in being a love poem by Donne which seriously explores a particular and consummated relationship, but does not offer us an ideal or "patterne" of love. Rather, it rises to a climax of affirmation, collapses in doubt, and ends equivocally. These characteristics are reflected in certain syntactic features, notably the incidence of personal pronouns, repetition, and the objective complement, and in a related use of theological metaphor. (JH)

4259. Kerins, Frank M. "Donne's 'A Valediction:Of Weeping,' 10-19." *Expl* 32:Item 71.

Donne's globemaking image in "A Valediction: Of Weeping," lines 10-19, is a necessary prelude to the development of the "tear as world" conceit. Within this image, the metaphor, "That which was nothing" is clearly a vehicle for the "round ball" rather than a description of the tear. It is only after lines 14-16 that the tension caused by this seemingly unrelated image is relaxed. Here one sees it as an analogy for the tear conceit. The syntax of lines 14-15 must be clarified to show that Donne is indeed speaking of his tear and not hers. The conceit culminates in the flood imagery of lines 17-18. His "tear world" is dissolved by reflecting her tears in it. Paradoxically, his "heaven" is dissolved as well because her image in his tear is also flooded. (FMK)

4260. Kerrigan, William W. "The Fearful Accommodations of John Donne." *ELR* 4:337-63.

The notorious carnality of "Batter my heart" and "Show me dear Christ" results from the logic of accommodated speech. God can only be known through anthropomorphic metaphors and, since the *anthropos* is a fallen creature, the vehicles of such metaphors will turn perverse when predicated of the deity. Although Protestants were united in their scorn for visual anthropomorphism, Luther defended anthropomorphism of the word. In this tradition Donne the preacher "opened" accommodated language in order to display the fearful distance between human signification and divine reality. As a poet he wooed God within the terms of a marital triangle until, having arrived at the lustful consequences of this conceit, he equated rape with restored virginity and adultery with fidelity. These equations, successfully in "Batter my heart" and less so in "Show me dear Christ," enact the tragic but necessary premise of his devotional life: God is perfect by definition despite the fact that each definition of God is imperfect. (WK)

4261. Kolin, Philip C. "Donne's 'Obsequies to the Lord Harrington':Theme, Structure, and Image." *SoQ* 13:65-82.

Donne's "Obsequies to the Lord Harrington" incorporates Donne's own meditations on the ravages of mutability, the vices of the world, and the difficulties in securing virtue. Through a series of 8 questions and answers, Donne passes through a dialectic of doubt to belief. Harrington is set up as the heavenly guide whose earthly life can serve as an ideal for man. The poem deals as much with imitating virtuous models as it does with criticizing man's flawed instruments for doing so. Hence, the directional and measurement images show how mortal, physical tools can, through a process of accommodation, be used to search for a higher and more lasting achievement. The sun dial, the last and most important image, allows Harrington to function as a source of inspiration as well as a reflector of the greater glory of Christ. (PCK)

4263. Lein, Clayton D. "Donne's 'The Storme':The Poem and the Tradition." *ELR* 4:137-63.

Although critics commonly view Donne's "The Storme" as a major early effort in realistic description and expressionistic form, the poem in reality is a sophisticated variation upon the ancient rhetorical tradition of the epic storm. This topos had a vigorous revival in the Renaissance, particularly in the hands of Erasmus and Rabelais. Donne rejected the pattern of his Renaissance predecessors, however, relying instead upon the major classical models in Virgil, Ovid, Seneca, and Lucan. Every significant aspect of the poem's form relates to the epic rhetorical tradition.

By radically seizing for himself, however, the role of the epic hero, Donne was able to redirect the tradition toward self-definition and hence flood the poem with his own private mythology. The craft of the poem lies in its brilliant coordination of details from the rhetorical tradition with the instinctive metaphoric gestures of his creative imagination. (CDL)

4269. Miller, Clarence H., and Caryl K. Berrey. "The Structure of Integrity:The Cardinal Virtues in Donne's 'Satyre III'." *Costerus* N.S. 1:27-45.

The main reason for the clarity and integrity of Donne's "Satyre III" is that it is carefully structured according to the pattern of the cardinal virtues: fortitude, temperance, prudence, and justice. Based on Plato's division of man's faculties into rational, irascible, and concupiscible, the framework of the four virtues was elaborated by medieval and Renaissance writers and became a focus for discussing the relation between nature and grace, with which Donne opens his poem. "Satyre III" depicts the irrational "courage" of irreligious adventurers, the irrational pursuit of religion by analogy with extravagant amorists, the rational effort to achieve religious truth, and the unjust claims of civil power over the religious conscience of the individual. This structure is also reflected by variations in diction, imagery, and sentence structure. An examination of the structure helps to explain the conflicting emotions and the moral integrity of Donne's satiric *persona*. (CHM & CKB)

4273. Newton, Richard C. "Donne the Satirist." *TSLL* 16:427-45.

Recent criticism of Donne's Satyres tries to save them from the traditional charges of moral anarchy and self-indulgence. Donne knew the charges were potentially valid, and the Satyres constitute Donne's exploration of his own satiric character. The first Satyre reveals a compulsion toward satire but projects that compulsion on to the Humorist. In the second Satyre Donne uneasily acknowledges that his satiric "perfect hate" is his own, but not until the third does he come to see the satiric vision as necessary and honorable. In the fourth and fifth Satyres he enters society, accepts his own necessary presence in the satiric scene, and finally arrives at a satiric vision which includes all of society but which is neither anarchic nor self-indulgent. Having achieved a balanced satiric vision, Donne abandons the genre, but not the wise skepticism which his exploration of it has achieved. (RCN)

4274. Nichols, Olivia M. "Donne's 'A Lecture upon the Shadow'." *Expl* 32:Item 52.

John Donne, educated from childhood in the art of rhetoric, applies its principles in "A Lecture upon the Shadow." The poem is a deliberative, deductive argument patterned on Cicero's arrangement for the classical oration. The speaker's selection of tropes and figures enhances the sun-and-shadow imagery as he seeks to persuade his lady that love will fade into its own darkness unless it is openly acknowledged in the light of honesty. (OMN)

4276. Ong, Walter J.,S.J. "Gospel, Existence, and Print." *MLQ* 35:66-77. [Rev. art. on Gale H. Carrithers,Jr., *Donne at Sermons:A Christian Existential World*, and James Gray, *Johnson's Sermons:A Study*.]

The relationship of the Christian sermon to other verbal discourse is perplexing because of Christian belief regarding the incarnation of the Word of God, Who is both Word and Person and, moreover, a completely free gift of God to man. Donne's preaching seeks to involve preacher and congregation in an existential and transcendent relationship. The sermon cannot in its aims be contained within either rhetorical or esthetic frames. As rhetoric, the sermon is concerned with practical, existential decisions, but decisions made through God's grace, over which the preacher knows he and his congregation have no direct control. As part of the liturgy, the sermon is not drama or other creative "play," but rather the people's "work" (*leit-ourgia*). Samuel Johnson's forty-odd sermons, ghost-written by a layman for clergymen to preach and now studied in James Gray's new *Johnson's Sermons*, register a shift in psychological structures prepared for by writing and matured by print: existential oral *engagement* becomes indirect, as a writer attuned to print relates vicariously to an absent audience. (WJO,SJ)

4277. Otten, Charlotte F. "Donne's 'The Extasie,' 6." *Expl* 32:Item 58.

Donne's "fast balme" in "The Extasie," line 6, is a plant rather than "a steadfast, or a fastening, warm moisture" which springs from the lover's hands. The Renaissance herbalists show (as do Pliny and Virgil) that balme is a plant which, when rubbed on hives, attracts bees, keeps bees together, and nourishes them. Balme's cementing qualities are also evident from its Renaissance use as a vulnerary which "glueth together greene wounds." Donne, therefore, uses balme as a fragrant glue rubbed on lover's hands to form an indivisible graft. (CFO)

4279. Ousby, Heather D. "Donne's 'Epithalamion Made at Lincolnes Inne,' 90." *Expl* 32:Item 49.

The word "t'embowell" in line 90 of Donne's "Epithalamion made at Lincolnes Inne" (1595?) contains two puns. As one editor has noted, Donne is playing on the sexual implications of the word. He is also, however, punning on "bowel" in the sense of "offspring" and thus implying that the couple will produce an heir. (HDO)

4290. Smith, M. van Wyk. "John Donne's Metempsychosis." *RES* 24(1973):2-25,141-52.

Donne's *Metempsychosis: The Progress of the Soul* is essentially a satiric beast fable on the rise to power and resulting political corruption of Robert Cecil, Secretary of State under Elizabeth I and James I. Not only was Cecil the most envied and hated man of his day but he formed a suitable focus for private dissatisfactions and public concerns that Donne shared with some followers of the Earl of Essex and Sir Walter Raleigh. The frequent Renaissance interpretation of metempsychosis as a moral cycle of reward and retribution is sardonically inverted in Donne's poem: the ascent from plant through brute to man is characterized by a moral descent from beast to beastliness. Metempsychosis provided Donne with both a moral pattern of the protagonist's education in malfeasance, and a narrative pattern for a series of satirico-allegorical vignettes on the protagonist's activities. This pattern is complete in the poem as it stands. *Metempsychosis* is a finished poem, the promises of Donne's introductory Epistle being part of his satiric jest. (MvanWS)

4292. Sullivan, Ernest W.,II. "Post Seventeenth-Century Texts of John Donne's *Biathanatos*." *PBSA* 68:373-90.

Analyzes the textual deficiencies of the anthology selections of *Biathanatos* edited by Evelyn Simpson, John Hayward, Robert Hillyer, H.W. Garrod, Charles Coffin, Timothy Healy, and Helen Gardner and the full texts edited by Augustus Jessopp, J. William Hebel, and Charles Mark. Corrects or verifies much of the incorrect or unproved bibliographical information dealing with the description and authority of the 17th-century texts of *Biathanatos* in these editions. (EWS)

4294. Tourney, Leonard D. "Convention and Wit in Donne's *Elegie* on Prince Henry." *SP* 71:473-83.

Donne's "Elegy upon Prince Henry" is one of the great funeral poems of the 17th century. Yet few critics have explained Donne's intention and fewer have interpreted the strange method of his solemnities: the fusion of wit, erudition, and extravagant praise that gives the poem its distinctive character. The poem may be understood through an understanding of the social premises and rhetorical conventions of Renaissance funeral poetry and a careful analysis of Donne's argument. Such an analysis reveals the mechanics of Donne's wit, his debt to elegiac convention, and the poem's fundamental seriousness and integrity. (LDT)

4295. Waller, G.F. "John Donne's Changing Attitudes to Time." *SEL* 14:79-89.

Donne's changing attitudes to time have a revealing place in his age's intellectual revolution. His early poems concentrate upon discrete moments in the flux of experience, deliberately avoiding any metaphysical context except the lovers' own commitment. Between c.1605 and his ordination, and then in his later *Sermons*, however, Donne retreats into traditional orthodoxy. The early poems celebrate the moment, but the moment never lasts, and perhaps his vivid apprehension of time in his love poems is, however striking and powerful, oddly limited by its very strength. Donne's later religious development and capitulation to religious orthodoxy have their roots in the very strengths of independence and isolation that his early poems demonstrate. (GFW)

Dryden. 4299. Armistead, J.M. "The Narrator as Rhetorician in Dryden's *The Hind and the Panther.*" *JNT* 3:208-18.
In *The Hind and the Panther* Dryden assumes the narrative posture of a poet-rhetorician in order at once to divert attention away from Dryden-as-Catholic and to draw the reader into his religiously political vision of things as they ought to be in later seventeenth-century England. As rhetorical narrator, he manages the reader's attitude through sheer poetic and rhetorical skill —that is, by manipulating the poem's three modes (argument, allegory, and myth) to convey his meaning to the corresponding levels of the reader's awareness: understanding, senses, and "conscience." The presence of such an active, competent narrator reinforces the poem's meaning with an impression of poetic integrity that is not automatically identified with Dryden the despised turncoat. Thus, an effective *ethos* is created despite Dryden's own poor "image" in the public mind. (JMA)

4300. Black, James. "Dryden on Shadwell's Theatre of Violence." *DR* 54:298-311.
Argues that Dryden's *MacFlecknoe* has no single "occasion," but is a continuation, in a satirical idiom, of the critical controversy that Dryden and Shadwell had been conducting for years. The poem is more of a piece with Dryden's dramatic criticism than is generally realized—extensive illustrations from Shadwell's plays are used to show how Dryden has isolated and recreated the mode of Shadwellian drama. In the sense that the poem is "dramatic" and leaves Shadwell "confirmed in full stupidity" as practitioner of a now-ridiculous kind of drama, it can be considered Dryden's own version of *The Rehearsal.* (JB)

4305. Duggan, Margaret. "Mythic Components in Dryden's 'Hind and Panther'." *CL* 26:110-23.
Allusion to classical myth ties together references in *The Hind and the Panther* to beast lore, history, and contemporary event; makes possible Christian parallels to the situations of Graeco-Roman myth; and thus helps to make the poem a coherent whole. The Panther—*pan-thera* who includes the negative aspects of all the other fierce animals of the poem—is linked with wrongdoers from the *Metamorphoses* who are monstrous, illegitimate, sexually inconstant or perverse, hypocritical, unjustifiably aggressive, and ultimately self-destructive. These qualities parallel those Dryden has assigned to Protestantism in general and especially to the Latitudinarian Anglicanism of his own day. The Hind, on the other hand, is connected with a number of clearly superior figures from the *Metamorphoses* who are sinned against or affronted by unworthy characters but who ultimately triumph. The positive qualities derived from such admirable Ovidian figures are like those of Roman Catholicism as Dryden presents it. References to myth, both Christian and Ovidian, control and direct meaning in the poem, and so aid in creating Dryden's own myth, a configuration which is both subtle and precise. (MMD)

4309. Fujimura, Thomas H. "The Personal Element in Dryden's Poetry." *PMLA* 89:1007-23.
Although Dryden is generally regarded as a public poet concerned with public themes, in the last 15 years of his life he turned to more private themes to justify himself and his career. We must be aware of the autobiographical element to appreciate such poems as: the "Ode to Oldham," the "Ode to Mrs. Killigrew," the epistle "To Congreve," and "Alexander's Feast." These poems are meaningful if read with awareness of them as personal revelations and affirmations of Dryden the man. (THF)

4313. Kishi, Tetsuo. "Dryden and Shakespeare." *ShStud* 10(1971-72):39-51.
When Dryden adapted *Troilus and Cressida*, he was eager to make his Cressida faithful to Troilus unlike Shakespeare's Cressida. Actually Dryden's Cressida is faithful only on the psychological level and she is little better than Shakespeare's Cressida. He was bothered with the fact that Shakespeare's play was lacking in a point from which one can get a unified vision of the whole action. Consequently he tried to write a genuinely classical tragedy. He was not aware, however, that in a classical tragedy the kind of viewpoint he had in mind is supposed to exist outside man, and he put it inside his characters. Although Dryden was urged to adapt Shakespeare by the modern aspects of the bard, the result was even more modern than the original because of his preoccupation with the psychology of his characters. (TK)

4317. Martin, Leslie M. "The Source and Originality of Dryden's Melantha." *PQ* 52(1973):746-53.
Melantha in Dryden's *Marriage à la Mode* derives from Madeleine de Scudéry's Berisa in *Grand Cyrus*. The scene (III.i) in which Melantha laments an affront by Princess Amalthea and endures rebukes for her extravagant behavior also occurs in the romance and verifies *Grand Cyrus* as Dryden's source. Dryden transforms the negative implications of Berisa's violations of *précieuse* decorum into a fundamentally sympathetic rendering by emphasizing Melantha's spontaneity, humanity, and vitality. The addition of French diction culled from the vocabulary of *préciosité* enables him to satirize foreign corruptions of English manners and speech and to domesticate Berisa's "passion of the Court" in an idiom intelligible to the contemporary audience. Finally, Dryden reverses the character's function: in the romance an affirmation by negative example of *précieuse* social ethics, she becomes in *Marriage à la Mode* a witty but damaging comment on *préciosité* itself. (LM)

4319. McHenry, R[obert] W.,Jr. "The Importance of Right Reason in Dryden's Conversion." *Mosaic* 7,iii:69-86.
A major factor in Dryden's conversion to Roman Catholicism is the concurrent alteration in his assumptions on the traditional Anglican use of right reason. 17th-century Anglican use of "right reason" was closer to those who argued for "innate ideas." But Dryden moves increasingly away from these innatist assumptions, as can be seen in his rejection of them in his source for "Religio Laici," Charles Wolseley's *The Reasonableness of Scripture-Belief* (1672). Moreover, in the Roman Catholic "Hind and the Panther," Dryden eliminates all appeals to right reason; he comes to associate it with the dissenters' reliance upon private inspiration. Because he rejects this Anglican use of reason, Dryden turns to what he considers the more stable authority of Rome. His conversion originates in his theoretical assumptions, not in his political conservatism, for his changed view of reason significantly contributes to his religious change. (RWM)

4324. Staves, Susan. "Why Was Dryden's *Mr. Limberham* Banned? A Problem in Restoration Theatre History." *RECTR* 13,i:1-11.
Dryden's comedy, *Mr. Limberham; Or, The Kind Keeper*, was performed in March 1677/78, but according to Dryden himself the play "was permitted to be acted only thrice." Examination of the arguments which have been advanced to explain why *Mr. Limberham* was banned shows that there are insuperable objections to most of them. *Mr. Limberham* was not stopped because it was too obscene or because it was too effective as a general satire on keeping. Nor was the play stopped because Limberham was taken to represent Shaftesbury or any other prominent member of the country party. Dryden did not intend Limberham to represent Lauderdale. It is possible that some members of the audience decided to apply the character of Limberham to the Earl. (SS)

4325. Stringer, Gary. "Ease and Control in Dryden's Prose Style." *SHR* 8:303-16.
If one seeks a syntactical explanation of Dryden's particular prose excellence, he discovers two (apparently) contradictory impulses. Dryden employs stylistic techniques that impart a relaxed, spontaneous character to his style while he also consciously strives for restraint and control. Accordingly, the essential Dryden consists in a blending of these opposite syntactical tendencies: he never lets freedom run rampant, nor control become stiff and brittle. A further feature that bespeaks Dryden's desire to communicate both lucidly and memorably is the skillful interplay between the abstract and the concrete, a goal achieved most memorably by the complementary devices of the figure and the maxim. (GAS)

4328. West, Michael. "Shifting Concepts of Heroism in Dryden's Panegyrics." *PLL* 10:378-93.
Dryden's *Heroique Stanzas* treats Cromwell as a charismatic hero. Although he alludes to Aristotle's ethical doctrine of comprehensive heroic *magnanimity*, he is more influenced by the distinctive Aristotelian concept of transmoral *heroic virtue*. This quality underlies Cromwell's transcendent and quasi-divine status. It explains Dryden's peculiar emphasis upon Cromwell's ultimate inability to express his transcendence in action. As with

the superheroes of *Annus Mirabilis* and the heroic drama, deeds cannot embody supramoral essence. Panegyrics of the 1680s, however, reveal Dryden's discontent with the possible abuse of this concept to justify a moral monster. In *Eleonora* he draws upon Thomistic doctrine to develop a new concept of heroism. Like *Alexander's Feast*, *To Sir Godfrey Kneller* suggests that transcendent heroic virtue is at best an ideal esthetic fiction, not an historical reality. Dryden's post-Revolutionary dedications explicitly reject this ideal to develop instead a protosentimental concept of Christian heroism stressing common humanity even more than magnanimity. (MW)

Farquhar. 4335. Jordan, Robert J. "George Farquhar's Military Career." *HLQ* 37:251-64.
A considerable part of Farquhar's energies in the period March 1704 to March 1706 went into his career as an army officer. Military records in various libraries provide details of the raising of the regiment (in which Farquhar was active), describe his presence at a Dublin Court Martial in July 1705, and give evidence for his departure from the regiment early in 1706. They also make possible some tentative guesses at the dates of his recruiting drives through Shrewsbury and Lichfield, and of his Dublin performance in *The Constant Couple*, as well as providing a few shreds of evidence concerning his relationship with the Duke of Ormonde, a relationship that is further complicated by a hitherto overlooked (though quite accessible) printed source, which attributes Farquhar's lieutenancy to the Duke, under somewhat discreditable circumstances. Provides background material to *The Recruiting Officer*, which Farquhar wrote during this period. (RJJ)

Fletcher, J. 4341. Forker, Charles R. "*Wit Without Money*:A Fletcherian Antecedent to *Keep the Widow Waking*." *CompD* 8:172-83.
Fletcher's *Wit without Money* forms a hitherto unnoticed link between two London scandals which involved the baiting of rich widows. Both incidents were likely subjects for satirical treatment on the stage, the latter being the basis for the lost play *Keep the Widow Waking* by Dekker, Webster, Rowley, and Ford. *Wit without Money* differs significantly in tone and audience appeal from the lost play as inferred from ballads and other evidence. Elements of plot and auspices of production suggest that Fletcher's more sophisticated piece may have influenced Dekker and his collaborators in their cruder effort. (CRF)

Ford. 4344. Rosen, Carol C. "The Language of Cruelty in Ford's '*Tis Pity She's a Whore*." *CompD* 8:356-68.
In *The Theater and Its Double*, Artaud envisions staging Ford's '*Tis Pity She's a Whore* without regard for text. In '*Tis Pity* the power of words to inflict wounds and to ritualize action resounds throughout. The abuse of Annabella by her husband in Act IV and the appearance of Giovanni bearing his sister's heart in Act V are both instances of Ford's fusion of poetry and plot into a vital poetry of the theater. Other moments of ritualized cruelty are similarly augmented by the duplicity of words. A reading of Maeterlinck's translation of '*Tis Pity* (the version familiar to Artaud) eliminates the possibility of justifying Artaud's scorn for Ford's language on the basis of an unfaithful adaptation. For the ruthless poetic force of Maeterlinck's translation intensifies this drama of the broken taboo. (CCR)

Halifax. 4352. Faulkner, Thomas C. "Halifax's *The Character of a Trimmer* and L'Estrange's Attack on Trimmers in *The Observator*." *HLQ* 37(1973):71-81.
Examination of *The Character of a Trimmer* written by George Savile, Marquis of Halifax in 1684 and the prolonged attacks on political and religious moderates made by Sir Roger L'Estrange in *The Observator* (1681-87) beginning on 13 November 1682 reveals that the tone used by L'Estrange's Trimmer persona is quite similar to Halifax's characteristic tone of studied moderation and the conciliatory attitudes advocated by L'Estrange's Trimmer are very much like those policies recommended in the *Character*. L'Estrange's conception of a Trimmer covers every shade of moderate opinion on political and religious issues, and a review of

Halifax's policies shows that he is precisely the sort of moderate who fits L'Estrange's definition. The most important evidence of the connection is found in the implicit attacks made on L'Estrange in Halifax's *Character* and in a letter written by Sir William Coventry to his nephew on 26 January [1685] in which he anticipates L'Estrange's reaction to the *Character*. Halifax recognized that L'Estrange's attacks on Trimmers were applicable to the moderate party which the Marquis informally led; consequently the *Observator* was undoubtedly instrumental in the genesis of the *Character of a Trimmer*. (TCF)

Herbert, G. 4359. Charles, Amy M. "Mrs. Herbert's Kitchin Booke." *ELR* 4:164-73.
The household account book of Magdalene Herbert, the mother of Edward, George, Henry (and seven other Herberts), provides a unique view of the life of the household shortly after Mrs. Herbert moved from Oxford to Charing Cross in 1601. Carefully kept by the steward John Gorse and frequently reviewed and signed by Mrs. Herbert, it records not only the expenses of food and drink and housekeeping purchases, but also unexpected details about the life of the family. Gorse records who was present at both dinner and supper and what food was served. The family was seldom without guests—and even without guests there were generally more than 25 persons at meals. The account, which covers 21 weeks in all, is kept in detail from the day before Easter until early July, when the family dispersed for the summer, leaving only the two youngest boys, Henry and Thomas, in residence. Invaluable in recording daily life in the Herbert household, the book affords evidence about whom the Herberts knew, what the sons studied, and how they lived when they first settled in London. (AMC)
4364. Higbie, Robert. "Images of Enclosure in George Herbert's *The Temple*." *TSLL* 15:627-38.
The use of enclosure imagery in Herbert's *The Temple* forms one of the unifying patterns. The enclosure represents man's acceptance of his proper limitations; but to pass beyond his earthly enclosures and reach God he needs God's grace. Herbert thus leads us from man-made enclosures to a divine enclosure, the temple, by transforming his imagery, turning man's enclosure into a prison. He makes us feel the poem's limitations and look beyond them to the ideal harmony and simplicity he cannot directly express, the ideal form which *The Temple* as a whole is meant to suggest. He teaches us that man must surrender his rational, acquisitive desire for self-enclosure if he is to be admitted into God's house, which is often pictured as a container of sweet things on which the Christian can finally feast, in an image representing the Eucharist. (RGH)
4371. Morillo, Marvin. "Herbert's Chairs:Notes to *The Temple*." *ELN* 11:271-75.
F.E. Hutchinson's notes on Herbert's references to chairs in "The Pilgrimage" and "Mortification" misleadingly identify them with stationary seats rather than modes of conveyance, the sense which the context of allegorical journeys in both poems requires. Although the *OED* fails to document the sense of "chair" as a kind of litter for the infirm or wounded, the usage is amply confirmed by citations from Shakespeare's plays. (MM)
4375. Sharp, Nicholas "Herbert's 'Love'." *Expl* 33:Item 26.
George Herbert's "Love" (III) is literally a dialogue between a guest, or communicant, at the eucharistic meal and the host, or communion wafer, in which Christ is really present. This literal level of meaning should be recognized before any allegorical or anagogical exegesis of the poem. (NAS)

Herbert of Cherbury. 4378. McFarland, Ronald E. "The Rhetoric of Optics in Lord Herbert's Poems to Diana Cecil." *M&H* 5:215-28.
In his series of six poems to Diana Cecil concerning the color black, Edward, Lord Herbert of Cherbury has produced an effective poetic consideration of the physics and metaphysics of optics. Lord Herbert's scientific interests are indicated in his *Autobiography*, and his library included several contemporary treatises concerning optics. In the poems to Diana Cecil, Lord Herbert used various notions about the theories of light, vision, and color in order to effect a transition between the physical

perception of Diana's black-haired, dark-eyed beauty and the metaphysical perception of her inner beauty. He produces an optical metaphor which provides continuity and describes the metaphysical in terms of the physical. (REM)

Heywood, T. 4394. Cary, Cecile W. "'Go Break This Lute':Music in Heywood's *A Woman Killed with Kindness*." *HLQ* 37:111-22.
The lute sequence in Heywood's *A Woman Killed with Kindness* culminates many references to music which illumine the play. The tri-partite Boethian division of music, the music-love relationship, and the emblematic significance of particular instruments are relevant to the analysis. Heywood's heroine's discordant lute (*musica instrumentalis*) reflects her interior discord (*musica humana*) which separates her from heavenly concord (*musica mundana*). Music is present as a symbol of marital harmony from the Frankford marriage to its dissolution. The lute itself strengthens the sense of Anne Frankford's departure from harmony and reason. Nonetheless, earthly music is never totally reasonable and only approximates heavenly music; therefore Anne must break her lute, bidding farewell to earth's happiness. Such ambiguity about music appears throughout but is most noticeable in the wedding and lute scenes. However, once Anne's lute is broken, Heywood abjures musical references, allowing the Frankford marriage to be reinstated without the ambiguities of earthly music. (CWC)
4395. Hooper, Gifford. "Heywood's *A Woman Killed with Kindness* Scene xiv:Sir Charles's Plan." *ELN* 11:181-88.
Critics have consistently misinterpreted the proposal of Sir Charles in scene xiv of Heywood's *A Woman Killed with Kindness* as an offer to prostitute his sister in payment of a debt of honor. The text shows that Sir Charles at no time contemplates anything dishonorable (e.g., xiv.61), and Susan affirms throughout the scene her determination not to sacrifice her honor (e.g., xiv.84-88). But Susan does agree to make a concession. What exactly is it? What Sir Charles requests and Susan is ready to accept is "marriage" to Sir Francis, the sacrifice of virginity, not honor. "The Thirtieth Nouell" in Tome II of Painter's *The Palace of Pleasure*, on which Heywood may have based his subplot, supports this interpretation of Sir Charles's proposal, and mentions specifically the one set of circumstances in which Charles's sister might tolerate loss of virginity: in marriage. (AGH)

Hobbes. 4403. Selden, Raman. "Hobbes and Late Metaphysical Poetry." *JHI* 35:197-210.
Traditionally, Hobbes's esthetics has been linked with developments in neoclassical poetry. However, the theories of wit found in "Elements of Law" (1640) have a greater affinity with late metaphysical poetry. Hobbes's early mechanistic conception of mental imaginings has a deep structural affinity with Cleveland's mechanized and associative method of developing "trains" of images. By noting an analogy between Hobbes and Cleveland the critic can avoid an over-simple view of the "decadence" of late metaphysical poetry. (RS)

Jonson. 4405. Angell, C.F. "A Note on Jonson's Use of Sir Edward Dyer's 'My mynde to me a kyngdome is'." *PLL* 10:417-21.
Jonson refers to Dyer's familiar lyric "My mynde to me a kyngdome is" twice in his early plays. In *The Case Is Altered* Juniper and Onion, the two servingmen, believe themselves natural noblemen. They deceive and steal in order to fulfill their aspirations. Both are punished for their appetitiveness. Macilente, in *Every Man Out of His Humour*, while abjuring Dyer's view, nevertheless imposes his will on the other characters because he considers his superior intelligence entitles him to superior privilege and position. Macilente goes unpunished for his wilful acts, but he points the way to those later Jonson characters like Volpone who will be punished for imposing their wills upon the world. (CFA)
4415. Dutton, A. Richard. "The Significance of Jonson's Revision of *Every Man in His Humour*." *MLR* 69:241-49.
Commentators have remarked upon a change of tone and an apparent change of temper in Jonson between *Volpone* and *Epicoene*. A change does occur, but it does not tend toward greater indulgence; it can be identified in the adoption of fully realized, contemporary London settings for the comedies. This seems deliberate and lends significance to the revision of *Every Man in His Humour*, which is clearly related. The London coloring is not incidental but helps tighten the structure and focus the satire for the contemporary audience. Jonson's concern, however, is not verisimilitude, but exposure of folly (illusion) —moral realism. His drama is generated in the friction between the actualization of character and setting and the exposure of illusion. This principle is not as integral to the revised *Every Man in His Humour* as it is to later plays, and the revision is significant as an insight into his maturing technique. (ARD)
4416. ——— "*Volpone* and *The Alchemist*:A Comparison in Satiric Techniques." *RMS* 18:36-62.
Comparison of *Volpone* with *The Alchemist* challenges the assumption that the contemporary realism of *The Alchemist* accompanies a decline in Jonson's "moral pupose" as a dramatist. *Volpone* is an experimental work, ironically mocking the audience's expectations. Selfish materialism reigns, ensures Volpone and Mosca's fall, but is reinforced by the Avocatori. The Would-bes are central, drawing the audience into the Venetian nightmare, testing their complacency, while the "metempsychosis-play" and mountebank-scene ironically challenge audiences' tastes and discrimination. The audience is implicated within the process of satiric judgment. These principles are expanded in *The Alchemist*, which identifies uncritical elements in its own audience with its "gull" characters. (ARD)
4418. Fowler, Alistair. "The 'Better Marks' of Jonson's 'To Penshurst'." *RES* 24(1973):266-82.
Ben Jonson's "To Penshurst" is a more complex and a more religious poem than many have thought. It contrasts Robert Sidney's Penshurst, a great center of patronage, with certain prodigy houses (ambitious show-places) that had spectacular architectural features. In lieu of these, Penshurst has "better marks": symbolisms of moral (and poetic) order. Thus, Jonson arranges his description of Sidney's estate according to several patterns or structures: temporal, hierarchical, and numerical. In the temporal structure he praises Penshurst in relation to the three parts of time. In the hierarchical structure he puts visitors and residents in a significant sequence of ascending order of value. And in the numerical structure he arranges the provisions of the estate according to patterns conveying a theological symbolism. In such ways Jonson persuades us that the Penshurst estate is as well-ordered a structure as the programmatic prodigy houses. Similarly, the emblematic images show it to be harmonious and well-ordered iconologically, without being overidealized. (ADSF)
4419. Friedberg, Harris. "Ben Jonson's Poetry:Pastoral, Georgic, Epigram." *ELR* 4:111-36.
Ben Jonson's choice of the epigram as his primary poetic form results from his determination to demonstrate poetry's capacity for mirroring the empirical world rather than for creating imaginative other worlds. The epigram is a dependent form, tied by its function as inscription to a site or subject in ordinary reality. Jonson reinforces its generic function by reducing his epigram to the act of naming the good man ("On Lucy Countesse of Bedford"). Naming stresses language's capacity for designating at the expense of its capacity for abstracting or creating new ideas. This links Jonson to the linguistic revolution begun by Bacon, while making him suspicious of metaphor. In "To Penshurst" generic categories replace the grammatical categories of "Bedford," while retaining the same structure: poetry is an act of predication which links quality to substance. In "Penshurst" Jonson superimposes natural and literary landscapes to express Penshurst's values without compromising its locus in fact. (HF)
4421. Gardiner, Judith K. "Infantile Sexuality, Adult Critics, and *Bartholomew Fair*." *L&P* 24:124-32.
A re-examination of *Bartholomew Fair* indicates that a psychological interpretation can help solve the current critical crux about its structure and tone. Three old men in the play who repress youth are humiliated and punished. The play is structurally unified by parallel Oedipal enactments and the play violates the conventions of New Comedy. The undefended infantile and

sometimes "perverse" character of the sexuality in the play creates its special atmosphere and explains the controversy between the "moralists" who view this material as sinful or threatening and the "vitalists" who identify with the fair world's unrepressed lusts and aggressions. (JKG)

4422. Gianakaris, C.J. "Jonson's Use of 'Avocatori' in *Volpone*." *ELN* 12:8-14.
Jonson's knowledge of Venetian history and Italian usage was such that he could use the term "Avocatori" accurately in *Volpone*, despite its seeming to be in error. Scholars today observe that "Avocatori" in English does not mean judges or magistrates, as Jonson clearly meant the word to imply in *Volpone*. By applying to *Volpone* the work of Contarini concerning Venice, as it was known at the end of the 1500s, scholars have devised tortured rationalizations to excuse Jonson's apparent lapse in translating or in word choice. A closer look at Venetian legal history, however, substantiates Jonson's use of "Avocatori" as judges. During the Venetian republic in the early Renaissance avocatori possessed judgmental power and could mete out punishments. Jonson therefore was justified in his word choice. (CJG)

4431. Kifer, Devra. "Too Many Cookes:An Addition to the Printed Text of Jonson's *Staple of Newes*." *ELN* 11:264-71.
Between the performance of *The Staple of Newes* in 1626 and the printing of the play in 1631, Jonson added a passage in which he punningly identified the fat and jovial cook Lickfinger with the gaunt and ascetic jurist Sir Edward Coke. There is no discernible resemblance between the two, nor is there any hint of this identification in any other part of the play; but there is one character who does bear a striking resemblance to Coke—the avaricious kill-joy Pennyboy Senior. The evidence points clearly to the conclusion that Jonson had originally drawn Pennyboy Senior as a full-length caricature of Coke and some years after the play was performed added the specific identification of Coke with Lickfinger in order to protect himself from the charge that he had engaged in vicious personal satire. (DRK)

4433. Kossick, Shirley. "Ben Jonson:Some Aspects of His Life and Work." *UES* 11 (Mar 1973):4-11.
The complexity of Ben Jonson's world is reflected in his life and work. The contrasts and paradoxes of the era—growing capitalism, increased interest in the classics, science, and education, alongside poverty, illiteracy, recurrent outbreaks of plague, and such pseudo-sciences as alchemy—are echoed in the literary scene in general and in Jonson's many-sided art. Capable of the most delicate tenderness, sensitive appreciation of achievement, and lyrical courtliness, his more characteristic expression is abrasively satiric. Austere as his comment often is, Jonson was also attracted to the extravagance of the masque. He contributed, too, to the development of the anti-masque which in his hands afforded an opportunity both for comic invention and for diversifying and extending the masque proper. In his plays Jonson combines his knowledge of the classics with a profound feeling for contemporary life and idiom. *Volpone* and *The Alchemist*, possibly his most outstanding achievements, illustrate the prodigious range and flexibility of Jonson's art. (SGK)

4436. Levin, Lawrence L. "Replication as Dramatic Strategy in the Comedies of Ben Jonson." *RenD* 5(for 1972):37-74.
In his comedies, Jonson designed a central analogue that reflects upon the play's denouement and conclusion. The early comedies, excluding *Every Man Out of His Humor*, contain one episode that prefigures a later unraveling of the plot by a justice figure. Analogues in the comedies are discussed. (LLL)

4445. Oates, Mary I. "Jonson's 'The Under-wood,' LXX." *Expl* 33:Item 6.
A convenient starting point for an explication of Ben Jonson's *Under-Wood* LXX ("Cary-Morison Ode") is the triad of myths he deploys at the beginning, middle, and end. The ode, an elegy on Henry Morison, who had died at twenty-one, is addressed to his friend, Lucius Cary, and each myth provides a different perspective on Cary's loss. The first is the story of the Saguntine Infant, who returned to his mother's womb rather than face Hannibal's sack of the city, the tiny physical circle he describes is an analogue of both his and Morison's "complete" lives. The second is a reference to Pindar's version of the Castor-Polydeuces

myth, and the mutual devotion of the "Dioscuri" parallels Cary's and Morison's own. The third boldly asserts that the two friends will be themselves heroes to future generations, as the Dioscuri have been for those past. These myths move in ever-widening circles, from the Infant's tiny one, to the two "spheres" of the Dioscuri, to the single "circle of perfection," that unites both friends in heaven: all epitomize Jonson's vision of an "immortal friendship." (MIO)

4450. Ribeiro, Alvaro. "Sir John Roe:Ben Jonson's Friend." *RES* 24(1973):153-64.
Information about the life of Sir John Roe (1581-1606), one of Ben Jonson's closest friends during the years 1603-06 and author of nine poems previously attributed to John Donne, has been available to scholars only in the notes to editions of these two poets (Gifford, Chambers, Grierson, Herford and Simpson). These meager pieces of evidence have given rise to misconceptions and speculation on the part of some literary historians. In particular, Barbara N. De Luna maintains in her *Jonson's Romish Plot* (Oxford, 1967) that Roe implicated Jonson in the Gunpowder conspiracy, a circumstance which prompted him to write *Catiline* in an attempt to exonerate himself. Examination of Roe's occasional verse and the facts of his complete life and career, especially those preserved in hitherto unpublished sources, render this theory untenable. Indeed, the evidence shows that Roe was stationed in the Low Countries prior to and during the uncovering of the Plot. He returned to London after November 1605 and there died of the plague in Jonson's arms, a fact which adds extra poignancy to Jonson's epigrams on Roe. The parish register of St. Clement Danes in the Strand reveals that Roe was buried on 17 January 1606. (AFVR)

4455. Shibata, Toshihiko. "On the Palinodial Ending of *Cynthia's Revels*." *ShStud* 10(1971-72):1-15.
The instances in which the palinode is incorporated into plays are rare. Jonson's *Cynthia's Revels* is probably the sole example in English Renaissance drama. Jonson did not repeat its use because popular playwrights derided his pedantry in the war of the theater. In his age the ideal of courtly love had gradually been superseded by that of conjugal love, and his imagination was essentially of a monolithic kind. Yet the dual view of the world implicit in this narrative device is not altogether heterogeneous in the general climate of Elizabethan plays. (TS)

4456. Smith, Bruce R. "Ben Jonson's *Epigrammes*:Portrait-Gallery, Theater, Commonwealth." *SEL* 14:91-109.
Jonson's collected *Epigrams: First Book* represent the best English Renaissance exercise in a genre that attracted poets of the early 17th century just as sonnets had attracted poets a decade earlier. No one was better aware of this distinction than Jonson himself. Jonson invites us in his preface to stand back and survey the design of his whole collection. "Portrait-gallery," "theater," and "commonwealth" are three metaphors he hands us as a guide. What we see is a lively moral drama that juxtaposes fools and heroes, vice and virtue, ridicule and homage, low style and high style. No other English epigrammatist offers such a complete and unified moral vision. (BRS)

4463. Wescott, Robert. "Volpone? Or the Fox?" *CR* 17:82-96.
Ben Jonson presents Volpone to us in the stereotype of the wily Fox, with such success that he is traditionally and apparently unquestionably considered to be one. Close examination of crucial passages reveals however that Volpone casts himself in the role of the Fox, acting it out for unexpectedly deep and complex psychological reasons: to gratify his conceit, to supply his need to exercise power, and ultimately to nourish his profound misanthropy. This conjectural portrait of Volpone is verified when it leads to a consistent reading of the seduction scene; it resolves some vexing questions associated with that scene. Jonson has poured much of his own scorn for a contemptible humanity into Volpone's speeches; in qualifying Volpone he is castigating, or at least probing, the misanthropic elements of his own scorn. (RW)

4464. Williams, Mary C. "A Tale of a Tub:Ben Jonson's Folk Play." *NCarF* 22:161-68.
In *Tale of a Tub* Jonson uses settings, characters, plot, and imagery, as well as proverbs, and country customs, to create a folk atmosphere which is vigorous and good-humored, though thoroughly unsentimental. In spite of a plot based on rival

wooing, love is irrelevant, and the folk spirit is one of hearty approval of nature's impersonal life force. Set on a cold St. Valentine's Day, the play illustrates St. Valentine's Day and 16th-century wedding customs. Country characters speak in rustic language sprinkled with proverbs, familiar expressions, and superstitions. The plot structure resembles a country dance, as Jonson suggests in calling his heroine "the Lasse from Dargison." (MCW)

Locke. 4470. Schankula, H.A. "A Summary Catalogue of the Philosophical Manuscript Papers of John Locke: Additions and Corrections." *BLR* 9:81-82.
Further authorities cited, and some additions and corrections to the *Catalogue* published in the *Bodleian Library Record*, Vol. 9, No. 1, Feb. 1973. (HASS)

Lovelace. 4472. Clayton, Thomas. "Lovelace's 'Cupid Far Gone,' 28-30." *Expl* 33:Item 32.
In Lovelace's "Cupid Far Gone" Cupid becomes "polymorphous perverse" and runs amuck, ending his un-Senecan ramble in a comically half-demonic and perhaps playfully blasphemous as well as classical-Herculean harrowing of hell. There is some apparent difficulty with the "Argos"—as often with Pluto/Plutus—and its context in lines 28-30. What Lovelace or his printer has done is to present a resonant figure in "Argos" (the herdsman) for an "Argo" mainly intended, in a number of senses, primarily the ship of the Argonauts and the constellation, which Cupid promises Charon even as he takes Cerberus as an English country gentleman's hunting-dog in the hearty sports of venery. (TC)
4473. —— "Some Versions, Texts, and Readings of 'To Althea, from Prison'." *PBSA* 68:225-35.
Lovelace's "To Althea" circulated far more widely in his ownnn day than in the seven texts his major modern editor prints, describes, or refers to in his Oxford English Text, and the textual situation of the poem is typical of the kinds of problems of authority and transmission presented by so many 17th-century lyrics. The textual data of "To Althea, from Prison" suggest a unique complex of typical corruptions in a process often involving oral-aural transmission and memorial transcription, the strong possibility of earlier and later authorial versions, and the near certainty of a final authorized version in which the crucial variant ("gods" vs. "birds" in l. 7) retains a critical entropy as well as poise. (TC)

Marston. 4478. Hamilton, Donna B. "Language and Theme in *The Dutch Courtesan.*" *RenD* 5(for 1972):75-87.
Throughout Marston's *Dutch Courtesan* we are reminded of how accurately skill in language use indicates the moral qualities that characters possess. Characters guilty of hypocrisy, lust, and greed all abuse language. They in turn become the targets of those whose morals are more firmly grounded and whose speech, as flexible and communicative as it is entertaining, always reflects their self-control. The attacks, led by Freevill against Malheureux and by Cocledemoy against Mulligrub, first take a variety of verbal forms. But when the fools fail to respond, Freevill and Cocledemoy forsake the attempts to reform them by appealing to their reason through language and resort instead to physical devices of disguise and manipulation, means which are able to elicit a response from the irrational and morally numb victims. Marston's plot complication, far from avoiding the play's moral issues, actually helps to complete the statement of its controlling ideas. (DBH)
4480. Houser, David J. "Purging the Commonwealth: Marston's Disguised Dukes and *A Knack to Know a Knave.*" *PMLA* 89:993-1006.
Marston's *The Malcontent* and *Parasitaster* are examined in the light of an analysis of *A Knack to Know a Knave* (1592). Marston's plays share with the earlier play details of form that involve not only the disguised authority figure noted by other critics but also his declaration of purpose, the source and sort of vice he observes, the means by which his particular discoveries are given expanded significance, and the technique and result of the final exposures. The study of the formal pattern of these elements provides the link between Marston's plays and an earlier example of disguise

as the dramatic device upon which the plot turns. (DJH)
4484. Salomon, Brownell. "The Theological Basis of Imagery and Structure in *The Malcontent.*" *SEL* 14:271-84.
The Calvinistic doctrines of predestination, divine grace, and human depravity form the basis for the imagery and structure of Marston's *The Malcontent*. Calvinism affords insight into the poet-playwright's worldview, suggesting that his decision to forsake legal and theatrical careers to become an Anglican priest was not anomalous but consistent with lifelong beliefs. His fideistic tendencies were shared by many in the Established Church. It deepens our understanding of the functional use of these ideas in the play. Recurrent thematic images of excrement, effete sexuality, and animalism, and *contemptus mundi* valuations of men depict man's helplessness without supernatural aid. But, divine mediation of the natural and supernatural worlds is expressed through dramatic structure in the Pauline-Augustinian-Calvinist repentances of Aurelia and Pietro. (BS)

Marvell. 4488. Adkins, Joan F. "Neoplatonism in Marvell's 'On a Drop of Dew' and 'The Garden'." *BRMMLA* 28:77-92.
The thematic structure of Marvell's "On a Drop of Dew" repeats Plotinus' concept of the emanation and the return. The dewdrop occupies a central position between the phenomenal world and the spiritual world. The evaporation of the dewdrop by the sun symbolizes the soul's rejection of earthly imperfection and a return to immutability. The persona of "The Garden" contracts the multiplicity of Nature into the Mystical One. The natural garden, perceived as a reflection of the Universal Soul, gives way to the recreating mind; after the separation of body and soul, the garden, transmuted into an ideal garden, is eternal. Neoplatonic themes thus reveal poetic structure: a progression of sense, mind, and spirit. (JFA)
4491. Clayton, Thomas. "A Note on Marvell's Tone." *SCN* 32:7-8.
Marvell's restraint of tone, ambiguities of expression, and ambivalence of attitude in his non-satirical poems make him uniquely elusive among the complex contemporary poets he most nearly resembles. Marvell's art is much of the matter of his nature, as his nature is of his art, and he writes at large of the ethos of imaginative man in creative action when his highest sublunary faculties are engaged. A significant corollary of his idiom is the complex of attitudes he expresses toward physical love between man and woman. (TC)
4492. Crook, Nora C. "Marvell's 'The Definition of Love,' 25-26." *Expl* 32:Item 73.
A famous example of Marvell's use of the concealed Latinate pun occurs in his *Horatian Ode* where he plays on the two meanings of "acies" (i.e., "axe's edge" and "eyesight"). Another such pun occurs in "The Definition of Love" where the word "angle" is intended to evoke a passage in Horace's Ode IX, Book I. There "angulum" means "a place of amorous assignation," and this meaning, carried over into Marvell's poem, adds a poignant resonance to what one might suppose to be merely an apt metaphysical image. (NCC)
4495. Herron, Dale. "Marvell's 'Garden' and the Landscape of Poetry." *JEGP* 73:328-37.
"The Garden" recapitulates the process of divine inspiration whereby the poet is lifted up for a glimpse of original perfection and returned to his ordinary state in order to record, refine, and share his vision through his art. Marvell presents a witty frame of reference whereby the reader can refer the garden experience to the art of poetry. In the first four stanzas, the poet withdraws into a wild garden where he will be granted a special vision; he leaves behind him the ordinary world and the symbols of its achievements. In stanzas 5-6 the speaker's body is imprisoned below on the grass as his mind and soul prepare to ascend in two separate phases to a mystical encounter with divine perfection. In the end, mind and body are reunited abruptly and returned to the lapsarian world. (DH)
4497. Kalstone, David. "Marvell and the Fictions of Pastoral." *ELR* 4:174-88.
This essay traces the relationship between Marvell's "Damon the Mower" and Virgil's Second Eclogue. (DK)
4504. Quivey, James. "Marvell's Couplet Art:'Last Instruc-

tions to a Painter'." *ELWIU* 1:28-36.
Though often damned as excessively difficult to read, Andrew Marvell's "Last Instructions to a Painter" is vital, kaleidoscopic, impudent, charming satire. In part the poem's success in these respects is achieved through skilled couplet manipulation. The norm couplet, lacking polish and careful balance and occasionally lapsing into near-doggerel, combines with the rapid, unordered presentation of an enormous number of subjects to reflect the blustery confusion of Parliament's 1666 Excise Debates and the chaotic ineptness of England's navy in the 1667 Medway embarrassment—major subjects of the poem. When Marvell seeks special emphases and particular burlesque effects, he deviates from the norm couplet and achieves desired effects through combinations of prosodic irregularities such as run-on lines, open couplets, hypermetrics, atypical rhymes. He uses similar prosodic devices in order to point tone and tempo shifts in the poem. (JRQ)

4505. Schwenger, Peter T. "Marvell's 'Unfortunate Lover' as Device." *MLQ* 35:364-75.
The last line of Marvell's "The Unfortunate Lover"—"In a Field *Sable*, a Lover *Gules*"—may be identified as a device. Devices, partaking of both armorial and emblematic elements, are distinguished from both by the nature of their meanings. Their cryptic style is characteristic of Marvell's poem as a whole, which may be read as the expression of a love frustrated and forbidden by its very nature. The contrast between the tumult of images in the body of the poem and the final static device may be seen as a comment on the sacrifice involved in translating the personal agony into an impersonal artifice. (PTS)

4509. Wilson, A.J.N. "Andrew Marvell's 'The First Anniversary of the Government Under Oliver Cromwell':The Poem and Its Frame of Reference." *MLR* 69:254-73.
The eulogy celebrates Cromwell's greatness in quite distinct aspects, seen successively in quite distinct terms. For Cromwell as architect of the new constitution of 1653—the first and obligatory theme—the frame is Hellenic tradition about the *polis*, its origin and role. An abrupt change comes when the following paragraphs presage Cromwell's leadership in armed struggle against Papal ascendancy in Europe; the frame now is Protestant eschatology and biblical allusion. Next, in a passage of alternate biblical and classical allusion, the Lord Protector appears as an Augustus-like ruler, praised in terms of the orthodox view of the Princeps in the Augustan age. Finally, Cromwell as organizer of the resurgent naval might of England is praised in language reminiscent both in spirit and detail of Rome, the Roman drive for power and glory in it. From all this and the temper of particular political references the panegyric appears to appeal now to one, now to a quite different outlook on the affairs of the English nation. (AW)

4511. Zwicker, Stephen N. "Models of Governance in Marvell's 'The First Anniversary'." *Criticism* 16:1-12.
Marvell's *The First Anniversary* celebrates the consolidation of Cromwell's power as Protector. Marvell sought analogues for Cromwell in biblical prophets, patriarchs, and judges. Variously, Cromwell is revealed as David the psalmist, Elijah the prophet, Noah the patriarch, and most significantly Gideon the judge. Protector and judge are paralleled in their careers as in their spiritual lives so that humility before the Lord justifies political action. The rejection of kingship is a crucial element in the narrative of both careers, an act that demonstrates personal humility and God's governance of the nation. Further, Gideon as an Old Testament type of Christ the judge and Cromwell as correlative of that figure invoke the eschatological model of Christ as judge destroying the wicked, defending the Elect and defeating Antichrist. The model of biblical judge suits Cromwell's temporal and apocalyptic roles in the poem, allowing for England's meaning as Elect Nation and for Cromwell' millennial significance. (SNZ)

Massinger. 4514. Yamashita, Hiroshi. "The Printing of Philip Massinger's Plays." *ShStud* 10(1971-72):16-38.
Several bibliographical problems of *The Duke of Milan* (Q₁, 1623) and *The Maid of Honour* (1632) are discussed. Examines sheet B in *The Duke*, which might be the original as well as a cancel, and McIlwraith's compositor determination in *The Maid*; it would

seem incorrect for some pages. The nature of the printer's copy of these two quartos is also discussed. It is probable that both of them were set from the autograph, although the copy of *The Duke* was possibly a scribal transcript of the autograph. (HY)

Middleton. 4517. Duffy, Joseph M. "Madhouse Optics:*The Changeling.*" *CompD* 8:184-98.
The Changeling by Middleton and Rowley centers on the predicament of Beatrice-Joanna who disastrously "sees" the world in terms of her own desires. Her visionary attempt to manage reality leads to her damnation, but also enables her to become a figure of tragic greatness. The play iself, through its central characters and action "sees," the ordinary world as a potentially more lunatic environment than an asylum. (JD)

4521. Kistner, A.L. and M.K. "*The Spanish Gipsy.*" *HAB* 25:211-24.
In *The Spanish Gipsy*, Middleton and Rowley combine a Christian philosophy of sin, repentance, expiation, and rebirth with a concept of self and the loss of identity which is a strikingly modern comment on role identification and integrity of being. They underline their chief subject, loss of identity, with characters unable to recognize each other, with disguises, and with an entire act conducted in nearly total darkness which is symbolic of the moral confusion of the characters. They reinforce these themes by tension created between opposing meanings of *noble, gentleman, honor*, and *friend*, and they emphasize the moral darkness and its opposites, truth and light, through imagery. (ALK & MKK)

Milton. 4537. Ayers, Robert W. "The Editions of Milton's *Readie & Easie Way to Establish a Free Commonwealth.*" *RES* 25:280-91.
Masson and Clark supposed that the first edition of Milton's *Readie and Easie Way to Establish a Free Commonwealth* was composed 21-29 Feb. and both believed that the work was published on 3 March. Internal evidence argues that the body of the work was written 18-21 Feb. and that the preface was written on 21 Feb. or early on the morning of 22 Feb. Internal and external evidence together indicate that the work was published early in the final week of February. Clark says that the second edition was composed between 16 March and 25 April 1660, probably between 9 and 22 April. It was published, Masson said, sometime in April, while Clark said that it appeared probably in the last six days before the Restoration of 1 May. But the evidence indicates composition between 16 and 27 March with publication between 27 March and 17 April. Proper dating of particularly the second edition is certainly important to understanding the politically allusive text and to the chronology of Milton's writings. (RWA)

4542. Berry, Boyd M. "Puritan Soldiers in *Paradise Lost.*" *MLQ* 35:376-402.
One paradox in *Paradise Lost*, that characters are busy yet do not conclude their business, is best illuminated by Puritan military sermons which portray a *miles Christi* ceaselessly drilling—not winning or even fighting. Not a "doctrine" but one embodiment of a revolutionary attitude, the Puritan soldier's intransitive, massed formations simultaneously emphasize God's omnipotence yet demand unconstrained, joyous commitment from God's agents. Milton's God dramatizes this revolutionary outlook when he sends his angels on missions strategically impossible from a worldly, timebound perspective. He permits them to "stand still," just as he makes an Eden which Adam and Eve must ceaselessly prune, as a way joyously to affirm faith. Milton even muted the acts of the Son and Father. Foreshadowing, episodicity, reiteration reinforce the pattern and show Milton's consistently revolutionary commitment informing the whole poem. (BMB)

4543. Black, James. "The Return to Pandemonium:Interlude and Antimasque in *Paradise Lost.*" *WascanaR* 9:139-98.
In *Paradise Lost* Milton transcends genres and overleaps the critics' problem of whether epic and tragedy were the same or different things. The incident of Satan's return to hell in Book x is an example of *Paradise Lost*'s consciously dramatic quality. Satan attempts a *coup de théâtre* and there is dramatic suspense. But Satan, attempting a travesty performance of "The Harrowing of Hell," is made to fail both as hero and as actor and is hissed by

his audience. He and they are last seen as participants in a grotesque animated tableau—the antimasque to Paradise's graceful masque of innocence. Thus *Paradise Lost* comprehends both epic and drama and also synthesizes several kinds of drama in one "advent'rous song." (JB)

4544. Blessington, Francis C. "Maia's Son and Raphael Once More." *MiltonQ* 8:108-13.

Milton's use in *Paradise Lost* of Mercury's visit to Aeneas (*Aen.* IV. 219-78) has not been fully investigated. In language, structure, allusion, and imagery, Virgil's scene has had as much influence upon Raphael's visit as any biblical source and more influence than any other classical source. Both Mercury and Raphael descend from heaven because of a prayer in order to warn men to be on guard against enemies, to be free from passion, to seek a higher type of love, to elevate their lives to higher states of being, and to be mindful of their offspring. The parallel between the two messengers is strengthened by Milton's use of verbal echoes and imagery. (FCB)

4549. Boswell, Jackson C. "Samson's Bosom Snake." *MiltonQ* 8:77-80.

In *Samson Agonistes* the serpentine imagery is all-pervasive. Most of these herpetological references and allusions are easily understandable; but when Samson calls the sumptuously be-decked Dalila a "bosom snake" (l. 763) readers invariably stop to check the notes for clarification. Bosom snakes are found in the *Aeneid*, Spenser, Greene, Nashe, Lodge, Deloney, and Painter; indeed there is a picture of a bosom serpent in Whitney's *Emblemes*. All of these bosom snakes descended from a she-viper of Aesop. Milton's usage of the metaphor takes on deeper meaning when we consider the special place of snakes in Germanic lore, in Eastern and Mediterranean mystery religions, and in Hebraic traditions. Samson had ample mythological precedent for embracing one who must have appeared as attractive to him as Satan's serpent did to Eve. (JCB)

4551. Brodwin, Leonora L. "Milton and the Renaissance Circe." *MiltonS* 6:21-83.

Milton's life-long preoccupation with the Circe myth, where noted, has been misjudged through reference to the allegorized Circe of Renaissance mythographers. Milton distinguishes the three Homeric temptations and focuses upon the higher appeals, which his successive treatments reformulate in increasingly elevated moral terms. *Elegy I* defines the second, sexual temptation, its rural setting reappearing in *L'Allegro*, *Lycidas*, *Paradise Lost*, and *Paradise Regained*; the third temptation is defined as festivity and mirthful art in *Elegy VI* and as ignorant happiness in *Prolusion VII*. In *Comus* these temptations are reformulated to include marriage and a devotional enjoyment of worldly good. Comus' temptation approximates Adam's unfallen condition in *Paradise Lost*, and uxoriousness now constitutes the Circean temptation to needed patience. Finally, in *Samson Agonistes*, the regained patience which redeemed Adam becomes the ultimate temptation of Circe, a figure who has always embodied, for Milton, the temptation to renounce higher obligations for the simpler fulfillments of ordinary humanity. (LLB)

4554. Calhoun, Thomas O. "On John Milton's *A Mask at Ludlow*." *MiltonS* 6:165-79.

Milton's *A Mask at Ludlow* is about the conflict among children, adolescents, and adults. The adolescents are distinguished from children and adults by their immediate concern with the problems of erotic love. For the children, eros is primarily a subject for fantasy and for the adults, it is a threat to morality and family unity. Lady Alice, age 15, sings to Echo and seeks an escape from the perplexing, sensuous world in which she is lost. But, in confronting Comus, she must face the demands of erotic love directly. The children and adults combine forces to suppress the erotic dilemma of adolescence. They overcome Comus, and the Lady is released from her own emotions and the trial of growing up. Nature grants her no liberty, but the kind of apotheosis she had earlier wished for Echo—a return to Father and family. (TOC)

4555. Camé, Jean F. "Images in Milton's *Areopagitica*." *CahiersE* 6:23-37.

Milton considered his *Areopagitica* as an essential element in the great fight for liberty which then took place. Milton wants to convince both the Parliament and his readers; his images are therefore part and parcel of his argument. He endeavors to mention things his readers know and therefore draws heavily upon everyday images. Books being living creatures, Milton derives images from life, death, the body, illness, remedies. He remains faithful, however, to the kind of images he had already used and which he was to use throughout his life, e.g., those borrowed from the bible, literature, and mythology. Images centering around the theme of light and darkness are less frequent than is thought by critics who do not make a clear enough difference between figurative and non-figurative style. (JFC)

4557. —— "Myth and Myths in Milton's *Comus*." *CahiersE* 5:3-24.

In *Comus* (1634) Milton tells the story of an initiation occurring at night in a forest; this is the mythical aspect of the masque: many mythological references confirm this basic mythical pattern. "Myth" is a constant element in all civilizations. A basic mythical pattern consists in loss, followed by initiation which includes a virtual or real death followed by rebirth. In *Comus*, the Attendant Spirit heralds the theme by leaving Heaven. Then the first quester, the Lady, appears, lost in a forest which looks like a labyrinth. She has to face the monster (Comus) and to undergo a sort of death when she is "chain'd up in Alabaster" (660). Helped by her brothers who have undergone a similar initiation, and by Sabrina, she finally defeats the monster and can now, being fully initiated, enter her father's mansion. (JFC)

4559. Cipolla, Elizabeth M.C. "Pastoral Elements in Milton's Latin Poems." *UES* 10,iii(1972):1-16.

Three Latin poems are discussed. In the *Elegia quinta* the return of spring is equated with a return of the Golden Age as this idea occurs in classical and Renaissance poetry. The elegy describes a resurgence of literary and sexual power and expresses a youthfully exuberant pride in scholarship. In *Mansus*, a verse tribute to an Italian nobleman who had befriended him, Milton employs pastoral imagery and conventions to suggest an English poetic tradition in which he aspires to find an honored place. The *Epitaphium Damonis* follows closely the tradition of the bucolic death lament but pastoral devices are used only when they do not violate good sense or the sincerity of Milton's grief. The rich and elaborate pastoral allegory—a language in itself—is used with restraint to accentuate emotion and cannot always be interpreted literally. The poem is viewed within the context of the pastoral tradition and many allusions are traced to their sources to show Milton's eminently artistic adaptation of a conventional form as a vehicle of genuine emotion. (EMCC)

4560. Clark, Ira. "Christ on the Tower in *Paradise Regained*." *MiltonQ* 8:104-07.

The tower scene in *Paradise Regained* gathers major Miltonic polarities, theological points, dramatic elements, and image clusters in one emblem embodying Christ's mediation between man and God, his mystical union of man and God. Christ's standing on the tower while Satan is falling is paradoxically both essentially active and integrally metaphorical. By commending himself to God's plan, Milton's Son of Man passes a test for faithful obedience to God. As he does he activates the Son of God in himself and supplants Satan as the triple-officed mediator in the middle air; he also embodies Christian exaltation by humiliation. (IC)

4562. Cohen, Michael. "Rhyme in *Samson Agonistes*." *MiltonQ* 8:4-6.

The absence of an insistent pattern of rhyme in *Samson Agonistes* is evidence that Milton did not want to be subject to the tyranny of a particular rhyme scheme throughout, but the sparing use of rhyme in the drama serves many functions. Internal rhymes underscore thematic words in many passages, end rhymes give epigrammatic force to individual couplets, and more extended passages of rhyme further Milton's imitation of classical models by reproducing choric melody. Intentional discords, or unrhymed lines within rhyming passages, give a mournful and elegiac effect to the choric lines after Samson's death. (MMC)

4563. Colaccio, John J. " 'A Death Like Sleep':The Christology of Milton's Twenty-Third Sonnet." *MiltonS* 6:181-97.

Milton's "late espoused Saint" appears at the center of two planes of spiritual movement, horizontal and vertical, each culminating in God and corresponding to the traditions of Christian typology and Christian Neoplatonism. On the former, she reveals Christ's redemptive self-sacrifice, subtly fulfilling the sacrifice ethos of pagan and Jewish myth and history. On the latter, she descends the Neoplatonic order seeking to "embrace" her beloved through grace. That the persona fails to recognize the import of the saint is due to the Thomistic-Neoplatonic doctrine of intellectual blindness and man's desiccated will to choose "higher" objects of love. The vision breaks at the word "delight," as does Adam's dream of Eve in *P.L.* VIII.474-80, signifying in the context of the Thomistic idea of dilection the persona's archetypal error. The persona's still "fancied sight" causes him to "wake" to the Christian Neoplatonic dream life of mortality. (JJC)

4569. Cumberland, Sharon, and Lynn V. Sadler. "Phantasia: A Pattern in Milton's Early Poems." *MiltonQ* 8:50-55.
Milton's concept of "phantasia" encompasses two manners of vision: high "phantasia," which is divinity seen by man in its full glory; and low "phantasia," which is divinity in its frightening aspect or an absence of the divinity and a focus on the self. Man's general state is middle "phantasia"—postlapsarian distancing with limited understanding of the divine. The degrees of "phantasia" are degrees of faith or of its lack. Unsaved "phantasia" is the imagination inturned on the self and cut off from God. Fallen "phantasia" is that of the faithful man who is still at a distance from God, as a result of his imperfect understanding since the Fall. High "phantasia" is that of the true visionary, who can be lifted and who, like the poet-priest, can aid in lifting the faithful man to a clear vision of divinity. Taken together, they demonstrate a definable pattern in Milton's early poems. (LVS)

4575. Elliott, Emory. "Milton's Biblical Style in *Paradise Regained.*" *MiltonS* 6:227-41.
Through the very words and phrases of Scripture Milton draws into *Paradise Regained* essential details of the encircling framework of Christ's total career and teaching, and he thereby puts the particular episode of the temptations into a biblical perspective. Many allusions recall biblical passages which emphasize Christ's humanity. Other allusions serve to point up the superior exegetical principles which enable Christ to make Satan appear foolish in his misinterpretations of the Scriptures. Throughout the debates between Christ and Satan allusions to the epistles of Paul and to the Book of Revelation also provide a structural tension between the restraint and self-discipline needed in this world which are stressed in the Pauline allusions in the poem's early books and the eternal reward or punishment of the next world which are stressed in the allusions to Revelation which increase near the poem's conclusion. (EBE,Jr)

4576. Farwell, Marilyn. "Choosing by Ambiguity: A Reconsideration of the Fall in *Paradise Lost.*" *WascanaR* 9:213-20.
The Fall in *Paradise Lost* presents serious problems for the unity of the poem. The choice Adam is asked to make between Eve and God is troublesome because either choice is detrimental to the poem. An alternative is dramatically and theologically both desirable and necessary. Adam learns cognitively and experientially that God is a God of love, one who works good out of evil and that he, Adam, must imitate that pattern. This is the same process of learning which the Son experiences in Book III. Thus, when Adam is presented with Eve's sin, he has enough knowledge to follow the pattern of the Son, to offer himself for another with faith in God that he will not be destroyed. He falls not because he chooses Eve but because he accepts the Satanic dichotomy which Eve presents to him. When this approach to the Fall is taken, the poem is no longer severed by the otherwise conflicting dramatic and theological elements. (MRF)

4577. Fee, William W. "Of Reformation in England—and America." *MiltonQ* 8:82-85.
Milton believed that government could be entrusted only to men of integrity and that popular wisdom and virtue were essential to the survival of freedom. He saw education as necessary to national integrity, and morality as the most important component of education. As Milton set aside his literary studies in order to write on matters of immediate national concern, so today's scholars and teachers have a responsibility to contribute to the raising of moral standards, particularly through the formulation of a more constructive curriculum, including greater attention to the personal example as well as the writings of Milton. (WWF)

4578. Fisher, S.A. "Milton's *Paradise Lost.*" *Expl* 33:Item 15. [On Raphael.]
Milton knew that the correct color for seraphs was red. Thus Raphael, a seraph, turns red with passion when Adam asks (in Book VIII of *Paradise Lost*) about angelic intercourse; he has an erotic response to Adam's question. Modesty is an unimaginable virtue in an unfallen creature; to flush, not blush, with active love is more angelic. This reinforces, not checks, Adam's passion. (SAF)

4582. Forker, Charles R. "Milton and Shakespeare: The First Sonnet on Blindness in Relation to a Speech from *Troilus and Cressida.*" *ELN* 11:188-92.
Milton's sonnet on his blindness (no. 19) appears to echo Shakespeare's *Troilus and Cressida* at I.iii.85-94, a part of Ulysses' well-known speech on degree. In addition to the verbal links between the two works, there would seem to be a significant contextual and associational relationship. Ulysses seeks to explain Greek weakness and irresolution by setting petty egotism and self-serving discontentment against a cosmological backdrop, by altering perspective and by enlarging the context to embrace a view of higher and more universal authority. This expansion of context is exactly the poetic strategy that various commentators on sonnet 19 have noted in relation to both the thought and the technique of the poem. (CRF)

4591. Goldman, Jack. "The Name and Function of Harapha in Milton's *Samson Agonistes.*" *ELN* 12:84-91.
A close examination of *Samson Agonistes* and a careful comparison of it with the Hebrew original and with relevant rabbinical glosses reveal that Milton must have intended Harapha not as a personality but rather as a personification of pagan haughtiness and moral depravity, a symbol of Samson's other self, that aspect of his own personality that he was destined to vanquish before he could emerge, in his death, as a Hero of Faith. In employing Harapha in this manner Milton gives evidence of his deep understanding of the Hebrew originals. (JG)

4594. Griffin, Dustin H. "Milton's Evening." *MiltonS* 6:259-76.
Evening is an epitome of Eden, leisurely, harmonious, creative, self-renewing, inter-animate, sustained by divine presence. By contrast, evenings in Virgil and Renaissance pastoral are often brief, damp, threatening. Milton focuses on evening as a calm, quiet time, as a gradual process rather than the hurried end of the day. Although Satan flatters Eve by suggesting that she is the evening cynosure, the narrative voice denies this anthropocentric view, and presents evening as an instance of the inter-animate unity of all creation. Not so much a precarious balance between day and night, evening is a moving moment, a "grateful vicissitude," just as Eden itself is marked not by physical and moral stasis, but by ceaseless change. After the Fall, as a measure of all that is lost, evenings become Virgilian, cold, damp, perilous. (DHG)

4602. Hoyle, James. "'If Sion Hill Delight Thee More': The Muse's Choice in *Paradise Lost.*" *ELN* 12:21-26.
In the invocation to *Paradise Lost*, why might Milton's muse take more delight in Mount Sion than in Mount Sinai? Milton's source in Spenser for his association of the three mountains of his invocation—Oreb-Sinai, Sion, and Helicon—occurs in the three-part simile for the "highest Mount" in Faery Land from which Redcross surveys "The new Hierusalem" (*F.Q.* I.x.53-54). In Spenser, Sinai is the Old Testament mount of "death" under the "bloudy letters" of the Old Law; the Mount of Olives is the mount of peace and life under the New Law; and Helicon is the home of the muses, Christianized to play heavenly notes. In *Paradise Lost*, however, it is necessary to distinguish between the geographical-historical Mount Sion, which was profaned by the devils, and the Sion of the spirit of everyman of the Epistle to the Hebrews 18-22. (JH)

4603. Huguelet, Theodore L. "The Rule of Charity in Milton's Divorce Tracts." *MiltonS* 6:199-214.
To reconcile Christ and Moses on divorce and to prove that the Scriptures sanction divorce for incompatibility, Milton needed a

principle of hermeneutics. He discovered "the Rule of Charity" which became his "loadstarre" of exegesis. It is likely that he discovered his key to Scripture in 1641-42 when he applied Ramistic method to exegesis. He observed that doctrinal charity becomes the "supreme axiom" in the method of Scripture, or the art of Divinity. Hence, by the axiom of charity, a literal, merciless interpretation of Christ's words on divorce would invert the Law and the Gospel and violate the Divine dialectics of Scripture. Milton's confidence in his divorce argument was bolstered by his perception of Divine method behind "the all-interpreting voice of Charity." (TLH)

4606. Hunter, William B.,Jr. "John Milton:Autobiographer." *MiltonQ* 8:100-04.
Although Milton wrote no express autobiography, as many other Puritans did, he evidently considered his published works to imply such a life history. The lack of evidence for a climactic experience, common with members of the Reformed Church, suggests that Milton never experienced it but rather saw his life as a continuing spiritual test (WBH,Jr)

4609. Hurley, C. Harold. "The Cheerful Man's 'Sorrow':A Key to the Meaning of 'L'Allegro,' 45–46." *ELN* 11:275-78.
Critics have long debated the meaning of lines 45-46 of Milton's "L'Allegro." Several commentators conclude, on the basis of punctuation and syntax, that L'Allegro—not the Lark, Mirth, or Dawn—comes to the window, but they are uncertain why he comes "in spite of sorrow" and to whom he bids good-morrow. The difficulties disappear, however, when the lines are applied to L'Allegro who seeks to avert melancholy by enjoying the day's pleasures. L'Allegro's melancholy bent has been frequently observed. Samuel Johnson and Thomas Wharton called attention to L'Allegro's melancholy, and modern critics note similarities between "L'Allegro" and Burton's *Anatomy of Melancholy* which suggest that L'Allegro's activities are antidotes for melancholy. The poem reveals that L'Allegro comes to his window, but the object of his "bid good-morrow" is less explicit. J. LeGay Brereton's conjecture that L'Allegro, following established custom, comes to greet the new day is borne out by the poem. Anxious to assuage melancholy's "eating Cares," L'Allegro awaits the pleasantries of the day. (CHH)

4611. Jacobs, Laurence H. "'Unexpressive Notes':The Decorum of Milton's Nativity Ode." *ELWIU* 1:166-77.
Milton's doubting question to his Muse, "Say, heavenly Muse, shall not thy sacred vein / Afford a present to the infant God" suggests one resolution to the argument about the purpose of the Nativity Ode, whether it celebrates the mystery of the Incarnation or asserts Milton's Puritan and Platonic rejection of the doctrine. Throughout the Ode Milton displays a variety of poetic styles, dictions, conventions, and traditional images, self-consciously testing their power to render the significance of the Incarnation. This testing explains the seemingly inappropriate borrowings from *The Tempest*, Jonsonian masque, and Elizabethan pastoral, as well as a number of images showing the inexpressability of the Incarnation. The Ode shows the ability of poetry to render the mystery of the Incarnation, particularly in its effects upon history and nature, while acknowledging the limited powers of poetic language for rendering transcendent religious concepts. (LHJ)

4619. Kessner, Carole S. "Milton's Hebraic Herculean Hero." *MiltonS* 6:243-58.
Samson Agonistes is unique in its treatment of the Herculean hero so prevalent in Renaissance drama. Unlike other Renaissance dramatists whose conception of the Herculean hero derived from traditional versions and who portrayed Hercules in all his *areté*, Milton's conception rested on the much more humanized hero of Euripides' *Heracles*. Comparison of *Heracles* with *Samson Agonistes* reveals many similarities in theme, structure, and character. (CSK)

4620. Kohn, Terry K. "Landscape in the Transcendent Masque." *MiltonS* 6:143-64.
The treatment of landscape contributes both to Milton's artistic integration of traditional masque elements and to the philosophic content of *Comus*. The Wood functions as a metaphor for earthly existence. Neptune and Sabrina inhabit mythological landscapes possessing both symbolic and realistic qualities. While conventional masque scenery "discovered" the masquers in a purely

mechanical way, Milton gives to his natural setting an intensified reality that illuminates theme and discovers identity in a deeper sense. The characters reveal themselves through their reactions to the landscape, and these responses support and clarify the masque's central concerns of temperance, the power of virtue, and the proper attitude toward nature. The "happy climes" of the epilogue transfigure the vistas of earth and climax the movement of physical and mental expansion precipitated by the triumph of virtue in the Wood. (TKK)

4623. Kuby, Lolette. "The World Is Half the Devil's:Cold-Warmth Imagery in *Paradise Lost*." *ELH* 41:182-91.
Traces a set of images in *Paradise Lost* which until now either has not been discussed or discussed. Cold-warmth imagery, still another thread in the incredibly close weave of the epic, is interesting not only for its own sake, but for what it implies about Milton's view of the spiritual and the material. The imagery is a buttress to the argument for Miltonic dualism. (LK)

4624. Landy, Marcia. "Language and Mourning in 'Lycidas'." *AI* 30:294-312.
In "Lycidas" Milton explores the nature of creativity and experiences a transformation of his feelings of loss, anger, and despair into affirmation and hope. "Lycidas" moves from the poet's experience of anger to exploring the disorganization of the present. The mourning process culminates in the mourner's successful working through of his painful feelings. Each phase in the mourning ritual can be documented in the poem and reveals Milton's awareness of the importance of confronting separation and loss. The images reveal the ambivalence which he experiences. That Milton ties the creative process to the awareness of loss and the necessity of recovery is a further stage in his understanding of poetry and language as a vehicle for regaining a sense of personal, religious, and cultural affirmation. (ML)

4630. Lewalski, Barbara K. "Milton on Women—Yet Once More." *MiltonS* 6:3-20.
Milton's Eve participates fully in the entire range of prelapsarian human activities. Milton's portrayal of the first marriage reflects his abiding belief that the prime end of marriage as defined in the Genesis story is human companionship, not progeny or the relief of lust. Most important, despite his acceptance of the commonplace of Eve's inferiority to Adam in the natural hierarchy, Milton structured the temptation episode to manifest that she, like the Lady in *Comus*, was "sufficient to have stood." What is profound and enduring in Milton's treatment of the first man and woman is his recognition of the capacity and responsibility of each to make crucial, individual decisions defining his or her life and of the depth and intensity of their need for each other to give that life human shape and to make it endurable. (BKL)

4632. Lieb, Michael. "Milton and the Metaphysics of Form." *SP* 71:206-24.
Milton's outlook as a writer is greatly indebted to his concern for the subject of metaphysics. An understanding of that distinction leads to an increased appreciation of his attempt to reconcile the apparent discrepancies between Platonic and Aristotelian metaphysics. Both points of view cause Milton's metaphysics to maintain the integrity of the phenomenal world from the vantage point of a supraphenomenal perspective. The repercussions of this posture have an immense bearing upon Milton's conduct in both prose and poetry. Such dichotomies as external-internal, visible-invisible, corporeal-incorporeal, and body-spirit take on new meaning. Reconciling Platonic and Aristotelian metaphysics, Milton is able to give credence to these dichotomies by maintaining that they do not exist. He is also able to assert the reality of the transcendent by emphasizing the inescapable presence of its opposite. (MJL)

4635. Lindenbaum, Peter. "Lovemaking in Milton's Paradise." *MiltonS* 6:277-306.
In *Paradise Lost* Milton took the unusual stand of asserting that Adam and Eve engaged in sexual relations while still in Eden before the fall. Any importance that the relative distinctiveness of such a stand implies is in turn reinforced further by the enthusiastic outbursts of the poem's usually calm narrator when he touches upon the subject of our first parents' nocturnal lovemaking (in Book IV) and on the related subject of the naked Eve's physical attractiveness. What amounts to an instance of

Milton's personal emphasis in the poem, then, encourages the reader as well as Adam to view sexual love as the "sum" of prelapsarian bliss (VIII.522); and when love of Eve proves to be the cause of Adam's fall, we are prompted to appreciate his decision as complex and difficult, even while we judge him mistaken in placing his love of Eve before obedience to God. The difficulty that Milton's own insistence upon prelapsarian sexual love works into Adam's decision is typical of the poet's presentation of prelapsarian life generally. Life in Milton's relatively difficult Eden is not as much significantly different from our postlapsarian existence as a pastoral image of our present complex life in small. (PL)

4636. Long, Anne B. " 'She May Have More Shapes Than One':Milton and the Modern Idea That Truth Changes." *MiltonS* 6:85-99.
Thomas Kuhn describes any given scientific framework of thought as an allegory which is "true" only in the sense that it permits creative work. Controversies in science lead to new formulations of truth. When contradiction arises, individuals should wait patiently for the new paradigm. Milton similarly believes that God accommodates truth to man's abilities. *Areopagitica* suggests that truth changes and that conflicts between opposing truths lead to a wider vision. *De Doctrina* details the radically different characteristics of God's dispensations. In *Paradise Lost* Milton feels free to choose the scientific paradigm which allows him creativity. He depicts conflicts between characters who have explored fully their particular dispensations and who must acknowledge at the moment of conflict the need for a wider truth. Because the creature can never know absolute truth, his patient waiting must be prompted and sustained by a positive and soul-testing allegiance to truth. (ABL)

4641. McQueen, William. "*Paradise Lost* v, vi:The War in Heaven." *SP* 71:89-104.
By presenting the beginning of his plot in the middle of *Paradise Lost*, Milton achieves perspectives on Satan's rebellion which would not be possible in a straight chronological presentation of the action. The heroic is evoked once more in the war in Heaven but it is almost immediately qualified. The first day's battle presents the conflict in the epic tradition of military heroism. The introduction of artillery on the second day introduces a new mode of battle and a different tone, as the action coarsens to a kind of celestial farce presided over by God. On the third day the heroic mode is completely transcended. Satan's destructive power is overwhelmed and rendered ridiculous by God's greater power; his disobedience is countered by the Son's obedience. The obtuseness of Satan's delayed recognition of the power that he opposes, the farcical action, and the crude, coarsened tone of his speeches heighten the harmonious depiction of the Godhead, which receives its most effective evocation in the poem in the account of Creation which immediately follows. (WAM)

4642. Miller, Leo. "Milton, Fichlau, Bensen and Conring: Addenda to the Life Records of John Milton." *PBSA* 68:107-18.
Replying to a 1649 dissertation *De Summae Potestatis Subjecto* by Naaman Bensen, divine right absolutist student at Helmstedt University, John Fichlau in his *Consideratio Juridico-Politica de Imperio Absolute et Relato Considerato* (1650) uses distinctive arguments also found in Milton's later *Defensio Pro Populo Anglicano* (1651), each deriving independently from common sources such as Bodin. Bensen's rebuttal *Exercitatio Politica de Summae Potestatis Subjecto* (1651) incorporates, passim, attacks on Milton's *Defensio* as parricidal, villainous, impious, filthy, and horrible, in contrast to Salmasius "the great" (*summus*). Ten quotations about Milton from Bensen (1651) and five from Conring's writings of various date are now added for the first time to those formerly tabulated by William Riley Parker, *Milton's Contemporary Reputation*, and J.M. French, *Life Records of John Milton*. (LM)

4643. ——— "Salmasius's *Responsio*:Addenda to the Milton *Life Records*." *N&Q* 21:95.
Supplementing the 1660 Heinsius-Spanheim correspondence on Salmasius's *Responsio*, as given in French's *Life Records of John Milton*, are two more letters by Heinsius to Spanheim, 2 Dec. 1660 and 28 Jan. 1661, printed in *Sylloge Nova Epistolarum Varii Argumenti*, 5 vols., 1760-69, an anthology of 17th- and 18th-

century correspondence. Heinsius notes that he has incurred Salmasius's hostility by his remark that Milton defended the worse cause well, Salmasius the better cause badly. Also mentioned elsewhere among these letters are Carlo Dati, A. Coltellini, V. Chimentelli, F. Barberini, C. Arnold, and Emeric Bigot. (LM)

4644. Mollenkott, Virginia R. "Milton's Technique of Multiple Choice." *MiltonS* 6:101-11.
Milton presented his readers with two or more possible interpretations of certain situations in order to avoid committing himself on issues where he himself was doubtful, to recognize the mysteries of the universe, to make his plot more intriguing, to create a bridge between Hebraic mythological exclusiveness and Hellenic richness, and to provide ironic commentary on the human condition. Always the technique has the effect of drawing the reader into more active participation through choice. (VRM)

4648. Newmeyer, Edna. "The Language of a 'Butchers Stall':Wordsworth on Milton's Description of Abel's Sacrifice." *MiltonQ* 8:69-72.
In a rare marginal note on *Paradise Lost*, Wordsworth faults Milton for "inelegant" diction; the alleged lapse occurs in his description of the sacrifices offered by Cain and Abel (*PL*, XI. 429-43) and concerns one detail: "The Inwards and thir Fat, with Incense strew'd." Milton draws on Mosaic Law to explain the Lord's rejection of Cain's offering. The instructions in Leviticus on the offerings reveal that Cain was negligent, and Abel punctilious, in the performance of the prescribed rites. Cognizance of Mosaic Law by Adam and his sons would not have struck Milton as anachronistic because exegetical tradition held that the rituals later embodied in the Laws dictated to Moses by God were inherent in "the doctrine of true godliness . . . naturallie engrafted" in Adam and passed on by him to his sons. Since the "Butchers stall" details were the words of God, Milton would hardly have considered the diction inelegant. (EN)

4658. Peter, Brother Baldwin. "Milton's Hell Hounds and the Children of God." *MiltonQ* 8:1-3.
Satan, Sin, and Death in *Paradise Lost* are an infernal trinity which parodies the Trinity. The Hell Hounds encircling Sin (II.653-66, 790-804, 861-63, 873) complete the parody. The dogs are the offspring of Satan, Sin, and Death and have as their counterpart Adam and Eve, who are the children of God and made in his likeness. The Hell Hounds are also a parody of the Christian concept of the children of God. The trinitarian image "*Cerberean* mouths" suggests a distortion of the divine image in man. It mocks Satan's attempt to imitate God and serves as a mockery of Adam and Eve's attempt to affect godhead. (BBP)

4663. Revard, Stella P. "Vision and Revision:A Study of *Paradise Lost* 11 and *Paradise Regained*." *PLL* 10:353-62.
The blind spots exhibited by the first Adam in *PL*, when he is set upon the visionary mount by Michael, shadow forth by contrast the clairvoyance of that second Adam who, in *PR*, is set by Satan upon a similar mount. Both Adam and the Son are tried not only by the problems of man's mortal nature, but also by the lures of false luxury and false glory. Adam shrinks from death, is dazzled by the bevy of fair women, and cannot understand the spectacle of men seeking glory in battle. The Son, in contrast, accepts death, dismisses the luxurious table of Satan, and demonstrates how those who seek glory in war destroy themselves and pervert God's glory. Though Adam finally learns to endure and hope, his visionary experience transforms nothing of his own or mankind's future. The Son of God, however, by turning away from Satan's vision, transforms it, and in response the wilderness blossoms as he said it might. His vision has triumphed, fulfilling what Adam dreamed but could not make real. (SPR)

4668. Safer, Elaine B. "The Socratic Dialogue and 'Knowledge in the Making' in *Paradise Regained*." *MiltonS* 6:215-26.
An examination of the dialogue form in *Paradise Regained* illuminates Milton's method of educating the reader by involving him as an indirect participant in a Platonic-Socratic dialectic between Christ and Satan. Plato's dialogues use an oblique method of suggesting enigmatic answers that arise from surface contradictions; riddles and questions that make the reader unable to distill a set doctrine from them; myth, allegory, and fable to move toward poetic truths. The overall pattern of the dialogues is

from darkness to light. In *Paradise Regained*, the debate between Christ and Satan follows the Platonic pattern. As Christ exposes Satan's definitions, the reader gradually progresses from ignorance to awareness. Christ's sharp rebuff of the temptation is a barbed method of cautioning the reader against yearning for codified wisdom, an anathema to the dialectic process itself. The dialectic encourages us to distinguish between knowledge simply taken over and knowledge which is achieved through "much arguing" and "many opinions." (EBS)

4672. Scoufos, Alice-Lyle. "The Mysteries in Milton's Masque." *MiltonS* 6:113-42.

In *Comus* Milton used both stock characters and stock plot. Taking his cue from the liturgical text which the *Book of Common Prayer* listed for St. Michael's Day (Revelation xii.7-13), he turned to the plot of the Woman Wandering in the Wilderness which had been the subject of the Advent plays of medieval drama. The Woman from Revelation xii was first dramatized in the 12th-century *Ludus de Antichristo* in which she was named Ecclesia (following the tradition of biblical commentaries). Milton appears to have known the work of Reformation playwrights who exploited the older Advent plays. The Advent plays had ended with the Archangel Michael winging to the rescue. Milton's Attendant Spirit functions in a similar way to confront Comus who has inherited the attributes of the seductive Antichrist. (ALS)

4673. Shaheen, Naseeb. "Milton's Muse and the *De Doctrina*." *MiltonQ* 8:72-76.

There are five invocations in *Paradise Lost* and *Paradise Regained* directed to the biblical Holy Spirit. A reading of the *De Doctrina* shows Milton to be making a distinction between God and the Holy Spirit. He admits uncertainty about the nature and origin of the Holy Spirit but firmly contends that the Spirit is inferior to God and should not be invoked in the way that God is invoked. No basis exists for interpreting Milton's poetry only in the light of the *De Doctrina*, especially when to do so contradicts Milton's clear identity of his Muse in the epics. Thus to insist that a single statement in the *De Doctrina* taken out of context is an absolute and binding gloss on the epics is quite unwarranted. (NS)

4674. Shaw, William P. "Milton's Choice of the Epic for *Paradise Lost*." *ELN* 12:15-20.

Milton chose the epic genre for *Paradise Lost* because he realized the epic genre would include the vital elements of tragedy. Sidney, Scaliger, Tasso, and others propagated the view that the epic genre was the supreme poetic mode because it was the most inclusive mode—including all the other genres within its scope. Milton, therefore, did not have to scuttle his early perception of the fall of man as a tragedy. His choice of the epic made it possible to describe the cosmic and theological subjects surrounding the fall, which tragedy would not contain. But his choice of the epic also made it possible to incorporate and approximate the form and substance of tragedy within the larger, epic framework. In Book ix of *Paradise Lost* Milton isolates and dramatizes the central episode of the fall and changes "Those Notes to Tragic." (WPS)

4685. Stackhouse, Janifer G. "Early Critical Response to Milton in Germany:The *Dialogi* of Martin Zeiller." *JEGP* 73:487-96.

When Martin Zeiller included a summary of the dispute between Claudius Salmasius and John Milton in his publication *Ein Hundert Dialogi, oder Gespräch Von unterschiedlichen Sachen zu erbaulicher Nachricht auch Nutzlichem Gebrauch und Belustigung* (1653), he carried off nothing less than a journalistic scoop. His discussion is the first known commentary about Milton in the German language, preceding what has heretofore been accepted as the first German commentary by 8 years. The same year marks the date when Milton's original influence in Germany as a political theoretician could extend beyond those able to read previous criticism written in Latin about his treatise. (JGS)

4686. Steadman, John M. "Milton's 'Summa Epitasis':The End of the Middle of *Samson Agonistes*." *MLR* 69:730-44.

Re-examines the problem of the plot structure of *Samson Agonistes* against the background of Renaissance critical theory concerning the relationship between the point of highest tension (*summa epitasis*) and the catastrophe. In lines 1348-49 Milton

appears to locate this point. In *Samson Agonistes*, as in Milton's dramatic sketches for other biblical tragedies, the epitasis is his own invention and serves not only to complicate the action and arouse suspense but also to prepare for the final catastrophe. (JMS)

4687. Stollman, Samuel S. "Milton's Dichotomy of 'Judaism' and 'Hebraism'." *PMLA* 89:105-12.

Milton shows concurrently "powerful judaistic motifs" and "anti-judaistic motifs." He advocated liberty of conscience but was silent during the debate on the Readmission of the Jews. Milton's views may have evolved or changed but he was doctrinally consistent. He dichotomized the Old Testament constellation of personae and concepts into "Judaic" motifs which he rejected and "Hebraic" motifs which he adopted. He took Paul's antithesis of the Law (the Flesh) and the Gospel (the Spirit) and applied it within the Hebrew Bible itself. The "Judaic" complex is that which is human, relevant to the Jews as a people inclined to servitude, and the "external" aspect of the Mosaic Law, also a form of bondage. The "Hebraic" complex is divine, universal, and the "internal" Scripture equated with freedom and, ultimately, Christian liberty. The "Hebraic" motif supplies a continuity for the Scriptures. The dichotomy accords with Milton's philosophy (Plato's and Aristotle's dualisms) and with his methodology of structural and imagistic contrasts. (SSS)

4688. Thompson, Claud A. "'Coded' Signatures:A Printer's Clue to the Bibliographical Tangle of The *Doctrine and Discipline of Divorce* (1644)." *PBSA* 68:297-305.

There is a pattern of stop-press correction in the 1644 quarto of Milton's *The Doctrine and Discipline of Divorce* which indicates that purposeful textual corrections were made in the inner and/or outer formes at one or two stages during the printing of 6 of the 11 full sheets in that edition. In some copies, as many as five gatherings are "coded" with a period or a colon in one of their signatures to indicate that corrections have been made in a sheet during printing. These "punctuated" signatures suggest an uncommon concern with textual accuracy in the revised edition of *DDD*. They also enable one to identify the corrected sheets in any extant copy of the 1644 quarto. (CAT)

4690. Tobin, J.J.M. "Milton's *Samson Agonistes*, 19-20." *Expl* 32:Item 77.

There is a singular and striking reference to "hornets" in Milton's *Samson Agonistes*, 19-20. On the surface level the stinging creatures are the pangs of conscience from which Samson suffers throughout the drama. There is, further, the folk-etymology connecting "hornet" with "horn," and in the 16th and 17th centuries "horn" and cuckold are universally associated. In the 17th century a cuckold is a husband whose wife has cheated or tricked him by unfaithful behavior not necessarily sexual in nature. Samson sees Dalila as just such a wife. The hornets of his mind originate directly from his having been cuckolded. Milton's known practice of associating the charms of female beauty with entrapment by net or chain suggests the homophonic wordplay on "whore-nets" and "hornets." Hence entrapment and the cause of that entrapment appear in the pun "whore-nets," the thought of which hurt is present in the sting of "hornets." (JJMT)

4691. Ulreich, John C. "Typological Symbolism in Milton's Sonnet xxiii." *MiltonQ* 8:7-10.

Typological symbolism provides an approach to Milton's sonnet on his "late espoused Saint" by clarifying the vexed allusion to "Purification in the old Law." The image of ritual purification refers to the old letter of Leviticus and to the new spirit of Luke. Classical, Hebraic, and Christian images are organized typologically, to reflect a movement from external, dream-like shadows to internal, visionary truth, foreshadowing a final revelation of Christ as the "glad husband" of his purified bride. Milton has also expressed a tragic sense of loss, the pattern of which is also typological, for the dramatic form of the poem finds its closest analogue in the myth of Orpheus. (JCU)

4695. Waters, D. Douglas. "Milton's Use of the Sorcerer-Rhetorician." *MiltonQ* 8:113-16.

With the exception of *Samson Agonistes*, the sorcerer-rhetorician appears not only in *Comus* but also the major poems. Milton used sorcery as a metaphor for false rhetoric, a technique which implies an interest in the sorcerer-rhetorician. Whereas Comus is a sorcerer who is in league with devils, Satan and Belial are devils who are both sorcerers and rhetoricians. The growing emphasis of the sorcerer-rhetorician helped Milton achieve a greater flexibility and imaginative freedom within the Renaissance conventions of witchcraft and indicates the limitation of those critical views that stress the "degeneration" of Satan as an epic character. (DDW)

4699. Welcher, Jeanne K. "The Meaning of Manoa." *MiltonQ* 8:48-50.

Manoa in Milton's *Samson Agonistes* comes directly from the Bible. "Manoah" is used in the Bible as a justified retreat for those who have fulfilled their commitment. It is the specific antithesis of "agonistes," but with no pejorative connotation. Manoa is truly father to what must be Samson's first thought: has he struggled long enough? Samson's refusal does not signify that Manoa's offer is evil, but that it is inappropriate now. In fact, Samson explicitly anticipates going to a resting place—death. When Manoa learns that Samson has died, Manoa brings the poem full circle: now he will build the proper resting place for his son. (JKW)

4703. Wilson, Gayle E. "Decorum and Milton's 'An Epitaph on the Marchioness of Winchester'." *MiltonQ* 8:11-14.

An analysis of "An Epitaph on the Marchioness of Winchester" reveals that Milton carefully observed "decorum" in the presentation of his subject's merits. He casts his praise of Jane Paulet into the form of a demonstrative oration, develops it in terms of the *topos* of descent, and embellishes it with the appropriate allusions and rhetorical figures. (GEW)

4705. Wittreich, Joseph A.,Jr. "Milton's 'First' Illustrator." *SCN* 32:70-71.

Suzanne Boorsch has established that Henry Aldrich, not John Baptist Medina, is the designer for the first, second, and twelfth illustrations first appearing in the 1688 Tonson edition of *Paradise Lost*. This requires a reassessment of these designs. The Satanist controversy has its inception in the spirit of contention between Aldrich and Medina and, subsequently, between Aldrich and engravers like Pierre Fourdrinier who sought to alter the artist's conceptions, fracturing the close relationship between a design and Milton's text by moving the illustration into closer line with the orthodoxies that Milton's text violates. (JAW)

4706. —— "Review of Year's Work:Beyond New Criticism: Literary History, Literary Criticism, and Milton Studies, 1973." *MiltonQ* 8:15-21.

The book-length studies of Milton issued in 1973 suggest that Milton criticism is moving significantly beyond the New Criticism. The Old Criticism, which New Criticism sought to replace, is still too much with us, however, as suggested by Kirkconnell's *Awake the Courteous Echo*, and by Kelley's edition of *De doctrina christiana*. *Achievements of the Left Hand*, ed. Lieb and Shawcross, and *The Prison and the Pinnacle*, ed. Rajan, shows Miltonists combining the various "criticisms" and binding them irrevocably to literary history. In harness, literary history and literary criticism, both immensely sophisticated, are bringing Milton studies to a new level of consciousness. (JAW,Jr)

4710. Woolrych, Austin. "Milton's Political Commitment: The Interplay of Puritan and Classical Ideals." *WascanaR* 9:166-88.

Milton was at the same time a humanist scholar and a radical puritan who believed that in all matters of faith the Holy Scriptures had sole and absolute authority. When he sacrificed for many years his vocation to become a great Christian poet in order to serve the cause of the English Revolution with prose polemics, there was an obvious possibility that these two strains in his thought would conflict. Religious and scriptural arguments dominated his earlier tracts, and their preponderance diminished somewhat as his early millenarian hopes faded and his official employment immersed him in matters of state. Thereafter the prevalence of the one strain or the other tended to be determined by his intended audience and by his subject-matter. But in his last major prose tract, *The Readie and Easie Way*, the two are found once more in close counterpoint. (AHW)

Oldham. 4716. Brooks, Harold F. "The Chief Substantive Editions of Oldham's Poems, 1679-1684:Printer, Compositors, and Publication." *SB* 27:188-226.

Mary Clark printed the original editions of the 4 collections of Oldham's poetry and the second (revised) edition of the first collection. The publisher, Hindmarsh, was probably the pirate of his *Satyr against Vertue*, 1679. For using this bad text in *Satyrs upon the Jesuits* 1681 and perhaps for the piracy, Hindmarsh was satirized by Oldham, who supplied errata for a third issue. The second had added "A Satyr Upon a Woman." The first was set by two compositors; L, lavish with italics, set sheets B and C, and identifiable stints in D and E, where compositor M came back to his assistance. Exceptionally, E was not, it seems, set seriatim. In the other volumes, no features preclude M being sole compositor; equally, two or more, having similar habits, might be responsible. The evidence analyzed comprises the orthography of Oldham's autographs and of the prints; composition from extant printed copy; the treatment of verse-lines too long for the compositor's measure. Propensity to recognized types of error is noted, and varying rates of error are estimated. (HFB)

Otway. 4718. Durant, Jack D. "'Honor's Toughest Task': Family and State in *Venice Preserved*." *SP* 71:484-503.

In *Venice Preserved* Otway demonstrates through analogy the political realities most basic to domestic quiet. Placing the demands of rash heroic action at odds with the profounder demands of marital and familial integrity, he insists that tranquility in the state presupposes loving mutual trust among the members of the political family, that stability inheres in this trust. His dramatic means are complex ones, generating far-reaching psychological and moral implications. But in functioning consistently to recommend the high values of family unity, they point as well to a unity binding the political and domestic actions of the play. (JDD)

4719. McVicker, C.D. "Balzac and Otway." *RomN* 15(1973): 248-54.

The English restoration dramatist Thomas Otway, by the adaptation of certain historical facts to his tragedy *Venice Preserved*, influenced Balzac in the *Histoire des treize*, in *Ferragus*, and especially in the creation of the character of Vautrin. Balzac quotes from the French version of the play in the meeting of Vautrin, alias Carlos Herrera, with the young Rubempré, then on the verge of suicide; in the relationship of the two friends, Pons and Schmucke; and in the meditation of the founder of the *Société des Treize* on the value of the philosophy of Otway. The influence of Otway tends to negate the theory of Vautrin's homosexuality, and tends to support the theory of Balzac's misogyny in the later part of his life. Furthermore, even though the theory of homosexuality in the case of Vautrin has been proposed by various scholars, there seems to be no novelistic evidence to support it. Neither do supposedly historical sources provide any sound evidence of sexual deviation. Finally the theory of Otway's influence helps to clarify the intentions of Balzac in regard to human relationships, particularly in the later novels. (CDM)

4720. Whitworth, Charles W. "The Misfortunes of Romeo and Juliet:Richard Penn Smith's 'Revival' of Otway's *Caius Marius*." *CahiersE* 6:3-7.

Otway's *History and Fall of Caius Marius*, a "clumsy patchwork" of Plutarch and *Romeo and Juliet*, remained popular for several decades, until revivals of the Shakespeare play in the 1740s drove it from the stage. In 1831, the American playwright Richard Penn Smith produced a play on Caius Marius and the Roman Civil Wars. Though he had considerable classical learning and had read widely in Elizabethan dramatic literature, he also knew Otway's forgotten play. A comparison of the plays leaves no doubt but that Smith lifted whole passages, sometimes verbatim, from Otway. He also borrowed from Shakespeare and Jonson, of whom echoes and direct quotations are readily found in Smith's play. The editor of Smith's *Caius Marius*, while referring to Otway's play, does not give the least hint of Smith's wholesale plundering. (CWW)

Reynolds. 4726. Hobbs, Mary. "Drayton's 'Most Dearely-Loved Friend Henery Reynolds Esq'." *RES* 96(1973):414-28.

Evidence, chiefly original, is provided to identify Henry Reynolds as of Holton St. Mary, Suffolk; the Lord Chamberlain's secretary,

c. 1606-13, having possibly served Essex previously; schoolmaster in the parish of St. Mary Axe, c. 1614-c. 1624; of St. Katherine Coleman, c. 1624-30; and at Chichester, 1630-31; after which he lived in London until his death in 1635. He had at least two daughters, Bathsua and Ithmara. Besides his printed works, Reynolds wrote a Latin treatise on communications , *Macrolexis*. He was Chapman's friend as well as Drayton's and knew Henry King: nine of his sixteen short poems are preserved among six manuscripts containing good copies of King's poems, particularly the Stoughton Manuscript (in private hands), Folger MS. V.b.43 and John Wilson's songbook, Bodley MS. Mus.b.1. Ten poems set to music by Henry Lawes (nine attributed in *Ayres and Dialogues* indexes) are listed and located, with two unprinted stanzas from his manuscript songbook. Eight other poems are printed out from the Stoughton Manuscript and one from B.M. MS. Add. 25707 (also related to Henry King). (MH)

Rochester. 4729. Fabricant, Carole. "Rochester's World of Imperfect Enjoyment." *JEGP* 73:338-50.
Rochester's literary work bears constant witness to the profound limitations of sexuality. It does so both through its thematic preoccupation with impotence and joyless lust and through its bleak, eminently nonerotic language, which betrays any vision of sensual plenitude. Rochester goes far beyond the other Restoration Court Wits in creating a cosmic vision predicated upon what he perceives as the body's total inefficacy: its inability to fulfill even the most basic human desires. His writings bitterly subvert the libertine ideal rather than merely qualifying it with sophisticated cynicism or pornographic humor. We can most fully appreciate Rochester's distinctiveness in this respect by comparing his poem, "The Imperfect Enjoyment," with other contemporary versions of the impotence theme. (CF)

Shadwell. 4743. Fisher, Alan S. "The Significance of Thomas Shadwell." *SP* 71:225-46.
Shadwell's adaptation of Shakespeare's *Timon* in 1678 was his first explicitly Whiggish play, but the changes he makes there to advance his party's cause resemble what he had been doing with comedies all along. The hero of Shadwell's *Timon* is Alcibiades, a literal-minded, honest rake, exactly like the Whig leader, Buckingham. Shadwell takes Shakespeare's complicated morality and simplifies it radically into its inconsistent parts. He ignores this inconsistency, however, because both sides of it are "good sense" in their ways, and he was confident that nothing that is good sense can be wrong. This same confidence is a constant of Whiggish thinking generally, and it is the primary element of Shadwell's comic vision. The world of Shadwell's comedies is resolved the way a Whig politician would resolve his own: miracles are unnecessary where good sense (and money) are abundant. (ASF)
4744. Ross, J.C. "An Attack on Thomas Shadwell in Otway's *The Atheist*." *PQ* 52(1973):753-60.
Daredevil, the "atheist" in Thomas Otway's black comedy *The Atheist; or, the Second Part of The Souldiers Fortune* (London, 1684), and the plot-element involving him constitute a dramatic libel upon Shadwell. This explains a reference in the dedication to the extreme hostility the play aroused in part of its audience. Daredevil has such Shadwellian qualities as bumptiousness, love of drink, and a rakish past; and a wound causes him such terror of death and damnation that he makes a confession of past misdeeds. Items from 8 January to 8 February 1682 in such newspapers as Nat Thompson's *The Loyal Protestant*, reflecting on Shadwell's links with Catholicism in the past and present status as a Whig "True Protestant Poet," refer to an occasion when injury in a fray terrified him into making a written recantation of his "Atheistical Opinions." Otway's possible motives for making dramatic capital of this incident include political hostility of Tory against Whig, professional exasperation with a man who ridiculed contemporary modes of tragedy, and personal animus against an ex-friend whom he blamed for leading him into dissolution. (JCR)

Snawsel. 4748. McLean, Andrew. "Another English Translation of Erasmus' *Coniugium*:Snawsel's *Looking Glasse for Maried Folkes* (1610)." *Moreana* 43-44:55-64.
Snawsel's *A Looking Glasse for Maried Folkes* (1610) combines a translation of Erasmus' *Coniugium* with a catechistical dialogue on the duty of husbands and wives. Little is known about the translator, a Yorkshire gentleman whose sons attended Cambridge. Examples from the Latin original and Snawsel's translation concern an anecdote paralleling More's courtship of Jane Colt and illustrate how the translator uses picturesque and proverbial sayings to maintain a colloquial idiom. Snawsel's changes in translation affect expression rather than meaning. (AMM)

Traherne. 4756. Dees, Jerome S. "Recent Studies in Traherne." *ELR* 4:189-96. [Rev. art.]
Over 110 studies on Thomas Traherne have been published since 1945. Though all of his works have been studied, scholars and critics have continued to concentrate primarily on *Centuries of Meditations* and the poems, and have most recently been concerned with examining Traherne's thought in relation to the intellectual background of the 17th century and with discovering structural principles in his works. Standard editions of *Centuries, Poems, and Thanksgivings* and of *Christian Ethicks* have appeared, and a new manuscript of "Select Meditations" was discovered. (JSD)
4758. McFarland, Ronald E. "From Ambiguity to Paradox: Thomas Traherne's 'Things'." *WascanaR* 9:114-23.
The apparent vagueness of the diction in Traherne's poetry results from his tendency to use some words which have variable or indefinite semantic reference. His frequent use of "thing(s)" exemplifies Traherne's ability to move from the inherent ambiguity of the term toward definition in the religious and philosophical context of the poems. First, Traherne distinguishes between true and false things, but he discovers that his perception of true things in the universe does not insure felicity. After this discovery Traherne attempts to disregard things in favor of thoughts. In the poems entitled "Thoughts (I-IV)" Traherne brings about a paradoxical resolution of the semantic and philosophical problem with the declaration that "Thoughts are Things." (REM)

Vanbrugh. 4767. Olshen, Barry N. "The Original and 'Improved' Comedies of Sir John Vanbrugh:Their Nineteenth-Century London Stage History." *RECTR* 13,i:27-52.
The Confederacy was Vanbrugh's only play to have survived in anything like its integrity in the early years of the 19th century, though it never attained the position of a regular stage piece. To *The Relapse* goes the achievement of having the most varied stage history of any comedy of its period. Its stage career includes two late 18th-century adaptations: Lee's *A Man of Quality* and Sheridan's *A Trip to Scarborough*, the latter surviving into the 19th century; and two late 19th-century adaptations: Hollingshead's *The Man of·Quality* and Buchanan's *Miss Tomboy*. The most popular of the comedies was *The Provok'd Husband*, which is actually more Cibber's play than Vanbrugh's. (BNO)

Vaughan, H. 4770. Bourdette, Robert E.,Jr. "Recent Studies in Henry Vaughan." *ELR* 4:299-310.
Since 1945, detailed study of the major influences on the poetry of Henry Vaughan has modified the older judgment of Vaughan as a "poet of stanzas, lines, or even half-lines." Critics have used varied sources to demonstrate the real unity in individual poems. Much of the criticism has been devoted to arguing the primacy of one influence in Vaughan's work, sometimes at the expense of his distinctive ability to reshape his sources to his own purposes. A few critics have discussed the importance of the secular poems both as poems and as convincing evidence of a continuous, rather than disjunctive, artistic development. Examination of Vaughan's "poetics"— particularly its Jonsonian, allegorical, or meditative base—indicates a particularly useful area of study. Detailed criticism of Vaughan's extensive corpus is still limited to a few of the better-known poems. Though a definitive study of Vaughan is still needed, Simmonds' book is an important contribution, particularly as it emphasizes Vaughan's poetics and some of the lesser-known poems. (REB,Jr)

4777. Pollock, John J. "The Divided Consciousness of Henry Vaughan." *PLL* 10:422-24.
Vaughan's *Silex Scintillans* reveals the poet's "divided consciousness," that is a paralysis of the will or lack of decisiveness evident at key points in a number of the poems. The contradiction between the words "invisible" and "dim" in the final line of "The Night" is perhaps the most striking example of Vaughan's tendency to draw back from the total renunciation of self that he continually strives for and yet fails to attain. Evidence from "The Starre" indicates that Vaughan may well have been aware of his peculiar propensity for self-contradiction. (JJP)

4778. Rudrum, Alan. "An Aspect of Vaughan's Hermeticism:The Doctrine of Cosmic Sympathy." *SEL* 14:129-38.
Vaughan's vision of the world is deeply influenced by the hermetic philosophy and his best poems are those which express the hermetic trinity of God, Man, and Nature. His earlier poems draw upon hermetic lore; only his mature religious verse fully expresses the hermetic trinity. The distinction of Vaughan's poems is related to the hermetic philosophy, in that it provided a structure which answered more fully to his temperament than did a straightforward Christianity. The network of relationships in hermetic cosmology provided Vaughn with a system of metaphors and enabled him to achieve exactness of expression. (AWR)

4779. Sandler, Florence. "The Ascents of the Spirit:Henry Vaughan on the Atonement." *JEGP* 73:209-26.
Vaughan can be described as a Neoplatonist, having affinities with the Cambridge Platonists and Traherne. Vaughan inclines to the Johannine tradition; he sees Nature and History and all phenomenality as the "veil" of the *noumenon* while the Atonement becomes the revelation of the essential relationship between man and God, and its effect Deification. "Man's fall and Recovery" and "The Passion" evidence confusion on Vaughan's part between Pauline and Johannine views. His more characteristic poems of Atonement are "The World" and especially "The Night," where the Atonement is assimilated into the pattern of the Descent and Ascent of the Logos and the Spirit. (FS)

4780. Wanamaker, Melissa C. "Discordia Concors:The Metaphysical Wit of Henry Vaughan's *Silex Scintillans*." *TSLL* 16:463-77.
Since the ancient idea of *discordia concors*, a yoking of opposites, later became equated with the paradoxical kind of wit so pervasive in 17th-century English literature, application of the principle affords an approach to understanding metaphysical wit. Analysis of Vaughan's use of the concept in *Silex Scintillans* reveals it as a later variation of the Donnean manner of yoking opposites. For Vaughan, however, the process toward truth is perhaps even more complicated than Donne's. The first step is one of division: the perception of discord within the seeming concord of the natural world. Once such falsity is recognized, the poet is able to transcend this world and achieve regeneration poetically through the second stage of *discordia concors*, in which opposites are yoked to create paradoxes that reflect true spiritual rebirth. (MCW)

Waller. 4781. Höltgen, Karl J. "Why Was Man Created in the Evening? On Waller's 'An Apologie for Having Loved Before'." *MLR* 69:23-28.
Edmund Waller argues in "An Apologie for Having Loved Before" that as man was created in the evening and first saw the stars, then the moon, and at last the full splendor of the sun, so he will love several women until he finds the one of perfect beauty. The Christian tradition knows nothing about man's creation in the evening. The Talmud, however, relates that he was created on the eve of the Sabbath. The Talmud was well-known to 17th-century scholars, and Waller enjoyed, according to an unpublished poem by Sir Justinian Isham, the reputation of a learned man. A volume of the fifth edition of *Poems*, 1886 (British Museum, C.28.c12[1]), contains hitherto unnoticed manuscript annotations important for future work on Waller. They were transcribed from a copy belonging to Bishop Atterbury, who used Waller's manuscript. Atterbury provides a variant text of the poem and refers to an Arabian legend on Abraham. The legend accounts for further details of Waller's argument and proves that the lover's progress from inferior to perfect beauty is a profane version of man's spiritual progress toward God. (KJH)

Webster. 4783. Champion, Larry S. "Webster's *The White Devil* and the Jacobean Tragic Perspective." *TSLL* 16:447-62.
In Jacobean tragedy no significant character is untainted, and since there is no fully articulated transformation in the protagonist, a pervasive moral ambivalence obtains throughout the tragedy. Webster achieves this perspective in *The White Devil* by utilizing the major antagonists as the central characters of internalization and by methodically and consecutively emphasizing the corruption of the major characters surrounding Vittoria along with the pitiful impotence of the few with moral integrity. The structure commands admiration of Vittoria's courage and perseverance in the face of a dilemma from which her inability to escape becomes ever more certain; and, although she never repents in the full sense of the word, she does achieve tragic dignity and, for the spectators, a meaningful anagnorisis. Moments before her death she acknowledges the moral justice of her fate in a corrupt society; moreover, her resolution provokes Flamineo to perceive the nihilism to which a life of unchecked passion ultimately leads. (LSC)

4787. Hogan, Jerome W. "Webster's *The White Devil* v.iv.118-121." *Expl* 33:Item 25.
When in John Webster's *The White Devil* Flamineo declares that sometimes he has felt the "maze of conscience" in his breast (v.iv.121), he is referring to the state of bewilderment caused by a guilty conscience and not the weapon "mace," as Samuel M. Pratt contends (*Expl*, 29, 1970, Item 11). Support for this reading comes from the play itself and from works on moral theology published during the Renaissance. (JWH)

4788. Kelleher, Victor M.K. "Notes on *The Duchess of Malfi*." *UES* 10,ii(1972):11-15.
Critical response to *The Duchess of Malfi* tends to oversimplify and thereby to impoverish the play. An analysis of the problem areas in the drama clearly indicates the subtlety and complexity of Webster's vision. Bosola is usually regarded as a man of flawed virtue. Yet he is an enigmatic figure who acts out each of the many facets of his personality with equal vigor. We come close to understanding his depth when we regard him, not as either basically virtuous or evil, but as a fate figure. In contrast to Bosola, the Cardinal and Ferdinand are much more than the irrational forces they are usually taken to be. An examination of their actions and language reveals that Ferdinand is motivated by incestuous desire and the Cardinal by a Machiavellian lust for power. The Duchess, too, is a complex figure. She is not from the outset a symbol of virtue: her character develops throughout the first four acts. Paradoxically, her final state of perfection is achieved only through a process of error. (VMKK)

Wilson, J. 4793. Otten, Robert M. "Son of Ben, Son of Brugis:A New Source for John Wilson's *The Projectors*." *RECTR* 13,ii:55-57.
Recent criticism asserts that Jonson's *The Devil Is an Ass* is the major influence on Wilson's *The Projectors*. Such a statement fails to consider how Wilson used Brugis's polemic pamphlet, *The Discovery of a Projector*, as a source for the characters, the projects, and the projecting cant in the play. Wilson simply provides names for Brugis's types: Gotam, Sir Gudgeon Credulous, Squeeze, Suckdry, and Mrs. God-goods. From Brugis Wilson takes the list of projects which his characters promote. Wilson's witty heroes, Jocose and Driver, exploit these projectors' greed by dazzling them with the jargon that Brugis had noted was the projector's self-justification for a seemingly hairbrained idea. (RMO)

Wither. 4794. Calhoun, Thomas O. "George Wither:Origins and Consequences of a Loose Poetics." *TSLL* 16:263-79.
Discusses the means by which a loose style emerged in the poetry written by George Wither between 1612 and 1628. In *Britian's Remembrancer* (1625-28) Wither abandons the conventional origins of his loose style in order to shape his poem according to the vision of immorality, mutability, and death which actually lies behind the voices of satiric, elegaic, and pastoral poetry. Wither intends a poem based on the conditions of personal experience,

not on the artfices of literary conventions. As a consequence he creates a digressive, amorphous, self-destructing book. As a post-mortem, justifications are offered for the loose style drawn from the principles of Peter Ramus and Wither's translation, *The Nature of Man.* (TOC)

Wycherley. 4797. Weales, Gerald. "William Wycherley." *MQR* 12(1973):45-58.

The small amount of biographical information we have about Wycherley suggests that he accepted, even embraced the mores of his time. The surprising thing about him is that he interrupted a life devoted to the pursuit of position and wealth to write four plays that are the strongest satiric attacks to come out of the Restoration, sardonic looks at the kind of social-sexual -financial scramble to which he apparently gave his life. (GW)

VIII. EIGHTEENTH CENTURY

Bibliography. 4801. Rogal, Samuel J. "Principal Eighteenth-Century British Titles in the *Index Librorum.*" *LC* 39:67-75. A historical summary of the *Index librorum*, a synopsis of the Tridentine Regulations (1564), a list of the principal editions of the *Index librorum* published between 1660 and 1800, and a selected listing of titles published in England (as well as translations of these works published on the Continent) and included in Catholic Indexes issued between 1668 and 1827. (SJR)

General and Miscellaneous. 4804. Berry, Christopher J. " 'Climate' in the Eighteenth Century:James Dunbar and the Scottish Case." *TSLL* 16:281-92. Examines the particular argument of Dunbar in the Scottish context based upon 18th-century widespread use of the concept of climate. This context is interesting for two reasons: (1) the Scots' enunciation of a broad sociological approach to social phenomena; and (2) the impact on the Scots of Hume and Montesquieu, especially concerning the apparent contradiction between Hume's advocacy of "moral causes" and Montesquieu's of "physical causes." Examines Dunbar's own attempted reconciliation between these two, based on the role of "local circumstances." Dunbar's theory exemplifies not only the widespread interest in climate, but also links together the two major ordering principles of climate and progress. (CJB)

4821. Ewert, Leonore H. "The Implication of 'Writation'." *PQ* 52(1973):775-76. The *OED* defines the 18th-century coinage "writation" as "poor and insipid writing." This informal term of criticism "appears seldom in printed form: however, as it is to be found, several times, in the unpublished correspondence of Elizabeth Montagu (1720-1800), it is used to register objection to semantic innovations concomitant to the linguistic revolution of that period. Montagu attempts to dismiss highly individual usage as a "mushroom growth" and a "novel jargon." Even Dr. Johnson's style is criticized as being ostentatious and perhaps dangerous "writation"—a term invented, according to this bluestocking, by Lord Cobham. (LHE)

4822. Formigari, Lia. "Language and Society in the Late Eighteenth Century." *JHI* 35:275-92. Linguistic theories of the 18th century reflect belief in the existence of a "natural" man, who is not a product but a point of departure of history. Both language development and universal history are therefore the unfolding of man's essential attributes: thought and sociality. In the new approach, the task of anthropology is to describe man's self-creation. In this process labor has an essential role. Man's relation to nature is mediated by productive relations that mediate individual relations and language as well. (LF)

4824. Goldberg, S.L. "Augustanism and the Tragic." *CR* 17:21-37. Although the Augustan age is often regarded as having been "utterly incapable of attaining the tragic" (in the words of F.R. Leavis), this view is based upon a conventional conception of the art of Pope and Johnson. Johnson's, for example, is more questioning and uncertain than his critical principles might suggest. The wholly self-involving integrity with which he acknowledges the irreconcilable conflicts of human existence, his sense of life being doomed to be its own nemesis, and his recognition that men must "make" the power to know all this and to live by their knowledge of it mark the art of "the Vanity of Human Wishes" as genuinely tragic. And as in Johnson, so in Pope and other writers: the tragic was attained not in the

externally conceived "tragick" forms of the age, but in those looser forms, where the writer could engage less conventionally, and therefore partly unselfconsciously, with those areas in which individual moral choice, social forces, and universal "fate" all intersected. (SLG)

4825. Gossman, Lionel. "Literary Scholarship and Popular History." *ECS* 7:133-42. The attempt to consider the 18th century as a unity and the proposal that it be considered "from the bottom up" (East Central Regional Conference of the American Society for 18th Century Studies, 3rd annual meeting, 1972) is questionable from the point of view of the literary scholar on two counts: in general, it is by no means clear how different historical series (history of literature, political history, history of technology, etc.) are related, and in the particular case of literature, it is likely that the folk culture and the literate culture constitute two distinct systems which cannot be considered as a single whole. Indeed, the literate culture of the 18th century in Europe emphasized discontinuities and especially the barrier between it and popular culture. In the end, it may appear questionable whether "18th-Century Studies" themselves are a valid field of inquiry. (LG)

4847. Ogden, John T. "From Spatial to Aesthetic Distance in the Eighteenth Century." *JHI* 35:63-78. The concept of distance received the attention of 18th-century English scientists, poets, and philosophers. Their treatment extended its meaning beyond a concept of space and time to include psychological and esthetic meanings. The expanding meaning of distance may be understood in the context of the changing understanding of space and time in the philosophies of Locke, Hume, and Kant. Distance provided the 18th century with a means of exploring the relationship between subjective and objective realms of experience. (JTO)

4849. Palmer, Nancy and Melvin. "English Editions of French *contes de fées* Attributed to Mme d'Aulnoy." *SB* 27:227-32. In spite of an English vogue for French fairy tales in the early 18th century, the bibliography of the French *conte de fée* in England has remained confused. Part of the confusion has resulted from the fact that a 1699 collection of fairy tales is regarded today as a bibliographical ghost. There are reasons to believe, however, that the book did in fact exist and that it contained four fairy tales, all by Mme d'Aulnoy. The main obstacle to an accurate account of the French fairy tale in England, though, is the fact that 28 of the tales attributed in England to Mme d'Aulnoy are by 4 other French authors. This study tabulates the contents of the four collections attributed to Mme d'Aulnoy and indicates correct authorship of the fairy tales they contain. (NBP & MDP)

4857. Smyser, Jane W. "The Trial and Imprisonment of Joseph Johnson, Bookseller." *BNYPL* 77:418-35. The Law Reports in the London *Times* of 1798-99 and Howell's *State Trials* are the chief means by which the confusion and obscurity hitherto surrounding Johnson's trial and imprisonment can be dissipated. The government's prosecution of Johnson was perhaps the most important in a chain of convictions against Gilbert Wakefield for writing *A Reply to Some Parts of the Bishop of Landaff's Address to the People of Great Britain* and against three London booksellers, Johnson, John Cuthell, and Jeremiah S. Jordan, for selling the *Reply.* The story, with all its ramifications, is in itself an interesting and cautionary tale; it shows that Johnson, whether free on bail or imprisoned, lost none of his eminence and power in the eyes of such writers as Coleridge and Wordsworth. (JWS)

4864. Winter, David. "Girtin's Sketching Club." *HLQ* 37: 123-49.

In 1799 a group of young artists whose chief member was the watercolorist Thomas Girtin formed a sketching club whose purpose was to establish in England a school of historic landscape painting by the selection of subjects from poetry. The group drew from contemporary poetry and literature and the selections show the members' tastes to lie with the naturalistic rather than the ideal. Their procedure coincides with the theories of Lessing, Burke, and Reynolds, as well as a larger movement in the 18th century that associated painting and poetry. In a new twist to the doctrine of *ut pictura poesis* it was the quality of poetic imagination that the club sought to appropriate, and its practice places the club firmly within the early development of Romantic landscape painting. (DW)

4865. Winton, Calhoun. "Recent Studies in the Eighteenth Century." *SEL* 14:458-75. [Rev. art.]

Discusses the major scholarship and criticism published on the literature of the Restoration and the 18th century during 1973 and early 1974. (CW)

Biography and Autobiography. 4872. Korshin, Paul J. "The Development of Intellectual Biography in the Eighteenth Century." *JEGP* 73:513-23.

Biographers before 1700 seldom focused on a subject's intellect, except for occasional fleeting observations. And the large biographical compendia of the century after 1700 yield little of this. The modest 18th-century beginnings of intellectual biography may be found in the neglected tradition of the *ana*-book, a nearly forgotten genre which started in the Renaissance and flourished in the 17th and 18th centuries. They are primarily collections of the sayings of the learned, intended to present a comprehensive picture of the thought of a single famous individual, usually a scholar or humanist. The style of inquiry these books fostered continues to actuate modern biography. (PJK)

4873. Rogers, Pat. "The Memoirs of Wharton and Samens: Authorship and Authority in Eighteenth-Century Biography." *BNYPL* 77:224-35.

It is necessary to study the provenance of historical sources such as political biography with the same care accorded to manuscript and archive sources. An illustration is provided by the frequent citation of the *Memoirs of Wharton* (1715) as the work of Richard Steele. In fact, both this biography of Thomas, Lord Wharton, and a parallel work dealing with John, Lord Somers (published 1716) can be identified on a variety of grounds as the work of the Whig historian and miscellaneous writer John Oldmixon. It follows that the books should be regarded, not as authoritative inside studies, but as offshots of the Whig pamphleteering industry of the day. (PR)

Criticism. 4875. Bogel, Frederic V. "Structure and Substantiality in Later Eighteenth-Century Literature." *SBHT* 15:143-54.

English literature of the later 18th century is dominated by an awareness of the insubstantiality of experience. For some writers, like Burke, it is the substantiality of the external world that is threatened; for others, like Boswell, it is primarily the self. For Sterne, it is both. Substantial experience is often expressed by structural patterns related to paradox, but the later 18th-century concern with insubstantiality finds expression in patterns of a different kind: patterns of doubleness (like dilemma and contradiction) and of singleness (in which one of two terms usually existing in tension is elaborated while the other is suppressed). Underlying these structural patterns is a mode of vision that is destructive of substantial experience. In the later 18th century, the Augustan effort to recover the substantial paradoxes of the Renaissance is abandoned and, in effect, each half of a formerly paradoxical union is independently pursued. (FVB)

Drama and Theater. 4886. Rogal, Samuel J. "Thomas Lowndes' 1777 Listing of Dramatic Works." *RECTR* 13,i:53-58.

The 1777 London edition of *The Dramatic Works of Colley Cibber* contains two lists—found in the first and fourth volumes, respectively—of books, collections, and plays printed for Thomas Lowndes (1719-84) in Fleet Street. The list in volume one comprises 212 items, of which only 18 are works of dramatic literature. The one in the fourth volume contains 111 single volume plays to sell at 6d. each; of these, 86 belong to the period between 1660 and 1777.
SJR

Periodicals. 4892. Fairer, David. "Authorship Problems in *The Adventurer*." *RES* 25:137-51.

New manuscript material makes it possible to supplement existing knowledge as to the authorship of several *Adventurers* and to suggest answers to a few problems of identity created by the paper. Bonnell Thornton's authorship of the "A" papers finds support in a letter from Joseph Warton written three days after the first "A" paper; the letter from "Night" in no. 27 was probably contributed by Catharine Talbot; Elizabeth Carter is almost certainly the problematical "authoress" and Johnson's second "friend," and papers 33 and 42 should perhaps be assigned to her. An unpublished letter shows that the "Z" papers were not solely the work of Joseph Warton but were considered something of a family enterprise: his brother Thomas shared the authorship of no's 51 and 57 (possibly contributing no. 71 himself) and their young governess-sister Jane is the most likely author of the controversial 87th paper. Prints for the first time from manuscript the letter from John Payne to Joseph Warton, 2 Feb. 1754, and proves that Jane Warton was the anonymous author of *Letters Addressed to Two Young Married Ladies, on the Most Interesting Subjects* published by Dodsley in 1782. (DF)

4897. Tierney, James E. "*Museum* Attributions in John Cooper's Unpublished Letters." *SB* 27:232-35.

Although scholarship has for some time credited Cooper with a large role in the production of Dodsley's *Museum; or Literary and Historical Register*, the evidence for such a judgment has been slim. Examination of the author's unpublished correspondence with Dodsley certifies Cooper's prolific contribution to the periodical. Under the pseudonyms, "Philaretes," "Musophilus," and "Philoptochus," Cooper contributed 19 essays and 3 poems to the *Museum*, as well as another essay which appeared without a by-line. (JET)

Poetry. 4901. England, A.B. "Further Additions to Bond's Register of Burlesque Poems." *SB* 27:236-40.

Six poems which are not included in the "Register of Burlesque Poems" at the end of Bond's *English Burlesque Poetry 1700-1750* (New York, 1932; reissued 1964) are described and their bibliographical details are given. (ABE)

4906. Rizzo, Betty. "Found:Joseph Lewis, Elusive Author of *Mother Midnight's Comical Pocket-Book*." *BNYPL* 77:281-87. [Foll. by Arthur Sherbo, "Another Reply, This Time to Betty Rizzo," 288; and Editor's Note, 289–90.]

Mother Midnight's Comical Pocket-Book (1753), a sixty-four-page pamphlet of comic, satiric, and romantic verses and songs, is derived from Mrs. Midnight's (Christopher Smart's) successful periodical *The Midwife* (1750-53). The verses in the pamphlet use themes and techniques of Smart and although one poem, "The Author's Acrostic," provides the signature "Joseph Lewis," Arthur Sherbo has attributed the pamphlet to Smart because of internal evidence and because no Joseph Lewis had been found to exist. However, there is an interesting letter in the British Museum from Lewis to Goldsmith (1773) providing clues that Lewis was indeed the author of the pamphlet. A reply by Arthur Sherbo and an "Epigraph" by the journal editor are published following the article. (BR)

Prose Fiction. 4923. Sherbo, Arthur. "A Postscript to *Studies in the Eighteenth-Century English Novel*." *JNT* 4:226-32.

In *Studies in the Eighteenth-Century English Novel* (East Lansing, 1969) Sherbo attempted to show that certain phrases and turns of phrases that had been characterized as idiosyncratic of one or another 18th-century novelist (Defoe and Fielding particularly) were actually part of a long tradition of narrative, one which even extends to today. In this Postscript he adduces further evidence, in the form of a number of additional examples, both from prose and poetry, of what in his original study he called the economical statement, the identifying parenthetical statement, and the disclamatory parenthetical statement. The longevity and similarity of these statements conduces to the belief that they are traditional rather than idiosyncratic. (AS)

4928. Wolff, Cynthia G. "The Problem of Eighteenth-Century Secular Heroinism." *MLS* 4,ii:35-42.

When, in the 18th century, the secular world began to dominate literature, religious options for heroism were no longer available to authors wishing to describe strong women. The turning point might be Richardson's *Grandison*, which postulates marriage as woman's goal. Novels after *Grandison* accepted this domestication of women and developed a language of sentiment to describe their heroines. The difficulties thus presented to authors who wished to portray strong heroines can be demonstrated by Austen's problems in rendering Emma. (CGW)

Satire. 4930. Bloom, Edward. "Apotropaic Visions:Tone and Meaning in Neoclassical Satire." *HLQ* 38:35-52.

Authorial detachment in satire is illusory, for its ultimate effect depends on persuasive observation of the follies and vices being criticized. Satire may be regarded as analogous to propitiatory sacrifice. Vicariously it is an instrument of disintegration through which the discomfiture, even destruction, of a scapegoat is intended paradoxically to reintegrate a community fragmented by shame and guilt. This apotropaic purpose depends for success upon a language and tone that the reader may be urged to relate to regenerative goals. The measure of good satire is good intention well and amply argued. (EAB)

4932. Lockwood, Thomas. "On the Relationship of Satire and Poetry after Pope." *SEL* 14:387-402.

During the later 18th century, the idea of "poetry" and the idea of "satire" increasingly come to be treated as incompatible, in theory and practice both. The various answers to the famous question of whether Pope was truly a poet indicate how two different definitions of poetry could produce different answers to the question of the status of satiric poetry as poetry. As the idea of "true" poetry narrows in the late 18th century to exclude satiric poetry, and as the idea of "poetic" begins to crystallize as the opposite of "prosaic," satiric poetry itself undergoes a kind of identity crisis. The result in the satiric poetry of this period is a general lack of confidence in the traditional assumptions of the genre. Some of this poetry entertains self-conscious doubts about the validity or efficacy of satire, thus moving in the direction of satire-satirized; other satiric poems increasingly incorporate the newer styles of "true" poetry—either as the object of ridicule, in parody, or seriously, thus bringing about a strange mixture of conventions. (TL)

Translation. 4934. Kent, John P. "The *Diable Boiteux* in England:The Tonson Translation and the Fake Chapter." *PBSA* 68:53-63.

Lesage's *Diable boiteux*, published by the Widow Barbin early in 1707, was a success, with a second and third impression required within the year and a completely new edition in 1726. There were at least ten editions in English during the 18th century, two of which were published by Jacob Tonson, one in 1708 and the translation of the revised version in 1729. The Tonson products are important for two reasons: one, they endured; two, in both there is a chapter which is a fake, that is to say has no original from which it was translated, a chapter which is a figment of the ingenious translator's imagination. The fake chapter has been continually reprinted, most recently in 1927. The Tonson version, despite the illegitimate chapter, is a good translation; vigorous and colloquial, it deserves the popularity with which it has been received. (JPK)

Addison. 4935. Rogal, Samuel J. "Joseph Addison (1672-1719):A Check List of Works and Major Scholarship." *BNYPL* 77:236-50.

This checklist contains the primary works attributed to Addison —including his contributions to periodicals—and critical and

biographical commentary published from his death to the present. (SJR)

4938. Salter, C.H. "Dryden and Addison." *MLR* 69:29-39.

Addison's views on drama, wit, ballads, *Paradise Lost*, and the "Pleasures of the Imagination" are summarized. They were largely anticipated by Dryden whose influence he tried to conceal. In particular, pleasure and imagination are the cardinal ideas of Dryden's criticism. Various recent attempts to represent Addison as substantially influenced by Bacon, Descartes, Hobbes, and Locke, and as the founder of Romantic or psychological criticism, are mistaken. Addison is commonly an Ancient, Dryden a Modern. (CHS)

Akenside. 4940. Smith, Lyle E. "Akenside's 'A British Philippic':New Evidence." *PBSA* 68:418-27.

Akenside's "A British Philippic" exists in three versions, each containing substantive variants; but only two of the three texts are unmistakably filiated. Textual as well as circumstantial evidence suggests that the poem printed in the *Gentleman's Magazine* is the earliest version, the one printed in folio titled "The Voice of Liberty; or, A British Philippic" is its middle version, and the one printed in folio titled "A British Philippic" is its final version. (LES)

Blake. 4949. Adamson, Arthur. "Structure and Meaning in Blake's 'The Mental Traveller'." *Mosaic* 7,iv:41-58.

The structure of Blake's "The Mental Traveller" is a metaphor for historical processes, the "creator" a male, the "created" a female. Time reversals indicate the separation of mind and body, time and space, humanity and nature, etc.. as they are manifested in culture. Historical cycles correspond to human psychology. Blake's insight regarding a movement from the "corporeal" to the "mental" is metaphorically identical to Spengler's theory of history in *The Decline of the West*. The poem moves through two cycles of a larger one, from a primitive-pastoral setting and state of mind to the rational-civilized ones. Man moves from a body womb to a mental womb, from nature and garden to society and city, both states being containment by the female. (AHA)

4953. Baine, Rodney M. and Mary R. "Blake's 'The Marriage of Heaven and Hell,' Plate 9." *Expl* 32:Item 50.

Among Blake's paradoxes in *The Marriage of Heaven and Hell*, perhaps the most misunderstood is the Proverb of Hell "The tygers of wrath are wiser than the horses of instruction." Throughout *The Marriage* Blake insisted that every animal, and by implication every man, should remain true to his own individuality. Tigers are not wiser than horses; but tigers which follow their own wrathful nature are wiser than perverted "horses of instruction," which do not. (RMB & MRB)

4956. Blaydes, Sophia B. "Blake and Smart as Poets of Vision." *WVUPP* 21:23-35.

The works of Smart and Blake were rejected by their age because of the poets' ideas. Smart's visions of joy and harmony cast him as a religious enthusiast, a threat and embarrassment to society. Blake's vision, that man's creativity freed man from the restraints of law and tradition, cast him as a dangerous non-conformist. Blake's visions came from private inspirations. Smart's came from God's works—the Bible and nature. In Smart's *Song to David* and "Reason and Imagination" and Blake's *Marriage of Heaven and Hell*, they explain their visions. Both applaud man's imagination, but Smart believed that man's imagination needed reason's anchor. While Blake valued man's imagination, he rejected reason because it restricted and destroyed man's energy and creativity. Both poets and their visions are accepted today; their isolation from the late 18th century has helped to define its rigidities and to suggest a flexibility in our own. (SBB)

4957. Borck, Jim S. "Blake's 'The Lamb':The Punctuation of Innocence." *TSL* 19:163-75.

Most 18th- and early 19th-century grammarians argue that punctuation should be interpreted in a rhetorical fashion in order to assist the reader's understanding of the poem. Yet the two most frequently used modern editions of Blake's works reflect differing editorial approaches to the complex problem of presenting a readable text, Keynes's regularizing Blake's punctuation and Erdman's adhering to a completely faithful copy. Thus two texts are presented which admit different readings of the same poem, particularly when read within the context of 18th- and 19th-century theories about the utility of punctuation. If these theories are applied to a reading of Blake's "The Lamb," Keynes's text is not as helpful as is Erdman's, especially if the poem's complex syntax is interpreted in conjunction with its logical syllogisms, difficult rhymes and consonances, and imagistic progressions. (JSB)

4958. Carey, Frances A. "James Smetham (1821-1889) and Gilchrist's *Life of Blake.*" *BlakeN* 8:17-25. [Illus.]
The spiritual intensity of Smetham's visual art was compared by Rossetti with that of Blake, and it was this affinity that prompted him to recommend Smetham as a draftsman for Gilchrist's *Life of Blake*, then later, to suggest the incorporation of Smetham's review of the *Life* in the second edition. The relationship between Smetham and Blake is perhaps most eloquently expressed by the unofficial cycle of marginal illustrations with which Smetham annotated his own copy of Gilchrist in 1867. These miniature pen drawings were conceived by the artist as *monuments* to his thoughts. For Smetham *monumentalism* operated as a commentary on the life of Blake beneath which was concealed his own spiritual history. (FAC)

4961. Connolly, Thomas E. "*Songs of Innocence*, Keynes (1921) Copy U, Keynes-Wolf (1953) Copy U." *BlakeN* 7:88-89.
This copy of Blake's *Songs of Innocence*, located in the Houghton Library at Harvard University, has been hitherto inaccurately described. Two pulls of pl. 29 "The Little Black Boy" as well as one pull each of three plates of *Experience* (pl. 29 Title page to *Experience*, pl. 30, "Introduction" to *Experience*, and pl. 37 "The Chimney Sweeper" of *Experience*) are included in this copy. Also bound in this volume are excerpts from the "Prologue" to *The Canterbury Tales* with modernized versions on facing leaves. The copy and further pencil notes are described. (TEC)

4971. Essick, Robert N. "Blake in the Marketplace, 1972-73." *BlakeN* 7,iii(1973-74):52-59.
The 1972-73 sales of works by Blake and his circle showed some decline in quality compared to 1971 but a considerable increase in quantity. Blake's commercial engravings are attracting greater interest partly out of necessity as the more important works become scarce. (RNE)

4974. —— "*Jerusalem* 25:Some Thoughts on Technique." *BlakeN* 7,iii(1973-74):64-66.
In *BlakeN* (1972) Dierdre Toomey reports the discovery of three states of plate 25 of Blake's *Jerusalem*. In all probability the variations in black relief lines are due to differences in inking and printing rather than intentional changes on the copperplate, and thus do not constitute different states. There is no easy means of adding new relief lines to a relief etching, and even if Blake had known such a method he would not have used it to produce the minor changes Toomey describes when he left unrepaired the large erased areas on *Jerusalem* plate 3. (RNE)

4977. Fletcher, Ian,ed. "John Todhunter's Lectures on Blake, 1872-1874." *BlakeN* 8:4-14. [With introd.]
In January 1960 some of Todhunter's literary manuscripts were presented to the University of Reading. Among the unpublished manuscript material at Reading are four lectures on Blake which form part of a cycle on the English poets delivered at Alexandra College, Dublin. In these lectures, dated 31 October 1872, 5 November 1872, 10 March 1874, and 12 March 1874, Todhunter identifies Blake's avant garde qualities and presents a synthetic view of Blake's moral vision. (IF)

4980. Goslee, Nancy M. " 'In Englands green & pleasant Land':The Building of Vision in Blake's Stanzas from *Milton.*" *SIR* 13:105-25.
Often miscalled "Jerusalem," the untitled lyric Blake included in the two earlier copies of *Milton* in fact anticipates the direction taken by his two final prophetic books, *Milton* and *Jerusalem*. In the lyric, Blake uses more public symbols than in those longer visionary works to dramatize the speaker's turn from a private questioning to a public assertion of vision. Blake shows the speaker's attempts to realize prophetic vision in the actual landscape of "Englands . . . Land." The speaker's fusion of diverse traditional sources into his own image of poetic power suggests a way of moving beyond the "dark Satanic Mills" to the

building of Jerusalem "here." (NMG)

4983. Green, Richard G. "Blake and Dante on Paradise." *CL* 26:51-61.
Dante and Blake share conceptions of recaptured beatitude which are at times strikingly similar. The Redeemed of Blake's prophetic writings as well as the souls in the *Paradiso* are depicted as flame-enclosed, and for both writers the flames are an index of the fusion of emotional passion and mental cognition, two human attributes which are severed in the "fallen" world of mortality. Blake, like Dante, furthermore regards the fire as an emblem of the love and mutual self-sacrifice which is ubiquitous throughout Eternity, in the same way that self-directed appetite, personified by Blake's "Spectre" and by Dante's lion and she-wolf in the opening canto of the *Inferno*, blocks man's quest for divine illumination. Blake and Dante view Paradise as a timeless, spaceless realm, in which incessant energy coexists with repose, in which each moment perpetually resurrects itself as an Immediate and hence Eternal Now, in which man's mind has willed itself into a restoration of his true humanity and physicality, and in which all seemingly inanimate objects represent his physicality, which comprehensively constitutes the body of Christ encompassing all creation. (RGG)

4986. Helms, Randel. "Ezekiel and Blake's *Jerusalem*." *SIR* 13:127-40.
Blake's *Jerusalem* is related to the Book of Ezekiel. Following Ezekiel, Blake patterns his poem after a three-part structure depicting the moral and physical decay of Albion, his entanglement in a "War of Blood" with Lucah (France), and the imaginative labors of Los to restore him to his former unity. But Blake's use of Ezekiel is also ironic. He deliberately reverses some of Ezekiel's geography, and pointedly disavows Ezekiel's call for sacrifices in the new Temple. To Blake, Jerusalem will be restored not by "Laws of Sacrifice for Sin" but by the labors of the inspired imagination. (RH)

4987. —— "Proverbs of Heaven and Proverbs of Hell." *Paunch* 38:51-58.
Many of the Proverbs of Hell in William Blake's *Marriage of Heaven and Hell* are ironic inversions or satiric imitations of proverbs in the Old Testament. This essay lists and discusses the particular examples. (RH)

4988. Hoover, Suzanne R. "The Public Reception of Gilchrist's *Life of Blake.*" *BlakeN* 8:26-30. ["Gilchrist's *Life*:A List of Reviews and Articles," 31.]
Gilchrist's *Life of Blake* (1863) took the form of a polemic, presenting Blake as the victim of unjust neglect by his own and succeeding generations; readers of the book were strongly challenged to make a new assessment. Seventeen reviews are known to have been published before 1866. The majority of these assessments were favorable, in spite of widespread reservations. Among Blake's works included in the biography, the *Songs of Innocence* and *Illustrations of the Book of Job* were most highly praised. Toward the end of the 1860s several articles and quasi-reviews appeared in other periodicals. (SRH)

4992. Johnson, Mary Lynn. "Emblem and Symbol in Blake." *HLQ* 37:151-70.
Blake's adaptation of allegorical figures and motifs in emblem literature to his own symbolic purposes brings into being a point of contact between allegory and myth, emblem and symbol. Blake's transfiguration of the emblem is evident in the contrast of his "Aged Ignorance" from *The Gates of Paradise* and the Rose, Sunflower, and Lilly from *Songs of Experience* with traditional treatments of these figures. Blake fuses allegories of Sense versus Faith and Time versus Love in his design of Aged Ignorance clipping the wings of visionary Youth. Against the tradition that Cupid willingly wounds himself on the thorns of love, Blake's "My Pretty Rose-tree" ridicules Petrarchan masochism and sexual possessiveness. The emblematic sunflower represents the lover's longing for his beloved or the soul's desire for God; but in Blake's "Ah! Sunflower," aspiration itself is a form of confinement. In "The Lilly," an ironic reconsideration of the conventional lily surrounded by protective thorns, Blake presents the true stain on virginity as its defensiveness. Blake's wing-clipper, rose, sunflower, and lily are emblematic figures, but they are emblems with all the subliminal implications and resonances

of symbols. (MLJ)

4994. Keynes, Geoffrey. "The Blake Trust Gray Catalogue and the Blake Trust Facsimiles." *BlakeN* 7,iii(1973-74):64-66.
G.E. Bentley (*BlakeN* 24) questioned the accuracy of all the facsimiles of Blake's Illuminated Books issued by the Blake Trust because he had detected minor defects in the Catalog of the Tate Gallery exhibition of the Illustration to Gray's Poems. This catalog was a mass-produced volume in which the color plates were printed by a four-color offset machine process. Bentley's evidence is therefore irrelevant as a basis for criticism of the hand-colored facsimiles done for the Blake Trust. The Trustees are satisfied that these are as near true facsimiles as is possible. (GK)

4995. Lefcowitz, Barbara F. "Blake and the Natural World." *PMLA* 89:121-31.
Although most critics have stressed William Blake's "mystical" disdain for the phenomena of objective reality, his responses to nature are both frequent and varied. While not following any lineal order of development, these responses may be said to assume a hierarchical order once we examine them in their overall context. The hierarchy ranges from mere description of nature in a manner reminiscent of the 18th-century physico-theological poets through a consideration of nature as an aspect of human perception and an aspect of human will. Finally, nature may be transmuted into art through the shaping power of the imagination, or in Blakean terms, through an inward confluence of Los and Christ. (BFL)

4997. Macmillan, Malcolm K. "Dialogue Between Blake and Wordsworth." *BlakeN* 8,i-ii:38-41.
Before his mysterious disappearance 11 July 1889 Malcolm Kingsley Macmillan wrote a dramatic dialogue between Blake and Wordsworth. The dialogue was written in Rome before 17 April 1889 and left unfinished. In the dialogue Blake and Wordsworth meet in Elysium and engage in a dispute concerning the place of Nature, God, and the passions in their respective arts and the value of Lord Byron's poetry. (IF)

5004. Murray, Roger. "Blake and the Ideal of Simplicity." *SIR* 13:89-104.
Late Augustans felt simplicity resulted from restraint in ornament; but Blake worked out an alternate ideal of simplicity based on a sublime particularity variously associated with the Bible, Homer, Milton, Thomson, MacPherson, and mythic art in general. Blake abjured Augustan practice in particularity, metaphor, predication, and modification; and in general, content/style dualism, on which ornamentalist style theory was based. The prophetic works should be read not as naturalistically particular or ornamentally chastened verse, much less as prose or poetry manqué, but as poetry of particularized vision, poetry exhibiting the sublime simplicity of unadorned myth. (RNM)

5007. Pearcy, Roy J. "Blake's *Tyger* & Richard Crashaw's Paraphrase of Thomas of Celano's *Dies Irae*." *BlakeN* 7:80-81.
Blake's *Tyger* shows some marked similarities with Crashaw's *Hymn of the Church in Meditation of the Day of Judgment*. Both poems treat the same subject of divine wrath in the same metrical form, and there are further detailed correspondences in both diction and imagery. Blake certainly knew Crashaw's works, and may have recalled his *Hymn* when composing the *Tyger*. Recognition of the possible influence of the *Hymn* on the *Tyger* emphasizes the apocalyptic nature of the latter poem, and may help explain certain of its enigmatic images and its general thematic concerns. (RJP)

5008. Reisner, Thomas A. "Blake's 'To Tirzah'." *Expl* 33:Item 3.
The name of William Blake's mythological character Tirzah has been generally explained as a topographical reference to Tirzah, the capital of Israel and the earthly counterpart of the heavenly city, Jerusalem. Even E.D. Hirsch, who cites 1 Kings xv.11 and 34 in support of this derivation, however, confesses surprise at Blake's choice of Tirzah, rather than of Babylon, as the antithesis of Jerusalem. Blake's choice becomes clearer when the name is taken into account: *tirzah* in Hebrew means "kill," as in *Lo tirzah*, the commandment "Thou shalt not kill." This lexical sense accords well with the function of Tirzah in Blake's short lyric. The "mother of [our] mortal part," she symbolizes both man's natural

fear of death and the law which is its formulaic expression. It is Tirzah who binds man's soul in a corruptible body, by equating physical with spiritual extinction; and conversely it is Jesus whose death sets man free, by permitting him to be "Raised a Spiritual Body." (TAR)

5010. Roberts, Peter. "On Tame High Finishers of Paltry Harmonies: A Blake Music Review & Checklist." *BlakeN* 7:91-99.
Blake held strong views regarding musical creativity. He was antagonistic toward compositions not essentially simple and melodic. However, his prophetic overview indicated his recognition of the need for a marriage between the inspired and the rational. Musical settings of Blake texts and recordings currently available are surveyed and evaluated both from a tentative "Blakean" view and current musical standards. A checklist of published musical settings of Blake texts and commercial recordings is included. (PER)

5020. Taylor, Gary J. "The Structure of *The Marriage*: A Revolutionary Primer." *SIR* 13:141-45.
By Blake's time the primer had taken on the form of a pious elementary school book made up of woodcut illustrations, short poems, dialogues, hymns, proverbs, catechism, the Lord's Prayer, and the Ten Commandments. This veritable mosaic of piety may have influenced the mosaic form of *The Marriage*. This striking similarity between Blake's illustration of plate two and the so-called "Tree of Knowledge" frontispiece is but one instance of several parallels. (GJT)

5021. Taylor, Peter A. "Blake's Text for the *Enoch* Drawings." *BlakeN* 7:82-86.
Five of Blake's drawings after the apocryphal *Book of Enoch* have been explained by Allan R. Brown who sees them as reflecting the whole Blakean cycle. Brown, however, did not use the only translation of *Enoch* available to Blake, but one published some 85 years after Blake's death. Brown, in addition, took liberties even with this later text, by not indicating omissions and by interpolating some passages into others. The language of the later translation leads Brown to interpret some details of Blake's drawings in a way that Blake could not have intended. Furthermore, the recent discovery by John E. Grant of a 6th *Enoch* drawing will lead us to reformulate our notions about how the individual drawings relate to one another. (PAT)

5022. Trawick, Leonard. "Nature and Art in *Milton*: Afterthoughts on the 1973 MLA Seminar." *BlakeN* 7,iii(1973-74):67-68.
The 1973 MLA Seminar "Perspectives on Blake's *Milton*," based on five papers published in *BlakeS*, skirted the poem's expression of Blake's critical or esthetic ideas. Blake believes that reality is mental, and the corporeal world exists only "in the mind of a fool." Nevertheless, the senses are the necessary vehicles of thought and vision. Jesus, "the imagination in every man," incarnates the ineffably spiritual into sensuous form that can lead man to salvation. Milton's descent in Blake's poem parallels Christ's incarnation; the struggle, purification, and reunion with his emanation that Milton undergoes constitutes Blake's separation of the eternal, valid parts of Milton's life and work from the parts marred by esthetic and doctoral error. (LMT)

5026. Wardle, Judith. " 'Satan not having the Science of Wrath, but only of Pity'." *SIR* 13:147-54.
In his *Essay on Epic Poetry* Hayley praises political and literary freedom, but he takes the conventional view that "British Freedom" was established in 1688; and although he rejects "System" in literary theory, much of the poem deals with the rules of epic poetry. His long discussion of epic "machinery" is self-contradictory and inconclusive. In rejecting satire and all forms of allegory, Hayley opposes Blake. Hayley's idea of epic is a poetic version of the sentimental novel, pathetic but not sublime. (JFW)

5029. Williams, Porter, Jr. " 'Duty' in Blake's 'The Chimney Sweeper' of *Songs of Innocence*." *ELN* 12:92-96.
Although "The Chimney Sweeper" of *Innocence* is one of Blake's finest expressions of visionary joy, doubts are sometimes raised over the tone of the admonitory lines associating the spiritual security of the sweepers with their efficient performance of cruel duties. Actually the disturbing lines ironically express Blake's indignation and compassion. From the viewpoint of the enslaved

children, the sweeper's advice about duty is realistic and kind, but a reader should feel Blake's shock over conditions which make such advice necessary. Later works support this reading and reinforce several attitudes toward duty implicit in the song. (PW)

5030. Wilton, Andrew. "A Fan Design by Blake." *BlakeN* 7,iii(1973-74):60-63.
Publishes a watermark on the reverse of a known Blake drawing in the British Museum, hitherto thought to be by another hand. Wilton associates the design particularly with illustrations engraved by Blake after Stothard in about 1782 and proposes that year as the approximate date of the drawing. (AW)

Boswell. 5038. Lustig, Irma S. "Boswell and the Descendants of Venerable Abraham." *SEL* 14:435-48.
Among many other evidences of Boswell's religious curiosity is his attendance at the two major London synagogues 3 and 4 April 1773. His responses to the services changed markedly from distaste and condescension to sympathy for the "outcast" congregants. Boswell's attitudes raise biographical and historical questions to which answers are sought in contemporary records, diaries, letters, and pamphlets. A review of Hebrew ritual explains the "barbarisms" which the many other visitors also disdained, and a history of the Jews since the resettlement in England suggests why they were still exotica. (ISL)

5040. Nussbaum, Felicity A. "Boswell's Treatment of Johnson's Temper:'A Warm West-Indian Climate'." *SEL* 14:421-33.
In the *Life of Johnson* Boswell reconciles apparent inconsistencies in Johnson's personality without violating truth. Boswell exercises care to counteract the force of Johnson's violent temper by emphasizing his more endearing qualities. Manuscript revisions show Boswell's pattern of softening Johnson's conversational roughness and making his ferocity less offensive throughout the *Life*. Especially in shaping the journal account of a dinner at Dilly's, 15 April 1778, Boswell thoroughly rearranged the order of topics discussed in order to disclose how Johnson's alternating anger and kindness resembled an unpredictable tropical climate. Close study of the sources for the making of the *Life* and the manuscript revisions reveals that Boswell's structural changes provide an authentic pattern of balances. (FAN)

Butler, J. 5064. Johnson, Clifford "Joseph Butler, Laodicean Rationalist?" *MLS* 4,ii:78-85.
Butler's *Analogy of Religion* (1739) refutes the deists by showing that a "religion of nature" followed to its logical conclusion would coincide with Christianity; that is, Christianity is "analogous" to a system derived from reason. Butler is sometimes seen as being lukewarm because of his rationalizing approach, but actually his rationalism is necessary in order to meet the deists on their own ground. (CJ)

Cowper. 5073. Boyd, David. "Satire and Pastoral in *The Task*." *PLL* 10:363-77.
The underlying structural principle of *The Task* is the alternation of satiric and pastoral poetry. Whenever Cowper suspects his moral security to be threatened, he interrupts the *apologia* for pastoral withdrawal which is the professed subject of the poem, abandons the *persona* of a rural recluse, and adopts the antithetical role of a public satirist. The constantly shifting satiric vision of urban society in the poem, the tonal modulations, the rhetorical maneuvers, are all determined primarily by the histrionic demands of Cowper's self-presentation and by his attempt to disguise his pastoral withdrawal, actually a retreat from the moral complexities of society, as a superior mode of moral action. (DVB)

Defoe. 5083. Baine, Rodney M. "Daniel Defoe and *Robert Drury's Journal*." *TSLL* 16:479-91.
Since 1885, when S.P. Oliver argued that Robert Drury's *Journal* was a work of fiction, possibly by Defoe, most Defoe scholars have disagreed only on whether, as "Transcriber," Defoe merely revised Drury's account, or whether he created the entire work. Since the publication in 1961 of Secord's *Robert Drury's Journal* proved conclusively that much in the account was biographically

and historically accurate and could have come only from Drury himself, the theory that the work is Defoe's fiction is no longer tenable. Careful examination of the book, however, shows that the alleged similarities between it and Defoe's known work are conventional ones which could easily be matched in other contemporary writers. Moreover, striking differences in style and in ideas show that Defoe was neither author nor Transcriber. (RMB)

5097. Leranbaum, Miriam. "'An *Irony Not Unusual*':Defoe's *Shortest Way with the Dissenters*." *HLQ* 37:227-50.
A close study of Defoe's *Shortest Way* from various points of view shows that it is not properly a satire, but a "banter," or deception. A survey of general satiric practices reveals that Defoe's work only speciously conforms to satiric models, and a rhetorical analysis of his pamphlet indicates that it is organized so as to depart from its inflammatory polemical models only in degree of intensity, not for purposes of distortion or caricature. Defoe strove for authenticity and his contemporary readers ought to have been deceived. Defoe later named his particular models and an examination of these shows how closely he followed their particular phrasing and rhetoric. He himself calls the work a "banter" and an examination of this term and his other remarks about the pamphlet suggests that we do well to trust his own sense of its style and purposes and his reasons for refusing to include signals to its fictional character. A hoax of precisely a decade earlier that was highly successful in victimizing a High-Church spokesman may have given Defoe both the idea for his own hoax and (misleading) assurance of like success. (ML)

5100. McVeagh, John. "Rochester and Defoe:A Study in Influence." *SEL* 14:327-41.
Rochester was Defoe's favorite writer. His audacious witty thought impressed Defoe despite his notorious reputation as libertine and cynic and filtered into Defoe's mind where it can be seen in several of the latter's minor writings. There it clashed with the political optimism and religious belief which Defoe had been trained to accept and wished to believe in. The result is an amalgam of skepticism and faith which tug at one another and disturb the clarity of some Defoean writings and dominate the vision of man conveyed in the major novels. (JM)

5102. Mitchell, Velma M. "Charles Eaton Burch:A Scholar and His Library." *CLAJ* 16:369-76.
The Charles Eaton Burch Collection, acquired by Howard University in 1952, contains rare and interesting books about Defoe, eighteenth-century literature, and other men of letters. The Collection represents Burch as a teacher, bibliophile, and a scholar. There are copious notes for the classes in 17th- and 18th-century literature that he taught while also serving as Chairman of the English Department at Howard. Among the numerous rare editions in the Collection are volumes from many limited editions. A typical volume is copy 227 of 250 copies of the St. Giles Edition of Daniel Defoe. There are also present many of the fourteen articles, often containing new and valuable information about Defoe and also disproving findings of earlier scholars, that Burch contributed to the Defoe bibliography. Probably the most valuable item in the Collection is a hand-written manuscript which Burch hoped would be the definitive study of Defoe. (VEMM)

5105. Olshin, Toby A. "'Thoughtful of the Main Chance': Defoe and the Cycle of Anxiety." *HSL* 6:117-28.
A number of riddles about Defoe and his works continue to be intriguing. The question of irony in *Moll Flanders* is still being debated and the ending of *Roxana* has never fully satisfied the critics. Defoe's life, recently reconsidered by Sutherland, still appears to contain a number of surprising transitions. When Defoe's career and his fiction are viewed through the insights of psychoanalytic criticism, however, a unified pattern becomes evident: a strong oral drive which never received complete gratification appears to have produced a recurring state of intense anxiety relieved by a temporary satiety. This pattern is symbolically portrayed in the anxiety-ridden pattern of the lives of Moll and Roxana. A psychohistorical dimension becomes visible when one places Defoe in the early 18th-century setting of England's aggressive commercialism where trade frequently followed the same checkered pattern of wealth followed by

bankruptcy. (TAO)

5106. Peterson, Spiro. "Defoe in Edinburgh, 1707." *HLQ* 38:21-33.

An important autograph letter dated 6 May 1707, now on deposit in the Scottish Record Office, provides a rare glimpse of Defoe shortly after the Union Treaty went into effect. Although on the surface enigmatic, the letter gathers considerable historical and biographical significance when connected with the Union and Defoe's activities through the extant letters, memoirs, diaries, and newspapers. The background of the letter can be cautiously pieced together. Early in the year 1707, Defoe could view himself confidently as "perfectly unsuspected," but by April he was known in Edinburgh to be a hired agent employed by the English ministry to manage the Scots into an acceptance of legislative Union. The letter writer, John Sandilands, informs Sir John Clerk about a worrisome "paper bearing [Defoe's] Character." Certainly unfavorable, the Character must have been motivated, partly at least, by the discovery of Defoe's true role during the events leading to the Union. Strong reasons also exist to believe that the "paper" must be *The Review Review'd. In a Letter to the Prophet Daniel in Scotland*. (SP)

5108. Rogers, Pat. "Defoe as Plagiarist:Camden's *Britannia* and *A Tour thro' the Whole Island of Great Britain*." *PQ* 52(1973):771-74.

The main source for Daniel Defoe's *Tour* of Britain (1724-26) has usually been identified as John Mackey's *Journey* (1714-23). A much more important aid to Defoe was William Camden's *Britannia*, as edited by Edmund Gibson in 1695. Defoe raided *Britannia* in almost every portion of his work. Borrowing may take the form of paraphrase, metaphrase, or verbatim quotation. It may be acknowledged, but more commonly it is not. The most striking parallelisms involve a protracted theft from Camden or Gibson, though there may be a slight modification of details to cover up the theft. In one instance, Defoe prints word for word a section of Gibson's text, running to almost 1000 words. A close study of Defoe's borrowing habits reveals his ability to transform the material and make it his own. (PR)

5110. Siegel, Sally D. "Everyman's Defoe:Paradox as Unity in *Robinson Crusoe*." *Thoth* 14:51-56.

Critics tend to view Defoe's *The Life and Adventures of Robinson Crusoe* as a type of spiritual odyssey, adventure story, or economic treatise. A more inclusive interpretation that accounts for religion, adventure, and economics is suggested by focusing on Defoe's penchant for offering something to everyone as illustrated in his treatment of Crusoe's "original sin." (SDS)

Dodsley. 5120. Gray, James. "'More Blood Than Brains': Robert Dodsley and the *Cleone* Affair." *DR* 54:207-27.

Dodsley's tragedy *Cleone* opened at Covent Garden on 2 December 1758 in an atmosphere of controversy and excitement. Dodsley successfully combined his literary, editorial, diplomatic, and business talents in achieving this popular tour de force, even after Garrick had rejected the play as too "cruel, bloody and unnatural" for the tastes of a Drury Lane audience. Dodsley also consulted a succession of literary advisors, including Pope, Chesterfield, and Johnson, all of whom favored the piece. Johnson, who thought it contained "more blood than brains," nonetheless supported it warmly, even giving his advice at rehearsal and leading the applause on opening night. Critical opposition to *Cleone*, apparently headed or inspired by Garrick, failed to prevent the triumph of the piece, which won a special place in 18th-century theater history. (JG)

Fielding, H. 5131. Guthrie, William B. "The Comic Celebrant of Life in *Tom Jones*." *TSL* 19:91-105.

In *Tom Jones*, Fielding suspends his moral judgment and offers a comic celebration of life. Fielding's festive comic spirit controls the atmosphere of the novel, determines the narrator's attitudes toward characters and events, and shapes the traditional comic conclusion. In Fielding's comedy of celebration, the narrator and Tom Jones may be considered celebrants. The narrator establishes the festive atmosphere by extensive use of the feasting and drinking motifs, especially in combination with satire. The narrator's affirmative view of sexuality contrasts with Allworthy's

moralistic pronouncements. (WBG)

5139. Kropf, C[arl] R. "Educational Theory and Human Nature in Fielding's Works." *PMLA* 89:113-20.

Fielding was familiar with the major issues and theories treated in the educational literature of his day and also recognized that various theories of education found their basis in various theories of human nature, the raw material with which education deals. In *The Fathers*, one of Fielding's lesser known-plays, he assumes that education is all-powerful in forming character, but in *Joseph Andrews* the entire question of education and human nature is treated with ironic ambivalence. In *Tom Jones* education is irrelevant to character development, and the Nightingale episode reads like a specific reversal of the theme of the earlier play. In the course of these three works Fielding reverses his position, beginning with the assumption that human nature may be defined as a tabula rasa and concluding that human character is predetermined. In *Amelia* Fielding compromises between these extremes in a manner reminiscent of Locke's position in his *Some Thoughts concerning Education*. (CRK)

5142. Moss, Harold G. "Satire and Travesty in Fielding's *The Grub Street Opera*." *ThS* 15:38-50.

Fielding's *The Grub-Street Opera* contains an unusual and puzzling mixture of satire on Walpole, the Royal Family, and contemporary theater. The motives behind this combination of novelty in his attack on George II and imitativeness in his music and drama can be understood only in the light of contemporary censorship practice: like Gay in his ballad operas and the authors of *The Craftsman*, Fielding hoped to avoid conviction for libel by making possible for himself a defense should he be indicted. A "disguise" which amounted to extensive borrowing of music and lyrics from the popular musical entertainment of the time would have permitted Fielding to defend himself by arguing that his satire was only a travesty of other satires. (HGM)

5144. Olivier, Theo. "*Pamela* and *Shamela*:A Reassessment." *ESA* 17:59-70.

Both Fielding and Richardson are moralists and entertainers, albeit with different approaches. Critical preoccupation with Richardson's conscious moral purpose has closed our eyes to contemporary valuation of him as an entertaining writer. The structure of *Pamela* suggests a constant duality of intention toward Mr B.; this indicates that Richardson has woven a tale of suspense that is also amusing and moralistic. *Shamela* is overvalued as an exposé of *Pamela*; it is a slight, though amusing, piece of bawdy parody which soon loses sight of *Pamela* and develops toward the truly Fieldingesque strength of *Joseph Andrews*. (TO)

5147. Rundus, Raymond J. "*Tom Jones* in Adaptation:A Chronology and Criticism." *BNYPL* 77:329-41.

This study lists, describes, and evaluates 17 authenticated adaptations and cites a dozen more non-authenticated adaptations of Henry Fielding's *Tom Jones*, from George Colman's *The Jealous Wife* (1761) to Joan Macalpine's *Tom Jones* (1966), with particular attention given to comic operas by Poinsinet and Philidor (1765, 1766), Joseph Reed (1769), and Courtneidge and Thompson (1907 bicentennial); Pierre-J.-B. Choudard Desforges' two verse comedies (1782, 1787); Robert W. Buchanan's "Sophia" (1886); and John Osborne and Tony Richardson's film adaptation (1963). While recognizing the previous bibliographical and critical studies done by Carl Waldschmidt in 1906, by Wilbur Cross in *The History of Henry Fielding* (1918), by Lawrence Price in a 1942 *JEGP* article on the German stage adaptations, and by G. Ross Roy on the French stage adaptations (1970), the present study essentially completes and corrects Cross's bibliography and provides a critical evaluation of each authenticated adaptation. (RJR)

5148. Schonhorn, Manuel. "Heroic Allusion in *Tom Jones*: Hamlet and the Temptations of Jesus." *SNNTS* 6:218-27.

Tom Jones resembles Hamlet and can be seen as a surrogate of the Prince, for Fielding's hero embodies that one essential quality of the 18th-century Hamlet: filial piety. The performance of *Hamlet* that Tom watches in London, then, recalls for the reader that most positive trait which makes Jones a true measure of the Prince. In addition, Fielding's less than comic hero assumes the mantle of Jesus, not only because of his forty days in the wilderness beyond Paradise Hall, but because of his three temptations: Molly, Jenny, and Lady Bellaston. (MS)

5151. Stevick, Philip. "On Fielding Talking." *CollL* 1:19-33.

By his commentary in *Tom Jones*, Fielding draws the reader into an epistemological exercise, inducing the reader to share in knowing, in suspending judgment, and in framing individual events within the universal experience of mankind. In the process, Fielding creates a "voice" which is a remarkable imitation of spoken conversation. The "voice" creates its own authority, articulating the rules of the work in which that authority is contained; it creates the possibility of a peculiar kind of range, in which the vulgar and the elevated, the transitory and the classic, can all be contained; and it sustains itself by a constant play of "self-interference." (PS)

5152. Vopat, James B. "Narrative Technique in *Tom Jones*: The Balance of Art and Nature." *JNT* 4:144-54.

The narrative principle of Fielding's *Tom Jones* (1749) is to demonstrate the necessity of applying the control of art to nature. The principle is metaphorically represented in the description of Paradise Hall in which the values of art give order and meaning to natural energy. Tom's experiences in the novel restate the metaphoric implications of Paradise Hall. Life in *Tom Jones* is essentially predacious and the lesson of Tom's experience is that "Good Nature" must be balanced by self-control. However, it is the narrator himself who most fully embodies the art of control in the novel. The narrator's primary action is to create fictional order, to apply the framework of history to experience. It is the very consciousness of the narrator's own design which finally makes the statement of art in *Tom Jones* so compelling and convincing. (JBV)

Garrick. 5156. Allen, Ralph G. "*A Christmas Tale*, or, Harlequin Scene Painter." *TSL* 19:149-61.

In *A Christmas Tale*, Garrick's scene designer, P.J. DeLoutherbourg, reveals himself to be more than simply a facile creator of new stage spaces. His unusual paintings and bizarre lighting effects reveal his Harlequin ability for making tame fancies seem unpredictable and strange. DeLoutherbourg's skill was often his own subject, requiring only the slightest of literary supports. *A Christmas Tale*, indeed, was written to order to fit some scenes designed by him nearly a year earlier. (RGA)

5158. Tierney, James E. "The Dating of a Garrick Letter." *PBSA* 68:170-72.

In their standard edition of Garrick's letters Little and Kahrl misdate the actor's 14 October 1756 letter to Dodsley as 18 October 1759. This misdating is clear from both internal and external evidence provided by two other letters exchanged between the two men. The first, a letter from Dodsley to Garrick written on 18 October 1756, is obviously a response to this Garrick letter, for it quotes some of Garrick's words exactly. The second, a letter of 18 October 1756 from Garrick to Dodsley (Little and Kahrl recognize this date) certifies the date of the Dodsley letter as well as the chronology of the correspondence, for it, in turn, quotes exactly from the Dodsley letter. Since the Garrick letter in question was originally dated only "Thursday," it doubtless was written on the previous Thursday to Dodsley's; that is, on 14 October 1756. (JET)

Garth. 5159. Sena, John F. "Samuel Garth's *The Dispensary*." *TSLL* 15:639-48.

Garth's *The Dispensary* goes beyond attacking the apothecaries to comment on the moral quality of contemporary society. Garth adopted the mock-heroic form as an effective means of defining the values of his world. By placing contemporary men and events in the context of an heroic society and by viewing the disparity between the present situation and the classical ideal, he provided his readers with satiric perspective and a sense of proportion. The poem is replete with scientific lore, personal encomia, social observations, literary reflections, and descriptive passages of high poetic merit. Garth's personal commitment to the dispensary project, however, prevented any long lapses from the central theme, which resulted in a decline in *The Dispensary*'s popularity as interest in the apothecary-physician quarrel diminished. (JFS)

5160. ——— "The Letters of Samuel Garth." *BNYPL* 78:69-94.

Although Samuel Garth (1661-1719) achieved prominence in the 18th century as a physician, poet, and political activist, little is known of his personal life. This is largely attributable to the paucity of surviving documents. In fact, the only extant personal papers of Garth are these 31 letters. The letters constitute a primary source for biographical information. (JFS)

Gay. 5164. McIntosh, William A. "Handel, Walpole, and Gay: The Aims of *The Beggar's Opera*." *ECS* 7:415-33.

Though there is considerable parody of Italian opera and some political satire as well, the overriding concern of John Gay in *The Beggar's Opera* is with the foibles and vices of polite society. Mistakenly, critics for some two centuries have fantasized an enmity between Gay and Handel, when in fact the two men's friendship can be traced to the early 1720s when they, along with Pope and Arbuthnot, spent time with Chandos at Canons. Both belonged to the Burlington House coterie, and both are numbered among subscribers to the other's works. No less mistaken is the view that Gay was in open conflict with Walpole. Even if the minister had not subscribed to Gay's works and attended his plays, it is rash to suppose the playwright would do anything to provoke the man who could bring him absolute ruin. Gay's failure to secure preferment at court emerges as the most likely basis for the play, in which he attacks the society he felt had betrayed him. Despite his protestations of stoicism to Swift, Gay's appointment as gentleman usher to an infant changed his view of the world, and it is this new vision of vice and stupidity that lies beneath the comic façade of *The Beggar's Opera*. (WAM)

5166. Owen, Joan H. "*Polly* and the Choice of Virtue." *BNYPL* 77:393-406.

Though Gay's *Polly* has been largely ignored or briefly glossed as a sequel, the consonance of its dramatic and ethical integrity needs yet to be stated. The play, like the Second Series of *Fables*, exhibits Gay's need to resolve in a sequel the ambiguities of a first production. Here he returns to the ethical fable of *The Beggar's Opera*, the myth of Hercules' Choice between Virtue and Pleasure, which had been left suspended in Macheath's reprieve. This time, Gay makes Polly and Jenny iconic contestants in the Herculean fable by a clever dramatic allusion to Dryden's *All for Love*. The result is a novel revision in which Polly as Virtue becomes a militant strategist and judge of a mock Antony and Cleopatra. In Gay's creative iconography, Polly cast between a Man of Pleasure and a Man of Virtue suggests a new sexual democracy of ethical responsibility. (JHO)

5167. Rogers, Pat. "Satiric Allusions in John Gay's Welcome to Mr. Pope." *PLL* 10:427-32.

In 1720 Gay wrote a poem to welcome Pope back from Greece. This poem was suppressed for more than half a century. A reading of the verses in the light of contemporary attitudes toward George I suggests a reason for this long delay in publication. Gay constructs his work around the framework of a triumphal entry, such as George I had made in 1714 when he traveled to London from Hanover. In particular, Gay makes repeated play with the view that the King was an absentee monarch. Gay appears to write simply a friendly message of welcome to Pope; but at the same time he offers a veiled rebuke to the King for his slowness to return to his realm at this critical juncture. (PR)

Gibbon. 5169. Porter, Roger J. "Gibbon's *Autobiography*: Filling Up the Silent Vacancy." *ECS* 8:1-26.

While Edward Gibbon has usually been considered the epitome of stability and certitude, the man who marched through life with a clear direction, his *Autobiography* reveals a considerable regret, disappointment, and rationalization. He constantly worries that his commitment to a life reputedly conceived from the start as fixed and well-defined has been bought at the expense of other kinds of experience. His *Autobiography* seeks a focus in which his partial sense of loss may be seen in a perspective permitting him to accept his situation with tolerance, even when life does not live up to his hopeful image of it. His book dramatizes the reconciliation of a self-congratulatory tone with regret for what might have been. The language of natural decay gets into his writing about the self, suggesting he sees his own life in terms similar to those he uses about the Empire. His imagery and tone testify to a precarious balance, and he defends himself against an even more somber view of human nature than he does allow. (RJP)

5170. Trevor-Roper, H.R. "An Unpublished Letter of Edward Gibbon." *BLR* 9:100-01.
Transcript of, and brief comment on, a letter written 8 May 1762 by Gibbon from Blandford (where he was serving with the Hampshire militia) to Thomas Becket, his publisher and book supplier, ordering various books. (HRT-R)

5171. Voth, Grant L. "Gibbon and the Christian Soldier: Tonal Manipulation as Moral Judgment." *SEL* 14:449-57.
There is a distinct change in tone, from amused to judgmental, in Section v of Chapter xv of Gibbon's *Decline and Fall*. Gibbon manages this change in tone not so much by using different stylistic devices as by altering the manner in which he treats the early Christians. Where he earlier presents them as eccentric, in Section v he treats them as both normal and despicable in motivation and action. The metaphor which ties together the two tones is that of the Christian soldier; and it is precisely the point at which the soldier changes from defensive to offensive tactics that Gibbon ceases to be amused and begins to be judgmental. The change in tone is a weapon of attack and an explicator of the attack. (GLV)

5173. Ziegler, Robert J. "Edward Gibbon and Julian the Apostate." *PLL* 10:136-49.
In the second volume of *The Decline and Fall* Gibbon attempted to produce an impartial and balanced account of Julian the Apostate. This was a difficult objective: study of this emperor's life had customarily been partisan. Gibbon, however, maintained an independent posture, rejecting especially the anticlerical praise for Julian voiced by such freethinkers as Shaftesbury and Voltaire. Gibbon's Julian, despite some important differences, basically resembles that of la Bléterie, whose biography of the apostate was in accord with the clerical opinion of the 18th century. (RJZ)

Godwin. 5175. Hunter, Parks C., Jr. "William Godwin's Lengthy Preoccupation with *Antonio*." *KSJ* 23:21-24.
Godwin worked for a longer period on his blank-verse tragedy *Antonio, or the Soldier's Return* than has previously been recognized. The first mention of the play under the name "Antonio" appears in Godwin's Journal for 5 January 1799. It has been assumed that the play occupied Godwin's time for only 23 months. Instead, the first entry on the play in the Journal is for 26 June 1797, under the name "Alonzo." As such, the play partially occupied Godwin until 20 December 1798, when he completed the first draft. In its next stage, under the name of "Antonio," the revision occupied Godwin from 5 January 1799 to the end of the year. Godwin became obsessed with the revision of the play and worked almost exclusively on it during 1800. Preoccupied for the incredibly long period of three and a half years by a very poor play, Godwin became the victim of a totally unrealistic opinion of its worth. (PCH)

Gray. 5192. Hinnant, Charles H. "Changing Perspectives on the Past:The Reception of Thomas Gray's *The Bard*." *ClioW* 3:315-29.
Analysis of Gray's historical attitudes reveals that the complaints of his contemporaries concerning "The Bard" were based upon more than the poem's alleged obscurity. Although Gray shared many of the historical prejudices of 18th-century Englishmen, the poem's lack of success can be traced to his familiarity with earlier chronicles. Like most readers of his time, Gray viewed history as the story of liberty; the majesty of the bard's prophecy is deepened by the fact that he is the embodiment of patriotic virtue. But the minstrel's indictment of Edward's massacre of the bards offered nothing at the time to admirers of Edward's reign. Similarly, Gray's attempt to revive the historical myths of earlier eras made little sense to readers versed in mid-18th-century English history. (CHH)

5196. Jones, Myrddin. "Gray, Jaques, and the Man of Feeling." *RES* 25:39-48.
The allusion to Shakespeare's Jaques in the 26th stanza of Gray's "Elegy" plays an important part in establishing the nature and identity of the poet pictured there. Jaques is represented as both the melancholy man and the critic of society. 18th-century critics, actors, and painters also regarded him, favorably, as a "man of feeling": a solitary moralist, deeply moved by injustice. *As You Like It* became the period's favorite Shakespeare play, and the character of Jaques was altered to suit the age's predilection for the sentimental satirist. Gray's "Elegy," similarly, has denounced the arrogant and insensitive, and friends recognized, in the poet of the closing stanzas, characteristics common to both Gray and Jaques. The figure of Jaques thus images and unites all the elements Gray wishes to establish for his poet: the critic of society, the man of feeling, the solitary and anguished outsider, seeing and denouncing the pains and injustices of life with stern and compassionate clarity. (MMJ)

5201. Moore, Judith K. "Thomas Gray's 'Sonnet on the Death of Richard West':The Circumstances and the Diction." *TSL* 19:107-13.
The language of Gray's "Sonnet on the Death of Richard West" deliberately echoes and modulates the language of Gray's earlier "Noontide" and of Richard West's ode on the spring addressed to Gray, and thus parallels the sequence of communication and isolation that is the pattern of Gray's and West's correspondence. Gray's friendship with West functioned for Gray as a vital social bond, and the sonnet on West's death is a response to the alienation of the poet from the proper interdependence of society. The allusions of the poetic diction to love and harmony thus apply conventional themes ironically to the poet's unique situation, with the result that the formal poetic diction here serves quite personal and private ends. (JKM)

5203. Sugg, Richard P. "The Importance of Voice:Gray's *Elegy*." *TSL* 19:115-20.
Gray's "Elegy in a Country Churchyard" affirms the importance of the poetic voice in man's perennial quest for immortality. Personifications based on speech and hearing, and images and evocations of sound, emphasize the life/speech death/silence association. The speaker's praise of the "living lyre" and his allusions to other poets suggest the preeminence of the poetic voice among the sounds of life. Gray, by creating the independent voice of the "Elegy" to speak on the mortality of poets and the immortality of poetry, has made the "Elegy" his own epitaph. (RPS)

Hartley. 5208. Hatch, R[onald] B. "David Hartley:Freewill and Mystical Associations." *Mosaic* 7,iv:29-39.
Hartley's argument in *Observations on Man*—that all of man's actions and beliefs can be explained in physiological terms—led him to a mystical view of the "ultimate Happiness of all Mankind" and the "Necessity of human Actions." Hartley's philosophy takes him beyond the assumptions of British empiricism into ideas that are usually associated with early 19th-century Romantics. Hartley maintains that the doctrine of necessity does not oppose man's free will but is a component of freedom. Yet Hartley's belief led him to affirm that ultimately man is not a "real" cause, but a part of the "one only, infinite Cause." Hartley looked forward to the day when the discoveries of science would enable man to progress beyond "the Idolatry of the Creature" to a knowledge of his union with the universe. (RBH)

Hume. 5213. Colver, A. Wayne. "The 'First' Edition of Hume's *Essays and Treatises*." *PBSA* 68:39-44.
The Strahan ledgers cast considerable light on the circumstances leading to the publication of the first collected edition of Hume's philosophical writings and make it possible to account for the large number of variant issues that appeared between 1753 and 1756. Three of these issues are identified and described, including the earliest and the latest; the alleged delay in the publication of the second volume (containing the *Philosophical Essays concerning Human Understanding*) is also explained and doubt is cast on the possible existence of a 1754 printing of the *Philosophical Essays*. AWC

5218. Hay, Eldon R. "A View of Miracle—with Apologies to David Hume." *IR* 31,i:41-51.
Hume's remarks on miracle, satirical and critical, are found in the

well-known passage in *An Inquiry concerning Human Understanding*. These comments are used as the basis for a contemporary apologetic for the concept of miracle. Miracle happens now, or it does not happen at all. Mere reason is insufficient to convince us of the veracity of Christianity; yet faith is neither non-rational nor anti-rational. Apologetics distinguish miracle from nature in describing God's activity as *against nature* (contranaturalism), *beyond our present knowledge of nature* (preternaturalism), *above nature* (supernaturalism). The views of Macquarrie, Tillich, and Bultmann point to a more adequate view—personal, existential, significant. (ERH)

5223. Price, John V. "Hume's 'Account of Stewart':An Important Presentation Copy." *Bibliotheck* 6(1973):199-202.
In 1745 David Hume defended his friend Archibald Stewart, Lord Provost of Edinburgh, against charges of collaborating with Prince Charles Edward Stuart in the '45 Rebellion. He published anonymously a defense of Stewart, entitled *A True Account of the Behaviour and Conduct of Archibald Stewart, Esq*; Hume presented a copy to Stewart inscribed "By David Hume Esqr who was under great Obligations to Provost Stewart." This gesture recalled Hume's obligations to Stewart when he supported Hume in his application in 1745 for the Chair of Ethics and Pneumatical Philosophy at Edinburgh University. The presentation copy points to a closer relationship between the men than hitherto known. (JVP)

5224. —— "The First Publication of David Hume's *Dialogues Concerning Natural Religion*." *PBSA* 68:119-27.
David Hume's *Dialogues concerning Natural Religion* was published posthumously in 1779 in two editions. The first edition appeared without any imprint other than the date, while the second edition carried a London imprint. Hume had entrusted the publication of his work to Adam Smith and William Strahan, both of whom eventually declined to publish the work. The responsibility for publishing then fell upon Hume's nephew. Hitherto, scholars have thought that the first edition was printed in London and published by Robinson. New evidence indicates that the first edition of the *Dialogues* was published in Edinburgh, not in London, and that its publication was attended with more difficulties than heretofore known. (JVP)

Johnson, S. 5228. Amis, George T. "The Style of *The Vanity of Human Wishes*." *MLQ* 35:16-29.
Much of the power of Johnson's *Vanity* derives from its creation of a sense not simply of control, but of a controlling personality which unites the fragmented and non-linear structure of the poem. The metrical and syntactic structure of the couplets, and certain matters of diction, in particular, a high incidence of words derived from colloquial French rather than Germanic sources, contribute to this sense. It is thus heroic verse, but in particular, heroic speech, the voice of one who uses control and detachment to view unflinchingly the horrors of the human condition. The much-debated conclusion is the culmination of this enactment of heroism. It is a mature and austerely Christian rejection of both easy answers and despair, which limits reasonable "solutions" to the psychological. (GTA)

5232. Clayton, Philip T. "Samuel Johnson's *Irene*:'An Elaborate Curiosity'." *TSL* 19:121-35.
Analysis of Johnson's *Irene* as a Neoclassical tragedy, of its adherence to the rules concerning the three unities, *liaison des scènes*, and poetic justice, reveals that Irene is the play's heroine and not Aspasia as has been suggested. Multiple patterns of contrast emphasize the importance of Aspasia; however, Aspasia functions as a virtually immutable standard by which to judge Irene's tragic fall. Consideration of the play's adherence to the rules concerning unity of action and poetic justice clearly establishes Irene as the heroine. Although the cold diction of *Irene* probably vitiates its dramatic effect, nevertheless, its fundamental design is artful and sound. (PTC)

5233. Cormican, John D. "Samuel Johnson's Struggle with His Personality as Revealed in His Prayers." *BSUF* 15,iii:19-25.
Johnson's prayers revealed an awareness of the human weaknesses which marked his failure to live an absolutely Christian life and evoked feelings of guilt and fear. Johnson's real obsession was with reason; he was torn between his belief in man's

rationality and the necessity for a Christian to believe things beyond reason. Johnson's struggle with his sins made him aware that reason did not prevail in all aspects of his life. Similarly, the failure to control his sins and the awareness of his religious doubts made him fear death. Before his death, however, he made the "leap to faith" which allowed him to accept himself and the limitations placed on reason by the human condition. (JDC)

5237. Folkenflik, Robert. "Johnson and 'An Essay on Elegies'." *BNYPL* 77:189-99. ["A Reply" by Arthur Sherbo, pp. 200-04.]
Arthur Sherbo's attribution of "An Essay on Elegies" to Samuel Johnson is disputed. The style of the essay is not Johnsonian: neither diction nor syntax corresponds to the prose works of Johnson, and nothing accounts for such radical differences except the conclusion that "An Essay on Elegies" was not written by him. A reply by Arthur Sherbo is published following the article. (RF)

5243. Jemieliity, Thomas. "Samuel Johnson, the Second Sight, and His Sources." *SEL* 14:403-20.
Two possible sources for Johnson's analysis of the second sight in the *Journey to the Western Islands* are Martin's *Description of the Western Islands* and the pseudonymous *Treatise on the Second Sight* (Edinburgh, 1763). His at least indirect knowledge of the *Treatise* came from several of his Highland hosts who contributed incidents of, and opinions about, the second sight for the *Treatise*. Johnson, however, shares neither the avowedly polemic purpose of the *Treatise* nor its bias. Both men proceed similarly: definition, general characteristics, and objections. Their attitudes differ markedly: for Martin, second sight is fact, for Johnson, only possibility. (TJJ)

5255. Radner, John B. "Samuel Johnson, the Deceptive Imagination, and Sympathy." *SBHT* 16:23-46.
A number of Johnson's efforts as a practical moralist can be best appreciated if we keep in mind his claim in *Rambler*, 60 (1750) that "all joy or sorrow for the happiness or calamities of others" is produced by an act of imaginative projection. Johnson regarded sympathy as a major basis for what little virtue and happiness there is in human life. He neither argued that such sympathy proves that men are naturally benevolent nor claimed that all sympathy is utterly selfish. His psychological explanation for sympathy combines two analyses that were associated during his lifetime with the argument that sympathy involves no genuine concern for the welfare of others; but he was chiefly attracted to this explanation because it rooted sympathy in deliberate efforts of attention, reflection, and imaginative projecton, and not simply in passive sensibility. In urging readers to extend their compassion and overcome their envy, he assumed that every man can respond sympathetically to the feelings of others if, and only if, he thoughtfully projects himself into their situations. (JBR)

5256. Ramage, John D. "The Politics of Samuel Johnson:A Reconsideration." *SBHT* 15:221-40.
If one reassesses Samuel Johnson's politics, one must deal with Donald Greene's *Politics of Samuel Johnson*. While Johnson's early political views and actions served to promote the growth of democracy, his political thinking underwent a substantial change toward a more authoritarian view. (JDR)

5260. Siebert, Donald T.,Jr. "Johnson as Satirical Traveler:*A Journey to the Western Islands of Scotland*." *TSL* 19:137-47.
Johnson's *Journey to the Western Islands of Scotland* has been viewed both as a loosely organized travel book reflecting little more than scrupulosity of observation, and as a work with the subtleties and architectonics of literary art. Informing Johnson's chronological account is a clear sense of his privileged point of view, the vantage of the satirical traveler, who can see things as they are because he sees them without the blinders of theoretical expectation, national interest, or simply familiarity itself. Johnson exploited his unique position as an open-minded and open-eyed foreign visitor from London to create a travel book of satirical power, whose purpose, in the main, is to oppose fads and shibboleths. (DTS,Jr)

5261. —— "Johnson's *The Vanity of Human Wishes*, 79-90." *Expl* 32:Item 63.
In Johnson's poetry an amazing richness of detail always buoys up the grandeur of generality. In lines 79-90 of *The Vanity of*

Human Wishes, the ever-malleable and glittering frame of gold, adorning the "painted face" of the great statesman, is emblematic of the false standards of value the poem exposes. Johnson's synecdochic reduction of the great man to his portrait— later stripped of its honorific frame and degraded by kitchen grime and coarse jests—and the reduction of the great man's toadies to passive sheep poured in his door suggest that false ambition likewise shrinks men into things without free will, reason, and dignity. (DTS,Jr)

Lillo. 5278. Marshall, Madeleine F. "Millwood and Marwood:Fallen Women and the Moral Interest of Sentimental Tragedy." *Mary Wollstonecraft Jour.* 2,ii:2-12.
In the morality of sentimental tragedy, as exemplified in Lillo's *The London Merchant; or, The History of George Barnwell* and Lessing's *Miss Sara Sampson*, moral evil is real and complex. Lillo's Millwood and Lessing's Marwood strongly defend themselves and bitterly criticize the evil of the "good" people of the plays. As in sentimental comedy, where a carefully reserved exemplary heroine gains her desired ends, so in sentimental tragedy, virtue is right reason and rarely attained in this world. The fallen woman, formerly the butt of ridicule, is the victim of sexual injustice. According to Millwood, the male sex has made her an evil, mercenary woman. Marwood knows that she and Sara are alike victims of Mellefont. (MFM)

5279. Pedicord, Harry W. "George Lillo and 'Speculative Masonry'." *PQ* 53:401-12.
The success of Lillo's *The London Merchant* has continued to baffle critics. It is now possible to attribute the genesis, initial success, and long life of this domestic tragedy to the tradition, teachings, and constant active support of the Ancient Order of Free and Accepted Masons. Close study of the drama shows that the ballad plot, characterizations, and dialogue are paraphrases of ritual and lectures within the lodge hall. Subsequent success of the play on the Continent shows continued Masonic support through the enthusiasm of Diderot and Lessing, the latter a lodge member in Hamburg. (HWP)

Malone. 5285. Lancashire, Anne. "Warburton's List and Edmond Malone:A Non-Existent Relationship." *SB* 27:240-48.
Malone's 1778 list of 34 "ancient plays" which apparently had been preserved, by 1778, in name only, was not in part derived from Warburton's list of manuscript plays supposedly once in his possesison. Malone used other sources: especially the 1759 sale catalog of Warburton's books and manuscripts, and Malone's own annotated copy of Langbaine's *An Account of the English Dramatick Poets*. The first scholar to transcribe and publish Warburton's list was apparently George Steevens, who also seems to have contributed to Reed's *Biographia Dramatica* most of the information it contains on Warburton's plays and list. Finally, Steevens provided information suggesting that the present British Museum MS. Lansdowne 807 passed almost directly from Warburton's possession to that of William Petty, first Marquis of Lansdowne. (AL)

Manley. 5288. Snyder, Henry L. "New Light on Mrs. Manley?" *PQ* 52(1973):767-70.
There is a petition in the Sunderland manuscripts at Blenheim Palace signed by Maria Williamina Manley who would seem to be the writer Mary Delariviere Manley. Dated 24 December 1706, it carries the plea of the petitioner to the Queen for a pardon, so that she can be released from Newgate where she is imprisoned for debt. Evidence is provided to support the identification of the petitioner as the writer. If correct, it fills in a gap in Manley's life for which her biographers have not been able to account. (HLS)

Mason. 5289. Yost, George. "The Celtic and Dramatic Background of Mason's *Caractacus*." *RECTR* 13,ii:39-54.
English interest in first-century battles of the Celts and Romans involving the Celtic leaders Caractacus and Boadicea extended over a long period. After Fletcher's *Bonduca*, each succeeding play—Hopkins' *Boadicea*, Glover's *Boadicia*, and Mason's *Caractacus*—shows in its structure adaptations from its dramatic predecessor or predecessors. Fletcher makes a sympatic balance of the Celtic and Roman ancestors of the British and contrasts the magnanimous male and intransigent female Celtic leader. He establishes the practice of having a noble and villainous character on the same side of the conflict, as well as of having a chief in love with a British woman. Hopkins and Glover take one or the other of Fletcher's pairings or contrasts and make it the center of action. Mason discards the Celtic female leader and finds his paired opposites in two young Celtic men. (GY)

Mickle. 5291. Letzring, Monica. "Mickle, Boswell, Liberty, and the 'Prospects of Liberty and of Slavery'." *MLR* 69:489-500.
"Prospects of Liberty and of Slavery," an uncompleted poem by William Julius Mickle (1734-88) and the correspondence with James Boswell concerning it reveal the process by which Mickle developed the liberty theme that was to become significant in his major work, his translation of the Portuguese epic *The Lusiad*. The poem, on the model of such popular poems as Thomson's *The Seasons* and "Liberty," was to include historical narration, pictorial description, and moral generalization relevant to contemporary England. Mickle finally abandoned the poem, realizing that in his *Lusiad* he could develop the same theme on a grander scale using the same techniques but with greater assurance of favorable reception. Boswell, who had assisted Mickle with various literary and personal problems, was particularly interested in the "Prospects" because it was to include lines on the House of Auchinleck and on the Corsican struggle for independence with which he was then concerned. (ML)

North. 5292. Millard, P.T. "The Chronology of Roger North's Main Works." *RES* 24(1973):283-94.
After being in the custody of North's son until 1779, the collection of manuscripts by Roger North (1653-1734) disappeared. They surfaced again in the 1830s when one batch appeared in a country auction and another was discovered on sale as waste paper. Dawson Turner and James Crossley quarrelled over their possession and Crossley won. At Crossley's death they passed into public collections. Internal and external evidence reveals that North worked on his *Examen* c. 1710-13 and that the biographical works were in hand for sometimes as long as thirty years. In each case, however, a date can be established at which the work was in a reasonably finished state: *Francis North* 1714, *Dudley North* 1709, *John North* 1715, "General Preface" 1718, and the *Autobiography* post-1707. Quotations from North and Johnson illustrate the remarkable resemblance between the biographical theory of the two, although North wrote at least thirty-five years before Johnson. (PTM)

Pope. 5298. Aden, John M. " 'The Change of Scepters, and impending woe':Political Allusion in Pope's Statius." *PQ* 52(1973):728-38.
Pope's translation of the first book of Statius' *Thebaid* is a veiled allusion to the Revolution, the Jacobitical exile, the Williamite usurpation, the folly of those that promulgated these things, and the prospect of no better to come in Hanover. Pope's Statius is his first experiment with political satire under the screen of translation or imitation. The *Thebaid* is implicitly rich in English parallel for the period of Pope, a story of civil strife and contending royal claimants. Pope takes this analogue and presses it home in manipulation of the Latin text toward English application. As he does later, Pope counts not only on the satire of commission but of omission as well, counting on his reader to recall the whole original as well as noticing his explicit tamperings with that original. (JMA)

5299. Adler, Jacob. "An Essay Upon Projects." *CE* 34(1973): 1061-66.
William D. Schaefer and John Gerber have both suggested, in slightly different ways, that members of our profession should write articles about literature which would be of interest to the general literate public, perhaps after the model of *Scientific American*. In order to examine some aspects of the value of these suggestions, I have sought a work which on the face of it would be of relatively little interest to non-professionals, and have tried to find various approaches for writing articles about it which might

arouse non-professional interest. I offer suggestions for articles on *An Essay on Criticism* in terms of various aspects of prosody, of rules and literary expectations then and now, of standards for the good critic, and of what makes a critic bad, then and now, of the meaning of "nature," then and now, and a number of other aspects of the poem. The purpose of these suggestions is not to put them all forth as examples of articles assumed to be workable, but rather to sketch out the range of possibilities in connection with one unlikely poem, and thus to help readers decide whether the original suggestions of Schaefer and Gerber are viable. (JHA)

5307. Cornelia, Marie. "*The Rape of the Lock* and the Romace Tradition." *ConnR* 8,i:84-89.
In *The Rape of the Lock* Pope mocks the heroic poem and the romance tradition as well. Pope makes satiric use of the *amour courtois* as it had come down to him from the troubadours and the *Roman de la Rose* through the Petrarchan sonneteers. The Baron, preparing his campaign to win Belinda's lock, is an exemplar of the lover's suppliant posture toward the gods. The game of Ombre is couched in battle terms, as is the Hampton Court fracas, and this follows the tradition of battle imagery so commonly used by Petrarch and other sonneteers in their treatment of love. As for Belinda herself, the compleat belle, she is also the Rose, intent upon exercising *daunger* to preserve *honour*, and *honour* is as ambiguous in Pope's poem as it had been in the Rose Garden. But there is no ambiguity in the poem's ending. Along with Beatrice and so many other ladies of the romance tradition, Belinda and her lock are stellated, in the heavens, through the poem. (MC)

5309. Dash, Irene. "The Touch of the Poet." *MLS* 4,ii:59-64.
Pope's edition of Shakespeare's *Works* (1725) has long been condemned for its subjective, unscientific approach. Because Pope was a poet, however, he transcended the limitations of his methodology. This is particularly apparent in *The Winter's Tale* where one of those unorthodox techniques—the innumerable small scene divisions—reveals a unity beneath the seeming diversity, illuminates obscure areas of text, and suggests the theatrical potential of the play. Pope's scenic units influenced mid-18th-century adaptors and led subsequent editors to explore the subtle nuances of language. (IGD)

5313. Gosselink, R.N. "The 'Dissolving Antithesis':Technique in *The Rape of the Lock*." *HAB* 24(1973):191-96.
Pope's use of the antithesis and its corollary, the list with an incongruous item, for purposes of irony is amply documented in recent criticism; however, a few antitheses produce a double thrust of irony: (1) the irony of the opposition of values in the ideal heroic world and in the real world of mannered social action, and (2) the antithesis dissolving into a further irony. A proper understanding of the social and literary milieu of Pope's time shows that the antitheses between Bibles and billet-doux, counsel and tea, and prayers and masquerade dissolve to prove more apparent than real. (RNG)

5317. Hotch, Ripley. "The Dilemma of an Obedient Son: Pope's *Epistle to Dr. Arbuthnot*." *ELWIU* 1:37-45.
In *An Epistle to Dr. Arbuthnot* Pope examines his doubt about his mission as a satirist. His compulsion to write has made his life a long disease, and he has to justify his choice of profession to himself in order to justify it to others. The poem begins with an apparent retreat from duty into childish irresponsibility. Pope bears a superficial resemblance to the dunces who attack him; they, however, are not only irresponsible, but disobedient to their parents when they try to become authors. Pope can therefore define his obedience through opposition to them. Whatever pain his obedience causes he accepts the duty laid on him from birth to be a poet. By the end of the poem, Pope's retreat has become an emblem of his strength and an image of his obedience to the ideals of his parents. (RH)

5323. Korkowski, Eugene. "Scriblerus' Sinking Opera:*Peri Bathous* XIII." *L&P* 24:80-88.
In *Peri Bathous* XIII Pope and Arbuthnot sabotage Martinus Scriblerus' "Project for the Advancement of the Bathos" by arranging double-entendres that reduce the "advancement" to a bowel movement and show "division of labor"—whether in Aesopian fable, in cabinet-making, in organ building, in language manufacture, or in the clock-making and diving-bell inventions of Thomas Tompion—to be a variant of the digestive-eliminative,

work-producing process. But in using such ingenious wordplays to parody "modern projectors" of naive schemes, Pope and Arbuthnot narrow their audience and put self-amusement uppermost. The psychological spring for this self-amusement is a wish to show themselves "civilized" by symbolically shoving shame-arousing feces toward their rivals in learning, the "mechanists" or "moderns," making the latter appear "uncivilized." (EBK)

5324. Kroll, Barry M. "The Relationship of the Supernatural Machinery to Humoral Doctrine in *The Rape of the Lock* (1714)." *Thoth* 14:45-50.
In *The Rape of the Lock*, Pope consistently links each spirit to a key humoral element and its appropriate state of personality. He connects the sylphs with the element air and a sanguine humor, the gnomes with earth and a melancholy humor, the nymphs with water and a phlegmatic humor, and the salamanders with fire and a choleric humor. In the course of the poem, Belinda assumes each of the four dispositions, and Pope satirizes her affectation. Pope's moral, the essence of Clarissa's lines, is that none of the affected dispositions represent a properly human personality. (BMK)

5325. Kropf, C[arl].R. "Miscreation:Another Miltonic Allusion in *The Dunciad*." *PLL* 10:425-27.
In the first description of Dulness' creative powers in Book I of his *Dunciad* Pope refers to "a warm Third day" (I.57). This is an allusion to the warm third day of creation as Milton describes it in *Paradise Lost* (I.276-81). Pope's passage describing Dulness' creation (I.54-78) alludes to Milton's description at numerous points. The effect of the allusion is to introduce Dulness, at her first appearance, as a satanic figure, an agent of miscreation. (CRK)

5328. Lawler, Traugott. " 'Wafting Vapours from the Land of Dreams':Virgil's Fourth and Sixth Eclogues and the *Dunciad*." *SEL* 14:373-86.
The *Dunciad* parodies Eclogue 4: in both, a mother and son herald a return to the age of Saturn. Pope's imagery of birth and childhood stresses this relationship. His allusions to Eclogue 6 center on the stories of Hylas and Gallus: Smedley disappears from "the Strand" like Hylas and, like Gallus, receives in the other world symbols of poetic inheritance. The Gallus episode transfers the theme of regeneration of Eclogue 4 to Eclogue 6; where its instrument in 4 is the divine child, in 6 it is poetry. The *Dunciad* celebrates poets such as Smedley who destroy, not create, and thus inverts Eclogue 6 as well as Eclogue 4. Since the poems form a unit in Virgil, Pope rightly draws on both. "Mock-pastoral" is generally appropriate to the *Dunciad*, since pastoral regularly celebrates poetry and poets; and the pastoral style also allowed Pope to oppose a beauty of his own to the sordid writing of the dunces. (TL)

5333. Mengel, Elias F.,Jr. "The *Dunciad* Illustrations." *ECS* 7:161-78.
Since they appear to be more or less enigmatic and extraneous to the poem, the seven plates brought together from editions of the *Dunciad* (1728-43) have been virtually ignored by Pope's editors and critics. In one way of looking at them the *Dunciad* illustrations satirize the visual aids of dullness in such works as "on Out-side merit but presume," but a closer look proves that these mock emblems image the wit of the poem and are as much a part of it as the mock critical apparatus. Not only do they illustrate particular passages and themes, but they also reflect its mock heroic mode by using visual equivalents or approximations of the epic style. (EFM,Jr)

5338. Rogers, Pat. "Faery Lore and *The Rape of the Lock*." *RES* 25:25-38.
The Rape of the Lock is a fantastic and surreal work, as well as a social satire. Pope builds on a native English tradition of rustic "faery" lore, deriving from earlier writers such as Shakespeare, Spenser, and Drayton. His revisions of the poem were possibly influenced by William Diaper's *Dryades* (1712), which utilizes the same tradition. The mythology of the poem displays a contest between the aerial sylphs and the earthly gnomes; the contribution of the gnomes to the poem's imaginative logic is greater than has been realized. (PR)

5340. Rudat, Wolfgang E.H. "Belinda's 'Painted Vessel':

Allusive Technique in *The Rape of the Lock*." *TSL* 19:49-55.
Discusses the allusive associations radiating from several passages in *The Rape of the Lock* and focuses on the picture of the "painted Vessel" gliding down the Thames. The picture is a parody of Shakespeare's description of Cleopatra's barge. The ship becomes the woman's body as it had been described in Ovid's *Ars amatoria* and in Ausonius' *Cento nuptialis*, the latter consisting of verse fragments taken from Virgil. On a more private level of *The Rape*'s mode of existence, Pope uses Virgilian allusions to establish a link with Ausonius' obscene poem and write a physiological mock-epic. (WEHR)

5342. Trimble, John. "Clarissa's Role in *The Rape of the Lock*." *TSLL* 15:673-91.
Clarissa is a richly paradoxical figure functioning as both surrogate and object of irony. Only when one grasps her prudish character can one reconcile her with the poem's generalizations about woman's nature. Far from patly clarifying *The Rape*'s putative moral, Clarissa ironically complicates and enriches it. She does this by adopting unwittingly some of the conventional values of her modish world, by demonstrating that good sense doesn't necessarily exclude self-interest and vanity, and by parodying a speech that threatens to trivialize her basic concerns. In sum, Clarissa only heightens our sense of the paradoxicality of the beau monde, and it was this sense, perhaps above all, that Pope wished to leave with us. (JRT)

Richardson, S. 5359. Leibowitz, Judith. "The Poetics of Salvation in *Clarissa, La nouvelle Héloïse*, and *Die Leiden des jungen Werther*." [F 26]:242-45.
The salvation or deification of self through abnegation changes during the 18th century to the glorification of an assertive and passionate self. Richardson's Clarissa achieves salvation in Christian terms solely through the quality of her feelings. In *La nouvelle Héloïse* (1761), by adding an ethic of social responsibility to the earlier sentimental criterion, Rousseau attempts to justify the passions. Goethe's Werther glorifies the passionately assertive self without need of religious or social justification. This secularized, esthetic model anticipates the "religion" of the Romantic self that dominates the early 19th century. (JL)

Shaftesbury. 5375. Sherman, Carol. "In Defense of the Dialogue:Diderot, Shaftesbury, and Galiani." *RomN* 15(1973): 268-73.
Certain passages of Diderot's *Apologie de l'abbé Galiani* constitute a poetic of the dialogue as a literary form. He approved of the use of the latter as a vehicle for the expression of philosophic ideas and he enumerated the qualities it should possess in order to persuade or instruct most surely: an impartial or a skeptical tone, absence of intervention by the author, and natural characters who have their own varied points of view and in whom the reader may recognize himself. These strictures echo the rules that Shaftesbury laid down in his *Characteristics* for the practice of philosophical dialogue. The dates of his preparation of the abbé's *Dialogues* and of his own subsequent defense of them correspond to the dates of composition of his first dialogue works Diderot often went so far as to avoid representing the defeat of the opinion he wished to attack. It seems that Galiani's example and Shaftesbury's lessons were at least partly responsible for the hermeticism or apparent impartiality of Diderot's best literary creations. (CS)

Sheridan, R.B. 5381. Durant, Jack D. "Prudence, Providence, and the Direct Road of Wrong:*The School for Scandal* and Sheridan's Westminster Hall Speech." *SBHT* 15:241-51.
The School for Scandal is often said to lack moral substance; but, when studied in relation to Sheridan's famous Westminster Hall speech (1788), the play is seen to give form to some of Sheridan's insights into vice and virtue. The moral world of the play is comparable to that described in the speech. In most features of villainous motive, the character of Hastings parallels that of Joseph Surface. Charles Surface's spontaneous filial piety finds explanation in the speech; and the speech explains in moral terms the inevitable failure of Joseph Surface's complex stratagems. In arguing that villainies can succeed only if they are conducted with singleminded "prudence," Sheridan echoes Lady Sneerwell's

charge that Joseph Surface falls victim to his own great "avarice of crimes." (JDD)

5382. Jason, Philip K. "A Twentieth-Century Response to *The Critic*." *ThS* 15:51-58.
Sheridan's *The Critic* is not only a burlesque criticism of misguided tastes, disreputable theatrical policies, and poor dramatic construction, but also an investigation into the relative truths and realities of art and life. By exposing the weaknesses of Puff's *The Spanish Armada*, Sheridan underscores the artificiality of all drama, including his own first-act frame. Through Sheridan's handling of the rehearsal format, a multiple perspective is achieved: the audience is confronted with the reality of the characters in Puff's play, the reality of the actors performing parts in Puff's play, and the reality of actors playing actors playing parts in Sheridan's play. These concentric realities are held in contrast with our own sense of life, promoting tensions and reverberations that are intuitively felt and which demand rational analysis. (PKJ)

Smart. 5388. Rizzo, Betty. "A New Prologue by Christopher Smart and a Forgotten Skirmish of the Theatre War." *PBSA* 68:305-10.
30 to 50% of the occasional poetry in the *Midwife*, the monthly magazine edited by Smart for John Newbery, has not been accounted for. One set of verses, a prologue, can be credited to Smart based on the prompt book of Richard Cross of Dury Lane Theatre. John Hill, author of the *Inspector*, a daily column in the *London Daily Advertiser*, waged a journalistic war with Fielding, Garrick, the actor Henry Woodward, and Smart in 1752. The four planned a production at Drury Lane of Fielding's farce *The Mock Doctor*, in which Woodward would take off John Hill, and Smart would write a prologue to advertise the proceedings. It was forbidden by the Lord Chamberlain, but appeared soon after in the *Midwife*. (BWR)

5390. Williamson, Karina. "Christopher Smart in the Song-books." *RES* 25:410-21.
Eighteenth-century songbooks and collections provide an important source of textual information about Smart's poetry and demonstrate his popularity as a song-writer in the period. The rise of the London pleasure-gardens as musical centers stimulated a great increase in the production of songs. Smart's songs conform to the types favored at these resorts, the "ballad" and the "art song," and many of them were set to music by popular composers such as Thomas Arne and William Boyce. The earliest text of some of Smart's poems are found in these composers' collections, and they show significant variants in the text of others. They also provide evidence which helps toward the attribution of anonymous songs to Smart; two discussed here are "Gay Florimel of noble birth" and "When gentle Harriot I first saw," both set by Arne. A checklist of Smart's songs, with details of publication, is appended. (KW)

Smollett. 5396. Copeland, Edward. "*Humphry Clinker*:A Pastoral Poem in Prose." *TSLL* 16:493-501.
The discrepancy in tone between the caustic satire of Smollett's early novels and the good-humored, benign tone of *Humphry Clinker* has always puzzled critics. This shift in tone can be accounted for in part at least by the novel's debt to the 18th century's broadened concept of the conventions of the pastoral. In England, Gay's *Shepherd's Week* (1714) though conceived as "mock pastoral" was approved by Dr. Johnson as "just representations of rural manners." In Scotland, Ramsay turned pastoral drama and poetry to an expression of national pride. Smollett's numerous experiments in mock pastoral and traditional pastoral forms in addition to the specific references in *Humphry Clinker* to pastoral ideals support the claim that his last novel may itself be subject to the order and conventions of "a comic pastoral poem in prose." (EWC)

5401. Gassman, Byron. "*Humphry Clinker* and the Two Kingdoms of George III." *Criticism* 16:95-108.
Smollett's *Humphry Clinker* (1771) may be seen as a product of Smollett's feeling that George III's accession in 1760 had provided England almost a last opportunity to realize the Augustan vision that had long tantalized the literary imagination. Smollett's

expedition travels largely through the kingdom that he felt George had actually inherited, an England being ruined by the venality and tasteless ostentation of vulgarians such as Pope's Timon. But Smollett also creates an image of the mythic Augustan kingdom envisioned by many disgruntled Englishmen who had hoped that George, as a patriot king, could reverse England's moral decay. Smollett's vision of George's England as a realm beneficently ruled by a patriot king is really only an enlargement of the classical concept of the rural patriarchy as the ideal social organization. Smollett senses that this ideal kingdom is probably beyond historical realization, but he succeeds in briefly incarnating it in the hospitality, generosity, and wise husbanding of nature associated with Bramble's life at Brambleton Hall and with the estate of the Dennisons, encountered near the end of the novel. (BG)

5405. Pannill, Linda. "Some Patterns of Imagery in *Humphry Clinker*." *Thoth* 13,iii:37-43.
The nature of the symbolic journey in Smollett's *Humphry Clinker* has been interpreted as a movement from sickness to health, city to country, and progress to primitivism. This journey may also be interpreted as the movement from disorder to rational order in society and in Matthew Bramble's family of unrecognized son and unattached females. This disorder is evident in the images of hell, monsters, and disharmony. More importantly, animal images are emblems of this irrationality. But when the predatory animal role is transferred from the females to the males as Matthew's sister Tabby and servant Win find husbands, order is restored and these images all but disappear from the novel. (LSP)

5408. Preston, Thomas R. "The 'Stage Passions' and Smollett's Characterization." *SP* 71:105-25.
Smollett nearly always projects the internal emotional states of his characters by depicting only their external, bodily reactions. These "stage passions" explain his adaptation of the same external signs to different emotions, for paradoxically the signs could be reduced to formulas that applied to nearly all emotions indiscriminately. Against their background it becomes clear that Smollett's characterization does not yield introspective, Jamesian individuals, but universal types whose emotional life is meaningful primarily in relationship to a context of causes, effects, moral relevancy, and social implications. (TRP)

5410. Siebert, Donald T.,Jr. "The Role of the Senses in *Humphry Clinker*." *SNNTS* 6:17-26.
Critics have puzzled over the function of unsavory imagery in Smollett's fiction, particularly imagery of taste and smell. In *Humphrey Clinker* there is a counterbalancing imagery of pleasant sensation and that sensory experience is not merely the stuff of comedy but indeed the basis of the novel's thematic commentary. Smollett's imagery can be fully understood and appreciated only in a Lockean context. In Locke the senses are the gateway to knowledge and ultimately to subtle ratiocination and sophisticated judgments; in the novel, Matthew Bramble constantly puts implicit faith in the testimony his own sharp senses provide. What most condemns Baynard's way of life are Bramble's vivid sensations of discomfort, just as the opposite attractions of physical well-being most recommend Bramble's own country seat in Wales. (DTS)

Sterne. 5418. Banerjee, Chinmoy. "*Tristram Shandy* and the Association of Ideas." *TSLL* 15:693-706.
Neither Locke's theory of pathological association nor his notion of the rational "train of ideas" helps one to understand the psychological order underlying *Tristram Shandy*. The "eccentric" mind of Tristram, in terms of which the work is organized, as well as the comic minds of Toby, Walter, and Susannah are illuminated by the psychological and esthetic formulations of Hume and Gerard which seem to provide a theoretical basis for Sterne's "truth." *Tristram Shandy* is not a comedy of abnormal understandings illustrative of Locke, but is a comedy of a human nature which Locke failed to observe. (CCB)

5420. Brienza, Susan D. "Volume VII of *Tristram Shandy*—A Dance of Life." *UDR* 10,iii:59-62. [Foll. by Thomas M. Columbus, "Postscriptum: 'A Dance *with* Death; a Dance *of* Life'." 63.]
Volume VII of *Tristram Shandy* celebrates the dance of life, not the dance of death. The journey through France both symbolizes and affects the life-giving movement away from death and toward sexual rejuvenation. In Paris every mention of eating or clothing contains a sexual allusion. Sexuality, merged with circularity in "the ring of pleasure," plays a role in this volume. The sexual dance means motion, and motion to Tristram means life. Tristram does not succumb to the still point of death but rejects Death as a partner at the beginning, and escapes it by his dance through France. (SDB)

5428. Golden, Morris. "Sterne's Journeys and Sallies." *SBHT* 16:47-62.
Sterne saw and created life as equivocal zigzags along a road from birth to death. The journey, together with its blunting or diversion, is his plot core in images. On his journey, the Sternian Quixote rides his Rosinante, the projection by which his mind expresses its earthly part. To direct it and himself properly, he must have maps of the psychological and social worlds. For this real world of experience the sentimental memory—the record of feeling—stimulated by scenes or gestures is the best signpost to the retrospect and, therefore, the scope of life. His motivating impulses arise from internal irregularities and indicate defects and delusions. (MG)

5440a. Park, William. "*Tristram Shandy* and the New 'Novel of Sensibility'." *SNNTS* 6:268-79.
Beginning with *Tristram Shandy* in 1759, the conventions of the English novel begin to change. Narrators become increasingly less reliable; heroes become men of feeling; heroines are not subject to rape; distresses become "delicate" rather than physical; protagonists spend more time within their families; and the families and "custom" are more severely criticized. The change in convention may be best seen by examining the works of authors who wrote before and after 1760, particularly Mrs. Lennox, Cleland, and Smollett. One should perceive the novels of the 1760s-70s as a type of novel—the novel of sensibility—and as one of the period styles within the history of the English novel. (WP)

5443. Tripodi, Vincenzo. "Immagini di grazia nella traduzione di Ugo Foscolo del romanzo sterniano." *FI* 8:223-39.
Foscolo demonstrates his own distinct poetic elements in the translation of Sterne's *A Sentimental Journey through France and Italy by Mr Yorick*. The variations of adjectives and nouns develop classical images of beauty, which are chaste and full of lyrical sensibility. The selection of different verbs delicately reveals the passionate soul of the characters. The addition of new syntactic elements molds a mythical version of beauty. Foscolo's new metaphor depicts, with subtle color, the modest innocence of the characters. Sometimes, his translation achieves a rhythmic unity and modulation in the sentence structure. (VT)

Swift. 5447. Anselment, Raymond A. "*A Tale of a Tub*:Swift and the 'Men of Tast'." *HLQ* 37:265-82.
The issues of taste developed in the *Tale's* Apology question the literary discrimination of both Jonathan Swift and his detractors. In particular, the extreme praise given to Marvell's now largely forgotten satire is perplexing. An analysis of the Apology indicates that Swift valued the precedent set by Marvell's work. In transforming sterile animadversion into innovative satire, *The Rehearsal Transpros'd* successfully blends an urbane and often witty humor with the serious subject of religion. But the example provides more than a justification for Swift's own tack; both satires explore a common interest in the theme of taste. In each case the immediate concern with manners and propriety is subsumed into more encompassing satires of reductive and dangerously solipsistic visions that originate from prideful claims to self-sufficiency. Although Swift's comic exuberance and ironic complexity are unique to the *Tale*, his exploration of enthusiasm and its various categorizations of madness are anticipated in Marvell's satire. Swift's adaption, however, is consonant with the *Tale's* vision, and provides the final justification of his own taste. (RAA)

5448. Beauchamp, Gordon. "Gulliver's Return to the Cave: Plato's *Republic* and Book IV of *Gulliver's Travels*." *MichA* 7:201-09.
R.S. Crane has offered the most fruitful suggestion for understanding Gulliver's experience in Book IV by adducing a parallel

between that voyage and Plato's Allegory of the Cave: Gulliver among the Houyhnhnms approximates Plato's cave-dweller released from the illusions of his dark world. Crane fails, however, to pursue the parallel and thus does not account for Gulliver's final misanthropic stance. The purpose of Plato's allegory was to stress the social obligation of the one who had escaped to enlightenment; this responsibility is abdicated by Gulliver, who becomes the object, rather than the medium, of Swift's satire. Gulliver's personal failure to live up to the reasoned perfection of the Houyhnhnms, however, does not negate their function as a Utopian ideal. Like the rational societies of Plato and More, that of the Houyhnhnms offers a critical model for assessing the shortcomings of actual societies. (GLB)

5452. Bryan, Margaret B. "Swift's Use of the Looking-Glass in *Gulliver's Travels*." *ConnR* 8,i:90-94.
The four passages in *Gulliver's Travels* (1726) in which Gulliver looks at himself in a looking-glass provide a yardstick for measuring his deterioration throughout the book into ultimate madness. At first sanely able to laugh at his "ridiculous" image in the Brobdingnagian mirror, Gulliver next finds his mirror image so "despicable" that he refuses to look at it, and in the third passage views himself with "horror and detestation." The fourth and climactic mirror passage contains in its one sentence a miniature Great Chain of Being, one which, as Gulliver describes it, is the mirror image of the 18th-century standard. At bottom are the Yahoos of Gulliver's own family, "docible animals"; next he places himself, a "human creature" who must be tolerated; third come the brutal English Houyhnhnms whose "Persons" are to be respected; and at the top is the "noble" "whole Houyhnhnm Race." After averting his eyes from his unendurable reflection in the third mirror passage, Gulliver here prefers the inverted mirror image to reality and thus is revealed as hopelessly mad at the end of the book. (MBB)

5455. Cohan, Steven M. "Gulliver's Fiction." *SNNTS* 6:7-16.
The strong and universal appeal of *Gulliver's Travels* comes from its psychological structure. Swift offers us a pattern for confronting basic fears and desires. Thus each of Gulliver's four voyages is an intensified projection of some human impulse; taken together, the four voyages correspond to four stages of psychological progression, embodying man's own development from an immature consciousness of self to a more mature consciousness of society and other men. (SMC)

5459. Fischer, John I. "Apparent Contraries: A Reading of Swift's 'A Description of a City Shower'." *TSL* 19:21-34.
Swift's "A Description of a City Shower" depicts a shower which is simultaneously a terrible flood. The poem forces us to recognize that what we call meaning is less certain than we usually assume. Thus, though the poem's fragmentary character reminds us that the great flood legends of western literature were generally disbelieved by the beginning of the 18th century, the "Shower" nevertheless recaptures the import of those legends by teaching us the limits of our capabilities. Swift's poem also recovers that grace implicit in the greatest of those legends, Noah's flood, by demonstrating that our felt worth as living beings is consistent with an admission that life possesses a power and an integrity independent of us. (JIF)

5460. Fisher, Alan S. "An End to the Renaissance: Erasmus, Hobbes, and *A Tale of a Tub*." *HLQ* 38:1-20.
In *A Tale of a Tub* Swift asserts a curious personal presence which one senses in the brilliant irrelevance of his analogy-making. The analogies are at their best when Swift is describing something wicked or dangerous, and they add an atmosphere of having fun, just at those points in the *Tale* where Swift's contemplation seems bleakest. The effect is paradoxical, as if a free intellect were attesting a world where determinism and mindlessness are the only realities. Paradoxes remind one of Erasmus, but if Erasmus obliterated meaningless distinctions in the light of a higher truth, Swift obliterates distinctions which are not meaningless—the very distinctions on which civilization depends. Swift senses that we can, alas, no longer see the truths Erasmus saw. Between Swift and Erasmus lies Hobbes, whose reduction of human qualities to mechanism Swift found strangely unanswerable. But if Swift cannot answer Hobbes, he can subvert his system. The Digression on Madness purports to support Hobbist premises and argues

them with buffoonish enthusiasm into paradox, just the kind of discourse Hobbes found most wrong. (ASF)

5461. —— "Swift's Verse Portraits: A Study of His Originality as an Augustan Satirist." *SEL* 14:343-56.
Swift's satirical portraits in verse seem less interested in their subjects than in some process of corruption Swift associates with their subjects. His satire destroys the man but cannot negate the corruptive force the man exemplifies. It offers no positive ideal save the high-spirited anger of the poet himself, who is not so overcome with inevitable evils that he must cease to hate them ingeniously. Thus his portraits are at the same time both clever and bitter, and this is an interesting blend. Such bitterness makes comfort about existing affairs impossible, but the cleverness allows us at least to feel we know what to call our enemies. Swift's major satires offer this blend, too. With it Swift shifts the force of satire's "correctiveness" away from the external world, where he knows it will do no good, to the perceiving mind (his and his reader's) where—perhaps—it may. (ASF)

5462. Fitzgerald, Robert P. "The Structure of *Gulliver's Travels*." *SP* 71:247-63.
The vitality and wide appeal of *Gulliver's Travels* may be explained in terms of its structure, which is formed by the analogous intertwining of two ideas: (1) the value of society is equivocal; (2) the value of knowledge is equivocal. Each of the four Parts of the *Travels* asserts this structure in a different way, the four Parts cohering by a system of oppositions and mediations. Seeing the work in these terms shows how it is unified, has bearing on some of the common critical controversies about the book, such as the debate over the Houyhnhnms, and helps to explain its mythic appeal and its appeal to children. (RPF)

5465. Irving, William H. "Boccalini and Swift." *ECS* 7(1973-74):143-60.
The Augustan essayists and Swift in particular are indebted to the forgotten Italian writer Boccalini. Satirical fables, allegorical devices, the use of implication and irony, images, and mannerisms of style show definitely that Boccalini's attitudes and ideas were actively circulating when *A Tale of a Tub* was published. Swift's insistence on the need to probe beneath the surfaces, his delight in scatological imagery, his paradoxical hesitations between hope and despair in matters of social reform, his feeling for the need for stability in political affairs, his recognition of human dignity, his scorn for critical rules, for chasing faults in writers, all these themes and more appear in Boccalini as in Swift, and often in forms that are curiously similar. Swift was not borrowing consciously from Boccalini, but the two writers were temperamentally sympathetic, and these ideas were the currency of the age, stamped early and emphatically by Boccalini, and later even more emphatically by Swift. (WHI)

5472. Lockwood, Thomas. "Swift's *Modest Proposal*: An Interpretation." *PLL* 10:254-67.
It is misleading to interpret the "Modest Proposal" as a fictionalized imitation of, and attack on, the so-called "economic projector." The "Proposal" lends itself only awkwardly to that view; nor does the evidence of Swift's earlier Irish papers support it. A better concept is that Swift ironically attributes to his putative audience, the "publick," an inhuman and pervasive moral indifference, and in doing this effectively forces the reader to relive, as a comic-horrifying literary experience, the emotional and moral extremes of Swift's own personal experience in the Ireland of the 1720s. (LT)

5473. Meek, Jay. "Swift's *A Modest Proposal*, Paragraph 10." *Expl* 33: Item 11.
Swift's narrator, in the tenth paragraph of "A Modest Proposal," proposes reserving 20,000 children for breed, one-fourth of whom will be male, and concludes erroneously that the ratio among breeders would be one male for every four females. The narrator's arithmetical miscalculation serves as a miniature index to his rational, as well as ethical, fallibility. (JM)

5480. Patterson, Anne E. "Swift's Irony and Cartesian Man." *MQ* 15:338-51.
Although the heterogeneous nature of Gulliver's third voyage diminishes its story interest, it is now known to be far more than vague, pointless satire of mathematicians. The "Voyage to

Laputa" focuses Swift's satire on the peculiarly Cartesian form of the "new science." Descartes conceived of nature as mechanism, exempting humanity alone by virtue of its complex, diverse actions and unique ability to produce meaningful speech; his disciples took the obvious next step of including man in the universal mechanism. Swift attacks this dehumanization by illustrating how the Laputan narrowness of view restricts man's activities and makes him an automaton, while the Baconian Balnibarbians, who have seized upon the Cartesian methodology, systematically strip language of all meaning. Along with language the functions of the mind are reduced to the purely mechanical, thus placing man far below the level of Swift's "animal rationis capax." Finally, Swift's attack on the reductionism implicit in the "new science" has special ironic relevance to the cybernetics, semantics, behaviorism, genetic engineering, lobotomizing of our own age—the true age of Cartesian man. (AEP)

5481. Patterson, Emily H. "Swift's Marginal Allusions to the Atterbury Case." *Anglia* 92:395-97.
Swift indicates belief in the innocence of Francis Atterbury, Bishop of Rochester, through three separate notes to the Earl of Strafford, the Earl of Clarendon, and Baillie of Jerviswood, which he penciled into the margins of Clarendon's and Burnet's works of history. In each of these marginalia Swift holds up Atterbury's 1723 conviction for Jacobite treason against the example of an innocent person's conviction on unproved charges and his sentence to banishment or death. Swift's three references indicate that he was not content merely to condemn the illegality of the procedures used to convict Atterbury, but that he was asserting Atterbury's innocence. (EHP)

5483. Probyn, Clive T. "Gulliver and the Relativity of Things:A Commentary on Method and Mode, with a Note on Smollett." *RMS* 18:63-76.
Critical discussion of the theme of relativity in *Gulliver's Travels* has been almost entirely concentrated on narrow source study of the physical rationale. The travel-book genre within which *Gulliver's Travels* is set, however, offers the theme of moral relativity. Swift attacks the insularity and prejudiced conde-scension of the travel-book and repeats its arguments in satirical form. Aspects of moral status and social hierarchy also fall under this heading and are in marked contrast to the theme as broached in Dryden and in Smollett's *Humphry Clinker*, where Swift's fears of social mobility leading to moral anarchy are treated with a more benign response. Swift's use of the list and of Gulliver as spokesman are indicators of this theme and strategic elements in Swift's attack on European complacency. (CTP)

5488. Real, Hermann J. " 'That Malignant Deity':An Inter-pretation of *Criticism* in Swift's *Battle of the Books*." *PQ* 52(1973):760-66.
The interpretation of *Criticism*, patron deity of the Moderns, presupposes an acquaintance with the history of two different ideas. These are, first, the theory of humors, and, second, the classical ideal of the *vir bonus*. The description of *Criticism*'s outward appearance and of her environment is based on the doctrines of 17th-century humoral pathology. The physical and mental defects which are reflected both in the goddess herself and in her offspring indicate that *Criticism* suffers from morbid melancholy. This as well as her descent (*Pride* is her mother and *Ignorance* her father) let her become the incarnation of complete intellectual and moral decay. The satire gains in intensity when contrasted with the implicit norm. This is provided by Quintilian's *vir bonus dicendi peritus*, which, though originally the definition of the ideal orator, by the end of the century had become qualities necessary in the poet and critic. Thus the nature of *Criticism* is revealed as the complete inversion of the ideal: *dea mala iudicandi imperita*. Though the whole episode is patterned after the description of Envy in Ovid's *Metamorphoses*, Swift's devel-opment and refinement of the model are quite original. (HJR)

5495. Smith, Frederik N. "Swift's Correspondence:The 'Dra-matic' Style and the Assumption of Roles." *SEL* 14:357-71.
In his correspondence Swift plays easily with many of the devices common to his published satires. The most important element of his style is its extremely loose syntax; he avoids periodicity in order that the sound of his voice may emerge unencumbered by overt rhetoric. What Swift aims at is not the depiction of a

thought but a mind thinking. In the studied casualness of Swift's style an idea typically begets another, or is qualified or contradicted by what follows. This loose style is especially apt for the projection of a mind in a certain mood or for showing a certain type of mind. Swift's loose style serves the double function of making his persona transparently credible while at the same time undermining that persona with a broken, hesitating syntax. (FNS)

5496. —— "The Epistemology of Fictional Failure:Swift's *Tale of a Tub* and Beckett's *Watt*." *TSLL* 15:649-72.
Working on his novel *Watt* Beckett recalled vividly the *Tale* and used its radical fragmentation of narrative form as a model for his own work. Both books emphasize their own failure as novels in the traditional mold and go on to demonstrate the failure of language, logic, and mathematics as a means of coming to grips with the world. For Swift the problem is the misuse of these tools of understanding; for Beckett the problem is the tools themselves. Yet both authors push themselves to the outer limits of thinking, into that strange territory where art and life, meaning and absurdity border on one another. In that rare atmosphere fiction fails, but in the failure of their fiction Swift and Beckett discover the limits of art as well as the limits of the human mind. (FNS)

5497. Spiller, Michael R.G. "The Idol of the Stove:The Background to Swift's Criticism of Descartes." *RES* 25:15-24.
Swift's satire of Modernity in *A Tale of a Tub* and *The Battle of the Books* draws on criticisms common in the latter half of the 17th century. In referring to Descartes as an exemplar of the modern intellectual revolution, Swift sees him as mad, fanatical, and introverted, a view transcending most contemporary criticisms of Descartes, which go no further than accusations of pride, atheism, or charlatanism. One earlier writer, Meric Casaubon (1599-1671) provides an attack which links Descartes' experimental philos-ophy with religious fanaticism: in his *Treatise Concerning Enthusiasme* (1656) he sees Descartes' philosophical originality as a species of mystical enthusiasm; and his unpublished ms. treatise "On Learning" (1667) supplies a fuller criticism, which is that of Swift. The similarity of Casaubon's views to Swift's suggests that Casaubon represented an attitude widespread enough to be picked up by Swift in the last quarter of the century. (MRGS)

5499. Tyne, James E.L.,S.J. "Swift and Stella:The Love Poems." *TSL* 19:35-47.
The eleven poems that Swift writes for Esther Johnson are love poems of considerable distinction. When addressing Stella, Swift disguises the deep affection that throbs beneath his seemingly dispassionate lines by insisting that they are poems of "Friend-ship, not love." Everywhere he implies that she is above all else a person of "masculine" good sense and good humor. Yet Stella's specifically feminine qualities are also celebrated, especially in many touching sickroom scenes, and Swift's real feelings for Stella are best reflected in his transformation of the conventional metaphors of other love poets. In spite of all his admiration, the Dean never forgets that Stella is merely human and consequently imperfect. This clear-eyed awareness, however, does not detract from, but rather paradoxically enhances, all that is said in praise of Stella. (JLT)

5500. Tyne, James L.,S.J. "Swift's Mock Panegyrics in 'On Poetry:A Rapsody'." *PLL* 10:279-86.
The lines Swift addresses to George II and Sir Robert Walpole in "On Poetry: A Rapsody" are complex and devastating. Swift apes both the stylistic mannerisms and the sycophantic stance of the laureates, Eusden and Cibber, to parody their literary ineptitude and to satirize the King and the Minister. While exploiting this defect for his own satiric purposes, Swift simultaneously weaves into his lines significant verbal echoes from the encomia that Horace and Virgil directed to Augustus Caesar and Maecenas. As Swift's more biting lines indicate, the man chiefly responsible for the alleged triumph of dullness and depravity is the brazen Walpole. (JLT)

5501. Uphaus, Robert W. "*Gulliver's Travels, A Modest Proposal*, and the Problematical Nature of Meaning." *PLL* 10:268-78.
Re-examination of *Gulliver's Travels* and *A Modest Proposal* demonstrates that they are works whose largest subject is the problematical nature of meaning. Readers sense a certain

uneasiness and disorientation in response to *A Modest Proposal* and *Gulliver's Travels* because Swift continually enlarges our consciousness by creating a variety of occasions where we are led to expect one kind of meaning which is presumed both to exist within the text and to be essentially separable from our lives, only to have this expectation violated by Swift's persistent attempts to move back and forth from a seemingly closed system of coherent fictional references to the open and problematical world of experiences and expectations. (RWU)

5503. Zimmerman, Everett. "Gulliver the Preacher." *PMLA* 89:1024-32.
In his satires, Swift often has his persona say true things for reprehensible reasons. The satire then becomes primarily a study of the moral implications of the relationship of the speaker to his proposals. In *Gulliver's Travels* the persona presents a view of man's evil that is generally in accord with the traditions of Christianity and of satire. But Swift shows us Gulliver's immoral intentions. Although Gulliver pretends that he wants to reform us, his pretense is a strategy for disguising his own evil. (ELZ)

Wilkes. 5519. Moureau, François. "Sur une lettre de Diderot à John Wilkes publiée dans le *Courier du Bas-Rhin*." *DHS* 6:277-85.
Discusses a recently discovered text of a letter from Diderot addressed to the celebrated politician, John Wilkes, in 1768, which hitherto was only known in an English version published in 1805. Recalling the interest Diderot had shown in Wilkes, Moureau compares the two texts. He concludes that the French text in all probability corresponds to the original of the letter written by Diderot. (FM)

Wollstonecraft. 5520. Boos, Florence S. "The Biographies of Mary Wollstonecraft." *Mary Wollstonecraft Newsl.* 1,ii(1973):6-10.
William Godwin's *Memoirs* of Wollstonecraft remained the most complete biography until Ralph Wardle's careful *Mary Wollstonecraft: A Critical Biography* (1951), which added material from Wollstonecraft letters and historical background on feminism. Two more biographies have recently appeared, Margaret George's *One Woman's Situation: A Study of Mary Wollstonecraft* (1970) and Eleanor Flexner's *Mary Wollstonecraft: A Biography* (1972). George's biography mixes effusion and condescension in language heavy with psychoanalytic jargon, but avoids serious

treatment of her ideas. Flexner's *Mary Wollstonecraft* adds historical documentation on the Wollstonecraft family and varies Wardle's interpretations well, but limits itself generally to biography; Wardle is somewhat rambling in style and includes fewer background data, but his comments on everything Wollstonecraft wrote are one of the best features of his book. Since two good biographies now exist, a collected edition of Wollstonecraft's own letters might be useful, along with further studies of Wollstonecraft as intellectual and writer. (FSB)

5523. Poston, Carol H., and Janet M. Todd. "Some Textual Variations in the First Two Editions of *A Vindication of the Rights of Woman*." *Mary Wollstonecraft Jour.* 2,ii:27-29.
Although the exact publication dates in 1792 are uncertain, Wollstonecraft had a few months to consider her *Vindication of the Rights of Woman* before she revised it for the second edition. The differences between the two editions are mainly in punctuation and grammar, few changes reveal Wollstonecraft's growing assurance in her own unconventional opinions. In particular, Wollstonecraft tempers her idea of male superiority, reducing it in the second edition to the possibility that men are larger and stronger than women. In the second edition, too, she expresses a slightly less favorable attitude toward nature than she expressed in the first edition. (JMT)

5525. Todd, Janet M. "The Language of Sex in *A Vindication of the Rights of Woman*." *Mary Wollstonecraft Newsl.* 1,ii(1973): 10-17.
One of Wollstonecraft's aims in *A Vindication of the Rights of Woman* (1792) is the substitution as a political concept of the rights of humanity for the rights of man, and the substitution of human ideals of excellence for masculine ones. Wollstonecraft reveals the ambiguity in the term "man" and suggests that the restrictive meaning of "man" as male is frequently understood in place of the generic meaning; when society is described as based on the nature of man, Wollstonecraft asserts that this nature is man's alone, not woman's. She sees men and women distinguished by a language that enshrines men's eulogistic concepts of themselves and their pejorative concepts of women. In her social analysis she mocks this distinction when she states that soldiers, seemingly the most "manly" of people, resemble women because of their similar artificial environment; they are therefore the most "womanly" of men. (JMT)

IX. NINETEENTH CENTURY

General and Miscellaneous. 5544. Brogan, Howard O. "The English Romantics:Revolution, Reaction, and the 'Generation Gap'." *JGE* 26:111-24.
Wordsworth, Coleridge, and Southey were in the beginning so sympathetic to the French Revolution that they were held up in the Tory *Anti-Jacobin* as examples of ridiculously naive and self-deceptive revolutionary partisans, even as they were in the very process of losing their confidence in the Revolution as it was diverted into foreign conquest. After their conversion to conservatism under the impact of disillusioning events, they were again assailed for being traitors to their own earlier idealism! Such generational conflict might then, as well as now be mitigated by Blake's doctrine of eternal forgiveness—in this case of the excesses in Innocence of revolutionary youth and in Experience of conservative age—by attributing such sins to the States of Youth and of Age rather than to the individuals passing—as all of us must—through these stages. (HOB)

5547. Clubbe, John. "Romanticism Today." *Mosaic* 7,iii:137-50. [Rev. art. on Abrams' *Natural Supernaturalism*, Peyre's *Qu'est-ce- que le Romantisme?* and Beaty's *Light from Heaven*.]
Romanticism is as much a European phenomenon as it is a congeries of national movements, and it is folly to try to understand so complex and varied a phenomenon without seeing how it evolved within social, political, and cultural manifestations, within currents of ideas, that transcend national borders. Three recent studies of Romanticism are considered in detail in the light of this thesis: M.H. Abrams, *Natural Super-Naturalism: Tradition and Revolution in Romantic Literature* (1971); Henri

Peyre, *Qu-est-ce-que le romantisme?* (1971); and Frederick L. Beaty, *Light from Heaven: Love in British Romantic Literature* (1971). Although none of these books falls wholly within the field of Comparative Literature, *comparatistes* will benefit from the informed awareness manifest in them of European culture in the Romantic age. (JC)

5553. Efron, Arthur. "Bostetter's Critical Method:The Romantic Truth-Tellers." *Paunch* 38:13-31.
Contrary to Hartman's view (*MP*, Nov. 1965), Bostetter did not lack the ability to see poetry as going beyond the "reality principle." Hartman also missed the systematic nature of Bostetter's criticism. Four principles are involved: poetry by any particular poet involves a philosophy, which must be evaluated as to its truth; the personal experience of the poet either becomes incorporated into his philosophy or it wrecks his poetry; individual poems, however great, should be re-evaluated in the light of the major poetic and philosophic confrontation that the poet attempts in a poem that is crucial to his development; protecting the poet from criticism of his world view actually disparages the poet's life and work. Implicit in Bostetter's charge that the Romantics were "ventriloquists" for their own cosmic sense, is the corrective that they also show how poetry is epistemologically foolproof from their own needs to use it. Like Lawrence saying that "you can't fool the novel," Bostetter is saying that you can't fool poetry either. (AE)

5560. Gemmett, Robert J. "The Beckford Book Sale of 1804." *BNYPL* 77:205-23.
William Beckford (1760-1844), author of *Vathek*, was one of the

most singular and exotic book collectors of the 19th century. Beckford disposed of portions of his library on four occasions during his lifetime. The first of these sales, held by Sotheby's in 1804, seems to have been previously unnoticed by Beckford's biographers, but original sale-catalogs are in the British Museum and the Harvard University Library. The catalog is transcribed in full and the title page reproduced in facsimile. Of special note in the catalog are the many examples of Beckford's early reading, his taste for histories, travel books, and the Classics which formed the backbone of his education by private tutors, and his interest in books on magic and the black arts, which reflect a different side of Beckford's personality and are reminiscent of the divided taste that became a trademark of his life and writings. (RJG)

5587. Richards, Emma S. "English Romanticism and the Latvian Poet Jānis Rainis." *JBalS* 5,ii:126-35.

In *The Religious Philosophy of Jānis Rainis, Latvian Poet*, Ziendonis reveals the influences shaping the work of Rainis: the revolutionary spirit of his epoch, the interest in mythology and folklore, the view of nature as a part of religious experience, and the use of poetry as an instrument for achieving social change. Examples drawn from the work of Blake, Shelley, Wordsworth, and Coleridge illustrate similar influences characterizing the English Romantic period. The link between the earlier English poets and Rainis is their acquaintance with German culture. (ESR)

5593. Stephens, Fran C. "Cottle, Wise, and *MS. Ashley 408*." *PBSA* 68:391-406.

The British Library MS. Ashley 408 (in part, Coleridge's *Poems on Various Subjects*) is a heterogeneous group of materials combined by Coleridge's publisher. It has been inaccurately described in every previous account. The first item in the MS, the "Advertisement," exhibits bibliographical similarities to the Gutch Notebook and to four leaves now bound in the "Rugby" MS. The second item in the MS, an interleaved printed text of "Religious Musings," is similar to the Wordsworth Library (Grasmere) MSS. Verse 42 and 43. The third item, "Notes," is actually proofs for the 1796 edition. (FCS)

5594. Taylor, Dennis. "Natural Supernaturalism's New Clothes:A Recurrent Problem in Romantic Studies." *WC* 5:33-40.

However we describe the poem's relation to reality, the question persists: how does this creative model continue to hold true to a world where "every moment is a new and shocking / Valuation of all we have been"? This question brings poet and critic together in a common endeavor to find a formulation of that which makes all formulations immediately traditional. We find in the romantic answer to these questions a critical or creative finesse: reacting against "imitation" while relying on it; identifying the hope of romantic sincerity with its illusory achievement; making organic continuity depend on creative dialectic and vice versa; proclaiming a novelty that defends itself as a tradition. (DT)

5596. Temple, Ruth Z. "Truth in Labelling:Pre-Raphaelitism, Aestheticism, Decadence, Fin-de-Siècle." *ELT* 17:201-22.

The key terms for "schools" of literature and painting in the later 19th century have been used by historians of the period with so little precision and consistency that they have lost their usefulness. These terms represent tendencies which are not perfectly distinct, but the lack of any systematic attempt to distinguish one from another, together with a disquieting scarcity of correct information, has produced a deplorable blur. A sampling of literary encyclopedias, histories, and special studies of one or another of the movements documents the confusion. One cause of inexactitude may be prejudice: most of the terms had, originally, for the general public, a pejorative connotation —were, indeed, bestowed by adversaries—and this has persisted. Moreover, most arose in France, seldom a recommendation to English critics. Some suggestions toward a more precise nomenclature follow. (RZT)

5597. Tye, J.R. "Malleus Maleficorum:The Reverend W.F. Barry, D.D., 1849-1930." *ELT* 16(1973):43-56.

Catholic antagonism in England toward European literary realism and decadence in the late nineteenth century found its most powerful voice in the Rev. W. F. Barry. Initially in the *Dublin Review*, but principally in the *Quarterly Review* during the nineties, Barry subjected the major French and some German

writers, as well as Wagner, Ibsen, Kipling, and minor English writers, to a systematic and penetrating theological and literary analysis. Sharing Pope's vision of a Europe threatened with eternal night, he presented the sequence of 19th-century literature as moving inevitably from Rousseau's exaltation of the Ego toward raging moral chaos and the end of civilization. Barry's apocalyptic attitudes became more tempered by the end of the decade, however, when he contributed less frequently to the *Quarterly*. By its range and rigorous theological consistency, his criticism provided a formidable element in the critical spectrum of the nineties and a model for the specifically Christian critics of the 20th century. (JRT)

5600. Widmer, Kingsley. "The Good Academician:E.E. Bostetter." *Paunch* 38:3-12.

A discussion of the writing and teaching of Bostetter, with particular attention to the arguments and quality of *The Romantic Ventriloquists* (Seattle: Univ. of Washington Press, 1963). Bostetter succeeded in criticizing the Romantics with standards that are often those of the Enlightenment. (KW)

Criticism. 5606. Munday, Michael. "John Wilson and the Distinction Between Fancy and Imagination." *SIR* 13:313-22.

John Wilson wrote 14 articles for *Blackwood's Magazine* between 1817 and 1830 in which he used the terms Fancy and Imagination. Wilson used these words in a sense normally associated with Coleridge's definition in *Biographia Literaria*. Wilson believed that Imagination was superior to Fancy, and that it was both an organ of perception and an organizing and synthesizing force. For him the Imagination was an active power which worked alongside the conscious will in an effort to create art from the materials provided by life itself. Neither *Biographia Literaria* nor the work of Stewart or Schelling provided Wilson with his definition of Fancy and Imagination. His intimacy with Coleridge seems the likliest source of his thinking. (MMM)

Periodicals. 5639. Ward, William S. "Index and Finding List of Serials Published in the British Isles, 1789-1832:A Supplementary List." *BNYPL* 77:291-97.

Some 177 periodicals, newspapers, and other serials are listed as a supplement to *Index and Finding List of Serials Published in the British Isles, 1789-1832*, which was published in 1953. The supplement has been made possible especially because of the publication of the *British Union Catalogue of Periodicals* and its supplements and also of the third edition of the Union List of Serials, both of which have been published since the *Index*. Most of the titles did not appear in either the *ULS* (2nd ed) or in the *Index*, but a few did and are repeated here in order to give fuller bibliographical information or in order to gear the *Index* to *BUCOP* and to the new acquisitions listed in *ULS* (3rd ed). (WSW)

Poetry. 5643. Beckson, Karl. "A Mythology of Aestheticism." *ELT* 17:233-49.

Central to late 19th-century Estheticism is the Religion of Art and Beauty. Constructing a mythology upon such a vision of art, the Esthetes venerated certain literary figures and regarded a work of art as both sacred ritual and Eucharist. As symbolic priest, the poet or artist presides over the Mystery of Transubstantiation, as Joyce's Stephen Dedalus later envisions the act of "transmuting the daily bread of experience into the radiant body of overliving life." Mediating between the worlds of fact and imagination, the poet-priest has the power to create eternal Beauty, to provide a vision of that transcendent reality, the world of Being. His salvation lies in his capacity to create an enduring work of art, to become one, as Yeats said, with "the artifice of eternity." (KB)

5645. Doggett, Frank. "Romanticism's Singing Bird." *SEL* 14:547-61.

By the early 19th century, the singing bird had become an image of the poet's creativity. For poets of the first half of the century, the singing bird suggested that poetry was an overflowing of joyous internal creativity. In the second half, the image intimated that poetry was a flowering from buried anguish. This implication from the Philomela myth influenced Arnold, Swinburne, Bridges. Hardy's "The Darkling Thrush," while retaining in its winter scene the association of the lyric voice with bitterness, revived the concept of lyricism evinced by the earlier romantic poets. (FD)

5650. Haworth, Helen E. " 'A Milk-White Lamb that Bleats'? Some Stereotypes of Women in Romantic Literature." *HAB* 24(1973):277-93.

One major stereotype of women in Romantic literature is to be found in an early sonnet by Keats, in which a young girl is described as a "milk white lamb that bleats / For man's protection." Young Romantic heroines are always described in this way, as submissive, dependent, and incredibly beautiful. In adulthood, such girls had two apparent futures—that of wife and mother, or of a "fallen dove." Some writers, such as Blake and Shelley, saw the latter role as a result of the age's insistence on chastity as the one prime virtue for women; and this same insistence on chastity is perhaps one reason for the age's sexual reticence. Many writers of the period deplored its emphasis on youth and beauty and argued that to best fulfill their roles as wives and mothers women needed an education. (HEH)

5651. —— " 'The Virtuous Romantics'—Indecency, Indelicacy, Pornography and Obscenity in Romantic Poetry." *PLL* 10:287-306.

The Romantic period was concerned about "indecency" and "indelicacy" because it was thought that literature could influence people's behavior. Prudishness is found in Taylor's refusal to publish emendations to "The Eve of St. Agnes" that would make the sexual consummation more explicit; in the critical uproar about "licentious Moore's" *Poetical Works of the late Thomas Little*; in Bowdler's editions of Shakespeare and Gibbon; and in critical reactions to reprints of earlier English literature and translations from the classics. It is found in the public silence and private comments about Burns's anonymous *Merry Muses of Caledonia*, which until very recent years would have been termed both "obscene" and "pornographic." (HEH)

5656. Nelson, James G. "The Nature of the Aesthetic Experience in the Poetry of the Nineties:Ernest Dowson, Lionel Johnson, and John Gray." *ELT* 17:223-32.

Esthetic experience in the poetry of the 1890s is characterized by its intensity and results in "one's burning with a hard, gem-like flame." Although much of the significant poetry of the 1890s follows the paradigmatic form of Keats's "Lamia" up to a point, what happens after the encounter with beauty in the poetry of Gray differs significantly. Gray, in "Mishka," values the emotion, the mood, the psychological state resulting from the moment of encounter for its own sake. It was often the aim of the esthetic poet to explore the impact of beauty on an observer. (JGN)

5660. Starzyk, Lawrence J. " 'The Fiery Consciousness of His Own Activity':The Poet as Outcast in Early Victorian Poetic Theory." *TSLL* 16:109-34.

Early Victorian critics eventually came to recognize the impossibility of poetry dealing with the needs of society in an age so markedly unpoetical. The times militated against the poet having any position whatever in the social structure. The poet could hope to find significance only in the consciousness of his own activity as it was distinguished from the activity of the masses. Ironically, the age's own characteristic introspection gave the ultimate sanction to the self-conscious awareness enforced upon poet and critic alike. By adopting as a critical assumption the pervasive dialogue of the mind with itself, the poet could make of himself in seclusion a relevant instrument of the modern spirit. (LS)

5661. Timko, Michael. "Arnold, Tennyson, and the English Idyl:Ancient Criticism and Modern Poetry." *TSLL* 16:135-46.

Arnold's rejection of Tennyson reflects a basic disagreement with and a misunderstanding of Tennyson's poetic matter and manner. Arnold resented Tennyson's "Philistinism," his "genuine British narrowness," which was the basis of his popularity. More important, Arnold seems not to have understood Tennyson's use of the genre of the domestic idyl and he denounced *Dora*, one of the idyls, for reasons that seem to ignore Tennyson's reasons for employing that form. In his relationship with Tennyson, Arnold abandoned his generally consistent role of objective critic to air a personal reaction to the work of a contemporary. (MT)

Prose Fiction. 5675. Keech, James M. "The Survival of the Gothic Response." *SNNTS* 6:130-44.

The Gothic novel should be reconsidered, not on the basis of its methods but on the particularized response it evokes. It creates an effect of fear, characterized by the vague presentiment of danger and evil, by the intensity of its effect, by a pervasive ominous atmosphere. This fear is also developed by the frightening supremacy of power over weakness. The traditional trappings are not the defining elements of the Gothic; rather, the traditional Gothic novels, from Walpole to Maturin, use different devices but produce a common effect. (JMK)

5682. Reed, John R. "The Public Schools in Victorian Literature." *NCF* 29:58-76.

Public schools are not prominent in Victorian fiction despite their great social importance. This anomaly reveals a division of opinions about children. Imaginative writers largely preferred the Romantic notion that children were innocents threatened by experience to the Victorian educational theory that saw children as ungoverned creatures to be shaped into adults as soon as possible. Writers who disapproved of the schools and their educational philosophy presented both unfavorably in their fiction and implied or stated a corresponding criticism of the society that public school values fostered. Those who approved of the schools created a new kind of juvenile hero, patterned on the manly ideal of the public schools and incorporating the independent qualities of the unregimented child, in an apparent attempt to combine public school values with romantic adventure. (JRR)

5687. Tomlinson, T.B. "Love and Politics in the Early-Victorian Novel." *CR* 17:127-39.

The novels considered all have weaknesses which reveal a gap between their love-stories and political action or theme. In each novel, there is a split between an informed but truncated inquiry into sociological and political issues and thinly conventional love-stories. The failures in each novel are therefore not simply matters of "style" or "technique." (TBT)

Arnold, M. 5698. Douglas, Dennis. "Matthew Arnold's Historic Sense:The Conflict of Greek and Tyrian in 'The Scholar-Gipsy'." *RES* 25:422-36.

The concluding metaphor in "The Scholar-Gipsy" has not one but many historical "sources." Its questionable hypothesis of trading rivalry between Phoenician and Greek in the Aegean echoes Grote, and Roman historiographic tradition, and anticipates Arnold's treatment of the dialectic of Hebrew and Hellene in *Culture and Anarchy*. In both texts, the influence of Liberal Anglican historians is strong. The imaginative eclecticism, critical and informed, of the use of history in "The Scholar-Gipsy" reflects the influence of thinkers like Coleridge and Niebuhr on Arnold's generation. Indeed, the very shakiness of the poem's logic suggests the ambivalencies of the conflict-ridden 30s and 40s. The polemical deftness of *Culture and Anarchy* strikes the keynote of an age of reconciliation. Heine's aside on the interaction of Hebraic and Hellenic influences in post-Renaissance Europe had been previously picked up by Stanley and Goldwin Smith. (DD)

5703. Monteiro, George. "Addendum to Davis' *Matthew Arnold's Letters*." *PBSA* 68:65-66.

A 6 August 1884 note to J.B. Gilder, listed as unpublished, was published in *The Critic*, 5 (30 Aug. 1884), 97. (GM)

5704. O'Sullivan, Maurice J.,Jr. "Matthew Arnold:Un Milton jeune et voyageant." *MiltonQ* 7:82-84.

While the importance of Milton's influence on the poetry of Matthew Arnold has been widely acknowledged and well documented, the cursoriness with which the Victorian's prose examines the Puritan's philosophy and theology has discouraged attempts to define the precise nature of their disagreements. Despite its pronounced admiration for Milton's formal achievements, Arnold's criticism tends either to disregard or disparage Milton's subjects. The objections to *Paradise Lost* in Arnold's prose are echoed in a passage near the end of "Dover Beach" which offers both an agnostic critique of Milton's version of Christian optimism and an undespairing, if somber, substitute for it. (MJO'S)

5707. Siegchrist, Mark. "The Role of Vivian in Arnold's *Tristram and Iseult*." *Criticism* 16:136-52.

Efforts to understand the relation between the main plot of Arnold's *Tristram and Iseult* and the story of Merlin and Vivian with which it closes have had difficulty relating the figure of Vivian to either or both of the two Iseults. Vivian does not represent the experience of either Iseult, but instead embodies the unnaturally powerful force of passion that precipitates the poem's tragedy. Vivian is no victim of passion—she is its agent. As a sorcerer. the fairy Vivian is as unnaturally fatal as the potion that has reduced the lovers to isolation and death, and through the complexity of its description of Vivian in terms of forest landscape, the emblem ironically associates her with the green world of the paradise the lovers had hoped to find in passion. By its assertion that the wisest as well as the most heroic are helpless to resist passion, and by its context that undercuts its own effectiveness as a warning, the end-emblem completes one of Arnold's most negative treatments of the theme of passion as a possible solution to the dilemmas of modern life. (MS)

Austen. 5727. Jason, Philip K. "Off-Stage Characters in Jane Austen's Novels." *SHR* 8:55-66.
The off-stage characters in Austen's novels provide a background or milieu in which the major characters move. They give that world a sense of roundness and verisimilitude, provide a measure or touchstone for the values under discussion in the novels and help to delineate the on-stage characters in terms of those values, and they aid in the development of the plot. They add to the sense of unity by complementing and supplementing the contrasted characters of major interest. In many cases, the important off-stage characters are related to those on the stage in such a way that the free will of the latter is limited. (PKJ)
5728. Joukovsky, Nicholas A. "Another Unnoted Contemporary Review of Jane Austen." *NCF* 29:336-38.
Text of a hitherto unnoticed review of Austen's *Pride and Prejudice* in the *New Review* for April 1813. (NAJ)
5730. Lauber, John. "Jane Austen's Fools." *SEL* 14:511-24.
The essential characteristic of the fool as a literary type is a fixed or "mechanical" quality. His words and actions are a set of close variations upon a single theme. Fools are essential to Austen's novels as a source of comedy, as agents sometimes blocking and sometimes unwittingly advancing the heroine's desires, and to offer the sharpest possible contrast to the heroine's qualities. The fool is aware of externals only; he lives a life of ceremony in contrast to the life of feeling experienced by the heroine. The power of fools is limited, they form a subsociety but not the world, they characteristically defeat themselves. (JL)
5734. McMaster, Juliet. "Surface and Subsurface in Jane Austen's Novels." *ArielE* 5,ii:5-24.
Charlotte Brontë's criticism of Jane Austen was that she could not depict strong feelings, and restricted her view to "the surface of the lives of genteel English people"; and subsequent studies have acknowledged that Austen's business is with the head rather than the heart. Although she does not dwell explicitly on vehement emotion, she presents feelings by indirection and by a subsurface level of implication. So a polite conversation on matters of general import can be informed with intense personal emotion. When Edmund Bertram and Mary Crawford discuss the functions of a clergyman, they are essentially considering marriage, and Fanny witnesses a veiled courtship; when Captain Wentworth discourses aphoristically on the virtues of firmness, he is giving vent to his bitterness at losing Anne Elliot; and so on. Austen's irony can work as a device for rendering strong feeling by suggestion and indirection. (JM)
5743. Weinsheimer, Joel C. "*Mansfield Park*:Three Problems." *NCF* 29:185-205.
In Jane Austen's *Mansfield Park* the formal antithesis of Fanny Price and Mary Crawford paradoxically obscures, rather than clarifies, their distinction. Austen relinquishes the technique of "reciprocal illumination" between these characters and with it the communal values this technique embodied. Similarly problematic is the novel's tripartite standard of evil: how or whether Austen reconciles social cohesion with personal feeling must be clear, however, if the reader is to sanction the pious rigor of the novel's conclusion. Finally, though Fanny idealizes the Park and its inhabitants, the extent to which Austen validates her heroine's vision is open to question. The iniquities of the Crawfords are mirrored in those of the Bertrams; that Mansfield represents an objective ideal appears, therefore, to be a delusion. The lack of clarity in these crucial areas suggests that in *Mansfield Park* Austen may have overreached herself. (JCW)

Blackmore. 5757. Sutton, Max K. "The Mythic Appeal of *Lorna Doone*." *NCF* 28:435-49.
Blackmore's *Lorna Doone* (1869) is a romance with large mythic dimensions. The abducted heroine resembles Persephone, and the hero's experience invites comparison with initiation into the obscure Mysteries honoring Persephone and Demeter at Athens and Eleusis. Lorna falls into the Doones' power at the start of winter; she next appears to the hero, John Ridd, near the start of spring. John's task is to rescue her from Carver Doone who tries to force her into submission during the Great Winter. John's initiation consists of facing not only the brutality of the Doones but also the potential for it within himself. His temptation is to use his strength as rashly as Hercules or as cruelly as his antagonist. He expresses the inner conflict and movement of his life through analogies with seasonal changes and features of the landscape. Following the shooting of Lorna at the altar, hero and villain almost drown together: John barely escapes after offering mercy to his enemy. This triumph over his passion for revenge marks the passing of his greatest test. The bride's recovery signifies his purification; her return gives John a vision of felicity that is comparable to the joy and hope which Cicero received from his initiation into the Mysteries. (MKS)

Blackwood's. 5758. Marin, Clive A. "*Blackwood's*." *MQ* 15:417-28.
Blackwood's was a 19th-century publishing house which put out *Blackwood's Magazine*, and a number of important novels and histories. Founded by William Blackwood in 1817 in Edinburgh, as a response to the Whiggish *Edinburgh Review*, *Blackwood's Magazine* was first edited by J.G. Lockhart (Scott's son-in-law) and John Wilson. It soon became noted for its Tory irreverence and its scholarly criticism. Thomas de Quincey was one of the early contributors, as were Sir Walter Scott, James Hogg, and John Galt. As the 19th-century progressed, *Blackwood's* became more respectable, attracting such authors as George Eliot and Joseph Conrad. The House also put out books by R.D. Blackmore, Bulwer Lytton, and Charles Reade. *Blackwood's* was read by politicians and became identified with the British Empire; it put out military histories and sponsored journals of exploration —Richard Burton and John Speke were published by the House. (CAM)

Brontë, C. 5768. Langford, Thomas A. "Prophetic Imagination and the Unity of *Jane Eyre*." *SNNTS* 6:228-35.
The three pictures in Chapter xiii of *Jane Eyre* are prophetic and consistent with the atmosphere of dreams, visions, and premonitions which characterize Jane's life as a whole. The pictures reflect the melange of experience of Jane's traumatic past, but in her sensitivity to that experience and to the world of the spirit, she is able to portray also the future storm for which the past has prepared her. Embraced in the scope of the pictures are three major sections of the novel and the three most crucial situations in Jane's life. (TAL)
5771. Yeazell, Ruth B. "More True than Real:Jane Eyre's 'Mysterious Summons'." *NCF* 29:127-43.
The "mysterious summons" calling Jane Eyre back to Rochester is an outward sign of a crucial transformation in Jane herself. Obsessed from the first by the desire for both independence and love, as Rochester's servant Jane feels an intense conflict between these two deeply felt needs. Rochester's proposal promises complete union between the lovers, but in *Jane Eyre* passion which tends toward the total identification of two selves can lead only to death. After the discovery of Bertha Mason, Jane might become Rochester's mistress, but only at the intolerable price of her own integrity and independence. Jane at last finds her identity and wins economic and psychic independence at Marsh End; only after these changes—in the plot and in the self—does Rochester's summons come. The dialectic of *Jane Eyre* thus

demands that love must be grounded on the separateness of two independent selves. (RBY)

Brontë, E. 5773. Daley, A. Stuart. "The Moons and Almanacs of *Wuthering Heights*." *HLQ* 37:337-53.
Emily Brontë's careful and precise attention to chronology in *Wuthering Heights* is an integral part of her novelistic method. The incongruity between the fictive dates and the actual dates assigned to the events of the novel has hitherto been puzzling. Moreover, the structure and chronology of *Wuthering Heights* relies upon moon phases, particularly three harvest moons. The data demonstrate that while Emily did not use the almanacs of 1784, 1800, 1801, and 1802, those of two years of her childhood, 1826 and 1827, closely match the time sequences of the novel and thus link it to the Gondal poems and the Young Men's Play. The intricately articulated movements in the chronology of the action of whole weeks or months, moon cycles, sunsets, and the movable feast of Easter agree remarkably with the almanacs of these two years, 1826 and 1827. Without this reading of the daily and seasonal changes measured by the sky, sun, and moon, *Wuthering Heights* would have lacked much of its firmness and symmetry of texture. (ASD)

5781. Scrivner, Buford, Jr. "The Ethos of *Wuthering Heights*." *DR* 54:451-62.
Within each individual there is something unchanging, essential, yet each must exist within a world where external circumstances, the demands of social convention or the inexorable workings of flux, may contradict or thwart this inner quality of being. Contrastive groupings of character, of details of setting, and of metaphor in Brontë's *Wuthering Heights* express this dualism: Lockwood and Edgar Linton contrasted with Heathcliff; the moors and Wuthering Heights itself as opposed to the elegant Thrushcross Grange; Catherine's comparison of her love for Edgar to the foliage of the trees, her feelings of identity with Heathcliff to the rocks beneath. From this dualism emerges the necessity of controlling and manipulating the external to allow fulfillment, expression of the interior. The central ethical failure, the tracing of whose consequences constitutes the main plot line, is Catherine's decision to marry Edgar, making impossible the external realization of the fundamental unity of being between Heathcliff and herself, yet most of the characters are involved in the same dilemma and represent different attempts at solution. (BS,Jr)

5782. Sucksmith, Harvey P. "The Theme of *Wuthering Heights* Reconsidered." *DR* 54:418-28.
The Victorian context of *Wuthering Heights* is relevant to any reconsideration of the novel's central theme. When we take Victorian attitudes toward sex, love, and marriage into account, the novel is seen as a great work of visionary art which presents the tragedy of modern man with regard to his instinctive life. This tragedy is concerned with what man has abandoned, and must abandon, if civilization is to proceed (represented by the Catherine-Heathcliff relationship), with what man has exchanged for it in Victorian times (represented by the Catherine-Edgar relationship), and with the compromise man must achieve (represented by the relationship between the younger Catherine and Hareton), a compromise perhaps being realized in our time. Brontë's anguish about this problem is a characteristic 19th-century anguish, but if we are today more optimistic about the possibility of happiness in certain areas of sexual experience we should bear in mind that in other instinctual areas, notably the aggressive, civilization permits us increasingly less gratification. (HPS)

5783. Thomson, Patricia. "*Wuthering Heights* and *Mauprat*." *RES* 24(1973):26-37.
While the literary sources of *Wuthering Heights* have been much stressed, the possible influence of French fiction has been ignored. George Sand's novel *Mauprat* (1837) bears striking resemblances to Brontë's *Wuthering Heights* in theme, characterization, atmosphere, and the romantic subjectivism of natural description and may well have been one of its sources. The subject of *Mauprat* is the ferocious, obsessive love, in life and beyond the grave, of Bernard, for his beautiful, imperious cousin, Edmée. Roche-Mauprat (his early home) and the Château of

Sainte-Sévère (Edmées) parallel the primitivism and civilization of Wuthering Heights and Thrushcross Grange—a parallel underlined by imagery of hell and heaven. Like Heathcliff, Bernard overhears Edmée confess her contempt for his savagery and does not stay to hear her admission of her sense of the inevitability of their love and shared identity. In *Mauprat* love is shown as eventually a civilizing force—as for the second generation in *Wuthering Heights*—but unlike that of Heathcliff for Catherine. (PT)

5784. Viswanathan, Jacqueline. "Point of View and Unreliability in Brontë's *Wuthering Heights*, Conrad's *Under Western Eyes*, and Mann's *Doktor Faustus*." *OL* 29:42-60.
Point of view is used as the basis for a comparison of the three novels. Analyzes the common features of the narrators' position and the various narrative techniques which enable the reader to go beyond the narrators' comments. (JV)

Brontës. 5790. Slattery, Eugene E.M. "The Brontës:Refined Gothic." *UES* 12,iii:24-27.
In *Jane Eyre* Charlotte Brontë reshapes the Gothic genre by using symbolism which calls for a mature and complicated response. In *Wuthering Heights*, Emily uses two main narrators and a number of "tertiary" narrators who all play a part in the events they relate. Charlotte's technique is more conventional as she makes use of one narrator only to give the novel its peculiar coherence. This coherence is strengthened by the heroine's character being consistent from childhood to adulthood. Emily's elemental characters—except for Lockwood—do not have the same type of consistency. (EEMS)

5791. Wilson, F.A.C. "The Primrose Wreath:The Heroes of the Brontë Novels." *NCF* 29:40-57.
The Brontë sisters reject the convention by which a dominant male presides over a submissive female. Charlotte Brontë substitutes the ideal of an androgynous hero and determined heroine: the man, without relinquishing masculinity, has to exhibit a singularly gentle or "feminine" sensibility, and his energetic partner joins him in an equal and plastic relationship. Both Anne and Emily Brontë learned from Charlotte, though Emily learned unwillingly. In the first part of *Wuthering Heights* the androgyne does not appear, and the heroine has to choose between the brutally virile Heathcliff and the effeminate Edgar. Each shows his unworthiness, and the androgynous Hareton subsequently becomes the romantic hero. (FACW)

Browning, E.B. 5798. Zimmerman, Susan. "*Sonnets from the Portuguese*:A Negative and a Positive Context." *Mary Wollstonecraft Newsl.* 2,i(1973):7-20.
Elizabeth Barrett Browning's *Sonnets from the Portuguese* (1850) is more closely allied to the Song of Songs than it is to conventional sonnet cycles. In the love poetry of Sidney, Shakespeare, and Wyatt, the enthralled poet-lover seeks to regain his sovereignty; Love is his enemy. Elizabeth Barrett too is vanquished by love; her abasement before a human lover is excessive. Yet other lovers (Petrarch, Dante, Sidney, Wyatt) raise their souls from earthly love to spiritual love or philosophy. In contrast, she seeks to lower her soul from heaven to earth. In the Song of Songs the love of the bridegroom for the bride is analogous to the coming of spring to the dead land and to Christ's saving love for mankind. Elizabeth Barrett shares many characteristics with the black bride, and there are strikingly close verbal parallels between the two epithalamia. The woman preparing for marriage is very different from the courtly lover; for her, subordination is better than sovereignty and earthly love is a proper subject for celebration. (SZ)

Browning, R. 5804. Burr, Michael A. "Browning's Note to Forster." *VP* 12:343-49.
Critics have recently accepted the notion that a note by Browning in the "mill" copy of *Pauline* was written to John Forster. The note is read as an apology from the author to his friend for the "confessional" character of the poem. In fact, the note could not have been addressed to Forster, and, far from being a veiled admission that the poem is confessional, the note supports Browning's life-long contention that *Pauline* is "dramatic in

principle." (MAB)

5816. Goldfarb, Russell M. "Hiram H. Horsefall & Company:The Audience for Mr. Sludge, the Medium." *RS* 41(1973): 192-200.

When Robert Browning's dramatic monologue is read with an awareness of the poem's cultural context, then attention shifts from Mr. Sludge toward his audience. Sludge has too often been identified with Daniel Dunglas Home, the best known medium of the nineteenth century. Biographical considerations should hinder us from seeing Sludge as Home and reading Browning's poem as an instrument in a vendetta. Hundreds of mediums practiced in England and America during the 1850s and early 1860s, a time when spiritualism was enormously popular. "Mr. Sludge, 'The Medium,'" however, berates its audience more than it berates the medium. The poem attacks people who attended séances and encouraged mediums. (RMG)

5818. Guerin, Wilfred L. "Browning's 'Cleon':A Teilhardian View." *VP* 12:13-23.

The speculations of Pierre Teilhard de Chardin, scientist and religious thinker, which have already been used to provide commentary on Tennyson's *In Memoriam*, Hopkins' poetry, and Dante's *Divine Comedy*, can do the same for Browning's "Cleon." Cleon seems to approach such Teilhardian ideas as the increase of consciousness, the personalization of creation, love as energy, and the movement toward the Christosphere. Cleon of course rejects these inchoate insights, but it appears that Browning might have had ideas similar to those which Teilhard would articulate in the 20th century. (WLG)

5825. Hyde, Virginia M. "The Fallible Parchment:Structure in Robert Browning's *A Death in the Desert*." *VP* 12:125-35.

Tripartite structure in Robert Browning's "A Death in the Desert" corresponds to the "three souls" of Johannine doctrine outlined in the poem. The entire work is a scale model of the historic church with diverse but intercepting units which are admittedly vulnerable to reductive factual analysis. The prologue introduces physical evidence of Christian origins, a "parchment" guarded by an early-century hermit. This parchment comprises the following monologue which contains multiple viewpoint and indeterminate personae, all ranged about the central figure, St. John, in a manner allowing for the Higher Critics' contention that cults of scribes had written New Testament books in the apostle's name. This composite intellectual exercise is probably the first dramatic monologue featuring an institution's voice. In an epilogue, the crisis in faith extends to a modern skeptic and a supplicant for spiritual power able to transcend apparent feelings of an earthly structure. Dramatic action arises in the prologue, the parchment's guardian handing the document across the centuries to the archetypal skeptic Cerinthus and the epilogue's fervent speaker. Browning unifies the poem through a continuous theme, the cohesiveness of selfless love, and the rudimentary plot embracing past, present, and future. (VMH)

5826. Hymes, Allan. "'A New Rule in Another World': Guido's Experience of Death in *The Ring and the Book*." *Thoth* 14:3-11.

Doubt is an essential theme of Browning's *The Ring and the Book*. Murderer of the innocent Pompilia and her parents, Guido faces execution, yet never faces the utter nothingness of death. He believes that after death there will be "a new rule in another world" not much different from that here on earth. Opposed to Guido stand first, the Pope, who believes that man must "strive" for his goal in life, never certain of the outcome of any human endeavor, and second, Caponsacchi, the hero-priest, who has faced his own doubts about himself as man and priest. (ADH)

5844. Machann, Clifton. "The Wise-Wrenn Copy of Browning's *Helen's Tower*." *PBSA* 68:432-34.

Browning's *Helen's Tower*, a two-page pamphlet consisting of a single sonnet which is currently cataloged in the Wrenn Collection at the University of Texas as an offprint from the type set up for an 1870 reissue of *Helen's Tower, Clandeboye*, is probably a torn leaf from an 1892 edition. Evidently, Wise misrepresented it to Wrenn. (CM)

5850. Neufeldt, Victor A. "Browning's 'Saul' in the Context of the Age." *JEGP* 73:48-59.

"Saul" is a visionary poem, in part autobiographical, but also an address by the poet-prophet to a mid-19th-century man concerning his spiritual darkness. The poet adopts the stance of the Old Testament prophet, but sees with New Testament and 19th-century eyes. Browning can only offer his contemporaries the possibility of regeneration after he has resolved certain religious questions and defined his own beliefs. In "Saul," Browning traces the inability of primitive religious thought to satisfy the needs of the soul, then presents his vision of a revitalized Christianity, not to be found in the chapel, that will reunite God and man and re-establish the sense of God's immanence. In this process art and religion have become one. The poetic art has become the vehicle of salvation and the poet God's spokesman—that is, Carlyle's hero poet. (VAN)

5851. O'Sullivan, Maurice J.,Jr. "'Up against the Shambles' Gate:Robert Browning and the Loss of Leaders." *Mosaic* 7,ii:101-08.

The dissonance in idea, tone, and rhetoric among three of Browning's political poems suggests that the traditional view of his political philosophy, which holds that his liberal optimism never essentially altered, has ignored both the influence of skepticism on his work during the late 1840s and his inability to synthesize it successfully with the ideals of his youth. While an early poem "The Lost Leader" (1843) presents his pre-skeptical, enthusiastically populist position, a work of the next decade "The Patriot," written after his disillusioning Florentine experiences, inverts much of the former poem. By 1885 in "Why I Am a Liberal," Browning could only create an equilibrium between the attractions of optimism and skepticism by resorting to an elaborate, uneasy, and unsatisfying rhetoric. (MJO)

5858. Priestley, F.E.L. "The Central Paradox in Browning." *HAB* 24(1973):87-97.

For the last forty years, much Browning criticism has dealt with the "conflict" defined by Duckworth, either in terms of the poet's psychological problems or of his esthetic problems as derived by critics from a study of the "Essay on Shelley." The psychological criticism is concerned with Browning the man rather than with his poetry and tends to reduce the poetry to biographical document. It also tends, in its search for a simple formula, to hide Browning's real complexities. The second approach, in taking the "Essay on Shelley" as a complete and simple poetic manifesto, also over-simplifies the complexity of the poet's activity. Moreover, a close study of the essay reveals basic flaws in the usual interpretations. A much more important clue to Browning's poetic theories and the problems he comes to face in his poetic practice is to be found in comments in *Sordello* on the three types of poet, and in an analysis of the implications in relation to the function of poetry. For Browning, there is ultimately an unresolvable conflict between the function of the poet as seer, and his function as Maker-see. (FELP)

5861. Russo, Francine G. "Browning's 'James Lee's Wife':A Study in Neurotic Love." *VP* 12:219-34.

Analysis of diction, imagery, syntax, and grammar in Browning's "James Lee's Wife" shows that the failure of her marriage has roots in her personality. She is passive and excessively dependent on her husband, a woman who feels powerless and who attributes power to everything outside herself. The desire to retain what she depends upon reveals itself in images of grasping and possessiveness; her sense of powerlessness shows itself in more and more intense images of entrapment and suffocation. She uses her highly idealized vision of love, shown by biblical and literary allusion, to validate her need to be totally absorbed in, and to absorb, her husband. (FGR)

5863. Scheer, Thomas F. "Mythopoeia and the Renaissance Mind:A Reading of 'A Grammarian's Funeral'." *JNT* 4:119-28.

Previous readings of Browning's "A Grammarian's Funeral" have tended to ignore the self-awareness of the Grammarian's students. Close reading of the poem, however, reveals that the students are neither the Grammarian's dupes who ingenuously praise him nor unconscious detractors who damn him while speaking his elegy. Rather, the students consciously present the Grammarian to the people of the town and "vulgar thorpes" as a man of learning and pity though they recognize that he is, in fact, a pedant, "dead from the waist down." In their balancing of scholarship and the senses, this world and the next, the students are prototypes of

Browning's famous Renaissance figures. (TFS)

5868. Siegchrist, Mark. "Browning's *Red Cotton Night-Cap Country*:The Process of Imagination." *VP* 12:137-52.

Browning's *Red Cotton Night-Cap Country* presents an imaginative penetration to the truth beneath a contemporary French scandal. It has been faulted on the distance of the speaker from his material and on the incongruously jovial tone in which he approaches the tragedy. The poem depends on these very discrepancies to create a gap between the perceiver and his subject, the crossing of which provides a measure of the imaginative power capable of performing such a feat. This faculty of sympathetic projection is what Browning considered to be the source of poetry, and the poem is so specifically a record of the process by which dramatic monologues are created that by the end of the poem it is implied that the speaker is none other than Browning himself. In thus displaying Browning's poetic faculty at work discovering significance in the most uncompromising raw experience, the poem is a demonstration of his artistic method free from the ambiguities of dramatic impersonation. (MS)

5869. —— "Pollyanna or Polyanthus:Clara de Millefleurs in Browning's *Red Cotton Night-Cap Country*." *ELN* 11:283-87.

In his exploration in *Red Cotton Night-Cap Country* of motivation submerged beneath lurid human action, Browning suggests the moral ambiguity of his hero's paramour by a complex floral imagery, the various implications of which are concentrated in the lady's name—Clara de Millefleurs. The French *millefleurs* echoes the Greek *polyanthus*, the beautiful but suspiciously artificial cultivation which is the flower most associated with her. These dubious connotations of sensuality and sophistication are reinforced by two other meanings of *millefleurs*—a carnivorous bog-plant and a medicine made of cow's urine—and all these innuendos are deepened by the possible irony of the purity implied by "Clara" and the spurious aristocracy implied by "de." By providing the heroine of his moral mystery story with a name so rich in various negative implications, Browning deftly hints at possibly treacherous depths beneath her attractive surface. (MS)

5872. Sonstroem, David. "On Resisting Brother Lippo." *TSLL* 15:721-34.

Browning's Fra Lippo Lippi does not deserve as lenient a hearing as many readers give him. The poem's extensive network of thematic contrasts offers too strenuous a contest of ideas to encourage simple approval of Lippo. Moreover, the disreputable setting counts against him, and the guard's compromising his trust in succumbing to the wayward monk serves as a gentle reminder to the reader not to do likewise. Lippo's preference for darkness, his inconsistent professions, his imperceptiveness with respect to points of view and ways of life other than his own, his boundless effrontery, etc., should all serve to temper the reader's delight in his undeniable vitality and charm. (DAS)

5884. Ziegler, Heide. "Browning's 'The Bishop Orders His Tomb at Saint Praxed's Church,' 76-79, 98-100." *Expl* 32:Item 45.

Robert Browning's dramatic monologue "The Bishop Orders His Tomb at Saint Praxed's Church" presents us with a textual problem, as far as the references to the late Latin of Ulpian and to the even later Vulgar Latin form *elucescebat* in lines 76-79 and 98-100 are concerned. The use of different types of Latin, each representing a different stage from Classical to Vulgar Latin, reflects the bishop's implicit value judgments about his predecessor. (HZ)

Butler. 5891. Bisanz, Adam J. "Samuel Butler:A Literary Venture into Atheism and Beyond." *OL* 29:316-37.

Butler's life-long endeavor to come to terms with the problems of faith and reason, Christianity, and iconoclasms is to be considered an integral part of his literary work, of which the two "Erewhons" are but two outstanding examples. Butler's religious peregrination from orthodox theism to atheism and ultimately toward a transcendental vision of polytheism is discussed. At the same time, the development of Butler's thought is analyzed against the background of what later became known as the philosophy of pragmatism. (AJB)

5893. Copland, R.A. "Butler's Metaphorical Man." *AUMLA* 42:163-74.

Butler contributed to the debate on evolution. Like Shaw he rejected the explanations of Darwin and reasserted the earlier evolutionists' belief in the operation of will and intelligence within the organism. This made easily for an anthropomorphism like Shaw's, the events of evolutionary history being accounted for metaphorically as though they involved human motivation. But Butler's metaphors were drawn from a narrow social range. Taken together they develop their own logic and appear not merely to convey but to promote Butler's thinking. The writing becomes both witty and serious: all life has been impelled by a belief in private enterprise and inspired by the ambition to become a decently educated, sober-minded English gentleman. (RAC)

Byron. 5895. Allentuck, Marcia. "Byron and Goethe:New Unpublished References by Henry Gally Knight." *PQ* 52(1973): 777-79.

After commenting on the puzzling aspects of the Byron-Goethe relationship, Allentuck quotes from an unpublished letter at the Huntington Library by Henry Gally Knight, which details a visit to Goethe after Byron's death and sheds new light on Goethe's complex responses to Byron. (MEA)

5896. Ashton, Thomas L. "*Marino Faliero*:Byron's '*Poetry* of Politics'." *SIR* 13:1-13.

Romantic political poetry synthesizes metaphors at once political and prophetic, precisely because prophecy is a metaphor of evolving consciousness. In *Marino Faliero*, the insult scrawled on the Doge's throne is both an explicit summary of the sexual politics of Venice, and an indictment of oligarchy. Byron's Doge discovers that prophecy's words are made true by historical things. Evolving consciousness of freedom's truth enables the Doge to integrate individual and national identity, private and public husbandry, and to summon the Adriatic storm-tide of revolution, as he discovers his true role in inevitable historical process. (TLA)

5901. Blackstone, Bernard. "Byron and the Levels of Landscape." *ArielE* 5,iv:3-20.

Byron's nature poetry is distinguished by its humanism, by interchange between man and landscape, city and countryside, on a number of levels from the georgic to the mythical. His imagery of snowflakes, crystals, flowers, and rocks projects a strength/weakness oxymoron extending into human relationships. The approach is "emblematic" along horizontal-vertical lines, with strongly sexual overtones. Contact with Mediterranean landscapes modified his earlier "hard primitivism" approach, but love continues to be seen as the ruling cosmic principle within a cyclic pattern of man emerging from, and returning to, his mother earth in physical-spiritual interchange. His sea poetry explores similar levels, in which the delights of merging and dominating are included in a context of freedom. (BB)

5906. Brogan, Howard O. " 'Byron So full of Fun, Frolic, Wit, and Whim'." *HLQ* 37:171-89. [B's personality.]

Byron's manners have long been held against him as reflecting upon the tone of his works as well as of his life. This unfavorable conception is based upon a few accounts written by biased observers and by scholars indignant at his supposed mistreatment of Lady Byron, Claire Claremont, Hunt, Keats, and the Shelleys. An examination of opinions expressed by many observers from his childhood until his death, including Lady Byron and the Shelleys, supply overwhelming evidence that on the whole Byron's manners were fascinating as well as gentlemanly, reflecting a stable character beneath a mercurial personality, and helping to explain the distinctive quality of his work. (HOB)

5919. Eggenschwiler, David. "The Tragic and Comic Rhythms of *Manfred*." *SIR* 13:63-77.

Byron's *Manfred* makes a unified esthetic effect through two complementary rhythms: the tragic represents the movement of life as necessary, coherent, and catastrophic; the comic represents it as arbitrary, episodic, and inconclusive. Manfred senses tragic inevitability but he also recognizes nature's incoherence, and tries to escape fate through an arbitrary suicide. Although the rhythms alternate throughout, the tragic grows stronger and finally dominates. In his triumphant defeat Manfred finds an essential self that cannot be changed by the arbitrary spirits, the vagaries of chance, or his own changing impulses, but he also destroys that part of himself which can experience the comic rhythm of life.

(DE)
5937. Miller, Edmund. "Byron's *The Vision of Judgment*, Stanzas 48-51." *Expl* 33:Item 4.
When St. Peter calls George III a "Guelph" in stanza 49 of Byron's *Vision of Judgment*, he is being ironic as well as arcane. George III was a Guelph by descent from the medieval German house whose strong support of the papacy brought its name to apply to any supporter of the papacy in the dispute of the Guelphs and the Ghibelines. Perhaps Byron calls his devil "Satan" in this poem as a kind of response to Southey's charge that he was the chief of a "Satanic" school of poetry. (EM)
5941. Parker, David. "The Narrator of *Don Juan*." *ArielE* 5,ii:49-58.
Byron's *Don Juan* owes its unity to the narrator's being a version of the rogue. Byron successfully exploits his posturing habit in *Don Juan* in the multiple narrative voices which suggest the unifying presence of a rogue narrator. The poem is more profitably considered as rogue literature than as absurd literature because of its robustness. The narrator's aristocratic temperament and style do not prevent him from being a rogue. Rogues always have affinities with aristocrats and gentlemen. The multiple styles and ramshackle grace of the verse are also evidence of roguery. (DP)
5956. Spence, Gordon W. "The Moral Ambiguity of *Marino Faliero*." *AUMLA* 41:6-17.
Marino Faliero does not clearly indicate Byron's moral attitude toward his subject, though the dramatis personae are concerned with the morality of their actions. Marino Faliero's conduct is open to conflicting interpretations. He has a generous intention, but his motives are ambition and revenge. He creates the terms on which he demands to be judged but his rhetoric does not absolve him of his guilt. Israel Bertuccio is a mirror-image of Faliero's resentment and revenge and Bertram is a mirror-image of his humane feeling. These two sides of the Doge's character come into conflict when, in passing sentence upon the senators, he balances their public vices against their private virtues. (GWS)
5957. Sperry, Stuart M. "Byron and the Meaning of *Manfred*." *Criticism* 16:189-202.
In recent years Byron's *Manfred* has been read as a play of personal and psychological catharsis, a purgation necessary to the ironic detachment of his later verse. This insight has never been amplified fully in terms of the play's dramatic structure or the history of its composition. Revising the final act, Byron made several major changes, the most important of which was to add the grim, Mephistophelian spirit who comes to claim Manfred as his victim at the close. Structurally the play is an exercise in sustained negation in which Manfred successively rejects all spiritual authorities of the world, pantheistic, Manichean, or Christian. The culminating struggle between Manfred and the infernal spirit dramatizes Byron's confrontation with a more insidious power—the character of the Byronic hero, a role he had long enacted and on which he compulsively relied for the particular energy of his verse. *Manfred* dramatizes Byron's struggle for psychological liberation from the powers of Nemesis which made *Don Juan* possible. (SMS)

Carlyle. 5993. Campbell, Ian. "Carlyle, Pictet and Jeffrey Again." *Bibliotheck* 7:1-15.
Carlyle in his twenties suffered a crisis of conscience (connected with religious doubt) and a crisis of transition between interest in scientific and mathematical studies, and his new historical and ethical German interests. A missing article on Pictet, composed in 1819, has eluded scholars but Pictet's book is here identified for the first time, the effect on Carlyle analyzed, and its significance to Carlyle at a crucial point in his career analyzed. Pictet's work was on the history of celestial perturbation attributable to interplanetary gravitation: Carlyle's scientific interest (and his long-standing admiration for Newton) were involved, but the dry and unimaginative tone of the work he was studying repelled him—and may have helped complete the abandonment of such studies. (IC)
5996. Dibble, Jerry A. "Carlyle's 'British Reader' and the Structure of *Sartor Resartus*." *TSLL* 16:293-304.
The British Reader in *Sartor Resartus* is the repository of a well-defined set of British attitudes toward Germans and Germany with which Carlyle was familiar. *Sartor Resartus* is a carefully constructed labyrinth designed to take the British Reader from one stage of consciousness to another, from understanding to reason, and it is the Reader's progress and the changes in his attitude that the organization of the book reflects. It becomes possible to account for the particular kind of objections the Editor addresses to his audience, the sequence of materials he presents, and for the final chapters of the book as well. The chapters on "Dandies" and "Tailors" are a formal parody of the fictive world created in *Sartor Resartus* and are thus a humoristic way of indicating to the Reader the nature of the illusions generated by his original point of view. (JAD)
6011. Tarr, Rodger L. "Thomas Carlyle's Growing Radicalism:The Social Context of *The French Revolution*." *Costerus* N.S. 1:113-26.
Carlyle's *The French Revolution* transcends the bounds of historical record, and on one level at least may be viewed as a social prophecy in which he expands upon the moral dicta of *Sartor Resartus* and anticipates the social theories of *Past and Present*. His stated purpose was not to write merely a factual account of the French Revolution, but rather to interpret the insurrection within the context of the "Condition of England." Specifically, in *The French Revolution* he attacks laissez-faire economics, warns against the artificial division of the aristocracy and the indigent, and counsels that revolt, however justified, does violence to justice. These themes permeate the whole of Carlyle's history as he assumes the role of a prophet warning England about the consequences of materialistic despotism and moral corruption. The history, then, becomes a forum for Carlyle's sociomoral theories, and as such is important in tracing the rise of his radicalism during the 1830s. (RLT)
6012. ——. "Thomas Carlyle's Libraries at Chelsea and Ecclefechan." *SB* 27:249-65.
Contains an annotated bibliography of Carlyle's libraries at Chelsea and Ecclefechan. Pertinent bibliographical information is given for each entry, followed by symbols to identify the special characteristics of each entry with particular attention given to the extent of marginalia and, where possible, the date when Carlyle acquired each book. The bibliography is divided into sections to facilitate reference, and it is accompanied by a critical account of the history of Carlyle's library. (RLT)

Carpenter. 6020. Richards, Max. "The English Whitman." *ArielE* 5,iv:40-55.
In "Summer Heat," "By the Shore," "Spending the Night Alone," "Squinancy-Wort," and "As to You O Moon," Edward Carpenter shows himself to be more than "Whitman and water" or merely a bard of social prophecy for Utopian readers in six languages. These and other pages of *Towards Democracy* (1883-1905) have a freshness, vividness, play of mind and sympathy, that merit comparison with Whitman and Lawrence (and at times Wordsworth). Carpenter's mystical experience gives him ground for a radical idea of human equality and for establishing an intimate personal relation between poet and reader. He wrote to Nature's dictation, often windily, yet charmingly and with a nobility not always without strength. (MR)

Coleridge, S.T. 6043. Delson, Abe. "The Symbolism of the Sun and Moon in *The Rime of the Ancient Mariner*." *TSLL* 15:707-20.
In "The Ancient Mariner" the sun and moon function alternately favorably and unfavorably, sometimes changing their association in the same scene. Their chief cumulative attribute is of an instability so pervasive as to suggest betrayal. That Coleridge could have seriously presented such a view in one of the landmarks of English romanticism, and contrary to the attitude set down in other poetry written at the same time, may appear suspect. On the other hand, Coleridge was in a state of emotional, intellectual, and physical flux during the period of composition; the genre of the ballad of the supernatural would offer protection against being attacked for the theme; and some of the entries made at the time in his notebooks show ideologically skeptical moods that could have found imaginative embodiment. (AD)

6044. Dendurent, H.O. "The Coleridge Collection in Victoria University Library, Toronto." *WC* 5:225-86.
An analytic description of an important collection of MSS, rare books, and documents relating to Coleridge. The collection also contains considerable resources for the study of Coleridge's family and his literary and intellectual friends—Robert Southey, William and Dorothy Wordsworth, Charles Lamb, and dozens of lesser contemporaries. The material is listed and briefly described in three parts. Part I (440 items) describes works by Coleridge in book form, in anthologies and others' works, in newspapers, and in MS or transcript. This last category is further subdivided to include poems, collected writings, dramatic pieces, prose works, sermons and lectures, letters, notebooks, marginalia, miscellaneous notes, and table talk. Part II (330 items) describes Coleridge association items: books in the Coleridge library, letters to Coleridge, Malta documents, documents relating to Coleridge's writings, other bills and documents, contemporary reviews and assessments, and material collected for scholarship and criticism and Coleridgeiana. Part III (371 items) describes the material relating to other members of the Coleridge circle: verse and other writings, correspondence, miscellaneous writings, documents, and general miscellaneous items (such as photographs) found in the collection. (HOD)

6047. Fleissner, Robert F. *"Hwæt! Wē Gardēna:*'Kubla Khan' and Those Anglo-Saxon Words." *WC* 5:50-58.
"Kubla Khan" is typologically related to *Beowulf*, and fifteen parallels are considered, but to think of them as determining any historical indebtedness is perilous; nonetheless, if the poem was composed in an unconscious state, then actual influence would scarcely matter, particularly if dreams are understood pneumatologically. The last section of the poem, in any case, was most likely composed after the dream was over. Precedent for the analogy is seen in terms of Cowper's *The Task*, which has passages that may be designated "Beowulfian" as well as Xanaduvian. The last line of "Kubla Khan" may read "drank" (not "drunk") "the milk of Paradise." (RFF)

6048. ——— "'Kubla Khan' as an Integrationist Poem." *NALF* 8:254-56.
In the light of recent papers suggesting that "The Rime of the Ancient Mariner" details the Englishman's conscience concerning the enslavement of black people, it helps to examine "Kubla Khan" as a dream-vision about racial integration. As such, the Abyssinian maid relates to the other imagery in the poem of the reconcilement of "contraries." Far from representing the fear of miscegenation, she stands for the anima. It is notable that the book Coleridge was reading before he composed the poem, *Purchas His Pilgrimage*, was a continuation of Leo Africanus' *The History and Description of Africa*. On an archetypal level, the fertility of the poem suggests the African jungle ("forests ancient as the hills," for example). Such a "mythic" interpretation has advantages over the more narrowly autobiographical Freudian readings. (RFF)

6053. Haeger, J.H. "Coleridge's Speculations on Race." *SIR* 13:333-57.
The as yet unpublished Coleridge manuscripts include at least five separate writings on race. The pattern of these speculations indicates a connection with the ideas on "lower" biological forms in *Theory of Life*. Earlier fragments demonstrate Coleridge's grasp of the theoretical issues as he reviews questions of taxonomy. But two fragments turn away from analytical investigation in favor of synthesis as Coleridge discusses "degeneration" from original white purity and anticipates the concepts of a master race, the white man's burden, and moral progress. Inclusion of such ideas in the plan for his grand system seems an error, since it puts into codifying framework what Coleridge himself recognized as theory. (JH)

6055. Hoheisel, Peter. "Coleridge on Shakespeare:Method Amid the Rhetoric." *SIR* 13:15-23.
Coleridge saw the plays of Shakespeare as Romantic dramas, imaginative incarnations of moral ideas through which we contemplate an eternal truth. These ideas unify a specific play through the development of either a moral aberration or a moral wholeness in a character. Language, imagery, and characterization are controlled by the idea of human nature which

Shakespeare chooses to embody. The Coleridgian approach to Shakespeare's plays is to seek out the moral idea which is incarnated in the attitudes and actions of characters, thereby illuminating the permanent condition of mankind. (PH)

6071. Passler, Susan M. "Coleridge, Fielding and Arthur Murphy." *WC* 5:55-58.
A probable analogue for the description of nature in "Kubla Khan" is Fielding's description of Allworthy's estate in *Tom Jones* (I. iv), but it seems equally likely that Coleridge had in mind Arthur Murphy's metaphoric description of the plot of *Tom Jones* in his "Essay on the Life and Genius of Henry Fielding, Esq." In Murphy's "Essay," his assessment of the plot of *Tom Jones* employs the metaphor of a pent-up river flowing underground through caverns until it shoots up, meanders through the country, and then flows into an ocean. The verbal similarity between this description and lines 19-28 of "Kubla Khan" is greater than the similarity between the poem and *Tom Jones* and it is highly probable that Murphy's work is a relevant analogue. (SMP)

6072. Patterson, Charles I.,Jr. "The Daemonic in *Kubla Khan*:Toward Interpretation." *PMLA* 89:1033-42.
Kubla Khan seems to be a poem about demonic poetry, a strain that reappears intermittently, and thus the search for spiritual and philosophic meanings in the poem could be relinquished. From this point of view, *Kubla Khan* appears neither as a fragment nor as a poem about evil. (CIP,Jr.)

6073. Paul-Emile, Barbara T. "Samuel Taylor Coleridge as Abolitionist." *ArielE* 5,ii:59-75.
Deals with the evolution of Coleridge's opinion on the issue of black slavery. His writing on the subject is divided into two periods. The first, during which he supports abolition, extends from 1792 to 1798. From 1808 to 1833 there is considerable change in his opinion on the issue and his mature opinion becomes strongly conservative. He begins to see society as hierarchical by divine plan and moves from all drastic change fearing that it would lead to great social disorders and upheavals. (BP-E)

6074. Pradhan, S.V. "Coleridge's 'Philocrisy' and His Theory of Fancy and Secondary Imagination." *SIR* 13:235-54.
Coleridge's writings reveal the existence of a fully-worked out philocrisy, i.e., an analysis of the functions of the mind—Reason, Understanding, and Sense—and of the faculties of Fancy and Imagination that mediate between these functions. The functions and faculties are arranged hierarchically in his "scale." The "scale" and the theory of the Primary Imagination can be integrated to yield Coleridge's theory of knowledge. The "scale" offers a general theory of the genuses, Fancy and Imagination, while *Biographia Literaria* offers a special theory of their literary species. It also suggests the possibilities of other species of Fancy and Imagination such as Fancy in science and the philosophic Imagination. (SVP)

6081. Weinberg, Alan M. "Samuel Taylor Coleridge (1772-1834):A Duo-Centenary Tribute." *UES* 10,iii(1972):17-20.
Coleridge's quest for unity in multeity pervades his work and reflects the integrity and comprehensive nature of his thought, finding expression in his organic theory of life and art. While the value of his prose works should not be underestimated, Coleridge's large and vital intelligence is best approached through his poetry, for it is as a poet that Coleridge is likely to win the widest acclaim. In conclusion, cognizance must be taken of the central importance of religion for Coleridge: the existential grounds of Coleridge's faith are consistent with his overall need to live out his general philosophy in daily life. In this way Coleridge's search for the oneness of life became "a real and distinct possibility." (AMW)

6082. Zall, P.M. "The Cool World of Samuel Taylor Coleridge:Implacable Christian." *WC* 5:169-73.
Wordsworth's lawyer Edward Christian wielded enormous influence as an arch-conservative spokesman for the legal privileges of the universities. Among these privileges was the right to receive free copies of each book copyrighted in Great Britain, a right seldom invoked until 1812, and more particularly 1814 when Christian's copyright law adopted by Parliament created chaos in the book trade, chiefly among the publishers of costly, specialized, multi-volumed editions. At the same time, the donation

provisions of the law required the dissemination of "worthless" books that otherwise would have come from the press stillborn. (PMZ)

6083. —— "The Cool World of Samuel Taylor Coleridge: Bawdy Books and Obscene Ballads." *WC* 5:59-64.
In complaining against literature that tended to "inflame the fleshly appetites" Coleridge expressed the spirit of an age (1797-1817) that saw a new form of "democratic" censorship to protect the morals of a new mass reading class. The Society for the Suppression of Vice and its powerful ally, Lord Chancellor Eldon, effectively banished bawdry from the streets and shelves of the nation. (PMZ)

Crabbe. 6093. Hatch, Ronald B. "George Crabbe, the Duke of Rutland, and the Tories." *RES* 96(1973):429-43.
It has long been argued that when Crabbe was appointed domestic chaplain to the Duke of Rutland, his "Liberal opinions" proved unacceptable to the Duke of Rutland who was a "Tory." This belief has led scholars to hypothesize that Crabbe was forced to modify his poetry in the 1780s in order to make the sentiments acceptable to his patron. This argument, however, has little basis in fact: it results largely from a false model of British political life at the time and an incomplete understanding of Rutland's political and social beliefs. Although in late 1782 and 1783 Crabbe seems to have experienced some delicate situations at Belvoir Castle, this in no way influenced the concerns of his poetry. (RBH)

De Quincey. 6104. Herbert, Christopher. "De Quincey and Dickens." *VS* 17:247-63.
The works of De Quincey and Dickens show affinities of theme and technique. These affinities center in their treatment of psychological themes and have their origins in their lifelong preoccupation with the childhood experience of living as waifs in the streets of London. Each shows a deep concern with the function of memory and with the internal hazards it entails. For De Quincey memory represents the chief faculty of individual bereavement and loss. This sense of loss is in turn a function of the feeling of personal guilt. By this avenue he reaches his hypothesis of the "Dark Interpreter," the alien self that lives covertly and menacingly within the psyche. This pattern of themes, then, can be seen to underlie many of Dickens' novels. (CCH)

6105. Janzow, F. Samuel. "The English Opium-Eater as Editor." *Costerus* N.S. 1:47-82.
The identification of Thomas De Quincey's political and literary contributions to the *Westmoreland Gazette* during the 16 months of his editorship, 1818-19, is less difficult than may be supposed. An examination of De Quincey's *Gazette* yields convincing evidence that the editorials are his work, and that he wrote or prepared many other articles for his journal. A listing of his *Gazette* writings includes 90 articles from his editorial column, 33 articles and essays from outside his column, one article in the form of an anonymous letter to the press, 4 "articles" of the "essays-in-footnotes" type, 15 abstracts and abridgments, 35 uniquely De Quinceyan "classified extracts," 16 excerpts from non-De Quinceyan sources with added editorial comment by De Quincey, four "reviews" consisting of extracts from the works reviewed, one translation, and 18 editorial notices—some 217 items, more than half of which are original work. Attribution to De Quincey of the great majority of these writings ranks as "positive"; that of the rest either as "probable," or as "possible." (FSJ)

De Vere. 6107. Fackler, Herbert V. "Aubrey deVere's *The Sons of Usnach* (1884):A Heroic Narrative Poem in Six Cantos." *Éire* 9,i:80-89.
Unlike preceding versions of the Deirdre legend, De Vere's retelling is at once faithful to the materials of the legend, full of correctly-handled ancient customs, possessed of narrative integrity and careful development, and psychologically realistic. Using the best sources available to him, he followed the rationale of Victorian medievalism, reorganizing, reinterpreting, and re-integrating elements of plot and thematic emphases. In his

sources he found suggestion and outline; his art lies in his filling-in and his addition of structural coherence to the legend. (HVF)

Dickens. 6117. Beasley, Jerry C. "The Role of Tom Pinch in *Martin Chuzzlewit*." *ArielE* 5,ii:77-89.
Tom Pinch stands at the very center of Dickens' *Martin Chuzzlewit*. The simple-hearted servant supplies an obvious contrast to the arch-hypocrite Pecksniff and functions as a moral barometer by which all of the narrative's major characters must be measured if they are to be fully understood. Pinch's devotion to a false image of Pecksniff makes him guilty, like most of the people in his world, of a wrong-headed vision of life. This failure of vision constitutes a form of selfishness, and Pinch's successful struggle with it provides absolutely essential commentary on the experience of the novel's other characters. (JCB)

6145. Feltes, N.N. "Community and the Limits of Liability in Two Mid-Victorian Novels." *VS* 17:355-69.
Mid-Victorian novels present the changing experiences of "community" in a variety of ways. The dramatic relations among Eliot's characters in *The Mill on the Floss* reflect the values of early industrial capitalism, whose common form of commercial enterprise was a partnership. By the mid-1850s, however, the laws governing commercial organizations had been amended to allow the joint-stock company, with limited liability. Dickens' *Little Dorrit* (1856-57) reflects the contemporaneous public debate over liability. "Liability" is a useful concept for the historical critic to measure the increasing effect on "community" of "alienation." (NNF)

6148. Fleishman, Avrom. "Master and Servant in *Little Dorrit*." *SEL* 14:575-86.
Dickens' *Little Dorrit* develops a pattern of human relationships akin to those Hegel described in the dialectics of master and servant: not only do masters gain from their servants but the latter receive satisfactions from—and even become emotionally dependent upon—their masters. The extreme instance of servitude is the title-figure herself, and her constant self-abnegation in behalf of others marks a limit of ethical behavior—approaching the model of Christ's charity. Yet the workings of the plot show servitude or self-sacrifice a lesser thing than reciprocal love. The denouement encourages a view of men and women related not by superiority and inferiority, exploitation and sacrifice, but by the mutual gifts of mature love. (AF)

6153. Gardner, Joseph H. "Dickens, Romance, and *McTeague*:A Study in Mutual Interpretation." *ELWIU* 1:69-82.
Previous commentary on Dickens' influence on *McTeague* has focused on its melodrama, grotesques, and symbolism, but "mutual interpretation," as opposed to traditional "source studies," reveals a deeper and more significant Dickens influence. In the dentist Norris is able to achieve a Dickensian mode of characterization and interpretation of human experience that extricates him from the cul-de-sacs of "scientism" that entrap him in such dreary exercises as *A Man's Woman*. Moreover, Norris absorbs from Dickens a tendency to associate distorted attitudes toward money with grotesque or perverse sexuality that provides him the basis for the characterization of Trina, the relationships between her story and the novel's sub-plots, and much of its symbolism. (JHG)

6157. Hannaford, Richard. "Fairy-Tale Fantasy in *Nicholas Nickleby*." *Criticism* 16:247-59.
Despite conflicting modes of pantomime, melodrama, and fairy-tale fantasy in *Nicholas Nickleby*, the novel achieves design and thematic unity through Dickens' reliance upon fairy-tale motifs. Pantomime is a source of much broad comedy and melodrama of emotional extravagance, but fairy tales represent a vision of a secondary world where, instead of a bewildering and corrupt everyday reality, one discovers simplicity, justice, and a respect for the most essential human values. The world of Faërie is contrasted with a dull and ugly commercial world, and the primary structural unity in the novel depends upon a plot-of-fortune in which Nicholas seeks for success while combatting brutalizing forces at work in society. The plot-of-fortune, *peripetea*, and the intervention of the fairy godfathers (the Cheerybles) reveal that if Dickens wants to create a world of good

cheer and benevolence, he must rely upon values which exist outside ordinary experience—in Faërie. (RH)

6168. Kennedy, G.W. "Dickens's Endings." *SNNTS* 6:280-87.
Dickens' endings show a steady progression toward subtlety and variety through his career. The most important common structural feature in Dickens' endings is the presence of a private domestic sanctuary in which the surviving benevolent characters can find permanent refuge. The characters within these sanctuaries come to live, at the conclusions of the novels, in a special order of mythical time marked by a constant round of ritual celebrations. Often Dickens indicates this time-shift by emphasizing the near-agelessness of the benevolent characters after the main action of the novel is completed. Dickens also changes from the normal narrative past-tense to the present-tense. The domestic refuges that exist in this mythical time become arenas, isolated from the corruption of the surrounding society and untouched by the grinding effects of ordinary time, in which unconditionally virtuous action is possible. (GWK)

6174. Lane, Lauriat, Jr. "Dickensian Iconography: 1970." *DR* 54:130-35.
The different forms and orders of Dickensian iconography and their assistance in the appreciation of his art are enumerated. Even bric-a-brac can lead the serious critic to ask what in Dickens' character calls forth such a response. The actual portraiture of Dickens suggests something of his development. Closer to Dickens' writings are photographic and other pictorial images of his England. The original illustrations to his books have the greatest significance but their exact importance remains debated. The critics address these questions and see the illustrations' role as incorporating and summarizing the theme and spirit of a particular novel. (LL)

6178. Marten, Harry P. "The Visual Imaginations of Dickens and Hogarth: Structure and Scene." *SNNTS* 6:145-64.
The Hogarth-Dickens correlation in matters relating to the creative imagination is discussed. An exploration of Hogarth's own criticism and *A Rake's Progress* and *Industry and Idleness*, together with an examination of Dickens' *Nicholas Nickleby* and other novels, helps us comprehend the similar ways in which the whole of each artist's work affects the perceiver. The works of both men are spatio-temporal and progress through interrelated, yet distinct, visual frames. The Hogarthian-Dickensian grotesque is what we perceive in *Industry and Idleness*, *Bleak House*, and other creations of the two men in which reality and unreality, fact and symbol, comedy and terror, are blended. (HPM)

6188. Palmer, William J. "The Movement of History in *Our Mutual Friend*." *PMLA* 89:487-95.
Dickens' *Our Mutual Friend* is an existential novel dealing with the struggles of the central characters to place existence before essence. This theme of self-definition involves characters singularly preoccupied with analyzing the deadness of past history and with rejecting the impositions of the past upon the present and the future. Boffin's historical reading and Lizzie Hexam's visions in the symbolic fire both reveal the necessity of change if there is to be an existential future. The main protagonist, Eugene Wrayburn, faced with the Shakespearean-Sartrean decision of whether or not to be in his sexual relationship with Lizzie, chooses to reject the pornographic cliches of Victorian sexuality and establish an existence for himself outside of the atrophied "society" of the novel. *Our Mutual Friend* is an optimistic statement of Dickens' belief in the power of the individual to regenerate a dead world. (WJP)

6189. Parker, Dorothy. "Allegory and the Extension of Mr. Bucket's Forefinger." *ELN* 12:31-35.
Critics have interpreted tag gestures and phrases in novels as shorthand devices for characterization unchanging in their meaning. Dickens, who employs this device frequently, brings an entirely new scope to it in *Bleak House* where Detective Inspector Bucket is first identified with punitive hand gestures. While Bucket is working for Tulkinghorn, Dickens is ambivalent about him, so the tag gestures mostly depict affable menace. Then, gradually, Bucket's tag gestures become associated with those of Allegory, the painted figure on the ceiling of Tulkinghorn's law office. As they shift, Bucket moves away from the heartless legalism that clings to him as Tulkinghorn's minion to become a minister of justice. At the end, when Bucket is engaged on his search for Esther's dying mother, the same gestures show warm human charity. Thus Dickens uses an old rigid device to reveal character and amplify the novel's meaning in a new and flexible manner. (DEP)

6194. Pratt, Branwen. "Sympathy for the Devil: A Dissenting View of Quilp." *HSL* 6:129-46. [*The Old Curiosity Shop*.]
Dickens describes Quilp, the comic villain of *The Old Curiosity Shop*, through animal images, implying that he is not man, but beast. The portrayal of Quilp is often ambivalent and ultimately compassionate. Cast as the Marchioness' father in the novel's original plan, he demonstrates affection as well as hatred, and his cruelty stems from a pitiable envy of those who are lovable as he can never be. Quilp's exaggerated badness allows us to admit our own antisocial feelings through identification with a fellow (though a much worse) sinner. He seems to serve also as an authorial wish fulfillment, acting out to absurdity his creator's desires for freedom. Dickens first describes Quilp's burial at a crossroads, with a stake through his heart—the traditional laying to rest of demons and suicides. But the author relents, and tells us it is rumored that Quilp's wife and his errand boy secretly gave the body a Christian burial. This final forgiveness of Dickens' devil brings Quilp back from outer darkness into the human community, and implies the author's own wish to believe that even unredeemable wickedness can be redeemed by Christian love. (BBP)

6210. Smith, Sheila M. "John Overs to Charles Dickens: A Working-Man's Letter and Its Implications." *VS* 18:195-217.
Prints and annotates a long letter of 20 July 1840 from the carpenter John Overs to Dickens giving Overs's critique of Carlyle's *Chartism*. This working man's reaction to Carlyle shows Overs's lively independence of mind often expressed in vigorous language and suggests that Overs influenced the character Will Fern in the *Chimes*, and gave him some of the rebellious fire for which Dickens was criticized. Fern is also unlike Overs's letter in his abject gratitude for guidance and condescension from those "above" him. A scrutiny of Overs's relationship with Dickens suggests the novelist's limited conception of the working man as an object either of pity or of guilt. (SMS)

6223. Tick, Stanley. "The Decline and Fall of Little Nell: Some Evidence from the Manuscripts." *PCP* 9:62-72.
John Forster is generally given the credit he claims for suggesting to Dickens the sad ending of *The Old Curiosity Shop*. Midway through the serialization, we are told, when Dickens "had not thought of killing her," it was Forster who pointed out that the young heroine should not survive her adventure. Study of the manuscript suggests that Dickens had, quite early in the work, considered Nell's death as a possible conclusion for the novel. Perhaps Dickens's decision to have Nell die was influenced by his friend's advice, but several crossed-through passages in the manuscript show that the notion of her death was entertained long before Forster spoke up. (ST)

6231. Waddington, Patrick. "Dickens, Pauline Viardot, Turgenev: A Study in Mutual Admiration." *NZSJ* 1:55-73.
Dickens probably first met Pauline Viardot during her opera seasons in London in the late 1840s; but their friendly relations date from his stay in Paris during the winter of 1855-56. He came to be a great admirer of her art. Partly through the Viardots Dickens also met Turgenev. Some rare information on their literary relations is presented in this article, which also includes three hitherto unpublished letters of Dickens to Pauline Viardot, a note from Dickens to Turgenev's English translator, and some previously unused details from the diaries of George Sand. (PHW)

6235. Wees, William C. "Dickens, Griffith and Eisenstein: Form and Image in Literature and Film." *HAB* 24(1973):266-76.
Montage and visual representation, concepts readily understood in the context of cinema, are relevant in understanding aspects of literature as well. Eisenstein was the first to bring these similarities between film and literature to light, most notably in his essay "Dickens, Griffith and the Film Today," in *Film Form*. Close examination of Dickens' writings, Griffith's films, and the writings and films of Eisenstein himself validate Eisenstein's

insights. Further validation comes from a comparison of montage and metaphor, and in this context similar formal elements can be found in Haiku, Imagist poetry, Eisenstein's shooting scripts, and passages in Dickens' novels. (WCW)

6237. Westburg, Barry. " 'His Allegorical Way of Expressing It':Civil War and Psychic Conflict in *Oliver Twist* and *A Child's History*." *SNNTS* 6:27-37.

In *Oliver Twist* we find fragments of an historical drama involving, primarily, the conflict surrounding the careers of Charles I, Cromwell, and Charles II. Several names of characters suggest an "allegory"—and by reading *Twist* with the aid of *A Child's History* we can interpret the personal significance that Cromwellian civil war acquired for Dickens. In opposing a facile, lying Charles I and an honest, inarticulate Oliver Cromwell, and by weaving their story into that of an innocent child (Twist) and his deceptive tormentors (Monks and Fagin), Dickens explored the complex sources and limits of his own creativity. He superimposed two stories of character-oppositions, and created an implicit dimension where both purely good and evil characters emerge equally atrocious and yet equally justified. (BW)

6243. Wolfe, Peter. "The Fictional Crux and the Double Structure of *Great Expectations*." *SAQ* 73:[335]-47.

Great Expectations has two overlapping structures—the formal three-part break, which marks the stages of Pip's growth, and an acausal web of climaxes strung around random events in Chapters i, viii, and xxxix. The dynamism created by these two overlapping structures rays out to include within its tensional orbit not only Pip and Victorian society but also humanity at large. (PW)

6248. Zambrano, A.L. "The Style of Dickens and Griffith:*A Tale of Two Cities* and *Orphans of the Storm*." *Lang&S* 7:53-61.

The films of David Wark Griffith owe an incalculable debt to Charles Dickens. Because Dickens saw the novel as an essentially dramatic form, his style creates vivid characterization and visual motifs to convey theme. This style is reflected in Griffith's *Birth of a Nation* or *Intolerance*, and Griffith acknowledged that the inspiration for his cinematic innovations came from Dickens' novels. However, Griffith's world is slightly more simplistic and melodramatic, and while *Orphans of the Storm* draws many of its incidents from *A Tale of Two Cities* and often parallels its thematic development, the film remains essentially limited in scope. Because Griffith believed the cinema's appeal was intrinsically emotional, he presented the French Revolution in terms of physical danger and deprivation, climaxing with Danton's daring last-minute rescue of the heroine from the guillotine. Dickens instead uses biblical motifs and striking symbols to augment the thematic implications of his novel, ending on a note of resurrection and spiritual rebirth. (ALZ)

Disraeli, B. 6250. Schwarz, Daniel R. "Art and Argument in Disraeli's *Sybil*." *JNT* 4:19-31.

Disraeli's *Sybil* is organized as a comprehensive indictment of a society that neglects its working poor. Disraeli creates an omniscient narrator who conceives himself both as the conscience of England and as a prophetic voice who imagines the possibilities of England's redemption by means of a revived monarchy, a responsible aristocracy, and a resurgent Church. Sybil represents the spiritual potential of religion and Charles Egremont represents the potential of a morally responsible aristocracy. The narrator re-educates the reader to understand that Morley's reductive view of an irrevocable division between the privileged and the common people derives from paranoid class hatred. (DRS)

Dodgson. 6251. Anderson, Irmgard Z. "From Tweedledum and Tweedledee to Zapo and Zépo." *RomN* 15(1973):217-20.

Fernando Arrabal owes Lewis Carroll the inspiration for various accessory episodes dealing with Alice and certain animals. One chapter of Lewis Carroll's *Through the Looking Glass* supplied Arrabal with the entire vital substance of *Pique-nique en campagne*. Tweedledum and Tweedledee have become Zapo and Zépo; Alice has lent her traits to M. and Mme Tépan; and the Walrus and the Carpenter are re-embodied in Arrabal's stretcher-bearers. A close correspondence between the ideas and the actions of Carroll's characters and those created by Arrabal is unmistakable. Only the seriousness of the situation has increased: Alice's concern over a brotherly spat in "Tweedledum and Tweedledee" has intensified into Arrabal's bitter condemnation of senseless warfare. (IZA)

6260. Miller, Edmund. "Lewis Carroll's Genealogical Oversight in 'The Tangled Tale'." *ELN* 12:109-11.

There is a mathematically simpler solution to the genealogical puzzle in Knot II. A Governor of Kgovjni with the right family connections need not invite anyone at all to his dinner party. (ECM)

Dowson. 6266. Steinmann, Theo. "The Two-Dimensional Structure of Dowson's 'In Tempore Senectutis'." *CP* 7,i:49-53.

In Dowson's "In Tempore Senectutis" every key word has multiple functions in a pattern of correlations. Different terms for the past change the focus. The perspective opens up from an individual vision to a global view, as the separate entities man and woman become the matrimonial unity "us." Numerous repetitions suggest the permanence young love projects into life, and the hardly noticeable changes reflect the slow decay of growing older. The rhyming words are interlocked and their juxtaposition sums up certain themes of the poem. They mark the rhythm in the progression of thought and sentiment. (TS)

Eliot. 6292. Ermarth, Elizabeth. "Incarnations:George Eliot's Conception of 'Undeviating Law'." *NCF* 29:273-86.

George Eliot stresses individual choice and responsibility in her fiction yet the far-reaching consequences of every action and the growing weight of conditions seem to mock the idea of freedom. Her idea of cultural law actually reinforces the notion of personal liberty. Natural law is deterministic but cultural law only determinate. Every determinate condition constitutes a cultural "law" in Eliot's sense. The only "undeviating law" is the law of facticity, the only rule, to perceive the "hard unaccommodating Actual." Law in her sense probably derives from Feuerbach's anti-Hegelian notion of time and from Spencer's nonteleological idea of progress as increasing differentiation. (EE)

6293. —— "Maggie Tulliver's Long Suicide." *SEL* 14:587-601.

Eliot makes it clear in *The Mill on the Floss* that the social norms of St. Oggs exert a heavy influence on Maggie's development. This has long been obvious but less obvious, perhaps, is the fact that the norms Maggie struggles with are sexist. They are norms according to which she is an inferior, dependent creature who will never go far in anything and which consequently are a denial of her full humanity. Years of such denial teach Maggie to repress herself so effectively that she cannot mobilize the inner resources that might have saved her. By internalizing crippling norms, by learning to rely on approval, to fear ridicule, and to avoid conflict, Maggie grows up fatally weak. In place of a habit of self-actualization she has learned a habit of self-denial which Philip rightly calls a "long suicide." (EE)

6295. Fulmer, Constance M. "Contrasting Pairs of Heroines in George Eliot's Fiction." *SNNTS* 6:288-94.

George Eliot's employment of contrasting pairs of heroines exemplifies her concern for moral lessons; through dramatic scenes involving two young women with different attitudes and characteristics, she preaches the negative effects of selfishness and the broadening, positive effects of sympathetic understanding. In each case the women do and say things which indicate very clearly that one is distinctly more mature morally than the other. This moral distinction lies in their different capacities for sympathy. (CMF)

6299. Higdon, David L. "Failure of Design in *The Mill on the Floss*." *JNT* 3:183-92.

Between 1850 and 1890, English and American fiction experienced a crisis in form: numerous major authors found themselves unable to conclude their novels in ways satisfying to their audience and their art. Nowhere are the problems more evident than in the conclusion to George Eliot's *The Mill on the Floss*. By recovering the structural design of this novel, now obscured by modern publication practices, we can discover an emblematic "embrace scene" permeating the entire work and successfully providing a sense of unity. However, we can also see that George Eliot, like her contemporaries, so committed the action, idea, and structure of her work to "openness" that their demands were irreconcilable with the conventional closed ending. (DLH)

6300. —— "Sortilege in George Eliot's *Silas Marner*." *PLL* 10:51-57.

By using the drawing of lots, a common form of sortilege, as the inciting event in *Silas Marner*, George Eliot focused her novel's concern with chance and providence and also provided an accurate glimpse of primitive religious practices. Belief in sortilege causes the Lantern Yard congregation to deny essential human love and sympathy. Five key scriptural texts related to sortilege are discussed and numerous examples of the practice are provided from Moravian and Methodist sources. (DLH)

6301. Hollahan, Eugene. "The Concept of 'Crisis' in *Middlemarch*." *NCF* 28:450-57.

George Eliot's attention to the importance of crisis in a plot is shown partly by 15 occurrences of the word "crisis" in the second half of *Middlemarch*. Most significant among these occasions is a definition of "crisis" as "that concentrated experience which in great crises of emotion reveals the bias of a nature, and is prophetic of the ultimate act which will end an intermediate struggle" (ch. lxxiv). The plot is generated by the character, decisions, and actions of Will Ladislaw. In a series of similar events, Will boldly asserts his independence from fragmenting, delimiting social pressures; in the crisis itself, Will tells Mr. Brooke, "I shall stay as long as I like. I shall go of my own movement, and not because they are afraid of me" (ch. li). Presented in somewhat encomiastic terms, Will is nevertheless central to the theme: that in a time of cultural change and fragmentation when widely sanctioned guiding visions have disappeared, the individual's innate desire for wholeness forces him to devise his own vision of completeness. (EH)

6308. Quick, Jonathan R. "*Silas Marner* as Romance: The Example of Hawthorne." *NCF* 29:287-98.

Discusses the influence of Hawthorne's *The Scarlet Letter* on Eliot's *Silas Marner*. *Silas Marner* stands apart from the realist tradition in which Eliot is mainly located. Autobiographical evidence is first introduced to display Eliot's interest in Hawthorne's writing and career. Similarities between the structural, thematic, and stylistic features of *Silas Marner* and *The Scarlet Letter* are discussed, reflecting at every point the preoccupation of each author with the romancer's art. George Eliot saw even more clearly than Hawthorne that the prose romance offered artistic freedom from the strict confinements of realism. (JRQ)

6309. Roazen, Deborah H. "George Eliot and Wordsworth: 'The Natural History of German Life' and Peasant Psychology." *RS* 41(1973):166-78.

Despite the Wordsworthian nature of George Eliot's interest in common life, there are important differences in the two writers' approaches to rustic subjects. Wordsworth observes and admires such figures from a distance; his real interest is in what they can mean to him, in his own imaginative powers. While Eliot's portraits are more rounded, her common-life characters are less "common" than Wordsworth's. Some reasons for Eliot's reluctance to write at length about peasants may be inferred from an early article, "The Natural History of German Life" (1856), in which she adopts the fundamentally un-Wordsworthian view that for the peasant, "custom holds the place of individual feeling." While her total description of the peasant does not apply to any major characters in her subsequent fiction, several aspects of peasant psychology and behavior outlined in her essay are relevant to later protagonists, and the essay can be used to help clarify similarities and differences in the two writers' approaches to peasant subjects. (DHR)

6310. Rogal, Samuel J. "Hymns in George Eliot's Fiction." *NCF* 29:173-84.

George Eliot's fiction yields both examples of others' hymns and metrical versions of Psalms, as well as commentary on attitudes toward hymnody and psalmody. Hymnodists and psalmodists represented in the fiction include John Hopkins, William Whittingham, Thomas Ken, Isaac Watts, and Charles Wesley.

Illustrations of their divine odes represent not only various aspects of the controversy raging within the Anglican Church during the early 19th century concerning the movement from psalter to hymnal, but serve also to point out the prejudice among Anglicans (especially in rural parishes) against dissenting and evangelical sects. Generally, the hymns in George Eliot's fiction represent her own religious traditionalism; although she set out to capture the drama of Evangelicalism among middle- and lower-class Britons, she, herself, never drifted far from the religious establishment. Thus, the hymns and Psalms in her fiction parallel the essence of her religious belief: the middle ground of positivism that encompassed both conformity and dissent. (SJR)

6315. Sullivan, William J. "Music and Musical Allusion in *The Mill on the Floss*." *Criticism* 16:232-46.

At each stage of Maggie Tulliver's progress in *The Mill on the Floss*, George Eliot introduces music: sometimes as metaphor or commentary to define the nature of Maggie's emotional life; often as literal, meaningful narrative event; and as a series of allusions to musical works which illuminate the developments of the plot. References to music in the abstract, to singing or listening to music, or to the psychological effects of music, establish the excessive power of Maggie's emotional life and the consistency of her responses to apparently disparate life-situations. Eliot articulates the components of Maggie's "triple world of Reality, Books, and Waking Dreams" which are at once a complex psychological definition and an insight into the structural composition of the novel. Significant allusions to works by Handel, Keble, Thomas à Kempis, Haydn, and Bellini emphasize the patterns of the "triple world" and introduce characters and incidents correlative with those of the novel. (WJS)

6316. —— "The Allusion to Jenny Lind in *Daniel Deronda*." *NCF* 29:211-14.

The allusion to Jenny Lind in Chapter v of *Daniel Deronda* calls attention, not only to the qualities of Gwendolen Harleth's voice, but to certain negative aspects of her character as well. Although it might be considered as praise of Gwendolen's vocal abilities, the allusion is almost certainly also intended as a comment on her egotistic motives and limited esthetic perceptions. There is good evidence to believe that Eliot wrote the review of Henry Chorley's *Modern German Music* which appeared in the *Leader* on 29 April 1854, a review which focused on Chorley's estimate of Jenny Lind's technical accomplishments and motivational failures. Chorley's presentation of Jenny Lind parallels Eliot's presentation of Gwendolen Harleth, and his criticism of Jenny Lind parallels Klesmer's criticism of Gwendolen. It seems likely, therefore, that the 1854 review suggested some of the details for the novel. (WJS)

6320. Wing, George. "The Motto to Chapter XXI of *Daniel Deronda*: A Key to All George Eliot's Mythologies?" *DR* 54:16-32.

The motto to Chapter xxi of *Daniel Deronda* is an image describing the power of ignorance. It was written by Eliot herself, imitating the style of the King James Bible. The motto has minimal application to the chapter but it illuminates the entire work. The power of ignorance is also influential in her other novels and has a damaging effect on certain individuals. Its strength dissipates from the center toward the periphery, bringing distress to a whole group. (GW)

6321. Witemeyer, Hugh. "George Eliot, Naumann, and the Nazarenes." *VS* 18:145-58.

Adolf Naumann, the German painter of *Middlemarch*, has escaped the scrutiny applied to Eliot's other characters. Naumann's historical prototypes are identified, Eliot's knowledge and evaluation of Nazarene painting is summarized, and Naumann's place in the historical pattern of *Middlemarch* is clarified. Naumann combines attributes of the Nazarene painters. Eliot admired the revival of early Christian iconography which helped ignorant observers like Dorothea to understand Medieval and Renaissance art; however, she disliked the archaism and the Catholic religious aims of Nazarene painting and had no use for the elaborate allegorical German history paintings which came into fashion in the 1830s and 1840s. Naumann's theory and practice of history painting have affinities with Mr. Casaubon's reductive Christian mythography. Naumann's career thus reflects the historical pattern of aspiration and failure established by the careers of the major characters in *Middlemarch*. (HW)

Evans, C. 6323. Jenkins, David. "Community and Kin: Caradoc Evans 'At Home'." *AWR* 24,liii:43-57.
Caradoc Evans was born into a rural community in southwest Wales. One way to understand a community is to see it as its members see it. This article places Evans in the context of his natal community, the community being understood as its members understood it. (DJ)

6324. Williams, Trevor. "Caradoc Evans's 'Sayings':An Approach to the Style of His Later Work." *AWR* 24,liii:58-66.
From the outset of his literary career Caradoc Evans' prose style was extremely terse. This terseness tended to reflect that limited moral and spiritual universe of his characters. His later work, however, sacrifices clarity to the pursuit of epigrammatic precision. Examples of epigrammatic sentences, or "sayings," which he was able to insert into his text almost at random are presented. (TLW)

Froude. 6333. McCraw, Harry W. "Two Novelists of Despair:James Anthony Froude and William Hale White." *SoQ* 13:21-51.
Markham Sutherland, the hero of Froude's *The Nemesis of Faith*, reluctantly takes holy orders but is fired from his first job for heresy. Seeking peace in Italy, he meets an unhappily married Englishwoman with whom he falls in love. But when her child accidentally dies, the guilt-stricken Markham attempts suicide, only to be stopped by a Newmanite figure who steers him into a monastery where he dies more miserable than ever. The moral seems to be that "all kinds of religious faith are equally impossible, and yet so is a successful life without faith." In Hale White's *The Autobiography of Mark Rutherford*, the restless and high-strung hero leaves a fundamentalist seminary for unsuccessful jobs in teaching, lay preaching, and publishing; his quests for certainty and friendship are aggravated by bouts of melancholia but helped by encounters with Wordsworth's poetry, a militant but kindly rationalist, and various sympathetic women. He ends in a resigned and tolerant humanism. (HWM)

6334. Mulhauser, Frederick L. "An Unpublished Poem of James Anthony Froude." *ELN* 12:26-30. [Incl. text of the poem, "Confessio fidei. Killarney an hour before Sunrise."]
Froude is well known as a historian, editor, and biographer but not as a poet. An unpublished poem of his in a letter of 1848 to A.H. Clough demonstrates Froude's early interest in writing poetry and contributes to the background of Froude's best-known novel, *The Nemesis of Faith*. (FLM)

Gosse. 6356. Gracie, William J.,Jr. "Truth of Form in Edmund Gosse's *Father and Son*." *JNT* 4:176-87.
Edmund Gosse's *Father and Son* reveals a story unknown or at least unacknowledged by the author himself. Proposing to render a life with "scrupulous" fidelity to truth, Gosse combines the techniques of autobiographical literature with fiction to create a remarkable portrait more valuable for what it implies than for what it states. Gosse intends to relate the emergence of an esthetic soul from a hostile environment, but his blend of autobiographical narrative and fiction and his reliance on highly mannered metaphorical language and a tightly controlled dramatic structure reveal more than he knew. (WJG)

Hardy, T. 6369. Baker, Christopher P. "The 'Grand Delusion' of Jude Fawley." *CLQ* 10:432-41.
The cause of Jude Fawley's misfortune and downfall is not adequately explained by Hardy's contradictory philosophy. An answer may be found in the character of Jude himself: Jude's actions at four major decision-points reveal a habit of ignoring his own awareness that he is seeking goals he realistically cannot obtain. Jude's self-knowledge is too great to assign responsibility for his actions solely to an overriding fate or social order. His delusion springs from his own refusal to seek goals which are more suited to his own abilities than the grand schemes which he entertains but consistently fails to achieve. (CPB)

6380. Cassis, A.F. "A Note on the Structure of Hardy's Short Stories." *CLQ* 10:287-96.
Examines the structure of Hardy's short stories written in the tradition of the *ecrivain* rather than those written in the tradition

of the *raconteur*. The short stories are carefully structured around an "idea"—life's little ironies. The elaborate structural pattern is deliberate, and Hardy expresses his views through the structure of his stories rather than through explicit statements. To illustrate Hardy's deliberate construction, a comparison is made between the two versions of "The Waiting Supper." In tracing the elaborate structural pattern in the short stories, Hardy's use of incidents, the beginnings, and endings of his stories are also examined. (AFC)

6402. Edwards, Duane. "*Tess of the d'Urbervilles* and *Hippolytus*." *MQ* 15:392-405.
Thomas Hardy's *Tess of the d'Urbervilles* resembles Euripides' *Hippolytus* in a number of ways. For example, Tess is very much like Phaedra and Angel is like Hippolytus. The structure of *Tess* reveals that Tess, like the characters in *Hippolytus*, is partially responsible for her own fate although circumstances work to her disadvantage. Thus Tess falls into reveries at five critical junctures in her life. In doing so, she is unable to make decisions or exert her will. So she deserves to suffer, but at the same time she, like Phaedra and Hippolytus, suffers more than she should. In Hardy's novel there is some compensation for this: Angel undergoes recognition and becomes a better man. But in the novel neither Theseus nor Hippolytus himself benefits from his own or from Phaedra's death. Ultimately, then, Hardy's novel is less pessimistic than Euripides' play. (DDE)

6404. Fass, Barbara. "Hardy and St. Paul:Patterns of Conflict in *Jude the Obscure*." *CLQ* 10:274-86.
A consideration of Hardy's statement in *Jude the Obscure* that it concerns the deadly warfare between flesh and spirit focuses on St. Paul's relation to the novel. St. Paul did not conceive of the human dichotomy dialectically, and tracing his influence on *Jude* leads one to believe that Hardy despaired of reconciling the opposing forces of paganism and Christianity. Moreover, Matthew Arnold's *St. Paul and Protestantism* provides a link between St. Paul and the Victorian debate concerning Hebraism and Hellenism. Arnold leads to another influence on *Jude*, Heinrich Heine, also interested in the social consequences of man's dual nature. Hardy could distinguish between Arnold, who wished to reconcile Hebraism and Hellenism, and Heine, who despaired of union. It is Heine's view that triumphs in *Jude*, for it is his conception of the struggle that comes closest to St. Paul's. (BF)

6418. Hornback, Bert G. "Thomas Hardy:The Poet in Search of His Voice." *VP* 12:55-63.
Thomas Hardy's best poetry is characterized by his use of a natural, personal voice. When his poems are unsuccessful it is often because he is hiding himself and his personal feelings behind a mask of irony. Hardy always insisted that he was not a pessimist but a "meliorist." The meliorist Hardy speaks in his best poems in a voice very different in a number of ways from the Oz-like voice he adopts in his other poems. In this huge majority of his poems, Hardy's irony is not just in his subject or theme, but in manner, tone, even in the language of the poems. He hides himself and his feelings behind the safety of harshness, linguistic objectivity, and formal, often stilted diction. It is as though he writes to avoid communication in these poems. Hardy's best poems, however, speak in a different voice, and the irony which makes pessimism is replaced by the meliorist's compassion. In these poems Hardy the philosopher disappears; the latinate and cacaphonously polysyllabic diction is discarded; the form of the verse, however stark, seems natural; and the disguise of irony, of objectivity, is abandoned and subjective feeling is allowed in its place. (BGH)

6419. Horne, Lewis B. "Hardy's Little Father Time." *SAQ* 73:[213]-23.
Little Father Time's presence in *Jude the Obscure* dramatizes the way in which Jude moves in awareness from an older era characterized by traditional modes of perception into a modern one. Little Father Time is a product, representative, and victim of Modernism. Little Father Time and the child Jude share like traits, some belonging to the child-figure of Romantic tradition, but these traits bring forth different effects largely because the periods of time to which each child belongs have different qualities. Little Father Time's suicide, in design an act of

renunciation intended to aid, pushes Jude into a full recognition of the force of Modernism, drawing him through a kind of rite of passage. The nature of this act is illuminated when viewed in terms of ritual actions described by Emile Durkheim in *The Elementary Forms of Religious Life*. (LBH)

6420. Hyman, Virginia R. "The Ethical Dimension in Hardy's Novels." *ELWIU* 1:178-92.

Deriving his ideas about ethics from Comte, Darwin, Huxley, Spencer, Mill, and particularly Leslie Stephen, Hardy believed that men's attitudes and feelings were changing, and that his fiction could accelerate such change by evoking and reinforcing the proper responses. Associating subjectivity, romantic idealism, and the desire for personal happiness with egotism, and an objective perspective and empathy with altruism, he believed, like Stephen, that the more "advanced" attitude would be brought about either directly through suffering or vicariously, "by the pain we see in others reflected in ourselves." While the earlier novels trace his characters' evolution from egoism to altruism, the later ones present the tragic consequences of failure to make the appropriate adaptations. Trapped by their idealizations and subjectivity, Hardy's tragic characters cannot move forward. However, the very failure of response in the characters evokes the proper kind of response in the reader. (VRH)

6428. Kozicki, Henry. "Myths of Redemption in Hardy's *Tess of the d'Urbervilles*." *PLL* 10:150-58.

On levels of myth and ritual, we see Tess as the ritual sinner in a double cycle of guilt, sacrifice, and redemption. She is the mythic sacrificial victim-hero, whether in the Greek-tragedy pattern or the Judeo-Christian. Angel is the modern intellectual and he realizes in Tess's wedding-night revelation the resurgence of the demonic metaphysics that he had rejected with his father's Evangelicalism and a demand upon him for an imitation of Christ. His collapse is the fragility of Romantic "religion," that drives Tess as scapegoat into the wilderness where, in a folding of one cycle over the other, Alex returns again as agent. (HK)

6436. May, Charles E. "*Far from the Madding Crowd* and *The Woodlanders*." *ELT* 17:147-58.

Most critics have asserted that Hardy's *Far from the Madding Crowd* and *The Woodlanders* are traditional pastorals with the following characteristics: the male protagonists (Gabriel and Giles) are true Arcadians at one with nature; the antagonists (Troy and Fitzpiers) are anti-pastoral forces who break up the rural values; the female protagonists (Bathseba and Grace) first err in choosing anti-pastoral forces, but are finally reunited with nature at the end of the novels. A closer look at *Crowd* and *Woodlanders* reveals that because Hardy's vision of reality was incompatible with the mythus which gave rise to Greek and Elizabethan pastoral, the result is a distortion of pastoral, or grotesque pastoral. Images of nature's death and decay pervade both works. Gabriel and Giles bow to social laws rather than natural ones. Troy and Fitzpiers represent efforts to transcend the decayed natural world. The true organic conclusions of the two fables occur when Bathseba, in a pestilent swamp, and Grace, in a violent storm, come to an existential awareness of the value-lessness of the natural world. (CEM)

6438. Mickelson, Anne Z. "The Family Trap in *The Return of the Native*." *CLQ* 10:463-75.

Hardy's characters lead solitary lives in an indifferent universe and appear caught in some trap—*The Return of the Native* dramatizes the family trap. Mrs. Yeobright's possessive love results in her son's inability to form any lasting relationship with a woman. Clym suffers from the threat of emasculation, failure of marriage and of purpose. Hardy develops the complexities of family feeling and the special loyalties they evoke by becoming a kind of third voice attempting to understand the actions of mother and son. He probes into Mrs. Yeobright's bewilderment in attempting to meet her son's confused demands and the proliferation of roles she assumes. He also demonstrates that Clym's efforts to realize his masculinity and virility are doomed because of the intense mother-son relationship. The relationship with Eustacia affords Hardy the opportunity to explore psychological processes of guilt, fear, and discovery. (AZM)

6440. Morgan, William W. "Form, Tradition, and Consolation in Hardy's 'Poems of 1912-13'." *PMLA* 89:496-505.

Hardy's "Poems of 1912-13" constitute a formal elegy over his first wife, Emma. The twenty-one lyrics are thematically unified, and the sequence is given overall form and structure by the persona's organized perception of time. Within the sequence the narrator focuses upon recent past, present; then distant past, recent past, present. This five-part temporal model serves as the form of the elegy. It is likely that he wrote this sequence in full consciousness of the great elegies preceding his, for he adapted many of the conventions of the elegiac tradition to his own artistic needs. The traditional consolation of perpetuity outside time and space, however, he denied, and for it he substituted the consolation of full emotional and intellectual comprehension of the couple's experience together. This limited consolation, based upon the persona's organized perception of time, is the logic of grief for Hardy's godless universe. (WWM)

6443. Murfin, Ross. "'Channel Firing':An Introduction to Hardy's Special Cosmos." *Thoth* 13,iii:27-36.

Hardy's poetry derives much of its color and life from rural traditions and traditional ballads. At the same time, these Dorset or "Wessex" poems direct the reader toward philosophical questions about the nature of the universe. "Channel Firing" effectively uses traditional ballad lore, rhythms, images, and themes to raise abstract questions about the nature of a cosmos in which such tragic, even grotesque, tales could seem plausible. Hardy introduces an ineffectual personal God—a God whose impotence is due to the fact that he is not an omnipotent creator but, rather, the creation of man's hopeful theologies. Identical to the God of some of Hardy's other poems the God of "Channel Firing" is "A form for praying to" whom "we can no longer keep alive." (RCM)

6448. Page, Norman. "Thomas Hardy's Forgotten Illustrators." *BNYPL* 77:454-64.

The illustrations which accompanied nearly all Hardy's novels on their first appearance have since that time been almost entirely neglected. Hardy took considerable interest in the work of his illustrators and on occasion supervised it closely. The relationship of illustrations to novel is examined in several instances, and the work of three artists is given special consideration, the complete record of Hardy's illustrated novels being summarized more briefly. (NAP)

6465. Springer, Marlene. "Invention and Tradition:Allusions in *Desperate Remedies*." *CLQ* 10:475-85.

A major aspect of Hardy's fictional style is his abundant use of allusions. In *Desperate Remedies* Hardy uses his allusive patterns to give flatteringly subtle clues to plot, while on a more academic level he utilizes ironic references which furnish consistency and complexity to the portrait of Manston. When action and conversation come dangerously close to making Manston too sympathetic for the role of sensation-antagonist, the allusions artfully undercut him and foreshadow his defeat. Moreover, these allusive techniques become permanent, extremely useful devices of his later style—as evidenced by Sergeant Troy's allusively enhanced similarity to Manston, or by the Hellenic-Hebraic dichotomy allusively outlined in *Jude the Obscure*. (MAS)

6467. Sullivan, Tom R. "The Temporal Leitmotif in *Far from the Madding Crowd*." *CLQ* 10:296-303.

Hardy articulated in his discussions of evolutionary meliorism a behavioral standard for man compatible with temporal concepts made current by 19th-century scientific thought. 19th-century science was dominated by geological and biological discoveries which made man aware of cosmic, as opposed to clock, time. Hardy's discussions of evolutionary meliorism urge man to be reasonable and patient in his efforts to effect change for the better. Such patience required man to be in proper accord with cosmic time, to see himself and his moment in time in relation to the eons required for evolutionary development. Clear fictional embodiment of the idea may be seen in Hardy's use of images associated with time as indexes to character in *Far from the Madding Crowd*. We are shown through imagery that the rustics and Gabriel Oak achieve the proper relationship with cosmic time. Temporal imagery associated with Troy, Boldwood, and Bathsheba reveals varying kinds and degrees of dislocation from the rustic norm. (TRS)

Hazlitt. 6481. Jones, Stanley. "Haydon and Northcote on Hazlitt:A Fabrication." *RES* 24(1973):165-78.
The entry for 3 August 1826 in Benjamin Robert Haydon's diary recounting a visit to James Northcote and repeating their denigration of the departed Hazlitt is fictitious. Haydon hated Northcote and avoided him; the calumnies had already appeared in earlier entries in the diary; the interlocutors mention Haydon incidentally as if he were an absent third person; and finally, Hazlitt was in Paris at the time. Haydon modeled this dialogue upon Hazlitt's own "conversation" with Northcote, "Boswell Redivivus, No. 1.," lately published in the *New Monthly Magazine*. His pride was offended by Hazlitt's remarks on the necessity of a contemporary popularity as a prerequisite for posthumous fame. After a seventeen-year feud with the Royal Academy, Haydon had lost confidence and recently made overtures: he now took Hazlitt's words for a criticism of his own attitude, and this dialogue is his furious answer. At least two of Haydon's accusations in it are demonstrably shaky. (SSJ)

6484. Ready, Robert. "Hazlitt:In and Out of 'Gusto'." *SEL* 14:537-46.
Hazlitt wants "gusto" to describe pictorial rather than literary effects. The sensual quality of "gusto" cannot adequately characterize a writer's success in putting intense abstractions into words. "Interest" is a term which Hazlitt favors in specifically literary contexts to denote the poet's sympathetic knowledge both of things and of their relative importance to readers. This interest, this knowledge, underlies gusto. The sympathetic awareness of what object interests others is prior to any attempt to convey the "power or passion defining the object." Gusto, then, is a sign of the greatest interest. (RR)

Henley. 6487. Cohen, Edward H. "A 'Lost' Henley Poem." *PBSA* 68:172-74.
Henley's "Ballade R.L.S." is an unflattering portrait of Robert Louis Stevenson, apparently lost to its author near the end of his life and heretofore unknown to scholarship. The work is significant as new evidence of the waning of the Henley-Stevenson friendship long before their celebrated quarrel of 1888. (EHC)

Hogg. 6492. Georgas, Marilyn. "A New Source for Hogg's *Justified Sinner*:Greville's *Life of Sidney*." *NCF* 29:338-45.
The antinomian controversy in the Scottish church during the first quarter of the 18th century provided theme and atmosphere for Hogg's *Justified Sinner*. A plot source is found in a passage from Greville's *Life of Sir Philip Sidney* in which Sidney and the powerful Earl of Oxford have a tense confrontation on a tennis court. This episode provides the pattern for George Colwan's main confrontation with his antinomian half-brother Robert Wringhim Colwan. Repetition and expansion are Hogg's main methods of adaptation. He has a series of tennis court confrontations, and adds a street fight between the followers of the half-brothers, and an eventual duel between the two. Hogg shaped it to show the "elect" party, Robert, actually to be the evil party, for whom George's innocent boyish game of tennis became a crime that justified punishment by murder. (MDG)

Hopkins. 6497. Bump, Jerome. "Hopkins and Keats." *VP* 12:33-43.
The role played by Keats in Hopkins' development has long been neglected, even in such extensive studies as Ford's *Keats and the Victorians*. Keats's influence was so pervasive in his early poetry that he had to struggle, often harder than Tennyson, Arnold, Swinburne, or Meredith, to make his own poetry unlike Keats's, a process of maturation that is almost archetypal among Victorian poets. Many of the weaknesses of his early poetry are the typical weaknesses of Victorian poetry and are related to the attempt to imitate Keats's early poetry: love of sensations for their own sake, lack of concentration and construction, overemphasis on pictorial stasis, a superficial response to nature, and a dreamy subjectivity relying on conventional allusiveness and precious diction rather than objective correlatives. As his letters reveal, like other Victorian poets Hopkins preferred to criticize these weaknesses in Keats rather than in himself, yet his projections of how Keats

would have changed if he had lived are justifications of his own development away from Keats. (JFAB)

6498. ——. "Hopkins, the Humanities, and the Environment." *GaR* 28:227-44.
Creative literature like the poetry of Gerard Manley Hopkins can expose our categorical dualisms as fictions which we have taken literally and replace them with new fictions more congruent with a larger reality. From 1875 to 1879 Hopkins achieved an extraordinarily unified vision of God, man, and nature and created new words, rhythms, and metaphors to communicate it. Later, assigned to various Victorian cities, he directly confronted industrial and urban pollution and lost his unifying vision. His later poetry eloquently expresses our own elegaic response to our deteriorating environment and reveals the danger of the narcissistic preoccupation with the individual-in-isolation which has dominated Western art in the last two centuries. (JFAB)

6503. Cornelia, Marie. "Images and Allusion in Hopkins' 'Carrion Comfort'." *Renaissance* 27:51-55.
The poetic technique used by Hopkins in his "Carrion Comfort" is one of allusion and reverberation. The poem stirs echoes in the memory, which upon examination prove to originate in the Scriptures. The key images of the sonnet appear first in lines 5-8. Derived from Psalms, Job, Isaiah, and Jeremiah, they are the image of a "terrible" one with "lionlimb" and "darksome, devouring" eyes, and the image of the fan or winnow with its accompanying tempest. In the octave, as in the Old Testament, these images connote destruction. But, executing a superb volta, Hopkins in the sestet introduces the New Testament use of the winnow as the loving instrument of salvation which separates wheat from chaff and leaves the good grain "heaped" "sheer and clear." This leads finally to the realization that he against whose power the poet has been fighting is not Satan the enemy but "(my God!) my God." (MEC)

6507. Fox, Judith H. "*The Queen of the Air*:Transformation of Myth in Ruskin and Hopkins." *VP* 12:335-42.
Hopkins' "The Blessed Virgin compared to the Air we Breathe" contains debts to Ruskin. In *The Queen of the Air* Ruskin compares the goddess Athena to the air, describing at length the physical and spiritual powers by which the air, personified and worshiped by the ancient Greeks, enlivens, protects, and inspires man to virtue. While Hopkins relies upon *The Queen of the Air* for his structural simile and for many thematic and verbal details, he skillfully combines it with the doctrine of St. Bernard that all grace comes to men through Mary, and he infuses the poem with his own joyful devotion to and praise of the Virgin. (JHF)

6519. Richards, Bernard. "Hopkins' 'To Oxford'." *Expl* 33:Item 24.
Alison G. Sulloway's reading of lines 15-22 of Gerard Manley Hopkins' second sonnet "To Oxford" in *Gerard Manley Hopkins and the Victorian Temper* (1972) is adversely criticized. Her interpretation is that Hopkins willfully redecorates an Oxford chapel, in his mind's eye, to make it conform to his new-found admiration for Gothic architecture. It seems much more certain that the poem celebrates the pleasures to be gained from the phenomenal facts of optical illusion. (BAR)

6520. Richards, Bertrand F. "Meaning in Hopkins' 'Carrion Comfort'." *Renaissance* 27:45-50.
An explication of Gerard Manley Hopkins' "Carrion Comfort" demands close examination of the language of the poem. In no other way can meaning be determined. Words must be thoroughly defined and appropriate definitions chosen. Word groups must be examined as they combine into larger units of thought. The underlying syntax must be determined. Finally, ambiguities, ironies, and symbolic uses must be considered. The resolution of these difficulties reveals a possible explication: The seemingly incoherent outcry of the poet against his God becomes the reasoned and rational statement and response of the traditional sonnet. The octave states the poet's despair at being unable to understand God's apparent injustice to man. The sestet states that only his frailty—his human weakness—has led him to suppose that the will and purposes of God are to be judged by human standards. His resignation to the will of God is his true conversion. (BFR)

6524. Scott, Charles T. "Towards a Formal Poetics:Metrical

Patterning in 'The Windhover'." *Lang&S* 7:91-107.
After re-examining certain formal characteristics of Hopkins' "The Windhover" and pointing out the inadequacy of certain traditional conclusions about these formal charactersitics, a reanalysis of the metrical pattern of the poem is given by utilizing the Halle-Keyser theory of the iambic line. A revised format for the poem, which is defensible in terms of linguistic and stylistic considerations, and which is also iambic in its metrical patterning, is presented. Hopkins achieved a masterful interweaving of the Old English alliterative tradition and the iambic tradition by suggesting the appearance of the one while actually adhering to the principles of the other. (CTS)

6528.   Thomas, Alfred,S.J. "Hopkins' 'The Windhover'." *Expl* 33:Item 31.
The kestrel in Hopkins' "The Windhover" verges on self-transcendence. Some Greek philosophers held that whatever fulfills itself becomes divine, its *theion* appearing. In Marsh's *Lectures on the English Language*, a book Hopkins consulted, we are given examples of certain Greek authors using the term *to Theion* absolutely for the Divine Being. This fact confirms this sonnet's Christocentricity and reinforces the view that the kestrel symbolizes Christ, the poem's real "underthought." (AT)

Hunt, L. 6533. Stam, David H. "Leigh Hunt and *The True Sun*:A List of Reviews, August 1833 to February 1834." *BNYPL* 77:436-53.
From August 1833 to February 1834 Leigh Hunt contributed almost daily book reviews for *The True Sun*. These reviews, which Hunt had thought lost, were collected by Alexander Ireland and mounted in two bound volumes which are now in the Newberry Library, Chicago. This article includes some brief excerpts from Hunt's *True Sun* reviews together with a complete list of all books reviewed by Hunt for *The True Sun*. (DHS)

Hutton. 6534. Tener, Robert H. "Hutton's Earliest Review of Arnold:An Attribution." *ELN* 12:102-09.
It is a mistake to assume that Hutton's criticisms of Matthew Arnold begin in the 1870s, for strong internal evidence can be marshalled for his authorship of the review of the 1853 *Poems* in the *Inquirer* of 3 December 1853. First, Hutton was a contributing editor of the *Inquirer* at that time. Moreover, this review contains passages paralleling his characteristic views on poetry as well as several of his favorite allusions and quotations, a quotation from an anonymous article by his best friend, Walter Bagehot, being particularly telling for attribution. (RHT)

Keats. 6542. Anderson, Norman A. "Corrections to Amy Lowell's Reading of Keats's Marginalia." *KSJ* 23:25-31.
In an appendix to the second volume of her 1925 biography of John Keats, Amy Lowell transcribed marginal annotations that Keats had made in several books in his personal library. Her transcriptions provide a valuable record of Keats's thinking about his reading; however, they also include some omissions, mis-readings, and incorrect identifications in four of the volumes. The corrections concern mainly marginal comments that reflect Keats's intelligence as a reader, his spontaneous thoughts inspired by his reading, and his impatience with certain authorial foolishness. (NAA)

6544.   Bell, Arthur H. " 'The Depth of Things':Keats and Human Space." *KSJ* 23:77-94.
Space, shaped according to his emotional and intellectual concerns, serves Keats in his poetry and letters as a metaphoric language by which to describe and re-enact the intuitional "feel" of his insights. Keats's imagination sizes upon vistas of limitless space when expressing a sense of disorientation and frustration. Purposiveness and exhilaration, on the other hand, call to his mind images of structure such as the "Mansion of Many Apartments." Keats's spatial imagery lends conceptual direction and emotional atmosphere to its context. (AHB)

6545.   Brogan, Howard O. " 'The Cap and Bells, or ... The Jealousies'?" *BNYPL* 77:298-313.
The two chief lines of critical interpretation of the poem "The Cap and Bells," both of which depend on the identification of the emperor Elfinam being the political identification of George IV,

are questioned. The literary identification of the emperor points to Lord Byron when separating from his wife. Both rest upon a brief passage which was probably a late addition. However, numerous details in the poem point toward an interpretation personal to Keats. These include many allusions to his reading, some apparent references to non-literary personal relationships—including Elfinam's strange Man-Tiger-Organ and especially his jealous love for Fanny Brawne. This jealous love indeed seems central to the significance of the poem and accounts for Keats's preferring to entitle it "The Jealousies." (HOB)

6552.   D'Avanzo, Mario L. " 'Ode on a Grecian Urn' and *The Excursion*." *KSJ* 23:95-105.
Wordsworth's description of Grecian myth in the fourth book of *The Excursion* underlies the general character of Keats's Ode. The manner in which Keats adapts Wordsworth's sublimities reveals the inventiveness and greater vividness of the younger poet. The urn as symbol distills and objectifies most of Wordsworth's ideas on art, imagination, immortality, and religion. Keats assigns art the role that Wordsworth gives nature. Because he did not accept the permanence and perfection of nature, Keats ascribes to ideal art the form and spirit harboring truth and beauty. The urn is equivalent to Wordsworth's nature. (MLD)

6564.   Jones, Leonidas M. "Edward Holmes and Keats." *KSJ* 23:119-28.
Examines a letter by Edward Holmes Keats in the *Morning Chronicle* of 27 July 1821. The letter reports incidents from Keat's first meetings with Hunt and Benjamin R. Haydon. It also shows that John Taylor reported to Keats the substance of William Blackwood's devious attempt at conciliation on 31 August 1820 and Keats's angry rejection of that attempt. After Keats's death, Holmes combined journalistic and musical careers. *A Ramble among the Musicians of Germany* (1828) includes an elegiac passage linking the deaths of Keats and Beethoven. *The Musical Times* of 1849 preserves an argument by Keats about *Paradise Regained* not recorded elsewhere. (LMJ)

6575.   Pannill, Linda. "Keats's *Lamia*:A 'Knotty Problem'." *Mary Wollstonecraft Newsl.* 1,ii(1973):17-24.
The woman-serpent figure in Keats's "Lamia" (1820) may be interpreted as Potentiality, the uncreated cosmos which the hero Lycius shapes to his vision and needs as the poet shapes the materials of experience or the mythic creator the female chaos which preceded the universe. Lamia's womanhood is as important symbolically as her serpenthood. The mythic associations of amorphousness and mystery connected with the serpent complement the portrayal of Lamia as, alternately, a beast, a woman of "old Adam's seed," and a goddess. All of these are variations on the images of woman in myth and literature. Lamia's transformations are determined by the ways in which she is viewed by Lycius, and her final change into a snake occurs when he is forced to see her not as woman but as "serpent." (LP)

6576.   Pereira, Ernest. "John Keats:Three 1819 Odes." *UES* 9,iii(1971):1-9.
An evaluation of "To Psyche," "On Melancholy," and "On Indolence." Attention is given to form, setting, theme, the equation of natural and poetic processes, and the "distillation" of images from earlier poems. An intensely subjective exploration of imaginative experience, "To Psyche" suggests the disillusion following attempts to create a lasting reality from "the wreath'd trellis of a working brain." In "On Melancholy" Keats turns from the wished-for "stasis" to acquiescence in the transience of beauty and joy. Rejecting traditionally "romantic" attitudes, his Melancholy revitalizes the jaded sensibility because it comes naturally—with the sudden sharpness of an April shower. The article emphasizes sensory values, paradox, and the poem's significance in Keats's development. Structurally weak and uneven in tone, "On Indolence" presents an amalgam of ideas and images culled from preceding poems and letters, and its interest is mainly biographical. (EP)

6577.   —— "Realms of Gold:A Visit to Keats' House and the Memorial Library, Hampstead." *UES* 12,i:1-18.
The history of Keats House is traced, focusing on Keats's tenancy and his relationship with Charles Brown, the Brawnes, and the Dilkes. The growth of the Keats Collection and the steady rise of the poet's reputation are explored. Some personal relics are listed,

with rather more attention being given to the Keats letters and other MS material. Keats's marginal comments in the books he read are noted and his personal library and the various special collections housed at Hampstead are discussed. The scope of the survey widens to include the resources of the Keats-Shelley Memorial in Rome and other repositories of Keats material. There are numerous illustrations and description is supplemented with biographical and critical comment aimed at placing Keats's association with Hampstead in the wider context of his poetic development. (EP)

6579. Primeau, Ronald. "Chaucer's *Troilus and Criseyde* and the Rhythm of Experience in Keats's 'What can I do to drive away'." *KSJ* 23:106-18.
Keats's repeated references to *Troilus and Criseyde* in letters and his allusions in poems beginning as early as *Endymion* suggest a significant Chaucerian influence at crucial stages in his development. Drawing on his reading of *Troilus*, Keats's "What can I do to drive away" further exemplifies his growing interest in man's need to accept and act in accord with "the sweetness of the pain" wherein lies the fullest realization of human potential. Modern criticism on Chaucer and Keats has provided the insights and terminology necessary for a more complete understanding of how Keats transformed the themes and techniques he found in *Troilus* into his own distinctive thematic and stylistic patterns. (RP)

6583. Smith, Louise Z. "The Material Sublime: Keats and *Isabella*." *SIR* 13:299-311.
Keats rejects romance filtered of reality's "disagreeables" and values romance balancing sensibility and detachment. In the *Epistle to Reynolds*, Keats seeks the balance of imaginatively perceived beauty and truth in reality. Keats's syntactically ambiguous "material sublime" affirms that romance should arise from the sublime in the real world and from external matter, not sensibility. Yet imagination, inadequately supported by philosophy, cannot harmonize the *Epistle*'s "disagreeables." *Isabella* embodies in narrative form the theory of romance defined in the *Epistle*. Detachment created by digression and juxtaposition affords Keats the wisely passive imaginative acceptance of a tragically near-equal balance of love and destruction. (LZS)

6585. Stephenson, William C. "The Fall from Innocence in Keats's 'Lamia'." *PLL* 10:35-50.
Keats's "Lamia" is a psychological drama with imagistic and dramatic overtones from *Paradise Lost*. Part 1 traces Lycius's awakening into the imaginative state of lover's bliss and Part 2 his relapse into the practical state of mind, characterized at its lowest by Corinthian society and at its highest by Apollonius. Lycius, "in self despite/Against his better self," initiates his own downfall by seeking to possess Lamia. His fall is presented dramatically with parallels to Book 9 of *Paradise Lost*. Before Lycius's fall, Lamia is a positive enchantress, or projection of Lycius's nobler self, initiating and fulfilling her lover's faith, just as initially Apollonius is a projection of Lycius's baser self. Once Lycius falls, Lamia and Apollonius reverse roles. (WCS)

Kingsley, H. 6596. Croft, Julian. "Is *Geoffry Hamlyn* a Creole Novel?" *ALS* 6:269-76.
Henry Kingsley's *The Recollections of Geoffry Hamlyn* is an Englishman's fantasy of what Australia could have been in the mid-19th century. The landscape is the Promised Land, the settlers Patriarchs, and the social system is feudal and based on caste. By reviewing the French, Spanish, and specialized West African meanings of "creole," the word is redefined in English to describe the attitudes toward caste of the main characters in the novel. A creole is a resident of Australia whose primary allegiance is to the mother-culture and who despises the indigenous colonial culture. Creoles and non-creoles in the novel are distinguished by body-type, language, and social attitudes. None of the characters is a private figure for they are stereotypes of imperial virtue or convict depravity. The novel's importance lies in this social view rather than in any esthetic merit. (JCC)

Kipling. 6602. Harrison, James. "Kipling's Jungle Eden." *Mosaic* 7,ii:151-64.
Jungle life in Kipling's *Jungle Books* is strongly Edenic in character. Yet it is also strikingly unedenic in certain respects. An earlier, seasonless, vegetarian paradise, before the coming of death and law, portrayed in "How Fear Came," is on the whole unfavorably compared with a meat-eating, life-and-death present, subject to law. Indeed, it is the balance between a ruthless vigor and a restraining law which constitutes the Edenic for Kipling. The jungle, then, embodies an Edenic equilibrium in its simplest, natural form, which man as individual and species must outgrow, but to which Mowgli retains the right of re-entry at will, and which can therefore be recreated at every level of life, even as the jungle itself must periodically and postlapsarianly recreate it. (JH)

Landor. 6617. Kestner, Joseph. "The Genre of Landor's *Gerbir*: 'Eminences Excessively Bright'." *WC* 5:41-49.
Consideration of Landor's *Gebir* (1798) involves explication of its simultaneous Latin version, *Gebirus*. An analysis of the English and Latin versions of 1803 accounts for the style of the English and reveals the most important source for the genre of the work, the "Peleus and Thetis" of Catullus, the greatest epyllion of ancient literature. Because the epyllion is itself a miniaturizing genre, literary devices like elision, polyptuton, syncope, anaphora, and diminutives reflect the concern of the epyllion for compression; Landor's English version, therefore, cannot be analyzed by the standards of epic. Furthermore, *Gebir/Gebirus* incorporates not only the stylistic but also the thematic qualities of the epyllion, especially its attention to temporality rather than epical timelessness. (JAK)

6618. Lloyd, Bernard. "A Famous Swansea Romance." *AWR* 24,liii:92-95. ["Rose Aylmer."]
One of the most famous short poems in the English language—"O what avails the sceptered rose, O what the form divine"—was inspired by a meeting on Swansea beach and the subsequent brief romance that Landor had with Rose Aylmer. Family opposition to the romance caused her to be sent to India where she soon died. Landor carried the memory of her with him for many years, though he subsequently married. Landor lived in Swansea from about 1795 to 1801, before moving to live many years in Italy. From there he often wrote back to English friends in nostalgic vein regarding his memories of the natural beauty of Swansea beach and the Gower coast. (BBL)

Marryat, F. 6634. Pickering, Sam,Jr. "'The most "Harum-scarum" sort of novel we have ever encountered': Marryat's *The King's Own* and Shandyism." *ESA* 17:71-77.
Examines Frederick Marryat's adaptation of Sterne's "Learned wit" in *The King's Own*. Like *Tristram Shandy*, Marryat based *The King's Own* on John Locke's principle of association. The major character is his harlequin-like narrator, a figure forever intruding into the narrative in order to call attention to the art of the novel and away from the story. (SFP,Jr)

Meredith. 6638. Baker, Robert S. "*The Ordeal of Richard Feverel*: A Psychological Approach to Structure." *SNNTS* 6:200-17.
The London chapters of *The Ordeal of Richard Feverel* have been condemned by Meredith's critics as forming a repetition of the Raynham section. Richard's experience in London is related to his early years at Raynham, the roots of his later career being traceable to his early education. In London he experiences an important and psychologically complex extension of his experience at Raynham and is skillfully connected by Meredith to his childhood attachment to Lady Blandish and his traumatic night visitation by his mother. Meredith's novel is structured around a series of incremental repetitions as Richard encounters a series of women all of whom exhibit similar characteristics. (RSB)

6644. Holt, Carolyn D. "Sir Austin and His Scrip: A New Approach to *The Ordeal of Richard Feverel*." *JNT* 4:129-43.
The Ordeal of Richard Feverel presents a contrast of two authors with two approaches to art and experience: Meredith himself, and his character Austin Feverel, whose writings dominate the world of the novel. Sir Austin's *Scrip* is a force for reductiveness, oversimplification, the enemy of what he himself calls "God's great array of Facts"—that is, Meredith's great array of Facts. Meredith's novel creates the inclusiveness against which the

aphoristic mentality is judged. Because Meredith successfully resists the temptation to confront Sir Austin's categorizing with categories of his own—because he can use it, instead, as a means of realizing complex character—the reader is cautioned against freezing Meredith's *Ordeal* to critical categories such as comedy and tragedy. (CDH)

6646. Maxwell-Mahon, William D. "The Pattern of Egoism: A Comment on George Meredith's Major Novel." *UES* 10, iii(1972):21-35.

Between *The Ordeal of Richard Feverel* (1859) and *Beauchamp's Career* (1867), Meredith had acquired a reputation for obscurity as a result of his complex form and intellectual expression. With the appearance of *The Egoist* (1879), however, his real worth was recognized by his contemporaries. The Prelude to *The Egoist* is Meredith's *Apologia Pro Vita Sua*. There he summarizes the comic principles that give his fiction form, and the theory of Egoism that underlines his artistic thought and expression. The relevance of the Prelude to the novel itself is borne out by the study of plot and characters. Sir Willoughby Patterne, the central figure, bears a significant resemblance to Sir Austin Feverel. His egoism makes him the unconscious destroyer of his own happiness and that of his companions. Clara Middleton, the novel's heroine, is the type of character Meredith had been working toward in *Sandra Belloni*, *Vittoria*, and *Rhoda Flemming*. She embodies his conception of the feminine ideal. (WDMM)

Mill, J.S. 6653. August, Eugene R. "Mill as Sage:The Essay on Bentham." *PMLA* 89:142-53.

John Stuart Mill's "Bentham" demonstrates how Mill operates as a sage using both logic and art to awaken the reader to a new perception of reality. Mill creates a sense of disappointment arising from Bentham's great promise and limited performance, both as thinker and as man. Constructing an image of himself as a whole thinker, Mill thereby underscores Bentham's position as half-thinker. He also creates an elaborate portrait of Bentham as a great father-teacher-hero-God figure, only to reveal Bentham's inability to perform these roles adequately. By heavy use of negatives, Mill suggests that Bentham's thought has little positive value. Finally, the essay's structure undermines all of Bentham's philosophical contributions. Deriving from Carlyle's "Boswell's Life of Johnson," Mill's earlier writings on Bentham show him refashioning Carlyle's language and developing the ironic techniques used in "Bentham." Although Mill has no clear-cut theory of prose artistry, in practice he writes as a complex logician-artist, using prose as an imaginative medium. (ERA)

Morris. 6666. Reed, Michael D. "Morris' 'Rapunzel' as an Oedipal Fantasy." *AI* 30:313-22.

William Morris' dramatic poem "Rapunzel" has been described by Robert Stallman as a "rite of passage" myth. A psychoanalytic content gives the myth its appeal and governs our response to the poem. This psychoanalyti c level contains and develops, through primal scene imagery, a positive oedipal fantasy. This fantasy, however, creates anxiety, for it includes the fear of the father. Our response to this anxiety is managed or sublimated by the absence of action at the poem's turning point. The Prince never confronts the Witch, he is not blinded by thorns as in various versions of the fairy tale, but is magically transported to the tower and happiness with Rapunzel (Guendolen). This defensive management is further supported by the thematic meaning of the poem which emphasizes purity and patience and the necessity for true love to be non-violent. But this defensive management allows the reader to participate in the fulfillment of the child's incestuous desire for the mother, a point which seems to explain why the Victorians described the poem as bewitching. (MDR)

6667. Sadoff, Dianne F. "Imaginative Transformation in William Morris' 'Rapunzel'." *VP* 12:153-64.

A recent critic, rescuing Morris' "Rapunzel" from critical neglect, thinks the poem a Victorian quest for mature adulthood, but a fresh look at the poem reveals Romantic dialectic and transformation. The process of the poem transforms dream into reality: the Prince's dream of a beautiful woman becomes "real life," and Rapunzel's dream of sexual climax becomes symbolic physical fulfillment. But this transformation does not merely invert the poem's central themes; in the "dreamy" harper's song, the singer loses Guendolen and retains only memories of her, whereas in his newly constituted reality, the Prince gets the best of dream and reality—Guendolen in the flesh. The poem transforms itself through the power of poetic inspiration to create desire, through the power of the human imagination to create its own fulfillment, and through the power of love and sexuality to transform lovers and the world around them. (DFS)

Newman, F.W. 6671. Winslow, Donald F. "Francis W. Newman's Assessment of John Sterling:Two Letters." *ELN* 11:278-83. [Incl. text of letters.]

From a collection of letters acquired by the Philadelphia Divinity School, addressed by Francis W. Newman to Moncure Conway, two have been chosen for publication because of their interest to students of 19th-century literature. They give Newman's personal assessment of his friend John Sterling, and, as such, add to our knowledge of Sterling, a knowledge by and large restricted until now to the biographies of Hare and Carlyle. The letters are reproduced in their entirety, with a brief introduction and appropriate annotation. (DFW)

Newman, J.H. 6676. Johnston, John H. "Newman and Nineteenth-Century Reform." *WVUPP* 21:48-53.

In the *Tamworth Reading Room* letters Cardinal Newman entered into a public controversy—the methods and aims of popular education—which reveals the fundamental values behind his conservatism and apparent lack of interest in educational reform. Newman would approve of no reform, no system of popular education which was not religious in principle. The "moral improvement" sought by the establishment of a secular library at Tamworth could not be achieved through a mere access of physical knowledge: "To know is one thing, to do is another; the two things are altogether distinct." (JHJ)

Oxford Movement. 6685. Pfaff, Richard W. "The Library of the Fathers:The Tractarians as Patristic Translators." *SP* 70(1973):329-44.

Among the less well-known literary enterprises of the Oxford Movement is the Library of the Fathers, a series of translations of patristic writings which ultimately ran to 48 volumes. Begun by J. H. Newman and E. B. Pusey in 1836, it was ambitiously conceived as buttressing the Anglican claim to substantial concord with the Fathers, to the discomfiture, presumably, of Roman Catholics and Protestants alike. The series enjoyed considerable prosperity in the 1840s and early 1850s, but declined thereafter, through a combination of financial difficulties and defections from the movement. The most important undertaking of the Library of the Fathers was a translation of much of Chrysostom, and Augustine, Gregory the Great, Cyril of Jerusalem, and Athanasius were also treated at length (Newman's study of the latter being, of course, instrumental in his conversion to Rome); but it never reached anything like the scope originally projected for it. Its failures as well as its successes mirror those of its parent movement. (RWP)

Pater. 6690. Court, Franklin E. "Virtue Sought 'As a Hunter His Sustenance':Pater's 'Amoral Aesthetic'." *ELH* 40(1973):549-63.

In *Plato* (1893) Pater discusses the relationship between virtue and the "relative spirit": virtue is a force "relative" to "every several act, and to each period of life, in regard to each thing we have to do, in each one of us." In "Diaphaneite" (1864) he claims that to live in "Imitatio Christi" is to have the fair-mindedness to see a thing as it really is and to judge it, relatively, in terms of what it does best. The "eternal worth" of a man, he argues in the Wordsworth essay (1874), must be judged with equal forbearance. The concept reappears in *Marius* (1885) and "Emerald Uthwart" (1892), specifically. It is also integrally related to his role as a critic of the arts: his critical vision refuses to admit absolutes; his concept of virtue is devoid of any considerations of a presupposed knowledge of or force for evil in this life, a stance that accounts largely for the noticeable absence of villains and intentional villainy in his fiction. (FEC)

6693. Schuetz, Lawrence F. "The Suppressed 'Conclusion' to *The Renaissance* and Walter Pater's Modern Image." *ELT* 17:251-58.
Speculation over Pater's motives for suppressing the "Conclusion" in the second edition of *The Renaissance* has focused on Mallock's caricature of him as "Mr. Rose" in *The New Republic* or on Pater's concern for reputation and position. Correspondence indicates that Pater decided to withdraw the "Conclusion" prior to 15 November 1796; thus Mallock's satire could have had little influence, for only the initial installments had appeared at that time. Thomas Wright, Pater's biographer, has also exaggerated the influence of Pater's loss of the Oxford Proctorship in 1874 due to Jowett's displeasure with *The Renaissance*. Pater's 1888 note that his principles had been misinterpreted reflects the wording of a letter from John Wordsworth which mistakenly attacked the "Conclusion's" philosophy. This letter and the misinterpretation it represented probably determined Pater's decision to withdraw the "Conclusion" on ethical grounds. (LFS)

Peacock. 6697. Brogan, Howard O. "Romantic Classicism in Peacock's Verse Satire." *SEL* 14:525-36.
Peacock's satire reveals romantic sympathy checked by a classical sense of the absurdity of romantic excess. In *Paper Money Lyrics* he assails greed resulting in economic panic and the hypocritical award of chivalric honors to the newly rich. In the mingled verse and prose satire of his fiction he finds greed to be the chief frustration of healthy young love, as well as a factor in the brutality of war and one explanation for the increasing conservatism of Southey, Wordsworth, and Coleridge. Self-interest can also result in the absurd romantic posturing which Peacock especially attributes to Shelley and Byron. (HOB)

Pritchard. 6709. Adams, Sam. "Thomas Jeffery Llewelyn Pritchard." *AWR* 24,lii:21-60.
Prichard was pleased to be thought "the first Welsh novelist" on the basis of his *Twm Sion Catti* (1828)—an expansion of Welsh traditional tales. Certainly he is an important Anglo-Welsh antecedent. Though Welsh-speaking and culturally nationalistic, he wrote in English. He never rose above the level of a literary hack, but achieved some popularity between 1824, when he published a volume of poems, *Welsh Minstrelsy*, and 1839, when he brought out an enlarged *Twm Shon Catty*. He sold his books in his own "bookshop" in Builth Wells, and door-to-door in South Wales. Little is known of his origins and life, but he was for a time a touring actor. In his declining years he wrote *Heroines of Welsh History* (1854), which failed miserably. Rescued from poverty by a local newspaper, he died in January 1862 of burns he received when his clothing caught fire in his Swansea home. (SA)

Reade. 6710. Muller, Charles H. "Charles Reade and *The Cloister and the Hearth*:A Survey of the Novel's Literary Reception and Its Historic Fidelity." *UES* 9,i(1971):18-26.
In 1861 *The Cloister and the Hearth*, after the preceding low ebb of Charles Reade's reputation, struck the reading public as well as the American and English press like a tidal wave. In America the novel swept the continent, rapidly passing through eight editions within a few weeks after its first appearance. Many English reviews paid tribute to Reade's reputation by placing him in the foremost rank of writers. The *Westminster Review* reviewed the novel together with and at the expense of Dickens' *Great Expectations*. An important reason for the vast success of the novel and its lasting fame is that Reade's Baconian methods of research and Keanian notions of realism were well suited to the antiquarian research necessary in the resuscitation of a past era. Reade also presents a convincing picture of the past by exploring the novel's fifteenth-century milieu through his characters. He so fully enters into the age he describes that reviewers unintentionally complimented him by raising the objection that he told his tale as if he were a prejudiced partisan of the fifteenth century. (CHM)

Rolfe. 6713. Jones, G.P. "Frederick Rolfe's Papal Dream." *Mosaic* 7,ii:109-22. [*Hadrian the Seventh*.]
Hadrian the Seventh is in the dream-vision mode, functioning on three levels: the personal, public, and artistic. The personal dream of ascending to the papacy allows Rolfe to indulge in vicarious self-aggrandizement and provides him with a forum for confessional self-vindication and a metaphor for expressing his disregarded potential. The public dream consists of the provision through his revolutionary Pope of Draconian solutions to what Rolfe has presented as the besetting problems of contemporary Church and State, solutions which serve to expose and criticize actual political circumstances. The artistic dream is the unobtrusive verbal pattern which ironically disclaims the reality of the novel, thereby providing a distancing and evaluative formula which forestalls the reader's skepticism and modulates his response to the substantive personal and public dreams. (GPJ)

6714. ——— "Literalism and Beyond:The Characterization of Public Figures in *Hadrian the Seventh*." *JML* 3:928-50.
Hadrian the Seventh uses a factual matrix of public figures and affairs as the basis for a satirical critique of the contemporaneous international situation and out of which to generate Rolfe's own set of anti-democratic solutions to international sociopolitical problems. The novel's proximity to public actuality lulls the reader into accepting sweeping solutions through gradual modifications of actuality. The major political character is a private personality, Jerry Sant, who is pressed into service as a public symbol of the venality of socialism and by extension of democracy. Sant is almost certainly a caricature of an obscure Scottish socialist by the name of George Gerrie. This explains the counterproductive vituperativeness of the characterization of Sant. Contrasting with the controlled blending of political fact and fictional speculation that Rolfe accords to the public sphere of concern, the characterization of Sant is so distorted by animosity as to frustrate Rolfe's polemical objectives of discrediting the principles represented by the character. (GPJ)

Rossetti, D.G. 6719. Bentley, D.M.R. "The *Belle Assemblée* Version of 'My Sister's Sleep'." *VP* 12:321-34.
The text of the *Belle Assemblée* version of Rossetti's "My Sister's Sleep" offers valuable insights into his poetic development in the days of the Pre-Raphaelite brotherhood. When revising the poem in 1849 he made the addition of several stanzas and details which, in their characteristically Pre-Raphaelite fusion of the realistic with the symbolic, reflect his taste and practice in painting at this time. Although, in 1869, Rossetti would excise many of the Christian images and allusions from "My Sister's Sleep" the unequivocally religious orientation of the early versions of the poem parallels such paintings as the "Girlhood of Mary Virgin" and raises the question of how much the poet-painter was affected by his contact, from 1843 onwards, with the Oxford Movement. (DMRB)

6720. Berry, Ralph. "Rossetti as Painter." *Mosaic* 7,iii:151-55. [Rev. art.]
Rossetti's talent for both painting and poetry might have inhibited greater achievement in either field, and Victorian taste for combinations of verbal and visual expression might have contributed to Rossetti's uncertainty. His painting exploits certain technical limitations, just as his career shows him well able to make the most of his productions. But Rossetti's great achievement was to project a dramatized image of self. His earlier paintings show lovers in a situation of intense solitariness: the later ones refine the idea to a single portrait of a woman with whom the relationship of the artist is implied. (RB)

6723. Gitter, Elisabeth G. "Rossetti's Translations of Early Italian Lyrics." *VP* 12:351-62.
A comparison of Rossetti's translations of early Italian lyrics with the originals shows that he removed or altered whatever he thought would mar his translations. He frequently omits or blurs conventional tropes and moral and philosophical meanings, emphasizing pictorial, dramatic, and emotional effects instead. Trying to duplicate the vernacular of high style, he chooses words that convey an antique patina without always reflecting the ruggedness of the Italian. Although Rossetti never strays far from the originals, he does change their emphasis, thus transforming them into Victorian poems. (EGG)

6725. Keane, Robert N. "Rossetti:The Artist and 'The Portrait'." *ELN* 12:96-102.

"The Portrait" was composed about 1847, considered for publication in 1861, possibly revised, and then buried with Rossetti's wife in 1862. Since "The Portrait" deals with themes central to much of Rossetti's work, it is useful to see how the poem is changed from an imaginative youthful poem of light and love to a darker, more melancholy poem colored with suggestive allusions to the personal experience of the mature poet. (RNK)

6730. Pittman, Philip M[cM]. "The Strumpet and the Snake: Rossetti's Treatment of Sex as Original Sin." *VP* 12:45-54.
It has been fashionable to assume that the appearance of sex in Rossetti's poetry manifests his psychogenic weakness, or an unnatural prurience, or both. Rossetti's treatment of sex in his art is consistently both natural and healthy; indeed it is the center of a rigid moral structure. Love between man and woman, and the sexuality that it implies, is a persistent concern in Rossetti's poetry. But physical love is never presented as an end admirable of and for itself. Rossetti's treatment of the love theme almost always implies a story, and the story almost always suggests a moral. In the figure of Lilith, as she appears in both the longer poem "Eden Bower" and the sonnet "Body's Beauty," his moral stance is most patently clear. Lilith is damned because her exercise of love is merely physical—animal, and self-gratifying; she is both sterile and sodomistic. Her counterpart is Eve, who is herself fruitful and through whom Eden is fructified and given significance. Eve is the embodiment of the principle of creativity in love; her fecundity counterbalances Lilith's barrenness; her love for Adam, and all that it implies, emphasizes and condemns Lilith's hate. (PMcMP)

6732. Tyzack, Charles R.P. "*King Arthur's Tomb*: The Versions of D.G. Rossetti and William Morris Compared." *Trivium* 8(1973):127-32.
A comparison of D. G. Rossetti's painting *King Arthur's Tomb* with William Morris's poem of the same title reveals a difference in the treatment of the two protagonists, Lancelot and Guinevere. The conflict between passion and repentance, which Rossetti has externalized in the two figures, Morris portrays taking place within Guinevere's consciousness, thus reducing Lancelot to a relatively passive and unimportant figure. In neither case does the conflict find any resolution. Morris's Guinevere expresses a characteristic 19th-century dilemma since religion can provide no solution to the problem of guilt: her penitence has no positive content, no forgiveness is offered, and she can only find release in self-destruction. For both writer and painter love is the one sure positive value; yet for both it is tainted by the guilt of sexuality, and Guinevere becomes a figure of temptation and destruction. (CRPT)

Ruskin. 6734. Alexander, Edward. "*Praeterita*: Ruskin's Remembrance of Things Past." *JEGP* 73:351-62.
Ruskin began to publish his autobiography, *Praeterita*, in July 1885, by the method of part-issue. *Praeterita* modified the public image of Ruskin's personality from one of prophetic dogmatism to one of sweet reasonableness. Because Ruskin conceived *Praeterita* as atonement for sins against his parents, and because he was determined to maintain silence about things painful to remember, much of importance is omitted from the book. Places were more decisive than people in forming Ruskin's mind and vocation. His first view of the Alps is the key episode in *Praeterita*; the book is built on systematic contrast between the great cities of Europe and the squalor of London; and its imaginative quest is fulfilled by the beauty of Scotland. But the unique value of *Praeterita* lies in his pristine clarity of vision, which offers a technique for recovering and recreating the past. (EA)

6735. Beeton, Douglas R. "John Ruskin: An Essay on Research." *UES* 11,iii(1973):12-24.
The value of literary manuscripts for critics is examined with particular reference to the work of John Ruskin, and more specifically, volume I of *Modern Painters*. The manuscripts dealt with are those in the Pierpont Morgan Library of New York, the most relevant being the two bound exercise books described as the "Brantwood" note-book by Cook and Wedderburn in the Library Edition of Ruskin's works. The manuscript version of *The Poetry of Architecture* gives scope for considering the significance

of the amendments Ruskin introduced even at the outset of his career. The first draft of the beginning of *Modern Painters* shows how alterations and discarded passages give light to Ruskin's perception of the function of the artist. It becomes clear that his work, far from being the product merely of impulse, was, to use the words of Cook and Wedderburn, "in some measure the result of infinite pains." A few of the unpublished, apparently fugitive, letters and notes in the collection of the Pierpont Morgan Library show how the "background" to the writer provides further understanding. (DRB)

6736. Burd, Van Akin. "A Week at Winnington: Two New Ruskin Letters of 1864." *ELN* 12:38-43.
From Duke University come two hitherto unpublished letters by Ruskin written during a week's visit at Winnington Hall near Northwich, Cheshire, between 20 and 26 May 1864. These letters determine more accurately the dates of Ruskin's visit and demonstrate the motives behind his interest in Margaret Alexis Bell and her school for girls. Ruskin had found at Winnington the freedom he lacked at home. He also found among the affectionate girls the love he had missed in his marriage and more recently in Rose La Touche from whom he was separated. In the first letter, written on Friday 20 May, the day of his arrival at Winnington, Ruskin tells his mother about the warmth of his reception at the school. For an unidentified correspondent Ruskin records in the second letter his disappointment over the adverse reception of his ideas and writings. Together the letters allow us to feel again the restlessness and despondence of these middle years of Ruskin's life. (VAB)

6743. Landow, George P. " 'I heard of a delightful ghost': A New Ruskin Letter." *PQ* 52(1973):779-83.
John Ruskin's previously unpublished letter to A. I. Woodhouse (3 Jan. 1876) reveals his interest, at a crucial point in his spiritual career, in any evidence of a life after death. (GPL)

6744. Maxwell-Mahon, William D. "John Ruskin: Social Scientist." *UES* 11,iii(1973):1-11.
Ruskin's socialism was as much the outcome of his character and special interests as it was an expression of the ethical temper of Victorianism. He saw art as a medium for the social improvement of mankind, and *Modern Painters* reflects this conviction. With *The Seven Lamps of Architecture*, he reached the center of his social theory: any employment should embody both the creative and the functional ideal of society. Ruskin's best work, in style and execution, was *The Stones of Venice*, as is seen from the examination of a representative passage describing St. Mark's Square. The esthetic principles put forward in this work were given practical expression through Ruskin's association with the Working Men's College, his lecture tours in the Midlands, and the didacticism of *Unto This Last* and *Fors Clavigera*. But theory often outran practice, never more so than in his formation of the Guild of St. George. (WDM-M)

Scott. 6756. Hafter, Monroe Z. "The Spanish Version of Scott's *Don Roderick*." *SIR* 13:225-34.
The Vision of Don Roderick was translated (1829) because of Scott's prestige and his having tied the medieval Spanish success over the Moorish conquerors of the Visigothic monarchy to the popular revolt against Napoleon's invasion. The translator, Agustín Aicart, felt constrained to transform Scott's sharp attacks on Spain's religious fanaticism, hypocrisy, and cruelty into praise for her Christian virtues, and to shift Scott's disdain for Carlos IV on to Manuel Godoy. The broadly liberal original is thereby changed into a defense of altar and throne, characteristic of the conservative pattern of Spanish Romanticism during the period of Fernandine absolution. (MZH)

6758. Hahn, H.G. "Historiographic and Literary: The Fusion of Two Eighteenth-Century Modes in Scott's *Waverley*." *HSL* 6:243-67.
Begun in 1805 but not published until 1814, Scott's *Waverley* has its conceptual roots in 18th-century historiographical theories such as the cyclical notion, the evolving society idea, and the emblem-making/allusion practice. All reflect that century's main historiographical aims—the specifying of perspective and motive-force. Likewise, Scott's literary techniques are more traditional than innovative. Such traditions simplified the novel for the

reading public. When blended in *Waverley*, both techniques generate the prototype of the historical novel. (HGH)

6768. Wood, G.A.M. "Scott's Continuing Revision:The Printed Texts of *Redgauntlet*." *Bibliotheck* 6(1973):121-98.
There were five editions of Sir Walter Scott's *Redgauntlet* (1824) published in his lifetime. The first edition contains defects and there are over a thousand substantive and major accidental variants between the 1824 first edition, the three editions of 1827, and the Magnum opus edition of 1832 (here listed). Scott worked with a copy of the 1827 octavo reprint of *Redgauntlet* when he was revising the novel for the Magnum opus edition, for which the 1827 octavo also served as printers' copy; and the variants to be found in the 1827 duodecimo edition are textually of little importance. Though the Magnum opus edition prints Scott's final authorized version of *Redgauntlet*, it is also a reprint of a reprint of an inadequate and inaccurate first edition. (GAMW)

Shelley, P.B. 6776. Bean, John C. "The Poet Borne Darkly: The Dream-Voyage Allegory in Shelley's *Alastor*." *KSJ* 23:60-76.
The main theme of Shelley's *Alastor* is the poet-hero's dissatisfaction with pantheism and his consequent search for direct knowledge of the transcendent world. The dream-voyage section is a coherent allegory that explores the limits of human knowledge by contrasting Shelley's hope of vision with his certainty of earthly disintegration. The sea-crossing becomes an allegory of the heroism and danger inherent in being a visionary. At the conclusion of the journey, the scene in the "silent nook" brings the visionary and the nihilistic moods into a tentative balance and reaffirms the ambiguity of the poet's quest. (JCB)

6777. Bennett, James R. "*Prometheus Unbound*, Act I, 'The play's the thing'." *KSJ* 23:32-51.
Act I of *Prometheus Unbound* is properly read through the perspective of psychological realism because it deals primarily with the way man thinks and acts in history. It is divided into four scenes to portray the growth of Prometheus from man as he is to the imagined initial stage of the breakthrough into man as he ideally might be. I.v.1-305 is climaxed by Prometheus' renunciation of his ancient cursing nature. I.ii.306-442 dramatizes the blindness of every other character to the meaning of Prometheus' abandonment of vengeance. I.iii.442-634 confronts Prometheus with the Furies, climaxing Prometheus' thousands of years of suffering. I.iv.635-833 presents Prometheus as almost fully changed, determined now to be "the saviour and the strength of suffering man." This development parallels the play as a whole, which spirals up and away from man as he is to man as he joyfully might be in a reconstituted world. (JRB)

6791. Hartley, Robert A. "The *Uroboros* in Shelley's Poetry." *JEGP* 73:524-42.
The *uroboros*, or encircling serpent, an important symbol in Shelley's poetry, has been viewed as simply a symbol of eternity. An examination of Shelley's use of the symbol, his sources, and its contemporary significance reveals that it can be better understood as a symbol of time and universal change. In Shelley's works the *uroboros* appears in the context of revolution and historical change; in his sources it is representative of the revolutions of the universe, time, and change; and the *uroboros* is a radical emblem in the American and French revolutions and in the English reform movement of Shelley's day. (RAH)

6800. Lees, Daniel E. "Shelley's 'Medusa' and Hegelian Synthesis." *UES* 12,iii:1-3.
Shelley's creative power in handling difficult esthetic subject matter can be seen in his poetic treatment of a painting in the Uffizi Gallery. In "On the Medusa of Leonardo da Vinci in the Florentine Gallery," Shelley's subject presents a paradox: the severed head of the Gorgon still writhes with living snakes. Does she live or die? The problem is solved by casting the poem in terms of Hegelian synthesis. The first two stanzas illustrate the thesis of the poem: death; the second two present the antithesis: life; and the final stanza provides the synthesis: life-in-death. (DEL)

6807. Pollin, Burton R. "Godwin's *Memoirs* as a Source of Shelley's Phrase 'Intellectual Beauty'." *KSJ* 23:14-20.
The last two words of the title of Shelley's "Hymn to Intellectual Beauty" suggest to many readers a Platonic origin for the basic poetic concepts that is not easy to reconcile with the empirical or utilitarian implications of the poem. It is likely that Shelley derived the adjective "intellectual" directly from a moving passage describing Mary Wollstonecraft at the end of the 1798 edition of Godwin's *Memoirs* of his wife. This derivation also clarifies other concepts of the poem and helps to date the writing of the "Hymn." Later, for a translated passage from Plato's *Symposium* in his "Speculations on Morals," Shelley again used the phrase without any warrant in the original Greek—further evidence of Godwin's influence. (BRP)

6812. Reisner, Thomas A. "Some Scientific Models for Shelley's Multitudinous Orb." *KSJ* 23:52-59.
Critics of *Prometheus Unbound* have proposed a variety of possible sources for Shelley's motif of the "multitudinous orb" (IV. 236-279), ranging, on the one hand, from Ezekiel's vision to certain passages in Dante and Milton, and, on the other, from Erasmus Darwin's *Botanic Garden* to Sir Humphry Davy's atomic hypothesis. None of the "scientific" models proposed so far appears particularly convincing. The figure of the multitudinous orb finds a more satisfactory prototype in the work of two 18th-century scientists, Leonhard Euler and the Marquis de Laplace, each of whose texts on Equinoctial Precession Shelley may be assumed to have read. (TAR)

6819. Scrivener, Michael H. "Bostetter's Case Against Shelley." *Paunch* 38:40-50.
In Chapter v of *The Romantic Ventriloquists* (1963) Bostetter offered a depreciation of Shelley that was infuriating, but also insightful. Bostetter raised the problem of the Romantic revolution—its definition, and Shelley's relationship to it. Bostetter asked to what extent was Shelley's poetry contributing to the project of human liberation and to what extent was it an indulgence of neurotic evasion and self-delusion. However, his valid insights into the problematic areas of Shelley's poetry were marred by an antagonistic tone, as though Bostetter were having a personal quarrel with Shelley. There are also other problems with Bostetter's analysis: his neglect of Shelley's psychological problems, the historical context, and the inherent difficulties of visionary poetry. (MHS)

Southey. 6826. Antippas, Andy P. "Four New Southey Letters." *WC* 5:91-96.
A letter to Charles Danvers discusses details of publication of the *Annual Anthology* I (1799). Another letter, to John May, takes up personal matters concerning Southey's brother and his cousin. The recipient of the third letter is unknown; its subject is probably *Madoc*. The final letter is addressed to Thomas Clarkson who sent Southey a copy of his *Researches Antidiluvian* for review. (APA)

6828. Bernhardt-Kabisch, Ernest. "Southey in the Tropics:*A Tale of Paraguay* and the Problem of Romantic Faith." *WC* 5:97-104.
The dialectical and experiential "faithless faith" of the greater Romantics is replaced in Southey's work by a *mauvaise foi* at once dogmatic and deprecatory. The late poem *A Tale of Paraguay* is typical of earlier narratives in its transformation of the Pantisocratic ideal of Southey's youth into missionary paternalism and in its ambiguous treatment of religion. Christian doctrine is at once inculcated as an answer to the problem of death in the state of nature and impugned as monkish superstition. Southey merely short-circuits the contradiction by sentimentally asserting that "death is best"; he does not resolve it dialectically and experientially in the true Romantic way. (EBK)

6830. Curry, Kenneth. "Southey's Portraits." *WC* 5:67-71.
Several of Southey's portraits are owned by such institutions as the National Portrait Gallery (London), Bristol City Art Gallery, Balliol College (Oxford), and the National Gallery of South Africa (Capetown). Other portraits are privately owned, and still others are known to have been drawn or painted only because of a reference in a letter or from having been exhibited at the Royal Academy. Some confusion exists from contemporary engravings which were not reproduced from an authentic portrait. The article concludes with a brief history of each portrait, its present location when known, and a reference to a good reproduction. (KC)

6833. Morgan, Peter F. "Southey:A Critical Spectrum." *WC*

5:71-75.

A succinct analysis of Southey's views of prose, particularly historical writing and literary criticism, with the related areas of philosophy and satire is presented. Southey himself writes history, but his distrust of philosophy includes a distrust of the philosophy of history. His own aim is to present the factual truth vividly and didactically. As he distrusts the philosophy of history, Southey has little time for intellectual satire and criticism, especially contemporary reviewing. On the other hand, he himself possesses critical values and defends his own practice as a reviewer. (PFM)

6834. Ober, Kenneth and Warren U. "Zukovskij and Southey's Ballads:The Translator as Rival." *WC* 5:76-88.

Zhukovski's genius is clearly illustrated in his 1831 translations of five ballads by Robert Southey. Occasionally sacrificing the advantage Southey derives from monotone and understatement, Zhukovski strengthens the ballads by providing concrete and vivid images, editorial comments, and supplementary details which bring the ballads into sharper focus. A personal and immediate involvement with his themes and characters and a real talent for choosing the right setting, the precise image, and the effective additional detail enable Zhukovski to successfully translate Southey's ballads. (WVO & KHO)

6835. Proudfit, Charles L. "Southey and Landor:A Literary Friendship." *WC* 5:105-12.

Although the literary friendship between Southey and Landor is one of the less celebrated among Romantic writers, the correspondence that it evoked over 35 years provides a history of psychological interdependence and intellectual stimulation which both writers considered to be one of the most important aspects of their lives. A review of their correspondence during these years of friendship reveals that Landor earned Southey's dedication of *Kehama* to him and that Landor's choice of Southey as the ideal poet-critic in four of the Imaginary Conversations expresses his respect and admiration for Southey's literary expertise. (CLF)

6836. Stanton, Michael N. "Southey and the Art of Autobiography." *WC* 5:113-19.

Robert Southey wrote a fragmentary autobiography in epistolary form, covering only the first 17 years of his life. The autobiography is largely objective and externalized. It is garrulous and colorful and bears out Southey's contention that the genre should concern itself with domestic history, life, and manners. Its account of Southey's literary development shows him to be a poet who takes his inspiration from books and not from the world outside. Southey's autobiography is an attempt to recapture the past perfectly and thus overcome time and death. In places, his account becomes a catalog of deaths, illnesses, and misfortunes. (MNS)

6837. Volz, Robert, and James Rieger. "The Rochester Southey Collection." *WC* 5:89-91.

The Robert Southey Collection in the Rush Rhees Library at the University of Rochester holds most of the lifetime editions and numerous holographs. These include the original drafts of the 17 "Autobiographical Epistles" to John May, the correspondence with Anna Eliza Bray and Sir Humphrey Fleming Senhouse, Senhouse's 1838 diary of his continental tour with RS and Crabb Robinson, the unnoted translations from Michelangelo, the MS of "The Devil's Thoughts," and the modestly entitled "Fragment of Kehama M. S. S." Association items and miscellaneous letters round out the collection. (RRV & JR)

6838. Zall, P.M. "The Gothic Voice of Father Bear." *WC* 5:124-28.

Southey's authorship of "The Three Bears" has been called in doubt in recent years with the discovery of an anterior version written by a country gentlewoman, Eleanor Mure. Yet, Southey's story, included in *The Doctor* (and reprinted here), made no pretense to originality but rather prided itself as an example of stories currently told among the peasantry. Southey even used distinctive type fonts to signify how the story should be read aloud. His real contribution was in recording the process of oral composition, for his version catches the well known tale in its transitional phase—with a fox, or "vox," giving way to a "vetch," or old woman (who later becomes golden haired); and three bears who, whatever their domestic relations may be, are all male. (PMZ)

Stevenson. 6851. Ward, Hayden W. " 'The Pleasure of Your Heart':*Treasure Island* and the Appeal of Boys' Adventure Fiction." *SNNTS* 6:304-17.

The most remarkable feature of *Treasure Island* is its insistence on the continuity and compatibility of boyish and adult experience, on the submergence of adult moral perspective in a boy's point-of-view. In the boy-hero, Jim Hawkins, Stevenson makes exploratory pragmatism seem compatible with moral idealism, and disregard for the adult's conception of duty the prerequisite of an effective defense of the good. The boy-hero becomes a providential agent whose powers adults recognize as morally and physically superior to their own. The ethics of *Treasure Island* account for Stevenson's sudden great popularity in the 1880s and 90s, when the uncertainties of an imperalist foreign policy and complex domestic problems in both Britain and the United States made readers eager for a fiction that equates a boy's practical powers with moral superiority, that makes individual freedom compatible with social order. (HWW)

Swinburne. 6863. Murfin, Ross C. "Athens Unbound:A Study of Swinburne's *Erectheus*." *VP* 12:205-17.

Erechtheus is a lyrical drama which, through myth and symbolic action, dramatizes the human soul as it undergoes a crisis in world-view. Swinburne directs the reader's attention toward the underlying symbolic structure of the poem by creating deliberate inconsistencies in plot, characters, and event. He describes a time-between-times in which the soul wavers between subservience to the gods or a revolutionary declaration of its own divinity. A symbolic battle takes place upon an equally emblematic landscape lying between land and sea, night and day, seed-time and harvest. Both battle and landscape indicate that the soul's annihilation of the man-made gods will bring about a time of hesitation, fear, and inner conflict. Princess Chthonia's willingness to die for Athens suggests both the reconciliation with nature and the establishment of mature, human wisdom which result from the agnostic choice. (RCM)

6864. Paley, Morton D. "The Critical Reception of *A Critical Essay*." *BlakeN* 8:32-37. [On S's *William Blake*.]

The first book-length critical study of Blake was *William Blake* by Swinburne. Nine reviews appeared in the periodical press, all within a year of publication. At times the reviewers long for the less threatening Blake presented by Gilchrist, and the predictable dismissal of Blake's visionary qualities also occurs. Still, Swinburne's essay forced even the unsympathetic reviewers to consider Blake seriously, and Moncure D. Conway's review in the *Fortnightly* and the anonymous notice in the *Broadway* are highly discerning. (MDP)

6867. Sypher, Francis J.,Jr. "My Dear Ulrica . . .': Swinburne's Earliest Letter." *QJLC* 31:92-96.

Swinburne's earliest letter, dated Capheaton, 5 December 1848, to Ulrica Fenwick, is here transcribed and reproduced by photograph, together with pictures of places mentioned in it: Capheaton, the home of Sir John Swinburne, and the Pantheon Bazaar in London. Cancellations in the letter (perhaps made at the suggestion of a familial censor) indicate Swinburne's eager affection for the daughter of his tutor. (FJS)

Tennyson, A. 6882. Goslee, David F. "Character and Structure in Tennyson's *The Princess*." *SEL* 14:563-73.

Tennyson's *The Princess* typifies the paradoxical relation of character and structure in all his narratives. Ida stands at the center of a neat and artificial nest of frames, each of which is apparently manipulated by a character in the frame enclosing it. Ida, however, cannot be manipulated. Instead, she structures the goals, the curriculum, even the threatening statuary of her university to escape from her fairy-tale world into the relative freedom of history. Through her visions she breaks up not only her own confining world, but the confining structure of the poem itself. This conflict of character and structure thus usurps the central place of interpersonal conflicts in a more traditional narrative. (DFG)

6898. McSweeney, Kerry. "The State of Tennyson Criticism." *PLL* 10:433-46. [Rev. art.]

Consideration of seven recent books on Tennyson substantiates two propositions: Tennyson is a peculiarly difficult poet to write about well or to assess accurately; there is an ever-present temptation for critics to forsake the rigors of genuine critical discourse for the sonorities of moralistic commentary. Different critical approaches are assessed; the central aspect of Tennyson's artistic growth is discussed; and the rapidly growing critical consensus concerning the greatness of *Idylls of the King* is scrutinized from a negative point of view. (KM)

6900. Morris, Celia. "From Malory to Tennyson:Spiritual Triumph to Spiritual Defeat." *Mosaic* 7,iii:87-98. [The *Idylls of the King* and the *Morte d'Arthur*.]

Tennyson's "The Holy Grail" shows the erosion of Christian belief in the 19th century and the spiritual crisis that erosion caused. The world of the *Idylls of the King*, one that believes in sin but not in salvation, becomes a world of despair. We see this more clearly when we compare Tennyson's poem to *Le Morte d'Arthur*. To the characters in Malory, the Church's mysteries and rituals are real and efficacious. Their Quest is holy and attainable. Their counterparts in Tennyson use the Quest to evade their duty. Malory's Launcelot largely succeeds in participating in Holiness. Pursuing the Quest for moral reasons, Tennyson's Lancelot fails. Like Percivale, he is overcome by a sense of sinfulness and unworthiness no rituals can help him master. In Malory, Percivale fights for his salvation. In Tennyson, Percivale despairs. "The Holy Grail" pays mere lip service to faith in spiritual guidance and the possibilities of repentance, Divine forgiveness, and Grace. (CM)

6905. Priestley, F.E.L. "Locksley Hall Revisited." *QQ* 81:512-32.

A careful reading of Tennyson's Locksley Hall poems makes evident the dramatic skill with which the poems are composed. Both adolescence, in the first poem, and old age, in the second, are viewed from a complex attitude—with sympathy, with amusement, with mixed approval and disapproval. The second poem, by completing the narrative of the life begun in the first, throws a richly ironic light on the young man's judgments and fancies, adding new dimensions and depths. At the same time, it exploits dramatically both the contrasts of youth and age and also the elements that persist in the character. (FELP)

6906. Puckett, Harry. "Subjunctive Imagination in *In Memoriam*." *VP* 12:97-124.

Using the subjunctive, Tennyson sets up a series of imagined worlds, which are then frequently overthrown or qualified, so that *In Memoriam* moves gradually through a series of flawed imaginings to a higher quality of imagination at the conclusion. Early in the poem the flawed images are usually those of imagined loss or despair, which the poet overthrows in order to recover the will to live and love. But more important are the shabby or extravagant hopes which appear rather early in the poem and continue well into the latter half. These, too, are overthrown as the poet moves toward more perfect images of hope, finally displacing one act of the will (hoping) with another (loving). This process of a gradually perfected imagination, leading to a perfected will, is far more important and more interesting than any set of truths or beliefs that might be gleaned from *In Memoriam*. (HP)

6908. Rosenberg, John D. "Tennyson and the Landscape of Consciousness." *VP* 12:303-10.

Among Tennyson's finest achievments are his mythical landscapes that symbolize states of human consciousness. The dreamlike quality of his vision, combined with his ability to see at close range, rendered his dreams more vivid than our realities. *In Memoriam* is intensely personal and yet is the archetypal presentation of the Victorians' "tense dialogue of faith in mortal combat with doubt." Tennyson maintained throughout his career powers of keenest observation combined with an abnormally keen awareness of the anomalous state of man. His characteristic note is one of ambivalence between certainty and doubt, past and present, illusion and reality. (JDR)

6915. Shaw, W. David. "Tennyson's Late Elegies." *VP* 12:1-12.

Set in desolate scenes, unremittingly stark and minimal, several of Tennyson's late elegies—verses like his lines "To the Marquis of Dufferin and Ava" (1889), "In the Garden at Swainston" (1870),

and "Crossing the Bar" (1889)—use a deliberately impoverished but oblique style, first perfected in two early elegies written shortly after Hallam's death: "Break, Break, Break" and "On a Mourner." The deaths of Sir John Simeon in 1870 and Tennyson's son Lionel in 1886 overwhelm the poet with a sense of the barren emptiness of the world. Though the attenuated diction of the plain style is appropriate to the imminence of death, it affords a striking contrast to the ceremonial richness usually associated with Tennyson, even in other late poems like "Demeter and Persephone" (1887) and the classical pieces, "To Virgil" (1882) and "Frater Ave Atque Vale" (1883). There is a clarity of outline in the late elegies, a grand austerity of style and thought, as Tennyson returns to the barrenness of *In Memoriam*, composing a poetry of epitaph and inscription. (WDS)

6916. Spatz, Jonas. "Love and Death in Tennyson's *Maud*." *TSLL* 16:503-10.

In the climax of *Maud* love becomes an inspiration for hate and a license for the hero to commit the violence that he has always condemned. *Maud* must be seen as Tennyson's unconscious insight into the relation between love and aggression. The narrator's love for Maud is a neurotic pattern of behavior that protects him from a conscious recognition of his violent desires and later justifies the murder he has committed. Love becomes the only acceptable alternative to impotence and despair on the one hand and an unbearable burden of guilt on the other. It finally comes to symbolize all of the ideals in whose name man perpetuates his barbaric acts. The hero's state of murderous sublimation at the end of the poem is the prototype of man's "adjustment" to an aggressive and bestial society. (JS)

6917. Staines, David. "Tennyson's 'The Holy Grail':The Tragedy of Percivale." *MLR* 69:745-56.

The ten-year delay (1859-68) in the continuation of Tennyson's *Idylls of the King* was a consequence of the poet's inability to find an appropriate means of incorporating the Grail story into his distinctly 19th-century Arthurian poem. Using Malory as a resource rather than a source, Tennyson altered the traditional concept of the Grail story so that the unsuccessful quester, Percivale, is now the center of the treatment. In the idyll, the only idyll which uses the dramatic monolgue rather than omniscient narration, Percivale narrates his version of the quest so that the failed quest becomes personal tragedy, told, most effectively, by a narrator too blind to see the full meaning of his own narration, "So spake the King: I knew not all he meant." The completion of three more idylls within one year of the completion of *The Holy Grail* suggests Tennyson's personal satisfaction with his unique presentation of the Grail story. (DS)

6928. Ward, Arthur D. " 'Ulysses' and 'Tithonus':Tunnel-Vision and Idle Tears." *VP* 12:311-19.

Tennyson paired Ulysses and Tithonus so that each highlights attractions and inadequacies of the other's personality and moral position. Ulysses' moral, emotional "tunnel-vision" refuses to recognize whatever would frustrate his purpose. Tithonus' madness, by contrast, is passive and circular, as his repetition of words and ideas demonstrates. While Ulysses' ego devours or obliterates everything outside it, Tithonus' ego passively conforms to its surroundings and seeks its own obliteration in sexual union with Eos. Ulysses' incapacity for love has crippled his capacity for action; Tithonus' incapacity for self-reliant action has crippled his capacity for love. (ADW)

Thackeray. 6934. Cabot, Frederick C. "The Two Voices in Thackeray's *Catherine*." *NCF* 28:404-16.

Thackeray's inability to sustain an ironic voice can be considered a major cause of the failure of *Catherine*, his first novel, appearing serially in *Fraser's Magazine* in 1839-40. His ostensible narrator, "Ikey Solomons, Esq., Junior" does not duplicate the success of his model, the narrator of Fielding's *Jonathan Wild*, because he confronts his reader at once as a parodist-clown and as a stern preacher. Too often he utters Thackeray's own moral and critical ideas. He goes too far when he suggests that the reader is no better than the criminal characters in his own tale. In *Catherine* Thackeray intended to depict criminals as they really are. For his heroine he chose a woman who murdered her husband and dismembered his body: but his attempt to achieve ironic distance from her is undercut by his developing interest in her as a literary character. (FCC)

6938. Harden, Edgar F. "The Challenges of Serialization: Parts 4, 5, and 6 of *The Newcomes*." *NCF* 29:3-21.

Parts 4, 5, and 6 of Thackeray's *The Newcomes*, which make up the earliest unit of the surviving manuscript, offer important evidence for our understanding Thackeray's problems and achievements as a serial novelist. Part 4, which was written four months before its appearance in January 1854, proved too long to be printed and presented Thackeray with the choice of cancelling some of the manuscript or transferring the final scene to the following installment. He chose to do the latter and therefore had to write additional material to fill part of the space created by the transfer—additions that enhanced his narrative. In Part 5, which was completed before Part 4 went to press, the deferral produced a text that once again could not be printed in full; in this instance he was prompted to make deletions that significantly improved the novel's artistry. Part 6 was sent to the printer from Italy in two segments; misunderstandings and delays threatened the monthly installment's appearance, but these difficulties were overcome by good fortune, the help of a friend, and Thackeray's own commitment to his art. (EFH)

6942. McMaster, R[owland] D. "The Pygmalion Motif in *The Newcomes*." *NCF* 29:22-39.

An informing theme of Thackeray's *The Newcomes* is the aspiration to shape the actual world according to ideal figments of the imagination. Colonel Newcome, inspired by a romantic daydream from his own past, devises an imaginary paradise to make his beloved son happy. Enthralled by his fiction and trying to impose that dream upon life, the Colonel brings on disaster. Parallel attempts by several other characters reflect the same structural theme. Ethel patterns her own life according to contradictory fictions, sordid or pastoral, to suit her mood or company. Supporting imagery oscillates ironically between pastoral and commercial, elegant artifice and mundane reality. Systems of allusion and illustration (including the drawings) stress the tension between an inclusive vision of life as conventional repetition or inherited form and the individual's sense of his life's fresh uniqueness. The theme has at least two dimensions: the moral (in fallen humanity's attempt to recollect and refashion the paradisal), and the artistic (in attempts to impose form upon, and make art out of, the resisting raw material of life). (RDM)

6950. Shillingsburg, Peter L. "Thackeray's *Pendennis* in America." *PBSA* 68:325-29.

Bibliographers attribute to the Harper edition of Thackeray's *Pendennis* a textual superiority over the first London edition in book form because the Harper edition contains paragraphs and two illustrations suppressed from the first London edition. The facts are that the New York edition contains nothing which is not in the first London edition in book form, and there is little substantial difference between the first London edition as it was issued in parts (1848-50) and in book form (1849-50). The paragraphs in question were "suppressed" for the first time in the unillustrated "Cheap edition" of 1856. (PLS)

6954. Sutherland, John A. "The Expanding Narrative of *Vanity Fair*." *JNT* 3:149-69.

The full form of Thackeray's *Vanity Fair* did not emerge immediately. Thackeray began by writing a work different in outlook and simpler in scope. As a result the early sections of the narrative, and more especially the manuscript, offer some useful insights into Thackeray's changes of mind as he wrote. The first major problem was his relationship with his heroine Becky; it was not until Chapter viii that he managed to establish a stable attitude to her. In addition the character of George Osborne gave problems. It was not for some time that Thackeray came to see him as a villain. Correspondingly George's counterpart, Dobbin, was in the nature of a narrative afterthought. The evolution of both these characters witnesses to Thackeray's increasingly confident social analysis of his age and its snobberies. Of particular interest are the so-called "Vanity Fair" interpolations. These moral apostrophes which Thackeray added to his narrative are, however, rather more complex and evasive than they are often taken to be. (JAS)

6957. Wolff, Cynthia G. "Who Is the Narrator of *Vanity Fair* and Where Is He Standing?" *CollL* 1:190-203.

In seeking the moral center of *Vanity Fair* critics accept the narrator's claims to omniscience and moral reliability and assume that the different levels of discourse used by the narrator constitute controlled, self-conscious irony. Though the narrator's language is sometimes ironic, the several levels of discourse also indicate his confusion, ambivalence, or disingenuity. The true irony of the novel is not verbal but structural, and the narrator seems helpless either to comment on this irony or even to notice it. The narrator's own limitation becomes the most significant moral element of the novel. (CGW)

Thomson. 6959. Noel-Bentley, Peter C. " 'Fronting the Dreadful Mysteries of Time':Dürer's *Melencolia* in Thomson's *City of Dreadful Night*." *VP* 12:193-203.

The image of Dürer's *Melencolia I* at the end of Thomson's *City of Dreadful Night* resolves every major theme and image of the poem. The development of the image from the male personage of 1857 through the female statue of "A Lady of Sorrow" and Melencolia herself in "The 'Melencolia' of Albrecht Dürer" in the 1860s to the final manifestation of Melencolia in *The City of Dreadful Night* parallels Thomson's development from orthodox Calvinist to despairing atheist. (PCN-B)

Todhunter. 6962. Tolley, Michael J. "John Todhunter:A Forgotten Debt to Blake." *BlakeN* 8:15-16.

Todhunter was an imitator of Blake in his early collection of poems, *Laurella* (1876). This forgotten debt is recovered and the interesting preface to *Laurella*—recording interviews with a Blake-like character—is quoted in part. (MJT)

Trelawny. 6963. Allentuck, Marcia. "An Unremarked Drawing of Edward Trelawny." *KSJ* 23:24-25.

The Department of Rare Books and Special Collections of McGill University in Montreal possesses a heretofore unremarked portrait of Edward Trelawny by Edward Bird. Allentuck analyzes the drawing and relates it to other paintings of Trelawny by other artists. This is the only portrait of Trelawny thus far discovered in North America. (MA)

Trollope, A. 6965. Aitken, David. "Anthony Trollope on 'the Genus Girl'." *NCF* 28:417-34.

Anthony Trollope's feminine characters are invariably drawn in accordance with a set of fixed, rather conservative ideas about women. The only possible career for a woman is marriage because "superior power has settled" the matter for us. Women are by nature strong to endure but not to aggress. They are inclined by very instinct to lives of service, sacrifice, and submission. Above all, they are creatures of feeling. Their passions can be formidable, but the character of feminine passion is such as to compel women to marry and take second place in the family and society. The woman who rebels against this, as many of Trollope's most striking and sympathetically rendered heroines do, will inevitably find that her heart will defeat her. So the arguments of militant feminism are in vain. Woman is born to her destiny, and cannot, in the very nature of things, escape it. (DA)

6969. Glavin, John J. "Trollope's 'Most Natural English Girl'." *NCF* 28:477-85.

Anthony Trollope is capable of using complicated, continuous metaphor in the development of his narrative. In *Framley Parsonage* (1860) the love story proceeds and is enriched by an on-going analogy to the seasonal development of the natural world. Lucy Robarts, the romantic heroine, first appears at the winter solstice as the dead earth in the grip of winter. Lufton, who becomes her lover, is the "sun" of her universe. As the plot of the novel proceeds from winter to spring to summer she is gradually warmed and enlivened by his influence. Finally, after undergoing a ritual experience of disappearance and almost death, similar to initiation and fertility rites, she emerges mature and willing to respond to his love. Trollope's consistent deployment of the metaphor suggests that Lucy's vitality, in both her claim on the reader's sympathy and within the novel's thematic structure, derives from her intimate connection with the processes of natural, and ultimately, sexual life. (JJG)

6973. Hall, N. John. "An Unpublished Trollope Manuscript on a Proposed History of World Literature." *NCF* 29:206-10.
Among the Trollope family papers in the University of Illinois Library survives a 1300-word manuscript in which Anthony Trollope proposes, outlines, and supplies guidelines for writing a history of world literature. Trollope never came to write the work, even as he broke down in his resolve to write a "History of English Prose Fiction." One cannot date the manuscript precisely, but evidence points to early composition, c. 1840. The proposal exudes a naive, youthful confidence about an undertaking of staggering dimensions: some 19 chronological divisions (5 before Christ) and 12 main subject divisions, encompassing every kind of writing from poetry and history through theology and the fine arts. The present text, which includes Trollope's list of 10 "Bibliographical Books to be read," renders the manuscript exactly as Trollope wrote it except for some minor changes in punctuation. (NJH)

6974. —— "Letters of Thomas Adolphus Trollope to Henry Merivale Trollope, 1882-92." *LC* 39(1973):106-24.
110 letters from Thomas Adolphus Trollope, Anthony's older brother, to Henry Marivale Trollope, Anthony's older son, survive among the Trollope family papers in the University of Illinois Library. Excerpted here, the letters show Thomas Adolphus carrying on his writing career and compiling his memoirs. Along with the literary talk and family news Thomas Adolphus sprinkles outbursts against the policies of Gladstone. Inevitably, however, the letters concerning Anthony are of most interest: the intimate replies to his nephew's detailed accounts of the stroke, illness, and death of his father; the advice for the publication of the posthumous *Autobiography*; and the subsequent and continuing concern over the next ten years for Anthony's reputation. (NJH)

6976. Halperin, John. "Politics, Palmerston, and Trollope's Prime Minister." *ClioW* 3:187-218.
Anthony Trollope's ambivalence toward party politics is reflected by the awe in which he held some politicians and the House of Commons itself, and the savage satire with which he attacked others who succeeded chiefly by the playing of political games. His ideal statesman is a man who puts honesty and integrity above political expediency, even at the risk of failure. Trollope's parliamentary novels demonstrate what he admires and what he dislikes in the political arena, and why. Trollope preferred even misguided weakness in a political leader who was honest—and, preferably, aristocratic—to real political expertise in a party leader whose success depended upon sham, cunning, and deceit. The reader who may want to know specifically who is actually who in Trollope's political novels, however, may well find himself stymied by the novelist's usual practice of taking characteristics of several different men for each of his political portraits, and his tendency to draw upon public rather than private conduct in creating his fictional personages. (JH)

6982. Levine, George. "Can You Forgive Him? Trollope's 'Can You Forgive Her?' and the Myth of Realism." *VS* 18:5-30.
Anthony Trollope's fiction represents an acceptance of the conventions of 19th-century realism. Despite a critical awareness of the limits of the imagined society, his works accept the need for compromise with the unwritten rules of that society. In *Can You Forgive Her*, Trollope pushes the realistic myth to the point at which other writers were forced to break with the traditions of realism. Trollope, however, leaves his characters in the contingent, compromised world of the realistic myth, and implies in the very structure of the novel, the satisfactoriness of the conditions he has dramatized as inadequate. (GL)

6984. McMaster, Juliet. " 'The Meaning of Words and the Nature of Things':Trollope's *Can You Forgive Her*?" *SEL* 14:603-18.
Alice Vavasor and not Glencora is the central character in Trollope's *Can You Forgive Her?*, since she most clearly embodies the novel's major concern with the relation of language to experience. Trollope's characterization of her is not only a subtle psychological study but is conceptually central to the thematic patterning of the novel. In her unexpected vacillations between her two fiancés, she reflects a morbid disjunction between doing and saying, fact and theory, experience and expression, that is a

sickness, to different extents, of other characters like George Vavasor and Glencora, as well as in politics and the world at large. Trollope enlarges on this theme by reference to modes of expression, means of self-delusion, and the difficulties of communication. (JSMcM)

6991. Waddington, Patrick. "Turgenev and Trollope:Brief Crossings of Paths." *AUMLA* 42:199-201.
Turgenev and Trollope first met at George Eliot's London home in 1871, when Turgenev and his friends the Viardots were refugees from the Franco-Prussian conflict. The two may not have read each other's works, but Trollope liked Turgenev well enough to invite him to the Athenaeum Club. They met again in London ten years later, when Turgenev was the guest of honor at a dinner given by Ralston and attended by several English novelists and journalists. Here again Turgenev and Trollope had little impact on one another; but their deaths gave rise to obituaries in which they were compared. One such notice defined Trollope's art as "informative" and Turgenev's as "suggestive"; but most British commentators were as ignorant of the latter's works as Trollope had probably been. (PW)

6992. West, William A. "The Anonymous Trollope." *ArielE* 5,i:46-64. [On *Fortnightly Rev.* art. "On American Literature" and 3 novels intended for anon. pub.: *Nini Baltaka, Linda Tressel,* and *The Golden Lion of Granpère*.]
Trollope wrote two novels which were published anonymously. In his *Autobiography* Trollope offers his analysis of the disguise he assumed in order to assure that the authorship of the novels should remain undetected. West's analysis begins with Trollope's comments, but goes beyond his rather cursory remarks by tracing the ways in which the tales are departures from Trollope's usual, expected range in subject matter and themes. They suggest, in fact, a willingness on Trollope's part to experiment with subjects quite unlike those dealt with in the earlier Barchester novels. West examines the new materials in the two novels, and concludes by noticing that they appeared just before *The Last Chronicle of Barset* and *He Knew He Was Right*; which suggests that the anonymous tales are indeed important to Trollope's development insofar as they lead the way to the expanded range of his later, darker fiction. (WAW)

6993. Witting, Ellen W. "Trollope's Irish Fiction." *Éire* 9,iii:97-118.
From Trollope's experiences in Ireland came his four Irish novels, two comic Irish tales, and various works which take place partly on Irish soil. An exploration of the relationship between what Trollope saw in Ireland and the shape and effectiveness of all his major Irish fiction reveals that the gradual blurring of his vision of Irish experience is reflected in the form of each succeeding Irish novel. (EWW)

White, W.H. 6998. Hughes, Linda K. "Madge and Clara Hopgood:William Hale White's Spinozan Sisters." *VS* 18:57-75.
Spinoza's concepts of the relation between virtue and intellect and the control of the passions through adequate ideas underlie White's characterization of the sisters in *Clara Hopgood*. Initially Madge is an exponent of instinct who indulges in passion and becomes pregnant. Her intellect reasserts itself and her virtue increases. Clara is a consistent spokeswoman for the intellect, hence her life is a paradigm of Spinozan values. The sisters demonstrate the superiority of reason over impulse. The structure of the novel is also Spinozan, moving from a dualistic opposition of Clara and Madge to a monistic pattern of harmony between them. (LKH)

Wilde. 7006. Marcus, Jane. "Salomé:The Jewish Princess Was a New Woman." *BNYPL* 78:95-113. [Illus.]
Wilde's *Salomé* is a genuine tragedy, a great work of art which has been obscured by the pornographic nature of Beardsley's drawings. English and American audiences have not shared the European and Russian recognition of the revolutionary themes in the play. Illustrations from Beardsley, Moreau, Alexandra Exter, and Anja Silja, singing the role of Salomé from a production of the opera, reinforce the point that Salomé was the icon of the ideology of the Decadents, that Wilde's play was an original political and esthetic rewriting of the legend. (JCM)

7010. O'Brien, Kevin H.F. "'The House Beautiful':A Reconstruction of Oscar Wilde's American Lecture." *VS* 17:395-418.
No known manuscripts of "The House Beautiful," used by Wilde on his lecture tour in 1882, survive; however, Wilde's tour received coverage in American and Canadian newspapers, and a collation of the accounts of the lecture produces a credible rendering of the piece. Textual reconstruction provides a review of the decorative tastes of the Esthetic Movement as interpreted by Wilde, indicates that Wilde was influenced by Ruskin's and Morris' attempts to bring beauty into the lives of the middle class, and its sincerity, social concern, and talk of the connection of art and morality provides an interesting contrast to Wilde's later flippancy, Philistine baiting, and artistic isolationism. (KHFO)

7011. Parker, David. "Oscar Wilde's Great Farce:*The Importance of Being Earnest*." *MLQ* 35:173-86.
In Wilde's *The Importance of Being Earnest* the characters all seem selfish, and it is hard to defend them morally; however, Wilde's comic vision justifies this. As in Restoration comedy, the protagonists are selfish for symbolic purposes. They are rogues, in a farce which poses questions about human identity. Wilde is concerned with Nothingness, with absurdity in human existence. These things are explored in the verbal texture of the play, in the paradoxes, in the plot, and in the action. A sense of the insubstantiality of human identity throws stress on impulse. In their changeability, their attitudes to love, their scorn of theory, consistency, simplicity, and verifiable truth, the characters demonstrate the fluidity of human identity. The major characters are either protean or imposers of fantasy on the world. Minor characters are consistent and erroneously believe they know the truth. The play is admirable because it tackles the concerns of fashionable theories about farce, the drama of the absurd, and Existentialist theories of identity with wit, intelligence, and an appetite for life. (DP)

7012. Pollin, Burton R. "The Influence of 'The Ancient Mariner' upon 'The Ballad of Reading Gaol'." *RLV* 40:228-34.
Wilde's "The Ballad of Reading Gaol" appears to be markedly dependent upon Coleridge's "Ancient Mariner" for images, phrases, tone, and metrical structure. The parallels, for which a large number of specific textual passages are given, are far too numerous to have been the product of Wilde's memory or minor similarities of circumstances. His significant references in his other works and correspondence and his reading of Coleridge's poem in prison indicate his conscious use of the earlier ballad. The fundamental differences, however, in philosophic orientation furnish an explanation for the discrepancies and inconsistencies in Wilde's poem. (BRP)

7013. Portnoy, William E. "Wilde's Debt to Tennyson in *Dorian Gray*." *ELT* 17:259-61.
Striking parallels in the characterization, thematic substance, and imaginal technique of "The Lady of Shalott" (1842 version) and the "Sibyl Vane" episode of *The Picture of Dorian Gray* (1890) indicate Wilde's extensive borrowing from Tennyson. Both works depict the career of a beautiful woman who is impelled by her love for a handsome young man to abandon her esthetic isolation for the realm of nature or life. This portion of *Dorian Gray* is replete with close reproductions of the imagery and phraseology of Tennyson's poem whose cumulative effect is to corroborate the thesis of relationship proposed here. Both works employ shadow, mirror, and music images in defining the worlds of art which their respective heroines inhabit. (WEP)

Wordsworth, W. 7020. Beauchamp, Gorman. "Wordsworth's Archetypal Resolution." *CP* 7,i:13-19. ["Resolution and Independence."]
In "Resolution and Independence" Wordsworth recreates four shifting psychological moods which give rise to two questions: what activates the dejection and what enables the poet to come to terms with it? Biographical speculation has obscured the answer to the first question: the poet is plunged into despair by the tragic potential of human existence, the dread of falling from happiness to misfortune. He is rescued by his vision of the leech gatherer, which seems to him almost providential. This wanderer-figure symbolizes the wholeness of nature and the eternal sufferer who has yet managed to prevail. The encounter provides resolution

because the leech gatherer is an archetypal figure who serves to reintegrate the disintegrating personality. (GB)

7021. Birdsall, Eric R. "Wordsworth's Revisions to *Descriptive Sketches*:The Wellesley Copy." *WC* 5:9-14.
Of the few copies of the first (1793) edition of Wordsworth's *Descriptive Sketches* which survive, among the most interesting is one in the Wellesley College library which contains unique revisions, most made by Wordsworth himself. Since the poet continually revised the poem, it is difficult to know precisely when the revisions were made. But collation of the manuscript changes with other versions of the poem and comparisons to the Wordsworths' letters and journals suggest that the Wellesley copy is the "Sarah's copy" of the poem referred to in an 1814 letter and that it was used to prepare the excerpts from *DS* reprinted in the 1815 edition of the poems. It seems that this copy served as the basis for the 1820 edition of the poem and that it was the one the Wordsworths took along as they retraced the progress of the poem on their tour of the continent late in 1820. The appendix to the article is a list of the revisions in this unique copy and is important because very few of the changes appear in deSelincourt's edition of the *Poetical Works*. (ERB)

7022. Brantley, Richard E. "Spiritual Maturity and Wordsworth's 1783 Christmas Vacation." *SEL* 14:479-87.
The lines from *The Prelude* in which Wordsworth recalls his father's death (XI.345-97, 1805) reflect a biblical doctrine of particular significance to the Evangelical Movement: God hastens spiritual maturity through chastisement of pride. When his discontented spirit yields to loving reproof from a chastening God, he bows in humility and thereby pays to the Father of spirits the reverence formerly due to the father of his flesh. His Evangelical terminology, then, is more than casual; for this particular passage, in which God's mediated and unmediated presence is central. suggests that a theology at once traditional and vital survived in and helped to shape his new kind of verse. (REB)

7023. Braun, Theodore E.D. "Diderot, Wordsworth, and the Creative Process." *CLS* 11:151-58.
Diderot's conception of the creative process, as expressed in the *Paradoxe sur le comédien* has significant affinities with Wordsworth's conception of it, as expressed in the Preface to the second edition of the *Lyrical Ballads* and in the Preface to his *Poems*. Analysis of the texts shows that Wordsworth, in discussing poetry, and Diderot, in discussing acting, were really speaking of artistic creation in general. The major difference in their views is related to the role of sensibility; yet even here Diderot's ambiguity reflects an implicit grasp of the distinction which Wordsworth was to make explicitly between poetic and human sensibility. (TEDB)

7024. Brier, Peter A. "Reflections on Tintern Abbey." *WC* 5:5-6.
The actual ruins of Tintern Abbey have more to do with the meaning of Wordsworth's poem than critics have suggested. Covered with greenery, the Christian ruin reveals Wordsworth's natural religion. (PAB)

7029. Dings, John. "Bostetter on Wordsworth." *Paunch* 38:32-39.
Bostetter's criticism of Wordsworth gives real attention to the increasing contraction of the poet's social vision: his mistrust of reform grounded in his refusal to see the suffering of other people either as real suffering or as having social causes. The limitation of this criticism is that it treats social vision abstractly, and not as an engagement with a concrete social reality. For example, whereas Bostetter lambastes the "Old Cumberland Beggar" as a defense of beggary and an act of callous, selfish projection, we can resituate the poem within contemporary Poor Law discussions and within the actual life of a community, as recollected by Wordsworth, and see it as a complicated and touchingly impotent attempt to defend a humane but obsolescent idea of social order against a brutal and progressive one. (JD)

7033. Ferguson, Frances C. "The Lucy Poems:Wordsworth's Quest for a Poetic Object." *ELH* 40(1973):532-48.
The ordering which Wordsworth gave to the Lucy poems reveals a quest motif in which the quest itself seems increasingly to distance the poet-speaker from Lucy. Although the first three

Lucy poems are classified by Wordsworth as "Poems Founded on the Affections," the final poems which are "Poems of the Imagination," cast doubt upon the status of the earlier poems as love poems written about a real person. Lucy appears in diminishing form through the course of the poems, finally seeming never to have been born. As a group, the Lucy poems suggest a radical questioning of mimetic theories of poetry which attempt to correlate poems with real objects in the natural world. Wordsworth's quest for a poetic object—Lucy—undermines such theories by moving through stages of increasing knowledge of Lucy to the awareness that Lucy is essentially both unattainable and unknowable. (FCF)

7035. French, A.L. "The 'Fair Seed-Time' in Wordsworth's *Prelude*." *CR* 17:3-20.
Readers of Wordsworth's *The Prelude* have never quite known what to do with the "visionary" passages. One reason for this problem is that the term "visionary" has been made to include all kinds of passages, some of which are "visionary" in ways which are indeed suspect. The best of these passages, however, render experiences of the otherness and alienness of Nature which were so profoundly disturbing that Wordsworth often tried to discount them by suggesting that they could be regarded as ethically profitable and could thus be connected with his conscious adult beliefs about Man and Nature. This explains why the verse celebrating those conscious beliefs is so inferior to that celebrating the awed terror and disorientation the rendering of which is, in fact, the chief strength of *The Prelude*. (ALF)

7040. Griska, Joseph M.,Jr. "Wordsworth's Mood Disturbance:A Psychoanalytic Approach to Three Poems." *L&P* 24:144-52.
Between 1798 and 1804 Wordsworth exhibited symptoms of a psychosomatic illness. As a child Wordsworth experienced traumas, some of which brought on suicidal fantasies, and an even greater number of adulthood crises which may have precipitated these symptoms and which aroused anxiety that perhaps he lacked the ability to succeed as a poet. This anxiety manifested itself in his poetry from 1798 to 1807, especially in "Resolution and Independence," "Intimations of Immortality," and "Elegiac Stanzas" where the poet attempts to reconcile his longing to write visionary poetry with an apprehension that nature is abandoning him. (JMG,Jr.)

7041. Hassler, Donald M. "Belief and Death in Wordsworth's *Peter Bell*." *BNYPL* 77:251-57.
Peter Bell is among Wordsworth's most stark poems. It expresses a dark side of Wordsworth's belief that should be noticed more and that should assure the poem a more respected place in his canon. The redemption of Peter's mind is accomplished entirely by means of the association of ideas, and this materialistic psychology is the source of the skepticism in the poem. All movement is simply valuable as movement. This implication of associationism can be seen vividly in David Hartley's near quantitative description of God as the sum of all movement. Since Wordsworth's usual stated beliefs are at odds with the quantitative leveling of a theory such as associationism, his belief must be based on some variety of transcendentalism. The world of the poem is exclusively "a world of death." (DMH)

7043. Hill, Alan G. "New Light on *The Excursion*." *ArielE* 5,ii:37-47.
The affinities between Wordsworth's "conventional" poem *The Excursion* and Minucius Felix's early Christian dialogue *Octavius* suggest that the two works are connected. A definite link between them can be established because Wordsworth borrowed Coleridge's copy of *Octavius* over a long period of time. Detailed comparison between the structure and temper of the two suggests that Wordsworth was influenced in important respects by Minucius Felix. (AGH)

7045. Holland, Patrick. "Wordsworth and the Sublime:Some Further Considerations." *WC* 5:17-22.
The publication of Wordsworth's fragmentary essay "The Sublime and the Beautiful" demands a much more precise application of 18th-century theory of the sublime to Wordsworth's poetry than appears in Albert O. Wlecke's *Wordsworth and the Sublime*. In that essay Wordsworth insists on the importance for the mind of looking at the forms of Nature

steadily and understanding the laws by which they affect the mind. These laws are those of the Sublime and the Beautiful. Lines 716-29 in Book VII of *The Prelude* foreshadow the theory of the sublime laid out in "The Sublime and the Beautiful." Wordsworth treats the mind as if it possessed spatial qualities. In *The Prelude* Wordsworth treats phenomena and men as paradigmatic of the mind, for both possess those qualities needed to impart a sense of the sublime—"simplicity," "duration," and "power." (PH)

7048. Jaye, Michael C. "Wordsworth at Work:MS.RV Book II of *The Prelude*." *PBSA* 68:251-65.
Ms. RV is the earliest manuscript of Book II of Wordsworth's *Prelude* and has been given little attention by Wordsworthians. The manuscript—a fair copy in the hands of Dorothy Wordsworth and Sara Hutchinson with initial drafting and thorough revision by Wordsworth himself—reveals Wordsworth's most important work at a critical early stage in its long and complex history. The most important factors governing the expansion of the poem from one book to two were Wordsworth's return to England from Germany in the spring of 1799, his relationship with Coleridge who was anxious for Wordsworth to return to work on *The Recluse*, Wordsworth's own ambivalence toward the never-to-be-written *Recluse*, and his desire to continue to trace the forces that shaped his poetic being. (MCJ)

7051. Kaufman, Paul. "John Peace to William Wordsworth: Four Unpublished Letters." *ELN* 11:193-99. [Incl. texts of the letters.]
These four hitherto unpublished letters, 1839-45, given in 1923 to the Bristol City Library by Gordon Wordsworth (the poet's grandson), express an appealing, lifelong devotion of John Peace to Wordsworth. Their significance lies in the disclosure of the complement to the seven published letters of Wordsworth to the librarian of the Bristol Library Society. The identity and personality of Wordsworth's correspondent emerge for the first time. Here is an epistolary portrait of the shy old bachelor who walked perhaps a hundred and fifty miles (both ways) just to see his friend receive the honorary degree at Oxford. Something of the rapport between them appears in the poet's revelation to Peace of the intensity of his sorrow over the death of his daughter—overt expression apparently limited otherwise to his immediate family and Miss Fenwick. (PK)

7052. Kirkham, Michael. "Innocence and Experience in Wordsworth's 'The Thorn'." *ArielE* 5,i:66-80.
"The Thorn" is about innocence and experience, considered as successive and simultaneous conditions. The story of Martha Ray is a fable of man's fall from the state of psychical and social concord and initiation into the pains of adult living. The thorn symbolizes at once age and a (stunted) childhood, linking the attainment of maturity with decay of innocence. Martha's child is like an internalized memory of the innocence that was once the external medium in which she existed. The general theme secretes also an inner drama concerning the relation of Wordsworth the man to Wordsworth the boy, and the poet to the source of his poetry. (MCK)

7054. Kroeber, Karl. " 'Home at Grasmere':Ecological Holiness." *PMLA* 89:132-41.
Wordsworth's "Home at Grasmere" expresses a conception of home as a territorial sanctuary. The holiness of Grasmere Vale consists in the possibility for ecological wholeness which it provides. The enclosure of the valley liberates the poet's psychic potency, because there he is encouraged to be receptive to multiple dimensions of experience. Through such openness he is consciously able to reintegrate his being into the enduring rhythms of natural existence, thereby articulating his unique individuality. "Home at Grasmere" embodies Wordsworth's ideal of what poetry should be, namely, the realization through language of the intrinsic poeticalness of commonplace actuality. This true poetry liberates man from the prison of mere perception, revealing how individuals—by fitting themselves to nature and fitting nature to themselves—can give unique expression to the unified, interdependent wholeness which is life, the expression being a fulfillment rather than a negation of fundamental inherent tendencies of natural process. (KK)

7062. Mellown, Muriel J. "The Development of Imagery in

'Home at Grasmere'." *WC* 5:23-27.

In Wordsworth's "Home at Grasmere" descriptions of personal experience lead to metaphors which suggest the poet's visionary insight into man and nature. This sequence of experience, metaphor, vision is evident in the three basic themes of the poem: relationship, paradise, and voyage. In each of these Wordsworth passes from literal to figurative and symbolic levels. Descriptions of literal relationships prepare for metaphors which express the fundamental union of man and nature in terms of a family bond. In the second theme, the poet's boyhood dream of an actual paradise at Grasmere suggests paradise metaphors indicating the mature man's awareness of the glories of the human mind. The actual voyage to Grasmere leads to the culminating voyage metaphor which sets forth Wordsworth's intention to explore the human mind. The consistent development of these basic themes and images forms a principal unifying element within the poem. (MJM)

7063. Minot, W.S., John I. Ades, and Gordon K. Thomas. "Notes on Wordsworthian Puns." *WC* 5:28-32.

Examples of punning in Wordsworth's poetry are found throughout the sonnet "Composed upon Westminster Bridge," in which he combines such ambiguous words as "composed," "fair," "touching," "lie," and "lying" with the symbolism of bridging to describe his attempts to unify in the imagination the contrasting sights and ambivalent feelings produced in him by London. The sonnet thus restates in summary form the struggle for "Composure and ennobling Harmony" described in detail in *Prelude* VII. At the end of the struggle the poet stands, successfully, in the center of the span uniting opposite sides of the river—composed, upon Westminster Bridge. (GKT)

7064. Nabholtz, John R. "The Integrity of Wordsworth's 'Tintern Abbey'." *JEGP* 73:227-38.

"Tintern Abbey" is frequently regarded as ambiguous in its thematic content and uncertain in its structure. Wordsworth's suggestion about the "odic transitions" in the poem resolves these objections. The poem opens with a picture of the union and reciprocity between man and nature. The first "turn" (ll. 1-57) considers one side of that union, the primacy and power of nature. The second "turn" (ll. 57-111) defines the emerging power and independence of the mind. The third and final "turn" (ll. 111-59) moves the strengths of the mind from union with the natural scene to reciprocity with another human being. It is in human relations that the mind's strengths reach their fulfillment and simultaneously fulfill nature's initiation of the process. The mind is here dramatized defeating mortal limitations by preserving in memory, even against death, the rich growth of human experience. (JRN)

7068. Olivier, Theo. "*The Lyrical Ballads* and the 'Preface'." *Theoria* 43:63-72.

Coleridge and early reviewers of the *Lyrical Ballads* distinguished the poems from the theoretical expression of their experimental purpose. Wordsworth's poetic judgment is thoroughly sound, and the expressed aim, "to keep the reader in the company of flesh and blood," is virtually all he need have said of his attempt to change the focus of poetry. His real concern is with the lapsed values of men; he had learned to care about men and to recognize the value residual in simplicity, and this is why he wanted to be "a man speaking to men." Consideration of the ballads shows this concern clearly in the constant revelation of the worthiness of simple beings and their actions. (TO)

7074. Pulos, C.E. "The Unity of Wordsworth's Immortality Ode." *SIR* 13:179-88.

An apparent structural contradiction in Wordsworth's Immortality Ode may be resolved by recognizing that its light symbolism embodies not one central concept, as usually assumed, but two main concepts. The first, the "visionary gleam," functions in both halves of the poem and the other, the "light," functions only in the second half. What survives "in our embers" is not the "visionary gleam" that has fled like an adolescent illusion but the "light," the child's intimations of immortality which are "Truths that wake, / To perish never." (CEP)

7077. Robinson, Jeffrey. "*The Prelude*, Book XIV, and the Problem of Concluding." *Criticism* 16:301-10.

The Prelude is written under the assumption that the events of the poet's past have led meaningfully to the poet's present, that, by means of his past, he has finally achieved the stature of a major visionary poet. The Mt. Snowdon passage is the climax of this movement toward complete imaginative maturity; however, the poem concludes with the uncertainty of one who senses that his assumption might be ill-founded. This is reflected in the uneasy and ambivalent ways he treats his sister Dorothy and Coleridge. This is not only a psychological ambivalence but an esthetic one concerning the nature of a poem's conclusion when the poem demands the (external) response of a listener in order to be concluded. (JR)

7078. —— "Unpublished Letter of William Wordsworth to Henry Robinson of York." *WC* 5:15-16.

Presents an unpublished letter of William Wordsworth to the solicitor Henry Robinson of York on 19 May 1829, and includes a few remarks about Henry Robinson and his relations with Wordsworth. (JR)

7085. Spiegelman, Willard. "Wordsworth's *Aeneid*." *CL* 26:97-109.

Wordsworth's 1823 translation of the first three books of *The Aeneid* exemplifies his poetic strengths and weaknesses as well as the peculiar response he has to Dryden's *Aeneid*. Challenged and restricted by Dryden's example, Wordsworth attempts to master the heroic couplet, a form of which he soon tires and upon which he partly bases his decision not to complete the poem. Wordsworth's "matter-of-factness" in translating is often superior to Dryden's freedoms with the original, but Wordsworth's effort to remain literally faithful to the Latin often results in stilted or euphemistic English verse. A comparison of the two renderings of the Laocoon episode (II. 199-227) shows the relative merits of each translator. One other possible reason for Wordsworth's not finishing the epic is his reluctance to do a full-scale version of the Dido tragedy in Book IV. His treatment of her at the end of Book I suggests a lack of sympathy with her dilemma and an unwillingness to treat the facts of sexual passion as vividly as Virgil or Dryden. A similar reluctance is shown even in more ordinary passages of sensuous description. (WLS)

7090. Stone, C.F.,III. "Narrative Variation in Wordsworth's Versions of 'The Discharged Soldier'." *JNT* 4:32-44.

Three versions of the discharged soldier episode provide a unique perspective on Wordsworth's narrative art in *The Prelude*. The first version (winter 1798) reveals little about the poet's relation to his past. Instead it develops the dramatic possibilities inherent in the encounter between the soldier and an 18 year-old lad. When Wordsworth decided to include this in *The Prelude* he eliminated the dramatic emphasis, enhancing instead the mystery this encounter has even in recollection. The third version, prepared for *The Prelude*'s posthumous publication, suppresses the second's perspective, emphasizing now the soldier's dignity and endurance, a consolation for an aging poet. Each version makes clear Wordsworth's sense of the difference between dramatic narration centered on subject matter and monodramatic narration centered on the narrator. (CFS)

encounter has even in recollection. The third version, prepared for *The Prelude*'s posthumous publication, suppresses the second's perspective, emphasizing now the soldier's dignity and endurance, a consolation for an aging poet. Each version makes clear Wordsworth's sense of the difference between dramatic narration centered on subject matter and monodramatic narration centered on the narrator. (CFS)

7093. Swearingen, James E. "Wordsworth on Gray." *SEL* 14:489-509.

Wordsworth's choice of the sonnet on West is a condemnation neither of Gray nor of that poetry in which he was himself rooted. The similarities between the two poets, along with Wordsworth's more traditional conception of the relation of the creative mind to nature, point to the essence of the attack in the Preface. The weakness in Gray is a lack of the passion which weds the mind to nature. In the lines of the sonnet itself Wordsworth finds two "styles," one expressing personal anguish and another referring to nature. What Wordsworth sees as a lack of sincerity in the lines on nature derives from Gray's feeling divorced from a nature whose joyful renewal offers no consolation in the face of human mortality. Wordsworth's understanding of nature is thus the more traditional of the two. (JES)

7099. Wilson, James D. "Tennyson's Emendations to Wordsworth's 'Tintern Abbey'." *WC* 5:7-8.

In his personal copy of Wordsworth's six-volume *Poetical Works* (1849) Tennyson added marginal comments to "Tintern Abbey." These comments serve as emendations of sorts, as they attempt to refashion Wordsworth's poem. Most of the emendations were aimed at shortening the poem: Tennyson objected to frequent repetition of the word "again" (lines 2, 4, 9, 14); he deleted lines 6-8, replacing them with a single line he composed himself, "That makes a lone place lonelier"; and he substantially shortened lines 35-48. As a critic of Wordsworth's poetry, Tennyson here reveals a surprising insensitivity to those elements of verse which Tennyson handles well in his own work—notably sound echoes and melody. (JDW)

Yonge. 7103. Stark, Myra C. "*The Clever Woman of the Family*—And What Happened to Her." *Mary Wollstonecraft Jour.* 2,ii:13-20.

Charlotte Yonge's novels are revealing documents for the feminist scholar. They bear witness to the reality of the Victorian cult of the family, that elevation of the domestic into the epic, in the culture and in the novel. Works such as *The Daisy Chain* or *The Clever Woman of the Family* testify to the prevailing religious beliefs concerning the imperative nature for women of duty, self-sacrifice, and obedience that helped form this cult. These conceptions led to a rigid definition of woman's role and nature that kept her passive and submissive. The orthodoxy of the Angel in the House explains the position of women in the 19th century as well as the lost promise of early feminism. (MCS)

X. TWENTIETH CENTURY

General and Miscellaneous. 7125. Labriolle, Jacqueline de. "Fortune ou infortune de Claudel dans les pays anglophones? (1912-1972)." *RLC* 48:55-77.

Examines the reception of Paul Claudel's works in Great Britain and the United States. (JdL)

7129. Parrinder, Patrick. "Historical Imagination and Political Reality:A Study in Edwardian Attitudes." *ClioW* 4:5-25.

The Edwardian intelligentsia was homogeneous and politically committed, yet its ideology was characterized by the aloofness and fatalism of a "Darwinian" version of history. In fiction, the "England's destiny" novelists, Wells, Kipling, Forster, Ford, and Galsworthy, portray not a dramatic process of historical change but a symbolic vision of its inevitability. Edwardian social thought shows similar contradictions. Masterman's *Condition of England* (1909) is an imaginative essay rather than a Liberal political blueprint. Sociologists like L.T. Hobhouse and Graham Wallas were divided between Fabian activism and a transcendent optimism. Beatrice Webb tried far more strenuously for consistency. The failure of the campaign for the Minority Report, and the Webbs' late incarnation as apologists for Stalinism, were deeply ironic. Even the Webbs reflected the passive attitudes of their contemporaries. The Edwardian synthesis of politics and historical imagination was shortlived, for soon artistic modernism and post-War visions of history as nightmare came to mock the optimism of bourgeois politicians. (PP)

7131a. Thale, Jerome. "The Making of the Edwardian Age." *Mosaic* 7.ii:25-43.

Examines the literary and imaginative dimensions of the "Edwardian age." With the coming of the war the Edwardian age began to be invented. At first images—the lamps going out—are created; these develop into plots—the ironic contrast between pre-war complacency and the horror of the war; then plots promote the creation of more images, and provide a form to contain them. The creation of the Edwardian age affords a pure, non-controversial example of the workings of the imaginative process. It makes clear the large non-cognitive element in the creation of such myths and the extent to which the process of literary invention is itself a cause of such myth. (JT)

Criticism. 7134. Gibbons, Tom. "Modernism and Reactionary Politics." *JML* 3:1140-57.

Attention has often been drawn to the reactionary political opinions of such literary Modernists as Yeats, Eliot, Pound, and Wyndham Lewis. The readership and influence of these men of letters were however negligible compared with those of eugenic scientists. After 1880, as the result of the spread of evolutionary ideas, the need for a new elite social class was increasingly taken for granted by men of various shades of political opinion. The reactionary politics and elitism of writers like Kipling and "the men of 1914" must be judged in terms of the pseudo-scientific assumptions of their age. (THG)

7137. Wasson, Richard. "From Priest to Prometheus:Culture and Criticism in the Post-Modernist Period." *JML* 3:1188-202.

Analyzes a trend toward a new materialist criticism. Cultural criticism is moving from the enclosed formalism of the new critics and to a criticism represented by Sontag, Hamilton, Frye, Marcuse, Brown, and Raymond Williams in which culture is a whole way of life and in which literary criticism is mystified. Art represents the force of revolutionary Eros, the desire for what Marx would call species being. (RHW)

Drama and Theater. 7139. Bryan, George B. "Dear Winston's Clever Mother:Lady Randolph Churchill and the National Theatre." *ThS* 15:143-70.

The recipient of recent historical attention, Lady Randolph Churchill is not renowned as a theatrical personage; yet her exertions in behalf of a British national theater are colorful as well as descriptive of some facets of Edwardian life. In 1908 the Shakespeare Memorial National Committee was formed to create a theater in the dramatist's memory, and Mrs. George Cornwallis-West (as Lady Churchill then was) was among the adherents. Between 1909 and 1912, she wrote and produced a drama, staged a sumptuous ball, helped to acquire a building site, argued for a national acting school, and created an exhibition called *Shakespeare's England*—all in aid of the National Theatre. Her efforts were conceived in gargantuan scale, and *Shakespeare's England*, particularly, failed in the same measure. World War I redirected her efforts, but her deeds in behalf of the National Theatre were not negligible. (GBB)

7145. Ditsky, John M. "All Irish Here:The 'Irishman' in Modern Drama." *DR* 54:94-102.

Certain British and American playwrights of the past century have attached special abilities and responsibilities to characters filling "Irish" roles. Synge's Mahons are stereotypes of the dispossessed Irishman. The clash of dreamer with reality is epitomized in O'Neill's Paddy, *The Hairy Ape*, and Cornelius' Melody, *A Touch of the Poet*, while Arthur Miller's Kenneth, *A Memory of Two Mondays* brings the heightened sensitivity of the representative Irishman to pathetic levels. In O'Neill's *The Iceman Cometh* and Pinter's *The Birthday Party*, the Irish characters are special emissaries of Death itself from coping with extraordinary burdens of exile, dreaming, and poetic gifts. (JMD)

7146. Elvgren, Gillette,Jr. "Documentary Theatre at Stoke-on-Trent." *ETJ* 26:86-100.

In an attempt to develop theatrical forms in Great Britain that spring from the historical, industrial, and cultural roots of a community, theaters are presenting documentary plays on such diverse subjects as the coal workers in Newcastle and the Inland Canal System around Nottingham. The Victoria Theater under the direction of Peter Cheeseman has produced more documentaries than any other theater in England. Cheeseman has utilized the flexibility of the round stage in creating documentaries that have the episodic flow of the cinema. He has discovered audio techniques that replace the more traditional film support given to documentary efforts, and has developed a variety of techniques in creating theatrical metaphors for objective, factual material. (GAE)

7148. Jurak, Mirko. "Commitment and Character Portrayal in the British Politico-Poetic Drama of the 1930s." *ETJ* 26:342-51.

In the 1930s the Group Theatre produced a number of politico-poetic plays. They are Auden's *The Dance of Death, The Dog Beneath the Skin, The Ascent of F6,* and *On the Frontier* by Auden and Isherwood; MacNeice's *Out of the Picture;* and Spender's *Trial of a Judge.* These plays share many political, philosophical, and social attitudes, as well as similarities in genre and style. The governing class in the plays is morally corrupt and preparing for war, whereas the rebels struggle against oppression only in pronouncements. Artists and other intellectuals live in a world of illusions and are often obsessed by guilt feelings. They are afraid of active participation in life lest absolute humanistic ideals be destroyed. The ideal of love is unrealized although it is shown as one of man's highest values. (MJ)

7151. Moss, Leonard. "A Check List on the Theory of Tragedy, 1900-1970." *BNYPL* 77:407-17.

This bibliography lists books and articles published in English and written by 20th-century authors who have tried to define tragedy as a literary genre and a philosophical concept. It excludes essays dealing with theorists writing before 1900, except Hegel and Nietzsche; with individual playwrights and novelists; and with the preliterate origins of tragedy. (LM)

7155. Riley, Michael M. "Interview with Jack Pulman, English Screenwriter." *SHR* 8:471-84.

Pulman explains his approach to the practical and artistic problems of adaptation as he discusses his cinematic versions of *Portrait of a Lady, The Golden Bowl, David Copperfield,* and *Jane Eyre.* Declaring that *The Golden Bowl* was the most difficult work to adapt, Pulman explains that it presented particular challenges because so much that is important exists only inside the minds of the characters. In commenting upon James's use of ambiguity Pulman discusses the advantages of using a narrator in film. He speaks of the screenwriter's sense of dramatic necessity and structure and the possible conflict with his desire to be faithful to the novel he is dramatizing. (MMR)

Periodicals. 7168. Johnson, Abby A. "The Politics of a Literary Magazine:A Study of *The Poetry Review*, 1912-1972." *JML* 3:951-64.

For 60 years, the internal politics of the Poetry Society have determined the nature of the *Poetry Review*, official journal of the largely British organization. A strong conservative majority (1912-61) demanded that the editor publish conventional verses, preferably by Society members. It urged him to support poets seeming traditional and to criticize those appearing unorthodox. In 1962, the disgruntled minority consolidated its power and assumed control of the Society and *Review*. The *Review* soon began to look like a modern, even an avant-garde, magazine. This alienated most of the members who had survived the upheaval in the Society following Spark's editorship. At the same time, it attracted new and sophisticated readers, persons who would never have supported the old *Poetry Review*. (AAJ)

Poetry. 7179. Eriksson, Pamela D. "British and American Poetry Since 1945." *UES* 12,i:27-41.

The survey begins with British poetry of the 1950s discussing *The Movement* poets, Philip Larkin, Thom Gunn and *The Group* and emphasizing the largely academic nature of the poetry of this time. American poetry of the 1950s is more explorative and experimental as evidenced by the Projectivism movement started by the Black Mountain Poets, the Beat poets, such as Allen Ginsberg and Sylvia Plath. British poetry of the 1960s is no longer "academic" but is catholic in presentation and in content tending toward naiveté in some of the Underground and Liverpool poets. (PDE)

7190. Pryor, Ruth. " 'Wisdom is hid in crumbs':Vernon Watkins and Dante." *AWR* 24,lii:94-101.

Examines Watkins' use of the poems of Dante in his poetry. Special attention is given to Watkins' adaptation of *terza rima* to the English language and some reference is made to his unpublished work. (MRP)

7197. Wade, Stephen. "Idris Davis and Proletarian Liter-

ature." *AWR* 24,liii:26-30.

Idris Davies, in his particular social milieu within English literary life in the mid-20th century, created a new variant on an archetypal generic mode of poetry. He explored the proletarian element in this genre by employing a ready-made type of Anglo-Welsh writing. In this poetic style Idris Davies made a place for himself in the history of Anglo-Welsh modern verse and in the traditional, Victorian, English verse. (SPW)

Prose. 7198. Noppen, J.P. van. "Spatial Metaphors in Contemporary British Religious Prose." *RLV* 40:7-24.

A vocabulary study of British religious prose in the 1960s reveals that a topological, static, and vectorial concept of space prevails. The interesting places are the intersections between this world and the divine and the places of Man and God. The latter loci define bi-polarities like above/beneath and in/out. The vertical polarity is used in the supernatural projection of theism that extrapolates a transcendent God to an outside heaven. The value attributed to the various spatial categories reflects the theological climate. The study of the metaphorical twist in religious language may thus yield insight into theology from a new perspective. (JPvN)

Prose Fiction. 7211. Smith, David. "Underground Man:The Work of B.L. Coombs, 'Miner Writer'." *AWR* 24,liii:10-25.

The attempt of a miner to write about his own people was acclaimed in the 1930s. For the serious historian such writing proves doubly revealing—an analysis of its literary shape and intentions is as valuable as its content. B.L. Coombes provides insights into the industrial society of South Wales in the early 20th century. (DBS)

Allingham. 7223. Peters, Margot, and Agate N. Krouse. "Women and Crime:Sexism in Allingham, Sayers, and Christie." *SWR* 59:144-52.

Stereotyped characters and sexist attitudes are found throughout the conservative British detective novels of Margery Allingham, Dorothy Sayers, and Agatha Christie. Hero-worship of the aristocracy is the basis for the attitudes of male superiority and female inferiority in the works of Allingham and Sayers: "where you have knights you've got to have ladies." Christie emphasizes plot rather than character. Her women are stereotyped—naive girls, addle-brained sex symbols, social aberrants. Competent, independent women are frequently portrayed as sexless or destructive. But Christie is not as sexist as Sayers and Allingham, for Christie occasionally suggests that a woman can be fulfilled without youth, beauty, or husband. (CTW)

Auden. 7233. Daalder, Joost. "W.H. Auden's 'The Shield of Achilles' and Its Sources." *AUMLA* 42:186-98.

"The Shield of Achilles" is not obviously based on Homer's Greek (*Iliad* xviii, 368-617), but chiefly on Chapman's version of the passage, *Achilles Shield.* Study reveals that Auden is deliberately opposing Chapman's praise of Achilles, Thetis, Hephaestos, and war, while drawing on Chapman's positive picture of, e.g., the harvest dance to make that a symbol of the unity of Greek civilization. The absence of sacrifice shows our lack of Christianity, and Auden refers to Milton's *Paradise Lost,* Book xi, to show how fallen militaristic man is. He further alludes to Genesis and Exodus to emphasize this and shocks us into a renewed awareness of the New Testament. (JD)

7238. Hyde, Virginia M. "The Pastoral Formula of W.H. Auden and Piero di Cosimo." *ConL* 14(1973):332-46.

W. H. Auden's *Bucolics* (1951), referring directly to the Renaissance painter Piero di Cosimo, sheds light on the moralized landscape which activates Auden's "pastoral" scenes from "Paysage Moralisé" through the religious *Horae Canonicae* and later poems. Piero's *Landscape with Animals* and *Discovery of Honey* (or *Feast of Bacchus*) illustrate "hard primitivism" in opposition to traditional pastoral mythologies of a prehistoric Golden Age or Eden. Both the poet and the painter show man at a crossroads between pre-history and modern time. Auden and Piero find innocence only in the bestial condition preceding human consciousness but uphold the necessity of the quest for urbane perfection. Auden emphasizes progress through a balanced "middle way," and his imagery rises from Bacchanalian to spiritual social constructs. His landscapes comprehend man's original absorption in nature, the flux of history, and a movement toward an ultimate stability transcending both. The poems' iconography conforms frequently to that of Piero's paintings. (VMH)

7242. Johnson, Wendell S. "Auden, Hopkins, and the Poetry of Reticence." *TCL* 20:165-71.

Auden believed that an artist could and should be reticent about intimate concerns. For him the most intimate concerns were sexual and religious. He was disturbed by Hopkins' tendency to display his personal feelings, especially his religious feelings. But Auden, who decided not to publish some of his most personally revealing verse, came to understand the difficulty of the Victorian poet's isolated life and the psychological necessity for his expressing private emotions in poetry. Nevertheless, Auden masked his own emotions, and he wanted none of his intimate letters to be published and no life of himself to be written. (WSJ)

7251. Rees, Samuel. " 'What Instruments We Have':An Appreciation of W.H. Auden." *AWR* 24,lii:9-18.

The word "instruments," from Auden's elegy "In Memory of W.B. Yeats," may be used to describe his own critical and poetic legacy: instruments for psycho-surgical probing and cutting; for recording and measurement of a culture's health and weather; for orchestration into the collected poetry of over 40 years. (SR)

7252. Sarang, Vilas. "Articles in the Poetry of W.H. Auden." *Lang&S* 7:77-90.

The frequency of definite and indefinite articles in Auden's poetry shows significant changes in correlation with changes in his relationship to his audience. In the volumes of the 1930s the frequency of definite articles is very high. In the volumes since 1940, the occurrence of definite articles has gradually diminished. Correspondingly, the frequency of indefinite articles has risen. The use of the indefinite article normally implies a general class of subjects and is associated with a colloquial manner. The fact that, in later editions, Auden has suppressed definite articles in his early poems confirms the change in his attitude, and also shows that he uses articles with an awareness of their impact. (VGS)

Bennett. 7292. Riemer, Werner W. "Arnold Bennett:A Check List of Secondary Literature." *BNYPL* 77:342-57.

In this check list, 412 items of secondary literature on Arnold Bennett have been collected for the first time. They deal exclusively with or contain significant references to the English novelist and his work. The publication dates of the entries range from 1903 to 1973. The article is divided into three sections. Part I contains bibliographical information on 124 "Books and Pamphlets," published between 1911 and 1972. Part II, "Articles and Chapters in Books," lists 262 items from 1903-1973. The final section on "Master's Theses and Doctoral Dissertations" includes 26 entries dating from 1930 to 1970. (WWR)

Bolt. 7301. Fehse, Klaus-Dieter. "Robert Bolts *A Man for All Seasons*:Eine Interpretation." *NsM* 26(1973):131-40.

In *A Man for All Seasons*, his first and very successful attempt at writing a modern history play, Bolt has chosen a presently non-controversial subject, the life of Thomas More, to make his characters "theatrically big without embarrassment." The most obvious structural device is the use of the Brechtian-ty pe figure of the Common Man who is primarily intended "to draw the audience into the play," i.e., to point out the significance of More's behavior for modern man. There is a careful grouping of characters, based on the principle of contrast, with More and Cromwell as antagonists. In contrast to the Elizabethan play *Sir Thomas More* which treats the downfall and death of More within the framework of the medieval conception of degree and order, Bolt portrays "Thomas More, a Christian Saint, as a hero of selfhood." From the modern dramatist's point of view the historical conflict presents itself as a conflict between selfhood and commitment, private conscience and public duty. (In German) (K-DF)

Bowen. 7304. Davenport, Gary T. "Elizabeth Bowen and the Big House." *SHR* 8:27-34.

Elizabeth Bowen's Anglo-Irish origins are perhaps the most important influence on her work. The "big house" comprises a world which becomes the imaginative center of her finest novels. Two non-fictional works, *Bowen's Court* and *The Shelbourne*, constitute her most affectionate view of the big house tradition; her fiction almost invariably deals with its decline in the hands of a corrupt gentry. *The Last September* shows the betrayal of the tradition by ugly snobbery. The culture of the big house is a spiritual anchor of high potential in *The Heat of the Day*, but again proves ineffectual because its powers are mismanaged by the gentry. Bowen's ideal is an adaptable sort of nobility that is able to assimilate and in turn strengthen the democratic modern world. (GTD)

Burgess. 7324. Fitzpatrick, William P. "Black Marketeers and Manichees:Anthony Burgess' Cold War Novels." *WVUPP* 21:78-91.

In *Honey for the Bears* and *Tremor of Intent* Burgess explores the impact of his basically Manichaean world view as it influences human relationships from the personal to the international level. Redefining evil as that which is without true commitment, Burgess parades before the reader a reprise of solipsistic neutrals who form a microcosm of contemporary villainy. The plight of Burgess' heroes, Paul Hussey and Denis Hillier, is not merely to overcome the external wickedness that confronts them at every turn, but to conquer their inclination to accept neutrality instead of engagement. Both novels emphasize Burgess' position that morality is not the office of nations or races, but rather of individuals. (WPF)

Campbell, R. 7333. Beeton, Douglas R. "Roy Campbell." *UES* 10,iii(1972):43-50.

The South African poet Roy Campbell brought great vigor to all his activities, which ranged from bull-fighting and soldiering, to the creation of zestful poetry. In the poem "The Serf," which seems to explode with the force of his imagery, he associated himself with the common man. The energy of a primitive people is again captured in "The Zulu Girl." In the long poem "The Wayzgoose" he is highly satirical about many aspects of life in South Africa. The last half of Campbell's life was spent in Spain and Portugal; the Iberian peninsula—its physical aspects and its literature—was reflected in works such as the sonnet sequence "Mithraic Emblems." "The Flaming Terrapin" is a long symbolic statement describing the biblical deluge. Campbell's sense of imagery and color is expressed in "The Zebras," and his love of common things in "Choosing a Mast." "Autumn," one of his best poems, reveals a masterly use of fiercely vivid imagery. (DRB)

Cary. 7342. Seltzer, Alvin J. "Speaking Out of Both Sides of *The Horse's Mouth*:Joyce Cary vs. Gulley Jimson." *ConL* 15:488-502.

Whether they see Gulley Jimson as moral hero, rogue, or victim of society, most critics of *The Horse's Mouth* have assumed Joyce Cary's identification with his charismatic hero, thus missing the many clues to Cary's ambivalence toward Gulley and the problem of artistic freedom. The frequent references to Hitler are strategically placed to provide an ironic counterpart to Gulley's amoral charm, and this context—along with Gulley's murder of Sara—forces us to modify our impressions of Gulley's innocence, re-evaluate his convictions, and challenge his immunity, as artist, from conventional mores. Because Gulley's attempt to transcend reality results in his trespassing upon the very values he most cherishes, we must finally see the novel as a testing ground rather than a tract for unlimited individual freedom. (AJS)

Clarke, A. 7372. Redshaw, Thomas D. "His Works, a Memorial:Austin Clarke (1896-1974)." *Éire* 9,ii:107-15. [Contains bibliog. of C's works.]

The most fitting and most enduring monument to the late Irish poet Austin Clarke (1896-1974) is the entire edifice of his work. The narrative and lyric poems, the verse dramas, the Celtic Romanesque prose romances reflect the dominant, sometimes obsessive concerns of Clarke's long and wandering career as

Romantic bard, London scrivener, and finally as the *ollamh* of Dublin. His highly crafted poems seem now to stand as the single poetic achievement linking the one world of Yeats to that opposite one of Patrick Kavanagh. Clarke's canny labors brought the defining and reviving energies of both worlds into the "new" Irish poetry of the 1960s. Perhaps the one poem from Clarke's deft hand that best exemplifies such an assertion is his *Mnemosyne Lay in the Dust* (1966). A checklist of his publications and a selective list of 34 critical articles about them are included. (TDR)

Colum. 7378. Campbell, Douglas S. "Padraic Colum's Celebration of Littleness." *Éire* 9,iii:60-68.
Colum's poetry rises above peasant verse because he attempts to fuse imagination with popular traditions, to express divine as well as human drama, and to present a romantic but conscious affirmation of a medieval rural Irish folk ethic. At bottom, the romantic in Colum's verse is a sensibility to the infancy of a nation. The three main characteristics of his concept of this national ethic are oral literature, scholarship, and the "correspondences" between the cosmos and the language of the oral literature. Fragments and revisions of two poems, "Reminiscence" and the "Basket Weaver," manifest quite well Colum's celebration of littleness. The former presents a sort of primary epic hero and the latter contains an archetypal persona. Although not significant in themselves, both are given significance as examples of a healthy, vital, medieval style of life. (DSC)

Conrad. 7385. Adams, Barbara B. "Sisters under Their Skins:The Women in the Lives of Raskolnikov and Razumov." *Conradiana* 6:113-24.
Conrad patterned many elements of *Under Western Eyes* after Dostoevski's *Crime and Punishment*. This similarity can be traced in the relationships between the male protagonists and the women in their lives. Women form the primary motive for action in these men who cannot act without their sexual-saintly stimulus. They are feared and loved, untouched and untouchable. Both Raskolnikov and Razumov are obsessed with real mothers and an unobtainable symbolic Mother Russia. Raskolnikov's mother moves him to a destructive act, just as Victor Haldin's mother moves Razumov, his murderous proxy, to a self-destructive act of confession. Lesser female characters relate to these men in similar ways. In a reversal of the usual roles, the women in these novels act; the men, Razumov and Raskolnikov, re-act. (BBA)

7388. Brebach, Raymond T. "The Making of *Romance*, Part Fifth." *Conradiana* 6:171-81.
The stages of development of *Romance* suggest what Ford learned from Conrad and give some details of the mechanics of their collaboration. Brebach examines *Seraphina* (Ford's independent version of the novel); "Synopsis of *Seraphina*: A Romance"; *Romance*, first proofs; Conrad's and Ford's revision of these proofs; "First Revise" proofs of the novel's last three pages; Ford's revisions of these proofs; and *Romance: A Novel*. A progressive elimination of the element of chance and a tightening of plot structure is indicated. Conrad's corrected proofs reveal his concern to clarify action and to keep plot developments clearly before the reader. Ford's corrected proofs indicate that he was able to recognize Conrad's intentions and carry them a step further, and that on short notice he was able to produce prose of a higher quality than Conrad could under similar circumstances. (RTB)

7389. Bruss, Paul S. "Conrad's 'Youth':Problems of Interpretation." *CollL* 1:218-29.
Criticism of Conrad's "Youth" has centered upon whether the young Marlow matures. Evidence in favor of maturation usually derives from Marlow's responsible handling of his crew during the several *Judea* disasters; evidence against, from the romantic escapism which characterizes his outlook. By isolating the young Marlow's stay in Falmouth, we can locate the terms of the growth which allow the elder Marlow to adopt an ironic and skeptical view of his *Judea* experience without jeopardizing his appreciation of that voyage's essential significance. (PSB)

7390. ——— "Marlow's Interview with Stein:The Implications of the Metaphor." *SNNTS* 5(1973):491-503. [On *Lord Jim*.]
Near the middle of *Lord Jim* Marlow introduces Stein as a man who has withdrawn into the catacombs of his insect collections; at the end he recounts how greatly Stein ages following his encounter with the embittered Jewel. Both passages point to Stein as a character who, since his retreat from Celebes, fails to enjoy intimate involvement with people and life. It is only when Stein responds to Marlow's plea for help, however, that this philosopher fully reveals the problems inherent in his withdrawal. For then, in a series of subtle metaphors, Stein articulates a rigid philosophy of balance and harmony which thoroughly belies the vision of contingency and emptiness at the core of Conrad's early fiction. (PSB)

7397. Cuthbertson, Gilbert M. "Freedom, Absurdity, and Destruction:The Political Theory of Conrad's *A Set of Six*." *Conradiana* 6:46-52.
Three themes unify Conrad's short fiction in the collection, *A Set of Six*: freedom, absurdity, and destruction. His protagonists anticipate the "absurd heroism" of Camus's Sisyphus and his revolutionary analysis in *The Rebel*. Conrad may not evaluate absurdity as the existential thinker does, but he recognizes it as a political phenomenon to be reckoned with. Conrad's political theory in dealing with freedom and equality reflects a Burkean conservatism. The political theorist can synthesize these diverse intellectual traditions with the aid of literary criticism. (GMC)

7399. Daleski, H.M. "Hanging On and Letting Go:Conrad's *The Nigger of the 'Narcissus'*." *HUSL* 2,ii:171-96.
The voyage of the *Narcissus* enacts the journey of life in a godless universe. The structural principle of the novel is contrast, and Conrad examines contrasting attitudes to life. Conrad is concerned with the drift of meaninglessness and the drift toward death. Though the crew panics and opts for drift when the *Narcissus* is struck by the storm, the captain keeps his head and proves that the ship can be steered to its chosen destination. The drift to death is dramatized in the illness of Jimmy Wait, which both he and the crew refuse to acknowledge. But when Jimmy dies and Belfast pushes his unmoving body into the sea, this acceptance of death is followed by the springing up of a wind—and the ship, no longer drifting, heads for home. (HMD)

7400. Davis, Kenneth W., Lynn F. Henry, and Donald W. Rude. "Conrad's Trashing/Thrashing Sails:Orthography and a Crux in *The Nigger of the 'Narcissus'*." *Conradiana* 6:131-33.
The holograph manuscript and the fragmentary typescript of Conrad's *The Nigger of the "Narcissus"* provide evidence that Conrad confused the phonemes "T" and "Th." Such evidence provides a basis for determining a crucial reading in Chapter v of the novel. (KWD, LFH, & DWR)

7401. Davis, Roderick. "Under Eastern Eyes:Conrad and Russian Reviewers." *Conradiana* 6:126-30.
The remarkable success of *Under Western Eyes* in Russia is discussed in contrast to the indifference accorded it in England. Four reviews have been located in Russian journals, two from 1912, when the first translation appeared, and two from 1925, when the work was translated anew. These reviews are summarized and analyzed to illustrate the divergent responses of the critics to Conrad's knowledge of Russia, his imaginative abilities, his political and psychological perceptivity, and his general artistry as a novelist. A concluding comparison is made between pre- and post-revolutionary viewpoints that seem implicit in these reviews and that indicate the novel's endurance beyond its immediate historical context. (RD)

7408. Geddes, Gary. "*The Rescue*:Conrad and the Rhetoric of Diplomacy." *Mosaic* 7,iii:107-25.
Conrad's *The Rescue* is replete with allusions to innuendo and tone of voice. Speech can bridge the separateness of men, but it is as capable of destroying as redeeming its user. What Conrad seems to be working at is a language of notation, in which speech functions simultaneously at both the real and the symbolic levels. He explores not only the nature and psychology of speech as it exists in the epic universe of *The Rescue*, but also the related concept of diplomacy in human affairs and the idea of the gentleman. D'Alcacer embodies the principle of style and plain-dealing that is associated in Lingard's mind with genuinely aristocratic behavior. (GG)

7416. Higdon, David L. "The Conrad-Ford Collaboration." *Conradiana* 6:155-56.

The Conrad-Ford collaboration has three significant dimensions: textual, psychological, and esthetic. On how many novels did Ford actually collaborate with Conrad? What impelled Conrad to offer to collaborate with at least seven authors? What artistic innovations did the collaboration produce? This introduction raises the questions the special issue of *Conradiana* explores. (DLH)

7417. Hollahan, Eugene. "Beguiled into Action:Silence and Sound in *Victory*." *TSLL* 16:349-62.
Analysis of Conrad's *Victory* reveals that the main thematic subject of inaction and action is developed by means of a complex motif introduced and underscored by frequent repetition of the words "silence" and "sound." The story is a dramatization of the human predicament arising from the desire for quiet withdrawal from active life. The contrast between silence and sound is shown in the setting, atmosphere, and mood. Conrad organizes *Victory* so as to illustrate through the characterizations the thematic polarities of inaction and action. Psychological, moral, and metaphysical profundities are developed by means of the interaction of the characters in terms of the silence-sound motif. The plot structure dramatizes the inaction-action thematic subject in the experiences of Axel Heyst. Heyst is temperamentally and philosophically committed to silence, but twice he breaks the silence when he is beguiled into action, first by Morrison and then by Lena; finally, he must choose once and for all between inaction and action, and he suffers a moral defeat when he cannot explicitly declare his love for Lena. (EH)

7422. Kehler, Joel R. "The Centrality of the Narrator in Conrad's 'Falk'." *Conradiana* 6:19-30.
There is a dual movement within Conrad's "Falk": two deliberately juxtaposed patterns of action. While Falk moves through the simple comedic pattern to the formulaic triumph and apotheosis at the conclusion, the narrator progressively pierces the comic masquerade of events to expose the awful emptiness that lies beneath. "Falk," then, is at bottom a conscious and grotesque parody of a comedy, for the world is left in the hands of archetypal forces in nature: Falk and the niece are no less. Their marriage represents the impersonal joining of atavistic male and female principles: one active and hot, the other passive and cold. Only two such creatures could inherit the earth envisioned by the depths of the story. (JRK)

7423. Kennard, Jean E. "Emerson and Dickens:A Note on Conrad's *Victory*." *Conradiana* 6:215-19.
The juxtaposition of coal and diamonds with the practical and the mystical in the opening pages of *Victory* suggests that Joseph Conrad was alluding to Emerson's "Wealth" and Dickens' *Hard Times*. The images relate the themes of *Victory* to the 19th-century quarrel over the idealistic and the realistic, and demonstrates that, by means of Dickens, Conrad was responding to the inadequacies of Emerson's analysis. (JEK)

7427. Lippincott, H.F. "Sense of Place in Conrad's *The Rover*." *Conradiana* 6:106-12.
Conrad's *The Rover* reflects an acute sense of place, the French Côte de Provence near Toulon. The opening 30 pages of the novel depict an actual journey from Toulon to the tip of the Giens Peninsula which Conrad himself could have taken as a young boy. The journey assumes symbolic value as it parallels the search of Peyrol, the old ship's captain, for the places he knew as a child and the nature of his personal identity. The island of Porquerolles, where Peyrol thinks he was born, acts as a fixed point of geographical reference to orient the reader to the subsequent sea action, at the same time that the island is a recurring symbol of human limitation. (HFL)

7431. Martin, Joseph J. "Edward Garnett and Conrad's Reshaping of Time." *Conradiana* 6:89-105.
Conrad's greatest stride toward the mature method was made in the story "Karain" which was reshaped according to Garnett's advice. Evidence from Conrad's letters and from Garnett's critical writings, and particularly from an analysis of Turgenev's "A Lear of the Steppes," suggests that the striking parallels in chronological structure between "Karain" and the Turgenev story were the result of Garnett's having persuaded Conrad to imitate Turgenev's method. In reshaping "Karain" Conrad solved the important recurring problem of how to treat inherently melo-

dramatic material in a psychologically resonant and seemingly inevitable manner. "Karain" is a clear prototype of *Lord Jim* and subsequent novels in which Conrad violated conventional chronology to create a highly meaningful "disorder." (JJM)

7432. Martin, W.R. "Compassionate Realism in Conrad and *Under Western Eyes*." *ESA* 17:89-100.
Russia gave Conrad the opportunity to present a vision of man's moral choices: confronted by brute fact, the naive idealist must retreat into sentimentality, remain in cynicism, or move on to an attitude that is both compassionate and realistic. *Under Western Eyes* shows characters fixed in these various stages of moral development, and traces Natalia's (and Razumov's) progress through them all toward the compassionate realism already reached by Tekla. Conrad's artistic purposes are directed at a Western complacency that supposes that the extremes of Russian politics have been safely and permanently transcended by the jejune order and *gemütlichkeit* of Geneva. (WRM)

7435. Meixner, John A. "Ford and Conrad." *Conradiana* 6:157-69.
The relationship of Conrad with Ford was the most useful, seminal, and important of Conrad's literary connections. The argument rests on Ford's practical usefulness: in prodding Conrad to compose his personal memoirs, in supplying him with plot ideas, in actual writing, and in financial backing; on the ground-breaking effect of their three collaborations on Conrad's other work; and, most importantly, on the artistic and moral support Ford provided for Conrad's vulnerable psyche. The character and dynamics of the relationship are examined as are the forces that made for their eventual falling-out. Their split was not a disaster for Ford, but the separation was calamitous for Conrad. (JAM)

7436. Messenger, William E. "Conrad and His 'Sea Stuff'." *Conradiana* 6:3-18.
Conrad's intense dislike of being thought of as a sea writer resulted from his inner knowledge that he had, in a small and temporary way, abdicated his artistic responsibility in assuming that very role in his early quest for popularity, in emulation of Marryat and Cooper and because of Edward Garnett's advice. The dilemma of writing for popular success and writing according to the dictates of artistic conscience are seen most clearly in *The Nigger of the "Narcissus"* and *The Rescue*. (WEM)

7441. Nettels, Elsa. "The Grotesque in Conrad's Fiction." *NCF* 29:144-63.
The grotesque in Conrad's fiction manifests itself in two forms: in the appearance and actions of grotesque characters who effect the destruction of the protagonist's illusions; and in the sinister and dream-like quality the world assumes once his sense of security has been destroyed. Most of Conrad's grotesque figures, such as James Wait, Kurtz, Gentleman Brown, Nikita Necator, Mr. Jones, and Ortega, are identified by extreme physical abnormality, which is usually the sign of spiritual deformity and often of madness. Resembling non-human forms—animals or mechanisms—they seem both fearful and comic. Their two important functions are to project in distorted form the repressed irrational side of the protagonist's nature and to assist in the transformation of his world into an alien and sinister place. (EN)

7449. Renner, Stanley. "A Note on Joseph Conrad and the Objective Correlative." *Conradiana* 6:53-56.
Both Eliot and Conrad speak of Conrad's early work in the terminology of the objective correlative. Eliot praises the "new groups of objects" and "new feelings" in the language of the earlier Conrad, while Conrad implies that in his other work of that period he found the right formula. Conrad could be adopting the terminology of Eliot's Hamlet paper published in the *Athenaeum* in 1919. But the more interesting question is to what extent Conrad influenced Eliot in formulating the concept of the objective correlative and in creating his own works. Clearly Conrad's fiction made a deep impression on Eliot. The fact that Eliot saw Conrad's earlier fiction in the context of the objective correlative, together with certain general similarities between *The Waste Land* and *Heart of Darkness*, suggests that in both method and vision Eliot may have owed Conrad a fairly significant debt. (SR)

7451. Rose, Charles. "*Romance* and the Maiden Archetype."

Conradiana 6:183-88.

Rose discusses the idealization of the heroine in Conrad and Ford's *Romance*. Due to this idealization, or the sublimation of a maiden anima figure, Conrad and Ford were able to evade an exploration of the anima in its perilous complexity. Moreover, the sublimation was one way of disguising a symbiotic relationship in which Conrad used Ford to perpetuate his heroic fantasies and Ford used Conrad to foster the illusion that Conrad was heroic, an illusion he later put to use in creating Edward Ashburnham. By investing their heroine with a mystique, they were committing themselves to a male mystique of dubious authenticity. (CR)

7457. Saveson, John E. "Conrad, *Blackwood's*, and Lombroso." *Conradiana* 6:57-62.

Conrad's knowledge of the theories of the criminologist, Cesare Lombroso, mentioned in *The Secret Agent*, could easily have come from his reading of four long editorial articles on anarchists in *Blackwood's* which appeared from 1899 to 1907. Terms, descriptions, character analysis, and themes are shared by the articles and the novel. Some of these have no counterpart in Lombroso. (JES)

7467. Stallman, Robert W. "Checklist of Some Studies of Conrad's *The Secret Agent* since 1960." *Conradiana* 6:31-45.

An annotated bibliography of 73 studies of Conrad's *The Secret Agent* published 1960-72. (RWS)

7468. Stark, Bruce R. "Kurtz's Intended: The Heart of *Heart of Darkness*." *TSLL* 16:535-55.

Europe, not the Jungle, is the source of the moral darkness in Conrad's "Heart of Darkness." It follows from this ironic reversal that the Sepulchral City, the Intended's house, and the Intended make up the Inner Circle of the tale's Infernal System whereas the Company's Jungle stations, Kurtz's station, and Kurtz make up its outer circle. When Kurtz finally realized the central role of the Intended in his own "intentions" and their black consequences, he condemned both as "the horror" and thus became the intensely tragic hero of the story. Marlow, however, does not see this, lies, and is thus condemned to repeat a story that he does not completely understand. But if Kurtz's last words include some vision of this white woman's central role in his own black deeds, then Marlow did not really lie when he told her Kurtz's last word "was your name." This woman actually has two symbolic names: the first represents what Kurtz intended to do; the second the "horror" that these intentions became. (BRS)

7469. Steinmann, Theo. "Lord Jim's Progression Through Homology." *ArielE* 5,i:81-93.

Through the other male protagonists in *Lord Jim*, Conrad illustrates Jim's potential destinies and his intrinsic inability of self-assessment. The French lieutenant reflects a Jim who would have done his duty without romanticizing his actions, thus becoming a dull and uninteresting character. Captain Robinson replaces his notions about duty and honor by a cynical sense of proportions. Stein has gone through Jim's trials and tribulations, but he manages to reconcile romanticism and efficient realism. Jim never outgrows the easy and yet paralyzing morality of his father and cannot cope with unprecendented situations. Gentleman Brown is a negative print of Jim's basic attitudes. While Jim has become the slave of a self-developed set of values, Brown has liberated himself from moral restraints. Accident or fate have determined which of all these personae Jim was to become. (TS)

7476. Vidan, Ivo. "An Unusual Hungarian Reference to Conrad." *Conradiana* 6:225.

The note identifies an allusion to Conrad's "The End of the Tether" in Gyula Illyes' *Ebed a Kastelyban* [*Mid-day Dinner at the Hall*], (1961), a Hungarian novel. (IV)

7478. —— "More on 'One of Us'." *Conradiana* 6:225.

This note suggests that the "one of us" phrase in *Lord Jim* is further explained by its appearance in a 10 July 1899 letter of Conrad to H.D. Davray. (IV)

7480. Walt, James. "Conrad and James Huneker." *Conradiana* 6:75-88.

Music and literary critic James G. Huneker became acquainted with Conrad's work and pioneered in building Conrad's U.S. reputation. He admired Conrad partly because he was a Pole, partly because he was a romanticist in an age dominated by realism, partly because he seemed to have brought something unique to the sea tale: a gift for psychological analysis. Huneker went beyond admirers like Mencken in recognizing that Conrad's early Malaysian stories were overcolored and that he had showed a restrained and superior art in *Under Western Eyes*. The psychological acumen of Conrad, Huneker observed, was conspicuous in his women characters as well as in his men. (JW)

7482. Wasserman, Jerry. "Narrative Presence: The Illusion of Language in *Heart of Darkness*." *SNNTS* 6:327-38.

As storyteller in Conrad's *Heart of Darkness*, Marlow's primary medium is language, and one of the things he learns in the Congo is that words can falsify as well as illuminate. In discovering that language is a necessary component of the barrier between civilized man and the horror and darkness, Marlow also dicovers its essential superficiality and the profound truth of transverbal experience. In order to make both his and Marlow's audiences "see," Conrad reverts to an alternate strategy: presenting Marlow as the physical and visual embodiment, the objective correlative, of his verbal narrative. The result is that the style of the novel, insofar as it is inclusive of Marlow's narration, is the theme. (JW)

7487. Wiley, P.L. "Two Tales of Passion." *Conradiana* 6:189-95.

The subtitles of both Conrad's *The Nigger of the "Narcissus"* and Ford's *The Good Soldier* designate these works as "tales." Much dispute here has been provoked by the seeming ambiguous or inconsistent behavior of the narrators. Contrary to customary practice in the modern novel the narrator of a tale is not bound to the roles of analytical autobiographer or eyewitness but enjoys freedom in the effective arrangement of a story told orally and addressed to the semblance of a communal audience. These essential features are evident in Conrad's work and, with appropriate modifications, in Ford's as well. In both instances apparent contradictions or abrupt shifts in narrative consistency may be attributed to the effort to render an experience of passion. (PLW)

7488. Zabierowski, Stefan. "Conrad's Polish Career: 1896-1968." *Conradiana* 6:197-213.

Traces the reputation of Conrad in Poland through three main stages. Received with good will from the first, Conrad was early considered a fascinating personality who created interesting characters, then as a remarkable artist, and finally as a profound thinker. (SZ)

Davies, W.H. 7491. Rabinowitz, Ivan I.A. "Words in Themselves Ordinary: A Comment on Five Poems by W.H. Davies (1871-1940)." *UES* 12,i:22-26.

Because Davies writes simply he has been ignored by critics who prefer riddles to answer and educated guesses to untutored truths. Davies' best lyrics are miniature representations of a greater harmony. In many lyrics he establishes a connection between universal concord and human love. Lyric design captures and enacts universal design. In the poem "Names," his most explicit statement of the relationship between celestial ordination and the everyday life of man, Davies uses the simple act of naming as an image of harmony and as an explanation of his belief in the simple power of song. (IAR)

Eliot. 7512. Bailey, Bruce. "A Note on *The Waste Land* and Hope Mirrlees' *Paris*." *T.S. Eliot Newsl.* 1,ii:3-4.

In her long and fragmented bilingual poem *Paris* Mirrlees anticipates phrasing and even some of the subject matter and so-called structural innovations of Eliot's *The Waste Land*. Both append their poems with Notes and juxtapose fragments of songs, snatches of conversation, literary allusions, and original poetry which finally climax in accelerated cacophony. Mirrlees' poem also shares a number of details with the published and draft versions of *The Waste Land*, including uses of a spring setting, crowing cock, American slang, king-fishers, and urban rivers. Eliot had good reason to be acquainted with Mirrlees' poem before 1922, for it was one of the nine books (including Eliot's *Poems*) printed by the Woolfs from 1917 to 1920. (BFB)

7513. Barry, John B. "Eliot's 'Burial of the Dead': A Note on the Morphology of Culture." *ArQ* 30:63-73.

In *The Waste Land* Eliot views the events of history as comprising a self-contained antithesis culminating in a divine act. "The

Burial of the Dead" traces modern sterility and drift to the loss of the objective fear of death. Indeed, the will to endure among the inhabitants of the wasteland retains a sinister potency through separation from a mother-landscape in which the idea of religious destiny is vested. Evidence for the lack of corporeality of home or place is the dry abstract language which follows the Starnbergersee holiday episode. The spiritual powers employed by Eliot are not intended as prophecies of regeneration but reveal the evaporation of a background to which all religion is form-bound. Shakespeare's lines from *The Tempest*, recalling a sea-change, suggest the subordination of extrinsic fate to the interior struggle redeemable only by a divine act. Rebirth cannot be founded in the world as nature (vegetation myths) which accounts for the latent sense of guilt and irony in the poem. Only by a transcendence of experience, never the work of the mind alone, can there be liberation from time. (JB)

7518. Bugge, John. "Rhyme as Onomatopoeia in 'The Dry Salvages'." *PLL* 10:312-16.
In the sestinalike section 2 of "The Dry Salvages," the third of the *Four Quartets*, Eliot makes the rhyme scheme of each of the sestets do the work of onomatopoeia. Its succession of sounds echoes the repetitive cadence actually produced by the sea breaking in waves upon the beach. The effect is a continuous auditory image that underscores and clarifies the symbolism of the sea. Viewed without prospect of Incarnation the sea is an eternity of endless becoming, meaningless flux. But the impact of sea upon land also bespeaks the crucial impingement of the Timeless upon the temporal which is the Christian's only hope of redemption from "mere sequence." (JB)

7525. Donker, Marjorie. "*The Waste Land* and the *Aeneid*." *PMLA* 89:164-73.
The *Waste Land* has important connections with the *Aeneid* beyond those of a shared mythic configuration. These connections are primarily literary and we receive them as Gilbert Highet describes the allusions of symbolist poets—in hints, nuances, phrases repeated in a dream. So Eliot evokes the concatenation of events in the first six books of the *Aeneid*, and like Virgil he reformulates the literary monuments of the past as a comment upon the present age. Images of *The Waste Land*—the drowned Phoenician sailor, the lady of situations, the man with three staves, the Wheel, the card that is blank, Mrs. Equitone—have conspicuous analogues in the *Aeneid*. Significantly, Anchises' great sermon in the sixth book of Virgil's poem is not only a recapitulation of Aeneas' own purgatorial experiences as quester but also suggests the movement of *The Waste Land* as a series of trials by water, wind, and fire. In sum, *The Waste Land* assumes the central importance of Virgil; Virgil is for Eliot, as he was for Dante, a guide and an inspiration. (MJD)

7527. Duffey, Bernard I. "The Experimental Lyric in Modern Poetry:Eliot, Pound, Williams." *JML* 3:1085-103.
The Waste Land, The Cantos, and *Paterson* represent a kind of lyric that may be called "experimental" and be understood as a poetic exercise that assumes an indeterminate and personal state of feeling to be the substance of its expression. Within such indeterminacy, the poet finds objects for his imagery that seem to be compelled by the state of feeling with which he grapples. His expression may well contain argument or other reference, but its poetic adequacy will be determined by his success in finding and manipulating properly affective objects. (BID)

7529. Dzwonkowski, F. Peter,Jr. " 'The Hollow Men' and Ash-Wednesday:Two Dark Nights." *ArQ* 30:16-42.
In T.S. Eliot's "Hollow Men" the hollow men are trapped in the desert of the time world and tantalized by a vision of spiritual possibility utterly beyond their grasp. They wander purposelessly in the dark night of an asceticism which, because they have no will, merely curses them with pain and leads neither to mystical unity nor to renewed spiritual health but rather to desperation and defeat. In *Ash Wednesday*, the speaker first perceives the unreality and emptiness of life in the time world. He then wills to enter the dark night in quest of a relationship with timelessness and, after a struggle of the will against temptation, achieves the mystical vision. The true achievement of the speaker is not the mystic moment but enduring spiritual health while he continues to exist in the world of time. The will of the speaker distinguishes

him from the hollow men and renders the waste land meaningfully habitable. (FPD,Jr)

7530. Egri, Péter. "T.S. Eliot's Aesthetics." *HSE* 8:5-34.
As a social critic, T.S. Eliot condemns the economic and social symptoms of what he calls "whiggery" and promotes the idea of a Christian society. In his literary criticism the exceptional sensibility of the poet-critic frequently clashes with the conception of the critic-poet. The need to find his poetic predecessors leads him to a just rehabilitation of neglected poets, but also prompts him to launch unjustified attacks against Shakespeare, Milton, and Shelley. Eliot's contradictory view of life and art finds an adequate expression in the imagistically free and paradoxically sharp treatment of his poetic form. He feels harmony banal and only considers the dissonant form becoming art. In his plays the concrete and abstract approaches are in conflict. (PE)

7536. Ewen, D.R. "Eliot, Bantock, and Education." *T.S. Eliot Newsl.* 1,i:7-9. [Rev. art.]
Bantock's *T.S. Eliot and Education* is a recapitulation and summary of his previous writings on Eliot's views on education, plus two elementary biographical and critical chapters. Both authors deny that formal education can develop whole personalities. Both ignore the questions raised in avowedly secular societies, and in societies based on non-Christian religions, with non-classical cultural histories. Bantock's book is a tribute of gratitude to a poet who helped him to construct his values, and who lends authority to Bantock's views on education. (DRE)

7537. Fleissner, Robert F. "The Browning of T.S. Eliot." *T.S. Eliot Newsl.* 1,i:6-7.
Certain contrasts and comparisons between "My Last Duchess" and "Prufrock" suggest themselves: among them, the tonal quality descriptive of *la pourriture noble* of the esthetic movement, the confusion of Life and Art on the part of the speaker, and the similar evasive quality leading to an ironic effect. Prufrock is Browning's Duke *manqué* in that he accepts the role of "attendant lord," taking upon himself as it were the regular title bestowed upon the younger son of a duke. The contrast between the Duke and "Lord" Prufrock helps to illumine what Eliot has created. (RFF)

7538. Frank, Armin P. "Eliot and Babbitt:A Note on Influence." *T.S. Eliot Newsl.* 1,ii:7-9.
Babbitt's influence on Eliot is said to be profound, intimate, and direct, and noticeable even in those areas where Eliot went on to break with Babbitt's teachings. Yet important views and procedures even of the early Eliot differ absolutely from central ones of Babbitt's. Thus, Babbitt's philological method of distinction by definition and historical derivation and Eliot's non-historical procedure of contrasting quotations from poems have no common procedural basis. An important group in Eliot's "classical" tradition, and one model of his own poetry, the Metaphysical Poets, to Babbitt are "Romantics" and, therefore, harbingers of depraved modernity. There is, therefore, room and need for a reappraisal of Eliot's relationship with his background, despite Howarth's indispensable *Notes on Some Figures Behind T.S. Eliot* . (APF)

7540. Giles, Richard F. "A Note on April." *T.S. Eliot Newsl.* 1,i:3.
Eliot's use of April in the opening line of *The Waste Land* is further explained by an examination of the etymology of "April" and of Herrick's use of April in two poems. This examination reveals the rich connotative value of this single word. (RFG)

7542. Gordon, Lyndall. "*The Waste Land* Manuscript." *AL* 45:[557]-70.
By examining the paper T.S. Eliot used, together with a variety of biographical and textual clues, it is possible to date the fragments of *The Waste Land* and to read them in the order in which they were composed. At first, Eliot collected material for a spiritual autobiography. He began in 1914 with three visionary fragments. At the end of that year, he imagined a flawed would-be saint's ordeal by fire. Between 1916 and 1919, there followed a stream of fragments, superficially linked to London, but stressing private experience—an incompatible marriage, a sense of sexual sin, a sense of the futility of material life, a longing to be transformed and to discern an ideal meaning that continually eluded him. The first draft, completed at Margate in November 1921, remained a

personal record but, with the second draft at Lausanne, Eliot began to overlay private emotions with more contemporary detail. In the end he obscured his original vision. (LFG)

7544. Hargrove, Nancy D. "Landscape as Symbol in T.S. Eliot's *Ash Wednesday*." *ArQ* 30:53-62.

In *Ash Wednesday* T.S. Eliot dramatizes the human soul in its attempts to turn from self and make a commitment to God. The six sections of the poem alternate between views of struggle and visions of attainment, with the last section setting forth the final conflict and suggesting the triumph of the spirit. Eliot uses rural landscape as a major symbol in communicating the complexities of this struggle between flesh and spirit. In each section landscape is analyzed in terms of meanings and sources, both personal and traditional. Personal settings suggest that which the protagonist hopes to reject, giving immediacy to the agony of renunciation; traditional settings convey that which the protagonist hopes to affirm, communicating the universality and stability associated with spiritual fulfillment. Dante and Tennyson are the leading literary sources for these traditional settings. Thus, this highly complex use of landscape is a brilliant, though subtle, rendering of theme through symbol; as such, it further demonstrates Eliot's mastery of symbolism. (NDH)

7545. Hays, Peter L. "Commerce in *The Waste Land*." *ELN* 11:292-94.

T.S. Eliot's antipathy to commerce, the way in which material pursuits preclude spiritual concerns, appears in *The Waste Land* and provides a unifying theme even though the word "commerce," like the hanged god, does not appear. Eliot uses at least four and possibly five of the definitions listed in the OED for the noun "commerce." Taking the least likely first, "commerce" was an 18th-century, stylish English card game. The term, of course, means buying and selling, mercantile dealings; it also can mean sexual intercourse. "Commerce" also refers to other forms of communication, conversation, and exchange between people and places. And, finally, it signifies converse with God. Thus the term, with its multiple meanings, pervades the poem, serving to unite it while commenting upon it, as does the image of the Fisher King. (PLH)

7555. Knapp, James F. "Eliot's 'Prufrock' and the Form of Modern Poetry." *ArQ* 30:5-14.

A depth-psychological analysis of Eliot's "The Love Song of J. Alfred Prufrock" illustrates the way in which changing patterns of culture and new conceptions of the nature of human experience were reflected in the formal innovations of modern poetry. Eliot's poem abandons many familiar literary conventions in order to portray the inner life of a man struggling to free himself from his own psychological defenses. As Prufrock moves closer to a conscious acknowledgment of his yearning and his fear, he manifests a series of defensive maneuvers which finally become so strong that he can safely say exactly what he wants, because he knows he will never try to have it. Eliot embodies this movement in techniques which perfectly mirror the processes of avoidance, distortion, regression, wish-play, and rationalization which constitute Prufrock's experience. (JFK)

7562. McCarthy, Patrick A. "Eliot's *Murder in the Cathedral*." *Expl* 33:Item 7.

Parallels between the first three temptations of Thomas Becket in *Murder in the Cathedral* and the temptations of Christ in Luke iv.1-13 demonstrate that Becket anticipates and easily rejects the three Tempters because he sees himself as a type of Christ. Becket recognizes the dangerous pride which has led him to consider himself as a Christ figure when the Fourth Tempter, who expresses Becket's real desire, urges him to seek glory through martyrdom. (PAM)

7568. Montgomery, Marion. "The Awful Daring:The Self Surrendered in *The Waste Land*." *ArQ* 30:43-52.

In T.S. Eliot's *The Waste Land* Tiresias unites the other personages of the poem, and in him the sources of Homer, Sophocles, and Dante are united. The key concepts of light and seeing center in Tiresias. He reveals the level of the personal in the poem, the necessity of self-love corrected. The tone of self-condemnation, of a severe turning inward, leads to the heart of darkness, the inclusive darkness the poem tries to dispel. Eliot's original epigraph from Conrad ties the modern world to Dante's vision, for *The Waste Land* dramatizes the attempt to move off the point of suspended spiritual death which Eliot saw as pervasive. The poem requires that the awareness live again every detail of desire, temptation, and surrender through the memory. After writing *The Waste Land*, Eliot sees that every moment requires a continual surrender. If personality is extinguished for the sake of poetry, it may be extinguished for the sake of person as well, through a giving which involves a continual act of spiritual rescue by grace's descent into the opened, continually new person. Eliot's poetry reveals the shadings of a mind continually turning to the light and so enlightened, and at every moment threatened by darkness. (MM)

7571. Naples, Diane C. "Eliot's 'Tradition' and *The Sound and the Fury*." *MFS* 20:214-17.

In *The Sound and the Fury* Faulkner used themes and techniques commonly associated with Eliot's mythical method to extend the scope of the novel. The myth that begins the legend of Kadmos and his Theban line (three brothers make separate searches for their sister, Europa, who has been kidnapped by Zeus transformed into a bull) may have suggested the structure of the novel. Broken taboos and subsequent curses, like those in Frazer's *The Golden Bough*, are keys to the decline of a family in *The Sound and the Fury*. Moreover, Faulkner's novel is informed by a vision of mythical time that is akin to Eliot's "present moment of the past" in which the artist must live. (DCN)

7582. Rodgers, Audrey T. "Dance Imagery in the Poetry of T.S. Eliot." *Criticism* 16:23-38.

What emerges from the variety of dance images in Eliot's poetry is an insistent pattern of opposites: the dance as a ritual of transcendence, a symbol of unity, a celebration of human and cosmic harmony on the one hand; and, on the other, a symbolic *danse macabre*—the rhythmic gestures of futility that constitute activity in the modern world. Eliot's waste land poetry abounds in images of degraded rituals: the devitalized circling of "The Hollow Men," the dancing bear of "Portrait of A Lady"; but early in Eliot's poetry, the glimmering presence of another dance suggests elevation and expiation of suffering. *Ash-Wednesday* prefigures the fullest expression of dance as harmonizing motion in the *Four Quartets*. Here, Eliot gathers into one condensed and many-faceted image all the reconciling motifs of the dance. Implicit in Eliot's use of dance imagery are the rich meanings accrued through time; but his distinctive contribution lies in his juxtaposition of opposites. The dance image contributes to the total design of Eliot's poetry and heightens the sense of irony we have come to associate with his vision of the world. (ATR)

7583. —— "'He Do the Police in Different Voices':The Design of *The Waste Land*." *CollL* 1:48-63.

The structure of *The Waste Land* is mythic because it is conceived, emerges, and takes final shape from the perspective of the poet as seer. What the poet-Tiresias sees is the substance of the poem: the opposition of sacred and profane, the quest for regeneration in a dead society, the affirmation of unity amid the debris of the wasted land. His vision dictates the order of the elements of the poem: each section documents his attempt to retrieve the regenerative fragments from a meaningful past. Through recollection, he succeeds in freeing himself from his dead world. (AR)

7584. —— "The Mythic Perspective of Eliot's 'The Dry Salvages'." *ArQ* 30:74-94.

The *Four Quartets* reflects Eliot's use of the mythic perspective as a questing intelligence that unifies all the antithetical elements of the poem. In each Quartet, the speaker explores the possible routes to the Still Point; discovers fugitive illuminations in and out of time; and concludes by affirming the dignity of striving. "The Dry Salvages" illustrates the structural pattern repeated in the other poems: the metaphor of the journey, the purgatorial hope and despair, the divine intercessor, the call for prayer and sacrifice, and the experience of achieving the Still Point. Elements of the mythic consciousness that provide the structural unity of the poem include: a belief in an indivisible and self-contained world capable of transcending time and change; the affirmation that beginnings and ends are the same; and the assertion that rebirth begins with symbolic death. Thus the celebration of unity-in-diversity and the purgatorial experience, suggested in the epigraphs, define the mythic perspective that encompasses and holds in tension the apparently disparate elements of experience in each of the Quartets, while at the same time ordering the whole. (ATR)

7586. Rother, James. "Modernism and the Nonsense Style." *ConL* 15:187-202.

Elizabeth Sewell was among the first critics to explore extensively the relationship between Symbolism and Nonsense and to document the impact of that relationship on the poetry of Eliot. In the light of this research, it is possible to argue that Eliot was not the only modernist to develop a style heavily dependent upon the strategies of the classical Nonsense writers. Clearly the use of language as "closed system" indicates that Wallace Stevens availed himself of these techniques. Unlike conventional satire, the Nonsense style illuminates a world in which it has become increasingly difficult to say anything clearly or convincingly. As a result, both Nonsense and the numerous varieties of modernism influenced by Lewis Carroll and Edward Lear are obsessed with the growing disparity between words and things, meaning and reality. (JR)

7587. Rozsa, Olga. "T.S. Eliot's Reception in Hungary." *HSE* 8:35-44.

Hungarian criticism on Eliot began in 1931 with writings with a religious approach and dealing almost exclusively with Eliot's conversion to Anglo-Catholicism. At the end of the 1930s critiques appeared which gave sensitive and detailed descriptions of the formal aspects of his poetry, but ignored his ideological background. In 1949 the first Marxist critique judged him severely, emphasizing only the reactionary character of his poetry and literary criticism. From 1949 to 1957 no critique on Eliot appeared. Since then Marxist writings have prevailed though religious articles have also been published. (OR)

7591. Schuchard, Ronald. "T.S. Eliot as an Extension Lecturer, 1916-1919." *RES* 25:163-73,292-304.

Using new materials to reconstruct the details of Eliot's wartime teaching experience, the syllabuses for the Extension courses that Eliot taught for Oxford, the University of London, and the London County Council from 1916 to 1919 are made available here. His five courses on Elizabethan, Victorian (2), modern English, and modern French literature were crucial in his development as a poet-critic. Providing a partial basis for his later essays and a storehouse of allusions for his poetry, Eliot's courses initiated one of his most prolific and influential periods of critical and creative activity. The syllabuses give needed substance to much existing criticism and provide significant information for future Eliot studies. (RS)

7600. Surette, P.L. "The Music of 'Prufrock'." *HAB* 25:11-21.

In "The Music of Poetry" Eliot claims as a natural resource for poetry "the use of recurrent themes" as in music. "Prufrock" depends for its structural organization upon a very close analogy to sonata form. This analogy accounts for the peculiar division of the poem into four dissimilar parts by horizontal lines of suspension points, and perhaps for the designation, "Love Song." Recognition of the musical analogy reveals the sources of the poem's enigmatic quality and suggests that the compositional unit for Eliot is the stanza or strophe, a completed poetic movement of relatively short compass which can be endlessly reiterated and varied. (PLS)

7604. Torrens, James,S.J. "Charles Maurras and Eliot's 'New Life'." *PMLA* 89:312-22.

In the late 1920s, when T.S. Eliot was haunted by Dante's *Vita nuova* and by the Earthly Paradise cantos of the "Purgatorio," he was also very much under the influence of Charles Maurras, the French monarchist and anti-Romantic. He found in Maurras the "criterion" he was searching for—a sense of "order" that would save the poetic sensibility from mere emotional self-indulgence. In 1928, Eliot translated an old essay on criticism by Maurras which argued that readiness for impression must be matched by a capacity for selection. Eliot had Maurras very much in mind when he sat down to write his own essay on Dante, and, by a special dedication, he tied the essay very tightly to Maurras, whose treatise on Dante he knew. "Ash Wednesday," too, with its interplay between the yearning, regretting sensibility, and the expiatory frame that controls it, is a mirror of both Eliot's Dante

essay and the esthetics of Maurras. (JST,SJ)

7607. Watt, Donald. "Eliot, Huxley, and 'Burnt Norton, II'." *T.S. Eliot Newsl.* 1,ii:5-7.

Eliot's "Burnt Norton, II" was perhaps spurred by Huxley's earlier poem, "The Burning Wheel" (1916). The two writers were acquaintances at Garsington during and after World War I. Eliot knew of Huxley's verse, although in the late 1920s and 1930s he became increasingly critical of Huxley's thought. Similarities of theme, figure, and structure suggest that Eliot may be disagreeing with the position Huxley takes in "The Burning Wheel." Eliot's specific objection, "And do not call it fixity," seems to refer directly to Huxley's choice of language at a parallel point in "The Burning Wheel." (DW)

Empson. 7619. Maxwell-Mahon, William D. "The Early Poetry of Empson." *UÈS* 10,i(1972):12-22.

William Empson's poems can be divided into poems written between 1927 and 1933 and those written after 1933. The earlier poems show a lack of visual imagery and are largely imitative of Donne and the metaphysical school. An exception is "Sea Voyage," in which scene and philosophical situation are presented as an integrated image. Empson's metaphysical borrowings can be seen in "Arachne"; and his use of contemporary scientific ideas is apparent in "Plenum and Vacuum," which deals with a finite though unbounded universe. The "Letter" poems are also examples of scientific analogy; they are unsuccessful because the feeling is obscured by elaborate conceits. In "To an Old Lady," Empson reveals a social sensitivity more reminiscent of Pope's urbanity than the "tough reasonableness" of Donne and his school. This shift in sensibility is also apparent in "This Last Pain." The "singing line" quality of the verse is the result of a poetical harmony between feeling and thought. (WDMM)

Ford. 7637. Lentz, Vern B. "Ford's Good Narrator." *SNNTS* 5(1973):483-90. [On *The Good Soldier.*]

John Dowell, the first person narrator of Ford's *The Good Soldier*, is a self-conscious narrator fond of reflecting on the art of storytelling. Ford has made Dowell a spokesman for ideas which he took very seriously, and as such Dowell must be seen as a totally reliable narrator. By addressing his story to a specific listener, Dowell creates a narrative framework within which the central action of the novel occurs. This frame gives Dowell-the-narrator a concrete narrative presence; it is in this role that Dowell both utters Ford's critical views and is himself the ideal narrator. (VBL)

7638. Mohay, Bela. "F.M. Ford's Contribution to the Theory of the Novel." *HSE* 8:51-66.

Ford became fully aware of, and elaborated on, his own principles of impressionism when he saw them threatened and attacked by the vorticist movement and the aftermath of World War I. The main features of the technique of impressionism are specified, and an attempt is made to explore the moral, social, and historical aspects of Ford's world outlook, to set them in historical context, and to contrast them with naturalism. Impressionism in England was an aristocratic middle-class trend among the intellectuals that aimed at reforming the middle-class that seemed to be in crisis at the turn of the last century. (BM)

7640. Moser, Thomas C. "From Olive Garnett's Diary: Impressions of Ford Madox Ford and His Friends, 1890-1906." *TSLL* 16:511-33.

Olive Garnett, unsuccessful fiction writer, younger sister of Edward Garnett, and close friend to Ford Madox Ford, faithfully kept a diary from 1890 to 1906. Olive's diary shows that Ford was colorful, attractive to women, and given to telling tall tales. The diary records Ford's romantic elopement with Elsie Martindale in March 1894 and the first years of their marriage. Finally, Olive gives first hand reports of the initial symptoms of Ford's nervous breakdown in London in March 1904; she also gives vivid pictures of him weeping and staggering under the July sun on the Salisbury plain, then departing for treatment in Germany in early August. The coincidence of dates and images with crucial events in *The Good Soldier* suggests that Olive may have been present at the germination of Ford's masterpiece. (TCM)

Forster. 7648. Beeton, Douglas R. "The Creed of Connection." *UES* 12,iii:28-30. [Rev. art.]
In examining the new Abinger edition of Forster's *Howards End*, the value of the book is reassessed. Despite its weaknesses, particularly in the portrait of Margaret and in the overassertiveness of catch-words such as "only connect," the book is seen as a remarkable 20th-century statement on Romantic faith. The companion volume *The Manuscripts of* Howards End is examined for the considerable light it throws on the published work. (DRB)

7649. Bolling, Douglass. "The Distanced Heart:Artistry in E.M. Forster's *Maurice*." *MFS* 20:157-67.
E.M. Forster's posthumously published novel *Maurice* provides yet further evidence of the author's artistic control and restraint. With its homosexual themes and concerns, *Maurice* put special pressures on Forster's artistry and self-control. A careful reading of the novel reveals how well the author rose to these challenges. *Maurice* is in no sense a work thematically or symbolically compromised by Forster's homosexuality; rather, the latter exerts energy and direction within a larger vision of man's relationship with the spiritual, the natural, and the societal. Forster's protagonist, Maurice, emerges as a credible figure through the distancing brought to bear on him. Style, tone, and imagery work together to give the novel adequate unity. (DB)

7655. Goonetilleke, D.C.R.A. "Colonial Neuroses:Kipling and Forster." *ArielE* 5,iv:56-68. [On K's earliest stories and F's *A Passage to India*.]
Nightmarish experiences are a characteristic aspect of European life in the colonies. As "The Dream of Duncan Parrenness" and "The Phanton Rickshaw" show, Kipling is aware that not all these nightmarish experiences relate to specifically colonial fears such as racial fear. But in "The Gate of the Hundred Sorrows" and "The Strange Ride of Morrowbie Jukes," he deals with specifically colonial nightmarish experiences—Misquitta's deterioration into opium-addiction and Jukes's "going native." In *A Passage to India*, Forster also handles colonial neurosis during and after the Marabar Caves episode, and through it he makes a "passage to more than India." (RG)

7656. Hanquart, Evelyne. "The Manuscript of Forster's *The Longest Journey*." *RES* 25:152-62.
At E.M. Forster's death, the MSS. of most of his major works were found, and they offer an interesting field of investigation. *The Longest Journey* MS., e.g. shows some lacunae with respect to the published version and most of the time at crucial points of the plot-line, which might not be purely irrelevant. The MS. also presents several alternative versions of some sequences besides a rather extensive rejected chapter. These various aspects of the MS. are examined, briefly analyzed, and discussed in the light of the published text, in order to give a better understanding of this novel as a whole and of Forster's creative process at work. (ECRH)

7657. Hotchkiss, Joyce. "Romance and Reality:The Dualistic Style of E.M. Forster's *Maurice*." *JNT* 4:163-75.
In E.M. Forster's *Maurice*, thematic dissonance—the conflict between two modes of coping with life—is reinforced by stylistic tension. Two distinct styles are operative: one, which is termed "plain," is used for purposes of realistic description and the other, which is termed "elevated," occurs in passages that are intended to show a dimension to experience beyond the commonplace. The plain style is satiric in intent; elevated style creates an atmosphere of romance. The elevated mode is heightened and more artificial and literary in diction and in the employment of metaphor and imagery. Sentence structure in the elevated mode is more complex. The plain mode is a substantive style. The swift alterations from style to style work admirably to build a sense of tension between the worlds of romance and reality—and it is this tension which is, ultimately, the main subject of the novel. (JMH)

7659. Kennard, Jean E. "*A Passage to India* and Dickinson's Saint at Benares." *SNNTS* 5(1973):417-27.
An essay by Goldsworthy Lowes Dickinson in *Appearances* may be a previously overlooked source of E.M. Forster's *A Passage to India*. In this essay Dickinson describes a visit to a holy man at Benares in whose house hangs a picture of a symbolic tree which symbolizes the cyclical journey of the soul. This explanation has close parallels to the structure of *A Passage to India*. That Forster

was thinking of this Hindu analogy of the progress of the soul when he wrote *Passage* is further suggested by the numerous references to trees in the novel and by the name given to its chief representative of Hinduism, Professor Godbole. (JEK)

7661. McDowell, Frederick P.W. "E.M. Forster and Goldsworthy Lowes Dickinson." *SNNTS* 5(1973):441-56.
The relationship between Forster's *Dickinson* and Dickinson's "Recollections" is now apparent. Forster's book continues the record beyond the "Recollections" and supplies details of Dickinson's public life, though Forster declined to discuss Dickinson's homosexuality in any explicit way. In *Autobiography* the secular saint of Forster's biography is supplemented by the frustrated, sexually obsessed man. Both books are necessary for a portrait of Dickinson. The experience of love sharpened Dickinson's discriminative powers and makes the book his best. His work is discussed; and despite its intermittent interest, it does not fulfill the claims made for it by Sir Dennis Proctor. (FPWM)

7670. Turk, Jo M. "The Evolution of E.M. Forster's Narrator." *SNNTS* 5(1973):428-40. [On *A Room with a View, Howards End,* and *A Passage to India*.]
Forster's narrator evolves from the omniscient type of commentator to one more subtle and unobtrusive, but never thoroughly effaced. His role changes from that of a "Stage Manager" in the early *A Room with a View*, to a mediator speaking almost as one with the central character in *Howards End*, to that of an observer with penetrating social and psychological insight, plus a growing awareness of the metaphysical, in *A Passage to India*. The narrator's values evolve from emancipated but authoritative opinions to a broader, more tolerant view of humanity that is still satirically perceptive but whose omniscience is unpresumptuous. Forster's narrator in *A Passage to India* conveys a sharp picture of man's social and political inadequacies coupled with tentative hope for better relations among men. (JMT)

Fowles. 7673. DeVitis, A.A., and William J. Palmer. "*A Pair of Blue Eyes* Flash at *The French Lieutenant's Woman*." *ConL* 15:90-101.
In *The French Lieutenant's Woman* Fowles draws upon Hardy's *A Pair of Blue Eyes*. The striking plot similarities—elopement and ambiguous return, followed by the formation of a doomed love triangle—as well as the similarities of character and melodramatic situation signal Hardy's influence. A more meaningful proof lies in the manner in which the patterns of imagery of *The French Lieutenant's Woman* echo those of Hardy's novel. The motifs of fossils, eyes, and of the intersubjective look are recast in Fowles's novel from their original mold. In *A Pair of Blue Eyes* Hardy gives his characters autonomy in choosing their own destinies—he perceives that man must define his own existentiality or else allow a conspiracy of circumstances to fossilize his existence. Fowles, however, writes not such a mimetic novel as one in which plot, characters, and imagery, although influenced by Hardy, display the knowledge of an additional century of observation of man's struggle to master the circumstances of life. He portrays a particularly mid-20th century Sartrian awareness—the necessity of choosing self-definition over fossilization. (AADeV & WJP)

7677. Rankin, Elizabeth D. "Cryptic Coloration in *The French Lieutenant's Woman*." *JNT* 3:193-207.
There are in John Fowles's novel *The French Lieutenant's Woman* several digressions which seem to detract from the unity of the novel. Such intrusions actually serve to reinforce the concepts of freedom, evolution, obsolescence, and survival which form the thematic basis of the novel. The novel is primarily the story of a conventional Victorian gentleman's evolution into an existential hero, but it is also concerned with the evolution of the novel from conventional omniscient narrative to existential *nouvelle roman*. The author-narrator repudiates control over his characters as a kind of "cryptic coloration" under cover of which his conventionally narrated novel may survive, or succeed, in a literary world which has evolved into a wrongheaded imitation of the existential universe. Couched in these terms, the narrative digressions merge with the story of the evolution of Charles Smithson and unify the various elements of the novel. (EDR)

Galsworthy. 7681. Banerjee, Jacqueline. "Galsworthy's 'Dangerous Experiment'." *AWR* 24,lii:135-43.

Lacking the courage of his contemporaries, and of his own early convictions, John Galsworthy was unable to find in his flirtation with the passions any positive alternative to the materialism of his society. The moral overtone in his novels became more and more obvious, and he gradually retreated from biting satire of the propertied classes to a half-hearted faith in their potential for good. Thus the fictional world of the Forsytes and their peers (*The Forsyte Saga*, 1922; *A Modern Comedy*, 1929; *End of the Chapter*, 1935), despite its impressive historical authenticity and sweep, grew increasingly superficial and proved ultimately dissatisfying—not only to such severe critics of Galsworthy as D.H. Lawrence and Virginia Woolf, but also to Galsworthy himself. (JPB)

Graves. 7697. Cohn, Alan M. "Glanville-Hicks's *Nausicaa* and Graves (Higginson D76)." *Focus* 4:71-73.

A consideration of the available evidence indicates that the published libretto for Peggy Glanville-Hicks's opera *Nausicaa* (Higginson D 76), which is based on Robert Graves's *Homer's Daughter*, was written by Glanville-Hicks, but with Graves's assistance. (AMC)

7701. Ormerod, David. "Graves' 'Apple Island'." *Expl* 32:Item 53.

The apparently obscure images of Robert Graves's "Apple Island" may be elucidated by reference to the mythology (or symbology) of his *The White Goddess*. The central theme of the poem concerns the lover's worship of a cruel yet fascinating mistress, and recalls the White Goddess' ritual yearly slaughter of her consort. The mistress of the poem is associated with natural forces suggestive of femininity, violence, and danger (the sea and the moon), while the lover's helplessness is linked to the male's efforts to impose his own patterns on nature. In *The White Goddess* the apple is identified with the quince, and the quince itself with the round mirror of the mermaid, herself representing the bitter-sweet nature of love. The quince is also sacred to sea-born Aphrodite, and the island of the title suggests Cyprus as well as Hesperides and Eden. It also recalls the ancient menace of ritual sexual assaults upon male intruders in all islands sacred to female divinities. The last stanza of the poem, fusing the various female images of destruction, unites the themes of male dread and female power in the final image of the halved apple, an emblem of the Goddess' immortality. (DO)

7702. Simon, Myron. "The Georgian Infancy of Robert Graves." *Focus* 4:49-70.

Like other members of the Marsh circle, Graves adopted the stance of poetic independence and dedication; thus, his personal discovery of Skelton's poetry in 1915 was more closely related to his Georgianism than is usually supposed. Graves also derived from the Georgians his sense of the kind of realism legitimately practiced by a poet. Under Georgian influence, Graves endeavored to give clear expression to his unmediated insights, so that he regarded mastery of technique as a functional requirement of the true poet. (EM)

Greene, G. 7705. Brock, D. Heyward, and James M. Welsh. "Graham Greene and the Structure of Salvation." *Renascence* 27:31-39.

Graham Greene's *The Power and the Glory* focuses on the conflict between theoretical and actual humanitarianism and emphasizes the imperfection inherent in man's limited existence. The lieutenant seeks to perfect the imperfectible and, consequently, frustrates his own ends. By stripping away the mechanical and administrative trappings of the church, he unconsciously exposes the essential goodness of Christianity based upon the ideals of love and charity personified by the fallen priest. As an exercise in naturalistic hagiography, the novel suggests that the priest finally mirrors the mystery of Christ's selfless incarnation, and the ending indicates the continuity of faith, the true martyrdom of the whisky priest, the omnipresence of grace in the modern world, and an analysis of the efficiency of contemporary Christianity. (DHB)

7706. Cassis, A.F. "The Dream as Literary Device in Graham Greene's Novels." *L&P* 24:99-108.

All Greene's novels narrate dreams, and with *The Heart of the Matter* Greene confines the narration of dreams to those of his central characters. The dreams narrated reveal what appears to be a conscious and deliberate effort on Greene's part to utilize the dream as a literary device, to create atmosphere, to introduce the reader to the level of the unconscious in his characters, to familiarize him with the most secret and conflicting impulses, and to reveal the absolute reality of a character undergoing emotional strain. Greene sometimes uses the dream to influence the course of action and to ensure the reader's acceptance of the change in the course of action. There are also the rare occasions when one can interpret the dream as a subtle unobstrusive authorial comment. (AFC)

7710. Davis, Robert M. "From Standard to Classic:Graham Greene in Transit." *SNNTS* 5(1973):530-46. [Rev. essay on G crit.]

The collected edition of Greene's novels and the volume of his film criticism represent a necessary stage in forming a final estimate of the nature and value of his achievement. The four secondary works under review—a checklist of criticism, a collection of previously published essays, and two critical books—for the most part add bulk rather than substance to Greene criticism. First-rate criticism of Greene remains to be written. (RMD)

7725. Muller, Charles H. "Graham Greene:The Melodramatic Character." *UES* 12,iii:31-37.

In *The Heart of the Matter* Greene has most successfully adapted melodrama and the pattern of the thriller for the psychological exploration of character. The novel is unique since in it Greene has dramatized inaction. Melodramatic interest in Scobie, the protagonist, stems from his imprisonment to the excess of the emotion of pity which inhabits the will to act. Scobie's suicide is the one positive action which finally is to evade all action. (CHM)

7726. —— "Graham Greene and the Absurd." *UES* 10, ii(1972):34-44.

In Greene's "post-Catholic" novels there are figures who embody a belief in progress. Opposed to these are the main characters who not only represent the antithesis of progress, but who contradict Teilhard de Chardin's notion of "noogenesis"—the belief in man's intrinsic power to attain a higher goal through an evolutionary process. In *The Quiet American*, Fowler, a part of the flotsam of humanity, exposes the absurdity of Pyle's rational belief in a Third Force. Since all rational dogmas must end in contradiction, one has no choice but to weigh up the radical absurdity of the universe. This triumph of the absurd over the rational has its best expression in *The Comedians*. The symbols Greene uses to depict the comedy of the absurd are those of a game of chance and of the clown. What finally emerges is that only those who are committed to some form of belief—whether trivial or grandiose—preserve a measure of human dignity in the face of the absurd. (CHM)

7727. —— "Graham Greene and the Justification of God's Ways." *UES* 10,i(1972):23-35.

There is little suggestion in Graham Greene's novels that he is offering a justification of God. In *Brighton Rock* the vindication of evil in the form of Pinkie, a juvenile Satan, would seem to preclude the belief in a God who is unlimited both in goodness and in power. It is arguable, however, that Greene presents a "theodicy" on the basis that evil is itself proof of God's existence. In *The Lawless Roads* he states that during his childhood he found the most intimate symbols for heaven in the cruelty and casual violence of the modern Inferno of daily life; and so Pinkie's ravaged universe presupposes the existence of a heavenly counterpart. The book's "theodicy" is also evident in its allegorical implications. That Rose, the innocent waitress, can respect and value Pinkie's goodness, and the divine Grace which her love symbolizes. Herein lies the significance of the poison images: Pinkie's evil is a sickness, a poisoning of the potential good, and Rose represents the divine Grace that is able to heal, or save. (CHM)

7728. —— "Graham Greene's New Novel." *UES* 12,i:67-69.

In Greene's *The Honorary Consul* the characters all act a part, believe in illusions, and are bogus figures, with bogus titles. Charley Fortnum is "not a proper Consul." There are also bogus "doctors," like Doctor Humphries; "Father" Rivas, as the renegade priest is called, is another bogus title. With these characters Doctor Eduardo Plarr is forced to play a serious role in the comedy of the absurd. Plarr has the perspective of *l'homme absurde*; he is unable to become involved, to commit himself to any belief or to any part of the Absurd since he understands, and sees through, the nature of the comedy. (CHM)

Hughes, T. 7757. Bouson, J. Brooks. "A Reading of Ted Hughes's *Crow*." *CP* 7,i:21-32.
Hughes creates a Crow-mythology to replace the Judeo-Christian myths and makes Crow operate on several levels in the imaginary shamanistic flight through the world of myth and legend. He is malleable and easily becomes St. George, Oedipus, Hercules, and Christ. Further, Hughes, acting as the shaman, becomes the Crow. Crow is witness to the creation of the world, is the demon who sets it awry, and the victim and scapegoat symbolically dismembered and reintegrated. The poet delves into unconscious racial memories and experiences and expresses the ceaseless repetition of creation and destruction. (JBB)
7766. Ries, Lawrence R. "Hughes' 'The Hawk in the Rain'." *Expl* 33:Item 34.
Hughes is interested in the perspective the animal world provides for examining the human condition. This approach is evident in "The Hawk in the Rain," where the real subject of the poem is the speaker. Unlike the hawk who finds a release from struggle in an acceptance of the forces of nature, man resists these forces and is destroyed by them. Only in death does man achieve such union. The hawk, however, reaches a still point which unifies his being with nature. Although the hawk, like man, will eventually be destroyed, the quality of his death is superior to man's, for the hawk's fall to earth results in the final natural union of "his heart's blood with the mire of the land." (LRR)

Hulme. 7768. Primeau, Ronald. "On the Discrimination of Hulmes:Toward a Theory of the 'Anti-romantic' Romanticism of Modern Poetry." *JML* 3:1104-22.
While Hulme rejects the "escapism" and "sloppy thinking" of many romantics, his own epistemology and his esthetic are indebted to a tradition which his terminology rejects. Hulme simply rejected some romantic attitudes because he wished to emphatically support others. What he sees as "classical" generally corresponds to what he considers "the best" in the romantics after he had purged them of "split religion" or "moaning" and "whining." It is therefore more accurate to read Hulme as an "anti-romantic" romantic who contributed to a tradition that lasts with some distinct modifications into the modern period. (RP)

Huxley, A. 7769. Allentuck, Marcia. "Aldous Huxley on Mark Gertler:An Unremarked Essay." *PBSA* 68:180-83.
An essay which Huxley wrote on the work of Mark Gertler, the Bloomsbury painter and friend of Lawrence, in 1937 is unlisted in the two Huxley bibliographies extant. This note adumbrates the relationship between Huxley and Gertler, analyzes Huxley's essay, and reproduces it in full. (MA)
7770. Baker, Robert S. "Spandrell's 'Lydian Heaven':Moral Masochism and the Centrality of Spandrell in Huxley's *Point Counter Point*." *Criticism* 16:120-35.
In Huxley's *Point Counter Point* Maurice Spandrell's fixation on his mother and his shock at her marriage to Major Knoyle are developed in such a way as to manifest a number of distinct pathological symptoms that for Huxley are emblematic of modern European society. Spandrell's "masochistic prostitutions" are intimately connected with his attempt to resurrect the virginal mother of his youth in the form of an absolute Augustinian God, while his endeavor to destroy whatever prospects life holds out to him corresponds precisely with Freud's definition of moral masochism. Huxley's novel is thematically structured around the four fundamental relationships (to parent, lover, death, and God) that govern a man's life and in their unfolding define his character. Spandrell's role is the only one in *Point Counter Point* that embraces in a detailed way all four. His death scene is an endeavor to reunite himself with his pubescent idol (his mother) but, in reality, his death is associated with the torpid mysticism of

Marjorie Carling and the adolescent sensuality of Burlap. (RSB)
7772. Bonicelli, Elena. "Libertà dell'Utopia, Utopia della libertà in Aldous Huxley." *RLMC* 26(1973):307-14.
In *Brave New World* Huxley criticizes the dangerous, alienating tendencies of the modern world and prophesizes chilling results. The schema proposed by the author is that of the traditional utopia but his intention is to recreate conditions for the wide accessibility of the genre. Certain cues in the book anticipate the modern literature of science fiction. The ideology which underlies the whole novel nevertheless prevents it from becoming a decidedly new form: polemics and ideological exasperation lead the author to disregard the unusual and incisive, stylistic and imaginary solutions which, barely outlined, are immediately abandoned. (EB)
7781. Vitoux, Pierre. "Aldous Huxley and D.H. Lawrence:An Attempt at Intellectual Sympathy." *MLR* 69:501-22.
Huxley's temporary endorsement of Lawrence's views is manifested in the creation of the character of Rampion in *Point Counter Point*. But the novel is also influenced in depth by Carl Jung's description of psychological types: attitude-types (introvert and extrovert) and function-types. This framework is used creatively by Huxley to organize the counterpointing (in characterization and conflicts). Rampion is included in it as an example of the successful balance of functions, but also as an extreme representative of the type of the introvert. After trying to systematize this ideal of functional completeness in *Do What You Will*, Huxley will react against what then appears to him as Lawrence's obscure vitalism—a reaction that will contribute to his final adoption of the perennial philosophy. (PV)

Joyce. 7813. Broes, A.T. "Shakespeare in *Finnegans Wake*." *HAB* 25:304-17.
In *Finnegans Wake*, Joyce confesses through his alter ego, Shem, that he "did but study with stolen fruit how cutely to copy all . . . various styles of signature." One of the authors whose "signature" appears most frequently in the *Wake* is Shakespeare. L.A.G. Strong, William Peery, and M.J.C. Hodgart have taken turns at identifying his "entrances and exits" in the novel. They have overlooked, however, hundreds of other references to his plays. Broes gives a play-by-play listing of these, according to act, scene, and line. (ATB)
7834. Delany, Paul, and Dorothy E. Young. "Turgenev and the Genesis of 'A Painful Case'." *MFS* 20:217-21.
James Joyce was reluctant to acknowledge any indebtedness to Turgenev. In part, he criticized Turgenev just to annoy Stanislaus Joyce, who considered him a better writer than Tolstoi. In "A Painful Case," known to be a satire on Stanislaus, Joyce made the joke more appropriate by borrowing heavily from the plot and characterization of Turgenev's story "Clara Militch." The hero of both stories is a withdrawn intellectual who, through pusillanimity, causes the death of a woman who seeks his love. Joyce also was indebted to "Clara Militch" for its handling of one of the major themes in *Dubliners*, the connection between the living and the dead. (DP & DEY)
7840. Eckley, Grace. "Ohio's Irish Militia and Joyce's *Ulysses*." *Éire* 9,iv:102-16.
Contradicts the assertion that Myles Crawford of the Aeolus chapter in Joyce's *Ulysses* suffers from mental decay. The "sense" in his outburst about his North Cork Militia and Spanish officers winning victories in Ohio is found in three sources: the historical significance, in Ohio, of the name Crawford; the name and activities of the Civil War general Don Carlos Buell; and the existence of the Tenth Ohio, the "Cincinnati Irish" regiment. The "Soldier Poet" of Ohio in the Civil War was William Haines Lytle, whose declamatory verse connects with the rhetorical qualities of the Aeolus chapter. (GE)
7854. Gabler, Hans W. "Towards a Critical Text of James Joyce's *A Portrait of the Artist as a Young Man*." *SB* 27:1-53.
Four documents with bearing on the textual history of Joyce's *Portrait* are described and analyzed: a set of tearsheets, galley- and page-proofs of the first printing of the novel serialized in *The Egoist*, London; a typewritten list of corrections for the second book edition; the printer's copy of the second book edition; and fragments of the typescript which intervened

between the authorial manuscript and the first printing and which had been believed to be entirely lost. (HWG)

7878. Herring, Phillip F. "Experimentation with a Landscape:Pornotopography in *Ulysses*—The Phallocy of Imitative Form." *MFS* 20:371-78.

Discusses erotic topography (including the love-voyage) and provides a historical survey, with examples from the *Roman de la Rose*, Sidney, Spenser, Shakespeare, Carew, Donne, Milton, Blake. A brief overview of the 20th century ends with an example from West's *Miss Lonelyhearts*, and a comparison of D.H. Lawrence and Joyce on the way they view a natural setting. Herring discusses the importance of directional movement in *Dubliners*, anatomical-cartographical design in *Finnegans Wake*, the suggestive sprawl of Dublin's harbor, and, more fully, the erotic-topographical configuration of *Ulysses* and its thematic implications. (PFH)

7893. Kelleher, Victor M.K. "'The Fingernails of God':A Comment on James Joyce's Aesthetic." *UES* 9,i(1971):14-17.

In *A Portrait of the Artist as a Young Man*, Stephen Dedalus claims that "The Artist, like the God of creation, remains within or behind or beyond or above his own handiwork, invisible, refined out of existence, indifferent, paring his fingernails." It is frequently assumed by critics that this is a statement of Joyce's own esthetic. But an analysis of Joyce's ironical presentation of character and event reveals that there is some affinity between his and Stephen's esthetic positions: at the moral level, in particular, Joyce is intent upon remaining "invisible" or inscrutable. Nonetheless, this obvious parallel between author and Stephen's "God of creation" should not be pushed too far. Far from being "indifferent" to his artistic creation, he is highly concerned about its moral structure. The word "indifferent," in fact, refers not to Joyce, but to Stephen, whose esthetic, like his character, contains disturbing elements of hubris. (VMKK)

7900. Klein, James R. "Lotts, Horse Piss, and Rotted Straw." *CE* 34(1973):952-75.

After a stay in a psychiatric ward, I decided I had not understood James Joyce's *A Portrait of the Artist* until I had gone crazy. I hadn't understood that Stephen had nearly lost contact with reality, had used words as a handhold on reality, and finally had gone crazy in a socially acceptable way by becoming a writer. Words are real, but I also went crazy on words as Stephen nearly had. I had become so divorced from my life story that I had ceased to be myself. Trying to "invent" an esthetic, I had so lost my way that my scribbled notes became the Word. But words were equally important to my recovery. "Insanity" is to "sanity" what an incoherent written expression is to a coherent one. The poet creates not only the world of his poem and a moment of his reader's consciousness but his very self. Horses of monstrous revery rear up out of words, yet only words may harness them. In revising his writing the writer revises himself. A writer must learn that he cannot leap to liberation on the word arcs of his imagination but must build the incarnation of his liberty by mortaring word brick to word brick. (JRK)

7901. Kloss, Robert J. "The Function of Forgetting in Joyce's 'Clay'." *HSL* 6:167-79.

Maria's forgetting of the plumcake on the tram, in James Joyce's "Clay," has rarely been considered in terms of motivation and selectivity. Maria intends to reward the children, with whom she identifies and to punish Joe and his wife by depriving them of her gift. Hostility on her part is consistent with her own emotional conflicts and with the atmosphere of the tale. The forgetting of the cake, like that of the stanza, is related to Maria's frustrated sexuality. Thematically linked are the misplacing of the corkscrew and nutcracker. The four missing things are connected additionally by being "openers," either physical or psychical. Examination of the reasons for forgetting opens us up to our own inner conflicts so that we stand revealed to ourselves—in a Joycean sense, "epiphanized." (RJK)

7907. Lane, Mervin. "A Synecdochic Reading of 'Wandering Rocks' in *Ulysses*." *WHR* 28:125-40.

The individual sections of the "Wandering Rocks" chapter in Joyce's *Ulysses* are synecdochic reversals of the main chapters. Exegesis of each of the sections in their relation to the "parent" chapters demonstrates that in its use of form, personages,

contexts, and situations the "Wandering Rocks" or "Street" chapter is made up of reversals, inversions, and contrasts within and between the sections themselves, as well as in relation to the main chapters of the book. (ML)

7923. Maddox, James H.,Jr. "'Eumaeus' and the Theme of Return in *Ulysses*." *TSLL* 16:211-20.

The "Eumaeus" chapter of Joyce's *Ulysses* affords a unique perspective on the mental processes of Stephen and Bloom in the closing chapters of the book. "Eumaeus" is characterized by mistaken or confused identities. The most prominent example of this confusion is Murphy the sailor. Murphy is Ulysses the dissembling narrator, but more generally he reminds us of many narrators. He raises in Bloom's mind the idea of returning to Molly. As a composite character, Murphy epitomizes the "return" of mythic types to be reincarnated in the present. The two heroes themselves make mistakes of identity, but in ways which lead them toward the truth. (JM)

7946. Norris, Margot C. "The Language of Dream in *Finnegans Wake*." *L&P* 24:4-11.

The language of *Finnegans Wake* is necessitated by the requirements of a dream work which accommodates modern Freudian dream theory. Joyce devised a "double talk," a flow of language capable of expressing contradictory thought simultaneously, to depict the conflicting relationship between the dreamer's conscious and unconscious impulses. The result is a novel prose-poetry which illustrates psychoanalyst Jacques Lacan's contention that poetic tropes serve as linguistic analogues to certain dream processes. The obscurity of *Wake* language is a function of the theme of guilt in the work: in dream, the defense against guilt prompts the use of devious means and disguises in order to hide certain meanings while providing cues for their discovery. (MCN)

7951. Pearce, Richard. "Experimentation with the Grotesque:Comic Collisions in the Grotesque World of *Ulysses*." *MFS* 20:378-84.

In *Ulysses*, Joyce extends both the limits of the novel and the tradition of the grotesque by embodying one of the most dramatically potent and threatening forces in the novel's medium. The opening of "Circe" is examined to show how Joyce brings the novel's medium into its drama, and how the medium becomes an unknowable, unpredictable, and unreasonable force. Collision, the basis of Eisenstein's theory of montage, is one of the novel's basic dynamics; it is illuminated by a model of Eisenstein's first film. The major collisions in *Ulysses* are between characters, between the medium and the reader, and between the medium and Leopold Bloom. (RP)

7952. Petroski, Henry. "What Are Pomes?" *JML* 3:1021-26.

There is evidence that Joyce's *Pomes Penyeach* was a more important and serious effort for him than is commonly held. Although the poems may be read as the sentimental lyrics of an ageing man in exile and not poems of Everyman seeking universal truth, apparently for Joyce they were a consolation in a time of self-doubt and loneliness. If one is aware that, besides being a fruit and the slang of his contemporaries, a "pome" is a ball of precious metal which celebrants of Mass filled with hot water and placed on the altar in cold countries to warm their hands so they might not fumble the sacred elements, the small book's verses assume a new dimension. One can readily see in them a constant evocation of youth and Dublin to warm the heart of a lonely artist writing his last and most ambitious work looking for the universe in a dark womb. (HP)

7962. Raisor, Philip D. "Grist for the Mill:James Joyce and the Naturalists." *ConL* 15:457-73.

Joyce was a serious student of the 19th-century naturalistic movement, but he treated it as raw material for his own works. He considered Ibsen to be the founder of the movement, and in 1899-1906 Joyce read the writers who, he felt, were Ibsen's descendants. Joyce's own comments on the naturalists indicate that in reading their works he was less concerned with a theory of Naturalism than in attitudes and techniques which would serve his own esthetic ends. Although determining the extent and operations of Naturalism in Joyce's thought and works is complicated by divergent definitions of Naturalism, the presence of Scandinavian, German, English, Irish, Russian, Italian, and French naturalists is clearly discernible. The point at which Joyce is closest to the naturalists is in their mutual agreement that individual details contain within them their own shape and meaning, and, therefore, are not dependent upon myth for their significance. (PR)

7981. Scott, Bonnie K. "Joyce's Schooling in the Field of George Moore." *Éire* 9,iv:117-41.
While Joyce was developing artistically, he shared common Dublin ground with George Moore. Though his adolescent enthusiasm for Moore turned to cynicism, Joyce betrayed great familiarity with Moore's work in continuing criticisms. Moore scorned Joyce, probably finding the youth's beginnings in Zola and Symons too familiar for comfort. In interpreting Ireland, Moore anticipates many of Joyce's images and themes. He also anticipates Joyce's interest in the human mind—both in its experience of external trivia and internal content of guilt and Freudian dream. In borrowing, Joyce frequently improves upon his master, making internal and external experience flow together and representing not just Irish people but humanity. (BKS)

Larkin. 8017. Blum, Margaret. "Larkin's 'Dry-Point'." *Expl* 32:Item 48.
Philip Larkin's "Dry-Point" deals with conception, birth, life, death, and the afterlife. Larkin devotes an unrhymed quatrain to each of the four phases of man's existence. He uses a dry-point-etching metaphor throughout the poem, except in the first three lines of the last quatrain, where he turns to imagery more suitable to the subject matter of the quatrain. The bleak joylessness of man's earthly existence is contrasted with the hoped-for bright serenity of death and the ensuing life after death. (MMB)

8020. Naremore, James. "Philip Larkin's 'Lost World'." *ConL* 15:331-44.
Although Philip Larkin's early poems in *The North Ship* (1945) were influenced by Yeats, Larkin says that the real starting point in his career came a year later, when he read Thomas Hardy. While the surface mannerisms of his work changed, his major themes and the essential conflicts in his personality remained. Thus in "Sad Steps" and "Waiting for breakfast" he rejects his romantic illusions only to turn back and lament the "strength and pain" of youthful idealism. This ambivalence can be found earlier in *The North Ship*, which is romantic yet filled with moments of emotional impotence and the desire to withdraw from life. If Larkin's isolated, voyeuristic persona has been implicit in his work from the beginning, so also, in his later, "anti-romantic" poems he remains painfully aware of "that much mentioned brilliance, love." Sometimes this conflict leads him into moods of emotional paralysis or misanthropy, but in his best poems, such as "Church Going" or "The Whitsun Weddings," he is prompted to speak in more hopeful terms. At some level Larkin may be aware that his literary philosophy is the flawed antithesis to modernism's flawed thesis: his work is free of the anti-human barbarism which is the dark side of Yeats, but it also shows his longing for the "passionate intensity" of the poems he admired in his youth. (JN)

Lawrence, D.H. 8024. Baker, James R. "Lawrence as Prophetic Poet." *JML* 3:1219-38.
Lawrence's poems (especially those written after 1918) offer an evolutionary picture and synopsis of Lawrence's diagnosis of modern mentality and society, his short range predictions, and his far-reaching prophecies. Both diagnosis and predictions are negative. Since our salvation must be post-apocalyptic, the prophetic poems are largely positive, projecting reconciliation of civilization and nature. Lawrence's concerns foreshadow those found in the work of contemporary psychologists, philosophers, sociologists, cultural historians, anthropologists, and professional futurologists. (JRB)

8029. Beards, Richard D. "*Sons and Lovers* as *Bildungsroman*." *CollL* 1:204-17.
Like his counterparts in other apprenticeship novels, Paul Morel is forced to face four essential choices in his quest for self-realization: he must select a vocation, find a mate (or the ideal of one), clarify his religious perspective and, finally, accept his identity. Paul's quest to be an artist is counterpointed by his family's economic struggle; his search for the right mate typifies

the *Bildungsroman* protagonist's instrumental use of members of the opposite sex as he or she works toward the ideal. Paul's increasing awareness of the mystical universe results in an identity in which he accepts his place in that living cosmos. (RDB)

8034. Burwell, Rose Marie. "Schopenhauer, Hardy, and Lawrence:Toward a New Understanding of *Sons and Lovers*." *WHR* 28:105-17.
Integration of the information available concerning Lawrence's reading of Schopenhauer and its relationship to his essay on Hardy explains the complex desire of the narrator to "have it both ways." Paul Morel breaks with Miriam Leivers and with Clara Dawes not because "his mother holds his soul," but because he has unconsciously identified with the father that he cannot consciously admire. By the novel's end Paul has gained confidence in himself as a man and an artist and he has learned for the first time that he can prosper without the assistance of the women who have invaded his life since birth. When Paul moves toward the "city's gold phosphorescence" he moves with certainty toward a fuller integration of the opposites represented by his mother and father that have warred within him. (RMB)

8045. Davis, Patricia C. "Chicken Queen's Delight:D.H. Lawrence's 'The Fox'." *MFS* 19(1973):565-71.
"The Fox" is a reflection of Lawrence's need to fight the female's influence. He looks for his weapon in the demonic. Henry, by killing the fox, assumes in totemic fashion its powers. In Lawrencian terms he faces the ultimate threat: not one female opposing him, but two, existing in close conjunction. He succeeds in separating them, but in killing Banford he destroys what is feminine in March. Instead of there existing the hint of a lesbian relationship, we have strong overtones of male homosexuality: Henry's interest in March is specifically an interest in her masculine side. As if he suddenly realized the ominous turn his creation was taking, Lawrence attempts to dilute this threatening new current by a sudden revision in March's character. He introduces into her personality a kind of femaleness which never existed before. The story thus exudes a curious schizophrenic quality: it begins in an atmosphere of well-sustained tension, but ends in depleted fashion on a false psychological note. (PCD)

8048. Ditsky, John M. " 'Dark, Darker Than Fire':Thematic Parallels in Lawrence and Faulkner." *SHR* 8:497-505.
The dark forces, the powers of flesh and blood attuned to the rhythms of Nature herself, have found similar stylistic expression in the works of Lawrence and Faulkner. Focus upon a specific passage in *The Rainbow* suggests parallels in Faulkner's novels: the "hawk"-faced artist of *Mosquitoes* seems predicted; the rhythmical reaping of Dewey Dell and Lafe in *As I Lay Dying* seems adumbrated; the sonic brilliance of *Sanctuary*'s rape scene seems foreshadowed; and even the existential realizations of *Wild Palms* can be found in embryo. (JMD)

8056. Green, Eleanor H. "Blueprints for Utopia:The Political Ideas of Nietzsche and D.H. Lawrence." *RMS* 18:141-61.
The similarity in political theory between Nietzsche and Lawrence is striking enough to suggest that Nietzsche exercised a strong influence over Lawrence's thought. Both men were "heroic vitalists" who stressed the importance in their utopian state of a strong leader, a hierarchical social structure, the total submission of the lower orders to their superiors, the subjugation of women to men, harsh discipline and military training for boys, and a powerful and spontaneous interrelationship between man and the natural forces of the universe. It is in Lawrence's "leadership" novels that Nietzschean political ideas are most fully used and developed. (EHG)

8067. Hinz, Evelyn J. "D.H. Lawrence and 'Something Called *Canada*'." *DR* 54:240-50.
In *Lady Chatterley's Lover* Canada is introduced as the land toward which liberated lovers turn their gaze. Lawrence's use of Canada is best explained in terms of his own practical search for the ideal land, a search that took him from one country to another and which always ended in disappointment. An early version of the novel suggests that it was his increasing disillusionment with other promised lands which prevented him from putting Canada to the test. It was also because Canada could be used as the projected residence for his lovers. (EJH)

8071. Humma, John B. "Melville's *Billy Budd* and Lawrence's 'The Prussian Officer':Old Adams and New." *ELWIU* 1:83-88.
D.H. Lawrence did not know about Melville's *Billy Budd* (not published until 1924) when he wrote "The Prussian Officer" (1913). Yet his characterizations of the orderly and the captain closely parallel Melville's characterizations of Billy and Claggart just as the central action in "The Prussian Officer" closely conforms to that in *Billy Budd*. In both stories the younger men are "unconscious" types (unfallen Adams), whose free, spontaneous behavior arouses the jealousy of the two officers—self-conscious, hyper-rational types (fallen Adams) who have repressed their instincts. Resentful of the instinctual, animal natures of Billy and the orderly, Claggart and the captain both assume the role of Satan in attempting to subvert the innocence which is the chief abiding quality of these two reflections of their former selves. That innocence, which renders Billy and the orderly vulnerable, also insures their victory over the officers. Though they both die, neither one is "defeated." (JBH)

8109. Stammler, Heinrich A. "Apocalypse:V.V. Rozanov and D.H. Lawrence." *CSP* 16:221-44. [Sum. in Fr.]
Compares the work and thought-worlds of D.H. Lawrence and V.V. Rozanov and discusses Rozanov's influence on Lawrence. (HAS)

8075. Kleinbard, David J. "D.H. Lawrence and Ontological Insecurity." *PMLA* 89:154-63.
R.D. Laing's concept of ontological insecurity and Erik Erikson's analysis of identity confusion contribute to an understanding of Lawrence's characterization in *The Rainbow* and *Women in Love*. Will Brangwen's fear in the *The Rainbow* that he will dissolve into nothingness without Anna is typical of individuals suffering from ontological insecurity. This anxiety ramifies into webs of mutually contradictory feelings. For example, Will's fantasy of merging with Anna clashes with his fear of losing his identity. Anna embodies for Will an unconscious fantasy of his mother; this displacement is the root of the contradictions and conflicts in which he becomes entangled. This fantasy system proliferates into role and identity confusions. Will wishes to be absolute master of his home and child-servant of his wife's matriarchy. Simultaneously in his relationship with his little girl, Ursula, he is an affectionate father, a sadistically destructive sensualist, and a child seeking parental support. These dissonant impulses and roles exacerbate Will's sense of his unreality, incoherence, and general impotence. (DJK)

8079. Lee, Robin. "Darkness and 'A Heavy Gold Glamour': Lawrence's *Women in Love*." *Theoria* 42:57-64.
The major theme of *Women in Love* is the search for indiviual authenticity within a social community, and the characters present different ways of confronting this search. Chapter ix reflects the structure of the novel and in patterns of imagery evokes Lawrence's moral judgments. The linked images of "darkness," "gold," and "whiteness" suggest three aspects of the search for authenticity and community by Gerald Crich and Gudrun Brangwen. Lawrence also uses these images to suggest to the reader a symbolic, almost mythic dimension to the novel, which is not perceived by the characters. In this way, Lawrence's novel evokes a concrete situation and also suggests the mysterious inner life of individuals and an historical process in the outer world. (RHL)

8093. Raddatz, Volker. "Lyrical Elements in D.H. Lawrence's *The Rainbow*." *RLV* 40:235-42.
The Rainbow is the result of Lawrence's constant search for a language that could adequately transform his ideas and feelings into literary expression. In his concept of the "immediate present," he dismisses the established dimensions of time and space and introduces the lyrical rhythm which is unnoticeable, unobtrusive motion that pauses on the moment and makes it seem eternal. Along with the lyrical rhythm goes the synesthetic flux of sensations. Man's existence is natural, not civilized; his feelings correspond to his natural surroundings, and his intellect is dominated by his sensitivity. The creative implications of the lyrical approach are revealed in the theme of rebirth through sexual and spiritual fulfillment. (VR)

8109. Stammler, Heinrich A. "Apocalypse:V.V. Rozanov and D.H. Lawrence." *CSP* 16:221-44. [Sum. in Fr.]

Compares the work and thought-worlds of D.H. Lawrence and V.V. Rozanov and discusses Rozanov's influence on Lawrence. (HAS)

8110. Stein, Robert A. "Finding Apt Terms for Lawrence's Poetry:A Critique of Sandra Gilbert's *Acts of Attention*." *WHR* 28:253-59. [Rev. art.]
Gilbert's attempt to gain admiration for Lawrence's poetry in terms of his "acts of attention" is not the right track to take. Gilbert distinguished what Lawrence came to set aside as matter for poetic exploration. In this regard, Gilbert contributes needed clarification yet carries things too far. (RAS)

Lehmann, R. 8132. Coopman, Tony. "Symbolism in Rosamond Lehmann's *The Echoing Grove*." *RLV* 40:116-21.
Interpretations of *The Echoing Grove* usually focus on the character of Rickie, stressing the fact that he is eventually rejected by both his wife and his mistress. A close reading shows that Rosamond Lehmann subtly points to a form of "reconciliation" between the three characters. The scene with the rat at the opening of the novel suggests the importance of the relationship between human beings. Furthermore, Rickie's cuff-links are a recurrent motif in the different parts of the novel: after his death they become the property of his wife, next of their son. Finally, the various connotations of the title skillfully suggest that the unhappy past experiences should be discarded so that a "reconciliation" might follow. (TC)

8133. Gindin, James. "Rosamond Lehmann:A Revaluation." *ConL* 15:203-11.
Notes the recent absence of critical interest in Lehmann's work and deals critically with the six novels (*Dusty Answer*, 1927; *A Note in Music*, 1930; *Invitation to the Waltz*, 1932; *The Weather in the Streets*, 1936; *The Ballad and the Source*, 1944; *The Echoing Grove*, 1953) and the single volume of short stories (*The Gypsy's Baby*, 1945). The typical Lehmann heroine, her sensitivity, her position in the family and in middle-class society, her desire to break away in order to find herself are discussed. The rebel is, however, constantly interested in and determined by personal and social history. The attempt at self-discovery is never fully successful, and Lehmann offers no consolation. Lehmann's work is defended against the "limitations" reviewers had found, her thematic inconclusiveness, her "feminine" quality, her focus on prose style. Her work has been neglected because it is not easily teachable or extrapolated into a message, and it has been too simply consigned to perspectives of childhood and adolescence. (JG)

Lessing. 8138. Joyner, Nancy. "The Underside of the Butterfly:Lessing's Debt to Woolf." *JNT* 4:204-11.
To the Lighthouse and *The Golden Notebook* bear strong resemblances in style and theme. While Woolf splices the events of two days together by the casual mention that ten years have passed, Lessing ranges over a long period of years but in the middle includes a minute account of the events of a single day. Rather than focusing on one person through a number of characters' minds, as Woolf does, Lessing uses a variety of attitudes of a single person through the device of the notebooks. Thematically, both novels center upon the difficulties of a creative woman, and in both there is an explicit hostility toward men. Even the device of using the repetitive "I" to indicate men's excessive egotism appears in both books. The conclusions of the two novels sharply diverge, however, for Lily Briscoe discovers with relief that the achievement of her art means more to her than a conventional life, while Anna Wulf presumably gives up her art because of her inability to live independently. (NJ)

8140. Markow, Alice B. "The Pathology of Feminine Failure in the Fiction of Doris Lessing." *Crit* 16,i:88-100.
Examination of the etiology of feminine "failure" in Lessing's fiction suggests that it is rooted in a diseased male/female relationship, which is symptomatic of a larger neurosis. Both Lessing's "free" and traditional feminine characters betray neurotic-psychotic symptoms, in part, because they are caught in transition between two conflicting ideologies. Though they demonstrate cognitive awareness of the constricting effects of adherence to the old mythology of domesticity, Lessing's feminine

characters illustrate her own ambivalence about roles in the form of nostalgia. A permanent lassitude characterizes these traditionalists, yet Lessing's "free" women are equally devitalized, primarily because they are self-destructively committed to romantic love. (ABM)

8142. Porter, Dennis. "Realism and Failure in *The Golden Notebook.*" *MLQ* 35:56-65.
Doris Lessing's *Golden Notebook* appears at first sight somewhat disappointing on account of the conventional character of its realism. The work's developing complexity soon makes it clear that Lessing is challenging the fictional techniques in which she seemed to put her initial trust. Further, the acknowledgment of the inadequacy of its own techniques is thematically linked to a more generalized sense of failure, which is both personal and sociohistorical. It follows, therefore, that the structural cumbersomeness and the untidy realism of *The Golden Notebook* are willed. The apparent failure of the literary imagination to control its material is symptomatic of a general malaise. If *The Golden Notebook* does not display the elegant mastery of Gide's *Counterfeiters*—the classic example of the novel probing the limits of its power to represent reality—it is because Lessing's strengths are of a dourer, non-esthetic kind. She chooses to employ the techniques of conventional realism to suggest the formlessness and grainy texture of our collective living, while at the same time she questions the appropriateness of such techniques. (DDP)

Lowry, M. 8179. Bareham, Terence. "After the Volcano: An Assessment of Malcolm Lowry's Posthumous Fiction." *SNNTS* 6:349-62.
Lowry's last novels reveal strands of his art still developing and expanding. *Dark As the Grave Wherein My Friend Is Laid* and *October Ferry to Gabriola* differ from the earlier work since their heroes are able to begin a process of self-redemption. *October Ferry* is the most "complete" in this sense: by the end of the book the tone is one of hope and reconciliation. Even the images and leitmotifs, which at first sight seem identical to those in the earlier work, have been transmuted by a new emphasis on love, stability, and family unity. This sense of retreat from the abyss of despair gives some indication of Lowry's design in the unfinished cycle of which all his novels are parts. Links with the contemporary short stories also help to fit *October Ferry* into a place much more significant than that hitherto granted it in the Lowry canon. (TB)

8182. Cross, Richard K. "*Moby-Dick* and *Under the Volcano*: Poetry from the Abyss." *MFS* 20:149-56.
Lowry's *Lunar Caustic* (1963) is about "a man's mystical identification with Melville" and contains many Melvillean echoes, whose nexus is the hero's confrontation with his own white whale, the forces that menace his sanity. Specific sources are less important than "linked analogies," the ways the two writers' affinity of mind expresses itself in *Moby-Dick* and *Under the Volcano*. Readers who bring conventional novelistic expectations to these books often complain that one cannot see the forest for the symbols. Lowry shared Melville's belief that "some certain significance lurks in all things," and in order to specify its nature both developed meditative modes that enabled them to inspect objects from a number of angles. The volcano and the whale become all-encompassing repositories of meaning, intrinsic or imposed. That the scaffolding used in constructing the two works remains partially visible matters far less than the grandeur of scale and design of these poetic cathedrals, whose naves are the world. (RKC)

Moore, G. 8226. Cary, Meredith. "George Moore's *Roman Expérimental.*" *Éire* 9,iv:142-50.
Moore used three genres to write about his native land. A comparison of the essays and sketches of *Parnell and His Island*, the short stories of *The Untilled Field*, and the autobiography *Hail and Farewell* clarifies the exile's view of Ireland. It also reveals Moore's development of a type of autobiography designed to include the best qualities of journalism and fiction while avoiding the shortcomings of both. His autobiographical theory suggests the influence of Zola's postulation of a "scientific novel." (MC)

Murdoch. 8239. Goshgarian, Gary. "Feminist Values in the

Novels of Iris Murdoch." *RLV* 40:519-27.
Discusses Murdoch's basic feminist values and aims as adumbrated in her philosophical writings and dramatized in her fiction. Murdoch's feminist analysis of male-female relations is directly concerned with the artificial myths and mystiques of womanhood that have denied women recognition as free, independent, and contingent human beings. Her novels do not explore the forthright belief in female inferiority but the subtler effects of men building exalted fantasies about women. Her analysis also points to some of the psychological motivations behind men's raising women to the plane of the inessential. Herein lies the comic irony in her works: the rueful apprehension of the gap between male illusion and the reality of himself and his beloved. (GG)

O'Casey. 8259. Ayling, Ronald. "Ritual Patterns in Sean O'Casey's *Within the Gates.*" *Theoria* 43:19-27.
Detailed textual analysis of an episode in Scene i of *Within the Gates*, in which the heroine meets the Salvation Army Officer, illustrates O'Casey's experimentation in dramatic form, his use of liturgical and choric effects, and his success in heightening superficial idiomatic speech. The play's movement from realism to ritual is related to a basic technical problem in modern drama: the need to realize deeper planes of consciousness within banal contemporary situations and language. O'Casey satirizes dogmatic extremes in religion and atheism while conveying a profound spiritual experience in terms of refashioned biblical imagery and Anglican liturgy. *Within the Gates* (in its two published versions) is O'Casey's most ambitious dramatic experiment, taking formal innovations in *Juno and the Paycock* and *The Silver Tassie* further than before while also looking forward, in its failures as its successes, to later fantasies like *Cock-a-Doodle Dandy*. (RA)

8262. Lowery, Robert G. "O'Casey, Critics and Communism." *Sean O'Casey Rev.* 1,i:14-18.
Throughout his life, O'Casey's Communism was the source of great controversy. Many of his admirers saw his Communism as a foible, while others saw it as the philosophy in which lay his strength and undying optimism. While it is true that O'Casey's poverty was a major contributory factor in his political development, it was his laboring experience in the workshops and factories of Dublin that crystalized the class-conflict in O'Casey's mind. It is no accident that participation in the 1913 Strike in Dublin was to O'Casey his finest moment. (RGL)

8264. Murphy, Maureen O.R. "Sean O'Cathasaigh agus Conradh na Gaeilge." *Sean O'Casey Rev.* 1,i:18-19.
An early Gaelic League enthusiast, O'Casey broke with the League over its reluctance to interfere in religious or political issues, a policy too narrow for his broader interests in social and national reform. He was particularly angered by the League's silence in the Michael O'Hickey case. While he criticized the language policy of both the League and the government, he remained a fervent enthusiast for the Irish language. (MM)

8266. Siegmeister, Elie. "A Long, Long Road." *Sean O'Casey Rev.* 1,i:22-32. [Foll. by the orig. score of "The Dublin Song."]
The difficulty of making an opera out of O'Casey's *The Plough and the Stars* is monumental. O'Casey's drama is not the typical, neatly-packaged play, but a flaring, panoramic, quasi-Elizabethan combination of poetry, earthly humor, fantasy, bitter tragedy, and blunt realism, with a generous helping of traditional music thrown in. The characters must be developed through songs, arias, scena's, and ensembles. But an adaptation runs the risk of deleting some measures here and adding others there, using part of the third movement in the middle of the second, changing the opening and committing in general other mayhem. The unity of the juxtaposition of differing elements in O'Casey's play is achieved through the logic of the music drama. Just as the characters who start by living in separate worlds are forcibly thrown together by the cataclysm of war, wounds, and human compassion, so the various strands of the music, sharply separated in Act I, begin to interpenetrate in Act II and finally merge in Act III. (ES)

O'Faolain. 8270. Harrod, L.V. "The Ruined Temples of Seán

O'Faolain." *Éire* 9,i:115-19.
Sean O'Faolain's stories frequently center around remembered brief moments. For O'Faolain the memories are "scraps of a ruined temple," often the moments just before disillusionment or failure. O'Faolain's early stories looked back to the "days of vision" during the Irish Civil War; his more recent stories seem to make the "vision" a universal experience. Two studies, Maurice Harmon's *Sean O'Faolain: A Critical Introduction* (Notre Dame, 1966) and Paul Doyle's *Sean O'Faolain* (N.Y., 1968), deal with the issues of O'Faolain's work. Doyle's book ignores O'Faolain's biographies and travel books, while Harmon's argues that the biographies lead to the creative work. Harmon ultimately suggests that O'Faolain is most successful in the short story form because his "misfit heroes" are incapable of sustaining full relationships with society. The "ruined temples" are best handled in a form that, according to Frank O'Connor's *The Lonely Voice* (N.Y., 1963), is "remote from the community—romantic, individualistic, and intransigent." (LVH)

Orwell. 8275. Bonifas, Gilbert D. "Notes sur la genèse de *Down and Out in Paris and London.*" *Annales de la Fac. des Lettres et Sciences Humaines de Nice* 18(Dec 1972):57-64.
Orwell's critics seem to believe that he went down and out among tramps only on his return from Paris, in 1930 and 1931. Yet, while in France, he published on 1 January 1929 in a left-wing newspaper, *Le Progrès Civique*, an article entitled "La journée d'un tramp," which is so circumstantial that, obviously, Orwell must have had first-hand knowledge of the daily life of a tramp prior to writing it. This, therefore, puts his first experiences among vagrants back to 1927. Moreover, a detailed stylistic and lexical analysis of the French article (the English original has been lost) proves beyond doubt that Orwell later cannibalized it to write his better-known essays on tramps: *The Spike* and *Down and Out in Paris and London.* This, again, induces us to believe that the latter works recount experiences which took place in 1927 and not in 1930-31. (GDB)

Owen. 8296. Breen, Jennifer. "Wilfred Owen:'Greater Love' and Late Romanticism." *ELT* 17:173-83.
In his early poetry Wilfred Owen often adopted the subjects and techniques of late Romantic poets such as Coventry Patmore, Swinburne, and Wilde. After his initial period as a front-line officer in France during World War I, he began to compose original poems which transcended the language and attitudes of late Romanticism. Previous critics have not noticed that in two of his important pieces—"Greater Love" (1918) and "Cramped in that Funnelled Hole" (1917)—Owen parodied Swinburne's "Before the Mirror" (1866) and Tennyson's "The Charge of the Light Brigade" (1854) respectively. He thus evoked the actuality of modern warfare and also exposed, by ironic mockery, several inadequate aspects of late Romantic culture. (JB)

Paget. 8303. Cary, Richard. "A Slight Case of Plagiary, Part I:Berenson, Paget and Anstruther-Thomson." *CLQ* 10:303-24.
Following publication of their two-part essay on "Beauty and Ugliness" in the *Contemporary Review* (1897), Lee and Anstruther-Thomson were accused of plagiarism by Berenson, who claimed they had extracted their concepts from talks with him about his theory of "tactile values" and instructive visits to galleries with him. The two outraged women immediately repudiated his charge and demanded unqualified apologies. Berenson quickly withdrew from the front line, leaving Mary Costelloe to defend his position. The voluminous correspondence, debating point for point in the controversy, is here reproduced. (RC)
8304. —— "A Slight Case of Plagiary, Part II:Rainfall on the Perimeter." *CLQ* 10:442-61.
Part I of this essay, in the March 1974 issue of *CLQ*, recounts the outraged reactions of Vernon Lee (Violet Paget) and Clementina Anstruther-Thomson and their demands for an apology from Bernard Berenson for his accusation of plagiarism in their theory expressed in "Beauty and Ugliness," *Contemporary Review*, 72 (Oct.-Nov. 1897). This sequel traces the ramifications and repercussions of their argument to the further reaches of their

social and intellectual cliques in England, France, and Italy. Quotation and documentation is predominantly from hitherto unpublished letters and memoirs in the Colby College collection. (RC)

Peake. 8307. Rome, Joy J. "Twentieth-Century Gothic: Peake's *Gormenghast.*" *UES* 12,i:42-54.
In his *Gormenghast Triology* Peake emphasizes the grotesque and the menacing, blending wonder, mirth, horror, and repellent neurosis. The main device for setting the mood of *Titus Groan* (1946) is the stranglehold of tradition and meaningless ritual. *Gormenghast* (1950) sustains the dimension of magic while focusing on seemingly disparate elements: a satire on education, a burlesque of the Romance genre itself, and the extermination of the evil rebel. *Titus Alone* (1959) sees the hero forsaking the sterility of the old established world for the scientific, industrialized, totalitarian state. (JJR)

Pinter. 8320. Dukore, Bernard F. "The Pinter Collection." *ETJ* 7:81-85.
The title of Harold Pinter's play *The Collection* refers to a dress designers' collection at Leeds, where two of the characters may have committed adultery; it also refers to what the spectator sees and hears on the stage. The play's four characters are mixed to form six matching couples. The couple who know whether adultery occurred are the only couple not appearing onstage. Pinter's refusal to write a scene between them is a dramatic stratagem rather than a dramatic deficiency, for the dramatic issue is not the truth about what happened at Leeds, but the question of how one character, through knowledge, may dominate and control another. (BFD)
8332. Tener, Robert L. "Uncertainty as a Dramatic Formula." *HAB* 24(1973):175-82.
Pinter shows that everyday language communicates indirectly man's primitive and biological impulses and his narrow view of reality. Human behavior, propelled more by impulse than by reason, is not consistent with the linguistic labels applied to reality. Pinter develops this inconsistency in *The Lover, The Homecoming, The Caretaker* by creating a dramatic determination anchored in man's primitive impulses, sense of relationships, and fear of the unknown. Man's linguistic internalization of his responses to his environment Pinter relates to a room which releases man's inner self. In the three plays Pinter develops a dramatic formula by relating the ambiguity derived from the biological and primitive self with a middle or lower social class perception of reality. In *The Lover* multiple definitions of male-female relationships occur with no category being fixed. In *The Homecoming* man's desire to be fixed opposes his always becoming. The language Ruth uses enables her to fracture her fixed existence. In *The Caretaker* the room frees Aston's and Davie's inner selves and sets them in conflict with each other. Thus the plays reveal a quest for identity and the mythologies of reality man fears. (RLT)

Richardson, D. 8354. Rose, Shirley. "Dorothy Richardson's Focus on Time." *ELT* 17:163-72.
Dorothy Richardson's concern with time as a modern "problem" is reflected particularly in a series of occasional essays written for an obscure magazine *Focus*, as well as in *Pilgrimage*. She sees in the regular cycle of the natural world the refutation of time-as-enemy. Her view of time's movement is complemented by the stability of the essential in man and nature. Time, therefore, is not an erosion but rather an accretion or harvest of life. (SR)

Russell, B. 8356. Montgomery, Marion. "Lord Russell and Madame Sesostris." *GaR* 28:269-82. [R, Eliot, and Huxley.]
In *Antic Hay* (1921), Aldous Huxley satirizes the London literary social world of Lady Ottoline Morrell, frequented by such notables as Huxley, Lawrence, Woolf, Eliot, and Russell, who introduced Eliot to it. *Antic Hay* makes more substantial for Eliot's reader the milieux in which he wrote *The Waste Land.* Mr. Scogan (Russell) would coldly reduce people to integers of force, useful to superior "Directing Intelligences" who are to fashion the future, though he sees "no ultimate point of existence." Scogan

participates in his hosts' charity fair, telling romantic lies to dull peasants, disguised as "Sesostris, Sorceress of Ecbatana." The young poet Denis Stone, a Prufrock, puzzles the weekend world, his principal concern the one Eliot long struggles with: whether the world outside individual awareness can be touched at all. Denis discovers that "The individual . . . is not a self-supporting universe," nor are the consequences avoidable by taking "a very good train at 3:27." Denis's uneasy relationship with Scogan and the aimless intellectual world of London carry strains more somberly echoed in Eliot's "Game of Chess," where we meet Eliot's Sosostris. (MM)

Shaffer, A. 8367. Glenn, Jules. "Anthony and Peter Shaffer's Plays:The Influence of Twinship on Creativity." *AI* 31:270-92. The protagonists of many plays by the twin playwrights Anthony and Peter Shaffer manifest the personality traits of twins even though these characters are not twins. Analysis of Peter Shaffer's *Equus, White Lies, The White Liars,* and *The Public Eye* confirms this observation. Examination of the characteristics of twins shows their influence on the authors' creativity. The presence of disguised twins in plays can appeal to the audience and enhance the esthetic experience. (JG)

Shaw, G.B. 8372. Berst, Charles A. "The Craft of *Candida.*" *CollL* 1:157-73. Critics have contended that Shaw is overly intellectual as a dramatist, his genre is the play of ideas, his characters are Shavian mouthpieces, his structures are loose, and his dialogue is verbose and undisciplined. A close analysis of *Candida* reveals contrary evidence: in this play emotions and characterization are far more important than ideas, the characters are complex individuals greatly removed from Shaw, the structure is extremely tight, and the dialogue is dramatic and economical. (CAB)

8387. Hugo, Leon H. *"The Doctor's Dilemma* at the Court Theatre." *UES* 10,ii(1972):29-33. *The Doctor's Dilemma* was the eighth of eleven plays by George Bernard Shaw produced by the Vedrenne-Barker management at the Royal Court Theatre, London, in the 1904-07 seasons. Contemporaty letters and newspaper articles indicate that Shaw publicized his "quarrel" with William Archer about Shaw's ability to write a deathbed scene. Other letters indicate Shaw's concern about the cost of the production. Shaw was extremely busy: for example, his duel with H. G. Wells about the management of the Fabian Society took place at this time. Shaw's notebooks reveal that about a week before production there was a quarrel with the *Daily Express* about the premature disclosure of the plot of the play. Newspaper notices of the play were mixed; however, the public liked it. (LHH)

8388. Kelley, Nora. "A Sketch of the Real Lucy Shaw." *Independent Shavian* 8:12. Although Shaw's biographers agree that Shaw himself was an unreliable source for a true picture of the members of his own family, they have accepted his portrayal of his oldest sister, Lucy. His own letters, those of Lucy, Mrs. Pat Campbell, and other mutual friends indicate a woman more in the mold of Shaw's fictional heroines. Born in 1853, she shared Shaw's early life until she left for London with her mother in 1872. She commented often on her brother's work, praised his generosity to her and repeatedly referred to his concern for her health. He was with her when she died. Thirty years later, he honored her memory by a bequest to her devoted nurse. (NMK)

8395. Mason, Michael. *"Caesar and Cleopatra:*A Shavian Exercise in Both Hero-Worship and Belittlement." *HAB* 25:1-10. Caesar is Shaw's idea of the political genius, Cleopatra his epitome of political viciousness. A supreme realist, Caesar combines the qualities of brute, woman, and god. This concept implies the rejection of masculine idealism, but stresses Caesar's grasp on reality. Under his tutelage Cleopatra matures, retaining, however, all the weaknesses of a cruel and limited nature, which will lead to her downfall with Antony. The corruption of Cleopatra's Court and her parasitism on Caesar are apparent everywhere. Shaw distorts history. In glorifying Caesar he has debased Cleopatra to a level beneath contempt. (MAM)

8400. Nickson, Richard. "G.B.S. Versus U.S.A." *Independent Shavian* 13:13. Bernard Shaw's opinions and practices run so contrary to those of Americans in general that it comes as a surprise to find an argument by a Supreme Court Justice (William Douglas) to be thoroughly Shavian. But the bulk of our population continues its wasteful beefeating habits—spreading them throughout the world—at the cost of widespread malnutrition and starvation, flying in the face of the vegetarianism of Shaw. Clive Barnes, drama reviewer of *The New York Times,* has long compounded the difficulty of mounting a Shaw production on Broadway; and the MLA membership survey and the 1972 *MLA International Bibliography* reflect a corresponding diminution of attention to the works of Shaw. (RN)

Sillitoe. 8422. Nardella, Anna R. "The Existential Dilemmas of Alan Sillitoe's Working-Class Heroes." *SNNTS* 5(1973):469-82. The central characters of Sillitoe's fiction attempt to define themselves as being in a post-Kantian universe where life and identity are constantly threatened by both personal and impersonal forces. Arthur Seaton of *Saturday Night and Sunday Morning* fights the forces of dehumanization by drinking heavily, having affairs with married women, and longing to retreat into nature. Frank Dawley of *The Death of William Posters* flees his boring job and chaotic family life to become in *A Tree on Fire,* a Marxist committed to social action. The Marxist philosophy that permeates the two latter works is a logical progression from *Saturday Night and Sunday Morning:* an outgrowth of an existential view of the universe where man must now try some action to change or better the world. (ARN)

Synge. 8450. Gutierrez, Donald. "Coming of Age in Mayo: Synge's *The Playboy of the Western World* as a Rite of Passage." *HSL* 6:159-66. Synge's *The Playboy of the Western World* evinces modernist literary qualities when viewed as an ironic initiation passage ritual. The male conflicts in the play invert the coming-of-age ritualism of initiand, initiator, and community in such a manner as to dethrone the father-"initiator," deride the community (Mayo village), and base the protagonist Christopher Mahon's maturation on his confrontation with, and alienation from, society. This ironic reversal of initiation roles is intensified into satire by the community romantically idolizing Christy for being a parricide. The disillusionment of the community with the romance of patricide culminates in Christy's exposure to the ordeal of communal scorn and retribution. By presenting Christy's domination over his father under the stress of public hostility, Synge effects an ironic ritual activity which undermines the authority of society to guide youth into adulthood. The implication emerges that in modern society maturity is consolidated despite rather than with the support of society. (DG)

8458. Solomon, Albert J. "The Bird Girls of Ireland." *CLQ* 10:269-74. The Inishmaan girls in J.M. Synge's *The Aran Islands* (1907) are frequently suggested as a direct literary prototype for James Joyce's wading-girl in *A Portrait of the Artist as a Young Man* (1916). George Moore's use of a similar situation in *Hail and Farewell: Salve* (1912) suggests that he too should be considered in the progression of the image. The girl represents a particular vision of life and art for each artist. As the vision grows in complexity from Synge to Moore to Joyce, the respective images grow in subtlety and intricacy—culminating in Joyce's masterful description of the representative of secular beauty. (AJS)

Thomas, D. 8464. Gates, Barbara T. "Thomas' 'In My Craft or Sullen Art'." *Expl* 32:Item 68. The poet-narrator of Dylan Thomas' "In my craft or sullen art" makes associations between lunacy, love, and poetry that recall Theseus' speech in Act V of *A Midsummer Night's Dream.* Exercising his art under a moon that "rages" and suggests the poet's own connection with lunacy, the narrator claims to write only for the "common wages" of lover's hearts. He assumes, as does Theseus, that the imaginations of lovers are akin to those of poets and thus sees lovers as a fit audience for his art. Later, however, his references to the "proud" man who stands apart from the "raging" moon of lunacy, and to the "towering" dead as well, emphasize those for whom the poet does not write. If one bears Theseus' tone in mind, as well as the apparent sincerity of Thomas' narrator, the irony of the conclusion to "In my craft" is subtly reinforced. (BTG)

8467. Page, Christopher. "Dylan and the Scissormen." *AWR* 24,lii:76-81.
Memories of Christmas and *Return Journey* attest to Thomas' acquaintance with *Struwwelpeter*, a book of nursery rhymes first published in the 19th century, with text illustrations last revised in the first decade of the 20th. He recalls a particular illustration in *Memories of Christmas*: a horrific tailor severing the thumbs of a screaming child with a gigantic pair of scissors. The notebook poems contain a number of images in which scissors mutilate flesh. The standard themes—death, sex, destruction, etc.—are involved. Various poems published in Thomas' lifetime contain unmistakeable allusions to the scissorman. The savage and vindictive figure becomes a felicitous personification of violent themes. A short story, "School for Witches," centers upon the scissorman who has become a tinker and mender of blades. Sexual sadism, mutilation, brutality, and heavily charged, turbulent symbolism characterize the work. These usages attest to the influence of the mental world of Thomas' childhood upon the writings of his adolescence and maturity. (CCP)

8468. Sunderman, Paula. "Dylan Thomas' 'A Refusal to Mourn':A Syntactic and Semantic Interpretation." *Lang&S* 7:20-35.
Some critics stress that Dylan Thomas' poem "A Refusal to Mourn" reflects Thomas' concern with the Christian theme of immortality, while others claim it concentrates solely upon a paganistic regeneration. The most promising approach to the meaning of the poem is through an analysis of the inter-relationship of syntax and semantics. Two models, those of Levin and Hill, were used to analyze the poem's linguistic features, the interrelationship of linguistic and extralinguistic features, and the relation of the poem to its cultural matrix. The results show, first, that an analysis of the poem's linguistic features can resolve its structural ambiguity. Second, the interrelated pattern of syntax and semantics explicitly relates the poem to its cultural milieu of classical and Judeo-Christian tradition; and, third, this pattern clearly demonstrates the poem's central theme: Thomas' Christian affirmation of immortality. (PWS)

Tolkien. 8474. Nored, Gary. "*The Lord of the Rings*—A Textual Inquiry." *PBSA* 68:71-74.
Certain features of a "new" oversized edition of Tolkien's *The Lord of the Rings* lead one to suspect that this edition is not altogether new. Firstly, type font, batter, and other details are the same in both editions. Secondly, a mail order form is duplicated in both editions, even though the price quoted is incorrect for the large edition. Finally, a diagonal rule test gives negative indications of change between the editions. The large edition appears to be a photo-enlargement of the small one, the text of which is derived from Houghton Mifflin's revised second edition (c. 1965). Nonetheless, this is not the latest text; in fact, in 1966 Allen and Unwin also issued a second edition. Collation of the Allen and Unwin second edition with Houghton Mifflin's second reveals extensive authorial emendation. Therefore, the reader seriously interested in examining Tolkien's latest text will do well to obtain that of Allen and Unwin. (GVN)

Waugh, E. 8481. Blayac, Alain. "The Evelyn Waugh-Dudley Carew Correspondence at the Humanities Research Center, University of Texas, Austin." *EWN* 8,ii:1-6.
Catalogs and analyzes the Carew-Waugh material at the University of Texas. Each Waugh letter to Carew is summarized. The letters reveal Waugh as boy-leader at Lancing and Oxford, as energetic thinker engaged in diverse activities, and as self-assured and confident. They demonstrate a pugnacity and self-assurance which conflict sharply with the anguish and doubts expressed in his personal diaries. (PAD)

8484. Duer, Harriet W. "Pinfold's Pinfold." *EWN* 8,i:3-6.
Pinfold literally means a place to confine animals. Waugh's use of

it in *The Ordeal of Gilbert Pinfold* explains the book's meaning. At the beginning Pinfold is imprisoned by voices, and his ill body has trapped his soul. His ultimate victory is one of soul over body analyzed in secular terms. Angel and the Hooligans have used language to close in the hero, but he fights back using language as his weapon. The voices finally disappear when he receives two enlightened analyses. Pinfold's belief in the voices was not a medical problem, but a sickness of the soul. (HWD)

8486. Greene, Donald. "Sir Ralph Brompton—An Identi-fication." *EWN* 8,iii:1-2.
In *Unconditional Surrender*, the last volume of the *Sword of Honour* trilogy, the character of Sir Ralph Brompton appears. Elegant and sinister, Brompton holds a governmental office and exerts considerable power behind the scenes. He appears several times in the novel and propagates leftist views. The recent publication of Nicolson's *Portrait of a Marriage* confirms that Brompton is a portrait of Sir Harold Nicolson. Both Brompton and Nicolson began as diplomats, had careers as men of letters, were active in politics, and were homosexuals. (PAD)

8487. Heath, Jeffrey M. "Apthorpe Placatus?" *ArielE* 5,i:5-24. [On *Men at Arms* and *The Ordeal of Gilbert Pinfold*.]
Examines the country house, the double, and the comic macabre which shape Waugh's fiction. By means of the house motif Waugh establishes an antithesis between the City of God and the counterfeit City of Man. The protagonist who wishes to escape from the condition of a cartoon in the fraudulent city must first recognize and then destroy what is fraudulent in himself. If a Waugh hero tries to escape without taking significant moral action, a pernicious double tightens its grip and intensifies the hero's anguish. The comic macabre punishes those who are fraudulent, clarifies blurred moral distinctions, and paves the way for right action. (JMH)

8488. ———. "*Vile Bodies*:A Revolution in Film Art." *EWN* 8,iii:2-9.
Vile Bodies uses many cinematic techniques. The force of such use is metaphoric. *Vile Bodies* is organized around a life film of John Wesley by a British Company, Wonderfilm. The company deals with stories of English history in which lesser imitators have succeeded Catholicism. Wesley's Methodism represents a feebler duplicate, while Mr. Isaacs of Wonderfilm is the archetypal exploiter of religion. Waugh looks upon the later history of England as a film of imitative cycles in which the Reformation became the Anglican Revolt. *Vile Bodies* blends its theme —conversion—with the operative metaphor—cinematic inver-sion. (PAD)

8489. Johnson, Joseph J. "Counterparts:The Classic and the Modern 'Pervigilium Veneris'." *EWN* 8,iii:7-8.
The structurally central chapter in *Decline and Fall* is called "Pervigilium Veneris." It is a satirical transformation of the anonymous Latin classic of the same title. Margot's weekend party finds her, like her ancient counterpart Venus, sleeping for three nights. Lord Parakeet is a modern Bacchus while Peter Best-Chetwynde is Cupid. Margot's reappearance closely parallels Venus's arrival as nature blooms. Both the chapter and the Latin poem are composed of corresponding bird and animal imagery. The cyclical nature of Waugh's controlling metaphor reinforces his modernized and sterilized version of the seasonal cycle of change which ends the classic poem. (PAD)

Wells. 8499. Ingle, Stephen J. "The Political Writing of H.G. Wells." *QQ* 81:396-411.
H.G. Wells is not taken seriously today as a social-political thinker. Though what he had to say was unquestionably relevant for his contemporaries, many critics have dismissed him as being irrelevant in the modern context. Wells was an outstanding social critic and his early imaginative writings such as *The Time Machine, The War of the Worlds, The History of Mr. Polly*, and *Tono Bungay* provided a perfect vehicle for what he wanted to say. Wells forsook these imaginative works and began to concentrate on rather lifeless novels with an obvious political "message" and on encyclopedic historical and biological texts. If we examine Wells's message rather than the media he chose to develop it, we find a body of social criticism and advanced political thought on subjects as relevant as multi-national

companies, pollution, birth control, and nuclear weaponry. (IJS)

Woolf, V. 8523. Deiman, Werner J. "History, Pattern, and Continuity in Virginia Woolf." *ConL* 15:49-66.
Virginia Woolf's historical perspective is discussed in *A Writer's Diary* and the novels *The Voyage Out, Night and Day, Jacob's Room, Mrs. Dalloway, The Waves,* and *The Years,* as well as in *A Room of One's Own* and "A Letter to a Young Poet," where both literary and personal continuity are emphasized. Different characters are emblematic of history or as questers after historical pattern and vision. An extended analysis is devoted to *Between the Acts,* which represents the culmination of the historical theme. A parallel in theme and vision connects the novel to "Thoughts on Peace in an Air Raid," also written during the Battle of Britain, and the undated essay "Evening over Sussex: Reflections in a Motor Car." Woolf's historical consciousness became the springboard for belief even in the face of absurdities of war, insanity, and suicide, and her perceptions of patterns of history offered a kind of redemption from time and affirmed a continuum into the future. (WJD)

8542. Quick, Jonathan R. "The Shattered Moment:Form and Crisis in *Mrs. Dalloway* and *Between the Acts.*" *Mosaic* 7,iii:127-36.
Form and meaning in Woolf's *Mrs. Dalloway* display an interdependence that is unusually crucial. The logic of her use of expressive form is that, since a full, stable consciousness of the unity of experience is always elusive, the form which labors to express that consciousness and its imparted meaning constantly faces disintegration. Committed to this formal principle, Woolf could in no way isolate problems of formal unity from crises of meaning. Her deliberate subjection of both fictive elements to the same rigorous test marks the uniqueness of her novels in the experimental fiction of the 1920s. Examination of Woolf's fragmentation of her narrative through repeated disruptions of spatial and temporal relationships demonstrates why her chief preoccupation—the deterioration of human communities—required this rigorous association of form and meaning. (JRQ)

8543. Richardson, Betty. "Beleaguered Bloomsbury:Virginia Woolf, Her Friends, and Their Critics." *PLL* 10:207-21. [Rev. art.]
Recent writings on Virginia Woolf and the Bloomsbury Group are examined. Criticism of Woolf ranges from commentary in feminist writings, for which she is a pop cult figure, to traditional critical works in which her stream of consciousness and linguistic techniques are re-examined. New work by Lytton Strachey has been published, as has a volume of E.M. Forster's short stories, primarily homosexual in orientation. A complete edition of Bertrand Russell's fiction is available, as are the writings of Dora Carrington; both are peripheral to Bloomsbury. Some new biography has appeared, and a single work provides intellectual background to Woolf's writings, although, as yet, not enough attention has been paid to Bloomsbury as part of a larger intellectual climate in the early decades of this century. (BR)

8546. Rubenstein, Roberta. "Virginia Woolf, Chekhov, and *The Rape of the Lock.*" *DR* 54:429-35.
Woolf's admiration of Russian writers appears in several of her major essays and in a curious unpublished MS review of a new edition of Pope's *Rape of the Lock.* The unlikely juxtaposition of Russian literature and Pope can be explained by Woolf's literary preference for the complexities of the soul over the frivolities of the dressing table. The contrast developed between the two reveals Woolf's characteristic critical method of viewing one work against another and the opportunity to trace her own "stream of consciousness" associations as she moves from the "Russian mist" to the large virtues of Russian hearts, to the contrasting smallness of Pope's imagined world, to the pettiness of Pope's personality. Adjusting her focus, she attempts to identify the virtues of *The Rape of the Lock,* but her lack of sympathy toward Pope and his "diseased soul" (an attitude repeated in *Orlando*) and her susceptibility to the Russian mood interferes with critical objectivity. The review concludes with Woolf's ambivalent recognition of the English tendency to distort the judgment of their literature by exalting and exaggerating the virtues of Russian writers and their works. (RR)

8549. Shields, E.F. "The American Edition of *Mrs. Dalloway.*" *SB* 27:157-75.
A collation of the American and the English editions of Woolf's *Mrs. Dalloway* two first editions reveals numerous variants. On its own request, Harcourt printed the American edition from a special set of English page proofs which had been revised by Woolf. An examination of the revised page proofs shows that Harcourt attempted to follow Woolf's directions. On its own authority, Harcourt at times changed the punctuation, principally in cases involving the use of the ellipsis mark and the use of quotation marks with a comma or period; Harcourt also accidentally omitted three section divisions. The overwhelming majority of variants originated, however, with Woolf herself. (EFS)

8551. Snow, Lotus. "The Heat of the Sun:The Double in Mrs. Dalloway." *RS* 41(1973):75-83.
In her Introduction to the Modern Library edition of *Mrs. Dalloway,* Virginia Woolf comments that in the first version of the novel Clarissa Dalloway had no double: Septimus Warren Smith did not exist. After briefly reviewing the history of the double in literature, an attempt is made to explain why Woolf provided Mrs. Dalloway with a double. The method employed is analysis of the recurrent imagery, both structural and integral, uniting Clarissa and Septimus. Structural images are those of time and space by which Woolf creates not only the framework of the novel but also the conditions of human existence, continuity and flux. Integral images are those which demonstrate the oneness of Clarissa Dalloway and Septimus Warren Smith despite their divergent circumstances and choices. For the former Woolf appears to be indebted to Roger Fry, as quotations from his theories of the source of the esthetic emotion demonstrate. The integral images portray the single identity of the two characters in their responses to life and to death. (LAS)

Yeats, W.B. 8559. Allen, James L. "Charts for the Voyage to Byzantium:An Annotated Bibliography of Scholarship and Criticism on Yeats' Byzantium Poems, 1935-1970." *BNYPL* 77(1973):28-50.
The mass of secondary material on Yeats's Byzantium poems makes necessary a guide and directory. A major controversy in much of the critical material on the poems is whether purification of the soul or the creation of art is symbolized. Better analyses suggest that both levels of interpretation can obtain simultaneously. These and other published points of exegesis and evaluation are surveyed in this annotated bibliography of 132 entries. (JLA)

8561. ——. "Unity of Archetype, Myth, and Religious Imagery in the Work of Yeats." *TCL* 20:91-95.
A single mythic pattern pervades Yeats's work, the quest for or the achievement of union between man and God. Although this pattern occurs in the poems, plays, and prose in numerous versions, almost all of them can be seen as variants of the universal "monomyth," the archetypal journey motif. (JLA)

8572. Dalsimer, Adele M. "Yeats's Unchanging Swift." *Éire* 9,ii:65-89.
Although in the early years of his creative life, Yeats held Georgian Ireland and its chief spokesmen in low regard, in 1896 he read and reviewed favorably Richard Ashe King's *Swift in Ireland.* This work, published in the New Irish Library series, so impressed Yeats that it provided the image of Swift that appeared in Yeats's writing thirty years later. King's image of Swift as a prophet unheeded in his time, tormented and maddened by the political scene around him, was one with which Yeats was readily able to identify. Furthermore, Yeats found Swift's political thought extremely congenial to the contemporary Irish scene, and saw sufficient personal similiarities between himself and King's portrayal of Swift to use King's Swift as a symbol of his own position in modern Ireland. The Swift that appears in such poems as "Blood and the Moon," "The Seven Sages," "Parnell's Funeral" and the play *The Words Upon the Window-Pane* is based on the portrait of Swift that Yeats found 30 years earlier in King's biography; at the same time the image suggests Yeats's own position in Ireland in the early 20th century. (AMD)

8575. Estrin, Barbara L. "Alternating Personae in Yeats'

'Lapis Lazuli' and 'Crazy Jane on the Mountain'." *Criticism* 16:13-22.

"Lapis Lazuli" has been a pivotal poem for a critical attack on the *Last Poems* and on Yeats himself. A common assumption of the negatively oriented critics is that the speaker in the poems is the poet. Another, and more useful, approach to the concluding works is to suppose that the speaker in each of the poems represents simply a poetic persona adopted by Yeats to reflect one aspect of his multiple vision. The active and exhilarated persona of "Lapis Lazuli" can be contrasted to the passive and somewhat defeated persona of "Crazy Jane on the Mountain," neither voice representing the completed picture. While "Lapis Lazuli" presents a demonic longing for destruction and an exultation in death, "Crazy Jane on the Mountain" laments the shortness of human duration. In "Lapis Lazuli" the speaker emerges the androgynous creator of his opus, while in "Crazy Jane on the Mountain," the persona acknowledges the limitations of her own, merely human, power. The personae in both poems present aspects of the movements toward Life and Death outlined in Yeats' *Vision*. (BLE)

8585. Hirschberg, Stuart. "Why Yeats Saw Himself as a 'Daimonic Man' of Phase 17: A Complementary View." *ELN* 11:202-05.

Studies of the sources and structure of Yeats's "system" have overlooked the fact that Yeats was not being arbitrary in placing himself in Phase 17 of the "Great Wheel" of personality types described in Book I of *A Vision* (1937). A comparison of Yeats's natal horoscope with the system of representation delineated in *A Vision* reveals the fact that Yeats chose Phase 17 because it corresponded to the geometrical alignment of the sun and moon within his own horoscope. (SH)

8586. —— "Yeats and the Meditative Poem." *Éire* 9,iv:94-101.

"Meditations in Time of Civil War" is the title given to a series of seven poems that Yeats wrote at Thoor Ballylee, his "ancient tower," during the summer of 1922 while civil war was raging in Ireland. Traditionally, the discipline of meditation encompasses a three-fold process in which a problem is evoked by the memory, explored by the intellect, and finally transcended by the will. Within the sequence Yeats adopted the format of the meditative exercise in an attempt to resolve the conflict between his private ideals and the public and political concerns that arose as a consequence of the civil insurrection then being waged between Republicans and Free Staters. (SH)

8587. —— "Yeats' 'The Phases of the Moon,' 118-123." *Expl* 32:Item 75.

The involuted syntax of Robartes' description of the three last phases of the Great Wheel in W.B. Yeats's "The Phases of the Moon" can be understood to mean that just as Phase Fifteen offered an escape between Phases Fourteen and Sixteen so the way of the Saint (Phase Twenty-Seven) offers an escape of self-renunciation midway between the Hunchback and Fool. (SH)

8589. Holberg, Stanley M. " 'Sailing to Byzantium': A New Source and a New Reading." *ELN* 12:111-16. ["The Story of Conn-eda; Or the Golden Apples of Lough Erne."]

A partial source of the golden bird in Yeats's "Sailing to Byzantium" may be the bird in "The Story of Conn-eda; Or the Golden Apples of Lough Erne" in *Fairy and Folk Tales of the Irish Peasantry*, edited by Yeats in 1888. The connection between the two birds suggests a significant distinction between the triviality of the form of the artificial bird and the importance of its song. The speaker chooses this *objet* as the form of his next incarnation because he wants this form to be removed as far as possible from involvement in living, thus dying. Still, he wants to have the power to sing of the time-bound and the timeless. (SMH)

8591. Huberman, Elizabeth. "To Byzantium Once More: A Study of the Structure of Yeats's 'Byzantium'." *ELWIU* 1:193-205.

Although a number of critics have questioned the logical order of the stanzas in Yeats's "Byzantium," comparison with earlier and later poems, study of earlier drafts, and close analysis of the emotional, rhetorical, and musical development of the poem demonstrate that the final structure is both inevitable and convincing. Like so many of Yeats's poems, this one is

ambiguous; it vacillates between the real and the ideal. But under the ambiguity, as indicated, for example, by the increased chill of the Byzantium setting, when compared to that in "Sailing to Byzantium," or by the parallels between the spirits' dance in the fourth stanza and the process of "dreaming back" described in *A Vision*, there is a definite disillusion with the ideal and a withdrawal from it, until the movement from the ideal becomes, in the pivotal fourth stanza, a decisive turn toward the real, the "fury and the mire of human veins." (ELH)

8594. John, Brian. " 'To Hunger Fiercely after Truth': Daimonic Man and Yeats's Insatiable Appetite." *Éire* 9,i:90-103.

By "Daimonic man" W.B. Yeats means that self most aware of the tragedy of existence and, therefore, also most capable of completeness. Consummation of self depends upon frustrated desire, hungry appetite, defeated action: the discipline of the Mask. The imagery of appetite is crucial and its multifariousness reflects the change in Yeats's style and vision: the images of apples, bread, bitter crust, and hollow cheek prove most significant. Yeats found similar images and principles in Dante, Carlyle, William Morris, and folklore, bringing all together in a mythic pattern true for history and for individual men. The image of the consuming and consumed heart is central. Yeats's acceptance of this vision's necessity makes him condemn the Irish present, "read" his own life symbolically, and affirm with Crazy Jane his fierce appetite and his inevitable hunger. The nature of Yeatsian tragedy depends upon the heart's fearful consumption leading to a corresponding joyful consummation of self. (BJ)

8595. Johnston, Dillon. "The Perpetual Self of Yeats's *Autobiographies*." *Éire* 9,iv:69-85.

Yeats's *Autobiographies* depicts his development through infancy, separation from the family, association with various groups, and self-identification. Chronology and progression of plot are obscured by several deliberate effects. First, within its four stages the plot is organized geographically or dramatically, moving between places or groups rather than from one period to the next. Secondly, sub-sections of the book often conclude with rhetorical questions, metaphorical statements, or lines from Yeats's latest poetry. Such complex terminations obscure distinctions between the autobiographer and his youthful self-versions and project an image of Yeats as a perpetual enquirer, who finds not answers but questions of a more complex nature. Ultimately, Yeats associates himself with Shelley's Ahasuerus. By ironically undercutting his ending in "Trembling of the Veil," Yeats suggests the perpetuity of his self's patterned course of seeking and finding and seeking again on a higher level. (DJ)

8599. Kuehn, Nandini P. "Yeats' 'The Indian to His Love'." *Expl* 33:Item 23.

An understanding of Yeats's use of Indian mythology is essential to grasp the full meaning of "The Indian to His Love." Reference to Kama, the Indian God of Love, were overt in early versions of lines 12 and 16 (see *The Variorum Edition*). The parrot is traditionally Kama's vehicle and thus belongs with the other references in the poem as a symbol of love. Its raging at its own image is in deliberate contrast to the serene confidence with which the lovers seek perfect love. The poem therefore implies that such perfection, while it attracts lovers, also paradoxically antagonizes them. Hence "The Indian to His Love" presents an antithesis and questions the possibility of lovers ever achieving perfect love. (NPK)

8602. Marcus, P.L. "Yeats and the Image of the Singing Head." *Éire* 9,iv:86-93.

The "old Gaelic legend" on which Yeats based his early story "The Binding of the Hair" and his dance plays *The King of the Great Clock Tower* and *A Full Moon in March* was almost certainly an incident from the Irish annals involving a royal bard named Donnbo who is slain in battle but whose severed head keeps his promise to sing for his lord. The love relationship in Yeats's story and plays was not present in this source. It seems likely, therefore, that Yeats modified the Donnbo story by blending it with incidents which happened to have a traditional Irish analogue. (PLM)

8611. Perrine, Laurence. "Yeats' 'On a Political Prisoner,' 19-24." *Expl* 32:Item 64.

The ambiguous lines 20-22 of Yeats's "On a Political Prisoner" should be construed to read that the bird sprang out of the nest on a lofty rock to stare at the cloudy canopy. (LP)

8628. Vanderwerken, David L. "*Purgatory*:Yeats's Modern Tragedy." *CLQ* 10:259-69.

Yeats's structural method in *Purgatory* provides the key for understanding the play's modernity. By reworking traditional materials and by undercutting conventional expectations, Yeats partially redefines tragedy for 20th-century man. The two protagonists, the physical and historical environment, and the nature of the tragic situation reflect Yeats's attempt to reorient our understanding of tragedy. In particular, *Purgatory* comments on the development of two traditional elements of tragedy: the source of absolutes and the nature of tragic recognition. (DLV)

8632. Wheeler, Richard P. "Yeats' 'Second Coming':What Rough Beast?" *AI* 31:233-51.

The historical reality that Yeats imagines in "The Second Coming" is significantly shaped by an unconscious inner reality of fears, longings, and defenses. The power that readers have found in the poem is tied to inner conflicts and ways of mastering them. The cultural powerlessness and disintegration presented in the first stanza builds psychologically on an overwhelmed infant's helplessness in situations of traumatic magnitude. Other defenses against helplessness are made available which promise a kind of mastery. (RPW)

Young, A. 8638. Maxwell-Mahon, William D. "Andrew Young:The Man and His Work." *UES* 9,iv(1971):1-4.

Andrew John Young drew upon childhood memories of Dalmeny, an estate outside Edinburgh, for such topographical works as *A Prospect of Flowers* (1945), *A Prospect of Britain* (1956), and *The Poet and the Landscape* (1962). While studying at Edinburgh University, Young wrote *Songs of Night*. Although he dismisses this work as juvenilia, it is evidence of natural poetical talent. Between 1920 and 1931, Young had seven small books of verse published. He was recognized by the literary world only after the appearance of *Winter Harvest* in 1933—for which he received the Benson Medal for poetry. Young's verse is traditional in form; in theme and subject it is devotional and pastoral, reflecting his religious calling and love of nature. The influence of Young's religious calling is most apparent in two works: *Nicodemus* (1937) and *Out of the World and Back* (1952-58). The pastoral element in his verse can be seen in "On the Pilgrims' Road," "In December," "The Dead Crab," and "The Dead Mole." (WDMM)

AMERICAN LITERATURE†

I. GENERAL

General and Miscellaneous. 8641. Arrington, Leonard. "Mormonism:Views from Without and Within." *BYUS* 14:140-53.

The conflict between Mormon and anti-Mormon ideals produced three basic changes in the image of Mormonism in literature. The first image of Mormonism arose from the debate over the integrity of Joseph Smith. Mormons won this first image-battle. During the days of isolation in the Great Basin, Mormon pioneers, preoccupied with subduing a hostile environment and temporarily forgetful of the value in using literary means to express religious truths, lacked literary aggressiveness and failed to counteract the massive amounts of stereotyped propaganda produced by anti-Mormon writers. Hence non-Mormons won the literary battle, and the national image of Mormonism became that of an emotional, fanatical, and dictatorial religion. Beginning in the 1930's, however, production of a vast quantity of imaginative literature by Mormons themselves helped significantly to reverse the negative image of earlier years, exemplifying again the power of the artistic and imaginative arts in winning sympathy for a cause. (LA)

8645. Banta, Martha. "American Apocalypses:Excrement and Ennui." *SLitI* 7,i:1-30. [Emerson, Poe, N. West, Crèvecoeur, Mailer, *inter alia*.]

The image of America as the destined site for the Apocalypse permeates the writings of Nathaniel Ward, de Crèvecoeur, Emerson, Thoreau, Poe, Twain, Adams, and Mailer. Redefinitions given the mind's scope by William James help join the apocalyptic imagination and the belief in America's cosmic role with a gothic vision of existence. For some writers, external historical events and subjective responses to the American context promise the future fulfillment of a perfect plan master-minded by a gothic god or the Transcendentalist All-Soul. For others, fear of matter or boredom may result in the tragic annihilation of human existence. (MB)

8651. Broderick, John C.,et al. "Recent Acquisitions of the Manuscript Division." *QJLC* 30(1973):295-337. [Incl. letters of Marian MacDowell and MSS of a number of Amer. lit. figures.]

Personal papers and literary manuscripts acquired by the Library of Congress in 1972 included additional papers of Marian (Mrs. Edward) MacDowell, founder of the MacDowell Colony. Her correspondence includes numerous letters of Edwin Arlington Robinson, Hamlin Garland, and Thornton Wilder. The Frederick Douglass papers contain few manuscripts of his early writings but several of the later ones. The Crosby N. Boyd collection included a manuscript of Samuel L. Clemens ("A New Cabinet 'Regulator'"). And the Waldo Pierce papers contain information about Ernest Hemingway and Maxwell Perkins. Other acquisitions in the fields of science, history, and politics are also listed. (JCB)

8654. Clark, William B. "The Serpent of Lust in the Southern Garden." *SoR* 10:805-22.

The "myth" of miscegenation in Southern fiction since the Civil War is analyzed. Analysis of Joel Chandler Harris' "Where's Duncan?" enables one to schematize the myth into the following motifs: (1) a narrative pattern involving guilt and retribution; (2) a tendency to identify miscegenation with the sins of slavery and racial caste in general; (3) the dual role of victim and avenger played by the mulatto character; and, (4) "the search for Self" resulting from the ambiguous racial identity of the mixed-blood character. Drawing on such primary sources as abolitionist tracts and fugitive slave narratives, the genesis of the myth is treated and its recurrence in important Southern writing up to the present is traced. (WBC)

8658. Cooke, Gwendolyn J. "How Students Feel about Black Literature." *NALF* 8:293-95.

Sixteen classes of senior high school students filled out a questionnaire after reading two units utilizing literary works by black and white writers and after presenting creative projects. Although a majority of the experimental subjects had read black literature prior to the experimental treatment, the majority of the reading had been completed independently of school. Moreover, there was not a consistent policy in either of the English departments concerning the teaching of black literature. This study indicates that students' immediate reaction to assigned black literature is both positive and negative. However, if discussion focusing on the literary work is chaired by a sensitive and objective teacher, the immediate negative attitude of students can be changed. Some students will read black literature voluntarily after it has been introduced to them in a classroom. (HH)

8671. Hasley, Louis. "Black Humor and Gray." *ArQ* 30:317-28.

Black humor reflects disbelief in the intelligence controlling the conditions of life. It deepens the shades of blackness seen earlier in Hawthorne, Poe, Melville, and Twain. It combines humor and pessimism, employs extreme incongruities, and carries an overall sense of metaphysical disillusion and nihilism. Often the authorial detachment and playfulness necessary to literary humor is absent.

---

† *Festschriften* and Other Analyzed Collections are listed in the first division of this volume. "F" numbers in brackets following a title refer to these items.

The black humorist is inclined to blame the universe rather than rational, irrational, and non-rational behavior of man. Deep down, he reflects a hopeless dream of ideality. (LH)

8675. Inge, M. Thomas. "Richmond, Virginia, and Southern Writing." *MissQ* 27:371-73. [Introd. to spec. issue on this topic.] Examination of the extent to which the quality of life in Southern urban centers has influenced the sensibilities of their artists. In the three essays which follow, three scholars examine the importance of the city of Richmond in the careers of Glasgow and Cabell and explore their relationship to the Southern Literary Renaissance. They also suggest that there are meaningful relationships between the urban writer and his environment which merit further exploration. (MTI)

8678. Kelly, R. Gordon. "American Children's Literature:An Historiographical Review." *ALR* 6(1973):89-108. Presents an argument for the evidential significance of children's literature in the historical reconstruction of past patterns of belief. Traces the development of histories of children's literature from the late nineteenth century to the present. Surveys the most significant literary and historical scholarship which has been done on American children's literature in the generation following the Civil War and identifies possibilities for further work in the field. (GRK)

8679. ―― "Literature and the Historian." *AQ* 26:[141]-59. If literary works are to be useful to the historian, he must have a basis for construing the meaning of literary texts and specifying the social domain for which generalizations based on literary evidence may be considered valid. Both problems are clarified by adopting a concept of culture defined in terms of rules for ordering behavior. Historical meaning is culturally circumscribed, and generalizations based on literary evidence are limited by the spatial and temporal boundaries of belief systems. (RGK)

8696. Parker, Hershel, with Bruce Bebb. "The *CEAA*:An Interim Assessment." *PBSA* 68:129-48. After a survey of the organization and later history of the Center for Editions of American Authors, this review-essay focuses on volumes so far published with the Center's seal, commenting on the book design and the arrangement of editorial material in the individual editions, the nature of textual discoveries and problems which have arisen, and the contributions to biography and literary history. Final judgments are avoided, since half the completed CEAA work still awaits publication. Some of the most profound effects of the CEAA may always be immeasurable, as in what may follow from the developing of higher scholarly standards by many of the editors and their associates. (HP)

8699. Rollins, Peter C. "Film and American Studies:Questions, Activities, Guides." *AQ* 26:[245]-65. The American Historical Association, the American Studies Association, the Popular Culture Association, the MLA, the ALA have all directed attention and resources to film-related activities. As a result, new journals such as *Film and History, Journal of Popular Film, Literature/Film Quarterly* have flowered. Basic facts about this new field are provided because graduate study normally includes little or no guidance about how to approach this contemporary historical document and art form. (PCR)

8706. Spiller, Robert E. "History of a History:A Study in Co-operative Scholarship." *PMLA* 89:602-16. [On *Lit. Hist. of the U.S.* and the Amer. Lit. Group of the MLA.] The American Literature Group, MLA, was committed to a history of American literature as an expression of an evolving American culture. It developed the theory that our culture was transplanted mainly from Western Europe, but was indigenous as shaped by a moving frontier. In 1938, a committee was appointed to plan a cooperative literary history. The project then split. The

Group undertook long-term fact-finding while historical reinterpretation was taken over by 55 historians and critics. *Literary History of the United States* was first published in 1948 and is now in its fourth edition. A reconstruction of the theory and history of this unique experiment in cooperative scholarship from documents in the Universities of Pennsylvania and Wisconsin is made. (RES)

Special Bibliographies, Check Lists, and Dictionaries. 8734. Davis, Charles E., and Martha B. Hudson. "Humor of the Old Southwest:A Checklist of Criticism." *MissQ* 27:179-99. A bibliography of criticism on Southwest humor and humorists, divided into three parts: the first consists of general studies which have appeared in periodicals; the second, general studies from books; and the third, both books and articles on individual authors. (CED & MBH)

8745. Rosenberg, Roberta. "Checklist of Lewis Leary's Work." *EAL* 8:298-304. A checklist of the literary criticism, essays, and poetry written by Lewis Leary through 1973. (RR)

Afro-American. 8759. Stern, Frederick C. "Black Lit., White Crit?" *CE* 35:637-58. White critics and teachers, dealing with materials by and about black writers, are not only crossing cultural boundaries but are dealing with materials from a culture for which the white world has long been a racist, oppressive, "Other." White criticism must understand that the black world will determine its own esthetic destiny, without reference to or concern about white opinion. Nevertheless, rejecting the possibility of useful white criticism about black literature is invalid, because such a rejection denies the function of art as a means of communication. White criticism of black materials is possible, if whites will accept certain *caveats*. Furthermore, at this moment, black and white critics may have different functions. Black criticism may need to focus upon the separation of black art from the white world. White criticism, however, must find the relationships between black and white art, primarily for the sake of whites, so that we can understand and overcome our complicity in and dehumanization by our white racism. (FCS)

American Indian. 8763. Bevis, William. "American Indian Verse Translations." *CE* 35:693-703. The commercially available anthologies of American Indian verse in translation are reviewed and several of the most recent are criticized on the basis of freedom of translation and unjustified pretense to "documentary" value in their titles, covers, and formats. Several poems are compared to original oral "texts" and an argument is made for more literal translation of Indian verse. (WWB)

8765. Sayre, Robert F. "A Bibliography and an Anthology of American Indian Literature." *CE* 35:704-06. Much is to be learned about American Indians by going to long-forgotten books and journals, many of which have been reprinted. *The Indians and Eskimos of North America*, a bibliography compiled by Jack W. Marken (Dakota Press, 1973), lists nearly 3,000 works by and about Indians which were in print as of 1972. *Literature of the American Indian*, ed. Thomas E. Sanders and Walter W. Peek (Glencoe Press, 1973), is an anthology of Indian writing. It has defects but contains a great variety of material. *Seven Arrows*, by Hyemeyohsts Storm (Harper and Row, 1972), is an excellent textbook, in the form of a novel, for learning how to understand traditional Indian teachings. (RFS)

II. SEVENTEENTH AND EIGHTEENTH CENTURIES

Bibliography. 8811. Clancy, James T. "Native American References:A Cross-Indexed Bibliography of Seventeenth-Century American Imprints Pertaining to American Indians." *PAAS* 83(1973):287-341. A shortage of bibliographical guides to the American Antiquarian Society's *Early American Imprints, 1639-1800*, ed. Clifford K.

Shipton, has handicapped the full utilization of this collection. The present bibliography lists every known 17th-century book, pamphlet, and broadside published in Ameirca which has been found to refer in any way to Native Americans. The entries are cross-indexed into three main sections. The first lists in a roughly chronological order the entries which comprise the substance of the index. Within the second section the entries are organized under the Native American tribes to which they refer. The third section comprises a geographical indexing of the entries. (JTC)

8813. Harlan, Robert D. "David Hall and the Townshend Acts." *PBSA* 68:19-38.

Concludes an examination of the effects of British colonial policy and American reaction to that policy upon the career of David Hall, the Philadelphia printer, publisher, bookseller, and stationer. Hall's close identification with the colonial opposition of the Townshend Acts is in contrast to his somewhat reluctant association with the patriotic program during the Stamp Act crisis. The reasons behind his actions also differed. Political convictions dominated his behavior during the Townshend Acts crisis while financial considerations were paramount during the Stamp Act crisis. (RDH)

8815. Stern, Madeleine B. "Saint-Pierre in America:Joseph Nancrede and Isaiah Thomas." *PBSA* 68:312-25.

Joseph Nancrede (1761-1841), French-born bookseller-publisher of Boston, published between 1796 and 1797 the first American editions of the major works of Bernardin de Saint-Pierre, French philosopher-botanist-poet-artist. The project was grandiose, involving multi-volume sets, engraved illustrations, French, English, and bilingual editions. The mechanics of producing French books in American editions is illuminated in a series of 6 letters from Nancrede to his printer Isaiah Thomas of Worcester. The American publication of Saint-Pierre's writings introduced the philosophical romanticism of a distinguished French writer and thus accelerated American understanding of French thought. (MBS)

General and Miscellaneous. 8818. Beck, Leonard N. "Dominique de Blackford:Plagiarist." *PBSA* 68:427-32. [Fren. text on Amer. pub. in Italy.]

Dominique de Blackford's *Précis de l'état actuel des colonies angloises* has been described as compiled from William Douglass' *A Summary, Historical and Political, of the . . . British Settlements in North America* and Peter Kalm's *Travels.* Except for some minor interpolations, this booklet is in fact a direct plagiarism of Gottfried Achenwall's *Anmerkungen über Nordamerika und über dasige Grossbritannische Colonien aus mündlichen Nachrichten des Herrn Dr. Franklins.* (LNB)

8822. Cohen, Sheldon S. "Student Unrest in the Decade Before the American Revolution." *ConnR* 7,ii:51-58.

Surveys the nature and extent of student dissent in the 9 colonial colleges during the decade preceding the American Revolution. Collegiate manuscripts, records, and considerable secondary writings indicate that most instances of student unrest during this period involved non-political matters; but there was considerable awareness of contemporary political events on the campus and students, in several cases, were confronting their faculty in a struggle for greater personal freedom and respect. It is inferred that these confrontations influenced the young scholars in the various roles they assumed during the ensuing rebellion. (SSC)

Periodicals. 8842. Barnes, Timothy M. "Loyalist Newspapers of the American Revolution, 1763-1783." *PAAS* 83(1973):217-40.

The article examines three features of Loyalist newspapers: (1) names and dates of printers accompanied by a short biography, (2) a list of Loyalist essayists, and (3) the location of a microprint and one original copy. (TMB)

Bradford. 8852. Scheick, William J. "The Theme of Necessity in Bradford's *Of Plymouth Plantation.*" *SCN* 32:88-90.

In *Of Plymouth Plantation* Bradford frequently refers to the function of necessity in the experience of the Pilgrims. These references comprise a thematic element in the history. Increasingly Bradford realizes that his previous interpretation of necessity as manifestations of divine providence beneficially directing the colony, particularly with regard to the land decision of 1623, may have unwittingly accommodated human ambition arising from the evil necessity of innate depravity. (WJS)

Bradstreet. 8854. Eberwein, Jane D. "The 'Unrefined Ore' of Anne Bradstreet's Quaternions." *EAL* 9:19-26.

Bradstreet's quaternions provide insight into her development as a poet, both psychologically and technically. These debates among the Elements, Humours, Ages of Man, and Seasons allowed her to refresh her English education, converting facts into useful knowledge, and to experiment with various logical and rhetorical structures. By giving control to the tensions which characterized her writing—particularly the pull between emotional delight in the multiplicity of this world and intellectual assertion of its vanity, the quaternions made possible the achievement of her better known poems, written after *The Tenth Muse.* (JDE)

8855. Requa, Kenneth A. "Anne Bradstreet's Poetic Voices." *EAL* 9:3-18.

The poetic voices of Anne Bradstreet reveal the conflict between the role of the poet and what she would consider were the roles she was expected to fulfill. When she attempts to speak as a public poet in her elegies or in "The Four Monarchies," she imitates writers whom she considered great but becomes self—conscious because she feels that she is a Puritan woman intruding into the domain of men. Similarly, when she creates other public speakers, as in her Quaternions, she cannot allow them to become adequate surrogates for her own public voice. The result is that the major public poems are flawed: rather than well—made conclusions, she provides only abrupt halts, in which she confesses her inadequacy to fulfill the role of public poet. On the other hand, the private poems are so close to what she considered were her true vocations of housewife and mother that she is not self-conscious as poetic speaker, is not imitative, and is in control of her various verse-forms, her metaphoric language, and her poetic structures. (KAR)

8856. ———— "Anne Bradstreet's Use of DuBartas in 'Contemplations'." *EIHC* 110:64-69.

Du Bartas *Divine Weekes* must be seen as an important source for Anne Bradstreet's "Contemplations," for such similarities as the two speakers' perspectives, locations, and actions, their apostrophes to the sun, and the nightingale indicate her use of Du Bartas. That she apparently turned to her study rather than the out-of-doors suggests she was more interested in the lessons derived from her poem than in trying simply to portray the new landscape. Perhaps to her, as to Wigglesworth in "God's Controversy with New England," America appeared a "waste and howling wilderness" that the godly could transform into a pleasant park. Importing details from Du Bartas was her attempt to form what was wild and external into her controlled emblems. (KAR)

8857. Waller, Jennifer R. " 'My Hand a Needle Better Fits':Anne Bradstreet and Women Poets in the Renaissance." *DR* 54:436-50.

Women writers increased in number during the 16th and 17th centuries, and it is instructive to see Bradstreet not just as New England's first major poet but as the culmination of a century or more of development, as the English Renaissance's most important woman poet. Despite some exceptions, 17th-century women writers are characterized by a sense of inadequacy and unease, an assumption that they have a largely suspicious audience, and a cautious and derivate use of educational material in their work. Bradstreet's great advantage was that her environment both limited and encouraged her poetry; love, domesticity, marriage, and religion were the material of her verse, and the strength of her verse grows from her accepting the limitations on her life and subject-matter. (JRW)

Brown, C.B. 8858. Bell, Michael D. " 'The Double-Tongued Deceiver':Sincerity and Duplicity in the Novels of Charles Brockden Brown." *EAL* 9:143-63.

Brown's four best known novels present a contest between 18th-century ideas of order and forms of energy which threaten this order. This energy is political and psychological, but it is also specifically associated with the literary imagination in general and with the writing of fiction in particular. Brown shared his contemporaries' fear of the power of fiction. He feared its artificiality, leading even the most avowedly sincere writer into "artful" duplicity. He also feared the consequences of exposing the mind to illusory pictures of life, thereby unsettling its balance and weakening its ability to distinguish between actual and imaginary. Thus both Carwin (in *Wieland*) and Ormond (in *Ormond*) are associated in their villainy with literary art. Carwin's ventriloquism upsets Clara Wieland's faith in Lockean order and drives her brother insane. In his first two novels Brown's fears about fiction are expressed mainly in the figures of his villains. In *Edgar Huntly* and *Arthur Mervyn* these fears come, as well, to dominate narrative structure. Both novels turn, finally, on questions of narrative reliability. It is this narrative self-conscious—this sense that literary order is particularly threatened by the sources and nature of its own energy—that makes Brown's novels so interesting to the student of later American fiction. (MDB)

8862. Hedges, William. "Charles Brockden Brown and the Culture of Contradictions." *EAL* 9:107-42.
Current commentary on Brown goes too far in dismissing his political and philosophical concerns, overemphasizes the psychological implications of his work, and often exaggerates his novelistic subtlety. It too easily assumes that he is the originator of a "dark," significantly "American" tradition in fiction. As a corrective we need a view that is alert to the cultural relevance of his fiction and which remains skeptical of his craftsmanship in fiction. In such a view *Wieland* shrinks in importance; *Ormond* suffers from Brown's failure of nerve; *Arthur Mervyn* and *Edgar Huntly* embody his major achievement, the creation of a distinctively American hero, one whose failure fully to realize his own identity reflects American cultural contradictions. (WLH)

8866. Reid, S.W. "Brockden Brown in England:Notes on Henry Colburn's 1822 Editions of His Novels." *EAL* 9:188-95.
Brown's success among English readers culminated in 1822 with Colburn's editions of the Dunlap biography and of *Wieland*, *Ormond*, and some shorter works. Alongside Newman's issues of Brown's other fiction in 1821, Colburn's editions resulted in something like a "complete" Brown long before Brown's countrymen were supporting his fiction in American bookstalls. Examination of Colburn's 1822 editions shows that, although he apparently treated Brown as just another three-decker novelist, his reprints contain an extraordinary number of alterations of words, phrases, and whole sentences. Since these changes cannot be Brown's, they suggest not only that Colburn saw a need to edit Brown's works before publishing them, but also that he found them commercially worth such editorial effort even though in Brown's homeland there had been insufficient financial support of America's first professional novelist. (SWR)

8868. Rodgers, Paul C.,Jr. "Brown's *Ormond*:The Fruits of Improvisation." *AQ* 26:[4]-22.
Brown composed *Ormond* rapidly under pressure from his publisher and without benefit of planning or opportunity to revise. He started work with only a vague notion of his heroine and villain and relied upon his powers of improvisation to generate "story." When inspiration failed, he bided time by developing marginal characters or by shifting dramatic focus to his narrator. He made three attempts to activate his villain's villainy, each time changing his conception of Ormond. The tale is a mishmash of promising formal and thematic initiatives, no one of which engaged Brown's attention long enough to organize the book. (PCR,Jr)

8869. Soldati, Joseph A. "The Americanization of Faust:A Study of Charles Brockden Brown's *Wieland*." *ESQ* 74:1-14.
Charles Brockden Brown's *Wieland; Or, The Transformation* (1798) is the American Gothic successor of the Faustian tradition. Theodore Wieland's fantasy that he can soar above human frailty is characteristic of the Faustian's anguished Icarian striving, which is the result of his Narcissistic self-enamoration. Attempting to dwell in the ethereal realms of God, Wieland brutally murders his wife and children. After being stripped of the delusions of self, he commits suicide. The savagery of Wieland's Faustianism—its utter violence and total destructiveness—sets him apart from his European predecessors and reflects the New World's violent temper, pointing the way for protagonists of numerous later American novels. (JAS)

8870. Witherington, Paul. "Charles Brockden Brown:A Bibliographical Essay." *EAL* 9:164-87.
Brown scholarship is increasing rapidly, and rather unevenly. The Hemenway-Keller "Checklist" (*PBSA*, July-Sept., 1966) is still valuable, but aging. A new edition of Brown's works underway at Kent State University will include pieces previously unprinted with the novels, but no stories or letters. Biography is still the weakest part of Brown scholarship, most critics relying too heavily on Dunlap's early *Life*. Criticism has clustered in three major periods: the period immediately following Brown's death, the end of the 19th century when realism and naturalism were being debated, and the period following World War II when Brown became a subject for formalistic and archetypal criticism. Recent increase in the number of Brown dissertations suggests that Brown scholarship has not yet reached its peak, but critics still over-emphasize the major works and traditional approaches, anthologizing rather than distinguishing. (PW)

8871. —— "Charles Brown's Other Novels:*Clara Howard* and *Jane Talbot*." *NCF* 29:257-72.
Brown's themes of restraint and benevolence and his moral tone dominate all his novels. Gothic egos and artists or artist surrogates are condemned and converted to social ends, whatever the cost to these individuals or Brown's technique. That Brown's self-defeating view of art is consistent is shown by the motif of the evil benefactor, a deadly man in the early novels and, in later novels, an uncompromising woman clutching the hero to the heart of society. *Clara Howard* and *Jane Talbot* are logical ends of Brown's quest for form. They are tightly structured and the letter form creates good effects of suspense, irony, and shifting points of view. *Jane Talbot* offers Brown's most believable villain, Frank, and Jane, his most interesting woman character. Caught between his esthetic vision and his moral conservatism, Brown ended his writing career not knowing that the form he had found in his last two novels was his most effective compromise. (PW)

Cooke. 8874. Arner, Robert D. "Clio's *Rhimes*:History and Satire in Ebenezer Cooke's 'History of Bacon's Rebellion'." *SLJ* 6,ii:91-106.
In his "History of Bacon's Rebellion," Cooke unites the perspectives of the historian and the satirist in his persona. As historian, the speaker interests himself in telling the story and in evaluating the Rebellion by means of historical allusions, most of which are to the Puritan Revolution. This approach to his subject also provides him with the "view from above" typical of the satirist's vision and engenders a sense that the follies of mankind are particular only in their manifestations, but constant and universal in their origins and their tendency to recur. Cooke's conservative politics are more properly seen from the critic's vantage point as a function of his speaker's conservatism; they determine the imagery the speaker employs to characterize the actors in his drama. (RDA)

Edwards. 8882. Scheick, William J. "Family, Conversion, and the Self in Jonathan Edwards' *A Faithful Narrative of the Surprising Work of God*." *TSL* 19:79-89.
A Faithful Narrative is informed by a family motif derived from Edwards' concern over the dereliction of parental control of youth and his perception of the disregard of adults for the authority of their ministerial spiritual father. This motif is directly related to the theme of the work, for conversion occurs when the proper familial environment has been established. Conversion is best understood with regard to a posteriori effects upon the inner self. Edwards' concern with the self is evident in his similes based on nature and in his image of insularity implying an identity between the converted self, the community, and the family ideal. (WJS)

Eliot. 8885. Miner, Kenneth L. "John Eliot of Massachusetts and the Beginnings of American Linguistics." *HL* 1:169-83.
The Indian Grammar Begun (1666) of John Eliot of Massachusetts (1604-90) constitutes the first published account of an "exotic" language that can rightfully be called scientific. The first portion of the argument treats Eliot's English-based orthography and the problems it poses in the description of a language completely different from English. Eliot's use of a "morphophonemic" transcription is presented. Eliot's *The Logick Primer* (1672) is

suggested as a source of particular insight into the Puritan understanding and use of logic. Having speculated about the impact that Jesus College, Cambridge, may have had on Eliot's linguistic accomplishments in his analysis of an Amerindian language, the author concludes that Eliot deserves to be called the true founder of American linguistics, in particular since he anticipated modern use of levels of representation by more than a century. (KLM)

Fiske. 8886. Bray, James. "John Fiske:Puritan Precursor of Edward Taylor." *EAL* 9:27-38.
Tree of life imagery appears in the poems of Edward Taylor and John Fiske who both used the tree of life as an apocalyptic image. In Fiske's poetry exploration of the image is circumscribed by his adherence to tenets of Ramist logic and Covenant Theology. Fiske managed partially to resolve the difference between image, theology, and logic by creating a threefold dialectic structure and incorporating it into the form of an anagram. Extending the image, Fiske, like Taylor, created images which fit inside a single metaphoric infinite body representing Christ. Anticipating Taylor, he found ways to extend tree of life imagery by linking it with other Puritan concepts. But because of his dialectic circumscriptions Fiske failed to realize the potentials of his image as fully as did Taylor. Taylor explored the image more completely by positing a direct personal relationship with Christ, by supposing a reciprocal union with Christ, and by linking images together in introspective associations which anticipate the techniques of *symboliste* poetry. (JB)

Franklin. 8890. Kushen, Betty. "Three Earliest Published Lives of Benjamin Franklin, 1790-93:The *Autobiography* and Its Continuations." *EAL* 9:39-52.
The three earliest book length lives of Benjamin Franklin published outside the United States appeared within three years of his death. The texts of these lives were genetically related and succinctly demonstrated the influence of Franklin's *Memoirs*, his *Autobiography*, had in shaping for good or ill all future accounts of his social, business, and political activities. In order of their publication they were: *Memoirs of the Late Dr. Benjamin Franklin* (1790), *Mémoires de la vie privée de Benjamin Franklin* (1791), and *The Private Life of the Late Benjamin Franklin* (1793). The latter two were comprised of Part I of Franklin's own *Memoirs* plus a continuation by another author. These biographies set the pattern of characterization, both laudatory and derogatory, followed in all later lives down to the 20th century. In the art of self-education and natural philosophy Franklin was unstintingly praised; in the practice of politics severely criticized as hypocritical and self-aggrandizing. (BSK)

Freneau. 8898. Kyle, Carol A. "That Poet Freneau:A Study of the Imagistic Success of *The Pictures of Columbus*." *EAL* 9:62-70.
Freneau's *The Pictures of Columbus* (1774) succeeds in the large formal device announced in the title: the "pictures" of the new world structure this mythical epic of the discovery of America. The first set of pictures depend upon the image as idea, on the Platonic image-making faculty of the mind. The first seven sections pre-picture the Columbian adventure. Pictures VIII through XIII translate the concept to actual poetic imagery. Picture XIV moves from image to act: the actual discovery occurs. In the "terrible" pictures XV through XVIII, the act reverts once more to imagined pictures as the legend of Columbus haunts the coasts of the new world. (CAK)

Hammon. 8901. Palmer, R. Roderick. "Jupiter Hammon's Poetic Exortations." *CLAJ* 18:22-28.
An appraisal of Jupiter Hammon as a black preacher, pacifist, and poet is presented. Like King David in his Psalms, Hammon made similar exhortations to his audiences in his poetry and advocated such moral qualities as patience, devotion to duty, obedience to authority, avoidance of violence, and other similar conduct. Hammon's writings provided the climate to practice Christianity which eventually awakened in the minds of all its followers the concept that all men are equal before God and man.

(RRP)

Jefferson. 8907. Gittleman, Edwin. "Jefferson's 'Slave Narrative':The Declaration of Independence as a Literary Text." *EAL* 8:239-56.
Despite memorable analyses by Tyler (1897) and Becker (1922), the Declaration's literary significance has been ignored. Jefferson systematically developed an idea first broached in his 1774 *Summary View*: oppressive tyrannies deliberately reduce colonists to slaves. Accordingly, the Declaration is a self-conscious slave narrative in which syntax, diction, and form dramatize facts of enslavement. Abstract "they" modulates to personal "we," creating an extraordinary slave community. A slavery myth determines the grievance strategy. Fictional "causes" deriving from Jefferson's moral imagination make "facts" hyperbolically instructive. "He" (George III) tyrannizes "we," culminating in the draft slavery-grievance—an apocalyptic vision more horrible than slavery itself—deleted by Congress. The absence of this climax commits a later generation to completing Jefferson's slave narrative. The 20th-century "we," now black-and-white, need to redefine and de-mythologize ourselves. (EG)
8909. Skallerup, Harry R. "'For His Excellency Thomas Jefferson, Esqr.':The Tale of a Wandering Book." *QJLC* 31:116-21.
Corrects and amplifies Sowerby's *Catalogue of the Library of Thomas Jefferson*, entry no. 3816. Although listed in the index of the first catalog of the Library of Congress, *A Complete Collection of Tables for Navigation and Nautical Astronomy* (London, 1805), by Joseph Mendoza y Rios, it apparently was not among the books that Thomas Jefferson sold to Congress in 1815. The book eventually became the property of the U.S. Naval Lyceum (a private library which flourished in Brooklyn, New York, 1834-88) and was acquired by the U.S. Naval Academy when the Naval Lyceum was disbanded. The existence of the book outside of the Jefferson Collection at the Library of Congress could indicate that perhaps a few other "missing" books of Jefferson's may have followed similar paths and possibly still survive. (HRS)

Johnson, E. 8910. Gallagher, Edward J. "The Case for the *Wonder-Working Providence*." *BNYPL* 77(1973):10-27.
Reviews the history of Edward Johnson's *Wonder-Working Providence of Sions Saviour in New England* (1653) from publication to the present, and then attempts to place it in its contemporary setting so that its unique qualities may be seen. (EJG)

Mather, C. 8914. Bercovitch, Sacvan. "'Nehemias Americanus':Cotton Mather and the Concept of the Representative American." *EAL* 8:220-38.
Cotton Mather's life of John Winthrop, "Nehemias Americanus," fuses two notions of the exemplary man: hagiographic or christological, and historical or soteriological. The fusion rests on basic premises of New England Puritanism: first, the tendency to conflate the covenants of grace and community (linking personal and corporate salvation); second, the emphasis on a distinctive experience and locale, whereby not only the errand but the New World is described in terms of sacred history. As a result, the meanings of country, saint, and church come to reflect one another, and "America" itself is invested with the status of visible sainthood, itself becomes a Nehemiah *redivivus*. Against this background, the essay explores the interaction of rhetoric and reality, biography and historiography, in Mather's concept of heroism, one which blends figuralism, realism, and eschatology in defining a man who is uniquely heroic because he is a representative American. (SB)
8916. Stein, Stephen J. "Cotton Mather and Jonathan Edwards on the Number of the Beast:Eighteenth-Century Speculation about the Antichrist." *PAAS* 84:293-315.
In colonial America Cotton Mather (1663-1728) and Jonathan Edwards (1703-58) shared a fascination with the apocalyptic figure of the beast in Revelation 13:18 and with the interpretation of its mysterious number 666. Both men evaluated an earlier explanation of the number proposed by Francis Potter (1594-1678), an English divine active in the period of the English Civil

War. They agreed with him that the identification of the beast was an important theological task. Mather and Edwards found Potter's interpretation based upon the extraction of the square root of 666 ingenious and plausible. Their own apocalyptic speculation reinforced the traditional pattern of anti-Catholicism in 18th-century America and indirectly contributed to the development of a cultural disposition to transform secular conflicts into religious crusades. (SJS)

Morton, T. 8919. Arner, Robert D. "Pastoral Celebration and Satire in Thomas Morton's *New English Canaan.*" *Criticism* 16:217-31.

In his *New English Canaan*, Thomas Morton employed two different but interrelated comic voices, both of which derive from Greek phallic songs and survive as the voice of May Lord and the Lord of Misrule in folk festivals still celebrated during the Renaissance. The function of the first voice is to praise the fertility of the land as imaged by the phallus (maypole); and when that symbol is destroyed the second voice, the voice of the satiric Lord of Misrule, dominates the book. This shift in voices is matched by a shift in imagery from the green and gold of pastoral New England to the dark, bleak Underworld of Puritan New England. At the end of the book, Morton shifts once more into the voice of the prophet, implicitly acknowledging that the festive point of view has failed in the New World. (RDA)

Taylor, E. 8934. Jones, Jesse C. "A Note on the Number of Edward Taylor's *Preparatory Meditations.*" *EAL* 9:81-82.

In a 1939 edition of Edward Taylor's poems, Thomas H. Johnson states that there are 217 Peparatory Meditations; most scholars since that time have echoed Johnson's figure. Donald Stanford, however, in his 1960 edition of Taylor's poems, does not mention a specific number of Meditations. An examination and comparison of the two editions reveals erratic enumeration by Taylor and editorial disagreement between Johnson and Stanford concerning "rough draft" or "separate version" status of some poems. Because of such complexities, to insist on 217 or any other figure as *the* number of Preparatory Meditations is oversimplification. (JJ)

8935. Reed, Michael D. "Edward Taylor's Poetry:Puritan Structure and Form." *AL* 46:[304]-12.

Because of his use of the metaphorical or baroque conceit, Taylor has often been characterized as the last of the English metaphysical poets. However, while the English metaphysicals used the conceit to demonstrate similarity where the less poetic saw only difference, Taylor employed the conceit to establish and maintain the difference between the divine and the human while casting the divine truth in a form intelligible to men. Further, the structure of Taylor's poetry was equally influenced by Puritan doctrine. Following the American Puritan rigidified and codified fear of hypocrisy and pride, Taylor cast the final stanzas of his *Preparatory Meditations* in a hypothetical mode to maintain a crucial position between spiritual despair and pride. (MDR)

Tyler. 8941. Dennis, Larry R. "Legitimizing the Novel:Royall Tyler's *The Algerine Captive.*" *EAL* 9:71-80.

The early American novel often masqueraded as history, biography, or journal, or if it did not resort to such subterfuge claimed, nevertheless, to be founded on fact. Tyler's *The Algerine Captive* (1797) claimed to be a history, but a close reading of the novel reveals its concerns with the necessity for such misrepresentation. In large measure, the novel was an attempt to map out the legitimate arena for fiction. Through a comic confounding of genres, Tyler, abetted by the use of a persona, showed that fiction can make valid statements about the human condition, particularly man's enslavement to romantic illusions. Tyler's didacticism and nationalism tended, to some extent, to undermine the authority of his position.

Wheatley. 8952. Silverman, Kenneth. "Four New Letters by Phillis Wheatley." *EAL* 8:257-71.

Four letters written by Phillis Wheatley between 1772 and 1774, published here for the first time, call attention to her place in the international missionary movement. All are addressed to the English philanthropist John Thornton, a member of the so-called Clapham Sect, which devoted itself to abolition, evangelism, and the plight of the poor. The letters disclose the efforts of Thornton, Ezra Stiles, Samuel Hopkins, and others to employ Phillis as a missionary in the Gold Coast town of Annamaboe. Feeling herself more a Bostonian than an African, Phillis declined the role. The letters also reveal her interest in the American Indian missionary work conducted by the Monhegan preacher Samson Occom, and the missionary interests of John and Susanna Wheatley. In one letter Phillis states that John Wheatley granted her freedom three months before his wife's death. The undercurrent of strain in the letters is traceable to the anti-intellectualism of the movement, which led Thornton, and Phillis herself, to subtly derogate her poetry. (KS)

III. NINETEENTH CENTURY, 1800–1870

General and Miscellaneous. 8964. Irwin, John T. "The Symbol of the Hieroglyphics in the American Renaissance." *AQ* 26:[103]-26.

In 1882 Jean François Champollion deciphered the Egyptian hieroglyphics and his discovery exercised profound influence on the literature of the American Renaissance. Champollion discovered that the hieroglyphics were, for the most part, phonetic signs, and thus that the relationship between sign and significant in Egyptian writing was not necessary and emblematic but arbitrary. Emerson and Thoreau, in spite of Champollion's scientific reading of the hieroglyphics, continued to treat the hieroglyph of the world as a metaphysical emblem, often using misreadings of Champollion's work to back up their arguments. Hawthorne and Melville treated the hieroglyph of the world as essentially indeterminate and thus capable of bearing any interpretation projected on it in the act of knowing. (JTI)

8973. Shurr, William H. "Typology and Historical Criticism of the American Renaissance." *ESQ* 74:57-63. [Rev. art.]

Describes Ursula Brumm, *American Thought and Religious Typology* (1970); Sacvan Bercovitch (ed.), *Typology and Early American Literature* (1972); and Kathleen Raine and George Mills Harper (eds.), *Thomas Taylor the Platonist: Selected Writings* (1969). We are now in a position to abandon the term "symbolism" as anachronistic in analyzing the works of the American Renaissance. Historically the classic American authors were heavily influenced by a native tradition of typological criticism, deriving from biblical criticism as practiced by writers of the Colonial period. At the turn of the 19th century this essentially Platonic method of perception was given new stimulus and direction by the widely received translations of the Neo-Platonists by the Englishman Thomas Taylor. (WHS)

Afro-American. 8979. Bell, Bernard W. "Literary Sources of the Early Afro-American Novel." *CLAJ* 18:29-43.

In reacting to a gallery of Sambos and Babos and projecting their own vision of the black American identity, William Wells Brown and his contemporaries turned to the literature at hand for models. The slave narratives provided a bridge between the oral and literary worlds. Like the narratives, the early novels are characterized by Christian values, melodrama, and moral fervor. Equally important is the Bible. Traditionally, blacks have compared their oppression to that of the Jews. Aside from allusions to the Hebrew patriarchs and prophets, the most frequent adaptations are of the myths of Moses and the Second Coming of Christ. While abolitionist literature and the Bible provided their most vital mythological system, Southwestern frontier humor, the plantation tradition, and the dime romances were also significant models for early black novelists. (BWB)

Drama and Theater. 8983. Harbin, Billy J. "Hodgkinson and His Rivals at the Park:The Business of Early Romantic Theatre in America." *ESQ* 76:148-69.

Under the management of William Dunlap (1766-1839), and with such skilled, popular performers as John Hodgkinson (1765-1805), Anne Brunton Merry (1768-1808), and Thomas Abthorpe Cooper (1776-1849), the Old American Company at the Park attracted sufficient audiences to sustain the operation. Although Dunlap and his actors chose a repertory which reflected popular audience tastes, the theater was not to become a fully successful commercial operation until after 1810. (BJH)

8984. McDermott, Douglas. "Touring Patterns on California's Frontier, 1849-1859." *ThS* 15:18-28.
California's theater between 1849 and 1859 has never been properly understood because the geographic, economic, and demographic relationships among San Francisco, the central valley towns, and the mining camps have never be explained. Serious attention has been given to San Francisco, but the other areas have been treated cursorily. Yet, because of the dispersion of population and wealth, theater in San Francisco could not have existed as it did unless players had toured the other areas. Theatrical troupes played first in San Francisco for as long as 6 months. From there they would go to Sacramento. Then they had two alternatives: remain in the central valley, playing in Marysville and Stockton before returning to San Francisco; or travel into the Sierra Nevada Mountains and tour the mining camps, reappearing in a month or two in a valley town before returning to the coast. (DM)

8985. Montilla, Robert. "The Building of the Lafayette Theatre." *ThS* 15:105-29.
The Lafayette Theatre was built in 1825 by Charles W. Sandford in the Canal Street district of New York City. Plans of the Lafayette published in 1825 show that it was designed as the home of a circus. The Lafayette's huge double stage was the largest in the nation. By 1826 the Lafayette had been converted by its owner into an amphitheater by replacing the riding-ring with a seating pit and adding full-scale equestrian dramas to the daily bills. But the opening of a sumptuous rival house, the Bowery Theatre, in 1826 prompted the owner to undertake further refinements of the Lafayette beginning in 1827. With the completion of the alterations of 1827-28 the Lafayette was fully converted from a minor circus arena into a regular melodramatic theater that was generally acknowledged to be one of the largest and most splendid places of amusement in the nation. (RBM)

8986. Reardon, William R. "The American Drama and Theatre in the Nineteenth Century:A Retreat from Meaning." *ESQ* 76:170-86.
An overall lack of meaning in the 19th-century American theater was the outgrowth, in part, of two major factors. The first influence stemmed from the economic problems for theaters which resulted from striking organizational changes and growth. The second influence came from the less than felicitous nature of national topics as content for the drama. The economic factor is traced backwards into the final years of the 18th century by examining critical statements throughout those years and by paralleling them with varied theatrical changes as they occur. At this point, the Barbary Wars are discussed in detail as an example of a national topic and are correlated to the points made about economics. (WRR)

8988. Stoddard, Roger E. "A Catalogue of the Dramatic Imprints of David and Thomas Longworth, 1802-1821." *PAAS* 84:317-98.
The catalog records 429 editions of 347 British and American plays issued in New York City by David Longworth, the first American publisher to specialize in plays, sometimes in partnership with and eventually succeeded by his son Thomas. Also included are descriptions of three play catalogs, a biography of an actor, a theatrical magazine, and four collections of which the most noteworthy is *The English and American stage*, 40 vols. (1807-12). (RES)

Periodicals. 8992. Carson, Barbara H. "Proclus' Sunflower and *The Dial*." *ELN* 11:200-02.
The name of *The Dial* offers another instance of the influence of Neoplatonism on the New England Transcendentalists. Bronson Alcott, who named the journal, read widely in Thomas Taylor's translations of the Neoplatonists. In Taylor's notes to Jamblichus'

Life of Pythagoras, Alcott discovered Proclus' description of the sunflower's symbolic representation of the sun on earth. This analogy coincided perfectly with Alcott's belief that the human soul reflects, on earth, its divine source. Therefore, Alcott adapted Proclus' trope in his writings, changing the sunflower (implicitly or explicitly) into a "soul-flower" and associating that with a sundial. His most significant use of the Neoplatonic symbol appeared in the first of his "Orphic Sayings" in the first issue of *The Dial*. His adaption of Proclus' trope here suggests not only the source of the name of *The Dial*, but also Alcott's estimation of the celestial purpose of that publication. (BHC)

8994. Haberland, Paul M. "The Reception of German Literature in Baltimore's Literary Magazines, 1800-1875." *GAS* 7:69-92.
Scholarship concerning the reception of German literature in America during the 19th century concentrates on the major Northern cities, Boston, New York, and Philadelphia. It neglects the appraisal of German literature in Baltimore, gateway to the South. A systematic search through 19th-century Baltimore's literary magazines reveals a fascinating chronological development of opinion regarding German authors and their works. Early in this period Baltimoreans consider German literature morally pernicious and tasteless. The Civil War introduces a hiatus of concern, but a renewed interest follows the War's conclusion. (PMH)

8997. Sederberg, Nancy B. "Antebellum Southern Humor in the *Camden Journal*:1826-1840." *MissQ* 27(1973-74):41-74.
Knowledge of the genre of Southern antebellum humor can be greatly enhanced by examinations of local newspapers of the period. Sederberg compiles and analyzes the humorous material in the *Camden Journal* (South Carolina) from 1826 through 1840. The humorous sketches are discussed under the categories of Crockett and Other Brag Anecdotes; Courting Anecdotes; Religious Anecdotes; Political Anecdotes; and Lawyers, Doctors, Teachers, and Miscellaneous Customs. Trends are discussed and these are related to such factors as editorial policy and the availability of such humorous anecdotes. The greatest gains in sophistication occur in the categories of courting sketches and professional and miscellaneous customs. Appendices contain a detailed history of the *Camden Journal* and a chronological listing by category of abridged versions of the humorous sketches. (NBS)

Prose Fiction. 9004. Marler, Robert F.,Jr. "From Tale to Short Story:The Emergence of a New Genre in the 1850's." *AL* 46:[153]-69.
The short story as an independent genre emerged during the 1850s; the composite fictional worlds of the three leading authors demonstrate a broad shift from Poe's overt romance and verisimilitude to Hawthorne's neutral ground of actual and imaginary and thence to Melville's mimetic portrayals and reliance on facts for the profound probing of everyday reality. (AT)

9013. Weidman, Bette S. "White Men's Red Man:A Penitential Reading of Four American Novels." *MLS* 4,ii:14-26. [Brown's *Edgar Huntly*, Cooper's *The Last of the Mohicans*, Simms's *The Yemassee*, and R.M. Bird's *Nick of the Woods*.]
The essay explores four works of fiction in which white American authors of the 19th century treat the figure of the Indian. Charles Brockden Brown, in *Edgar Huntly* (1799), explores the terror of the unknown self projected onto the wilderness and its inhabitants; James Fenimore Cooper, in *The Last of the Mohicans* (1823), concerns himself with a sense of lost possibilities. The dominating emotion in William Gilmore Simms's *The Yemassee* (1835) is triumph. For Robert Montgomery Bird, in *Nick of the Woods* (1837), the predominant emotion is hate-filled anger, the response of men goaded beyond their abilities to resist brutalization. (BSW)

9014. Wilson, James D. "Incest and American Romantic Fiction." *SLitI* 7,i:31-50. [W.H. Brown, C.B. Brown, Poe, Hawthorne, Melville.]
Sibling incest furnishes the American "dark" Romantics W.H. Brown, C.B. Brown, Poe, Hawthorne, and Melville a means to expose as dangerously naive the sentimental conception of man as a "belle âme." The solipsistic individual, cut off from institutional

means of channeling illicit passion, discovers his narcissistic infatuation with his sister to be inevitably self-destructive; any attempt to regulate one's life according to a personal morality divorced from the demands and compromises required in an emergent social order is doomed. Poe and Melville explore the consequences of solipsism on the artistic temperament. With all novelists, the treatment of solipsism raises disturbing political questions. (JDW)

Alcott, B. 9019. Myerson, Joel. "Bronson Alcott's 'Scripture for 1840'." *ESQ* 77:237-59.
This is the first publication of a journal Alcott kept during 1840. It was unaccountably missed by Shepard in his 1938 edition of Alcott's *Journals*. Major portions of this selected edition present new and valuable information about Emerson; about Alcott's mental state at the time he moved to Concord; about the founding of Brook Farm; and about the English Transcendentalists, including unpublished letters from Alcott to Charles Lane and J. Westland Marston. (JM)
9020. Stoehr, Taylor. "'Eloquence Needs No Constable': Alcott, Emerson, and Thoreau on the State." *CRevAS* 5:81-100.
Examines the political rhetoric used by Alcott, Emerson, and Thoreau in their reaction against the state. On the arrest of a black man named Anthony Burns as a result of the Fugitive Slave Act, Alcott reacted by saying, "Why are we not within?" The anti-slavery movement gradually lured the transcendentalists out of their individualism into partisan statements and acts. Reacting against the Fugitive Slave Act Emerson vowed, "I will not obey it, by God," and Thoreau wrote "Slavery in Massachusetts." (TTS)

Boker. 9026. Gallagher, Kent G. "The Tragedies of George Henry Boker:The Measure of American Romantic Drama." *ESQ* 76:187-215.
All of Boker's plays departed from the patriotic verse tragedy that Americans had been writing. Taken together they constitute a record of how a playwright struggled to master the dramatic form. *Calaynos* explores the personal error of a protagonist who denies the domain of the emotions and misjudges because of that shortcoming. With *Anne Boleyn* Boker attempts the tragedy of suffering, centering all interest in the character of Henry's second wife. In *Leonore de Guzman* and *Francesca da Rimini*, Boker weds his growing ability to create drama with two strong protagonists whose commitment to honor and actions carry the tragedy through to consummation. (KGG)

Browne, C.F. 9028. Cracroft, Richard H. "Distorting Polygamy for Fun and Profit:Artemus Ward and Mark Twain Among the Mormons." *BYUS* 14:272-88.
Mark Twain's and Artemus Ward's humorous use of their popular materials about the Mormons shows not only their own adherence to the anti-Mormon myth so prevalent, but it also reveals clearly that it was Artemus Ward, not Twain, who realized and utilized the Mormon materials to greater advantage. Mark Twain probably learned a great deal about handling his Mormon material from Ward. Both writers hit the sensitivities of English-speaking people regarding world opinion about Mormonism. (RHC)

Clarke. 9031. Myerson, Joel. "'A True & High Minded Person':Transcendentalist Sarah Clarke." *SWR* 59:163-72.
Sarah Freeman Clarke's letters provide a valuable viewpoint on the life and times of the New England Transcendentalists. Clarke was content to watch and absorb the artistic and philosophic contributions made by her distinguished peers—Hawthorne, Fuller, Alcott, Emerson, and Ripley. (CTW)

Cooke, P. 9032. Tucker, Edward L. "Philip Pendleton Cooke and *The Southern Literary Messenger*:Selected Letters." *MissQ* 27(1973-74):79-99.
The start of the literary career of the Virginia author Philip Pendleton Cooke coincided almost exactly with the beginning of the magazine which brought him some recognition, *The Southern Literary Messenger*. These letters, previously unpublished, throw light on what the editors of the magazine were interested in and

what they were attempting to do. Letters to various editors of the magazine show difficulties, especially financial, facing the publication, and they indicate the part that Cooke, as a typical contributor, played in the history of the magazine. They also show how Edgar Allan Poe, one of the editors, and Cooke, who did not know each other personally and neither of whom had any close literary friends, were, nevertheless, associated. (ELT)

Cooper. 9035. Cosgrove, William E. "Family Lineage and Narrative Pattern in Cooper's Littlepage Trilogy." *ForumH* 12,i:2-8.
Cooper's Effingham and Littlepage novels retain family unity and estates through many generations in order to show the necessity of a refined aristocracy to a civilized America. Overcoming threats to such family unity determines structure as well as theme in these novels. In *Home as Found*, the marriage of Eve to Paul Powis ties two wealthy lines of the Effingham family into a tidy, familial knot. In *Satanstoe*, *The Chainbearer*, and *The Redskins* four generations of the Littlepage family are perpetuated as each young narrator journeys to the family estate and successfully claims his land and his wife. (WEC)
9037. Denne, Constance A. "Cooper's Artistry in *The Headsman*." *NCF* 29:77-92.
Usually considered primarily as a sociopolitical work, *The Headsman*, however, both demonstrates Cooper's artistry and suggests much about his method of creation. Setting is intrinsic to its complex artistic design and structures its action through the device of a journey. As the characters move from low to high, there is a change in their fortunes which corresponds directly or inversely to the metaphor of the progress. Cooper constructs a unitive form in which all of the diverse elements have meaning, but he also endows each situation with sufficient dramatic conflict, in ascending intensity, to justify the implicit requirements of the structuring metaphor. The journey is a real one, yet its events are subsumed into one dominant symbolic action, the perilous journey that is the human condition. The values Cooper enunciates are meaningful not only to the characters of the tale but also to the larger humanity they represent. Through his artistic use of setting, Cooper translates his moral vision of society as a "community of mutual support" into fictional terms and communicates that vision analogically. (CAD)
9039. Kligerman, Jack. "Style and Form in James Fenimore Cooper's *Homeward Bound* and *Home as Found*." *JNT* 4:45-61.
In *Homeward Bound* and *Home as Found*, Cooper focuses on the social and political problems of America. He relies on the diction and patterns of action of the sentimental novel, updated to fit a more relevant topic. Cooper's style and its relation to the elements of fiction fragment his attempts to unify his version, except didactically. His diction in characterization tends to be conceptually abstract, since in his characters he embodies the principles that struggle in the world of Cooperstown around him. In passages which depict action, he relies heavily on the vocabularies of concrete realistic representation and sensational clichés he developed in the novels of the mid-1820s. (JK)
9043. Schachterle, Lance. "The Three 1823 Editions of James Fenimore Cooper's *The Pioneers*." *PAAS* 84:219-32.
James Fenimore Cooper's *The Pioneers* appeared in three separate authorized editions in 1823. The first New York edition, published by Charles Wiley, was typeset in the fall of 1822 during a yellow-fever epidemic. The text suffered accordingly, and Cooper quickly revised it, perhaps even before its appearance on 1 February 1823. On 26 February 1823 John Murray published the novel in London, using as copy text sheets of the Wiley edition which contained some authorial revisions. But more significantly, a second Wiley edition appeared soon after the first. This edition, long regarded as a "reprint," is demonstrably a new edition; set for the most part from new type, it contains over 700 emendations of substantives. Many of the Murray revisions appear also in the second Wiley text, strongly suggesting that the revisions in the later New York edition were made by Cooper himself. (LES)
9047. Vance, William L. "'Man and Beast':The Meaning of Cooper's *The Prairie*." *PMLA* 89:323-31.
The language, action, setting, and characterization of *The Prairie*

cohere around the idea of man as one species of animal among many. On one level, man is a hunter, dominating the other beasts upon whom he is dependent for food and clothing. On another level, man is a scientist subjecting the beasts to study, classification, and control. On a third level, the novel observes man as an animal of ambiguous identity. The various groups of characters exemplify differing varieties of humanity. The barbaric Indians and the angelic Inez are opposing extremes in dehumanizing characterization. Ellen and Paul display the conflicting demands of feeling, reason, and conscience on the typical middle ground of human nature. In the most dramatic aspect of the romance, the Bush family is forced by pressure of extraordinary circumstance from a brutal, lawless existence into a troubled consciousness of human guilt, justice, and mortality, Finally, in the aged and dying Leather-Stocking is represented a rare example of a fully human life achieved at the most primitive remove from mere animality. (WLV)

Davis, John. 9051. Kribbs, Jayne K. "Setting the Record Straight on the Real John Davis." *PBSA* 68:329-30.
John Davis has long been considered American by scholars because of his total commitment to the American experience in several of his works. For this reason Davis is listed in *American Literary Manuscripts*, with 75 libraries and historical societies across the country reporting materials by him. This information is inaccurate. There are no extant manuscripts, documents, or letters by Davis in America. (JKK)

Drake. 9058. Slater, Joseph. "The Case of Drake and Halleck." *EAL* 8:285-97.
John Rodman Drake and Fitz-Greene Halleck, known and loved in the mid-19th century as the American Keats and the American Byron, are now unread and almost forgotten. They deserve kinder treatment from anthologists and literary historians, not just for what they were once quaintly thought to be but for what their best poems really are. Drake's humorous fairy tale, *The Culprit Fay*, the impudent lampoons and merry celebrations of life in New York which both young men wrote for the newspapers as "Croaker" and "Croaker, Jun." in 1819, and Drake's masterpiece, the gently satiric tale *Fanny* of 1821, belong in the sparkling but neglected tradition of American light verse. (JS)

Dunlap. 9059. Zipes, Jack. "Dunlap, Kotzebue, and the Shaping of American Theater:A Reevaluation from a Marxist Perspective." *EAL* 8:272-84.
William Dunlap and August von Kotzbue played a vital role in the historical development of American theater; yet, scholars generally dismiss their works as *kitsch* (trivial art). A re-evaluation from a Marxist perspective reveals the ramifications of their relationship up to the present. First, it is important to note that Kotzbue and Dunlap shared similar views on theater as a moral institution but often compromised themselves to support the status quo and the hegemony of the ruling classes. A close study of the comedies *Der Opfertod* and *The Italian Father* (and other dramas) supports this contention. Furthermore, Kotzbue and Dunlap contributed to the growth of the well-made play in the 19th century which, in turn, gave rise to commercial theater. (JZ)

Emerson. 9063. Barbour, Brian M. "Emerson's 'Poetic' Prose." *MLQ* 35:157-72.
An analysis of Emerson's thinking about language and literature suggests that he was unreceptive to any quality except lyric intensity. His interest in words was not in their ability to enact and thus create a meaning; he saw them as pointing beyond themselves to The Real. His own prose strove to rush the audience past the human world of moral relationships and moral knowledge to a purer realm. Hence his writing is "poetic" in a highly limited sense: it moves not toward the realized concrete, but toward the intense abstract. This has severe implications for him as a moralist. As Henry James said, "there were certain complications in life" that Emerson "never suspected." His prose, while uplifting, is short on what J.R. Lowell called "ponderable acquisition," and the wisdom Emerson imparts is the refined product of an attention diverted from the world of intractable

moral complexity (say, the novelist's world), so that what endures is not so much his wisdom as the strength of character that kept the vision fixed. (BMB)
9075. Doherty, Joseph F. "Emerson and the Loneliness of the Gods." *TSLL* 16:65-75.
The phenomenology of Emerson's dark side emerges from the logic of epistemological assumptions in *Nature*. His identification with the Godhead as Ground of Being culminates in the detached consciousness of "Experience." Emerson's original expansive vision of affirmation contains its own principle of inner destruction within a logical flaw that collapses his dream of freedom into a nightmare of lonely self-enclosure. He discovers that when the self becomes All, then consciousness becomes trapped in endless acts of hermetic self-referral. To become the Ground of Being ironically excludes one from any beings outside the self. (JD)
9085. Lindner, Carl M. "Newtonianism in Emerson's *Nature*." *ESQ* 77:260-69.
Emerson's *Nature* contains many Newtonian metaphors and analogies. A systematic examination reveals Emerson in the process of moving from Enlightenment concepts to the origins of the American Romantic tradition. The principle of correspondence was reinforced by the concept of the world as divine mechanism, following directly from Newton's laws of gravitational astronomy. Newton's theory of gravity permitted Emerson to recognize parallels between the spiritual and physical worlds, and metaphor for articulating his vision. Unity, the Oversoul, and poetic vision could all be expressed through gravitational centrality. (CL)
9098. Sowd, David H. "Peter Kaufmann's Correspondence with Emerson." *ESQ* 75:91-100.
In February of 1857, Emerson received a letter from Peter Kaufmann of Canton, Ohio, initiating what was to become a rather intensive correspondence. In all, Kaufmann, a Hegelian philosopher and self-styled reformer, wrote 10 letters to Emerson, including a "lengthy Epistle" of some 80 pages, designed to introduce Emerson to his life and thought, and Emerson replied with five letters to Kaufmann. In Emerson's five brief responses, his large, uniformly generous nature is exhibited. But no less important is the fascinating portrait the letters paint of a little-known Midwestern philosopher holding forth on the frontier, vigorously asserting an affinity with Emerson's thought that, in fact, was more perceived than actual. (DHS)
9099. Steinbrink, Jeffrey. "Novels of Circumstance and Novels of Character:Emerson's View of Fiction." *ESQ* 75:101-10.
If Emerson tended to scorn "Novels of Circumstance," he was often generous in his praise of "Novels of Character." The novel of circumstance deals almost exclusively with externals, with materialistic trappings rather than elevating universals. Aiming merely to entertain the impressionable middle class, it is morally derivative, not formative, and therefore abdicates the didactic responsibility incumbent upon all good literature. Novels of character, conversely, involve the reader deeply in an investigation of human personality itself, thereby enhancing his view of permanent and perennial truths. Fiction, Emerson allowed, can provide genuine—even transcendental—insight. (JS)

Hawthorne. 9115. Bales, Kent. "The Allegory and the Radical Romantic Ethic of *The Blithedale Romance*." *AL* 46:[41]-53.
Hawthorne's *Blithedale* has at its core an allegory defining the radical romantic values against which the actions of the community, and especially of Miles Coverdale, are to be judged. The allegory also analyzes the psychological needs of the central characters. Coverdale is necessarily central in both cases, for the allegory is Hawthorne's principal signal that Coverdale's judgment cannot be trusted and that he does not speak for his creator. To a degree he is an alter ego, for like his creator he feels ambivalent about romantic radicalism. However, by making Coverdale unaware of the allegory which his narrative embodies, Hawthorne separates himself from his narrator: unlike Coverdale he feels the attraction of radical romantic values strongly enough to put them at the heart of his romance in the relatively definitive form of allegory. (KB)
9116. —— "*The Blithedale Romance*:Coverdale's Mean and

Subversive Egotism." *BuR* 21,ii(1973):60-82.

In *The Blithedale Romance* Hawthorne uses an unreliable narrator to confess and condemn his own apostasy from the radical romantic values of Brook Farm and its fictional counterpart, Blithedale. This ironic strategy is perfectly equivocal: readers unsympathetic to radical romantic values find the narrator, Miles Coverdale, to be sympathetic and reliable rather than the unperceiving Judas that he is. Only readers sharing to some extent the professed values of the community will hear the confession and join in condemning Coverdale. His mind is conventional, his expression trite. He respects received wisdom when the circumstances call for imagination and daring invention. Because he believes that all is fated, that history has a single future and he but one role to play in realizing it, he accepts what happens. Thus alienated from the Blithedalers' goals of remolding history and self, he indulges in sadistic games and fantasies. Compared to him the putative villain, Hollingsworth, is far more attractive. (KB)

9118. Berthold, Dennis. "Hawthorne, Ruskin, and the Gothic Revival:Transcendent Gothic in *The Marble Faun*." *ESQ* 74:15-32.

Early in his career Hawthorne disliked Gothic architecture because of its over-elaborate, artificial designs and its gloomy, Roman Catholic associations. He gradually became an enthusiastic admirer of the Gothic. When Hawthorne visited the cathedrals of England and Italy, he enjoyed them as beautiful icons of transcendent religious meaning. In *The Marble Faun* Hawthorne used a Gothic backdrop for Donatello and Miriam's reunion scene. Understanding the symbolic value associated with the Gothic reveals that the statue of Pope Julius III and the Gothic facades of the buildings in the Square of Perugia constitute an architectural metaphor for the paradox of the fortunate fall. (DB)

9122. Byers, John R.,Jr. "*The House of the Seven Gables* and 'The Daughters of Dr. Byles':A Probable Source." *PMLA* 89:174-77.

The House of the Seven Gables may owe a considerable debt to Eliza Leslie's "The Daughters of Dr. Byles," a sketch of the two spinster great-granddaughters of Increase Mather in *Graham's Lady's and Gentleman's Magazine* (Jan., Feb. 1842). Both Hepzibah Pyncheon and the Misses Mary and Catherine Byles reside in black ancestral homes shaded by giant trees and furnished with portraits, chairs, and tables from another age. Hepzibah, who physically resembles Catherine, lives, like the aged sisters, under the imprint of the past, seldom venturing into the world; she simply awaits the return of her brother, whose miniature she cherishes and whose prison sentence has kept him away for thirty years, as the Misses Byles await the return of their nephew, whose portrait hangs prominently in the parlor and whose self-imposed exile has lasted forty years. Hawthorne closes his romance as Leslie closes her essay, with the exchange of a temporal home for one of eternity. (JRB,Jr)

9127. Chambers, Jane. "Two Legends of Temperance: Spenser's and Hawthorne's." *ESQ* 77:275-79. [On "The Birthmark."]

A source of Hawthorne's "The Birthmark" is found in Spenser's *The Faerie Queene*. Hawthorne's emphasis upon Georgiana's birthmark as a tiny red hand grasping her heart recalls Ruddymane's bloodied hands at the breast of his dying mother. In each tale, the hero nobly but blindly attempts to remove the stigma of mortality from a being whose near perfection evokes an admirable but potentially fatal compassion. Each author shows that the stain of mortality is mankind's link with God and thus the prerequisite for salvation. Spenser's Guyon is a romantic hero who, guided by the Palmer (Reason), learns this lesson quickly and maintains balance. Hawthorne's Aylmer, however, is a tragic hero who ignores his Palmers, loses the crucial balance between heart and head, and becomes a true victim of Excess. (JC)

9142. Fogle, Richard H. "Hawthorne's Variegated Lighting." *BuR* 21,ii(1973):83-88.

Common daylight is most important to Hawthorne but never all-sufficing. There are always other lights to be considered, and he tries continually to achieve a proper adjustment between them. His fullest exploration of visionary light occurs in "The Custom House," and sketches such as "A Select Party" and "The Hall of Fantasy" furnish important instances of his variegated lighting

arrangements. Hawthorne is tentative, continually aware of modifications, of the possible effects of particular contexts and circumstances. He understands synthesis rather than imagining it; he uses Romantic concepts critically and eclectically. He is committed to wholeness and comprehensiveness and accuracy according to his lights, which are remarkably variegated. He bent over a little too far backwards to do justice to the light of common day, which was of all lights least congenial with his natural instincts. (RHF)

9146. Graham, John. "The Restored Passages in the Centenary Edition of *The Blithedale Romance*." *HAB* 24(1973):110-14.

The editorial restoration of three passages in the Centenary edition of *The Blithedale Romance* may be questioned on both textual and literary grounds. Textual Editor Fredson Bowers admits that the deletions made by Hawthorne in manuscript "undoubtedly represent his final intentions," but, The speculates, the excisions may have been the responsibility of E. P. Whipple or, more probably, Sophia Hawthorne. Bowers offers no positive evidence to support either alternative. Undemonstrable conjecture, therefore, became the fundamental editorial basis for rejecting both the authority of the manuscript and Hawthorne's final intentions. Bowers further asserts that the reasons for deletion "could not have been literary." An examination of the three passages, however, indicates that Hawthorne could well have excised them for literary reasons. (JG)

9147. Greenwood, Douglas. "The Heraldic Device in *The Scarlet Letter*:Hawthorne's Symbolic Use of the Past." *AL* 46:[207]-10.

Critics have misinterpreted the final sentence of Hawthorne's *The Scarlet Letter*: "On a Field, Sable, the Letter A, Gules," thinking the sentence itself is an epitaph on the common tombstone of Hester and Dimmesdale. Hawthorne merely asserts that on this tombstone is a shield with the letter *A* on it. A look at two other places in the novel where Hawthorne uses coats of arms reveals his conscious, symbolical use of the heraldic device to signify Hester's and Dimmesdale's past sins and present redemption. (DMG)

9154. Hijiya, James A. "Nathaniel Hawthorne's *Our Old Home*." *AL* 46:363-73.

Using a consistent and evocative set of symbols, artfully plotting his narrative, and freely inventing details, Hawthorne fashions in *Our Old Home: A Series of English Sketches* (1863) what could almost be considered his fifth romance. The book compares American democracy with English aristocracy and finds the latter wanting. In the first chapters the narrator sees the mother country as a dream, an Eden of elegant gardens and cathedrals. But later he discovers the hell of slums and poorhouses which stand behind the palaces. With some regret he turns his back on Europe and affirms the moral superiority of egalitarian America. (JAH)

9158. Jarrett, David W. "Hawthorne and Hardy as Modern Romancers." *NCF* 28:458-71.

Hardy's reading of Hawthorne's *The House of the Seven Gables* (1851) is illustrated in *The Hand of Ethelberta* (1875-76), and this reading influenced *A Laodicean* (1881). This influence is examined in the uses made of photography in each work, in the uses made of the railroad, and, most important, in the manipulation of the conventions of the romance form. For example, each work is dominated by the central archetype of the Gothic romance, the mansion in decay, and contains an "orphan-of-the-castle" heroine, a usurpation, and a betrothal symbolizing a compromise between progress and tradition. Hardy simplifies Hawthorne's romance by making Somerset the hero and Dare the villain, whereas Hawthorne's Holgrave, from whom they stem, is complex and self-contradictory: in these contradictions Hawthorne symbolizes the uneasy relationship between novel and romance. Hawthorne is more concerned to assert the romance's independence of the novel, Hardy to demonstrate how he can employ romance conventions without losing his identity as novelist. (DWJ)

9163. Lefcowitz, Allan. "*Apologia* pro Roger Prynne:A Psychological Study." *L&P* 24:34-44.

Chillingworth's function in *The Scarlet Letter* masks an under-plot within which complex Oedipal themes and motivations are at work. His physical disability is a personal symbol of isolation that cannot be dissolved by union with a woman. The villain in the romantic plot is seen, from this point of view, to be as passionate as and no more sinful than his partners in the triangle. When Chillingworth focuses his jealousy on Dimmesdale rather than upon Hester, the course of his behavior indicates homosexual longings reduplicating earlier complusions brought on by rejecting mother figures. (AL)

9168. Martin, Terence. "Hawthorne's Public Decade and the Values of Home." *AL* 46:[141]-52.

Hawthorne went abroad in 1853 with a sense of home so ingrained that he could sport with it even as he relied on it. As his French and Italian Notebooks demonstrate, Rome challenged this idea of home and evoked within Hawthorne dramatic feelings of attraction and repulsion; perhaps to temper the claims of Rome, he stressed the idea of the centrality of London when he later converted portions of The English Notebooks into the essays of *Our Old Home*; however, Hawthorne remained wedded imaginatively to strategies he had developed as a writer in New England. (TM)

9169. Mathews, James W. "Hawthorne and the Periodical Tale:From Popular Lore to Art." *PBSA* 68:149-62.

Scholars have minimized the influence of contemporaneous periodicals on Hawthorne's tales. In his earliest works he exploited native materials, particularly witchcraft, and evidently revised and refined in order to insure publication. An example of early influence is Whittier's "Powow Hill," which could have been a source for "Young Goodman Brown." Among his works treating New England history, Hawthorne was more sympathetic toward native characters when local publication was involved. He also adapted the sketch and the sentimental domestic tale, several of these demonstrating obvious periodical influence. "Egotism; or, the Bosom Serpent" is another prominent example of Hawthorne's adaptation of a periodical source. After he had mastered the tale, Hawthorne abandoned this genre for the novel. In his last tale he revived one of his early subjects—witchcraft —with a shift in emphasis. "Feathertop" allegorically decries pandering to popular taste and values. (JWM)

9171. McDonald, John J. " 'The Old Manse' and Its Mosses:The Inception and Development of *Mosses from an Old Manse*." *TSLL* 16:77-108.

The unity of *Mosses from an Old Manse* derives from the biographical unity of the period when Hawthorne and his bride lived in the Manse at Concord. Those years had a definite tone for Hawthorne, a tone which he captured in the preface to *Mosses*. The identification of this tone of life also draws attention to a pivotal phase of Hawthorne's lifelong concern with the problem of finding a "neutral ground" between reality and imagination. Hence "The Old Manse" points both to the facts of the Hawthornes' "real" life in Concord and to the effects which these facts were having on his implied theory of fiction. (JJM)

9195. West, Harry C. "Hawthorne's Magic Circle:The Artist as Magician." *Criticism* 16:311-25.

The pervasive presence in his works of images and motifs of the magic circle, and of dramatic patterns based upon conjuration and exorcism, suggests that Hawthorne conceived of the creative process in terms of the black art. In his fiction the magic circle symbolizes the self, the soul, the imagination, and the source of poetic truth, and often physically insulates a creative individual from the debilitating effects of "the Present, the Immediate, the Actual." The creative process involves an initial retreat from reality to a sacred precinct within the contours of the fiction, signifying the artist's retreat inward to the source of his vision. Imbued with a vision of reality from the perspective of the soul, the artist may then, like a magician, conjure out of his imagination characters as avatars of his vision, project meaning and significance upon their interaction, and thus exorcise his soul of the conflict between poetic truth and objective reality. (HCW)

9197. Wheelock, Alan S. "The Burden of the Past." *EIHC* 110:86-110.

Hawthorne viewed the past as a pernicious force in society for he saw that the influence of the dead over the living was disproportionate to the former's status. Salem provided Hawthorne with the most corporeal symbols of the intrusion of the past into the present—those dark and "beetle browed" houses that had survived the town's Puritan origins. He made use of these buildings as the palpable presence of the past in the present; as the settings for any story overshadowed with a history of guilt and early sorrow, and as an extension of the personality of its occupants. Hawthorne's three-way exploitation of the old house image is analyzed while his characteristic ambivalency about the ultimate value of the past in human society is examined. A case is made for the influence of Hawthorne's early environment on the nature and tone of his fiction as well as on his personality and social relations. (ASW)

9199. Yoder, R.A. "Transcendental Conservatism and *The House of the Seven Gables*." *GaR* 28:33-51.

Transcendental Conservatism tempers the American Adam with the legacy of Burke and the English Romantic poets who shared his reverence for the historical imagination. Both Emerson and Hawthorne felt the need for a detached vantage-point from which Uriel's prophecy that "evil will bless" appears true. Emerson's visionary archangel returns as the seer in *Seven Gables*, first as Clifford who cannot shake his linear predilections, and then as Holgrave, who in his own second growth fully comprehends the circles of nature and Burke's principle of organic change. Bancroft's natural dialectic is acted out when Phoebe and Holgrave wed the principles of permanence and progression (called "property" and "persons" in Emerson's *Politics*), and their union reiterates the crossings, patchwork, and general "inter-mixture" that has been nature's conservative method throughout the romance. In the new Eden, Wordsworth's imagination is restored, and Holgrave's transformation is the kind of "apocalypse of the mind" that has figured large from *Nature* to our current fables of renewal. (RAY)

Henson. 9200. Doyle, Sister Mary Ellen,S.C.N. "Josiah Henson's Narrative:Before and After." *NALF* 8:176-82.

Comparison of the 1851, 1858, and 1876 editions of Henson's slave narrative offers significant insights on his developing character and on the slave narrative as a developing genre and forerunner of black fiction. The first edition is brief, factual, and simply narrated, designed to inform the public about slave experience. The later editions add new events and expand others by detailing the actions, characters, and dialogue. They enlarge the accounts of Henson's inner reactions and reveal, by shifts in language, his growing sense of self-importance and satisfaction, linked to self-deception and manipulation of others, both black and white. His personality developments suggest the permanent psychic damage done to an intelligent natural leader by bondage and subjugation. Nevertheless, this unifying focus on Henson's character and the sparse, well-integrated commentary give a literary quality which makes the narrative a forerunner of the best developments in black fiction. (MED)

Holmes. 9203. Garner, Stanton. "*Elsie Venner*:Holmes's Deadly 'Book of Life'." *HLQ* 37:283-98.

Oliver Wendell Holmes's *Elsie Venner* was written in reaction to the fatality of the romances of Hawthorne and Melville. He subjected a Hawthornesque girl to the scientific scrutiny of the realist. A daughter of Eve, Elsie inherits serpentine characteristics, but they are temporary; as she reaches womanhood, love may "bring her right." The intended agent of her metamorphosis is, appropriately, a Brahmin medical student. But Holmes's philosophical intention was frustrated by his psychological perceptions and by the vitality of his creation. Elsie's serpentinism magnifies her muliebrity until she is an "over-womanized woman" with a sexuality too powerful for the hyper-refined Bernard. Unable to respond to her plea to "love me," he kills her by rejecting her. Holmes's melioristic point having been lost, Bernard is sent—with some contempt on Holmes's part-back to the tepid society which has forced him into an unanticipated determinism, but his novel did succeed in bringing to an end the period of the moral romance and initiating the era of realism. (SG)

Irving, W. 9210. Fraser, Howard M. "Change is the Unchanging:Washington Irving and Manuel Gutiérrez Nájera." *JSSTC* 1(1973):151-59.

A comparative study of Irving's influence on Manuel Gutiérrez Nájera indicates a basic revision in the literary sensibilities of the 19th century. Irving's "Rip Van Winkle" is a fundamentally comic vision of colonial America's metamorphosis into a Republic. The protagonist mirrors the attitudes and pace of his town and his century coming face to face with the onrushing future. Nájera's "Rip-Rip" transforms the central character into a tragic victim of brutal, cosmic forces. In his nightmarish parody of the original, Nájera anticipates the sense of life's anguish and despair brought about by catastrophic change, itself a theme of 19th- and 20th-century literature. (HMF)

9211. Harbert, Earl N. "Washington Irving's *Conquest of Granada*:A Spanish Experiment that Failed." *ClioW* 3:305-13.

Of Washington Irving's three most significant Spanish books, *A Chronicle of the Conquest of Granada* alone was written as a literary experiment. In that work Irving sought to mix sound history and romantic story-telling and to form a unique combination which would appeal to many readers of both history and fiction. The publication history of *Granada* shows that its author failed in this attempt and that he gradually lost sight of his original purpose. (ENH)

9216. Ringe, Donald A. "Irving's Use of the Gothic Mode." *SLitI* 7,i:51-65.

Irving's use of the Gothic mode may be understood in terms of the intellectual system that informs the opinions of Geoffrey Crayon. Crayon himself does not accept supernatural phenomena as objectively real, but considers them rather the result of deceptive vision, the creation of superstitious minds, or the effect of immersing oneself in Gothic fiction. Each is assigned a specific narrator, sometimes as much as twice removed from Crayon—a device which allows for a wide variety of effects, from rollicking humor to true horror. (DAR)

James, H. 9218. Feinstein, Howard. "The Double in *The Autobiography* of the Elder Henry James." *AI* 31:293-315.

Henry James Senior's autobiography, *Immortal Life, Illustrated by a Brief Autobiographical Sketch of the Late Stephen Dewhurst*, was included by William James in his father's *Literary Remains*. According to William his father was subject and author of the autobiography. The Dewhurst pseudonym is justified on theological, structural, historical, and psychological grounds. The name's significance derives from Swedenborgian sources and shows James's spiritual qualities. There are significant differences between Dewhurst and James and analysis reveals Dewhurst as a significantly developed alter ego. They connect James's lifelong struggle with his natural self-hood, quest for vocation, and failure to complete his autobiography. (HMF)

Lippard. 9221. Pollin, Burton R. "More on Lippard and Poe." *PoeS* 7,i:22-23.

Supplements two recent articles on George Lippard with the text of Lippard's review of Poe's *Prose Romances* of 1843 in *The Citizen Soldier* of Philadelphia and with completions for Lippard's obituary notice of Poe in *The Quaker City*. Both are in the strain of vindication and adulation. Lippard's five satirical articles in a series called "Literary and Political Police" in *The Quaker City* are described, chiefly for their Poe content. Poe is the "Justice on the Bench of the Police Court" before whom various political and literary offenders are being tried and sentenced. The reports indicate various attitudes shared by Poe and Lippard. (BRP)

Longfellow. 9223. Allaback, Steven. "Longfellow's 'Galgano'." *AL* 46:210-19. [Reprs. 1853 poem.]

In May 1953, Longfellow published a poem in *Putnam's Monthly* entitled "Galgano," a verse translation of a tale from *Il pecorone* by Giovanni Fiorentino. This article includes the text of that poem, notes, and introductory comment. (SLA)

9226. Lefcourt, Charles R. "Longfellow et la culture italienne." *RLV* 40:243-48.

Longfellow's poems and prose demonstrate his love for Italy. *Outre-Mer* contains numerous references to customs and legends he had become acquainted with as a young traveler. *Hyperion* and *Kavanagh* both contain references to celebrated Italians. Longfellow's interests broadened to include Dante, and in his 10 sonnets accompanying his translation of *The Divine Comedy*, he shows a profound understanding and an immense respect for Dante. After his voyage to Italy in 1868, Longfellow wrote a series of poems based on areas he had visited, and in his *Tales of a Wayside Inn* he borrows from Boccaccio and adapts entire sections from Cellini. (CRL)

9229. Smith, C.N. "Emma Marshall and Longfellow:Some Additions to Hilen's *Letters*." *JAmS* 8:81-90.

For some 30 years Longfellow exchanged letters with Emma Martin Marshall, a prolific English Victorian author of historical fiction and children's stories. Longfellow's first letters to Marshall, though polite, were perfunctory in tone, but gradually his tone became more cordial. Marshall valued her epistolary relationship with Longfellow, though she never met him. Four letters from Longfellow to Marshall are included by Hilen in *The Letters of Longfellow*. The texts of other letters and a few fragments were first published by Beatrice Marshall in her biography of her mother, *Emma Marshall* (1900). These are reprinted in an appendix to the article with explanatory notes. (CNS)

Melville. 9231. Adler, Joyce. "Melville's *Benito Cereno*: Slavery and Violence in the Americas." *Science & Society* 38:19-48.

"Benito Cereno" foreshadows a tragic fate for the United States of the 1850s if it fails to see the nature and violent potential of the master-slave relationship. Melville uses colors as the dynamic opposites of the master-slave relationship which in the Americas took on the white/black coloration irrelevant to it in essence. The philosophical realities of the relation are expressed by poetic means alone: structure, layers of irony beneath the surface ironies, accumulations of echoes and shadows, and historically-meaningful symbols including those Melville shares with Babo in their strange partnership of subtle imaginations which speak only by indirection. (JSA)

9238. Baym, Nina. "The Erotic Motif in Melville's *Clarel*." *TSLL* 16:315-28.

In Melville's *Clarel*, the erotic situation introduced in the frame is carried through the entire poem as an important aspect of its theme and action. Clarel thinks that sexual love is inherently impure and that his erotic feelings will separate him from God. When Ruth becomes accessible to him, he flees from her, embarking on a pilgrimage. The dilemma remains with him and is complicated by the idea of homosexual love as a resolution of the tension between earthly and profane love. Celibacy and homosexuality are both rejected by the young hero who is finally anxious to return to Ruth. His very wavering proves, however, to have been fatal. Ruth has died in his absence. A lover of women, the poem shows, cannot be a Christian, while a Christian cannot love women. Losing both God and women, Clarel suffers a nervous collapse. (NB)

9241. Berkeley, David S. "Figurae Futurarum in *Moby-Dick*." *BuR* 21,ii(1973):108-23.

The theme of Melville's *Moby-Dick* is prophesying the destruction of modern civilization by its having substituted adherence to the truths of theoretical science and the applications thereof in the conquest of moral and spiritual evil in place of reliance on the truths of the Christian church. Melville's understanding of Christian typology as reflected in his works is defined. The sea, the ark, the monster, and shipwreck are discussed, showing the sources of these types and antitypes. Berkeley discusses the Christian typological apprehension that the sea is the world, the bottom of the sea is Hell, the ark is the church, the monster is Satan, crossing the sea is baptism, and shipwreck is perdition. For *Moby-Dick* the significant change in this paradigm is the substitution of the *Pequod* for the ark, implying a secularized technological means for annihilating ultimate evil instead of, as with the ark, simply bearing its occupants over the sea to the safe port of Heaven. The sinking of the *Pequod* is therefore a shadow of coming things. (DSB)

9250. Canaday, Nicholas,Jr. "Melville's 'The Encantadas': The Deceptive Enchantment of the Absolute." *PLL* 10:58-69.
The ten sketches of "The Encantadas" dramatize Melville's conviction that an absolute perspective on life is never valid and, when acted upon, is always dangerous. The first four sketches are primarily descriptive, stressing varying perspectives and curious specimens of natural creatures; and the next two present the ambiguities of historical events. The seventh, eighth, and ninth sketches are narratives based upon legend: uncertainties in man's functioning as political being, domestic creature, and malignant evil-doer. The last sketch, a brief farewell to the clutter of this belittered world, concludes with the idea of mutability expressed in an epitaph of sailors' doggerel. (NC,Jr)

9253. Cohen, Hennig. "The 'Famous Tales' Anthologies: Recognition of Melville, 1899." *PBSA* 68:179-80.
It has been generally accepted that Melville's literary reputation, especially in the United States, was at a point of "near-oblivion" near the turn of the century. The inclusion of selections from three of his works in what seems to have been a successful publication series, carefully edited and produced, is an argument to the contrary. (HC)

9258. Eberwein, Robert T. "The Impure Fiction of *Billy Budd*." *SNNTS* 6:318-26.
The poem "Billy in the Darbies" which concludes *Billy Budd* embodies the meaning implicit in the narrator's activity. The poem contains speculations on the physical reality of death. The counterpart of the poet's work appears in the narrator's intellectual and metaphysical speculations on the meaning of the events he describes. The poet uses inappropriate language and refers to persons outside the narrative. The narrator employs biblical allusions ignored by his audience, argues defensively for his own veracity, and resorts to conjecture on the issues of Claggart's nature, Vere's madness, and the final interview between Billy and the Captain. Although romance and pure fiction allow one to create reductive visions of life, true art, the impure fiction of *Billy Budd*, refuses to simplify. Melville seems to be saying that all genuine art begins and ends in speculation. (RTE)

9260. Fisher, Marvin. " 'Bartleby,' Melville's Circumscribed Scrivener." *SoR* 10:59-79.
Employing an expressionistic Wall Street setting, Melville dramatizes in "Bartleby" a hierarchical society with distinct class and caste divisions. For Bartleby the experience in this office corroborates the dead-end existence he has known previously, and his ultimate demise in the Tombs culminates the metaphorical quality of his life in America. Melville's story suggests that Bartleby has no claim to the whole truth, nor does the narrator. In fact, the point-of-view extends the meanings of the story to demonstrate the linked failure of community, communication, and communion. Bartleby's reaction to these shortcomings embodies the pathology of schizophrenia, which stems from the character of the existing society and the susceptibilities of the sensitive individual. (MF)

9262. —— "Prospect and Perspective in Melville's 'Piazza'." *Criticism* 16:203-16.
As an introductory story rather than an essay Melville's "The Piazza" is more closely related thematically and technically to what follows than is "The Old Manse," after which the "The Piazza" may have been modeled. The actual piazza which Melville added to his house in Pittsfield "to enjoy the calm prospect" provides the metaphor by which Melville offers a foretaste of the five following *Piazza Tales*. It provides the narrator's standpoint for putting the world into perspective. Melville achieves his perpective by a series of allusions to painting, literature, religion, and theater—all realms of the imagination. But as the narrator tests his assumptions against empirical reality he is forced to abandon his more dangerous or distorting illusions while affirming another kind of illusion—that which enables art to unmask the deceptions of the world.

Beginning with the bright gildings of the visual and verbal picturesque, he is forced to recognize that "truth comes in with darkness," and almost accidentally he deepens his understanding of the world, the function of art, and the role of the artist. (MF)

9274. Hennelly, Mark. "Ishmael's Nightmare and the American Eve." *AI* 30:274-93.
Melville's *Moby-Dick* dramatizes one of the most pervasive themes in American literature—the Adam's flight from his Eve. Prompted by his own split-personali ty and Oedipal leanings, the American Adam projects his guilt upon Eve. With the reinforcing biases of Puritanism and the frontier ethic, he then flees her duality but can no more escape it than he can his own. In *Moby-Dick*, Ishmael's nightmare prefigures the major structural, symbolic, and character concerns of the novel. Structurally, the dream introduces an antipodal design which attempts to reconcile female commitment with male withdrawal, the womb with the tomb, finite time with eternity, and tolerant relativism with prejudicial absolutism. It also anticipates the figurative content of the novel's sexual, natural, and classical imagery. Lastly, and dramatizing the latent message of the dream, the *Pequod*'s crew and especially Ishmael and Ahab all flee from the ambiguity of their Eves back on shore. It is only at *Moby-Dick* 's conclusion that the castrating mother of the dream is finally reconciled with the alma mater, the *Rachel*. (MMH)

9277. Hillway, Tyrus. "Melville's *Education in Science*." *TSLL* 16:411-25.
Though not equipped with an extensive knowledge of science when he began writing, Melville consulted scientific works in the preparation of his early works. *Mardi* shows considerable knowledge of contemporary ideas in science obtained from popular literature of the time. *Moby-Dick* demonstrates a discriminating choice of scientific authorities. Hillway traces the sources and growth of Melville's scientific knowledge from his earliest "Scientific class book" to the era of evolution. (TH)

9279. Idol, John L.,Jr. "Ahab and the 'Siamese Connection'." *SCB* 34:156-59.
Unlike Ishmael and Queequeg who fashion a social bond, a "Siamese connexion" in Melville's words, Ahab welds his crew to him by using such ligatures as economic or psychological bonds. Though he felt the tug of a "Siamese connexion" in his association with Pip after the latter went insane, Ahab tied unbreakable cords to Fedallah and the malicious side of nature. In pursuing his metaphysical goals, Ahab rejected human ties and all felicity therein. Scorning the limitations of groping, puzzled humanity, an ungodly, vindictive side of Ahab labored to forge bonds with what seemed the essence and form of deity. (JLI,Jr.)

9290. McCarthy, Paul. "Elements of Anatomy in Melville's Fiction." *SNNTS* 6:38-61.
The anatomy as described by Frye and Stevick is an important genre in Melville's long fiction. *Mardi* shows such elements and also illusions of speech, essay passages, and a flexible, expansive development. In *White Jacket* the narrator provides catalogs, classifications, essays, and allegoric figures in various typical sequences. *Moby Dick* includes anatomy elements in early land chapters and increasingly thereafter. Satiric classifications, intellectual play, mixing of the sophisticated and primitive, masterful essay chapters, and other elements appear in the novel. *The Confidence Man* is in typical sequences an over-all vision as is evident in humor characters, unconventional ideas, stories-within-a-story, stark descriptions, and comic and satiric scenes of con-man and victim. (PMC)

9292. McElroy, John H. "Cannibalism in Melville's *Benito Cereno*." *ELWIU* 1:206-18.
Melville gives varied and emphatic instructions to the reader in "Benito Cereno" to pay attention to what is being left out of the excerpts from the title-character's deposition; and not until one heeds these authorial directions can he perceive that the secret of Babo's power is the threat of ritual cannibalism that he uses against the Spaniards. The reader's experience in the deposition continues Delano's experience of half-truths and innuendoes in the first part of the story. What Melville dramatizes through Cereno's desire to remain silent in court about the cannibalism is the compulsion of a man who knows from experience the necessity to forgive his enemies in order to keep from being

overwhelmed by the evil in man's history. In the end he fails, as the court drags from him the whole truth and takes its officially sanctioned vengeance against Babo, whose severed, gory head is the final image of the narration, a symbol of civilized "cannibalism" that complements the symbolism of the skeleton and expresses Melville's despair over man's inability to find redemption through Christian forgiveness. (JHM)

9295. Milder, Robert. "Melville's 'Intentions' in *Pierre*." *SNNTS* 6:186-99.

Melville conceived *Pierre* as a variation on the popular romance and changed his intentions only after he was well into the book. Though this interpretation has been ably defended, the unities of structure and theme and the complex ironies which pervade the novel indicate that Pierre's journey from complacency to despair was implicit in Melville's intentions from the first. (RM)

9299. Monteiro, George. "Melville Reviews in *The Independent*." *PBSA* 68:434-39.

Hitherto unrecorded are *The Independent*'s reviews of Melville's *Typee*, *White-Jacket*, *The Confidence-Man*, and *Battle-Pieces*. Its review of *Moby-Dick* was recorded in 1972. All five reviews are reprinted. (GM)

9300. —— "Melville's 'America,' I." *Expl* 32:Item 72.

In "America" Melville's reference to "Brazilian" in the lines "As rolled Brazilian billows go / Voluminously o'er the Line" constitutes a puzzle to the modern reader. Denoting the color red, the term derives from the name for the dye extracted from brasil-wood. Both Webster's *Dictionary* (1847) and the *Oxford English Dictionary*, for example, so define *brazil*. In at least three poems—"My first well Day—since many ill," "A Moth the hue of this," and "I asked no other thing"—Emily Dickinson employs the term in the same way. (GM)

9305. Quirk, Tom. "Saint Paul's Types of the Faithful and Melville's Confidence Man." *NCF* 28:472-77.

Perhaps the most perplexing aspect of Melville's *The Confidence-Man: His Masquerade* is the identity of the confidence-man himself. Identifications of the confidence-man have ranged from the suggestion that he is the "Devil" in disguise to the belief that he may be a "Christ-figure." There seems to be substantial textual evidence, however, that the confidence-man actually masquerades as the "types of the faithful" as described by Paul in I Corinthians xii.28. Thus, the deaf-mute masquerades as an apostle, Black Guinea as a prophet, John Ringman as teacher, the "man in gray" qualifies as a worker of miracles, the "Yarb-Doctor" poses as a healer, the P.I.O. man masquerades as a helper, and the man with the "traveling cap" pretends to be an administrator or governor. Finally, Frank Goodman is fluent in a number of languges and upon occasion, makes certain apostolic gestures which help to identify him as the eighth type of the faithful, one who speaks in a "diversity of tongues." (TVQ)

9306. Reck, Tom S. "Melville's Last Sea Poetry:John Marr and Other Sailors." *ForumH* 12,i:17-22.

Melville's poetry is generally disregarded in favor of his reputation as a fiction writer. However, since he wrote exclusively verse during his later years when economic and other problems were eliminated, his poetry should be examined as a key to Melville's mind. Particularly his sea poetry, and specifically the volume *John Marr and Other Sailors*, gives good information about his changing temper toward the issues of God and the universe during his final years. (TSR)

9309. Ross, Morton L. "*Moby-Dick* as an Education." *SNNTS* 6:62-75.

A proper appreciation of *Moby-Dick* begins with the full experience of its remarkable intricate play of pedagogy. Melville begins by training the landlubber reader in the minutiae of an esoteric subject, using Ishmael's sensibility to transform the necessary facts from discrete items in objective inventory into the play of stimuli within specific human experience. He further strengthens the reader's growing sense of experiential knowledge by the skillful use of kinaesthetic procedures, the effects of which engage us in the actions of the whaling voyage. At the center of this increasing sense of competence is a sensuous apprehension of the great whale, and its major aim is an acute perception of the whale's enormous power. (MLR)

9310. Rowland, Beryl. "Melville Answers the Theologians:

The Ladder of Charity in 'The Two Temples'." *Mosaic* 7,iv:1-13.

Had this story been read and understood, it would have offended reader's sensibilities in ways undreamed of by the editor and publisher of *Putnam's Monthly*, who rejected it in 1854. Briggs and Putnam disapproved of Melville's use of facts; they failed to realize that he was using expository data to create a literal dimension for an extended allegory which propounded an unpalatable thesis having little to do with Grace Church. At a time when ecclesiastical ordinances were the subject of fierce controversy both in England and America, Melville was making use of contemporary commentary to re-examine the essentials of the Christian dogma itself. (BR)

9318. Stafford, William T. "A Whale, an Heiress, and a Southern Demigod:Three Symbolic Americas." *CollL* 1:100-12.

Moby-Dick, *The Wings of the Dove*, and *Absalom, Absalom!* reveal particularized statements about the American nationalistic experience through symbolic Americas as represented by Melville's whale, James's Milly Theale, and Faulkner's Thomas Sutpen. Although these symbolic Americas are characteristically differentiated, they possess in common a view of an idea of "America" that is somehow cosmic in scope, perpetual, and prophetic. As prophecy these older Americas predict recent Americas: a land that destroys those who would madly destroy it, an ideal of selflessness that may well be self-serving, and a rendered tragic heritage that prescribes racial harmony—current problems of ecology, self-righteousness, and racism. (WTS)

9320. Sten, Christopher W. "Bartleby the Transcendentalist: Melville's Dead Letter to Emerson." *MLQ* 35:30-44.

The fact that "The Transcendentalist" in collection had been sent to Hawthorne's home, where in 1850 Melville read some of Emerson's prose, permits the suggestion from internal evidence that he patterned his scrivener and lawyer in "Bartleby" after the essay's idealist and materialist. In this light the story becomes a satiric condemnation both of the idealist's refusal to compromise with the imperfect material world's demands and of the materialist's blindness to the spiritual world's redemptive potential. Both philosophies *in extremis* are dismissed as variations of "self-interest," but the lawyer's example implies the need to assert the materialist's premise—that the material world cannot be denied—and then to engage the tragic struggle to realize a better world by continually testing one's image of the ideal and one's perception of the material against one another. Bartleby, symbol of the ideal world, can and does save the man who employs him, but the lawyer, despite overtures of brotherly love, cannot save the man who refuses to be employed in the material world. (CWS)

9321. —— "The Dialogue of Crisis in *The Confidence-Man*:Melville's 'New Novel'." *SNNTS* 6:165-85.

An examination of the narrator in *The Confidence-Man* reveals that he encourages suspicions of the confidence-man's avatars while withholding the proof necessary for just accusations. An examination of each encounter discloses that its consequence is hidden permanently from view. Portraying ambiguous situations which demand both skepticism and confidence, Melville awakens us to the liabilities of each alternative: the risk of confidence is loss of fortune, face, or life itself; the risk of skepticism is loss of moral integrity. Because no satisfactory middle course exists, the state of crisis is perpetual for those who seek to be both practical and moral. (CWS)

9327. Thomas, Joel J. "Melville's Use of Mysticism." *PQ* 53:413-24.

A close study of the mystical episodes in *Mardi*, *Moby-Dick*, and *Pierre*, reveals a change in Melville's attitude toward transcendentalism, from an early hostility to a gradual acceptance of the transcendental quests contained therein. *Mardi* contains an overt rejection of Emersonianism on the basis of its philosophical optimism and essential egoism. In *Moby-Dick* the rejection of Emersonianism is replaced by a search into a more Kantian Transcendentalism. Contained within the mystical episodes of *Pierre* is Melville's most overt defense of the heroism, however futile, of the transcendental quest. Recognizing this fundamental shift in attitude helps to avoid the inconsistencies manifested in several otherwise excellent critical studies which have adopted a monolithic view of Melville's attitude toward Transcendentalism.

(JJT)

9332. Turco, Lewis. "American Novelists as Poets:The Schizophrenia of Mode." *EngR* 25,iii:23-29.

Due to the dichotomous confusion in English that the mode of poetry is verse and that everything else is simply prose, American novelists have come to believe that prose works may not be considered poetry. As a result, many novelists have turned to writing verse poetry and in doing so have performed poorly in the unfamiliar verse mode. If poetry were defined as "language art," whether written in prose or verse, this problem might have been avoided, and the novelists might have seen that those language experiments they performed in their novels or other prose works were in fact their true poetry. (LT)

9333. Vaught, Carl G. "Religion as a Quest for Wholeness: Melville's *Moby-Dick*." *JGE* 26:9-35.

Melville's *Moby-Dick* is a complex allegory which illustrates the human quest for wholeness. The quest may begin anywhere and it begins with the particularity of the one who undertakes it and includes a constant reference to the dimension of experience which gives life meaning and significance. Despite its positive orientation, it is true that the quest for wholeness leads inevitably to discord. At the conclusion of the novel, positive and negative dimensions of the quest come together when Moby-Dick snatches Ahab up from his surrounding context, Queequeg crosses his arms and vanishes into the sea, and Ishmael finds salvation in the coffin which emerges from the intersection of Moby-Dick's plunge into the ocean and the water which surrounds him. (CGV)

9336. Watson, Charles N.,Jr. "Melville's Fiction in the Early 1970's." *ESQ* 20:291-97.

Critical and interpretive studies of Melville's fiction testify to the continuing appeal and protean quality of his work. He is seen variously as romantic ironist (John Seelye, *Melville: The Ironic Diagram*), religious quester (Martin L. Pops, *The Melville Archetype*), democratic humanist (Ray B. Browne, *Melville's Drive to Humanism*), and working literary craftsman (Alan Lebowitz, *Progress into Silence* and Howard P. Vincent, *The Tailoring of Melville's "White-Jacket"*). Finally, William B. Dillingham's *An Artist in the Rigging* stresses the thematic continuity of the narratives prior to *Moby Dick*. Despite such multifaceted attention and a certain amount of repetitiveness, there are still some needs, chief among them being the need for a new literary biography. (CNW,Jr)

Poe. 9352. Boos, Florence and William. "A Source for the Rimes of Poe's 'The Raven':Elizabeth Barrett Browning's 'A Drama of Exile'." *Mary Wollstonecraft Jour.* 2,ii:30-31.

In January 1845 Poe published a critical review of E.B. Browning's 1844 *A Drama of Exile, and Other Poems*; in it he lauded her as superior to all poetic contemporaries, but mixed praise with condescension for her inexact rhymes and supposed lapses from good taste. Considering this archness it is interesting that several lines from "A Drama of Exile" strongly suggest the refrain of "The Raven." "The Raven" was first published in the early months of 1845, and the chronology strongly suggests the possibility that E.B. Browning's before/door/nevermore rhymes received an unexpected harmonic overtone in literary history. (FB)

9353. Burns, Shannon. " 'The Cask of Amontillado':Montresor's Revenge." *PoeS* 7,i:25.

Montresor's guidelines and methods for revenge in Poe's "The Cask of Amontillado" coincide with popular ideas about Italian revenge. Montresor gives Fortunato no hint of impending revenge, is willing to bide his time before avenging, desires to "punish with impunity," must remind Fortunato of his wrong, and takes great pleasure in tormenting his victim. Poe stresses Montresor's family and Montresor must avenge any insult to his family, especially from a Mason. Thus, Montresor addresses the bones of his ancestors. They know the nature of Montresor's soul, and to them, to the name Montresor, Fortunato has been sacrificed. (SB)

9355. Carringer, Robert L. "Circumscription of Space and the Form of Poe's *Arthur Gordon Pym*." *PMLA* 89:506-16.

Circumscription of space is a fundamental and necessary feature of Poe's fictional universe of negative possibility. That his

characters are almost always narrowly circumscribed suggests their severely limited prospects and interests. Diminished space also represents withdrawal into self, and Poe's centers of diminished space often contain symbols of that destructive core of the inner self which continually threatens the moral and rational being of the Poe protagonist. In undertaking *The Narrative of Arthur Gordon Pym*, Poe was committing himself uncharacteristically not only to the representation of movement in space but also to an objective mode of development, outward and ongoing testing and discovery of self in the infinite possibilities of space. The curious form of *Arthur Gordon Pym* is the result not so much of careless incompetence (as recent scholarship has suggested) as of fundamental conflict between psychological inclination and the formal requirements of an unfamiliar genre. But this work is of special interest, since *Arthur Gordon Pym* is a first effort in an important line of experimentation in American fiction, the transformation of an undistinguished form, the sea narrative, into a vehicle of major literature. (RLC)

9363. Fisher, Benjamin F.,IV. "To 'The Assignation' from 'The Visionary' and Poe's Decade of Revising." *LC* 39(1973):89-105(to be cont.).

Reprinting the original 1834 *Godey's* text of "The Visionary," later renamed "The Assignation," may provide useful material for study of Poe's tales, particularly as they indicate his habits of composition and revising. Most previous students seem to comment on the first version, but actually cite a later appearance (there were four altogether). Several other early tales have been reprinted from obscure periodicals; now it is time to have available "The Visionary." Commentary on the original text is included. (BFF)

9365. Flory, Wendy S. "Usher's Fear and the Flaw in Poe's Theories of the Metamorphosis of the Senses." *PoeS* 7,i:17-19.

Poe suggests that the senses persist after death until the individual is metamorphosed into a state of "ultimate life," but, if so, the senses must experience the decomposition of the body. Poe confronts this as the theme of premature burial. Usher's hypersensitivity indicates his imminent metamorphosis, but his fear is negative, prompting him to rely on the reason which for Poe is inferior to the apprehensions of the senses. Usher's fear that he will find some degree of life in Madeline's "corpse" prevents him from acting to free her and is responsible for the shock which finally kills him. Madeline, representing the physical body, and Roderick, the senses of that body, must die together, the brother falling dead beneath the now dead body of his sister. (WSF)

9366. Forclaz, Roger. "Edgar Poe et les animaux." *RLV* 39(1973):483-96.

Poe's love for animals is demonstrated by the role of faithful companions assigned to dogs in his fiction. Poe is also concerned with the problem of instinct: he even contends that instinct is superior to reason. The sagacity evinced by many animals gives them an ominous character; they become a source of terror and mystery in Poe's fiction and are often used for their symbolic value. By their demonic nature, they are a manifestation of the grotesque. The alienation which is characteristic of the grotesque is also expressed by the transformation of humans into animals, as in *Hop-Frog*. Poe's treatment of animals reaches a climax in *The Conqueror Worm*, where the human condition is represented in terms of images borrowed from animals. (RF)

9373. Hubert, Thomas. "The Southern Element in Poe's Fiction." *GaR* 28:200-11.

Poe is a Southern writer not because of local color elements but by virtue of qualities peculiar to the Southern literary imagination. The Ciceronian dimension of his prose style, for instance, along with his supreme verbal confidence, marks Poe as a Southern writer. More importantly, certain of Poe's views, as expressed in his fiction, are Southern. His chivalric attitude toward women is a case in point. What might be called Poe's agrarianism, which stemmed in part from his antipathy to industrialism, is also a Southern concern. Industrialism, which he saw as reflecting man's desire to dominate nature, ends by both upsetting the natural order and by creating havoc in the political realm. The radical democrat, incognizant of natural hierarchy, becomes a blind leveler and reformer. Poe directs some of his satire at both political and intellectual extremists and evinces no sympathy for such notions as progress and perfectability. He did, however, show great interest in genuine scientific inquiry. (THH)

9375. Idol, John L., Jr. "William Cowper Brann on Edgar Allan Poe." *PoeS* 7,i:24-25.
William Cowper Brann, publisher of *Brann's Iconoclast*, knew something of Poe's work both as a critic and poet. By comparing Poe's achievements to that of other poets, Brann sought to deny Poe an honorable position among poets of whatever era or nationality. Brann's remarks are most conveniently available in *The Works of Brann the Iconoclast*. (JLI,Jr)

9378. Jannaccone, Pasquale. "The Aesthetics of Edgar Poe." *PoeS* 7,i:1-13. [Orig. pub. in Ital. in 1895. Tr. Peter Mitilineos.]
Poe gave a new direction to esthetics in the U.S.A., which was still bound by the school of Pope and Goldsmith. He congratulated himself primarily on the originality and loftiness of his poems. Examining the various fragments in which his doctrine is dispersed, one integrates it and discovers the sources of his opinions. He believed that the task of composition was to express an inner vision, reflecting a superior light coming from above. This is the highest peak of ideality, stemming from German idealism through Coleridge. At the same time, Poe insisted that composition must employ sound and rational techniques, pointing out that originality is more a matter of work than inspiration. (PM)

9384. Miller, John C. "The Birthdate of John Henry Ingram." *PoeS* 7,i:24.
When Ingram's publications of Poe's *Works* and a two-volume biography of the poet merited inclusion of his name in leading British reference volumes, his birth year first appeared as 7 October 1849, the day and year of Poe's death, and then as 16 November 1849, this last date persisting to the present. But certified copy of Ingram's birth certificate, furnished to the Treasury Department when he received a Civil Service commission in 1868, shows his birthdate to be 16 November 1842. Further proof is in Ingram's unpublished letter to Mrs. Sarah Helen Whitman, dated 6 March 1874, stating that he is then 31 years old. Miller conjectures that Ingram's early identification with Poe and his life-long conviction that he had been chosen to redeem Poe's besmirched personal reputation led Ingram to falsify his birth year to coincide with Poe's death year. (JCM)

9389. Ostrom, John. "Fourth Supplement to *The Letters of Poe*." *AL* 45:[513]-36.
Supplements to or corrections for the 1948 and 1966 editions of *The Letters of Edgar Allan Poe*. Included are three new letters in full, three new fragments, and nine first collected, including several from auction and sale catalogs. Textual and bibliographical notes accompany the letters. New data relate to letters previously printed, such as possible forgeries, location of originals, identification of correspondent, possible new address for Poe, and new or corrective material for the check list of letters to and from Poe. (JWO)

9394. Pollin, Burton R. "Another Source of 'The Bells' by Poe: A *Broadway Journal* Essay." *MissQ* 27:467-73.
Poe revised "The Bells," of May 1848, into the much more effective version of 112 lines, presumably of February 1849. Both were published in the *Union Magazine* late in 1849. The revision may be explained by the fact that he donated a copy of the *Broadway Journal* to Sarah Helen Whitman in October 1848, first going carefully through it marking errors and memorable passages. In the two volumes he would have come upon an essay "The Broadway Carnival," which is full of holiday images relating to sleigh bells; these he could have incorporated into his new version of his poem—as suggested by many parallels, which are specifically traced. As to whether the anonymous author of the prose piece could be Poe himself, it is possible he wrote the essay as editorial filler, although the style is not distinguished. (BRP)

9398. ——— "Poe, Freeman Hunt, and Four Unrecorded Reviews of Poe's Works." *TSLL* 16:305-13.
Freeman Hunt, founder and editor of the very successful *Merchants' Magazine* of New York, was a friend of Poe from 1845. Both frequented the salon of Anna C. Lynch, and Hunt performed the services for Poe of receiving his important mail after Poe moved to Fordham and of testifying to his character in the 1847 libel case. C.F. Briggs and, later, Poe published many full and favorable reviews in the *Broadway Journal* of successive issues of Hunt's magazine, and Hunt lavished praise in previously unnoticed reviews of Poe's work. The full text of these reviews is given. (BRP)

9401. Reeder, Roberta. "'The Black Cat' as a Study in Repression." *PoeS* 7,i:20-22.
In Poe's "The Black Cat" the narrator's account of his behavior is a case of repression of instinctual psychic energy which bursts forth in uncontrollable destructive power. Man's rational tendencies are represented by the animus, his intuitive, instinctual tendencies by his anima. The cat and the narrator's wife become symbolic representations of the narrator's anima, which he is trying to destroy. In his attempts to destroy both the cat and his wife, he succeeds in destroying himself as well. Had he had positive feelings toward his wife and cats, toward the instinctual side of his personality, he might have found this side of him the source of profound intuitions and creative acts. (RR)

9402. Rees, Thomas R. "Why Poe? Some Notes on the Artistic Qualities of the Prose Fiction of Edgar Allan Poe." *ForumH* 12,i:10-15.
Poe's popularity lies in his artistic skill rather than in his subject matter alone. Unlike most of the writers contemporaneous with Poe, who depended on conventional rhetorical rules, Poe uses modern scientific methods to engage his readers' interests and thus avoids the ornate rhetoric and archaisms vitiating much 19th-century writing. The specimens adduced from Poe indicate that his better stories are marked by concision, immediacy, precision, and concreteness of detail. (TRR)

9407. Sands, Kathleen. "The Mythic Initiation of Arthur Gordon Pym." *PoeS* 7,i:14-16.
Poe's *The Narrative of Arthur Gordon Pym* achieves unity through the mythic rite of passage. The consecutive plots form an initiation culminating in the hero's penetration into the mysteries of the universe. In the shipwreck narrative, Pym undergoes separation, endures physical and moral trials, and achieves manhood before his rescue. The polar narrative repeats this motif as Pym enters the uncertainties of initiation into shamanism in which the dramatic events of the narrative symbolize an inner journey toward psychic liberation. Pym endures rather than controls his real and symbolic journey toward undefined goals, guided by the semi-savage priest Peters. (KMS)

Prescott. 9415. Brotherston, Gordon. "An Indian Farewell in Prescott's *The Conquest of Mexico*." *AL* 45(1973):348-56.
Prescott does not finally deny the European right to conquest in America but complicates his position in *The Conquest of Mexico* by emphasizing the excellence and cultivation of Nezahualcoyotl, ruler of Tezcoco in the 15th century. One of the poems he attributes to Nezahualcoyotl was taken from García y Granados' *Tardes americanas* (1778); the value of the Otomi "original" and Spanish translation printed there has been disputed. On inspection the first half of the original turns out to be palpably more Indian than the second. Not only did Prescott place more emphasis on the Europeanized second half but he contrived by further adjustment to make Nezahualcoyotl actually renounce temporal power in the poem and predict "the extinction of Indian dynasties for ever." (GB)

Stowe. 9427. Brandstadter, Evan. "Uncle Tom and Archy Moore: The Antislavery Novel as Ideological Symbol." *AQ* 26:[160]-75.
The Slave; or, Memoirs of Archy Moore by Richard Hildreth was published in 1836 and served as a literary model for *Uncle Tom's Cabin*. A comparison of the two novels provides insights into the influence of *Archy Moore* on Stowe. An analysis of the reactions to the two novels by contemporary readers reveals much about antebellum attitudes on race, religion, and literature. (EDB)

9429. Jobes, Katharine T. "From Stowe's Eagle Island to Jewett's 'A White Heron'." *CLQ* 10:515-21.
In Stowe's *The Pearl of Orr's Island* Jewett found specific impetus to define her own artistry. Stowe's Eagle Island episode (ch. xvi) consists of a brief narrative in which a sensitive girl protests a

boy's despoiling an eagles' nest and of an authorial comment on the crucial role played by the girl, an innately gifted artist-seer, in the spiritual/natural conflict dramatized in the episode. The comment indicates that she conceives of the artist as essentially a minister. Evidently stirred by the episode, Jewett rewrote it twice, revealing in her revisions a clear independent conception of the artist. She moves from Stowe's ministerial dialectic and didacticism toward more personal and lyric artistry. Jewett's sensitive child-artist is seeker before seer; her child seeks self-definition and spiritual insight through nature, not in opposition to it. Jewett's changes to gentle questing and to integral use of New England setting manifest growing maturity in artistic self-awareness. (KTJ)

9430. Lebedun, Jean. "Harriet Beecher Stowe's Interest in Sojourner Truth, Black Feminist." *AL* 46:359-63.
The relationship between Stowe and Sojourner Truth suggests that Stowe's interest in civil rights extended to women as well as to blacks and that the influence of Sojourner Truth may be seen in Stowe's fiction. Unlike other feminists of the pre-Civil War era, Sojourner was black (an ex-slave) and illiterate. She attracted the attention of the public for her outspoken performances as an orator, and she earned Stowe's admiration for her courage and piety. After the two women met and conversed in 1853, Stowe wrote the introduction to the new edition of Sojourner's life-story. Later, Stowe presented in *The Minister's Wooing* a character named Candace who resembles Sojourner in her dynamic manner and feminist ideals. (JL)

9432. Miller, Randall M. "Mrs. Stowe's Negro:George Harris' Negritude in *Uncle Tom's Cabin*." *CLQ* 10:521-26.
Through George Harris in *Uncle Tom's Cabin*, Stowe revealed an attachment to heroic means to secure black freedom and an appreciation of the great variety of slave personality types that survived in the American South. Harris emerged as the dominant spokesman for black manhood in the book. In this capacity he served Stowe's purpose to espouse her solution to the racial dilemma of emancipation of the ignorant slaves. Harris urged his black brothers to join him in colonizing Africa. This solution outraged Negro abolitionists. More vexing to Stowe, however, was the question of Harris' strong traits of intelligence and creativity. In her *Key to Uncle Tom's Cabin* Stowe defended her character portrayal by emphasizing that Harris' positive qualities were the inheritance of his white father. Harris, the mulatto, was only half a man, suggesting that with his black qualities alone he could never prosper or survive in white society. This racial bias in the *Key* negated the meaning of Harris in *Uncle Tom's Cabin* and led to the portrayal of Harris and the other characters of energy and enterprise, mulattos all, as whites in the popular stage versions of the 19th century. (RMM)

Thoreau. 9438. Adams, Raymond. "Henry Thoreau, Concord, Mass." *TSB* 128:3-5.
Henry Thoreau eagerly identified himself with Concord, Mass. His observations of nature were virtually confined to his native town, where he gave the hills or streams or trees nicknames as though they were friends. Thoreau spoke the dialect of Concord and enriched his writing with local phrases and allusions. Finally, he wrought the intimate attitude toward local life and nature and the idiom of the town into his own prose style. (RA)

9443. Bickman, Martin. "Flawed Words and Stubborn Sounds:Another Look at Structure and Meaning in *Walden*." *SHR* 8:153-62.
Walden uses landscapes and journeys to chart shifts and conflicts within a consciousness associated with the author, and focuses on language itself as a medium where these conflicts can be enacted and perhaps reconciled. The extended descriptions of the pond suggest the way artistic language both reflects and transforms reality. Close readings of passages like the wood-chopper and iron-horse episodes show how Thoreau creates a clear disjunction between fact and symbol and juxtaposes them to graph a constantly repeated journey between a centripetal fascination with pure art and a centrifugal attraction toward the ineluctable specificity and multiplicity of the outside world. (MB)

9444. Borst, Raymond. "Thoreau Advertisements from *The Atlantic Monthly*:1862-1868." *TSB* 129:4-6.

This compilation of the advertisements and announcements in *The Atlantic Monthly* offers new information about the publication of Thoreau's books and magazine articles. It is now possible to date exactly when his books were "in preparation," "in press," and finally "just published." All books are priced and the results of the Civil War and the post-war inflation are evident. All of the posthumous Thoreau books of the 1860s are included in these *Atlantic* advertisements. The excerpts from the reviews by magazines, newspapers, and the leading literary critics of the day provide an additional source of contemporary opinion of Thoreau's popularity and reputation. (RRB)

9445. Boudreau, Gordon V. "Thoreau and Richard C. Trench:Conjectures on the Pickerel Passage of *Walden*." *ESQ* 75:117-24.
On the Study of Words, by the English divine and philologist Richard Chenevix Trench, was a shaping factor in the formulation of the pickerel passage in "The Pond in Winter" chapter of Thoreau's *Walden*. Three times in journal entries for January 1853 Thoreau acknowledges "borrowings" from Trench's *Study*. He does not, however, acknowledge a borrowing in the entry of 25 January 1853 which is the basis of the pickerel passage in *Walden*. Key words in the journal passage—"topaz" and "conjecture" —not only identify *Study* as a source, but also provide a revealing conjecture of the sometimes convoluted manner by which Thoreau achieves a symbolic richness of meaning and lucidity of expression. The shift from "topaz" to "pearl" in the genesis of the passage effects a symbolic center not only of the pickerel passage in *Walden*, but also, by extension, of *Walden* itself as a pearl of great price. (GVB)

9453. Carson, Barbara H. "An Orphic Hymn in *Walden*." *ESQ* 75:125-30.
When Thoreau's "Smoke" was published in *The Dial* in 1843, it and a companion-piece were given the common heading "Orphics." "Smoke" earned this designation because it shares specific points of form, imagery, and ideas with the *Hymns of Orpheus*. Thoreau read widely about Orphism and translated a number of the Orphic hymns from the Greek. His use of his Orphic hymn "Smoke" in *Walden* underscores this self-conception through the Orphic light imagery and expression of the Orphic desire for ascent to the Apollonian realm. The poem also indicates Thoreau's progress in his ritual quest and his resolution of the conflict between the Apollonian and the Dionysian sides of his nature. (BHC)

9454. D'Avanzo, Mario L. "Fortitude and Nature in Thoreau's *Cape Cod*." *ESQ* 75:131-38.
Thoreau's narrative explores the relationship between man's spirit and nature. Nature shapes his spirit in fortitude, the virtue that sustains man and supports the other virtues. Man's spiritual adaptation and survival in a hostile universe are examined. *Cape Cod* continues Thoreau's probing of man's ability to firm, strengthen, and perfect his soul in nature's midst. The "excursion" takes him through many sea sketches, histories, facts about the land, and character portrayals, all of which fill out the theme of fortitude and give the work unity. It is a spiritual journey as much as a geographical account. (MLD)

9455. Fenn, Mary G. "Susan Loring on Thoreau." *TSB* 129:1.
Susan Loring's paper on her friendship with the Emersons recently surfaced in Concord, Massachusetts. The Lorings lived on Main Street near Thoreau and Ellery Channing. When little Susan Loring visited at the home of her best friend Edith, Edith's father, Ralph Waldo Emerson, would often take them off to the woods and fields. One day they went on a berry-picking expedition, Emerson driving the children in a hay wagon while his friends, Channing, Moncure Conway, Henry Thoreau and his sister, Sophia, followed in a carryall. Conway spent the day teasing the children until Emerson answered their desperate appeal for help by suggesting they pinch Conway. If that didn't work Emerson would horsewhip him. As Emerson waved the whip in a threatening manner the girls set upon Conway and pinched him until he retired in defeat. (MGF)

9461. Harding, Brian R. "Swedenborgian Spirit and Thoreauvian Sense:Another Look at Correspondence." *JAmS* 8:65-79.

Interpretations of the Swedenborgian theory of correspondence current in Thoreau's day included the belief that the lost union of Spirit and Nature could be recovered, by the self-reflective consciousness, through an awareness of the physical roots of the language used to express the moral and spiritual life. This belief offered Thoreau a way of discovering meaning in his observations of the natural world and suggested to him an alternative to the ecstatic union of Self and Nature he had experienced in his youth. In his journals Thoreau recorded the occasions when his recognition of the correspondence between the physical and the spiritual took the form of response to the metaphors latent in language. In his essays and his book-length works, Thoreau's philological application of correspondential theory made possible a thematic use of verbal wit intended to demonstrate the derivation of spiritual meaning from physical fact. (BRH)

9465. Harding, Walter. "Thoreau and Ecology." *TSB* 123(1973):6.
The *Oxford New English Dictionary Supplement* citation of Thoreau for the word "ecology" is based on a mis-reading of Thoreau's handwriting given in Harding and Bode's *Correspondence of Henry David Thoreau*. The word was not coined until four years after Thoreau's death. (WH)

9467. Harding, Walter,ed. "More Excerpts from the Alfred Hosmer Letter Files." *TSB* 123(1973):6-7.
The Hosmer Collection in the Concord Free Public Library contains a wealth of unpublished information about Thoreau. Among the letters herein reprinted are one by Eben Loomis reminiscing about his friendship with Thoreau; one by A. M. Sampson, one of Thoreau's earliest admirers; and several by Samuel Arthur Jones on Thoreau's imprisonment. (WH)

9470. Hibler, Richard. "Thoreau and Epicurus." *TSB* 129:1-3.
Thoreau and Epicurus shared many metaphysical and axiological ideas. Both were amateur scientists who sought ultimate truth in the circumspect examination of nature. Each developed an axiological system emphasizing a conduct of life following a similar pattern. Epicurus, an advocate of restrained hedonism, taught the philosophy of eudaemonia (happiness) found in mental joys tempered with forbearance and moderation. Like his predecessor, Thoreau lived with ascetic restraint, seeking food for the mind and renouncing material possessions. Both philosophers followed the dictum *Lathe Biosas* which means "to live in obscurity." Each withdrew to a life of introspection and reflection freed from societal business, political, and social obligations. Statements from Thoreau and Epicurus in their writings share the cynical hostility each felt toward life amidst the multitude. (RWH)

9471. Hill, Douglas B.,Jr. "Getting to *Walden*:The Strategies of Thoreau's Thought." *BSUF* 15,ii:14-26.
In "Civil Disobedience" and "Ktaadn," Thoreau records his discovery of, and reaction to the presence of power—in the State and in Nature, respectively. Although the experiences that inspired these pieces occurred while he was living at Walden Pond, and while he was completing the final draft of *A Week on the Concord and Merrimack Rivers*, neither jail nor mountain appears, except incidentally, in the two full-length works. Moreover, the implications of the experiences are almost totally submerged in the elegiac and celebratory energies of *A Week* and *Walden*. By employing in each work a self-consistent persona, with a single task to perform, he is able to choose deliberately poetic truth over experimental truth. (DBH,Jr)

9474. Jacobs, Edward C. "Thoreau and Modern Psychology." *TSB* 127:4-5.
Thoreau's pond-cove analogy to the development of the mind in "The Pond in Winter" in *Walden* (1854) anticipates Jung's discoveries. Jung stresses that conscious and unconscious mind must achieve a state of interdependence—"individuation"—for psychic wholeness. For Thoreau the conscious mind develops as it separates itself from the unconscious mind. The cove must contend with the collective unconscious, its "storms," and "tides," and with that conscious life of which it is becoming a part, those "promontories of the shore." Success leads to a cove of "sweet" seawater—individuation. Failure results in a "dead sea." Two reasons explain our failure to form a cove of "sweet" seawater.

Either we are "poor navigators," never finding our way out of the deep waters into a harbor cove, or we steer for a sterile cove and, cut off from the "natural currents" of deeper water, we become entrapped in "the dry docks of science." (ECJ)

9483. Orth, Michael. "The Prose Style of Henry David Thoreau." *Lang&S* 7:36-52.
Thoreau's prose style in *Walden* is a romantic style identifiable by symbolism and organicism. Organicism appears in the rhetorical strategies and structures, and also syntactically in paratactic sentences with many terminal free modifiers. Symbolism appears in trophes that create reality by restructuring perception. Close analysis of several hundred words from the chapter "Spring" in *Walden* shows that Thoreau adapts various personas and uses them to juxtapose seemingly incongruent facts, thus forcing new relationships to our attention. Morphological and scientific diction combine with shifts from literal to metaphorical meaning to make us experience the imaginative creation of a world. Thoreau's schemes are even more distinctive. His sentences have a mean length of 26.4 words, opposed to a belletristic mean of 22.7; but more significantly, his T-units (syntactic units which could be punctuated as independent sentences) are exceptionally long, while his base clauses are exceptionally short. Even more striking, 51 percent of the words in the test passage are in free modifiers—a very large proportion. A high proportion (36 percent) of these free modifiers appear at the ends of sentences. All of these characteristics reinforce the highly paratactic and experimental nature of Thoreau's style. (MPO)

9486. Rhoads, Kenneth W. "Thoreau:The Ear and the Music." *AL* 46:[313]-28.
Music existed for Thoreau on several disparate though connected levels of perception. Thoreau preferred the wild, free music of the untutored outdoor musician to the formal music of the concert hall. He conceived a music transcending the limitations of instruments and performance and heard music in the phenomena of nature. He commanded an acute sensory perception and sound was his primary medium of correspondence with nature. Music became for Thoreau symbolic, a metaphor expressing the principles of universal creation and spiritual reality. (KWR)

9488. Scheick, William J. "The House of Nature in Thoreau's *A Week*." *ESQ* 75:111-16.
Images relating to the architectural features and internal decor of man's home comprise a structuring motif for Thoreau's *A Week on the Concord and Merrimack Rivers*. At the center of this motif is an emphasis on the sequential opening of doors: first that of the artificial house, then that of nature and the rambler himself, and eventually that of the spiritual mansion. Such domestic imagery was intended to appeal subliminally to the reader, conveying a sense of ease with nature derived from an unconscious identification of nature with the comforts of home. (WJS)

9496. Uhlig, Herbert. "Improved Means to an Unimproved End." *TSB* 128:1-3. [T's thoughts in light of Darwinian philosophy.]
Thoreau and Darwin were contemporaries who influenced the thinking of more than one generation. Their views, although arrived at independently, often ran parallel. Life to each was an experiment. They both expressed optimism that the human race would eventually improve. Darwin's view led to man himself partially directing his continuing evolution. Thoreau would have agreed, but he would probably have insisted that random choices and blind destruction of traditional routes are senseless. More important, he would have emphasized, is the choice of the right routes leading to worthwhile goals; using improved means, but only to reach improved ends. (HHU)

9497. Volkman, Arthur G. "A Mythological Rainbow." *TSB* 129:7.
In the chapter on "Baker Farm," Thoreau reported in *Walden* that "Once it chanced that I stood in the very abutment of a rainbow's arch," a remark that aroused skepticism among critics. Charles R. Anderson has pointed out in *The Magic Circle of Walden* that, under certain circumstances, such an experience is possible (p. 136). (AGV)

9500. Werge, Thomas. "The Idea and Significance of 'Economy' Before *Walden*." *ESQ* 77:270-74.
The word "economy" in *Walden* refers not only to austerity but to

four traditional connotations of the word: the economy of Nature; the economy of Nature as the expression of God, its author; the economy of the Christian soteriology; and the economy of style and truth in Scripture and in the judicious handling of doctrine. The "Oeconomy of Heaven" (Jeremy Taylor) of which the Western religious tradition speaks sees the full realization of man's economy in the divine process by which his salvation is accomplished. *Walden* draws on these meanings of economy and, even when changing them for its own purposes, renews and re-emphasizes their traditional significance. (TW)

9501. West, Michael. "Scatology and Eschatology:The Heroic Dimensions of Thoreau's Wordplay." *PMLA* 89:1043-64.
Thoreau's puns reflect the widespread philosophic interest in language that flourished in mid-century America. Influenced by Wilkinson's *The Human Body and Its Connection with Man* (1851), Thoreau's covert scatological puns embody in style his philosophy of play, blending estheticism and stoicism in the concept of life as an heroic game. (MW)

Whitcher. 9512. O'Donnell, Thomas. "The Return of the Widow Bedott:Mrs. F.M. Whitcher of Whitesboro and Elmira." *NYH* 55:5-34.
Often dismissed as merely another collection of dialect "Yankee papers," Whitcher's *The Widow Beddott Papers* is actually an attack on the pettiness, hypocrisy, and bad manners common tao village life in America in the 1840s. Whitcher's native Whitesboro, a bustling canal village in central New York, was given to reform crazes and fads that drifted westward on the Erie. Borrowing a thin story-line from Trollope's *The Widow Barnaby*, Whitcher satirized her neighbors' shortcomings in her first sketches, published in *Neal's Saturday Gazette*. Later, as a clergyman's bride in Elmira, she encountered even shoddier manners and morals, and excoriated her new neighbors in more sketches in *Godey's*. (TFO'D)

Whittier. 9516. Trawick, Leonard M. "Whittier's *Snow-Bound*:A Poem about the Imagination." *ELWIU* 1:46-53.
Whittier's *Snow-Bound* owes much of its continuing interest and value to its complex yet coherent treatment of imagination in the manner of the British Romantics. The poem shows the power of imagination to project life and meaning into a cold, dead external world—to "half-create," as Wordsworth says. In the poem snow symbolizes three kinds of estrangement: loss of a sense of kinship with nature, failure of communication with other men, and separation from loved ones by time. The open wood fire opposes snow as a symbol for imagination which is able to overcome these privations. Yet Whittier also mistrusts the imagination as delusory, and in the end indulges in its warming light only after he feels he has satisfied the moral demands of his time. (LMT)

IV. NINETEENTH CENTURY, 1870–1900

Drama and Theater. 9527. Powers, Edward C. "Tommaso Salvini:An American Devotee's View." *ThS* 15:130-42.
Tommaso Salvini's portrayal of Othello was probably the most controversial ever to be seen in 19th-century American theaters; yet it was also among the most popular. Theater historians seeking explanations for the success of Salvini's much altered conception of Shakespeare's tortured Moor, spoken in Italian, have available to them a heretofore unpublished response to it by a contemporary who witnessed over fifty such performances, Thomas Russell Sullivan. His manuscript is a careful record to striking visual details and memorable acting in a Salvini *Othello.* For Sullivan, the impressive qualities were Salvini's uninhibited expression of the passion and violence so often only implied in Shakespeare's dialogue, the joy of hearing a language with its own inherent beauties of sound, and the sheer novelty of seeing an actor totally committed to the demands of his role. (ECP)

Adams. 9546. Harbert, Earl N. *"The Education of Henry Adams*:The Confessional Mode as Heuristic Experiment." *JNT* 4:3-18.
The Education of Henry Adams has commonly been studied as an example of autobiography or self-revelation. Yet the incompleteness and distortion of fact show that Adams makes use of a method that alters the confessional mode by replacing revelation with contrived disguise. Personal experience becomes the material for experiment rather than a cause for confession. As a result the careful reader, and not the writer, is the center of authorial attention in the most important passages. (ENH)

9550. Stark, Cruce. "The Historical Irrelevance of Heroes: Henry Adams's Andrew Jackson." *AL* 46:[170]-81.
In *The History of the United States During the Administrations of Thomas Jefferson and James Madison*, Henry Adams insisted that the nature of a democracy precludes heroes, that prominent figures must be viewed as representatives of forces at work among the people. Ignored in the scholarly concern with such types in Adams' *History* is the type of the "hero" himself. No figure so represented the man of action as Andrew Jackson; and in his historical generalizations, Adams agrees with conventional attitudes toward Jackson. Through his presentation of historical detail, however, Adams adroitly undercuts the significance of the man of action. (CFS)

Alger. 9554. Scharnhorst, Gary F. "The Alger Problem:The Hoax About Horatio Revealed." *BSUF* 15,ii:61-65.
The first biography of Horatio Alger by Herbert R. Mayes in 1928 was uncritically accepted and became the basis for later erroneous versions of Alger's life. A later biography heavily dependent upon Mayes, written by John Tebbel (1963), appeared contemporaneously with the most well-researched biography to date, that of Ralph Gardner. Tebbel's effort was praised and Gardner's scorned, however, since the "definitive" Mayes biography supported the former. Mayes has recently admitted that his original biography was a hoax, thus revealing the need to interpret the Alger myth by employing a non-psychoanalytic method. (GFS)

Bellamy. 9555. Cornet, Robert J. "Rhetorical Strategies in *Looking Backward.*" *MarkhamR* 4:53-58.
Little has been written about Bellamy's *Looking Backward* as a piece of persuasive literature, a work with its own peculiar rhetorical problems and solutions to those problems. Bellamy's primary rhetorical problem was to find a means of presenting his practically realizable utopia that would vitiate the potential charge against his work of incredibility, and then to make the work palatable to his American, nominally Christian, audience. To realize this end, Bellamy employed two principal strategies. The most general strategy Bellamy used was to shift the burden of credibility away from the utopian world of the 20th century, largely by making it, not the 19th, the book's ostensible audience. Secondly, Bellamy cast West's experience in the form of displaced Christian myth. It is by this strategy that Bellamy used what Burke considers the fundamental principle of rhetoric, "identification." That is, he identified his utopian plan with the pattern, familiar to his audience, of Christian redemption signified by grace for individual persons and millenial completion for the world. (RJC)

9556. Gildzen, Alex. "The Anonymity of Edward Bellamy's First Book and Other BAL Variants." *PBSA* 68:63.
The Kent State University Library copy of Bellamy's *Six to One: A Nantucket Idyl* includes the author's name on an advertisement on the inside front cover. *BAL* intimates the author's name was not listed until the 1890 reprint. Bellamy's postscript is absent from KSUL's *Looking Backward ... Thirty-Fifth Thousand.* KSUL's *The Duke of Stockbridge* has a variant binding. (AG)

Bierce. 9562. McLean, Robert C. "The Deaths in Ambrose Bierce's 'Halpin Frayser'." *PLL* 10:394-402.
Although "The Death of Halpin Frayser" is most frequently viewed as a traditional Gothic tale, Bierce provides the basis for a rational, psychological explanation of events without destroying

the supernatural quality of the story. "Halpin Frayser" is therefore in the mainstream of the distinctly American or ambiguous Gothic. Bierce presents apparently supernatural events at the same time that he provides other evidence to explain them rationally. Employing a fair but practiced deception, Bierce leads readers to believe that Halpin Frayser is slain by the apparition of his dead mother. In reality, Frayser slays his mother in guilt and revulsion over their incestuous relationship. Jaralson, Frayser's father posing as a San Francisco detective, strangles his son in vengeance. (RCM)

9563. Monteiro, George. "Addenda to Gaer:Reprintings of Bierce's Stories." *PBSA* 68:330-31.
To Joseph Gaer's *Ambrose Gwinett Bierce: Bibliography and Biographical Data* (1935) can be added three reprintings: "An Occurrence at Owl Creek Bridge," *Current Literature*, 21 (Mar. 1897), 237-39; "A Horseman in the Sky: The Sentry's Shot," *Current Literature*, 18 (Sept. 1895), 258-59; and "A Psychological Shipwreck," *New York Times Magazine* 25 Feb. 1968), p. 113. (GM)

Cable. 9567. Campbell, Michael L. "The Negro in Cable's *The Grandissimes*." *MissQ* 27:165-78.
The Grandissimes is a social novel: Cable treats the conditions and the structure of early 19th-century New Orleans society. By making four black characters function organically in his plot, Cable is able to give an authentic and balanced treatment of the race problem. Through the characters of Bras-Coupé, Clemence, Palmyre, and Honoré Grandissime ("free man of color"), Cable suggests the infinitely various ways in which a society based on a slave economy stifles and emasculates the members of the slave caste. (MLC)

Chesnutt. 9571. Andrews, William L. "The Significance of Charles W. Chesnutt's 'Conjure Stories'." *SLJ* 7,i:78-99.
Chesnutt's "conjure stories" exhibit a mastery of the major features of southern local color fiction while often expanding or transcending the limitations of traditional local color writing. Chesnutt adhered to local color conventions in his focus on the customs and culture of ante-bellum central North Carolina and in his use of Uncle Julius as ex-slave narrator for his stories. But he made a valuable contribution to Southern literature by eschewing sentimental and unrepresentative stereotypes of whites and blacks and by offering more realistic assessments of the average white's and black's deeper concerns. (WLA)

9573. Dixon, Melvin. "The Teller as Folk Trickster in Chesnutt's *The Conjure Woman*." *CLAJ* 18:186-97.
The tales which make up *The Conjure Woman* are verbal contests which the teller Julius uses to accomplish many interrelated goals. Julius, a folk trickster, establishes a thematic unity in the novel which describes his successful attempts at fulfilling material and psychological needs by telling folktales that describe similar trickery and need fulfillment through conjuration. He uses verbal trickery to assert his masculine identity and maintain an oral power over his employers that slavery and postbellum race relations suppressed. Julius' use of mask and trickery in folkore accomplishes what Chesnutt does in his similar use of the fictive medium of the novel—a commentary on the realistic struggle of his contemporary blacks. (MD)

9575. Hemenway, Robert. " 'Baxter's Procrustes':Irony and Protest." *CLAJ* 18:172-85.
"Baxter's Procrustes" was Chesnutt's response to the racist presumptions that a black author who writes successfully of white characters will automatically validate his talent. Although a story about white people exclusively, "Baxter's Procrustes" explores the habits of mind which could confuse whiteness with art. Chesnutt exposes thinking that distorts reality into the shape of preconceptions, the literary philosophy that equates truth with subject matter. The satire of the story is directed at the refusal of the Rowfant Club, a Cleveland literary society, to grant Chesnutt membership. (REH)

9576. ——— "Gothic Sociology:Charles Chesnutt and the Gothic Mode." *SLitI* 7,i:101-19.
The psychology of the Gothic mode has a sociological aspect, since the color imagery evoking the primal response coincides with the mythology of race prevalent in Western culture, leaving racist fantasies to reverberate in the Gothic effect. This illustrates why Charles Chestnutt found the Gothic tradition inappropriate for his collection of stories, *The Conjure Woman*, even though the tales are filled with the occult and the supernatural. Instead, Chestnutt's stories prove that "conjure," a black system of belief in animistic nature, becomes a positive set of rituals, a force for life opposed to the death forces of slavery and white racism. Chestnutt's proof depends upon subverting the Gothic psychology, thereby reorienting the imagery traditionally associated with supernatural phenomena. (REH)

Chopin. 9581. Koloski, Bernard J. "The Swinburne Lines in *The Awakening*." *AL* 45:[608]-10.
The two lines of poetry quoted by the newspaperman Gouvernail during the party scene late in Chopin's *The Awakening* (1899) constitute the beginning of Swinburne's sonnet, "A Cameo," from his early volume *Poems and Ballads* (1866). The sonnet is part of a series of poems which explore aspects of man's attitude toward death, and Gouvernail's quoting from it suggests that the newspaperman is alert to the essence of what is happening about him. The lines reinforce the atmosphere of impending death which is often noticeable in the novel. (BJK)

9582. Milliner, Gladys W. "The Tragic Imperative:*The Awakening* and *The Bell Jar*." *Mary Wollstonecraft Newsl.* 2,i(1973):21-27.
Studies the theme of women's imperative drive to fulfill her potentialities in Chopin's *The Awakening* and Plath's *The Bell Jar*. Woman's awakening to her self and her abilities, only to be denied fulfillment because of social attitudes and biology, can lead to tragedy when the bell jar of despair descends, as it does for these women heroes and their creators in Victorian and modern society. With the use of imagery and poetic structure these novels depict the frustration of the desire for self-realization that drives Edna Pontellier to suicide and Esther Greenwood to madness and attempted suicide, just as it drove Chopin to write the feminist novel that destroyed her life as a writer and the writer Plath to self-destruction. (GWM)

Clemens. 9587. Agrawal, I.N. "Mark Twain's Visit to Allahabad." *IJAS* 3,i(1973):104-08.
Mark Twain's visit to Allahabad toward the end of the nineteenth century was of historic importance. He had come to India in order to collect material for a book of humorous observations on travel. Twain was welcomed at the Railway Theatre on the evening of 3 February 1896. On this occasion he gave his well-known *At Home* and captivated the audience with his special brand of humor. Twain's own impressions of Allahabad have been recorded in *More Tramps Abroad*. Twain visited the Fort area and was touched by the innocent laughter and the simple faith of the common Indian pilgrims. The sight of the pilgrims carrying the holy water of sacred rivers to their far-off homes was meaningful to this visitor from the western world. Twain's irrepressible humor, however, asserted itself when he entered the Allahabad Fort built centuries ago by the great Moghul Akbar. As he stood on the ramparts of the Fort he saw the ash-besmeared mendicants squatting all over the area of the fair. His total impression now included a sense of primitive joy which he had experienced during his early Mississippi days. (INA)

9589. Baum, Joan. "Mark Twain on the Congo." *MTJ* 17,ii:7-9.
King Leopold's Soliloquy is remarkable because it is relatively unknown even though its subject matter bears direct testimony to the "unspeakable" horrors recorded in Conrad's *Heart of Darkness*. It is an indictment of atrocities committed in the Congo not only by powers overtly coveting its wealth but by those professing humanitarian goals. With the intention of showing the challenge to his divine authority and the exaggerated nature of the claims against him, Leopold succeeds in indicting himself instead. His complaint is the most effective witness to his arrogance and cruelty. Twain's premise is that to certain historical events there can be no neutral observers; his conclusion is that the craving of the Congo illustrates once again the triumph of "the damned human race." (JB)

9591. Berger, Sidney. "New Mark Twain Items." *PBSA* 68:331-35.
The variants in the first English edition of *Pudd'nhead Wilson* (Chatto & Windus, 1894) become explicable by examining the publisher's letter files of their correspondence with Frederick J. Hall of C.L. Webster & Company, Clemens' American publisher. One letter states that Chatto & Windus had in their possession part of the *Century Magazine* serialized version which had begun to appear the year before the English edition was published. In this and a second letter, they were requesting more copy from the *Century*. Such a discovery, coupled with information gleaned from the collations, proves the English edition to be derivative, and of no authority. (SEB)

9595. Brogan, Howard O. "Early Experience and Scientific Determinism in Twain and Hardy." *Mosaic* 7,iii:99-105.
While Hardy and Twain grew up in very different circumstances, each was subjected to a simple rural environment close to untamed nature and a society notable for folk superstition and rather grim religious convictions. Each began writing in a Romantic vein, soon moved from that to Realism, and ended in bleak allegorical Naturalism. Similar development of writers so dissimilar in personality seems to have resulted from their gradual acceptance of the deterministic view of the world dominant in the science of their time, but this acceptance was fostered by the psychological set given to each from the pervasive influence of folk superstition and religious predestinarianism playing upon a sense of guilt acquired from unfortunate family relationships. (HOB)

9597. Burg, David F. "Another View of *Huckleberry Finn*." *NCF* 29:299-319.
The ending of the *Adventures of Huckleberry Finn* is successful for Mark Twain's essentially antimoral metaphysics predicated the correct form his novel should assume. This point has been obscured by critics who argue that the novel's main theme is a quest for freedom. Its main theme is simply flight. This distinction determines our judgment of Huck's decision to rescue Jim from bondage at the Phelps farm. His decision results from a sound heart's rejecting conventional morality, without positing either a higher morality or a renunciation of slavery. Huck's choice serves the primary value of compassion and underscores the consistent irony of life. (DFB)

9599. David, Beverly R. "The Pictorial *Huck Finn*:Mark Twain and His Illustrator, E.W. Kemble." *AQ* 26:[331]-51.
Mark Twain's relationship to his illustrator, E.W. Kemble, during the hectic pre-publishing days of the *Adventures of Huckleberry Finn* reveals more than answers to the mystery of the "defaced" illustration on page 283. While corresponding with Kemble and Charles Webster, Twain comments on his understanding of the influence of illustration on the "genteel" audience of the 19th century. Also, Twain states interesting ideas concerning Huck's personality and the character of his "charming" Missouri folk, the violence of certain episodes in the novel, and the ambiguous morality of other scenes. (BRD)

9608. Gaston, Georg Meri-Akri. "The Function of Tom Sawyer in *Huckleberry Finn*." *MissQ* 27(1973-74):33-39.
The ending of *The Adventures of Huckleberry Finn* has been the center of controversy for years. Analysis of the function of Tom Sawyer shows that the ending is structurally and thematically appropriate and the novel has an organic unity. As the story proceeds, Tom emerges as the real antagonist: if he is not always part of the action, his spirit is. Thus when he materializes in the last part, he reveals himself as the primary villain. Because Huck has traveled a long distance from his original worship of Tom, he can eventually assert his independence of Tom's corrupt morality and sentimental view of life and art. The ending is not therefore a happy one, however. Twain stresses his pessimism through the circular structure of the novel and the ubiquitous nature of Tom's sinister spirit. In the end we must conclude that Huck's quest for true freedom is futile. (GG)

9614. Hill, Hamlin. "Who Killed Mark Twain?" *ALR* 7:119-24. [On T scholarship.]
A wealth of newly released materials makes it possible for both the literary biographer and the critic to reassess and re-evaluate the life and career of Mark Twain. Many possibilities and areas for future research are cataloged; however, the essential dilemma is that the current state of Mark Twain scholarship is marked by dullness, stale repetition, and intellectual torpor. Unless future scholars in the field are willing to offer ingenious, provocative, and challenging studies of their topic, Mark Twain will be "killed" by their tedious research. (HH)

9621. Krauth, Leland. "Mark Twain:At Home in the Gilded Age." *GaR* 28:105-13.
The often slighted novel *The Gilded Age* reveals at once that Twain's normative center is domesticity, a value shared by both the West and the East. Reflecting his own domestic circumstance, Twain makes the value of home and family a touchstone in his fiction throughout his career. In fact for Mark Twain the symbolic Fall of Man is the fall from the loving security of home into the threatening, lonely world of adult reality. While most of his major works, including the finally despairing *A Connecticut Yankee in King Arthur's Court*, simply affirm domesticity, toward the end of his career Twain traces the debasement and corruption of the family in *Pudd'nhead Wilson*. Twain's last great effort, however, his *Autobiography*, is once again a testament to home and family at the same time it is a moving record of Twain's personal loss. (LK)

9622. Leary, Lewis. "Mark Twain Did Not Sleep Here: Tarrytown, 1902-1904." *MTJ* 17,ii:13-16.
In spite of having been claimed a fellow-citizen who owned a residence in Tarrytown, New York, by local newspapers, Mark Twain seems never to have lived there. It may seem likely that he and his daughter Jean did go more than once to see the place which Mrs. Clemens had bought in 1902, while her husband was away on a Caribbean cruise with Henry Huttleston Rogers. Twain had thought that his wife's health might prosper at the Tarrytown hillside estate, and that his daughter Jean, who enjoyed horseback riding, might find the recreation and health which she sought. But Mrs. Clemens' health took the family to Florence. After she died there, the Tarrytown house was sold in January, 1905, without the Clemens family ever having been in residence. (LL)

9624. Lee, L.L. "Mark Twain's Assayer:Some Other Versions." *MarkhamR* 4:47-48.
Mark Twain, in *Roughing It* (1872), tells the story of the rascally assayer who, to satisfy his speculating customers, always overassayed their specimens. In 1956, Austin and Alta Fife, in *Saints of Sage and Saddle*, retell, as authentic folklore, the story of the assayer. But, in 1873 (or 1879), a certain Clark Johnson M.D. published *Seven and Nine Years among the Camanches [sic] and Apaches*, a book purporting to be the autobiography of "Edwin Eastman" who, captured by the Comanches, learned the secret of a great herbal medicine—"Eastman" includes, with stylistic changes that ruin the humor, Twain's assayer story as well as other events of *Roughing It*. The purpose of the hoax was, of course, to sell "Dr. Clark Johnson's Indian Blood Syrup." (LLL)

9626. Long, Timothy. "Mark Twain's Speeches on Billiards." *MTJ* 17,ii:1-3.
Both Paine's biography of Mark Twain and his collection of the humorist's speeches contain an anecdotal speech on billiards, in two slightly different versions. The version in the collected speeches is obviously incomplete and extracted from a longer talk. Both speeches were given by Twain at a billiard tournament held during April 1906 at the old Madison Square Garden. Twain gave the version of the speech from the biography on 17 April 1906, after a celebrated game between Willie Hoppe and George Sutton. During the course of the billiard tournament the San Francisco earthquake and fire occurred. The officials of the tournament arranged for an exhibition on 24 April 1906 for the benefit of the victims of the disaster. The advertisement for the occasion mentioned that Twain had been asked to speak, and the version of the anecdote from the collected speeches belongs to this date. (TL)

9635. Nibbelink, Herman. "Mark Twain and the Mormons." *MTJ* 17,i(1973-74):1-5.
Mark Twain's *Roughing It* differs considerably from contemporary Western travel narratives, especially in its treatment of the Mormons. Most writers saw America as the triumph of Christianity and democracy; and they self-righteously denounced

Mormonism for its despotism, heterodoxy, and polygamy. With an ironic temper remote from these conventional attitudes Mark Twain developed a mode of narration for humor and social comment that juxtaposes presumed opposites so as to reveal their underlying similarities, thereby exposing flaws or inconsistencies in both. Thus, he can deflate the prevailing moral tone while at the same time poking fun at the Mormons. Occasionally, he seems unable to submerge his social criticism in humor, and instead of a humorously ambivalent narrator he becomes a consciously ironic commentator. Even where Mark Twain engages in diatribe, however, he continues his ironic comparisons of institutions and cultures that reveal the irrational nature of all men. *Roughing It* provides early evidence that the humorist who deflates the jingoistic platitudes of democracy to reveal the common nature of humanity cannot be divorced from the skeptic who isolates himself by questioning all social values. (HWN)

9636. Pauly, Thomas H. "The 'Science of Piloting' in Twain's 'Old Times':The Cub's Lesson on Industrialization." *ArQ* 30:229-38.

Twain demonstrates in "Old Times" an acute sensitivity to the age of industrialization in which he lived. His recollections of the steamboat and "the science of piloting" involve an interplay of wonder and disillusionment that is much more complex than any progression from the former to the latter. The scientific knowledge which the cub is required to learn destroys the river's grandeur, yet it also adds to the awesome stature of his pilot-teachers, thereby causing a redirection, rather than a rejection, of the boy's romantic sensibility. When further technological advances topple these gods, there are still compensations. Unlike these former teachers and idols, Twain's experienced narrator who describes his lesson in "learning the river" has achieved a level of understanding that enables him to see beyond the immediate dangers of hidden snags and the less obvious perils of industrialization. (THP)

9646. Weaver, William. "Samuel Clemens Lectures in Kentucky." *MTJ* 17,ii:20-21.

As a part of the joint lecture tour with George Washington Cable, Samuel Clemens lectured in Kentucky during the last week of 1884 and the first week of 1885. Kentuckians welcomed Clemens with great enthusiasm and were pleased with his performances. (BLW)

9647. Wilson, James D. "*Adventures of Huckleberry Finn*: From Abstraction to Humanity." *SoR* 10:80-93.

The Christianity of Widow Douglas and Miss Watson, the romanticized chivalry of Tom Sawyer, the hedonism of Pap, the sentimental and brutal code of vengeance adhered to by the Grangerfords, and the inhuman, inflexible pride of Sherburn provide for Huck a series of ideal codes of behavior. He tries each code, before discovering all inadequate to meet the demands of his intuitive moral nature, his environment, and his companions. Huck learns the necessity of abandoning abstract ideals and clings to the enduring values of love, compassion, and self-sacrifice. The ending of the novel serves the thematic function of illustrating the continued isolation of the orphan who has developed a moral code determined by human needs. (JDW)

9648. Wilson, Mark K. "Mr. Clemens and Madame Blanc: Mark Twain's First French Critic." *AL* 45:[537]-56.

The first Continental criticism of Twain's work was an 1872 *Revue des Deux Mondes* article by Marie-Thérèse Blanc. Blanc reflected the values associated with the genteel tradition. Totally unsympathetic with Whitman, she was scarcely more responsive to what she considered the crude humor of Mark Twain and assured French readers that both the man and his work were best suited to uncultivated America. It was this cultural condescension, far more than her translation of his "Jumping Frog," that triggered Mark Twain's well known retranslation of the sketch. In an 1875 review of *The Gilded Age* Blanc again attacked Twain as lacking refinement, and this second snub rankled so bitterly that the humorist made an angry reference to it some twenty years later. At a meeting between Twain and Blanc in Paris in 1879, he seems to have taken delight in assuming the role of buffoon she had attributed to him in articles which had already made a significant contribution to his angry store of loathing for the French. (MKW)

Crane. 9650. Autrey, Max L. "The Word Out of the Sea:A View of Crane's 'The Open Boat'." *ArQ* 30:101-10.

In "The Open Boat" the climactic struggle of the four men to reach the shore offers two views of human nature: (1) man as a proud and independent individual, demonstrated by the oiler's effort to save himself, and (2) man as a pawn of fate, represented by his companions' acceptance of their insufficiency. The oiler rejects the elemental world of the sea and fails to reach the rational world of the land, and his efforts illustrate man's inconsequential endowment. The captain, cook, and correspondent acknowledge their limitations by seeking aid in their struggles. As a result of their own experiences and the example of the oiler's death, the survivors become interpreters; however, their knowledge reveals only the insignificance of man and futility of life. Crane supports his theory that man has the paradoxical alternatives of action based on ignorance and resulting in self-destruction or passivity derived from knowledge and leading to self-negation. Emphasizing the latter, Crane insists that the symbolic sea does not demand death, only submission. (MLA)

9652. Burhans, Clinton S.,Jr. "Twin Lights on Henry Fleming:Structural Parallels in *The Red Badge of Courage*." *ArQ* 30:149-59.

Crane's *The Red Badge of Courage* is built on two twelve-chapter halves, each developing through a prelude to battle, a combat experience, and an effort to comprehend that experience. In each half, Crane describes the battlefield and Henry's motivations and actions in identical imagery, defining war and Henry's role in it as non-rational, non-volitional, and non-individualistic. Crucially, this is Crane's language, not Henry's; we experience with Henry but understand through Crane's subtly ironic point of view. Crane defines Henry's motivations and behavior in equally subconscious and emotional terms, whether Henry is running from combat or toward it. Henry learns from his two contrasting experiences that he must protect his image as a hero by denying and hiding his earlier fear and flight and that death is a meaningless triviality for special individuals like him. Conditioned by his society's Homeric, romantic, and nationalistic concepts of war and manhood, Henry's self-evaluation is not Crane's, and is an ironic comment on Henry's society and its values. (CSB,Jr)

9656. Gollin, Rita K. " 'Little Souls Who Thirst for Fight' in *The Red Badge of Courage*." *ArQ* 30:111-18.

In Stephen Crane's *The Red Badge of Courage* soldiers are presented as ignorant men absorbed in petty quarreling; Wilson and Jim Conklin nearly fight in the opening pages. Wilson later tries to make peace among three squabbling soldiers, but only deflects their rage on himself. One of these soldiers plans to fight Wilson, but is himself later mortally wounded. One soldier treads on another's hand, an apparently trivial incident resulting, perhaps, in amputation. In the central incident a confused Henry is struck by an enraged Union soldier, receiving the wound others think he earned heroically. Henry's later courage is only another form of irrational pugnaciousness. Even the cheerful soldier's account of a friend killed by an enemy bullet while speaking angrily to another Union soldier extends the novel's pattern of meaningless quarrels and human waste. This ironic pattern recurs throughout Crane's fiction. (RKG)

9659. Karlen, Arno. "The Craft of Stephen Crane." *GaR* 28:470-84.

At age eighteen Stephen Crane announced his allegiance to the spirit of Naturalism, with its bias that the grimmest truths are truest. But his audacious gift for language, his poetic idiosyncrasy, contradicted his stance as recorder of things-as-they-are. In his early works, such as the short novel "Maggie," the poet and observer were so in conflict that the results were flawed masterpieces. A decade later, just before he died, Crane was reconciling his poetic gift and bitter Naturalism, so that they served each other; the result was some of the finest prose in American literature. Crane's development, then, was like that of many other literary masters who began as Realists or Naturalists: following an essentially extraliterary theory, he improvised and invented stylistically to achieve his ends and became a founder of "modernism," to be claimed as a predecessor by Pound and

Hemingway. (AK)

9662. Kinnamon, Jon M. "Henry James, the Bartender in Stephen Crane's 'The Blue Hotel'." *ArQ* 30:160-63.

The bartender in "The Blue Hotel" is Henry James; biographical details of the Stephen Crane-Henry James relationship and the role of the bartender within the fabric of the story point to this conclusion. Crane intended to ridicule the James lifestyle by portraying the barkeeper with Jamesian traits: a man who assumes a passive role in life and who abhors violence. (JMK)

9664. Kyles, Gillian G.M. "Stephen Crane and 'Corporal O'Connor's Story'." *SB* 27:294-95.

A Crane manuscript fragment in the Special Collections of Columbia University Libraries known by the inscription on its verso as "Corporal O'Connor's Story" had been thought to be a surviving part of a very early draft of *The Red Badge of Courage*. Transcription of this barely legible manuscript proves it to contain notes on the activities of the Avon (N.J.) Seaside Assembly probably taken while Crane was a cub-reporter for the *New York Tribune* in the summers of 1890-92. Delsarte, the French drama teacher, and his American disciple, Steele MacKaye, are both mentioned in the fragment. Crane published an 1892 piece mentioning a Madame Alberti and her students at the Seaside Assembly who studied Delsarte's methods and who came to be known as the "Delsarte girls." The significance of the inscription on the verso is unknown although by evidence of paper and calligraphy it might be associated with another early Crane unfinished short story about the Twelfth Cavalry and the Indian wars. (GGMK)

9665. LaFrance, Marston. "Stephen Crane Scholarship Today and Tomorrow." *ALR* 7:125-35.

Presents the results of 80 years' growth in Crane studies divisible into three periods: from 1896 to 1900, from 1921 to 1950, and from 1950 to present. The first period produced five valuable pieces by George Wyndham, Herbert P. Williams, Willa Cather, Edward Garnett, H.G.Wells; the second only an unpublished thesis by Jean V.E. Whitehead Lang. Since 1950, the best known schools of Crane criticism, the naturalistic, psychological, and symbolic, flourished especially during the fifties. Recommended subjects are the differences between naturalism and an ironic view of life, and Crane's recurring image patterns. Other schools, smaller but critically more promising, are concerned with Crane's style, poetry, social thought, and the native sources for his work. Crane's most ignored major works are "Death and the Child" and "War Memories." Other areas needing investigation are Crane's newspaper sketches, poetry, his influence on Conrad, the pre-*Maggie* work, the social climate of Asbury Park and Ocean Grove, and his disappearance in Havana in 1898. (ML)

9667. Mayer, Charles W. "Stephen Crane and the Realistic Tradition:'Three Miraculous Soldiers'." *ArQ* 30:127-34.

Stephen Crane inherited the realistic tradition in America. His impressionism, as illustrated by "Three Miraculous Soldiers," is a means of vivifying a world of appearances and illusions that man must dispel in order to function in a meaningful way. In their attack upon the romantic mind, James, Howells, and Twain focused upon individuals who need to "know" things that are ontologically knowable, things that may be perceived, organized, and assessed in a real and consequential world. Like his predecessors, Crane exploits the motif of illusion vs. reality in all his major works. In "Three Miraculous Soldiers" an ordinary scene of war is metamorphosed by a rebel girl's romantic imagination into a magician's world of strange images and distorted fragments. In the violent climax this world dissolves and she perceives that war is suffering and death, heroism only sympathy for those in trouble. (CWM)

9668. Maynard, Reid. "Red as Leitmotiv in *The Red Badge of Courage*." *ArQ* 30:135-41.

The color red pervades much of the description in Crane's *The Red Badge of Courage*. As a unifying leitmotif red is a dominant color in descriptions of battles, and it is the pervasive color of the cosmos described in some of the novel's thematic passages. Red images can be grouped into various clusters such as blood imagery, fire imagery, animal imagery, demon imagery, and emotion imagery. Animal imagery dramatizes the Darwinian-Spencerian survival theme of the war microcosm, while demon imagery suggests that the eternal human conflict is a hellish affair enacted within the infernal shell of existence. Not only is red a recurring leitmotif symbolizing struggle, but it is also a leitmotif of transformation since it extends the microcosm of the battle ground into a cosmic reality. Both time extension and space extension are effected, and we see that universal struggle extends through all time as well as through all space. (RNM)

9670. Monteiro, George. "Stephen Crane's 'Yellow Sky' Sequel." *ArQ* 30:119-26.

Crane's "Moonlight on the Snow" continues the principal themes of "The Bride Comes to Yellow Sky." Beyond parodying certain conceptions of the American West, it focuses on the paradoxes inherent in the transformation of a relatively simple social and political unit into a more complex entity in the national system. Drawing upon *The Adventures of Huckleberry Finn* as well as Scott's *The Fair Maid of Perth*, "Moonlight on the Snow" anatomizes the way in which the collective desire to speculate in land values affects the more primitive mores of a town which favors clan loyalties over justice by law. (GM)

9671. Peirce, J.F. "Stephen Crane's Use of Figurative Language in 'The Blue Hotel'." *SCB* 34:160-64.

Crane's use of figurative language is skillful in "The Blue Hotel." The reader is made to suspend disbelief through powerful descriptions of action, place, and weather in a series of developing images. Crane's genius lies in his choice of the telling word to elicit reader response. Personification and hyperbole are used with consummate skill, synesthesia with excellent effect, metonymy with subtlety, but synecdoche only conventionally. Many animal images and similes are used. His use of onomatopoeia is largely conventional, but his use of irony is effectively brutal. (JFP)

9673. Rechnitz, Robert M. "Depersonalization and the Dream in *The Red Badge of Courage*." *SNNTS* 6:76-87.

The intention of the final paragraphs of Crane's *The Red Badge of Courage* is ironic. Henry Fleming may come to consider his actions "in spectator fashion," but he fails to "criticize them with some correctness." His failure is caused by his willingness to adopt the official army version of reality which is equally remote from actuality. He is forced to that adoption because of the failure of the transcendental synthesis of matter and morality. Without that synthesis, individual perception becomes fragmentary and atomistic and cannot compete with the socially sanctioned version of reality. In adopting that version, Henry becomes more the soldier and less the human being. The confused tone of the final paragraphs is caused by Crane's yearning to believe in the Emersonian dream of anarchic freedom, that dream which is the product of the transcendental synthesis. (RMR)

9674. Simoneaux, Katherine G. "Color Imagery in Crane's *Maggie:A Girl of the Streets*." *CLAJ* 18:91-100.

Crane's *Maggie: A Girl of the Streets* reflects a portrayal of his visual and emotional world. Consistently, Crane associates certain colors with certain characters, their hopes and fears, and with aspects of their environment. In the novel the strong colors red and black are used more often than other colors. Black is primarily associated with Maggie; red with her mother and her brother; red, black, blue, and white with her lover; and yellow with her environment. Black is related to death; red to anger and violence; and yellow to the coarseness of the environment. (KGS)

9679. Zambrano, Ana Laura. "The Role of Nature in *The Red Badge of Courage*." *ArQ* 30:164-66.

A three-fold use of Nature emerges in Stephen Crane's *The Red Badge of Courage*. Always colored by Fleming's own emotional perception, Nature amplifies Fleming's emotions, and serves as an extension of his state of mind. Nature sheds its innate indifference and passivity, and in his eyes seems to rejoice, rebuke, or strengthen him. Through this recurring re-evaluation Nature becomes an active, unifying force in the novel. (ALZ)

Crawford. 9680. Brumbaugh, Thomas B. "The Facile Francis Marion Crawford." *MarkhamR* 4:70-71.

Francis Marion Crawford (1854-1909), son of the distinguished American sculptor, Thomas Crawford, was a prolific and popular novelist at the turn of the 19th century. A newly discovered letter written in 1892 to his publisher, Sir Frederick Macmillan, reveals something of his facile working method. *Mario's Crucifix*, for example, was written in ten days. Crawford's Anglo-Indian novel, *Mr. Isaacs*, was accomplished from 5 May to 15 June 1882, although he made two journeys during that time. In such cases, he concludes, the labor is no less, and "the result is often better." (TBB)

Dickinson. 9685. Goudie, Andrea. "Another Path to Reality: Emily Dickinson's Birds." *CP* 7,i:31-38.
Dickinson's poems involving birds are personal responses to both the observable and perceivable realities of life. Using birds as metaphors, she presents her acute awareness of loneliness, her absorption with man's enigmatic position in an indifferent universe, and her keen perception of her ecstatic response to life. With equal effectiveness she uses birds to convey her passionate anger, her stoic acceptance of life's rigor, and her wistful longing for the days that used to be. She also uses metaphors involving birds to express her jauntily thoughtful optimism, to define hope, to affirm her personal strength of will, and to exult in the triumphant will of all mankind. (AKG)
9686. Hagenbüchle, Roland. "Precision and Indeterminacy in the Poetry of Emily Dickinson." *ESQ* 74:33-56.
Dickinson sees the world as process and life as a continuous crisis. The resultant break between poet and world largely excludes the use of metaphor and favors metonymy. Dickinson's concentration on the elusive "critical" moments of experience becomes apparent in the epigrammatic shortness; the description of unstable phenomena; the elliptic style. She achieves *absence présente* through negation, oxymora, ambivalent genitive appositions, asymmetrical structures, and the disappearance of objects into "Circumference." Dickinson relates the incommensurable realms of finite and infinite "Compound Vision," simultaneously recording the spatio-temporal world with utmost precision while throwing a veil of indeterminacy over the timeless realm of eternity, which can only be inferred, not proved. (RH)
9689. Hill, Archibald A. "Figurative Structure and Meaning: Two Poems by Emily Dickinson." *TSLL* 16:195-209.
"The Soul Selects" has been often written about, and various meanings suggested for "close the Valves of her attention / Like Stone." Among the suggestions, the image "bivalve mollusc" proves to be part of an ordered series of analogies moving from larger to smaller. The final analogy suggests that the "chosen One" is like the grain of sand that becomes a pearl. The series of integrated analogies offers more parallels than the other possibilities, and so constitutes the better hypothesis of meaning. In contrast, in "It dropped so low" the images and analogies are disorganized and even contradictory. Thus, study of parallels quantified and in series offers a worthwhile tool for recovery of meaning and esthetic evaluation, since the tightly knit structure of the first poem shows it to be superior. (AH)
9699. Monteiro, George. "The One and Many Emily Dickinsons." *ALR* 7:137-41. [On D scholarship.]
Identifies and discusses several of the major strands in the scholarship on Emily Dickinson's life and poetry, particularly the work of the last twenty years (post-Johnson), and concludes with suggestions as to what remains to be done in Dickinson studies. (GM)
9704. Perrine, Laurence. "Dickinson's 'The Robin Is the One'." *Expl* 33:Item 33.
The three stanzas of Dickinson's "The Robin is the One" are organized, explicitly or implicitly, by four progressions—one of sound, one of activity, and two of time: (1) limited staccato notes, full-throated song, silence; (2) reporting on advancing spring, mating, sitting on eggs; (3) early March, early April, early May; morning, noon, evening. (LP)
9706. Pollak, Vivian R. "Emily Dickinson's Literary Allusions." *ELWIU* 1:54-68.
Through quotation and proper name allusions, Emily Dickinson signals the most direct kind of exploitation of literary sources in her poetry. Dickinson borrows most frequently from popular sources such as the Bible, generally avoiding references to high culture works attributable to a single author. The only author to whose work she alludes through quotation or proper name attribution more than once in her poems is Shakespeare. The

Bible is the only literary source Dickinson exploits continuously and in depth for metaphoric allusion. Her allusions aim at obliterating the edges between literature and life. Dickinson's desire is to identify past and present, Amherst and Judea, the sacred and the profane. She uses literature most successfully as refracted mental experience and is drawn by plot situations which function as objective correlatives of her own feelings. (VRP)
9707. ——. "Emily Dickinson's Valentines." *AQ* 26:[60]-78.
Of the 5 remaining poems of Dickinson's youth, the most ambitious are two comic valentines, "Awake ye muses nine" and "'Sic transit gloria mundi.'" These poems are engaging emblems of her early humorous verse and of that comic bias which yielded the witty conjunctions of her art. Dickinson's poems, written at ages 19 and 21, reveal more about her development as an artist than has been previously supposed. She burlesques a variety of literary forms and attitudes to which she was herself deeply attracted. The 1852 valentine is freer in its departures from valentine conventions than is her 1850 verse. Both poems contain the germs of that potentially creative ambivalence between acceptance and rejection which characterized Dickinson's relationships to other people, to society, to nature, and to God, and which included her emerging perception of herself as well. (VRP)
9708. Porter, David. "The Crucial Experience in Emily Dickinson's Poetry." *ESQ* 77:280-90.
Living after things happen is the crucial enterprise in Dickinson's poetry. The poem beginning "After great pain" is a paradigm of this preoccupation. Dickinson drew her peculiar power from an habitual backward-looking perspective. It is the experience around which the most important portion of the canon coheres. Premonitions, assaults, and crucial arrivals are metaphorical openings to this retrospective consciousness. Visitations thus inaugurate the period of afterward and constitute a main structural element in the poetry. Dickinson's art of the aftermath yielded the strategies of dislocation by which we identify her unique voice: the bonding of contradictory words, paradox junctures, freakishly precise images, and structural instability. (DP)
9712. Walz, Lawrence A. "Dickinson's 'Summer Has Two Beginnings'." *Expl* 33:Item 16.
Once the reader perceives the relevance of the final line of "Summer Has Two Beginnings" the seriousness of Dickinson's poem becomes evident. In stanza 1 Dickinson depicts two summers: the "real" summer, which begins in June, and a summer of the mind, which is brought to life in the speaker's memory ("begins") in October. This paradoxical distinction underlies the whole poem. Stanza 2 reveals that Dickinson's speaker prefers the mental construct to the real thing—at least momentarily. The witty tone, sustained in this stanza, is undercut in the final stanza. Here Dickinson reminds the reader that the month of October is the season of death. One can prefer it to June, and can prefer the mind-summer to real summer, but one must remember that eventually he will be dead for an eternity which is definitely not "deciduous." The reader is shocked by the final line—a *memento mori*—into recognition of a truth, and the poem now becomes an unusually subtle *carpe diem* poem. (LAW)
9715. White, William. "Emily Dickinson's *An Amazing Sense*:Addendum to Buckingham." *PBSA* 68:66-67.
A hitherto unrecorded edition of Dickinson, *An Amazing Sense: Selected Poems and Letters of Emily Dickinson*, Selection and Introduction by J.R. Vitelli (Bombay: Popular Prakashan, 1966, [xvi], 96 pp.), has escaped the attention of collectors and bibliographers. It contains a Preface by Manning Hawthorne, Cultural Affairs Officer, Bombay; Vitelli's Introduction; Reading Suggestions; 135 poems and 17 letters (from editions of this material edited by Thomas H. Johnson and Theodora Ward); annotations to the letters; and an Index of Poems. Its publication is designed mainly to introduce Emily Dickinson to students in India; the editor was Visiting Professor, University of Bombay, 1964-65. (WW)

Eggleston. 9718. Underwood, Gary N. "Toward a Reassessment of Edward Eggleston's Literary Dialects." *BRMMLA* 28:109-20.
Because Eggleston has been regarded as a respectable dia-

lectologist, critics have assumed the authenticity of his literary dialects. A thorough critical study is overdue, and it should compare Eggleston's representations of dialects with accurate records of 19th-century English. In the absence of such a definitive study, *The Mystery of Metropolisville* provides material for a tentative reassessment. In this novel Eggleston represents characters from Vermont, Indiana, and Illinois as speaking in dialect, but he fails to distinguish Hoosier English from that of New England. This failure raises serious questions about Eggleston's skill. (GNU)

Fuller, H.B. 9725. Swanson, Jeffrey. "A Checklist of the Writings of Henry Blake Fuller (1857-1929)." *ALR* 7:211-43. This checklist provides the most comprehensive listing to date of Fuller's writings, both published and unpublished, excluding the correspondence. Nearly 40 items are listed here for the first time, and the exact location of many others, previously known only from incomplete clippings or general references, has here been established. In addition to novels, short stories, poems, plays, and essays, the published items listed include over two hundred book reviews, editorials, travel reports, and other brief pieces. Manuscripts of a number of these items have been located, and manuscripts of all of Fuller's unpublished works, including his personal diaries, are listed and briefly described. Manuscript collections are indicated throughout the checklist. (JAS)

9726. —— "'Flesh, Fish or Fowl':Henry Blake Fuller's Attitudes Toward Realism and Romanticism." *ALR* 7:195-210. Over a period of fifty years Fuller wrote hundreds of essays and book reviews. A general survey of this material, largely ignored by critics, reveals a curious pattern concerning his response to the question of realism in fiction. In the 1870s and 1880s he ridiculed the popular romance and endorsed Howells' realism, even though his own first novel, *The Chevalier of Pensieri-Vani* (begun in 1886), was conceived as "an idealistic travel-fiction." In the 1890s he began to criticize realism, even though his *Cliff-Dwellers* (1893) was acknowledged as a major contribution to that movement. By 1900, he rejected realism and championed the "vitality" of romanticism. He adhered to this position until his death. Given this eccentric response, critics have been uncertain how to classify Fuller, though typically they have labeled him either a realist or romanticist. (AJS)

Garland. 9731. Grover, Dorys C. "Garland's 'Emily Dickinson'—A Case of Mistaken Identity." *AL* 46:219-20. Garland's supposition that he met Emily Dickinson in person in 1902 may be a case of mistaken identity rather than the fantasy it has seemed. Though Emily Dickinson died in 1886, Garland in *Companions on the Trail* (1931) records that in 1902 they met and talked about writing. It may have been that the woman was in fact Martha Gilbert Dickinson, a niece of Emily Dickinson. Garland, writing at the age of 71, probably got his Dickinson women confused. (DCG)

Harris, J.C. 9734. Crawford, John W. "Bred and Bawn in a Briar Patch—Deception in the Making." *SCB* 34:149-50. The device of deception in folk literature is very prominent and serves as one of many archetypal motifs. We see it in ancient Greek literature, as well as in British and American from the Middle Ages to the 20th century. Brer Rabbit and Flem Snopes epitomize the common trait of folk deceivers—all good ones are "bred and bawn in a briar patch." (JWC)

Hay. 9746. Vandersee, Charles. "The Great Literary Mystery of the Gilded Age." *ALR* 7:245-72. [On *The Bread-Winners*.] When the *Bread-Winners* was serialized in the *Century* magazine for six months, beginning August 1883, the American reading public became caught up in a curious guessing game. *The Bread-Winners*, concerning the social aspirations of a working class girl, immediately achieved and retained nationwide attention as the plot expanded into a "social study" of labor unrest during the 1877 railroad strikes. When the serial had ended and the book version had been selling for a few months the number of proposed authors totaled at least 25. Though most of the persons are now forgotten, several were quite plausible in their day, and a few made outright denials. John Hay, a Cleveland businessman, was one who denied authorship. Though evidence kept turning up that linked him with the novel, he never admitted any connection. Thus the book and his two outspoken defenses of it never stood in his way to appointment as Secretary of State. His secret foray into fiction was not officially revealed until 1907, two years after his death. (CV)

Herne. 9748. Saraceni, Gene A. "Herne and the Single Tax:An Early Plea for an Actor's Union." *ETJ* 26:315-25. James A. Herne was an American actor, manager, and playwright who became preoccupied with social reform in 1889 when Hamlin Garland introduced him to Henry George's system of political economy. The single tax promised the achievement of individual human freedom through social and spiritual elevation. On this basis Herne attempted to stimulate the formation of an actors' union as early as 1889, inadvertently incurring the condemnation of Harrison Grey Fiske in the pages of the *New York Dramatic Mirror*. (GAS)

Howells. 9752. Crowley, John W. "The Sacerdotal Cult and the Sealskin Coat:W.D. Howells in *My Mark Twain*." *ELN* 11:287-92. W.D. Howells sensed a profound conflict between the values of his native West and those of his adopted East. In *My Mark Twain* this conflict is manifested in Howells' divided loyalties between Mark Twain (the sealskin coat) and the Boston literati (the sacerdotal cult). In his ambivalent account of Twain's notorious speech at the Whittier Birthday Dinner, and in several other incidents which focus the meaning of this climatic scene, Howells betrays both vicarious delight and guilty shock over Twain's aggressions against genteel Boston. And although Howells asserts his common heritage with Twain in the "vast Mississippi Valley," he also assesses the degree of his cultural disinheritance from the West in his role as heir-apparent to the New England tradition. Howells' underlying fear throughout is that, like the deadbeats in Twain's speech, he has become an impostor of a "littery man." (JWC)

9757. Hilton, Earl. "Howells's *The Shadow of a Dream* and Shakespeare." *AL* 46:220-22. In *My Literary Passions* Howells specifically excluded *Pericles* and *The Winter's Tale* from his general admiration for Shakespeare. Yet the name of the heroine in *The Shadow of a Dream* (1890) seems drawn from *The Winter's Tale*. Hermia is a modification of Hermione, Shakespeare's heroine, and her last name, Winter, is drawn from the play's title. The initial situation in Howells's novel appears to be from the same source. Further study of the relation between the play and the novel, and between other Shakespearean tragi-comedies and other Howells works of the 1890s should shed new light on Howells's mood and mind in that period. (ERH)

9760. Marler, Robert F.,Jr. "'A Dream':Howells' Early Contribution to the American Short Story." *JNT* 4:75-85. Howells' little-known short story "A Dream," published in 1861 in the *Knickerbocker*, is his first fiction to show mature craftsmanship. During the 1850s, the enormous quantity of magazine tales produced a composite world of fiction marked by its decadent romanticism. In reaction, realistic representation increasingly gained acceptance, and Howells' "A Dream" stands as a capstone to this development. Though Howells and subsequent commentators have said "A Dream" is the first chapter of his unpublished novel "Geoffrey Winter," a comparison reveals that the story and the first chapter are not the same. Rather, the novel's manuscript shows the young Howells struggling toward a theory of realism that would counter the conventions of popular romance. (RFM,Jr)

9764. See, Fred G. "The Demystification of Style:Metaphoric and Metonymic Language in *A Modern Instance*." *NCF* 28:379-403. Howells' use of language in *A Modern Instance* calls the conventional forms of fiction into question and presents a new literary style in which the romantic ontology is displaced by the representation of a wholly secular universe. This style, that of literary realism, assembles according to a metonymic principle which is in opposition to the primarily metaphoric assembly of romantic language. The metaphors of the romantic style replicate the teleological structure of a theocentric universe by providing analogies between the realms of matter and spirit. In realism, however, the metaphoric style gives way to a linguistic mode that reflects those discrete attributes of experience whose significance is exhausted once they are arranged by empirical perception. What Howells does is to show that Bartley Hubbard violates the structure of language when he forces Marcia Gaylord to respond to an irresponsible erotic overture. By forcibly changing her written answer of "No" to the "Yes" which he desires of her, Bartley symbolically destroys the integrity of all language. This rupture serves Howells as the sign of parallel fragmentations in culture and its institutions: the church, the law, journalism, marriage, and the family constellation, as well as language. (FGS)

9768. Vanderbilt, Kermit. "Howells Studies:Past, or Passing, or to Come." *ALR* 7:143-53.
Howells scholarship has moved through two distinct periods since the end of World War II. The first stage ran its course into the middle sixties. This was a time for essential spadework, highlighted by the Gibson and Arms *Bibliography*; the two-volume biography by Edwin Cady; and the *Mark Twain-Howells Letters*, edited by Smith and Gibson. Studies explored Howells' relation to Italy, native realism, European realism, social and political thought, and painting. Since then the emphasis in Howells studies has shifted to a consideration of Howells' fictional world as the expression of an ambivalent social conscience and a modern sensibility. The gradual resurrection of Howells as one of the giants of our literature now appears nearly completed as each of the scholarly 32 volumes of the "Selected Edition of W.D. Howells" makes its appearance from Indiana University Press. (KV)

James, H. 9777. Boardman, Arthur. "Mrs. Grose's Reading of *The Turn of the Screw*." *SEL* 14:619-35.
Analysis of the rhetoric of James's "The Turn of the Screw," focusing on Mrs. Grose, the most important rhetorical element in the work after the governess, shows that the ghosts are ghosts, emanations from a cosmic force, rather than projections from the mind of the narrator. (AB)

9779. Bouraoui, H.A. "Henry James's *The Sacred Fount*: Nouveau roman avant la lettre?" *IFR* 1:96-105.
James's *The Sacred Fount* (1901) has proved enigmatic to critics, several considering it a self-parody. James's assertion that it has "its own little law of composition," however, is borne out by its self-reflection on the art of fiction, relating it to James's essays and his *Stories of Artists and Writers*. In this context, it anticipates the French "nouveau roman." The Jamesian artist figure's perceptions of "vampirical" love affairs among his fellow guests at an English country house are effectively demolished on the literal level. But a Jamesian ambiguity plays on their possible esthetic validity and the novel is a parable of the novelist's power "to guess the unseen from the seen." (HB)

9785. Corradini Ruggiero, Claudia. "Henry James as a Critic:Some Early French Influences." *RLMC* 26(1973):285-306.
Henry James's 1865 review of Matthew Arnold's *Essays in Criticism* provides initial clues to his early critical thought and introduction to French literature. That same year he identified the ideal critic as being the Swiss writer Edmond Scherer. James's 1876 essays on Baudelaire, Balzac, and Flaubert show Scherer's persisting influence, but are also in agreement with the French critic Ferdinand Brunetière's ideas. A close textual analysis, however, proves that only Scherer directly influenced James, while Brunetière himself followed in Scherer's footsteps. (CCR)

9787. Davidson, Arnold E. "James's Dramatic Method in *The Awkward Age*." *NCF* 29:320-35.
There are obvious contrasts in James's *The Awkward Age* that often expose certain characters. The manner in which one character is compromised can then be compared to the compromising or, sometimes, the validation of other characters. Emphasizing dramatized action and structuring the novel around calculated contrasts, James demonstrates that things are not always what they seem, that a social judgment is not synonymous with a moral one. This enables both James and the reader to

penetrate the dubious sophistication which gilds Mrs. Brookenham's circle to see the spiritual bankruptcy that actually characterizes it, to look beyond Nanda's social setbacks to see her as an individual who is aware and thus morally alive. (AED)

9793. Field, Mary Lee. "Henry James's Criticism of French Literature:A Bibliography and a Checklist." *ALR* 7:379-94.
Presents a bibliography of all the reviews, articles, notes, and essays James wrote about French fiction. Each of the critical works is listed in chronological order and identified with the number which Edel and Laurence assigned in *Henry James: A Bibliography*. The bibliography also gives information about reprints of James's criticism of French fiction. A checklist, arranged alphabetically by author's last name, of all the French authors and their works which James singled out for comment in his criticism is also included. (MLF)

9794. Fletcher, Pauline. "The Sense of Society in *The Ambassadors*." *ESA* 17:79-88.
In James's *The Ambassadors* the real subject matter is the conflict of different cultures and social values as reflected in Strether's internal struggles. Each of the remaining characters embodies a single aspect of American or Parisian society, and through them James shows a keen sense of the economic and political forces underlying each culture. Strether is the only character who develops a consciousness which to some extent transcends social conditions. He achieves a detachment which allows him to judge both Paris and Woollett, but only at the cost of great personal loneliness. (PCF)

9804. Houston, Neal B. "Henry James's 'Maud-Evelyn': Classic *Folie à Deux*." *RS* 41(1973):28-41.
Critics view "Maud-Evelyn" as James's treatment of the sense of the past or as the inevitable man-woman conflict. However, the characteristics of *folie à deux* as defined by Alexander Gralnick may be applied to Marmaduke and the Dedricks in "Maud-Evelyn." These characteristics are: (1) Association, in which the primary and secondary agents have had a long association together; (2) Dominance and Submission, in which the primary agent is dominant and the secondary agent is submissive; (3) Relationship, in which the agents possess a close relationship; (4) Pre-Psychotic Personality, in which the victim of *folie à deux* possesses predisposing personality characteristics associated with the aberration; (5) Sex and Age, in which a younger person is especially susceptible to delusion; (6) Type of Delusion, in which the victim's orientations are suspiciousness and credulity; and (7) Homosexuality. James anticipates clinical definition of *folie à deux* and succeeds in his literary presentation of the psychosis. His identification of the malady in "Maud-Evelyn" extends, as well, to characters other than Marmaduke. Their delusions lead them in mad pursuit of a lost little girl in a pinafore. (NBH)

9805. Johannsen, Robert R. "Two Sides of *Washington Square*." *SCR* 6,ii:60-65.
An examination of James's *Washington Square* in terms of its two carefully constructed motifs reveals craftsmanship in the novelist's arrangement of descriptive and figurative language. The novel's early motif, one which portrays the Sloper home as a fortress amid chivalric concerns, is comically disposed of and replaced by a motif which associates the tragic effects of domination and sacrifice with the Sloper home in its later sanctified form. Characters ultimately reject the comic unrealities of the chivalric romanticism of the first motif and overcome the tragic effects of its ritualistic successor; readers and characters alike dismiss these romantic motifs which have originated in and developed from initial visual perceptions of Washington Square itself and arrive at a realist's view of the Square and life. (RRJ)

9806. Johnson, Lee Ann. "James's Mrs. Wix:The 'Dim, Crooked Reflector'." *NCF* 29:164-72.
Henry James uses the role of Mrs. Wix, the governess in *What Maisie Knew*, as a vehicle for his social satire. She serves not, as has been suggested, as a figure of evil nor as a serious standard of respectability but rather as a source of humor and irony in the novel. In her over-zealous attempts to develop Maisie's "moral sense," she exposes her own weaknesses and those of others as well. Throughout she functions as a comic figure whose limited moral vision provides a sometimes humorous, sometimes penetrating insight into the tainted world of Maisie's parents, and

whose frequently ill-timed and misguided advice reveals that she is a harmless but ridiculous old woman. (LAJ)

9807. —— "The Psychology of Characterization:James's Portraits of Verena Tarrant and Olive Chancellor." *SNNTS* 6:295-303.

An examination of Henry James's methods of depicting the two female principals in *The Bostonians* reflects his struggle to move from romance to realism in his first social novel. The characterization of Verena relies heavily upon elements of romance which are incongruous in the realistic setting James establishes. Moreover, James's dependence upon antithesis as a technique of developing the two women causes Verena, originally intended as the heroine, to pale in contrast to Olive. The rendering of Olive is sympathetic yet critical, with James emphasizing the ambivalence and complexity of her feelings. Olive emerges as the true heroine of the novel. (LAJ)

9809. King, Mary J. "The Touch of the Earth:A Word and a Theme in *The Portrait of a Lady*." *NCF* 29:345-47.

The single word "touch" recurs throughout *The Portrait of a Lady* to such an extent that the one syllable alone tells subtly yet effectively of the complexity of human existence. From James's first rather whimsical introduction of the word through the names "Archer" and "Touchett" to his mention of Caspar Goodwood's powerful touch in the final scene of the novel the word argues persuasively for the theme of freedom blunted by the entanglements of human relationships. Behind the novelist's playful manipulation of language is the patient, methodical construction of a web of human relationships within which all of his characters will later become entangled. (MJK)

9814. Lemco, Gary. "Henry James and Richard Wagner:*The American*." *HSL* 6:147-58.

This comparative analysis of Henry James's *The American* and Richard Wagner's opera *Lohengrin* is an outgrowth of the mythic critical concepts of Northrop Frye. The approach utilizes mythic considerations in its singular investigation of the relation between literature and music, or music and ideas. Contrary to those interpretations which have denied the influence of myth in James's work, Christopher Newman of the *The American* reveals striking similarity to Wagner's legendary hero, Lohengrin. The demand for implicit and unquestioning faith permeates the sensibilities of both protagonists as each embodies the authors' conceptions of a spiritual force incarnate in a world fraught with conflict and hypocrisy. (GL)

9815. Ling, Amy. "The Pagoda Image in Henry James's *The Golden Bowl*." *AL* 46:383-88.

The pagoda image which begins the Princess half of James's *The Golden Bowl* has been considered difficult to interpret, yet it is a very important metaphor. Internal evidence would indicate that an article by C.F. Gordon Cumming, "Pagodas, Aurioles, and Umbrellas," published in *The English Illustrated Magazine* of 1887-88 was James's source for facts about pagodas. Symbolically, by its smoothly tiled exterior and its keeping her at a distance, and by the fact that pagodas in China stored the remains of saints and other precious objects, the pagoda in Maggie's garden represents her growing awareness of the "outlandish" (adulterous) yet seemingly considerate behavior of the Prince and Charlotte. (AL)

9816. Lohmann, Christoph K. "Jamesian Irony and the American Sense of Mission." *TSLL* 16:329-47.

James's international fiction treats the characteristic American sense of mission with subtlety and irony. In Christopher Newman, the protagonist of *The American*, James presents the archetypal American as seeker and discoverer of culture and as proselytizing missionary of a redemptive New-World faith. In *The Ambassadors* the ironic mode becomes more pointed as James subtly employs the diction of Christian religion and pursues a strategy of repeated and unexpected reversals. Strether's original mission is to save Chad; then he decides to save Madame de Vionnet instead; and finally he turns out to be saved from the narrow moralism that at first had been the very foundation of his mission. James's treatment of his major characters in these novels suggests his increasingly astute analysis of a form of American idealism that is always in danger of turning into jingoism and imperialistic arrogance. (CKL)

9819. Macnaughton, W.R. "Turning the Screw of Ordinary Human Virtue:The Governess and the First-Person Narrators." *CRevAS* 5:18-25.

The governess in Henry James's "Turn of the Screw" is important both because of the effects she helps him create and because she is a person whose actions must be observed and judged by the reader. She combines roles similar to those played by many of James's first-person narrators. What also links her to other narrators is the difficulty she has in discerning and interpreting the evidence upon which she must base her actions. The ambiguity resulting from this situation helps explain the story's ability to stimulate so many different readings possessing their own peculiar validity. (WRM)

9822. Monteiro, George. "Addendum to Edel and Laurence: Henry James's 'Two Old Houses and Three Young Women'." *PBSA* 68:331.

James's essay was first published in *The Independent*, 51 (7 Sept. 1899), 2406-412, 10 years prior to what has been hitherto recorded as its first appearance—*Italian Hours* (1909). (GM)

9826. Nettels, Elsa. "The Scapegoats and Martyrs of Henry James." *CLQ* 10:413-27.

In his portrayal of characters who see themselves as sacrificial victims, Henry James inverts the traditional concepts of scapegoat and the martyr. His protagonists who aspire to martyrdom are not witnesses who choose to die that they may affirm religious or political faith but victims of psychological need which drives them to imprisoning relationships in which they desire either to master another person, as does Olive Chancellor in *The Bostonians*, or to submit themselves to the will of others, as does Hyacinth Robinson in *The Princess Casamassima*. James's two principal scapegoat figures, Lambert Strether in *The Ambassadors* and Maggie Verver in *The Golden Bowl*, are not passive victims but active seekers of their own and others' good who willingly accept the burden of the scapegoat and in so doing enjoy a sense of personal worth and relief from the burden of guilt their own feelings and acts have imposed upon them. All four protagonists, Olive, Hyacinth, Strether, and Maggie, exemplify James's concept of suffering as the price one must pay for experience and wisdom. (EN)

9828. Page, Philip. "The Curious Narration of *The Bostonians*." *AL* 46:374-83.

The pecularities which characterize *The Bostonians* can be attributed in part to James's attempt to encourage the active participation of his readers. James's narrator omits as much as he includes and eschews consistency and predictability in his attitudes toward the principal characters. James further unsettles his reader by calling attention to both the narrating and the reading of the novel. The narrator is unusually self-conscious, he is defensive about his manipulations, he has ambivalent attitudes toward the reader, and he admits the limitations of his language and his narration. These strategies frustrate the reader but also necessitate his participation in the novel. (EPP)

9830. Pearce, Howard D. "Witchcraft Imagery and Allusion in James's *Bostonians*." *SNNTS* 6:236-47.

In James's *Bostonians* witchcraft imagery and echoes of words like spell, charm, and possession produce complex reactions to characters who are engaged not merely in a melodramatic love conflict but in ambiguous magical rites. Allusions to demonic beings and supernatural transactions further intensify the tragi-comic struggle for possession of the innocent, Verena Tarrant. Goethe's *Faust* provides a referent for Olive's attempt to gain from Verena a commitment. Even more darkly suggestive are associations of Olive with Coleridge's Geraldine. These metaphorical appeals to the supernatural point up the tendency in James's characters to generate supernatural sanctions for their very basic human needs. (HDP)

9833. Reynolds, Larry J. "Henry James's New Christopher Newman." *SNNTS* 5(1973):457-68.

A close examination of the revisions in Christopher Newman's character for the New York edition of *The American* reveals that James created a new Newman in the revised novel by subtly endowing his hero with more intelligence in comic situations; more warmth and sensitivity in his relationships with Claire, Valentin, and Mrs. Bread; more knowledge and maturity in almost all of his associations with others; a greater appreciation of European culture and art; and more reasonableness and self-possession in his contemplation of revenge. The nature of these changes indicates that James recognized the unsympathetic nature of Newman's character in the earlier version of the novel. (LJR)

9836. Rodgers, Paul C.,Jr. "Motive, Agency, and Act in James's *The Aspern Papers*." *SAQ* 73:[377]-87.

The tale James tells in *The Aspern Papers* appears to follow his notebook *donnée* so closly that we well may wonder at his emphasis, in the preface of 1908, upon the artist's need for freedom from restricting "facts" in developing his idea. The paradox is only apparent, however, for the tale differs profoundly from the notebook anecdote. A sensitive reconstruction of the speechless Juliana's actions and motives following her midnight confrontation with the narrator suggests strongly that she anticipates the thoughts and actions of both Tina and the narrator after her death (Section IX). When we note that she destroys her will shortly before her death, thereby freeing Tina to offer the papers to the narrator, our suspicion hardens into certainty. It is the dead Juliana, in the final analysis, who frustrates the narrator. James's subtle departures from historical fact create a degree of plot unity, irony, and thematic impact wholly lacking in the anecdote. (PR)

9838. Sabiston, E. "The Prison of Womanhood." *CL* 25(1973):336-51.

Henry James's Isabel Archer in *The Portrait of a Lady* (1881) is often seen as the prototype of recent portraits of young women. However, her predecessors include Austen's Emma Woodhouse (1816), Flaubert's Emma Bovary (1857), and George Eliot's Dorothea Brooke (1871-72). In all four works society imposes even more severe limitations upon women than upon men and the imaginative heroine is nourished upon books rather than upon life. The heroine's "provincialism" prompts her to seek ultimate values, but also imposes a frustrating ignorance upon her. Her mixture of aspiration and ignorance dictates her author's alternating tenderness and irony; even, at times, predisposes him to judge her actions by the same criteria he might apply to his own artistic endeavors. For all four women the inescapable prison is neither the provinces nor marriage nor ignorance, but the prison of womanhood. (EJS)

9842. Shelden, Pamela J. "Jamesian Gothicism:The Haunted Castle of the Mind." *SLitI* 7,i:121-34.

Gothic echoes are heard in several of James's ghostly tales as well as in some of his non-ghostly novels. In "The Jolly Corner" (1908), the Gothic devices function as emblems of the protagonist's psychological and spiritual condition. The American counterpart of the medieval castle, the house, serves as the objective correlative of the psyche, while it also images the internal *Doppelgänger*. Brydon, searching for the self that might have been, finds only an aspect of the self that is; but his horrified recoil preempts recognition and awareness of the "ghost" which he "scares up" in the convoluted apartments of his mind. (PJS)

9848. Stein, Allen F. "The Hack's Progress:A Reading of James's 'The Velvet Glove'." *ELWIU* 1:219-26.

The traditional reading of "The Velvet Glove" is probably the main reason for its neglect. According to this reading, John Berridge, the renowned author who refuses to write a complimentary preface for the most recent potboiler of a beautiful authoress, reveals an admirably unswerving dedication to literature. Read in these terms, the story fails to convince because Berridge, himself, the sentient center, is not a compelling embodiment of artistic integrity, nor does James mean him to be one. Instead, he is a self-deluding hack who, unable to cope with the humiliation into which his infatuation with the authoress leads him, attempts to re-establish his self-esteem by assuming a pompous pose of outraged honesty. Perceived accurately, then, Berridge becomes a marvelously comic figure and "The Velvet Glove" emerges as a work of subtle character revelation in the best Jamesean tradition. (AFS)

9853. Tintner, Adeline R. "Henry James Criticism:A Current Perspective." *ALR* 7:155-68.

Defines a current and personal perspective on the state of Henry James studies, and includes a sketch of the availability of

Jamesian material with emphasis on recent facts revealed in the final volume of Edel's biography. Tintner discusses fashionable trends and suggests that attention should now focus on what James did with his literary heritage rather than what he said about it. James is a writer of the greatest ingenuity and nothing occurs by accident in his work. This viewpoint is encouraged by such recent studies as those that situate James in his cultural milieu, resulting in a demonstration of his technical devices without falling into the current shibboleths of "structuralism." The need to pay attention to the neglected later novels and stories and to avoid the old chestnuts is stressed. James the Edwardian and James the Georgian deserve and require attention (*The Finer Grain* suite, *The Outcry*, *The Autobiographies*). (ART)

9855. —— "Octave Feuillet:*Le petite comtesse* and Henry James." *RLC* 48:218-32.

Henry James's published criticism of Feuillet's fiction in the 1860s-70s does not begin to measure the life-long effect his work had on James's literary imagination. Particularly, in his *Notes of a Son and Brother* (1914) James relates how his brush with a French marquise and her servants supplied him with the real model for the heroine of Feuillet's *La Petite Comtesse* reincarnated in his own fiction in the Princess Casamassima, thus initiating James's habit of reuniting in his imagination his observation and knowledge of life with his knowledge of literature. (ART)

9857. —— "Sir Sidney Colvin in *The Golden Bowl*:Mr. Crichton Identified." *CLQ* 10:428-31.

Henry James has written into the character of Mr. Crichton, "the custodian of one of the richest departments of the great collection of precious things" in the British Museum, a recognizable portrait of his friend, Sidney Colvin, Keeper of Prints and Drawings there from 1884 to 1916. Like him, "whom everyone knew and who knew everyone," he was the host of a literary and artistic center, and occupied a lodge contiguous to the Museum. Like him Crichton is described as being interested in acquiring for the nation distinguished collections as well as being sympathetic to the private collector, especially to his ladies. James develops Crichton as a minor *ficelle* who introduces Maggie to the records of her husband's family as well as to the Bloomsbury area where she discovers the secret of the flawed bowl. Fanny Assingham is a sly tribute in both name and character to Fanny Sitwell who became Colvin's wife during the year that James was writing *The Golden Bowl*. (ART)

9859. Tomlinson, T.B. "An American Strength:James's *The Ambassadors*." *CR* 17:38-58.

Often James is naive about the "items of high civilization" he finds lacking in American life but present in England and Europe. In some scenes in *The Ambassadors* itself, such as Strether's first meeting with Gloriani, his presentation of an American confronting a representative of one of the older cultures is weakly sentimental. On the other hand, the great single strength of *The Ambassadors* is that it establishes distinctively American qualities as rivaling, and in some ways exceeding, those thrown up by older civilizations. (TBT)

9863. Yeazell, Ruth. "The New 'Arithmetic' of Henry James." *Criticism* 16:109-19.

In *The Golden Bowl* (1904) James uses the Assinghams' comic dialogue both to parody and to defend the late style. In Fanny, James carries to an absurd extreme that obsessive analysis of character and motive which pervades his novels. Fanny thus becomes a parody of the artist himself, and Bob, with his blunt and impatient responses, a parody of commonsense critics of the late style like William James. Bob begins by undermining Fanny's verbal proofs with literalistic commentary, but is finally converted to the Jamesian style and vision. Distressed by the suffering and guilt which the bare truth causes Fanny, he joins in her effort to create sustaining fictions. The Assinghams hence reflect Maggie's own effort to save the world by speaking of it as if it were safe. Thus James also dramatizes the purpose which such language serves—the maintenance of a fragile order and harmony in a world in which reality is often terrifyingly disruptive. (RBY)

James, W. 9865. Chesnick, Eugene. "William James:Fictions and Beliefs." *SAQ* 73:236-46.

In *The Will to Believe* and *The Varieties of Religious Experience*

James is hard-pressed to defend the possibilities of religious belief against the threats of the new scientific method. He must argue that religion cannot be reduced to its neurological components but must be understood as a lived experience, while denying any such experiences for himself. For the students for whom *The Will to Believe* was intended, James provides a pep-talk, plays upon their feelings to keep them from losing their Christian faith and their faith in their own abilities to act effectively. He deals cautiously with the scholars and clerics who are his audience for *The Varieties of Religious Experience* because he knows that a defense based on the testimony of mystics and popularizers is certainly suspect. (EC)

9868. Suárez-Galbán, Eugenio. "Torres Villarroel y los *Yo* empíricos de William James." *RomN* 15(1973):274-77.
In his autobiography (1743-58), Torres Villarroel sees and divides the selves in much the same way as William James in *The Principles of Psychology* (1890). Like James, Torres interprets the empirical selves as material, social, and spiritual, as can be observed from Torres' self-analysis. (ES-G)

Johnston. 9872. Voyles, Jimmy P. "Richard Malcolm Johnston's Literary Career:An Estimate." *MarkhamR* 4:29-34.
Richard Malcolm Johnston is an important figure in the history of the United States, particularly so in that of the South. He bridges the gap between two schools of fiction, humor and local color, thus filling an important role in the continuity of American literature. His portraits of middle Georgia and its customs seem complete and authentic. Gentle humor pervades his work, redeems much of it from sheer boredom, and reveals the levity and wit with which the common people of middle Georgia faced life on a rugged frontier. (JPV)

King, G. 9875. Bush, Robert. "Charles Gayarré and Grace King:Letters of a Louisiana Friendship." *SLJ* 7,i:100-31.
Grace King described Charles Gayarré's character and way of life as he suffered poverty and neglect in Reconstruction Louisiana. Their friendship produced in her the desire to carry on in his tradition as regional historian. In 1886 her objection to his proposed publication of details of cruelty to Negroes in the early 19th century generated a quarrel between them. King's generation felt it necessary to defend the old régime by suppressing facts that might harm its cause in history. The rise of King's reputation as writer coincided with the decline of Gayarré's. (RB)

Lanier. 9878. Antippas, Andy P., and Carol A. Flake. "Sidney Lanier:Some Unpublished Early Manuscripts." *PBSA* 68:174-79.
Nine manuscripts at Tulane University differ considerably, in substantive readings, from the text as presented in the Centennial Edition of 1945. (WBT)

Miller. 9881. Moyne, Ernest J. "Joaquin Miller and Baroness Alexandra Gripenberg." *MarkhamR* 4:68-70.
During a transcontinental tour of the United States in 1888, Baroness Alexandra Gripenberg, Finnish author and a leader in her country's woman suffrage and temperance movements, met many American writers. In Hartford, Connecticut, she met Charles Dudley Warner, Harriet Beecher Stowe, and Mark Twain; in Chicago she was introduced to Robert Ingersoll; and in Oakland, California, she became acquainted with Joaquin Miller. She was so deeply impressed by Miller that she noted in her diary everything concerning him. Although she was disturbed by his warmth of feeling toward her, she was fascinated by his conversation and felt a spiritual affinity with him. In a letter home, she wrote that Miller was without a doubt the most brilliantly gifted of all the men she had ever met. This emotional overestimation of Miller's genius as a man she later corrected in a reasoned evaluation of him as a poet in her *A Half Year in the New World* (1889). In her informal diary account of her meeting with Miller, as well as in her formal published one, Baroness Gripenberg has left us an excellent firsthand description of an eccentric and fantastic American writer who is now all but forgotten. (EJM)

Murfree. 9884. Carleton, Reese M. "Mary Noailles Murfree

(1850-1922):An Annotated Bibliography." *ALR* 7:293-378.
Mary Noailles Murfree (1850-1922), under the pseudonym "Charles Egbert Craddock," is one of the most prominant regional writers of the period. She contributed significantly to the early development of American literary realism. Part I of this bibliography gives a complete listing of Murfree's primary works, including the short stories, novels, and essays. This section also lists and locates the unpublished manuscripts and the correspondence to and from Murfree. Part II presents annotations, chronologically arranged, of book reviews and commentary from contemporary literary journals, notices in advertising and reviewing magazines, and biographic and critical material from the late 19th and 20th centuries. (RMC)

Norris. 9889. Graham, D.B. "Frank Norris's Afternoon of a Faun." *PLL* 10:307-12.
A literary source for the concluding scene of Chapter i of Norris' *The Octopus* (1901) is Stéphane Mallarmé's poem "L'Après-midi d'un faune: églogue" (1876). Norris might have known Mallarmé's poem directly or through J.-K. Huysman's discussion of it in *À Rebours* (1884), though there is no external proof to indicate knowledge of either work. The scene in *The Octopus* contains both an allusion to a faun in a state of semiconsciousness and an adaptation of the situation of Mallarmé's poem to fit Norris's fictional strategy. Both works are forms of pastoral emphasizing a tranquil rural landscape, meditative rhetoric, and the predominance of mood over action. (DBG)

Whitman. 9914. Girgus, Sam B. "Culture and Post-Culture in Walt Whitman." *CentR* 18:392-410.
Like modern radicals and avant-gardists such as Brown, Laing, and Pollock, Whitman attacked conventional forms of cultural order and structure. His radical attitude toward culture anticipated modern culture as many contemporary humanists see it. Such humanists describe contemporary culture as "beyond culture," "post-humanistic," or "paratactical." Much of Whitman's prose and poetry function as "paratactical strategies" that subvert traditional structures of time, space, language, consciousness, sex, and politics. As in the later cases of Yeats, Pound, and Eliot, the paratactical or avant-gardist proclivity to abjure conventional forms in art encouraged a tendency in Whitman to expound potentially anti-democratic ideas. However, Whitman's deeper democratic instincts and his belief in the importance of culture as a foundation for democracy cause him also to ascribe an almost religious significance to culture. (SBG)

9927. Lozynsky, Artem. " 'Us Three Meaning America': Whitman's Literary Executors." *PBSA* 68:442-44.
On at least one occasion, Whitman's American disciples were worried that Whitman's literary execuctorship might fall into British hands. An unpublished letter from one American disciple, R.M. Bucke, to another, H. Traubel, proves this fact. (AL)

9929. Martin, Robert K. "Whitman's 'The Sleepers,' 33-35." *Expl* 33:Item 13.
Whitman's "The Sleepers" has been misinterpreted because of a failure to properly understand the French terms and their significance in the overall erotic imagery of the poem and the use of this imagery in the construction of a total metaphor for the relation of the self to the world. Lines 33-35 of the poem depict the hidden genitals which are briefly glimpsed as the poet imagines a game of hide-and-seek. The genitals themselves are a metaphor for the self and the coy relation of the poet-self to his readers and thereby to the world. (RKM)

9938. Reid, Alfred S. "The Structure of 'Song of Myself' Reconsidered." *SHR* 8:507-14.
Whitman's "Song of Myself" is a lyrical poem of faith in human perfectibility. To express the image of the Self's awakening from stasis to growth, Whitman organizes the poem into five parts: (1-7) an initial definition of Self; (8-19) a catalog of self-identities according to jobs, class, age, geography; (20-25) a second definition of Self, now with a name, "Walt Whitman, a cosmos"; (26-47) a second catalog, stressing expansion through the four senses of hearing, touch, physical incorporation, and motion; and (48-52) a concluding restatement. The form is that of a large dual envelope; three definitions enclose two different kinds of

illustrative catalogs. (ASR)

9954. White, William. "Errors in *Leaves of Grass*, Comprehensive Reader's Edition." *PBSA* 68:439-42.
As the Comprehensive Reader's Edition of Whitman's *Leaves of Grass*, edited by Blodgett and Bradley is likely to be the standard edition of this work, 28 textual misprints are pointed out, 8 of them corrected in the W.W. Norton & Co. paperback reprint of that edition. There are 32 stylistic errors in the table of contents, and 11 other mistakes in footnotes and the index (4 corrected in the Norton reprint). (WW)

9958. Wrobel, Arthur. "Whitman and the Phrenologists:The Divine Body and the Sensuous Soul." *PMLA* 89:17-23.
Whitman turns to the phrenological concept of the soul as the agent that makes the physical self susceptible to the spiritual and the infinite. He insists that it is the soul's office to translate the sensuous data apprehended by a physiologically endowed man perfectly attuned to the universe into the spiritual truths that are integral in the mystic union of all Being. So closely does Whitman identify robust health with spiritual awareness that this forms the basis of his materialistic monism, arguing that the body and the soul are merged into an indivisible One. Since the body is the soul, the sensible is in fact the suprasensible, and matter is mind, dualism represents no problem. A single identity is achieved when the active soul "charges" the surrounding universe and perceives the ideal in the actual. Major phrenological ideas also inform Whitman's unique equalitarian transcendentalism, his sensual mysticism, and his poetic catalogs where the persona, fusing with a cumulative imagery, signals his union with the larger Oneness where all contradictions are resolved. (AW)

V. TWENTIETH CENTURY

General and Miscellaneous. 9968. Bush, Robert. "Dr. Alderman's Symposium on the South." *MissQ* 27:3-19.
In 1903 Edwin Anderson Alderman, President of Tulane, in preparing an address for delivery at Johns Hopkins, asked about 25 U.S. intellectuals to send their views on the contribution of the South to American character. Answers that came from historians, college presidents, professors, and writers from various sections form a symposium on the South. Frederick Jackson Turner admired the founding fathers as well as Jackson and Calhoun, but few Southern leaders of the second half of the century. Ellen Glasgow concentrated on states' rights. W.P. Trent emphasized the Southern contribution of "pure art" in poets like Poe, Lanier, Hayne, and Timrod. Ashton Phelps wrote on the masterful literary style of plain men like Andrew Jackson. G.P. Alexander cited the lack of the mercenary and the presence in Southern character of "sweetness, dignity, and courtesy." C. Alphonso Smith believed the South's romanticism was its greatest contribution. (RB)

9994. Long, Richard A. "The Outer Reaches:The White Writer and Blacks in the Twenties." *SLitI* 7,ii:65-71.
During the 1920s a number of white American writers used the black man and black folk life as elements in their work. This apparent flourishing of interest in blacks, accompanied by the work of black writers which comprises the Harlem Renaissance, gives to the period a superficial abundance of interest in blacks which later events showed to be fugitive. The attitudes of the white writers to their subjects was essentially patronizing, the only stance acceptable to the white reading public of the era. (RAL)

10019. Soderbergh, Peter A. "The South in Juvenile Series Books, 1907-1917." *MissQ* 27:131-40.
Series book authors, who were Northerners invariably, plied their readership with views of Southern history, values, and habits that fell far short of reality. The overall stance toward Dixie can only be described as patronizing. Since series books were the major mass medium for youth prior to 1920, it is reasonable to conclude that the stories were influential in the reinforcement of stereotypic attitudes. (PAS)

Afro-American. 10031. Budd, Louis J. "The Not So Tender Traps:Some Dilemmas of Black American Poets." *IJAS* 3, i(1973):47-57.
Black poets in the United States are confronting difficult problems in trying to forge a poetry worthy of their unique needs and goals. Even Gwendolyn Brooks sometimes agrees with those younger poets who spurn mainline Western culture; more positively these poets—such as Imamu Ameer Baraka (LeRoi Jones), Don Lee, and Nikki Giovanni—call for original forms and themes freed from white influence. However, totally new forms are now hard to devise, and a majority of literate blacks are committed to the English language while Africa as unifying symbol and source threatens to fragment when embraced closely. Militant poets also call for returning their art to the people—that is for winning a mass audience and serving the cause of black liberation. However, a poetry pitched for the masses may prove narrow and finally unsatisfying to those with a sophisticated sense of poetic expression. Still, in the hands of genius, dilemmas may lead to brilliant solutions. Black artists today are creating much fresh, compelling poetry. (LJB)

10032. Clayborne, Jon L. "Modern Black Drama and the Gay Image." *CE* 36:381-84.
Modern black drama in the United States is a social and political art form which reflects much of the militant thought in the black community; yet, despite the progressive and liberated tone of most modern black plays, gays and homosexuality are presented in stereotypical terms. Established playwrights like Imamu Amiri Baraka and Ed Bullins, as well as lesser known black dramatists, conceive of gays as weak, corrupt perverts and equate the state of America with their conception of gays. Modern black playwrights have avoided the implications of Gay Liberation, seemingly unaware that the limp-wrist, lisping, misogynistic male and the deep voiced, cigar smoking, man-hating female stereotypes of homosexuals are no more realistic than the superstitious, lazy, dull-witted stereotype of blacks. (JLC)

10034. Dance, Daryl C. "Contemporary Militant Black Humor." *NALF* 8:217-22.
The works of contemporary black American writers reflect their disillusionment with Christian religion, the American dream, and rational appeals. Symbolic and real murders of whites permeate militant black literature, and many of the black characters can realize themselves only after destroying whites. The black hero doesn't mind dying. In much militant black literature the scenes replete with the sound of machine guns and the flow of human blood are wildly comic as are many similarly grisly episodes in the Uncle Remus tales. The laughs inspired in these works by the murders and humiliation of whites and Uncle Tom Negroes may not be funny to some, but to the militant young blacks they are extremely funny. Contemporary militant black humor, like the folk literature from which it springs, is intended for the blacks—to awaken them to their heritage and a sense of self pride and to move them to revolution. (DCD)

10042. Govan, Sandra Y. "The Poetry of the Black Experience as Counterpoint to the Poetry of the Black Aesthetic." *NALF* 8:288-92.
Considers whether or not one can perceive poetry that comes from the black experience as separate from the poetry which has emerged in the development of the black esthetic. An attempt to pinpoint the differences between the two genres leads to a review of contemporary black critics. A cursory examination is made of various poets and poems which reflect the black esthetic perspective. The philosophical basis of what was labeled the poetry of the black experience is surveyed as are the poets and the poems that typify this perspective. With the exception of the concept of the artist's responsibility to community, one might well say that the poetry of the black experience and the poetry of the black esthetic are "the changing same." (SYG)

10047. Jaskoski, Helen. "Power Unequal to Man:The Significance of Conjure in Works by Five Afro-American Authors." *SFQ* 38:91-108. [Douglass, Chesnutt, Gaines, Petry, McClellan.]
In works by Douglass, McClellan, Chesnutt, Petry, and Gaines, the literary presentation corresponds with folklore research that

reports conjure as a body of beliefs non-Western in origin and highly suspect by the dominant Anglo-Christian culture. Conjure represents a source of learning and power available to members of an oppressed group. Chesnutt, in *The Conjure Woman*, and McClellan in "Annette," associate conjure with the enforced ignorance of slavery and regard it as destructive unless cautiously used for disinterested purposes. Douglass, however, offers in two autobiographies a perspective similar to that in Petry's *The Street* and Gaines's "A Long Day in November": conjure may provide support and power when legal, social, or religious resources of the dominant community fail, and it is associated with new integrity and independence in the individual as well as positive identification with the Afro-American community. (HJ)

10049. Johnson, Abby Ann and Ronald M. "Forgotten Pages:Black Literary Magazines in the 1920's." *JAmS* 8:363-82. Some of the inner dynamics of the Harlem Renaissance emerged in black literary periodicals. Founded by Locke and Gregory, *Stylus* was to encourage a new black literature. In publishing *Black Opals* Fauset had similar intentions. He wanted older black writers to encourage young blacks living in the Philadelphia area. Edited by Gordon, the *Saturday Evening Quill* issued the writings of the Boston Quill Club from 1928 to 1930. Founded by Thurman, *Fire* and *Harlem* neither published the efforts of a literary society nor encouraged conventional patterns in black writing. *Fire* seemed too new to many readers and never survived its first number of November 1926. With *Harlem*, issued only in November 1928, Thurman tried unsuccessfully to appeal to a wide variety of black readers. By the end of the decade, *Stylus* alone remained, primarily because it received support from the University and influential black writers of the day. (AAAJ & RMJ)

10061. Rodnon, Stewart. "Black Belles-Lettres." *NALF* 8:191-96. [Rev. art.]
Twenty-four recent volumes of black belles-lettres may be divided into 7 categories: history, politics, religion, language and communication, psychology, education, and music. In general almost all the authors find themselves in intellectual retreat from the violent excesses of black-power struggles which seem to have reached their height in 1968-69. In the history category, the effort continues to correct distortions and to emphasize black intellectual accomplishment. The black-politics books contain as a major theme the idea that hope for black equality lies now primarily in the improving political arena. In religion, one study examines the Black Muslim movement and the other discusses the historical and present role of the black Christian minister. The relatively untapped riches of black language and black communication in general are now the subject of intensive and overdue scholarly interest. Two black psychiatrists have produced important popularized works on the black psyche. The books on education argue for intellectual honesty and the pursuit of excellence and against the watered-down programs prepared and run by misguided educators. The single volume on black music, while technically brilliant and well-researched, demonstrates an unpleasant anti-white bias. (HH)

Criticism. 10074. Douglas, George H. "Alfred Kazin:American Critic." *ColQ* 23:203-16.
Alfred Kazin is sometimes seen as having grown out of the liberal, sociological conditions of criticism that flourished in the 1930s. He is better seen as belonging to the tradition of historical criticism which was represented so well in America by writers like F.O. Matthiessen, Van Wyck Brooks, and Edmund Wilson. Kazin's phiolsophy as a critic is that only the man who is alive both to literature and the historical life of a particular people can write deeply and meaningfully about literature. His attempt has always been to avoid the twin fanaticisms of sociological criticism and formalism. (GHD)

10075. Inge, M. Thomas. "Recent Southern Literary Criticism:A Review Essay." *AppalJ* 2:46-61.
While many Northern and Western critics of American literature appear to feel that the investigation, exploration, and exhumation of Southern letters by Southern critics have produced parochial and imaginatively limited commentaries, a review of recently published books indicates that they are misinformed. Critical

studies and collections of essays by Holman, Davis, Cowan, Rubin, Sullivan, and Raper reveal that a host of critics have freed themselves from any sentimental bias toward their homeland or its culture and are capable of viewing Southern literature with an honest and perceptive gaze. (MTI)

Drama and Theater. 10078. Brown, Lloyd W. "The Cultural Revolution in Black Theatre." *NALF* 8:159-64.
The term "black revolutionary theater" describes a militantly anti-integrationist, anti-bourgeois theater emphasizing black cultural revolution, possibly involving physical rebellion. The contemporary black playwright presents stereotypes critically, in order to subvert stereotypical patterns and perception and to symbolically restructure perceptual values. LeRoi Jones's *Black Mass* exemplifies the extent to which cultural perceptions shape the meaning and function of art. In *The Slave* Jones integrates the dramatization of black self-perception with the esthetic issue. Other black revolutionary dramatists present stereotypes affecting black self-perception, repulsive because they represent one-dimensional images which cramp the perceptions and values of real people, black and white. Critics who remain ignorant of the kind of reality presented in black revolutionary theater are irrelevant. (HH)

10095. Rich, J. Dennis, and Kevin L. Seligman. "The New Theatre of Chicago, 1906-1907." *ETJ* 26:53-68.
Founded 8 October 1906, the New Theater of Chicago became America's first subscription endowed theater. Established in response to increased commercialism and theatrical syndication, prominent Chicago citizens designated themselves The Musical and Dramatic Direction and became the producing agency of the New Theater. Though Chicago had created similarly sponsored ventures in both art and music, the New Theater failed and was closed 20 weeks after it opened. The venture served as a model for more successful subsequent efforts. Close analysis of the artistic and economic management of this Chicago theater reveals not only the reasons for its failure but also many of the reasons which have plagued the "Art" (Little) Theater Movement in America. (JDR & KLS)

Periodicals. 10113. McFarland, Ronald E. "A Survey of Poetry in the Periodicals." *CE* 36:475-76. [Poets and teachers rank periodicals according to the quality of the poetry they publish.]
Constitutes the results of an opinion survey of 65 poets and teachers of contemporary poetry who were asked to indicate which periodicals (including trade, literary, and little magazines) presently publish the highest quality poetry in America. The results are listed in four categories and, combined with other sources of information, a few of which are listed, may be of use to teachers, librarians, or poets who wish to identify the outlets of current good poetry. (REM)

Poetry. 10130. McElrath, Joseph R.,Jr. "Plumbing the Swamp:The Modern Mode of Self-Pity." *SHR* 7(1973):53-65.
A personal protest against the fashionable "modern" tendency toward self-pity and preoccupation with the "darkness" of life, of which the contemporary poets Stanley Plumly and Rod McKuen are significant spokesmen. Thoreau is given praise as a spokesman for a more constructive life-vision which gained wide acceptance in America in the 1960s. (JRM,Jr)

10137. Nassar, Eugene P. "Illusion as Value:An Essay on a Modern Poetic Idea." *Mosaic* 7,iv:109-23.
Criticism has, in general, blurred the importance of the idea of "Illusion as Value"—of the necessity for the mythologizing of life even in the absence of belief—in the poetry of Stevens, Hart Crane, Auden, Yeats, Frost, William Carlos Williams, and Pound. The prevalence of the philosophy of "as-if," the "play-principle," the "formal ordering," in the modern poetic consciousness is a reaction to the demythologizing of modern life, and the willingness to accept such a philosophy is to a large extent a definition of what makes modern poetry modern. (EPN)

Prose Fiction. 10157. Aldridge, John W. "The American Novel at the Present Time." *RLV* 40:122-31.

One sees two significant developments in contemporary American prose literature: an attempt through the use of the combined effects of fiction and journalism to depict the incoherence or grotesqueness of current history (the New Journalism or Nonfiction Novel) and an attempt to reflect the grotesqueness through the use of burlesque, political caricature, comic-strip buffoonery (Black Humor or Dark Comedy). Works by Mailer, Capote, and Wolfe illustrate the first development, and works by Barth, Heller, Pynchon, and others illustrate the second. These developments suggest that the novel is adjusting to the changed circumstances of modern life by evolving into new forms. (JWA)

10164. Bessière, Jean. "L'Amérique hors texte:Sémantique du roman international (1920-1935)." *Degrés* 4(1973):f-f24.
Through a semiological study of an account of the first expatriation and an account of the *Lost Generation*, the semantics of the international novel were established. From *The Sun Also Rises* to *Tropic of Cancer* significancy seems to be the product of distance placed between the signifier and the signified. This expression of displacement in space or time is interpreted in terms of cultural psychoanalysis. (JAB)

10168. Browning, Preston M.,Jr. "The Quest for Being in Contemporary American Fiction." *ForumH* 12,i:40-46.
Alienation from the primordial sources of life is expressed in the novels of Styron and Updike, as well as in the fiction of the black humorists. Both *Rabbit, Run* and *Lie Down in Darkness* express the anguish of persons caught in a seemingly inescapable vortex of nonbeing. In *Catch-22* Chaplain Tappman's encounter with Captain Flume and his mystical vision of Yossarian, squatting naked in a tree, adumbrate a possible escape from the unreality and absurdity which pervade the world of the novel. In Pynchon's novel, Oedipa Maas may discover only the demonic potentialities behind the obvious "just America." (PMB)

10172. Carter, Paul A. "Rockets to the Moon 1919-1944:A Dialogue Between Fiction and Reality." *AmerS* 15,i:31-46. [Science fiction.]
Science-fiction writers in the United States, Britain, and Germany allied themselves with the early rocket experimenters to combat public skepticism concerning space flight. An investigator like Robert Goddard, although condemned by news media as a visionary or a fraud, received vindication in the American science-fiction pulp magazines that were established at the end of the 1920s. In the late 1930s, science fiction dealing with interplanetary travel began to shift away from technology and to take account of political, sociological, and even religious dimensions of the question. Astronautic enthusiasts in 1944 had mixed feelings about the V-2 rocket weapon, torn between their satisfaction that space flight had been shown to be possible and their aversion to the Nazi regime which had accomplished it. Science fictionists have not shared in the general letdown which followed the actual lunar landings of 1969-72, although some of them foresaw that it might happen. (PAC)

10174. Cook, Sylvia. "Gastonia:The Literary Reverberations of the Strike." *SLJ* 7,i:49-66. [Novels by Fielding Burke, Grace Lumpkin, Myra Page, Mary Heaton Vorse, S. Anderson, William Rollins.]
Six proletarian novels were based on a strike by textile workers in Gastonia, North Carolina in 1929: *Strike!* by Mary Heaton Vorse; *Call Home the Heart* by Fielding Burke [Olive Tilford Dargan] *Gathering Storm* by Myra Page; *Beyond Desire* by Sherwood Anderson; *To Make My Bread* by Grace Lumpkin; and *The Shadow Before* by William Rollins, Jr. The necessity for Marxist authors to demonstrate the reasonableness and inevitability of communism for the urban South ran counter to the irrationality shown by the poor whites in the strike and conflicted with the comic and grotesque image of the poor white's literary reputation. (SC)

10181. Fox, Hugh. "Standards:Some Subjectivities on Fiction." *SHR* 7(1973):183-90.
The primary weakness of most New York commercial fiction is its symmetrical predictability in both form and content. Fiction should create an authentic "experience" for the reader, it should experientially "teach," but in order to do this it must extend, probe, reveal life and not merely record its surfaces. (HBF)

10183. Gollin, Rita K. "Understanding Fathers in American Jewish Fiction." *CentR* 18:273-87.
The commonplace that most American Jewish fiction is characterized by a strong mother and ineffectual father is untrue. Repeatedly in the novels and short stories of Henry Roth, Philip Roth, Malamud, Bellow, Singer, Gold, and Potok, the mother plays a minor role, while the father is the chief conveyor of moral wisdom to his son. In the course of understanding their fathers, the sons learn compassion and moral responsibility. These reciprocal patterns of responsible self-awareness are crucial to the structure of American-Jewish fiction. (RKG)

10187. Hartman, Geoffrey H. "The Aesthetics of Complicity." *GaR* 28:384-88.
The French *nouveau roman* differs from the American novel after World War II in reflecting programmatically on its premises and on the nature of fiction generally. The American novel continues to extend the domain of realism and does not change from being that "loose and baggy monster" Henry James complained about. There is more complicity, in the American novel, with itself: the French novel, after passing through the *roman d'aventure* of the 1930s—inspired, in part, by Conrad, Hemingway, and "l'âge du roman americain"—has returned via the slyly prevailing influence of James and Gide to a purifying reflection on the relation between novelist and detective, novelist and licensed voyeur. When we compare Malraux's *Man's Fate* of the 1930s with Robbe-Grillet's *Jealousy* of the 1950s, we see how suspicious of itself and the intimist mode of novel-writing the French tradition has become. A new consciousness of the reader, as a partner in the fiction being created, or someone to be seduced by it, is evidenced. Fictional techniques are no longer viewed as neutral or productive of newness, but as deeply or covertly ideological. (GH)

10202. Lyons, John O. "The College Novel in America:1962-1974." *Crit* 16,ii:121-28.
The college novel remains a vigorous if not a distinguished form. A list of 80 examples supplement the original bibliography of 200 novels. The conventions of the form have not changed significantly; the students are still angry and the professors still befuddled. The novels written from the vantage of the first tend to be *Bildungsromane*, and those from the second to be satirical novels of manners. The campus upheavals of the late 1960s resulted in reportorial accounts, but also produced several fictionalized versions of those confrontations. (JOL)

10214. Reilly, John M. "Images of Gastonia:A Revolutionary Chapter in American Social Fiction." *GaR* 28:498-517.
Six novels published within five years of the textile workers' strike of 1929 in Gastonia, North Carolina significantly illustrate self-conscious attempts to adapt ideology to literature and, thus, afford us the chance to study the general problem of ideology in fiction as well as the compatability of historical materialism and the novel. The unsuccessful work of Myra Page in *Gathering Storm* results from formula overwhelming the dialectic of character, and Sherwood Anderson's *Beyond Desire* has insufficient grasp of collective experience. The best of the novels, though, explore the consciousness of a character becoming class conscious (Fielding Burke's *Call Home the Heart*), achieving commitment (Mary Heaton Vorse's *Strike!*), or discovering the social dimension of personal troubles (William Rollins' *The Shadow Before*). The unique features of these successful experiments in radical writing derives from a radical understanding of the drama of character in a socioeconomic context. (JMR)

10218. Russell, Charles. "The Vault of Language:Self-Reflective Artifice in Contemporary American Fiction." *MFS* 20:349-59.
Contemporary experimental American fiction is self-reflective with respect to its analysis of the nature and limits of linguistic meaning. Two dominant directions in this self-reflective literature can be noted. One, represented by Pynchon, Kosinski, Brautigan, and Sukenick, focuses on the epistemological roots of the artwork. It inquires as to how experience is filtered through consciousness and language. The other, represented by Nabokov and Barth, emphasizes the prescriptive structures of literary language. The literary experimentation of the two movements centers on a free-flowing improvisation of language with silence, and the parody of all semiotic structuring, respectively. (CRR)

10222. Small, Robert C. "The Junior Novel and Race

Relations." *NALF* 8:184-89.
Most junior novels dealing with race-relations in America have been published during the last decade. An analysis of a number of these works in terms of their controlling messages, contrived plots, weak characterization, sentimental tones, and distorted picture of race-relations leads to the conclusion that, although generally admirable in intent, they are poor in execution. The authors present a stereotypical picture of the problem and the individuals it involves. These authors also present seemingly easy solutions and do so in a didactic and sentimental style. Although there are exceptions, such as Lorenz Graham's *South Town* (1958) and Frank Bonham's *Durange Street* (1965), the majority of such works are so bound up by the moral they try to present that they fail as literature. (RCS,Jr)

Agee. 10234. Kramer, Victor A. "Premonition of Disaster:An Unpublished Section for Agee's *A Death in the Family*." *Costerus* N.S. 1:83-93.
Agee's final book, *A Death in the Family* (1957), was not complete at his death. Unpublished materials which accompany the composite manuscript are of value because they clarify published sections and suggest what directions Agee may have followed had he continued to write this autobiographical narrative. The previously unpublished section presented here (designated "Premonition") was excluded from the published book, possibly because it is exclusively about the parents in *A Death in the Family*. It deals neither with the time immediately surrounding the death of the father, nor with the experiences of the child Rufus. This unfinished section, however, provides additional detail; and while it is unclear what Agee might have decided about the employment of this passage within a completed manuscript, the section extends the characterization of the parents by providing background in support of their actions. The passage is rendered in diplomatic transcription, with no emendations. (VAK)

Aiken. 10241. Tabachnick, Stephen E. "The Great Circle Voyage of Conrad Aiken's Mr. Arcularis." *AL* 45:[590]-607.
Because Conrad Aiken's corpus comprises an integrated whole of ideas and images, his individual works can lose full significance when read in isolation. His "great circle" voyage and its accompanying images of Pole Star, sea-gulls' cries, and freezing temperatures appear in his poetry and prose, and symbolize the journey into the self, the acceptance of past traumas, and the rebirth of the self in love. This pattern of images becomes especially pervasive and important in the play *Mr. Arcularis.* (SET)

Albee. 10250. Quinn, James P. "Myth and Romance in Albee's *Who's Afraid of Virginia Woolf?*" *ArQ* 30:197-204.
Whenever the dramatist presents philosophical concepts in artistic forms, he runs the risk of reducing his work to lifeless rhetoric. Edward Albee is one of the few dramatists of our time who is capable of achieving the esthetic balance between his irrational existential assumptions and the rational artistic forms he employs. In *Virginia Woolf* Albee presents his existential vision by an ironic parody of romantic mythic modes and roles. Using an inversion of the romantic form, the author parodies the ideals of Western civilization. All the "illusions" man has erected to eliminate the differences between self and others and to escape the existential burden of his freedom and loneliness come under attack. The dramatic action reflects the psychic development of unauthentic personalities in the exorcism of their illusions. With little assurance that the night journey into themselves will resolve their problems, Albee's characters are left with the anguish of responsible choice. (JPQ)

Baldwin. 10274. Bell, George E. "The Dilemma of Love in *Go Tell It On the Mountain* and *Giovanni's Room*." *CLAJ* 17:397-406.
In *Go Tell It on the Mountain* (1953) and *Giovanni's Room* (1956) Baldwin sees the possibility of love within the theological or psychological context of a morality based on fear, guilt, and corruption as slight indeed. Gabriel, the "man of God," embodies the oppression that such a theological orientation brings. As

husband and "lover," father and brother, and church leader, he is seen as incapable of love. David's failure to find love is largely due to his conscience which is formed in the traditional puritanical morality not unlike that espoused by Gabriel. But to contend that the novels give no solution to the dilemma of love is to miss their inherent optimism, for they affirm the quest for love. (GEB)

10276. Dance, Daryl C. "You Can't Go Home Again:James Baldwin and the South." *CLAJ* 18:81-90.
Baldwin in his quest for his identity finds that he, like most black Americans, must first discover his origins, his home. After much searching, he discovered that the black American must accept that his roots are in America, specifically in the South. Ironically, at the same time he experiences a sense of self-realization upon the discovery of his home, he finds that he can never go home again. America, specifically the South, offers discovery of his identity, threatens to rob him of his manhood, and denys him peace and rest. (DCD)

10277. Goldman, Suzy B. "James Baldwin's 'Sonny Blues':A Message in Music." *NALF* 8:231-33.
"Sonny's Blues" tells of two black brothers' struggle to understand one another. The older brother, a straightlaced Harlem algebra teacher, is the unnamed narrator who represents everyman's brother; the younger man is Sonny, a jazz pianist who, when the story opens, has just been arrested for peddling and using heroin. As in so much of Baldwin's fiction, chronological time is upset and the subject creates its own form. Four time sequences mark four movements while the leitmotifs of this symphonic lesson in communication are provided by the images of sound. Musical terms along with words like "hear" and "listen" give the title a double meaning. This story about communication between people reaches its climax when the narrator finally hears his brother's sorrow in his music, hears, that is, Sonny's blues. (HH)

10278. Gounard, Jean-François. "La carrière singulière de James Baldwin:1924-1970." *RUO* 44:507-18.
Prior to 1970 Baldwin seems to have gone through three different stages in his literary career. In the first stage, he accepted his condition as a black man in America and was thus able to talk freely about it to white America. The second stage was very difficult since he had to accept American life in all its forms and complexities and identify with them. In the third stage, Baldwin had to choose between being a spokesman and prophet for the civil rights movements as in *The Fire Next Time* and remaining an artist as in *Go Tell It on the Mountain*. (J-FG)

10282. Wills, Antony A. "The Use of Coincidence in 'Notes of a Native Son'." *NALF* 8:234-35.
An autobiographical writer is confronted with the problem of bringing form to his usually fortuitous set of experiences—a problem made greater than with the novelist because of the nonfiction writer's need to preserve truth to fact. Baldwin solves this problem in *Notes of a Native Son* by making the most of various coincidences: his birthday, the birth of his brother, and the death of his father all occurred on the same day and in close proximity to a racial riot. He evolves from these coincidences an intricate series of interrelationships, including symbols of death and rebirth and multiple ironies. The intensity of the effect produced on the reader is greater than the sum of the parts and recreates the trigger which released Baldwin's own shift of attitude. Esthetic unity thus reflects back on life itself. (AAW)

Barnes. 10283. Baxter, Charles. "A Self-Consuming Light: *Nightwood* and the Crisis of Modernism." *JML* 3:1175-87.
Barnes' *Nightwood* incorporates several problems connected with the Modernist movement. Dr. Matthew O'Connor serves as a spokesman for these questions and becomes a mouthpiece for the novel itself. O'Connor tries to give therapy to a would-be aristocrat and to a sexual invert. His therapy fails because he himself suffers from these difficulties; also, his language is pitched at so high an artistic level that no one can listen to him. His language, characteristic of Modernism, grows more brilliant in inverse proportion to its effectiveness. Finally, his collapse, after *Nightwood* has explained its condition through him, seems to be part of the collapse of the entire literary enterprise of Modernism.

(CMB)

Barth. 10285. Farwell, Harold. "John Barth's Tenuous Affirmation:'The Absurd, Unending Possibility of Love'." *GaR* 28:290-306.
John Barth insists on the ambiguity of love in all his writing, apparently seeing in love the image of the absurdity of the world. His fiction offers a continuing, if tentative, acceptance of love as a relative value that one might possibly affirm. At the end of *The Floating Opera* (1956) Todd Andrews suggests that values less than absolute might still be worth holding, and the novels which follow seem dramatic reworkings of Todd's tenuous affirmation, especially with reference to love. With the short fiction published in *Lost in the Funhouse* (1968) and especially "Menelaiad," Barth's affirmation of love becomes clearer; the story of Menelaus constituting something of a turning point. Barth never simplifies his view of love; the ambivalence of love remains one of his basic themes. Increasingly love has become the chief analogue for creativity itself, the lover and artist being more intimately linked. (HF)
10289. Janoff, Bruce. "Black Humor, Existentialism, and Absurdity:A Generic Confusion." *ArQ* 30:293-304.
The term "black humor" has caused confusion in critical terminology and understanding. Labels such as "the existential novel," "novel of the absurd," "nightmare fiction," and "the anti-novel" have been used interchangeably with black humor. The problem arises from the inability to distinguish between the black humorists as a loose novelistic school and the existential novelists. Despair resulting from an intuition of the absurd is a theme common to both groups of writers. There are two areas of generic distinction, however. The first deals with the comic perspective and the second with philosophy. (BLJ)

Bellow. 10335. Bolling, Douglass. "Intellectual and Aesthetic Dimensions of *Mr. Sammler's Planet*." *JNT* 4:188-203.
Bellow's *Mr. Sammler's Planet* has been attacked for its failure to bring thematic and symbolic energies together to achieve overall unity. The novel employs a controlled bifurcation as its method rather than a more conventionally conceived novelistic unity. The reversible figure-ground drawing and paintings from Klee's "bar-period" interest provide examples which clarify Bellow's intent. The reader must come to terms with two major patterns in the novel without attempting to subordinate one to the other as plot to sub-plot, for example. The two dominant strands are Mr. Sammler's intellectualizings and speculations and the farcical pursuit of Govinda Lal's purloined manuscript. (DTB)
10339. Fuchs, Daniel. "Saul Bellow and the Modern Tradition." *ConL* 15:67-89.
Saul Bellow's work is based on a creative repudiation of modernism. Modernist archetypes like the artist hero, the criminal, the visionary are criticized, inverted, burlesqued, in an *oeuvre* which is totally conscious of its literary antecedents. Bellow attempts an assessment of human possibility which is political in the broadest sense, replacing ideology with civility, hysteria with common sense. The modern tradition derived from an esthetic ideology capable of monumental effects but open to the charge of a failure of heart. Works by Stendhal, Flaubert, Dostoevski, Rimbaud, Joyce, Mann, Eliot, Lawrence, and Gide are also discussed. (DF)
10341. Hux, Samuel. "Character and Form in Bellow." *ForumH* 12,i:34-38.
The formal structure of Bellow's novels tends toward irresolution of conflicts, an open ending which seems to invite a sequel. Rather than an unintended esthetic weakness, this chosen structure is necessitated by two facts: (1) Bellow's novels typically depict a character trying to create an identity for himself, and (2) identity in Bellow's view is never achieved definitively as long as a human is alive to choose and will and grow. Consequently, Bellow's plots remain open as a structural analogue to the openness and growth of his protagonists. (SH)
10344. Mellard, James. "*Dangling Man*:Saul Bellow's Lyrical Experiment." *BSUF* 15,ii:67-74.
The contours of the lyrical novel are drawn by the protagonist's point of view. In *Dangling Man* encounters are presented in dramatic scenes absorbed by Joseph's imagination and conveyed to us in the journal. There is a clear and climatic order that, once grasped, leads us to the meaning of Joseph's consciousness's recurring encounters with characters, events, and scenes. The images of the guide, the attacker, and the fallen man, for example, are linked in Joseph's imaginative experience with the image of Vanaker. Vanaker is the objective correlative for those spiritual craters Joseph must come to terms with before he can choose to go to war. (JMM)

Berry. 10353. Morgan, Speer. "Wendell Berry:A Fatal Singing." *SoR* 10:865-77.
Wendell Berry is one of the first significant agrarians to write of farming. Berry's poetry ultimately derives from a practical metaphysic, a way of acting according to the ground of being. The poet seeks a deep knowledge and acceptance of time and death as a perfecting current in his life. The development of Berry's attitude toward death from his earliest book *The Broken Ground*, through *Openings*, *Farming: A Handbook*, and *A Country of Marriage*, shows a movement from facile defiance of mortality toward a sense of the balance between life and death, light and dark, possession and relinquishment. Berry poetically witnesses the discoveries of his own life as farmer in a nature proclaiming limits as well as blessings—a life that lives in the shadow of death. (SM)

Bishop, J.P. 10368. Hayhoe, George F. "John Peale Bishop's Theory of Poetry." *MarkhamR* 4:34-38.
John Peale Bishop developed a poetic theory which attempted to synthesize the traditional discipline of the poet's craft and the originality of modern experimentation in literature. An examination of Bishop's reviews and essays, as well as examples of his own poetic practice, reveals a concern with many problems which face the poet in our own century: the problem of diction, the importance of verse in poetry, obscurity in modern literature, and the relation of poetry to the arts of painting and music. Though Bishop's premature death prevented him from developing a systematic theory of poetry, his *Collected Essays* (1948) is a testimony to his taste and his exclusive concern with truly literary values. (GFH)

Bourne. 10373. Silet, Charles L.P. "A Note on Randolph Bourne." *BNYPL* 77:274-75.
Randolph Bourne contributed an unsigned nine-page supplement "American Independence and the War" to the April 1917 issue of *The Seven Arts* (1916-17). In a letter to the author Louis Untermeyer, one of the journal's Advisory Editors, confirmed that the anonymous piece was by Bourne. This supplement contains the crux of the arguments Bourne leveled against American participation in World War I and thereby provided the genesis for his series of anti-war essays which appeared in the pages of *The Seven Arts* during the summer and early fall of 1917. These essays, in which Bourne foresaw the dangers of American involvement in the European war, were to form his last significant body of work before he died of influenza in the epidemic of 1918. (LPCS)

Brautigan. 10376. Hearron, Thomas. "Escape Through Imagination in *Trout Fishing in America*." *Crit* 16,i:25-31.
Brautigan's *Trout Fishing in America* deals with man's need to escape from the city into the wilderness. Instead of the new land just beyond the mountains, the novel shows campgrounds so overcrowded that only the death of one of the campers makes a campsite available. Trout streams are disassembled and offered for sale in wrecking yards. Despite this situation, imaginative escape is still possible. The novel thus traces the development of the narrator's imaginative faculty, and its metaphorical structure offers the hope that imagination can transmute reality to allow man the escape that he needs for his survival and salvation. (TH)
10377. Hernlund, Patricia. "Author's Intent:*In Watermelon Sugar*." *Crit* 16,i:5-17.
Richard Brautigan's *In Watermelon Sugar* gives a negative effect which is probably intentional. The novel contains four time sequences, intertwined and fragmented. Unravelled, they reveal a

utopian society, fully developed by Brautigan's mixture of fantasy with familiar setting. The sections of the novel focus on three deaths, recounted by a nameless, unreliable narrator. He and his society react to death, as to life, by avoiding violent or unpleasant emotions. Although they claim their life is suitable and good, it is unrewarding and lacking in pleasant emotions. Brautigan's techniques of repetition and juxtaposition neutralize the possibility of gratification from sex, eating, or pride in the society. (PH)

10378. Leavitt, Harvey. "The Regained Paradise of Brautigan's *In Watermelon Sugar*." *Crit* 16,i:18-24.
The novel as a utopian instrument, the analogues to the Garden of Eden, and natural determinism create a coherent structure for *In Watermelon Sugar*. A vision of a rustic good life in a post-industrial society based on the destruction of and rejection of materialistic-technological society forms the utopian structure. The garden-like setting, Adam and Eve prototypes, the rejection of knowledge, apple imagery, the Cain and Abel prototypes, the new world created out of the debris of the past—all provide a Genesis for a new world rising out of the chaos of the past. Absence of a deistic force coupled with an acceptance of, and integration into nature, provide the moral sustenance of the novel's social order. (HRL)

10380. Vanderwerken, David L. "*Trout Fishing in America* and the American Tradition." *Crit* 16,i:32-40.
Brautigan's *Trout Fishing in America* finds its place in the idealist and romance traditions of American fiction. Brautigan's America is an imaginative ideal. Through methods of juxtaposition, discontinuity, and "careful disorderliness," Brautigan measures the current gap between ideal America and real America and, historically, the distance we have spiritually fallen since 1776. Structurally, Brautigan's use of traditional seasonal metaphors parallels and reinforces the main thematic concerns. Although the novel records loss upon loss, Brautigan's imaginative vision transforms real America, returning us to an ideal America —"often only a place in the mind." (DLV)

Brooks, G. 10383. Hansell, William H. "Gwendolyn Brooks's 'In the Mecca':A Rebirth into Blackness." *NALF* 8:199-207.
In "In the Mecca" Brooks demonstrates her full acceptance of a black mystique and of the black artist's necessary involvement in his community. The poem examines the repercussions of a child's disappearance—and ultimate murder—on a ghetto family and community. Mrs. Sallie Smith's discovery that her child is missing begins a frantic search through a large apartment building, The Mecca. It is a microcosmic view of black America. There are Northerners and Southerners, old and young, militants and Toms, charlatans and would-be saints; some think only of escape, some try not to think, and some plot bloody revenge. And more prominent than any of these is Alfred, who undergoes a profound transformation. He enters as an aloof intellectual who has casual love affairs and drinks until everything seems just as it should be. At the end, having reassessed the meaning of Leopold Senghor, the black heritage, and his own role, Albert rejects his old ways and affirms the need for racial change in America. In sum, his transformation constitutes a rebirth into blackness. (WHH)

Bullins. 10392. Jackson, Kennell,Jr. "Notes on the Works of Ed Bullins and *The Hungered One*." *CLAJ* 18:292-99.
Ed Bullins' earlier short stories are varied in their content and format. *The Hungered One* clearly prefigures his later work. The realism is truncated in its vision, limited in its analysis of the society from which the characters emerge, and fails to reveal the dynamics of the society which thwart and maim his characters. (KAJ,Jr.)

Burke. 10397. Gallo, Louis J. "Kenneth Burke:The Word and the World." *NDQ* 42,i:33-45.
According to Burke, man's invention of symbols stems directly from his use of language which, in turn, arises metabiologically; that is, the forms of language correlate exactly with the rudimentary metabolic processes of the human body. Artists utilize symbols to cleanse the sin and guilt of both themselves and their societies. Art, therefore, becomes a strategic manufacturing of symbols. Symbolic action occurs when a symbol "moves" an audience, the symbol being by nature dramatic. Drama functions as a concretized dialectic since it, too, involves the antagonism of opposites and seeks a final resolution (or synthesis). Artists strive to capture this synthesis in their works because it promises a perfection not found in "reality." (LJG)

Cabell. 10405. Duke, Maurice. "Cabell's and Glasgow's Richmond:The Intellectual Background of the City." *MissQ* 27:375-91.
During the 19th century Richmond, Virginia was a kind of literary center below the Potomac. Cabell and Glasgow were born and raised there, and thus the city, its reading tastes, its theater, and its writing tradition influenced their thinking as well as their writing. (MD)

Cain. 10415. Reck, Tom S. "J.M. Cain's Los Angeles Novels." *ColQ* 22:375-87.
James M. Cain's reputation suffers because of quarrels over his content, which deals with the sordidness of human nature. Yet the subject offers serious statements, and the style is a perfect correlation to the content and the characters. Cain's novels are particularly adept in diagnosing the behavior patterns of failure and self-destruction in America's lower socioeconomic classes during the 1930s. *The Postman Always Rings Twice* documents a life of greed and base sexuality on the outskirts of the city. *Mildred Pierce* traces the economic rise but moral failure of a woman caught up in her own obsessive ambition. *Double Indemnity* shows how character flaws bring on disaster in the insurance business. Cain's novels are good social criticism, specifically about Los Angeles, and are valid psychoanalyses of stupid and criminal actions. (TSR)

Cather. 10421. Ditsky, John. "Nature and Character in the Novels of Willa Cather." *CLQ* 10:391-412.
Willa Cather's novels indicate a logical triple division of her use of the land to define or develop character: as embodiment of history or witness of the past; as source of hope and reflection of human dreams; and as shaper of individual development, especially in terms of orientation to art. Study of the appearance of these three strains in all of Cather's novels reveals a remarkably consistent and thoroughly understood approach to nature that parallels Cather's altering view of man and history. (JMD)

Cleaver. 10448. Felgar, Robert. "*Soul on Ice* and *Native Son*." *NALF* 8:235.
In *Soul on Ice* Cleaver has given us a theory of sexual roles in black and white American culture which explains the sexual dynamics of Wright's *Native Son*. Cleaver proposes four basic sexual types: the Omnipotent Administrator (the white man of power, alienated from his body), the Ultrafeminine (the white woman as Southern Belle), the Supermasculine Menial (the black man as phallus), and the Amazon (the brutalized black woman). The corresponding characters in Wright's novel are Buckley as the Omnipotent Administrator, Mary Dalton as the Ultrafeminine, Bigger Thomas as the Supermasculine Menial, and Bessie Mears as the Amazon. Seen from the perspective of Cleaver's myth, Wright's characters take on an added dimension. (RF)

Conroy, F. 10450. Ramsey, Roger. "The Illusion of Fiction in Frank Conroy's *Stop-Time*." *MFS* 20:391-99.
An autobiography may be modified in its tone by the illusion of fiction it creates, the sense that it is "invented" as well as recorded. Frank Conroy's prose, in his *Stop-Time*, makes use of several fictional techniques to direct the reader to the non-literal, ambiguous, and suggestive levels of his own experience while at the same time recounting a rather mundane surface adolescence. The title, the prologue and epilogue, the "stop-time" moments, the use of the first person and the name of the author, the patterns of imagery and their consistency, the shifting tense, and the wordplay—these techniques raise the autobiography to artifice, ambiguity, and literature. (RR)

Crane, H. 10462. Simon, Marc. "CALM Addendum No. 4:Hart Crane." *PBSA* 68:69.

Reports a variant typescript text of "For the Marriage of Faustus and Helen." (WBT)

Cullen. 10471. Copeland, Catherine H. "The Unifying Effect of Coupling in Countee Cullen's 'Yet Do I Marvel'." *CLAJ* 18:258-61.

In "Yet Do I Marvel" Cullen has systematically employed types of coupling other than rhyme to give the poem the unity necessary for the communication of his idea. He accomplishes this by using two types of equivalences. They are designated as Type I, which emphasizes position and the syntax of parts of constructs, as well as whole constructs; and Type II, which uses extra-linguistic factors such as phonics and semantics. By using them as a mixture of comparables and opposites, he adeptly portrays his difficulty in accepting the dilemma which he is experiencing. (CHC)

Cummings. 10474. Davis, William V. "Cummings' 'no time ago'." *RS* 41(1973):205-07.

In many of Cummings' poems, theme is most explicitly evidenced in form. In "no time ago" Cummings "fractures" his theme in order to re-create and visually indicate, in the form, the mystery of the experience he is attempting to detail. The thematic center of the poem is bounded by open-ended parenthetical stanzas which structurally "flop over" on the statement of the central stanza and thus suspend it between the "gasps" of the parentheses. The unexpected and mysterious visionary meeting with Christ is thus both thematically stated and structurally shown. (WVD)

10475. ——— "E.E. Cummings's 'except in your'." *ELN* 11:294-96.

E.E. Cummings' "except in your," like the Elizabethan and Metaphysical hyperbolic love poems to which it is related, makes its case through an exactingly formal structure and a carefully maneuvered theme which balance and parallel one another. The parenthetical and non-parenthetical portions of the poem suggest Cummings' dual thematic and structural argument. (WVD)

10477. Everson, Edith. "Cummings' 'That which we who're alive in spite of mirrors'." *Expl* 32:Item 55.

A key to the interpretation of E.E. Cummings' poem "that which we who're alive in spite of mirrors" is discovered in the manner in which it both uses and undercuts the Shakespearean sonnet form. Syllable count, rhyme scheme, and division into quatrains and concluding couplet comply with the form, although this fact is nearly obscured by metrical roughness and eccentric spacing. The first lines of the quatrains reveal the poem's central statement, which appears in full only in the concluding couplet: "(and that which we die for lives / as wholly as that which we live for dies)." This paradox is clarified when "die" and "live" are seen to be parts of one vital process and are related to the idea of sexual love. If renaissance poets often wrote of the "death" of sexual union, Cummings goes even further, so that "dying" and "living" become one in a dynamic cycle of renewal. Self-giving is said to be accompanied by rebirth just as, on the level of Cummings' esthetic, destruction is prerequisite to creation. (EAE)

10480. Nadel, Alan M. "Cummings' 'When faces called flowers float out of the ground'." *Expl* 32:Item 47.

E.E. Cummings' "when faces called flowers float out of the ground" is a celebration of spring. The poem uses active verbs in a structure as subtly intricate as a spider's web to create an interval world that parallels the one about which it speaks. The first line in each of the three stanzas rhymes and relates to the end of winter. The second lines state an equation of gerunds and the third lines counterpoint the first two by emphasizing the motif of "keeping." The center lines all restate the main theme and contain, within them, parenthetical reiterations. A word contained in each of these parentheses becomes the first word of the last three lines of its respective stanza. This makes the stanzas parallel in structure but unique in content. The final lines, which deal with the open image of "dancing mountains," are tempered by the constriction of full parentheses and their rhyme link to the third ("keeping") line. This linking of opposites underscores the temporal nature of experience and its subsequent intensity.

(AMN)

10482. Oliver, William I. "*Him*—A Director's Note." *ETJ* 26:327-41.

Analyzes Cummings' play *him* and investigates the problems it poses to a director. (WIO)

10485. Sülzer, Bernd. "Möglichkeiten linguistischer Interpretation im Unterricht:E.E. Cummings' 'Poem No. 151'." *NsM* 26(1973):153-57.

Geoffrey N. Leech's linguistic approach is applied to E.E. Cummings' "Poem No. 151." This approach is suitable for teaching as it directs the pupils' attention on aspects of the method and does not overemphasize aspects of content. The interpretation follows a sequence of fixed steps. In the first pass the poem is divided into sections in order to make it "legible." The next step deals with the analysis of composition, including an inquiry into ambiguity, level of style, register, deviations (grammatical, geographical, and of register), and redundancy. The last step, appreciation, contains an analysis of the function of alienation as employed in the poem and of the high degree of poetic encoding as a device to avoid the banality of poetic conventions of the past and of the everyday usage of the present. (In German) (BS)

10486. Weinberger, G.J. "Cummings' ')when what hugs stopping earth than silent is'." *RS* 41(1973):136-39.

In ")when what hugs earth than silent is" Cummings illustrates love-transcendence being effected by means of winter and death (as opposed to the more conventional spring and rebirth). The complexity of the language reflects both the mysterious nature of the process in general and the particular problems which arise because of the winter setting: i.e., the lovers must, paradoxically, pass through a state of "unbeing" before they can attain their goal. (GJW)

10487. ——— "E.E. Cummings's Benevolent God:A Reading of 'when you are silent, shining host by guest'." *PLL* 10:70-75.

Cummings' approach to God is of a tentative nature, in keeping with his view that anything or anyone either measurable or completely definable is of little value. The sonnet "when you are silent, shining host by guest" serves as a celebration of the love of an essentially unknowable God for the individual, for "every" man and for nature. Structurally a Shakespearean sonnet, the poem moves from God's silence (ll. 1-4), to his speaking (ll. 5-8), to his synthesis of motion and rest (ll. 9-12), and to the effect of this synthesis on sublunary existence. (GJW)

10488. West, Philip J. "Medieval Style and the Concerns of Modern Criticism." *CE* 34(1973):784-90.

If one analyzes Cummings' "All in green went my love riding" in class according to the methods of oral formulaic criticism and in view of medieval theories of poetic architectonics, he will have opportunity to reinterpret the poem with more insight, to demonstrate the value of medieval literature to creative writers as well as to scholars, to give his students an understanding of oral formulaic theory, to explore the basis of medieval esthetics, to speculate on the validity of interdisciplinary approaches, to explore the edges of transformational-generative theory, and to combat the condescension frequently encountered when a lettered audience deals with the literature of an oral society. (PJW)

Cuomo. 10489. Bryant, Jerry H. "The Fiction of George Cuomo." *ArQ* 30:253-72.

Departing from the stand of most contemporary theorists and practitioners of the novel, George Cuomo writes fiction that not only ranges through the traditional forms but also can be "interpreted." He imitates the early picaresque of Thomas Nashe and the late of Henry Fielding, the social novel of Charles Dickens, and—partly tongue-in-cheek, partly seriously—the surrealism of Kafka. What ties his fiction together is the moral and behavioral concerns with which he confronts his characters. In the four novels he has written since 1963—most significantly *Bright Day, Dark Runner* (1964)—he blends ironic comedy with earnest moral purpose to dramatize the main problem of his characters: finding strength to permit them to deal with the surprises, the absurdities, the ironies of a life pervaded by chance. The main source of that strength, Cuomo suggests, is close relationship with other people and the past from which they spring. Cuomo is an oddity in serious contemporary American fiction, for his approach is positive without being childishly or sentimentally sanguine. (JHB)

Davidson, D. 10493. Dessommes, Lawrence. "The Epistemological Implications in 'The Ninth Part of Speech'." *MissQ* 27:21-32.
Donald Davidson's verse letter dedicated to Louis Zahner questions the nature of eduction, rejecting the modern view that is more concerned with economics of consolidation, method, and life adjustment than with quality, matter, and truth. The persona seeks answers from his former teacher, Louis Zahner; his absence occasions the letter, wherein the speaker answers his own question. He says that education should link ideas with things by means of the imagination; one learns thereby the proper attitude toward reality. This principle is also basic to art, especially poetry. The persona illustrates by using two anecdotes retold by a lady schoolteacher. In each an element of nature, a wildcat and a wolf respectively, upsets the schoolteacher's everyday routine so that she has to take account of nature as well as her abstract patterns. Thus the poet suggests the necessity of union between theorems and things for a true view of reality. (LD)

Dickey. 10511. Lindborg, Henry J. "James Dickey's *Deliverance*:The Ritual of Art." *SLJ* 6,ii:83-90.
In presenting a middle-aged graphic artist in a rite of passage in which he must kill a man, Dickey develops in *Deliverance* several stages of the creative imagination; these stress the reality which grows out of the artist's illusions. In the book's culminating scene an organic relation to nature is established. The artist's mind is one with nature and he has the Emersonian capacity to project himself as a creator-god. The design which emerges from this union reveals that the underlying forces of nature are indifferent to and transcend individuality. (HJL)
10514. Stephenson, William. "*Deliverance* from What?" *GaR* 28:114-20.
James Dickey's *Deliverance* outwardly promotes its ritual initiation into manhood theme concerning the transference of power from master to apprentice yet simultaneously exploits another theme concerning the antinomian's potential initiation into the brotherhood of man. The outer theme emphasizes Ed's and Lewis's deliverance from mediocrity; the inner theme is their failure to be delivered to anything more than their own futile images of personal freedom. Lewis, the antinomian, is the hero of the outer theme; Drew, the artist, is the scapegoat hero of the inner theme. Dickey wants to believe it is Lewis's influence that saves Ed, whereas the novel tells us it is Drew's. Perhaps Dickey sees what Drew sees, that the brotherhood of man can be built only on a saner view of what it is that keeps men together: music and law, not the antinomian urge to escape man's limitations and build a new society in the wilderness. (WCS)

Didion. 10517. Geherin, David J. "Nothingness and Beyond: Joan Didion's *Play It As It Lays*." *Crit* 16,i:64-78.
Play It As It Lays is a serious philosophical novel dramatizing two differing responses to an existential encounter with absurdity and the void: one character, B Z, gives up and kills himself; the other, Maria Wyeth, chooses life, even though it must be led, at least temporarily, in an institution where she is being treated for an "emotional breakdown." But in her Sisyphus-like refusal to give in, the novel rejects nihilism. The philosophical theme is combined with a bleak and satirical picture of contemporary America and an intense and vivid psychological portrait of a modern woman whose emotional experiences have led her to an awareness of nothingness. (DJG)

Donleavy. 10519. Morse, Donald E. " 'The Skull Beneath the Skin':J.P. Donleavy's *The Ginger Man*." *MichA* 6:273-80.
Donleavy's *The Ginger Man* reflects both halves of the Epicurean maxim: "Eat, drink, and be merry, for tomorrow we die." Donleavy accomplishes the difficult task of creating a wildly comic work at whose center is a fundamentally unattractive hero whom the reader, nevertheless, hopes will win against the world's

high odds. Part of *The Ginger Man*'s comedy arises from the contradictions within Dangerfield, part from the unique narrative technique, and part from the several parodies of Christian salvation and hope. At the core of the novel, as in the *Satyricon*, lies death and impermanence. (DEM)

Dos Passos. 10527. Diggins, John P. "Visions of Chaos and Visions of Order:Dos Passos as Historian." *AL* 46:[329]-46.
Dos Passos' two distinct attitudes toward history in two different phases of his career are analyzed. As a radical novelist, Dos Passos saw history as contingent and chaotic; as a conservative narrative historian, he conceived the American past as rational and coherent. Diggins discusses the changes in Dos Passos' vision of historical reality as he moved from writing novels to writing history; the ideological difficulties Dos Passos encountered in trying to invoke his conception of colonial America; the theoretical and interdisciplinary problems a historian encounters in analyzing the work of a novelist who "does" history. (JPD)
10535. Vanderwerken, David L. "Dos Passos' *Streets of Night*:A Reconsideration." *MarkhamR* 4:61-65.
Dos Passos' *Streets of Night* is his most tightly constructed work and it is thematically consistent with his major work. Structurally, *Streets of Night* establishes a series of triangular relationships, beginning with the three main characters—Macdougan, Taylor, and Wendell. Within character's consciousness appear internal triangles, which seem to owe much to Freud's division of the human psyche, consisting of the character as an ego, and two figures that objectify the id and the super-ego. The conflict between the desire for freedom and internal restraints provides the energy of the novel. Thematically, *Streets of Night* deals with the failure of each character to live authentically, duped by an illusory belief that life is a determined circle, and that each is chained to a "meaningless round," with no escape possible. Numerous images of wheels and circles reinforce the characters' sense of enclosure. Ultimately, Dos Passos suggests, America itself has lost its vitality, with its inhabitants walking a circular treadmill like mules. (DLV)

Dreiser. 10544. Forrey, Robert. "Dreiser and the Prophetic Tradition." *AmerS* 15,ii:21-35.
The religious spirit in which Dreiser wrote can be characterized as prophetic, which is more concerned with now than hereafter, with social justice rather than salvation, and with the spirit rather than the letter of religious law. The best example of his prophetic writing is in the magazine *Ev'ry Month* in which, in the late 1890s, he wrote a column of moralistic reflections which he signed "The Prophet." Though he later turned against religion, he retained as a novelist his strong, religious compassion and late-19th-century Social Gospel spirit. It may be more accurate to see Dreiser coming out of the prophetic religious tradition than out of naturalism, which is only to say that the Bible and the prophets had more influence on him than any novel he read. (RF)

DuBois. 10557. Turner, Darwin T. "W.E.B. Du Bois and the Theory of a Black Aesthetic." *SLitI* 7,ii:1-21.
As editor of *The Crisis* for a generation, DuBois urged blacks to avoid the stereotypes expected by whites, select black subjects, portray them truthfully in black styles, and preserve the African heritage. Defining "Negro Art" as "the expression of millions who share common memories and experiences," he argued that such expression, if worked into art, would be "new, unusual, splendid." Although vague definitions of beauty and truth sometimes weaken applications of his theories, DuBois established the prototype for the black arts theorist who insists that black art must be "reviewed and acclaimed by our own ... judgment," must have "a Negro constituency," and must "grow out of the inmost heart and frank experiences of Negroes." (DTT)
10558. Walden, Daniel. "DuBois' Pan-Africanism, a Reconsideration." *NALF* 8:260-62.
DuBois' analysis of the problem of colonialism bears close scrutiny even now. Although his influence on the Pan-African movement was primarily intellectual, he deserves credit for "giving reality to the dream" of Pan-Africanism; he threw himself into one conference after another to protest against the colonial

system, racial prejudice, and exploitation. As pamphleteer, polemicist, educator, leader, sociologist, and historian, he popularized ideological positions. (HH)

Dunbar. 10559. Lee, A. Robert. "The Fiction of Paul Laurence Dunbar." *NALF* 8:166-72.
Neither an unflawed folk author nor a damp Uncle Tom, Dunbar presented popular mythic versions of 19th-century black life, while occasionally expressing outrage at racism. Seeking white approval, Dunbar nonetheless worked protest into his tales. Dominated by works in which slavery is presented as mutually beneficial to master and slave, the collections contain a number of tales, such as "The Lynching of Jube Benson," which present the live sexual and psychic issue behind racial sadism. Dunbar's novels may be equally divided into "raceless" and "racial" categories; in the latter category, *The Fanatics* indicts both Civil War parties, while *The Sport of the Gods*, an astringent piece of black naturalism, is more combative in tone and racial awareness than earlier works. (HH)

Dunne. 10564. Mann, Georg. "Call for Mr. Dooley." *Éire* 9,iii:119-27.
The decline in the popularity of Finley Peter Dunne's Mr. Dooley columns is usually attributed to his use of Irish dialect. More surprising is their popularity in spite of Dunne's use of materials only intelligible to Irish Americans, as demonstrated by examples from the columns. Dunne's Irishness was an integral part of his humor and his inclinations, and he played a minor role in Irish-American affairs. His neglect is unjustified. (GM)

Eberhart. 10568. Cooney, Seamus. "Eberhart's 'Experience Evoked'." *Expl* 32:Item 39.
Contrary to Bernard F. Engel's view in his Twayne book on Eberhart, "Experience Evoked" contains no specific Christian symbols, the "garden" is not a cemetery, nor is "cry" an imperative verb. Rather, the poem surveys attitudes to and ways of living in the presence of death. Whether people resist death in "savagery," either as terror-stricken babes or after having lived in energetic protest against the doom of mortality, or whether they embrace it as part of a natural cyclic process containing hints of renewal, after having enjoyed the world as a garden, the "harsh shroud" awaits them all indifferently. (SC)

10569. Eberhart, R. "Eberhart's 'Experience Evoked'." *Expl* 32:Item 76.
In his reply to Seamus Cooney on his criticism of "Experience Evoked" (*Expl*, 32, 1974, Item 39) Eberhart corrects his assumption that "Sewing" (line 5) was an error for "Sowing." Cooney criticized Bernard F. Engel on "old Rose" (line 5), and Eberhart replies that he thought he was thinking of the Romances of the Rose. Eberhart remarks that neither Engel nor Cooney had noted a strategy of reductive grammar in "Now come to me all men" (line 1) to "Come" (last line), the reductive device being used at the beginning of each set of five lines, and in the last line. Eberhart also points out a similarity in the conclusions of the comments by Engel and Cooney. (RE)

Ellison, R. 10588. Pryse, Marjorie. "Ralph Ellison's Heroic Fugitive." *AL* 46:[1]-15.
In order to free ourselves from the same formlessness of invisibility that the narrator of Ellison's *Invisible Man* experiences, we must reintegrate our awareness of historical, literary, and sociological aspects of the changing American identity which lead to Invisible Man's self-realization. The novel explores the road North as the historical road to freedom. This theme of escape from the South runs through white as well as black fiction. Yet as *Invisible Man* indicates, the Southern heroic fugitive tests the "negative capability" of the total American identity. Ellison's narrator chooses "symbolic action" as method and response to the lack of reality he finds in a white world. Allegory becomes Ellison's "underground." Finally, as a social outcast, Invisible Man searches for recognition and inclusion. He finds that in refusing to hide his social stigma, by displaying his visibility, he can affirm invisibility and his own humanity. (MLP)

10593. Scruggs, Charles W. "Ralph Ellison's Use of The *Aeneid* in *Invisible Man*." *CLAJ* 17:368-78.
Ellison's parody of the *Aeneid* in a specific scene of *Invisible Man*, the narrator's encounter with Sybil echoing Aeneas's encounter with the Sybil of Cumae in Book VI, suggests a possible approach for understanding the underground experience of his hero. Like Aeneas, the Invisible Man emerges from the Underworld with a new sense of direction. Aeneas learns of Rome from his father's ghost, and Ellison's hero now understands the dying words of his grandfather, and, by implication, his role in recreating America. Also, the Aeneas-Invisible Man parallel calls attention to an important theme in the novel. Unlike Odysseus the Invisible Man must find a new home; he can never return to the one he has left. (CWS)

Faulkner. 10601. Ackerman, R.D. "The Immolation of Isaac McCaslin." *TSLL* 16:557-65.
Isaac McCaslin's reappearance in old age in "Delta Autumn" illuminates the oppositions central to Faulkner's art. By allying himself totally with the natural world in his early manhood, Ike suffers a symbolic immolation which forms the foundation for vision and the truths of the heart while at the same time disabling him for action in the civilized world. Alliance with Old Ben is also alliance with the snake, with pariah-hood, with death. Ike's dealings with Roth's octoroon mistress in "Delta Autumn" are not illustrative of biased ineffectuality but rather of the tragic chasm which Faulkner envisions between nature and civilization, heart and mind, black and white. In "Delta Autumn" Ike bears witness to this division. (RDA)

10602. Adams, Richard P. "At Long Last, *Flags in the Dust*." *SoR* 10:878-88.
Although Douglas Day's edition of *Flags in the Dust* may not be a reliable text, it is considerably longer than *Sartoris*, and it probably comes closer to being the book Faulkner intended to write. It certainly provides a fuller description of Yoknapatawpha County, especially in the aspect represented by the rise of the poor-white Snopeses. It does not replace *Sartoris*, but it is an addition to the Faulkner canon that will help us to understand how Faulkner, after a long and often stumbling apprenticeship, achieved, with seeming suddenness, the pinnacle of his writing career in *The Sound and the Fury*. (RPA)

10603. Behrens, Ralph. "Collapse of Dynasty:The Thematic Center of *Absalom, Absalom!*" *PMLA* 89:24-33.
Absalom, Absalom! achieves mythic significance and universality through Faulkner's deliberate use of parallel between Thomas Sutpen's attempt to found a dynasty in the Old South and the attempts of ancient Hebrew rulers to establish their kingdoms. The choice of title for the novel, as well as numerous analogies between Faulkner's plot and incidents in the prophetic books of the Old Testament, particularly II Samuel, indicate that Faulkner intended the biblical accounts of dynastic failures to illuminate and strengthen his theme. In attempting to find reasons for the failure of Sutpen to establish his Southern dynasty, critics have advanced four tenable theories. One theory finds Sutpen's innocence the principle reason for his failure; another sees hubris as the cause of failure; still a third theory contends that the socioeconomic injustices of the pre-Civil War South, magnified in the character of Sutpen, account for the failure. The fourth and most tenable theory, considered too briefly by critics, indicates that the very concept of dynasty is so basically flawed that failure is inherent in the design itself; or, more broadly still, that men erroneously persist in the mythic hope that they can establish permanent dynasties, though historically none has succeeded. (RB)

10626. Cowan, James C. "Dream-Work in the Quentin Section of *The Sound and the Fury*." *L&P* 24:91-98.
A consideration of the literary use of dream-work, the principles of condensation, displacement, and dream symbols, together with psychoanalytic concepts of Oedipus complex and death wish, helps to illuminate Faulkner's structural and stylistic devices in the Quentin section of *The Sound and the Fury*. On the day of his suicide, Quentin's conscious mind registers immediate sensory impressions, while visual images, voices, and odors out of the past impinge on his consciousness in association with present stimuli. Although Faulkner's technique would seem incoherent in

conventional narrative, it is understandable in terms of the logic of dream-work. The reader must proceed analytically, piecing together scraps of evidence from Quentin's sensory impressions, his fragmented reveries, and his free associations to each. Examination of five selected passages illustrates Faulkner's technique. (JCC)

10629. Dahl, James. "A Faulkner Reminiscence:Conversations with Mrs. Maud Falkner." *JML* 3:1026-30.

The reminiscence is of the approximately ten visits in the home of Mrs. Maud Falkner. Her temperament, her prejudices, her artistic talents, and her ideas about the literary work of her sons, William and John, highlight the piece. Of particular interest are her thoughts on the race question, her praise of Caroline Barr (whom she identified as the Dilsey of Faulkner's work), and her remarks on the relationship between the world of Faulkner's fiction and real life within the Falkner family and in Oxford, Missippi in the 1950s. (JD)

10640. Geffen, Arthur. "Profane Time, Sacred Time, and Confederate Time in *The Sound and the Fury*." *SAF* 2:175-97.

Faulkner links key events in *The Sound and the Fury* to significant dates in Confederate history and its commemorations by employing both the conventional anniversary pattern and an unusual "day-before" structure. Since Confederate time in the novel is really a form of failed sacred time, one's understanding of it—and the day-before pattern—depends on determining how Faulkner uses profane and sacred time. The thrust of Faulkner's design asserts the particular moribundity of Confederate civil religion while also affirming the inescapability of its tragic and unrewarding pattern. (AG)

10643. Graham, Don B., and Barbara Shaw. "Faulkner's Small Debt to Dos Passos:A Source for the Percy Grimm Episode." *MissQ* 27:327-31.

One of Faulkner's sources for the Percy Grimm chapter in *Light in August* is the "Wesley Everest" sketch by John Dos Passos in the December 1931 *New Masses* (retitled "Paul Bunyan" in *1919*). Faulkner's name Percy Grimm echoes Dos Passos' proto-fascist Warren O. Grimm. Parallels between the two episodes include superpatriotic fervor, flight, castration, Christ symbolism, and a sense of horror growing directly out of fascist tendencies present in American assumptions of political and racial superiority. (DG & BS)

10644. Gresset, Michel. "Faulkner's 'The Hill'." *SLJ* 6,ii:3-18.

The second of Faulkner's early prose sketches, published on 10 March 1922, constitutes the best possible threshold to his "apocryphal county." Faulkner evinces many important choices: not only the future simple protagonist, but time (sunset) and place (the hill-and-valley motif), movement arrested in the fascination of timelessness, and the imminence of a possible revelation are there. Yet the most illuminating comment on the pregnancy of the piece lies in Faulkner's own criticism of the time, where "development" is stressed as the major quality in organic art. (MAG)

10653. Hult, Sharon S. "William Faulkner's 'The Brooch':The Journey to the Riolama." *MissQ* 27:291-305.

"The Brooch" reveals a characteristic Faulkner theme, that of the sexually crippled male agonized by his fantasy of the ideal female. Howard Boyd's obsession with William Henry Hudson's *Green Mansions: A Romance of the Tropical Forest* displays his need to find in one woman, Rima, both the maternal and the erotic female principles which in real life are contained in two women, the mother and the wife. Howard's impasse is symbolized by the brooch which his mother transfers to his wife, for it then precludes his attainment of mature sexual freedom. His suicide becomes a symbolic return to the infantile state where the maternal and the erotic merge. (SSH)

10656. Johnston, Kenneth G. "The Year of Jubilee:Faulkner's 'That Evening Sun'." *AL* 46:93-100.

In "That Evening Sun" Faulkner's intention was to measure the promise of the 1863 Proclamation by the reality of the blacks' life in Mississippi at the turn of the century. Faulkner's error concerning the age of Quentin Compson, the story's narrator, and his choice of names for Nancy's common-law husband are not flaws; rather they are functional elements which point up Faulkner's thematic intent and link the story with the ideas of

bondage, freedom, and jubilee. Quentin's 1889 birth date establishes the time of events in the story as 1898, and the time of narration as 1913. Thus "That Evening Sun" is a jubilee story told in the year marking the 50th anniversary of the Emancipation. The names which Faulkner used for Nancy's husband, Jubah and Jesus, strongly suggest that he deliberately constructed his story on the jubilee-bondage motif. (JGJ)

10660. Kobler, J.F. "Faulkner's 'A Rose for Emily'." *Expl* 32:Item 65.

Faulkner's handling of Emily Grierson's name in "A Rose for Emily" reveals the attitude of the citizens of Jefferson toward her. Except for five references to her as "Poor Emily," she is always called "Miss Emily," an appellation which establishes the paradoxical feelings of respect through the title and of familiarity, perhaps even superiority, through the given name. During the Barron courtship she is called "Poor Emily" because she is seen with an undesirable alien and has lost all right to the respect indicated by "Miss." The word "Poor" is always capitalized as a title. After burying "Miss Emily" and discovering the skeleton of Homer, the townfolk no longer call her by any name. Faulkner's title illustrates both the respectful side, with "A Rose," and the ordinary, down-to-earth side, with just plain "Emily." (JFK)

10661. Korenman, Joan S. "Faulkner's Grecian Urn." *SLJ* 7,i:3-23.

Faulkner's fondness for Keats and for the "Ode on a Grecian Urn" may stem from the similarity between the ambivalent attitude toward time and change expressed in the ode and Faulkner's own attraction to and rejection of immunity from time. Faulkner creates characters who seek the sort of stasis enjoyed by the figures on the Grecian urn. He treats most seriously and ambivalently those characters whose desire for stasis is bound up with a longing for the past. The author recognizes his protagonists' tendency to romanticize the past and their consequent inability to tolerate life in the present; at the same time, he presents these characters with great sympathy. As a Southerner trying to reconcile his loving allegiance to his heritage with his awareness of the need for change, Faulkner finds in Keats's ode the expression of conflict he understands. (JSK)

10668. Lilly, Paul R.,Jr. "Caddy and Addie:Speakers of Faulkner's Impeccable Language." *JNT* 3(1973):170-82.

The "Addie" section of *As I Lay Dying* dramatizes Faulkner's theory about the nature of language. Caddy and Addie are speakers who—in very different ways—transcend the limits of narrative form. They demonstrate that utterance cheapens language's poetic life. Both are "unvirgin" speakers who epitomize the virgin-pure quality of the poet's "absolutely impeccable, absolutely perfect" language. Caddy is for Faulkner "too beautiful" for words; she functions instead as a hypothesis of impeccable (because silent) speech. Addie, however, is dead when we hear her voice in the "Addie" section. She has escaped not only life but the peccable nature of language. Addie's jar symbolizes (as do other images of containment) the tension between space and enclosure that constitutes this novel's problematical narrative form. Addie's revolt against the "shape" of language is an extreme version of Faulkner's restlessness with conventional ways of narrating: if feeling is corrupted by the "shape" of language, perhaps the purest speaker might escape the stringencies of narrative form (PRL)

10673. Martin, Carter W. "Faulkner's *Sartoris*:The Tailor Re-Tailored." *SCR* 6,ii:56-59.

William Faulkner's source for the family name which gives the title to his first Yoknapatawpha novel, *Sartoris* (1929), may be local, but he chose it for its aristocratic sound, which he himself enhanced by altering Mississippi practice and placing the emphasis on the first syllable. Faulkner seems from the novel's context to be aware of the implications of the allusive quality of the name as it refers to Carlyle's *Sartor Resartus*. Pervasive clothing imagery contributes to the novel's thematic concern with the relationship of past to present, especially as understood by the protagonist, young Bayard, who is unable to emerge from the pastness of the Civil War and World War I. The irony of the allusion to Carlyle's clothes philosophy is that Bayard fails to arrive at the balanced acceptance of the past and present; he refuses to clothe himself in "The Everlasting Yea." (CWM)

10677. McElrath, Joseph R.,Jr. "*Pylon*:The Portrait of a Lady." *MissQ* 27:277-90.

Faulkner significantly chose a pylon, not pylon*s*, as his initial metaphor. *Pylon* is not primarily the story of the Reporter's encounter with the flyers. The primary focal object is Laverne. Faulkner reveals the personality of his main character obliquely, actively engaging his reader in the task of evaluating various characters' responses to Laverne. (JRM)

10684. Messerli, Douglas. "The Problem of Time in *The Sound and the Fury*:A Critical Reassessment and Reinterpretation." *SLJ* 6,ii:19-41.

There has been no attempt made to solve seeming inconsistencies which appear in Faulkner's *The Sound and the Fury*. These inconsistencies center around the character of Dilsey, for, while to those who believe she represents Faulkner's moral order, Dilsey is seen to "transcend" the linear time of the Compson family, critics such as Sartre see her "transcendence" to mean that "Faulkner wants to forget time," and see in this desire a vision of despair. Indeed, in a Bergsonian context Dilsey's "transcendence" is meaningless. However, if one considers the novel in the light of a philosophy such as Eugène Minkowski's, it is Caddy who is at the center of the novel, for she acts out of a sense of the "now" while the rest of the characters revolve around her: Benjy, who has no sense of time, Quentin, who values only the past, Jason, who lives only for the immediate future, and Dilsey, who lives a life grounded in a future "beyond life," a future which gives the flux of life which Caddy represents meaning. (DJM)

10685. Middleton, John. "Shreve McCannon and Sutpen's Legacy." *SoR* 10:115-24.

In *Absalom, Absalom!* (1936) the past does not come fully alive for Quentin until Shreve urges him to tell about the South. Shreve, the outsider, is at first skeptical and detached, but is gradually drawn into the reconstruction of the Sutpen legend until he becomes literally a part of it. Once completely engaged, he retains his apparent ironic detachment as a mere pose. Shreve's detachment and objectivity exist only in his freedom from the traditions and prejudices of the South. Because he, unlike Quentin, can live emotionally in the imagined past without being trapped by it, he alone finally confronts the full implications of Sutpen's legacy. (JM)

10687. Milum, Richard A. "Faulkner and the Cavalier Tradition:The French Bequest." *AL* 45:[580]-89.

Faulkner's work reflects as a source French cavalier tradition which roots itself in contact by his characters with people of French descent and with centers of French culture. Early examples of such contact involve the experience of Faulkner's Indians—Ikkemotubbe and Issetibbeha—with the Parisian adventurer, the Chevalier Soeur Blonde de Vitry, and the impact exerted upon the new settlement of Jefferson by the Old Frenchman, Louis Grenier. Perhaps more important are the experiences of Thomas Sutpen in the French West Indies, and the legacy of his captive French architect, a contribution which reaches far beyond Sutpen's individual story. In each case, the bequest is decadent, encouraging tendencies toward excess, display, and moral license. As such it contends with the powerful Calvinistic demands of sacrifice and responsibility, thus becoming, as a part of the cavalier tradition in general, a major element of dramatic conflict in Faulkner's work. (RAM)

10688. —— "Ikkemotubbe and the Spanish Conspiracy." *AL* 46:389-91.

A historical allusion in Faulkner's "Red Leaves" places the unlikely relationship between Ikkemotubbe (Doom) and the Chevalier Soeur Blonde de Vitry within context of the "Spanish Conspiracy" of 1795-1797. De Vitry was apparently involved in the attempt to separate a large part of the American frontier from the U.S. in order to create a buffer for Spain against westward expansion. De Vitry's assistance in the *coup* by which Doom becomes the new Chief of his tribe is thus an effort to establish an ally in the area under contention. The ultimate failure of the plot ended the relationship between the aboriginal Indian chief and the sophisticated Parisian adventurer. The allusion provides a new dimension of irony by reducing the fortunes of De Vitry, Ikkemotubbe, and the rest of his Chickasaw tribe to the status of minute pawns in the foreign policy of at least two nations. (RAM)

10689. Minter, David. "Faulkner and the Uses of Biography." *GaR* 28:455-63. [Rev. art.]

Joseph Blotner's *Faulkner* provides a complete picture of Faulkner's daily life. Since Faulkner's fiction was not in any simple way autobiographical, however, Blotner's work raises the issue of the usefulness of biography. Blotner enlarges our understanding of Faulkner's fiction by locating models and sources in local and familial history and by tracing the development of stories and novels through careful examination of manuscripts. Blotner also clarifies our sense of the basic rhythm of Faulkner's career, and particularly of the two big problems it poses—the advance of the late 1920s and the decline of the 1940s. (DM)

10692. Moses, Edwin. "Faulkner's *The Reivers*:The Art of Acceptance." *MissQ* 27:307-18.

Faulkner develops the theme of *The Reivers*—the importance of recognizing and accepting things as they are, and accepting responsibility for one's actions—in three ways: (1) Point of view: the vast difference in perspective between the 67-year-old narrator and the 11-year-old hero. (2) Allusion: the casual and comic reference to people, events, and issues central to earlier novels of the Yoknapatawpha sequence. (3) Rhetoric: the ironic use of heavily charged language in comic situations to undercut the importance of the characters' passions and struggles. (EPM)

10695. Murphy, Denis M. "*The Sound and the Fury* and Dante's *Inferno*:Fire and Ice." *MarkhamR* 4:71-78.

Some of the specific structural and philosophical similarities between *The Sound and the Fury* and the *Inferno* are demonstrated. Dante's influence is not only possible but is supported through a close comparison of both works. Parallels are drawn between the identical Holy Week dates of both, of Benjy's relationship to the idiots found in the Vestibule Cantos, of Quentin's situation and its similarity to those found in the Wood of Suicides, and of the comparison between Jason and the traitors to their kindred who are trapped in the frozen center of Hell, the Ninth Circle. Caddy functions in a paradoxical way as an inverted Beatrice character to the Compson brothers, and there are also many similarities between her fate and Francesca da Rimini. While the Christian and moral references in the Dilsey section are obvious and persistent, these refrences in the other three sections (especially to suffering and punishment) are as equally pervasive, if not quite as obvious. This philosophical pattern is related to the ordering principle of the four chapters taken as a whole. This structure is circular, and joins the ordering forces, Benjy and Dilsey, with the disruptors, Quentin and Jason, who are philosophically and structurally surrounded. (DMM)

10702. Palmer, William J. "Abelard's Fate:Sexual Politics in Stendhal, Faulkner and Camus." *Mosaic* 7,iii:29-41.

The castration of an individual, either literally or symbolically, by a power group is a recurring metaphor appearing in the literatures of different countries. Stendhal, Faulkner, and Camus are existential novelists who employ the metaphor of castration to image their novel's societies' methods of devitalizing the individual. In *The Red and the Black* through the use of phallic imagery Julien Sorel's social and existential castration is represented. When he rebels against "Abelard's fate," for the first time showing his potency as an individual, the novel's society must destroy him. In *Light in August* an individual attempts to define himself in a society even more overtly reactionary than Stendhal's France and here literal castration is his punishment. Again sexual imagery defines the protagonist's dilemma. Camus in *The Stranger* also objectifies the theme of revolt by means of sexual analogy. Meursault is imprisoned, cut off from the sea, forced to accept a sterile alternative to healthy sexuality. In each novel the attempted destruction of virility parallels the attempted usurpation of selfhood. (WJP)

10703. Parker, Hershel. "What Quentin Saw 'Out There'." *MissQ* 27:323-26.

Critics of Faulkner's *Absalom, Absalom!* have shown what Quentin Compson learned at Sutpen's in September, 1909: he learned that Charles Bon was Sutpen's son. Critics have not decided how Quentin learns what he learns, but many assume that either Clytie or Henry tells him. Close reading indicates that he pieced the puzzle together himself after seeing the Sutpen face on Jim Bond. Faulkner's own language stresses not what Quentin heard at Sutpen's but "what he had seen out there." (HP)

10709. Reed, Richard. "The Role of Chronology in Faulkner's Yoknapatawpha Fiction." *SLJ* 7,i:24-48.
Numerous chronological problems in Faulkner's Yoknapatawpha fiction preclude the construction of a single, unified chronology. Faulkner himself recognized the existence of the problems and the necessity of chronological ordering. Some of the chronological inconsistencies are simply mistakes, most, however, are the result of other causes, including the author's concept of time, his deliberate attempts to complicate chronology, the complicated manner in which the fiction was composed and published, and the dynamic nature of Yoknapatawpha County as it evolved in Faulkner's mind. When the various events of the individual works are arranged in sequence, the reader discerns subtle relationships, the evolution and dissolution of cultural patterns and human values, and a chronicle that corresponds to the history of the South and the nation. (RR)

10714. Rome, Joy J. "Love and Wealth in *Absalom, Absalom!*" *UES* 9,i(1971):3-10.
The focus of attention is on Thomas Sutpen, the central character of William Faulkner's *Absalom, Absalom!* He is born into a poor family and devotes his life to the unscrupulous pursuit of wealth. Faulkner tries to understand the events of history in terms of the human experience which has produced them. He maintains that man has an innate dignity and the spiritual strength to endure great hardships. Values such as love and honor enable man to arrive at ultimate self-fulfillment. The pursuit of wealth is evil when it causes a man to thwart the self-fulfillment and humanity of others. Brief examination of the novel's structure and language shows how these illuminate the heroic figure of Sutpen. The attitudes of Rosa Coldfield and Mr. Compson are explored and contrasted and, by piecing together the story from the conjectures of the various narrators, Sutpen's failure then emerges—it lies in his renunciation of pity and honor. Sutpen is a symbol of the malaise of the South. (JR)

10716. Ross, Stephen M. "Conrad's Influences on Faulkner's *Absalom, Absalom!*" *SAF* 2:199-209.
Absalom, Absalom! owes part of its psychological power to Faulkner's familiarity with Conrad's fiction. The narrative structure of Mr. Compson's chapters resembles the structure of *Lord Jim*, and the story-telling scenes evoking Marlow's and Mr. Compson's narrations echo each other in tone and imagery. The letter Quentin receives from his father serves a similar structural purpose as Marlow's packet to the "privileged man," in continuing the search for a "final" explanation of Jim and Sutpen. Quentin even more closely resembles the Marlow of "Heart of Darkness." Both relive their journeys into moral darkness as they retell them. Just as Marlow steams up the Congo to find the dying Kurtz, Quentin travels to Sutpen's Hundred to discover Henry Sutpen, who has committed an unpardonable crime against one of darker skin. Marlow and Quentin seek explanations for how such crimes could be committed, and both are fascinated and appalled at what they find. (SMR)

10726. Taylor, Walter. "Horror and Nostalgia:The Double Perspective of Faulkner's 'Was'." *SHR* 8:74-84.
"Was," the first story in *Go Down, Moses* (1942), mirrors Faulkner's beliefs that "There is only the present moment, in which I include both the past and the future," and that "there's not too fine a distinction between humor and tragedy." The dominant mood of "Was" is one of sentimental nostalgia about the southern past; but the story also contains brief but significant suggestions of the tragedy of slavery. Faulkner yokes these two moods together without reconciling them, producing a sensation of stasis. Such artificial fusion of attitudes has puzzled readers but it also accomplishes a major objective: the creation of a sense of the presentness of the past. (WT)

10731. Wagner, Linda W. "*As I Lay Dying*:Faulkner's All in the Family." *CollQ* 1:73-82.
When Faulkner's *As I Lay Dying* is viewed as Addie Bundren's story, the characters Anse, Rev. Whitfield, and Cora Tull become obvious ironic foils for the more sympathetic members of the family. The determinant of character throughout most of the novel is the character's use of words; the easy rhetorician is

suspect. Only action, physical movement, is worth human effort. Dividing the novel into sections according to its natural rhythmic breaks provides helpful insight into its characterization. Each of the seven-part divisions brings the reader to a new point of information before mood changes and the plot-line continues. (LW)

Fauset. 10741. Feeney, Joseph J.,S.J. "Greek Tragic Patterns in a Black Novel:Jessie Fauset's *The Chinaberry Tree*." *CLAJ* 18:211-15.
Fauset's *The Chinaberry Tree* uses techniques of Greek tragedy to add universality and horror to a story of domestic love among comfortable blacks in a small north Jersey town. The novel combines elements of a suspense novel and a Greek tragedy. Fauset maintains suspense by concealing this relationship from the reader at a loss to tragic irony. She also uses occasional Greek images and references, and the tragic dimension arises naturally out of her plot. (JJF,S.J.)

Ferlinghetti. 10742. Hopkins, Crale D. "The Poetry of Lawrence Ferlinghetti:A Reconsideration." *ItalAm* 1,i:59-76.
Many poets associated with the "Beat" generation of the 1950s have received little consideration other than in connection with that subject. Lawrence Ferlinghetti deserves to be separated from the stereotypes of "Beat" poetry. His work displays both a knowledge and use of literary tradition and an important and innovative treatment of contemporary life. Ranging from lyric to social protest, Ferlinghetti's writing deals with many of the major themes of modern literature and amounts to a significant contribution to 20th-century American poetry. (CDH)

Field. 10745. Smith, Duane A. "Eugene Field:Political Satirist." *ColQ* 22:495-508.
Eugene Field spent two years (1881-83) as managing editor of the *Denver Tribune* at a time when both Colorado and Denver were growing and politics was the game of the rich mining men. Sharp-witted Field found it all fascinating, especially politics and he thrived in the environment. Political satire was a versatile weapon in that day, especially in the newspapers and Field matured to become one of the best practitioners in Colorado. Everything was fair game to him, from local and state to national politics and his writings have left behind an interesting impression of the times. (DAS)

Fitzgerald, F.S. 10762. Eble, Kenneth. "*The Great Gatsby*." *CollL* 1:34-47.
Fitzgerald's *The Great Gatsby* has a greatness of theme, one which illuminates the American past and present but which also has the power of myth to convey meaning independent of time, place, and the particulars of the narrative. The novel is a truly efficient novel, particularly suited in that respect to being regarded as the great American novel. Its moral dimensions still touch the American sense of decency and fair play. The depiction of the real and the ideal is in some ways an American preoccupation but also an embodiment of the Romantic vision beyond its appearance in America. (KE)

10768. Humma, John B. "Edward Russell Thomas:The Prototype for *Gatsby's* Tom Buchanan?" *MarkhamR* 4:38-39.
Between April 1924, when Fitzgerald left New York for the Riviera with three chapters completed, and October, when he completed *Gatsby*, Fitzgerald radically reconceived the novel. He had met the Gerald Murphys in Paris en route to the Mediterannean. From them he may have learned of Edward Russell ("Ned") Thomas, who had been the first husband of Linda Lee. The parallels between Ned Thomas-Tom Buchanan and Linda Lee-Daisy Fay are both numerous and close. Both Ned Thomas and Tom Buchanan were philanderers. Linda Lee and Daisy Fay were both Southern belles, daughters of well-to-do Louisville bankers. Both were 18 when they married. The marriages themselves offer striking parallels: they were continually on and off the rocks, with both husbands inclined to buy off their sins with gifts of expensive jewelry. The precise details of these parallels, taken in their entirety comprise an intriguing speculation. (JBH)

10781. Moyer, Kermit W. "Fitzgerald's Two Unfinished Novels:The Count and the Tycoon in Spenglerian Perspective." *ConL* 15:238-56.
The nature of Spengler's influence on Fitzgerald's later work has remained obscure—in part because critics have ignored or misunderstood the four completed episodes of the unfinished medieval serial-novel, *Philippe, Count of Darkness*, in which the Spenglerian themes are rehearsed. *Philippe* records the birth of Western culture through the saga of a Faustian noble who competes for power with the local priesthood and with a neighboring robber baron and who ultimately sacrifices his soul to the dictates of his will-to-power. In *The Last Tycoon*, Monroe Stahr repeats this prototypal pattern as civilization declines: he is the noble's heir, "the last of the princes," who also trades his soul for power and who tries to guard his empire from the socialist "priests" and the profit-hungry robber barons of a decadent age. If Fitzgerald's historical perspective remained Spenglerian in these two unfinished novels, his sense of decline gave way to a fuller sense of eternal recurrence, and his historical focus shifted from death to the eternal juxtaposition of death and rebirth. (KWM)

10784. Prigozy, Ruth. "The Unpublished Stories:Fitzgerald in His Final Stage." *TCL* 20:69-90.
Fitzgerald's unpublished stories reveal much about his artistic and emotional struggles in his last years. They show him reaching for new rhetoric, plots, and characters to replace the outworn techniques of his early years as a writer. The unpublished stories are transitional, standing between the full-blown romantic pieces of the 1920s and the brief, elliptical efforts of his last two or three years. His middle-period stories deal with themes he had treated earlier, but rhetoric, characterization, plots—particularly endings —are weak and melodramatic. (RP)

10792. West, James L.W.,III. "Matthew J. Bruccoli's *F. Scott Fitzgerald:A Descriptive Bibliography*." *Costerus* N.S. 1:165-76. [Rev. art.]
Bruccoli's bibliography of Fitzgerald is the best full-dress bibliography of a major American writer in print. There are, however, shortcomings and inconsistencies in Bruccoli's compilation—chief among them the scant attention to the papers and bindings and the slighting of negative and inconclusive evidence. This review provides a lengthy list of corrections, additions, and queries, together with suggestions for a projected augmented edition of the bibliography. (JW)

Frost. 10803. Basler, Roy P. "Robert Frost:Lobbyist for the Arts." *QJLC* 31:108-15.
Robert Frost's official association with the Library of Congress and semiofficial association with the entire Washington governmental establishment began with his appointment as Consultant in Poetry for 1958-59 and continued with his appointment as Honorary Consultant in the Humanities in 1959, until his death on 29 January 1963. He came to Washington with an avowed purpose: to make "the politicians and statesmen more aware of their responsibility to the arts." (RPB)

10824. Fleissner, Robert F. "Frost's 'Moon Compasses'." *Expl* 32:Item 66.
The final three dots in "Moon Compasses" may stand for "as with Donne," since Frost's calipers roughly approximate the action of the feet of Donne's compass figure ("So love will take between the hands a face . . ."), but they also reflect the romantic tendency to leave the poetic meaning open-ended, thereby pointing to the riddle of the circularity at the end of "A Valediction: Forbidding Mourning"—probably the inspiration. (RFF)

10832. Greiner, Donald J. "Robert Frost, the Poet as Critic:An Analysis and a Checklist." *SCR* 7,i:48-60.
During the 20 years of neglect between Frost's high school poetry and the publication of *A Boy's Will* (1913), he formulated a critical theory which he believed would help him "do something" to American literature. Yet he never gained the reputation as a theoretician. One reason was his refusal to collect his essays and opinions on poetic theory. Another is that his statements as a practical critic of other writers' work lack the value of his comments about theory. Thus Frost's reputation as a poet-critic should rest upon his theories about poetry. The checklist notes letters, interviews, essays, lectures, and memoirs. (DJG)

10835. Harris, Kathryn G. "Robert Frost's Early Education in Science." *SCR* 7,i:13-33.
Frost always chose friends he could share scientific interests with. He set up an observatory at home, did experiments after school in a chemistry laboratory, and read widely in science books of all sorts. In college years Frost studied the scientifically-informed philosophies of William James and Henri Bergson. At the Derry Farm he taught his children the constellations, botanical processes, and wild flower identification. The poems reflect Frost's "astronomical view of things," as Randall Jarrell stated. Frost maintained a lively interest in new scientific discoveries and mystified scientists with his understanding. His scientific knowledge was background for his theories about poetry and was often the material of his poems. (KGH)

10837. Henry, Nat. "Frost's 'Stopping by Woods on a Snowy Evening'." *Expl* 32:Item 33.
In supporting his note on Frost's "Stopping by Woods on a Snowy Evening" (*Expl* 27, 1968, item 7) with quotations from John Ciardi's analysis ("Robert Frost: The Way to the Poem," *Saturday Review*, 12 April 1958), Earl Wilcox, pressing the "death wish" implication of "sleep," indicates that he was not aware of Frost's quick rebuttal at his poetry reading a week later (19 April 1958). Frost tagged a number of his selections with wry comments plainly related to getting back at his "friend" Ciardi: "I have the kind of intelligence that likes saying two things in one, but wanting the second to be clear"; "My apparent intention *was* my intention"; "It's not intention splashing a paper with ink and folding it—that's fun, but it's nonsense"; "When I write about death, I know it"; "It's just that; never mind what they tell you." Frost's clearly-pointed rejection of the "death" association ("It means enough without its being pressed") implied his persistent, but largely ignored, plea for avid explicators to stop "pressing." (NH)

10845. Lindner, Carl M. "Robert Frost:'In the American Grain'." *ColQ* 22:469-79.
In theme and temperament Robert Frost demonstrates his affinity with the American Romantic tradition. Like Melville and Emerson, Frost confronts a natural setting in search of answers. He explores earlier concepts, such as correspondence and compensation, as his "I's" discover themselves through their struggles against internal and external limitations. Man is inevitably and repeatedly thrown back upon his own particular and peculiar resources. While Frost's poetic voice is undeniably his own, his artistic methods and metaphysical concerns are clearly in keeping with the New England Romantic tradition. (CML)

10850. Miller, Lewis H.,Jr. "The Poet as Swinger:Fact and Fancy in Robert Frost." *Criticism* 16:58-72.
Textual analysis of "Birches," "Mowing," and "The Wood-Pile" reveals Frost's strategy for coming to terms with an unalterably alien nature and for providing a solution to the central problem—as Frank Kermode describes it—confronting serious artists of our century: "How to do justice to a chaotic, viscously contingent reality and yet redeem it?" Frost's response to this question lies in his dazzling facility for offering his readers a sustained vibrancy or swing between a world of fact and a world of fancy. Such facility is readily apparent in "Birches," a poem which, in its form and content, provides a demonstration and assertion of the manner in which Frost proceeds as a poet. The figure for Frost's poetic, as it is manifested and exhibited in "Birches," is meticulously applied to "Mowing" and "The Wood-Pile" in order to establish a pervasive tendency in vintage Frost to insist on the discontinuity and dissonance of human experience while at the same time offering redemptive fictions which soften, without distorting, the hard, contingent facts of the "pathless wood." (LHM)

10852. Monteiro, George. "Unlinked Myth in Frost's 'Mending Wall'." *CP* 7,i:10-11.
In the final lines of "Mending Wall" the poet's meditation moves back through time toward the shadowy ancient rites which lie behind the farmer's own annual ritual. Frost limits himself to hinting vaguely at the myth which links current-day New England

farmers with their ancient counterparts. That he does not make the mythic parallel explicit, either by allusion or direct statement, differentiates his characteristic poetic practice from that of such Modernists as Eliot and Pound. (GM)

10855. Perrine, Laurence. "The Sense of Frost's 'The Self-Seeker'." *CP* 7,i:5-8.
Frost's poem "The Self-Seeker" portrays a man who is bravely, wisely, and successfully coming to terms with the altered condition of his life. He knows that he must avoid bitterness over his accident and therefore refuses to bicker with the Company over damages. The epithet "Broken One" is literal and ironical: he is broken in body but not in spirit. The title is also literal and ironical. In the usual sense of the term, the protagonist is the opposite of a self-seeker: he refuses to waste his life squabbling over money. In a deeper sense, however, he is seeking to preserve his essential identity; he is a seeker "of" self. (LP)

10860. Sanders, David A. "Words in the Rush of Everything to Waste:A Poetic Theme in Frost." *SCR* 7,i:34-47.
By setting powers of concentration against natural attrition, the poetic virtuosity Frost often treats lightly becomes a tactic for imaginative survival. In "Spring Pools" and "Hyla Brook" striking figures and images point obliquely to the defense they marshal against time, as rhythm and sound lend iconicity to a language already committed, narratively, to change. "The Oven Bird" alludes more overtly, through the bird's revelation of loss "in all but words," to what only the poet can "make of a diminished thing." "A Hillside Thaw" surprisingly calls us to witness the figurative "magic" that first illuminates, then eclipses, nature's own. (DAS)

10862. Schutz, Fred C. "Frost's 'The Witch of Coös'." *Expl* 33:Item 19.
The analysis in *Expl* 28, 1969, Item 40 of Frost's "The Witch of Coös" is not persuasive in its argument that the narrator is intellectually limited, literal-minded, and imperceptive. His remark that the Witch "hadn't found the finger-bone" does not carry implicit belief that such bones exist; the remark is negative (she "hadn't") and therefore carries not corroboration but indirect rebuttal. Similarly his confirmation of the name (Toffile) on the mailbox does not establish his belief in the Witch's story, but rather only that Toffile (not the ghost) may be real. The narrator serves not as historian of the story, reporting simply what he can verify and what he cannot. If he makes any judgment at all, it lies in his use of the epithet "old-believers" which he applies to Mother and Son in the introductory frame, his phrase implying a cautious, reserved, even derisive attitude toward the pair. The limited verifications of the narrator actually serve to force the reader to make his own conclusions about this intriguingly rich story. (FCS)

Gaines. 10879. Bryant, Jerry H. "Ernest J. Gaines:Change, Growth, and History." *SoR* 10:851-64.
Ernest J. Gaines writes about a region of America from which myths may be drawn, and he has that talent for creating a character that has a broad visceral appeal. In *Catherine Carmier* and *Of Love and Dust*, social, spiritual, and political change are prevented by the inlaid conservatism of the old plantation blacks. In *The Autobiography of Miss Jane Pittman*, change becomes growth, and both are embodied in the character of Miss Jane. Her history shows the political triumph of the human spirit, and it is through her as an "unhistorical" personage that we can best understand our other history. (JHB)

Glasgow. 10890. Duke, Maurice. "The First Novel by a Glasgow:Cary's *A Successful Failure*." *Ellen Glasgow Newsl.* 1,i:7-9.
Ellen Glasgow's elder sister Cary Glasgow McCormack wrote and published an amateurish novel a few years before her sister began her literary career. *A Successful Failure: An Outline* deals with several themes Ellen Glasgow later amplified in her own work. There is, therefore, the possibility that the novel may have influenced Ellen Glasgow. (MD)

10894. MacDonald, Edgar E. "Glasgow, Cabell, and Richmond." *MissQ* 27:393-413.
In post-Civil War Richmond, Georgian morality, Victorian prudery, and Confederate veneration produced a society that exalted deception into a way of life, producing a dual image of truth that disturbed the impressionable youth of Glasgow and Cabell. Glasgow early rejected the hypocrisy she associated with her father's creed and proceeded to describe Richmond in realistic detail, scorning the romantic approach of popular fiction. Cabell was more directly affected by the prevailing mores of Richmond when his name was associated with the murder of a profligate cousin. Both came to realize that their rejection and later compromises were universal patterns for the sensitive. Richmonders enjoyed the notoriety that the two writers created, but treated them with the indifference the Southerner generally accords the artist, subscribing to the belief that life is experience, not art. (EEM)

10895. Scura, Dorothy M. "Glasgow and the Southern Renaissance:The Conference at Charlottesville." *MissQ* 27:415-34.
A meeting of Southern writers proposed by Glasgow took place in Charlottesville at the University of Virginia 23 and 24 October 1931. Among the thirty attending the Conference were Glasgow, Faulkner, Cabell, Green, Tate, Anderson, Gordon, Johnston, Davidson, Phillips, Bishop, and Henderson. The planned topic, "The Southern Writer and His Public," was largely ignored during two days of round-table discussions and social events. The meeting resulted from a realization among Southern authors that a rebirth of letters was occurring in their region. (DMS)

10896. —— "One West Main." *Ellen Glasgow Newsl.* 1,i:3-6.
In 1887 Ellen Glasgow moved to the Greek Revival mansion on the corner of Main and Foushee Streets in Richmond, Virginia, where she died in 1945. After 1916 Ellen Glasgow was mistress of One West Main. She furnished the home with old family pieces and fine, 18th-century antiques. It became the place where she claimed she "had suffered most," but it was also the setting of her elegant entertainments. (DMS)

10897. Steele, Oliver. "Ellen Glasgow's *Virginia*:Preliminary Notes." *SB* 27:265-89.
Notebook 2 in the Glasgow Collection in the Alderman Library of the University of Virginia is essentially devoted to preliminary notes for Glasgow's *Virginia*. These notes show some significant things about the process of composition and about Glasgow's conceptions of the characters, themes, and actions of the novel. It is clear from these notes that she had originally planned a place in the novel for Cyrus Treadwell which would have given his ruthless rise to financial success a thematic importance equal to that of the tragic life of the heroine. (OS)

Goyen. 10900. Philips, Robert. "Secret and Symbol:Entrances to Goyen's *House of Breath*." *SWR* 59:248-53.
The symbols in Goyen's *House of Breath* and the secrets of the protagonists afford two ways of understanding the novel and sharing the author's intentions. The secrets involve the pubescent desires of Boy, Walter Warren Starnes' cancer, the liver disease of Jessy Gancheon, Folnet's aberrant behavior, Christy's illegitimate birth, and the absence of sex from his marriage to Otey. Goyen's symbols invoke the elements of air, earth, and water for association. The novel's secrets and symbols suggest that "ambition and lust have torn the house of breath asunder, and it remains a splendid but surely a fallen house." (CTW)

Hansberry. 10915. Willis, Robert J. "Anger and the Contemporary Black Theatre." *NALF* 8:213-15. [H, L. Jones, Garrett.]
Protest is implicit in most contemporary plays by black American dramatists. While not forgoing artistry, dramatists such as Hansberry, Baraka (LeRoi Jones), and Garrett are replacing the stereotype "nigger" image of buffoonery and low comedy with angry characters designed to forge black consciousness into a literature that speaks not only for the black man but also for the experiences of all Americans. (HH)

Harris, C. 10918. Simms, L. Moody,Jr. "Corra Harris on Southern and Northern Fiction." *MissQ* 27:475-81.
Reprints Corra Harris' 1904 essay (in *The Critic*) "Fiction, North and South" and gives introductory material by the editor. Harris,

a Southerner, praised Northern fiction and strongly criticized the achievements in fiction of her native region. Her explanations for this phenomenon varied, ranging from the impact on both North and South of climate and education to the Southern penchant for sentimentality and the Northern interest in "the human problems of the times." (LMS)

Hartmann. 10920. Knox, George. "A Complex Fate:Sadakichi Hartmann, Japanese-German Immigrant Writer and Artist." *GAS* 7:38-49.
Carl Sadakichi Hartmann's career is an inversion of the Horatio Alger "myth," a youth rising through adversity to recognition as art and photography critic, cultural entrepreneur, King of Bohemia, but finally aged Pierrot dying disillusioned and forgotten. Born in Japan of German-Japanese parents, reared in Hamburg, and exiled to America in his teens, he pursued a multifarious life, often pondering his role as immigrant of mixed origins in: the *Autobiography, Esthetic Verities, 1000 Happy Moments*, etc., all unpublished. Precociously prolific, he was nevertheless lost in obscure publications. (GAK)

Hayden. 10932. Novak, Michael P. "Meditative, Ironic, Richly Human:The Poetry of Robert Hayden." *MQ* 15:276-85.
Afro-American poet Robert Hayden has not received the critical response his work deserves despite the current interest in the literature of black Americans. Hayden has often stressed that he wants his work to be judged as poetry and not in some special category reserved for black artists. There is no denial of race in Hayden's work and some of his finest work confronts his central theme of suffering and hope through the subject of the experience of being black in America. "A Ballad of Remembrance" shows Hayden facing an agonizing choice in a surreal New Orleans between accommodation, hate, and love. The poem ends when he chooses the way of love as the way out of the dilemma America has created for him. "Middle Passage," Hayden's most ambitious poem, recreates the horrors of the slave trade. But even in the darkest chapters of Afro-American history Hayden looks to those heroes who strove to change their own and their peoples' lives. (MPN)

Hazard. 10933. Burt, C.R. "Addendum to Baird and Greenwood:Hazard." *PBSA* 68:74-75. [Bibliog. info. on *A Transplanted Puritan*.]
Caroline Hazard's *A Transplanted Puritan* (New York, 1927. 26 pp.) is an addendum (numbered 1143a) to Newton D. Baird and Robert Greenwood, *Annotated Bibliography of California Fiction, 1664-1970* (Georgetown, Calif.: Talisman Literary Research, 1971). This volume was printed at the Harbor Press in New York. (CRB)

Heller. 10935. Hasley, Louis. "Dramatic Tension in *Catch-22*." *MQ* 15:190-97.
Joseph Heller's *Catch-22* presents a pattern of dramatic tension between harrowing incidents of war and a counterpointing humor. The humor itensifies rather than alleviates the horror and irrationality of war. The actions, motivations, and narrative strategy are unabashed, often surrealistic, absurdity. War is not only irrational in the abstract but reduces to irrationality everyone engaged in it. The responsive reader experiences a kind of rapid, ecstatic, anguished shuttling between outrageous humor and preposterously shattering events. Dialogue, narrative, description, and introspective characterization continually enhance the artistry of presentation. *Catch-22* is a contemporary classic both of humor and of war. With its bitterly ironic humor, it resists the wrongs suffered in this life by the insufficiently guilty. For these wrongs Heller holds both men and the inscrutable Deity responsible. (LH)
10938. Nagel, James. "Two Brief Manuscript Sketches: Heller's *Catch-22*." *MFS* 20:221-24.
Among the many pages of notes, outlines, and manuscript Joseph Heller assembled during his years of work on *Catch-22* are two brief sketches which appear to be early conceptions of a hospital scene which was to become a short story entitled "Catch-18" and later the first chapter of one of the most important recent

American novels. These sketches reveal early stereotypic ethnic characterization; indeed, in at least one early draft, Yossarian is said to be Jewish. In the process of revision, however, the ethnic qualities of the characters were submerged and their unusual dimensions developed into the richness of character now evident in *Catch-22*. (JEN)
10942. Standiford, Les. "Novels Into Film:*Catch-22* as Watershed." *SHR* 8:19-25.
In order to successfully adapt novels into film, the filmmaker must avoid slavish reproduction of the story line to the exclusion of more subtle concerns of his medium. If illustrating is the paramount concern during adaptation, the product is likely to be little more than a talking book. As in fiction, story line should provide only the skeleton for full artistic exploitation within the medium. Mike Nichols anticipated the shortcomings of plot illustration approach when filming *Catch-22*. In place of a rambling, predominantly humorous narrative, he substituted a tight, somber progression of scenes moving to Yossarian's moment of decision. Nichols' film differs from the novel, but he maintains the serious theme, cuts repetitive jokes, approximates Heller's style through dialogue and non-sequitur arrangement of scenes, juxtaposes humor sharply against carnage. (LAS)

Hemingway. 10949. Bell, H.H.,Jr. "Hemingway's 'The Short Happy Life of Francis Macomber'." *Expl* 32:Item 78.
Robert Wilson's treatment of Margot Macomber in Hemingway's "The Short Happy Life of Francis Macomber" is often misunderstood and misinterpreted because we fail to see the author's application of the hunter's code on the human level. This code forbids a hunter to leave a wounded animal in the brush because he is in pain and because he may maul any unsuspecting party who stumbles upon him. Wilson views Margot Macomber as a wounded animal after she kills her husband when she becomes aware that he, having found himself, will leave her. The hunter in Wilson will not permit him to leave her in the brush of civilization without breaking her spirit so that she won't ruin the lives of any other men. It is for this reason that he "kills" her with five verbal shots at the end of the work. (HHB,Jr)
10963. Crozier, Robert D.,S.J. "For Thine Is the Power and the Glory:Love in *For Whom the Bell Tolls*." *PLL* 10:76-97.
The symbolic structure of Hemingway's *For Whom the Bell Tolls* is based on St. John of the Cross's concept of *La Gloria* and the mystical experiences of the dark nights of sense and spirit. General perspectives in the work of St. John of the Cross provide understanding of the textual allusiveness which broadens the context within which this work is to be considered. The two experiences of *La Gloria* in the work focus the mystical experience of the dark nights of sense and spirit through appropriate sense imagery in the first experience and through spiritual imagery in the second. (RDC)
10967. Doody, Terrence. "Hemingway's Style and Jake's Narration." *JNT* 4:212-25.
In *The Sun Also Rises*, Jake does not have the autonomy to make his narrative unequivocally his. Jake's expression varies with time and circumstances, and the prose changes to embody Jake's different states. Yet there is no formal recognition that Jake informs the prose with his own developing consciousness. Jake performs like Nick Adams of "Big Two-Hearted River," whereas his real agency is closer to Nick Carraway's. For Jake sees in Romero a purity or heroism not unlike that which Carraway sees in Gatsby. This ability to define Romero defines Jake, who is more selfless toward his rival than Hemingway can be toward his narrator. Hemingway intrudes on Jake's narration and leaves Jake problematically ironic, caught in the apparently unrecognized conflict between the artistic purpose and moral significance of Hemingway's style. (TD)
10980. Kerrigan, William. "Something Funny about Hemingway's Count." *AL* 46:87-93.
Count Mippipopolous in *The Sun Also Rises* shares the sexual impotence of the narrator. This detail, communicated by the code phrase "something funny" long after the Count has departed from the novel, reveals the darker ironies of Chapter VII, raises new questions about the untoward satisfactions of Lady Brett, underscores the Count as a model for Jake, and sharpens the aura

of transcendent nonchalance at the end of the book. Jake at the dinner table in Madrid, sated with food and wine, evokes the epicurean ambience of Count Mippipopolous, comfortable at last with the stoic belief that his debility is, insofar as anyone need know, "something funny" indeed. (WWK)

10982. Koontz, Leah Rice. "My Favorite Subject Is Hadley." *ConnR* 8,i:36-41. [Interview with first Mrs. H.]
Hadley, the first Mrs. Hemingway, recalled with both seriousness and wit her life with Ernest Hemingway in Paris in the 1920s. She told anecdotes of his personality, his working habits, his mother, their son, Bumby, and their landlady, Madame Chautard, whom both detested. She commented on the famous quarrel with Ernest when he went to Constantinople on assignment, the consolation gift of an amber necklace, and the later desolation of her losing the suitcase containing his manuscripts. Among their many Paris friends she spoke frankly of Harold Loeb, Duff Twysden, Ford Maddox Ford, Gertrude Stein, Lincoln Steffens, and Pauline Pfeiffer. She gave credit to Hemingway for changing her from a shy girl, interested mainly in music, to a woman who had the key to the world. His life-long admiration for her is expressed in his work. They remained friends until his death. (LRK)

10989. Merrill, Robert. "Tragic Form in *A Farewell to Arms*." *AL* 45:[571]-79.
Hemingway called *A Farewell to Arms* a tragedy, but his critics have found it to be unacceptable as a tragic work in Aristotelian terms. What is unique in Hemingway's tragic design is that his hero's mistaken actions do not "cause" his doom, yet the novel still has a tragic effect. The novel's characters and events are used to create tragic expectations throughout the novel, expectations satisfied by the novel's conclusion. Hemingway has portrayed his hero and heroine as something more than innocent victims. While not "responsible" for what happens to them, they are aware of the consequences should they choose to love, for the world of this novel is such that lasting happiness is impossible in it. Tragic tension arises between what we desire for Hemingway's lovers and what we know will be their fate. (RM)

10993. Monteiro, George. "The Education of Ernest Hemingway." *JAmS* 8:91-99. [The influence of H. Adams' *Education* on H.]
Despite Hemingway's denigration of Adams's *Education* and his characteristic denial that he had read it, much of Hemingway's work from the Nick Adams stories of *In Our Time* through *Winner Take Nothing* betrays the unmistakable influence of Adams's book. The biblical cast of the opening chapter of the *Education* has intriguing ties with *The Sun Also Rises*, and the "death of love" theme of *The Sun Also Rises* and *A Farewell to Arms* is anticipated by Adams's account of the disappearance of sex as a human force. In *Winner Take Nothing* several stories revolve around Adams's themes of Christianity, sex, and acedia. "A Clean, Well-Lighted Place" is heavily indebted to Adams's chapter on "The Dynamo and the Virgin." (GM)

10999. Oldsey, Bernard. "Of Hemingway's *Arms and the Man*." *CollL* 1:174-89.
Two key questions about *A Farewell to Arms* revolve around Hemingway's selection of a title borrowed from George Peele and his earlier fictional treatments of thematic motifs which became the bases of the novel. His selection of the title emphasizes his choice between Marlowe's bitter irony and Peele's lyric romanticism. The title helps account for the dialectic movement of the novel—from romance to realism to idyllic tragedy. As for Hemingway's own war experiences, and the various ways in which he made use of them in fiction, the critical reader discovers in these the proper answer to how autobiographical Hemingway's fiction is. (OB)

11003. Prizel, Yuri. "The Critics and *The Old Man and the Sea*." *RS* 41(1973):208-16. [Rev. art.]
Since its publication in 1953 Hemingway's *The Old Man and the Sea* has been subjected to a variety of interpretations, diverging widely at the first glance. A more careful examination, however, shows that most of those interpretations actually reach similar conclusions and the differences are more those of terminology rather than of reading. The main schools of interpretations may be divided into Christological, existentialist, archetypal, and psychological. Of these four, the first three stress the concepts of

man's dignity, his unity with nature, and the need for individual struggle, differing from each other only in terminologies because of different frames of reference. The fourth group, the psychologically oriented one, not only disagrees with the former three, but its advocates are unable to come to an agreement among themselves as to the meaning of *The Old Man*. This disagreement undermines the validity of psychological interpretations of *The Old Man*. (YP)

11007. Rosen, Kenneth. "Ten Eulogies:Hemingway's Spanish Death." *BNYPL* 77:276-77.
The reception of Spanish critics to Ernest Hemingway's death in 1961, as evidenced in the ten articles listed here which were published in leading Spanish journals, offers a view of the man and his work that supports the contention that the author's final act was perfectly consistent with the philosophy expressed in his writings. The articles listed here might be a productive starting point for anyone trying to evaluate Hemingway's work in light of the criticism now flowing out of both Asia and Europe as well as the United States. (KMR)

11012. Somers, Paul P.,Jr. "The Mark of Sherwood Anderson on Hemingway:A Look at the Texts." *SAQ* 26:[487]-503.
From an analysis of Hemingway's "My Old Man" and Anderson's "I Want to Know Why," which demonstrably influenced it, it is evident that the two writers share the use of interjections for emphasis; polysyndeton, or the linking of sentences by "and"; repetition and understatement. Whereas in matters of syntax and repetition, Anderson was in a way Hemingway's fellow pupil to Gertrude Stein, in the employment of understatement Anderson showed him a way to convey immediacy and emotional intensity, a way he employed in much of the best of his later work. (PPS,JR)

11018. Walcutt, Charles C. "Hemingway's *The Sun Also Rises*." *Expl* 32:Item 57.
The main characters in Hemingway's *The Sun Also Rises* are damaged people who, in a spiritually damaged world, are making heroic efforts to fend off that world and to maintain control of their precarious nerves. The Count and Romero have, in different ways, come to terms with the world. The others are trying, each in his way, and succeeding to various degrees. Jake is doing best with the hardest situation. Below him are Bill, Brett, Mike, and, far below, Cohn, who does not understand the situation at all. (CCW)

11019. Warner, Stephen D. "Hemingway's *The Old Man and the Sea*." *Expl* 33:Item 9.
Often passed off as gratuitous reflections, the five dream sequences involving lions on the beach in Hemingway's *The Old Man and the Sea* are an index of irony in the volume's narrative. For the reader, the narrative represents a tale of adventure and endurance; for Santiago, the events are mundane. By comparing the attitudes taken by the reader, the boy, and Santiago toward the dream sequences, the entire narrative may be understood to represent an ironic inflation of Santiago's world. (SDW)

Herrick. 11030. Franklin, Phyllis. "The Influence of William James on Robert Herrick's Early Fiction." *ALR* 7:395-402.
Herrick's earliest published work reveals much about his undergraduate concern with self-development and failure—particularly with the psychology of failure as suggested in the work of William James. Herrick accepts the existence of a stream of consciousness, the importance of habit in the early establishment of character, and the role of attention and will in the development of strong (and therefore moral) character. (PF)

Heyward. 11031. Shirley, Wayne D. "Porgy and Bess." *QJLC* 31:97-107.
Heyward's novel *Porgy* as adapted for the stage by Dorothy and DuBose Heyward forms the basis of George Gershwin's opera *Porgy and Bess*. Two attempts to adapt *Porgy* for the musical stage preceded Gershwin's opera: one, a parody with lyrics by Dorothy Fields and music by James Francis (Jimmy) McHugh made it to the stage as part of *Blackbirds of 1928*. The first-draft typescript of the libretto written by DuBose Heyward for Gershwin, now in the Library of Congress, shows the problems faced in adapting a play to the operatic stage and suggests some of the differences between the legitimate stage and the operatic stage. (WDS)

11032. Slavick, William H. "Going to School to DuBose Heyward." *SLitI* 7,ii:105-29.

In *Porgy*, Heyward sees the essential rhythm of black life defined by faith, community, and the common history of suffering. The characters of Catfish Row are unready for the modern world, yet must face the pressures of white society and the demands of fate. The marks of Heyward's realistic treatment are a primitivism rooted more in his characters' American experience than in the atavistic echoes of African drums. In *Mamba's Daughters* through faith, perseverance, and love, Mamba and Hagar make possible the granddaughter's success. Lissa understands her racial heritage and unites it with the discipline of high art as her song gives voice to the race's experience of suffering, longing, and joy. In a parallel white plot, the son of an old Charleston family feels something of Lissa's creative urge but subordinates it to economic success, only to recognize, in the end, that Lissa chose the better part: life. (WHS)

Hughes, L. 11043. Cobb, Martha K. "Concepts of Blackness in the Poetry of Nicolás Guillén, Jacques Roumain and Langston Hughes." *CLAJ* 18:262-72.

A comparative study of Guillén, Roumain, and Hughes to investigate the extent to which their poetry reflects the continuities and parallels of black life experiences conceptualized thematically as: (1) confrontation (blackness in a hostile society); (2) dualism (dilemma of being both black and American); (3) identity (search for one's humanity and one's heritage); and (4) liberation (the struggle for freedom). (MKC)

11044. Dandridge, Rita B. "The Black Woman as a Freedom Fighter in Langston Hughes' *Simple's Uncle Sam*." *CLAJ* 18:273-83.

In *Simple's Uncle Sam* Hughes depicts the black woman fighting against racial injustice in a variety of ways. The female relatives of the main character, Jesse B. Semple, include: (1) Joyce, an accomodationist; (2) Lynn Clarisse, a non-violent integrationist; and (3) Minnie, a militant black nationalist. The tactics they employ as freedom fighters enable them to function as counterparts to Booker T. Washington, Martin Luther King, and Malcolm X, respectively. Hughes's inclusion of female figures, instead of male ones, enables him to make amends for the oversight of black American writers in general who have failed to depict the black woman as a freedom fighter. (RBD)

Ignatow. 11051. Mills, Ralph J.,Jr. "Earth Hard:The Poetry of David Ignatow." *Boundary* 2:373-429. [Foll. by "Nine Poems by David Ignatow," 431-41.]

David Ignatow emerges with the publication of *Poems 1934-1969* as one who has developed a deliberately flat, prosaic style that gives his work its distinctive character and who has made himself a "metaphor for the community," exploring with deliberation both his inner life as a representative modern urban man and the life of the city around him. His is a poetry which begins without benefit of religious consolations or ideological foundations, which increasingly searches through the elements of experience for human values in a period that is rapidly dispensing with them. (RJM,Jr)

Jackson, S. 11055. Nebeker, Helen E. "'The Lottery': Symbolic Tour de Force." *AL* 46:100-07.

The ambivalent critical appraisal accorded Shirley Jackson's short story, "The Lottery," is rooted in the critics' failure to perceive that the story is actually two stories and themes fused in one fictional vehicle. The symbolic level reveals a summary of man's past and a prognosis for his future. Ultimately the symbols coalesce to indicate that the ritual of the lottery, rather than providing a channel for the release of man's repressed cruelties, actually serves as the genesis of cruelty—cruelty not rooted in man's inherent emotional needs at all. Man, Jackson says, is a victim of his unexamined and hence unchanging traditions. Unless he becomes aware of the horror of his ritualistic, irrational actions, rejecting that which has long been perverted from its original intention, he is ultimately doomed. (HEN)

Jarrell. 11057. Ferguson, Frances C. "Randall Jarrell and the Flotations of Voice." *GaR* 28:423-39.

The elusiveness of Randall Jarrell's use of poetic monologues and his sense of the spoken voice through much of his poetry prompts a re-examination of his poetry in terms of the movements of voice (rather than in terms of thematic and tonal analysis). Jarrell's prose essay "Stories" establishes a pattern of interweaving between his voice and the voices of the storytellers whose stories are recounted; and this pattern leads away from the notion of voice as a means of effecting a shock of recognition or a moment of self-discovery. Rather, the disembodiment of voice becomes conspicuous as the outline of individual speakers blur. Although a poem like "The Death of the Ball Turret Gunner" uses a monologue in which the speaker apppears to be a "representative man," poems like "Jerome" and "Eighth Air Force" play upon the apparently arbitrary processes of linguistic association to dissolve the notion of a finally composed and static self. Finally, voice appears to register the loss of all individual consciousness, the abandonment of all objects of merely personal concern. (FCF)

11060. Richards, Bertrand F. "Jarrell's 'Seele im Raum'." *Expl* 33:Item 22.

Randall Jarrell's poem "Seele im Raum" portrays an insane woman recalling in a moment of sanity her experience. She has created the metaphor of an eland to explain to herself her derangement. Her isolation, withdrawal, and guilt are shifted to this antelope-like creature. The eland dies and with it die the outward manifestations of her psychosis but inwardly the struggle continues. The duality of mind and soul, not mind, is dead. The German word "elend" signifies her own state of wretchedness. Her only solution is to renounce the world, to retreat from reality, and to live in remembrance of the past. On a higher level the poet reveals his own crisis of belief. If one cannot believe, then there is no soul, only mind. Without belief, without soul, there is no just cause for mind or for existence; therefore, existence itself is wrong. The poet and his subject have each arrived at the same conclusion: to live without faith is to lead a meaningless existence. (BFR)

Johnson, J.W. 11084. Ross, Stephen M. "Audience and Irony in Johnson's *The Autobiography of an Ex-Coloured Man*." *CLAJ* 18:198-210.

To challenge his readers' stereotyped notions about blacks, Johnson creates the narrator of *The Autobiography of an Ex-Coloured Man* (1912) out of three conventional figures: the tragic mulatto, the sentimental love hero, and the hero of class. When the "ex-coloured man" passes for white, he succumbs to his white, middle-class background more than he flees the black race. Johnson aims this irony at the psychological burden of whiteness causing his mulatto's tragedy. He leads the reader to sympathize with the narrator both as a black seeking racial identity and as a conventional hero seeking love and his proper status in respectable society. Given the narrator's past and the America he lives in, the two sympathies prove incompatible. Johnson traps the reader in the same ironic dilemma of values which the narrator describes. (SMR)

Kerouac. 11107. Dardess, George. "The Delicate Dynamics of Friendship:A Reconsideration of Kerouac's *On the Road*." *AL* 46:[200]-06.

Not even Jack Kerouac's best-known book *On the Road* has been examined with care. When it is so examined, the book reveals its classic dramaturgic structure and a major use to which Kerouac put that structure, i.e., as the framework upon which a delicate, contradictory edifice of friendship might be built. This moves from the simple hero-worship of Sal for Dean to an exchange of roles whereby Sal assumes a position *in loco parentis* for Dean. By the end of the book Sal has realized the contradictory nature of his love for Dean. The narrator's language develops from deliberately simplified distinction-making to complex expansiveness. (GD)

Kesey. 11113. Leeds, Barry H. "Theme and Technique in *One Flew Over the Cuckoo's Nest*." *ConnR* 7,ii:35-50.

The success with which technique serves theme in Ken Kesey's

One Flew Over the Cuckoo's Nest (1962) can be emphasized through a close textual analysis of several central symbol patterns and the structural devices used to present them. In a narrative structure analogous to those of *The Great Gatsby* (1925) and *All the King's Men* (1946), the narrator, Bromden, develops under the tutelary example of the protagonist, McMurphy. The effective integration of prose style with narrative character underlines Bromden's progress back to sanity. His early hallucinations are metaphorically closer to truth than the perceptions of a sane person. Hands become symbolic extensions of male potency, and both the importance of a clear sexual identity and the pervasive pattern of Christ imagery attach to McMurphy. In the sterility of the ward and the American society it represents, his sexual vitality makes him loom as a figure of apparently mythic proportions. Yet, in sacrificing himself to expose and reverse the dehumanization of the inmates by the monolithic Combine, he shows himself to be "just a man," which is quite enough. (BHL)

Kosinski. 11119. Coale, Samuel. "The Cinematic Self of Jerzy Kosinski." *MFS* 20:359-70.
In *The Painted Bird, Steps, Being There,* and *The Devil Tree,* Kosinski develops the cinematic self, a character defined solely in terms of his own visual actions. The often fragmented texts of the novels suggest both the disconnection of consciousness and a series of visual scenes from a film. The cinematic character is unable to understand himself, for he exists only as he acts. He remains trapped in a discontinuous series of actions from which there is no escape and no time for reflection. In his attempt to find himself, he is constantly in danger of losing himself altogether. (SC)

11122. Richter, David H. "The Three Denouements of Jerzy Kosinski's *The Painted Bird*." *ConL* 15:370-85.
Kosinski's *The Painted Bird,* first published in 1965, was revised in 1966 and again in 1970. In all three editions its protagonist is driven to accept one ideology after another in order to make sense of the atrocities of which he is witness and victim; in all three he withdraws into hysterical muteness, taking refuge from humanity. All versions end with the boy rejecting his ideologies, achieving autonomy, and finding his place in society, but Kosinski's revisions are designed to alter our response to the boy's resocialization. The 1965 edition concludes with an epilogue describing the inevitable conflicts between the independent youth and his newly-collectivized state; the 1966 edition omits the epilogue entirely, and the tension between socialization and autonomy survives only in a few phrases; in the 1970 edition even these are excised or palliated. Each revision makes less ambiguous our relief at the Painted Bird's return to his flock, but the price of Kosinski's happy ending is a weakening of his savagely ironic portrayal of an inhuman humankind. (DHR)

Larsen. 11128. Youman, Mary Mabel. "Nella Larsen's *Passing*:A Study in Irony." *CLAJ* 18:235-41.
Larsen's *Passing* ironically develops the theme that there are spiritual values in the black heritage, but blacks can lose or forfeit their birthright. The irony is created by contrasting the two main characters. Clare Kendry "passes for white"; Irene Redfield remains black but rejects her true heritage. The novel develops Irene's middle-class world. She is obsessed with a need for economic security, middle-class morality, and class distinctions. Though Irene considers herself a race woman, she has rejected the true values of blackness (spontaneity, freedom, laughter) and in the process destroys Clare who seeks to reaffirm spiritual values by returning to a black world. The novel shows that Irene's middle-class black world is indeed sterile, non-humane, and therefore to be rejected. (MMY)

Levertov. 11135. Pryse, Marjorie. " 'The Stonecarver's Poem' —A Linguistic Interpretation." *Lang&S* 7:62-71.
Denise Levertov's "The Stonecarver's Poem" is ambiguous at the level of surface structure. Charles Fillmore's model of case grammar provides a theoretical basis for analyzing two possible reconstructions of the surface structure and choosing one as the only grammatically possible reconstruction. The transformational history includes John R. Ross's transformation "Gapping," which

reveals a syntactic basis for an interpretive metaphoric ration between parallel elements in the poem. There are two instances where a fully grammatical surface structure would require anaphoric *the*-deictic modifiers. Analyzing their omission indicates that the first line of the poem, "Hand of man," without *the*-deictics, may be interpreted as either "hand of Man" (universal man) or "(the) hand of (the) man" (the stonecarver's hand). Fillmore's case theory again provides the framework for revealing the process of creation as the interpretive semantic root of the two verbs implicit in the title, "carve" and "write," thus adding a third set of elements to the metaphoric ratio which models the interpretation of the poem—poet : poem :: stonecarver : stone violet :: god : Adam. (MP)

London. 11173. Forrey, Robert. "Male and Female in London's *The Sea-Wolf*." *L&B* 24:135-43.
Through the conflict between the effete intellectual Humphrey Van Weyden and the brutal sea captain "Wolf" Larsen in *The Sea Wolf*, London may have unconsciously played off his inner self against his public image of lone wolf adventurer. If Van Weyden is a latent homosexual who wants "to come out," then it is obvious why he cannot. *The Sea-Wolf* suggests that life, like a voyage on a sealer, is a vicious business in which the strong enslave or slaughter the weak, just as the sadistic seamen do the seals. Van Weyden chooses to toughen up rather than come out. (RF)

Long. 11204. Almon, Bert. "Woman as Interpreter:Haniel Long's *Malinche*." *SWR* 59:221-39.
Long's *Malinche* offers valuable insights into the proper relationship between man and woman. By presenting the story as a series of incidents, Long emphasizes its symbolic nature. The power-centered, chauvinistic, ruthlessly ambitious Cortés of Long's story is an embodiment of some traditional masculine qualities. He is contrasted with a woman who hopes that he will serve as a savior, a peace-giver for her people. Malinche represents a key archetype, "the comrade and advisor, i.e., the fellow human being." Because Cortés refuses the moral and spiritual realities Malinche wishes to interpret for him, their relationship fails. But Long suggests that men and women can work together as comrades and friends, with or without love and begetting, to create a better world. (CTW)

Lowell, R. 11211. Axelrod, Steven G. "Robert Lowell and the New York Intellectuals." *ELN* 11:206-09.
Robert Lowell's recent satiric poem "The New York Intellectual" (in *Notebook* and *History*) specifically caricatures the critic Irving Howe, and may also refer implicitly to another New York writer, Diana Trilling. Written before Lowell's departure for England, "The New York Intellectual" is his bitter farewell to what he viewed as the heartless intellectualism of the New York literary milieu. (SGA)

11214. Fein, Richard J. "*Lord Weary's Castle* Revisited." *PMLA* 89:34-41.
Lord Weary's Castle conveys Robert Lowell's sense of historical destruction during and immediately after World War II. His efforts to relieve his despair by integrating it with Catholic belief, with Classical themes, with his knowledge of European and American history only succeed in confirming the apocalyptic view. The religious poetry in particular seeks a redemptive state beyond the poet's consciousness of war and violence, but usually results only in confirming the sense of destruction. The nervous, insistent rhythms of the poetry are themselves expressions of Lowell's compulsion to deal with violence and aggressive intrusions on man's consciousness. Throughout the book, the poetry expresses pity for the victims of military aggressions. In *Lord Weary's Castle*, Lowell is disturbed by American military aggression from colonial Indian battles to World War II; it is a distraught sense of American experience that would continue to haunt his poetry in the following decades. (RJF)

11218. Lensing, George S. "Robert Lowell and Jonathan Edwards:Poetry in the Hands of an Angry God." *SCR* 6,ii:7-17.
Jonathan Edwards figures prominently in Lowell's "Mr. Edwards and the Spider" and "After the Surprising Conversions" from

Lord Weary's Castle (1946), "Jonathan Edwards in Western Massachusetts" from *For the Union Dead* (1964), and "The Worst Sinner, Jonathan Edwards' God" from *History* (1973). Lowell, speaking through his own voice or through the voice of Edwards in dramatic monologue, draws liberally from the essays and sermons of Edwards—establishing, at times, a deliberate ambiguity between his own voice and that of Edwards. For Lowell Edwards represents an oppressive Calvinistic morality, often with manic overtones, even as he stands almost heroically for the morally committed life which accepts nonetheless the fallen nature of man. (GSL)

Lytle. 11230. Joyner, Nancy. "The Myth of the Matriarch in Andrew Lytle's Fiction." *SLJ* 7,i:67-77.
While the South provides the setting for Lytle's fiction, his heroines are not matriarchs as that term is generally understood. The protagonist of "Jericho, Jericho, Jericho" is a strong woman, but she has sacrificed her femininity for the land and finally realizes that her empire will vanish with her death. The wife of "Mr. MacGregor" is divested of her power when her husband and a slave fight a duel over her, symbolizing the prevalence of the chivalric code and emphasizing the patriarchal system. Julia Cropleigh, the Eve figure in *The Velvet Horn*, more nearly fits the requirement of the matriarch as defining image, but she lacks the pre-eminently important quality of the ideal of the southern woman, chastity. (NJ)

Mailer. 11249. Merrill, Robert. "Norman Mailer's Early Nonfiction:The Art of Self-Revelation." *WHR* 28:1-12.
Mailer's early nonfiction is discussed as a preparation for Mailer's later work in this form and as a considerable achievement in its own right. The evolving, "personal" approach to nonfiction which has characterized Mailer's work in this form is examined. The individual essays given detailed attention are "The White Negro," "Superman Comes to the Supermarket," "In The Red Light," and "Ten Thousand Words a Minute." Each of these essays (except "The White Negro") deals with a specific national event, which Mailer describes in a highly personalized manner, so as finally to convey his sense of its emblematic importance, its relevance so far as the national condition is concerned. (RM)
11252. Seib, Kenneth A. "Mailer's March:The Epic Structure of *The Armies of the Night*." *ELWIU* 1:89-95.
Norman Mailer's *Armies of the Night* (1968) takes the framework of the Classical epic for its essential structure and employs the major features of the traditional epic in the narrative details of the book. *Armies* begins *in medias res*, posits an epic question, invokes the muse, employs heroic catalogs and elaborate similes, supernatural events, and a journey into the underworld. These details are not merely allusive and ornamental; they are functional and basic to Mailer's theme—the destiny of the United States. The march on the Pentagon becomes a historical event of the first magnitude, as the Trojan War was to Greece, and Mailer posits himself as the epic hero, standing both within and above his narration. Like Achilles, Mailer is a man of wrath; like Odysseus, a fool—but like both he is supremely human. His modern epic expresses through one incident the fate of an entire nation. (KAS)
11253. Siegel, Paul N. "The Malign Deity of *The Naked and the Dead*." *TCL* 20:291-97.
The island of Anopopei in Mailer's *The Naked and the Dead* is the mysterious world in which men live, a world working in unfathomable ways to confuse, terrify, and destroy them. The action and dialogue as well as the setting and atmosphere suggest the presence of a malign supernatural power which is unconcerned with the personalities and fates of individual men and reduces them to the point where they cease to be individuals. The climb up the mountain and the long haul of carrying the wounded Wilson bring to the men an epiphany in which they attain a fleeting vision of a cruelly indifferent deity. The experience in which Ridges and Goldstein had their protective illusions stripped from them and were left "naked," exposed to the numbness of despair, colors their whole future view of life. (PNS)
11256. Taylor, Gordon O. "Of Adams and Aquarius." *AL* 46:[68]-82.
Adams in the *Education* and Mailer as "Aquarius" of *Of a Fire on*

the Moon are author-protagonists whose personal consciousness of historical change is both method and theme. Both writers brood on the cultural and metaphysical implications of technological acceleration. If their symbols of technology are different—dynamo as against rocket—their responses are often similar. Both explore questions of historical transformation in terms of sensations of personal annihilation, a pose of "posthumous" detachment for each a means of self-involvement with his materials. For both a new psychology is implied in the events on which they focus, and each uses himself as a model for predicting and criticizing the mentality of a new age. Their "educations" in scientific theory produce in Adams's thermodynamics and Mailer's rocketry systems of metaphor dependent for imaginative force on each author's sense of the unresolved mysteries such theories purport to explain. Other subjects of common interest reinforce a reader's sense of affinity between Adams and Aquarius. (GOT)

Masters. 11266. Burgess, Charles E. "Masters and Some Mentors." *PLL* 10:175-201.
Personal intellectual encounters in his youth affected Edgar Lee Masters and his *Spoon River Anthology*. Masters' relationships with the intellectuals of the region of his youth are woven into the free-verse tales of his characters who speak from graves of a village cemetery that in many ways is representative of the world. A comparison of the works of these regional intellectuals with portions of *Spoon River Anthology* suggests Masters' debt to an obscure but considerable body of regional writings. (CEB)

McCullers. 11274. Presley, Delma E. "Carson McCullers and the South." *GaR* 28:19-32.
Carson McCullers' disregard of her own past lies at the heart of the fundamental problem she spent her life writing about—the perenially-thwarted search for identity. The early novels and stories were written by a pessimistic young woman who, like her protagonists, longed to transcend the environment of her frustrated childhood. Out of the early struggle emerged some literature of the first order, e.g., *The Heart Is a Lonely Hunter*. After abandoning the landscape of her agony, she transmuted her region into a lifeless emblem, e.g., *Clock without Hands*. She did not inherit a sense of tradition, and the record she left indicates she did not attempt to embrace a tradition well known to readers of Southern fiction. She built her life on the hope that, somehow, Paris or New York would reach down and rescue her from the cultural stagnation she felt and feared in the South. (DP)

McKay. 11277. Kent, George E. "Claude McKay's *Banana Bottom* Reappraised." *CLAJ* 18:222-34.
Although McKay's *Banana Bottom* is often praised for resolving identity problems raised in his earlier novels, repeated readings reveal both merits and flaws. A comparison with other Harlem Renaissance novels concerned with black identity indicates that, in moving the setting for the identity struggle to early 20th-century Jamaica, McKay escapes the highly tense identity tests provided by black confrontation with large numbers of whites in a place such as America. (GEK)
11278. Lee, Robert A. "On Claude McKay's 'If We Must Die'." *CLAJ* 18:216-21.
In McKay's "If We Must Die" the main rhetorical tension is between the "we" (the oppressed) and the "they" (the oppressors), and the modulations of tone toward each side provide the main structural basis. The "we" evolve from "hogs" through "kinsmen" to "men"; "they" devolve from "dogs" through "monsters" to a "murderous, cowardly pack." Other technical aspects, especially sound and musical devices, reinforce the opposition of the two forces. To read away from the poem's particular historical and social context is to reduce it. It is, therefore, crucial to see what is fundamentally racial in "If We Must Die." (RAL)

Merton. 11295. McInerny, Dennis Q. "Thomas Merton and the Awakening of Social Consciousness." *AmerS* 15,ii:37-53.
Merton was an important influence on the awakening of social consciousness among American intellectuals during the 1960s. His early thought was generally unconcerned with social issues,

but from the publication of *Disputed Questions* in 1960 until his death in 1968 he was to write extensively on the subjects of war and racial strife. He argued that no man of conscience can justify turning his back on social evils and hope to find salvation on exclusively private terms. He advocated intense social involvement. At the same time, however, he saw dangers in activity which degenerates into activism, whose fruit is violence. In the end, he struck a tenuous balance between social commitment and the pursuit of contemplation. (DQM)

Miller, A. 11302. Jacobson, Irving F. "The Child as Guilty Witness." *L&P* 24:12-23.
"I Don't Need You Any More" illustrates all three senses of "home" found in Miller's work: the interior harmony of earliest childhood; the reattained equivalent for this, when one feels oneself an integral part of society; and the conflicts, fears, and guilts of family life. Martin falls from unity into multiplicity and he tries to recapture or recreate the earlier state of unity. Caught between the maternal and the paternal worlds, and accepted by neither, he defines his exclusion as a heroic mission, making his isolation from the family his primary means for relating to it. Yet also, he regards himself as a guilty witness of family conflicts and hopes that his commitment to silence will keep his family unified. (IFJ)

Mitchell, M. 11309. Gaillard, Dawson. *"Gone with the Wind* as Bildungsroman or Why Did Rhett Butler Really Leave Scarlett O'Hara?" *GaR* 28:9-18.
Margaret Mitchell wrote *Gone with the Wind* from two time perspectives, the mid-1800s and the 1930s. At the intersection of these times in her imagination is the image of the Southern Lady. The point toward which the novel moves is the death of this image as a scenario for woman's social behavior. When the child-wife created by the Southern Lady matures, when the image of the Southern Lady is no longer viable, the parent-husband walks out. Instead of feeling the traditional response, sadness, at his departure, women readers should feel relief. (DFG)

Moore, Marianne. 11315. O'Sullivan, Maurice J.,Jr. "Native Genius for Disunion:Marianne Moore's 'Spenser's Ireland'." *CP* 7,i:42-47.
In "Spenser's Ireland" Marianne Moore combines a pride in her Irish heritage with a bewilderment at the intransigence so fundamental to that heritage. Borrowing material from both the distant and recent pasts, Moore directs our attention initially to Spenser's experiences, especially, we soon learn, to his frustration with Ireland's resistance to change, only to redirect us, in a footnote, to "Ireland: The Rock Whence I Was Hewn," a magazine article by Donn Byrne in which she found a wealth of incidental information and a wry viewpoint which helped to generate the self-conscious irony in her conclusion. (MJOS)

Moore, W. 11316. Christopher, J.R. "Moore Meaning:In Fact, a Lot." *RQ* 6:124-33.
Two stories by Ward Moore, "Lot" and "Lot's Daughter," published in *The Magazine of Fantasy and Science Fiction* in 1953 and 1954, are, respectively, an imitation and an inversion of the biblical narrative of Lot. The first story fuses the realistic style and texture of psychological fiction, a traditional science-fiction theme of the attempt to survive atomic warfare and the biblical model. "Lot's Daughter," on the other hand, while less successful as a realistic fiction and less exact as a biblical parallel, offers the irony and intellectualizing of a Fryean anatomy. (JRC)

Motley. 11322. Rayson, Ann L. "Prototypes for Nick Romano of *Knock on Any Door*:From the Diaries in the Collected Manuscripts of the Willard Motley Estate." *NALF* 8:248-51.
Motley got the character of Nick Romano in *Knock on Any Door* from an encounter with Joe Nuaves, a boy in the Denver Detention Home. This developed into an important relationship, the beginnings of which Motley first described in Volume xxv, 1937, of his diaries. Immediately following his initial visits with Joe, Motley wrote the short story "The Boy" inserted in Volume xxvi of the diaries, which closely details the actual events and

conversations recorded in Volume xxv. A year later Motley returned to Denver to visit Joe, and in 1941 Joe came to stay with Motley in Chicago. Through this friendship with Joe, Motley developed his first and most important fictional character, Nick Romano, counterpart to his own transformation into Grant Holloway, mentor to Nick. (ALR)

Nabokov. 11334. Joyce, James. "Lolita in Humberland." *SNNTS* 6:339-48.
A hitherto unexplored area of artistry in Nabokov's *Lolita* concerns his use of allusions to *Alice's Adventures in Wonderland* and to Lewis Carroll. These allusions provide insight into Nabokov's sense of fiction and his affinity for Carroll, as well as providing greater understanding about *Lolita*. Nabokov makes use of his knowledge of Carroll's fascination with Alice Liddell in writing *Lolita*. The Alice leitmotif pervades and even named Humbert Humbert's world—Humberland. (JJ)
11341. Reisner, Thomas A. "Nabokov's *Speak, Memory*, Chapter III, Section 4." *Expl* 33:Item 18.
In Chapter iii, Section 4, of *Speak, Memory*, Vladimir Nabokov recalls how his Uncle Ruka, a self-proclaimed "expert in decoding ciphered messages in any of the five languages he knew" impressed the Nabokov children by turning "the sequence '5.13 24.11 13.16 9.13.5 5.13 24.11' into the opening words of a famous monologue in Shakespeare. Although Nabokov does not identify it further, the passage in question comes from *Hamlet*, III.i.56, the words "To be or not to be" being concealed by means of a simple substitution cipher. (TAR)

Nin, Anais. 11353. Zaller, Robert M. "Anais Nin and the Truth of Feeling." *ASoc* 10(1973):308-12.
It is a commonplace that politics pervades our culture, yet the first four volumes of the *Diary of Anais Nin*, covering the years 1931-47, contain scarcely a mention of political events or personalities. Nin gives us the keenest analysis of dreams, daily events, personal encounters, but makes no attempt to place the Stalin purges, World War II, or the atomic bomb in the context of her life. Yet if she rejects history it is not because she is unaware of it. She rejects politics not as a condition, but as a solution. Nin perceives war as the mass projection of individual irrationality. It is only in the individual that the answer to war can be found. (RMZ)

Noguchi. 11355. Graham, Don B. "Yone Noguchi's 'Poe Mania'." *MarkhamR* 4:58-60.
Yone Noguchi's first published poems drew praise from some quarters but charges of plagiarism from others. The first attack, by Hudson in the San Francisco *Chronicle*, cited syntactical and vocabulary parallels between Noguchi's "Lines" and Poe's "Eulalie" and "The Sleeper." The most invidious attack was leveled in a satirical insert in an issue of the *Philistine* and presumably was written by Elbert Hubbard. Here the shade of Poe returns to heap abuse on the yellow-back journals *Lark*, *Chap-Book*, and *Philistine* for being taken in by the "most innocent Jap on the poetic turn-pike." On Noguchi's behalf Joaquin Miller and Gelett Burgess wrote letters defending him. Later Hubbard relented, indicating that his real target had been the *Lark* and its editors. In his autobiography Noguchi recounted how he had been so under Poe's influence in his youth that he had felt himself to be Poe's incarnation. The controversy left its mark, for Noguchi never reprinted in his volumes of poetry those poems so roundly condemned in the opening year of his poetic endeavors. (DBG)

Oates. 11358. Pickering, Samuel F.,Jr. "The Short Stories of Joyce Carol Oates." *GaR* 28:218-26.
Joyce Carol Oates has written four books of short stories in the past decade. In the first book *By the North Gate*, the stories depicted a relatively objective world. Gradually, however, the stories have become more romantic. Human experience has become subjective rather than objective. In order to understand the stories, readers have been compelled to use their imaginations creatively. In *Marriages and Infidelities*, Oates has moved so far into the romantic world of sensations and subjectivity that the

very form of her stories has become mysteriously subjective, resulting in romantic disorder. (SFP,Jr.)

11361. Waller, G.F. "Joyce Carol Oates' *Wonderlane*:An Introduction." *DR* 54:480-90.
Oates's fiction is preoccupied with the fragility of human personality and the threatening obsessions and violence lurking beneath the surface of contemporary life. *Wonderland* traces the development of a single personality through a series of rapidly changing environments, names, families, and jobs. The novel's most insistent concern is with the effects of radical discontinuity upon the personality. (GFW)

O'Connor, Flannery. 11364. Burns, Stuart L. "O'Connor and the Critics:An Overview." *MissQ* 27:483-95. [Rev. art.]
O'Connor criticism has flourished since her death, 11 book-length studies having appeared. Drake's monograph *Flannery O'Connor* was one of the first to state the main thematic thrust of her fiction; it set the standard for most subsequent criticism. Post-Drake criticism falls roughly into three categories: essentially explicative works; works in which a central thesis becomes the basis for readings of individual stories; works which subordinate interpretation of individual stories to an over-all thesis. Beyond Drake, the books in category three—by Hendin, Muller, and Stephens—are most valuable because they place O'Connor's fiction in new perspective. (SLB)

11368. Farnham, James F. "Disintegration of Myth in the Writings of Flannery O'Connor." *ConnR* 8,i:11-19.
Inadequate attention has been given thus far to the role played in Flannery O'Connor's works by myth in its secular sense and to the more naturalistic implications of mythlessness. "Myth" is used here to mean any overall explanation of life which gives the individual a context of meaning larger than himself, one in which he can place his experiences and thus derive, *a priori*, some supportive meaning for his life from his experiences. The essential situation of the O'Connor character is the disintegration of the myth of redemption and the spiritual devastation which results. From a wider focus, O'Connor's writing deals with the collapse of myth experienced by many in our age. Her "Southern" freaks thus become the type of modern man as displaced person in an existential vacuum and gain meaning far beyond the limits of the South or of her orthodox Christian belief. (JFF)

11372. Gossett, Thomas F. "Flannery O'Connor on Her Fiction." *SWR* 59:34-42.
Excerpts from O'Connor's unpublished letters are paraphrased. O'Connor speaks freely of her own problems as a writer and avoids discussion of symbolism in her fiction. Her tone is frequently humorous in her commentaries on her short stories "A Good Man Is Hard to Find," "Greenleaf," "Good Country People," "A Circle of Fire," "The Artificial Nigger," and "Everything That Rises Must Converge." (CTW)

11373. —— "Flannery O'Connor's Opinions of Other Writers:Some Unpublished Comments." *SLJ* 6,ii:70-82.
Paraphrases comments by Flannery O'Connor on contemporary writers—largely American, English, and French. The copyright on all of O'Connor's work, including her personal letters, is held by Mrs. Edward F. O'Connor who has refused permission to have any of her letters printed. Gossett and his wife have about 135 letters and postcatds from O'Connor, some of them written to them but most of them to other people whose identities cannot be disclosed. (TFG)

11375. Katz, Claire. "Flannery O'Connor's Range of Vision." *AL* 46:[54]-67.
Although most critics interpret the fiction of Flannery O'Connor as Christian allegory, psychoanalytic reading suggests that the recurrent pattern is dominated by conflict over the consequences of autonomy. Personal power is equated with rage against a parent so intense that to act autonomously is potentially murderous; but to yield autonomy elicits a fear of engulfment. Thus the dissolution of the ego's power, ultimately death and merger with the protective omnipotence of Christ, is the saving grace. This regressive fantasy shapes not only plot but imagery and narrative voice. As narrator O'Connor functions as an avenging Christ, sadistically humiliating her characters through aggressive caricature, punishing them while simultaneously

allowing them to express their rage. The imagery evokes primitive fears of devouring, destructive penetration, castration, so that even the landscape becomes a projection of sadistic fantasies. It is the terror of these fantasies, however mitigated by defensive wit and Christian resolution, that provides the source of imaginative power in her fiction. (CK)

11383. Smith, Anneliese H. "O'Connor's 'Good Country People'." *Expl* 33:Item 30.
In O'Connor's "Good Country People" Joy-Hulga compares herself to Vulcan to assert her lameness and because she seeks to control her environment. As Hulga-Vulcan she negates her mother's dream of Joy-Venus. O'Connor reveals her character's scant self-awareness and the ironic appropriateness of her self-image as Vulcan. (AHS)

O'Hara, J. 11387. Eppard, Philip B. "Addenda to Bruccoli: O'Hara." *PBSA* 68:444-45.
Seven items are added to Bruccoli's *John O'Hara: A Checklist*: an introduction to a Fitzgerald collection, two short stories, three published statements and interviews, and a published letter. (PBE)

Olson, C. 11417. Hallberg, Robert von. "Olson's Relation to Pound and Williams." *ConL* 15:15-48.
Charles Olson is often referred to as a disciple of Pound and Williams. He admired the *Cantos*' freedom from the confines of linear time and he concurred in Pound's conviction of the importance of historical and societal matters, though he had only contempt for Pound's particular interpretation of history. More the democrat, Williams kept his work open to a wider range of experience, but he failed to establish in *Paterson* an historical dimension comparable to that of the *Cantos*. Williams' argument that words must be shaved of their historically accrued senses left Olson unconvinced; Olson shared Pound's faith in etymology as an accurate index of the history of Civilization. Olson took much from both poets but he gave to his contemporaries enough to refine a strain of American poetry that extends beyond all three poets. (RMvH)

O'Neill. 11444. Grecco, Stephen R. "High Hopes:Eugene O'Neill and Alcohol." *YFS* 50:142-49.
Alcoholism retarded O'Neill's growth as a writer. Intellectually he was receptive to the idea of tragedy, but emotionally he was unwilling to recognize and accept his pessimistic insights about man's nature. The kind of internal lucidity he needed to transform these insights into genuine works of art was violated by his drinking. *Mourning Becomes Electra* is only superficially tragic, lacking as it does a full commitment to the tragic vision. During the mid-1930s, O'Neill underwent a period of introspection. No longer drinking, he began writing more honestly and profoundly. *The Iceman Cometh* epitomizes the "new" O'Neill. (SG)

11445. Highsmith, James Milton. " 'The Personal Equation': Eugene O'Neill's Abandoned Play." *SHR* 8:195-212.
O'Neill worked on "Personal Equation" from 1914 to 1917, but gave up on the project. The plot was cumbersome, and the major characters stiff, while the language represented some of O'Neill's worst. But some of the motifs suggested later achievements, the minor characters (especially the seamen) are vibrant, and the playwright's sense of theater is sure and effective. (JMH)

Petry. 11468. Shinn, Thelma J. "Women in the Novels of Ann Petry." *Crit* 16,i:110-20.
Ann Petry reveals a world in which the individual with the most integrity is often forced to become an expression of the very society against which he is rebelling. She shows that the weak are misled by illusions and stifled by poverty. For Lutie Johnson in *The Street*, the struggle for survival is so demanding that even her attempt to struggle also to preserve her values gives her more stature in failure than most people achieve in victory. *Country Place* and *The Narrows* show how inequities and illusions rob weak and strong alike of chances for personal development and the sense of security. (TJS)

Pharr. 11469. O'Brien, John, and Raman K. Singh. "Interview with Robert Deane Pharr." *NALF* 8:244-46.
Robert Deane Pharr does not at present believe that novels can lead to social reform because America is not ready to look at itself. In *The Book of Numbers* he wanted to motivate black militants to aid black people, but he doubts that the intended audience reacts to the book. Moreover, even if blacks did attempt to follow his advice, they would not be allowed to use capitalism in a black neighborhood. The only well-paying option for ghetto blacks is crime. But no kind of wealth would be enough alone: like all people, blacks want a piece of every action. Pharr emphasizes dialogue as the method of exchanging ideas between people. Pharr's background also includes working at manual labor, and only personal contacts, provided by friends, with university faculty and publishers enabled him to get *The Book of Numbers* published. *SRO*, like *The Book of Numbers*, is autobiographical, based on observations and experiences: *SRO* even contains inner chapters in journal form, "insights" intended to involve the reader directly in the SRO hotel. (HH)

Plath. 11478. Eriksson, Pamela D. "Some Thoughts on Sylvia Plath." *UES* 10,ii(1972):45-52.
A detailed discussion of two poems by Sylvia Plath: "The Stones" from *The Colossus* and "By Candlelight" published in *Winter Trees*. Biographica 1 discussion is avoided in an attempt to exorcise the myth and legend surrounding Plath's life and death. Too much attention has been given to the "Sylvia Plath cult" and the label "confessional poet" is restrictive and harmful. Emphasis is laid on Plath's technique and the excellence of her poetry. By avoiding all mention of her personal problems, it is shown that the poems have universal appeal, that Plath has tried to depersonalize herself in the two poems discussed, and that a knowledge of her life and neurosis may be useful for the serious student, but is not a prerequisite for an understanding and appreciation of her poetry. (PE)

11479. Himelick, Raymond. "Notes on the Care and Feeding of Nightmares:Burton, Erasmus, and Sylvia Plath." *WHR* 28:313-26.
A comparison of Plath's autobiographical *The Bell Jar* with Burton on melancholy and Erasmus on folly suggests differences between assumptions underlying 20th-century sensibility and that of the Renaissance. The centripetal movement of Plath's account of her breakdown culminates in the bell jar as image of the aborting of authentic life and "self" in social constrictions. The centrifugal sweep of the *Anatomy* not only sees psychological malaise as a condition of being fully human but a requirement of emotional maturity, a paradox Erasmus was exploring in his *Praise*. There the life-as-stage metaphor is made to posit a view of the relationship between self and society markedly different from those implicit in *The Bell Jar*. Acknowledging life to be a performance by fallen natures in a fallen world, and nevertheless affirming that performance, this older humanistic view was both tougher-minded and less romantically simplistic. (RH)

11480. Libby, Anthony. "God's Lioness and the Priest of Sycorax:Plath and Hughes." *ConL* 15:386-405.
Both Ted Hughes and Sylvia Plath regard poetry as magical invocation, often of a dark female force, "the Goddess" or "the Mother," that presides over the violent transformations, personal or cultural, that preoccupy both. This archetype resembles Robert Graves' white goddess or Robert Bly's Great Mother. Now, according to Hughes (and Bly), it returns to do battle against masculine consciousness in the psyche of our culture. The battle, enacted in Hughes's and Plath's poetry, is apocalyptic, as nature rebels against the distortions imposed by men. Like Hughes, Plath feels deep ambivalence toward the Mother, seeing herself as her victim in poems like "Medusa," or "Nick and the Candlestick." But when she wrote this poetry she was a mother too, and poems like "Fever 103°," "Lady Lazarus," and "Stings" indicate that she identifies with the Mother. Her poetry is unusual not so much because of her preoccupation with death, which she shares with countless modern poets, but her references to a mysterious rebirth, ascension not to redemption but to vengeance. (APL)

11489. Uroff, M.D. "Sylvia Plath's Women." *CP* 7,i:45-56.
In the course of Plath's poems, the women assume attitudes of increasing intensity toward their failed relationships with men. The women are transformed from thinkers to worriers to vicious plotters in their efforts to defend themselves against men who seem at first merely unruly, then turn into animalistic creatures and finally into predators. Plath's women are thinkers, not sexual objects, while her men are frequently imaged as merely physical creatures. The woman as thinker or spirit survives in Plath's late poetry in her exclusive purity only by destroying the brute men and the lower order of existence that they represent. (MDU)

Porter, K.A. 11490. Givner, Joan. "Katherine Anne Porter, Eudora Welty, and 'Ethan Brand'." *IFR* 1,i:32-37.
A comparison of Porter's "Theft" and Welty's "Petrified Man" with Hawthorne's "Ethan Brand" shows the use and limitations of the grotesque. All these stories deal with a deficiency which manifests itself in the failure to engage with others in vital relationships. Porter and Hawthorne carefully describe their protagonists' flaws and set them off by comparison with certain positive values. Welty chooses not to analyze her characters' spiritual states. She externalizes their flaws and underscores their deficiencies by evoking the grotesqueries of the freak show. Porter and Hawthorne use grotesque effects sparingly to give final emphasis to weaknesses which have been carefully explored. (JG)

11491. ——. "Porter's Subsidiary Art." *SWR* 59:265-76.
In Porter's letters fact and fiction are inextricably bound together. Her correspondence with Glenway Wescott and Monroe Wheeler has an artistic unity which suggests that it was a "deliberate exercise in the art of writing letters, and one which was regarded on both sides as being suitable for eventual publication." Her letters include factual commentary about her fiction and about her critical writing. When Porter describes the circumstances of her life or of her marriages to Albert Erskine and Eugene Pressley, she juxtaposes fact and fantasy, past and present, to create a special art form. (CTW)

Porter, W.S. 11494. Marks, Patricia. "O. Henry and Dickens:Elsie in the Bleak House of Moral Decay." *ELN* 12:35-37.
The epilogue which follows Jo's death in Dickens' *Bleak House* is the thematic and textual source for O. Henry's "Elsie in New York." In their efforts to maintain an independent livelihood, both Jo and Elsie are frustrated by self-righteous representatives of the mores of society. The uncouth Jo is forcibly persuaded to "move on" until he "moves on" into death; Elsie, innocently searching for a *modus vivendi*, is threatened with damnation until she is driven into prostitution. O. Henry's epilogue, which follow's Elsie's capitulation, is a paraphrase of the epilogue in *Bleak House*. (PM)

Pound. 11495. Atkinson, F.G. "Ezra Pound's Reply to an 'Old-World' Letter." *AL* 46:[357]-59.
A hitherto unpublished letter by Pound to Sir A.T. Quiller-Couch augments the known details of Pound's early days in literary London and adds considerably to existing knowledge of an incident referred to by Pound in a letter to Harriet Moore. In objecting to Quiller-Couch's proposed two selections from his poems for reprinting in *The Oxford Book of Victorian Verse* (1912) Pound mentions several other poems in a brief critical survey of his first four volumes. The letter is undated but internal evidence indicates mid-October 1912. (FGA)

11504. Burns, Gerald. "Intellectual Slither in the 'Cantos'." *SWR* 59:76-84.
The problems encountered in reading Pound's *Cantos* are explored. Pound's most damaging influence has been the assumption that the reading of his verse feels like studying. His "pure effect-writing" is immature; clarity of method is subverted; value—wisdom and judgment—in the *Cantos* is variable. Pound's credentials as a great poet are his negative insight—his ability to avoid the mistakes he saw around him—and his ability to write poetry in such a way that the most casual reader must take it seriously. (CTW)

11526. Jackson, Thomas H. "The Poetic Politics of Ezra Pound." *JML* 3:987-1011.
Very early in his career Pound was driven to see the destiny of art

and artists as tied to political problems. He conceives of reality as a system of dynamisms, and he values the idea of flow and fluidity in both poetry and politics. He extended his theory of poetic mastery into other realms of human endeavor in the concept of the creative man who masters various manifestations of the flow of natural energies from the most private to the most public. Poet and politician alike need a sense of the concrete, a sense for gradations, and agility of mind. Pound despised usury for its evasion and obliteration of these key values. He conceived of Mussolini as a great artifex, but the major figures of this sort in the *Cantos* are Malatesta, Jefferson, and Adams. In the later *Cantos* the rather arid focal artifex, Adams, is replaced when the center of the narrative energy becomes a poet's, and no longer a politician's, sensibility. (THJ)

11534. Materer, Timothy. "The English Vortex:Modern Literature and the 'Pattern on Hope'." *JML* 3:1123-39.
The English Vortex was the association of Wyndham Lewis, Pound, Eliot, the sculptor Henri Gaudier-Brzeska, and some of the finest abstract painters in pre-World War I England. The term "Vortex" was used by Pound to describe the focusing of cultural energy from all the arts in a single group. Lewis led the movement as editor of their journal, *Blast* (1914-15). The Vortex hoped to produce visual designs which would influence the appearance of everything from household utensils to the form of a city. World War I destroyed the movement, and efforts to revive it and plan a new program failed in the explosive political atmosphere of the 1930s. (TJM)

11558. Wilhelm, James J. "Guido Cavalcanti as a Mask for Ezra Pound." *PMLA* 89:332-40.
A study of Ezra Pound's translations of Guido Cavalcanti's *Rime* shows Pound's lifelong interest in the work of the Italian poet. A further tracing of Cavalcanti's rhetoric in the *Cantos* shows that Pound employed Cavalcanti in a twofold way: he related him to Neoplatonic philosophers through his use of light imagery, and treated him as an Aristotelian empiricist. He thus made Cavalcanti serve two apparently divergent aims, just as Pound's own work does. Although the modern poet's philosophic understanding of Cavalcanti is open to controversy, his poetic uses have accounted for some of the finest passages of the 20th-century epic. (JJW)

11560. —— "The Dragon and the Duel:A Defense of Pound's Canto 88." *TCL* 20:114-25.
Examines Pound's Canto 88 in the light of the work of Thomas Hart Benton, showing how Pound adhered closely to Benton's thought and writings. Pound's poetic enactment reveals not only a respect for historical integrity as viewed through one man's eyes, but a poet's eye for history, in which the forces of good, however defined, are ever challenged by the forces of disruption. (JJW)

Purdy. 11564. Baldanza, Frank. "James Purdy on the Corruption of Innocents." *ConL* 15:315-30.
The theme of "the corruption of innocents" contains as archetypal factors the innocent adolescent picaro, the corrupting elder, and occasional mentors who enforce the traditional moral system. Purdy has a personal interest in certain Spanish picaresque and English boy-adventure works that represent analogous treatments of this theme, though they are not to be taken as sources. *Celestina* (1499) handles the material as a moralizing Renaissance Humanist tract, whereas *Lazarillo de Tormes* (1554) and Cervantes' "Rinconete and Cortadillo" (1613) employ a moral neutrality as a vantage point for rich social observation. Stevenson's *Treasure Island* (1883) and *Kidnapped* (1886) and J. Meade Falkner's *Moonfleet* (1898) put the adolescent through more thrilling adventure, but often with the aid of mentors who guard a fixed code of ethics that grants the boy a reward. Purdy's "63: Dream Palace" (1957) has an "existentialist" moral ambiance that places the boy in an identity crisis and a love-hate ambivalence that represents an anguished, profoundly tragic contemporary vision of the picaresque dilemma. (FB)

11565. —— "James Purdy's Half-Orphans." *CentR* 18:255-72.
Purdy's characters are literal or figurative orphans whose sense of radical rootlessness constitutes one of his primary themes. The half-orphans—children who are reared by one parent or grand-parent—form a significant subgroup. Three of his stories ("Color of Darkness," "Why Can't They Tell You Why?" and "Home by Dark") deal with children who are obsessed by a fetishistic attachment to objects or symbols associated with the absent parent; three others ("Eventide," "Encore," and "Night and Day") focus on the lone mother as do the plays *Children Is All* and *Cracks*. Purdy's most recent long novel, *Jeremy's Version* (1970), gives the fullest and most trenchant treatment of the theme. (FB)

11566. —— "Northern Gothic." *SoR* 10:566-82.
James Purdy's achievement in handling Midwestern material can be seen by contrasting his work with that of the Establishment regional laureate, Sherwood Anderson. Both share a confrontational story structure, in which two lonely persons momentarily breach walls of isolation; but Purdy places far more emphasis on stylistic rigor. Both deal in feminine archetypes of the spinster, the town slut, and the domineering matriarch; for males, the central archetype is the questing adolescent; fathers are weak failures, replaced in function by a failed professional man. The difference lies in Anderson's implicit meliorism which assumes there is a liberation and a communion possibly available to these outcasts; Purdy presents with honesty the hopeless existential dilemma of alienated man. (FB)

11567. —— "The Paradoxes of Patronage in Purdy." *AL* 46:[347]-56.
In Purdy's novels and stories nearly all relationships are pervaded by the assumption of patron-protege roles. The wealth, maturity, and authority of the patron seek out and dominate the beauty, wit, and innocence of the young male in patterns that frequently entail sado-masochistic manifestations, both metaphorical and actual. This basically economic effort to bargain for love lends to most such relationships a bickering, acidulous tone. (FB)

Pynchon. 11569. Friedman, Alan J., and Manfred Puetz. "Science as Metaphor:Thomas Pynchon and *Gravity's Rainbow*." *ConL* 15:345-59.
Thomas Pynchon's *Gravity's Rainbow* (1973) is an attempt at understanding history and the world in the light of a metaphor from modern science. The image of the thermodynamics of life provides the metaphorical answer to Pynchon's question of whether order or chaos prevails in the physical and in the spiritual universe. Characters in an elaborately detailed world observe that life is a "thermodynamic surprise" because it goes against the general flow of physical processes to increasing disorder. They split into advocates of complete deterministic conspiracy (paranoia) or complete randomness (anti-paranoia) to explain the occurrence of life in a world where disorder seems to prevail. Yet the increase of order in living structures is made thermodynamically possible by greater disorder in other parts of the universe. Pynchon demonstrates analogically that neither world nor history should be seen as exclusively representing order or disorder. Every process, most notably life, functions by "entropy management," the necessary balancing and cyclical regeneration of order and disorder. Thus the universe produces a continuing variety of existence, and from this point of view, paranoia and anti-paranoia vanish as delusions of limited perspective. (MEP & AJF)

11570. Leland, John P. "Pynchon's Linguistic Demon:*The Crying of Lot 49*." *Crit* 16,ii:45-53.
Much criticism of Pynchon's *Lot 49* deals with problems of content and meaning. However, *Lot 49* attacks many of the critical and interpretive strategies which we have traditionally brought to bear on literary texts. Pynchon's novel explores the possibilities and limits of language and fiction and thus forces us to re-examine these traditional interpretive categories. As "meta-fiction," *Lot 49* is profoundly anti-mimetic—its words deny easy access to things, its symbols fail to symbolize, its allegorical correspondences crumble within a circular structure of words. Thematically, the concept of "entropy" is crucial to an understanding of the novel as a metaphor that speaks Pynchon's conception of the fictional process—that of writing as well as reading. (JPL)

11571. Ozier, Lance W. "Antipointsman/Antimexico:Some Mathematical Imagery in *Gravity's Rainbow*." *Crit* 16,ii:73-90.

In Pynchon's *Gravity's Rainbow* the development of characters Roger Mexico and Edward Pointsman is illustrative of Pynchon's improvement since his first two novels. The men, both scientists, are initially contrasted as lover (Mexico) and manipulative behaviorist (Pointsman). Pynchon produces a mathematical metaphor from probability theory that adds symbolic and intellectual dimensions to the characterizations: Mexico can accept life's indeterminacy implicit in the existence of probabilities, but Pointsman cannot. This metaphor has mythological, religious, philosophical, scientific, and historiographic overtones which invest the characters with complex significance both within and beyond their individual identities. (LWO)

11572. Patteson, Richard. "What Stencil Knew: Structure and Certitude in Pynchon's *V*." *Crit* 16,ii:30-44.
The structure of Pynchon's *V*. reflects one of the novels central themes, the limitations of knowledge. Two strands of narrative matter alternate—Herbert Stencil's search for V. and Benny Profane's aimless wandering. Each of the chapters in which Stencil seeks out V. is narrated in a different way, a tactic which implies an attempt to explore diverse methods of discovering and communicating knowledge. Each way of knowing tested is found to be inadequate. The effort to know—to establish or discover a pattern of causal connections—is defeated by an ungovernable tendency toward formlessness that permeates the entire universe. (RP)

11573. Pütz, Manfred. "Thomas Pynchon's *The Crying of Lot 49*: The World Is a Tristero System." *Mosaic* 7,iv:125-37.
In *The Crying of Lot 49* Pynchon asks if we can detect patterns of order in life and history, or are both subject to increasing disorder and entropy. Oedipa Maas begins her quest when she accidentally detects certain patterns of events which suggest that a highly organized conspiracy reaches from 16th-century Europe to present-day America. Consequently, the bits and pieces of her experience begin to fall into coherent patterns: history becomes a field of recognizable order and predictability. However, Oedipa Maas may only be imagining the forms of order and unity which she thinks she has discovered. Paranoia becomes the universal suspicion of the novel. Toward the end, Pynchon's treatment of the heroine's case suggests that the ambition to detect order in history and human experience, time-honored though it is, is a neurotic obsession and reveals modern man's final lapse into a state of paranoid delusions. (MP)

11575. Simmon, Scott. "*Gravity's Rainbow* Described." *Crit* 16,ii:54-67.
Presents an overview of Pynchon's *Gravity's Rainbow*, discussing the pun of the title, as well as the novel's themes and its dualistic and cinematic structure. A defense of Pynchon's characterization is provided in Freudian terms. The novel is divided into five interrelated plots: Slothrop's central quest, the schemes of members of the PISCES group, Weissmann's building of the 00000 rocket, Tchitcherine's obsession with killing Enzian, and Enzian's own building of a duplicate of the 00000. An index of the more than 300 characters is presented, providing a page listing for each mention or entrance as well as a gloss on the role of each major character. (SS)

11576. Wagner, Linda W. "A Note on Oedipa the Roadrunner." *JNT* 4:155-61.
Pynchon's *The Crying of Lot 49* recreates physically the speed that dominates our culture. The book moves from a mockery of conventional novel technique to a pace of frantic action. Pynchon creates sympathy for protagonist Oedipa Maas because she is faced with countless impossible situations, and yet she endures. Pynchon draws on the Oedipus legend, the mythic American dream, and current absurdist and existentialist literature in his various plot lines, but he still presents Oedipa as the perservering innocent whose attempts to create order to exist as an active human being, are doomed to failure in her paranoid and divisive culture. (LWW)

Ransom. 11582. Young, Thomas D. "A Kind of Centering." *GaR* 28:58-82. [Biog.]
In 1914 John Crowe Ransom returned to Vanderbilt University, from which he had graduated five years before. With the exception of a two-year period of service in the United States

Army he remained a member of the English department of Vanderbilt until he went to Kenyon College in the fall of 1937 The period 1914-20 is most significant in his literary career. No only did his first book of poems, *Poems About God* (1919), appear; but his introduction to the symbolist poets during his period of service in France and his systematic and analytical reading of contemporary poetry convinced him that he wanted to write poetry of a kind vastly different from that in his first volume. (TDY)

11585. ——— "Without Rank or Primacy." *MissQ* 27:435-45. [R as a public school teacher in southern Miss.]
After his sophomore year at Vanderbilt, Ransom dropped out of the university to secure a teaching position. A few months past his 17th birthday, therefore, he went to Taylorsville, a small farming and lumbering village in the southern part of Mississippi, to teach the 6th and 7th grades at a salary of $65 a month. Although he found life in Taylorsville crude "even for a young man who had grown up in the small towns of middle Tennessee," he "marvelled at the friendliness" of his pupils and their parents. Impressions of the quality of life enjoyed in this community made their way into the Agrarian essays he wrote twenty-five years later. (TDY)

Rechy. 11589. Giles, James R. "Religious Alienation and 'Homosexual Consciousness' in *City of Night* and *Go Tell It on the Mountain*." *CE* 36:369-80.
Largely because of its "sensational" subject matter and its obvious autobiographical elements, Rechy's *City of Night* is underrated artistically. The novel is, however, deceptively compact and tightly controlled. The major chapters are unified around the concept of a "confession" of pain and loneliness, the unnamed central character playing the role of a "priest" who hears these confessions. The main character feels conflicting needs to receive sexual tributes to his physical beauty from anonymous strangers and to listen to these same strangers' narratives of personal suffering. The confession motif works ironically in the novel since Catholicism is established as a negative, destructive force. A hostile father figure is another threatening force in the novel. Baldwin's *Go Tell It on the Mountain* parallels *City of Night* in several ways: a main character intimidated by a dehumanizing church, a brutal father figure, and confession as a unifying device. (JRG)

Reed, I. 11591. Duff, Gerald. "Reed's 'The Free-Lance Pallbearers'." *Expl* 32:Item 69.
Early in *The Free-Lance Pallbearers*, Ishmael Reed savagely parodies the deathbed scene in Ralph Ellison's *Invisible Man* in which the protagonist's dying grandfather advises his children how to survive through subterfuge in the enemy's country. Reed has the dying mother of Harry Sam, the white dictator, tell her son to ". . . always be at the top of the heap. If you can't keek um, butt um. If you can't butt um, bite um and if you can't bite um, then gum the mothafukas to death." Through this parallel Reed rejects Ellison's vision of coherence and tradition in the black American experience. (GAD)

11593. Schmitz, Neil. "Neo-HooDoo: The Experimental Fiction of Ishmael Reed." *TCL* 20:126-40.
Reed's experimental fiction breaks from the tradition of the "Neo-Slave Narrative" in Afro-American literature. Reed approaches his writing from the same metafictive angle that many modern Anglo-American writers take, but he has nonetheless striven to avoid their negative tone and philosophical despair. He has created an eclectic mythology, Neo-HooDoo, and through its values attempted a radical revaluation of black writing in the United States. But the satiric direction of his fiction is not always in harmony with Reed's mythologizing, and the result is a series of formal and thematic problems in his fiction. (NS)

Robinson. 11602. Baker, Carlos. " 'The Jug Makes the Paradise': New Light on Eben Flood." *CLQ* 10:327-36.
Offers a short history of the origin and publication of Robinson's "Mr. Flood's Party" and indicates some minor changes made by the poet between the version submitted to and rejected by *Collier's* and the final version which appeared in *The Nation* on 24 Nov. 1920. An unpublished notebook by Ruth Robinson Nivison,

the poet's niece, contains her view that the real-life prototype of Flood was John Esmond of Gardiner, Maine. Certain literary associations are traced which enriched the portrait of Flood: *The Rubaiyat of Omar Khayyam, The Song of Roland,* and a little-known poem by James Kirke Paulding, "The Old Man's Carousal," which had appeared in Stedman's *An American Anthology* (1900) to which Robinson was also a contributor. The essay includes passages from four hitherto unpublished Robinson letters. (CB)

11604. Cary, Richard. "Additions to the Robinson Collection:II." *CLQ* 10:385-88.

In each of the four issues of *CLQ* during Robinson's centennial year, 1969, appeared an installment of an annotated listing of association items in the Robinson collection at Colby College: books and periodicals inscribed by him, or presentation copies to him. An addendum to these lists was published in September 1971, and the current one describes 86 acquisitions since that date. (RC)

11605. —— "Robinson's Friend Arthur Davis Variell." *CLQ* 10:372-85.

Edwin Arlington Robinson had an exceptionally large number of close friends although he was known to be ungregarious. One of these not mentioned by any biographer or critic was Arthur Davis Variell, a boyhood chum of Robinson's who attained international fame as a doctor and epidemiologist. After total disconnection for more than two decades, Variell wrote to Robinson in August 1922. They met frequently thereafter, mostly in New York City, until September 1929. In that interval Robinson sent Variell at least 53 letters and one postcard, now in Colby College Library. Relevant excerpts from these hitherto unpublished letters are presented in this essay. (RC)

11606. —— " 'The Clam-Digger:Capitol Island':A Robinson Sonnet Recovered." *CLQ* 10:505-11.

This sonnet, signed only "R.", appeared in *The Reporter Monthly,* a four-page literary supplement in Robinson's home town newspaper the *Kennebec Reporter* on 26 April 1890. It has never been attributed to him in any bibliography or checklist. Close examination of circumstantial and internal evidence favors inclusion of the poem in the Robinson canon. (RC)

11607. —— "The First Publication of E.A. Robinson's Poem 'Broadway'." *AL* 46:[83].

In *AL* for January 1951, Edwin S. Fussell presented Edwin Arlington Robinson's "Broadway" as a previously unpublished poem, an error unfortunately perpetuated by William White in his *Supplementary Bibliography* of Robinson in 1971. "Broadway" was in fact published in the New York *Evening Sun* on 15 November 1918, with one significant difference in (stanza 1, l. 5) from the Fussell version. (RC)

11609. Cox, Don R. "The Vision of Robinson's Merlin." *CLQ* 10:495-504.

In his Arthurian poem *Merlin,* Edwin Arlington Robinson uses a motif of vision and reflection to create an interpretation of the fall of Camelot that departs significantly from the legend as it appears in his sources. Robinson alters the dramatic circumstances of the legend by creating a Merlin who is not entrapped by the seductive Vivian and is free to leave the paradise of Broceliande whenever he desires. Merlin goes to Vivian's Broceliande believing she can order and explain his world; he is mistaken, and his "imprisonment" ends when he discovers that his submission to Vivian is entirely voluntary. When Merlin learns that Vivian cannot order his world he sees that the ideal visions men have believed they have seen are reflected visions for they represent the desire of the self for order. It is believing in a truth that matters, not the ultimate validity of the truth. Merlin leaves Broceliande to become Dagonet's king, thereby establishing a framework of existence within which both he and Dagonet can function, their cosmos now in order. (DRC)

11611. McFarland, Ronald E. "Robinson's 'Luke Havergal'." *CLQ* 10:365-72.

Edwin Arlington Robinson's "Luke Havergal" may be shown to have been composed during the time that the poet was examining Dante's *Divine Comedy* in some detail. Robinson's letters also indicate that in the spring of 1895 he was reading the gospel of Luke with much pleasure, and it is only in this book of the New

Testament that the story of the prodigal son, later the subject of a poem by Robinson appears. This article suggests that the name of the title character is drawn from the story of the prodigal son, and that, like the biblical character, Luke Havergal is a type of the penitent sinner. Moreover, both the dramatic conditions of the poem and the imagery and personae suggest a situation comparable to that of Dante's protagonist at the entrance to Hell. (REM)

11612. Miller, John H. "The Structure of E.A. Robinson's *The Torrent and the Night Before.*" *CLQ* 10:347-64.

Unlike E.A. Robinson's later volumes that organized poems by stanza form, Robinson organized his first book of poems, *The Torrent and The Night Before* (1896), into an introduction and four thematic groups. The themes of the four main sections are art, death, light, and living in the physical world. The first announces Robinson's intention to be a poet. The second contemplates different attitudes toward death and concludes that death is an inevitable fact, neither to be ignored nor sought after. The third investigates the possibility of finding spiritual light in a dark world, and the final group deals with the question of how to live in this world. (JHM)

11613. Monteiro, George. " 'The President and the Poet': Robinson, Roosevelt, and *The Touchstone.*" *CLQ* 10:512-14. [Illus.]

Theodore Roosevelt's generosity toward E.A. Robinson in persuading Scribner's to bring out a second edition of *The Children of the Night* and in securing for the poet a place in the U.S. Customs Service in New York evoked in January 1906 a response from *The Touchstone,* a short-lived Chicago periodical. Along with its satiric account of Roosevelt's actions appear four illustrations (E.A.R. in "the daisy fields of Maine," "a New York attic," "the subway," and the "custom-house") and "John Rockefeller," a "revised" version of "Richard Cory" in "print for the first time in any magazine." (GM)

11614. Perrine, Laurence. "The Sources of Robinson's Arthurian Poems and His Opinions of Other Treatments." *CLQ* 10:336-46.

Discussion of Edwin Arlington Robinson's sources for his three long Arthurian poems—*Merlin, Lancelot,* and *Tristram.* Cites evidence for his use or knowledge of Malory, the Vulgate *Merlin,* Tennyson, William Morris, Joseph Bédier, Richard Wagner, Swinburne, Matthew Arnold, Richard Hovey, John Masefield, James Russell Lowell, Hermann Hagedorn, and *Gawain and the Green Knight.* Only Malory, the Vulgate *Merlin,* and Tennyson exerted a clearly demonstrable influence on Robinson's treatment. (LP)

11615. Sanborn, John N. "Juxtaposition as Structure in 'The Man Against the Sky'." *CLQ* 10:486-94.

The philosophical and esthetic problems of Robinson's "The Man against the Sky" may be partially resolved by reading the poem as unified by the juxtaposition of the two great philosophies of faith and reason rather than as a progression from hope to despair. The well-established notion that a work must have a clear beginning, middle, and end, according to Aristotle's definition, may not be appropriate to the structure of this poem. A coherent reading of the poem can be gained by supposing that E.A. Robinson was writing from a deep sense of the tradition of a poetic structure which juxtaposes two dissimilar ideas forcing a new understanding of relationship. This structure has an impressive ancestry including Ovid and Chaucer whose uses of the envoi, palinode, or retraction force the reader to review what came before from a far different point of view. Rather than developing faith and reason separately, Robinson interweaves various aspects of the two points of view throughout the poem. (JNS)

11616. Tuerk, Richard. "Robinson's 'Lost Anchors'." *Expl* 32:Item 37.

E.A. Robinson's language in "Lost Anchors" demands that the poem be set in a biblical context. Various parts echo Habakkuk ii.2, Job iii.3 and iii.11, and Hebrews vi.19. The last of these passages may provide the most important clue for unraveling some of the mysteries of the poem, for it implies that to lose one's anchor is to lose one's hope, thus to be set adrift in "The world of ships" in which man lives. In realizing his own lack of hope and in voicing his predicament, the old sailor makes his situation all the more disturbing. (RCT)

Roethke. 11620. Brown, Dennis E. "Theodore Roethke's 'Self-World' and the Modernist Position." *JML* 3:1239-54.
Roethke attempts a sympathetic personal quest for a new synthesis. The *Open House* poems assert an initially impermeable self cut off from external relations. The greenhouse poems proceed to symbolize the interpenetration (both "nauseous" and empathetic) of self and nature, while the more experimental poems in *The Lost Son* dissolve the normal divisions between subject and object into finally existential states. The new poems in *Words for the Wind* chart relationships between self and others through both overt argument and the dialectic set up between dramatized styles. Finally *The Far Field* marks a culmination of Roethke's expansion of the self-world through mystical transcendence. (DEB)

11623. Heringman, Bernard. "Roethke's Poetry:The Forms of Meaning." *TSLL* 16:567-83.
Objectively similar forms in Roethke's verse produce strikingly different emotional effects. Tracing the differences illuminates the interaction of a meter or a rhythmic device with other elements of form and, of course, with content. A pair of poems with such a contrast helps show how the poet achieves rhythm integral with feeling, and more complex integrations. Among his poems in traditional verse, the same meter, even the same stanza, can convey opposed feelings; similarly among free verse poems with the same rhythmic pattern, such as Roethke's diminishing close, or his cut-off effect. Roethke showed a great variety of expressive power, especially in his handling of iambic trimeter and pentameter and in his free verse. (BH)

11625. Libby, Anthony. "Roethke, Water Father." *AL* 46:[267]-88.
Roethke's mysticism convinces most when it remains nontranscendent, as in "North American Sequence." Then it is a mysticism of physical union with the world through immersion in water or liquid landscapes, and a mysticism of darkness and conflict as well as light. The imagery of immersion and elemental conflict dominates Bly, Dickey, and Plath. The consistent patterns of imagery shared by these poets may result from similar deep visions. Though he does not often go as far as the younger poets in exploring the mystical vision they all share Roethke anticipates the deep dreams of our deepest poets. (APL)

11626. Vanderwerken, David L. "Roethke's 'Four for Sir John Davies' and 'The Dying Man.'" *RS* 41(1973):125-35.
"Four for Sir John Davies" and "The Dying Man" can be regarded as companion poems, since both explore the possibilities and limitations of imaginative constructs as means of attaining transcendence. Although Roethke's speaker in the "Davies" sequence finds no validation in the natural world for correspondences between man and the universe, he argues that the imagination can create sustaining illusions of such correspondences—illusions that must be accepted on faith. However, in "The Dying Man," Roethke tests the resolution reached in "Davies" and finds it unsatisfactory. Taking Yeats, the creator of a belief system, as a model of the "Davies" position, Roethke concludes that the imagination's artifices are merely beautiful shams. Yet, given that the universe is naturalistic and that human endeavor is "The fury of the slug beneath the stone, Roethke asserts that a posture of defiance toward the human condition is not only viable, but, indeed, heroic. Despite the imagination's inability to transcend the void, man's greatness lies in his willful defiance of the "dark behind the sun." (DLV)

Roth, H. 11628. Lyons, Bonnie. "After *Call It Sleep*." *AL* 45:610-12.
The question of what happened after Roth's *Call It Sleep* (1934) has not been answered adequately. In fact, the existence of "If We Had Bacon" in *Signatures: Work in Progress*, 1, No. 2 (1936), a twenty page opening section of Roth's never-completed second novel, is virtually unknown. The fragment reveals Roth's ear for dialect and contains some of the stylistic brilliance of *Call It Sleep*. As Roth's focus on childhood in *Call It Sleep* enabled him to avoid analyzing current social realities and his own adult life, so financial and emotional dependence on Eda Lou Walton (an

NYU professor and poet ten years his senior) kept him from developing fully. Maxwell Perkins was impressed with the first part of Roth's second novel, submitted in 1935, but Roth soon found that he didn't want to write any more. Because of his financial dependence on Walton, no economic necessity compelled him to complete it. (BKL)

11631. —— "Roth's *Call It Sleep*." *Expl* 33:Item 10.
When the word *zwank*, which is the Yiddish for "tongs," appears in David Schearl's stream of consciousness during his near-electrocution at the end of *Call It Sleep*, it brings together several themes. In "The Cellar" David's mother answers his question about the existence of an afterlife by picking up a sugar cube with tongs and saying that her mind can stretch no wider than the tongs. The tongs here represent the mind's inability to grasp the mystery of life and death. Conversely, in "The Coal" the Rabbi tells David how Isaiah was purified by God's coal when an angel picked up a fiery coal with tongs and touched Isaiah's lip with it. In the biblical story the *zwank* is the means of reaching understanding or redemption. Finally, when the *zwank* apppears in "The Rail," these thematic threads are united and transcended. The tongs of David's mind stretch wider; David is purified by God's coal; the two *zwank* motifs coalesce. (BKL)

11632. Redding, Mary Edrich. "Call It Myth:Henry Roth and *The Golden Bough*." *CentR* 18:180-95.
The artistic complexity and revolutionary political implications of *Call It Sleep* result from the tension created when Roth balances his sacred Hebraic themes with a variety of pagan and folk elements derived from the agricultural myths described in Frazer's *The Golden Bough*. Oedipal attachments, impotency, tyranny, confrontations with reality, death, and rebirth, rejection of the old in favor of the new, and self-sacrifice—major themes in *Call It Sleep*—have their pagan counterparts in the myths of Dionysus, Vulcan, Aphrodite, Adonis, and the Fire-King, and their symbolic representations in folk beliefs are practices related to agricultural rites. Roth assimilates these spiritual, pagan, and revolutionary themes because he makes them part of a child's developing consciousness—a vehicle which affords almost limitless artistic and phenomenological possibilities. (MER)

Roth, P. 11640. Opland, J. "In Defence of Philip Roth." *Theoria* 42:29-42.
Roth's early fiction reveals a psychoanalytic interest in the minds of characters who are forced to act contrary to their self-conceptions, and a sociological interest in Jews threatened by assimilation into a Gentile world. Roth achieves notable success in a satiric mode and shows a penchant for dialogue. His stories "Goodbye, Columbus" and "Eli the Fanatic" exhibit these stylistic strengths, and in both cases present a Jew resisting strong temptations to deny his Jewish roots. *Portnoy's Complaint* represents a logical development in Roth's career: satiric in mode and colloquial in style, it is concerned with the mind of a Jew under pressure. (JO)

11642. Rodgers, Bernard F.,Jr. "*The Great American Novel* and 'The Great American Joke'." *Crit* 16,ii:12-29.
Comparison of the techniques of Roth's *Great American Novel* with those of the Southwestern humorists illuminates the strategies Roth has employed in his other comic fiction and suggests a thematic unity in his work. Roth's early view of art dictated that only after he had attempted to explore these contrasts through tragedy and pathos—and was dissatisfied with the results—could he turn to comic means. When he did decide to portray these incongruities comically, his knowledge of the earlier humorists came to the fore. (BFR,Jr)

Roth, S. 11644. Hamalian, Leo. "Nobody Knows My Names:Samuel Roth and the Underside of Modern Letters." *JML* 3:889-921. [Foll. by Samuel Roth, "Adrift in London:An Extract from *Count Me Among the Missing*," 922-27.]
Samuel Roth touched the careers of many important contemporary writers in one way or another. He published, with or without permission (usually the latter), the work of Eliot, Joyce, Lawrence, and others, and as a result, achieved a kind of notoriety that is unique in the literary world. As an outcome of his pornographic enterprises, he became the central figure of a court

case that led to the famous Roth decision on pornography and obscenity in publishing. He could have been a key figure in the Chambers-Hiss case since he had known Chambers and published his poetry. (LH)

Salinger. 11645. Bryan, James. "The Psychological Structure of *The Catcher in the Rye*." *PMLA* 89:1065-74.
Critics have commented upon Holden Caulfield's "neurosis," but none have accepted Salinger's apparent invitation to a psychoanalytical reading of the novel. As a step in that direction, Bryan examines a structural pattern of aggression and withdrawal, largely sexual, in Holden's behavior. The pattern is reinforced by characters such as Stradlater and Ackley, the episodic middle chapters, and the concluding Phoebe section. (JEB)
11646. Bufithis, Philip H. "J.D. Salinger and the Psychiatrist." *WVUPP* 21:67-77.
We can understand the essential nature of Salinger's young heroes by delineating the tension that exists between them and the psychiatrist character. Salinger's psychiatrist emphasizes man's sociobiotic attributes. Salinger's young heroes are chiefly interested in man's individual-spiritual nature. Indeed, the Glass heroes oppose adaptability with renunciation. But renunciation, they realize, is not enough; there must be something positive that one can offer the world. Buddy Glass, finds his identity and his mission in being an artist. And, as Holden Caulfied had done only unconsciously, he invokes art as a strategy against neurosis. Art is the transference of neurosis from self (subjectivity) into artifact (objectivity). Salinger suggests that it is not the psychiatrist but the artist who, by his life and work, can best tell us who and what we are. (PHB)

Santayana. 11654. Shaughnessy, Edward L. "Oliver Alden and Studs Lonigan:Heirs to Spiritual Poverty." *MarkhamR* 4:48-52.
The boy story in American literature often focuses on the moral insufficiency of youth to cope with its world. Repeatedly such fiction describes the conditions of spiritual impoverishment which circumscribe the boy's milieu. George Santayana and James T. Farrell treat precisely these conditions. Together, the vastly different but equally destructive moral environments represented in *The Last Puritan* and *Studs Lonigan: A Trilogy* can serve to suggest a pervasive cultural malaise. In his examination of the "genteel tradition" which Oliver Alden inherits, Santayana describes an ambience that effectively kills the hero's natural spontaneity. His Brahmin legacy is his spiritual death sentence. Farrell shows how "an ordinary American boy" withers under the conditions of moral inadequacy that blight his Southside Chicago neighborhood. Thus, because both protagonists are drained of the soul's potential before they can develop, their premature physical deaths are anti-climactic. That the philosopher Santayana and the naturalist Farrell should discover the same fate in their heroes constitutes a two-pronged commentary on American culture as spiritually lethal. (FLS)

Sarton. 11655. Taylor, Henry. "Home to a Place Beyond Exile:The Collected Poems of May Sarton." *HC* 11,iii:1-16. [Rev. art.]
May Sarton's generously inclusive *Collected Poems* (1974) reveals her view of poetry as a continuous process in which less successful poems contribute to a development which must be seen whole. This view of poetry is consistent with a skillfully-handled didactic tendency in Sarton's work. From *Encounter in April* (1936) through *A Durable Fire* (1972) the themes of feminism, love, modern technological brutality, and the search for roots are explored with increasing skill and profundity, to the extent that psychic risk becomes one of Sarton's most productive creative processes. (HT)

Schuyler. 11658. Peplow, Michael W. "George Schuyler, Satirist:Rhetorical Devices in *Black No More*." *CLAJ* 18:242-57.
Schuyler's *Black No More* is the first book-length satire by a black American. Critics apparently did not understand the nature and function of the satire nor what Schuyler was attempting. His favorite rhetorical devices included *reductio ad absurdum*, caricature, parody, and the picaresque narrative. His true genius is reflected in the manner in which he sustained his ironic tone, moving from the gentle chiding of a Horace to the savagery of a Juvenal. (MWP)

Selby. 11664. Wertime, Richard A. "Psychic Vengeance in *Last Exit to Brooklyn*." *L&P* 24:153-66.
The powerful impact of the violence in *Last Exit to Brooklyn* results from Hubert Selby's ambivalent—and ambivalence-inducing—manner of visiting justice upon his protagonists. We are made to feel as the novel moves forward that the harsh punitive actions are just. Our ambivalence results from Selby's handling of a group called the "psychic avengers," which consists of juvenile thugs who loiter at a restaurant called the Greeks. Their function as psychic avengers is brought out with climactic clarity in the brutal ending of "Strike," a story whose action reveals itself as being endopsychic. (RAW)

Sexton. 11667. Axelrod, Rise B. "The Transforming Art of Anne Sexton." *CP* 7,i:6-13.
Sexton's confessional poetic consists of a centripetal or inturning therapeutic mode and a centrifugal or visionary mode. Her early poetry of extremity reflects the disintegration of an elaborate system of personal and social abstractions. Realizing the essential emptiness of her self and her world, the poet searches within the self for the roots of a more genuine existence. In more recent volumes Sexton explores the myth of the estranged body (*Love Poems* 1969), the mythology of sexual maturity (*Transformations* 1971), and the myth of the alien other (*The Book of Folly* 1973). (RBA)

Sinclair, U. 11672. Muraire, A. "Searching for a Theatre in France:Upton Sinclair vs. Albert Camus, André Malraux, and Jean Vilar." *BSUF* 15,ii:77-79.
Sinclair wanted to become a playwright. In 1959 he couldn't find a publisher in the States for his latest play, *Cicero*. He tried to have it staged and published abroad, and wrote to Camus who, according to press reports, had been promised a theater by the French authorities. Camus found the play appealing but couldn't stage it, as it eventually turned out that he had no theater of his own. Sinclair then wrote to Malraux, "Ministre d'Etat chargé des Affaires culturelles," who put him in touch with Jean Vilar, who was then at the head of the "Théâtre National Populaire." Vilar kindly and respectfully declined Sinclair's offer on account of the lack of dramatic intensity in the play. Sinclair gave up. *Cicero* was to be his last attempt at playwriting. (AM)

Snyder. 11680. Hunt, Anthony. "Snyder's 'After Work'." *Expl* 32:Item 61.
Although found in the "Far West" section of his *The Back Country*, Gary Snyder's short poem "After Work" is essentially Oriental in impact. The first two lines suggest the techniques of a Chinese landscape painter. Moreover, sensuous and sensual sets of relational opposites—cold hands and warm breasts, nature's trees and civilization's axes, the masculine world and the feminine world—represent the yin-yang interdependence existing in a state of dynamic balance. The entire poem exemplifies this dynamic balance as he yokes specific aspects of Oriental culture with a situation dramatically set in America's Western mountains and forests. (AH)

Stegner. 11699. Jenson, Sid. "The Compassionate Seer: Wallace Stegner's Literary Artist." *BYUS* 14:248-62.
Wallace Stegner has been described as a non-religious humanist, yet his theory of literary art is based on a belief in literature which is like religious faith. He believes that esthetic experience is private, subjective, and mystical. It is never quite communicable and is not subject to empirical verfication. Art is knowledge of things as an experience. The proof of art is in the esthetic experience, and ultimately, we cannot explain the reader's experience any more than we can explain the creative experience. Stegner's literary artist is a special man; he is essentially a common man, who has uncommonly developed humility,

patience, and impartiality. He forgives easily and rebukes softly. For Stegner the primary aim of literary art is to celebrate the human spirit, and literature has become for many the source of values and wisdom. The writer and the reader are searching in obscure depths; they are dealers in mystery. When the writer reveals the truth, he is a seer; and these revelations (quoting Joseph Conrad) "bind men to each other,... bind the living to the unborn." (SJ)

Stein. 11702. Cooper, David D. "Gertrude Stein's 'Magnificent Asparagus':Horizontal Vision and Unmeaning in 'Tender Buttons'." *MFS* 20:337-49.
Three modes of written communication are revealed in examples provided by Henry James, Whitman, and Gertrude Stein as introduction to the central problem of assigning a workable category for such works as "Tender Buttons" and *Ulysses*. Jung's comments on literature supply a framework for discussing the problem, primarily one concerned with the tension of communication and the *meaning* normally expected to result from that tension. The problem is summarily solved by developing a residual category, that of horizontal visionary poetry, where ultimate meaning is subordinated to sense reaction as a way of understanding the type of poetry which defies (or ignores) the whole idea of *meaning*. (DDC)
11706. Schmitz, Neil. "Gertrude Stein as Post-Modernist:The Rhetoric of *Tender Buttons*." *JML* 3:1203-18.
In *Tender Buttons* Stein seeks to decreate traditional narrative by attacking its epistemological basis—the belief that discourse represents reality—and in so doing reconstitutes the act of writing as self-effaced play within the finite and yet open field of language. For all the asserted privacy of its meaning, *Tender Buttons* nonetheless invokes a creative response from the reader by urging him through the exuberance of its dislocated syntax to rethink his conventional view of language and discourse. (NS)

Steinbeck. 11732. Satyanarayana, M.R. "The Unknown God of John Steinbeck." *IJAS* 3,i(1973):97-103.
The epigraph for the novel *To A God Unknown* is a hymn from Rigveda. The hymn called "Hiranyagarbha-Prajapati Hymn" raises the question: "To whom shall we offer our sacrifice?" and answers that it is *Prajapati*, the Creator. Steinbeck uses this as a commentary on the pagan-Christian tensions of the story. Joseph, the hero, kills himself in sacrifice to bring rain for the drought-striken Nuestra Senora valley. He is initiated into the mystery of sacrifice by an eccentric *guru* (tutor). The final sacrifice and the numerous forms of worship practiced by the hero are characteristic of Hindu religion. The rock in the sacred grove can be identified with Lord Shiva of the Hindu Trinity. Compared to this ancient religion, Christianity is disadvantageously presented. The hero's wife Elizabeth is ambivalent in her views. His brother Burton is a narrow-minded Puritan who hates Joseph's paganism and considers the only good Christian, Father Angelo, idolatrous. The hero's sister-in-law, Rama, is a symbol of the Great Mother. Like him she does not profess any orthodox religion, let alone Christianity. (MRS)
11736. Spilka, Mark. "Of George and Lennie and Curley's Wife:Sweet Violence in Steinbeck's Eden." *MFS* 20:169-79.
Steinbeck's Miltonic view of women as exploiters of men's lust, and his alertness to the exploitability of such feelings in youthful heroes, has much to do with the force of his early social fiction. His effort to create blameless versions of murderous rage seems founded also in that adolescent dilemma. In *Of Mice and Men* the low threshold of rage in the idiot Lennie "Small" is indirectly exploited by his lordly friend George "Milton" so as to punish the aggressive sexuality of the boss's son Curley and his straying wife. In *Grapes of Wrath*, which begins with the return of the blameless murderer who must learn to control his easy rages for the rest of the novel and which ends with his commission of another blameless murder, Steinbeck finds a social situation more commensurate with his own inchoate anger. In *East of Eden* he finally relates such rages to parental coldness and accepts sexuality as the vulnerable human condition by which they are exploited. (MS)
11738a. Sweet, Charles A.,Jr. "Ms. Eliza Allen and Steinbeck's

'The Chrysanthemums'." *MFS* 20:120-14.
Previous criticism has failed to understand Steinbeck's story and more precisely Elisa Allen's motivation because it has not dealt with the structure of the story. Steinbeck juxtaposes the business deals of both Allens. Initially, Henry completes a transaction in which he receives nearly his own price. Elisa fails in her dealings with the itinerant fixer. Although she tries to bargain with the man on an equal basis and in a masculine manner, the fixer, realizing her liberated pride and the sexuality inherent in the would-be feminist, takes advantage of her. Discarding both the chrysanthemums and the aroused woman, he persuades her to pay for a job she admittedly could have done. Unable to function as an equal in this transaction, Elisa tries to regain her lost dignity through her husband in one of woman's traditional roles, the seductress. When Henry treats her to a token night out, she realizes her dreams of equality and dominance are impossible, and that she is only "an old woman." (CAS,Jr)

Stevens, W. 11741. Atchity, Kenneth J. "Wallace Stevens:'Of Ideal Time and Choice'." *RS* 41(1973):141-53.
"Of Ideal Time and Choice" (from "Three Academic Pieces") is, syntactically and etymologically, one of Wallace Stevens' most perplexing and challenging poems, indicating the arduous demands he makes upon his ideal reader. The poem consists of only two sentences, the first comprising the first eleven stanzas and concluding with a series of emphatic questions based on the opening series of paradoxical suppositions. The final stanza answers the questions in a statement about the existential identity of "the poet" that comprehends the very heart of Stevens' poetics—relating this poem to others like "Sunday Morning," "The Man with the Blue Guitar," "Notes Toward the Supreme Fiction," and "Anecdote of the Jar," in which Stevens consistently defines the necessary interdependence of imagination and reality. (KJA)
11746. Carrier, Warren. "Commonplace Costumes and Essential Gaudiness:Wallace Stevens' 'The Emperor of Ice-Cream'." *CollL* 1:230-35.
Williams' poem, "Tract," a set of anti-poetic instructions for a funeral, may have suggested a technique to Stevens. Shakespeare's *The Phoenix and the Turtle* may be a philosophical prompting. A comparison of the two sets of staging orders for a funeral shows similar structures, opposite tones and themes. Shakespeare's assertion that since the royal embodiments of Truth, Beauty, etc., are dead, their abstract existence has ceased, is contrasted to Stevens' contention that though his destitute female is dead, the Emperor of Ice-Cream ("an absolute good") lives on. (WC)
11749. Flake, Carol. "Wallace Stevens' 'Peter Quince at the Clavier':Sources and Structure." *ELN* 12:116-20.
"Peter Quince at the Clavier" may be better understood with reference to sources with which Stevens had elsewhere shown familiarity. A paradigm used by Schopenhauer in his essay "Our Relation to Ourselves" concerns the analogy of a "man of intellect" with a pianist. Stevens' musician is placed in a setting characteristic of Renaissance paintings and the scenario is emblematic with reference to both artistic and philosophic sources. Quince is like the musician described by Plotinus who is transformed by the beauty of his own creation into the lover and thence into the philosopher. Quince's "philosophy" is based on a theory of correspondences which has affinities with both French Symbolist and Renaissance theory. (CAF)
11751. Furia, Philip. "Nuances of a Theme by Milton: Wallace Stevens's 'Sunday Morning'." *AL* 46:[83]-87.
Certain lines in "Sunday Morning" recall Michael's description of the earthly paradise in Book XII of *Paradise Lost*. Stevens, however, makes a very un-Miltonic point. For Milton, the "earth shall all *be* paradise" when Christ returns to transfigure it into heaven. For Stevens, the earth shall "*seem* all of paradise" when man abandons his fictions of heaven and embraces this world—where death and change render experience beautiful and valuable—as preferable to any permanent and deathless paradise. By thus adapting Milton's language to his own different vision, Stevens displays his characteristic mode of allusion, or, to use his term, "nuance." The attitudes toward Milton implied in "Sunday

Morning" are similar to those expressed in Stevens' letters and criticism. (PGF)

11758. McDaniel, Judith. "Wallace Stevens and the Scientific Imagination." *ConL* 15:221-37.
Wallace Stevens' *The Rock* reflects his interest in the ideas of modern science and the ways in which they have affected most branches of modern thought. The specific scientific concepts used by Stevens are Einstein's theory of relativity, Gibb's work on probability and Planck's on causality. These theories radically altered the view of the physical universe as held in the 19th century by scientists who believed in the objective existence of a material world in which cause and effect, sequence, and prediction were possible. Stevens' first poem in *The Rock* negates this view by proposing one world of a personal subjective reality and another of an objective mathematical certainty which can only be represented in the last word of the poem, the single letter R. In several of these poems Stevens speculates on the question that concerned Planck late in his life: is there a central mind which created the order we observe? Other poems recognize that in modern life, as in modern science, there are no longer "impossible concepts," only probabilities. (JAM)

11759. McIlvaine, Robert. "Stevens' 'Frogs Eat Butterflies. Snakes Eat Frogs. Hogs Eat Snakes. Men Eat Hogs'." *Expl* 33:Item 14.
Wallace Stevens' "Frogs Eat Butterflies. Snakes Eat Frogs. Hogs Eat Snakes. Men Eat Hogs" is about an "indolent" man whose life has been reduced to the level of eating in order to go on living and eating. Stevens' clever title is the most commented on feature of the poem. This title was borrowed, in slightly modified form, from Ambrose Bierce's *The Devil's Dictionary*. In that book Bierce defines the word "Edible" as "Good to Eat, and wholesome to digest, as a worm to a toad, a toad to a snake, a snake to a pig, a pig to a man, and a man to a worm." Stevens' modification of Bierce's witticism is even more cynical than the original statement. While Bierce sees life as cyclic, with man himself at last as a victim, Stevens' arrangement is hierarchical with man at the top (or bottom) of the ranking. Stevens' implication is that a man who has no subjective or poetic sensibility is nothing more than a hog of hogs. (RMM)

11764. Mollinger, Robert N. "Stevens' 'A Thought Revolved'." *Expl* 33:Item 1.
From 1937 to 1942 Wallace Stevens was concerned with the real character of man and with the possibility of a belief in an ideal man, the hero, to replace a belief in god. The "thought revolved" in "A Thought Revolved" (1937) is his idea of man. The four subtitles of the poem show the progression of the poet's thoughts on this idea. "The Mechanical Optimist" refers to a woman who, though neither believing in a god nor an ideal hero, nonetheless sentimentally believes death to be a journey to a better land. Without any thoughtful basis, she mechanically and optimistically believes in a cheerful end. In "Mystic Garden & Middling Beast," the middling beast refers to the poet's view of man as a commonplace person. In contrast, however, the mystic garden is the mental space in which the poet possibly can conceive a new religious symbol—the hero. "Romanesque Affabulation" implies the falsity of this religious symbol which is presented in the poem's third section. Though pleasing (affable), the ideal hero is seen as artificial, medieval, and fictive. The fourth subtitle, "The Leader," is ironic. Man is flawed rather than ideal, and the hero is rejected. (RNM)

11767. Sastri, P.S. "Stevens, the Romantics, and Santayana." *IJAS* 3,i(1973):39-46.
Stevens was influenced by the British romantic poets and by the philosopher Santayana. The philosopher spoke of essence as against existence, while Keats sought fellowship with essence. The twin principles of skepticism and animal faith that Santayana emphasizes prevented Stevens' romanticism from becoming solipsistic. From this standpoint "Notes Towards a Supreme Fiction" is examined in detail. (PSS)

11771. Turco, Lewis. "Wallace Stevens:The Agonism and the Existentity." *CP* 6,i(1973):32-44.
An agonist is a theoretician of poetry—neither amateur or professional. He may write his theories of poetry in prose or in verse. If he writes essays primarily, we call him a critic. However,

many poets, such as Wallace Stevens, write their theories in verse, and we may call such writers "agonists." Wallace Stevens' "An Ordinary Evening in New Haven" which may be seen as a late example of Stevens' agonism regarding the nature of poetry is analyzed. Poetry was a substitute for religion for Stevens. It was an existential shield behind which an esthetic "mind of winter" might be developed in order to cloak the poet to protect him from psychic harm in a world hostile to concepts of God. (LT)

11772. Walker, Kenneth. "Stevens' 'The Idea of Order at Key West'." *Expl* 32:Item 59.
In Stevens' "The Idea of Order at Key West," the speaker meditates on how the imagination as metaphysics perceives order and meaning in the sounds of the waves and how the imagination as art makes from these sounds the ordered world of poetry. He explores these relationships and probes the nature of reality by personifying imagination as a woman singing and by questioning how her song relates to the sounds of the sea. The speaker interprets the intelligible sounds created in the imagination as a response to the sounds of the sea. He affirms that the song has a coherence beyond natural sounds and that it is not exclusively a product of the mind divorced from external influence. The speaker's subsequent perception of order in the lights dotting the harbor is caused by the mind's need for order and the imagination's power to create it from the disparates of experience. (KEW)

11773. ——— "Wallace Stevens as Disaffected Flagellant." *MarkhamR* 4:26-29.
The prominence of religious themes in Wallace Stevens' early poetry reflects his efforts to free himself from a belief in Christianity, which he could neither accept nor relinquish. The stages of his development are evident in his shift from an ironic treatment of Christian concepts to expressions of his emerging view that traditional beliefs in God are inadequate and his growing conviction that the age of Christian belief is past. He begins to treat Christianity as an illusion that, while it may provide security for some people, no longer has sustaining power for him. Freeing himself from his need for traditional religion, he evolves the idea of illusion as value and is able to commend Christianity if it is recognized as a fiction, a creation of imagination that brings order and meaning to reality. By exploring in poetry the validity of traditional Christianity, he attempts to fix the bearing of men in reality and establishes poetry as a sanction of life. (KEW)

11775. Woodman, Leonora. "'A Giant on the Horizon': Wallace Stevens and the 'Idea of Man'." *TSLL* 15:759-86.
Stevens' phrase "pure poetry" anticipates the development of a qualitatively changed man, sometimes called the "ultimate poem." Stevens' hope is based on the psychological assumption that consciousness obscures a vigorous, pre-rational psychic stratum destined to reassert its hegemony. His faith in the "sub-conscious" is revealed in "Owl's Clover," a poem which establishes his hierarchical view of the imagination. The fundamental "essential imagination," dressed in the mythological garb of an Ananke-subman identified as "pure poetry," represents the pre-rational archetypal imagination. Consciousness severed these ties, producing the secondary imagination through which man expresses his loss in art and myth. In fact, however, art and myth are inspired by the "essential imagination," or Ananke, agitating for a return to first origins. Thus, the idea of God is in reality the idea of man. Once man recognizes that he alone is the source and object of faith, he will dispense with the objects of the secondary imagination. (LW)

Styron. 11786. Eggenschwiler, David. "Tragedy and Melodrama in *The Confessions of Nat Turner*." *TCL* 20:19-33.
William Styron's Nat Turner is haunted by a post-Romantic tragic vision of life as irrational, contradictory, and terrifying. To overcome his fear, he creates simplified melodramas out of the stereotypes his culture provides. Nat's first, pastoral images of benevolent, morally pure white masters vs. filthy, animalistic black slaves are broken by repeated instances of the masters' animality and weakness. So, Nat inverts the pattern into a conflict between black messiah and depraved master. When this melodrama collapses, Nat is able to accept a religious faith that

transcends both his tragic vision and his melodramatic defenses. (DLE)

Swados. 11790. Marx, Paul. "Harvey Swados." *OntarioR* 1,i:62-66.
Harvey Swados' experiences with work and with the working man significantly inform most of his fiction, especially his most important short story "Joe the Vanishing American" and his last novel *Standing Fast*. While Swados has much compassion for the suffering and the aspirations of working-class families, he finds their politics abhorrent. Swados, like Solzhenitsyn, believes the writer is obliged to denounce evil, especially when it is clearly embodied in a leader. (PM)

Tarkington. 11793. Sorkin, Adam J. " 'She Doesn't Last, Apparently':A Reconsideration of Booth Tarkington's *Alice Adams*." *AL* 46:[182]-99.
Tarkington's *Alice Adams* (1921) is a significant and still entertaining minor work worth examining for illumination of its era and for illustration of the state of its formal literary tradition—the Howellsian social novel and ironic comedy of manners—in a period now known primarily for formal innovation. Despite personal limitation and a literary conservatism, Tarkington finds support in the inherent strength of his old-fashioned realistic method, and he renders his contemporary America with vividness as well as fidelity to social and historical realities. (AJS)

Tate. 11793a. Dupree, Robert S. "The Mirrors of Analogy: Three Poems of Allen Tate." *SoR* 8(1972):774-91.
Allen Tate's poetry presents the contrast between modern man, who sees the world as an inert structure of mathematically manipulable substances, and his ancestors, who knew a world of intricate relationships and analogies which linked past and present in an organic whole. In "The Last Days of Alice," he shows how the loss of analogy dehumanizes while it secularizes us. In "The Cross," he presents the inadequacy of a merely secular salvation which leads nowhere beyond the present. "The Mediterranean" continues these themes, but provides them with a historical dimension. In this poem he is concerned with the sense of place and continuity as an antidote to the modern lust for the mathematically infinite universe of pure space and time. This understanding comes to us through poetry, which provides a properly analogical mirror for the rhythms of life. It also emerges in the rich allusiveness of Tate's poems, where past and present are kept constantly relevant by the analogy with other poetic insights and other universes. (RSD)

Thurber. 11801. Hasley, Louis. "James Thurber:Artist in Humor." *SAQ* 73:[504]-15.
James Thurber's principal concerns were personal, domestic. He dealt with the civilized stupidities, cruelties, and perversities of men and women in short stories, sketches, fables, fairy tales, satires and in a play he co-authored. His principal reputation is based on personal experience essays, often illustrated by his sophisticatedly primitive line drawings. His most notable story, "The Secret Life of Walter Mitty," epitomizes two character types recurring frequently in his work —the shy, henpecked "little man" and the confidently dominating female. His fables, often satirically didactic, are the best and funniest of this century. His style is a model of contemporary American—supple, witty, unmannered, sensitive to nuances, marked by humor that ranges from the quietly subtle to the explosive. (LH)

11803. Lindner, Carl M. "Thurber's Walter Mitty—The Underground American Hero." *GaR* 28:283-89.
In "The Secret Life of Walter Mitty" James Thurber deals with a major American theme—the conflict between the individual and society. In Mitty's attempts to deal with social pressures and restrictions (represented by his wife), he follows in the path of Rip Van Winkle and Tom Sawyer. The qualities that Mitty dreamwishes for himself are those of the American frontier hero. The picture of Mitty is therefore simultaneously sad and amusing, for he is a man who is discontented, alienated, and doomed to a life of frustration. The American heroic tradition is as out of place in

contemporary society as Mitty's visions of himself in action are unrealistic. His only recourse, therefore, given his inability to cope with a complex world, is to turn increasingly inward. (CML)

Toomer. 11805. Blackwell, Louise. "Jean Toomer's *Cane* and Biblical Myth." *CLAJ* 17:535-42.
When Jean Toomer published *Cane* in 1922, he made a significant statement on the theme "Black is Beautiful." This work is an experimental novel in the vein of James Joyce's *Ulysses*, published the same year. Unity in *Cane* is achieved through imagery, characterization, and setting. Whereas Joyce relied heavily upon Homeric myth to imply analogies and correspondences, Toomer drew upon biblical myth to create the majestic and compelling metaphor which identifies the black people in America. Toomer strived to give identity to his race, and by his use of biblical myth, he lifted *Cane* to the realm of prophecy. (LB)

11806. Blake, Susan L. "The Spectatorial Artist and the Structure of *Cane*." *CLAJ* 17:516-34.
Jean Toomer's *Cane* is a sketchbook recording the quest of a creative persona to give form to the chaos of experience, which he gradually realizes resides within himself. The term "spectatorial artist," coined by Gorham B. Munson, suggests the development of the persona's relationship to his material, which progresses from spectatorial detachment in Part 1, to personal involvement in Part 2, to artistic detachment in "Kabnis." As the artist realizes that the conflict in each story parallels his own problem of shaping life into art, the characterization becomes more complex. Finally, in the creation and destruction of Kabnis, the spectatorial artist simultaneously relinquishes the compulsion to order the universe around himself and achieves the artistic creation. The progress of *Cane* dramatizes the paradoxical discovery that both personal unity and artistic creativity depend on submission to the apparent chaos of the universe. (SB)

11810. Fisher, Alice P. "The Influence of Ouspensky's *Tertium Organum* Upon Jean Toomer's *Cane*." *CLAJ* 17:504-15.
Jean Toomer published *Cane* in 1923; it is an interesting book, because it heralded the inception of the Harlem Renaissance, and because the language therein creates a sense of timelessness and universality of experience that borders on the mystical. Toomer consciously experimented with language in an attempt to develop or realize certain ideas within the esoteric philosophy of Peter Demianovich Ouspensky whose *Tertium Organum—A Key to the Enigmas of the World* influenced him. Toomer and his literary friends—Hart Crane, Waldo Frank, Gorham Munson, and Kenneth Burke—read and studied Ouspensky and his ideas in the early 1920s and were particularly inspired by Ouspensky's concept that only the poet can communicate both the mystical, emotional feelings of an experience and the concepts inherent in that experience. Toomer experimented with a language of the future elevating the racial consciousness of the book to a level of cosmic consciousness. Ouspensky also influenced Toomer with his concept of animated nature where Toomer's use of language reflects as well Ouspensky's influence in the areas of time, animation of material objects, cosmic consciousness, and cause and effect. (APF)

11812. Kopf, George. "The Tensions in Jean Toomer's 'Theater'." *CLAJ* 17:498-503.
In "Theater," a short story included in *Cane*, Jean Toomer expresses the dynamics of the American experience for blacks in a series of tensions and counter-tensions between values which may be classed as urban vs. rural, white vs. black, sympathetic and natural vs. inhibited and alienated. The major characters, Dorris and John, do not draw the reader's interest by what they do. Toomer rejects any narrative movement in favor of portrayal of psychological conflict between and within these two people. Stretched between poles of values, the characters are in fact incapable of effective action. He allows their tense, inner voices to speak and as they do so the significance of what these people say and want transcends the personal and expresses what Toomer felt the plight of the black consciousness to be as it moved northward during the great migrations early in this century. The final tension of "Theater" poses the characters between passivity and activity, liberation and bondage. (GK)

11813. Kramer, Victor A. "The 'Mid-Kingdom' of Crane's

'Black Tambourine' and Toomer's *Cane*." *CLAJ* 17:486-97.
The shared characteristics of Hart Crane's "Black Tambourine" and Jean Toomer's *Cane* suggest that it is possible that Toomer based parts of *Cane*, especially the final climactic section "Kabnis," on his knowledge of Crane's poem; yet even if this is not the case these two works illustrate each other. The idea of the modern black man bridging a gap between the culture of the past and the present is basic to both works. A similar setting and images related to "Black Tambourine" are found in "Kabnis." In both works the strength of black culture, which is apparently immobile, is emphasized. (AVK)

11814. Matthews, George C. "Toomer's *Cane*:The Artist and His World." *CLAJ* 17:543-59.
Jean Toomer's letter of 12 December, 1922 to Waldo Frank in which he explains that *Cane* (1923) could be viewed esthetically, regionally, and spiritually provides a basis for a closer examination of forms and themes in the work. Esthetically, Toomer employs stripped, clean lines in his sketches of the women in "Portait in Georgia" whose apparent economy of expression belies their technical complexities and richness. Regionally, Toomer's sketches of women, his vignettes of thwarted lovers, and his portrait of Kabnis focus attention on themes and attitudes concerning the North and the South in which misfortune, deprivation, and even death result when societal customs are violated. Spiritually, *Cane* points in the direction of an awakening or inner awareness on the part of such characters as Karintha, Dan, and Kabnis among others, while at the same time it shows the impossibility of their realizing it completely. It is to Toomer's unending credit, however, that his ability to transcend stereotypical images of black characters enabled him to depict life in a most sensitive and artistic manner in *Cane*. (GCM)

11815. McCarthy, Daniel P. " 'Just Americans':A Note on Jean Toomer's Marriage to Margery Latimer." *CLAJ* 17:474-79.
Jean Toomer's marriage to white novelist Margery Latimer in 1931 resulted in a national scandal that damaged Toomer's literary career. In the late 1920s, Toomer became a disciple of the philosopher Gurdjieff, and began to disseminate Gurdjieff's beliefs to friends and students. He met Latimer at one of these sessions, and the two were married. *Time* magazine learned of the marriage and publicized it in a defamatory article. Toomer's attempts to explain his position failed because his Gurdjieffian world-view did not allow him to see anything "wrong" with miscegenation. His comments about the potential for a "raceless" America were misunderstood and ridiculed. The scandal ended when Latimer died in childbirth in 1932, an incident which was described in a personal letter written by Mark Schorer. However, the scandal branded Toomer a radical and made it even more difficult for him to publish his works. (DPM)

11818. Riley, Roberta. "Search for Identity and Artistry." *CLAJ* 17:480-85. [On *Cane*.]
Toomer's *Cane* offers a subtle weaving of poems, short stories, and plays relating his impressions of the black experience in America. Toomer presents the endurance and vitality of the rural black in sharp contrast with the emptiness and loss of feeling characterizing the urban situation. He explores the feelings of affirmation, avoidance, denial, resignation, and strength in the black people who touch or fail to make contact with their racial past. (RDR)

11819. Turner, Darwin T. "An Intersection of Paths:Correspondence Between Jean Toomer and Sherwood Anderson." *CLAJ* 17:455-67.
Correspondence between Jean Toomer and Sherwood Anderson from 1922 to 1924 provides important insights into them and ironic background for their subsequent literary directions. After Anderson initiated the correspondence by praising Toomer's unpublished sketches at *Double Dealer*, Toomer wrote that he was flowering from seeds planted during his stay in Georgia and that Anderson's literary works had assisted his growth. When Anderson, characterizing Toomer's as the first "really Negro" writing he had seen, confessed his desire to write "out of" Negroes, Toomer commended Anderson's ability to evoke Negro beauty and emotion. Anderson failed to foresee the ironic divergence of their paths after 1924. In *Dark Laughter* (1925) Anderson created the black primitives he had proposed to

Toomer. In contrast, Toomer, already evading identification as Negro, never again created black characters. Instead, he expended his talents teaching and writing about the dilemmas of inhibited whites. (DTT)

Underwood. 11826. Jason, Philip K. "Wilbur Underwood: Hart Crane's Confidant." *MarkhamR* 4:66-68.
The career of Wilbur Underwood (1876-1935), a Washington, D.C., poet whose friendship with Hart Crane is noted by Crane's biographers, illustrates Crane's view of the poet's dilemma in America. During the 1890s, his poems appeared in significant periodicals and then in Stedman's *An American Anthology, 1787-1900* (1900). Achieving some critical acclaim but no popular following, Underwood labored in minor government posts. Underwood's *A Book of Masks* (1907) and *Damien of Molokai* (1909) were long out of print when young Hart Crane met him in 1920. Underwood directed Crane's reading and became a life-long confidant to Crane's personal crises. To Crane, Underwood's unrecognized talents and his dependence on sterile employments symbolized America's indifference to artistic values. During 1927-33 Underwood published three additional volumes. A number of his devotional poems, marked by careful craftsmanship and genuine emotion, continue to live in anthologies of religious verse. One piece, "I Do It Unto Thee," has entered our popular culture. Either attributed to others or printed anonymously, this poem, also known as "The Kitchen Prayer," appears on countless souvenirs and decorative items. Disdained by Underwood, it was not collected until the posthumous *Selected Poems* (1949). (PKJ)

Updike. 11827. Backscheider, Paula and Nick. "Two on *Couples*. [1.] Updike's *Couples*:Squeak in the Night." *MFS* 20:45-52.
Sex in John Updike's *Couples* can be understood as a complex metaphor for man's relation to and examination of religious faith. The movement in the novel is Piet Hanema's search for the "vote for happiness" in the world. He moves past the false gods (all related to sex in this novel) of the institutional church, Freddy's brand of humanism, Georgene's "post pill paradise," Angela's abstractness, and Foxy's communion to construct his own faith, "beautiful to him, a transparent hangar shaped by laws discovered within itself, minimal, invented, Piet's own." (PRB & NAB)

11830. Falke, Wayne. "*Rabbit Redux*:Time/Order/God." *MFS* 20:59-75.
Updike's *Rabbit Redux* sociologically explores the meaning of personal time for Harry Angstrom and of historical time for the United States. Both Angstrom and the nation have fallen from the innocence of an Edenic American dream, and both must understand that illusions of the past are harmful to the present. Both the individual and the nation must accept time (history) as inherent to men's affairs and accept loss and guilt. But such acceptance does not solve the problem of the lack of meaningful order to life. The novel suggests that the first moon walk demonstrates the sterility of technology and national aspiration, that the war in Southeast Asia is a way for white Americans to avoid confronting their hypocrisy and oppression of Indians and blacks. With Rabbit's conception of the disorder of the present and the past, he feels that only the conception of God would fully explain and justify the present, yet institutionalized religion has been as responsible for disorder as any other force. (FW)

11833. Gingher, Robert S. "Has John Updike Anything to Say?" *MFS* 20:97-105.
Updike's delicate, subliminal style has procured for him both admirers and detractors of strong convictions. His demonstrable exercise of stylistic grace tends to camouflage his own concern as a writer with more important issues. Some critics reduce him to a clever artisan who consciously or unconsciously hides his own artistic deficiencies, who dodges the larger issues by employing a bounty of stylistic refinement. What is sometimes mistaken for a mere overworked, pretentious style, a mask for an author who has nothing to say, actually reflects a unique, photographic ability to capture details that usually go unnoticed in fictional technique. Recent studies of Updike's fiction leave no doubt as to the extent

of his concerns—his treatment of sex, death, religion, and the married state. But in addition to his stylistic preciosity, the emotional vapidity and absence of realistic human conflict in his fiction tends to discredit his seriousness and, therefore, stature as a writer. (RSG)

11834. Griffith, Albert J. "Updike's Artist's Dilemma:'Should Wizard Hit Mommy?'" *MFS* 20:111-15.

In his short story "Should Wizard Hit Mommy?" in *Pigeon Feathers* (1962), John Updike uses a complex series of structural parallels between a commonplace, domestic story and a story-within-the-story to create a subtle parable about the artist's conflicts of roles in the modern world. Updike's protagonist, Jack, indulges himself with the pleasure of telling his four-year-old daughter Jo a naptime story, even though he senses the unspoken demand of his wife that he stop and help her with household chores. Resenting the implicit conflict between his creative inclinations and his practical responsibilities, Jack alters the usual formula for the animal fable he tells Jo: instead of having little Roger Skunk's problems solved by a wizard's magic spell, Jack has Roger's mother assault the wizard, reject his spell, and force Roger to live his life without magic escapes. The parallels in Jack's and Roger's situations reveal the dilemma of the would-be artist who is caught in a "cage," the "ugly middle position" between the prosaic realities of domestic life and the romantic fantasies of the creative imagination. (AJG)

11838. McCoy, Robert. "John Updike's Literary Apprenticeship on *The Harvard Lampoon*." *MFS* 20:3-12.

John Updike's undergraduate work on *The Harvard Lampoon* provided an invaluable literary apprenticeship. He accepted a scholarship to Harvard hoping to draw cartoons for the *Lampoon* and to use this experience as an entrée to the pages of *The New Yorker*. Starting as a freshman, Updike served in every major post on the *Lampoon*, including a year and a half as editor, supplying seven cover illustrations, over 100 cartoons and occasional drawings, 60 poems, and 25 articles and short stories. His cartoons were very skillfully executed, and he was rewarded with a year's postgraduate study at a drawing school in Oxford. His poems were usually brief. Some of his stories were surprisingly serious for a humor magazine, but most were broadly done, with a tone less satirical than bemused. Others contain indications of the verbal dexterity and the rich, purposeful style we have come to expect in Updike's writing twenty years later. (RM)

11839. McKenzie, Alan T. "Two on *Couples*. [2.] 'A Craftsman's Intimate Satisfactions':The Parlor Games in *Couples*." *MFS* 20:53-58.

The excellence of *Couples* rests in the intricate craftsmanship whereby Updike establishes character and milieu. This craftsmanship is especially evident in the two parlor games, "Impressions" and "Wonderful." In the first of these the characters call attention to various aspects of their milieu, reminding us how effectively Updike has established it. They speak of news, flowers, paintings, beverages, foods, and books, the very objects out of which they and their author have constructed their lives. In "Wonderful," on the other hand, their answers reveal not their environment, but their identities. Their revelations corroborate and intensify the characteristics they have acquired elsewhere. Thus Piet's "a sleeping woman," Foxy's "The Eucharist. I can't explain," and Freddy Thorne's " ...the human capacity for self-deception" are gnomic in themselves, but subtle, clear, and significant in the enlarged contexts of the rest of the novel. (ATM)

11840. Meyer, Arlin G., with some additions by Michael A. Olivas. "Criticism of John Updike:A Selected Checklist." *MFS* 20:121-33.

Although John Updike has not received as much critical attention as some of his contemporaries, his works have been widely reviewed and discussed. The "Updike Checklist" contains lists of Updike's published books and his uncollected stories, articles, reviews, and interviews. A list of general studies of Updike's works is followed by special studies of each of his individual works and page references to the general studies devoted to individual works. Criticism not in English, minor reviews, general studies in which Updike is only briefly mentioned, and discussions in standard reference works have been omitted. The bibliography indicates a wide variety of responses to Updike's work and a continuing debate as to his status among contemporary American novelists. (AGM)

11842. Regan, Robert A. "Updike's Symbol of the Center." *MFS* 20:77-96.

According to Updike's neo-Kantian semiology, since the mind can never assert anything beyond itself, certain concepts native to the mind do not "result from" experience but "condition" experience. Updike's symbol of the center is one such concept. The center is not a maieutic of experience but a mother of experience. And since all life—conceptual as well as phenomenal—is organic, the symbol of the center presupposes its efferent sibling, the circle. Like Jung's archetype of the "mandala," Updike's circle functions as a topographical vehicle of order. Order is a perceptual and psychological given—given, that is, through Grace. For the circle is the Incarnate Word of God. As artist, Updike exists "at" the center, and the order that results is a created order born of the principles of geography and ontogeny: the center is his fructifying "place," and the ordering circle its ultimate horizon. (RAR)

11843. Rosa, Alfred F. "The Psycholinguistics of Updike's 'Museums and Women'." *MFS* 20:107-11.

In "Museums and Women" John Updike uses an interesting technical device, sound or phonetic symbolism, as the basis for the theme of his story. Updike suggests that "museums" and "women" as words are naturally paired because the letters "m" and "w" are related in various ways; they are physically reflective of each other, parts of a greater whole as are man and woman, and are resonant consonants making the words in which they appear "hum." By pointing out the relationship between the words, he has also emotionally surcharged them for his readers. Updike sees the relationship of the words and what they symbolize as providential. This is a perceptual mode that is American, derived from his reading of Barth, and a part of his family heritage. (AFR)

11848. Vickery, John B. "*The Centaur*:Myth, History, and Narrative." *MFS* 20:29-43.

John Updike's *The Centaur* uses mythic materials in a distinctive manner in its narrative. In a 1968 interview Updike stressed that his works were deeply infused with historical awareness and attitudes, that he is primarily fascinated with the problems of narrative and story-telling, and that as a result he has been drawn to old sagas and myths for clues concerning the essence of the concept of "story." These views are corroborated by *The Centaur* which blends myth and history in its narrative. In doing so, the novel and its epigraph reveal that, for Updike, the writer, the story-teller, is the one who regularly includes both the conceivable and the inconceivable in his statements. The use of methods of ascription and elision, as well as metaphor, historical rationalization, and contemporary substitution enables Updike to blend the conceivable and the inconceivable and to tell the story of a story itself by deliberately calling attention to the narrative act and the fictive and existential roles of the narrator. (JBV)

11850. Waldmeir, Joseph. "It's the Going That's Important, Not the Getting There:Rabbit's Questing Non-Quest." *MFS* 20:13-27.

Updike's *Rabbit Run* is not a quest novel. Rabbit never knows where he is going; indeed, he has nowhere to go. The quest is at best a structural technique or motif; since it is never pursued, it can neither be successful nor unsuccessful. Updike's primary concern is with the social, philosophical, and religious conflicts which precipitate and motivate Rabbit's running. The social conflict between Rabbit and his family, for whom he presumably should feel and accept responsibility, is abstracted to the philosophical plane with the introduction of Reverend Eccles, who represents a social, pragmatic alternative to Rabbit's mystical, intuitional transcendentalism. Neither philosophical alternative is satisfactory as a resolution of Rabbit's dilemma: pragmatism is both sterile and impotent; transcendentalism, though not sterile, is equally impotent. And religion, that either represented by Eccles or Reverend Kruppenbach, has lost its way. (JJW)

Vonnegut. 11856. Abádi-Nagy, Zoltán. " 'The Skilful Se-

ducer':Of Vonnegut's Brand of Comedy." *HSE* 8:45-56.
Vonnegut puts traditional forms and devices to novel comic uses. *Cat's Cradle* is a satiric parable on three levels: 1) it is about the responsibility of science and politics; 2) "Bokononism" is a parody of religion as opium; 3) Vonnegut uses a paradigm and distorts it into parody. The fantastic element functions as a comic catalyst and as allegory in *The Sirens of Titan* since there is full agreement between Constant's and the Tralfamadorians' motives: the latter are the product of the former's obsession carried to absurdity. In Vonnegut's use comic mechanism exposes comic contrasts (the Shah in *Player Piano*) and a contrast can become a mechanism (the first pages of *Mother Night*). (ZA-N)

11857. Edelstein, Arnold. "*Slaughterhouse-Five*:Time out of Joint." *CollL* 1:128-39.
A reconstruction of the chronological sequence of Vonnegut's *Slaughterhouse-Five* reveals that every detail of Billy Pilgrim's space travel to Tralfamadore is present in Billy's terrestrial life. The space travel can then be seen as a fantasy that protects Billy from the horrors of his time-travel reliving of his war experiences. Escape in general and escape backward from tomb to womb in particular pervades the novel and culminates in Billy's geodesic womb on Tralfamadore. The implied Vonnegut of the first and last chapters creates an atmosphere in which we may judge Billy's retreat into fantasy. (AE)

11860. Messent, Peter B. "*Breakfast of Champions*:The Direction of Kurt Vonnegut's Fiction." *JAmS* 8:101-14.
Vonnegut's *Breakfast of Champions* is a novel of personal and societal despair. Man is a machine: American society is totally corrupt. Vonnegut's water imagery no longer suggests fertility but only a rigid sterility. The author himself enters his own novel, disillusioned and depressed in a meaningless world. Eventually a note of qualified optimism is sounded, but it appears a rather desperate and shallow escape on Vonnegut's part from the futility which surrounds him. The novel fails stylistically: in his attempt to broaden the range of fiction for an electronic age, the author traps himself between a desire to "shun storytelling," to give all facts equal weight, and a need to follow the development of the two major characters in the novel. (PBM)

Wagoner. 11866. Pinsker, Sanford. "The Achievement of David Wagoner." *ConnR* 8,i:42-47.
David Wagoner is still a poet very much "in-progress," but his contributions thus far make him deserving of serious study. In his first book—*Dry Sun, Dry Wind* (1953)—the influences of Theodore Roethke were considerable. However, his next volume (*A Place to Stand*, 1958), gave indications that a poetry involved with "instructions for *seeing*" was at hand. *Staying Alive* (1966) represented a major breakthrough, not only for Wagoner personally, but as a direction in contemporary poetry as well. Here Wagoner's voice is firmly his own and the wit of individual poems like "The Shooting of John Dillinger . . ." or the title poem, "Staying Alive," suggested a work of magical quality. In later volumes like *New and Selected Poems* (1969) and *Riverbed* (1972), Wagoner continued to explore the surprises that result from seeing contemporary society through wryly amused eyes. His verbal facility is anchored in the actual although his imagination transforms them in much the way that he performs—or writes about—"magic" acts. (SSP)

Warren, R.P. 11878. Vauthier, Simone. "The Case of the Vanishing Narratee:An Inquiry Into *All the King's Men*." *SLJ* 6,ii:42-69.
Examines the relationship of the two dependent images of narrator and narratee which shapes the process of self-knowledge embodied in Faulkner's *All the King's Men*. (SGV)

11880. Walker, Marshall. "Robert Penn Warren:An Interview." *JAmS* 8:229-45.
The interview comprises discussions held with Robert Penn Warren in 1969 through 1973. Warren answers questions about the early Nashville days of "The Fugitive," his involvement with the Agrarians, his long engagement with "All the King's Men" in its different versions. He considers the relation of his recurrent themes to an American tradition in literature. The interview traces the development of Warren's attitudes toward the South as

reflected in and prompted by his work. Warren talks about the processes of composing poems and prose. The interview concludes with a survey of the contemporary social and cultural situation especially in America. (MW)

West, M. 11897. McCallum, Gerald. "A Note on Morris West's First Novel." *ALS* 6:314-16.
A selected survey of various writings on the Australian novel indicates Morris West's first book *Moon in My Pocket* (published in 1945 under the name of Julian Morris) has been both badly neglected and wrongly criticized. Despite some romanticized and sentimentalized parts it is a taut, psychological, autobiographically flavored drama which traces with passion and understanding the torment of a young priest divided between God and a search for self-fulfillment. This quest is counterpointed against the celibacy and sterility of the priesthood and the quality of the novel coupled with its current relevance to arguments for a married priesthood are reasons why it should be republished and dramatized. (GKM)

West, N. 11900. Brown, Daniel R. "The War Within Nathanael West:Naturalism and Existentialism." *MFS* 20:181-202.
Nathanael West was suspended between the attitudes of naturalism and existentialism, sharing traits of each movement. Naturalism, Dadaism, and existentialism are all indebted to the same sources: Darwin, Nietzsche, Marx, and Freud (except for early naturalism). He shared the deterministic view of the naturalists, the one essential of the movement, and his comedy leads in the absurd humor of the existentialists. His bleakness ties him to both naturalism and existentialism. The cosmic nihilism of the existentialists and the condemnation of social determinants of the naturalists both result from social conditions, in the one leading to a sense of the absurdity of life, in the other leading to a demand for change. (DRB)

Wharton. 11906. Ammons, Elizabeth. "The Business of Marriage in Edith Wharton's *The Custom of the Country*." *Criticism* 16:326-38.
Undine Spragg's marital career in *The Custom of the Country* (1913) dramatizes Wharton's criticism of American leisure-class marriage. The Stock Market motif defines the book's satiric focus. Because Undine recognizes marriage as the stock exchange on which women negotiate themselves in return for status and wealth (and therefore power), she makes marriage her business in life. Undine excels at the commercial enterprise. When a marriage fails to bring her profit, she "unloads" and invests herself in a new and hopefully more remunerative partnership. Undine is no more exploitative than the culture which produces her. (EA)

11910. McDowell, Margaret B. "Viewing the Custom of Her Country:Edith Wharton's Feminism." *ConL* 15:521-38.
Edith Wharton's fiction dramatizes the shifts in attitude toward women between 1870 and the 1930s and reflects her own ambivalent attitudes on such controversial issues as divorce, abortion, careers for women, and the liaison outside marriage. She understood the need for elemental social change, especially in the relations between the sexes and improving the status of women. Though she wrote perceptively about working class and rural women, she also insists in her depictions of aristocratic women that oppression of women is society-wide. She exposes the suffering caused by the double-standard of sexual morality, the penalties which a male-oriented society exacts for a woman's "transgression," and the economic dependence and consequent inability of the middle class woman to achieve real fulfillment. (MBM)

11915. Wolff, Cynthia G. "Lily Bart and the Beautiful Death." *AL* 46:[16]-40.
Wharton's portrayal of Lily Bart in *House of Mirth* was influenced by the American Neoclassical school of portraiture and Art Nouveau which depict woman as a being whose function is to provide esthetic and moral influence. The supreme attribute of Lily's character is the capacity to render herself agreeable; her tragedy stems, however, from a too thorough-going attempt to achieve esthetic/moral perfection. Selden, a man of esthetic

inclinations and moral vanities, provides the impossibly demanding "audience" for Lily's performance. Ironically, success can come to Lily only through a total denial of self—that is, only through death—for only then can she maintain the unchanging esthetic/moral perfection that is demanded of a great work of art. Wharton's work is a satire of a morally bankrupt society that perverts both its notions of art and its notions of the feminine character. It is a criticism as well of all those works of art that estheticize women, their suffering, and their death. (CGW)

White, W.A. 11917. Dubbert, Joe L. "William Allen White: Reflections on an American Life." *MarkhamR* 4:41-47.
William Allen White published the Emporia Kansas *Gazette* from 1895 to 1944. Far more than just a newspaperman, White was active in Kansas politics as a liberal Republican who joined Theodore Roosevelt to form the Progressive Party in 1912. He wrote 20 books and hundreds of articles for leading publications. In substance White's works are an ideal example of faith in a national covenant, a belief that the nation can never deliberately go wrong although at times it may be distracted from the high purpose of God's plan which was America's solemn obligation to follow. Inspired by Emerson, White proclaimed a belief in progress that would eliminate the worst features of industrialism. Two of White's major heroes were Woodrow Wilson because of his efforts to internationalize the covenant idealism and Calvin Coolidge who endeavored to protect it at home during the materialistic 20s. (JLD)

Wiesel. 11920. Joseloff, Samuel H. "Link and Promise: The Works of Elie Wiesel." *SHR* 8:163-70.
Elie Wiesel's works portray a journey from the hell of Auschwitz and Buchenwald back to humanity. He avoids the temptations of becoming nihilistic, committing suicide, or going insane, and instead finds his own reasons for living and remaining humane. Wiesel's search takes him in two directions: as a survivor of the Holocaust, he feels an obligation to record the story of his family, teachers, and friends, his loved ones who were turned into ash in the crematoriums; as a man who feels alone in a world of hate and insanity, he discovers the possibility and the necessity of friendship. Ultimately Wiesel feels a link with individual friends sharing each other's questions and striving to ease each other's suffering, and also with the Jewish people, especially in Israel and the Soviet Union. (SHJ)
11921. Knopp, Josephine. "Wiesel and the Absurd." *ConL* 15:212-20.
Elie Wiesel was nurtured on orthodox Judaism, but later came to be influenced by French existentialism and especially by the writings of Camus. For the atheist Camus, the "absurd" arises from man's inability to contact absolute truth; for the orthodox Jew Wiesel, absurdity is engendered by God's failure to uphold his part of the covenant. Wiesel's protagonists share common ground with Meursault of *The Stranger* because, in response to Auschwitz, they sense the pointlessness of existence; however, they do not lose faith in God, but are compelled to grapple with the problem of his faithlessness to the Jewish people. The struggle results in rebellion against God which is an attempt to force God to fulfill his contractual obligation under the covenant. The narrator of *The Accident* attempts suicide, but the protagonists of Wiesel's later novels find a more positive expression for rebellion in their struggle to create happiness in spite of God's indifference to a world of misery. (JZK)

Wilbur. 11922. Taylor, Henry. "Cinematic Devices in Richard Wilbur's Poetry." *BRMMLA* 28:41-48.
Wilbur's poems and his prose comments on them suggest that he sometimes consciously employs cinematic techniques. This is especially true in poems where the debt to cinema is acknowledged ("Marginalia," "In the Elegy Season," "An Event," "Beasts," "The Undead"), but other poems ("Castles and Distances," "Walking to Sleep," "Tywater," "Beowulf," "The Pardon," "Merlin Enthralled") employ quite similar devices, to similar ends. The camera eye enables Wilbur to make rich but economical statements about what he sees, and to draw upon a recently-formed body of mythology. (HT)

Williams, J. 11926. Burke, William M. "The Resistance of John A. Williams: *The Man Who Cried I Am*." *Crit* 15,iii(1973):5-14.
Max Reddick, the protagonist of *The Man Who Cried I Am*, illustrates a central theme in Williams' fiction: the need of the black American to establish his dignity by resistance to the oppression that would deny it. Reddick learns that politics and history threaten him as a man, especially as a black American. His discovery of the Alliance Blanc and the King Alfred plan coupled with his terminal cancer lead him to recognize how trapped he is, politically and biologically. Nevertheless, Reddick makes his life count by resisting the overwhelming power of the Alliance Blanc. Through his attempt to expose the conspiracy and his subsequent death at the hands of the CIA, he asserts his private values against the nihilistic movement of history, thus preserving his individual worth as a black and as a man. (WMB)

Williams, W.C. 11941. Fiero, F. Douglass. "Williams Creates the First Book of *Paterson*." *JML* 3:965-86.
Creating Book One of *Paterson* (1946), Williams must convert a difficult immediate "local material" into a poetic matter of imaginative validity for the long poem. His decision to write a long poem set in the region of Paterson, New Jersey, can be located in about the year 1927. A study of a sequence of drafts of Book One at Yale University shows that Book One grew by a process of accumulation and pruning of passages—with the gradual insertion and development of elements of local history, letters received by Williams, key organizing metaphors, and "the fantastic," the myth of the giant and the Woman the Mountain. The imaginative force of the poem results from the emergence of the theme of the poet who struggles toward a solution of the details. The processes of the poetic act within a resistant environment become the poem's central concern. (FDF)
11942. Fox, Hugh. "The Genuine Avant-Garde: William Carlos Williams's Credo." *SWR* 59:285-99.
Williams sees the real function of the imagination as breaking through the alienation of the near at hand and reviving its wonder. *Kora in Hell* reflects Williams' view that the autonomy of the imagination should be encouraged, not restrained. *Spring and All* is a kind of credo of Williams' later work, suggesting that the "function of the imagination is to create a reality *more* 'real' than reality itself." *The Great American Novel* is an experimentation with avant-garde novel styles of the 1920s and a confrontation with the meta-reality and flat reality of words. In "The Descent of Winter" Williams presents examples of his objectivism and liberates prose from two kinds of complexity—that of traditionalism and that of the avant-garde. *A Novelette* reflects his rebellion against obscurantism and the *White Mule* trilogy his preference for actualism; his object-centrism is the key to *Paterson*. *Paterson* and the *White Mule* trilogy and short stories are experiments at "reaching objective reality employing subjectively overused communication symbols within the historical context of just as shabby social conventions." (CTW)
11944. Hardie, Jack. "Williams' 'The Well Disciplined Bargeman'." *Expl* 33:Item 20.
Williams' "The Well Disciplined Bargeman" (1948) is evidently a rejoinder to criticism of Wordsworth in Cleanth Brooks's *Well Wrought Urn* (1947). Brooks finds the sonnet "Composed upon Westminster Bridge" particularly well-wrought, but deems the "Intimations" ode unsuccessful. Brooks's specific criticism is of a piece with broad remarks concerning chaos and incoherence in the work of some modern poets. For Williams, then in the throes of composing his profuse poem *Paterson*, Brooks broaches a touchy subject. Williams' short poem comes to the defense of the ode's profusions. Some devices in Williams' poem are drawn from the ode itself. But the notion of "discipline" and the key images of river and barge are features of Brooks's explication of the sonnet. Williams turns the critic's own language and ideas against him. (JH)

Wilson, E. 11960. Monteiro, George. "Addenda to Ramsey's *Edmund Wilson*." *PBSA* 68:439.
One letter by Wilson and one about him were published in 1924 in *The Literary Review*, the weekly supplement of the *New York*

Evening Post. The Undertaker's Garland (1922) was reviewed in *The Reviewer* a Richmond, Virginia publication. (GM)

Wister. 11966. Shepherd, Allen. "Fair Harvard:A Note on Owen Wister's *Philosophy Four*." *MarkhamR* 4:52-53.
Though even in its day a decidedly minor work, Owen Wister's *Philosophy Four* (1903), a comic tale of undergraduate life at Harvard, articulates themes complimentary to those central in *The Virginian* (1902), his perdurable western romance. While they are not the 19th-century descendants of the Knights of the Round Table that the Virginian and his peers are, the twin heroes of *Philosophy Four*—vigorous, gentlemanly, modest, commonsensical, and Saxon—achieve a signal academic and moral victory over their hired tutor, who is effete, self-seeking, devious, ill-bred, and foreign. In their victory Wister offers a benign perspective on the saving virtues and graces of Eastern society, bridging the antinomy of East and West which had been a constant in American culture and in his own experience. (AGS)
11967. Swaim, Elizabeth A. "Owen Wister's *Roosevelt*:A Case Study in Post-Production Censorship." *SB* 27:290-93.
Bibliographical variations possible in ordinary 20th-century American trade books are exemplified by Wister's best-selling *Roosevelt: The Story of a Friendship*, publication of which was held up in June 1930 upon threat of a libel suit over the description of an innocuous hoax played on the President by a Charleston, South Carolina hostess in 1902. Already distributed pre-publication copies were recalled by Macmillan, and a new 16-page section, substituting 5 newly-written pages for the offending episode, was hastily printed and inserted, thus creating two variants of the first printing. (EAS)

Wolfe, T. 11969. Doten, Sharon. "Thomas Wolfe's 'No Door':Some Textual Questions." *PBSA* 68:45-52.
Recent studies of Wolfe's short fiction have not questioned existing texts or attempted to ascertain definitive texts for these pieces. Examination of the publication history, manuscripts, and typescripts of a short novel entitled "No Door" reveals, however, that problems concerning its text are numerous and deserve further study. (SSD)
11971. Gray, Richard. "Signs of Kinship:Thomas Wolfe and His Appalachian Background." *AppalJ* 1:309-19.
It is generally assumed that Wolfe had as little to do with the American South, and the Appalachian community in which he grew up, as he possibly could. This assumption involves a radical misreading of his work. His attitude toward "roots" expressed in his major fiction is examined as is Wolfe's deep creative interest in mountain life and culture. The problem of his "Southern-ness" is also considered. Wolfe's last, unfinished novel *The Hills Beyond* and its sources are analyzed in detail in order to show how toward the end of his life he was trying to make his past more relevant to his present; to forge a useable tradition for himself by adopting many of the themes he had discovered in local folktales, and many of the values he learned from the local community, and develop them into something more generally applicable and new. (RJG)
11973. Meehan, James. "Seed of Destruction:The Death of Thomas Wolfe." *SAQ* 73:[173]-83.
New medical evidence indicates that Wolfe was a victim of a rare fungus disease, coccidioidomycosis or desert fever. This new theory by a prominent medical specialist proposes that Wolfe picked up an air-borne fungus in the Southwestern deserts in early summer of 1938. Medical knowledge of coccidioidomycosis was scant at the time, thus Wolfe's doctors cannot be blamed for the outcome. Previous accounts of Wolfe's death are called into question, as are allegations that he had a "death wish" or was in previous poor health. (JJM)
11975. Walther, John D. "'Luke' Looks Homeward:An Interview with Fred W. Wolfe." *MissQ* 27:141-63.
Fred W. Wolfe, the last survivor of the renowned Wolfe family, reminisces about his late brother, Thomas. Wolfe comments on his own characterization as "Luke" in *Look Homeward, Angel*. He also discusses Tom's "autobiographical license," his attitudes toward fictionalized members of the Wolfe household and the Asheville community, his divided sensibilities regarding his

friends and literary acquaintances, his wavering sectional allegiances both North and South, and his ultimate need to resolve personal and literary conflicts. (JDW)

Wright, H.B. 11977. Ifkovic, Edward. "Harold Bell Wright and the Minister of Man:The Domestic Romancer at the End of the Genteel Age." *MarkhamR* 4:21-26.
Harold Bell Wright is an example of the domestic romancer who flourished just before World War I. The vogue of sentimental romance gave the middle-class audience an idealistic, Christian, and secure image of the American home to counter the new industrial America: non-WASP immigration, socialism, strikes, imperialism, divorce. Wright's minister-heroes reject evil city life and rejuvenate themselves in the simple, country homelife. But underneath Wright's euphoria is an unconscious fear that the rural society cannot survive. Happy endings notwithstanding, Wright introduces the railroad. In *The Shepherd of the Hills* (1907), the romance ends with ominous distant blasting. In *The Calling of Dan Matthews* (1909), the railroad is already there, and the town is ugly, corrupt. The minister-hero decides that the good men must control the machine. Looking for God behind the machine, he returns to the hills to mine the land, serving his fellow man. In Wright's pacific vision, America is an industrial pastoral, and middle-class America need not fear the new industrial age. (JEI)

Wright, J. 11978. Butscher, Edward. "The Rise and Fall of James Wright." *GaR* 28:257-68.
James Wright's early books *The Green Wall* (1957) and *Saint Judas* (1959) exhibited traditional forms and a penchant for laments. Though without much complexity of thought and sensibility, many of the poems in these volumes worked well to express their author's sense of isolated alienation. His strongest volume, *The Branch Will Not Break* (1963), depended upon a severe Neoclassic restraint and a series of original metaphors to keep its author's innate sentimentality in check. "Two Hangovers" can be viewed as a prototype for the other poems in the book, their strengths and weaknesses. *Shall We Gather at the River* (1968) demonstrated, however, a great decline as religious certainty became a closed cell for Wright's Whitmanesque celebrations and songs of social protest. This decline was continued into *The Collected Poems* (1972), where the new verses suggested an embarrassing absence of basic poetic skills. *Two Citizens* (1973) signified complete disaster as simplistic emotionalism overwhelmed his frail esthetic. (EJB)
11980. Henricksen, Bruce. "Wright's 'Lying in a Hammock at William Duffy's Farm in Pine Island, Minnesota'." *Expl* 32:Item 40.
A number of readers have failed to discern any logical relationship among the images in James Wright's "Lying in a Hammock" and have seen this poem as representative of a deterioration in Wright's style. Thom Gunn has said the last line is entirely meaningless. But there is a clear logical development in the poem, each image bearing a definable relationship to the theme of alienation and waste, which is clarified, as an epiphany, in the final line. (BCH)
11982. Van den Heuvel, Cor. "The Poetry of James Wright." *Mosaic* 7,iii:163-70. [Rev. art.]
This review of James Wright's *Collected Poems* traces, with an examination of the different books represented in the collection, the development of the poet's work from a human oriented, formal, "academically" constructed poetry, through a more objective concern for the things of the world, presented with a freer, more supple, yet disciplined, style, to its return to the human situation, still retaining and augmenting the exceptional mastery of the elements of the craft earned in the process. The poet's experience with and translation of the literatures of other countries is considered to have played an important part in that development. (CvdH)

Wright, R. 11983. Amis, Lola J. "Richard Wright's *Native Son*:Notes." *NALF* 8:240-43.
The dramatic conflict of Wright's *Native Son* takes place chiefly within the mind of Bigger Thomas who lives in a world of illusion

and dream sprinkled with colors of whites, blacks, and reds. To Bigger, all of life is conflict and issues, flooded with color, sound, sight, and fear over which he has no control. All of illusion comes in white and all of reality in black, so he cannot identify with his real self-image, which becomes tangled somehow in the world of "acting." Wright suggests that Bigger Thomas is an embodiment of the "black revolt against the injustices of the white caste society" and that this revolt often takes the form of crime against this same white society. Surrounded by this hostile white society, Bigger becomes the total embodiment of that society's hatred, prejudices, and resentments against the black man. Bigger becomes "natural man in the universe," man without Paradise, man without conscience, man without hope, love, or religion, man without a home, family, or friends. Bigger becomes "No Man." (LJA)

11986. Demarest, David P.,Jr. "Richard Wright:The Meaning of Violence." *NALF* 8:236-39.

"Between the World and Me" and *Black Boy* reveal violence in the human psyche and in race relations in America. The structure of the poem is a progress in identification and empathy that points to this theme. The black and white context of a lynch scene implies that racial violence done to any single black involves all blacks. No black can avoid awareness of white violence or identification with the victims. Wright develops this theme in less passionate terms in the autobiographic *Black Boy*, which is more about black family violence than about white violence. Several episodes show how the patterns of violence lend structure to *Black Boy*. In the scenes involving the cat and his uncle, black has been set against black. Both works hinge on a terrible tension between individual consciousness and race awareness. They thus expose a dual consciousness that has been seared into the black psyche by the violence of white America. (HH)

11988. Everette, Mildred W. "The Death of Richard Wright's American Dream:'The Man Who Lived Underground'." *CLAJ* 17:318-26.

Written after 15 years in the North, Richard Wright's "The Man Who Lived Underground" (1944) reveals through allegory, metaphor, and symbolism the futility of hope for "Everyblackman," represented by an innocent black's enforced, three-day existence in a sewer to escape being made a scapegoat by brutal police. His experiences in the sewer represent the ghetto life imposed on blacks by white society. Vignettes of life from this rat den elicit ironic truths about the falsity of the American Dream for blacks; distorted dreams reflect the man's plight and foreshadow the outcome—annihilation by fearful white society, after rejection, ironically, by blindly God-loving, conforming elements of his race. (MWE)

11989. Felgar, Robert. " 'The Kingdom of the Beast':The Landscape of *Native Son*." *CLAJ* 17:333-37.

One of the presiding metaphors of Richard Wright's *Native Son* is the lawless jungle, in which only the fittest survive. Given his belief in biological determinism, it is quite expected that he would suggest America's jungle ethics by using the wild forest as a radical metaphor. The black ghetto itself is the kingdom of the beast, ultimately created by white monsters, like Buckley. A pattern of animal imagery revolves around the Thomas family: Bigger himself is repeatedly described as a "black ape," Buddy is like a "chubby puppy," while Bigger makes Vera feel like a dog; and of course the Thomas's apartment is rat-infested. In the Dalton's house is the ubiquitous white cat Kate, who objectifies Bigger's guilt and fear. When the white beast is about to capture its prey, Bigger, he hides on top of a water tank, but the chill of a powerful jet of water "squeezed him like the circling coils of a monstrous boa constrictor." The white beast always captures its prey. (RF)

11990. Gounard, Jean-François. "Richard Wright as a Black American Writer in Exile." *CLAJ* 17:307-17.

Richard Wright's most powerful works were written when he was in close contact with the racial problems he knew best. His was a continuous search to understand and improve the lot of the non-white. From *Black Boy* (1945) to *White Man, Listen!* (1957) one can trace the evolution of a man whose first commitment was to the black American but who, because of his travels and experiences outside the United States, came to realize the worldwide implications of his concern. From his vantage point abroad, Wright gained a new perspective on racial problems that led to greater personal and literary maturity. He ventured into new forms of literary expression (humor, plays, haiku poetry), and developed a more accepting attitude toward the human condition. (JFG)

11991. Graham, Don B. "*Lawd Today* and the Example of *The Waste Land*." *CLAJ* 17:327-32.

Richard Wright's novel *Lawd Today* expresses naturalistic material in a form influenced by Eliot's *The Waste Land*. The novel's last section bears an epigraph from Eliot's poem, and certain formal techniques in the novel seem to parallel those in *The Waste Land*. A major pattern is the balancing of spring-rebirth against winter-death. Like the people inhabiting *The Waste Land*, those of Wright's city fail to find love and meet at every turn false beliefs, corrupted religion, Madame Sosostris-like prophets. The novel ends on a specifically Eliotic note: Jake figuratively drowns in a whirlpool while a fierce winter wind negates all hope of spring. (DBG)

11992. Gross, Seymour L. " 'Dalton' and Color-Blindness in *Native Son*." *MissQ* 27(1973-74):75-77.

The name Richard Wright gave to the white family in *Native Son* (1940)—Dalton—is of some critical significance. Since the two dominant symbolic strains in the novel are color and blindness, it was a fine stroke for Wright to have named a family which is blind to, or blinded by color, Dalton, for John Dalton was the discoverer of that optical distortion known as Daltonism or color-blindness. There is ample biographical evidence that the choice was deliberate, not a lucky accident. (SLG)

11994. Kim, Kichung. "Wright, the Protest Novel, and Baldwin's Faith." *CLAJ* 17:387-96.

James Baldwin's early controversy with Richard Wright concerning "protest" in literature centers on Bigger Thomas, Wright's protagonist in *Native Son*. In his creation of Bigger Thomas, Baldwin argues, Wright has further perpetuated the racist stereotype of the brutalized and dehumanized black American so dear to the white Americans rather than give a picture of the real black American in all his "disquieting complexity." The bases of Wright's and Baldwin's views are examined in turn; Baldwin's insistence on the irreducible complexity of the black American —as it is of all men—is seen to be based more on his hope and vision of what the black American might or ought to be in spite of his oppression rather than what he actually is in the ghettos of America. Hence his different view of him, especially so when compared to the views of Wright, and more recently of Eldridge Cleaver and LeRoi Jones. In the past few years, however, particularly since the murder of Martin Luther King, Baldwin has lost his vision of what the black American might or ought to be, and this seems to represent a more general loss of his faith in man, and more particularly in the American dream. (KK)

11996. Klotman, Phyllis R. "Moral Distancing as a Rhetorical Technique in *Native Son*:A Note on 'Fate'." *CLAJ* 18:284-91.

Wright purposefully uses the rhetorical technique of "moral distancing" in *Native Son* to separate the reader from his extreme proximity to the horrors of Bigger's life and those perpetrated by him. Wright wants the reader to be motivated into some form of constructive action, to aid black people by effecting economic and social change. We, therefore, become witnesses to the process by which Bigger is dehumanized by white society and are inevitably identified with that society in its culpability. (PRK)

11999. Siegel, Paul N. "The Conclusion of Richard Wright's *Native Son*." *PMLA* 89:517-23.

Both Max's courtroom speech in Richard Wright's *Native Son* and his final scene with Bigger have been grievously misunderstood. The numerous critics of the novel have regarded Max's speech as a Communist "party-line oration" whose propaganda is poorly related to the rest of the book. Bigger, however, finds a meaning in his life by accepting his feelings of hate. This is not a defeat for him, as critics have asserted. Hatred of the oppressor is a natural, human emotion which, used as the motor power of an idea driving toward a goal, can transform both the individual and society. As Max says, "The job in getting people to fight and have faith is in making them believe in what life has made them feel . . ." This is the belief Bigger finally acquires. With this belief comes a sense of comradeship with those whites such as Jan who have earned such comradeship in action. (PNS)

12003. Weiss, Adrian. "A Portrait of the Artist as a Black Boy." *BRMMLA* 28:93-101.
In *Black Boy*, Wright links the themes of survival and the emergence of the artist in a hostile racist environment through an emphasis upon the role of imagination in the experience of young Richard. Imaginative activity becomes a means of self-discovery and actualization in Wright's treatment of the Bluebeard incident. That experience provides Richard with a new sense of self and the world in which the vibrant inner reality strongly contradicts the bleakness of external reality. (AW)

Young, A. 12004. Bolling, Douglass. "Artistry and Theme in Al Young's *Snakes*." *NALF* 8:223-25.
Young's *Snakes* traces the spiritual evolution of the young black, MC, from his experiences in the Detroit ghetto to the moment of his departure from home for a new life. MC's tearing himself away from his loved ones and his background is itself something of a spiritual victory for him. Young shows us that MC's action is not simply one of youthful rebellion: it is also profoundly an affirmation of those he leaves behind and of his own deep needs and identity. MC's musical talent plays a major part in his rise from the degradations of the ghetto; but the love given the young man by his grandmother Claude is also crucial. *Snakes* is less a work given to the claims of black protest and "black esthetic" concerns than it is a disciplined evocation of the universals of human experience. (DB)

MEDIEVAL AND NEO-LATIN LITERATURE†

I. GENERAL

General and Miscellaneous. 12033. Bühler, Curt F. "Three Early Venetian Editions of Augustinus Datus and the Press of Florentius de Argentina." [F 120]:62-70.
The study analyzes three early editions of the *Elegantiolae* of Augustinus Datus. An examination of the texts of 19 editions shows convincingly that the earliest of the three Venetian editions was that printed and signed by Florentius de Argentina, previously judged to be the last printed. It was probably published about 1472. Some of the printing practices of this press are also reviewed and reveal problems the early printer had to face and his ways of solving them. (CFB)

12058. Peters, Edward M. "Editing Inquisitors' Manuals in the Sixteenth Century:Francisco Peña and the *Directorium Inquisitorum* of Nicholas Eymeric." [F 120]:95-107.
One of the most important activities of the Counter-Reformation papacy was the establishment of carefully edited printed editions of major monuments of ecclesiastical literature. In 1578 Francisco Peña, a Valencian canonist and later Dean of the Roman Rota, published a thorough edition of the *Directorium Inquisitorum* of Nicholas Eymeric, written at Avignon in 1378 and the most influential of all handbooks for inquisitors. Peña's edition of Eymeric's work consists as much of bringing the work up to date for the 16th century through the addition of many documents and *additiones* by the editor as presenting a careful critical edition of the text itself. (EMP)

Drama and Theater. 12081. Flanigan, C. Clifford. "The Liturgical Context of the *Quem Queritis* Trope." [F 114]:45-62.
The significance of the *Quem Queritis* dialogue for the history of the medieval drama has been obscured by an inadequate understanding of the liturgical form and function of a trope. In its troped form the *Quem Queritis* sought to explain the cultic significance of the Easter introit to which it was attached. It emphasized the way in which the liturgy was believed to render present again the events of the first Easter, thus enabling the medieval congregation to share in its soteriological benefits. The *Visitatio Sepulchri*, and perhaps other forms of the liturgical drama are primarily liturgical embellishments which by word, song, and gesture sought to make explicit the meaning of the liturgical celebration of Easter. (CCF)

12083. Hallwas, John E. "*Ordo ad Representandum Herodem*." *Expl* 32:Item 41.
The significance of the unusual order of presenting the gifts (gold, myrrh, frankincense) to the Christ-child in the Fleury *Ordo ad representandum Herodem* relates to the conventional symbolic interpretations for those gifts which are indicated in the play: gold is for a king, myrrh signifies burial, and frankincense indicates that he is truly God. In a play which reveals Christ's significance as the Savior, this order for the gifts illuminates the Infant's role

as the self-sacrificing Savior by reflecting the kingship-burial-divinity pattern that his life will assume. The unusual order also suggests the essential pattern into which human existence will be molded through the coming of Christ: life-death-eternal life. (JEH)

12085. Ogden, Dunbar H. "The Use of Architectural Space in Medieval Music-Drama." [F 114]:63-76.
In bringing together the text of a medieval music-drama and the plan of the church in which it was first performed, we perceive vividly the theatrical use of this architectural space. Recent archeological excavation of the Old Minster at Winchester gives us an idea of the staging area which Ethelwold had in mind when in the 10th century he described the performance of the *Visitatio Sepulchri*. On groundplans of two other churches, detailed textual rubrics permit us actually to trace the paths of the actors. (DHO)

12086. Rudick, Michael. "Theme, Structure, and Sacred Context in the Benediktbeuren 'Passion' Play." *Speculum* 49:267-86.
Comparison of the Benediktbeuern play with the Passion Play from Montecassino shows that the Benediktbeuern play is of a different kind, not a Passion Play, but rather a Palm Sunday (or Holy Week) Play. Evidence shows that the play was written to be performed within the Palm Sunday observance; its components are related to exegetical and liturgical commentary on its incidents and sacred context; the incidents and their order are apprehensible, not as a Passion narrative, but as a didactic structure concerned with the themes of Holy Week, specifically penitence and spiritual conversion. (MR)

Hymns. 12115. O'Malley, Jerome F. "A Survey of Medieval Johannine Hymns." *AnM* 15:46-73.
Investigates the 183 Latin hymns from the *Analecta Hymnica* written in honor of St. John the Evangelist. An analysis of the biblical and legendary motifs reveals chastity, John's relation to the Virgin Mary, and the contemplative life as the dominant motifs. The key to understanding the meaning of these motifs originates in the traditions of Eastern theology exemplified by Gregory of Nyssa. The use of the hymnodic motifs in the writings of Joachim of Flora and in relation to the Assumption of the Virgin Mary confirms the importance of the Johannine traditions for Western theology. (JFO'M)

Mysticism. 12206. McLaughlin, Eleanor. "The Heresy of the Free Spirit and Late Medieval Mysticism." *M&H* 4(1973):37-54.
Many historians today are still quoting medieval reports that the Free Spirits were in theory and practice antinomians and libertines, given to the most crass excesses of sensuality. A reason for the lack of unanimity on the nature of this heresy lies in the absence of a trustworthy body of sources for its history. No source material from the hands of the accused is known to exist. This paper offers a partial solution to that dilemma by presenting a new set of witnesses for the history of the heresy of the Free Spirit, an alternative to the typological accounts of inquisitor and

† *Festschriften* and Other Analyzed Collections are listed in the first division of this volume. "F" numbers in brackets following a title refer to these items.

chronicler. This new perspective is to be found in the orthodox mystics of the 14th and 15th centuries and is argued with reference to a representative sample of the evidence available: the *Mirror of Simple Souls,* an early 14th-century Beguine devotional treatise, and the sermons of Johannes Tauler. (EMcL)

Poetry. 12232. Wenzel, Siegfried. "The Moor Maiden—A Contemporary View." *Speculum* 49:69-74.
A new reference to the much debated Middle-English lyric "Maiden in the moor lay" has been discovered in a manuscript of Latin sermons preserved at Worcester Cathedral and probably written in the second half of the 14th century. The lyric is here called a "carol." The appearance of this reference makes it unlikely that the anonymous preacher who quoted it considered the poem as an allegory of the Blessed Virgin or of St. Mary Magdalene, as has been recently maintained. (SW)

Rhetoric. 12234. Banker, James R. "The *Ars dictaminis* and Rhetorical Textbooks at the Bolognese University in the Fourteenth Century." *M&H* 5:153-68.
Giovanni di Bonandrea, master of rhetoric from 1293 to 1321, initiated a dual instruction of *ars dictaminis* (art of letterwriting) and rhetoric at the University in Bologna. Throughout the 14th century Bolognese masters commented upon his epistolary treatise, *Brevis introductio ad dictamen,* and appropriated his practice of lecturing on the pseudo-Ciceronian *Rhetorica ad Herennium.* Giovanni taught the epistolary art to the unlearned notaries of the city and lectured on rhetoric to the law students of the University. Though the Bolognese masters continued to lecture on the classical text throughout the 15th century, interest in the epistolary treatise waned in the 1380s. (JRB)

II. MEDIEVAL LATIN LITERATURE

Arnulf of Orleans. 12300. Roy, Bruno. "Arnulf of Orleans and the Latin 'Comedy'." *Speculum* 49:258-66.
Arnulf of Orleans, known for his commentaries on classical authors, in his gloss on Ovid's *Remedia amoris* makes a comparison with "Pamphilus" implying that these comedies were intended to be performed. The allusions used in the literary controversy between Matthew of Vendome and the unknown author of the comedies *Miles* and *Lidia* suggests this author to have been Arnulf, Matthew's principal rival. Stylistic comparison of these two comedies with Arnulf's known works, while it cannot prove authorship, does show a certain continuity. (AGB)

Francis of Assisi. 12526. Carlson, Charles P.,Jr. "St. Francis and the Early Government of the Franciscan Order." *IR* 31,i:3-23.
Discusses St. Francis' control of the Franciscan order on the basis of several considerations: (1) A review of the constitutional history of other medieval religious orders indicates that some of the distinctive ideas embodied in the organization of the Franciscan Order were not as unique as Francis apparently assumed; (2) The Papacy manifested a very liberal attitude in permitting Francis to implement most of his ideas in founding the Order; and (3) Evidence is offered that Francis was not, strictly speaking, a reformer or "evangelical." (CPC,Jr)

Geoffrey of Monmouth. 12544. Keller, Hans E. "Two Toponymical Problems in Geoffrey of Monmouth and Wace: *Estrusia* and *Siesia*." *Speculum* 49:687-98.
Certain place-names in Geoffrey of Monmouth and Wace (Layamon) still elude identification, both in the formation of name as well as in their geographical location. *Estrusia* belongs to the first category, and linguistic data from French dialectology and Germanic studies are necessary to recognize that Geoffrey's *Estruenses* means "settlers along a river." The place of the decisive battle between Arthur and the Romans was known to be somewhere in Burgundy. Medieval documents show that Geoffrey must have thought of the Val Suzon. (HEK)

Ockham. 12687. Rhodes, Dennis E. "The Printer of Ockham." [F 120]:118-23.
The anonymous press which operated in Paris in July and August 1476 and which goes under the name of "The Printer of Ockham" printed five books: (1) the Dialogues of William of Ockham; (2) Nicolaus Panormitanus, *Processus judicarius*; (3) Aristotle, *Secreta secretorum*; (4) *De modo confitendi,* ascribed to St. Bonaventura, but written by Matthaeus de Cracovia; and (5) *Sermones*

moralissimi by de Haqueville. The last three are undated. The press is fifth in the order of Paris presses, and its types show a strong similarity with those of Caesaris and Stol. (DER)

Petrarch. 12731. Roche, Thomas P.,Jr. "The Calendrical Structure of Petrarch's *Canzoniere*." *SP* 71:152-72.
The ordering of the 366 poems in Petrarch's *Canzoniere* is numerologically oriented; the major division at poem 264 is intentional and is meant to coincide with Christmas Day as poem 1 is meant to coincide with Good Friday. Within this outer framework the groups of sonnets and the placement of non-sonnets adumbrate the progress of the Church year, emphasizing the seasons of Advent and Lent. (TPR,JR.)

Pseudo-Origen. 12752. Jennings, Margaret M. "The Art of the Pseudo-Origen Homily *De Maria Magdalena*." *M&H* 5:139-52.
Textual analysis of Pseudo-Origen's *De Maria Magdalena* reveals the confluence of scriptural, hagiographic, rhetorical, dramatic, and mystical elements. Biblical quotation, cadence, and allusion combine with rhetorical devices to form an artistically balanced discussion of the verse "Maria stabat ad monumentum foris plorans." Stylistic elements unite to characterize Mary of Magdala. Portrayed first from the viewpoint of the omniscient author and then through first person narration, Mary is utterly bereft. Her interior monologue at the core of the homily depicts how totally she suffered. Pseudo-Origen asks only our contemplation of Mary's loss and grief and our understanding of the joy which will be hers. (MMJ)

Thomas Aquinas. 12805. Dubruck, Edelgard. "Thomas Aquinas and Medieval Demonology." *MichA* 7:167-83.
Shaped essentially by the Middle Ages, our views of the devil, witchcraft, and sorcery stem from folk traditions dating back to "primitive" times. While he left no systematic treatise on demonology, Thomas Aquinas took a stand on several points of debate: demons exist as agents of evil (*maleficium*); people can be suspected of "implicit pact" with the devil or other supernatural agents; divorce can be granted if there has been intercourse with demons or evidence of impotence because of *maleficium*; there is no such thing as night flight; women are especially susceptible to the workings of the devil. Because of his statement on women above all, Aquinas is indirectly responsible for the institutionalized murder of thousands in the subsequent witch hunts and trials. (EDB)

III. NEO-LATIN LITERATURE

General and Miscellaneous. 12872. Dean, Ruth J., and Samuel G. Armistead. "A Fifteenth-Century Spanish Book List." [F 120]:73-87.
A 15th-century Latin manuscript of Boethius on the *Consolation*

of Philosophy in the library of the University of Pennsylvania contains on a fly-leaf a list of 20 books belonging to a private owner, drawn up by him in 1471. The titles are given in Spanish, but the collection was probably all in Latin, although one or two of the works may have been in the vernacular. Aristotelian translations and commentaries form about half of the collection. There are moral and theological treatises and two titles connected with preaching, while a dictionary and works on grammar and rhetoric complete the list. (RJD & SGA)

12873. Derwa, Marcelle. "Un aspect du colloque scolaire humaniste:Le dialogue à variations." *RLC* 48:190-202.
In the beginning the "colloquia scolastica" of the Humanists embodied a simple pedagogical method. The aim of such a method was to teach the correct Latin language and to protect the morality of the scholars or students. Through examples of Erasmus and Barlandus, it is demonstrated that, although they were good thinkers and writers, the Humanists transformed the simple "colloquia scolastica" into autonomous works written in a creative style and containing the highest teachings. (MD)

Erasmus. 12917. Becker-Cantarino, Baerbel. "Ronsard's 'Exhortations pour la Paix' (1558) and Erasmus." *RomN* 15:486-89.
"Exhortation pour la Paix" deals with man's destination as a peaceful being. These lines represent a topos from classical literature which Erasmus had employed in his spirited discussion of war and peace, his *Querela Pacis*, and in *Dulce Bellum Inexpertis*. Erasmus relegated war and warlike acts to the morally inferior world of the animals. For him man was to use his reason and human qualities to develop laws and organize society for his own protection. In his "Exhortation pour la Paix" of 1558 Ronsard gives an artistic rendering of Erasmus' arguments against war. (BB-C)

12920. Bietenholz, P.G. "Ambiguity and Consistency in the Work of Erasmus of Rotterdam." *WascanaR* 9:134-42.
An analysis of the occurrence and significance of ambiguity in the literary work of Erasmus. Chiefly Erasmus' correspondence from 1517 to 1520 was examined to determine his ambiguity and his consistency against the background of biographical fact, in particular his involvement in the controversies involving Reuchlin and Luther. (PGB)

12936. Fleischauer, John F. "A New Sixteenth-Century Translation of Erasmus." *PBSA* 68:164-66.
An unlisted copy of Erasmus' *De Civilitate Morum Puerilium* at the University of Pennsylvania library is identified as printed by John Walley, ca. 1550. The Pennsylvania copy, lacking both title page and colophon, contains both a Latin text and, curiously, an English text which is half the work of an anonymous translator and half that of Robert Whittinton. The anonymous translation is more fluent but less artful than Whittinton's earlier version. The Pennsylvania copy has been misplaced, so closer examination must wait; meanwhile, Fleischauer's copies of a portion of the text (duplicates of which are in the Houghton Library) are all that remain. (JFF)

12956. Logan, George M. "Erasmus' Intellectual Development." *HAB* 25:232-43. [Rev. art.]
Rabil's *Erasmus and the New Testament* and Thompson's *Under Pretext of Praise* prompt a reassessment of Erasmus' intellectual development. Rabil views this development as a dialectical process in which Erasmus articulates a series of resolutions of a conflict between childhood religion and adolescent humanism. The difficulty in this thesis is that Erasmus before his first visit to England in 1499-1500 exhibits no more than conventional interest in religion and seems content with the conventional reconciliations of literary study with religion. In fact, Erasmus' stay in England produced not only (as Rabil and others think) a resolution of the tension between religion and humanism but also the tension itself. After *The Praise of Folly* (1509), Erasmus' development continues in an essentially linear rather than dialectical fashion. His constant focus on morality, together with his growing skepticism of reason, leads him close to the pragmatic view that, on many of the subtler points of doctrine, one may as well believe whatever is most conducive to morality. (GML)

12976. Rebhorn, Wayne A. "The Metamorphoses of Moria: Structure and Meaning in *The Praise of Folly*." *PMLA* 89:463-76.
Following Moria's metamorphoses, Erasmus' *Praise* falls into three sections whose interrelationships generate its total meaning. Moving from section to section, Folly leads her auditors through a dialectic of conversion. At first ironic, Folly is the goddess of metamorphosis, a variant of Circe, offering men her gift of pleasurable illusion. She wants them to accept life as a comic play and attacks the "Stoic" for attempting self-divinization while rejecting the play of life. But in the satirical middle section, Folly betrays them by showing them the real tragedy of their lot. While revealing that one cannot separate life-preserving, pleasurable folly from destructive madness, by her transformation into a "Stoic" truth-teller, Folly prevents men from placing their faith in her benevolence. Thus, in the final section, she turns with them to Christian folly, the faith that leads men out of Plato's cave to God's unchanging, benevolent reality. Folly's final, ecstatic vision gives her followers a transcendent perspective redefining and including the comitragic visions of the first two sections. (WAR)

CELTIC LITERATURES†

VI. IRISH GAELIC

13140. Redshaw, Thomas D. "*Rí*, as in Regional:Three Ulster Poets." *Éire* 9,ii:41-64. [Seamus Heaney, Seamus Deane, John Montague.]
The Ulster "Troubles" have thrust upon such Ulster poets as Seamus Heaney, Seamus Deane, and John Montague the challenge to be poets of a region. This both hinders and helps their chosen celebrations of *pagus* and *paruchia*. The ten cantos of John Montague's *The Rough Field* (1972) not only form a response to the regional challenge, they also make up a "new epic." *The Rough Field* embodies its subject place with novel formal diversity by playing orthodox genres against Irish ones like the *aisling* or *dinnshenchus*. *The Rough Field* generates a fictive autobiography of the one persona by suggesting a symbolic psychomachia, thus richly enacting Montague's chief theme of consciousness bound, threatened, then freed. Seamus Deane's *Gradual Wars* (1972) also makes an American alliance. But Deane's very different craft and elegaic sense display Blake-like passions at the expense of a whole poetic structure. Seamus Heaney's *Wintering Out* (1972) consciously avoids direct experience of contemporary crisis, personal or not, by concentrating on Ulster placelore enriched by the metaphors of his early work. (TDR)

IX. WELSH

13164. Bisenieks, Dainis. "Welsh Myth in Modern American Fantasy." *AWR* 24,liii:130-34.
National myths remain alive through retelling, which American writers have done with the Welsh *Mabinogion*. Lloyd Alexander's five Prydain books (1964-68) adapt Welsh material to a tale of a hero's adolescence. Evangeline Walton retells the Four Branches of the Mabinogi in four novels. Kenneth Morris adds to the First and Second Branches material inspired by theosophy and bardism. The gods of a reconstructed Welsh pantheon test and send on quests the heroes Pwyll and Pryderi in *The Fates of the Princes of Dyfed* and Manawyddan in *Book of the Three Dragons*. (DB)

13166. Carson, J. Angela. "The Structure and Meaning of *The Dream of Rhonabwy*." *PQ* 53:289-303.

† *Festschriften* and Other Analyzed Collections are listed in the first division of this volume. "F" numbers in brackets following a title refer to these items.

The Dream of Rhonabwy is structured into four tripartite sections each of which consists of a pair of opponents and the messengers who approached them. Each pair of opponents is comprised of men whom one would expect to be in accord; however, in the *Dream* they represent instances of brother against brother. This pattern reflects a similar situation in Wales at the end of the 14th century when Owen Glyndwr tried to unite Wales and was hindered in his efforts by a diversity of opinion regarding the English and the proper attitude toward them. The nationalist and the pro-English positions reached the height of their tensions at the end of the 14th century, the era when we can conclude that *The Dream of Rhonabwy* was written. The date of the tale can now be advanced to 1385 at the earliest—and this on the basis of the identification of Heilyn Goch, the owner of the house where Rhonabwy took shlter; it is clear that Heilyn was an historical figure who was owner of a house in Dudleston, and who attained his majority about 1385. (JAC)

FOLKLORE†

I. GENERAL

History and Study of Folklore

Asia. 13268. Gupta, Sankar Sen. "A General View of Indian Folklore." *FolkloreC* 16:179-93.
The main tasks of folklorologists are to develop knowledge and skills that help one to study folk society and to assess the social implication of changing folklore. The inquisitive mind of the average Indian thirsts for knowledge. Even when living in dire distress, he fights for tradition and culture. The struggle for spiritual, moral, and traditional liberation helps him create folklore and new social order. A note on the men who made Indian folklore scholarly is provided. (SS)
13269. —— "A Note on 'Folklore and Folk Life in India'." *FolkloreC* 16:289-99.
A short survey of work of the folklorologists of the world and of India. Discusses the increasing acceptance of folklore and pays homage to pioneers in the field of folklore. (SS)
13270. —— "The Area, Scope and Objective of Folklore Study in India." *FolkloreC* 16:25-35,99-113,136-60.
Focuses on the techniques and importance of folklore study and provides a general introduction to the history of Indian folklore and a scientific way of studying it. The main genres, importance, and direction of Indian folklore (both ancient and modern) are discussed. Sen Gupta attempts to integrate the views of world-renowned scholars into the Indian perspective for the study of folklore and folk life in India. (SS)
13271. Kitahara, Michio. "A Theme of Japanese Culture." *FolkloreC* 16:283-88,299.
Many diverse aspects of Japanese culture often seem to be unrelated to each other in terms of a consistent theme. Several phenomena of Japanese culture which are superficially unrelated to sophisticated culture can be consistently seen in terms of a theme of manipulation. This theme appears to be especially useful in understanding Japanese ideas on man, suicide, hedonism, religion, the universe, science and technology, capitalism, achievement, perfection, art, and interpersonal relations. (KM)
13276. Siddiqui, Ashraf. "Some Foreigners' Contribution to Indian Folklore." *FolkloreC* 16:81-90,98.
An appreciation of the works on different aspects of Indian folklore of a few foreign scholars like Long, Crooke, Lewin, Carr, Hunter, and Dalton. Long's role as a proverbologist, Crooke's inspiration for going into the field for harvesting folklore, and Dalton's influence on generations of later scholars in projected ethnological studies are discussed. (AS)
13279. Sur, A.K. "Joie de vivre in the Folklife of Bengal." *FolkloreC* 16:330-33.
Sports, forms of entertainment and amusement such as Kabadi, Baich (boat racing), wrestling, lathi playing, swordsmanship, palagans, Kavigans, Akhrai and hap-Akhrain, Yatra and Putul nautch are discussed. (AKS)

Europe. 13336. Grobman, Neil R. "Adam Ferguson's Influence on Folklore Research:An Analysis of Mythology and the Oral Epic." *SFQ* 38:11-22.
Adam Ferguson commented on "traditionary fables" (oral epics), legends, tales, and mythology in *An Essay on the History of Civil Society*. Central to this work was a 3-stage system of unilinear cultural evolution: savagery, barbarism, and civility. Anticipating the 20th-century fieldwork of Parry and Lord on Homer's oral epic techniques, Tylor on unilinear evolutionism, and Boas on the mythology of preliterate societies, Ferguson focused on oral antiquities for valuable clues to each stage of man's development. (NRG)

South America. 13440. Ziomek, Henryk. "Rómulo Gallegos: Some Observations on Folkloric Elements in His Novels." *REH* 8:23-42.
Rómulo Gallegos drew perennial inspiration for his eight novels written 1920-43 from Venezuelan tradition. Through his pen, the native traditions relating to the Andes, the jungle, and the savanna reveal the very soul of his land. He recorded folk music, folk dancing, unusual customs, beliefs, and folkloric tales, legends, and stories, which had previously been preserved only in religious and communal rites, unrecorded poetry, music, and dance, and in the observance of old customs. Gallegos portrayed his characters through the use of these folkloric elements, and he incorporated into his works such unusual customs and beliefs as those concerning burial procedures and superstitious practices. (HZ)

Theory and Method

General and Miscellaneous. 13462. Prizel, Yuri. "Evolution of a Tale:From Literary to Folk." *SFQ* 38:211-22.
When a tale written by a professional writer is "adopted" by oral tradition, its structure and general make-up should change. One such transformation of a tale written by Pushkin is studied, and it is shown how it conformed to the rules of oral tradition. (YP)
13468. Utley, Francis L.(✠). "The Migration of Folktales: Four Channels to the Americas." *CAnth* 15:5-27.
Draws together some of the evidences of borrowing in folktales from the Old World to the New. Abstracts in four channels, from Europe across the North Atlantic, from Africa across the South Atlantic, from Northeast Asia via the Bering Strait, and from Southeast Asia across the South Pacific. Considering both pre- and post-Columbian borrowing, calls on both physical and cultural anthropology as witnesses to the route and relates this testimony to the recorded folktales in the Western Hemisphere. (FLU)

II. PROSE NARRATIVES

Myths and Legends

† *Festschriften* and Other Analyzed Collections are listed in the first division of this volume. "F" numbers in brackets following a title refer to these items.

Africa. 13571. Trieber, J. Marshall. "Creation:An African Yoruba Myth." *CLAJ* 18:114-18.
Presented is an adaptation of the Yoruba creation myth into

narrative form as the traditional tribal drummer and story-teller might recount it. After a conventionalized historical praise of the early Yoruba rulers and those who came before them back to the Nok, Trieber relates how Olodumare, chief of the Yoruba deities, ordered his lieutenant, Orisha-Nla, to scatter earth over the watery waste that then existed in the world and thus provide a place for man to dwell. (JMT)

North America. 13690. Holloman, William E. "The Ice-Cold Hand." *NCarF* 22:3-8.
The author's grandmother tells him an old tale in which a man deserts his fiancee, who dies soon after. One night, he passes the cemetery and meets her ghost. The ghost's touch makes him fatally ill. Later, the dead girl's image appears on his tombstone. A second version comes from someone still living near the same cemetery, and a third, collected 50 years earlier, appears in another collection. A comparison of dates and information from tombstones makes a relation between two people having the right names very improbable, but not entirely impossible. (WEH)
13699. Reid, John T. "Folkloric Symbols of Nationhood in Guatemala." *SFQ* 38:135-53.
Most of Guatemala's national symbols derive from the Maya-Quiché historical and legendary background of the Republic. Their extraordinary importance in creating a feeling of national identity is one aspect of the national emphasis on the pre-Columbian heritage. Particularly powerful symbols are discussed. The national symbology has been closely related to Guatemalan literature. (JTR)

Folktales

Africa. 13753. MacGaffey, Wyatt. "The Black Loincloth and the Son of Nzambi Mpungu." *RAL* 5:23-30. [Comp. analysis of Dadié's story and a Kongo dilemma tale.]
Two stories, one a recent literary work from the Ivory Coast and one a Kongo folktale of the turn of the century, are seen to have a common structure. They presume similar cosmologies, and their symbolic contents lend themselves in large measure to a common and consistent interpretation derived from Kongo rules. The comparison enhances the interest of both stories. (WM)

Asia. 13765. Agnihotri, Malti. "Why Prawn Has No Proper Lips:A Mizo Folktale." *FolkloreC* 16:276-77.
Mizos are inhabitants of the Assam area and now have their own State within India. This Mizo tale relates how a prawn cheated the villagers and escaped safely. (MA)
13770. Goswami, Praphulladatta. "Burmese Law Tales." *FolkloreC* 16:274-75,277.
Discusses a tale that has some amount of legal validity and which can be used by an advocate at a court of law. The tale narrates how the three claimants for a husband were judged in favor of one who protected him and how this decision was accepted by all. (PG)
13771. Gubler, Greg. "Kitsune:The Remarkable Japanese Fox." *SFQ* 38:121-34.
During the Meiji Era (1868-1912) in Japan, fox superstitions flourished in spite of the influx of modern technology and progressive ideas. Unusual twists to the superstition accompanied many of these developments. The types of foxes and their characteristics illustrate the remarkable nature of the Japanese fox and its exceptional powers, at least according to native perceptions of the period. By examining cultural studies of the era by Kunio Yanagida, the memoirs of Japanese diplomat Naotake Sato, and the observations of contemporaries, the claims of many Japanese for the uniqueness of the *kitsune* or so-called "Japanese fox" are outlined. (GG)

Europe. 13826. O'Shea, Edward. "Yeats's Revisions in *Fairy and Folk Tales*." *SFQ* 38:223-32.
In *Fairy and Folk Tales of the Irish Peasantry* Yeats has revised many of the folktales to make them conform to a principle of "generic integrity." The tales of William Carleton, T. Crofton Croker, and Samuel Lover, as Yeats found them, often violated this principle, therefore he removed the rationaliztions through selective editing. The result in one case is an entirely new version

of a tale by Samuel Lover. (EJO'S)

North America. 13853. Figh, Margaret G., and Margaret B. Kirkpatrick. "The Development of an Alabama Folktale." *SFQ* 38:109-20.
The 19th-century tale of the hole that will not stay filled reflects the emotional climate of the Reconstruction Period in southeast Alabama. Narratives analyzed in this article show the development of a legend growing out of folk interpretation of a natural phenomenon which has been accepted by many people as having supernatural significance. Variants have retained the dominant motif of a hole that remains empty as a constant reminder by a higher power of the guilt resulting from the hanging of an innocent man. All variants also indicate the universal need for a belief in the ultimate triumph of justice. (MGF & MBK)
13857. Schorer, C.E. "Indian Tales of C.C. Trowbridge:A Story." *SFQ* 38:233-41.
An unpublished manuscript of a 19th-century American Indian legend tells how a boy playing a musical top kills a girl by his indifference; then he finds a twin brother with whom he courts and tantalizes two haughty girls. In the comparative introduction, familiar elements pointed out include the ugly suitor, revenge upon haughty beauties, twin brothers playing pranks, and magic music. The strange elements include the attempt to get a bull frog to roar and the description of the musical top. (CES)
13858. ——— "Indian Tales of C.C. Trowbridge:The Fisherman." *SFQ* 38:63-71.
An unpublished American Indian legend tells how a young man avenges the murder of his aunt. While revenge by a young hero for wrong done to a woman is a familiar theme, unusual assistance is given in this tale by soldiers made from gourd seeds and guards who are wooden manikins. (CES)

Anecdotes, Jokes and Fables

General and Miscellaneous. 13865. Tallman, Richard S. "A Generic Approach to the Practical Joke." *SFQ* 38:259-74.
The practical joke or prank has received only scant attention from folklorists. As a genre, the practical joke is defined as an event which has the potential of becoming a story told about the event. A classification or checklist for the study of the practical joke focuses on the event as traditionally prescribed group and individual behavior. This classification is meant to be applied to the collection and analysis of practical joke stories, for it is not common for the field worker to have the opportunity to observe practical jokes as they happen within the tradition of an esoteric folk group. Three texts of practical joke stories are included and discussed briefly in terms of the suggested classification. (RST)
13866. Welsch, Roger L. "A Note on Practical Jokes." *SFQ* 38:253-57.
The membership of the American Folklore Society, which studies such things as humor and practical jokes, is not itself immune from the practical joke. (RLW)

North America. 13888. Dresser, Norine. " 'The Boys in the Band Is Not Another Musical':Male Homosexuals and Their Folklore." *WF* 33:205-18.
Results of a gay bar folklore study of male homosexuals indicate that negative social pressure keeps the men socially confined while at the same time they are contained from within through the attribution and acceptance of a particular image. This is accomplished by the stereotype depicted in jokes, pronoun switches, use of female names and labels, feminine mannerisms and expressions. Ironically, this kind of folklore which binds the male homosexual to his group becomes the element which serves to perpetuate his separation and non-acceptance by the dominant society. (NSD)
13893. Morrison, Monica. "Wedding Night Pranks in Western New Brunswick." *SFQ* 38:285-97.
Examines the dynamics of the "occasional" practical joke occurring at marriages in the Canadian province of New Brunswick. The two main expressions of the practical joke, the stories and the pranks themselves, are described and their relationship to other areas of custom examined. (MSM)

13896. Posen, I. Sheldon. "Pranks and Practical Jokes at Children's Summer Camps." *SFQ* 38:299-309.
Camp pranks, as examined at several children's summer camps, are categorized according to their content or focus. Practical jokes are examined in light of their function in context—similar pranks function differently, depending in part on the atmosphere in which they are played and the relationship between the parties involved. They can express affection or hostility, solidarity or factions. Camps display different attitudes toward practical joking. The occurrence of the same pranks at various camps is usually attributable to diffusion or common sources. (ISP)

13899. Scott, John R. "Practical Jokes of the Newfoundland Seal Fishery." *SFQ* 38:275-83.
The Newfoundland seal fishery requires certain forms of behavior which allow the men to live compatibly in confined quarters for extended periods of time. Three such diversions used by the Newfoundland sealers are play, song and story sessions, and practical jokes. The major discussion, on pranks, demonstrates the ways in which they provide diversion as well as enforce social controls without a need for direct confrontation between individuals. (JRS)

III. GNOMIC FOLKLORE

Proverbs and Sayings

Asia. 13926. Dua, Hans Raj. "Ethnography of Proverbs and Folk-lore." *FolkloreC* 16:300-13.
Treats proverbs in terms of categories of the sociocultural system. Many issues are raised with regard to the particular and universal properties of form and content of proverbs and the relationship between language, social reality, and cultural diffusion. Proverbs are also considered from the point of view of their functions within the theory of speech and speech behavior. (HRD)

13929. Niyogi, Tushar Kanti. "A Study of Tripuri Proverbs." *FolkloreC* 16:19-24.
Provides 35 Tripuri proverbs with their English parallels. Cultural diffusion may pin-point the polygenesis of these proverbs. Proverbs highlight sociocultural aspects, religious beliefs, and customs and express general truth. Tripuri is a language of the old inhabitants of Tripura State of India which is a border-state of West Bengal, Assam, and Bangla Desh. (TKN)

Europe. 13936. Brandes, Stanley H. "The Selection Process in Proverb Use:A Spanish Example." *SFQ* 38:167-86.
Folklorists have generally ignored the analysis of proverb use by single individuals. We utter only a portion of the proverb repertory found in our society. We are unaware of the total roster of available sayings and consciously and unconsciously screen the proverbs we do know in conformity with our particular life circumstances. This dual selection process is reflected in the unique ways that an old widow from the Castilian countryside uses proverbs from her village. (SHB)

North America. 13970. Hilliard, Addie S. "Shakespearean Proverbs in Chester County, Tennessee." *NCarF* 22:63-74.
The speech of the people of Chester County, Tennessee still contains proverbs and proverbial phrases very similar to those used by Shakespeare in his plays and poems. The early settlers, who were from North Carolina, came primarily from England. They had a number of common ties which bound them together: many accepted customs, their general philosophy of life, and their common language. Chester County, generally considered a rural area, has retained numerous folk expressions which are Elizabethan. (ASH)

13972. Mieder, Wolfgang. "The Proverb and Anglo-American Literature." *SFQ* 38:49-62.
Folklorists as well as literary critics have occupied themselves with the study of proverbs in literature. Such investigations require a meaningful methodology. A mere list of verified proverbs from an author's works does not suffice. A literary proverb study must also include an explanatory essay concerning the various functions of the proverbs in the text. Only the combination of such an essay with an alphabetically arranged proverb index will render worthwhile results. Because methodological rigidity has been lacking, the 144 items included in the bibliographical part of this study are of a highly varied quality. (WM)

Riddles

Europe. 13979. Fisher, Lynn V. "Esenin's Literary Reworking of the Riddle." *SEEJ* 18:20-30.
Folklore and the riddle play an important role in Sergei Esenin's poetry. His poetry has so far been studied in regard to actual use of folklore material, but the poet does not merely borrow from already existing material. He transforms the metaphor of riddle into simile and builds on his own imagery, changing the original riddle into an integral part of his lyric poetry. The majority of Esenin's images based on riddles deal with natural phenomena and a large number of them are concerned with the sun and moon. (LVF)

North America. 13986. Moore, Danny W. "The Deductive Riddle:An Adaptation to Modern Society." *NCarF* 22:119-25.
In order to survive in a complex society, a simple entertainment form, such as the riddle, must bend to that society's needs. While common riddles are regarded as children's amusement by most Americans, the deductive riddle, a brief mystery story, enjoys wide popularity among grownups, particularly college students. These puzzles spring from the murder mystery and spy thriller tradition. (DM)

Names

South America. 14015. Ramos, Alcida R. "How the Sanumá Acquire Their Names." *Ethnology* 13:171-85.
Sanumá name-giving is examined, exposing key features in the social structure. Personal names are described in terms of the domains from which they are derived and of the social aspects entailed in the practice of name-giving. In order to insure a coherent presentation of the data, the names under consideration have been divided into two groups: (1) names selected through a ritualized series of social actions that follow the birth of a new member, involving the killing of an animal in a ritual hunt and (2) names given by a number of alternative naming techniques that involve no special observances—these represent the majority of personal names on record. (LLBA)

Others

North America. 14020. Dundes, Alan. "The Henny-Penny Phenomenon:A Study of Folk Phonological Esthetics in American Speech." *SFQ* 38:1-9.
An examination of rhymed reduplicatives in English reveals definite patterning with respect to the pairs of initial consonants. Common pairs include /h/:/p/ and /h/:/d/ as in hocus pocus and humdrum. The apparent penchant for such pairs is reflected in names found in folktales and nursery rhymes. Thus Henny-Penny or Humpty-Dumpty may be said to indicate a folk esthetic judgment or phonological preference. This preference or Henny-Penny phenomenon may explain why certain idioms are borrowed (e.g., hoi polloi) or come into being in the first place (e.g., hot pants). (AD)

IV. FOLK POETRY

General

General and Miscellaneous. 14029. Rowland, Beryl. "The Oven in Popular Metaphor from Hosea to the Present Day." *AS* 45(1970; pub. 1974):215-22.
The oven is a natural metaphor for the womb; it is a figure which has its origins deep in the human psyche and in the culture of primitive communities. Many psychologists have observed that cooking is frequently equated with the process of pregnancy and birth and that the womb is the stove in which the child is baked. Whether *oven* as an isolated term for the womb has had a *sub rosa* existence is hard to determine. It certainly continued into this century in the phrase "bun in the oven." But this expression is now on its way out and the reason for its decline is not far to seek—it has not the emotional response of a taboo four-letter word. Pregnancy has become too respectable and commonplace to require metaphorical expression. (LLBA)

Oral Epics

Europe. 14094. Miletich, John S. "Narrative Style in Spanish and Slavic Traditional Narrative Poetry: Implications for the Study of the Romance Epic." *Olifant* 2,ii:109-28.
Examination of six types of closely occurring repetitions within traditional narrative poetry with a view to determining their total effect on the narrative style of the individual poem and of the genre in general. The study is based on a detailed analysis of 82 poems totaling 4,108 lines in Spanish, Serbo-Croatian, and Russian. Four different sub-genres are represented: the peninsular Spanish *romance* of the 16th century and the Judeo-Spanish *romance* of Morocco, the South Slavic *bugarštica*, the South Slavic *junački deseterac* or heroic decasyllable, and the Russian *bylina*. The six repetitive types can be divided into two principle categories, the "elaborate," which delays the narrative pace, and the "essential," which accelerates the flow of information. The narrative style of the four sub-genres are fundamentally "essential" but there is present a considerably pronounced retarding tendency, which results from the fairly high frequency of "elaborate" type repetitions. (JSM)

Ballads

Asia. 14123. Frankel, Hans H. "The Chinese Ballad 'Southeast Fly the Peacocks'." *HJAS* 34:248-71.
This anonymous *yüeh-fu* (ballad) tells in 355 lines the story of a young couple driven to double suicide by their elders. It must have been composed around the mid-third century A.D. The mode of presentation is divided between dialogue and objective narration. At three points the objective narrative briefly shifts to monologue. Such shifts occur when the ballad singer gives up his detached stance and impersonates the protagonist. This is one of the marks of the orally transmitted *yüeh-fu* genre. Other marks are formulaic language, stock characters, and typical uses of sounds and symbols from the natural environment. (HHF)

14124. Mahapatra, S. "Similes and Metaphors in Oriya Folk Ballads." *FolkloreC* 16:315-29.
A study of the similes and metaphors in Oriya folk-ballads collected in "Palligiti Sanchyan" by K.B. Das and in "Utkal Gaunli Gita" by C. Mahapatra. In addition to an introductory note, a selective list of similes and metaphors arranged according to their comparatum is provided. Most of the similes and metaphors appear to be artificial and are mere ornaments, yet they reflect typical Orissan nature, life, and culture and indicate the potentiality of the ancient Oriya language as a rich medium of expression. (SM)

Europe. 14128. Buchan, David. "Jamieson's Ballad Collecting: New Letters." *Bibliotheck* 7:16-20.
The National Library of Scotland has a letter, dated 25 December 1800, from Robert Jamieson to Robert Eden Scott. In it he describes his first meeting with Anna Brown, the ballad-singer whose repertoire was drawn on by Jamieson for his *Popular Ballads and Songs* (1806) and by Walter Scott for his *Minstrelsy of the Scottish Border* (1802 et. seq.); Jamieson mentions spending two days with Walter Scott and their coming to an editorial agreement; and he refers to his having received material from Percy's Folio MS. The Library also has a copy of a letter, dated 20 January 1802, from Jamieson to William Owen, a Welsh antiquary, which shows his interest in the social context of folksong. Printed here are the first letter in full, and an excerpt from the second, together with a brief commentary and notes. (DB)

14149. Reppert, James. "F.J. Child and the Ballad." [F 49]:197-212.
Child made a constant appeal to the original form of the ballad as a reference for merit. Itself an antique, the ballad has a traceable past; the plot line must be economical, reasonable, and logical; inconsistency is a mark of corruption. For Child, probability was a legitimization of taste. Frequently, often humorously, his criteria included an examination of motives for action in the ballad story. Ancient texts, as he called them, were best when drawn from material whose popular origin he could verify in foreign analogues. Child is here at his best. Difficulties appear in certain confusions and contradictions about ballad transmission as opposed to his statements concerning "declension in the rank and style of the characters." (JDR)

North America. 14166. Hawes, Bess L. "El Corrido de la Inundación de la Presa de San Francisquito: The Story of a Local Ballad." *WF* 33:219-30.
The known historical facts of the St. Francis Dam break of 1928 in the Santa Clara Valley of southern California provide only background to the individual perspective of the ballad-composer, a local Chicano farmer, who wrote his account of the disaster in the form of a *corrido*, a Spanish ballad form. The words and music of his *corrido* show close adherence to the compositional rules governing this song form and demonstrate the crucial importance of traditional models to the folk composer. However, this same quality of formalism also demonstrates that the primary function of the topical song in a rural or traditional community is to commemorate an event of significance. (BLH)

14167. Klymasz, Robert B., and James Porter. "Traditional Ukrainian Balladry in Canada." *WF* 33:89-132.
The Ukrainian folk ballad survives today as the most popular narrative folksong genre among Canadians of Ukrainian origin. A representative selection of eleven ballad items recorded in the field in the early 1960s are given in full and show that the Ukrainian-Canadian ballad corpus is largely conservative in form and content. The primary, overt function of the genre in its Canadian setting continues to be one of a vehicle for the transmission of a code of behavior. At the same time, the corpus also reflects moments of disenchantment, frustration, and dissatisfaction with these institutionalized patterns of conduct. As in the past, a stock of traditional musico-poetic techniques and devices is used to convey a wide variety of emotions and responses. (RBK)

Songs

Asia. 14199. Raha, Manis Kumar and Sunil Paul. "Deha-Tawa: Songs of the Baistom-Baudiyas of North Bengal." *FolkloreC* 14(1973):106-16.
A study of the songs of the Baistom-Baundiya sect who come from the ordinary peasant class of people. The songs are given in Bengali along with their English translations. (MKR & SP)

Europe. 14281. Rank, Inkeri. "The 'Song of Tapani' in Finnish Christmas Celebration." *WF* 33:133-57.
The ballad of Tapani (St. Stephen) was performed (Dec. 26) by a straw man (Tapani himself), a he-goat, a bear, and a crane in a procession. The date connected the legend of St. Stephen with the Nativity, King Herod, and related motifs. From St. Stephen as a kitchen boy in the English ballad arose the Scandinavian stable hand, reflecting ancient Norse Yuletide equine ceremonies. The

theme reached Finland in the 15th century or earlier. It was recreated and adapted to the Finnish oral tradition of rune-singing. Herod (Ruotus) is a typical Finnish farmer and Tapani his farm hand. To the portent of a speaking cock, the Finnish version added a bellowing bull and a budding sheath-knife handle. The ancient festival (early November) of Kekri, a deity of cattle and fertility, supplied the procession. Thus a pagan fertility ritual was incorporated into a Christian pageant. (IAR)

14289. Smith, G. S. "Modern Russian Underground Song: An Introductory Survey." *JRS* 28:3-12.
The underground song is currently one of the most vital and genuinely popular genres of Russian poetry. The incursion of the private tape recorder has meant that during the last 15 years underground songs have been preserved and circulated in the author's performance. The repertoire consists of narrative ballads of everyday life and personal lyrics; there are thematic and stylistic influences from gypsy song, criminal song, and some Western European traditions like the German cabaret song. The genre is dominated by Bulat Okudzhava, Vladimir Vysotsky, and Alexander Galich. (GSS)

North America. 14314. Abrams, W. Amos. "Horton Barker: Folk Singer Supreme." *NCarF* 22:141-53.
This brief biography and appraisal of a well-known folk singer, John Horton Barker, Chilhowie, Virginia, is the fifth in a series of essays prepared especially for *NCarF* by Abrams. Abrams reports on his past experiences and relations with those singers who serve as his subjects. He also reprints the songs they sang. Horton Barker, a blind balladeer, beloved by all who knew him, a debonair bachelor, sang for Eleanor Roosevelt at the White Top Mountain Folk Festival, the University of Chicago Folk Festival, and the Newport Festival. He also appeared on programs with the better-known singers of the past quarter of a century. (WAA)

14342. Hulan, Richard. "John Adam Granade: The 'Wild Man' of Goose Creek." *WF* 33:77-87. [Hymn composer.]
The first years of the 19th century saw a uniquely American vehicle of religious expression arise in the form of the camp-meeting. This new context for worship called for a new hymnody. Of the known authors of camp-meeting hymns, none was more influential than the Methodist evangelist John Adam Granade. Born in North Carolina about 1763, Granade moved to Tennessee in 1797. His conversion during one of the first camp-meetings was followed by a meteoric career of less than five years as a circuit preacher in Tennessee and Kentucky. In 1804 he published his *Pilgrim's Songster* (Lexington: Daniel Bradford). Of the thirty-one hymns we may confidently state were in that collection, twenty-four were used in popular camp-meeting songsters over the next forty years. A few may yet be heard in such conservative environments as *Sacred Harp* singing conventions and Primitive Baptist worship. (RHH)

Rhymes and Verses

Africa. 14400. Ọlajubu, Oludare. "Iwì Egúngún Chants—An Introduction." *RAL* 5:31-51.
Iwì Egúngún is a genre of the oral poetry of the Oyo Yoruba. It is chanted exclusively by members of the Egúngún (masquerade) cult during Egúngún performances. The Egúngún cult, an essentially male cult, is concerned with ancestor worship. The ancestors are believed to visit the people every year in the form of masqueraders to bless and entertain. Iwì is chanted by special types of masqueraders and by talented members of the cult in a special tone of voice. Iwì resembles Ìjálá and Rárà, two other genres of Oyo Yoruba poetry, because they draw from a common source of oral tradition for their composition. Iwì is, however, distinct from the two. Ìjálá sings the praise of Ogun (the god of iron) and its devotees—farmers, hunters, blacksmiths. It also sings of animal and plant life and the exploits of hunters in the bush. Rárà sings the praise of individual persons with the sole aim of attracting gifts. Iwì does not sing of any particular god, nor is it concerned with animal and plant life. It is not directed at single individuals with the sole aim of attracting gifts. It is in praise of man in general, man living and dead, man in society. (OOOO)

North America. 14417. Haviland, Virginia. "Who Killed Cock Robin? Depositions in the Collections of the Library of Congress." *QJLC* 30(1973):95-139.
In the history of traditional nursery rhymes—a substantial area for study in children's literature—one of the best known sequences of rhymes that has come down to us via oral tellings and in printed form is the truly "doleful" tale about the death of Cock Robin and sequel written-to-order verses which invented his earlier marriage to Jenny Wren. In a tracing of their history, the earliest recording of the death is noted to have been about 1744 and the "marriage" in 1806. Editions selected for illustration from the Library's large holdings of this nursery lore begin with the only known copy of a Boston edition, 1780, of *Cock Robin's Death and Burial*, which came to the Library as part of Frank J. Hogan's substantial gift of 86 rare children's books. Succeeding editions illustrated include an elaborated, larger chapbook edition of Boston, 1798, *The Death and Burial of Cock Robin; with the Tragical Death of A, Apple-Pie: The Whole Taken from the Original Manuscript, in the Possession of Master Meanwell*. Further editions illustrated show changes in printing, illustrative interpretation, language, content, and even point of view, developed as the verses were transmitted through the decades and across the Atlantic. (VH)

14418. Kloe, Donald R. "Buddy Quow: An Anonymous Poem in Gullah-Jamaican Dialect Written Circa 1800." *SFQ* 38:81-90.
Buddy Quow is a poem I.A. Beckles presented to General William Augustus Bowles. W.W. Pierson of the University of North Carolina photographed the poem and its translation in the 1920s while examining public documents in Spain. The photo-copy has been in the North Carolina Department of Archives and History where it was recently found. As Bowles became a general in 1789 and died in 1805 the poem has been given the date of c. 1800. By analysis of the poem it has been proven that the proper names used have their roots in the West African Tshi language. Additional study has shown that the language of the poem is Gullah, the language of the black slaves who lived along the South Carolina to Florida coast. (DRK)

V. FOLK GAMES AND TOYS

Children

General and Miscellaneous. 14428. Emrich, Duncan. "Children's Folklore in the Archive of Folk Song." *QJLC* 30(1973): 140-51.
The Archive of Folk Song, established in 1928 at the Library of Congress, contains a large collection for the study of children's folklore. Many noted scholars in the field have added to its holdings of field recordings and manuscripts and have edited longplaying records for the Library. To indicate the types of children's folklore represented, such genres as games, rhymes, riddles, and songs are illustrated with examples drawn from the archive. (DE)

VI. DRAMATIC FOLKLORE

Festivals and Rituals

Asia. 14503. Chattyopadhyay, Kumarananda. "Glimpse of a Carak Festival in Calcutta." *FolkloreC* 16:161-68.
Carak is a festival which, in spite of the all-pervasive forces of modernization, still finds breathing space in the stuffy, urban

climate. The Carak festival is held every year on the last day of the Bengali year, 30th Choitra (April), all over Bengal. Although the festival is popular in rural areas, it is on the wane in the cities. A description of a Carak festival which took place several years ago in Calcutta is used to point out the differences between rural and urban Carak festivals. (KC)

VIII. FOLK CUSTOMS, BELIEFS AND SYMBOLISM

General

North America. 14712. Hand, Wayland D. "Folk Beliefs and Customs of the American Theater:A Survey." *SFQ* 38:23-48.
The theater has its own unique body of beliefs, customs, and traditions, referred to as the Folklore of the Theater. This lore involves the actors themselves and all their activities, the theatrical premises, stage, properties, costumes, etc. Important in the creation and transmission of this occupational folklore are the relationships between the director, the actors, the stagehands, and many other backstage people and mascots, on the one hand, and the producers, management, and box-office people on the other. (WDH)

Medical Beliefs and Practices

Europe. 14738. Hultin, Neil. "Some Aspects of Eighteenth-Century Folk Medicine." *SFQ* 38:199-209.
William Buchan's *Domestic Medicine* (1769) discusses a number of traditional medical practices ranging from herbal and surgical to magical. Acutely aware of the limitations of scientific medicine, Buchan observed the "country people" for what he could learn from their practices. He was also aware of the psychological value of folk remedies and was conscious of the superstitions that account for many of the cures. (NCH)

North America. 14749. Betts, Leonidas J. "Folk Medicine in Harnett County." *NCarF* 22:84-94.
Assimilation of information gathered from three informants representing three socioeconomic levels—middle-class white, lower-class white, lower-class black—in a large rural community in North Carolina. There is little significant difference in the folk-medicine repertory of the informants. Further, patent medicines and increased medical services seem to be extinguishing folk cures. An appendix contains cures from each informant, cross-referenced with *Brown*. (LJB)

Religious Beliefs and Symbols

Bibliography and Discography. 14766. Yoder, Don. "Introductory Bibliography on Folk Religion." *WF* 33:16-34.
This bibliography, which accompanies "Toward a Definition of Folk Religion" (*WF*, 33, 1974, 2-15), lists 269 items in folk religion and folk belief. The list is alphabetized, with a topical author index covering: (1) basic approaches to religion, theory of folk religion, and definition of "folk religion"; (2) "superstition" and its definitions; (3) historical perspectives on folk religion in its stages of development; (4) folk religion in the present; (5) folk religion in a Catholic setting; (6) folk religion in a Protestant setting; (7) folk religion in Europe; (8) folk religion in the Americas; (9) folk religion in Asia; and (10) religious festivals and festivity in general. (DY)

General and Miscellaneous. 14771. Yoder, Don. "Toward a Definition of Folk Religion." *WF* 33:2-15.
"Folk religion," defined as the totality of those views and practices of religion that exist among the people of a complex society apart from and alongside the strictly theological and liturgical forms of the official religion, is a term used by scholars since the 1930s in American scholarship. German terminology (*Volksreligion, religiöse Volkskunde, Volksreligiösität, Volksfrömmigkeit*) appears to have been the precedent for the English

usage. Most influential of these terms is *religiöse Volkskunde*, coined in 1901, defined as the religious dimension of folk-culture, or the folk-cultural dimension of religion, It has been used widely in Europe where the discipline of *Volkskunde* has included not only verbal aspects of a culture but the entire range of social, spiritual, and material culture as well. In Anglo-American scholarship the term "folk religion" appears to have developed out of the work of anthropologists analyzing the mixture of cultures in Latin America. (DY)

Asia. 14827. Sur, A.K. "Religion in the Folk Life of Bengal." *FolkloreC* 16:197-212.
Hinduism is not merely a religion but a way of life. The *vratas* (vows) and *parvans* (festivals) are treated in detail with narration of associated legends. Special treatment is made of various feminine vratas (vows) and popular festivals. (AKS)
14828. —— "The Web of Religion in Bengal." *FolkloreC* 16:169-78.
Describes how religions such as Jainism, Ajivikism, Buddhism, and Brahmanism were superimposed on the bedrock of non-Aryan religion. Certain cults of folk origin such as those of Sitala, Sasthi, Basuli, Manasa, Chandi, etc., Gajan festivals of Siva and Dharma, the emergence of neo-Vaishnavism, the cults of the Bauls and the Kartabahajas, and the elements of synthesis in the religious culture of Bengal are discussed. (AKS)

Europe. 14867. Vīķis-Freibergs, Vaira, and Stephen Reynolds. "A Recent Study in Latvian Mythology." *JBalS* 5,iii:226-36. [Rev. art. on Haralds Biezais' *Die himmlische Götterfamilie der alten Letten*.]
Die himmlische Götterfamilie der alten Letten by Haralds Biezais discusses the sky-gods of Latvian folklore with Latvian folksongs or dainas as source material. Mythological personifications of the Morning Star, Thunder, the Moon, the Sun, Sun's daughters, and God's sons are members of an extended family of gods. The characteristics and activities of these deities are described and are essentially those of individuals in a peasant society. The criteria for Godhead are nowhere unambiguously defined and some defining characteristics fail to carry conviction. Consequently the attribution of divine status to some of the mythological figures can be questioned. (VVF)

North America. 14876. Gizelis, Gregory. "The Function of the Vision in Greek-American Culture." *WF* 33:65-76.
Religious visions are not only of private and accidental nature as folklorists and anthropologists have assumed, but they are also recurrent cultural phenomena. Visions of religious content are induced by austerities, frantic dancing, religious doctrines, and others' narratives of visions. In many small groups of the Greek community of Philadelphia the narratives of fellow-members of their society are the main source of inducement of religious visions. These visions serve the function of identification of the visionary with God and a small group. They also deem to be divine responses to human appeal for communion with God. Each particular version of the same vision serves the function of the visionary's identification with a specific small group. (GG)

Magic and Superstition

Asia. 14908. Bhowmick, P.K. "Functioning Secret Institutions." *FolkloreC* 16:41-61.
Deals with functioning secret institutions in West Bengal that are

connected with soothsaying and medicine men. Through this institution the common people tackle the supposedly invisible enemies causing trouble in their material life and try to overcome their difficulties. Discusses how the crystallized beliefs and elements of rituals connected with this type of institution constitute a functioning system, and how individuals are integrated with the system. (PKB)

14913. Gupta, Sankar Sen. "Talismans, Magic and Folk-Remedies." *FolkloreC* 16:233-66.
Deals with folk medicines and superstitions. The unreasoning awe with which the unscientific mind of early civilization looked upon birth, accident, and other mysteries of nature is discussed. If a living mind can influence and control another mind by suggestion, then a kind of telepathic, hypnotizing and controlling influence emanating from the spirit world may exist. (SS)

14917. Sur, A.K. "Magic and Shamanism in the Folk Life of Bengal." *FolkloreC* 16:267-73.
The beliefs and practices in Bengal concerning magic are an inheritance from prehistoric times. These beliefs and practices were early absorbed by Tantricism. Tantric incantations in connection with winning love of others, causing hatred and enmity between two persons, doing harm and evil to others, causing one's death, and extracting the venom of snake and dog bites are quoted. (AKS)

Customs

Asia. 14991. Sur, A.K. "Astrology in Folk Life in Bengal." *FolkloreC* 16:1-18.
The influence of astrology on the life of the people of Bengal is discussed with special reference to the choice of bride and bridegroom, marriage and post-nuptial, and post-foetal ceremonies. Elements of Hindu astrology are explained. (AKS)

14992. —— "Social Mores in the Folk Life of Bengal." *FolkloreC* 16:121-35.
The influence of the Austric and Dravidian speaking peoples on the socioeconomic life of Bengal is stressed. Penetration of Aryan culture into Bengal and development of the caste system are discussed. Social mores of the people of Bengal clustering around events in the life of a man or woman, from birth to marriage and death are discussed. Certain social ceremonies exclusive to Bengal are explored. (AKS)

Europe. 15043. Oinas, Felix J. "The Position of the Setus in Estonian Folklore." *JBalS* 5,i:18-25.
The folklore of the Setus, Orthodox inhabitants of southeastern Estonia (Setumaa), is similar to the folklore of the Ingrians and the Votes near Leningrad. The similarities appear in numerous epic and other songs and have been attributed to the relic status of Setu folklore, parallel development, etc. The reason for the close tradition between these groups is the direct connection that was maintained formerly by Lake Peipus and by land. Religious pilgrimages to Petseri monastery in Setumaa also contributed to the exchange of folklore. (FJO)

North America. 15080. Mathias, Elizabeth. "The Italian-American Funeral:Persistence through Change." *WF* 33:35-50.
One of the notable features of the South Philadelphia Italian-American community is the persistence of a southern Italian village funeral pattern. The village system of behavior surrounding death and burial has endured through the Italians' immigration from the agriculturally centered settlements of southern Italy to the urban community of Philadelphia, and the forms of the funeral have persisted for more than 100 years. The most striking characteristic of the funeral pattern, however, is that the pattern is borrowed. It is not the peasants' own traditional pattern which the immigrants chose to follow; instead the pattern is modeled after the system of the village *Signori*, the landowners for whom the peasants labored. In the southern Italian village the emphasis of the rituals surrounding the funeral had been on passage of the soul of the deceased; in America, the focus of inspiration shifted gradually away from avoidance of the soul's return toward the display of the body of the deceased. (EM)

South America. 15082. Dumont, Jean-Paul. "L'alliance substituée:La communication entre Créoles vénézuéliens et Indiens Panare." *Homme* 14,i:43-56. [Sum. in Eng.]
The system of communication established between the Panare Indians and the Creole peasants of Venezuelan Guiana is made up of the combination of three structures of exchange: linguistic, economic, and social. The Panare Indians and the Creoles indeed exchange messages, goods, and services, but no spouse is exchanged between the two societies. However, a social exchange is performed through the institution of *compadrazgo* which represents the exact reversal of marriage and ultimately serves the same structural function in the system. (LLBA)

IX. MATERIAL CULTURE

Folk Arts

General and Miscellaneous. 15170. Lange, Yvonne. "Lithography, an Agent of Technological Change in Religious Folk Art:A Thesis." *WF* 33:51-64.
Invented in Germany in 1798, lithography was a widely used process for the production of devotional prints by the early 1830s. Until then, single leaf woodcuts of Catholic saints that lacked perspective were the prototypes for flat painted religious panels called *retablos* in the southwest United States where figures in the round, known as *bultos*, also occur. With the advent of the cheap lithograph, a prototype that is conventionally termed two-dimensional but that optically shows three-dimensional forms in space, the *santero* (carver or painter of religious images) was unable to translate his vision into the traditional two-dimensional *retablo*. His solution was to carve the model. By the third quarter of the 19th century, *retablo* painting had given way completely to figures in the round. (YML)

North America. 15250. Welsch, Roger L. "Bigger'n Life:The Tall-Tale Postcard." *SFQ* 38:311-23.
The tall-tale postcard, which was popular in the United States 1905-15, is analogous but apparently unrelated to the oral tall tale. While such cards, featuring photographic juxtaposition, were produced and were popular throughout the country, they were primarily a prairie-plains phenomenon. (RLW)

Craft and Technology

Asia. 15271. Sur, A.K. "Technology in the Folk Life of Bengal." *FolkloreC* 16:65-76,91-98.
Technological achievement of the people of Bengal before the advent of Western influence is studied with special reference to agricultural practices and industries connected with oil crushing, sugar manufacturing, cotton spinning and weaving, silk rearing, iron smelting, steel making, and manufacture of conchshell products. (AKS)

Subject Index

1974 MLA ABSTRACTS
of Articles in
Scholarly Journals

Volume II

French, Italian, Spanish, Portuguese and Brazilian,
German, Scandinavian, Modern Greek, Oriental,
African, and East European Literatures

Compiled by

WALTER S. ACHTERT AND EILEEN M. MACKESY
*with the assistance of those whose
names appear in the staff list*

Published by

THE MODERN LANGUAGE ASSOCIATION OF AMERICA

1976

This is Volume II of three volumes of the 1974 *MLA Abstracts*. The three volumes are collected in a cumulative edition for libraries.

The *MLA Abstracts* is partially supported by a grant from the National Endowment for the Humanities.

1974 MLA ABSTRACTS

MLA Abstracts is a three volume annual following the arrangement of the MLA *International Bibliography*. This is Volume Two of the set, and includes sections on European, Asian, African, and Latin-American literatures. Volume One contains sections on General, English, American, Medieval and Neo-Latin, Celtic literatures, and Folklore; and Volume Three is devoted to linguistics. All three volumes are available separately to MLA members, or together in a bound "Library Edition."

The 1974 *MLA Abstracts* provides a classified, indexed collection of abstracts of journal articles on the modern languages and literatures to be used in conjunction with the 1974 *MLA International Bibliography*. All items for which abstracts appear in this volume are indicated by an asterisk preceding the item number in the appropriate volume of the 1974 *Bibliography*. Journals from which abstracts appear in this volume are preceded by an asterisk in the Master List of Journal Acronyms in the *Bibliography*.

The *MLA Abstracts* is intended to supplement the author, title listings in the annual *Bibliography* and thus provide for the scholar and student additional access to current scholarship. It is thought that a scholar beginning research on an author or topic will turn first to the appropriate sections of the *Bibliography* to obtain lists of all the items of possible relevance. Then the researcher may turn to the abstracts collections to learn more about the articles included there. The *MLA Abstracts* includes a subject index in which articles are indexed according to approaches, themes, genres, and special techniques. The index is intended primarily as a means of manual access into the collections. These terms will later be used in automatic retrieval of the abstracts data.

The abstracts have been set from tapes and will eventually be available for indexing and automatic retrieval. Spellings have been regularized within the body of the abstracts, but not in the titles of the articles.

Entry form follows that used by the *MLA International Bibliography*. Arabic numbers have replaced roman to denote the volume number of a journal. Undated items are understood to have been published in 1974. When an issue number of a journal is required for a given entry, it appears in lower case roman immediately after the arabic volume number. An arabic number preceded by F in square brackets following an entry title refers to an item listed in the *Festschriften* and Other Analyzed Collections division which begins this volume.

In the main, these abstracts have been prepared by the authors of the original articles, whose initials appear at the end of the abstract. Where an abstract has been prepared by another person, the abstractor's initials appear at the end of the abstract. Through a special arrangement, the MLA exchanges abstracts with *Language and Language Behavior Abstracts*. Abstracts ending with the initials LLBA have been supplied by *LLBA*. These collections could not have appeared without the generous assistance of the editors of the journals listed in the Table of Journal Acronyms and the thousands of authors who have prepared abstracts of their articles.

Staff for the 1974 *MLA Abstracts*

Staff of the *MLA International Bibliography*

TABLE OF CONTENTS
VOLUME II

TABLE OF JOURNAL ACRONYMS

ELT	English Literature in Transition (1880–1920)
ELWIU	Essays in Literature (Western Ill. U.)
Emily Dickinson Bulletin	
EngR	English Record
ESA	English Studies in Africa (Johannesburg)
ESQ	Emerson Society Quarterly
ETC: A Review of General Semantics (LLBA)	
ETJ	Educational Theatre Journal
EWN	Evelyn Waugh Newsletter
Expl	Explicator
FaN	Le Français au Nigeria
FHA	Fitzgerald/Hemingway Annual
FI	Forum Italicum
FLang	Foundations of Language (Dordrecht, Neth.) (LLBA)
FM	Le Français Moderne (LLBA)
FMonde	Le Français dans le Monde (LLBA)
FN	Filologičeskie Nauki (LLBA)
Focus on Robert Graves	
FoLi	Folia Linguistica (LLBA)
FolkloreC	Folklore (Calcutta)
ForumH	Forum (Houston)
FR	French Review
FsD	Fonetică și Dialectologie
FUF	Finnisch-ugrische Forschungen: Zeitschrift für Finnisch-ugrische Sprach- und Volkskunde
GaR	Georgia Review
GAS	German-American Studies
GL	General Linguistics
Glossa: The Journal of Linguistics	
GN	Germanic Notes
GQ	German Quarterly
GR	Germanic Review
GRM	Germanisch-romanische Monatsschrift, Neue Folge
GSlav	Germano-Slavica
GSLI	Giornale Storico della Letteratura Italiana
HAB	Humanities Association Bulletin (Canada)
Hasifrut: Quarterly for the Study of Literature	
HC	Hollins Critic (Hollins Coll., Va.)
HCompL	Hebrew Computational Linguistics
Hermathena: A Dublin University Review	
Hispania (U. of Mass.)	
Historiographia Linguistica	
HJAS	Harvard Journal of Asiatic Studies
HJb	Hebbel-Jahrbuch
HLQ	Huntington Library Quarterly
HR	Hispanic Review
HSE	Hungarian Studies in English (L. Kossuth U., Debrecen)
HSL	Hartford Studies in Literature
HUSL	Hebrew University Studies in Literature
IAN	Isvestija Akademii Nauk S.S.S.R., Serija Literatury i Jazyka (Moscow) (LLBA)
IBLA	Institut des Belles-Lettres Arabes Revue
IEY	Iowa English Bulletin: Yearbook
IF	Indogermanische Forschungen (LLBA)
IFR	International Fiction Review
IIJ	Indo-Iranian Journal (LLBA)
IJAL	International Journal of American Linguistics (LLBA)
IJAS	Indian Journal of American Studies
IncL	Incorporated Linguist (London) (LLBA)
Independent Shavian	
IR	Iliff Review (Denver)
ItalAm	Italian Americana
Italica	
ITL: Review of Applied Linguistics	

JAmS	Journal of American Studies
JAOS	Journal of the American Oriental Society
JArabL	Journal of Arabic Literature
JAS	Journal of the Acoustical Society (LLBA)
JBalS	Journal of Baltic Studies
JDSG	Jahrbuch der Deutschen Schiller-Gesellschaft
JEGP	Journal of English and Germanic Philology
JEngL	Journal of English Linguistics
JGa	Juanā Gaita (Hamilton, Ont.)
JGE	Journal of General Education
JHI	Journal of the History of Ideas
JIES	Journal of Indo-European Studies
JISHS	Journal of the Illinois State Historical Society
JML	Journal of Modern Literature
JNES	Journal of Near Eastern Studies (Chicago)
JNT	Journal of Narrative Technique
Journal of Ethnic Studies	
Journal of the International Phonetic Association	
JPS	Journal of the Polynesian Society (Auckland) (LLBA)
JQ	Journalism Quarterly
JRS	Journal of Russian Studies [Formerly *ATRJ*]
JSHD	Journal of Speech and Hearing Disorders (LLBA)
JSHR	Journal of Speech and Hearing Research (LLBA)
JSSTC	Journal of Spanish Studies: Twentieth Century
JWGV	Jahrbuch des Wiener Goethe-Vereins
KanQ	Kansas Quarterly [Formerly *KM*]
KFQ	Keystone Folklore Quarterly
Kivung: Journal of the Ling. Soc. of the U. of Papua and New Guinea (LLBA)	
KSJ	Keats-Shelley Journal
L&S	Language and Speech
Langages (Paris) (LLBA)	
Lang&S	Language and Style
LangS	Language Sciences
Language	
LanM	Les Langues Modernes
LATR	Latin American Theater Review
LB	Leuvense Bijdragen (LLBA)
LBib	Linguistica Biblica: Interdisziplinäre Zeitschrift für Theologie und Linguistik
LBR	Luso-Brazilian Review
LC	Library Chronicle (U. of Penn.)
LCUT	Library Chronicle of the University of Texas
LE&W	Literature East and West
LeS	Lingua e Stile (Bologna)
LHR	Lock Haven Review (Lock Haven State Coll., Pa.)
LimR	Limbă Română (București) (LLBA)
Lingua (Amsterdam) (LLBA)	
Linguistics	
Linguistique (Paris) (LLBA)	
Lithanus: Lithuanian Quarterly (Chicago)	
LL	Language Learning
LLBA	Language and Language-Behavior Abstracts
LOS	Literary Onomastics Studies
LP	Lingua Posnaniensis (LLBA)
LSoc	Language in Society
LURev	Lakehead University Review
LY	Lessing Yearbook
LyC	Lenguaje y Ciencias (Univ. Nacional de Trujillo) (LLBA)
MagN	Magyar Nyelvőr (LLBA)
MAL	Modern Austrian Literature: Journal of the Intl. Arthur Schnitzler Research Assn. [Supersedes *JIASRA*]
M&C	Memory & Cognition

M&H	Medievalia et Humanistica (North Texas State U.)
ManR	Manchester Review
Manuscripta	
MarkhamR	Markham Review
Mary Wollstonecraft Journal	
MDAC	Mystery and Detection Annual (Beverly Hills, Calif.)
MelbSS	Melbourne Slavonic Studies
Menckeniana	
MFS	Modern Fiction Studies
MichA	Michigan Academician [Supersedes *PMASAL*]
MiltonQ	Milton Quarterly [Formerly *MiltonN*]
MiltonS	Milton Studies
MinnR	Minnesota Review
MissQ	Mississippi Quarterly
ML	Modern Languages (London)
MLN	Modern Language Notes
MLQ	Modern Language Quarterly
MLR	Modern Language Review
MLS	Modern Language Studies
MNy	Magyar Nyelv (LLBA)
Monatschefte	
Moreana (Angers)	
Mosaic: A Journal for the Comparative Study of Literature and Ideas	
Mov	Movoznavstvo (Kiev) (LLBA)
MQ	Midwest Quarterly (Pittsburg, Kan.)
MQR	Michigan Quarterly Review
MS	Mediaeval Studies (Toronto)
MTJ	Mark Twain Journal
MW	Muslim World (Hartford, Conn.)
NALF	Negro American Literature Forum
Names	
NC	Nuova Corrente (LLBA)
NCarF	North Carolina Folklore
NCF	Nineteenth-Century Fiction
NCFS	Nineteenth-Century French Studies
NDQ	North Dakota Quarterly
NewL	New Letters [Formerly *University Review*]
NHJ	Nathaniel Hawthorne Journal
NK	Nyelvtudományi Közlemények (LLBA)
NLauR	New Laurel Review (The Pennington School, Pennington, N.J.)
NLH	New Literary History (U. of Va.)
NS	Die Neueren Sprachen (LLBA)
NsM	Neusprachliche Mitteilungen aus Wissenschaft und Praxis
NTLTL	Teaching Language Through Literature
NWZam	New Writing from Zambia
NYH	New York History
NZSJ	New Zealand Slavonic Journal
Oceania	
OcL	Oceanic Linguistics
OhR	Ohio Review
OL	Orbis Litterarum
OntarioR	Ontario Review: A North American Journal of the Arts
Orbis (Louvain) (LLBA)	
PAAS	Proceedings of the American Antiquarian Society
PADS	Publication of the American Dialect Society
PAPS	Proceedings of the American Philosophical Society
Paunch (Buffalo, N.Y.)	
PBML	Prague Bulletin of Mathematical Linguistics (Charles U., Praha) (LLBA)
PBSA	Papers of the Bibliographical Society of America
PCP	Pacific Coast Philology
PFr	Présence Francophone
PIL	Papers in Linguistics

PLL	Papers on Language and Literature
PMLA: Publications of the Modern Language Association of America	
PoeS	Poe Studies
PolP	Polish Perspectives
PPR	Philosophy and Phenomenological Research (LLBA)
PQ	Philological Quarterly (Iowa City)
Proceedings of the Comparative Literature Symposium	
Proceedings of the Pacific Northwest Conference on Foreign Languages	
Proof: Yearbook of American Bibliographical and Textual Studies	
QJLC	Quarterly Journal of the Library of Congress
QJS	Quarterly Journal of Speech
QQ	Queen's Quarterly
RAL	Research African Literatures
RALS	Resources for American Literary Studies
RdSO	Revista degli Studi Orientali (Roma)
RECTR	Restoration and 18th Century Theatre Research
REH	Revista de Estudios Hispánicos (U. of Ala.)
RELC	RELC Journal (Singapore)
Renascence	
RenD	Renaissance Drama (Northwestern U.)
RES	Review of English Studies
RevR	Revue Romane (LLBA)
RJŠ	Russkij Jazyk v Škole (LLBA)
RLC	Revue de Littérature Comparée
RLI	Rassegna della Letteratura Italiana
RLM	La Revue des Lettres Modernes
RLMC	Revista di Letterature Moderne e Comparate (Firenze)
RLV	Revue des Langues Vivantes (Bruxelles)
RNL	Review of National Literatures
RomN	Romance Notes (U. of N.C.)
RORD	Research Opportunities in Renaissance Drama
RPL	Revue Philosophique de Louvain (LLBA)
RQ	Riverside Quarterly (U. of Saskatchewan)
RS	Research Studies (Wash. State U.)
RUS	Rice University Studies
SAF	Studies in American Fiction
S&W	South & West
SAQ	South Atlantic Quarterly
SB	Studies in Bibliography: Papers of the Bibliographical Society of the University of Virginia
SBHT	Studies in Burke and His Time [Formerly *The Burke Newsletter*]
Scan	Scandinavica
SCB	South Central Bulletin
SCN	Seventeenth-Century News
Scottish Literary News	
SCR	South Carolina Review
SDR	South Dakota Review
SE	Slovenski Ethnograf (LLBA)
Sean O'Casey Review	
SeAQ	Southeast Asia Quarterly
SEEJ	Slavic and East European Journal
SEL	Studies in English Literature, 1500–1900
Seminar: A Journal of Germanic Studies (Victoria Coll., Toronto; and Newcastle U., New South Wales)	
Serif	The Serif (Kent, Ohio)
SFQ	Southern Folklore Quarterly
SFS	Science-Fiction Studies
SFUS	Sovetskoe Finno-Ugrovedenie/Soviet Fenno-Ugric Studies
SH	Studia Hibernica (Dublin)
ShakS	Shakespeare Studies (U. of Cincinnati)
ShawR	Shaw Review
SHR	Southern Humanities Review
ShS	Shakespeare Survey

SIL	Studies in Linguistics
SIR	Studies in Romanticism (Boston U.)
Skandinavistik	
SL	Studia Linguistica (Lund) (LLBA)
SlavR	Slavic Review (Seattle)
SLitI	Studies in the Literary Imagination (Ga. State Coll.)
SLJ	Southern Literary Journal
SlReč	Slovenská Reč (Bratislava) (LLBA)
SM	Speech Monographs
SML	Statistical Methods in Linguistics (Stockholm) (LLBA)
SNNTS	Studies in the Novel (North Texas State U.)
SoQ	Southern Quarterly (U. of So. Miss.)
SoR	Southern Review (Louisiana State U.)
Soundings: A Journal of Interdisciplinary Studies [Formerly *ChS*]	
SP	Studies in Philology
Speculum	
Spirit: A Magazine of Poetry	
SQ	Shakespeare Quarterly
SRC	Studies in Religion. A Canadian Journal
SRen	Studies in the Renaissance
SS	Scandinavian Studies
SSG	Schriften der Theodor-Storm-Gesellschaft
StCL	Studii si Cercetări Lingvistice (LLBA)
Studi Italiani di Linguistica Teorica Applicata	
Studies in 18th Century Culture	
STS	Scottish Text Society (LLBA)
Style (U. of Arkansas)	
Sub-stance: A Review of Theory and Literary Criticism	
SwAL	Southwestern American Literature
SWR	Southwest Review
Synthese (Dordrecht, Holland) (LLBA)	
TCL	Twentieth Century Literature
TD	Theatre Documentation
TDR	The Drama Review [Formerly *Tulane Drama Review*]
TESOLQ	Teachers of English to Speakers of Other Languages Quarterly
Theoria: A Journal of Studies in the Arts, Humanities, and Social Sciences	
Thesaurus: Boletín del Instituto Caro y Cuervo (LLBA)	
Thoth (Dept. of English, Syracuse U.)	
Thought	
ThR	Theatre Research/Recherche Theatrales
ThS	Theatre Survey (Amer. Soc. for Theatre Research)
Tlalocan (Mexico)	
TLL	Travaux de Linguistique et de Littérature Publiés par le Centre de Philologie et de Littératures Romanes de l'Université de Strasbourg (LLBA)

TN	Theatre Notebook
TNTL	Tijdschrift voor Nederlandse Taal- en Letterkunde (Leiden)
TPS	Transactions of the Philological Society (London)
Transactions of the Samuel Johnson Society of the Northwest	
Trivium (St. David's Coll., Lampeter, Cardiganshire, Wales)	
TSB	Thoreau Society Bulletin
TSE	Tulane Studies in English
T. S. Eliot Newsletter	
TSL	Tennessee Studies in Literature
TSLL	Texas Studies in Literature and Language
UCTSE	University of Cape Town Studies in English
UDQ	University of Denver Quarterly
UDR	University of Dayton Review
UES	Unisa English Studies
UP	Unterrichtspraxis
Vir	Virittäjä: Revue de Kotikielen Seura (Société pour l'Etude de la Langue Maternelle) (LLBA)
VJa	Voprosy Jazykoznanija (Moscow) (LLBA)
VLang	Visible Language
VMHB	Virginia Magazine of History and Biography
VMU	Vestnik Moskovskogo U. Ser VII. Filologija, Žurnalistika (LLBA)
VN	Victorian Newsletter
VP	Victorian Poetry (W. Va. U.)
VPN	Victorian Periodicals Newsletter
VR	Vox Romanica (LLBA)
VS	Victorian Studies (Indiana U.)
WascanaR	Wascana Review (Regina, Sask.)
WC	Wordsworth Circle
WF	Western Folklore
WHR	Western Humanities Review
WMQ	William and Mary Quarterly
WPL	Working Papers in Linguistics (Ohio State U.)
WPLUH	Working Papers in Linguistics (U. of Hawaii)
WVUPP	West Virginia University Philological Papers
WW	Wirkendes Wort (LLBA)
WWR	Walt Whitman Review
WZUG	Wissenschaftliche Zeitschrift der Ernst Moritz Arndt-Universität Griefswald (LLBA)
YCGL	Yearbook of Comparative and General Literature
YFS	Yale French Studies
Zambezia (Salisbury, Rhodesia)	
ZMF	Zeitschrift für Mundartforschung (LLBA)
ZPSK	Zeitschrift für Phonetik, Sprachwissenschaft und Kommunikationsforschung (LLBA)
ZRP	Zeitschrift für Romanische Philologie (Halle) (LLBA)

FESTSCHRIFTEN AND OTHER ANALYZED COLLECTIONS

Romance

Romance. 1. Benson, Larry D.,ed. *The Learned and the Lewed:Studies in Chaucer and Medieval Literature.* (Harvard Eng. Studies 5.) Cambridge: Harvard U.P. 405 pp. [In honor of Bartlett Jere Whiting; David Staines, "Bartlett Jere Whiting," 1-9; McKay Sundwall, "The Writings of Bartlett Jere Whiting," 389-402.]
Articles from this *Festschrift* are abstracted separately below.
6. Davidson, Clifford,ed. *Studies in Medieval Drama in Honor of William L. Smoldon on His 82nd Birthday. CompD* 8,i. Kalamazoo: Western Mich. U. 139 pp.
Articles from this *Festschrift* are abstracted separately below.
19. Kraft, Walter C.,ed. *Proceedings:Pacific Northwest Conference on Foreign Languages.* Twenty-fifth Annual Meeting, April 19-20, 1974, Eastern Washington State College. Vol. xxv, Part

1:*Literature and Linguistics.* Corvallis: Ore. State U. 296 pp. Articles from this *Festschrift* are abstracted separately below.
30. Rosaldo, Renato, and Robert Anderson,eds. *La literatura iberoamericana del siglo XIX:Memoria del XV Congreso Internacional de Literatura Iberoamericana, Universidad de Arizona, Tucson, Arizona, 21-24 de Enero de 1971.* Tucson: U. of Ariz. 279 pp.
Articles from this *Festschrift* are abstracted separately below.

Germanic

Germanic. 88. Miller, William E., and Thomas G. Waldman, eds., with Natalie D. Terrell. *Bibliographical Studies in Honor of Rudolf Hirsch. LC* 40,i. Philadelphia: U. of Pa. Lib., Friends of the Lib. 145 pp. ["Rudolf Hirsch Bibliography," 140-45.]
Articles from this *Festschrift* are abstracted separately below.

GENERAL ROMANCE LITERATURES†

General and Miscellaneous. 197. Mieder, Wolfgang. "The Proverb and Romance Literature." *RomN* 15:610-21.
A literary proverb study must include an explanatory essay concerning the various functions of the proverbs in the text. Only the combination of such an essay with an alphabetically arranged proverb index will render worthwhile results. Because methodological rigidity has hitherto been lacking, the 76 items included in the bibliographical part of this study are of a highly varied quality. They range from small notes to voluminous monographs, differing greatly in approach and value. Literary proverb studies have concentrated heavily on the authors of the 16th century. What is needed are comprehensive investigations of works of all centuries and modes. (WM)
205. Woodman, R.G. "Satan in the 'Vale of Soul-Making':A Survey from Blake to Ginsberg." *HAB* 25:108-21. [Eng., Fr., Ger. esp.]
In aligning the poet with what Blake called "the Devils party," the Romantics endowed Satan with creative powers and virtues lacking in the Satan of *Paradise Lost.* The moral and spiritual fervor of Blake's and Shelley's Satanism distinguishes it from the more orthodox Satanism of Baudelaire, Rimbaud, Genet, Joyce, and Ginsberg. The first four of these writers invest Romantic Satanism with those characteristics which belong to Satan proper. Their art explores a far more ambiguous conception of the revolutionary artist and his role in society. At its worst, Romantic Satanism in our time becomes the hysterical rhetoric of a spent power that parodies the poet-legislators championed by Shelley in his *Defence.* (RGW)

Drama and Theater. 207. Flanigan, C. Clifford. "The Liturgical Context of the *Quem Queritis* Trope." [F 6]:45-62.
The significance of the *Quem Queritis* dialogue for the history of the medieval drama has been obscured by an inadequate understanding of the liturgical form and function of a trope. In its troped form the *Quem Queritis* sought to explain the cultic significance of the Easter introit to which it was attached. It emphasized the way in which the liturgy was believed to render present again the events of the first Easter, thus enabling the medieval congregation to share in its soteriological benefits. The *Visitatio Sepulchri,* and perhaps other forms of the liturgical drama are primarily liturgical embellishments which by word, song, and gesture sought to make explicit the meaning of the liturgical celebration of Easter. (CCF)

Epic. 209. Miletich, John S. "Narrative Style in Spanish and Slavic Traditional Narrative Poetry:Implications for the Study of

† *Festschriften* and Other Analyzed Collections are listed in the first division of this volume. "F" numbers in brackets following a title refer to these items.

the Romance Epic." *Olifant* 2,ii:109-28.
Examination of six types of closely occurring repetitions within traditional narrative poetry with a view to determining their total effect on the narrative style of the individual poem and of the genre in general. The study is based on a detailed analysis of 82 poems totaling 4,108 lines in Spanish, Serbo-Croatian, and Russian. Four different sub-genres are represented: the peninsular Spanish *romance* of the 16th century and the Judeo-Spanish *romance* of Morocco, the South Slavic *bugarštica,* the South Slavic *junački deseterac* or heroic decasyllable, and the Russian *bylina.* The six repetitive types can be divided into two principle categories, the "elaborate," which delays the narrative pace, and the "essential," which accelerates the flow of information. The narrative style of the four sub-genres are fundamentally "essential" but there is present a considerably pronounced retarding tendency, which results from the fairly high frequency of "elaborate" type repetitions. (JSM)

Catalan. 232. Jernigan, Charles. "The Song of Nail and Uncle:Arnaut Daniel's Sestina 'Lo ferm voler q'el cor m'intra'." *SP* 71:127-51.
The first sestina, Arnaut Daniel's "Lo ferm voler q'el cor m'intra," has long interested romance philologists and scholars. Traditional critics of this difficult example of *troubar ric* have viewed the poem as a typical *canso,* a courtly love poem; yet certain sentences and phrases are so baffling as to defy interpretation on that level. The poem is really a comic tour de force, built on sexual double entendres centering on the six key words which are repeated seven times in the course of the poem. Line-by-line analysis reveals that almost every phrase can be interpreted on two levels, the courtly and the sexual. (CJ)

Provençal and Occitan. 292. Dumas, René. "Esprit Requien ami de Prosper Mérimée et lexicologue provençal." *RLMC* 27:12-21.
Dumas gives us a portrait of the scholar Esprit Requien in his role as a cultural intermediary. He examines Requien's relations with Mérimée and reveals that in writing *Colomba* Mérimée used information supplied to him by Requien. Living in Avignon, Requien was in a position to help Honnorat with his *Dictionnaire provençal-français.* More diligent in assisting his friends than he was in organizing his own œuvre, Requien left only a small volume of work, mostly brief pamphlets and articles. (RD)
293. Eckhardt, Caroline D. "Biblical Imagery in Bernart de Ventadorn's 'Lo tems vai'." *RomN* 15(1973):368-74.
In the sixth stanza of Bernart de Ventadorn's lyric *Lo tems vai e ven e vire,* the poet, describing his love affair, remarks "que so mostra l'escriptura," "since Scripture shows this." What Scripture shows, "so," has been taken as the subsequent idea (one good day outweighs many bad ones), but more probably applies to the

preceding idea (harshness will be followed by mercy). The poem as a whole reflects the experience of Job: the speaker is at first estranged, serving someone whose presence is manifested only as cruelty, but on the basis of the biblical sequence of affliction and redemption, he asserts that mercy will be forthcoming, and reaffirms his service. The object of Bernart's devotion is an earthly lady, however, and this biblical background functions primarily as analogy; the lady is identified with God only momentarily in the poet's claim that because God became merciful so will she. (CDE)

294. Fantazzi, Charles. "Marcabru's *Pastourelle*:Courtly Love Decoded." *SP* 71:385-403.
Marcabru's *pastourelle* "L'autrier, jost'una sebissa" is the prototype as well as the most finished exemplar of this hybrid genre of the pastoral line. In its marvelous antithetical structure, it becomes a forceful, dramatized statement of Marcabru's interpretation of *mezura* and *cortezia*. Through the candor of the shepherdess, Marcabru exposes the hypocritical ambiguity fostered by the propagators of the courtly ideal between true *fin'amors* and the more earthy *amor de cavalier*. (CF)

302. Levin, Richard. "A Second English *Enueg*." *PQ* 53:428-30.
There is an anonymous 16th-century sonnet in British Museum Add. MS 36529 which seems to derive from the *Enueg*, a continental verse form built around a catalog of complaints. In certain respects it resembles Shakespeare's Sonnet LXVI, hitherto regarded as the only English example of this form. (RLL)

307. Paden, William D.,Jr. "Bernart de Ventadorn, 'Lancan folhon bosc e jarric,' V.34." *RomN* 15(1973):375-77.
The words *per gelos folatura* do not give a clear reading, since *folatura* should be feminine and *gelos* is masculine. Instead of emending the MSS reading *pel* to *per*, we should emend *folatura* to *fol s'atura*. The passage may then be translated "I pray my lady not to leave me because of chastisement, nor to hesitate because

of that jealous fool to feel me in her arms." (WDP,Jr)

312. Saiz, Prospero. "Raimbaut d'Oranges's 'Assatz sai d'amor ben parlar,' 31-32." *Expl* 32:Item 46.
Lines 31-32 of Raimbaut d'Orange's *Assatz sai d'amor ben parlar* hold more irony than apparent on first interpretation. Strictly interpreted, they mean: "Keep your dwelling place from being like churches or ships." Commentators and critics, ignoring the ship, have suggested the exact opposite, interpreting them to mean "keep your houses as clean as a church" (Jeanroy) or "as hospitable as a church" (Pattison). This ignores the ship, which surely was not a clean place in medieval times, nor was it necessarily a hospitable one. Further, the people aboard a ship are a select few—the captain and the crew and they are all men. The suggestion, therefore, seems to be: do not make your house one for men only; include women in it—women of the worst sort. Contrary to the aspiring symbols of the church's steeple and the ship's mast, the suggestion is to "keep one's house grounded in reality" (and filled with loose women). (PS)

318. Sussex, R.T. "Joseph D'Arbaud, Poet of the Camargue." *AUMLA* 42:175-85.
1974 commemorates the birth of Joseph d'Arbaud. D'Arbaud belongs within the Mistral tradition: he left city life at Aix-en-Provence to reside for many years as a cattle ranch owner in this primitive country and writes both in French and in Provençal. His poems show a strong sense of the Latin and Arabic past and also of the gypsy tradition of Saintes-Maries-de-la-Mer: he knows intimately the daily care of horse and cattle and the birds and beasts that inhabit his landscape. He writes sparingly in verse or the novella form, but his greatest work is *La bête du Vaccarès* which recaptures the "panic" atmosphere of ancient mythology by recounting in the form of a "diary" the last days of a Greco-Latin rural deity, half-man, half-beast, in the Camargue in the closing years of the Middle Ages. (RTS)

FRENCH LITERATURE†

I. GENERAL

Bibliography. 322. Fiber, Louise A. "A Selected Guide to Journals in the Field of French Language and Literature." *FR* 47:1128-41.
The *Guide* contains an annotated list of over 90 scholarly periodicals publishing materials in the area of French language and literature. Included are interdisciplinary and pedagogical journals. Each entry carries a description of the journal and its publishing format. The *Guide* was compiled as an aid to the teacher, writer, advanced student, and libraries. (LAF)

General and Miscellaneous. 329. Allen, John R. "Methods of Author Identification through Stylistic Analysis." *FR* 47:904-16.
Although principles of author identification through stylistic analysis have been known for more than a century, they have been little used in the study of French literature, perhaps because many critics feel unqualified to undertake such research. Yet often the critic is the most qualified to use these methods: the amount of further training is minimal, as the critic's background enables him to formulate questions which can be studied with computational stylistics. This method isolates traits of style which shed light on previously unsolved problems of author attribution and literary history. Some criteria which can be used toward that

goal are: average word and/or sentence length, distribution of parts of speech, vocabulary choice, word length of parts of speech, vocabulary distribution, and relative entropy. Statistical tests already developed measure the significance of any traits observed. Given the proven effectiveness of computational stylistics in other fields, critics ought to examine the possibilities for applying these methods to the study of French literature. (JRA)

368. Wilson, Robert R. "Spenser's Reputation in Italy and France." *HAB* 24(1973):105-09.
Despite Spenser's great indebtedness to writers of the Italian romance-epic tradition, the *Faerie Queene* has never been adequately translated into Italian. Early translations, such as that by Mathias, are both incomplete and insufficient. Furthermore, there has never been a discussion of Spenser's work by Italian critics. Comment upon Spenser began in European criticism only after French critics toward the middle of the nineteenth century began to take note of him. This critical response was dominated by the opinions of Hippolyte Taine. An examination of critical writing on Spenser in Italian and French since the time of Taine shows that his assessment continues to have the weight of orthodoxy. (RRW)

II. FRENCH-CANADIAN LITERATURE

General and Miscellaneous. 406. Kattan, Naim. "Ecrire en français." *Boundary* 3:169-75.
Kattan presents a brief autobiography and explains why he has

chosen French as his literary medium. (NK)

Roy. 521. Mitcham, Allison. "The Northern Innocent in the Fiction of Gabrielle Roy." *HAB* 24(1973):25-31.
Gabrielle Roy's exploration of innocence and vulnerability is increasingly linked with her paradoxical conception of the northern wilderness. Despite its rigors, Roy feels, it is only in the

† *Festschriften* and Other Analyzed Collections are listed in the first division of this volume. "F" numbers in brackets following a title refer to these items.

harsh northern wilderness that human beings can hope to escape the "cage" or "trap" of contemporary civilization. Thus most of Roy's innocents find themselves in the predicament of having to make an almost impossible choice which Thaddeus, the wise old stone carver in *La Rivière*, defines as the essential human dilemma. Through her depiction of conflicting values, Roy shows that the innocent and vulnerable often possess heightened perceptions, such as the ability to dream. Roy's northern innocents have all retained this ability, which helps them to escape the contemporary world and provides them with a key to self-knowledge. For Pierre the artist and Thaddeus, dreams and the self-knowledge they provide are the basis of art. They enable Elas to transcend the squalor and frustration of life in the garrison of Fort-Chimo. (AM)

III. MEDIEVAL

General and Miscellaneous. 546. Haidu, Peter. "Making It (New) in the Middle Ages:Towards a Problematics of Alterity." *Diacritics* 4,ii:2-11. [Rev. art.]
The conventionality of medieval literature is a distinguishing characteristic that limits applicability of modern literary theory and stylistics. Medieval literature represents a larger category, that of cultural and historical alterity. Paul Zumthor's structural analysis in *Essai de poétique médiévale* is based on a recognition of alterity. Literary types are studied synchronically, materially, and according to typological characteristics. The principles of this typology are debatable, but result in a remarkable reorganization of literary production of five centuries. Two particular types are of critical importance: courtly lyric and romance, which are discussed in detail. Zumthor's basic limitation is simultaneously his virtue: a linguistic approach is most useful for lyric, less so for narrative and drama. Nevertheless, the *Essai* is now the major interlocutor in any dialogue about medieval literature. The American sense of the concrete and particular may serve as corrective to its abstraction, but Zumthor's is now the most important voice in the field. (PH)

Arthurian. 578. Matthews, William. "Where Was Siesia-Sessoyne?" *Speculum* 49:680-86.
The high-point of King Arthur's military career was his victory over Lucius and the Roman army at "Siesia" (Geoffrey of Monmouth). The name also appears as "Suison" (Wace), "Ceroise" (prose-*Merlin*), "Swesy" (Manning), and "Sessoyne" (Malory, alliterative *Morte Arthure*). The routes described for Arthur's expedition agree in all these works, and it is certain that the site of the battle was in Burgundy. Ten identifications have been proposed. Seven of these are unsuitable. The most likely candidate for "Siesia" is Val-Suzon. Midway between Langres and Auton, on the popular route, its topography, name forms, and historical associations make it suitable as the site for the battle that actually took place only in Geoffrey's mind. (WM)

579. Morgan, Alice B. " 'Honour & Right' in *Arthur of Little Britain*." [F 1]:371-84.
Lord Berners' translation *Arthur of Little Britain* shows that its French author was familiar with romance motifs, for this lengthy book is encyclopedic in its plot devices. The narrative, however, lacks conviction; the hero is only mildly challenged by his struggles to win the noble Florence, and the author's main concern seems to have been with issues of social decorum and moral choice. Examination of the romance's incidents, characterization, and dialogue shows how the elaborate plotting and fantastic events are combined with realistic issues of courtesy and morality. (ABM)

Chansons de geste. 585. Herman, Gerald. "A Note on Medieval Anti-Judaism, as Reflected in the *Chansons de geste*." *AnM* 14(1973):63-73.
Anti-Judaic sentiment prevails throughout the medieval French chansons de geste, much as it does throughout most of the other literary genres of the period. It is evident, in its simplest form, in the choice of epithets (*felon, traitre*, etc.) used by the *trouvères* to characterize various historical or fictional Jews. As a group, the Jews are condemned most bitterly for their historical role in the crucifixion of Christ, and, no less vehemently, for their blind adherence to erroneous beliefs. As active participants in the chansons de geste, they are seldom accorded a significant role and are portrayed, for the most part, as skilled swordsmiths or crafty seers. In those rare instances when a Jew assumes any particular relief in the medieval French epic, it is primarily as a ludicrous or an odious figure. In their depiction and characterization of Jews, the chansons de geste offer the reader an accurate gauge of popular anti-Judaic feeling in the 12th and 13th centuries. (GH)

Chansons de toile. 589. Scharff, Arthur B. "*Chanson de toile* or *Chanson d'histoire*." *RomN* 15:509-12.
Chanson de toile and *chanson d'histoire* both designate a distinctive group of medieval lyric poems. Both names were used by contemporary 12th- or 13th-century authors. Later other terms, such as romances, were applied to the songs, but these had little basis in logic and have now gone out of use. Investigation into medieval usage of the words involved in the two terms demonstrates that they have the same basic meaning. *Chanson de toile* proves to have a rather wide independent usage, while *chanson d'histoire* is rarely found except in connection with the other name. *Chanson de toile* is advocated as the standard name for the form. (ABS)

Drama and Theater. 599. Ogden, Dunbar H. "The Use of Architectural Space in Medieval Music-Drama." [F 6]:63-76.
In bringing together the text of a medieval music-drama and the plan of the church in which it was first performed, we perceive vividly the theatrical use of this architectural space. Recent archeological excavation of the Old Minster at Winchester gives us an idea of the staging area which Ethelwold had in mind when in the 10th century he described the performance of the *Visitatio Sepulchri*. On groundplans of two other churches, detailed textual rubrics permit us actually to trace the paths of the actors. (DHO)

Lais. 605. Beston, John B. "How Much Was Known of the Breton Lai in Fourteenth-Century England?" [F 1]:319-36.
Some English lays in couplets are translations of French lais. The English lays in tail-rhyme stanzas deal, however, with the same material as the longer romances in tail-rhyme stanzas. Their authors must have known the English couplet lays, but need not have known any French lais. Information in the prologue to *Le Freine* and *Sir Orfeo* and the prologue to the Franklin's Tale show scant knowledge of the French lai, explaining why the English lay-writers did not create a genre comparable to the French. (JBB)

Poetry. 606. Altman, Charles. "Medieval Narrative vs. Modern Assumptions:Revising Inadequate Typology." *Diacritics* 4,ii:12-19. [Rev. art.]
Claiming that medieval texts do not necessarily adhere to modern demands for unity, William W. Ryding, in *Structure in Medieval Narrative* (The Hague and Paris: Mouton, 1971), and Karl D. Uitti, in *Story, Myth, and Celebration in Old Fench Poetry, 1050-1200* (Princeton: Princeton Univ. Press, 1973), suggest that many 12th-century texts are organized around a basic duality, Ryding speaking of "bipartition" and Uitti of "epic binarism." Further analysis of the problems suggested by Ryding and Uitti suggests a distinction between two basic narrative types. The dual-focus form, so called because of its characteristic alternation between two opposed groups (as in the early *chanson de geste*), derives its meaning from division of space and subject substitution ($S_1P_1 \rightarrow S_2P_1$). In single-focus narrative a single individual is followed (as in Chrétien's *Yvain* and other romances), his change over time providing meaning through predicate transformation ($S_1P_1 \rightarrow S_1P_2$). (CFA)

Roman courtois. 620. Lee, Anne T. "*Le Bone Florence of Rome*:A Middle English Adaptation of a French Romance." [F

1]:343-54.

Le Bone Florence of Rome is a late 14th-century romance in Middle English tail-rhyme stanza. The author seems to have consciously altered the original with certain artistic considerations in mind. He has reduced the narrative from 6,000 to 2,000 lines, but in return he has provided more suspenseful plot development and more coherent dramatic focus. He has also omitted almost all reference to the supernatural which heightens the realistic atmosphere of his tale and renders his heroine more sympathetic by dramatizing her struggles on a human plane. Finally, the poet leaves out a great deal of lengthy and tedious religious material without, however, sacrificing the emphasis on the heroine as an exemplary figure. (ATL)

621. Spensley, R.M. "Allusion as a Structural Device in Three Old French Romances." *RomN* 15(1973):349-54. [*Floire et Blancheflor, Erec et Enide, L'Escoufle*.]

In the Old French romances of *Erec et Enide, Floire et Blancheflor*, and *L'Escoufle* the nature of the relationship between the hero and heroine is made clearer by an allusion to a more famous literary couple. The poet's aim is to contrast his own couple favorably with the well-known pair. Thus, Aeneas' failure to reconcile his public destiny with his relationship with Dido contrasts with Erec's success in reconciling his obligations to chivalry with his relationship with Enide. The dubious circumstances of the sophisticated Paris-Helen affair contrast with the innocence and simplicity of the Floire and Blancheflor relationship, and there is a similar contrast between Tristan and Yseut and the lovers in *L'Escoufle*. The allusions are instances of a type of composition in which the analogue or thematic parallel serves to reinforce the significance of the principal characters' behavior. (RMS)

Artus de la Petite Bretagne. 634. Oberembt, Kenneth J. "Lord Berners' Translation of *Artus de la Petite Bretagne*." *M&H* 5:191-99.

A comparison of *Arthur of Lytell Brytayne*—a translation completed sometime after 1496 by Sir John Bourchier, second Lord Berners—with its French source *Artus de la Petite Bretagne*. Berners' method of translation is a continuation of the typical 15th-century procedure—to keep very close to the sentence and to the language of the original. However, Berners translated into formal style the colloquial style of communing of his source and by so doing created a substantive difference between *Arthur* and *Artus*. The pose struck by the English characters is obviously more impersonal than that of their French counterparts. More important, the non-representational characterization produced by Berners' stylistic adjustment of direct discourse helps transfer the allegiance of the Little Arthur story from the mimesis of the French original to allegoresis. Berners' change of style was probably the result of his intent to write the kind of courtly English prose advocated by William Caxton. (KJO)

Aucassin et Nicolette. 639. Rea, John A. "The Form of *Aucassin et Nicolette*." *RomN* 15:504-08.

Although most scholars have regarded the form of *Aucassin et Nicolette* as unique, others have sought, and found, earlier texts with a similar alternation of prose and verse. But these parallels seem to offer no other apparent similarity to *Aucassin et Nicolette* which might have motivated the use of such a form. There did, in fact, exist an appropriate contemporary model, orally performed, which alternated verse with prose, and one which in addition presents other thematic and formal similarities to *Aucassin et Nicolette* such as might have motivated the author to adopt this form. (JR)

640. Schneiderman, Leo. "Folkloristic Motifs in *Aucassin and Nicolette*." *ConnR* 8,i:56-71.

Aucassin et Nicolette is interpreted as an allegory of initiation for adolescent males within the context of Provençval May Day customs. Using the concepts of psychoanalysis and anthropology, the motifs of adolescent self-assertion, rebellion, trial-by-ordeal, and wish-fulfillment are explored with reference to the characters and events of the medieval romance. Beneath the veneer of sophisticated courtly romance it is possible to discern an archaic sub-stratum of initiation rituals based on totemism and the cult of

fertility. This layer of meaning is only partly concealed, and is, in fact, obvious in much of the symbolism in the story. Special emphasis is given to non-rational elements in the narrative as indicators of primitive "survivals." (LS)

Baudouin de Sebourc. 643. Herman, Gerald. "A Fourteenth-Century Anti-Hero:Baudouin de Sebourc." *RomN* 15(1973):355-60.

Baudouin de Sebourc is one of the most "original" of the late medieval French epics, due not only to the poem's irreverent humor and satiric verve but also to the manner in which some of the principal characters are portrayed. The protagonist Baudouin, for instance, is depicted as the very antithesis of all that epic and romance tradition upheld as sublime in the figure of a hero. He is self-centered, impious, fickle, and unconcerned with such fundamental chivalric notions as honor and service to women. Baudouin's anti-heroism may have been intended as a parody of traditional aristocratic literature. (GH)

Bozon. 650. Shields, Hugh. "A Text of Nicole Bozon's *Proverbes de bon enseignement* in Irish Transmission." *MLR* 69:274-78.

A hitherto unidentified text of Nicole Bozon's *Proverbes de bon enseignement* exists in the Red Book of Ossory, Kilkenny, Ireland. Through a misreading of the MS title, this text was previously known as *Les Proverbis del Sibil*; the last word correctly reads *Bibil*, so that the proper title is *Proverbs of the Bible*. The Kilkenny MS provides some new textual variants of a work already published from nine MSS. Its particular interest, however, lies in the evidence it provides concerning the use of French in medieval Ireland and the part apparently played by the Franciscan order in the promotion of the language there. (HS)

Cent nouvelles nouvelles. 651. Lorian, Alexandre. "Deux cents nouvelles nouvelles." *HUSL* 2,ii:151-70.

The origins and beginnings of the French short story have recently been the object of an increasingly great number of publications, some of which are reviewed here. One of them, Dubis' *Les Cent nouvelles nouvelles et la tradition de la nouvelle en France au moyen âge* defines the "nouvelle" by examining the first French collection of stories (1462) and traces its national sources to the medieval *lai, fabliau* and *exemplum*; both method and documentation are valid, but the author's conclusions are not very startling. Another important publication is Livingston's posthumous transcription of Phillippe de Vigneulles's *Cent nouvelles nouvelles*, the only one complete and critical edition to date. The editor also tries to link each of these anecdotes to its possible sources: a personal experience, some vague literary model, and above all European folklore. (AL)

Chanson de Roland. 657. Crist, Larry S. "A propos de la *desmesure* dans la *Chanson de Roland*:Quelques propos (démesurés?)." *Olifant* 1,iv:10-20.

The received idea of Roland's failing by pride but redeeming himself by a good fight to the end after recognizing his failing is not part of the Oxford text nor does it belong to the period of the poem's composition. This French literature handbook topos of *démesure* as well as that of the Roland-preux/Olivier-sage opposition can be traced to their beginnings c. 1870. Roland is, on the contrary, to be understood as having taken up his cross, his duty as a means of calling Charlemagne back to his Christian duty, which he had shirked at the beginning of the poem. The *Roland* is thus a sort of allegory of the Christian life. (LSC)

659. Emden, Wolfgang G. van. " 'E cil de France le cleiment a guarant':Roland, Vivien et le thème du guarant." *Olifant* 1,iv:21-47.

Defends the interpretation of Roland as a *démesuré* against scholars who consider Roland as being without moral fault. The episodes and speeches which clarify the moral issues are examined against parallel or contrasting passages of the *Chanson de Guillaume* in which Vivien is given explicitly Christian attitudes. The implications of ll. 1161 and 1863ff. of *Roland*, where Roland respectively is acclaimed as *guarant* and accepts his inability to fulfill his obligations in that role and his responsibility for the disaster, are elucidated partly by means of a semantic study of the use of *guarant* and related words in both poems. Olivier is right to accuse the hero of erring, because of *démesure*, on the military and feudal level. (WGvE)

664. Keller, Hans E. "La conversion de Bramimonde." *Olifant* 1,i(1973):3-22.
The episode of Bramimonde's conversion to the Christian faith seems to be inserted into the *Song of Roland*, because the character of Marsile's spouse does not point toward a soul disposed to convert itself, as l. 3674 suggests. The name itself indicates violence, for it is derived from *braire* "to shout." Line 3674 is extraordinary because it is in striking contrast with the first half of the poem where the pagans are considered inferior human begins against whom the Christians wage a *bellum iustissimum*. The idea of a conversion by the queen herself shows the influence of Peter the Venerable on the poet, who must have belonged to the circle of his friend, Suger of Saint-Denis, for Peter had written the first treatise (about 1145) which pleads for convincing the pagans rather than exterminating them. But l. 3986 proves that the poem was revised in England, because the Christian name chosen by Bramimonde, Juliane, refers to the special cult of the saint in that country. (HEK)

671. Vos, Marianne C. "Ganelon's 'Mortal Rage'." *Olifant* 2,i:15-26.
Several implicit characteristics in the portrayal of Ganelon of *La Chanson de Roland* point to Judas Iscariot and thus to a New Testament figure. Admitting to the Judas figure theory one may go further and uncover aspects of Satan. Ganelon is closely related to Marsile and both epic characters pave the way for the arrival of the larger evil forces. There are no humorous or comic aspects surrounding the Count; he is a most serious, somber epic character. That Ganelon in all his duplicity predicts and fulfills the Divine Plan does not lessen epic suspense or the audience's sympathy with him. It is through him that this medieval epic is raised from a primitive transgression-vengeance pattern into a theodicy. (MCV)

Chrétien de Troyes. 690. Mahler, Annemarie E. "The Representation of Visual Reality in *Perceval* and *Parzival*." *PMLA* 89:537-50.
Art historical criteria are applied to equivalent descriptions—a portrait, an architectural complex, and a scene involving motion—in the *Perceval* of Chrétien de Troyes and the *Parzival* of Wolfram von Eschenbach. Chrétien's traditional rhetorical portrait of Blancheflor is a still, frontal, symmetrical image; his description of *chastel merveile* gives meticulous surface detail but instead of a logical spatial connection the parts are simply juxtaposed in the plane; Gavain's fight with the lion shows no real motion but breaks down into a series of still vignettes which represent rather than show the action. On the other hand, Wolfram's portrait of Condwiramurs is glimpsed from various angles and distances as she moves through space; *Schastel Marveile* is vaguely described but spatially self-consistent; motion in Gawan's lion fight is continuous both in space and time. Thus Chrétien's descriptions relate to the dominant tradition of medieval art which shows figures and objects in characteristic poses or arrangements outlined in the plane, Wolfram's to that uncommon strain which attempts to cope with natural relationships, particularly those of volumes in space. (AEM)

Fet des romains. 718. Beer, Jeanette. "French Nationalism under Philip Augustus:An Unexpected Source." *Mosaic* 7,ii:57-70. [*Li Fet des Romains.*]
Li Fet des Romains, a medieval translation of Caesar, Sallust, Suetonius, and Lucan, contains many intentionally anachronistic adaptations of its sources. Before the reign of Philip Augustus, popular interest in antiquity had been concentrated upon Alexander, Troy, and Thebes. The climate at the time of the Battle of Bouvines stimulated a new interest in the Roman *imperatores*. Specific comparison of Caesar and Philip is presumably intended to encourage the king in his dreams of territorial expansion. However, the anti-Gallic bias of Caesar's *Bellum gallicum* is converted in many cases to an apologia for Gaul. Topical references to the Anglo-Norman coalition with Otto IV and to the Greeks also reflect the new political situation of 13th-century France rather than the state of Caesar's Gaul. (JMAB)

Jean de Meun. 736. Barnett, John D.J. "Rationalism and Naturalism in Jean de Meung's *Roman de la Rose*." *UCTSE* 4(1973):45-55.
Those features which contributed to Jean de Meun's popularity in the Middle Ages also caused the rapid decline of his popularity. His rationalism is that of the Scholastic philosopher. Reason for him means Philosophy, and in extolling Reason he exalts his own position as "maître-ès-arts" against the landed and moneyed interests of his day. As he wrote (c.1275) his attitude toward the Aristotelianism of his day is interesting. Three theories have been propounded: (1) that he was a Christian Platonist of the type represented by the School of Chartres; (2) that he was a Latin Averroist; (3) that his position was that of St. Thomas Aquinas—a moderate Aristotelianism. In view of Jean's assertions concerning Providence, the theory concerning Aquinas seems the most tenable. On what grounds was he then attacked by Gerson and other theologians? Not for Averroism, as F. W. Müller asserts, but for his thoroughgoing naturalism, exemplified by his amoral teaching on sex. (JDJB)

Livre de Melibé et de Dame Prudence. 747. Palomo, Dolores. "What Chaucer Really Did to *Le Livre de Mellibee*." *PQ* 53:304-20.
Because Chaucer's Tale of Melibee has always been regarded as a near word-for-word translation of *Le Livre de Melibee*, his intentions in including it in *The Canterbury Tales* have remained obscure. Chaucer has consistently introduced techniques cited in medieval rhetorics for achieving "high style"—characteristics absent from the plain style of his source. But the rhetorical elegance is inappropriate to the vacuous content, and the unaltered "sentence" is consequently devalued by stylistic treatment. Chaucer both criticizes the treatise's pretentiousness and disproves the assumption that words are mere chaff concealing doctrinal truth. Chaucer satirizes the ordinary reader's attitude toward literature. In this way, the Tale of Melibee contributes to Chaucer's continuing commentary on the arts of reading and writing. (DJP)

Marie de France. 751. Fitz, Brewster E. "The Storm Episode and the Weasel Episode:Sacrificial Casuistry in Marie de France's *Eliduc*." *MLN* 89:542-49.
Using the sacrificial hypothesis of René Girard, it is shown that in Marie de France's *Eliduc* the sailor's speaking constitutes his becoming the perfect expiatory victim. The weasel episode provides a second sacrifice during which the partial victimization of Eliduc's beloved is reversed. (BF)

757. Pickens, Rupert T. "*Equitan*:Anti-*Guigemar*." *RomN* 15(1973):361-67.
Equitan has a definite function in the collection of Marie de France's *Lais*: it is an "anti-*Guigemar*" because its hero is essentially the same kind of man as Guigemar and experiences exactly the same kind of love, but is pushed by his destiny toward destruction, while Guigemar is redeemed. Love is an amoral force, an instrument of destiny, and appears "good" or "bad" only in terms of the fulfillment of a hero's destiny. (RTP)

Mort le roi Artu. 764. Bloch, R. Howard. "From Grail Quest to Inquest:The Death of King Arthur and the Birth of France." *MLR* 69:40-55.
From the perspective of its 13th-century author, the final sequel of the Lancelot-prose cycle, *La Mort le roi Artu*, seems to reflect a crisis in feudal values and institutions almost two centuries after the end of feudalism in France. The immanent procedure of trial by battle no longer produces adequate judicial meaning. In the first trial Lancelot successfully upholds what he recognizes to be a faulty cause; and in the second he manages again to prevail despite his own guilt according to the medieval formula for first-degree murder. While the hero's legal victories undermine the pragmatic basis of the "duel judiciaire," they also point to the inherent epistemological weakness of feudal justice. The author of

La Mort offers no apparent solution to the failure of any of the extra-civil institutions—trial by battle, entrapment, vendetta, and private war—to prevent the violence of private grievance from menacing the polity of the realm. (HRB)

765. —— "The Death of King Arthur and the Waning of the Feudal Age." *OL* 29:291-305.

La Mort Artu is discussed in terms of the rapidly changing social and philosophical ethos of 13th-century France. Although Arthur's kingdom is, politically speaking, a model of the feudal world, its values and institutions no longer function to insure the unity of the realm. (RHB)

Pèlerinage de Charlemagne. 771. Sturm, Sara. "The Stature of Charlemagne in the *Pèlerinage*." *SP* 71:1-18.

The structure of the *Pèlerinage de Charlemagne* suggests a focus for investigation of the poem's unity and its author's intent. Events in both Jerusalem and Constantinople serve to emphasize Charlemagne's superior stature, but rather than his personal worthiness, as Emperor, it is his literal stature which is demonstrated. The comic effect of the work, heightened by the epic pretext, is in the literal reading of the idea of imperial superiority. (SS)

Quinze joies du mariage. 775. Mermier, Guy. "La ruse féminine et la fonction morale des *Quinze joies du mariage*." *RomN* 15:495-503.

The nature and role of feminine ruse in the *Quinze Joies de Mariage* are analyzed and its moral function is discussed. The Prologue is the focus of the *Quinze Joies*; this perspective supports the theory that the book must clearly be distinguished from the traditional misogynous works of the period. (GM)

Roman de la Rose. 782. Baird, Joseph L., and John R. Kane. "*La querelle de la rose*:In Defense of the Opponents." *FR* 48:298-307.

Recent criticism concerned with the Quarrel over the *Roman de la Rose* has dealt harshly with the literary and argumentative efforts of Christine de Pisan and Jean Gerson. Accordingly, we are asked to believe that Christine was scarcely even interested in the Quarrel and that both she and Gerson were obviously over-whelmed and defeated, as a result of their literary naiveté. This view is untenable and is just as much a distortion as the earlier tendency to overvalue Christine's efforts. Christine de Pisan and Jean Gerson argue quite effectively, and there is no evidence to show that they were defeated. (JLB)

784. Caie, Graham D. "An Iconographic Detail in the *Roman de la Rose* and the Middle English *Romaunt*." *ChauR* 8:320-23.

The iconographic detail of Amant's sleeve-basting at the beginning of the *Roman de la Rose* signifies that Amant was deliberately in search of the God of Love and *fol amour* and that he did not come upon the Garden by chance. There is evidence both intrinsic to the poem and in patristic writings which explains the significance of sewing one's sleeves, a gesture which both author and medieval illustrators of the poem took great pains to describe in detail. Throughout the poem both Guillaume de Lorris and Jean de Muen describe well-sewn sleeves as a mark of those lecherous characters who have given themselves up to *fol amour* and are servants of the God of Love, who specifically demands that his servants have carefully stitched sleeves. In Scripture and in St. Jerome's writings there is evidence to show that the iconographic action of sewing one's sleeves signifies the deliberate preparation of a vain, worldly garment after the rejection of the seamless coat, symbol of purity and of the Passion. (GDC)

786. Hill, Thomas D. "Narcissus, Pygmalion, and the Castration of Saturn:Two Mythological Themes in the *Roman de la Rose*." *SP* 71:404-26.

Both the situation of the lover and the nature of human sexuality are defined in the *Roman de la Rose* in terms of allusion to specific classical myths—the story of Narcissus, Pygmalion, and the myth of the birth of Venus from the castration of Saturn. These narratives are discussed in terms of medieval mythographical commentary, arguing for a "gloss" which suggests that the poet is presenting the dreamer's explicitly sexual love for the rose as paradoxical and ambivalent. This paradox reflects a comic paraphrase of Augustine's definition of sexuality, in that Augustine grants that sexuality is necessary and yet insists that it is irrational. (TDH)

Roman de Renart. 794. Sands, Donald B. "Reynard the Fox and the Manipulation of the Popular Proverb." [F 1]:265-78.

The Middle Dutch poem *Reinaerts Historie* of circa 1375 is, from the point of view of narrative technique, inferior to its source, *Van den vos Reinaerde*, written some 100 years before. The later poem, however, in its satiric thrust is far more subtle than the earlier, chiefly through its utilization of popular proverbs. These are consistently in the mouths of scoundrels and hypocrites and their "truth" utilized to bolster dishonest argument. The internal audience is duped by proverbial "truth"; the external audience witnesses the technique and its effectiveness and may well come to assume certain unpopular attitudes toward popularly accepted proverbial "truth"—that a display of it is a cue that its user has dishonest motives. (DBS)

Sept Sages de Rome. 799. Runte, Hans R. "A Forgotten Old French Version of the Old Man of the Mountain." *Speculum* 49:542-45.

The Florence MS. Medicea-Laurenziana, Ashburnham 52 of ca. 1300 contains, within the framework of the *Histoire de la male marastre*, an account of "The Old Man of the Mountain" in which the two heretofore separate constituting motifs of the legend, the paradisiacal garden and the underground education, are combined for the first time. While the motif of underground education goes back to antiquity, its combination with the garden motif in the *Histoire* most certainly precedes all other examples presently known. (HRR)

Wace. 829. Keller, Hans E. "Two Toponymical Problems in Geoffrey of Monmouth and Wace:*Estrusia* and *Siesia*." *Speculum* 49:687-98.

Certain place-names in Geoffrey of Monmouth and Wace (Layamon) still elude identification, both in the formation of name as well as in their geographical location. *Estrusia* belongs to the first category, and linguistic data from French dialectology and Germanic studies are necessary to recognize that Geoffrey's *Estruenses* means "settlers along a river." The place of the decisive battle between Arthur and the Romans was known to be somewhere in Burgundy. Medieval documents show that Geoffrey must have thought of the Val Suzon. (HEK)

IV. SIXTEENTH CENTURY

General and Miscellaneous. 831. Atkinson, James B. "Naïveté and Modernity:The French Renaissance Battle for a Literary Vernacular." *JHI* 35:179-96.

Dante, Alberti, Lorenzo de'Medici, Bembo, and Speroni bequeathed to the French Renaissance a legacy that defended a vernacular by spelling out the substantive issues and establishing the perspectives through which to examine these questions. The use of the word *naïveté* considerably altered the tenor of the pro-vernacular debate in France. By discussing such topics as pronunciation, dialect, translation, and the unique quality of French in the light of *Naïveté*, Sebillet, Du Bellay, Ronsard, Montaigne, Estienne, and Pasquier—among others—developed a concept out of a term. As concept, *naïveté* helped to define what was particularly indigenous to them as writers and as Frenchmen. (JBA)

837. Butler, Johanna M. "More in Sixteenth-Century France." *Moreana* 42:21-22.

An allusion to More's execution and the Anglican schism appears in Diz. 147 of Maurice Scève's *Délie*, a Petrarchan sequence of love poems published in Lyon in 1544. No definitive answer has been given to the question—to what extent was the cultured public of the 16th century aware of contemporary international events and figures. Studies of 16th-century French private libraries show a striking lack of contemporary material. Such a reference to More and his drama by Scève, a provincial poet in a city with neither a royal court nor a university to serve as distribution center for international news, may be a significant indication of the degree of familiarity with contemporary events in England which could be expected of educated French society. (JMB)

838. Chavy, Paul. "Les premiers translateurs français." *FR* 47:557-65.

The learned men who, in the 12th or 13th centuries, concerned themselves with French translations were far from being naive. They had a fairly clear concept of what "faithfulness" should be. However, many a medieval translation appears untrue to the original. At least four sorts of reasons can be put forward to explain the "distortions" in such texts. For one, there is the didactic trend, which leads the translator to compile useful information from every source available. There is also the need for him to comply with the tastes of the less-educated public that reads only the vernacular. Conventions of literary style bring forth other factors of inaccuracy. Finally, early French translators were confronted with the intricate problem—encountered by translators of all times—of bridging the gap between widely separated cultures. In any case, they should not be judged by modern standards, but studied with respect to their own aims and means. (PC)

839. Clifford, Paula M. "The Grammarians' View of French Word-Order in the Sixteenth Century." *PQ* 53:380-88.

The 16th-century grammars of French may be more informative and of greater general interest than is often supposed. Their treatment of word-order illustrates the diverse approaches to a theory of the vernacular language at this time. (PMC)

840. Derwa, Marcelle. "Un aspect du colloque scolaire humaniste:Le dialogue à variations." *RLC* 48:190-202.

In the beginning the "colloquia scolastica" of the Humanists embodied a simple pedagogical method. The aim of such a method was to teach the correct Latin language and to protect the morality of the scholars or students. Through examples of Erasmus and Barlandus, it is demonstrated that, although they were good thinkers and writers, the Humanists transformed the simple "colloquia scolastica" into autonomous works written in a creative style and containing the highest teachings. (MD)

Drama and Theater. 870. Pinet, Christopher P. "The Cobbler in the French Farce of the Renaissance." *FR* 48:308-20.

The cobbler serves as an important comic stereotype in French farce of the Renaissance. His choice as the primary representative of tradesmen in these short, comic plays stems from his lowly social and economic status, as documented by guild laws and other historical accounts. The humble tasks performed by the cobbler and the difficulties he faces in trying to collect payment for work done make him the object of derisive laughter. Various myths and legends about the cobbler spring up in farce: he is a drunkard, a particularly jealous husband, he is lazy and sings from dawn to dusk. Later authors such as Bonaventure Des Périers and Jean de La Fontaine contribute to the cobbler's legendary status; Shakespeare uses him to intensify class conflict. Finally, Federico García Lorca takes the legend, adds a new psychological dimension to it, and demonstrates that the cobbler elicits a timeless and automatic laughter by his conformance to stereotyped bahavior. (CPP)

Du Bartas. 907. Arthos, John. "Du Bartas, Petrarch, and the Poetry of Deism." [F 46]:1-17.

The encyclopedic character of Du Bartas' writing displayed the almost inexhaustible resources of the theories of the Pléiade in France in the 16th century; but he made a special contribution of his own that was to be largely responsible for their continuing effects: through cultivating and extending the use of antitheses in the Petrarchan manner. He employed this device in referring all the features of organic and spiritual life and nature to the idea of a machine, in its nature as matter and its working. Through the

fullness of his use of the device and the language he developed for it he prepared the way for all those to whom the developments of deism were providing philosophic and ethical syntheses. (JA)

911. Requa, Kenneth A. "Anne Bradstreet's Use of DuBartas in 'Contemplations'." *EIHC* 110:64-69.

Du Bartas *Divine Weekes* must be seen as an important source for Anne Bradstreet's "Contemplations," for such similarities as the two speakers' perspectives, locations, and actions, their apostrophes to the sun, and the nightingale indicate her use of Du Bartas. That she apparently turned to her study rather than the out-of-doors suggests she was more interested in the lessons derived from her poem than in trying simply to portray the new landscape. Perhaps to her, as to Wigglesworth in "God's Controversy with New England," America appeared a "waste and howling wilderness" that the godly could transform into a pleasant park. Importing details from Du Bartas was her attempt to form what was wild and external into her controlled emblems. (KAR)

La Taille. 933. Smith, C.N. "Imitation and Invention in La Taille's *Courtisan retiré*." *RomN* 15:490-94.

After a review of the literary sources of La Taille's satire *Le Courtisan retiré* of 1573, the way in which the poet incorporated various incidents that relate the general theme to the particular conditions of the French court in the mid-16th century is discussed. The career of the Old Courtier has close similarities with that of Jacques d'Albon. La Taille's treatment of his material is such that his satire, though derived from a Spanish model, is made thoroughly French in tone and impact. (CNS)

Marot, C. 943. Françon, Marcel. "Sur les poèmes à forme fixe de Clément Marot." *RLMC* 27:5-11.

Note on a rondeau by Marot which is published erroneously with a complete line instead of a "rentrement," and on a sonnet containing a reference to the invasion of Provence by Charles V in 1536 and the invasion of Picardy by the imperial army. A remark upon the imprisonment of Clément Marot in 1526 is made. (MF)

Montaigne. 963. Limbrick, Elaine. "The Paradox of Faith and Doubt in Montaigne's 'Apologie de Raimond Sebond'." *WascanaR* 9:75-84.

Montaigne's "Apologie de Raimond Sebond" may be considered as a series of paradoxes, essays against the prevailing opinion of man, reflecting current philosophical and literary trends. The "Apologie" 's conflicts stem from its scholastic and Augustinian heritage. Montaigne examines and refutes the Renaissance concept of man in a Socratic manner. His metaphysical dilemma is analogous with that of Kierkegaard: the skeptic, in order to believe, must suspend reason. Faith becomes the supreme folly. Thus the major paradox of the "Apologie" is that skepticism leads to faith. The first series of paradoxes proving the superiority of animals over men draws mainly upon Plutarch and is influenced by Landi's *Paradossi* and Giraldi's *Progymnasa*. The paradox of a "learned ignorance" is both Socratic and Christian in inspiration, Cusa's *De docta ignorantia* being a likely source. Montaigne's concept of God owes much to the Platonism of Plutarch and St. Augustine. The final paradox is that the orthodox "Apologie" became a highly unorthodox, even irreligious, defense of Catholic faith. (EL)

Rabelais. 989. Clause, Odile. "Les mots et la vie chez Rabelais." *BRMMLA* 28:66-73.

Rabelais explored language by using a wide variety of means. His work is built like an infinite cycle—no end, no beginning—and its language appears like the human life cycle: a continuous chain of copulations, births, and deaths. This is especially noticeable in enumerations and coined expressions. Language for him is an immense world where all natural ways of creation are permitted, excluding the unnatural. This world, however, is often misleading and contradictory: language and literature are ambiguous. "Trinch," the message of the "Dive Bouteille," prolongs that ambiguity and brings the ending back to the beginning, the drinkers of the prologue, thus closing the endless chain of language and life. (OC)

999. La Charité, Raymond C. "Panurge's Heartbeat:An Interpretation of *Mitaine* (*Tiers Livre*, Ch XI)." *RomN* 15:479-85.
Analysis of Panurge's use of the word *mitaine* in chapter xi of the *Tiers livre* reveals that this particular image has contextual reverberations consistent with Rabelais's metaphoric practice in various episodes. The meaning of Panurge's heartbeat is one of sexual reference, which aptly expresses his excitement and expectation at the thought of marriage and an inquiry as to its outcome. (RCL)

1006. Simon, Roland H. "Les prologues du *Quart Livre* de Rabelais." *FR* (spec. issue 6):5-17.
In his prologue of 1548 to the *Quart Livre* Rabelais defuses his work in showing through the wildest example of authorial interpretation of a sign (the cover of a book he has just received) how it can be decoded into an inoffensive invitation to drink. He then launches into an open attack against those who have attempted to keep his books from the initiated for whom they were intended. Rabelais seems bent on proving to his detractors through mockery that they lack the key to the proper use of his materials. The author's diatribe is based upon a profound belief in the legitimacy of his purpose. On the other hand, the prologue of 1552, which has been retained in the successive editions, is on the surface a departure from such self-assured vindictiveness. It is devoted altogether to a series of anecdotes whose moral lessons drawn by the author praise moderation. However, the situation of the main characters in these anecdotes prove at close look to be so unbearable that it does away with any pretense of justification of moderation. This points directly to a need for a new reading of the *Quart Livre* as "anti-lecture." (RHES)

1007. Valette, Francis C. "Notes pour le commentaire de Rabelais." *RomN* 15(1973):323-27.
The phrase "redoubler au coulouoir" in the Loup Garou episode of the *Pantagruel* has been interpreted by Rabelais's editors as a fencing term describing an intricate maneuver of swordsmanship. This interpretation is not consistent with the text. "Coulouoir" designates the genitalia of the giant which Pantagruel is trying to hit with his sword. In the *Gargantua*, the word "hanicrochez" used to describe the tail of Gargantua's fantastic mare has been understood traditionally as meaning "similar to a hook." This word must be understood as "braided" in the manner it was customary to braid the tails of plowhorses. (FV)

Ronsard. 1011. Becker-Cantarino, Baerbel. "Ronsard's 'Exhortations pour la Paix' (1558) and Erasmus." *RomN* 15:486-89.
"Exhortation pour la Paix" deals with man's destination as a peaceful being. These lines represent a topos from classical literature which Erasmus had employed in his spirited discussion of war and peace, his *Querela Pacis*, and in *Dulce Bellum Inexpertis*. Erasmus relegated war and warlike acts to the morally inferior world of the animals. For him man was to use his reason and human qualities to develop laws and organize society for his

own protection. In his "Exhortation pour la Paix" of 1558 Ronsard gives an artistic rendering of Erasmus' arguments against war. (BB-C)

Scève. 1025. Lloyd-Jones, Kenneth. "Thomas More and Maurice Scève's *Délie*." *Moreana* 42:23-32.
Scève mentions More's death once in *Délie*. Many important contemporary personages and events are also referred to, but More's death is specifically related to Scève's spiritual and sensual rebirth through his love for Délie. Scève's special treatment of More—no other figure is so intimately or so intricately bound to the poet's situation—suggests a particular sympathy for aspects of the Utopian ideal. More's concepts for the necessary equilibrium of society and the nature and function of Virtue are echoed in *Délie*. One may conclude that *Utopia* played a seminal role in Scève's formation. (KL-J)

1029. Runyon, Randolph. "The Errors of Desire." *Diacritics* 4,iii:9-14. [Rev. art.]
Current semiotics research derives not only from Ferdinand de Saussure's foundation of a general science of signs but also from his secretive pursuit of "anagrams," hidden words he believed he had found in Latin verse. Jacqueline Risset, in *L'Anagramme du Désir* (1971), seeks to show that Scève's *Délie* is "a vast anagrammatic network" in this Saussurian sense. Unfortunately, her evidence is neither extensive nor convincing. Yet her claim for Scève's poem can be justified on the basis of other evidences. The appearance of the word "mercy" in fragmented form in dizain 76 of *Délie* is accompanied by a rigorous and fairly complex system governing the distribution of "M" and "Si" as first letters of the first lines of dizains. "Mer-cy" thereby emerges at numerous places in the text, like a Saussurian anagram, together with further instances of the speechlessness and the meteorological *serain* that appear to have caused its disintegration in dizain 76. (RPR)

Tahureau. 1032. Sommers, Margaret C. "Jacques Tahureau's Art of Satire." *FR* 47:744-56.
Jacques Tahureau's theory of satire is found in the *Dialogues non moins profitables que facétieux* published in 1565 and printed 13 times by 1585. Through his character Democritic, Tahureau declares that satire must combine didacticism and humor. It requires an author of sound moral character who cannot be ignorant, affected, or hypocritical. Using these criteria and a profound respect for human reason and its potential, Tahureau attacks Cornelius Agrippa. Agrippa's *De Incertitudine et Vanitate Scientiarum* (1537) according to Tahureau, presents fallacious and irrational arguments. Tahureau denounces Erasmus' use of self-parody and irony in the *Praise of Folly*. Erasmian satire distorts reality and confuses the reader. The *Dialogues* themselves illustrate Tahureau's satiric theory through their combination of definition, example, and rational debate with caricature, anecdote, and wordplay. (MPS)

V. SEVENTEENTH CENTURY

Drama and Theater. 1061. Brooks, W.S. "The Tradition of *Timocrate* and the History of the Marais Theatre in 1657." *MLR* 69:56-63.
Thomas Corneille's *Timocrate* ran for six months or 80 performances at the Marais theater during the winter of 1656-57 and was for a time performed by the Hôtel de Bourgogne in competition. Some recent critics have made suggestions which tend to invalidate the tradition, and a reappraisal is necessary. The first performance was earlier than these critics believe. The important assertion of Madame Deierkauf-Holsboer in *Le Théâtre du Marais* that the theater closed on 1 April 1657 allows *Timocrate* only a 3½ month run: she bases her findings upon a misinterpretation of a remark by Tallemant and a misunderstanding of part of Lancaster's *History of French Dramatic Literature*. The existence of part of the Marais troupe in Rouen in August 1657 is not proof of its break-up. Several plays, including others by Thomas Corneille, were performed at the Marais in spring 1657 or later. The tradition of concurrent performances at

both theaters also indicates that the Marais was functioning: this tradition is finally proved by a recently-discovered theater-placard fragment. *Timocrate* and other plays ran at the Marais beyond 1 April 1657, and the theater stayed open at least into 1658. (WSB)

1072. Sharkey, James M. "*La guerre comique*:A Dramatic Disputatio." *RomN* 15(1973):303-05.
La Guerre Comique by the "Sieur de La Croix" is an example of the disputatio, a Jesuit technique of argumentation, which is used to support the thesis that Molière is a "Térence resuscité." (JMS)

Arnauld. 1083. Carré, Marie-Rose. "Pensée rationelle et responsabilité morale:Le traité de sagesse dans *La logique* de Port-Royal." *PMLA* 89:1075-83.
La Logique de Port-Royal does not fit into any categories; indeed, the art of logic as an independent exercise of the mind seemed unacceptable to its authors. Writing at the end of the Aristotelian era and under the influence of Cartesian theories, Antoine

Arnuald and Pierre Nicole saw logical reasoning as justifiable only if it trains the mind to distinguish between good and bad. They believed in the existence of an immutable, eternal truth. Logic must train our word-using and concept-making faculty to acknowledge that the needs of man's soul belong to a much higher order of values than the science of "things," thus giving reason the strength to be "true" to its own nature. (M-RC)

Aulnoy. 1085. Palmer, Nancy and Melvin. "English Editions of French *contes de fées* Attributed to Mme d'Aulnoy." *SB* 27:227-32.
In spite of an English vogue for French fairy tales in the early 18th century, the bibliography of the French *conte de fée* in England has remained confused. Part of the confusion has resulted from the fact that a 1699 collection of fairy tales is regarded today as a bibliographical ghost. There are reasons to believe, however, that the book did in fact exist and that it contained four fairy tales, all by Mme d'Aulnoy. The main obstacle to an accurate account of the French fairy tale in England, though, is the fact that 28 of the tales attributed in England to Mme d'Aulnoy are by 4 other French authors. This study tabulates the contents of the four collections attributed to Mme d'Aulnoy and indicates correct authorship of the fairy tales they contain. (NBP & MDP)

Boileau. 1096. Lein, Clayton D. "Boileau, The Moderns, and the Topinamboux." *PLL* 10:21-34.
The full force of Boileau's fury at the Quarrel of the Ancients and the Moderns stemming from Perrault's *Le Siècle de Louis le Grand* (1687) emerges when we recognize the full meaning of allusions contained in two of his neglected epigrams—"Sur l'Academie." Boileau's immediate reaction was to assign Perrault's opinions on Modern progress to idiots and barbaric cultures—Hurons and "Topinamboux." This last group has never been sufficiently identified, although the 17th-century reader knew them as the most savage cannibals of the New World. (CDL)

Corneille, P. 1138. Reiss, Timothy J. "*Le Menteur* de Corneille:Langage, volonté, société." *RomN* 15(1973):284-96.
Corneille's *Le Menteur* proposes what one may term a *mise en crise* of (social) discourse. Dorante's lying appears as a constant effort to speak and to impose his will to avoid being subsumed within the social discourse of those around him. The discourse of the Other finally defeats him by opposing his own means to him (false letter, false rumors, tales). Clarice offers an alternative means of avoiding this loss of will while remaining within the exchange of social discourse: a totally gratuitous discourse, a "gift" which avoids the "trap" laid by the social. The third possibility offered is that of silence, a negation of society. The play can offer no solution whereby the individual can maintain his own will within a system of social exchange: one or the other must give way. *Le Menteur* thus casts into doubt both the possibility of society and Corneille's own previous theater of heroism. Language is finally unable to overcome the problems raised by a permanent opposition within the culture of I/other, inside/outside, individual/society—a series of contraries explicitly stated by a character within the play as the very basis of society's discursive exchange system. (TJR)

Corneille, T. 1152. Moravcevich, June. "Thomas Corneille's *Ariane* and Its Racinian Models." *RomN* 15:465-76.
Ariane represents a change in Thomas Corneille's conception of tragedy, which has frequently been termed Racinian by critics who are nonetheless reluctant to ascribe a real influence to Racine. Parallel passages from *Ariane* and Racine's *Andromaque* and *Bérénice* are discussed in order to support the claim that Racine's plays guided Corneille in the creation of a tragedy in which the primacy of passion determines the events and the development of the plot, thought and emotion fix the destinies of characters capable of arousing pity, and the expression of emotion sustains interest. (JM)

Descartes. 1168. Spiller, Michael R.G. "The Idol of the Stove:The Background to Swift's Criticism of Descartes." *RES* 25:15-24.

Swift's satire of Modernity in *A Tale of a Tub* and *The Battle of the Books* draws on criticisms common in the latter half of the 17th century. In referring to Descartes as an exemplar of the modern intellectual revolution, Swift sees him as mad, fanatical, and introverted, a view transcending most contemporary criticisms of Descartes, which go no further than accusations of pride, atheism, or charlatanism. One earlier writer, Meric Casaubon (1599-1671) provides an attack which links Descartes' experimental philosophy with religious fanaticism: in his *Treatise Concerning Enthusiasme* (1656) he sees Descartes' philosophical originality as a species of mystical enthusiasm; and his unpublished ms. treatise "On Learning" (1667) supplies a fuller criticism, which is that of Swift. The similarity of Casaubon's views to Swift's suggests that Casaubon represented an attitude widespread enough to be picked up by Swift in the last quarter of the century. (MRGS)

Guérin de Bouscal. 1184a. Hilgar, Marie-France. "Une tragédie de Guérin de Bouscal:*La mort d'Agis*." [F 19]:204-07.
Guerin de Bouscal's *La Mort d'Agis* and its dramatic technique and structure are analyzed in order to show the author's evolution toward classicism. The 1640-50 decade deserves particular attention because the modern conception of action in the theater imposes itself. The restrictions brought by the unities of time and place allow the in-depth psychological study of a crisis. (M-FH)

La Bruyère. 1191. Berk, Philip R. "*De la ville xxii*:La Bruyère and the Golden Age." *FR* 47:1072-80.
La Bruyère's "De la ville xxii" sets contemporary bourgeois ostentation against the pomp of Imperial Rome and the simplicity of the French past. The contrast between town life and a rural past is anticipated in the preceding entry, rare in La Bruyère's work for its ideal evocation of country life, and thus less a token of his real attitudes than his satirical intentions. These entries are modeled less on any observed reality than on classical literary motifs, particularly the Golden Age theme. The absence of laws and lawyers, the reference to the four metals associated with the Ages of Man, the use of the "negative formula" illustrate La Bruyère's parody of the Roman poets, but the closest parallel is Juvenal's ironic handling of the Golden Age theme, especially in Satire XI, whose repeated insistence on double standards for aristocrats and commoners is echoed at the end of "De la ville xxii." (PRB)

La Rochefoucauld. 1218. Weber, Joseph G. "The Personae in the Style of La Rochefoucauld's *Maximes*." *PMLA* 89:250-55.
Moralist literature of 17th-century France can be characterized by a human dialectic in which the author is in dialogue with himself or with an aspect of his personality, or in which there is a dialogue between the *moi* and *autrui* or between moral principles. In La Rochefoucauld's case, there is a stylistic withdrawal, an absence of intervention of the person of the author which allows for an imaginative interplay between the various personae in the style of the *Maximes*. This tendency creates an imaginary framework that supports an extended and more dramatic development of personification. In the successive versions of any given maxim personification is generally sharpened, and what emerges from the overall literary texture of the *Maximes* is a veritable dramatis personae of extraordinary diversity and vitality. By dramatizing moral values in their multifaceted, contradictory nature, the *moraliste* tries to resolve the paradox inherent in them, while at the same time allowing moral ideas the freedom to remain paradoxical. (JGW)

Malebranche. 1224. Beyer, Charles J. "Malebranche et l'esprit 'moderne' au début du dix-huitième siècle." *FR* 47:1081-84.
The idea of the continuous accumulation of knowledge by mankind makes the Ancients appear like children as compared to the Moderns. This is commonly considered the most original argument used by Perrault and Fontenelle in the "Quarrel" that started in 1687. It is, however, clearly developed as early as 1674 in Malebranche's *Recherche de la vérité*. He may have known a note in Latin written by Descartes, in which the same idea is explicitly formulated, and which in turn may have been inspired by a passage of Bacon's *Novum Organum* (1620). At any rate, this view of progress and modernity finds its first expression in the

Cartesian philosophy; the fact that Cartesianism ended up by being assimilated to old-fashioned scholasticism by the victorious "Moderns" thus appears a particularly ironical twist of history. (CJB)

Mareschal. 1232. Maubon, Catherine. "Pour une poétique de la tragi-comédie:La 'Préface' de la *Généreuse Allemande*." *RLMC* 26(1973):245-65.
The Preface to the *Généreuse Allemande*, a tragicomedy published in 1631, is a basic text for studying the history of early 17th-century French drama. The text deals with various points raised in the "Querelle des Anciens et des Modernes." In the name of freedom and relativity of taste Mareschal refutes the teaching of ancient forms and the tyranny of Aristotelian rules. His precise analysis reveals a profound sense of the theater. (CM)
1233. Porré, Helje. "The Mercer and the Philanderer:Comedy of Character in Early Seventeenth-Century Pastoral." *RomN* 15:459-64.
The Mercer in the anonymous *Le mercier inventif* and Hylas in *L'Inconstance d'Hylas* by Mareschal provide two examples of comedy of character in pastoral. The Mercer is lacking in morals, indecent in speech, with characteristics of both the conventional go-between and the parasite, but with a personality of his own. He is a colorful figure and a considerable source of humor. On the other hand, Hylas is a charming, elegant young man whose chief interest in life is flirting and love-making. The play's humor is never vulgar, but consists mostly of verbal fencing, invention, and wit displayed by Hylas and his protagonists in their encounters. Hylas rejects the *précieux* form of love with its unwavering constancy; instead he is firmly committed to philandering. (HP)

Molière. 1255. Gale, John E. "Proteus or Chameleon? A Note on *Tartuffe*." *SCN* 32:54.
Two lines from the speech in which Tartuffe defends Damis, who has just accused him of trying to seduce Elmiire (III.vi: 1098-99), reveal both the conscious irony with which Tartuffe expresses his power and the unconscious irony of his inability to function except in terms of identities bestowed upon him by others. The conscious irony consists of Tartuffe's use of "on" to represent the reasonable majority and the expansive phrase *tout le monde* to represent the mad minority. But, given the context, "on" can also be read as referring to any of Tartuffe's victims, and the line in which it appears becomes a statement of his willingness to personify their illusions, the better to dupe them. (JEG)
1264. Hope, Quentin M. "Place and Setting in *Tartuffe*." *PMLA* 89:42-49.
Place in Molière deserves attention. The more farcical plays have an outdoor, Italianate setting. In the higher-toned indoor comedies the characters inhabit concentric circles: props, set, house, city, province, universe. At the center of *Tartuffe* stands the intruder, Tartuffe himself. A sequence of entrance and exit scenes define the broader aspects of place in the play. Madame Pernelle's exit scene situates Orgon's family; a disputatious and gossipy household. Orgon's entrance reveals a person who has lost his sense of place. Conventionally in comedy the bourgeois father is happy to return from the hazards of the country to the security of his role as owner and master. To Orgon, however, the return means only reunion with Tartuffe. His entrance scene is balanced by his eviction at the hands of his protégé who changes places with him. Tartuffe's place is Orgon's house: his exits are false exits or strategic withdrawals, his return is triumphant until the regal denouement which sends him to the King's prison and Orgon's family to the King's palace where they will kneel in gratitude. (QMH)
1289. Potter, Edithe J. "Levels of Knowing in *M. de Pourceaugnac*." *OL* 29:87-92.
Molière's *M. de Pourceaugnac* is an exploration of the limits and methods of knowledge. It demonstrates that language and the senses, as means of knowledge, are inadequate. Appearances are flexible and may be distorted by manipulators. On the lips of impostors, speech becomes free from the exigencies of mimetic adherence to reality and capable of imposing its own distorted meaning on the nature of things. Sense perceptions and words interpose themselves between our understanding and reality

which often is whatever we can be persuaded to believe. (EJP)
1297. Scanlan, Timothy. "Molière's *Le misanthrope*, 1324." *Expl* 32:Item 43.
In l. 1324 of Molière's *Le Misanthrope* (IV.iii) there is a probably intentional wordplay on the French word *traits*, which can refer to "handwriting," as well as to "character traits." In the context in which the term is used, the two meanings are applicable and even complementary, since the character traits in question are Célimène's insincerity and infidelity, manifested in her handwriting, that is, in an intercepted love-note addressed to Alceste's rival. (TMS)
1300. Shaw, David C. "*Le misanthrope* and Classicism." *ML* 55,i:16-26.
Molière's *Le Misanthrope* has an almost racinian regularity and intensity. Although Alceste's problem is temperamental, not social, we laugh at him because he is the same as the others while claiming loudly to be different. By asking Célimène to feign love, Alceste demonstrates that his respect for truth is absolute only when he is not personally involved. This duality is characteristic of Alceste: he repeatedly fails to illustrate the principles violently expressed in the opening scene which seem to stem from narrowly subjective origins. His temperamental need to be singled out is constantly, and comically, frustrated. (DCS)
1305. Wadsworth, Philip A. "Recollections of Cicognini's *Gelosie fortunate* in *Le Misanthrope*." *PMLA* 89:1099-1106.
Molière's *Le Misanthrope* contains themes, characters, and speeches from the tragicomedy *Gelosie fortunate* by Giacinto Andrea Cicognini. The tragicomedy presents a striking combination of violent emotional conflicts and frequent humorous interludes which probably inspired some of the excesses of Alceste. The Italian source contributed also to the conception and configuration of characters around Alceste, particularly the affectionate and sensible relationship of Eliante and Philinte. (PAW)

Pascal. 1331. Heller, Lane M. "Note on a Pensée (Brunschvicg 107):Pascal and Montaigne." *OL* 29:216-20.
The source of Pascal's pensée "Lustravit lampade terras . . ." (Br 107), is found in Montaigne's "De l'inconstance de nos actions." Pascal states that there is little connection between his mood and the weather. He probes the question in a self-analytical notation like those that abound in Montaigne's *Essais*. He notes that the success or failure of "les affaires" fails to upset his equilibrium: he remains detached from everyday happenings in a kind of stoic *apatheia*. In the second half of the pensée, he admits that at times he thrives on the challenge to prove himself capable of shaping events to his ends. Ultimately, the train of thought set off by Montaigne's remark leads to a glimpse of that overweening pride Pascal strove to replace with humility. (LMH)

Racine. 1360. Cloonan, William. "Racine's Titles." *RomN* 15(1973):297-302.
While the characters who appear in the plays' titles need not all be tragic figures, they all do have a common function. In each play the title character serves as a catalyst for the other principal personages who define themselves and express their understanding of the play's crisis by their reactions to the title character. At the same time the title character's self-assessment determines his/her ability to deal effectively with the crisis. (WC)
1361. Coquillat, Michelle. "Phèdre, ou la liberté dans l'acte héroïque." *FR* 47:857-64.
The Racinian world is usually seen as the world of no-liberty, where the cartesian passions lead men. The main consequence of that is their passivity. This, in fact, is only an apparent level of comprehension. The Racinian hero expresses himself through a powerful desire of domination. The obstacles that seem to lie between him and what he desires are needed for without them he cannot fight for his liberty. Therefore, far from being a christian world, the Racinian universe has to be defined through a Nietzschean ethic, and appears extremely modern. Finally, Phèdre's character can be seen in sado-masochistic terms. (MSC)
1362. Duffy, Joseph M. "Subject and Structure as Cosmology in Racine's *Phèdre*." *Mosaic* 7,iv:155-70.
Phèdre is a verbal model of the confrontation with the universe undergone by its protagonist. The artistic imagination creates a

verbal universe containing energies that threaten its formal balance. In its totality, as well as in individual scenes and speeches, the drama both frees and attempts to circumscribe those energies. That imaginative universe is like the protagonist who in verbalizing her passion liberates its destructive force. The drama closes not because Phèdre dies but because like her it must bring itself to oblivion before its liberated energy shatters its structure. As with Phèdre's suicide the final return to silence is the drama's ultimate formal gesture of sustaining its own concept of order. (JMD)

1364. Evans, William M. "Does Titus Really Love Bérénice?" *RomN* 15:454-58.
In Roland Barthe's brief study *On Racine* (1964) the reader is given the impression that Titus does not love Bérénice. This impression is not consistent with an accurate reading of the play's text. If Titus does not love Bérénice, then Racine's play would at best be only a melodrama. Barthe's contention is refuted and several lines from the text are cited proving that Titus did indeed love Bérénice and that this love had to be forsaken to obey the higher law of the Roman state. (WME)

1365. Gilman, Donald. "'Le venin qui vous tue':Motif, Metaphor, and Mode in Racine's *Britannicus*." *RomN* 15(1973): 278-83.
The motif of poison and its metaphorical expression seem essential to the dramatic coherence and the delineation of plot and character in Racine's *Britannicus*. The first use of the image is figurative, describing either Agrippine's fear or the force of love. But the euphemistic use of this image assumes literal significance and emerges at the end as a technique for Racine to dramatize Néron's revealed character and Agrippine's ironic downfall. The recurrent motif of poison progressing from metaphor to motif and mode thus parallels the characterization of Néron as a *monstre naissant*, and allows Racine to tighten the tragedy's structural unity and to enhance, on the level of symbol and metaphor, the development of plot and character. (DG)

1366. Hall, H. Gaston. "Pastoral, Epic, and Dynastic Dénouement in Racine's *Andromaque*." *MLR* 69:64-78.
A neglected literary context is pertinent to assessment of the shape and values of Racine's *Andromaque*. Pastoral plays by Racan and Mairet furnish a dramatic structure, vocabulary, and conception of idealized love not characteristic of other Racinian sources. It is from Saint-Sorlin's *Clovis* that Racine took the substitution of children which deceived the wily Ulysses and allows Andromaque, after another successful stratagem, to have her son Astyanax-Francion—the ancestor of the French kings in the legend of the *Roman de Troie* kept alive in the epic tradition. The *translatio imperii* in the play from Troy to the line of French kings parallels the *translatio imperii* in the *Aeneid* from Troy to Augustan Rome. Significant differences from Racine's ancient sources reflect mainly pastoral values and the shift of dynastic

perspectives, in which Andromaque's stratagems represent a form of *pietas* comparable to Aeneas's deceit of Dido, and the device by which Joash is preserved in the Old Testament story of Athaliah. (HGH)

1374. Mishriky, Salwa E. "La transcendance de Bajazet." *RomN* 15(1973):306-13.
Racine's *Bajazet* demonstrates a struggle between the theme of "soumission" versus "indépendance." In order to understand the structure of the oriental society, we have to penetrate below the surface of the play. The tragedy is largely a story of the feminine world striving for dominance and the masculine world searching for personal liberty and integrity. One of the key words of *Bajazet* is the word *esclave* which allows Racine to associate the main theme of "esclavage" with the character of the hero. Bajazet is the apparent captive, but is actually a free person, even if in searching for his liberty, he becomes a tragic victim. Thus only the hero can safeguard his dignity from the vicissitudes of "esclavage" and transcend his essence. (SME)

Scarron. 1393. Conroy, Peter V.,Jr. "The Narrative Stance in Scarron's *Roman comique*." *FR* (spec. issue 6):18-30.
The complex problem of the narrator and his function in articulating the dual nature of Scarron's novel *Roman comique* is discussed. There are two distinct elements here: a serious, heroic love story narrated in the "tiroirs" and associated with the word "roman"; and a burlesque plot line involving the actors and their travels, to which we attach the modifier "comique." The principal distinction between these two inspirations is the largely comic narrator. More than simply a voice recounting the plot, the narrator participates in the actual formation and belongs to the very texture of the novel. His pseudo-intellectual digressions on subjects of literary import constitute, for example, one of the roles he adopts. His narrative style (2nd role) is largely responsible for the burlesque effects of disproportion and of ironic distancing throughout the book and finally, he tries to write himself the role of a minor personage. The three roles also double as reflections upon the novel itself. (PVC)

Sorel. 1402. Griffiths, Michael, and Wolfgang Leiner. "Some Thoughts on the Names of the Characters in Charles Sorel's *Histoire comique de Francion*." *RomN* 15:445-53.
Sorel's intention in his *Histoire comique de Francion*, to present a philosophy of life, is frequently expressed and emphasized, and as such the novel extends beyond the realm of romanesque divertissement. Even the choice of proper names for his characters has been carefully deliberated; and these names, by virtue of their historical, mythological, or etymological connotation, contribute, significantly, to the realization of the author's intention. (MG & WL)

VI. EIGHTEENTH CENTURY

Bibliography. 1420. Trenard, Louis. "Lumières et révolution, 1750-1820:Vingt-cinq ans de bibliographie." *DHS* 6:24-43.
Bibliography of the major works dealing with the development of thought and social and political history during this period. (LT)

General and Miscellaneous. 1434. Formigari, Lia. "Language and Society in the Late Eighteenth Century." *JHI* 35:275-92.
Linguistic theories of the 18th century reflect belief in the existence of a "natural" man, who is not a product but a point of departure of history. Both language development and universal history are therefore the unfolding of man's essential attributes: thought and sociality. In the new approach, the task of anthropology is to describe man's self-creation. In this process labor has an essential role. Man's relation to nature is mediated by productive relations that mediate individual relations and language as well. (LF)

1455. Mortier, Roland. "Les héritiers des 'philosophes' devant l'expérience révolutionnaire." *DHS* 6:45-57.
Investigates the reaction of those *philosophes* who were still alive in 1792-93. This investigation shows that they either opposed the Revolution or soon became suspect and were considered as liberal

opponents, with the sole exception of Alexandre Deleyre. The bitter hostility of Robespierre to the Encyclopedists shows the rift between the radicalism of the Jacobins and the liberalism of the philosophes, whose doctrines were to inspire the Constitution de l'An II and the political line of the Directoire. (RM)

1472. Trenard, Louis. "Lumières et révolution." *DHS* 6:3-23.
"Enlightenment" and "revolution" characterize, primarily in France, the emergence of a new society from the "Ancien Régime." France experienced, under 'Louis xv, an intellectual transformation, considered to be the cause of political, social, and economic movements at the end of the 18th century. This decisive evolution coincided with other elements which exacerbated the situation, such as repeated abortive attempts at reform, survival of the irrational and even of the mystical, unprecedented solidarity between the elite and the masses, transference of sentiment, etc. The Revolution, daughter of the Enlightenment, at times rejected the new way of thinking. (LT)

Drama and Theater. 1480. Sergi, Antonino. "*Phèdre* corrigée sous la Révolution." *DHS* 6:153-65.
Studies the copy of *Phèdre*, corrected by hand, which the actors

used for the productions of this play in 1793 and 1794; this unique copy is preserved in the library of the Comédie française. Racine's original lines are printed opposite the lines as altered by the revolutionary censor. The corrections are fewer and less fundamental than one might have expected, and without them it would not have been possible to present Racine's play during the Revolution. (AS)

Idéologues. 1482. Moravia, Sergio. "La société d'Auteuil et la Révolution." *DHS* 6:181-91.
Analyzes the political role played by a group of intellectuals who met in a country house near Paris belonging to Madame Helvétius, wife of the philosopher, following his death in 1771. These men constituted the intellectual and political group most directly connected with the perpetuation of the Enlightenment. Their activity during the Revolution demonstrated both the revolutionary spirit and the uncertainties and weaknesses of the group, following the rapid sequence of events. (SM)
1483. Regaldo, Marc. "Lumières, élite, démocratie:La difficile position des idéologues." *DHS* 6:193-207.
The birth of the intellectual is perhaps the most important social phenomenon of the 18th century. But the intellectual is a socially ambiguous being. This ambiguity can be seen clearly in the "Idéologues" of the *Décade philosophique.* Sincere republicans, they supported the ideals of liberty and equality, but they also defended property and free enterprise. They wanted government by an élite of experts. The plan for a constitution proposed by Amaury Duval in 1795 demonstrates this hesitation between democracy and elitism. Finally, before democracy can be attained, there must be a long process of national education. (MR)

Beaumarchais. 1507. Berthe, abbé L.-N. "Deux amis à la cour de Versailles:Une correspondance inédite de Beaumarchais et Dubois de Fosseux." *DHS* 6:287-97.
Beaumarchais and F. Dubois de Fosseux, the secretary of the Academy of Arras, knew each other well. They lived at close quarters for weeks, even months. One was equerry at the court of Versailles while the other, as secretary of the King's household, gave harp lessons to the daughters of Louis XV and organized highly appreciated concerts for them. The two liked each other and continued this friendship in a correspondence. A letter dated 12 December 1763—the earliest of the three extant letters from Beaumarchais to his young friend—shows clearly how close their friendship was. (L-NB)
1515. Rex, Walter E. "*Figaro*'s Games." *PMLA* 89:524-29.
Whereas literary sources and theatrical conventions such as the unities are quite important for the appreciation of Beaumarchais's *Barbier de Séville* and *La Mère coupable,* they prove curiously unhelpful when trying to approach the unique qualities of *Le Mariage de Figaro.* The special ambience of this play is related not to ordinary literary traditions, but to the separate category of children's games. From Chérubin's hide-and-seek in Act I to the grand game of blindman's buff in Act V, these are what give the action of the play its unity and also create the special quality of the fun in the play. Because of the time of life these games imply (i.e., childhood), there is also a special quality to the play's revolutionary overtones. Thus, in many senses, the end of the play represents the ushering in of a new age. (WER)

Berquin. 1518. Martin, Angus. "Notes sur l'*Ami des enfants* de Berquin et la littérature enfantine en France aux alentours de 1780." *DHS* 6:299-305.
Points out some research problems in a much neglected field of literary study in France—the history of children's books. The problems refer to the little known work of Arnaud Berquin, the creator of the first periodical for children in France (1782-85). Martin examines Berquin's debt to his German predecessor, C.F. Weisse, editor of *Kinderfreund* and reveals the conditions under which Berquin's periodical was edited and circulated. Numerous bibliographical references are provided. (AM)

Buffon. 1521. Anderson, Elizabeth. "More about Some Possible Sources of the Passages on Guiana in Buffon's *Epoques de la nature.*" *Trivium* 9:70-80.

Sonnini probably played the biggest role in supplying the documentation on Guiana contained in Buffon's *Epoques de la nature* (1778). The naturalist Laborda and the botanist Aublet are also among Buffon's informants and a more modest influence role is assigned to the surgeon Ollivier which strengthens doubts concerning the role of Dr. Artur. (EA)

Crébillon fils. 1537. Ebel, Miriam. "New Light on the Novelist Crébillon *fils.*" *FR* (spec. issue 6):38-46.
New evidence from two documents suggests that Crébillon fils was of a startlingly different mentality from that generally postulated. A sale catalog of his personal library (over 4,000 volumes, a third Italian) points to an owner of wide-ranging, unexpected curiosities, immune, however, to contemporary intellectual fashions. The library, besides reflecting a keen appetite for Greek and Roman classics, is strong in history, natural history, art, architecture, and travel. Authors with a taste for mixing jest with earnest abound. An inventory of possessions after death discloses a large print and drawing collection (over 7,000) by 16-18th century masters. (MDE)

Diderot. 1552. Braun, Theodore E.D. "Diderot, Wordsworth, and the Creative Process." *CLS* 11:151-58.
Diderot's conception of the creative process, as expressed in the *Paradoxe sur le comédien* has significant affinities with Wordsworth's conception of it, as expressed in the Preface to the second edition of the *Lyrical Ballads* and in the Preface to his *Poems.* Analysis of the texts shows that Wordsworth, in discussing poetry, and Diderot, in discussing acting, were really speaking of artistic creation in general. The major difference in their views is related to the role of sensibility; yet even here Diderot's ambiguity reflects an implicit grasp of the distinction which Wordsworth was to make explicitly between poetic and human sensibility. (TEDB)
1553. Brogyanyi, Gabriel J. "The Function of Narration in Diderot's *Jacques le fataliste.*" *MLN* 89:550-59.
Narration figures in Diderot's *Jacques le Fataliste* both as form, since the work consists largely of characters telling, or trying to tell, stories, and as theme, since much is said about narration, both by the characters and the narrator. For social inferiors such as Jacques, controlling a listener compensates for social inferiority. The struggle for the upper hand in the narrative game involves strategies such as interruption or inattention by the listener, digression, silence, or teasing by the narrator. The narrative situation thus gives rise to a master-slave struggle. (GJB)
1554. Chambart, Elaine. "The Function of the 'Lecteur' in Diderot's Non-Fiction." *ELWIU* 1:227-35.
Diderot is a "sophisticated" or "self-conscious" author who never forgets the reader's presence. He expresses artistically his rapport with the reader via first person narrative interruption. In his works of non-fiction, Diderot addresses the reader directly in order to digress, to praise or criticize animate and inanimate objects, and to inform us that he is cognizant of any objections that the reader might raise. He accomplishes the latter by using the rhetorical device of procatalepsis: anticipating the reader's challenges and disproving them. The *lecteur* whom Diderot invokes takes the form of either intimate friend or general public. As friend, he is never offended by the author; but as general public, he is sometimes a target for harsh verbal attacks. With the use of author-reader dialogue—unusual in non-fiction—Diderot dramatizes his philosophy, creates an atmosphere of intimacy, and renders didactic literature more enjoyable to read. (EC)
1555. Cherpack, Clifton. "Form and Innovation in Diderot's Drames." *SBHT* 15:253-64.
The failure of Diderot's *drames* as plays seems due to his use of the archetypal comic form, which, because of its characteristics and the expectations it engenders, was inappropriate to his theoretical goals. In this he seems to have followed a model provided by La Chaussée, but his predilection for the comic form and its conventions was more than the passive and passing acceptance of a successful formula. He made *Le Fils naturel* more typically comic than its Italian source and went out of his way to use comic conventions in *Le Père de famille.* The resulting failures illustrate Diderot's inadequate understanding of the relationship between form and "content" and between art and morality and

also some of the basic weaknesses of 18th-century esthetics. (CCC)

1579. Moureau, François. "Sur une lettre de Diderot à John Wilkes publiée dans le *Courier du Bas-Rhin*." *DHS* 6:277-85. Discusses a recently discovered text of a letter from Diderot addressed to the celebrated politician, John Wilkes, in 1768, which hitherto was only known in an English version published in 1805. Recalling the interest Diderot had shown in Wilkes, Moureau compares the two texts. He concludes that the French text in all probability corresponds to the original of the letter written by Diderot. (FM)

1586. Schwartz, Leon. "L'image de l'araignée dans *Le rêve de d'Alembert*." *RomN* 15(1973):264-67. French scholars recognize the importance of reasoning by analogy in the genesis of Diderot's ideas. One of the best-known analogies in the work that perhaps best demonstrates this process is the spider analogy in the *Rêve de d'Alembert*. Paul Vernière, in his edition of Diderot's *Oeuvres philosophiques*, has traced this analogy back to Diderot's *Salon de 1767*. However, its use there appears to have been only a reminiscence of the same image in a much earlier work, the article "Asiatiques" which appeared in the first volume of the *Encyclopédie* in 1751. The transformation of what was originally a mystical Persian Sufistic representation of God and the universe into Diderot's materialistic analogy with the brain and nervous system of the human body, and later in the same work into a Spinozist image of a material "God," demonstrates both how the analogical process in Diderot functioned and how the *Encyclopédie* contributed to his subsequent literary creativity. (LS)

1587. Sherman, Carol. "In Defense of the Dialogue:Diderot, Shaftesbury, and Galiani." *RomN* 15(1973):268-73. Certain passages of Diderot's *Apologie de l'abbé Galiani* constitute a poetic of the dialogue literary form. He approved of the use of the latter as a vehicle for the expression of philosophic ideas, and he enumerated the qualities it should possess in order to persuade or instruct most surely: an impartial or a skeptical tone, absence of intervention by the author, and natural characters who have their own varied points of view and in whom the reader may recognize himself. These strictures echo the rules that Shaftesbury laid down in his *Characteristics* for the practice of philosophical dialogue. The dates of his preparation of the abbé's *Dialogues* and of his own subsequent defense of the latter correspond to the dates of composition of his first dialogue works of this same nature. Diderot often went so far as to avoid representing the defeat of the opinion he wished to attack. It seems that Galiani's example and Shaftesbury' s lessons were at least partly responsible for the hermeticism or apparent impartiality of Diderot's best literary creations. (CS)

Gouges. 1619. Woshinsky, Barbara. "Olympe de Gouges' *Declaration of the Rights of Woman* (1791)." *Mary Wollstonecraft Jour.* 2,i(1973):3-6. This document is a feminist revision of the *Declaratio n of the Rights of Man* (1789). Olympe de Gouges, a minor playwright and pamphletist, died on the guillotine for her opposition to the Terror. Her feminism was also unpopular at the time: despite their egalitarian principles, revolutionary thinkers assigned a dependent, domestic role to women. It is this contradiction between the democratic ideals of the Revolution and its real treatment of women which Gouges criticized in her *Declaration*. She asserted that in the areas of civil and political rights and economic opportunity, the official *Declaration* sought to protect only the rights of "man." After pointing out the insufficienc ies of the original *Declaration*, she sketched a program of social reform which would lead to equality of the sexes. Gouges' vision of social justice appears far more revolutionary than that of her male opponents, but her egalitarian faith is a logical outgrowth of the Enlightenment tradition—a tradition she accused the Revolution itself of having betrayed. (BRW)

Holbach. 1622. Newland, T.C. "D'Holbach, Religion, and the *Encyclopédie*." *MLR* 69:523-33. A number of unsigned articles on religious topics in Diderot's *Encyclopédie* are now thought to have been written by the Baron d'Holbach (1723-89). A comparison of these articles with the sources used reveals that the Baron made several changes in order to expound his own theories, for example by altering or adding to his source material in order to make all religions appear as ridiculous or intolerant as Christianity. An alternative technique was to make the practices of foreign religions seem closer to those of the Catholic Church, thus implying criticism of the situation within France, although d'Holbach seems to have deliberately avoided drawing specific parallels. (TCN)

Houdar de La Motte. 1623. Raynaud, Jean-Michel. "Houdar de La Motte:Une lettre oubliée à Voltaire." *DHS* 6:245-48. Presents and reproduces a forgotten letter written in 1722 by Antoine Houder de La Motte, in the name of Cardinal Dubois, in answer to a letter from Voltaire (Besterman, D.116). Some precise details are given about textual and dating problems in the correspondence of 1722 and about Voltaire's journey to Cambrai and Brussels. (J-MR)

La Harpe. 1624. Landy, Rémy. "Des Lumières à la contre-révolution:Un drame écartelé, la *Mélanie* de La Harpe." *DHS* 6:143-52. La Harpe's *Mélanie* reads like an explicit attack on enforced and monastic vows in general. It expresses implicitly the struggle of the "noblesse de robe" against its own guilty conscience. This play had difficulty achieving the success which the Revolution seemed to offer it; in 1791-92, the violent acting of Monvel could not disguise its ideological timidity. In 1802, La Harpe, now reactionary and religious, rewrote his play. He replaced its social tragedy by an existential tragedy, and *Mélanie* finally found a coherence which the Enlightenment had been unable to give it. (RL)

Lesage. 1645. Kent, John P. "The *Diable Boiteux* in England: The Tonson Translation and the Fake Chapter." *PBSA* 68:53-63. Lesage's *Diable boiteux*, published by the Widow Barbin early in 1707, was a success, with a second and third impression required within the year and a completely new edition in 1726. There are at least ten editions in English during the 18th century, two of which were published by Jacob Tonson, one in 1708 and the translation of the revised version in 1729. The Tonson products are important for two reasons: one, they endured; two, in both there is a chapter which is a fake, that is to say has no original from which it was translated, a chapter which is a figment of the ingenious translator's imagination. The fake chapter has been continually reprinted, most recently in 1927. The Tonson version, despite the illegitimate chapter, is a good translation; vigorous and colloquial, it deserves the popularity with which it has been received. (JPK)

Marivaux. 1669. Zylawy, Roman. "Marivaux's Feminism in *La colonie*." [F 19]:208-11. Marivaux was frequently concerned with social issues. Among these was his interest in women's aspirations to equality and their desire for greater dignity. Of all his works, the play*La Colonie* is undoubtedly his most explicit expresssion of commitment to their cuase. In the early part of the century this play shocked the French public by its revolutionary tone. Marivaux is calling for professional and political rights for women. The age, of course, was quite unprepared for his bold and militant feminist rhetoric. In fact, even after revision to a much milder form, *La Colonie* failed on the Paris stage. (RIZ)

Panckouke. 1689. Tucoo-Chala, Suzanne. "La diffusion des lumières dans la seconde moitié du XVIIIᵉ siècle:Ch.-J. Panckouke, un libraire éclairé (1760-1799)." *DHS* 6:115-28. Examines the career of one of the most celebrated French editor-publishers of the 18th century, Charles Joseph Pancoucke. Discusses the complex relations between the defense of Enlightenment in a capitalistic sense and its political use by bourgeois democratic thought. Attention is also drawn to the conditions and consequences of the ideological opposition between Enlightenment and capitalism. (ST-C)

Rousseau, J.-J. 1703. Barny, Roger. "Jean-Jacques Rousseau dans la Révolution." *DHS* 6:59-98.

Like the philosophy of the Enlightenment in general, Rousseauism splintered during the Revolution. The democratic aspects of the *Social Contract* which had been used to support parliamentary doctrines now turned against them. Aristocratic influence led to an emphasis on other aspects or reinterpreted aspects initially favorable to the Revolution. These developments were helped by the abstract nature of the bourgeois universalism found in the *Social Contract*. If one does not claim the existence of an abstract truth of Rousseauism distinct from the use made of it, one can accept Lakanal's paradox "the Revolution taught us to understand the *Social Contract*," because the division of Rousseauism into contradictory doctrines corresponds to contradictions within Rousseau's thought. (RB)

1720. Ellrich, Robert J. "Rousseau's Account of a Psychological Crisis." *AI* 31:80-94.
Introduction to and translation of Rousseau's "Histoire du précédent écrit" in which Rousseau describes his obsessive fears concerning the preservation of the manuscript of his recently-finished *Dialogues*, his attempts to insure its preservation, and the evolution of his psychic state during the time of those attempts. The introduction explains and situates briefly Rousseau's account within the context of his life and psychic being. (RJE)

1737. Leibowitz, Judith. "The Poetics of Salvation in *Clarissa*, *La nouvelle Héloïse*, and *Die Leiden des jungen Werther*." [F 19]:242-45.
The salvation or deification of self through abnegation changes during the 18th century to the glorification of an assertive and passionate self. Richardson's Clarissa achieves salvation in Christian terms solely through the quality of her feelings. In *La nouvelle Héloïse* (1761), by adding an ethic of social responsibility to the earlier sentimental criterion, Rousseau attempts to justify the passions. Goethe's Werther glorifies the passionately assertive self without need of religious or social justification. This secularized, esthetic model anticipates the "religion" of the Romantic self that dominates the early 19th century. (JL)

1741. MacCannell, Juliet F. "History and Self-Portrait in Rousseau's Autobiography." *SIR* 13:279-98.
Rousseau repeated his autobiographical enterprise in his last three major works, varying the form among the history (*Les Confessions*), the self-portrait (*Les Dialogues*), and the reflection (*Les Reveries*). The logic of his choice of self-portraiture as successor to the historical, confessional form lies in Rousseau's relating of portraiture to figurative language. Both are, for him, non-representational, yet are nonetheless adequate for dealing with the ideal (non-empirical; not present) dimension of the self. No absolute distinction between the forms of history and self-portrait can, however, be made: Rousseau's history is composed of a series of self-portraits, and conversely, his self-portraits form, as he says of his style, "part of his history." (JM)

1742. ——— "The Post-Fictional Self: Authorial Consciousness in Three Texts by Rousseau." *MLN* 89:580-99.
The understanding of Rousseau's complex relationship to his *Julie ou La Nouvelle Héloïse* (1761) depends on the reading of his *Préface à Narcisse* (1752), the *IIe Préface à Julie* (1761) and *Les Dialogues* (1772). Rousseau reflects on the author-text relationship by examining and rejecting traditional personalistic (apology; narcissism) and moralistic (fiction as deceit or example) concerns, and discovers a paradox to "authorship." For Rousseau, the two terms, "author" and "work," are indistinguishable from each other in the sense that they are both "literary consciousness." (JFM)

1744. Misan, Jacques. "Jean-Jacques Rousseau et son image dans la Venise du Settecento." *RLMC* 27:113-18.
In 1768 Domenico Caminer founded in Venice *Europa letteraria*, a monthly journal in which Rousseau is the object of constant interest. This interest is expressed through articles on Rousseau's personality, work, and his polemics with his contemporaries. Study of his personality is by far the most developed of the three. Rousseau's work is of much less interest which is explained: (1) as arising from the difficulty which contemporaries have in seeing a fashionable writer's works as something apart from the writer himself; (2) as a consequence of the persecutions which his work earned him; or (3) a desire of the journal's editors to conceal their interest in ideas which were considered harmful and thus to ward off the repercussions of an ever-vigilant board of censors. (JM)

1746. Murphy, Patricia. "Fantasy and Satire in Rousseau's *La reine fantastique*." *FR* 47:747-66.
Most likely written early in 1756, before his break with the philosophes and before his "moral conversion" was complete, *La Reine Fantasque* shows Rousseau willing and able to use a popular literary device, the whimsical tale, in order to express both standard criticism of social types and behavior and some of his own ideas on the natural and the artificial, on education and on government. Examination of the form and content of this satire allows a better understanding of Rousseau's ability to work within conventions and go beyond them. The portrait of the Queen illustrates some of his most constant ideas about the nature of women. Although the story might seem an anomaly to those not familiar with the early stages of Rousseau's literary career, it is consistent with the many efforts he made to be accepted yet be his own man. (PM)

1752. Pickering, Sam. "The Sudden Rise and Fall of Rousseau's Reputation in Britain." *RS* 41(1973):268-77.
Rousseau's popularity in Britain coincided with latitudinarian dominance both of the Church of England and of literary criticism. The Sunday School Movement, the growth of evangelical religion, and the criticism of sensibility contributed to the decline in his popularity. By the end of the 18th century, Rousseau had become an almost mythological demonic figure. Instead of Richardson's equal, Britons now thought him the philosopher behind the French Revolution. (SFP)

Saint-Martin. 1774. Chaquin, Nicole. "Le citoyen Louis-Claude de Saint-Martin, théosophe révolutionnaire." *DHS* 6:209-24.
Shows the complexity of the political thought of Saint-Martin and emphasizes its fundamental difference from conservative thought. The Revolution, seen by Saint-Martin as a complete break with the past, called for an analysis of society, a redefinition of the concepts of liberty, popular sovreignty, etc., and of the role of collective action. The hesitations of Saint-Martin regarding the idea of the people and his unhappiness about the bourgeois consolidation of the Revolution raise questions familiar to specialists in the political thought of the Romantics. (NC)

Saint-Pierre. 1776. Garson, Ronald W. "Two Pastoral Romances: Longus' *Daphnis and Chloe* and Bernardin de Saint-Pierre's *Paul et Virginie*." *Trivium* 9:81-87.
Similarities of plot and style are the main features inviting a comparison of Longus' *Daphnis and Chloe* and Bernardin de Saint-Pierre's *Paul et Virginie*. Both novels trace the development and frustrations of young love in a rural setting. The psychological progression of the lovers toward awareness that their feelings are carnal as well as spiritual is meticulously traced. Pathos and rhetoric are common in both novels, with many humorous touches added in Longus' work. These, together with disciplined plot construction and a happy blend of plausibility and fantasy, have made him popular, while Bernardin's theorizing and alleged morbidity have made him less acceptable. (RWG)

1777. Stern, Madeleine B. "Saint-Pierre in America: Joseph Nancrede and Isaiah Thomas." *PBSA* 68:312-25.
Joseph Nancrede (1761-1841), French-born bookseller-publisher of Boston, published between 1796 and 1797 the first American editions of the major works of Bernardin de Saint-Pierre, French philosopher-botanist-poet-artist. The project was grandiose, involving multi-volume sets, engraved illustrations, French, English, and bilingual editions. The mechanics of producing French books in American editions is illuminated in a series of 6 letters from Nancrede to his printer Isaiah Thomas of Worcester. The American publication of Saint-Pierre's writings introduced the philosophical romanticism of a distinguished French writer and thus accelerated American understanding of French thought. (MBS)

Voltaire. 1785. Allen, Marcus. "Character Development in the *Oreste* of Voltaire and *Les mouches* of Jean-Paul Sartre." *CLAJ* 18:1-21.
Voltaire intended to prove his dramatic superiority over the

Greeks and, in the process, use the play as a vehicle for his political and social propaganda. Sartre had no desire to improve upon the tragic form. Like Voltaire, he saw in Orestes a vehicle for his philosophic views. Voltaire's *Oreste* remains fairly close to the Greek model while Sartre's hero undergoes a tremendous change—a change that is entirely necessary in order for Sartre to advance his ideas on human liberty. (MA)

1793. Curtis, Judith. "Voltaire, d'Allainval and *Le temple du goût.*" *RomN* 15:439-44.

One of the satiric responses to Voltaire's *Temple du goût* (1733) is d'Allainval's comedy of the same name, published the same year and never performed. In it we find stringent satire not only of Voltaire but of several of his friends. A key to the satire is found in an edition reported by the Soleinne catalog, which indicates that the characters in d'Allainval's play represent various actresses of Voltaire's circle; the Englishman Falkener, to whom Zaïre was dedicated; and the type of gentleman dilettante represented by Moncrif and the marquis de Surgères. The key is supported by research into Voltaire's interests at this period. (JC)

1800. Fazziola, Peter. "Candide Among the Bulgares: A Parody of Pascal's *Pari.*" *PQ* 53:430-34.

One major attempt to ridicule Pascal's thinking can be seen in Chapter ii of Voltaire's *Candide*, where the author resorts to parody in order to show the absurdity of Pascal's famous *Pari*. Candide finds himself in a situation which reflects that of man as viewed by Pascal. Both Voltaire's Candide and man, according to Pascal, find themselves chased from the earthly paradise and thrown into a dungeon. There, each is required to choose between two alternatives. Candide and the free-thinker in the *Pensées* would rather not make a choice and protest that the will is free. Yet, both are forced to choose, being told that the will is not free not to choose. Throughout, Voltaire uses, with only occasional variations, the same terms used by Pascal. In the end, only the king's grace can save Candide, as indeed, according to Pascal, only God's grace can save man. It is also apparent from *Candide* that the king saves only a few, as God, according to Pascal, saves only his few elect. (PJF)

1810. John, Elerius E. "Voltaire et la critique des religions révélées (d'après les *Lettres philosophiques*)." *FaN* 8,iii(1973):14-19.

Voltaire criticizes revealed religions in his *Lettres philosophiques*. The satire on religion in general and on Christianity in particular occupies an important place in these letters. Of the 25 letters, 7

concern revealed religion directly, while the 6 treating Science and English philosophy are full of unfavorable remarks against Christianity. Even in the other letters where emphasis is on literature, Voltaire does not conceal his anticlerical polemics. Voltaire rejects the Christian psychology based on these ideas but upholds the empiricism of Locke. Having skillfully criticized Christian dogmas he proposes new values based on human activity and free from metaphysical preoccupations. (EEJ)

1815. Lizé, Emile, ed. "Lettres inédites de Voltaire." *DHS* 6:249-58. [Seven letters, four to Grimm.]

An examination of some of the known manuscripts of the *Correspondance littéraire de F.M. Grimm* has already brought to light a certain number of unpublished letters written by Voltaire. Some hitherto unknown letters and passages discovered in the Gotha and Stockholm manuscripts and written by Voltaire to Desmahis, Huerne de la Motte, Grimm, and Linguet are published here. (EL)

1816. Magnan, André. "Le *Nouveau manuel épistolaire* de Chaudon et la correspondance de Voltaire: Lettres oubliées et notes critiques." *DHS* 6:259-75.

A description and inventory of the *Nouveau Manuel épistolaire* attributed to Louis-Mayeul Chaudon. It revealed, at its date of publication (1785-87), a good number of unknown letters from 18th-century writers, most of which have since been discovered in other sources. One can still extract from it four unknown letters of Voltaire and one addressed to him, as well as numerous indications relative to other texts of Voltaire's correspondence. (AM)

1835. Shillony, Helena. "*L'orphelin de la Chine* de Voltaire: Les limites de l'exotisme." *HUSL* 2:73-78.

L'Orphelin de la Chine (1755), Voltaire's adaptation of a Chinese drama translated into French by a Jesuit priest, affords an opportunity to assess the impact of exoticism on classicism. The vogue for *chinoiserie* appears as an attempt to widen literary and artistic horizons beyond the imitation of antiquity. His adaptation changed the exotic play into a trite love story between Genghis Khan and a Chinese lady. Voltaire's attempt to renew tragedy by turning to exotic plots and settings was bound to fail. The compelling structure of the genre, with its verse, its unities, its *bienséances*, destroyed those powerful and irregular features that made foreign drama attractive to a generation tired of classical French theater. (HS)

VII. NINETEENTH CENTURY

General and Miscellaneous. 1859. Bataillon, M[arcel]. "Jean Pommier comparatiste." *RLC* 48:5-11.

The late Jean Pommier, a renowned authority and subtle critic, liked to introduce the perspective of comparative literature into his studies of the sources of French literature. This is apparent in the various phases of his studies on Renan. Whether when dealing with problems of general literature, whether in his analyses of Chateaubriand's exoticism and Baudelaire's foreign inspirations, he often showed himself close to the spirit of the *RLC*. (MB)

1864. Clubbe, John. "Romanticism Today." *Mosaic* 7,iii:137-50. [Rev. art. on Abrams' *Natural Supernaturalism*, Peyre's *Qu'est-ce- que le Romantisme?* and Beaty's *Light from Heaven*.]

Romanticism is as much a European phenomenon as it is a congeries of national movements, and it is folly to try to understand so complex and varied a phenomenon without seeing how it evolved within social, political, and cultural manifestations, within currents of ideas, that transcend national borders. Three recent studies of Romanticism are considered in detail in the light of this thesis: M.H. Abrams, *Natural Super-Naturalism: Tradition and Revolution in Romantic Literature* (1971); Henri Peyre, *Qu'est-ce-que le romantisme?* (1971); and Frederick L. Beaty, *Light from Heaven: Love in British Romantic Literature* (1971). Although none of these books falls wholly within the field of Comparative Literature, *comparatistes* will benefit from the informed awareness manifest in them of European culture in the Romantic age. (JC)

1865. Corradini Ruggiero, Claudia. "Henry James as a

Critic: Some Early French Influences." *RLMC* 26(1973):285-306.

Henry James's 1865 review of Matthew Arnold's *Essays in Criticism* provides initial clues to his early critical thought and introduction to French literature. That same year he identified the ideal critic as being the Swiss writer Edmond Scherer. James's 1876 essays on Baudelaire, Balzac, and Flaubert show Scherer's persisting influence, but are also in agreement with the French critic Ferdinand Brunetière's ideas. A close textual analysis, however, proves that only Scherer directly influenced James, while Brunetière himself followed in Scherer's footsteps. (CCR)

1869. Garber, F. "The Structure of Romantic Decadence." *NCFS* 1(1973):84-104.

The 18th-century man of feeling, caught between desire and incapability, looked for modes of organizing experience which emphasized coherence and proportion. Rousseau was paradigmatic, discovering an Eden which was both paradisal enclosure and prison. Versions followed elsewhere in Rousseau, in Chateaubriand, Stendhal, and Huysmans. The enclosure also came to be a place within which one fed on one's own substance, endlessly generated in a process of cyclical self-consumption. The final parody is in Huysmans' decadent enclosure in *À rebours*, cut off from the analogy to organic nature which gave life to the Romantic enclosure. (FMG)

1879. Misan, Jacques. "Un foyer actif de l'italianisme au XIXe siècle: *La Revue de Lyonnais* (1835-1848)." *HUSL* 2:79-91.

A presentation of Italianisms in the provincial literary journal *La Revue du Lyonnais* (1835-48), directed by François-Zénon

Collombet, a former clergyman who left the Church in order to dedicate himself to lay work in the areas of Christian erudition, religious education, and literary criticism. He partakes of his journalistic talents with a homogenous team whose force resides in the constancy of a critical method made of catholicism, liberalism, and moderate romanticism. The results are convincing. The *Revue du Lyonnais* shows us the contemporary Italian literature in a rich and varied way, mentioning authors like Dante, Foscolo, Manzoni, and Pellico. (JM)

1880. Ricardou, Jean. "Le prisme d'Epsilon:Plutôt, de subdivisions prismatiques." *Degrés* 2(1973):d-d9.
Within the frame of a search for a theory of the French New Novel, the role played by certain operations in Claude Ollier's first five novels is explored. His first novel, *La Mise en scène*, develops according to the conflict between *dispersion* (time as a separating factor) and *conjunction* (resemblance as a uniting factor). His other novels obey the same two contradictory principles. The analyses lead to a conceptualization of intertextual relations (between the various elements of a given text), restricted intertextual relations (between the novels of a single author), and generalized intertextual relations (between the texts of different authors). Thus the text may be defined as a central *dispersion*, a pattern consisting of implicit parentheses, containing and contained in every line, indefinitely interlocking. (AH)

1881. Rossard, Janine. "Pudeur et amour romantique." *NCFS* 2:123-27.
Romantic love needs *pudeur* (modesty and/or reserve) to be romantic. With the early Romantics, *pudeur* does not create a harmonious relationship between man and woman, but unlocks too much of the characters' imaginations. With the more bourgeois Romantics it develops an inane mask of decorum. The Romantics show *pudeur* at work in young girls but, more originally, in young matrons and men. In all these characters hypocrisy is more unconscious than not but egotistical instincts prevail as love turns out to be either too individualized or too socialized under the imperfect impact of *pudeur*. (JR)

Balzac. 1940. Champigny, Robert. "Realism and Realities." *Diacritics* 4,i:2-6. [Rev. art.]
The stylistic features which Bernard Vannier, in *L'Inscription du corps*, notes in Balzacian portraits fit a perspective of interpretation which would avoid the distinctions between fictional individual, historical individual, and property. These confusions appear in the "realistic" requirements of verisimilitude, presence, and preexistence of the model. A mixture of styles contributes to a confusion between single text and independent testimonies. (RJC)

1954. Frappier-Mazur, Lucienne. "Balzac and the Sex of Genius." *Renascence* 27:23-30.
Only in the case of two groups is Balzac's portrayal of femininity directly influenced by his monistic theory of energy: women writers and malicious spinsters. Both may share the quality of genius, whether their creation is a literary work or machiavelian intrigues. Both are characterized by virginity, chastity, or at least childlessness; some degree of virility; hermaphroditic traits. A comparison with androgynous characters and/or male "geniuses" reveals that genius is indeed bisexual, mobilizes all the energy available and is concomitant in Balzac with his own longing for physical, bisexual parenthood. But whereas female geniuses are afflicted with monstrosity or destructiveness, male geniuses, apart from the criminal Vautrin, resolve their ambivalence into harmonious androgyny and creativity. Thus, intellectual conception in lieu of physical parenthood results in the highest forms of fulfillment in men, and conflict and polarity in women. (LFM)

1960. Haig, Stirling. "Dualistic Patterns in *La peau de chagrin*." *NCFS* 1(1973):211-19.
La Peau de chagrin is structured initially around the fundamental antinomy of possession and contemplation, of action and thought—represented by the magic skin itself—and is apparently resolved in dialectical fashion. The episode of Raphaël de Valentin's chance visit to the fantastic antique shop at the beginning of the novel, with its apparently random imagery and its proliferation of meaningless cultural debris, orchestrates in a highly structured presentation the antithetical and dialectical

concerns of Balzac's "philosophical study." (SH)

1962. Hayward, Margaret. "Balzac's Metaphysics in His Early Writings." *MLR* 69:757-69.
Scholars have commonly argued that Honoré de Balzac gradually developed his scientific and metaphysical system, evolving from an atheistic standpoint in his youth to a spiritualistic one inspired by Swedenborg. Swedenborg, it has been assumed, provided him in the 1830s with his religious views and his cosmogony. Reappraisal of early texts, however, shows the young Balzac to be, not an atheist, but a deist, who found his proof of God's existence and his cosmogony in an early reading (c.1820) of John Locke's *Essay Concerning Human Understanding*. (MJW)

1977. McVicker, C.D. "Balzac and Otway." *RomN* 15(1973):248-54.
The English restoration dramatist Thomas Otway, by the adaptation of certain historical facts to his tragedy *Venice Preserved*, influenced Balzac in the *Histoire des treize*, in *Ferragus*, and especially in the creation of the character of Vautrin. Balzac quotes from the French version of the play in the meeting of Vautrin, alias Carlos Herrera, with the young Rubempré, then on the verge of suicide; in the relationship of the two friends, Pons and Schmucke; and in the meditation of the founder of the *Société des Treize* on the value of the philosophy of Otway. The influence of Otway tends to negate the theory of Vautrin's homosexuality, and tends to support the theory of Balzac's misogyny in the later part of his life. Furthermore, even though the theory of homosexuality in the case of Vautrin has been proposed by various scholars, there seems to be no novelistic evidence to support it. Neither do supposedly historical sources provide any sound evidence of sexual deviation. Finally the theory of Otway's influence helps to clarify the intentions of Balzac in regard to human relationships, particularly in the later novels. (CDM)

1992. Ukoyen, Joseph. "Balzac et l'aristocratie." *FaN* 8, iii(1973):19-26.
In his presentation of the aristocracy in the *Comédie humaine*, Balzac makes no attempt to advance a theory or a definition of the nobility. His approach is descriptive and historical. He adopts the mythical origin of the nobility, according to which the French nobility resulted from the Frankish conquest of ancient Gaul, a feat perpetuated in the new name of the territory. This traditional nobility conforms to a strict hierarchy: at the head the king, the first gentleman or prince in his kingdom, followed by dukes, marquises, and counts and viscounts. The title of baron, the last rank, was originally given to all the nobles immediately beneath the king. Three great moments in French history, namely the Revolution and Empire, the Restoration, the July Monarchy, have left their mark on the evolution of the nobility: under the July Monarchy, the traditional nobility all but disappears, giving way to a spurious aristocracy and the bourgeoisie, which becomes henceforth the dominant element in French society. (JPU)

Baudelaire. 2018. Brench, Angela, and Henri de Briel. "The Marriage of Heaven and Hell:An Insight into the Duality of Baudelaire's Metaphysical Vision in *Les fleurs du mal*." *FaN* 8,iii(1973):26-33.
The obscurity of *Les Fleurs du mal* defies logical analysis and invites an intuitive approach to explain Baudelaire's metaphysical vision. His private journals insist on the hermetic qualities of language, hence its evocative power to express the synesthetic nature of objects and experiences. From ancient times language has possessed magical efficacy, a symbolic function in making the "correspondances" between physical and metaphysical reality. Mystery, sorcery, and exoticism are the tools with which Baudelaire forges this link. In the manner of many former secret schools and societies, including present-day Freemasonry, his reader is taken on a journey of initiation to an awareness of the cosmic structure imposed by the Grand Architect of the Universe. The poet is an "illuminé," he perceives the inherent duality in the essential unity of Creation. He aspires to a return to the primeval union of man with God through a fusion in his reflective consciousness of two opposing and yet complementary forces. (ADB & HTdB)

2021. Cottrell, Robert D. "Baudelaire's *Élévation* and the

Ptolemaic System." *RomN* 15:426-29.

In the first three stanzas of *Elévation*, Baudelaire evokes a spiritual ascension. Three features of the world defined within these stanzas seem to be derived from the Ptolemaic system: the nine spheres through which the poet's spirit passes; the sphere of the fixed stars through which his spirit moves before being immersed in the last region; the tenth and final sphere, which, like that of the Ptolemaic system is filled with fire. Baudelaire chose to describe the ascending motion of his spirit in terms of a system used for centuries by Christian writers to express the ultimate aspiration of the soul. (RDC)

2027. Kadish, Doris Y., and L. Brian Price. "A View from the Balconies of Baudelaire and Genet." *FR* 48:331-42.

Textual analysis of Baudelaire's poem "Le Balcon" and Genet's play of the same title reveals significant parallels of rhythm, imagery, structure, and vocabulary. The artificial nature of response to woman as a vehicle for transcendent goals provides the key to understanding Baudelaire's concept of space. A balcony serves as a point of departure for movement both within the confines of the room and outward toward the *au-delà*. This basic tension between concrete sensual reality and the *au-delà* emerges in the opening scenes of Genet's *Le Balcon* as an interplay between two spatial dimensions. Space plays a vital role in Tableau VIII. The balcony presents a view of characters in a state of illusion and the projection of this image into the depths of space. The inherent brevity of the peak experiences appears fundamental to both works. The "minutes heureuses" of the poem represent one isolated fragment of temporality. The peak moments in the first three tableaux of the play, as well as the group moment of exaltation on the balcony, are of necessity short-lived. Both poet and dramatist seem to suggest, however, that memory and the act of writing itself emerge as a revindication of human forces against the non-human passage of time. (DYK & LBP)

2052. Wickers, Janine N. "Baudelaire's 'Harmonie du soir'." *Expl* 33:Item 8.

The musical structure of Baudelaire's "Harmonie du soir" influences and determines the poem's ultimate meaning. The arrangement of the lines is almost fugal in that when a line is repeated, the line which follows it fills out the harmony of its meaning. The first stanza establishees the rhyme, structure, tone, and set of images for the entire poem. It fuses and harmonizes the sights, sounds, and smells of natural and religious images. The second and third stanzas continue to fuse scenic, musical, and religious images, while introducing elements of discord. The final stanza collects the images in the memory of the speaker and suggests that the entire poem is a musical, memorial Mass. (JNW)

Bertrand, Aloysius. 2057. Zecchi, Lina. "La produzione testuale nel poema in prosa:Lettura di 'Scarbo' di Aloysius Bertrand." *LeS* 8(1973):443-60.

The prose poem can be studied as a writing mechanism where syncretism, hybridism, and pseudo-morphosis tend distinctly toward the edification (or recovery) of an identity between writing/painting. The functioning and structure of this kind of text is brought out by the systematic analysis of the prose poem "Scarbo" by Bertrand. The problem of the production of a poetic text, the dichotomy between a book as an archeological (petrified) object and a book as a biological object (living organism), and the role of the reading public in the conservation of the literary product are approached. The rehabilitation of alchemy as a procedure and figure for the convergence of poetry and prose is discussed. (LH)

Chateaubriand. 2068. Goldschläger, Alain. "Sade et Chateaubriand." *NCFS* 2:1-12.

The philosophic and literary importance of Sade is unappreciated and subject to academic neglect. He seems quite distant from an orthodox writer like Chateaubriand, and yet both writers share the concept common to the early 19th century, that love is only possible through pain and anguish. The similar manner in which each writer explores the subjects of eroticism, sexuality, and criminality indicates their community of spirit. Sade, like Chateaubriand, was inspired by the English gothic novel in terms

of literary technique, although he evolved a more comprehensive and elaborate concept of nature. A comparative analysis of these two writers modifies and broadens our idea of a rigidly traditional Chateaubriand, and serves to humanize Sade by establishing more precisely his value as a man and writer. (AJG)

2077. Spininger, Dennis J. "The Paradise Setting of Chateaubriand's *Atala*." *PMLA* 89:530-36.

The landscape description of the New World that begins Chateaubriand's *Atala* has suffered from misguided criticism. The New World is "le nouvel Eden," adapted to a tradition of garden paradises, particularly that of Milton's *Paradise Lost*. While recalling its mythical model, however, the features of Chateaubriand's landscape simultaneously and ironically suggest a fallen condition by representing dualities in a state of tension. This ambivalence sets up a double relationship to the paradisiacal theme treated in the novel. The terrestrial paradise is recalled as the appropriate setting for another Fall. The conflicting properties of the symbolic locale do not achieve the expected synthesis and the story of the ill-fated lovers parallels the mythical Fall analogue. The emphasis then shifts to the celestial paradise, the religious (and Romantic) reconciliation of opposites. This remains tentative, however, for the final image of the novel is of the "new Eden" deprived of its sacred context, rife with dualities. (DJS)

Constant. 2081. Merken-Spaas, Godelieve. "Ecriture in Constant's *Adolphe*." *FR* (Spec. issue 6):57-62.

The role of *écriture* (the written word and the act of writing) in Constant's *Adolphe* shows that not only the spoken word but also the written word is hindered by constraint. There is violence inherent in the written word in its being used as a weapon to seduce Ellénore. The relationship between desire and *écriture* is examined. In *Adolphe*, *écriture* forms part of a movement (from silence to *parole* to *écriture*) which expresses the transition from nature to culture. (GM-S)

Dumas père. 2092. Bassan, Fernande. "Alexandre Dumas et le théâtre romantique." *FR* 47:767-72.

It is thanks to Alexandre Dumas the Elder that the French romantic drama triumphed with *Henri III et sa cour* (10 February 1829). This success encouraged the three other important romantics, Vigny, Hugo, and Musset, to write plays. The romantic theater grew through the reciprocal influence of these four men, whose "romantic" plays have many traits in common. Of the four, Dumas's theatrical works are the most abundant and varied. Taking at first his inspiration from Shakespeare and Walter Scott, Dumas introduced, with *Henri III*, violence and passion on the stage, as well as historical scenes, enhanced by beautiful sets and costumes—elaborate productions became the trade-mark of the romantic theater. Dumas wrote many historical dramas, but he also wrote modern romantic dramas—the first of which was *Antony* (1831)—where he introduced social criticism. He adapted dramas by Schiller and Shakespeare, and tried his hand at various types of plays: melodrama (*La Tour de Nesle*), *mystères*, fantastic plays, tragedies. As of 1839, melancholy not being compulsory anymore, he yielded to his cheerful nature and wrote good comedies; later he adapted many of his novels to the stage. (FB)

Duras, Claire. 2099. O'Connell, David. "*Ourika*:Black Face, White Mask." *FR* (Spec. issue 6):47-56.

Between 1815 and 1848 there appeared in France a fairly large number of literary works intended to advance the abolitionist cause. For the most part the authors of these works presented their heroes as superior in almost every imaginable way to normal white (or black) persons. In contrast to this tendency, Mme de Duras has given us a genuine black heroine in *Ourika* (1824). Mme de Duras is most modern in her analysis of the psychological disintegration of Ourika, a black girl rejected by white society because of her color. Like Frantz Fanon in *Peau noire masques blancs*, Mme de Duras traces her heroine's destruction through four basic stages: from feelings of inferiority through a period of insecurity to one of self-hatred and, finally, to despair. (DO)

Feuillet. 2100. Tintner, Adeline R. "Octave Feuillet:*Le petite *comtesse* and Henry James." *RLC* 48:218-32.

Henry James's published criticism of Feuillet's fiction in the 1860s-70s does not begin to measure the life-long effect his work had on James's literary imagination. Particularly, in his *Notes of a Son and Brother* (1914) James relates how his brush with a French marquise and her servants supplied him with the real model for the heroine of Feuillet's *La Petite Comtesse* reincarnated in his own fiction in the Princess Casamassima, thus initiating James's habit of reuniting in his imagination his observation and knowledge of life with his knowledge of literature. (ART)

Flaubert. 2104. Aubyn, F.C. "Madame Bovary Outside the Window." *NCFS* 1(1973):105-11.

Critics have defined the optics of Gustave Flaubert's *Madame Bovary* as essentially that of the view looking out of the window and down. Victor Brombert analyzes the window as a symbol of both imprisonment and liberation. The novel includes an additional optic that is almost equally important, that of Emma outside the window. Examples include that of Emma outside the shuttered windows of the abandoned pavilion near Tostes when she first asks herself why she married Charles. A second takes place during the ball at La Vaubyessard when a servant breaks a window to let in air and Emma notices the peasant faces outside the window. Another is that of Emma after the ball looking out a window but looking at the other closed windows of the chateau. Other characters including Léon, Rodolphe (he claims), and Père Rouault share this optic with Emma, an optic at once romantic and realistic. The romantic finds himself on the outside hoping to get in while the realist knows that we most frequently find ourselves outside the window of our own desires. In her refusal of this truth Emma loses all and sacrifices her daughter, the only innocent character in the novel. (FCSA)

2105. Bal, Mieke. "Fonction de la description romanesque:La description de Rouen dans *Madame Bovary.*" *RLV* 40:132-49.

In Flaubert's *Madame Bovary* the description of Rouen is a *diagramme iconique* because of the analogy between the relations holding between its elements and the elements of the (internal) reality (Emma). A term like *diagramme iconique*, however, does not indicate the reversibility of the relations mentioned—the description of Rouen is linked up with the whole of the novel, but the sub-parts occur elsewhere in the novel and then refer back to the description. The concept of *mise en abyme* (Ricardou) seems the most effective to analyze the description exhaustively. (MB)

2118. Fournier, Louis. "*Bouvard et Pécuchet*, comédie de l'intelligence." *FR* (spec. issue 6):73-81.

The misunderstanding of Flaubert's *Bouvard et Pécuchet* is rooted in a misappreciation of the genre of the work—which is comedy unmixed. It is impossible to ascribe to Flaubert the opinions of his "bonshommes.)" Many, including Sartre, have allowed themselves to discuss the "Dictionnaire des idées reçues" as a work of Flaubert, whereas it is made quite clear that it is the work of Bouvard and Pécuchet—and thus part of the vast comedy. Through his "bonshommes," Flaubert has diagnosed a "mal de l'intelligence" which marks his works, as well as modern Western thought. Bouvard and Pécuchet believe with blind faith in the absolute validity of human reason. (LF)

2135. Sabiston, E. "The Prison of Womanhood." *CL* 25(1973):336-51.

Henry James's Isabel Archer in *The Portrait of a Lady* (1881) is often seen as the prototype of recent portraits of young women. However, her predecessors include Austen's Emma Woodhouse (1816), Flaubert's Emma Bovary (1857), and George Eliot's Dorothea Brooke (1871-72). In all four works society imposes even more severe limitations upon women than upon men and the imaginative heroine is nourished upon books rather than upon life. The heroine's "provincialism" prompts her to seek ultimate values, but also imposes a frustrating ignorance upon her. Her mixture of aspiration and ignorance dictates her author's alternating tenderness and irony; even, at times, predisposes him to judge her actions by the same criteria he might apply to his own artistic endeavors. For all four women the inescapable prison is neither the provinces nor marriage nor ignorance, but the prison of womanhood. (EJS)

2137. Shriver, Margaret M. "*Madame Bovary* versus *The Woman of Rome.*" *NCFS* 1(1973):197-209.

In "Emma Unglued" (*SR*, 2 Dec. 1972) Alberto Moravia attacks Flaubert's *Madame Bovary*, finding the *bovarysme* of Emma clumsily superimposed. Moravia attempts to show that Emma cannot be motivated by the *insatisfaction romanesque* which Flaubert attributes to her. Moravia's denigration of Emma is explicable only when interpreted in the light of his own fiction. Contrasting *The Woman of Rome* and other of Moravia's novels and stories with *Madame Bovary*, one finds Moravia's women, animate with instinct alone, consistently unresponsive to the cultural impact of their ambience. Emma's response, therefore, seems to Moravia, as it did to Baudelaire before him, implausibly virile. That Emma should recall and identify with the heroines of novels avidly perused in convent days, Moravia deems a "cultural and ideological digression" on the part of Flaubert. Yet, like Emma, Moravia's own pivotal male protagonists consciously invest "real" life experiences with literary overtones. What is permissible for them, Moravia considers inadmissible in Emma, solely because she is a woman and, as such, must be denied even a minimal intellectual or metaphysical dimension, the exclusive prerogative of the effete introspective male. Though shedding little light upon Flaubert, "Emma Unglued" obiquely illumines Moravia's own fiction. (MMS)

Fromentin. 2152. Grant, Richard B., and Nelly H. Severin. "Weaving Imagery in Fromentin's *Dominique.*" *NCFS* 1(1973): 155-61.

Eugène Fromentin's *Dominique* is an anti-Romantic work that nonetheless has many Romantic aspects. It uses first-person narration, its subject is illicit passion, and an aura of fatality is at times present. In this context, imagery of weaving and embroidering appears at critical moments. Its function is clearly to suggest the woven fabric of our destinies. But the lesson preached is not that of a fatal Romantic passion but one of sober social responsiblity. When the protagonist is a victim of passion, the weaving imagery is negative: woven threads of passion that link people become horrible chains. When the hero finally realizes that illicit love must yield to social duty, the weaving imagery loses its negative value and appears in the idyllic form of a dutiful fiancée or wife making clothing for a family. Thus this imagery reinforces the explicit message of the narration. (RBG & NHS)

Gautier. 2155. Bassan, Fernande. "Une source bouddhiste possible d'un poème de Théophile Gautier." *NCFS* 2:24-28.

In 1838, at the age of 26, Théophile Gautier published, in his collection of poetry *La comédie de la mort*, the poem "L'Hippopotame," which has many points in common with the chant "The Rhinocerous" (by an unknown author), which appeared in an anthology of Buddhist Scriptures. This poem was translated into European languages, Nietzsche refers to it in an aphorism of *Morgenröte*. When we compare the Buddhist poem with Gautier's, we notice that the latter's is more exotic, in accordance with the romantic trend. In both works, the writers think that one should imitate the solitude and the courage of a pachyderm. In fact, Gautier's hippopotamus looks like a rhinoceros, with its thick skin and solitary walk. Gautier was always fascinated by Chinese culture and read extensively about it in his youth. He hired a Chinese professor for his daughter Judith who later published many books on Chinese literature. Considering the points in common between the two poems examined, and the interest of Gautier for China, he may have known and used the Buddhist poem. (FB)

2160. Cockerman, Harry. "Gautier:From Hallucination to Supernatural Vision." *YFS* 50:42-53.

Gautier was inclined to minimize the importance of intoxicants for the writer and his works on drugs have been seen as mere journalism, but the experience of intoxication has left its mark on areas of his creative work. Alcoholic intoxication is a much less important source of inspiration for him than opium and hashish, but it is all too easy to exaggerate the consequences of drugs for his creativity by placing excessive faith in the reliability of his own supposed accounts of his hallucinations. Since these more often than not use the same vocabulary, images, and impressions used in earlier works to describe visions and experiences he owed to art, literature, theater, or music, the most that can be claimed is that Gautier owed to drugs experiences that differ mainly in intensity rather than in kind from experiences already familiar to him. (HC)

2162. Dineen, R.M. "The Poetry of Théophile Gautier." *AUMLA* 41:50-63.
To counteract a pessimistic obsession with the impermanence of all life and beauty on earth, Gautier created a series of utopias. The first, in *Poésies*, takes the form of inactivity in a withdrawal from the world. On the failure of inactivity to combat the obsession, he tries its opposite with the topographical exoticism of *España*. This too proves ineffectual and the new utopia envisaged is the topographical and chronological exoticism of some of the *Emaux et Camées*, characterized by an insistence on the tangible permanence derived from the size and hardness of ancient monuments. This utopia also becomes unreal. The final solution appears at the end of *Emaux et Camées*. Gautier prefers pagan cremation to Christian inhumation, for the purifying dissolution of the fire transcends the horror of physical corruption. (RMD)

Hugo, Victor. 2184. Grant, Richard B. "Poem IV of Hugo's *Les contemplations*:A Problem in Interpretation." *RomN* 15:433-38.
For years, Poem IV of Book I of Hugo's *Les Contemplations* has been a subject for controversy. In the poem, Satan is juxtaposed to God's magnificent and bountiful universe. Earlier critical interpretations assumed that this juxtaposition was opposition, that Satan is excluded from divine joy, but recent critics have attempted to demonstrate that the poem is suggesting that even Satan is assimilated into God's harmony. By use of internal evidence and the place of the poem in the volume, Grant re-establishes the idea that Satan is indeed an envious and hostile outsider. (RBG)

Huysmans. 2207. Rossman, Edward. "The Conflict over Food in the Work of J.-K. Huysmans." *NCFS* 2:61-67.
The work of J.-K. Huysmans is marked by a conflict over food which he is able to solve only through the sacrament of the Eucharist. On the one hand eating is a savage, sadistic, neurotic act, an expression of mindless consumption; on the other it appears as the fraternal sharing of nourishment and ideas with fellow beings. Huysmans' characters, stand-ins for himself, oscillate between these contrary attitudes. In *En Route* the character Durtal, through his view of the Eucharist as an act of cannibalism on a cosmic scale, is finally able to achieve a more natural attitude toward food and eating. The devoured good of the Eucharist leaves nothing more to be desired, and ordinary food looses its power of fascination; it can henceforth be accepted naturally, without obsessive concern. Ironically, it is just this new, relaxed attitude toward food which poses a new threat to the author in the form of self-satisfaction. (EDR)

Laforgue. 2218. Giani Rotelli, Gabriella. "Sul testo di una poesia di Jules Laforgue." *RLMC* 27:119-21.
Compares the text of the Mercure de France edition of Jules Laforgue's "Devant la grande rosace en vitrail à Notre-Dame de Paris" with the text of the Pia edition. Of the numerous variants which may be found, the Pia edition notes only three. It says nothing about the origin of the discovered manuscript and, therefore, leaves open the problem of the double text. The poem "N'allez pas . . .," which in the Pia edition figures among the *poèmes inédits*, has already appeared in the Ateneo edition of Sergio Cigada. (GGR)

Lamartine. 2224. Willrich, Jacqueline L. "Jules Janin et Lamartine:Un aspect des relations entre Jules Janin et Lamartine, d'après des extraits de lettres inédites de Janin adressées à sa femme, de 1845 à 1856." *NCFS* 2:13-23.
Jules Janin's admiration for Lamartine goes back to his school days, when the *Méditations* came out. Later on, having acquired a literary reputation as a novelist and drama critic for the *Journal des Débats*, Jules Janin entered the circle of Lamartine's friends, and he introduced the poet to his wife Adèle. When Mme Janin

was absent from her home, the critic sent her a detailed account of the events of the day, mentioning the people he met. A letter in 1845 describes Lamartine as tired and preoccupied. Other letters mention Lamartine's political role and his failure to stay in power. At that time Janin fears that the poet's literary success in the past may be forgotten. After Lamartine's retirement from public affairs, Janin will encourage him to keep on writing. At one time Janin even compares his small contribution to the world of letters to Lamartine's fame with a rather open mind. The critic remained the poet's devoted friend until Lamartine's death in 1856. (JLW)

Mallarmé. 2264. Franklin, Ursula. "From Premonition to 'Réminiscence':A Prose Poem by Stéphane Mallarmé." *NCFS* 2:154-63.
"Reminiscence," a late piece of Mallarmé's prose poem cycle, *Anecdotes ou Poemes* of *Divagations*, constitutes a transformation of his early prose poem, "L'Orphelin." In "Reminiscence" Mallarmé's theme of orphanhood has become the anecdote of a symbolist piece celebrating the Hamlet-Igitur theme. The poem further marks a decisive stage in the evolution of the poet-persona in the prose-poem cycle, that of the Poet as Showman. The piece also reflects Mallarmé's notions on the theater, the ideal theater which is ritualistic and takes on the spiritual function of the dying Church. (UF)

2265. Goruppi-Moretti, Tiziana. "La critica mallarmeana nell'ultimo decennio (1962-1972)." *RLMC* 27:22-44,282-304.
Examines the development of Mallarmé criticism over the last 10 years. The delimitation of this period was motivated by the antinomic reading of Mallarmé's work by J.P. Richard and J. Derrida. Richard has proposed a "thematic" reading of the poet's complete works, basing his interpretation on the analysis of definite themes and their development. Derrida has proposed a type of reading based exclusively on "literal" interpretation, on the examination of linguistic and syntactic elements, independently of all semantic value. The article examines essays on Mallarmé which were written after the publication of Richard's book and the possible connections which later criticism has had with thematic criticism or the influences that it has undergone. (TGM)

2266. Graham, D.B. "Frank Norris's Afternoon of a Faun." *PLL* 10:307-12.
A literary source for the concluding scene of Chapter i of Norris' *The Octopus* (1901) is Stéphane Mallarmé's poem "L'Après-midi d'un faune: églogue" (1876). Norris might have known Mallarmé's poem directly or through J.-K. Huysman's discussion of it in *À Rebours* (1884), though there is no external proof to indicate knowledge of either work. The scene in *The Octopus* contains both an allusion to a faun in a state of semiconsciousness and an adaptation of the situation of Mallarmé's poem to fit Norris's fictional strategy. Both works are forms of pastoral emphasizing a tranquil rural landscape, meditative rhetoric, and the predominance of mood over action. (DBG)

2270. O'Meara, Maurice A. "La vision métaphysique et artistique dans *L'après-midi d'un faune*." *Lang&S* 7:138-42.
Mallarmé's use of metonymy and syntax in *L'Après-midi d'un faune* generates a poetic vision analogous to pointillist imagery and presents features that bring to mind the planetary structure of the atom. His subtle marriage of metonymic and metaphoric imagery produces an atmosphere in which the characters and objects of the Faun's world seem to disperse as energy particles which may be compared to the dots of color on a Seurat canvas. The poetic entity emerges cohesive, however, due to the elastic quality of the poem's sentences. (MAO)

2273. Rehder, R. " 'Une dentelle s'abolit' de Mallarmé." *NCFS* 1(1973):162-73.
"Une dentelle s'abolit" is representative of the later poetry of Stéphane Mallarmé, the poetry in which he came closest to accomplishing his purposes as a poet. An analysis of the poem reveals that all its images and ideas are developed from a single matrix. The poem is a perfect illustration of what Mallarmé meant when he spoke of "evoking an object little by little in order to show a state of soul." No simple statement of what the poem is about is possible. It exists between dream and reality, a poem of virtually intangible contingencies. Here Mallarmé has tried to

raise both the poem as a whole and individual words to the pitch of metaphor. (RMR)

Mérimée. 2294. Oliver, A. Richard. "The School for Mérimée:Four Letters from Charles Weiss." *SIR* 13:47-62.
Discusses four letters Weiss wrote to Mérimée about Charles Nodier which have never been published. This correspondence sheds light on Nodier's early youth in Besançon. Mérimée preferred to ignore the details, supplied by Weiss, that did Nodier credit and preferred the apocryphal interpretations of Nodier's doings as reported by Francis Wey. Mérimée's object in belittling Nodier was to discount his own literary debt to the man he succeeded in the Academy. (AO)
2295. Rosenthal, A. "Mérimée and the Supernatural:Diversion or Obsession?" *NCFS* 1(1973):138-54.
Prosper Mérimée was noted for his rationalism and skepticism; yet he sustained a lifelong interest in the supernatural and used the subject in over half of his fictional works. It has been suggested that this seemingly unlikely predilection was for him merely a diversion. It appears, however, that it sprang from a source far deeper than is readily apparent. As his correspondence has disclosed, Mérimée was capable of much deeper sentiment than was previously suspected, and his letters reveal a variety of fears and a nervous, superstitious disposition which was constantly concealed from public view. Despite his repeated denials of credulity in supernatural forces, he could never deny the possibility that they might truly exist. Mérimée was indeed troubled by his superstitious fantasies, and his literary treatment of the *fantastique* was a natural outlet for the repressed anxiety he felt. Haunted by the idea of fate and the presence of the unknown, his use of the supernatural in literature constituted the tangible form he gave to his fears. The number, variety, and consistent use of Mérimée's fantastic creations and the confessions in his correspondence indicate, not a diversion, but a veritable obsession. (ASR)

Michelet. 2301. Gossman, Lionel. "The Go-Between:Jules Michelet, 1798–1874." *MLN* 89:503-41.
Michelet's work, from the autobiographical writings to the histories and the books on natural history, invite interpretation according to a number of hermeneutic codes—philosophical, political, socioeconomic, psychoanalytical—and these interpretations in turn evoke each other, imparting to the texts something of the legendary quality Michelet himself admired in history and literature. Michelet's relation to history and his championship of the oppressed are questioned; behind both there is intolerance of otherness and desire for total control. (LG)

Musset, A. de. 2318. King, Russell S. "Musset:The Poet of Dionysus." *SIR* 13:323-32.
Nietzsche's concept of art as a product of a temporary reconciliation of the Dionysian and Apollanian tendencies affords a useful approach to Musset's poetry and particularly to "La Nuit de mai." This poem, a dialogue between the Apollonian Muse and the Dionysian Poet, is gradually transformed into a poem about art and creativity and mirrors the disharmony and unreconciled forces characterizing the romantic spirit. Musset's other poems and plays introduce related structures: the pervasive destruction of the will, art functioning as an escape mechanism, and the attempts to reconcile the will to act positively with Schopenhauerian pessimism. (RSK)
2327. Tappan, Donald W. "Musset's Murderous Rose." *RomN* 15:430-32.
According to most commentators, it is the "frelon" who dies in the imagery from the opening lines of "La Nuit de mai." The interpretation is grammatically indefensible and presents a preposterous picture. Rather, the rose dies, or will cease to be a flower, after the fertilization resulting from the visit of the hornet. The image is one of fecundity and is in perfect harmony with the the ambiguous theme of artistic creation/procreation with which Musset begins the poem. (DWT)

Nerval. 2330. Chumbley, Robert. " 'Delfica' and 'La différence':Toward a Nervalian System." *Sub-stance* 10:33-37.

The problem of the Nervalian sign is re-examined as the function of a system called *referance*. *Referance* is a rhetorical system marking the behavior of reference and referral deprived of repetition; it marks the absence of a differentiating system such as that of Derrida. This undefined space of *referance* is viewed as a transition between Foucault's categories of representation and signification. The confirmation and development of this system in "Delfica" suggests a new model of Nervalian discourse. (REC)
2331. Fine, Ellen. "Gérard de Nerval et le temps dans *Sylvie*." *NCFS* 2:128-41.
The two major categories in the thematic conception of time are its negation and exaltation. The first focuses on time arrested and a struggle against the destructive force of time. The second deals with continuity, circularity, co-existence of present and past both experienced and mythical. The ties linking the principal and retrospective narratives are clearly determined. The process of memory recall evokes a series of past images and events which are repeatedly recounted and subjectively interpreted by the narrator from different perspectives in time. There are also variations in "la durée" or tempo of the narration itself in which the time sequence is at times condensed, suspended, or accelerated. (ESP)
2339. Knapp, Bettina. "An Alchemical View of Gérard de Nerval's Tale *La marquis de Fayolle*." *NCFS* 1(1973):60-83.
An alchemical analysis of Nerval's "Le Marquis de Fayolle" in which the characters and events evolve in accordance with the three main transformatory phases which alchemists have depicted in terms of color: Chaos blackens, Dawn whitens, the Resplendent flame purifies. (BLK)
2343. Zuckerman, Phyllis. "Comedy, Tragedy, and Madness in Nerval's *Roman tragique*." *MLN* 89:600-13.
In the introduction to *Les Filles du Feu* Nerval explains his experience of madness through the story of a mad comedian who has assumed the pseudonym Brisacier and for whom comedy has disappeared. The story undermines the oppositions that govern Brisacier's tragic vision. He sees absolute differences between tragedy and comedy, real and symbolic violence, self and other, and truth and fiction, but events in the story make these terms indistinguishable from one another. Brisacier ultimately recognizes that he cannot play the role of Nero, Racine's tragic hero, even though it is his intense identification with this role that has driven him mad. (PWZ)

Nodier. 2344. Bell, Sarah F. "Charles Nodier's Knowledge of Modern Foreign Languages." *RomN* 15:421-25.
Charles Nodier's abilities as a linguist are known to be considerable, but apparently no systematic effort has been made to determine the extent of his knowledge of modern foreign languages. The matter is of interest because of the influence foreign countries or their literatures exerted on his work. Evidence demonstrates that Nodier had more than a little knowledge of Italian, knew some Spanish and English, and had a smattering of Illyrian, although it is unlikely that he knew any German. (SFB)
2345. Porter, Laurence M. 'Temptation and Repression in Nodier's *Trilby*." *NCFS* 2:97-110.
In Nodier's *Trilby* 3 exorcism ceremonies dramatize the struggle between Jeannie's moral sensibility and instinctive desire and illustrate the psychic mechanism of repression and its victory over her libido. Trilby can be interpreted as Jeannie's Jungian animus; the old monk Ronald as both her and society's super-ego. Banishing Trilby and his fellow-spirits denies repressed desires an acceptable, sublimated outlet. Nodier suggests that Jeannie is driven insane by an erotic obsession, that Trilby guides her to a higher mystical love which embraces all beings without disloyalty to any, and that in death Jeannie attains heroic stature by embodying the imaginative principle of the human spirit. (LMP)

Rimbaud. 2371. La Charité, Virginia A. "Rimbaud and the Johannine Christ:Containment and Liberation." *NCFS* 2:39-60.
The singular paradox which marks all of Rimbaud's poetry and which also takes into account all possible sources for his work is his effort to come to terms with the figure of Christ. In fact, Rimbaud's texts in *Poésies, Derniers vers, Une Saison en enfer*, and *Illuminations* are unified through his preoccupations with Christ as he is found in the New Testament writings of John. Rimbaud's

esthetic patterns parallel Johannine christological ones: rupture with known order, union of sign and thing signified, self-generation, binaries of opposition such as light-darkness and presence-absence, conjunction of ascent-descent, sound-sight, divine-human motifs, fusion of word and being. While Rimbaud scorns the didactic eschatological Christ of the Synoptic Gospels, he emphasizes the Johannine hypostatizations of the creative Word as the principle of cohesion expressed by light, love, and spirit. Although Rimbaud is ultimately contained by the concrete word as testimony, his poetry remains the first modern attempt to liberate man from historical verbal expression and reunite him with the creative force of his universe through poetry. (VALC)

2379. Peschel, Enid R. "Arthur Rimbaud:The Aesthetics of Intoxication." *YFS* 50:65-80.
Often Rimbaud simultaneously craves and condemns the effects of liquors, drugs, or transcendent beliefs. From these continuing conflicts he creates the beauty of his poetry, which has been described as a "Dionysian dance." With the concept of Rimbaud's "deliriums," happy laughter is intensified to wild enthusiasm, and "folie" is aggravated to raving, hallucination, illness, and insanity. Rimbaud's profound analysis of his exalted hopes and frustrated disappointment in love as a form of intoxication appear in *Délires I*. Three other important works epitomize Rimbaud's esthetics of intoxication: *Le Bateau ivre* exalts and debases the moral, esthetic, and spiritual aspects of his enterprise; *Matinée d'ivresse* portrays his hope and doubt in his religion of intoxication; and *Délires II* reveals language as a source and a symbol of his inebriation. For Rimbaud, the intoxicated and intoxicating quest for beauty necessarily implies love and poetry, as well as the antithetical grandeur of madness and defeat. (ERP)

Rostand. 2386. Williams, Patricia E. *"Cyrano de Bergerac* and French Morale in 1897." *SCB* 34:164-65.
The success of Rostand's *Cyrano de Bergerac* as drama is undeniable. However, a consideration of the morale of the French people in 1897 by means of a look at political and sociological events between 1870 and 1900 shows the desperate need of the French people for a titan hero with whom to identify. The courageous, heroic, captivating Cyrano was a timely and precise fulfillment of this need. (PEW)

2387. —— "Some Classical Aspects of *Cyrano de Bergerac*." *NCFS* 1(1973):112-24.
Edmond Rostand's undisputed chef d'oeuvre, *Cyrano de Bergerac*, is usually and justifiably termed a neo-romantic play: a return to the dauntless, poetic, and somewhat bombastic vein of Hugo's *Hernani* and its contemporaries. A careful study of Rostand's dramaturgy, however, reveals that the classical premises, those originated by Aristotle, are applicable to *Cyrano de Bergerac*. First, the term tragedy as defined by Aristotle is applied to the play; then, it is discussed according to six constituent elements of tragedy set forth by Aristotle. In summary, the image of tragedy is the structural framework for *Cyrano de Bergerac* on which is superimposed the constituents of romanticism. (PEW)

Sainte-Beuve. 2394. Marks, Emerson B. "Sainte-Beuve's Literary Portraiture." *ECr* 14:24-34.
The decline of Sainte-Beuve's reputation during the last half-century is owing chiefly to modern disapproval of biographical literary criticism, of which he is regarded as a pioneer exponent. The stigma of this label has led to a general neglect of his voluminous critical *oeuvre*, including many brilliant pages of appreciative criticism untainted by any trace of the personal or biographical heresies. Sainte-Beuve's modern reputation has also suffered from his having been so long hailed as a "scientific" critic, the natural historian of minds, whereas in fact the best portions of his work are valuable for their rare combination of humane erudition with esthetic sensitivity and explicative skill, not for the application of a naturalistic critical method. At their finest, Sainte-Beuve's critical essays are themselves minor works of art. The creative vein which had proven insufficient to make him a successful poet was turned to account in his literary portraiture. (ERM)

2395. Molho, Raphaël. "Modernité de Sainte-Beuve?" *ECr* 14:17-23.
Sainte-Beuve is ordinarily portrayed as a Neoclassic and the proponent of a historical criticism outmoded for modern times. Yet he is more modern than one might assume. He is among the originators of the idea of "reading," which considers the criticism of a work to be the simultaneous reconstruction of the work and its reader. Every critic recapitulates the work he annotates and expresses himself by his commentary. Fundamentally, like all the romantic generation, Sainte-Beuve did not believe in the stable and definite reality of man and things. Comprising unfathomable depths, carried away by the movement of the times, men and things possess neither coherence nor solidity. All that is left for a mind eager for rationality and clarity is writing. Constructing a solid building of words above the world's abyss is what is left to Sainte-Beuve. (RM)

2397. Mulhauser, Ruth. "A Legacy of Sainte-Beuve." *ECr* 14:55-63.
Sainte-Beuve played an active role in governmental action in 1846 and again as senator from 1865 to his death. In 1846, through a published article, he aroused public sympathy for the creation of the French School of Classical Studies in Athens and outlined the structure of such a foundation. Twenty years later, he played a similar role as spokesman to the government for the progressive university world on fundamental issues. Appointed senator in 1865, Sainte-Beuve represented what might be termed the "far left." He viewed his nomination as providing him a forum for making progressive views heard on vital issues. He made three speeches in the Senate in favor of freedom in the selection of books for popular libraries, freedom of the press, and academic freedom in teaching. (REM)

2398. Rigolot, François. "Sainte-Beuve et le mythe du XVIᵉ siècle." *ECr* 14:35-43.
Considerable textual evidence suggests that Sainte-Beuve's view of the 16th century is based on a fictional projection of conscious or unconscious obsessions. In his 1828 *Tableau de la poésie française*, he uses the 16th century as a polemic weapon to defend the Romantic credo. Later, the idea of esthetic progress leads him to view the French Renaissance as a testing ground for the masterpieces of the Neoclassical Age. Rabelais, both in the *Tableau* and the *Lundis*, is less a monk, a physician, and a scholar than an intoxicated word-monger whose stylistic debauchery lacks self-criticism and restraint. Yet, what Sainte-Beuve mostly admires in the 16th-century writers is their guilelessness and natural vigor as opposed, for instance, to the 18th-century affected naiveté and arrogant rationalism. Perhaps Sainte-Beuve needs to construct the myth of a spontaneous 16th century because it is only through the transposed past of literature that he can live the hugolian chaos of real life. (FR)

Sand. 2406. Thomson, Patricia. *"Wuthering Heights* and *Mauprat*." *RES* 24(1973):26-37.
While the literary sources of *Wuthering Heights* have been much stressed, the possible influence of French fiction has been ignored. George Sand's novel *Mauprat* (1837) bears striking resemblances to Brontë's *Wuthering Heights* in theme, characterization, atmosphere, and the romantic subjectivism of natural description and may well have been one of its sources. The subject of *Mauprat* is the ferocious, obsessive love, in life and beyond the grave, of Bernard, for his beautiful, imperious cousin, Edmée. Roche-Mauprat (his early home) and the Château of Sainte-Sévère (Edmées) parallel the primitivism and civilization of Wuthering Heights and Thrushcross Grange—a parallel underlined by imagery of hell and heaven. Like Heathcliff, Bernard overhears Edmée confess her contempt for his savagery and does not stay to hear her admission of her sense of the inevitability of their love and shared identity. In *Mauprat* love is shown as eventually a civilizing force—as for the second generation in *Wuthering Heights*—but unlike that of Heathcliff for Catherine. (PT)

Staël. 2414. Daemmrich, I.G. "The Function of the Ruins Motif in Madame de Staël's *Corinne*." *RomN* 15(1973):255-58.
The description of ruins in Madame de Staël's *Corinne ou l'Italie* forms a distinct literary motif fulfilling a double function in the

novel. Ruins appear as images for the personality, disposition, and mood of the main characters. The progressive portrayal of the ruins establishes the development of the protagonists' fate as well as their perception of it. The connection between ruins and Oswald's melancholy disposition becomes evident in Corinne's reversal of her pre-coronation song from joyous exuberance to melancholy reflection upon perceiving him. This contrast is strengthened by the shift from Corinne's exaltation of the grandiose and picturesque appearance of ruins and their preservation of the memory of the past to Oswald's pessimistic perception of the ruins. Corinne's change of mood from gaiety to despair on her moonlight walk among the Roman ruins and her final identification with their desolation summarizes the novel's movement. (IGD)

Stendhal. 2444. Kogan, Vivian. "Signs and Signals in *La chartreuse de Parme.*" *NCFS* 2:29-38.
Many characters in *La Chartreuse de Parme* are attentive to particular verbal signs and indices and to the various functions of communication which predominate in each of the three main sections of the novel. In the first section, which ends a little after the prediction of the Abbe Blanès, the referential function of language is primary and explains Fabrice's preoccupation with signs and omens, for Fabrice seeks to discover meaning in the world. In the second part of the novel, which culminates in the escape from prison, the code and means of communication are highlighted. Language becomes the mediator between man and the world. Fabrice in his tower exchanging light signals with Gina or playing the alphabet game with Clélia is a good illustration. In the last part of the novel it is the poetic function of language that is stressed. Poetic language is characterized by opacity, ambiguity, and parallelism. Clélia's vow is the best example; it marks the apotheosis of language in the novel. The progression then is one away from the universe that discourse is about and toward discourse itself. (VK)

2448. Palmer, William J. "Abelard's Fate:Sexual Politics in Stendhal, Faulkner and Camus." *Mosaic* 7,iii:29-41.
The castration of an individual, either literally or symbolically, by a power group is a recurring metaphor appearing in the literatures of different countries. Stendhal, Faulkner, and Camus are existential novelists who employ the metaphor of castration to image their novel's societies' methods of devitalizing the individual. In *The Red and the Black* through the use of phallic imagery Julien Sorel's social and existential castration is represented. When he rebels against "Abelard's fate," for the first time showing his potency as an individual, the novel's society must destroy him. In *Light in August* an individual attempts to define himself in a society even more overtly reactionary than Stendhal's France and here literal castration is his punishment. Again sexual imagery defines the protagonist's dilemma. Camus in *The Stranger* also objectifies the theme of revolt by means of sexual analogy. Meursault is imprisoned, cut off from the sea, forced to accept a sterile alternative to healthy sexuality. In each novel the attempted destruction of virility parallels the attempted usurpation of selfhood. (WJP)

2450. Pistorius, G. "L'humour dans le dernier roman de Stendhal." *NCFS* 1(1973):219-28.
Through an analysis of Stendhal's comic techniques the role that humor plays in *Lamiel* is discussed. *Lamiel* is full of comical incidents: the episode of firecrackers exploded behind the altar in order to simulate the fires of hell, Doctor Sansfin—the only caricature that is carried rather far—falling from his horse into the mud. Stendhal's favorite method is imitation. Not only does he reproduce the gestures of his characters, but also their tricks of speech. In many metaphorical turns taken literally we find another expression of comic irony. More sophisticated humor occurs in the forms of parody and burlesque. Humor used by Stendhal in *Lamiel* also involves social satire and mockery of bourgeois conventions. Cynical laughter becomes the answer for Lamiel herself, for whom ironical detachment is almost the only way to cope with reality. (GP)

2457. Talbot, Emile J. "Author and Audience:A Perspective on Stendhal's Concept of Literature." *NCFS* 2:111-22.
As a young man Stendhal held views on literature that were neoclassical in orientation from which he derived the belief that the proper subject of literature is man's internal life. He knew that such a literature makes demands on both the author and the reader which are different from those envisaged by neoclassical theorists. Since he considered great art to be based on an understanding of the interior life which is rooted in personal, emotional experience, he stressed the necessity of this experience as a prerequisite to both artistic creation and appreciation. It is through a capacity for emotivity and sensitivity, aided by the imagination, that a member of the audience becomes a co-creator. (EJT)

2458. ——— "Stendhal, the Artist, and Society." *SIR* 13:213-23.
Stendhal refused to accept the notion that the artist has a sociopolitical mission. He preferred to view the artist's presence in society in the broader context of the human condition and the problem of man's freedom. This is especially the case in *La Chartreuse de Parme* in which the poet Ferrante Palla appears mainly as a correlative figure who serves as a double to Fabrice. Stendhal's treatment of Fabrice's reaction to his imprisonment as a liberation from the fixation of society completes and poetizes Stendhal's thinking on this problem. (EJT)

Tristan. 2466. Collins, M., and S. Weil-Sayre. "Forgotten Feminist and Socialist." *NCFS* 1(1973):229-34.
Flora Tristan was an early French feminist of the 1830's and a socialist prophetic of Karl Marx. Her *Union ouvrière (Workers' Union)*, published four years before the Communist Manifesto, called for an international organization of all workers. Influenced by the English Chartists, she was the first to attempt to organize the French proletariat on the national level. Her feminism sprang from her personal experience as a woman who had to earn a living for herself, her mother, and her children after she separated from her husband. Her concern with women's right to work and to a decent salary was quite innovative at a time when most feminists were *bourgeoises* and detached from such issues. (MC & SWS)

Verlaine. 2481. Festa-McCormick, Diana. "Y a-t-il un impressionnisme littéraire? Le cas Verlaine." *NCFS* 2:142-53.
In applying the term impressionism to poetry one is aware that words evoke emotions and ideas. Many poets of various schools have created works where stream of consciousness prevails in free and changing association. Verlaine has been often characterized as an impressionist. His anti-intellectualism and musicality lend themselves to a fluidity of both movement and theme from which impressions emerge more clearly than thoughts. Images are suggested through movement, sounds, colors. The technique of placing and displacing, of showing and hiding, creates alternate pauses whereby dream and memory are confused. (DFM)

2492. Steisel, Marie-Georgette. "Verlaine's 'Il Pleure dans mon coeur'." *Expl* 32:Item 34.
In his poem "Il pleure dans mon coeur" Paul Verlaine methodically analyzes his state of *languor*. His mind has been sharpened by his high school literary formation in his *classe de rhétorique*; conditioned by years of methodical thinking, he writes his text according to the rules of a Cartesian rationalist. The quest in progress leads him to uncover, through the use of highly emotional terms, deeply seated moral and religious involvements, culminating in line 13: "C'est bien la pire peine" ("Indeed, it is the worst grief.") There the words are semantically charged with an almost double meaning: *c'est bien* could imply "it is good," "it's a good thing"; the superlative *pire* implies the greatest, and *peine* is charged with undertones of punishment. Thus, Verlaine conveys to the readers the sensorial and physiological impact of his own sorrow and condemnation. (M-GS)

Verne. 2499. Suvin, Darko. "Communication in Quantified Space:The Utopian Liberalism of Jules Verne's Science Fiction." *ClioW* 4:51-71.
Jules Verne's science fiction fits into Victorian "liberal utopianism," based on a diluted saintsimonism. Verne extends the Romantic "otherwhere" into a parallel world "otherwhen," interpolated into the imaginative space of classificatory science textbooks. Since quantified space and time are convertible,

Verne's extraordinary voyages are equivalents of the process of scientific reasoning solving the initial riddle, they are an epic of liberal communication. Quantified space is not a hierarchy of values, but a sum of kinetic objects; and Verne's plots and heroes return to bourgeois normality. However, the boy-scout mapping venture incorporates also escaping from the bourgeois world through traveling rather than arriving, through a miraculously clean space-machine (vehicle or island) and a trio of friends with loyal crew rather than women and class society. With the decline of liberalism in the mid-1870s, science turns destructive. Verne's dream of space was a flight from uncertain time, but it stands behind all science fiction about conquest of space and social engineering. (Includes bibliography.) (DRS)

Viardot. 2501. Waddington, Patrick. "Dickens, Pauline Viardot, Turgenev: A Study in Mutual Admiration." *NZSJ* 1:55-73.
Dickens probably first met Pauline Viardot during her opera seasons in London in the late 1840s; but their friendly relations date from his stay in Paris during the winter of 1855-56. He came to be a great admirer of her art. Partly through the Viardots Dickens also met Turgenev. Some rare information on their literary relations is presented in this article, which also includes three hitherto unpublished letters of Dickens to Pauline Viardot, a note from Dickens to Turgenev's English translator, and some previously unused details from the diaries of George Sand. (PHW)

Vigny. 2502. Haig, Stirling. "Conscience and Antimilitarism in Vigny's *Servitude et grandeur militaires*." *PMLA* 89:50-56.
Alfred de Vigny's *Servitude et grandeur militaires* is related to the historical and literary conjuncture of the 1830s, which saw the French army's Napoleonic grandeur sullied in the suppression of working-class revolts. *Servitude* is a characteristic Vigny triptych, but only the third tale, "La Canne de jonc," provides a morally determining lesson. Here the necessity of experience in the formation of conscience is emphasized. The hero of the tale, Captain Renaud, who throughout his career meets a series of negative and absent fathers (suggesting a metaphysical void that must be filled with human values), inadvertently kills a young Russian cadet during the campaign of France. Years later, Renaud is mortally wounded by a talionic reincarnation of the *enfant russe*, and expiates his crime in stoic silence. Conscience, as in Vigny's poetry, is attained in the grandeur and honor of silence and renunciation. (SH)

2506. Sokolova, T.V. "Alfred de Vigny and the July Revolution." *NCFS* 1(1973):235-51.
The July events and the behavior of the king during the Revolution induced in Vigny a critical attitude toward the "legitimate" monarchy of the Bourbons. The year 1830 marked the start of "the most philosophical epoch" in Vigny's life. He begins to consider social cataclysms as resulting from a social law. He ponders the higher meaning of revolutions. However, he still has many doubts and maintains a skeptical attitude toward the democratic movement of his time. Nevertheless his "tour d'ivoire" is not a way to escape society. He merely seeks isolation to concentrate his thoughts and to understand the events of his time. (MO,Jr)

Villiers de l'Isle-Adam. 2508. Hubert, Renée R. "Le domaine du fantastique et les limites de la science." *NCFS* 1(1973):174-81.
Villiers de l'Isle-Adam opposes a spiritual to a scientific attitude, an opposition which serves to define or delineate the domain of death. In "Le Convive des dernières fêtes" he shows the failure of a scientific explanation of death in the presence of a demonic occultism into which all previous scientific attempts are integrated. In "Les Secrets de l'échafaud" pinpointing the exact moments of death proves impossible, for the dying victim's reflexes remain impenetrable and the cold blooded scientist is affected by occult forces. In "L'intersigne" a bored aristocrat fails to recognize the meaning of his nocturnal visions. Unable to understand the divine signals, to communicate with the world beyond, the protagonist leads a very diminished existence. Centering around the presence of death, Villiers's stories stress the

inadequacy of the human mind and the necessity to believe in the supernatural. (In French) (RRH)

2509. Arnold, Ivor. "Villiers de l'Isle-Adam and *écriture-artiste*." *FR* 47:874-81.
Villiers de l'Isle-Adam's fictional descriptive style derives from that of the Goncourt brothers and draws on the general tendency in France to apply "art-for-art's-sake" methods to literature. The prose technique, *écriture artiste*, relies on devices of sentence-order and a variety of effects aimed at achieving phenomenological accumulation. Villiers's use of the technique is confined to nominalism, impressionistic sentence-inversion, noun-pluralization, anteposition of epithets, repetition and accumulation, and occasionally complex structures such as the *phrase à eventail*. Villiers also has recourse to the looser and more rhetorical Romantic style and his writing is not without doses of Parnassian density. The choice of style seems to be dictated by considerations of appropriateness within the convention of a general descriptive rhetoric of the time. (IAA)

Zola. 2517. Butler, R. "Zola Between Taine and Sainte-Beuve." *MLR* 69:279-89.
A study of Zola's reactions to Taine's critical method in articles and letters written between 1864 and 1869 leads one to challenge the view that Zola was profoundly influenced by Taine at this period. They reveal a growing hostility on Zola's part to what he saw as the dogmatic inflexibility of Taine's method. The evidence massively outweighs the single statement made by Zola in affirmation of Taine. Zola's insistence on the primacy of individuality in artistic creation finds support in the critical approach of Sainte-Beuve, whose opposition to Taine coincides with that of Zola. Taine's impact on Zola emerges as short-lived and limited, relevant only to Zola's crisis of maturity before the *Rougon-Macquart*. The more profound affinities between Zola's artistic temperament and the critical values of Sainte-Beuve are more authentic pointers to Zola's ultimate development as a writer. (RRB)

2520. Gerhardi, Gerhard C. "Zola's Biological Vision of Politics." *NCFS* 2:164-80.
The first of Zola's Rougon-Macquart novels introduces a number of themes recurring throughout the cycle. The adolescent Sylvère confuses love for the Republic with love for his girl friend. Zola's symbols so clearly underline this emotional confusion that a number of them read like post-Freudian clichés. His revolutionary characters are so obviously suffering from sexual or nutritional deprivation that one need look no further to explain the ardor of their campaign for justice. Zola's sociological explanations are by comparison weak and unconvincing. (GCG)

2524. Kamm, Lewis. "Zola's Conception of Time in *Les Rougon-Macquart*." *FR* (spec. issue 6):63-72.
Although previous criticism has emphasized a circular conception of time in Emile Zola's *Les Rougon-Macquart*, textual analysis of Zola's descriptive technique and dramatic presentation reveals instead his linear conception of time. Whether his vision and talent act as a camera panning the view, or, as in the "symphony of cheeses," he injects a fluid dynamism into his descriptions on the model of a piece of music, Zola describes things sequentially in the process of becoming. The dialectics of life and death and the literary devices of leitmotif and repetition signal new moments in the linear, eternal process of creation. Similarly, the suite of overlapping scenes and the succession of superimposed chapters illustrate Zola's tendency to present reality in a sequence of blocks which seem to arrest *le devenir* to depict individual moments. (LK)

2534. Petrey, Sandy. "Stylistics and Society in *La curée*." *MLN* 89:626-40.
As a social novel and a psychological study, *La Curée* is a unified textual representation of social reification. The thematic axis of Zola's assault on the corruption in the Second Empire's rebuilding of Paris functions as the stylistic and symbolic axis for his narration of Renée's incest and dissolution. The neutralized and alienated quality of existence in a society whose only values are monetary is apparent in the images, mythic allusions, descriptive terminology, and rhetorical devices which organize the language recounting Renée's affair with her stepson. (SP)

VIII. TWENTIETH CENTURY

General and Miscellaneous. 2558. Richard, Lionel. "*La Nouvelle Revue Française* devant l'Allemagne de 1909 à 1914." *Mosaic* 7,iv:71-98.

From 1909 to 1914 the *Nouvelle Revue Française* (*NRF*) published little on classical German literature. Discussion of contemporary German literature was limited to Rilke. On the other hand, the reviews of Félix Bertaux are very well informed: for example, he recommends the reading of Thomas Mann, although Mann was not translated into French until 1921. The *NRF* was never guilty of sterile nationalism: it was perceptibly ethnocentric, but remained open to foreign cultures and, in spite of the Germanophobia which was then in fashion, Germany occupied a significant place in the *NRF*. (LR)

Criticism. 2565. Antoine, Gérald. "La nouvelle critique:How Far Has It Got?" *Style* 8:18-33.

After a brief history of the French "Nouvelle Critique" school, the problematics of criticism are examined under four major questions: (1) critical method and objectivity; (2) criticism, the science of literature vs. a "literature about literature"; (3) thematic criticism vs. stylistic criticism; and (4) stylistic criticism vs. poetic criticism. Tentative classification of the movement is suggested and proposals are offered. (LLBA)

2573. Cohn, Robert G. "Nodes." *Diacritics* 4,i:34-41; ii:44-47.

The ancient concept of tetrapolarity becomes increasingly important in the modern era. According to this concept the four poles of a "cross" pattern interpenetrate in the same way as the two poles of a bipolar paradox do. The vertical and horizontal axes of the "cross" are thus both same and different. The concepts of modern physics, sexual differentiation, number, musical tones based on the octave, biological generation, and language all derive from this system. Derrida's critique of Rousseau can be defended against the demurrer of Paul de Man on these grounds. Grave deficiencies in Northrop Frye's *Anatomy of Criticism* result from his lack of core vision (in these terms). Georges Poulet, in his essays on Proust, fares better but misses some important points. Camus's *The Rebel* comes to grief on this plane. (RGC)

2574. Conley, Tom C. "Object, System, Absence." *Diacritics* 3,i(1973):19-25.

Since the mid-fifties French formalists have been building critical structures whose dimensions far surpass the thrust of a humanistic, creative impulse of art and literature. Theirs is a system destroying established categories and removing progressively degraded signifiers from the esthetic enterprise. Parallel to recent American art, formalism strips away the illusionistic bark of myths which have been characterizing man as alienated creature until function and total efficacy of symbolical activity are reached once again: "art degree zero." Negative approaches to the plastic medium since the nineteenth century are analogous, which Jack Burnham's work—*Beyond Modern Sculpture* and *The Structure of Art*—traces and proves. The object is transformed into system which becomes, through the critical act superseding all creative struggle, infinitely complex and ultimately absent. Concomitantly those who see *impasse*, petrification, or involution in recent art and criticism of France and America are those who hold to obsolescent values, unable to read the invisible yet evanescent iconography of creative and critical endeavors. (TC)

2584. Hamon, Philippe. "Narrative Semiotics in France." *Style* 8:34-45.

The situation of narrative semiotics in France is described and a bibliography as complete and as detailed as possible is set up. Narrative semiotics developed in the 1960s against the conceptual domination and the loose concepts of literary history and traditional critics, first under the influence of structural linguistics, then under the influence of semiotics liberated from the linguistic model. The main theoretical efforts in this field are those of Greimas, Barthes, Brémond, Todorov, Genette, Coquet, and Rastier. (LLBA)

2585. Helbo, André. "L'esprit et l'*alettre*." *Degrés* 1(1973):h-h12.

The notion of opening, in a semiotic sense, which is in opposition to the idea of closing, in a sociological sense, can be applied to contemporary arts. This contradiction, brought into view by the development of mass media, lies in the paradox of reading. Reading does not amount to participation in a communion but rather in a transaction; the consequences of this meeting concern the framework of temporality, the relation between language and life, and the rapport between criticism and creation. Contemporary life exacerbates this problem by emphasizing discontinuity. (AH)

2587. Klinkenberg, Jean-Marie. "Vers un modèle théorique du langage poétique." *Degrés* 1(1973):d-d12.

The search for definitive criteria of poetic language gives rise to a host of misunderstandings, for it is often done in a literary perspective. In a scientific perspective, it is less important to describe an object than it is to formulate a theoretical construct of this object. Among the proposed criteria, one of the most usual is that of divergence. A typology of the different approaches to this concept, a typology of the critiques referring to it, and a test of the counter proposals which are derived from it show the dangers of this definition at the same time that they lead to theorizing about the naive dichotomy between prose and poetry. The most satisfying of the theories of poetic language is that of Solomon Marcus, who is opposed to scientific language and lyric language. In a series of rigorous theorems, scientific language is defined as a language without homonymy but with infinite synonymy. Lyric language has infinite homonymy but no synonymy. This model, being both economical and strong, mathematically accounts for several characteristics recognized in poetic language. (AH)

Drama and Theater. 2607. Kilker, James A. and Marie J. "The Druon Affair:A Documentary." *ETJ* 26:365-76.

In the spring of 1973 a controversy involving politics, subsidies, censorship, and the arts took place in France. The new Minister of Culture, Maurice Druon, made known in a press interview his policy on state support of cultural activities, stating he would not use taxpayers' money to grant subsidies to individuals or organizations opposed to the very government from which they seek aid. Dissident artists took strong issue with the Minister's views. A record of the controversy is presented in translated documents. Louis Dandrel in *Le Monde* compares the financial aid given such leftist but artistically important organizations as the Théâtre du Soleil with politically favored groups. The controversy engendered overt recognition of a policy of government censorship that had already been covertly operative. (JAK & MJK)

2611. Miller, Judith. "Théâtre populaire de Lorraine:Regional Theatre." *ETJ* 26:352-64.

Jacques Kraemer founded the Théâtre Populaire de Lorraine in Metz, France, in 1963, to bring theater to the working class of the Lorraine region. The troupe's early productions of Molière, Marivaux, and Brecht denounced the social and economic injustices of the capitalist system without aiming at a particular target. After May 1968, radicalized by the month of strikes and social protest, Kraemer began writing pointed dramatic exposés of the iron and steel trusts which control the region's economy. The *TPL*'s later productions examine the region's moral and financial bankruptcy, racial prejudice, and power base. (JGM)

Poetry. 2631. Hubert, Renée R. "The Invasions of Poetry." *Diacritics* 4,i:21-25. [Rev. art.]

This review article seeks to establish the continuity of Mary Ann Caws's *The Inner Theatre* on Cendrars, Tzara, Péret, Artaud, and Bonnefoy who do not belong to the same movement or generation, and of Caws's approach which makes use of linguistics, poetics, art criticism, and psychology. Language viewed as the poet's linguistic consciousness constitutes a major unifying factor. This self-awareness relates to the abandonment of traditional distinctions such as prose and poetry, forcing the critic to seek new tools as each poetic text becomes autonomous or unrelated to others. The basic problem of the *Inner Theatre*, motion and immobility, is not restricted to a range determined by language. Visual perception, motion as an agent of transformation, motion as creator of spatial form, motion as synonymous with psychological motivation are recurring and evolving themes. Once defined, Caws's approach, with modifications, can be applied to poems by Michaux, where gesture becomes equivalent to immobility, by St. John Perse, where movement lies beyond tension, and Arp, where movement recapitulates past motion. (RRH)

2642. Onimus, Jean. "Ruptures et interférences dans le langage poétique." *Degrés* 2(1973):e-e9.

A stylistic analysis of Robert Guyon's "En regardant la mer" calls attention to elements of repetition which assure the coherence of the text, to verse structure, and to the progressive arrangement of silences. The placement of stops in the poem puts the reader in a state of insecurity and thus makes him openly receptive and attentive. Thematic interferences provoke ambiguities; a new coherence—poetic—thus emerges from apparent incoherence. (AH)

Prose Fiction. 2656. Hartman, Geoffrey H. "The Aesthetics of Complicity." *GaR* 28:384-88.

The French *nouveau roman* differs from the American novel after World War II in reflecting programmatically on its premises and on the nature of fiction generally. The American novel continues to extend the domain of realism and does not change from being that "loose and baggy monster" Henry James complained about. There is more complicity, in the American novel, with itself: the French novel, after passing through the *roman d'aventure* of the 1930s—inspired, in part, by Conrad, Hemingway, and "l'âge du roman americain"—has returned via the slyly prevailing influence of James and Gide to a purifying reflection on the relation between novelist and detective, novelist and licensed voyeur. When we compare Malraux's *Man's Fate* of the 1930s with Robbe-Grillet's *Jealousy* of the 1950s, we see how suspicious of itself and the intimist mode of novel-writing the French tradition has become. A new consciousness of the reader, as a partner in the fiction being created, or someone to be seduced by it, is evidenced. Fictional techniques are no longer viewed as neutral or productive of newness, but as deeply or covertly ideological. (GH)

2657. Kellman, Steven G. "Imagining the Novel Dead: Recent Variations on a Theme by Proust." *MLQ* 35:45-55.

The death of the novel has been the explicit theme of recent French fiction. Proust's magnum opus defines the tradition of the self-begetting novel; the novel creates itself at the same time as it creates a self, its central protagonist. The work of Jean-Paul Sartre, Michael Butor, Nathalie Sarraute, and Alain Robbe-Grillet further heightens this self-consciousness in prose which calls attention to its own artifice. Claude Mauriac's *La Marquise sortit à cinq heures* (1961) begets itself but concludes by contesting its own right to exist. Each of the narrators in Samuel Beckett's trilogy (1953) aspires to silence through words. Suicidal narratives, his novels create and sustain themselves in the very act of trying to destroy themselves. It is a fiction of the death of fiction. (SGK)

West Indian Literature. 2681. Baugh, Edward. "Questions and Imperatives for a Young Literature." *HAB* 24(1973):13-24.

During the last decade or so, there has been a growing ferment of discussion in the West Indies about the direction in which West Indian literature is developing and should develop. There has been a shift away from the general opinion that West Indian literature is necessarily rooted in English literature. This shift is an inevitable part of the compulsion toward self-asserti on. The dominant trend focuses on actual or desired black African connections. Individualism and introspection are suspect, and much is made of the ideas of "commitment" and "relevance" to "the society." Some of the major writers—V.S. Naipaul, Derek Walcott, Wilson Harris—are criticized because they do not seem to commit themselves sufficiently to the popular line. Their relevance is therefore questioned. However, they have made invaluable contributions to the debate. (EACB)

2696. Ikonné, Chidi. "René Maran, 1887-1960:A Black Francophone Writer Between Two Worlds." *RAL* 5:5-22.

The suggestion that René Maran took to writing as a result of his experience in the French Colonial Administration is very misleading. Maran was already a writer before he joined the Civil Service. He started publishing poems while still in high school. However, these poems, like all the others he wrote, hardly belong to black literature. This is also true, to some extent, of his *Batouala* which belongs essentially to the French genre of *roman colonial* and *exotique*. Nevertheless, his use of an aboriginal black man as a hero of the book also gives the French prize-winning novel a place among novels by the Negritude school of writers. The author's defense of French colonization and of Africans against the excesses of that same colonization places him among white French writers like André Gide, without depriving him of the bitterness of a man who believes that he is being discriminated against because of his color. René Maran was, therefore, a Frenchman in black skin—a man between two worlds. (CI)

2705. Ormerod, Beverley N. "Beyond *négritude*:Some Aspects of the Work of Edouard Glissant." *ConL* 15:360-69.

Edouard Glissant's work attempts to replace the notion of *négritude* with that of cultural synthesis. In *L'Intention poétique* (1969) he argues that *négritude* is an inappropriate ideal for the Caribbean, because its specific rejection of Europe ignores the continuing presence of European elements in the Caribbean, while its quest for African roots is impractical for Caribbean citizens. The Caribbean contains African, European, Indian, Amerindian elements, and its literature should attempt to reflect this racial and cultural variety. Glissant is concerned with the evocation and reinterpretation of Caribbean history in a quest to define the Caribbean heritage and encourage the establishment of a dynamic local culture independent of both Europe and Africa. His abstract views are translated into concrete literary artifact in terms of a tight symbology where the mountains of the Caribbean islands are equated with the freedom of the runaway slaves, the canefields of the flatlands denote slavery and plantation labor, and the sea beyond carries conflicting associations of untrammelled freedom, fatalistic acceptance of the past, and archetypal folk memories of the Middle Passage. (BNO)

2709. Smith, Robert P.,Jr. "Michèle Lacrosil:Novelist with a Color Complex." *FR* 47:783-90.

Michèle Lacrosil has done much to expose the surprising and shameful racial hierarchy based on the color of one's skin which still exists in the French Antilles where whites represent the ruling class, mulattoes the middle class, and blacks the subordinate class, socially and economically. Lacrosil has been preoccupied in a dramatic way with the problem of one's conscious and physical relationship with "Others" or the "Other." In her novels she evokes a universe overburdened with the social, political, and economical uneasiness of the French Antilles, against a background of slavery, colonialism and present-day instability. (RPS,Jr.)

Alain-Fournier. 2719. Sorrell, Martin R.M. "François Seurel's Personal Adventure in *Le grand Meaulnes*." *MLR* 69:79-87.

Le Grand Meaulnes is not just the work of Alain-Fournier, but also of the narrator François Seurel. Seurel's setting down in writing of the adventure is the culmination of his personal quest—he discovers himself as a writer. Seurel is a complex, independent person, and not two-dimensional as is sometimes claimed. His timidity and nervousness derive from his lameness and his repressed childhood. Consequently, Meaulnes becomes the focus for Seurel's physical and imaginative yearnings. Seurel increasingly tries to take over the adventure. However, unlike Meaulnes, he cannot accept the prosaic outcome; he needs a more "literary" one. The conclusion of the novel seems bleakest for Seurel, but his redemption lies in the very fact that he has wished to write down the adventure, thereby recreating it through art. (MRS)

Anouilh. 2722. Burdick, Dolores M. "Antigone Grows Middle-Aged:Evolution of Anouilh's Hero." *MichA* 7:137-47.

In *Antigone* Anouilh struck a tenuous balance between intransigent idealism and a morality of compromise. In *La Sauvage* the heroine's intransigent moral stance was linked to some shred of social meaning but in *Antigone* the idealist's position is a naked entity, shorn of content. Both antagonists have equal moral weight and evoke equal audience sympathy. Two later plays are then explored, to determine the evolution of Anouilh's idealism. In *Pauvre Bitos* the spokesmen for idealism and compromise are equally repellent. *Les Poissons rouges* shows the typical hero of Anouilh's later plays: a middle-aged playwright who survives but who has internalized the Antigone position in his struggle to protect "the honor of Man." (DMB)

2725. Jacobs, Gabriel. "The Antigone of the 'Résistance'." *AUMLA* 41:18-29.
Anouilh's *Antigone* deals with the conflict between idealism and expediency, refusal and acceptance. The choice between such positions was that faced by every Frenchman who lived through the Occupation. *Antigone* provoked heated arguments: was it a call to resist, or a call to collaborate, or neither? The delicate balance between the assertions of Antigone and those of Créon and Ismène, is evidence of a certain skepticism on Anouilh's part, but during the Occupation, such detachment was a luxury which no one could afford, for condoning collaboration by inaction represented only the illusion of refusing to choose. The treatment of the theme of refusal of the law could not but produce a political reaction, the nature of which was dependent upon the personal prejudices of the members of the audience, who *themselves* created the disequilibrium. (GJ)

2727. Spingler, Michael. "Anouilh's Little Antigone:Tragedy, Theatricalism, and the Romantic Self." *CompD* 8:228-38.
Anouilh's *Antigone* suggests that romantic self-assertion is a major reason for the decline of tragedy in modern drama. The audience sees Antigone both as sentimental heroine and as egocentric role-player. This double view occurs within the context of a tragic universe which has lost the traditional values which sustained it. Antigone's efforts to replace this discredited tragic universe with an interior world of personal values depends upon her maintaining her role as *la petite Antigone*. The chorus' detached view of the play contrasts with the sentimental portrait of the heroine creating a matrix within which Antigone's revolt and death appear absurd. (MS)

Apollinaire. 2729. Bermel, Albert. "Apollinaire's Male Heroine." *TCL* 20:172-82.
The Breasts of Tiresias by Guillaume Apollinaire consists of 16 loosely related scenes (an epic structure) and works by a series of theatrical transformations or miracles: the heroine Thérèse turns into a hero named Tiresias; her husband into a mother; objects such as a newsstand are animated, if not personified; and characters who are shot and killed instantly revive. Apollinaire also uses the assumed identity of his heroine-hero in order to mock the myth of Tiresias, that inhuman-seeming seer who has no stake in the life around him, by means of critical, political, and sexual comedy. (AB)

2752. Richter, Mario. "La 'Victoire' di Apollinaire." *RLMC* 27:177-209.
A detailed stylistic-thematic analysis demonstrates how, in Apollinaire's "Victoire," two different orders of experience are dramatically combined: (1) the first is bound to the human and artistic condition; (2) the second concerns life itself. "Victoire" is considered in light of the concrete context, of this circumstantial (literary and biographical) reality, which is the substance of its very life. It is an extraordinary answer to Breton and to the latest literary generation which thronged in admiration around the wounded poet and sought expression amid "barbarous" outbursts, especially in avant-garde journals. Perpetuity and change, past and future, uniqueness and multiplicity thus become the lyrical reason of a voice in search of itself, based on an ambiguity which is that of temporality. (MR)

Arp. 2764. Kotin, Armine. "Language Techniques in Jean Arp's French Poetry." *PLL* 10:159-74.
Arp's poetry can be divided into two periods, before and after 1957, on the basis of his experimental use of language. One of Arp's most original and most important stylistic inventions is the configuration technique which employs a limited vocabulary combined in "constellations" which are formed by chance but recur with a definite sense of pattern. Other techniques are modification of familiar idiomatic expressions to create new insight into the coded nature of language; sound association;

punning; and various kinds of semantic wordplay. He also uses faulted logic, resulting in surrealist images. (AK)

Arrabal. 2765. Anderson, Irmgard Z. "From Tweedledum and Tweedledee to Zapo and Zépo." *RomN* 15(1973):217-20.
Fernando Arrabal owes Lewis Carroll the inspiration for various accessory episodes dealing with Alice and certain animals. One chapter of Lewis Carroll's *Through the Looking Glass* supplied Arrabal with the entire vital substance of *Pique-nique en campagne*. Tweedledum and Tweedledee have become Zapo and Zépo; Alice has lent her traits to M. and Mme Tépan; and the Walrus and the Carpenter are re-embodied in Arrabal's stretcher-bearers. A close correspondence between the ideas and the actions of Carroll's characters and those created by Arrabal is unmistakable. Only the seriousness of the situation has increased: Alice's concern over a brotherly spat in "Tweedledum and Tweedledee" has intensified into Arrabal's bitter condemnation of senseless warfare. (IZA)

2766. Luce, Louise F. "The Dialectic of Space:Fernando Arrabal's *The Automobile Graveyard*." *JSSTC* 2:31-37.
The Automobile Graveyard belongs to the sub-genre of organic theater. With his "junkyard-in-the-round," Arrabal has created a unique cosmogony in which the dialectic between the staging elements and the energy thus released create an existential experience for the spectator which takes him back to the very origins of play, to the primordial, mythic recharging of the universe. Call it wasteland, wonderland, or nightmare, *The Graveyard* finds its most profound significance only in light of its internal dialectic. (LFL)

Artaud. 2780. Lyons, John D. "Artaud:Intoxication and Its Double." *YFS* 50:120-29.
Antonin Artaud's calls for a new dramatic language for his theater of cruelty are closely related to his fascination with the effects of various intoxicants. The impoverished and rational language of European theater is contrasted with the sign systems of Balinese and Mexican culture which induce heightened and unrational states of consciousness. Artaud ascribes to such cultures the gift of provoking trances in which the articulations of rational language are destroyed and the mind freed to combine ideas according to a new syntax, one which he felt he had experienced in opium and peyote dreams. Artaud's protests against regulation of drugs argue that despite such regulation the human mind will always find new ways to achieve an "abnormal lucidity." His own ambivalence toward opium apparently led Artaud to seek a superior intoxicant, one constituted by a new sign system for the theater. (JDL)

Aurier. 2788. Eruli, Brunella. "Tra realtà e sogno:I romanzi di Albert Aurier." *RLMC* 27:122-47.
Vieux and *Ailleurs* are two novels by Albert Aurier which appear contemporaneously, but reveal different artistic perspectives. While *Vieux* uses naturalistic models, *Ailleurs* is in the line of the new research of the novel, the anti-novel. This rapid change of esthetic orientation is due to the influence of the figurative culture of Aurier. Stylistic and thematic stratifications show the passage from naturalistic language to one dominated by a visionary reality. This rapid change of the narrative approach shows also that the real artistic movement advances through very intricate trajectories which absorb and use contradictory stylistic and thematic materials. (BE)

Aveline. 2789. Jacobs, Gabriel C. "La philosophie sans système:Extrait d'une interview avec Claude Aveline." *Trivium* 9:50-53.
Claude Aveline distinguishes two opposing lines of French philosophical development, one from Pascal to Barrès, the other from Montaigne to Anatole France. He asserts that it is the latter to which he finds himself most attracted, while admitting no formal philosophical training. He feels close to Bergson, Bachelard, and Jung, all of whom he considers great poets. He insists that they have little in common in their approach to life except that they are not bound by systems or dogma. He sees all systems as an oversimplification of the truth and thus concen-

trates the discussion on Montaigne and Pascal. (GCJ)

Bachelard. 2792. Bailey, Ninette. "Bachelard et la nouvelle critique:Une question de convenance." *ECr* 14:236-46.
The relationship established between Bachelard and French New Criticism is one not of influence but of suggestive parallels. Bachelard's later writings testify to a shift in his field of investigation which creates an overlap with the area explored by French New Criticism. From an analysis of the multiple cultural origins of literary images, Bachelard turns to consider the linguistic aspect of their formation, thus restricting his inquiry to the purely linguistic dimension of literature. Bachelard's rejection of the triple role of literature as a mirror of reality, an expression of subjectivity or a mere reaffirmation of existing statements indicates a further parallel with French New Criticism. (NB)

Barthes. 2821. Harari, Josué V. "The Maximum Narrative:An Introduction to Barthes' Recent Criticism." *Style* 8:56-77.
An attempt to present Barthes's recent literary production in view of his earlier attempts to establish himself as the leading French theoretician of literature. In the process of this presentation, the continuity of Barthes's critical theories is demonstrated, as well as the break that occurs in it from S/Z onward, and more abruptly in his most recent work *Le plaisir du texte*. By focusing on S/Z, an illustration of Barthes's textual analysis was made possible. The richness and validity of the typology of narrative Barthes offers in his study of Balzac's short story "Sarrasine" is highlighted. (LLBA)
2822. Lotringer, Sylvère. "Argo-Notes:Roland Barthes' Textual Trip." *Boundary* 2:562-72.
Barthes' definite style born under Existentialism, contained by Structuralism, now culminates in a bold textual practice. This itinerary is epitomized by two studies: *Critical Essays* (1963) and *Le Plaisir du Texte* (1973). The gradual discovery of linguistics still left unresolved the contradiction between Politics (Brecht) and Formalism (Robbe-Grillet). Literature must affirm meaning without defining it. The writer is an inductor of ambiguity: he generates indirection while the critic has to speak the indirect directly. Bringing the phonological model into the semantic field, Barthes thus discovers the *Logic of Relations* which will initiate structural analysis of narratives. Structuralist activity, however, setting up a series of infinite combinations simultaneously obliterates the ego's position in writing. Desire is what moves the vessel Argo: the deception of meaning constitutes the desire of a "subject" caught in language. Literature can frame this desire, but writing extracts desire from representation and, shattering language, uncovers the texture and pleasure of the text. (SL)

Bataille. 2832. Brée, Germaine. "The Break-up of Traditional Genres:Bataille, Leiris, Michaux." *BuR* 21,ii(1973):3-13.
In the 20th century in France, the classification of literary works by genres no longer covers a large mass of significant works now appearing. In fact, "genres"—novel, drama, poetry, essay—are, rather than distinct literary forms, modalities within basic new structures that encompass them. The narrative genres designated as "minor"—forms of autobiographical narrative, e.g.—have tended to constitute a frame for experiments in linguistic expression which deliberately aim at breaking down formal categorization. Recent histories of literature have reflected the situation, one of them grouping under the label "inventors" those writers whose work escaped genre classifications. They comprised most of the outstanding writers of the mid-century. A brief examination of the work of Georges Bataille, Michel Leiris, and Henri Michaux illustrates the trend, and leads to the conclusion that the literary unit considered today is the "text" or the "book" rather than the "genre." (GB)
2836. Kibler, Louis. "Imagery in George Bataille's *Le bleu du ciel*." *FR* (spec. issue 6):208-18.
Although Georges Bataille's ideal was to express his mystic experience, he is to be appreciated more as literary craftsman than as *guru*; in his fiction he does not achieve his ideal, but he does evoke the wonders of mysticism by relating it to eroticism. Bataille's use of imagery in the love scene between Henri Troppmann and Dorothea in *Le Bleu du ciel* (written in 1935,

published 1957) transforms the order of the "real" cosmos and creates a picture of the mystic world as Bataille most often imagines it—as the opposite of the physical world. Moreover, by means of imagery Bataille fuses the human elements of the scene with the mystic sphere and so suggests participation in a totality. Despite the immediacy of eroticism and the obscurity of mysticism, Bataille avoids sensationalism and imprecision, and he affords the reader an esthetic experience in which he perceives but does not participate in an erotic and mystic experience. (LK)
2838. Libertson, Joseph. "Bataille and Communication:From Heterogeneity to Continuity." *MLN* 89:669-98.
There is a diachronic dimension to the system represented by Bataille's discursive writings. This diachronic dimension is integral to the architecture of Bataille's system. Its fundamental index is a progressive appropriation and/or displacement of apparently heterogeneous terms, in the direction of an ontological context. The replacement of the system "homogeneity/heterogeneity," as elaborated in "La structure psychologique du fascisme" (1933-34) by the system "continuity/discontinuity' is discussed. (JL)
2839. ——— "Bataille and Communication:*Savoir, Non-Savoir, Glissement, Rire*." *Sub-stance* 10:47-65.
A multiplicity of dual oppositions structures Bataille's system. These oppositions are individually developed according to a stable, repeated configuration. The specificity of Bataille's categories, considered as a factor governing their substitutive invocations and multiple contexts, is perceptible only as a function of this specialized configuration of opposition. The purpose of this essay is to describe certain structures of opposition found in Bataille's text in the context of their relation to that zone of his system which may be termed "knowledge." (JL)

Bazin. 2847. Crant, Phillip A. "Un entretien avec Hervé Bazin." *FR* (spec. issue 6):253-60.
This interview contains the highlights of two meetings with Hervé Bazin on 5 and 6 January 1972. Bazin speaks intensely and freely about his poetry and his prose. He discloses some of his influences and friendships, including Mauriac, Camus, Valéry, and Montherlant. He discusses with intimacy his relationship to his literary work and his designs for his finalized Opus. Bazin also deals at length with the role of literature today, especially French literature vis-à-vis its political position in the world, and offers some challenging remarks on the character of the new novel. This exposure of Bazin demonstrates his wide literary experience and intellectual capacity which have placed him among the best of France's living novelists. (PAC)

Beckett. 2854. Brater, Enoch. "Beckett, Ionesco, and the Tradition of Tragicomedy." *CollL* 1:113-27.
Beckett's conception of humor is distinct from the classical idea of comedy in the tradition of Aristotle, Molière, and Meredith. Traditional comedy is rational, orderly, consolidating, and corrective. It implies a control which keeps the work within a recognizable, realistic framework. For Beckett these boundaries no longer apply; his is a black humor which lies in extreme distortion and farce. The tradition is that of Sterne, Swift, and Lewis Carroll. The theoretical basis for this tragicomedy is justified in the writings of Ionesco and Antonin Artaud. (EB)
2855. ——— "Noah, *Not I*, and Beckett's 'Incomprehensibly Sublime'." *CompD* 8:254-63.
Endgame retains an identifiable context of symbolism and poetic suggestion. Details from *Genesis* proliferate in the Hebrew-English puns and in the extended pattern of allusions lifted from the story of Noah and the Flood. In *Not I* Beckett uses the same mythology to short-circuit the connections between a given idea and a respondent idea. Auditor tempts us to think of the *nephilim*, the race of "wordless giants" destroyed in the biblical holocaust. Allusions to the Old and New Testaments confuse rather than establish a pattern of images "informing" the meaning of the text, so demonstrating not connections, but the appalling lack of them. (EB)
2856. ——— "The Empty Can:Samuel Beckett and Andy Warhol." *JML* 3:1255-64.
On an ideological level Beckett and Warhol practice a minimal

art involving a suspension rather than a clarification of meaning. The work of art becomes a *tabula rasa* whose elusive "significance" is pursued over and over again by the audience. *Endgame* is an esthetic object "anxious for definition." Familiar systems of criticism and interpretation begin to disfunction as a means toward understanding the work. All clues prove to be false clues. Art becomes a catalyst which forces us to confront ourselves in the act of esthetic evaluation. The well-wrought urn has become the empty can: a terrifying metaphor which "represents" our own contemporary isolation. (EB)

2857. —— "The 'I' in Beckett's *Not I*." *TCL* 20:189-200.
Not I is Beckett's drama about an elusive pronoun. Mouth insists that the tale it tells is about "she," not "I," hence giving the title of the play. *Not* I is also "not aye," what Beckett calls elsewhere "the screaming silence of no's knife in yes's wound." *Not* I, co-starring Auditor as ear, is also "about" Mouth, not eye. If we consider the pronoun in the title as Roman numeral, we see that the visual images exposed before us on stage are not I, but II. *Not* I yields the Jungian theory of the process of "individuation" necessary for the development of the ego. (EB)

2859. Busi, Frederick. "*Waiting for Godot*:A Modern *Don Quixote*?" *Hispania* 57:876-85.
Don Quijote and *Waiting for Godot* both deal with the theme of the futile vigil and the refusal to recognize common sense reality. Just as Don Quijote cannot admit that his Dulcinea is an ugly wench, so Didi entertains a similar disbelief about the nature of Godot. Their two subordinates, Sancho Panza and Gogo, typify the vulgar life forces through their actions as suggested by the symbolism of their names. The theme of interpersonality transference confirms a central theme of both novel and play: the ideal and the real tend to blur as the protagonists exchange roles. (FAB)

2862. Coetzee, J.M. "Samuel Beckett and the Temptations of Style." *Theoria* 41(1973):45-50.
Beckett's paradoxical art of zero—an art which tends mathematically toward the limit of silence—works by a series of "affirmations and negations invalidated as uttered" (*The Unnamable*). In the late fiction of the *Residua* the procedures of self-doubt and self-annihilation become more and more highly formalized. But linguistic analysis shows that even *Watt* (abandoned 1947) embodies at a stylistic level a binary *A-against-B* rhythm of doubt. The automatism of the style of *Watt* may be a reason why Beckett turned to writing in French. On the other hand, it is consistent with Beckett's conception of art as defeat that his late French work should have fallen into an automatism of style homologous with the English automatism of *Watt*. (JMC)

2864. Collins, P.H. "Proust, Time and Beckett's *Happy Days*." *FR* (Spec. issue 6):105-19.
Beckett's later works show more and more the influence of his early interest in Proust. *Happy Days* is close both in style and subject-matter to his monograph *Proust* (1931); and the central character of the play, Winnie, has many points of resemblance with la tante Léonie in the early part of Proust's *À la recherche du temps perdu*. Beckett's work on Proust shows that what interested him in the French writer was the problem of time, linked to the related questions of memory and habit, and it is just these three themes which reappear in *Happy Days*. But the treatment of these themes is totally different in Beckett's play; in particular, where Proust's narrator found a particular sense of "happiness" only in the negation of time through the rediscovery of the past by means of involuntary memory, Beckett's heroine finds her version of "happiness" solely in the present, for this is the only time when she can be sure she exists. (PC)

2880. Hubert, Renée R. "Microtexts:An Aspect of the Work of Beckett, Robbe-Grillet, and Nathalie Sarraute." *IFR* 1,i:9-16.
Attempts to establish relationships among the short texts of Sarraute, Beckett, and Robbe-Grillet; *Tropismes*, *Instantanés*, and *Textes pour rien* show respectively the writer in search of a relation between man and man, man and object, man and language, focusing on a time experience restricted to the present. Each exploration encounters obstacles which prevent a cohesive overall view. This accounts for fragmentation or discontinuity. All three writers relate to the void which results in contestation of continuity in perception and expression of self. (RRH)

2888. Lowenkron, David Henry. "A Case for 'The Tragicall Historie of Hamm'." *ArQ* 30:217-28.
Beckett's *Endgame* involves the demise of the tragic hero Hamm. Like Classical and Shakespearean tragic heroes, Hamm is larger than life in several dimensions, including chess, theater, language, relationships, and literary ancestors. Beckett attributes the *hamartia* to Hamm's birth, for which he is not responsible. This destroys naive views of poetic justice. Moreover, *arete* explains Hamm's courage when he faces his end without his props: a gaff, a dog, and a whistle. Tragically, Hamm becomes isolated from the community rather than incorporated into one; this is a result of his being part of Nagg's emotional generation while living in Clov's apathetic times. The villain is the entropic universe seen through the demonic imagery and the numerous references to nature's decay. This cosmic cruelty partially exonerates Hamm's nastiness. (HDL)

2891. Morot-Sir, Edouard. "Pascal versus Wittgenstein, with Samuel Beckett as the Anti-witness." *RomN* 15(1973):201-16.
Discusses the use of language and images in Pascal, Wittgenstein, and Beckett. (EM-S)

2897. Ormerod, Beverley. "Beckett's *Waiting for Godot*." *Expl* 32:Item 70.
In Beckett's *Waiting for Godot* the bare tree of Act I acquires fresh foliage in Act II—"four or five leaves" according to the English stage directions, while the French version specifies that the tree is covered with leaves. Critics have interpreted this foliation either as a symbol of hope, or as a satirical counterpoint to the image of the Tree of Life. In both versions of the play, however, the tree's true symbolic value would seem to derive from its own genus rather than from the sparseness or profusion of its foliage. It is a weeping willow, whose leaves are its "tears": thus it is the absence of leaves, not their presence, which denotes hope; and the return of the foliage in Act II ironically suggests that grief and suffering recur in an inevitable ongoing cycle. In the Bible the symbol of the Tree begins in the sorrow of Eden but ends with the promise of Calvary; Beckett's tree, on the contrary, first offers an illusory hope and ultimately signifies the perennial nature of human despair. (BNO)

2898. Parkin, Andrew. "Monologue into Monodrama:Aspects of Samuel Beckett's Plays." *Éire* 9,iv:32-41.
The mastery of stage monologue and monodrama is a characteristic of Beckett the playwright. Monologue as an important structural device is found in *Waiting for Godot, Endgame*, and *Play* while its tendency to create a type of monodrama is exemplified in *Krapp's Last Tape, Happy Days*, and *Not I*. Through monologue and monodrama Beckett dramatizes the isolation and the solipsistic cul-de-sac his characters inhabit. He also reveals new possibilities in the one-act form, such as the musical structure of *Endgame*, the cyclic nature of *Happy Days* and *Play*, and the dramatic continuum of *Not I*, which recalls the landscape of his previous drama. (ATLP)

2901. Prince, Gerald. "Didi, Gogo et le Vaucluse." *RomN* 15:407-09.
In *En attendant Godot*, the series of relatively precise allusions to the protagonists' past life in the Vaucluse has an important function, It helps underline the fact that it makes no difference whether one lives on an open road where everything is gray or in a beautiful closed valley, a garden where everything is red. Similarly, it makes no difference whether one lives out of society, without apparent ties or roots, or in a society dominated by M. Bonnelly, by a Good Lord ("Bon Eli"), a man who is kind and to whom one is attached ("bon et lie"). Circumstances may change; the human condition never does. (GP)

2902. Rabinovitz, Rubin. "Style and Obscurity in Samuel Beckett's Early Fiction." *MFS* 20:399-406.
Beckett feels that novelists give too much emphasis to narrative and too little to style. Moreover novelists have traditionally pretended that reality is easy to comprehend. For Beckett the form is designed to emulate the intricacy and deceptiveness of reality. Beckett mocks the omniscient posturings of writers who supply arcane details of a character's actions and thoughts. He undermines or parodies many of the fictional techniques for creating verisimilitude. In this fashion Beckett refutes the idea that to be credible, fiction must mimic the reality of the material

world. His search for reality is in the world of the inner self. (RR)

2910. Skerl, Jennie. "Fritz Mauthner's 'Critique of Language' in Samuel Beckett's *Watt*." *ConL* 15:474-87.

The philosophical background of Beckett's *Watt* must be re-evaluated, placing Mauthner in the position of primary influence whose "critique of language" informs Watt's quest, struggle, and failure. The theories of Wittgenstein and the logical positivists play a much smaller role than has been previously supposed. It is known that Beckett had read Mauthner's *Beiträge zu einer Kritik der Sprache* in the early thirties, and there are striking similarities between Watt's adventures and Mauthner's analysis of language in his *Kritik*. *Watt* illustrates Mauthner's general thesis and many of his specific propositions as well. Furthermore, there are explicit allusions to the *Kritik* in the novel. A close examination shows that Wittgenstein is relevant to the novel only when his *Tractatus* echoes Mauthner and that logical positivism is not an important part of the novel's philosophical background except for some incidental satire on the "verification theory of meaning." Watt's experience denies rather than illustrates Wittgenstein's "picture theory" and the major tenets of logical positivism. (JS)

2912. Smith, Frederik N. "The Epistemology of Fictional Failure:Swift's *Tale of a Tub* and Beckett's *Watt*." *TSLL* 15:649-72.

Working on his novel *Watt* Beckett recalled vividly the *Tale* and used its radical fragmentation of narrative form as a model for his own work. Both books emphasize their own failure as novels in the traditional mold and go on to demonstrate the failure of language, logic, and mathematics as a means of coming to grips with the world. For Swift the problem is the misuse of these tools of understanding; for Beckett the problem is the tools themselves. Yet both authors push themselves to the outer limits of thinking, into that strange territory where art and life, meaning and absurdity border on one another. In that rare atmosphere fiction fails, but in the failure of their fiction Swift and Beckett discover the limits of art as well as the limits of the human mind. (FNS)

2913. Smith, Stephani P. "Between Pozzo and Godot: Existence as Dilemma." *FR* 47:889-903.

Religion in *En attendant Godot* becomes a symptom of the dilemma of existence. The references to the thieves at the crucifixion at the beginning of the play opens a series of allusions to the arbitrary choices of fate which favor one of a pair. The tramps are faced with two undesirable and uncertain choices: they can wait for a Godot whose actions and existence remain in the domain of conjecture, or they can replace Godot with a real and present, but ridiculous and cruel Pozzo. The choice between Pozzo and Godot is a choice between an obviously erroneous and unsatisfying answer (the known gods of mythology) and a vaguely imagined possibility which can neither be affirmed nor denied (God). The tramps cannot know whether or not Godot will come; Pozzo does not fulfill their needs and expectations. At the end of the play Lucky remains with his personal diety and meaninglessly dispenses his energy in the service of a tyrannical and impotent master. The tramps remain without direction and continue to kill time, all positive action made impossible by their uncertainty. (SPS)

Bergson. 2921. Jones, Louisa. "The Comic as Poetry:Bergson Revisited." *NCFS* 2:75-85.

Bergson's *Le Rire* separates comic and lyric; modern poets combine them. Bergson describes tone mixtures, surprise word-plays, self-conscious language, etc.—all poetic today. Bergson remains limited by body/soul, subject/object, word/idea, artifice/natural assumptions but approaches synthesis of comic and poetic in examples and inconsistencies. (LEJ)

Blanchot. 2940. Batlay, Jenny H. "Analyse littéraire versus fiction romanesque:Réflexions sur *Le livre à venir* de Maurice Blanchot." *ECr* 14:247-54.

In *Le Livre à venir* Blanchot attempted to define the concept of "literary criticism," or rather than to define it, to express it, explore it, and eventually destroy it. His technique can be compared more to that of a creative writer than a critic, in the sense that he appeals more to the imagination of the reader than to his scientific knowledge of literature. His style and vocabulary are similar to a mystery writer's. The acts of reading and of writing are so inextricably mingled that the literary critic finds himself paradoxically writing even though not reading the book he is writing about. Another enigma in the work of Blanchot stems from his persistent questioning of the validity of literary criticisms, yet finding it impossible to discard: gratuitous, futile, but fascinating. Is this not, essentially, what life also is all about? (JHB)

Bosco. 2946. Prince, John. "New Light on the Origins and Symbolism of *Malicroix* by Henri Bosco." *FR* 47:773-82.

Malicroix by Henri Bosco, and indeed all his works, have undergone the hitherto unsuspected influence of Anglo-Saxon writers and contain a symbolic element which many critics have failed to recognize. After a period of relative eclipse, probably explained by the impossibility of classing them in any literary "family," Bosco's novels are enjoying a new popularity in France. Bosco considers *Malicroix* his greatest novel. It is mainly through declarations of the writer himself that the influence of Conrad and Kipling on the novel is established, as well as the existence of a marked symbolic content. However, this symbolism did not result from a premeditated decision but presented itself quite naturally to the author during the writing. A synthesis of the content of the novel permits us to establish the points at which these influences and this symbolism are evident. The presence of the latter disproves the opinion of many critics that the Bosco novels are nothing more than good regional literature. (JDWP)

2947. Van Grit, William. "Interview avec Henri Bosco." *FR* 47:882-88.

Bosco traces archetypal images, such as the house and earth, back to his childhood, his sense of mystery and his awareness of beneficent and maleficent forces in the universe. The central hero of his fiction is a solitary youth—Bosco himself—who shuns love and women because Bosco considers love a madness from which man must escape. He bases this idea on ancient philosophy and the Bible. He lists classical and romantic writers who influenced him, and traces his interest in the Rosicrucians, Albigenses, etc., back to the history of his native Provence. Although evil is omnipresent, good eventually overcomes evil as exemplified by his favorite novel *Malicroix*. Paradise is a symbol of happiness for mankind but Bosco considers it impossible because of ever-present war and evil. His message to his readers is to live according to the laws of nature and the earth. (PTO)

Breton. 2950. Balakian, Anna. "Breton and Drugs." *YFS* 50:96-107.

André Breton thought of surrealism as a form of benign intoxication, exhilarating and free of depressive aftereffects. He identified the poet-seer as one who in full possession of free will could expand his daily and literary reality. His medical studies had convinced him that man possessed natural powers of exaltation, blocked by cultural strictures, yet capable of release through nonpharmaceutical stimulants such as the practice of psychic automatism, the free play of eidetic associations, and love. In his own work he demonstrated his experience of terrestial paradise through the restoration of primal ties with the animal, vegetable, and mineral kingdoms, and the unification of the affective, intellectual, and sensory faculties which create for him a fully integrated universe. The ethical and political implications of Breton's hypothesis are that no government that ignores this crucial human need for psychic enrichment can ever hope to achieve a truly liberal society. (AB)

Burgart. 2955. Bishop, Michael. "Measurement upon Measurement:The Poetry of Jean-Pierre Burgart's *Failles*." *Mosaic* 7,iv:15-28.

In Burgart's poetic imagination self is beset with problems of duplicity, unrevealedness, and revulsion in his relationships with others and the phenomenal world. The word and the page become privileged objects of attention in a self-reflexive poetry where questions of being and wording are interwoven. Penetration into a magnetic yet anguishing obscurity might be achieved via direct rebirth into obscurity experienced as plenitude and transparency

—or via the makeshift of words. Yet words are deemed unable to cross the gulf between self and revealed obscurity. Questions of the locus and nature of self's being-with-the-world become obsessive. If self realizes its being via measurement, it is still condemned not to coincide with what is meant to express it. Self is reduced to measuring the dissociation, the "faille" between the "appel" and the "terme détérioré." Self commits itself to the solution of a problem pushed continually beyond solution by the poetic act that seeks to solve it. (MB)

Butor. 2959. Heck, Francis S. "Michel Butor, *Où, le Génie du lieu 2*." *IFR* 1,i:64-65.
Où, le Génie du lieu 2 embodies the form and the poetic verse, used in Butor's *Mobile* with a different subject matter: descriptions of people and customs of Korea, Cambodia, Santa Barbara (California), and Utah, where Mormon history is perpetuated in place names. The work deals with the ceremonies and customs of the Zuñi Indians, people representing the *génie du lieu* for Butor. The New Novel's preoccupation with time-distance is present in the ever-changing perspective of Mount Sandia at Albuquerque. Butor finds visits to other lands personally invigorating, especially if he can infuse their *génie* into Parisian life and culture. (FSH)
    2960. Helbo, André. "Discontinu et mobilité." *Degrés* 2(1973):m-m10.
The idea of *rupture* has always been defined by reference to its antonym. One ought to seek a more specific approach. After a critical survey—supported by the detailed refutation of the exegesis of Barthes—the perspective of Butor engaged in open and reflexive work goes beyond the yoke of a system to urge a reflection on the referent. (AH)
    2963. Larson, Jeffry. "The Sibyl and the Iron Floor Heater in Michel Butor's *La modification*." *PLL* 10:403-14.
In almost every passage of Michel Butor's *La Modification*, evoking the central character's present train trip from Paris to Rome, mention is made of the "tapis de fer chauffant" or iron floor heater. The fixture is mnemonically linked in the subliminal second-person narrative with Delmont's mistress, Cecile: it reminds him of his earlier trips between Paris and Rome with her. This memory triggers a long mental process which makes Delmont realize he cannot carry out his project of bringing his mistress back to live with him in Paris. The heater introduces Delmont into the underworld of his psyche in Sibylline fashion. Images associated with the heater recur in the Sibyl episodes of Delmont's nightmare. The iron floor heater assumes a mantic role to open up a new and more authentic future for Butor's traveler. (JKL)
    2969. Smock, Ann. "The Disclosure of Difference in Butor." *MLN* 89:654-68.
Butor remarks that fiction inscribes itself as a distance between the place where we read and the place we read about. Fiction marks a difference which allows the world to appear in two versions. But we ordinarily assume that the "real" version preceeded the "fictive" one, and we forget the interval in between without which there would appear neither a "fictive" nor a "real" world. The ordinary way of thinking about reality and fiction, presence and representation, reflects a certain way of considering the relations between blacks and whites, women and men, self and other. (AAS)
    2970. Spencer, Michael. "*L'ouverture* chez Butor." *Degrés* 1(1973):l-l 15.
Examines the development of Butor's work from *Passage de milan* (1954) to *Travaux d'approche* (1972) and discusses the role that the theme of chance plays in his works. (AH)
    2973. Warme, Lars G. "Reflection and Revelation in Michel Butor's *La modification*." *IFR* 1:88-95.
Léon Delmont's train journey from Paris to Rome describes a psychoanalytical processs through which the hero is forced to come face to face with himself and to attain a new awareness. The theme of reflection is emphasized by the numerous references to mirrors. The use of the second-person narrative shows the hero's attempt to externalize himself. The obsessive detail observations also serve to ward off an unwanted confrontation with the self; ironically, his observations of the fellow passengers deflect back to himself: they, too, turn into mirrors in which he can only see

himself and his own situation. The gradual undermining of the hero's rational defenses is completed in the dream sequences and just before arriving in Rome Delmont realizes that he has indeed been "on the wrong track." (LGW)

Camus. 2979. Brady, Patrick. "Manifestations of Eros and Thanatos in *L'étranger*." *TCL* 20:183-88.
Thanatos structures *L'Etranger*: death of the Mother, of the Other (the Arab), of the Self. These deaths are the only events which stimulate to lyrical life the neutral discourse of Meursault, walking embodiment of the death-wish, who reacts to life on the contrary with insensitivity and indifference (primacy of the inanimate). The principle of Eros is also given a significant role: in the relationships with the Mother (first love-object), with the Other (Marie), and with the Self (imaged in Nature, as opposed to Society, and in the narcissistic discourse of the *parole vide*). Furthermore, overt manifestations of Thanatos involve covert manifestations of Eros, a notable example being the killing of the Arab, surrogate Other violated together with the virgin silence of the sunlit beach. (PB)
    2985. Curtis, Jerry L. "Camus' Hero of Many Faces." *SNNTS* 6:88-97.
One of the most misunderstood of fictional characters is the elusive dialogist of Albert Camus's *La Chute*. Since Jean-Baptiste Clamence was intended to mirror Camus's contemporaries it is axiomatic that such a looking-glass was not meant to mirror an exclusive monolithic image of humanity. Rather Camus's hero must be understood as reflecting the multifarious absurdities of the human condition. At once prophet and false-prophet, Dantesque devil and Christian angel, both defender of noble causes and criminals' advocate, this hero of many faces inflicts upon man the just retribution of his own kaleidoscopic image. (JLC)
    2986. —— "Camus' Vision of Greatness." *OL* 29:338-54.
Analyzes Camus's concept of heroism. As a means of depolarizing the antipodean forces of both modern Christianity and contemporary Atheism, Camus invoked three Grecian figures —Sisyphus, Prometheus, and Nemesis—as paradigms from which he declined his own heroes. These legendary figures embody the absurdity, revolt, and moderation which correspond to stages in the development of Camus's own concept of greatness. The heroes are discussed in order to illustrate how they desire to transcend the absurdity of their various predicaments while realizing the impossibility of their quest. (JLC)
    2989. Durand, Laura G. "Thematic Counterpoint in *L'exil et le royaume*." *FR* 47:1110-22.
In *L'Exil et le royaume* "exile" means a state characterized by unhappiness, loneliness, and silence, while "kingdom" is the opposite condition of fulfillment, communication, participation. Each of the protagonists exemplifies one aspect of the many possible variations of meaning of the major themes, whose breadth of implication becomes clear only in a consideration of the stories in relation to and contrast with each other. Repeated use of certain motifs and imagery reinforces the thematic development of the central meaning: the necessity for communication and communion among humans, and for the acknowledgment and assumption of moral responsibilities. (LGD)
    2992. Gale, John E. "Does America Know *The Stranger*? A Reappraisal of a Translation." *MFS* 20:139-47.
Stuart Gilbert's 1946 translation of Camus's *L'Etranger* (1942) needs to be replaced. Based on the first edition, it does not take account of Camus's later excision of some metaphorical language in order to strengthen the contrast between the generally prosaic tone of the narrative and the more poetic language of moments of emotional stress. Furthermore, comparative study of syntax shows a tendency to substitute subordination for Camus's simple or coordinated sentences, thereby creating a sense of casuality which, as Sartre showed in 1943, Camus had consciously avoided. Several examples also show that whereas Meursault expresses himself in simple positive or negative language, Gilbert has him wordy and vacillating. The use of the *passé composé* and of indirect discourse confirms B.T. Fitch's 1960 thesis that the narrative is spoken by the imprisoned Meursault. Since the narrative tense distinction does not exist in English, it is all the

more important to retain indirect discourse as a sign of oral narrative, but Gilbert too frequently fails to do this. (EG)

3001. Keefe, Terry. "Camus's *La Chute*:Some Outstanding Problems of Interpretation Concerning Clamence's Past." *MLR* 69:541-55.
An examination of Clamence's account of his past in Camus's *La Chute* bears upon more general problems of interpretation. An attempt to reconstruct Clamence's past in relation to the sequences in which he relates events, and how forgotten events are remembered yields ambiguities and possible inconsistencies in chronology. (TK)

3008. Meyers, Jeffrey. "Camus' *The Fall* and Van Eyck's *The Adoration of the Lamb*." *Mosaic* 7,iii:43-51.
Van Eyck's *The Adoration of the Lamb* (1432) provides a visual representation of the theological framework of Camus's *The Fall*: the Christian answer to the problem of guilt. The painting provides a moral and religious reference for Clamence's confession of damnation. Since the novel's mode is completely ironic and thoroughly negative, an awareness of Van Eyck's vision of faith provides a firm contrast to Clamence's clever but evil reasoning. Both the painting and the novel illustrate Christian concepts by the opposition of the Fall of Man and the redeeming message of John the Baptist, both are allegories based on "revelations," and both concern the transference of guilt. (JM)

3009. Moses, Edwin. "Functional Complexity:The Narrative Techniques of *The Plague*." *MFS* 20:419-29.
Camus's narrator in *The Plague* is a reliable and exemplary figure but an amateurish ostensible author, who intrudes into the story and inaccurately claims to be entirely objective and to make no changes for artistic effect. Camus needs a narrator who will speak out of a deep involvement with his fellow citizens and with the plague experience. He must not be set off from his fellows by being referred to as "I," nor should he give the sense of regarding his fellows merely as characters. It would be impossible to gauge the degree of a truly anonymous narrator's involvement, and hence Camus progressively reveals Rieux's identity. Rieux's unconscious failures of objectivity reveal the personal nature of his struggle against the plague and further qualify him as an exemplary character. (EPM)

3010. Muraire, A. "Searching for a Theatre in France:Upton Sinclair vs. Albert Camus, André Malraux, and Jean Vilar." *BSUF* 15,ii:77-79.
Sinclair wanted to become a playwright. In 1959 he couldn't find a publisher in the States for his latest play, *Cicero*. He tried to have it staged and published abroad, and wrote to Camus who, according to press reports, had been promised a theater by the French authorities. Camus found the play appealing but couldn't stage it, as it eventually turned out that he had no theater of his own. Sinclair then wrote to Malraux, "Ministre d'Etat chargé des Affaires culturelles," who put him in touch with Jean Vilar, who was then at the head of the "Théâtre National Populaire." Vilar kindly and respectfully declined Sinclair's offer on account of the lack of dramatic intensity in the play. Sinclair gave up. *Cicero* was to be his last attempt at playwriting. (AM)

3016. Rosenthal, Bianca. "Camus and Nietzsche:Parallels and Divergences." [F 19]:232-35.
Nietzsche and Camus directed their critical and creative energies toward similar themes, often drawing identical conclusions. Nietzsche's nihilism resulted from his reaction against idealism and what he believed were the false values of Christianity. For Camus, death forces man to question whether life is worth living. As Camus points out, Nietzsche replied in the affirmative, stating that man, by living creatively in the face of nothingness, can overcome nihilism. Parallels can be drawn concerning ideas of Nietzsche and Camus. Their message can be summarized in the word "creation," which in a larger sense encompasses the totality of all being. (BR)

3019. Simon, Roland H. "Le rôle de l'écriture dans *La chute* de Camus et *Quelqu'un* de Pinget." *FR* 47:543-56.
A comparison of fictional autobiography in Camus's *La Chute* and Pinget's *Quelqu'un* shows that the written word falls short of translating the experience of living in its integrity. Various modes of language used by Clamence to involve his interlocutor in his confession of guilt are analyzed. The reader is both taken in by

the text and detached from it as he realizes the power of words to make him believe the unbelievable, to make him accept the unacceptable. At the end of the novel, the reader is caught between the false "certainty" of the fiction and the ambiguity of his own existence. The self-portrait of Pinget's character, denigrating style, using the basest vocabulary in its attempt to reach a concrete truth, paradoxically demonstrates that language tends to substitute itself for life. In both works, confession and self-revelation fail to convince the reader of their value beyond that of an exercise in writing. (RHS)

3020. Sterling, Elwyn F. "Camus' *L'étranger*." *Expl* 33:Item 28.
A recent article on the Gilbert translation of *L'Etranger* demands correction in the interests of accuracy and fairness. Gilbert did not gratuitously interpolate the sentence suggestive of masturbation by Meursault. The sentence appeared in manuscripts 1 and 2 and in a 1946 edition in French. Camus's subsequent deletion of the sentence may well have weakened the thematic structure of the *récit* at the point at which it occurred. Perhaps in accord with his notion of "corrected creation," Camus made a more important deletion in Part I which bears directly on the central question of Meursault's attitude. If Gilbert should not be faulted for including in his translation the masturbation line, other instances indicate that he did take unjustified liberties with the original text as argued in the article under discussion. (EFS)

3021. Sugden, Leonard W. "Meursault, an Oriental Sage." *FR* (spec. issue 6):196-207.
Among the allusions, literary and other, which Albert Camus clustered around the hero of *L'Etranger*, there is one which has been largely overlooked by critics and readers: the suggestion of an Oriental sage. Meursault's "strangeness" is at least partly due to the fact that he lies between two cultures, East and West. The quasi-mystical states of consciousness described by the author in his early essays, as well as in *L'Etranger*, are similar to the experiences of a Yogi, a spiritual absorption into nature which the Buddhists call Nirvana. The murder committed by the protagonist on the beach may be seen as a symbolic revolt, but, contradictorily, it is also a creative action, a search for unity. While the "myth" created in the novel is universally applicable, the Oriental ethic in itself is shown to contain the seeds of its own destruction. (LWS)

Céline. 3033. Alméras, Philippe. "Céline:L'itinéraire d'une écriture." *PMLA* 89:1090-98.
Changes in his expressed ideology subjected Céline's works to criteria that were not all literary. A study of the vocabulary, syntax, and architecture of Céline's 9 novels reveals a continuous evolution. The overall analysis indicates four different periods which do not reflect any ideological changes. The Célinian novels must be treated as a whole because their significance is impaired when considered separately. (PCA)

3055. Solomon, Philip H. "Céline's *Death on the Installment Plan*:The Intoxications of Delirium." *YFS* 50:191-203.
The substantive *délire* and the verb *délirer* are pervasive in Céline's novels. He rejects the intoxication of alcohol for that of delirium. The latter connotes certain modes of verbal expression: agitated or contrary to fact but also literary creation. In *Death on the Installment Plan* the delirium of the protagonist Ferdinand functions as narrative metalepsis, permitting a transition from the doctor of the social frame of the novel to the writer relating to his fictional childhood. In accomplishing this transition Ferdinand rejects escapist literature, exemplified by the *Legend of King Krogold*, for a more subversive form—that of Céline's novels with their attack against standard French and their bleak view of humanity. The respective deliriums of Auguste and Courtial des Pereires inform the delirium of the narrator. Auguste uses language as a weapon in a vain attempt to transform his son into a passive member of capitalist society. Courtial elaborates a linguistic utopia by means of a rhetoric of science. His utopia is destroyed when he tries to make his language operational. For both figures, escape from reality is possible only through insanity, of which delirium is an imperfect form. Ferdinand's delirium is superior to theirs because it permits him to become the "super-seer" as writer. (PHS)

Char. 3062. La Charité, Virginia A. "The Role of Rimbaud in Char's Poetry." *PMLA* 89:57-63.

Char is esthetically indebted to Rimbaud for his creative vision, teleology, and practice. The numerous thematic affinities between the two include a humanized harmonious universe, the attitude of revolt, the obligation of anguish, the poet as the initiator of action, and the concepts of poetic activity, love, experience, risk, man, nature. The poetic matter of their creative worlds is identical, but Char brings the necessary corrective of faith in human expression to Rimbaud's immature reliance on verbal expression. Where Rimbaud fails to synthesize the fragments, Char succeeds. It is Char's understanding of Rimbaud's work that enables him to evolve a poetic based first on life and second on theory. Char does not merely humanize the cosmos; he goes on to poeticize man. Technical similarities are equally numerous, but Char is disciplined; he rejects the equation of the act and expression in favor of an evocation of the activity through the effect of spontaneity, his theories of pulverization and crispation. (VAL)

Claudel. 3076. Cismaru, Alfred. "Paul Claudel and Boris Vian." *ClaudelS* 1,iv:34-40.

Boris Vian detested Paul Claudel. Although he alluded only rarely to Claudel in his work, Vian modeled his Father Saureilles of *Le Dernier des Métiers* after the Catholic writer. Father Saureilles, an effeminate and crooked prelate, according to Vian, embodies those characteristics which best describe Paul Claudel. In this, of course, he was wrong, yet his opinions are important to the literary historian because they are part of a contemporary phenomenon within the context of which any writer associated with the Church is viewed with suspicion. (AC)

3078. Erwin, John W. "Hero as Audience:*Antony and Cleopatra* and *Le soulier de satin*." *MLS* 4,ii:65-77.

The way Shakespeare and Claudel reduce their heroes to passive witnesses convinces audiences to experience their own freely chosen passivity as a source of power. Shakespeare can rely upon the close collaboration of a public, but Claudel must more elaborately stage theatrical mediation to educate audiences to authorize this apotheosis of response. (JWE)

3082. Gruenberg, Peter. "*La ville*:Une représentation à Bruxelles." *ClaudelS* 1,v:60-64.

The second version of Claudel's *La Ville* was staged in 1974 at the *Rideau* theater, Brussels. The merits of the staging and the message of the drama are examined. The "City" which is the center of the play is the Paris he hated in his youth. It is also the new city to be built on principles of justice and love. Avare, for example, is the personification of the whole Claudel-Rimbaud generation which revolted against arts and society, but he is not the last to have his voice heard. After the destruction of the city, Lâla reveals the roles that the destructor, the builder, the future kind will have to play in the reconstructed city, and the "irresistible hope" that she symbolizes with her being. The merit of the staging is that the Director Pierre Laroche created an atmosphere of a city that we all know; it may have been Paris of May 1968, or any other city at large which deploys unceasingly its spiritual and moral emptiness, hoping for better days to come. (MMN)

3088. Labriolle, Jacqueline de. "Claudel et les universités américaines." *ClaudelS* 1,iv:4-33; v:14-22.

From 1927 to 1933 Claudel served in Washington as Ambassador of the French Republic. He visited several American Universities and was granted 9 honorary degrees. From newspapers and many unpublished archives, we can learn how he was received and how this public life influenced his literary fortune in the English-speaking countries. Thematic analysis of his many speeches demonstrates the nature of the cultural and political problems he raised. This study is divided in two parts; this one, Part II, concerns Claudel's visit to Louisiana (1928), his rapport with the main Universities of the East Coast, and his journeys through Canada and New England (1929-30). (JCDeL)

3089. —— "Fortune ou infortune de Claudel dans les pays anglophones? (1912-1972)." *RLC* 48:55-77.

Examines the reception of Paul Claudel's works in Great Britain and the United States. (JdL)

3090. Lebel, Maurice. "Réflexions sur *Tête d'or, Les Perses*, et *Prométhée enchaîné*." *ClaudelS* 1,v:41-50.

Claudel's *Tête d'or* was staged for the first time in 1959 by Jean-Louis Barrault. Lebel, reminiscing this event, situates the drama in its historical context, and points out some of the possible influences on the young Claudel. The complexity of Claudel's drama, however, calls for a broader analysis. Lebel, analyzing along with *Tête d'or* Aeschylus' *Persae* and *Prometheus Bound*, underscores the relevance of the Greek tragedy and Claudel's roots in that tradition. These plays have a great deal in common: their purpose is moral lesson; they are dramatized epical poems; they introduce us into a universe which is situated beyond time and space; their heroes are imaginary supermen. Man's destiny is tragic, for he is unable to reach the object of his desire, although nothing less makes him happy. What is then the sense of our existence? (MMN)

3097. Nagy, Moses M. "*Conversations dans le Loir-et-Cher* at Carré Thorigny." *ClaudelS* 1,iv:50-59.

While two Parisian theaters successfully presented *L'Annonce faite à Marie* and Protée of Claudel, Carré Thorigny made the 1973-74 theater season of Paris even more "Claudelian" by giving a stage version of *Conversations dans le Loir-et-Cher*. Thanks to the courage and intuitive genius of Silvia Montfort, Claudel's rich prose became an enjoyable theater masterpiece. In all probability, Claudel had never thought of bringing his *Conversations* to the stage, but his book written in dialogue form is an open invitation to be uttered by actors. The book in its entirety would, of course, exceed the time limit alloted by the stage. Montfort selected a certain number of "conversations" in order to make one coherent and playable "conversation." (MMN)

3098. —— "*Paul Claudel-Louis Massignon 1908-1914: Correspondance*. Etablie et annotée par Michel Malicet. (Paris: Desclée de Brouwer, 1973)." *ClaudelS* 1,v:65-75. [Rev. art.]

Claudel's and Massignon's correspondence, sparkled by a religious question, starts in 1908. They were both fervent Catholics and were both tempted by the monastic life. Although Claudel does not hide his hopes that his young friend will be more persevering in his priestly vocation, one could not speak of proselytism on either side. There is, however, in this correspondence a crucial point which keeps the correspondents apart—the question of literature. Massignon has little or no appreciation for literature. Claudel cannot help feeling challenged in his literary endeavor, and so has to re-evaluate the very *raison d'être* of his writing. He writes, certainly not because *nulla die sine linea*, but because he feels that only poetry can penetrate some of the regions of the intellect. (MMN)

3104. Rigolot, Carol N. "The Paul Claudel-Saint-John Perse Correspondence." *ClaudelS* 1,v:51-59.

The extant correspondence consists of 19 letters from Perse and 9 from Claudel, supplemented by Claudel's commentary of *Vents* and Perse's memorial "Silence pour Claudel." They are grouped into two widely separated periods (1906-17; 1945-55), marking two important periods in Perse's life: the initiation of his diplomatic career and the beginning of his literary fame. Perse believed himself embarked with Claudel on a common quest for what he himself names the "divin." In his eyes, this sufficed to unite them. For Claudel there remained one barrier which he named the "agnosticisme total" of Perse. (CNR)

3107. Watson, Harold A., and Louise R. Witherell,eds. "Claudel's *The Bear and the Moon* on an American Stage. (A Taped Discussion)." *ClaudelS* 1,v:23-40.

This unrehearsed discussion, led by Richard Berchan, ranges over the full gamut of the translation and staging of this minor comedy and touches on such typical Claudelian themes as suffering/joy, light/darkness, animus/anima, hope/despair, dream/reality. Stimulated by questions from the audience following the performance, the cast offers insights into the characters and the humor of the play, while the translators and the director elaborate on the problems of rendering its symbolism and the verset on stage. (HMW)

3108. Whitaker, M. "Claudel, the Poet of *Les cinq Grandes Odes*—et l'Angleterre." *ESA* 17:101-06.

An attempt to dispel the misunderstandings which surround Claudel's work in England where Claudel is often read after Gide and seen through Gide's eyes. The English reader may toil to catch the tone of Claudel's life affirmation and explosive joy. To overcome this, a re-evaluation is suggested: Claudel's themes are placed in a wider European context and their meaning is illuminated from within his own world-view. (MW)

3109. Wiedner, Elsie M. "Philosophies and Stagings:Notes on Three Productions of 'La quatrième journée' of Paul Claudel's *Le soulier de satin*." *ClaudelS* 1,iv:41-49.

The Quatrième Journée of Paul Claudel's *Le Soulier de satin* has been omitted in production, included in truncated form, and presented as an entity. The production by Jean-Pierre Granval at Brangues (1972) perpetuated the approach of Jean-Louis Barrault in the first production of the whole play (1943), i.e., the Quatrième Journée is an independent restatement of the play's theme. The play is complete without it; conversely, it can stand virtually alone. In contrast, the play's production (as *Der Seidene Schuh*) by Gunther Fleckenstein and Theo van Alst (Muenster, Westf. 1958) assumed interdependency of the play and its final act. This interpretation stressed the development of the hero, whereas the French productions emphasized the significance of his relationship to the heroine. Details of production as well as over-all interpretation are determined by the basically philosophical decision on the presentation of Quatrième Journée. (EMW)

Cocteau. 3114. Hélein-Koss, Suzanne. "Rêve et fantasmes dans *Les enfants terribles* de Jean Cocteau." *FR* (spec. issue 6):151-61.

Making use of Gilbert Durand's study of the anthropological structures of the imaginary, a detailed analysis of Elisabeth's dream and Paul's hallucination reveals that the images constitute a symbolic network which underscores and condenses the development and theme of *Les Enfants terribles*. The various symbols reinforce one another, converging into a pattern, wherein fate assumes the form of Eros-Thanatos. Due to the inexorable law of Chronos, the innocent game-playing of the brother and sister can only result in incest or death. Elisabeth's dream in which she envisions a clearing in the forest foreshadows the fact that the purity of the brother-sister relationship can be recaptured through death alone. Paul's hallucinations, while in the throes of death, kaleidoscope the interlocking elements which have ordained his particular destiny. The hermaphroditic image of the ram's head with woman's hair, for example, indicates the dual nature of Paul's fate and refers both to his hero, Dargelos, and to his sister, Elisabeth. The ram, an archetype for the libido and death, as well as being a zodiacal symbol of fate, reflects the conflicting sexual forces which lead to Paul's suicide. (SHK)

3115. McNab, James P. "Mythical Space in *Les enfants terribles*." *FR* (spec. issue 6):162-70.

In *Les Enfants terribles* (1929) Cocteau presents two spaces which particularly fascinated him. They are the *cité* Monthiers, in winter, presided over by the school-bully Dargelos, and the dark, closed, womb-like room. The *cité* Monthiers is differentiated from surrounding reality and made into a sacred center. The appearance of Dargelos is an epiphany. His wounding of Paul, the schoolboy hero of *Les Enfants terribles*, is a supernatural event, a form of initiation. Paul is forced to leave school and stay at home, where he falls under the domination of his sister Elisabeth. Their bedroom duplicates in spirit the *cité* Monthiers of the beginning. Where Dargelos is for Paul a god who shows himself in the *cité*, Elisabeth becomes for him a priestess officiating in her temple: the room. At the end, when the two die, they rise to heaven in the "spirit" of the room. This last scene has much in common with the first. This assumption or ascent to heaven is a satisfactory conclusion to a myth which began with an epiphany, unfolded in a temple and is set, throughout, in sacred space. (JPM)

Colette. 3123. Fisher, Claudine G. "Solitude et liberté: Dilemme de Colette dans *La vagabonde*." [F 19]:212-16.

Colette's *La Vagabonde* deals with the dilemma of Renée Néré, torn between her fear of solitude and desire for freedom. She graduates from physical and concrete freedom to a higher plateau of freedom, a transcendance based on strength and pain. Her search takes her through the analysis of her marriage, divorce, her role in society, and relationship with her lover. She finally rejects

him to fulfill what she feels is her freedom. However, she remains a wanderer, a vagabond, a lonely woman hoping to achieve her own identity. (CGF)

Dabit. 3128. O'Connell, David. "Eugène Dabit:A French Working-Class Novelist." *RS* 41(1973):217-33.

Eugène Dabit (1896-1936), best known for his first novel *Hôtel du Nord* (1926), was also the author of another half-dozen works of fiction before he suddenly died of scarlet fever while touring the Soviet Union in 1936 as a member of Gide's entourage. Because *Hôtel du Nord* received the first *Prix du Populisme* in 1931, Dabit has usually been associated, in the histories and manuals of 20th-century French literature, with the "école populiste." Unfortunately, this linking of his name with French literary Populism has helped to deny him the wider audience that his fictional achievement deserves. Dabit wrote with compassion in a lean and disciplined style reminiscent of Gide's, but without any voluntarily imposed blindness with regard to the vices and human shortcomings of those members of his class who people his novels and stories. Serving no particular ideological point of view as a fiction writer, Dabit has furnished us with the most vivid literary portrait we have of the working masses of Paris on the eve of the advent of the Popular Front. (DO)

Deguy. 3131. Smock, Ann. "Re-turning Dissemblance:Readings of Two Poems by Michel Deguy." *Sub-stance* 10:17-31.

In "March qui déplie l'espace plié" Deguy turns over the chains of names to reveal the way their links alone conserve the nudity of a landscape they seem to burden down. Nudity is not unclothed presence, but the retreat of what Deguy calls "le même." This withdrawal into reserve leaves its trace each time a thing turns away toward something else and thus turns to us a different face. In "Un homme las du génitif" Deguy suggests that it is language's own misconstrual of its chain-like nature which makes it complicit with a violent heritage that can only be borne like a heavy yoke. As it draws the distant and the foreign into "our" sphere of resemblance, our language forgets the distantness at the heart of each thing which allows each to resemble. This distance is itself a forgetfulness, re-turning the disfigured figurativeness of language and re-disclosing the possibility of history as a peaceable circle dance. (AAS)

Desnos. 3138. Caws, Mary Ann. "Robert Desnos and the Flasks of Night." *YFS* 50:108-19.

The repetitive structures which are an insistent mark of the early writings of Robert Desnos depend on, and create in their turn, certain obsessive perceptions. The repeated elements play against their linguistic and conceptual variants to produce a cumulative effect greater than the sum of its parts—a result associated with mythical construction, primitive ritual, and incantation. Desnos acknowledges the necessity for the extinguishing of light and logic, and for the illumination of the bottle; but the recurring images of broken glass prefigure a final desertion of the dream by the poet, in favor of a sober reality from which are absent the extensive sequences of linguistic play, the obsessed passages focusing narrowly on one object, and the accumulated momentum of repeated elements with the accompanying deflections and denials. With the loss of the obsessive or intoxicated gaze and its related formal structures, the most valuable ground for clear-headed analysis is lost. (MAC)

Domenach. 3141. Santoni, Georges V. "Les intellectuels: Entretien avec Jean-Marie Domenach." *FR* 47:695-702.

In France, the term *intellectuals* used to refer to individuals engaged in defending innocent people or in criticizing the Establishment. Since the time of the Dreyfus incident when the term was created, the word has undergone a profound semantic evolution. French intellectuals have continued to redefine their roles and their obligations to society in light of an ever expanding body of knowledge and a growing number of non-manual workers. Jean-Marie Domenach, director of the periodical *Esprit*, closely resembles the classic intellectual according to the original French definition of the term. In this interview he discusses the evolution of his function within society. (GVS)

Du Bos. 3148. Bossière, Jacques. "Autour de Charles Du Bos:Critique et critiques." *ECr* 14:149-61.
The progress of critical reflection on Du Bos is traced through four essays by George Poulet, René Wellek, J.-P. Richard, and Angelo P. Bertocci. (JPB)

Duhamel. 3149. Hoch, Claire. "Georges Duhamel's Advice to Young Writers." *FR* (spec. issue 6):171-81.
Georges Duhamel, a physician turned writer, had a lifelong interest in the elements which go into making a writer and the means of disseminating his work. His advice grew from his own experience. He pointed to the manifold advantages of having a profession other than writing initially: it provides the writer with life experience, allows him time to see whether he has a message and a audience receptive to his ideas, affords him financial independence, and saves him from journalism. Duhamel found advertising for marketing a writer's work detrimental to artistic endeavor and demoralizing to the public taste. The artificial creation of demand for literary works through publicity contributes to the decadence of literature by its presumption that whatever can be sold deserves to be fabricated. (CH)

3151. Prince, Gerald. "Salavin et ses lecteurs ou le roman du roman." *FR* (spec. issue 6):182-88.
By studying the stylistic features of Georges Duhamel's *Journal de Salavin* one discovers that, contrary to what the hero claims, he is not writing only for himself but is in search of a sympathetic public. *Journal de Salavin* is the story of his failure. One by one, the readers comtemplated by Salavin are found to be unsatisfactory. At the end, the protagonist himself becomes a critical and disappointed reader of his diary and is forced to stop writing for lack of any audience. *Journal de Salavin* has been studied primarily from the philosophical, psychological, and moral points of view. Studied from a more formal point of view, it reveals itself to be a novel about narrative situation. (GP)

Duras. 3154. Bessière, Jean. "La discontinuité de *Moderato Cantabile*." *Degrés* 2(1973):o-o20.
In Duras' work a sole referent governs successively a romantic esthetic of separation, discontinuity, and vacancy. *Moderato Cantabile* elaborates on two abysses: (1) one which the rejection of intellectual denomination and that of representation of the mental universe produce; and (2) one which the use of form makes unavoidable. The first provokes a taking apart of romantic data and the second organizes the data without gathering it together. The multiplicity of signs does not inflict disparity but delineates their reciprocity. "To destroy, she said, Abahn Sabana David" identifies discontinuity with the sole destruction of the narration. Developing as some allegories do, re-establishing the relation between literary denomination and reality, the signs create out of the style the means for political and moral appeal. (JB)

3155. Bishop, Lloyd. "Classical Structure and Style in *Moderato cantabile*." *FR* (spec. issue 6):219-34.
Despite the use of many modern fictional techniques relating Marguerite Duras to the *nouveau roman*, the basic structure and style of *Moderato Cantabile* derive from classical principles of composition. The novel develops within a closed, "classical" space and approximates the focused structure of a classical tragedy: a limited cast; a tendency toward the unities and toward the *séparation des genres*; a psychological conception of action, although the psychology is presented with a modern phenomenological bias. Duras even observes the classical principle of decorum, violent action being handled by exposition rather than scenic presentation. Stylistically the novel exhibits a classical orientation, chiefly in the use of understatement. (LOB)

3156. Eisinger, Erica. "Crime and Detection in the Novels of Marguerite Duras." *ConL* 15:503-20.
Marguerite Duras's novels share the affinity of the *nouveau roman* for the themes and techniques of the detective story. Her basic theme, the interplay between love and destruction, leads to a reliance on the detective story, whose dual structure of crime and investigation mirrors Duras's parallel movements first toward violence, then communion. The investigation provides a solution to the mystery of otherness through an intense identification

between the detective and the criminal-victim couple. *Moderato cantabile* and *Dix heures et demie du soir en été*, in particular, recount the transformation of an aimless, self-destructive woman from first witness to a crime, to investigator, to potential victim, and ultimately, in the later novels such as *L'Amante anglaise*, to criminal. Duras's women, like Maigret, rely on a dampening of consciousness through drink, sleep, and hypnotic dialogue with a catalytic male helpmate in order to approach an understanding of the criminal's sensibility. (EME)

3158. Weiss, Victoria L. "Form and Meaning in Marguerite Duras' *Moderato Cantabile*." *Crit* 16,i:79-87.
In *Moderato Cantabile* (1958) Duras deals with the problem of modern woman's quest for passion in a boring world. By eliminating speech tags and introductory phrases, by quickly shifting scenes to keep the reader aware of what is happening at all the focal points of the story, Duras involves the reader in the tension Anne experiences. By contrasting the temporal freedom of Chauvin with Anne's own enslavement to boring routine, by restricting the narrative point of view to what the spectator's eye can see and his ear can hear, and by focusing on the uncertainty of Anne and her contemporaries, Duras deals with both a technique and a world view which are particularly modern. (VLW)

Ganzl. 3174. Goldsmith, Helen H. "*Fracasse '73*." [F 19]:222-25.
Serge Ganzl's *Fracasse* is particularly interesting because of the affinities of spirit which it has with the original *Capitaine Francasse*. While Ganzl has changed or reworked certain details of his model, and while he has enlarged the area of impact of symbols Gautier invented, yet Ganzl's startling use of masks, mannequins, machines, and music, his presentation of cruelty, and his projection of theatricality can be found in Gautier's novel. Ganzl admits the influence of such innovators as Artaud, Ionesco, and Adamov. (HHG)

Genet. 3180. Sherzer, Dina. "Les appellatifs dans *Le balcon* de Genet." *FR* 48:95-107.
The characters in Genet's *Le Balcon* focus frequently on terms of address such as pronouns, proper names, titles, and endearing nouns. Genet puts these elements to a literary use, since he exploits their resources in the play. The characters use titles in the creation and elaboration of the roles they invent, and thus the titles participate in the organization of the play as a whole by contributing to the establishment of the contrast between reality and illusion on which it is built. The switch from one type of pronoun to another type, or from one term of address to another, reveals the intimate feelings of the characters. The characters also use endearing terms of address to manipulate other characters. (DS)

3182. Stewart, Harry E. "The Case of the Lilac Murders:Jean Genet's *Haut surveillance*." *FR* 48:87-94.
Lilacs play an interesting and important role in both the 1949 and the 1965 definitive editions of *Haute Surveillance*. An accumulation of the isolated and apparently unrelated references to lilacs in the 1949 edition reveals a symbolism based on folkloric superstitions surrounding the lilac, a symbolism that Genet supplements in order to support the basic themes of his play. In both versions of the play, Genet moves from the lilac-flower-death symbol to the flower-criminal symbol. Fulfilling a statement in *Le Journal du Voleur*, Genet so bedecks his convicts with "flowers" that they disappear beneath them to become gigantic and new flower-symbols. Begining with the basic superstition, i.e., it is unlucky to take lilacs into a house for they will cause a death, Genet then creates a symbol which reflects the basic themes of the play—murder, betrayal, fate, sex, and the criminal-religious hierarchy. (HES)

Genevoix. 3185. Walling, James J. "*Raboliot*:A Major French Regional Novel." *ML* 55:182-88.
In *Raboliot* the philosophical content rests on an assessment of the interaction of environment and characters, but Genevoix's originality is mainly linguistic and stylistic. When transcribing peasant speech or unspoken thoughts, Genevoix gets convincingly

close to Solognot French in phonography, syntax, and vocabulary. Exotic lexical items include (1) dialect alternatives to standard French; (2) patois corruptions of standard French; (3) technical terms relating to specialized activities; and (4) names of lesser-known birds, mammals, flowers, etc. (JJW)

Gide. 3194. Brosman, Catharine S. "The Relativization of Character in *Les faux-monnayeurs*." *MLR* 69:770-78.
In *Les Faux-Monnayeurs*, Gide questions the 19th-century view of fictional character as an absolute. This questioning of character, which is related to the central theme of the book, falsity, takes place in connection with studies of hypocrisy and role-playing, Edouard's self-examination, and Bernard's search for his identity. Gide shows how hypocrisy and role-playing create a pseudo-character in which human possibility is atrophied. Edouard's comments on sincerity reveal the relativity and discontinuity of his own personality. Bernard discovers the existentialist position that character is to some degree a matter of free choice and that this choice is relative. Finally, Gide suggests and illustrates several techniques by which a novelist can render character in a less rigid manner and indicate its grounding in human freedom. (CSB)
   3208. McClelland, John. "The Lexicon of *Les caves du Vatican*." *PMLA* 89:256-67.
For Gide *Les Caves du Vatican* represents a break with the tradition of *La Porte étroite*. He is especially concerned that the novel's language be liberated from the orthodoxy imposed by current usage and thus there appear numerous extravagant names, exotic nouns, foreign words and phrases, argot, rare words, and lexical and semantic neologisms. This phenomenon can be explained only in correlation with Gide's systematic overturning of the standard narrative conventions of the Realist-Naturalist tradition in the novel. Gide realized that the revolution in thinking about language could play a role in freeing the novel from the existing restrictions of the public's expectations. By his esoteric vocabulary he forces the reader to remember that the novel's "story" is the author's invention and the characters his playthings. (JMcC)

Goldmann. 3242. Brady, Patrick. "Socio-criticism as Genetic Structuralism:Value and Limitations of the Goldmann Method." *ECr* 14:207-18.
The structuralist character of Goldmann's system is compatible with other forms of structuralism only if we define "structure" broadly, for example as a "hypothetical, heuristic model elaborated for the relational investigation of phenomena." Goldmann, however, locates the structure in the minds of the historically-located social group under investigation. Moreover, for such a group to develop such a structure it must be devoted to the *transformation globale* or the *maintien global* of the existing social order. The chief weakness of Goldmann's theory is that he claims that all great literature reflects such a *vision du monde*. This claim must lead either to the arbitrary exclusion from "great literature" of many brilliant writers or to an abusively socio-political interpretation of their perspective on reality. (PB)

Green. 3252. Libhart, Byron R. "Julien Green's Troubled American:A Fictionalized Self-Portrait." *PMLA* 89:341-52.
In Julien Green's works set in America there is an unusually close relationship between the personal tragedies and the national milieu, certain problems of American life seeming to engender the dilemmas that lead the characters to tragic outcomes. Yet these circumstances are not so typically "American" as suggestive of problems the French novelist himself, born in France of American parents, encountered during the three crucial years he reluctantly spent in America following World WarI. His lengthy *Journal* and some recent autobiographical works reveal that the principal dilemmas that torment his American characters relate to those which the unusual circumstances of his double nationality created for him: problems centering about the matters of national belonging and personal morality (relative to American puritanism). Green's American heroes are primarily transformations of himself, created partly to purge himself of his own tragic inclinations, partly to recapture a period of his life which, though fundamentally painful, had overtones of sweetness

because of his first sexual awakening. (BRL)
   3253. Matuschka, Michèle. "*L'autre* où le conflit de deux réalités." *FR* (spec. issue 6):235-44.
The concept of "la grâce dans le péché" (the belief in a specific grace granted to the sinner), pervading Julien Green's work for more than two decades, has taken on a new dimension in *L'Autre* (1971). Green uses an elaborate technique involving the juxtaposition of two similar narratives, almost exclusively centered around the motive of desire. However, a closer examination shows that the second narrative (Karin's) fulfills a broader function than its equivalent (Roger's), where the narrator's spiritual aspirations are constantly stifled by his erotic obsessions. In "mars-avril 1949" Karin becomes aware of the demands made upon her by the invisible One, "l'Autre." Thus at a deeper level the novel treats the progression of a spiritual awareness. But wider issues arise out of of the comparison of the two narratives. In the second, the theme of *atonement*, actualized in Karin's identification with Mary Magdalene, the great sinner of the Scriptures, marks the fundamental difference between Roger's simple conversion and the heroine's mystic experience. (MJM)

Guilloux. 3257. King, J.H. "Louis Guilloux's *Le jeu de patience*:Time and the Novelist." *Trivium* 8(1973):40-55.
The main interest of Louis Guilloux's *Le Jeu de patience* (1949) is in its temporal structure, its purposive disruption of chronology. The treatment of time in novels can be imagined as a spectrum, ranging from the subjective view of time (Proust) to the "chronicle novel" (Tolstoi), where objective, chronological time is the guiding narrative principle. Guilloux's novel is seen as a complex structure resulting from the tension between these two poles as felt by its narrator, who is simultaneously the chronicler of the life of a small town under the impact of the central historical events of the 20th century, and a novelist attempting to "humanize" history and the passage of time by allowing his work to be guided by the subjective, achronological workings of his memory. Particular attention is drawn to the possible ideological basis of Guilloux's narrative technique in this work, by means of a comparison with his earlier novel, *Le Sang noir* (1935). The difference is between a novel where time is corrosive and chaotic and one where it has a knowable direction and meaning in terms of history. (JHK)

Ionesco. 3260. Baciu, Mira. "Eugène Ionesco et la quête de l'authenticité." *PFr* 6(1973):44-53.
Just prior to his reception into the Académie Française, Ionesco published in "Notes retrouvée," a statement that literature in the 1970s had reached an impasse and was dying because its modes of expression were out of date. The seeds of this idea can be found in the first published work of Ionesco, *Nu* (*Non*), a book of and about criticism (Bucarest, 1932). Here he develops the concept that man, haunted by death, is unable to find expression of this panic in literature and criticism which are themselves dying, killed by a dead organism, language. Once destroyed, a new language should be found which will be capable of expressing human reality. But since authenticity of human expression lies within the self, and articulation is the first step toward removing the self from the self, the writer must accept the lie that expression is identical to concept. Even death, the single and true problem of man, becomes a lie through expression. Man's goal becomes then a quest for authenticity which is a transcendence of death. (MB)
   3271. Issacharoff, Michael. "Métaphore et métamorphose dans *Jacques ou la soumission*." *FR* 48:108-18.
The lighthearted surface of Eugène Ionesco's *Jacques ou la soumission* conceals a carefully conceived metaphorical structure which reveals the true poetic and philosophical qualities of the play. Ionesco makes a calculated use of a series of stylistic devices such as neologisms, alliteration, and the association or juxtaposition of contradictory terms, to transform the communication process. The normal system of signifier and signified is cunningly undermined and becomes a major source of comic and poetic effect. The action of the play advances through the use of a limited number of apparently merely comic metaphors that in reality form a subtle imagerial network with philosophical undertones. Food images are central and are linked structurally to

the themes of sex and conformism. A single image (*chat*) sums up the principal themes of the play—the breakdown of communication, sex, and matrimony as causes of conformism, and the bestiality of conformist human behavior. (MI)

Jacob. 3292. Schneider, Judith M. "Max Jacob on Poetry." *MLR* 69:290-96.
Although recent criticism emphasizes Jacob's contributions as an esthetician, the status of his "poetics" remains questionable. His theoretical writings contain fundamental contradictions reflected in the formal discontinuity of his *Art poétique* (1922) and his *Conseils à un jeune poète* (1945). The explanation of these contradictions lies in the diversity of Jacob's intellectual sources. His poetic theories derive from cubism and romanticism, as well as from personal religious beliefs originating in divergent theosophies. Jacob defines the poem either as an esthetic or as a mystical object, and, occasionally, as pure emotion. His theories link the experience of the poet and the reader to the revelations of the mystic, but Catholic orthodoxy makes him refute his own mystical implications. His terminology is symbolic and polysemic. He describes poetic execution contradictorily: as conscious and as automatic activity. (JMS)

Jouhandeau. 3293. Yeager, Henry J. "Jouhandeau, the Dialectics of Love." *PQ* 52(1973):783-88.
Marcel Jouhandeau, French novelist and essayist, explores his own intense relationship with God in his work. The personal code of conduct which results is an attempt to synthesize a powerful and complex sexuality with an equally strong Catholicism of mystical bent. The thrust of Jouhandeau's work becomes an apology for evil so as to justify its co-existence in himself with a thirst for union with God. He argues that all love is one. Thus love for any human becomes also love for God, and naturally the contrary. Several of Jouhandeau's preferred mystical writers express love for God in carnal terms, for example, Saint John of the Cross. Jouhandeau reverses the figure and speaks of the grossest physical relationships in terms of union with the Divine. It follows also that the more intense the carnal passion, the stronger the expression of love for the Almighty. (HJY)

Le Clézio. 3308. Cagnon, Maurice, and Stephen Smith. "Le Clézio's Taoist Vision." *FR* (spec.issue 6):245-52.
Le Clézio's writing displays affinities with many basic principles in Taoism. All being derives from the interpenetration and union of mutually opposed natural forces. Every concept contains within itself elements of its opposite; yet all oppositions are but variant aspects of a single underlying unity. Such interpretations of reality are evident in Le Clézio's style, in his themes, in his techniques of creating fictional characters, and in his overall philosophical orientation. Le Clézio adds to these ideas, however, an awareness of the inadequacy of words ever to express the complexities of totality, and of the artificiality of the dichotomies created and perpetuated by the abstractions and generalizations which are required by language. (CM & SS)

Maeterlinck. 3324. Hadar, Tayitta. "L'angoisse métaphysique dans *Les aveugles* de Maeterlinck." *NCFS* 2:68-74.
Maeterlinck's play *Les Aveugles* reveals through a study of its various elements, the author's very personal metaphysical vision of the world. The story of the play is simple: twelve blind men and women are waiting for a priest. He brought them here and asked them to wait for him while he went to search for bread and water. He lies dead on the stage, but they cannot see his body and therefore keep on waiting for his return. After they discover the body, they keep sitting and waiting, unable to do anything else. Through the use of elements of death and desolation—an old forest, an island surrounded by the sea, thorns, cold weather, funerary trees, characters dressed in dark colors—the play settles in an atmosphere of mystery and terror. The dialogues amplify the uneasiness. These blind people represent the human search for understanding. There are more questions than answers in the play. The mystery and terror have reached their peak. Death is not far and the waiting goes on. (TH)
3329. Riffaterre, Michael. "Decadent Features in Maeter-

linck's Poetry." *Lang&S* 7:3-19.
The title *Serres chaudes*, as a word group, or even as a compound word, is the semantic given that serves as a transformational model for the derivation of images, shaping the entire poetic discourse of the texts found in Maeterlinck's collection. That *serres chaudes* generates these poems cannot be explained by referring to the real hothouse, by the reader's familiarity with the thing itself, but rather by the oppositional semantic structures actualized in the compound word. The two basic binary oppositions that define the *serre chaude* structure, inside vs. outside and artifice vs. nature, are actualized either by variants within the descriptive system whose kernel word is *serre chaude*, or by variants obtained through transcoding into lexical systems or codes foreign to the *serre* system. The consistency of the transcodings accounts for the seemingly non-sensical strings of images: their significance resides in purely formal lexical associations that exclude the referential function whereby words are normally linked to reality. This constant transcoding points as well to the feature that defines *Serres chaudes* as a Decadent text, since it must be read as an icon of the artifice. (MR)

Malraux. 3333. Britwum, Kwabena. "Garine, the Self and the Tragic Theme in *Les conquérants*." *MLR* 69:779-84.
In *Les Conquérants* Malraux depicts the interaction between Garine's tragic fate and his self. Garine's deteriorating illness seems to suggest that his approaching death is inevitable at the outset. However, at three significant phases in his illness, he has the choice between staying at his post in the Chinese revolution and leaving for treatment in Europe. But he consistently refuses to leave in time and thus causes his own death because of his incurable attachment to revolutionary action. The tragic pattern becomes clear: Garine's double defeat contrasts with the revolution's success for which, ironically, he is partly responsible. The self causes Garine's doom but it also makes him a Promethean hero. (KB)
3343. Quintana, J. Terrie. "L'art ou l'homme? Sur un livre de Pascal Sabourin." *RLM* 355-359(1973):163-70.
La Réflexion sur l'art d'André Malraux: Origines et évolution is one of the few studies to take Malraux's ideas about art seriously. "Origines" refers to the intellectual climate of the period; the thought "evolves" as a literary theme. For Sabourin, art dominates all of Malraux's thinking: in his first writings, Western action is contrasted with Eastern intuition. The novels posit the individual as being in opposition to cultural traditions, to the world, and to history. This study is not without its weaknesses. In discussing *La Condition humaine*, for example, the author emphasizes Gisors' Chinese origins and thus interprets the Frenchman poorly; mixing up bits of dialogue and unaware of an important earlier text, he misinterprets Kama and the role of art in the same novel. A reading which is not as careful as it might be casts doubt on some of the author's conclusions. For Malraux, art is only one manifestation of the principal conflict between man and his destiny. (JTQ)
3344. Rowland, Michael L., and Sonja Stary. "Mask and Vision in Malraux's *L'espoir*." *FR* (spec. issue 6):189-96.
André Malraux's novel *L'Espoir* is the relation of a civil war which may be seen on two levels. Historically it is a depiction of the Spanish Civil War, and psychologically it is a representation of the civil war going on within Malraux's characters. This second civil war, like the historical struggle, is characterized by hypocrisy, idealism, chaos, and indecision. These aspects of the two civil wars show the parallelism between the two battles as well as the unity of *L'Espoir*. The imagery of mask and vision in *L'Espoir* encompasses not only the characters, who are disguised behind a mask and blinded by illusion, but also their equally illusory surroundings and the very action of the novel itself. (SGS & MLR)

Marcel. 3354. Cooper, Nina. "A Comparison of the Theatres of Gabriel Marcel and Jean-Paul Sartre." *HAB* 24(1973):98-104.
Two major contemporary existentialist philosophers, Jean-Paul Sartre and Gabriel Marcel, are also authors of theaters which, while ultimately dissimilar, are at points strikingly alike. Sartre's theater is a popular one and can stand independent of his

philosophy. Marcel's cannot. Baudelairean themes—*angoisse, spleen, exile, solitude*—dominate both theaters. Although characters in both are motivated by metaphysical anguish, Sartre's are exceptional beings in contrast to those of Marcel. In achieving self-awareness, Sartre's characters, driven by the concept of *faire*, use physical violence and cut themselves off from established society. Psychological violence is omnipresent in Marcel's theater. In trying to achieve an authentic identity, Marcel's characters accept the aid of the transcendent, *la grâce*, as Marcel conceives it. Whereas Sartre's characters achieve a valid existence but remain in solitude and *angoisse*, those of Marcel, with the effective intervention of the beloved dead who have become *présence*, find hope and reintegration into society. Both writers agree that the metaphysical conflicts which they dramatize are brought about by the domination of modern man by science and technology. For both the function of the dramatist is the redemption of man. Sartre uses the here and now, Marcel the transcendent. (NC)

Martin du Gard. 3374. Roswell, May. "*La gonfle*, Martin du Gard's Unstaged Farce." *RomN* 15(1973):197-200.
Roger Martin du Gard won the Nobel prize for his series of novels, *Les Thibault*. In minor works he treated subjects such as incest, homosexuality, and brutish degradation more freely than in the novels. Despite the success of his first peasant farce, *Le Père Leleu*, which eventually reached the Comédie Française, the author would not permit Louis Jouvet to stage his second one, *La Goufle*. He attributed his hesitation to the difficulties inherent in the use of peasant dialect, but the nature of the subject and plot were probably important factors in the decision. Such incidents as the exploitation of an imbecile girl and a projected infanticide might have proved unacceptable to contemporary audiences. This view is reinforced by the reception accorded to Martin du Gard's serious play, *Un Taciturne*, which treated discreetly of homosexuality. Serious questions were raised as to the suitability of such topics for the stage. (MR)

Mauriac, F. 3381. Kanawati, R[oda]. "L'enfer de la solitude dans l'univers mauriacien." *AUMLA* 42:202-06.
In Mauriac's world solitude is the dominant theme. Mauriac's characters try to establish contact with one another because every person exists only according to the image others have of him. This very life-giving image is almost never the authentic one, because it is always distorted by our own monstrous image. Hence, the greater the need to get to know one another intimately, the more terrible is the revelation that it is impossible and the infernal cycle is brought to an end only in perpetual silence, the tragic silence which falls between the tragic man and the mediocre, and more terrible, between the tragic characters on the same intellectual level. (RNK)
3388. Wildgen, Kathryn E. "Dieu et Maman:Women in the Novels of François Mauriac." *Renascence* 27:15-22.
François Mauriac's fictional characters are defined as morally good or bad in terms of their reaction to literature and to literary creativity. Good, attractive characters read novels, write poetry, or respond to poetic impulses in themselves and in others; the *abrutis* are immersed in business affairs, and often actively fear and despise literariness. Among the *abrutis*, women as a whole are the worst offenders. Baudelaire's "mère du poète" as described in "Bénédiction" is an important antagonist in Mauriac's world. Noémi Péloueyre, the angel of *Le Baiser au lépreux* (1922), insofar as she is a foil to Jean's meager attempts at poetry, is a despicable character, and the image we receive of her in the little-noticed separate work *Le Dernier chapitre du baiser au lépreux* is that of a shrewish, calculating businesswoman immersed in pecuniary speculation—and all because she "never read anything but her missal." (KEW)

Michaux. 3397. Kuhn, Reinhard. "The Hermeneutics of Silence:Michaux and Mescaline." *YFS* 50:130-41.
Textual analysis and comparative study of Michaux's works coupled with a close reading of Michaux's commentaries on his drug experiences brings into sharper focus the essential elements of the problematic relationship between drugs and creativity. The

effort to transcribe directly the hallucinations during the state of intoxication proves a failure. Michaux chooses instead to exploit the moment of detoxication during which he is conscious of the structures of the mental processes. He transforms this moment into *Paix dans les brisements*, which is a poetic reconstruction of the post-drug period, a depiction of thought coming into being and a mystic hymn. (RK)

Montherlant. 3411. Knutsen, Katharine A. "Symbolism in *Le cardinal d'Espagne.*" *FR* 48:343-48.
In *Le Cardinal d'Espagne*, Henri de Montherlant creates a symbolic network in which each symbol can be considered as one of two extremes, or as the intermediary between two other symbols. Spiritual or celestial symbols are at one extreme and infernal or profane symbols are at the opposite extreme. Mediocre, earthly symbols represent the compromise between these two extremes. A perceptive approach to this symbolic structure exists on two levels: first within the physical setting of the play, and secondly through an examination of the two principal characters. The importance of the relationship between Cisneros and Jeanne la Folle and the three levels of existence which reflect the elements of the triadic formation are shown through Montherlant's use of various symbols. (KAK)

Nin, Anaïs. 3426. Zaller, Robert M. "Anais Nin and the Truth of Feeling." *ASoc* 10(1973):308-12.
It is a commonplace that politics pervades our culture, yet the first four volumes of the *Diary of Anais Nin*, covering the years 1931-47, contain scarcely a mention of political events or personalities. Nin gives us the keenest analysis of dreams, daily events, personal encounters, but makes no attempt to place the Stalin purges, World War II, or the atomic bomb in the context of her life. Yet if she rejects history it is not because she is unaware of it. She rejects politics not as a condition, but as a solution. Nin perceives war as the mass projection of individual irrationality. It is only in the individual that the answer to war can be found. (RMZ)

Nizan. 3428. Suleiman, Susan. "Pour une poétique du roman à thèse:L'example de Nizan." *Critique* 30:995-1021.
Nizan's novels are privileged examples of the hitherto neglected genre of *roman à thèse*. *Aden Arabie* manifests the thematic structure of apprenticeship in its "exemplary" version; *Antoine Bloyé* manifests the negative or "anti-exemplary" version of the same thematic structure, while *La Conspiration* manifests both versions. *Le Cheval de Troie* manifests a different thematic structure; "antagonic" structure. All of Nizan's novels are *romans à thèse*, exhibiting the three distinctive features of the genre: presence of a binary value-system; an appeal to the reader to judge the characters and their actions according to the unambiguous value-system of the work; reference, either implicit or explicit, to a doctrine. (SS)

Péguy. 3435. Busi, Frederick. "The Image of Charles Péguy in Vichy France." *Renascence* 27:3-14.
Charles Péguy's career was steeped in controversy. His memory was kept alive by the devotion of his friends and son, Marcel, through the publication of the journal, *Les Cahiers de la Quinzaine*, which he had founded. A modest rebirth of interest in his work was noted in the 1930s. In his later career his followers observed a gradual shift on his part to nationalism, and this drift seemed to explain the renewed interest. Because of his ardent patriotism his name was often used by collaborationists during the German occupation of France. Through a process of very selective editing his name was held up as a model under the Vichy regime. Given the highlights of his actual career it would seem improbable that Péguy could be considered a harbinger of fascism. A careful analyis of his image under the Vichy years should put his convictions into an objective, more dispassionate perspective. (FAB)
3446. MacDonough, Richard B. "A Thematic Study of Péguy's *Tapisseries.*" *ClaudelS* 1,iv:60-70.
Péguy's poetic testament to mankind is contained in a cycle collectively entitled *Les Tapisseries*. These works indicate some of

the thematic threads which are woven into the substance of the poet's sincere, if somewhat controversial, Catholic belief. One such theme is that of woman, whom Péguy considers an indispensable instrument in mankind's salvation. A second theme is the Incarnation, which Péguy, as no author before him, has made a literary reality. Salvation is a third theme and perhaps indicates the primary concern of the poet. A fourth theme in the cycle is that of alienation, especially from a rationalistic and materialistic world which has forgotten God. (RBM)

Péret. 3456. Costich, Julia F. "The Poem in a World of Change:Péret's 'Quatre à quatre'." *RomN* 15:410-15.
The Surrealist world of Benjamin Péret is marked by continual change; this is concretized in his work in systems which reorient themselves before cause and effect can be linked. "Quatre à quatre," the opening text in the collection *De derrière les fagots* (1934), exemplifies this method as an approach to the interaction between text and reader. (JFC)

Pinget. 3467. Broome, Peter. "Robert Pinget's *Passacaille*." *IFR* 1:135-38.. [Rev. art.]
Robert Pinget's *Passacaille* contributes uniquely to the emerging pattern of the French *nouveau roman*, which has undermined the form of the novel, the role of the novelist, and the aspirations of language. It proposes a "plot" composed of hypotheses, variants, and blanks. The characters are equally unsubstantial, having only a verbal existence. The two main hurdles, time and words, prevent the text from reaching fruition and bring it into the absurd. Through its destruction *Passacaille* resurrects itself as the "poem-novel" in which repetitions act as refrains, tempo changes create waves of rhythm, and words acquire creative autonomy and suggestion. (PB)

Poulet. 3485. Léonard, Albert. "Critique et conscience." *ECr* 14:195-206.
Lansonian criticism was succeeded by a criticism of identification, with Du Bos, and by a criticism of consciousness, with Poulet and Richard. The French new criticism postulates the immanence of the literary work of art, an immanence co-extensive with its structures. To criticize is to explore a structuring consciousness which produces networks revealing a spiritual stream. This structural thinking is a radical departure from structuralist thinking, which is shackled by linguistics. To criticize is to go from the work to its author in order to discover how he relates to the external world. (AL)
3486. Thomas, Johannes. "G. Poulet und der Wahrheitsanspruch der Literaturkritik." *RLV* 39(1973):520-25.
One of Poulet's basic ideas is that the meanings of texts are produced by their readers, and that they represent the author's ideas. This assumption seems problematic to Poulet, because he postulates that any "subject" is defined by its ideas ("predicates") and cannot have "predicates" of other "subjects." As a solution, he proposes to imagine a second "subject" inside the reader-"subject," that produces the meanings of the text. The distinction between production and the content of the products destroys Poulet's "solution": The second "subject" is only a product of the reader-"subject," not a principle of production. Hence, Poulet's "phénoménologie" cannot justify any interpretation. (JT)

Prévert. 3488. Freilich, Joan S. "An Introduction to New Techniques of Literary Analysis." *NTLTL* 14,i:12-22. [Examples from Prévert.]
Three new methods of literary analysis now being taught in advanced language classes are stylistics, structuralism, and psychoanalytic interpretation. The use of stylistics in elementary classes is first illustrated through analysis of a French magazine advertisement, then through an analysis of Jacques Prévert's poem, "Il ne faut. . . ." The application of structuralist analysis to works read by beginning and intermediate students will also involve poetry. The structure, "constraint-rebellion-breakthrough" is traced through several of Prévert's poems. Psychoanalytic interpretation involves an attempt to elucidate the most fundamental affective concepts conveyed through the text. Anouilh's *Antigone* is used to illustrate how a strong emotional

current can underlie what is on the surface a philosophical work. (JSF)

Proust. 3492. Abbé, Derek van. "From Proust to Johnson: Some Notes after *Das dritte Buch über Achim*." *ML* 55:73-79.
Johnson's *Das dritte Buch über Achim* is evaluated, with incidental reflections on the stylistic and sociological points it raises. Notable is the weakness of the final political point of the fable. Indirectness appears to be Johnson's main method of criticizing East German communism; no overt criticisms are made. Unlike Proust, almost everything is left open at the end of Johnson's novel. Johnson is contrasted with Hermann Kant and with Joyce. Johnson is a master of compression, but there is a lack of clarity concerning the essential nature of his morality. (DDMVA)
3504. Clark, Priscilla C. "Proustian Order and the Aristocracy of Time Past." *FR* (spec. issue 6):92-104.
In search of an order to define his life and his vocation, the hero of *À la recherche du temps perdu* looks beyond the transience of individuals to the stability of social groups—to his family as a unit, to the Verdurin clan, the homosexuals, the Jews, and especially to the aristocracy, which in many ways subsumes society altogether. A closed milieu, the aristocracy assiduously cultivates its exclusiveness. Rooted in legend and history, it unconsciously prolongs the past into the present through gestures, language, attitude. The disintegration of the aristocratic order proves the vanity of the world and the necessity of turning inward, to find in the self the fictive order that will become *À la recherche du temps perdu*. (PPC)
3508. Finn, Michael R. "Proust and Dumas fils:Odette and *La dame aux camélias*." *FR* 47:528-42.
It is possible that Marguerite Gautier and *La Dame aux camélias* are sources for Odette de Crécy and *Un Amour de Swann*. Proust uses references to Dumas's *Francillon* (*RTP*, I,256-57), i.e., the plot parallels between the play and *Un Amour de Swann*, as a warning to Swann about Odette's infidelity. He never mentions Dumas's play in *À la recherche* and yet the story-lines of that play and *Un Amour de Swann* offer many thought-provoking analogies. (MRF)
3509. Fisher, Clarice. "Character as a Way of Knowing in *A la recherche du temps perdu*:The Baron de Charlus." *MFS* 20:407-18.
Examination of the baron de Charlus in *À la recherche du temps perdu* demonstrates the extent to which impressionism influenced Proust's depiction of character. Proust elaborates the problematic relation which exists between human beings as subjects and objects in time and space. What he emphasizes about character is the process through which we come to know one another. By the conclusion of *À la recherche du temps perdu*, the narrator as well as the reader has experienced Proust's lessons in the problems of knowledge and perception and, as a result, both have partially overcome their isolation. The baron, however, never bridges the distance between himself and other human beings. (CMF)
3525. Megay, Joyce N. "Proust et la Nouvelle Critique." *FR* (spec. issue 6):120-28.
After a partial eclipse in the 1930s and 1940s, Proust has again become the focus of critical investigation. The renewed interest in *À la recherche* is due partly to the posthumous publication, in the 1950s, of Proust's earlier works, and partly to the approaches of New Criticism, which not only depart from the methods of literary history, but in effect closely resemble Proust's own ideas regarding literary criticism. New Criticism considers the text as a system of signs. The "thematic" critics, Poulet and Rousset, reveal the hidden structural wealth of *À la recherche*, while pointing also to the ontological quest underlying the search for lost time. Blanchot's analysis, by stressing the dichotomy between life and art, gives added weight to Proust's contention that his novel is not autobiographical. The "structuralists" point to *À la recherche* as raising the question of the very possibility of literature, a question which is central to present critical thought. Thus the rediscovery of Proust is owing to the emphasis of New Criticism on the text as a closed system, rather than on the relevance of whatever message the work may contain. (JNM)
3533. Porter, Agnes R. "The Treatment of Time in Proust's Pastiches." *FR* (spec. issue 6):129-43.

In each of the eleven "Affaire Lemoine" pastiches, Proust creates a distinctive temporal universe derived from the model author's, and implies personal criticism of this conception of time and reality. The various universes represented may show time as forward-moving and purposeful; as an undifferentiated block; or as virtually static. Some are predominantly linear in their view of time; some cyclic; and some show a mixture of these two conceptions. An interesting aspect of several of the pastiches is the mixture of levels of time found in the play of humorous anachronisms, another expression of Proust's desire to escape from the limits of chronology. The time-concept of each pastiche is, furthermore, closely related to esthetic mastery. Those pastiche worlds showing an inadequate grasp of time have insufficient integration of reality and therefore an incomplete esthetic vision. Others have time concepts capable of forming the basis of a unified view of reality and a coherent esthetic. (ARP)

3542. Zants, Emily. "The Comic Structure of *A la recherche du temps perdu*." *FR* (spec. issue 6):144-50.
A comic form corresponding to the comic subject matter in *À la recherche du temps perdu* must be applicable to all major themes, if indeed the subject and form of *À la recherche* can be called comic. Bergson's idea that mechanical elements interfering with the individual life stream constitute comedy underscores two structural elements that can be found in Proust's means of self-discovery—including involuntary memory, dreams, and art—in his concepts of characterization such as multiple social selves, split personality, habit, and the effect of time, and in two aspects of structure: parallel situation and analogy. This analysis provides one manner of viewing the unity of the novel. (EZ)

Rivière. 3556. Eustis, Alvin. "Rivière's Crew:Crémieux, Fernandez, Arland." *ECr* 14:138-45.
The differences between Rivière and three of his collaborators on the *Nouvelle Revue Française* are discussed. The differences revolve around the conception of literature either as an active social and moral force or as a quasi-scientific archive of psychological discoveries. Rivière's maintaining of the second position places him in contradiction with these collaborators and with the *NRF* founders, Gide and Schlumberger, as well. The opposition centers, during Rivière's lifetime, in divergent attitudes toward Proust and Freud; after Rivière's death in 1925, it will appear again in the individual political reactions of NRF members to the February 1934 riots. (AAE)

3559. Peyre, Henri. "Jacques Rivière and the Pursuit of Truth." *ECr* 14:110-20.
The place of Rivière is at the very top of 20th-century French critics. Recent works on him have enhanced his stature, in contrast to recent would-be objective and dehumanized criticism. Rivière did not divorce literature from music and painting, and the appreciation of literary works from religious and ethical concerns. Paramount with him was the anguishing pursuit of sincerity and truth. Paradoxically, Rivière's growing preoccupation with psychological truth turned him into an advocate for the severing of literature from what he called moralism. (HP)

Robbe-Grillet. 3561. Carrabino, Victor. "Robbe-Grillet and Phenomenological Time." *RS* 41(1973):42-51.
Although 20th-century stream-of-consciousness novelists have made wide use of the Bergsonian duration, phenomenological time still remains to be explored in modern narrative. While Bergson understands the mind as a living organism, the phenomenologist conceives the perceiving consciousness as an entity devoid of psychology, for he is interested in "primitive formations" of time-consciousness. Merleau-Ponty, for example, reduces time to pure subjectivity. For him the subject is temporality. He states: "Time...arises from my relation to things.... We are the upsurge of time." Alain Robbe-Grillet—the most representative figure in the New Novel movement—has adopted the phenomenological time in his novels where the narrator acts as the only subjective time-consciousness. In his novels mechanical time gradually disappears. He presents a narrator who acts as a subject-temporality, hence time is created as the novel is created. (VC)

3562. Deneau, Daniel P. "Crouching Natives in Robbe-Grillet's *Jealousy*." *MFS* 20:429-36.
Descriptions of a single native and of a group of five natives are perhaps the most curious of the many repetitions in Robbe-Grillet's *Jealousy*. The single native is probably a "mirror image" of the unnamed narrator, the Eye of the novel. The Eye may focus on the single man and the group because he wonders about A...'s relationship with the natives on the plantation. Finally, the group of natives possibly suggests to the Eye that ultimately he may be able to place the human figures who obsess him into a fully comprehensible design. As the novel concludes, all natives disappear, the bridge stands empty, and the chaotic night and its monotonous sounds triumph. (DPD)

3563. ——. "Non-Functional Contradictions in Robbe-Grillet's *Jealousy*." *IFR* 1,i:62-64.
Jealousy contains several purposeless contradictions or tiny lapses, which probably would go unnoticed in a novel focusing less on minutiae and requiring less exact visualization. Among those listed, the most noteworthy is the spying narrator's inconsistent numbering system for A...'s bedroom windows. (DPD)

3571. Pugh, Anthony R. "Robbe-Grillet in New York." *IFR* 1:120-24.
Robbe-Grillet's *Projet d'une révolution à New York* presents the reader with the usual enigmas, and a partial solution on the traditional realistic level can be found. Robbe-Grillet introduces discussions with the reader about some of the puzzling details and at the same time invents details that cannot be explained. Through the intriguing patterns, as well as through the wit, it is clear that the book's coherence is imaginative rather than conceptual. The unifying principle is his claim that in a world where images of sex and violence bombard us, the only response possible is for our imagination to dominate. (ARP)

Roche. 3576. Leigh, James. "Reading *Compact*." *MFS* 20:437-46.
In Maurice Roche's *Compact*, characters and plot are replaced by a variety of typescripts, diagrams, and all possible verb tenses and personal pronouns. Relationships can be established, however, between certain pronouns and typescripts, which form generally cohesive series. Most consistent is the relationship between series-"Japanese doctor," a discourse always within quotation marks speaking of roaming the world in search of tatooed skins to buy; and series-"I," a first person discourse, the owner/user of such a skin. The result of series-"I"'s refusal of the doctor's offer—an ideogram branded onto his skin—is not the end of the book, however, and the search for characters thus demonstrates its ultimate futility. (JAL)

Saint-Exupéry. 3597. McKeon, Joseph T. "Saint-Exupéry, the Myth of the Pilot." *PMLA* 89:1084-89.
In his novels Saint-Exupéry wreathes the pilot in an aura of such hyperbole that the reader might find such exaggeration naive if not ludicrous. Yet the legend of the Saint-Exupéryian hero is not cased in a rigid matrix. In his works the imagery that forms the substance of the myth of the pilot undergoes a subtle transformation. For example, the legendary, mythological, and mystical character of the imagery in *Courrier Sud* is subtly altered. In the final pages of *Pilote de guerre* the metamorphosis is complete—the myth is dissipated in a profession of fraternal faith and through its hero, man is seen in his true perspective. (JTM)

3598. Parry, M. "A Symbolic Interpretation of *Courrier Sud*." *MLR* 69:297-307.
Saint-Exupéry's *Courrier-Sud* (1929) bears the imprint of Bergsonian metaphysics, both in the moral conflict it explores and the symbolic language through which this is expressed. Through the adventure of motion the hero apprehends the fundamental nature of life as unceasing flow and change; the novel traces his attempts to bring his subjective experience into line with this external reality. The chief symbols of movement are the train, the ship, and the sea. The major obstacle to self-unity is woman, whose values are diametrically opposed. The house, the lamp, and objects, symbols of materiality, domesticity, and permanence, express the essential nature of her world. The author resorts to an atmosphere of myth to suggest the inauthentic nature of of

Geneviève's world, thereby solving the hero's dilemma. (MMP)

Sarraute. 3606. Calin, Françoise. "*Le planétarium* de Nathalie Sarraute ou les tentations de l'apprenti-écrivain." *RomN* 15:401-06.

Creators in art and the creative act are Sarraute's real protagonists in *Les Fruits d'Or*, a novel about a novel, and in *Entre la Vie et la Mort*, where writers are the main characters—and in her other novels, especially *Le planétarium*, in which young Alain Guimiez strives to become a writer. Numerous obstacles interfere with the creative process in Guimiez's case. First of all, societal distractions, his fascination for literary salons, in particular the idle circle hovering around Germaine Lemaire. Secondly, his tendency to confuse art and reality, to turn his Aunt Berthe into a character in a novel. And, finally, as a necessary precondition to creating, he has to rid himself of his exquisite taste, his obsession with perfection. For, in art, perfection is a trap, a false concept which presupposes the existence of absolute esthetic criteria, determined once and for all. Will Guimiez become a Swann or an Elstir? a Charlus or a Vinteuil? In the end *Le Planétarium* appears to give him the benefit of the doubt. (FC)

3609. Groves, Margaret. "Nathalie Sarraute:*Vous les entendez?*" *IFR* 1,i:59-62.

Nathalie Sarraute's *Vous les entendez?* continues the exploration of human relationships present in all her novels and shows the weakening of the narrative thread. A single narrative sequence is repeated and varied to reveal the changing tensions of the relationships between father and children who are not "characters" but centers of consciousness presenting alternate movements of sympathy or hostility, attraction or repulsion. The voices heard are caught at the dawn of self-awareness and awareness of the other. Then language becomes uncertain and the text seems to be a crude translation of a more subtle reality beyond the powers of linguistic expression. (MG)

Sartre. 3616. Busi, Frederick. "Sartre on Flaubert." *RS* 41(1973):9-17.

In his study *L'Idiot de la famille*, Jean-Paul Sartre explores his obsession with the personality and career of Gustave Flaubert. Sartre sees Flaubert as the symbol of all that he is opposed to in art and politics. Sartre attempts to examine Flaubert's ambivalent relationship to the bourgeoisie from the perspective that combines Marxism and psychoanalytical insights. Flaubert's attitudes toward society, however, are too complex and puzzling for even Sartre to analyze. At first Sartre was irritated by Flaubert's position concerning the Paris Commune of 1871; later he devoted more attention to Flaubert's paradoxical role as an escapee from bourgeois society while still remaining a part of it. Sartre remains obsessed with Flaubert because he sees in him an artist like himself at odds with the world though at opposite ends of the political spectrum. The psychological problem that most intrigues Sartre is the fantasy world that Flaubert created in life and fiction in his attempt to accommodate his particular existence to its general spiritual and social surroundings. (FAB)

3629. Mohanty, Christine. "*Bariona*, the Germination of Sartrian Theater." *FR* 47:1094-1109.

The seminal influence of Sartre's *Bariona ou le fils du tonnerre* is demonstrated by comparing it to *Les Mouches*, *Le Diable et le Bon Dieu*, and *Les Troyennes*. *Bariona* and its successors are all based upon myth and all contain elements of the classic tragedy as well. Each of the main characters of *Bariona*, designated in the article as *le bâtard* (the hero), *la révoltée* (the heroine), *le salaud* (the establishment man), and *la dupe* (the people), have their counterparts in the comparative works. The obstacles awaiting these prototypes—the physical world, other people, and the concept of God—are encountered from the very genesis of Sartrean theater. In addition, the chief concern of the first play, man's liberty and concomitant *engagement*, is inherited by those that follow. (CAM)

3633. Pitts, Rebecca E. "*The Wall*:Sartre's Metaphysical Trap." *HSL* 6:29-54.

"The Wall" embodies those major moral and metaphysical themes which Sartre developed later both as artist and philosopher: authenticity and confrontation with death. Unquestion-ably "The Wall" deals with authenticity, or integrity but the question is whether Pablo makes an authentic decision or not. Confronted by the choice of betraying a Loyalist comrade's whereabouts or being shot, he does not doubt that he will not betray his friend but having spent a sleepless night in a death cell he is exhausted and in shock. When the moment comes, he mockingly sends his captors on a supposedly futile trip to the cemetery. But his comrade has also gone there to hide and is caught and shot. Most critics believe that Pablo is still authentic, the dénouement merely exemplifying the world's absurdity. Sartre's essay in *What Is Literature?* however, suggests that Pablo is guilty of betraying the "human"—admittedly a groundless set of values. The coincidence may be interpreted as an instance of unconscious telepathy: the story thus has implications for a world-view opposed to that of Sartre. (REP)

Schlumberger. 3642. Cap, Jean-Pierre. "Jean Schlumberger et la *Nouvelle revue française* 1909-1914." *ECr* 14:99-109.

For almost a quarter of a century, the *Nouvelle Revue Française* was the major weathervane, guide, and refuge of artistic creativity. Of the six writers who gathered around André Gide, the head of the movement, none contributed more than Jean Schlumberger to reshape the French literary landscape through the review and its subsidaries: les Editions de la *NRF* and its Théâtre du Vieux-Colombier. Not only was he the actual director of the *NRF* during its difficult first years, 1909-12, but in several key articles such as "Considérations"—the manifesto of the *NRF*—he expressed the guiding principles of the review. (JPC)

Simon, C. 3652. Mortier, Roland. "Discontinu et rupture dans *La bataille de Pharsale*." *Degrés* 2(1973):c-c6.

Claude Simon's novel is an example of the use of discontinuity as a literary device. The progress of the narrative is accomplished through lateral associations, related either to memory, or to visual experiences, or even to metaphors and purely linguistic connections. Image predominates over idea, and the whole structure is based on a codex of its own. Simon's various devices are analyzed and the importance of space is stressed. Every movement is reduced to an illusion, on an even level, in a halted world. The names also melt into a perplexing unity, symbolized by the manifold use of the person O (zero, circle, or pure metaphor). Each chapter returns to its starting-point, and so does the novel, reassuming the general purpose of inertia (in travel, battle, creation, or erotic action), not exactly as an everwinding circle, rather as a continuous spiral. (AH)

Suarès. 3661. Braun, Sidney D. "André Suarès and Henry Prunières:A Musical and Spiritual Affinity." *FR* 47:518-27.

The friendship between André Suarès (1868-1948) and Henry Prunières (1886-1942) has literary and biographical importance. As seen in the unpublished correspondence, their relationship came into being with the founding in 1920 of the *Revue Musicale* by the musicologist Prunières, who invited Suarès to contribute articles. In his search for literary affinities with music, and particularly those of poetry and music, Suarès stressed Wagner's and Debussy's contributions to Symbolism in France, while Prunières encouraged the publication in the *Revue* of *inédits* by authors ranging from Ronsard to Baudelaire. In spite of their frequent musical differences of opinion and despite the fact that Suarès leaned more toward German and French music there always prevailed in their relationship honesty, integrity, and mutual respect. (SDB)

Teilhard de Chardin. 3666. Kramlinger, Thomas. "The Salvation of the Natural World in the Thought of Teilhard de Chardin." *MichA* 6:313-20.

Teilhard de Chardin takes an ambivalent attitude toward the status of the natural world in the evolutionary eschaton, which he calls "Omega." According to some texts and arguments, the natural world will be present in its numerical identity; according to others, it will be present only as the intentional content of the exchange between communicating persons who alone will retain numerical identity. His statements for the latter position are the stronger—matter is "spiritualized" in the evolution of consciousness. (TLK)

Thibaudet. 3669. Rambaud, Henri. "Vues sur Albert Thibaudet." *ECr* 14:163-71.
Discusses the similarities and differences between Thibaudet and Du Bos, noting Du Bos's increasing popularity and the present indifference toward Thibaudet. Thibaudet's critical work can be divided into three stages: preparation of the great works, the great works, and the improvisations. Thibaudet was never interested in the person of an author primarily. His task was not to establish esthetic norms according to which he passes judgment or excludes. He sought to discover in literature families or relationships which counterbalance each other—hence the important role played by comparison and classification, the discovery of conflicts and peaceful coexistence, of parallels and dichotomies. (HTN)

Troyat. 3672. Boak, Denis. "The Case of Henri Troyat." *IFR* 1:143-46.
Discusses Troyat's novel *La Pierre, la feuille et les ciseaux* and includes a brief outline of his literary career. Troyat is in the tradition, not of a sterile naturalism, but of a broader realism. His best work is seen as his historical *romans-fleuves* set in pre-revolutionary Russia with conventional techniques and a style of classical elegance and sobriety. The work reviewed is a psychological novel treating three conflicting egoisms, set in contemporary well-to-do bohemian Paris. It is seen as a virtuoso performance, but falling short in significance of theme and depth of treatment from Troyat's best work. (DB)

Valéry. 3688. Enrico, Harold. "Between the Void and Pure Event: Paul Valéry's *Le cimetière marin* and Eugenio Montale's *Meriggi e ombre*." [F 19]:97-102.
Aside from structural differences, Valéry's *Le Cimetière marin* and Montale's sequence Meriggi e ombre from *Ossi di seppia* display a similarity of theme and of primary and secondary symbols and metaphors. These may be the result of a common Mediterranean heritage and a common Symbolist source and poetic climate rather than of imitation on the part of Montale, his work being first published in 1925 and Valery's in 1920. Both works present the poets torn between a desire to become part of an unattainable absolute on one hand and to remain part of a changeable life-process on the other. (HJE)

3706. Loubière, Joyce A.E. "Balzac: Le grand absent de chez Teste." *FR* (Spec. issue 6):82-91.
Balzac would appear to be the finest example of the novelist as castigated by Valéry, that is, the expansive writer who believes in the authenticity of characters he has arbitrarily created. Yet Valéry's correspondence shows that around 1894, prior to composing "La Soirée avec Monsieur Teste," he had seriously considered the aims and defects of Balzac's *Louis Lambert*. In fact, along with Auguste Dupin, Lambert is one of the authentic literary antecedents of Teste, and a close analysis of the texts reveals significant resemblances in the essential characteristics of the illuminist and the intellectual heroes. It is also evident that for the writing of "La Soirée," Valéry inverted all the usual Balzacian procedures, in a way that draws attention to the obvious necessity for a young 19th-century author in search of distinction to outdo his predecessor. (AEL)
3721. Shurr, Georgia H. "Artistic Creativity and Paralysis:

Valéry and Leconte de Lisle." [F 19]:217-21.
Leconte de Lisle in "Midi" and Valéry in *Le cimetière marin* are both drawn toward states of timelessness. Each wrestles with the temptation to embrace a state of pure passive contemplation. Each looks to "le Soleil" to symbolize this final timelessness. Both manifest signs that this is a search for liberation, for the highest development of human existence itself. The poems are seen as intensely intimate statements of the search for personal goals, couched in almost miraculously manipulated language, and concerned with almost identical moments in the lives of two quite different personalities. (GS)

Vian. 3736. Cismaru, Alfred. "Boris Vian's *Vercoquin et le plancton*." *SCB* 34:146-49.
Vian's vision of the novelist as a Rabelaisian rapporteur emerges from his first novel *Vercoquin et la plancton*. His descriptions of the world of the *zazous* and of business show their ludicrousness and prove that no activity can lead to lasting happiness. His fictional debut, an intriguing picture of the uncommitted French youth during the days of the occupation, establishes Vian as the "Pape spirituel des Bobby-Soxers," the apolitical for whom resistance meant dancing to American records in the course of unending *surprise parties*. (AC)
3737. ——. "*L'Equarrissage pour tous*: Boris Vian's Reproof of History." *BRMMLA* 28:49-56.
The invasion of Normandy by Allied forces in World War II is generally viewed by the French as an awesome, most serious event. Boris Vian, however, in *L'Equarrissage pour tous*, mocks the invading forces and reasserts the truism that an individual and his problems are infinitely more important than colossal happenings which are not of his own doing and which remain beyond his understanding. The plot of the play, relating as it does the *équarrisseur*'s attempts to cope with the complexities of choosing a husband for his daughter while a new world is being shaped outside, reveals admirably Vian's anticipation of an anti-war and anti-patriotism attitude which began to prevail here and abroad some two decades after the comedy was written. (AC)
3738. Easterling, Ilda-Marie. "Boris Vian: Merveilleux et invention poétique." [F 19]:226-31.
The world of Boris Vian is one of humanized plants, animals, things, or ideas, and mechanized human beings. Happiness for all is in total functioning, with music and love. Cruelty seems to be the keynote of some mysterious fatality that makes the lovers' time, the true life's time rush and leap away. To describe his own new universe, Vian plays with old beliefs—with the symbolism of shapes and colors—and he juggles with words, chops, rearranges, and lengthens them, sometimes insisting on their literal meaning, sometimes poking fun at their etymology. (I-ME)
3739. Gerrard, Charlotte F. "Vian's Priest as Showman in *Le dernier des métiers*." *FR* 47:1123-27.
In *Le Dernier des métiers* Boris Vian vigorously attacked religion. Sometimes ironic, Vian chose parody and satire for his theatrical portrait of a priest in *Le Dernier des métiers*. Drawing close parallels between the Church and the theater, Vian emphasized the hypocrisy of the central figure, Father Saureilles, an unholy and vicious performer of religious ritual. Vian used exaggeration for comic effects to ridicule organized religion because he associated Catholicism with money-making. *Le Dernier des métiers* expressed with sarcasm, humor, and theatricality Vian's constant opposition to dogma, insincerity, and pomposity. (CFG)

ITALIAN LITERATURE†

II. DANTE

3833. Acocella, Joan R. "The Cult of Language: A Study of Two Modern Translations of Dante." *MLQ* 35:140-56. [Ciardi, Sayers.]
John Ciardi and Dorothy Sayers have based their translations of

Dante's *Commedia* on a vision of the poem's language: to Ciardi a sparse, vigorous, virile language; to Sayers a highly varied language, combining the grand with the colloquial, the solemn with the comic. A comparison of their translations of the Ulysses canto *Inferno* XXVI, to the original reveals how much subtlety and grandeur the translators have sacrificed to these insistent emphases. Ciardi tends to vulgarize the original and thus radically diminishes the spiritual stature of Dante's Ulysses. Sayers distorts

† *Festschriften* and Other Analyzed Collections are listed in the first division of this volume. "F" numbers in brackets following a title refer to these items.

his language through exaggeration, inflating its solemnities with stiff archaisms and reducing its ironies to low comedy. As with Ciardi, the result is a cheapening of Ulysses and his Last Voyage. Both translators have their graceful moments, but both have failed to capture the complexity and dignity of the canto. (JRA)

3848. Bondanella, Peter. "Stylistics and Dante's Lyric Poetry." *FI* 7-8(1973-74):117-29. [Rev. art.]
Literary critics tend to be skeptical of quantitative stylistics, yet such methods, applied properly, can reveal much that the textual critic might overlook. Patrick Boyde's *Dante's Style in His Lyric Poetry* is a good example of such a method applied to the works of a major medieval poet. His method combines traditional rhetorical categories with modern statistical methods. The results of Boyde's study allow us to determine with accuracy the trajectory of the development of Dante's lyric style. (PEB)

3885. Green, Richard G. "Blake and Dante on Paradise." *CL* 26:51-61.
Dante and Blake share conceptions of recaptured beatitude which are at times strikingly similar. The Redeemed of Blake's prophetic writings as well as the souls in the *Paradiso* are depicted as flame-enclosed, and for both writers the flames are an index of the fusion of emotional passion and mental cognition, two human attributes which are severed in the "fallen" world of mortality. Blake, like Dante, furthermore regards the fire as an emblem of the love and mutual self-sacrifice which is ubiquitous throughout Eternity, in the same way that self-directed appetite, personified by Blake's "Spectre" and by Dante's lion and she-wolf in the opening canto of the *Inferno*, blocks man's quest for divine illumination. Blake and Dante view Paradise as a timeless, spaceless realm, in which incessant energy coexists with repose, in which each moment perpetually resurrects itself as an Immediate and hence Eternal Now, in which man's mind has willed itself into a restoration of his true humanity and physicality, and in which all seemingly inanimate objects represent his physicality, which comprehensively constitutes the body of Christ encompassing all creation. (RGG)

3925. Murphy, Denis M. "*The Sound and the Fury* and Dante's *Inferno*:Fire and Ice." *MarkhamR* 4:71-78.
Some of the specific structural and philosophical similarities between *The Sound and the Fury* and the *Inferno* are demon-strated. Dante's influence is not only possible but is supported through a close comparison of both works. Parallels are drawn between the identical Holy Week dates of both, of Benjy's relationship to the idiots found in the Vestibule Cantos, of Quentin's situation and its similarity to those found in the Wood of Suicides, and of the comparison between Jason and the traitors to their kindred who are trapped in the frozen center of Hell, the Ninth Circle. Caddy functions in a paradoxical way as an inverted Beatrice character to the Compson brothers, and there are also many similarities between her fate and Francesca da Rimini. While the Christian and moral references in the Dilsey section are obvious and persistent, these refrences in the other three sections (especially to suffering and punishment) are as equally pervasive, if not quite as obvious. This philosophical pattern is related to the ordering principle of the four chapters taken as a whole. This structure is circular, and joins the ordering forces, Benjy and Dilsey, with the disruptors, Quentin and Jason, who are philosophically and structurally surrounded. (DMM)

3949. Pryor, Ruth. "'Wisdom is hid in crumbs':Vernon Watkins and Dante." *AWR* 24,lii:94-101.
Examines Watkins' use of the poems of Dante in his poetry. Special attention is given to Watkins' adaptation of *terza rima* to the English language and some reference is made to his unpublished work. (MRP)

3958. Rolfs, Daniel. "Dante and the Problem of Suicide." *MichA* 6:367-76.
Dante's contradictory treatment of suicide appears at odds with his ethical system, which elsewhere judges pagan and Christian by the same standard. While all Christian self-murderers must pay the retribution portrayed in *Inferno* XIII, no pagan is mentioned here, despite the widespread occurrence of the act in antiquity. All pagan suicides in hell suffer for sins other than their way of death, while two, Lucretia and Cato, are even rewarded for their self-destructions. The most convincing argument remains that of D'Ovidio, that the poet, knowing voluntary death to have been the subject of a controversy which engaged the finest minds of antiquity, chose to suspend judgment on the issue of pagan suicide, and thus classified such heathens according to the motives which prompted them to take their lives. (DJR)

III. THIRTEENTH AND FOURTEENTH CENTURIES

General and Miscellaneous. 4006. Banker, James R. "The *Ars dictaminis* and Rhetorical Textbooks at the Bolognese University in the Fourteenth Century." *M&H* 5:153-68.
Giovanni di Bonandrea, master of rhetoric from 1293 to 1321, initiated a dual instruction of *ars dictaminis* (art of letterwriting) and rhetoric at the University in Bologna. Throughout the 14th century Bolognese masters commented upon his epistolary treatise, *Brevis introductio ad dictamen,* and appropriated his practice of lecturing on the pseudo-Ciceronian *Rhetorica ad Herennium.* Giovanni taught the epistolary art to the unlearned notaries of the city and lectured on rhetoric to the law students of the University. Though the Bolognese masters continued to lecture on the classical text throughout the 15th century, interest in the epistolary treatise waned in the 1380s. (JRB)

Poetry. 4022. Romeo, Luigi. "A Sociolinguistic View of Medieval Romance Erotic Poetry." *FI* 7-8(1973-74):81-101. [Mostly on Ital.]
The three levels of medieval Romance poetry (love, erotic, and pornographic) are intimately related to the language of the several cultures in which different social strata interact. The Poet, accordingly, uses proper linguistic devices, such as subject pronouns, as a function of both the language availability and the social levels. In the Sicilian School there is a clear correspondence between the chosen type of poetry and purely social situations independent of metric necessities and Provençal traditions. (LR)

Boccaccio. 4035. Cottino-Jones, Marga. "Observations on the Structure of the *Decameron* Novella." *RomN* 15(1973):378-87.
Postulates a basic definition of the *Decameron* novella, which may be at the same time flexible enough to be applied through a simple process of amplification or reduction to other similar narrative forms. Cottino-Jones discusses a specific tale of the earlier *Novellino* in a comparative correlation with the third novella of the First Day of the *Decameron* which is inspired directly by the former. As a result of this discussion, the decameronia novella is defined as a specially constructed structure, deeply related to the whole of the work and to the tone and mood of the specific day to which it belongs. It is carefully built on three narrative moments through which its essential element—the action—evolves. Specifically, it is the second moment, where the transformational process is realized, that constitutes the central narrative nucleus of the novella. Here the main characters—agents and objects—reveal their inner characteristics as participants in this process, through movements which are carefully and precisely controlled by an accurate use of syntax and lexicon. (MC-J)

4036. Ferreri, Rosario. "Ovidio e le *Rime* di G. Boccaccio." *FI* 7-8(1973-74):46-55.
Criticism has failed to indicate and evaluate Ovid's influence on Boccaccio's *Rime.* Textual scrutiny shows that Ovid's influence is actively present in the line of themes and situations and in the style of the *Rime.* The syntactical, morphological, and lexical levels are affected: clause structures, use of prepositions, and lexical innovations derive from Ovid. Ovid's influence combines with that of the early Italian love poetry and together constitute the two main literary components of the *Rime.* (RF)

4039. Kirkham, Victoria. "Reckoning with Boccaccio's *Questioni d'amore*." *MLN* 89:45-59.
Although the "Questioni d'amore" do not appear to belong in the

Filocolo, they constitute a carefully planned, thematically relevant digression. The line of questioning in Fiammetta's debate follows a numerologically significant sequence (6 + 1 + 6) because the 7th and central issue (whether love is good) is resolved with a negative ruling which is a poetic retraction. The allegorical episodes preceding and following the debate, courtly and Christian respectively, function as its frame passages, generating a structural unit in which retraction emerges both at the center and the end. (VEK)

4050. Utley, Francis L. "Boccaccio, Chaucer and the International Popular Tale." *WF* 33:181-201.
Attempts to bring together some of the more solid results of medieval literary study and modern techniques of folktale investigation, with illustrations from Chaucer and Boccaccio. The application of rich modern oral material as a tentative springboard for the study of the creative process in medieval literature raises theoretical problems. For Chaucer, Irish versions of Tale Type 1423 in which the supernatural interveners are Christ and the Virgin instead of Chaucer's Pluto and Proserpine are studied. For the Friar's Tale (Type 11186), another Irish version, Chaucer's conversion of the tale into an exemplum of Christian repentance is shown. For Boccaccio, an ancient exemplum, The Boy Who Had Never Seen Women (Type 1678), in the proem to the 4th book of the *Decameron* has been transformed from an exemplum on the dangers of concupiscence into a mock-exemplum on the natural aspects of desire. (FLU)

Cavalcanti, G. 4060. Wilhelm, James J. "Guido Cavalcanti as a Mask for Ezra Pound." *PMLA* 89:332-40.
A study of Ezra Pound's translations of Guido Cavalcanti's *Rime* shows Pound's lifelong interest in the work of the Italian poet. A further tracing of Cavalcanti's rhetoric in the *Cantos* shows that Pound employed Cavalcanti in a twofold way: he related him to Neoplatonic philosophers through his use of light imagery, and treated him as an Aristotelian empiricist. He thus made Cavalcanti serve two apparently divergent aims, just as Pound's own work does. Although the modern poet's philosophic understanding of Cavalcanti is open to controversy, his poetic uses have accounted for some of the finest passages of the 20th-century epic. (JJW)

Giacomo da Lentino. 4066. Vanasco, Rocco. "Lingua e tecnica della canzone 'Dolce cominciamento,' di Giacomo da Lentini." *LeS* 8(1973):431-74.
The formal aspect of Giacomo Lentini's "Dolce cominciamento" is brought out by the coordination of three levels of analysis: sounds and syntactic structures; vocabulary and rhetorical figures; themes, motifs, and formulaic expressions. Each level of analysis involves particular effects of sense. These effects accumulate progressively, the second level of analysis acquires its value in relation to the first, the third to both of these. The song, from the beginning, is structured at the level of signifier and achieves its unity via phonetic-syntagmatic-thematic equivalence. The song's orientation toward a formal order constitutes a kind of *habitus* which appears in the frequent symmetrical arrangements at the level of lexical distribution; the distribution of verbal elements, of nouns, of adjectives, and of adverbs; in the distribution of syntactic types in the stanzas; and the parallelism of the dialogue. From this progressive analysis it appears that the form of Lentini's song embraces and penetrates the "message" of the song and constitutes a deeper, more substantial meaning. (LH)

Petrarch. 4116. Earl, Anthony J. "The Ambiguities of Petrarch's *Rime*." *ML* 55:161-68.
Toward the end of his life, Petrarch revealed the ambiguity of his attitude toward the sonnets and other poems of the *Canzoniere*. The careful structure of the *Rime* suggests that this ambiguity also attaches to the poetic emotions and forms part of the poet's intentions. Love is treated both as carnal and spiritual, hence both as attainable and as suprahuman. The Platonism implicit in

hyperbolic adoration and in troubadouresque undertones creates further tensions between sexuality and artistic devotion, between loyalty to a lady beloved in poetry and loyalty to poetry expressed as love of a lady. The theme which unites these ambiguities is lyrical introspection. (AJE)

4127. Helterman, Jeffrey. "Masks of Love in *Troilus and Criseyde*." *CL* 26:14-31.
In *Troylus and Cryseyde*, Chaucer revised the conception of love found in Boccaccio's *Filostrato*. In *Troylus* there is a stripping away of attitudes that are called love until Troylus finally understands his love for Cryseyde. This process is analogous to the ascent through the levels of love in the *Vita Nuova* in which Dante adores first a *simulacrum* (the "screen lady"), then the god Amor, and finally Beatrice herself. Corresponding to these levels are love as courtly convention, love as metaphysical ideal, and finally love for Cryseyde. Only Troylus is flexible enough to proceed through all three stages of love. As Troylus matures, the style of the poem changes from Petrarchist (the rhetoric of Petrarch without the feeling) to Petrarchan (the form expressing the feeling). Troylus shakes off the limits imposed by Pandarus and becomes a far more selfless lover than Boccaccio's Troilo. The growth of Troylus explains his ascent at the close of the poem and a comparison with the *Filostrato* shows that the conclusion is fully integrated with the rest of the poem. (JAH)

4144. Ogle, Robert B. "Wyatt and Petrarch: A Puzzle in Prosody." *JEGP* 73:189-208.
Scholars have not yet satisfactorily explained the roughness of rhythm in Wyatt's translations of Petrarch's sonnets. Since Petrarch was well versed in Latin prosody and was a skillful composer of Latin verse, he probably experimented with the logaoedic measures of Horace and Catullus. If Wyatt was also aware of these meters, as his classical training would suggest he was, he may well have put them to test in his English adaptations. The frequent appearance, in Petrarch's sonnets and in Wyatt's translations, of one or another variation of the logaoedic rhythmical patterns leads to the conclusion that both poets were imitating these popular classical meters. (RBO)

4152. Regan, Mariann S. "Petrarch's Courtly and Christian Vocabularies: Language in *Canzoniere* 61-63." *RomN* 15:527-31.
The group of *Canzoniere* 61, 62, and 63 demonstrate how specific word meanings can change with context, revealing the clash of secular and religious values. These three poems form a "repentance cycle" sequence in which the speaker shifts roles from earthly lover to Christian penitent and back to earthly lover. In 61 the speaker joyously displays a full courtly love vocabulary. In the next poem the language of the suffering courtly lover is redefined by the new religious framework. As the speaker of 63 returns to honoring his "donna," a number of words given religious emphasis in 62 now possess courtly meanings. (MR)

4155. Roche, Thomas P., Jr. "The Calendrical Structure of Petrarch's *Canzoniere*." *SP* 71:152-72.
The ordering of the 366 poems in Petrarch's *Canzoniere* is numerologically oriented; the major division at poem 264 is intentional and is meant to coincide with Christmas Day as poem 1 is meant to coincide with Good Friday. Within this outer framework the groups of sonnets and the placement of non-sonnets adumbrate the progress of the Church year, emphasizing the seasons of Advent and Lent. (TPR,JR.)

St. Francis. 4173. Carlson, Charles P., Jr. "St. Francis and the Early Government of the Franciscan Order." *IR* 31,i:3-23.
Discusses St. Francis' control of the Franciscan order on the basis of several considerations: (1) A review of the constitutional history of other medieval religious orders indicates that some of the distinctive ideas embodied in the organization of the Franciscan Order were not as unique as Francis apparently assumed; (2) The Papacy manifested a very liberal attitude in permitting Francis to implement most of his ideas in founding the Order; and (3) Evidence is offered that Francis was not, strictly speaking, a reformer or "evangelical." (CPC,Jr)

IV. FIFTEENTH, SIXTEENTH, AND SEVENTEENTH CENTURIES

General and Miscellaneous. 4200. Gilbert, Felix. "Italian Collections of Letters in the Second Part of the Sixteenth Century." [F 88]:88-94.

Publication of collections of letters written by various authors was a new literary genre in the 16th century. Originally the purpose of these publications was to provide examples of good style in letter-writing. In the course of a few decades it was realized that letters could be an important source for the reconstruction of the events of the past and these collections began to serve primarily the needs of the historian. (FG)

4203. Hyde, Virginia M. "The Pastoral Formula of W.H. Auden and Piero di Cosimo." *ConL* 14(1973):332-46.

W. H. Auden's *Bucolics* (1951), referring directly to the Renaissance painter Piero di Cosimo, sheds light on the moralized landscape which activates Auden's "pastoral" scenes from "Paysage Moralisé" through the religious *Horae Canonicae* and later poems. Piero's *Landscape with Animals* and *Discovery of Honey* (or *Feast of Bacchus*) illustrate "hard primitivism" in opposition to traditional pastoral mythologies of a prehistoric Golden Age or Eden. Both the poet and the painter show man at a crossroads between pre-history and modern time. Auden and Piero find innocence only in the bestial condition preceding human consciousness but uphold the necessity of the quest for urbane perfection. Auden emphasizes progress through a balanced "middle way," and his imagery rises from Bacchanalian to spiritual social constructs. His landscapes comprehend man's original absorption in nature, the flux of history, and a movement toward an ultimate stability transcending both. The poems' iconography conforms frequently to that of Piero's paintings. (VMH)

Ariosto. 4285. Molinaro, Julius A. "Sin and Punishment in the *Orlando furioso*." *MLN* 89:35-46.

The relationship between sin and punishment in *Orlando Furioso* is examined to determine the nature of the connection between the two. Ariosto's punishment of sin, and its corollary, the rewarding of virtue, are built into the fabric of the poem just as is his all-pervasive irony. (JAM)

Boccalini. 4308. Irving, William H. "Boccalini and Swift." *ECS* 7(1973-74):143-60.

The Augustan essayists and Swift in particular are indebted to the forgotten Italian writer Boccalini. Satirical fables, allegorical devices, the use of implication and irony, images, and mannerisms of style show definitely that Boccalini's attitudes and ideas were actively circulating when *A Tale of a Tub* was published. Swift's insistence on the need to probe beneath the surfaces, his delight in scatological imagery, his paradoxical hesitations between hope and despair in matters of social reform, his feeling for the need for stability in political affairs, his recognition of human dignity, his scorn for critical rules, for chasing faults in writers, all these themes and more appear in Boccalini as in Swift, and often in forms that are curiously similar. Swift was not borrowing consciously from Boccalini, but the two writers were temperamentally sympathetic, and these ideas were the currency of the age, stamped early and emphatically by Boccalini, and later even more emphatically by Swift. (WHI)

Campanella. 4318. Reiss, Timothy J. "Structure and Mind in Two Seventeenth-Century Utopias:Campanella and Bacon." *YFS* 49(1973):82-95.

The utopia is generally considered as a stasis, putting a halt to history, of which it is the conclusion and upon which it is a commentary. Campanella's *City of the Sun* (1602-23) would be the exemplary model for such a view: with its geographically circular form, and its concentric organization, it is represented as the union of individual and city, of society and God. The process of its own signification is included in this microcosmic-macrocosmic entity, since it claims to arrive at the union of perfect knowledge and absolute being by a direct, unmediated reading of things. Opposed to it is Bacon's *New Atlantis* (1627), whose ideal is praxis, and which can only be viewed as the installation of a

history. It is a discourse whose main elements, the journey, the human viewing of things, the casting of intellectual "Light" (true knowledge) upon phenomena, present the dynamism of scientific experimentalism and possessive individualism. These two utopias thus reflect, at the level of discourse, the change in epistēmē which is occurring at this time. They also suggest that the utopia should not be seen as a thinking about an object, but rather as the objectivization of a mode of thought. (TJR)

Castiglione. 4327. Salamon, Linda B. "*The Courtier* and *The Scholemaster*." *CL* 25(1973):17-36.

Despite obvious differences Ascham's *Scholemaster* and Castiglione's *Courtier* share elements of humanist educational and esthetic theory. Their writers variously prescribe the physical, intellectual, moral, and social preparation of the future servant of prince and country. Thus in each the monarchical politics of the *speculum principis* are updated by common Renaissance concepts like Ciceronian eloquence employed in civic humanism; *grazia* and "good wit" have a similar nature and function. More distinctively, Castiglione's *sprezzatura* and Ascham's "comeliness" both express a decorum based on appropriateness and absence of affectation. Careful judgment in manners, in vocation, and in literary style is the hallmark of both the courtier and the civil gentleman. The apparent simplicity that conceals high art is their standard. Cultivation of the abstract faculty to appreciate such art is the joint contribution of Castiglione and Ascham to Renaissance educational theory. (LBS)

Cellini. 4331. Goldberg, Jonathan. "Cellini's *Vita* and the Conventions of Early Autobiography." *MLN* 89:71-83.

An understanding of the conventions of early autobiography can make Cellini's *Vita* more accessible to modern readers. Crucial differences in earlier attitudes about the nature of the self which render self-examination in the Renaissance objective, impersonal, and public affect Cellini's self-scrutiny. Spiritual traditions shape the prophetic rhythms of the *Vita*, its emphasis on conversion, and its use of other plot motifs frequently found in saints' lives. By Cellini's time, these models for self-understanding and these narrative techniques had been secularized in picaresque fiction. (JSG)

Folengo. 4361. Chiesa, Mario. "Sulle edizioni del *Orlandino* di Teofilo Folengo." *GSLI* 150(1973):323-32.

Discusses the hitherto unknown *editio princeps* of Teofilo Folengo's *Orlandino*, i.e., the De Gregori printing of July 1526. A comparison of variant editions shows that the Sabbio edition from the end of 1526 is the second revised and enlarged edition by the author and the Soncino edition of 1527 is only a *copia descripta* of the *editio princeps*. Other editions from the 16th and following centuries are discussed and criteria for a new edition of Folengo's poem are examined. (MC)

Machiavelli, N. 4382. Bonadeo, Alfredo. "Some Aspects of Machiavelli's Thought on War and Conquest." *WascanaR* 9:143-55.

Contrary to a common view that Machiavelli regards war among states as an indispensable means for survival, Machiavelli felt a deep-seated aversion for war. His anti-war stance is based mainly on the belief that an aristocratic or princely government cannot wage a war that is advantageous to the commonwealth as a whole. (AAB)

4389. Fido, Franco. "Appunti sulla memoria letteraria di Machiavelli." *MLN* 89:1-12.

Machiavelli's conversation with the great men of Antiquity in the letter of 10 Dec. 1513 to Vettori was probably suggested to him by a passage of Boccaccio's *Trattatello in laude di Dante*, and could reflect Machiavelli's idea of an existential analogy between his own and Dante's exile. A few years later this implicit and tragic comparison becomes a comic confrontation, a quarrel with the same Dante in the *Discorso o dialogo intorno alla nostra lingua*. (FF)

4401. Summers, Claude J. "Tamburlaine's Opponents and

Machiavelli's *Prince*." *ELN* 11:256-58.
In addition to being progressively ordered according to their abilities, Tamburlaine's opponents in Part One may also represent the different kinds of monarchs distinguished by Machiavelli in *The Prince*. Mycetes is a hereditary prince; Cosroe is an usurping "new prince;" Bajazeth is a conquering emperor; and the Soldan is unique in being an elected monarch. Thus, Tamburlaine can take his truce with the world after he defeats the Soldan because with that conquest he has triumphed over all conceivable kinds of princes. That Marlowe may have structured his play according to a principle based on kingship has obvious implications for further study of *I Tamburlaine*. In addition, this ordering of Tamburlaine's opponents may be evidence more concrete than any heretofore offered that Marlowe did in fact consult *The Prince* while writing *I Tamburlaine*. (CJS)

Pico della Mirandola. 4419. Grant, Patrick. "Donne, Pico, and *Holy Sonnet* XII." *HAB* 24(1973):39-42.
Donne read the works of Pico della Mirandola during the period when the Holy Sonnets were composed. It is probable that a passage from *Heptaplus*, v.6-7, which closely resembles "Holy Sonnet 12," is a direct source. Significant verbal parallels confirm the suggestion. A point of detail in the poem is illuminated by the comparison, and some light is thrown on the appeal, pessimistic as well as optimistic, that Pico offers to his Renaissance readers. (PJG)

Tasso, T. 4459. Daniele, Antonio. "Antonomie tassesche." *GSLI* 150(1973):202-32.
Analyzes in detail several madrigals by Tasso, singling out recurrent structures, in particular parallel formulas, from the parallel pronominal distinctions *io-tu* to the most complex thematical-metrical distinctions. The inquiry then considers some typical metaphors in Tasso's lyrical language, seeking to place them within the Petrarchan tradition and contemporary lyric poetry of the 16th century. Contemporary poetic theory, including that of Tasso himself, is discussed. In conclusion, the "rhythmic stylemes" are examined and an attempt is made to give an interpretation of them which—taking into account the contents of these madrigals and the fact that they were destined for the royal court—would place Tasso within the realm of Mannerism but would attribute to him traits which are already perceptibly Baroque. (AD)

V. EIGHTEENTH AND NINETEENTH CENTURIES

Decadentismo. 4580. Phillips, Paul M. "Decadentism: Decadence or Symbolism?" [F 19]:78-81.
Use of the term "decadentism" has increased considerably in Italian criticism of recent years; it is now employed to characterize much of late 19th- and 20th-century Italian literature. This expanded use of the term "decadentism" is mistaken since it can be too easily confused with the related words "decadent" and "decadence" which are derogatory and prejudicial. Furthermore, the term "decadentism" is ambiguous since various critics understand it in different and contradictory ways. It is not universal since it is not understood outside of Italy. Instead of using the term "decadentism," writers must employ and distinguish among the terms "symbolism," "decadence," and "existentialism" which, although they describe related literary phenomena, do not lead to the confusing and prejudicial judgments which the term "decadentism" can. (PHP)

Foscolo. 4596. Tripodi, Vincenzo. "Immagini di grazia nella traduzione di Ugo Foscolo del romanzo sterniano." *FI* 8:223-39.
Foscolo demonstrates his own distinct poetic elements in the translation of Sterne's *A Sentimental Journey through France and Italy by Mr Yorick*. The variations of adjectives and nouns develop classical images of beauty, which are chaste and full of lyrical sensibility. The selection of different verbs delicately reveals the passionate soul of the characters. The addition of new syntactic elements molds a mythical version of beauty. Foscolo's new metaphor depicts, with subtle color, the modest innocence of the characters. Sometimes, his translation achieves a rhythmic unity and modulation in the sentence structure. (VT)

Leopardi, Giacomo. 4647. Jonard, Norbert. "Leopardi et Camus." *RLC* 48:233-47.
Certain contemporary poets like Ungaretti have considered Leopardi as a prophet of the existential tragedy of modern times. Even Camus's name has been pronounced in connection with his pessimism, his perception of *ennui*, and his feeling of something closely related to the absurd. Jonard examines the themes common to both writers, whose philosophies proceed from the same lucid refusal of all illusions as well as from a revolt against *la condition humaine*. (NJ)
4661. Scorsone, María. "El tema de la muerte en Leopardi y Machado." *REH* 8:107-16.
Leopardi and Machado, in dealing with death, share points in common as well as some differences. Leopardi considers death as the only solution to life's disillusions and sufferings. Philosophically, for Leopardi, death is a part of living that should not be feared. His conclusions anticipate existentialism. Machado feels death is life's logical conclusion and he accepts it stoically. Machado and Leopardi share in common an existentialist concept of death as well as a negative attitude toward religious faith. The basic difference in the two is in their metaphysical concepts. Leopardi sees death as something negative, while Machado sees it as an aid to man's intellectual creativeness. (MGS)

Manzoni. 4699. Caserta, Ernesto G. "Manzoni's Theatrical Reform." *RomN* 15:516-21.
The dramatic reform proposed by Manzoni lies in the infusion into the action and into the conscience of the characters the knowledge of God and man's condition on earth and an awareness of their ethical responsibility to make their conduct conform to this truth. The dramatist must represent this historical drama of the human conscience in conflict with itself or with external forces. Manzoni's concept of tragedy as representation of reality is close to the classical, although with Manzoni we are in a Christian world and human history and destiny are viewed in the light of divine truth. (EGC)
4816. Radcliff-Umstead, Douglas. "The Transcendence of Human Space in Manzonean Tragedy." *SIR* 13:26-46.
Although the scene shifts throughout *Il Conte di Carmagnola* and *Adelchi*, there is a sense of spatial constriction since Manzoni's tragic characters come to realize that the struggle to dominate space on this earth is futile and that they must look to heaven for deliverance from the terrestrial battleground. The ultimate tragic locus for the Manzonian characters is their heart, usually the only place of refuge left to them. Spatial imagery reveals that in this world any rapprochement between men leads to compromise and annihilation. Inner peace comes with death, which brings celestial enlightenment. (OR)

Nievo. 4890. Jonard, Norbert. "Ippolito Nievo et George Sand." *RLMC* 26(1973):266-84.
Discusses the influence of George Sand on Nievo. Both Sand and Nievo wrote in the same genre (the rustic novel), but the social and political context of their writing differed. Jonard establishes parallels between *La petite Fadette* and *Il Varmo* and *L'Avvocatino* and measures the extent of Sand's influence on the *Novelliere campagnolo* or on novels such as *Angelo di bontà*. These works cannot be understood if one disregards French rustic literature, but neither can one neglect the Italian arcadian-pastoral tradition which was succeeded by the tradition derived from *La Nouvelle Héloïse*. Nievo's idealism, founded on goodness and spiritual union, is much more pronounced than the idealism of Sand whose socialism, however sentimental, is nonetheless evident. (NJ)

Parini. 4895. Tusiani, Joseph. "Giuseppe Parini, Poet of

Education." *Paideia* 3,i:26-33.
Parini's Ode "Education" revitalizes and reinterprets the ancient precepts of Greek education through the very thought and language of Rome. Employing as a background the Chiron-Achilles myth and purposely shunning any Christian correlation so as to prove that education has a sacrality of its own, Parini's teaching presents to young Carlo Imbonati the quintessence of such moral lessons as can be learned from Juvenal's *Satires* and Seneca's *De Clementia, De Ira*, and *De Providentia*—that feelings of piety do not diminish, but rather complement, the fiery nature of our impulses. (JT)

Verga. 4928. Andreoli, Anna Maria. "Verga e il racconto gnoseologico." *LeS* 9:341-50.
The *Novelle rusticane* appear to have a narrative form similar to the "choral" technique which Verga tried out in *I malavoglia*. In an analysis of the first story, "Il reverendo," the technical devices which structure it are discussed. The varying point of view gives the story its specific gnoseological character. In addition, similes and metaphors first appearing in "Il reverendo" set up a pattern of imagery which continues through the short stories that follow. (AA)

Verri, A. 4951. Wheelock, James T.S. "Alessandro Verri's Unpublished *Osservazioni* on Isidoro Bianchi's *Elogio storico di Pietro Verri*." *FI* 8:270-303.

Literary biography has flourished only in certain eras. One such era was the late 18th century. An excellent example of the genre is Isidoro Bianchi's *Elogio storico di Pietro Verri* (1804). The publication of a revised edition of a later biography of Pietro Verri (Nino Valeri, 1937; 1969) provides an opportunity to review the quality of Bianchi's *Elogio* in the light of subsequent scholarship. The "Osservazioni" are reproduced here, together with evidence of their effect on Bianchi's biography, in order to show their influence on the *Elogio* and as a vindication of the Verris' reputation following 20th-century attacks on the two brothers by Carlo Antonio Vianello. (JTSW)

Vico. 4955. Battistini, Andrea. "Vico e l'etimologia mito-poietica." *LeS* 9:31-66.
An analysis of Vico's attitude toward etymology throughout his writings leads to a reconstruction of the criteria which Vico adopts in the formulation of his personal etymologies. A comparison with the *Etymologicon Linguae Latinae* by Giovanni Gherardo Voss makes the peculiarities of his method clearer: whereas Voss creates the etymologies of Latin items by referring in most cases to semantic equivalents in foreign languages, Vico always seeks the original word within the same language, so that such vast semantic gaps open up between derivant word and parent word that nothing short of myths will serve to bridge them. (AB)

VI. TWENTIETH CENTURY

Drama and Theater. 5032. Longman, Stanley V. "Mussolini and the Theatre." *QJS* 60:212-24.
Benito Mussolini, the creator of the Italian Fascist state and its leader from 1922 to 1943, took the state as an extension of himself so that life, art, and politics merged. His regime abounded with examples of "para-theatre": staged events taking place in actual life for a calculated effect upon the public. He attempted to make his life "a work of art." His plays and theater ideas projected himself and his state onto the stage. Fascism itself was deeply theatrical in nature, twisting the Nietzschean Superman into a performer of a spell-binding myth to prompt a sense of national identification in his audience, the populace. Unfortunately, Mussolini as the protagonist in this drama could not maintain himself as its playwright as well, and thus he lost his grip on reality. He ended in tragedy much as the heroes in his plays ended. (SVL)

Bassani. 5087. Schneider, Marilyn. "Mythical Dimensions of Micòl-Finzi-Contini." *Italica* 51:43-67.
Bassani's setting of a Jewish community in pre-War Italy for his novel *Il giardino dei Finzi-Contini* meshes with the more intimate world of his young narrator's personal growth toward manhood. Micòl, whom he loves, is his primary guide; her aristocratic, religious parents enhance her mythic functions in the story, while her diseased brother sets in relief the wasteland of human nature above which she rises. The garden of the novel's title emblemizes her unextinguishable vitality. Although death pervades the narrative, Michòl resonates the spirit of life. Once "exiled" from her paradisial garden, the uncomprehending narrator wanders both geographically and physically until he attains "rebirth" as a mature young man. This moment is ritualized by his climbing over the garden wall. (MS)

Chiarelli. 5135. Vena, Michael. "Luigi Chiarelli:Profile of a Playwright." *ConnR* 7:57-63.
The originality of Luigi Chiarelli and his influence on modern theatre was acknowledged in his day by authoritative witnesses, but time has not been kind to him. Chiarelli's production can be categorized mainly along the lines of the *grottesco* genre, exemplified here by his comedy *La maschera e il volto* (*The Mask and the Face*). The play is one of the first successful attempts to rejuvenate Italian theater and to free it from the trammels of the customary "triangle" situations inherited from the 19th century. It is a biting satire exposing the conflict between empty social

conventions and inner feelings. The success of *La maschera* contributed to the favorable reception of Pirandello's plays. In fact, the *grottesco* marks the beginning of Pirandello's own evolution toward his "new" theater. (MV)

Fogazzaro. 5236. Finco, Aldo. "L'umorismo di Antonio Fogazzaro." *RomN* 15:522-26.
In all Fogazzaro's novels the author portrays a superhuman struggle between the force of the passions and the will to higher values. This battle is always presented under a comic mood which lets us penetrate deeply into the soul of every character. This humorism, which sometimes is tragic and cruel, is expressed in many instances through the Venetian dialect that adds beauty to every situation. (AF)

Montale. 5324. Machala, Susan P. "The Path to an 'Ordine Diverso':Three Poems by Eugenio Montale." *MLN* 89:93-109.
In Montale's poetry through a gradual transformation process, words and images become the events of a poem, the objective correlatives of the states which they symbolize, and poetry itself becomes this "other dimension." The transformation is traced through an evaluation of Montale's artistic premises and their application in three of his poems, each of which is representative of a major phase in this process. They are "Crisalide," "Casa dei Doganieri," and "Voce giunta con le folaghe." (SP-M)

Pirandello. 5446. Caserta, Ernesto G. "Croce, Pirandello e il problema estetico." *Italica* 51:20-42.
To contrast the esthetic theories of Croce and Pirandello has become for many critics a pretext to disparage Crocean esthetics. On the basis of a confusion of poetics with esthetics, Croce's criticism of Pirandello's art is often misinterpreted. A comparative analysis of the thought of Pirandello and Croce shows that although the two writers lived in very different worlds (psychological, moral, and intellectual), they nevertheless shared some basic esthetic principles, inherited from De Sanctis and developed by Croce, and they both believed in the dependence of literary criticism on esthetic doctrine. (EGC)

5453. Illiano, Antonio. "Interpreti della meridionalità di Pirandello." *RomN* 15(1973):221-25.
A survey of differing critical insights into the Sicilian traits of Pirandello's work. (AI)

5457. Licastro, Emanuele. "The Anti-Theatre in Pirandello: *The Man with the Flower in His Mouth*." *RomN* 15:513-15.

Pirandello's conversion of the short story "The Man with the Flower in His Mouth" into his homonymous play is most remarkable. Although he could have given the play theatrical movement by radically changing his text, Pirandello maintains a certain anti-theatricality by transcribing his story word by word. The changes would have destroyed the sense of intimacy necessary for expressing the private paradox of the dying protagonist who is made sensitive to the vitality of life by the approach of death, yet anguished by its approach which will soon deny him the privilege of living in its immediacy. The flower in his mouth is a cancer. (EL)

5462. Needler, Howard I. "On the Art of Pirandello:Theory and Praxis." *TSLL* 15:735-58.
Pirandello's theoretical statements in *L'umorismo* and in his preface to *Six Characters in Search of an Author* serve to define a unified critical approach to both his plays and his short stories. Pirandello made extensive metaphorical use of the relation of author and character, which provides the key to this approach. It allows a joint consideration of problems of characterization in the dramatic and fictional prose works. The theoretical argument makes use of a modified idea of Marxian praxis and gives rise to a suggestion for its redefinition in Pirandellian terms. (HIN)

5467. Rossi, Patrizio. "Tempo e memoria bergsoniani nell'*Enrico IV* di Luigi Pirandello." [F 19]:87-92.
Bergsonian philosophical schemes are used in *Enrico IV* where dramatic tension is constructed on the relation between memory and time. By comparing the development of the plot of *Enrico IV* with the ideas exposed in *Materia e memoria*, *Enrico IV* is seen as one of the best plays by Pirandello, although critics often point out that Pirandello is dealing with abstract ideas and not with emotions and feelings which are truly human. (PR)

Sanguineti. 5498. Frankel, Margherita. "*Capriccio italiano*:Un tentativo d'interpretazione." *FI* 7-8(1973-74):70-80.
Sanguineti's *Capriccio italiano* (1963) presents serious difficulties for an understanding of its meaning and scope. The distorted view provided by a dream atmosphere in which everyday facts intermingle with absurd, unnatural events; symbols and images drawn from myths, religion, current life, or the subconscious; literary references, stream of consciousness devices; logical associations sparkled by diverging semantic fields are all elements that compose the novel. The use of ungrammatical forms, of contorted and irregular syntactical structures, also makes the novel less accessible. This linguistic style is the author's effort to break the barriers of literary convention in order to express his very personal world and view of reality. (MF)

5500. Somville, Pierre. "Mosaïque et rupture:A propos d'un texte d'E. Sanguinetti." *Degrés* 2(1973):l-l 4.
Sanguineti's "Laborintus II" is composed of fragments from different literary works such as Dante's *Vita nuova* and of allusions to, for instance, Racine's and Robbe-Grillet's "labyrinths." On the frame of Ezra Pound's *Pisan Cantos*, the tone, rhythm, and lexical variations of this composition, as well as the tachycardic metrical punctuation, give an excellent example of patchwork. (AH)

Svevo. 5529. Godt, Clarence. "Svevo and Coincidence." *MLN* 89:84-92.
The mysterious coincidences which bring together different lives is a persistent theme in Italo Svevo's works. The lives of two persons who have scarcely or never met may be linked substantially but inexplicably in the mind of a third, as Emilio or Zeno. Unlike most of Svevo's characters, Zeno is not the victim of destiny's caprice: he habitually decides on a course of action and cites preposterous reasons why his conduct is inevitable. Svevo invents a narrative style which both creates and conceals Zeno's abdication of responsibility in confusing juxtapostions of phrases and sequences of ideas from which the logical connections are removed. (CG)

Tomasi di Lampedusa. 5556. Meyers, Jeffrey. "Greuze and Lampedusa's *Il gattopardo*." *MLR* 69:309-15.
Lampedusa has an intensely pictorial imagination and employs an extensive museum of art to visualize the major themes of *Il gattopardo*. He uses the literary interpretations of Diderot and the Goncourts to place Greuze in an esthetic and cultural tradition, and he incorporates Greuze's licentious hypocrisy, Diderot's moral self-deception, and the Goncourts' shrewd insight into the ambivalent character of Prince Fabrizio. Lampedusa makes Greuze's *Le Fils puni* reflect a personal and historical crisis: the death of the Leopard, his memories, his traditions, and his class. His use of Greuze's painting and the values it represents is a striking example of the great strength of *Il gattopardo*: Lampedusa's unusual ability to absorb and transform other works of art into his own traditional yet original masterpiece. (JM)

SPANISH LITERATURE†

I. GENERAL

Bibliography. 5626. Teschner, Richard V. "A Critical Annotated Bibliography of Anglicisms in Spanish." *Hispania* 57:631-78.
This bibliography annotates and analyzes 209 books, articles, parts of books, Ph.D. dissertations, etc., which deal with the influence of English on the Spanish of Mexico, Central America, the Caribbean, South America, and Spain. Entries are categorized geographically and topically; topical classifications include phonology, orthography, sports terminology, argot, and morphosyntax. The majority of studies are classified according to the region or nation they deal with: the largest number (50) bear on Puerto Rican Spanish, 28 deal with Mexican, 16 with peninsular Spanish, and smaller numbers with Argentinian, Chilean, Colombian, Venezuelan, Panamanian, Cuban, etc. (RVT)

General and Miscellaneous. 5632. Bell, Wendolyn Y. "Nomenclature and Spanish Literary Analysis." *CLAJ* 18:69-80.
Very frequently a new dimension may be added to character analysis through an examination of the expressive appellations used. While epithetical designations may reveal the attitude of the author or another "personaje" toward a given character, names and nicknames either harmonize with or stand in contrast to some salient aspect of the delineations. Keys to individual functions in the plot are thereby provided. Representative samplings of the various techniques are discussed as handled in major works from medieval times to the contemporary period. (WYB)

Sefardica. 5681. Armistead, S[amuel] G., I[acob] M. Hassan, and J[oseph] H. Silverman. "Four Moroccan Judeo-Spanish Folksong 'Incipits' (1824-1825)." *HR* 42:83-87.
A manuscript collection of Hebrew hymns compiled in Gibraltar and Tetuán in 1824-25 attests to the use of four Judeo-Spanish folksong *incipits* as tune indicators. Together with another 18th-century instance of folksong *contrafacta* in liturgical poetry, these four verses provide important documentation of North African Sephardic traditional poetry. (SGA, IMH, & JHS)

---

† *Festschriften* and Other Analyzed Collections are listed in the first division of this volume. "F" numbers in brackets following a title refer to these items.

II. LITERATURE IN SPANISH AMERICA

General and Miscellaneous

Drama and Theater. 5719. Blanco Amores de Pagella, Angela. "Manifestaciones del teatro del absurdo en Argentina." *LATR* 8,i:21-24.
The theater of the absurd is a contemporary manifestation of the fury of Dada which attempts to destroy the literary values of the text. The theater of the absurd tries to show the anguish of a world without permanent spiritual values in which man lives in total isolation. Griselda Gambaro, Eduardo Pavlovsky, and Julio Ardiles Gray can be classified as absurdists. The principal elements of their works are the grotesque, absurd behavior, illogic, and cruel humor, and the use of anti-theatrical devices such as signs and mannequins, while their main themes are anguish, time, the human condition, the mechanization of the world, and the lack of communication between human beings. (WRB)

Poetry. 5724. Litvak, Lily. "*Las mañanitas*:A Mexican *Alba* with a Provençal Element." *RomN* 15(1973):328-36.
"Las Mañanitas," a Mexican traditional song, is an *alba*, a type of love poetry about two lovers who, after spending the night together, separate at dawn. Litvak analyzes the several elements of the *alba* topos and especially the appearance of a third character, a night watchman linked to Medieval Provençal poetry who does not appear in this type of Spanish love poetry. (LL)

Literature before 1930

General and Miscellaneous. 5747. Bresie, Mayellen. "News-sheets Printed in Lima Between 1700 and 1711 by José de Contreras y Alvarado, Royal Printer:A Descriptive Essay and Annotated List." *BNYPL* 78:7-68. [Illus.]
112 printed items are identified, described, and placed in historical context. Most have not been listed in any previous bibliography of Peruvian printing. The collection is bound into a single volume located in the Rare Book Division of the New York Public Library. Three distinct types of materials are included: (1) pamphlets, including *relaciones*, or accounts of a single subject, (2) *noticiarios* (reprints, summaries, or excerpts of news from foreign gazettes), and (3) the *Diario de noticias sobresalientes en esta ciudad de Lima*, a local news-sheet. (MB)

Drama and Theater. 5769. Brokow, John W. "The Repertory of a Mexican-American Theatrical Troupe:1849-1924." *LATR* 8,i:25-35.
The troupe of Encarnación Hernández and his son-in-law, Carlos Villalongin, performed throughout northern Mexico and the southwestern United States from 1849 until it disbanded in 1924. Being typical of many Mexican companies, what we discover about it has wide-spread implications in Mexican theater historiography. The Latin American Collection at the University of Texas recently acquired an archive of 146 promptbooks used by this troupe which provides resources of some importance to researchers. This article provides a descriptive list of that archive. (JWB)

Arlt. 5800. Troiano, James J. "Pirandellism in the Theatre of Roberto Arlt." *LATR* 8,i:37-44.
Pirandello's *Ciascuno a suo modo* and *Sei personaggi in cerca d'autore* influenced Arlt in his *Trescientos millones* (1932) and *El fabricante de fantasmas* (1936) in the theatrical presentation of the autonomy of characters and the interplay of illusion and reality. Arlt's treatment of the relativity of madness and sanity as well as reality in *Saverio el cruel* (1936) is reminiscent of Pirandello's *Enrico IV*. Arlt does not merely reproduce imitations of Pirandello. Utilizing Pirandellian themes and techniques, he adapts them to his own bizarre literary style and Weltanschauung. He clearly distinguishes himself from Pirandello with the appearance of dream worlds, grotesque elements, and concern for social injustice. (JJT)

Barrenechea. 5812. Tomanek, Thomas J. "Barrenechea's *Restauración de la imperial y conversión de almas infieles*—The First Novel Written in Spanish America." *RLV* 40:257-68.
In the Biblioteca Nacional of Santiago de Chile is an unpublished manuscript "Restauración de la Imperial y conversión de almas infieles" written in 1693 by Father Juan de Barrenechea y Albis. A love story of Carilab and Rocamila is hidden within the 668-page manuscript, which contains accounts of Governor Alonso de Sotomayor's campaigns, discussions about interminable Araucanian wars, advice on how to restore churches in destroyed towns, prayers to St. Mary, referrals to Latin writers and the Church fathers. The narrative part shows the main features attributed to a novel. It is not an excellent novel, but it is the first full-fledged novel written in Spanish America. (TJT)

Darío. 5850. Forcadas, Alberto M. "El romancero español y posible influjo de algunos clásicos castellaños en 'Sonatina' de Rubén Darío." *REH* 8:3-21.
The French conception of "Sonatina" crumbles on a close comparison of the poem's themes, techniques, and even terminology, with parallels, analogies, and identities in Spanish poems, especially of the Romancero and of classics such as Quevedo. For example, the famous line of "Sonatina" "en el cinto la espada y en la mano el azor," could be attributed to a romance in *El villano en su rincón* of Lope de Vega. Most of "Sonatina"'s elements can be found in compositions included in the B.A.E. collection which the Nicaraguan said he had read carefully. Darío's interest in writing "Sonatina" might have been triggered by French readings, but the actual French influence in the poem is small. Although a dual influence in "Sonatina" can be admitted, the balance is decidedly in favor of the Spanish tradition. (AMF)

Gallegos, R. 5879. Ziomek, Henryk. "Rómulo Gallegos:Some Observations on Folkloric Elements in His Novels." *REH* 8:23-42.
Rómulo Gallegos drew perennial inspiration for his eight novels written 1920-43 from Venezuelan tradition. Through his pen, the native traditions relating to the Andes, the jungle, and the savanna reveal the very soul of his land. He recorded folk music, folk dancing, unusual customs, beliefs, and folkloric tales, legends, and stories, which had previously been preserved only in religious and communal rites, unrecorded poetry, music, and dance, and in the observance of old customs. Gallegos portrayed his characters through the use of these folkloric elements, and he incorporated into his works such unusual customs and beliefs as those concerning burial procedures and superstitious practices. (HZ)

Gamboa, Federico. 5880. García-Barragán, María-Guadalupe. "*Santa*, la novela olvidada que vuelve:Sus simbolismos e influencias sobre la literatura actual." [F 19]:184-88.
Federico Gamboa's *Santa*, formerly the most popular novel in Mexico, is today almost forgotten. *Santa* tells the very ordinary and human story of a humble girl who, seduced and abandoned, becomes a prostitute. *Santa* contains symbols that have passed unnoticed by its critics, the symbol of death being the most noteworthy of them. In 1965, at the centenary of his birth, Federico Gamboa was the subject of studies, honors, and praise from critics in his homeland and abroad; his novels are being republished and at the present time a well-known Mexican publishing house is preparing a new edition of *Santa*. (M-GG-B)

Garcilaso de la Vega, el Inca. 5885. Callan, Richard J. "An Instance of the Hero Myth in *Comentarios Reales*." *REH* 8:261-70.
Several primordial patterns of behavior are exemplified in the Viracocha episode as told by Inca Garcilaso. The Prince, banished for his unruliness (Withdrawal), was transformed by a vision of God Viracocha (Initiation), and came back to rescue the Kingdom from chaos (Return), a situation caused by the weakness of the King. Prince Viracocha's implied mandate was to

bring the Kingdom back to its original perfection. Tahuantinsuyo is the Land of Four Quarters and Cuzco, the World Navel. The king, who embodies the life principle, resides at the center because it is the point through which the potencies of life and order flow into the world. The Viracocha episode was the renewal of cosmic stability and a myth of rebirth, values which to the Incas were of greater significance than historical accuracy. (RJC)

Gutiérrez Nájera. 5894. Fraser, Howard M. "Change Is the Unchanging:Washington Irving and Manuel Gutiérrez Nájera." *JSSTC* 1(1973):151-59.
A comparative study of Irving's influence on Manuel Gutiérrez Nájera indicates a basic revision in the literary sensibilities of the 19th century. Irving's "Rip Van Winkle" is a fundamentally comic vision of colonial America's metamorphosis into a Republic. The protagonist mirrors the attitudes and pace of his town and his century coming face to face with the onrushing future. Nájera's "Rip-Rip" transforms the central character into a tragic victim of brutal, cosmic forces. In his nightmarish parody of the original, Nájera anticipates the sense of life's anguish and despair brought about by catastrophic change, itself a theme of 19th- and 20th-century literature. (HMF)

Huidobro. 5925. Schweitzer, S. Alan. "Conmovisión y mito en el 'Altazor' de Huidobro." *Hispania* 57:413-21.
Vicente Huidobro's *Altazor* (1931) is a lengthy poem whose several interrelated themes are contingent upon two central images: the poet's vision of an expanding universe and the developing consciousness of man as projected against the satanic myth. The world of physical creation and the conjectural, transcendental realm of "essence" are mysteriously contingent upon the evolving consciousness of the poet which is directly responsible to God. The poet-Satan protests his mortal existence to a God whose capricious and even malignant will is impervious to the suffering of man. Each canto prefigures the poet's fall from the Divine Grace into time and death. On the physical dimension the fall is conceived as an outward expansion of the poet's psyche toward the remote edges of outer space; on the mythical level, the poet falls from Paradise in a succession of circles which structure the inner hell of his torment and protest. The terminus of the poem is the madness of the protagonist in that his denial of the will of God occasions the disintegration of the poet's intelligence and precipitates the collapse of the physical universe. (SAS)

Larreta. 5932. De La Fuente, Albert. "'Artemis' de Enrique Larreta:Estructura e interpretación." *JSSTC* 1(1973):141-49.
The main conflict in Larreta's *Artemis* generates four dilemmas whose study leads to four levels of interpretation. On the allegorical level, the choice between the inner voice and the external demands of life corresponds to the respective cults of Artemis and Aphrodite. On the anagogical level, the primacy of mystical experience or the lack of it will determine the final outcome of the struggle between Artemis and Aphrodite. The literal and moral levels follow the solutions chosen for the other two. The structural analysis of *Artemis* reveals that this main conflict is developed in three increasingly dramatic scenes that converge upon an unexpected ending within a limited setting and time, and that the eternal struggle between Artemis and Aphrodite allows a comparison with Euripides' *Hippolytus*. Both Dryas and Hippolytus have a personal devotion for Artemis within the limitations of the Greek concept of *aidos* (L. *pudor*). (AF)

Lugones. 5948. Hardy, William. "Rhyme and Blank Verse: The Lugones-Marechal Polemic." *RomN* 15:605-09.
The polemic between Leopoldo Lugones and Leopoldo Marechal regarding rhyme and blank verse exemplifies the contrasting positions held by the traditional and *martinfierrista* schools of poetry active in the 1920s in Buenos Aires. Lugones and Marechal acted as spokesmen for the two groups and they exchanged their views in two important *porteño* periodicals: the newspaper *La Nación* and the literary journal *Martín Fierro*. While the criticisms of Lugones were often guarded and indirect, those of Marechal were blunt and direct, indicative of the polemical spirit of that period. (WH)

Martí. 5962. Sánchez, Myriam F. "Interpretación y análisis de 'Pollice verso' de José Martí." *Hispania* 57:40-47.
In "Pollice verso" José Martí asserts that moral, political, and social virtues constitute the only true shield of a people against misfortunes. The intention of instructing or teaching is evident throughout the poem by the use of axiomatic assertions, simple comparisons, and obvious logic. Diction, similes, images, figures of speech, and versification in free verse reinforce the theme. To avoid monotony or annoyance the poet uses the more flexible sprung rhythm and free verse lines which follow emotional rather than rhythmic units. His range of adjectives indicate that his theme is not merely rhetorical but a dictum for a day to day living. The poem becomes progressively declamatory and oratorical as it takes on a passionate convincing tone. Martí's success in achieving his aim rests mainly in the quality of sincerity which rings through the poem and intends to move the reader to take a position on the issue which the poet sustains. (MFS)

Poma de Ayala. 5980. Adorno, Rolena. "Racial Scorn and Critical Contempt." *Diacritics* 4,iv:2-7. [Rev. art.]
Colonial Spanish American literature has suffered from a scarcity of bona fide criticism; the critical treatment received by the *Nueva corónica y buen gobierno* (1615), by the Peruvian Felipe Guaman Poma de Ayala, documents the patterns of prejudice about racial origin and colonialism that have occupied editorial and textual studies of works by indigenous authors of the early colonial period. Textual analysis of the *Nueva corónica* reveals a highly complex work, one single feature of which is Guaman Poma's unorthodox use of the forms of European rhetoric. The "prologue," which follows the composition that it accompanies, and the exemplary biography of Inca and colonial viceroy, function in tandem to capsulize Peruvian history and formalize the utopian design, thus destroying the barrier between past and future by the rhetorical means of a complementary discourse. (RKA)

Sánchez, F. 5990. De Costa, René. "The Dramaturgy of Florencio Sánchez:An Analysis of *Barranca abajo*." *LATR* 7,ii:25-37.
Analysis of Florencio Sánchez' *Barranca abajo* reveals that the principal action concerns the protagonist's assertion of self in his efforts to retain his patriarchal position. The three-act form was advantageously used to represent the psychic anguish of Don Zoilo deepened by the loss of his estate, his civil standing, and finally, his family. The pattern is similar to that of *King Lear*. The dramatic question is why do the fallen patriarchs (Zoilo, Lear) prefer death? The series of misfortunes afflicting both fathers leads to their insanity and death, and the untimely demise of a faithful daughter (Robusta, Cordelia) is the final blow for both defeated men. (RD)

Silva, J.A. 5995. Ewing, Nalsy D. "Giacomo Leopardi y José Asunción Silva:Sus teorías poéticas." [F 30]:27-36.
Silva and Leopardi have much in common. First there is their attitude toward poetry itself, which they both consider to be the highest of the arts, lyric poetry being its highest expression. Both believed that art, especially poetry, should not be subservient to utilitarian ends, though both admit that poetry may coincidentally be "utilitarian." Each expresses the feeling that poetry cannot be created under the passion of emotions but only in calm recollection of passions previously experienced. Perhaps most striking are the similarities of their ideas about poetic diction. Both hold that poetic diction must be "vague" in the sense that the terms chosen should be susceptible to a variety of connotations. (Nd'AE)

Literature after 1930

General and Miscellaneous. 6042. Mason, Margaret L., and Yulan M. Washburn. "The Bestiary in Contemporary Spanish-Americna Literature." *REH* 8:189-209.
Juan Jose Arreola produced the first contemporary Spanish-

American bestiary of major significance, *Punta de plata*, later retitled *Bestiario*. Arreola considers animals a mirror in which man can see both the positive and negative aspects of himself. Neruda composed his "Bestiario" (1958) in verse. For Neruda, animals are the means by which man can establish a new relationship with reality. For Borges and Margarita Guerrero, in their *El libro de los seres imaginarios*, the bestiary provides the reader with an outlet for a capricious imagination without forcing a moral lesson upon the reader. Each of the Spanish-American bestiarists perceives animals and beast books differently. (MLM & YMW)

6043. Mead, Robert G.,Jr. "Images North and South of the Border:The United States and Latin America Today and Tomorrow." *Hispania* 57:320-29.
During their early national existence, Spanish-American authors tended to regard the people of the United States favorably, seeing in them an independent, energetic, democratic, and pragmatic character. Since the late 19th century, however, this image has deteriorated because of frequent U.S. military intervention and exploitative economic penetration in other hemisphere countries. Today most Spanish-American writers, notwithstanding some lingering admiration for Americans as individuals, dislike their governmental and corporate policies. Above all, they think it is difficult for Americans to understand cultures which are not born of ideals and values similar to their own. (RGM,Jr)

6050. Ruprecht, Hans-George. "Aspects du baudelairisme mexicain." *CLS* 11:99-122.
A contrastive comparison between the Mexican interpretation of Baudelaire's esthetics and Diderot's thoughts on style, Schlegel's understanding of "Magie" and Breton's idea of poetic analogies puts aspects of Mexican-Baudelairism into a post-romantic perspective. Apart from historically delineating this trend, emphasis is put on exploring the various strata of verbal art (phonological, lexical, syntactic, semantic) and the relation between Amado Nervo's and Tablada's lyrical discourse on the one hand and Baudelaire's poetics on the other. The focus is on the assimilation and the transmutation of Baudelaire's poetics by the Mexican modernists. (H-GR)

Drama and Theater. 6070. Dial, Eleanore M. "Alvaro Custodio and His Continuing Dream:The Teatro Clásico de México in the 1960's." *LATR* 7,ii:45-57.
Alvaro Custodio, founder of the Teatro Clásico de México (TCDM), broadened the scope of his activities from Spanish classical theater to include plays ranging from Magaña's *Moctezuma* II and Alvaro Custodio's own version of *El regreso de Quetzalcóatl* to *Hamlet* and Ruiz de Alarcón's *La verdad sospechosa*. He again presented *La Celestina*. He continued to bring his vision to the theater in Mexico and a major contribution during the decade was his imaginative use of historical settings, varying from pyramids to colonial churches or homes. Custodio also founded the Ediciones del TCDM which include his stage adaptation of Rojas' *La Celestina* (1968) and a bilingual edition of *Hamlet* (1968). (EMD)

6071. Ehrmann, Hans. "Chilean Theatre:1971-1973." *LATR* 7,ii:39-43.
Discusses theatrical development in Chile while Chile was under the regime of Unidad Popular. Emphasis in the theater was placed on social commentary and reform, in regard to thematic content as well as constituting the basis for evaluating "good" theater. Discussion of university theater and professional theatrical companies is included. As political polarization intensified and the middle class began opposing the Allende government, the "social content" plays were rejected and light comedies and escapist fare became the norm. Also, a tentative peasant and working class theater emerged, as in the Teatro Nuevo Popular. The content of these plays dealt with class struggle, with the ruling class opposing the workers and peasants. (CG)

6072. Neglia, Erminio G. "Una recapitulación de la renovación teatral en Hispanoamérica." *LATR* 8,i:57-66.
The real origin of the modern Spanish-American theater is discussed. Although sooner or later almost all national theaters in Spanish America experienced a dramatic revolution, only Mexico and Argentina have had the first and a more systematic theatrical

renovation. From the early 1920s to the beginning of WW II, Mexican and Argentine dramatists introduced modern themes and forms that would revolutionize the theater. One of the primary causes of this revolution was the new conception of reality and the preoccupation with human conflicts. Another potent force in bringing more freedom and imagination to the stage was the competition of the cinema. To survive, the theater had to change. New techniques were explored. The commercial theater suffered, but for dramatic art the impact was beneficial. (EGN)

6074. Schanzer, George O. "El teatro hispanoamericano de post mortem." *LATR* 7,ii:5-16.
In the last two decades a number of Spanish-American authors have written plays whose characters all or nearly all are dead before the curtain rises. Seven such plays by 7 authors from 5 countries are examined. They range from one-act to full-length plays and from those in a lighter vein to works of profound seriousness. Examination reveals that in spite of the great variety of treatment their authors seem to share a belief in human freedom and responsibility as well as in some continuity of existence. These ideas are deeply rooted in the popular Hispanic tradition. (GOS)

6075. Skinner, Eugene R. "Research Guide to Post-Revolutionary Cuban Drama." *LATR* 7,ii:59-68.
This bibliography represents an attempt to construct from existing general bibliographies and from personal research in the Cuban journals *Casa de las Américas, Cuba internacional, Cuba, revista mensual*, and *INRA*, a specialized bibliography on Cuban theater since 1959. It includes three types of entries: general bibliographies employed in gathering data, article- and book-length reports, and reviews of books and of plays published during the post-revolutionary period. Paragraph-length notices of plays in performance found in *Cuba internacional* and *Cuba, revista mensual* have not been included nor have titles of published plays. (ERS)

Prose Fiction. 6104. Siemens, William W. "The Devouring Female in Four Latin American Novels." *ELWIU* 1:118-29. [Fuentes' *Zona sagrada*, García Márquez' *Cien años de soledad*, Aguilera-Malta's *Siete lunas y siete serpientes*, Cabrera Infantes's *Tres tristes tigres*.]
There are four recent Spanish American novels in which an important role is played by women corresponding to the "devouring female" archetype. In Carlos Fuentes' *Zona sagrada* a femme fatale of the Mexican screen attracts even her 29-year-old son to drive him mad. Demetrio Aguilera-Malta has a novel entitled *Siete lunas y siete serpientes*, in which a young girl deliberately attracts men only in order to castrate them. Gabriel García Márquez' celebrated *Cien años de soledad* has its Remedios, *la bella*, whose very untouchable beauty drives men to madness and death, and in Cabrera Infante's *Tres tristes tigres* there are Vivian Smith Corona, whose very resemblance to the archetype frightens a man, and La Estrella, the enormous black siren whose voice is sufficient to captivate any male. All of these resemble the ancient moon goddesses, and it appears that in the face of today's feminism some primordial fears relating to the negative anima are being aroused. (WLS)

Benedetti. 6166. Mathieu, Corina S. "Aspectos del mundo burgués de Mario Benedetti." [F 19]:173-76.
With *Montevideanos* Mario Benedetti creates a portrayal of the Uruguayan bourgeoisie. Benedetti's concern with the moral crisis afflicting the tiny republic is often expressed in his essays. In *Montevideanos* and *La muerte y otras sorpresas*, his understanding of the shortcomings and frustrations of a middle class threatened by the nation's economic bankruptcy, coupled with his literary talent, create an artistic vision of a social reality. The bribery of public officials, the deadly routine of a government job, the multitude of class prejudices, the lack of communication between the sexes plague the lives of Benedetti's characters. (CSM)

Borges. 6180. Caviglia, John. "The Tales of Borges:Language and the Private Eye." *MLN* 89:219-31.
Borges' tales are designed to vanish under scrutiny, for reasons

that owe much to philosophical idealism and Jewish mysticism. George Berkley's idealism leads logically to the language of Tlön, which excludes nouns, since his theories deny the existence of the essences designated by nouns. In this light Borges' diction, which is rich in substantives, is seen to designate nothing. Analogously, his reliance on metonymy leads from specifics to abstract and non-existent genera. (JLC)

6192. Natella, Arthur A. "Symbolic Color in the Stories of Jorge Luis Borges." *JSSTC* 2:39-48.

A careful study of "El inmortal," "La muerte y la brújula," and "Las ruinas circulares" shows that there is a discernible pattern in the use of the colors grey, red, and yellow. Borges favors these colors to describe important immortal characters and eternal situations and circumstances. As such, these colors are symbols of eternity and can be an important key in understanding the basic but hermetic themes of these stories. (AAN,Jr)

6197. Sanders, Matthew R., and William Sanders. "Borges' Rabbinic *Extraordinary Tales*." *RomN* 15:602-04.

Borges' use of two anecdotes from Rabbinic literature in his *Extraordinary Tales* presents special problems for readers not familiar with this field, and demonstrates something of Borges' method in working with his sources. The published version of "The Restitution of the Keys" gives misleading documentation, and differs considerably from the Rabbinic original in a way that coheres with Borges' famous *Ficciones*. The other tale, "A Golem," amplifies the basic Talmudic text with details found in Rashi's commentary, shedding light on Borges' original intention with regard to the piece. (WS & MS)

6198. Scari, Robert M. "Aspectos realista-tradicionales del arte narrativo de Borges." *Hispania* 57:899-907.

The basic narrative technique in Borges is the concise delineation of the protagonist in a character portrait which is followed by the psychological analysis and thematic resolution leading to the climax. Since the treatment of moral experience is paramount, plot, mood, humor, suspense, and other such factors are much less significant here than they are in the philosophical, detective, and science fiction tales. Many of Borges's most widely admired narrative devices are absent from the realistic stories because they are not suitable to a type of narrative that seeks profundity rather than a display of ingenuity. (RMS)

6204. Wheelock, Carter. "Spanish American Fantasy and the 'Believable, Autonomous World'." *IFR* 1,i:1-8. [Esp. on B's "La trama."]

Tzvetan Todorov's *Introduction à la littérature fantastique* attempts to define the fantastic short story structurally, according to whether it maintains irrationality or dispels it within the text. But the fantastic can be defined only in terms of artistic effect. Fantasy is concentrated art, blatantly heretical. Art is amoral, areligious, and heuristic. By destroying the rational order aggressively, fantasy removes the behavioral injunctions of reason and convention. True fantasy is a hangover from primitive times when mythical thought made truth and fiction indistinguishable. (CW)

Carpentier. 6219. Ayora, Jorge. "La alienación marxista en *Los pasos perdidos* de Carpentier." *Hispania* 57:886-92.

Carpentier's *Los pasos perdidos* is a case of alienation as seen and described by Marx. In chapter i the protagonist is presented as an artist who has sold his soul to Capitalism. His art has been twisted into advertising and commercial making. In semiawareness of this process of prostitution, the protagonist lives as a completely alienated man. The development of the novel presents the gradual recovery of his soul and character. (JRA)

6229. Peavler, Terry J. "The Source for the Archetype in *Los pasos perdidos*." *RomN* 15:581-87.

While the nameless protagonist of Alejo Carpentier's *Los pasos perdidos* does re-enact the heroic cycle and while the author was careful to give his character mythic, universal significance, the structural model for the novel was not an abstract formula but a specific literary source—Poe's *The Narrative of Arthur Gordon Pym*. Analysis of the character relationships, the nature and results of the protagonists' adventures, the symbolic parallelism of the two works, and Carpentier's admitted love for the *Narrative* prove the extent of Poe's presence in Carpentier's novel. (TP)

Cortázar, Julio. 6250. Fein, John M. "Response/2." *Diacritics* 4,i:54-56.

Similarity of structure unites Cortázar's "Las babas del diablo" with its film version by Antonioni. The chaotic language of Cortázar's Michel is symptomatic of a severe mental disturbance. Since the cause of Michel's breakdown is his revulsion at the ugliness of reality progressively revealed through the enlargements of initially innocuous photographs, Cortázar's story can be interpreted as a modern morality tale. Other points of comparison are the expression of personality only through the medium of photography and the request by the woman for the return of the photograph, which serves as the basis for Antonioni's creation of the relationship between Jane and Thomas. These similarities suggest that Antonioni borrowed from Cortázar the narrator's unreliability. The movie's conclusion, the miming of a tennis game by the Rag Week students, and the final shot, reversing the technique of enlargement through a rapid diminution of Thomas until he disappears, place on the spectator the burden of ambiguity that Cortázar places on Michel. (JMF)

6253. Gonzalez, Eduardo G. "Cortázar:Figuras y limites." *MLN* 89:232-49.

"Lejana" (*Bestiario*, 1951) can be read as a paradigm for representational strategies at work in Cortazar's fiction. At its most formal level, "Lejana" establishes a polarity between anagram and palindrome. These word games represent divergent modalities of the way meaning is simultaneously disclosed and erased. They serve also as models to grasp the dialectical relationship that separates and unites other sets of contraries. (EGG)

6259. Gyurko, Lanin A. "Guilt and Delusion:Two Stories by Cortázar." *Crit* 14,iii(1973):75-90.

Julio Cortázar portrays individuals afflicted by delusions, hallucinations, and nightmares. These are expressive of the characters' alienation, guilt, or fear. At times the delusions of the characters act as a positive force while at other times fantasy is afflictive and destructive. Two stories, "La puerta condenada" and "Siestas," exemplify these contrasting functions of delusion. In the first, fantasy plays an ironically positive or compensatory role. A lonely woman, frustrated in her maternal desires, deludes herself into believing that she is a mother cradling a disconsolate child. The fantasy child allows the woman to diminish her anguish by exteriorizing it. "Siestas," on the other hand, demonstrates unexpurgated fantasy, the delusions of the guilt-obsesse d Wanda increase in force yet cannot be confided to anyone and finally drive her insane. Both narratives are ambiguous; in both Cortázar adopts the limited perspective of the puzzled or dismayed protagonist who never succeeds in solving the mystery by which he is confronted. (LAG)

6262. —— "Self-Deception and Self-Confrontation in Cortázar." *SHR* 8:361-73.

For Lucio Medina in Cortázar's "The Band," being forced to view a ludicrous performance by an incompetent band when he has paid for a ticket to see an artistic film is a traumatic experience that causes him to see his existence as a farce. Although he rejects his past life and abandons his society, he gains the possibility of constructing an authentic existence. In contrast, in "A Place Called Kindberg" (1971), the anguish of self-confrontation causes the protagonist to commit suicide. Marcelo's debility of will prevents him from breaking away from a materialistic, success-oriented existence that has both protected his emotionally unstable self and stifled it. In both stories, the plight of the protagonist is placed into an ironic perspective. (LG)

6263. —— "Self-Obsession and Death in Three Stories by Cortázar." *RS* 41(1973):234-51.

Death appears in many forms in Cortázar's fiction. In three of the stories from *Final del juego* (1964), "Una flor amarilla," "Relato con un fondo de agua," and "El rio," death is linked with extreme narcissism. The murders in the first two stories are acts of catharsis by which the protagonists attempt to rid themselves of fear and anguish that are largely self-induced. Their crimes serve only to compound their affliction. The exercise of the will leads the protagonist toward the assumption of the adverse fate that he has desperately attempted to avoid. Thus free will becomes an agent of fate, but fate turns out to be an inner determinism.

Delusion, hallucination, and nightmare devastate the characters from within. The external determinism in the form of a cosmic *fatum* postulated by the alcoholic in "Una flor amarilla" and that in the form of a dehumanizing social order by the recluse of "Relato" prove to be elegant rationales that these very self-defensive characters construct in order to deflect responsibility for their miserable fate away from themselves. All three narratives contain both literal and symbolic death. The protagonists live warped and hollow lives that are but another form of the death that they give to others. (LAG)

6289. Servodidio, Mirella d'A. "Facticity and Transcendence in Cortázar's *Rayuela.*" *JSSTC* 2:49-57.

In his portrayal of Horacio Quiroga in *Rayuela*, Cortázar situates himself within the mainstream of existentialist thought in viewing existence as dialectical and hence as involving tension and polarity. The twin terms "facticity" and "transcendence," used by both Heidegger and Sartre, are applicable to Oliveira who reveals himself to be an empirically determinate being who transcends his determinacy. The zigzagging trajectory of this character becomes more readily understandable when studied in the context of the irresoluble pull between these dual categories. (MES)

Donoso, José. 6314. Tatum, Charles M. "The Child Point of View in Donoso's Fiction." *JSSTC* 1(1973):187-96.

José Donoso uses the child point of view in his fiction to portray the loss of innocence and youthful vitality in his characters as they mature. The child narrator recreates the uncorrupted, fantasy-filled existence in which he is allowed to act out his feelings and instincts unfettered by social constraints while the reader views the adult world in the process of giving full expression to its pretentions, false values, anxieties, and complexes. By juxtaposing the two ages through point of view he makes us acutely aware of the glaring differences between the child's spontaneous unsocialized behavior and the falseness and sham of the adult's attitudes and rigidly confined self-expression. The characters in Donoso's fictional world become caught in a web of perverted values and aspirations which allows them to avoid facing the horrifying reality of their human condition. (CMT)

Fuentes, Carlos. 6318. Ciccone, Anthony J. "The Artistic Depiction of Fantasy-Reality in the Uncollected Short Stories (1949-51) of Carlos Fuentes." *JSSTC* 1(1973):127-39.

Discusses Fuentes' accomplishments as a short story writer and the significance of four of his uncollected short narratives with respect to his later career. "Pastel rancio," "Pantera en jazz," "El muñeco," and "Trigo errante" are considered. Significant attention is accorded to the artistic use of point of view, time, and space in the depiction of literary fantasy-reality in these stories. Since the theme of unreality-reality is a recurrent concern in much of Fuentes' art, the consideration of its use in these four narratives provides an insight into the scope and basis of some of his later literary achievements. (AJC)

6323. Gyurko, Lanin A. "Idealism and Moral Blindness in Two Stories by Fuentes." *RLV* 40:615-32.

Fuentes' two narratives, "La muñeca reina" and "Un alma pura," demonstrate the tragic consequences of the blindness of misguided idealists. In their single-minded devotion to imaginative, romantic, or social ideals, the protagonists inadvertently dehumanize and even destroy the lives of those with whom they come into contact. Carlos in "La muñeca reina" returns to the world of his youth in an attempt to find the creative center that his life is missing. The ingenuousness and the ardent idealism of Juan Luis in "Un alma pura" shield him from the recognition of his incestuous love for his sister Claudia. A sordid, brutal reality finally crushes both Carlos and Juan Luis, ineffectual dreamers whose ideals turn out to be mere self-delusions. (LG)

6327. —— "The Myths of Ulysses in Fuentes's *Zona sagrada.*" *MLR* 69:316-24.

In *Zona sagrada* Claudia devotes herself to creating and maintaining her myth as cinematic goddess in order to gain immortality. This myth is kept viable by the exploitation of those who are attracted to her and to her legend. Her neglected son, Guillermo, creates a myth of family reconciliation patterned on the myth of the homecoming of Ulysses. He is forced to accept a corruption of this myth developed in the *Telegonia* that signifies the collapse of his cherished fantasies. The role of Telemachus that he attempts to actualize is usurped by Giancarlo who betrays their friendship as he becomes the Telegonus who marries Claudia/Penelope. Claudia is an ambivalent personality, both redeeming and destroying mother, both Penelope and Circe. Forsaken by Claudia/Penelope, Guillermo is reduced to the Telemachus of the *Telegonia* as he falls under the power of Claudia/Circe. In his insanity, he feels himself transformed into a dog—the equivalent of the swine of Circe and the expressionistic form of the slavish adoration he has always evinced toward the mother from whom he now remains permanently isolated. (LAG)

6329. Hellerman, M. Kasey. "The Coatlicue-Malinche Conflict: A Mother and Son Identity Crisis in the Writings of Carlos Fuentes." *Hispania* 57:868-75.

Fuentes' writings illustrate a unique psychological trait of Mexican mothers, the Coatlicue-Malinche conflict. This trait is characteristic of women who, like Cortez's mistress, Malinche, have suffered a humiliating sexual violation. Mexican tradition despises the Malinche but entrusts to her son, the *hijo de la chingada*, the awesome task of restoring a utopian Mexican nation. The latter day Malinches in Fuentes' work exemplify the Coatlicue-Malinche conflict through their rejection of the circumstances surrounding their motherhood and through their identification with the enviable Coatlicue, virgin mother of the aggressive Aztec god, Huitzilopochtli. (MKH)

García Marquez, Gabriel. 6350. Müller, Gerd F. "*Hundert Jahre Einsamkeit* und der Mythus der ewigen Wiederkehr." *OL* 29:268-82.

In *Cien años de soledad* the chronological-teleological history of a geneology is broken up into a cyclical scheme, based on mythical structure, whereby the inherent mythical pattern shows obvious parallels with Giambattista Vico's generation theory. The story itself is presented as a magical account in which solitude appears as the central theme of the myth evoked by the author. On the basis of the mythical model the fantastic tale can be the illustration of a socially genuine situation—in the accelerated process of civilization man loses contact with his origin and the schism between the lost heritage and the progress of modern society cannot be overcome. (GFM)

6358. Siemens, William L. "Gabriel García Márquez and the Tainted Hero." *WVUPP* 21:92-96.

There is a distinct unifying element within Gabriel García Márquez' *La increíble y triste historia de la cándida Eréndira y de su abuela desalmada.* In each of these stories a male character appears corresponding initially to the general description of the universal hero of mythology. Each comes to a community in need, generally from an exotic location, and seemingly in possession of some special gift which can save the people. Yet in each case he fails, either because of moral disqualification or on account of some invincible weakness. The only strong, admirable persons in the work are several women and, ironically, a drowning victim of heroic proportions whose presence does transform the community. The villain of the melodramatic title story is a powerful woman, and when the hero at last succeeds in slaying her he is too weak to follow the fleeing girl. Nevertheless, the book ends with an intriguing image of the newly freed feminine spirit. (WLS)

6361. Tobin, Patricia. "García Márquez and the Genealogical Imperative." *Diacritics* 4,ii:52-55.

García Márquez' *One Hundred Years of Solitude* does not share the linear bias which informs our conceptualizations about time, knowledge, and narrative structures. The Western consciousness appropriates to mere chronological succession the significance of genealogical descent, whereby the past begets and legitimizes the present and predicts the future. *One Hundred Years of Solitude* features a genealogical family who through its generations are cheerfully ignorant in action and thought of any paternal legacy from the past. Approximating a mythical consciousness, the Buendías express a maternal accommodation of an abundant, chaotic, and indiscriminate reality, marked by non-linear manifestations in the family, of bastardy and incest; in time, of circularity and repetition; and in space, of juxtaposed fantasy and reality. Thus are the family, time, and story lines of the traditional novel all subverted in the service of a new, and more ancient, reality. (PLT)

Guillén, Nicolás. 6381. Cobb, Martha K. "Concepts of Blackness in the Poetry of Nicolás Guillén, Jacques Roumain and Langston Hughes." *CLAJ* 18:262-72.
A comparative study of Guillén, Roumain, and Hughes to investigate the extent to which their poetry reflects the continuities and parallels of black life experiences conceptualized thematically as: (1) confrontation (blackness in a hostile society); (2) dualism (dilemma of being both black and American); (3) identity (search for one's humanity and one's heritage); and (4) liberation (the struggle for freedom). (MKC)

Hernández, Juan J. 6394. Corvalán, Octavio. "Juan José Hernández and His City of Dreams." *IFR* 1:138-40. [Rev. art. of *La ciudad de los sueños*.]
La ciudad de los sueños treats social changes in Argentina in 1944-48. Hernández shows the twilight of an era and the impact of Peron's revolution upon the middle-classes. The narrative technique is a mixture of diary form, interior monologues, fictitious magazine clippings, newspaper headlines, telephone conversations, letters, and Eva Peron's speeches. The protagonist moves to Buenos Aires in search of a more exciting life and finds that the city conceals the same traits making life difficult for a single woman everywhere, bringing the final disillusion, love. Her story is a large metaphor of what the country endured between those years. (OC)

Marqués, René. 6426. Barrera, Ernesto M. "La voluntad rebelde en *Carnaval afuera, carnaval adentro* de René Marqués." *LATR* 8,i:11-19.
Crime and punishment are what man receives for having been born, having loved, and having sought the supreme ideal of liberty as the only true meaning for his existence. This existential vision of life develops at three levels of historical, mythical, and ontological content, through which one perceives the problematic coexistence of two cultures in conflict in Puerto Rico: the first of indigenous-Hispanic antecedence, representing tradition, and the other reflecting the impact of the modern North American lifestyle, which devours cannibalistically the essential values of the first. (EMB)
6429. Siemens, William L. "Assault on the Schizoid Wasteland:René Marqués' *El apartamiento*." *LATR* 7,ii:17-23.
The features of the existence of Marqués' two principal characters in *El apartamiento* reflect the characteristics of a schizoid individual. They are isolated from exterior reality in their apartment, with all their physical needs provided impersonally. When, after 20 years, there is dissatisfaction, their youthful creativity becomes incarnate in two characters who attempt to lure them from their circumstances. Their insecurity results in the appearance of two more characters representing the forces of repression, who manage to kill the other newcomers. The only hope is in the appearance of an Indian symbolizing "America's historical conscience," who is bound by the "inspectors" but finally set free by the two original characters. (WLS)

Paz, Octavio. 6550. Moody, Michael. "Imágenes en *Bajo tu clara sombra* por Octavio Paz." *RomN* 15:592-601.
Distinctive image patterns in the poem are discussed. The poem exhibits an archetypal structure that clearly imitates nature. A cyclical process provides the ritually significant stages through which the poem advances: birth, initiation, passion, death, and rebirth. Paz creates a highly personalized poetic vision through an intricate structuring of interlocking motifs. The poem accumulates meaning through the placement of similar images in diverse contexts (the blood image); the placement in opposition of image types that are commonly associated (fire and light); the close association or fusion of different image clusters (water and light, nature and light); and the use of the same image grouping to draw out different themes (light and nature). (MM)

Ríos Rey. 6573. Morris, Robert J. "The Theatre of Juan Ríos Rey." *LATR* 7,ii:81-95.
Juan Ríos Rey was one of the three principal dramatists in Peru from 1946 to 1960. Ríos cultivated a poetic and traditional dramaturgy free of national, social, and political influences. Of his 8 compositions, only the last is in prose and is not directly based on an acknowledged source. Of the others, written in a variety of verse forms, 4 are directly based on classical myth or legend, and 3 are inspired by 17th-century Spanish sources. A critical analysis and evaluation of each work, along with a concluding overview of his total dramatic production, is given to substantiate the claim that Ríos is one of the unrecognized patriarchs of the contemporary Peruvian theater. (RJM)

Roa Bastos. 6575. Gurza, Esperanza. "El exito del fracaso en *El trueno entre las hojas* de Augusto Roa Bastos." [F 19]:168-72.
In the last short story of *El trueno entre las hojas*, Roa Bastos confronts us with a universe at once real and absurd. Real, since things and characters are verifiable. Absurd, since everything seems to contradict itself. Even frail, short life expands and becomes eternal through the phantasmagoric music heard along the river, from the accordion of the deceased Solano Rojas. In the absurd universe, the bosses resemble and behave like the fauna of the jungle, and even exceed it in animality. Like exiles on foreign soil, the poor native workers toil and obey, fearing punishment and death. They, too, are "absurd," desperate, helpless men. (EG)
6576. Luchting, Wolfgang. "Time and Transportation in *Hijo de hombre*." *RS* 41(1973):98-106.
Augusto Roa Bastos (Paraguay, 1917-) in his 1959 novel *Hijo de hombre* uses a railway-carriage and a water-truck as a double metaphor of time, history, and progress. Both are related structurally as symbols of the Paraguayan oppresseds' courage and perseverance by the truck's driver, Cristóbal, being the son of the carriage's guardian, Casiano, by the manner of both vehicles' journey through time and space, and by the similarity of the circumstances and destinies of both the participants in the journeys and the vehicles themselves. Carriage and truck reveal Roa Bastos' special vision of history as progress. Wars interrupt this progress. Casiano's carriage, remainder and reminder of an earlier rebellion, twenty years later inspires a second one, which is inspired also by Cristóbal's feat in getting the water-truck to the front-line—at the expense of his own life and the life of those accompanying him. (WAL)

Rojas, Manuel. 6579. Param, Charles. "Humor and Manuel Rojas." [F 19]:177-83.
Discusses Rojas' great use of humor in its many forms, his reflections of real-life phenomena, and his possible reasons for such uses of humor. Rojas reveals his compassion for the unfortunate people of his life and times in several ways, among them his skillful use of humor to plumb the depths of their desolation. His humor gives a strong personal touch to his criticism of people and institutions. (CP)

Rulfo. 6580. Bruce Novoa, John D. "Some Answers about Rulfo's *La cordillera*." *Hispania* 57:474-76.
The publication of *La cordillera*, Juan Rulfo's follow-up to *Pedro Paramo* is in question, but it has not been published. In a 1969 interview, Rulfo, when asked why he had stopped writing, responded that he had not stopped writing, but had only stopped publishing. *La cordillera* exists but he refuses to publish it, only having allowed some fragments, reproduced here, to appear. Some critics have discussed the novel, and Gomez-Gil has even claimed its publication, an assumption negated by the fact that no mention of it has ever been made, and that both the supposed publisher and Rulfo deny it. Whether it will ever appear or not is still in question, but Rulfo still refuses to publish it. (Fragments of *La cordillera* are in Spanish.) (JBN)
6583. González, Alfonso. "Onomastics and Creativity in *Doña Bárbara* y *Pedro Páramo*." *Names* 21:40-45.
Naming in Rómulo Gallegos' *Doña Bárbara* and in Juan Rulfo's *Pedro Páramo* serves a more profound function than the mere symbolical. Names are an integral part of each author's

worldview. Onomastics in those novels present the reader with two different attitudes toward the phenomenon of "caciquismo" or political bossism. The names of persons and places in *Doña Bárbara* present the reader with a type of "caciquismo" which will vanish into oblivion as soon as progress is introduced as an alternative. The optimism of the author is reflected in the names he gives. Names in *Pedro Páramo* suggest an eternal "caciquismo" which is left unchanged by a revolution and by the death of the "cacique." The narrator communicates his pessimism through suggestions embodied in the names of characters and places. (AG)

6584. Lyon, Ted. "Ontological Motifs in the Short Stories of Juan Rulfo." *JSSTC* 1(1973):161-68.
Rulfo bases his short stories on the realities of his native Jalisco, Mexico. Each of the stories of *El llano en llamas* occurs in a limited geographical region and places man in an impossible situation, one in which he must confront the purpose of his beleaguered life. Several stylistic motifs illustrate Rulfo's concept of human existence; life as walking and continual movement, plaguing memory that imposes past errors on present existence, the futility of all human endeavor, and existence limited by physical darkness and restricted spiritual horizon. Together these motifs show man oppressed, thwarted, but never completely defeated. (TEL)

Sáinz, Gustavo. 6595. Gyurko, Lanin A. "Reality and Fantasy in *Gazapo*." *REH* 8:117-46.
In *Gazapo* Gustavo Sainz probes a volatile, contradictory world of adolescence, a realm on the borderline between reality and fantasy. The juveniles of the novel are authors, actors, and audience for their own productions. As storytellers they alter, embellish, parody, and search for the most dramatic and convincing manner of relating experience and thus bolstering their insecure identities. Sainz delights in demolishing established beliefs and preconceived norms. His art is one of whimsical contraries and incongruous juxtapositions. Chronological time, physical space, and continuity of character and episode are replaced by simultaneity, protean space, and arbitrary, multiple identities. Sainz's art of the preposterous affirms the joy of pure imaginative creation. (LAG)

Usigli. 6608. Rodríguez-Seda, Asela. "Las últimas obras de Usigli:Efebocracia o gerontocracia." *LATR* 8,i:45-48.
Usigli deals with different aspects of the conflict between generations. Whereas in *Los viejos* this confrontation is carefully

placed in the artistic milieu of drama critics and writers, with overtones to Usigli's own position within Mexican contemporary drama, in *¡Buenos días, señor Presidente!* it is developed in the realm of politics. Contrasting with the optimistic resolution of *Los viejos*, in which both old and young people will join forces against the mistakes of the world, in *¡Buenos días, señor Presidente!* a pessimistic tone prevails. The killing of Harmodio puts an end to the possibility of the establishment of a government ruled only by young people. (ACR-S)

Yáñez. 6626. Doudoroff, Michael J. "Tensions and Triangles in *Al filo del agua*." *Hispania* 57:1-12.
The subject of Agustín Yáñez' *Al filo del agua* (1947) is the collective consciousness of a small Mexican town on the eve of the 1910 Revolution, and its theme is the dissolution of a society. A central technique in the development of this theme is found in the structure and process of the plot. Virtually all of the characters are presented in interlocking groups of three. These triangles are subjected to a variety of forces which cause changes in them. The nature and rhythm of these changes affect the reader's perception and interpretation of the theme in specific ways. These changes determine the novel's overall design, which in turn conveys the sense of external stasis and increasing underlying instability, enriching the representation of an old social order on the brink of cataclysm. (MJD)

6628. Walker, John L. "Timelessness through Memory in the Novels of Agustín Yáñez." *Hispania* 57:445-51.
Since timelessness is inseparable from the flow of time, the timeless aspects of the personalities of fictional characters must be considered. Agustín Yáñez has played a prominent role in the development of the psychological aspects of the modern Mexican novel, where objective time is chronological and subjective time is internal. Either a cyclical flow or cessation of the flow can cause timelessness, as seen in the patient's feverish deliriums in *Pasión y convalecencia* (1943) but less in *Archipiélago de mujeres* (1943) whose stories are told through conscious memory. *Al filo del agua* (1947) deals with the futility of halting time's advance in the objective world, seen especially in the resulting insanity of some characters who try. The desire for fame's timelessness through composition of music is the theme of *La creación* (1959) but past timeless memories governing the protagonist's life ruin this. *La tierra pródiga* (1960) and *Ojerosa y pintada* (1959) show cyclical timelessness, expanding to the future. *Las tierras flacas* (1962) comments on timelessness through memory and recall. (JLW)

III. LITERATURE BEFORE 1500

Bibliography. 6629. Dean, Ruth J., and Samuel G. Armistead. "A Fifteenth-Century Spanish Book List." [F 88]:73-87.
A 15th-century Latin manuscript of Boethius on the *Consolation of Philosophy* in the library of the University of Pennsylvania contains on a fly-leaf a list of 20 books belonging to a private owner, drawn up by him in 1471. The titles are given in Spanish, but the collection was probably all in Latin, although one or two of the works may have been in the vernacular. Aristotelian translations and commentaries form about half of the collection. There are moral and theological treatises and two titles connected with preaching, while a dictionary and works on grammar and rhetoric complete the list. (RJD & SGA)

Romancero. 6660. Surles, Robert L. "El ciclo de Gaiferos: Herencia de la épica germánica." [F 19]:200-03.
Presents the Gaiferos legend of the Castilian *Romancero* as being thematic progeny of the Visigothic *Waltharius*-epic (the earliest extant version found in Anglo-Saxon fragments of the 8th century). The *romances* of the Gaiferos cycle represent the earliest of the *matiére de France* and several Golden Age stylizations, along with religious and emigré literary examples in the form of Sephardic and New World ballads. Having received early folkloric dissemination throughout the many literatures of Germanic tradition, the Waltharius/Gaiferos legend has come to permeate, as well, the Hispanic circumstance, both geographically

and temporally. (RLS)

Themes. 6665. Hall, J.B. "*Tablante de Ricamonte* and Other Castilian Versions of Arthurian Romances." *RLC* 48:177-89.
Scholars of Peninsular Arthurian literature have largely ignored the important modifications which the Castilian translators made to their sources. The present study seeks to remedy this by comparing the 13th-century Provençal poem *Jaufré* with the Castilian prose romance *Tablante de Ricamonte* which derives from it. The work of a disciple of Chrétien de Troyes, *Jaufré*, is a fairly lighthearted romance with numerous burlesque incidents in which both the hero and King Arthur are made to look ridiculous. In *Tablante de Ricamonte*, such episodes have been toned down or removed altogether. It is shown briefly how similar "ideological" modifications, aimed at presenting the chivalric way of life in a morally acceptable and elevated light, have been carried out in other Castilian Arthurian romances. (JBH)

Alfonso el Sabio. 6667. Davis, W.R. "Another Aspect of the Virgin Mary in the *Cantigas de Santa María*." *REH* 8:95-105.
Examination of the presentation and characterization of the Virgin Mary in the 13th-century collection of canticles by King Alfonso x, el Sabio, reveals how deeply concerned medieval man was with the Virgin, how intimately he identified with her, presenting her with virtually every human quality imaginable, yet

never being sacrilegious. Her actions and dialogue are discussed using numerous *cantigas* as examples of her human attributes. Clearly, the Virgin's emergence as a womanly figure dominates the church's divine representation, as medieval man causes her to participate in his secular world. (WRD)

6668. Hartman, Steven L. "Alfonso el Sabio and the Varieties of Verb Grammar." *Hispania* 57:48-55.

King Alfonso X of Castile and León (1226-84) is called Alfonso el Sabio because of the scholarly activity which he fostered at his court. He is thought to have supervised closely the work of his scribes as they wrote the Alfonsine treatises on history, astronomy, science, and law, and so he has been credited with "founding," standardizing, and stabilizing Castilian prose. However, a statisical examination shows that Alfonsine prose is internally inconsistent on certain items of verb morphology, and a diachronic comparison indicates that other such items emerge as temporary fashions which pass out of use shortly after the 13th century, returning to an earlier form. In view of these signs of inconsistency and impermanence of Alfonsine verb morphology, it would be well to redefine and perhaps further specify the contribution of Alfonso X to the history of Castilian. (SLH)

Amadís de Gaula. 6674. Mínguez Sender, José-M. "Algunos aspectos inéditos de la versión alemana del *Amadís de Gaula*." *BEG* 8(1970):63-68.

Discusses the German translation of *Amadís de Gaula* and comments on its popularity in the 16th and 17th centuries in Germany. (J-MMS)

Celestina. 6696. Forcadas, Alberto M. "Otra solución a 'Lo de tu abuela con el ximio' (Aucto 1) de *La Celestina*." *RomN* 15:567-71.

Menéndez y Pelayo suggested that "Lo de tu abuela con el ximio" could be a hint at Calisto's having a stain in his lineage. Green refuted this view in his " 'Lo de tu abuela con el ximio' *(Celestina, Auto 1)," HR* (1956). He concluded that the author of the first act of the *Comedia de Calisto y Melibea* was merely "deflating Calisto's magnification of the 'superiorité de la dame.' " Thus he ruled that Menéndez y Pelayo's assumption that "acaso la venganza del judío converso se cebó en la difamación de la limpia sangre . . .' now appears fantastic." But Don Marcelino's idea is closer to the truth because "ximio" hints at the Arabic "Maimo" (ape), the clue which leads to the "Maimon-ides" lover of Calisto's grandmother, a Jew. (AMF)

Cid. 6717. Montoro, Adrian G. "Good or Bad Fortune on Entering Burgos? A Note on Bird-Omens in the *Cantar de Mío Cid*." *MLN* 89:131-45.

An examination of traditional beliefs on bird-divination indicates that the "left" was not necessarily the evil side. The action of the *Cantar* shows the Cid passing from initial bad luck to final triumph. Therefore, the Cid's optimistic prediction must mean: "Things will go badly at first, but later we shall succeed." The right bird (which is the first to appear) forebodes troubles at the beginning of the hero's exile and the left one announces final victory. Thus the ride from Vivar to Burgos is a figure of the Cid's longer journey in exile. (AGM)

6721. Waltman, Franklin M. "A Literary Analysis by Computer." *Hispania* 57:893-98.

The application of a concordance program to a literary work, the *Cantar de Mío Cid*, in an attempt to resolve the polemic of authorship which has existed since 1929 is discussed. The concordance was used to ascertain if differences exist in the use of formulaic expressions, synonyms, syntax, or verb tenses. This program also gives statistical data such as sentence length, frequency of word occurrence, and alphabetical listing of words in descending or increasing frequency of occurrence. (FWW)

6722. —— "Synonym Choice in the *Cantar de Mio Cid*." *Hispania* 57:452-61.

A polemic has existed for several years as to whether there is one or more than one author responsible for the composition of the *Cantar de Mío Cid*. The viewpoints expressed by critics have been varied and numerous. The choice of particular synonyms within the poem are studied to determine if there is any great difference within the three parts of the poem. Synonyms were located by using a concordance print-out entitled *Concordance to Poema de Mío Cid*. Opinions of other critics are given first, followed by the presentation of the ideas expressed by Ramón Menéndez Pidal. Based on his beliefs, a scheme of verses is established with the study of synonym choices following. The study of synonyms, based on this scheme of verses, tends to disprove the existence of two poets. (FMW)

Gran conquista de Ultramar. 6729. Fitch, C. Bruce. "A Clue to the Genealogy of the *Gran conquista de Ultramar*." *RomN* 15:578-80.

A scribal error in MS. 2454 (Biblioteca Nacional), *Gran conquista de Ultramar*, the writing of an "o" over an already drawn "b" in a manner so that it is not readily visible, created a new word which was perpetuated in the next known edition (Salamanca, 1503). It is so highly improbable that the error occurred by chance that the only rational conclusion is that there is a direct line between the two. (CBF)

Libro de Alexandre. 6735. Willis, Raymond S. "The Artistry and Enigmas of the *Libro de Alexandre*:A Review Article." *HR* 42:33-42.

A review article of *The Treatment of Classical Material in the* "Libro de Alexandre," by Ian Michael (Manchester, 1970). The nature and thrust of the study are summarized and evaluated favorably. A few errors are corrected. A different interpretation is offered of the moral which Michael believes must be drawn from the exemplary punishment of Alexander the Great at the end of the Spanish poem. Castilian with a strong Riojan tinge is offered as an alternative to the dialect of the original, which Michael and others believe to have been Leonese. (RSW)

Manuel, Don Juan. 6742. Ayerbe-Chaux, Reinaldo. "El ejemplo IV de *El Conde Lucanor*:Su originalidad artística." *RomN* 15:572-77.

The *ejemplo* IV of *El Conde Lucanor* is a literary recreation of a well known medieval tale and represents a significant artistic achievement. A comparison of this *ejemplo* and its other European medieval versions reveals the superior qualities of the Spanish writer who transforms the guide lines he found in the collections of *exempla* of the preaching friars into a lively and colorful scene. (RA-C)

Martínez de Toledo. 6750. Sims, Edna N. "The Antifeminist Element in the Works of Alfonso Martínez and Juan Luis Vives." *CLAJ* 18:52-68.

Categorizes the most frequent portrayals of abstract negative female prototypes as presented by Martínez and Vives. The ill will of the male toward the female is apparent mainly in the judgments through which the authors interpret the reaction of society to the manifold vices of woman and is mainly concerned with the literary aspects of the problem. Martínez concentrates on the linguistic elements while Vives implies that woman causes man either to rise or fall. (ENS)

IV. LITERATURE FROM 1500 TO 1700

Drama and Theater. 6813. Garzon-Blanco, Armando I. "Note on the Authorship of the Spanish Jesuit Play of *San Hermenegildo*, 1580." *ThS* 15,i:79-83.

Newly discovered evidence in the University Library in Granada, Spain reveals the authorship of the 16th-century Jesuit play of *San Hermenegildo*. A copy dated Seville, 1591 has survived in the Royal Academy of History in Madrid, "Cortes" Collection, MS 386, and may be a copy of the original play produced for the inauguration of the Sevillian school of San Hermenegildo in 1580. Some critics attribute the authorship to the Sevillian playwright

Juan de Mal-lara. An incomplete, anonymous MS in an unpublished collection of documents in Caja A-40 in the University Library in Granada, describes the inaugural festivities of the school, including the production of the play. The play is described as a collaborative effort by Father Hernando de Davila, Father Cerda, and Don Juan de Arguijo. The play of *San Hermenegildo* became the prototype for other similar Jesuit plays in Europe and the colonies. (AIG-B)

6819. Parr, James A. "An Essay on Critical Method, Applied to the *Comedia*." *Hispania* 57:434-44.
Comedia criticism has traditionally been an imprecise and free-wheeling art, characterized by a generally positivistic orientation. The critical focus has now shifted to the thematic-structural method, which is generally sound but which stands in need of further refinement. To bring criticism more into the mainstream of modern theory and practice, one should: (1) learn to bring to bear intrinsic, extrinsic, and interdisciplinary approaches in order to extrapolate from a synthesis of these a clearer sense of the artistic accomplishment of the work; (2) seriously question the tendency of the poetic justice school to reduce imaginative fiction to the level of cautionary tales; (3) eschew judicial criticism with its attendant odious comparisons; and (4) strive to avoid the intentional fallacy. (JAP)

6823. Webber, Edwin J. "On the Ancestry of the Gracioso." *RenD* 5(for 1972):171-90.
Lope de Vega's reference to *La Francesilla* as "the first comedy in which the *figura del donaire* was introduced" probably contained more than the simple allusion to the dramatic Gracioso that is commonly assumed. The popular conception of wit as one of the requisites of the Renaissance gentleman had long since elaborated the stereotype of the *gracioso*—witty and urbane—courtier. In the mind of Lope, however, *gracioso* may have been virtually synonymous with *truhán* in the sense of "jester": the first connoting "fine wit" and the second, "buffoon." Lope was clearly speaking figuratively in referring to *la figura del donaire*, probably meaning "Wit personified" or "the Mask of Wit." With this phrase he could have been referring primarily to the *gracioso*, the preceding century's favored figure of wit, and secondarily to the Gracioso, the succeeding century's favorite comic character. (EJW)

Romancero. 6843. Foster, David W. "A Note on the Rhetorical Structure of the Ballad *Álora la bien cercada*." *RomN* 15(1973):392-86.
Edmund de Chasca's recent explication of the ballad, while focusing on intrinsic aspects of style and form, fails to emphasize sufficiently the rhetorical structure of the text, whereby an attempt is made to elicit audience sympathy for Moorish treachery against the Christians. This is accomplished principally by a bipartite structure which juxtaposes description and narration, attack and revenge, Christian villainy and Moorish righteous revenge, the multitudes and the solitary hero. The effect, as in other frontier ballads, is to "convince" the Christian audience of Moorish moral superiority. (DWF)

Themes. 6848. DeCosta, Miriam. "The Evolution of the *Tema Negro* in Literature of the Spanish Baroque." *CLAJ* 17:417-30.
Although the black was occasionally treated as a leitmotif in Spanish medieval literature, the *tema negro* became increasingly important in Baroque poetry, fiction, and drama. An analysis of terminology, racial epithets, physical descriptions, names, customs, and language reveals that writers of the period, such as Cervantes, Góngora, Quevedo, Benavente, Claramonte, and Ximénez de Enciso, portrayed the black through stereotypic literary archetypes—buffoon, soldier, noble savage, and scholar. Many of the literary techniques and themes (the African past, slavery, black beauty, song/dance, folklore, religious syncretism, and racial pride) foreshadow 20th-century *negrismo*. The treatment of the black in Spanish literature is indicative of a changed esthetic, a Baroque esthetic, with its emphasis upon caricature, conceptist conceits, linguistic anomalies and atypical archetypes. (MD)

Alemán, Mateo. 6854. Agüera, Victorio G. "Salvación del cristiano nuevo en el *Guzmán de Alfarache*." *Hispania* 57:23-30.
In his work(1599-1604) Mateo Alemán presented all the Catholic theses previously defined in the Council of Trent and used them on behalf of the *conversos* (of Jewish descent) in order to achieve for them the only equality they could claim: brotherhood in the Mystical Body of Christ. Alemn uses Guzmán as a vehicle for his thesis. After an apology of his father against gossipers who accuse him because of his Jewish background, Guzmán chooses the picaresque life, a path to anonymity and a means to avoid malicious gossip of his racial infamy. It is in the lowest of social statuses where he realizes the possibility of salvation because he is also a member of the Mystical Body. When he momentarily seeks honor and nobility, society will remind him of his dishonored *converso* situation. Finally, he repents with the prophetic warning that they will question the sincerity of his conversion. Certainly enough, the majority of critics today regard Guzmán's conversion as a strategy of the author to pass ecclesiastical censors. (VGA)

Calderón. 6871. Feal, Gisèle, and Carlos Feal-Deibe. "Calderón's *Life Is a Dream*:From Psychology to Myth." *HSL* 6:1-28.
Calderón's *Life is a Dream* shows parallel plots of two fathers (Basilio and Clotaldo) who do not recognize their children (Segismundo and Rosaura) as such. Astolfo, who abandons Rosaura, repeats the story of Clotaldo, who has abandoned Rosaura's mother. Rosaura and Segismundo must strive toward recognition by their fathers, recognition which is related, in Rosaura's case, to the restoration of her honor through marriage to Astolfo. Basilio and Clotaldo must accept the fact that a life cannot be entirely reduced to the dictates of reason. Life is a dream for one who loves a purely instinctual life, as does Segismundo at the beginning, just as it is for those who repress their instincts, as do Basilio and Clotaldo. The fathers of the play evolve in a direction counter to that of their children. Thus, in each of them, there is a final reconciliation of opposing forces within a person, the unconscious and the conscious. (GF & CF-D.)

6874. Friedman, Edward H. "Dramatic Perspective in Calderón's *El mayor monstruo los celos*." *BCom* 26:43-49.
In Calderón's *El mayor monstruo los celos* the conception of man's place in the universe is closely related to that of classical tragedy. The play demonstrates the impossibility of eluding the decree of fate, in this case the prediction of Mariene's death. Calderón conceives the work within a tri-partite hierarchical structure, based in descending order on fate, society, and the individual will. An internal agent, jealousy, provides a correlative for the dominant external agent, fate. Within this framework, the role of the artist becomes apparent through the interplay of conceptual and linguistic recourses. (EHF)

6878. Martin, Eleanor J. "Calderón's *La gran Cenobia*:Source Play for *La vida es sueño?*" *BCom* 26:22-30.
In *La gran Cenobia* Calderón may have found the inspiration for *La vida es sueño*. A study of the earlier drama reveals significant parallelisms with *La vida es sueño* in theme, situations, imagery, and characters. Critics have maintained that Calderón has frequently produced mature drama from revision of earlier works. Calderón corrects the dramatic immaturity of *La gran Cenobia* and attains greater sophistication in his *opus magum*. (EJM)

Cervantes. 6895. Bandera, Cesáreo. "Cervantes frente a Don Quixote:Violenta simetría entre la realidad y la ficción." *MLN* 89:159-72.
In the passage on *Tirante* the priest praises the realism of this novel, while condemning the author for being realistic without a purpose, without profiting from the incongruity of his realism within the traditional context of the chivalric novel. This passage serves also as a warning against taking Cervantes' own realm literally. The cervantine windmills, for example, are not in the novel because they are also in La Mancha. They are used to ridicule don Quijote's fantasies. (CB)

6911. Iventosch, Herman. "Cervantes and Courtly Love:The Grisóstomo-Marcela Episode of *Don Quixote*." *PMLA* 89:64-76.
In his celebrated quasi-bucolic episode of the first part of *Don Quixote*, Cervantes mocks and parodies the old school of the

Frauendienst, even as he levels his irony against a chivalric ideal that had come under increasing scorn since at least the end of the 15th century. Various elements are blended to achieve his story. Grisóstomo's suicide turns out to be incontrovertible as well as illustrative of the essentially Petrarchan although parodical character of the famous poem "La canión desesperada," while the generally bucolic although mixed and burlesque quality of the entire episode issues straight from a central theme of the Renaissance pastoral, the whole matter of man's freedom. The very term "canción desesperada," and probably other features of the long poem in Ch. xiv, derive directly from a 16th-century bucolic poet and fervent Petrarchist, Gutierre de Cetina. (HI)

Lazarillo de Tormes. 6996. Abrams, Fred. "Hurtado de Mendoza's Concealed Signatures in the *Lazarillo de Tormes*." *RomN* 15(1973):341-45.
For the past four hundred years since the publication of the anonymous *Lazarillo de Tormes* in 1554, the identity of the author has continued to perplex scholars. No attempt has yet been made to discover the author's identity through a cryptographic analysis of the text. The candidacy of Hurtado de Mendoza, ambassador to Carlos v, has always received strong support. Mendoza had some knowledge of cryptography as is evidenced by his use of ciphers in his diplomatic correspondence. Analysis of the initial sentence of the first *Tratado* reveals the presence of Mendoza's name and two of his pseudonyms "Danteo" and "Andrea." Either the presence of the concealed name and pseudonyms is purely coincidental; or, more plausibly, given his obsession with anonymity and his acquaintance with cryptography, Mendoza is indeed the author of the *Lazarillo*. (FA)

León. 7009. Kouvel, Audrey L. "Fray Luis de León's Haven:A Study in Structural Analysis." *MLN* 89:146-58.
Fray Luis de León's ode "Al apartamiento" is a structure of 13 stanzas divided into 2 symmetrical sections linked by a transitional stanza. The "mountain" metaphor of the first section is contrasted with the "sea" metaphor of the second; the concluding stanza echoes the opening one with slight variations. The poem represents two views of the poet's state: the inner will-directed struggle and the outer inevitable disaster. In the poem they are mirror images of each other and the imaginatively desired "haven" is the symbolic link. (ALK)

Mira de Amescua. 7014. Brown, Sandra L. "A Reconsideration of the Authorship of the *Don Alvaro de Luna* Plays." *Hispania* 57:422-27.
The irony inherent in Tirso's statement about the authorship of the plays in his *Segunda parte* (1635) has often been overlooked. In spite of the fact that humor is a hallmark of his literary style, Tirso's remark has been interpreted literally, in which case he is seen as the bogus author of eight of the twelve plays, including the two *Don Alvaro de Luna* plays. In recent years Mira de Amescua has received more notoriety than Tirso for the authorship of *Don Alvaro de Luna*. However, Mira's claim rests on grounds that are not altogether sound; in particular, the manuscripts ascribed to him are not positively trustworthy. On the basis of textual analysis, Tirso's right to the plays cannot be ruled out. The versification is normal for him, while the plot construction and characterization are not atypical. Moreover, the dramatization of the historical period of Alvaro de Luna as well as the reworking of scenes from Salustrio del Poyo, a lesser Golden Age dramatist, are not without precedent in his works. At the present time, the argument for Tirso's authorship of *Don Alvaro de Luna* cannot be categorically discounted. (SLB)
7015. Gregg, Karl C. "A Brief Biography of Antonio Mira de Amescua." *BCom* 26:14-22.
A summation of documentary information about the life of Antonio Mira de Amescua, in as clear a chronological sequence as possible, with minimal commentary or conjecture, is presented. The data indicate that Mira's literary productivity occurs between 1596 and 1632 and that he participated actively in intellectual circles during this span to the apparent detriment of his ecclesiastical career. (KCG)

Monroy y Silva. 7018. Ebersole, Alva V. "Nota sobre una obra de Cristóbal de Monroy y Silva (*Las mocedades del duque de Osuna*)." *RomN* 15(1973):314-17.
In *Las mocedades del Duque de Osuna* Cristóbal de Monroy y Silva (1612-49) presents one of the well-known gay blades of his own time, the Duque de Osuna, whose youth was more scandalous than the few scabrous episodes told in the play. The future Viceroy of Sicily and Naples is presented as a man amongst men whose practical jokes, once accomplished, were compensated for by payment to the unhappy victims. While attending a performance of a French play that mocks the arrogance of the Spanish king, the young Duke jumps on stage and interrupts the play. Condemned to die, he and his men are saved when he writes the king of France, his cousin, identifying himself as a *grande de España*. As a historical sidelight to the probable time of the first performance of the play, we note that the Duque de Osuna, who died in 1624, had at one time incurred the displeasure of the Conde-Duque de Olivares, so we can assume that the play could not have been presented until the fall from power of the Conde-Duque in 1643. (AVE)

Ruiz de Alarcón. 7035. Morton, John G. 'Alarcón's *La verdad sospechosa*:Meaning and Didacticism." *BCom* 26:51-57.
Critics and students of Ruiz de Alarcón's *La verdad sospechosa* have tended to focus attention on the frustrated liar motif and see punishment of the liar as crucial for understanding the play. The function of human reason in the passage from youth to maturity as understood through careful attention to motifs of youth, education, and innocence and through attention to a central thematic metaphor is a second important theme. Evidence in the play suggests that punishment is key neither to its meaning nor to its didactic thrust. While the crime-punishment pattern shapes the incidents, the play's resolution suggests the protagonist's successful passage to maturity. (JGM)
7036. Parr, James A. "Honor-Virtue in *La verdad sospechosa* and *Las paredes oyen*." *REH* 8:173-88.
Alarcón's presentation of "honor-virtue" emphasizes the Stoic-Christian ideal of self-mastery. Only those who have achieved a nobility based on self-discipline possess honor in the sense of moral worth. Both Don García of *La verdad sospechosa* and Don Mendo of *Las paredes oyen* lack nobility, and therefore honor, because of a lack of self-control. Their excesses are viewed as the effects of a common cause—a lack of self-discipline. The theme of appearance and reality facilitates exploration of the dichotomy between public and private honor. (JAP)

Salazar y Torres. 7040. O'Connor, Thomas A. "On the Authorship of *El encanto es la hermosura*:A Curious Case of Dramatic Collaboration." *BCom* 26:31-34. [S and Vera Tassis.]
Salazar y Torres died before he could complete his *El encanto es la hermosura*. Juan de Vera Tassis y Villarroel completed the play on orders from Carlos II or Mariana de Austria. An anonymous author, dissatisfied with Vera's conclusion, gave it a somewhat different ending, yet based on Vera's version. This anonymous variant was called *La segunda Celestina*, and until the 19th century editors had maintained distinct titles for the different versions. In the past century bibliophiles furnished conflicting information on the play. Mesonero Romanos, basing his criticism on original texts, stated clearly the evidence concerning Salazar's play and the variant endings. In the 19th century Dionisio Solís (1774-1834) adapted Salazar's play on Celestina, which indicates the play's perennial appeal. (TO'C)
7041. —— "The Curious Ending of *Elegir al enemigo*." *RomN* 15(1973):318-22.
At the conclusion of Salazar y Torres' *Elegir al enemigo*, Nise raises a discordant note when betrothed to Astolfo. She is punished through poetic justice for her deceptions and deceits; but Salazar is also intimating some concern, although ironically, about the *comedia*'s conventional marriages, which are supposed to restore social harmony. Her unharmonious protestation jars our senses and reminds us of the gulf that exists between the real world and that of art. (TAO)

Sánchez de Badajoz. 7043. McCready, Warren T. "Un verso de *La farsa moral* de Diego Sánchez." *BCom* 26:12-13.
The verse "Tempra.for:pru:for:justicia" (1160 in Weber de Kurlat's edition of the unique copy of the works of Sánchez de Badajoz) has not been correctly interpreted. The verse, spoken by Nequicia and consisting of the eight syllables required by the *redondilla* verse form, must be read literally. The context supports the assumption that Nequicia attempts to address the other characters by name (Tempranza, Prudencia, Fortaleza) but is cut off by their turning away. The form "pru" in the list of errata should probably replace the second "for" in the verse. (WTM)

Sepúlveda. 7047. Hathaway, Robert L. "The Serious Nature of Comedy:The *Comedia de Sepúlveda*." *BCom* 26:57-63.
The *Comedia de Sepúlveda*, presumably by Lorenzo de Sepúlveda, reflects seriously on love, honor, and beauty. This is considered unique at a time when intricate plots were only the vehicle for bawdy humor. But such humor exists in *Sepúlveda*; sexual imbroglios serve as Plautine counterpoint to the central love-honor conflicts. The playwright consciously chose the opening scenes to expound on the foolhardiness of amorous impetuosity, the misinterpretation of virtues inherent in feminine beauty, and struggles between filial duty and love's inclination, all pertinent to the theme of male culpability. Sepúlveda's technique argues that the play was written to be performed. (RLH)

Tirso de Molina. 7053. Brown, Sandra L. "Lucifer and *El burlador de Sevilla*." *BCom* 26:63-64.
In Tirso de Molina's *El burlador de Sevilla* Don Juan Tenorio stands out as a social counterpart to the biblical figure Lucifer. Don Juan is guilty of insubordination against God and society. As was the case with Lucifer, overweening pride is the cause of his downfall. The characterization of Don Juan as an arrogant and deceitful soul as well as the imagery associated with him link the *burlador* with the devil. (SLB)

7054. Cabrera, Vicente. "Doña Ana's Seduction in *El burlador de Sevilla*." *BCom* 26:49-51.
Upon confronting the ghost of Don Gonzalo in Tirso de Molina's *Burlador*, Don Juan says, "a tu hija no ofendi / que mio mis engaños antes." These words have been used to prove that he didn't seduce Doña Ana. This is erroneous because of his critical situation when saying the words and his treacherous nature. He must continue relying on his tendency to lie so that his final fall will have greater moral impact. Doña Ana's seduction contributes to the formal unity of the play by maintaining the consistency of Don Juan's personality and behavior, thus maximizing the effect of his only failure and reinforcing poetic justice. (VC)

7057. Fernández, Xavier A. "La pretendida caballerosidad de don Juan:Apostilla a un estudio de Charles V. Aubrun." *RomN* 15:564-66.
According to Aubrun, Don Juan acted like a gentleman in defense of Duchess Isabella when her life was threatened by the Spanish Ambassador. Unfortunately, the attribution of this noble trait to Don Juan is based on a spurious text of *El Burlador*, as edited by MacCurdy. (XAF)

7066. Sullivan, Henry W. "Was Gaspar Lucas Hidalgo the Godfather of Tirso de Molina?" *BCom* 26:5-11.
Seeks to establish a connection between Tirso de Molina and Gaspar Lucas Hidalgo, author of *Diálogos de apacible entretenimiento*. A Gaspar Ydalgo appears as the godfather of "Gabriel . . . hijo de padre incógnito" of the controversial San Ginés baptismal certificate advanced by Doña Blanca de los Ríos as the playwright's. Apart from coincidences of name, there are four facts that seem to link the two writers: a) the tripartite structure of Tirso's *Deleitar aprovechando* (1635), based ultimately on Hidalgo's *Diálogos*; b) Hierónymo Margarit of Barcelona printed the fourth edition of the *Diálogos* (1609) and the second edition of Tirso's *Cigarrales de Toledo* (1631); c) the satire of a poet-priest in the *Diálogos* (pt. I, Ch. iii); d) a cryptic pun in *La mujer por fuerza* (II,iv). (HWS)

Vega, Lope de. 7075. Case, Thomas E. "Seville and Lope's *Parte* Dedications." *BCom* 26:65-68.
Lope de Vega always expressed a fondness for Seville, a city he frequented in 1600-04. Years later, 1620-25, he dedicated a large number of plays to Sevillians, in *Partes XIII-XX*. In the dedication of *La hermosa Ester*, he mentions an early stay in Seville with his uncle, Miguel del Carpio. Recently, correspondence between Lope and a literary group in Seville seems to confirm his childhood and early schooling there. (TEC)

7077. Exum, Frances. "Lope's King Pedro:The Divine Right of Kings vs. the Right of Resistance." *Hispania* 57:428-33.
Lope de Vega's dramatic treatment of King Pedro I de Castilla reveals the medieval right to resistance of a people against a tyrannical ruler. In the *Audiencias del rey don Pedro, Ya anda la de Mazagatos, El médico de su honra, La carbonera*, and *El rey don Pedro en Madrid*, Lope invests his 14th-century king with the divine aura which later surrounded Spanish Hapsburg rulers. In *Los Ramirez de Arellano* he illustrates a political principle more pertinent to the historical reality of medieval Spain. Lope is careful to show that the Castilian people's support of Enrique's action is the will of God. (FBE)

V. EIGHTEENTH AND NINETEENTH CENTURIES

General and Miscellaneous. 7113. Hafter, Monroe Z. "The Spanish Version of Scott's *Don Roderick*." *SIR* 13:225-34.
The Vision of Don Roderick was translated (1829) because of Scott's prestige and his having tied the medieval Spanish success over the Moorish conquerors of the Visigothic monarchy to the popular revolt against Napoleon's invasion. The translator, Agustín Aicart, felt constrained to transform Scott's sharp attacks on Spain's religious fanaticism, hypocrisy, and cruelty into praise for her Christian virtues, and to shift Scott's disdain for Carlos IV on to Manuel Godoy. The broadly liberal original is thereby changed into a defense of altar and throne, characteristic of the conservative pattern of Spanish Romanticism during the period of Fernandine absolution. (MZH)

Prose Fiction. 7122. Goldman, Peter B. "Toward a Sociology of the Modern Spanish Novel:The Early Years." *MLN* 89:173-90. [First of two parts:1840-1900.]
The need for criticism to consider the extra-literary aspects of creativity and production is a fact which scholars are increasingly recognizing. Knowing whom the novel serves aids in the comprehension of the values and, ultimately, the esthetics which motivate and shape its creation. Of particular interest to Hispanists are the circumstances surrounding the rebirth of the novel in Spain. In the early 19th century the novel was disseminated by means of serial publication, often as a weekly adjunct of a periodical. The concept of the novel as the diversion of the poor is erroneous. Members of the newly forming middle class, whose jobs depended on functional literacy, i.e., the ability to read documents intelligently, were the principal reading public. (PBG)

Bécquer. 7139. Stuyvesant, Phillip W. "La búsqueda como símbolo de unidad en las obras de G.A. Bécquer." *REH* 8:300-12.
Bécquer's imaginative works reveal unity of purpose and expression in and between his poetry and prose. Three major phases are distinguished in the Bécquerian adventure: the call, the tests, and the defeat. The poet's call emanates from his need to give form to the vague sensations that tantalize his sensitivies. The narrative protagonist is also drawn to his adventure by undeniable circumstances. The poet's test is the frustrating quest for concise expression. The adventurer faces certain enigmatic situations that reappear throughout the "Leyendas." The failure of the poet and the protagonist to succeed marks man's limitations and illustrates the heroic aspects of mankind. (PWS)

Clarín. 7161. Lott, Robert C. "El estilo directo libre en *La Regenta*." *RomN* 15(1973):259-63.
Leopoldo Alas was aware of the presence in Galdós of the

naturalistic, Zolaesque style feature of free indirect style. In *La Regenta*, Alas used this essentially ironic-mimetic device in four ways: the ironical-critical blending of the author's narrative style and the characters' thoughts and words, the use of many words and phrases in italics to emphasize the characters' speech mannerisms, the reporting of real or imagined dialogues, and the psychologically revelatory, often dramatic, flashbacks. (REL)

Galdós. 7176. Bly, P.A. "The Use of Distance in Galdós's *La de Bringas*." *MLR* 69:88-97.
Pérez Galdós' *novelas contemporáneas* are generally regarded as accurate pictures of Madrid life. But in *La de Bringas* he deliberately distorts the perspective of his physical world. The Madrid Royal Palace, principal location for most of the novel, is viewed from unnaturally close or distant angles. The city of Madrid outside the Royal compound is summarily ignored in the first half of the novel, while detailed descriptions of locals suddenly abound toward the end. Other places in Spain or abroad are viewed exclusively from the epicentre of the Royal Palace. The aim of these unbalanced, abnormal physical perspectives seems to be to call the reader's attention to the absurd and sordid nature of the characters' lives, their actions, and their dwellings. Galdós' vision and technique come very close to those subsequently displayed by Valle-Inclán in his *esperpento* writings. (PAB)
7188. Durand, Frank. "The Reality of Illusion:*La desheredada*." *MLN* 89:191-201.
La desheredada by Galdós paves the way for his interest in the role of imagination and illusion. The fluctuating movement from reality to unreality begins with the opening scene of the novel which takes place in an insane asylum. The relationship between the insane asylum and the real world sets the stage for the protagonist's future actions. Illusions have a double significance for Galdós: they represent a subterranean world of interest to the realist, a basis from which to comment on the structure of society. By having his characters read romantic literature, Galdós extends his view of reality to include the illusions of his characters. (FD)
7192. Fedorchek, Robert M. "Social Reprehension in *La desheredada*." *REH* 8:43-59.
Forceful criticism of shortcomings in Spanish society is one of the dominant notes of Pérez Galdós' *La desheredada*, Public institutions are a failure because there is no genuine concern for human needs; when confronted with acute problems, Madrid officials decry the evils of the day with empty rhetoric. Galdós' use of irony and satire is superb when exposing the hollow bombast of their oratory and how their official indignation comes to naught after the knifing by Mariano Rufete. Personal failings are encompassed by the attitudes of *parecer* and *aparentar*, the desire to simulate well-being. Appearances are the foremost consideration in life for many individuals and illusions are substitutions for realities. (RMF)
7200. Hoar, Leo S.,Jr. "Benito Pérez Galdós and May Day, 1907." *RomN* 15(1973):238-45.
Benito Pérez Galdós' newspaper article "El 1º de Mayo" is only one of many articles or speeches of a political-social nature which the novelist produced at the outset of a new, more active political career as a *diputado* (1907-13). This piece has an even greater significance in connection with Galdós' creative process: it is an inspirational departure point for similar themes of social betterment presented with greater scope in his subsequent major works, mainly *novelas contemporáneas*, and also demonstrates further the dependence of the latter upon the former. (LJH)
7218. Willey, Jack R. "Guillermo Bruno:Una creación galdosiana." [F 19]:189-92.
Via a minute examination of the scant details provided by the dramatist for the reader in *Amor y ciencia*, Guillermo Bruno is presented as a literary creation. Wiley reveals the ways and methods selected by Pérez Galdós to give life to Bruno in order to make him a living personage. (JRW)

Hartzenbusch. 7222. Curry, Richard A. "Dramatic Tension and Emotional Control in *Los amantes de Teruel*." *WVUPP* 21:36-47.
Hartzenbusch faced a difficult literary problem as he penned his *Los amantes de Teruel* in 1837. How could he interest the Spanish public in still another dramatic version of the well-known legend of the Teruel lovers? Hartzenbusch includes additional secondary plot strands and new minor characters, all of which are integrated into the primary conflict and its resolution. Numerous temporal, spatial, and expository structural manipulations occur, especially those that promote tension or audience uncertainty. Frequent concise summaries of previously staged emotional confrontations force the spectator, especially toward the conclusion, to actively recall all of the play's tensions while even more accrue. Finally, a sonorous poetic language full of highly charged rhyme and hyperbaton promotes the involvement of the spectator's senses rather than his intellect. The diction functions to the same end as it includes abundant animal imagery and references to violence. (RAC)

Pardo Bazán. 7248. Schmidt, Ruth A. "Woman's Place in the Sun:Feminism in *Insolación*." *REH* 8:69-81.
Emilia Pardo Bazán's short novel *Insolación* reveals the feminist commitment of the author by a variety of artistic means. Gabriel Pardo, mouthpiece for the author in other novels as well, here is the chief vehicle for the expression of Pardo Bazán's belief that women should enjoy equality with men in 19th-century Spanish society. The reactions of the protagonist, Taboada Asís, and other characters, as well as their speech and actions make clear that *Insolación* is more than a charming love story. (RAS)

Rivas. 7255. Perri, Dennis. "Note on the Sources of 'El Alcázar de Sevilla'." *RomN* 15:556-59.
In "El Alcázar de Sevilla" the Duke de Rivas employs specific literary models to produce an original artistic unity. From the various versions of the murder of Fadrique, el maestre de Santiago, Rivas selects the elements most useful to his poetic intentions. The Duke seeks to depict the terrifying cruelty and insensitivity of Pedro I. The deviations from his basic model (Pedro López de Ayala's *Crónica de don Pedro el Primero*), underscore Pedro's vicious nature. Noteworthy are the modifications of the murder scene to produce a verbal image of senseless violence. The abrupt conclusion leaves the reader with a vision of Pedro's cruel indifference to human life. Rivas reflects the ability to mold his material according to his own artistic design. (DP)

Tamayo y Baus. 7259. Lassaletta, Manuel C. "*Un drama nuevo* y el realismo literario." *Hispania* 57:856-67.
The most characteristic features of Tamayo's *Un drama nuevo* (1867) reflect the mentality of realism. The theme of the drama—the coincidence of art and life—exemplifies the aim of realistic literature. This identification is revealed many times, besides the well known occurrences in the final scenes, when the role of the actors coincides with their problems as private individuals. Art and life superimpose themselves not only in the outward dramatic events, but even in the characters' inner emotions and in the events which took place before the raising of the curtain. (MCL)

Torres Villarroel. 7262. Suárez-Galbán, Eugenio. "Torres Villarroel y los *Yo* empíricos de William James." *RomN* 15(1973):274-77.
In his autobiography (1743-58), Torres Villarroel sees and divides the selves in much the same way as William James in *The Principles of Psychology* (1890). Like James, Torres interprets the empirical selves as material, social, and spiritual, as can be observed from Torres' self-analysis. (ES-G)

Valera. 7269. Quirk, Ronald J. "The Authorship of 'La gruta azul':Juan Valera or Serafín Estébanez Calderón?" *RomN* 15:560-63.
"La gruta azul y una jira en el vapor 'Colón'" is a short prose description of a day's outing on the Bay of Naples by Spanish officials and their guests. The Madrid newspaper *El Heraldo* published this account on 12 October 1849, and it was signed with the pseudonym "Silvio Silvis de la Selva." Manuel Azaña declared that Juan Valera wrote the essay, but Antonio Cánovas del Castillo and Jorge Campos have maintained that Serafín

Estébanez Calderón did. Information contained in a letter from Valera to Estébanez resolves this authorship problem in favor of

Estébanez. Moreover, Valera may have adopted the pseudonym "Silvio Silvis de la Selva" from Estébanez. (RJQ)

VI. TWENTIETH CENTURY

General and Miscellaneous. 7285. Romero, Héctor R. "La generación del medio siglo:Postulados y tendencias." *RLV* 40:371-74.
The Spanish writers of the 1950s can be studied as members of a generation. They all have the same attitude regarding the past, present, and future of Spain. Their themes deal with the social injustices of their time. They also turn to the style of French objectivism and American behaviorism. All these different techniques appear filtered through their own poetic nature giving us an objective novel influenced by the subjectivity and lyric temperament of the authors. (HRR)

7288. Vance, Birgitta. "The Great Clash:Feminist Criticism Meets Up With Spanish Reality." *JSSTC* 2:109-14.
While it is true, as many feminists maintain, that writers help to form society's attitudes in addition to simply reflecting them, it is *kunstwidrig* to demand from an author that, in a realistic work simply depicting the status quo, he falsify reality in order to better serve the Women's Movement. It is necessary to distinguish between those who distort reality in order to perpetuate the subjection of women and those who simply reflect it. In a recent article, Patricia O'Connor criticizes the depiction of Plinio, Spain's famous fictional detective, as anachronistic in his attitudes toward women. His attitude is simply that of the *machismo* rampant in all of Spanish society and excellently exemplified in the figure of Gregorio in *Nuevas amistades* (1961) by Juan García Hortelano. (BV)

Themes. 7305. Litvak, Lily. "La sociología criminal y su influencia en los escritores españoles de fin de siglo." *RLC* 48:12-32.
Studies the influence of the Italian criminalist school (Lombroso, Garofalo, Ferri) upon Spanish thinking at the end of the 19th century. Examines translations and studies published by the Spanish reviews on Italian criminology. Presents the original work of the Spanish criminalists and the influence of their doctrines on Spanish literature—especially in the works of writers such as Pardo Bazán, Unamuno, Baroja, Maragall, and, above all, Azorín. The debate concerning capital punishment is examined. (LL)

Baroja, Pío. 7400. Litvak, Lily. "Baroja y el medievalismo finisecular." *RLV* 40:269-82.
Traces the renewed attraction to the Middle Ages in Spain at the turn of the century and discusses the influence of these ideas in art, architecture, and literature. Focuses on the influence of the English Pre-Raphaelites in the medieval revival. The impact of the neomedievalist fashion on Pío Baroja is studied. His attraction to the Primitives, to the Pre-Raphaelites, his concern about the reconstruction of ancient buildings, and especially his conception of medieval architecture as an artistic and social ideal are discussed. (LL)

Benavente. 7409. Dial, John E. "Benavente:The Dramatist on Stage." *REH* 8:211-18.
Jacinto Benavente's concerns, prejudices, and preoccupations about the state of dramatic art find their way into his dramas of backstage life. Not all of his dramatists are capable of expounding intelligently on dramaturgy, nor were all meant to voice Benavente's ideas. Some dramatists, however, such as the one in *La vida en verso* (1951), do seem to be spokesmen for Benavente. Like their creator they are frequently witty, at times contradictory and elusive. Benavente is revealed as an artist with a deep personal attachment to the fantasy of drama who was endlessly fascinated by the mystique of the theater. (JED)

Bousoño. 7414. Predmore, Michael P. "*Teoría de la expresión poética* and Twentieth Century Spanish Lyric Poetry." *MLN* 89:202-18.

Several key assumptions and procedures of Bousoño are challenged: his principle of universality does not take into account the modern phenomenon of private poetry; his sense of the relative autonomy of the poem ignores the vital dependence of the individual poem upon the symbolic system of which it forms a part; and, in particular, his concentration upon an analysis of the single poem excludes the investigation of clusters of recurring images throughout a system of poems. One must look elsewhere, then, for an understanding of recurring imagery, private symbolism, and organic unity. (MPP)

Buero Vallejo. 7417. Brown, Kenneth. "The Significance of Insanity in Four Plays by Antonio Buero Vallejo." *REH* 8:247-60.
Eloy, in *Mito*; Goya, in *El sueño de la razón*; Irene, in *Irene o el tesoro*; and the Father, in *El tragaluz*, are characterized as mentally unsound, and judged insane. The requisites of insane actions—that they be "mad, idiotic, utterly senseless, and irrational"—are not at all fulfilled. Buero Vallejo's protagonists are much more than mere victims of mental disease. Eloy, Goya, Irene, and the Father express truth and hope under the guise of insanity. The denial of reality—the titles and subtitles play down the actuality of the events in the works—gives vent to an affirmation of unreality; the factuality of sanity is denied while the truth of insanity is affirmed. (KB)

Calvo-Sotelo. 7425. Poyatos, María B. "*La muralla* de Calvo Sotelo, auto de psicología freudiana." *Hispania* 57:31-39.
Demonstrates an unpremeditated symbolism in Calvo-Sotelo's *La muralla*. As in an Auto Sacramental, where metaphysical concepts are personalized, we see here a psychological auto, each basic Freudian category embodied in one of the characters. On these bases the play is considered as a single psyche whose mechanism can be seen functioning. We witness a moment of crisis in the struggle between the super-ego (Jorge, protagonist) and the unconscious (other characters), with the ego (Jorge's wife) in the middle. The super-ego, weakened by a trauma (theft), and burdened by a guilt complex when the traumatic experience is revived (heart attack), chooses his own destruction (restitution) to escape anxiety (terror of condemnation), but he encounters the instincts' strong opposition, finally supported by the ego, which causes his total collapse (Jorge's death). Jorge's implied redemption is consistent with Poyatos' conclusion, since the super-ego also attains redemption when—as a consequence of his collapse —it ceases to be responsible. (MBP)

Casona. 7427. King, S. Carl. "Symbolic Use of Color in Casona's *La sirena varada*." *RomN* 15(1973):226-29.
Demonstrates the effective use of color by Alejandro Casona in *La sirena varada*. Symbolic colors in this play are used as a parallel to the development of the thematic material. As the play develops the lighting changes from the initial red and green, symbolic of the pole of fantasy, to a clear white light at the end, symbolic of reason. A parallel to this use of light is found in the character of Sirena who imagines herself both blue and white, symbolic of fantasy and reason. The tension created by the conflict of these antagonistic colors causes dramatic tension. Consistent with Casona's philosophy that reality must be accepted the play ends with the dominance of the white light of reason and Sirena's necessary return to a real world. (SCK)

Cela. 7440. Busette, Cedric. "*La familia de Pascual Duarte* and the Prominence of Fate." *REH* 8:61-67.
A strongly deterministic vision of life permeates Camilo José Cela's *La familia de Pascual Duarte*. It manifests itself in the manner in which Pascual perceives himself, his life, and the roots of the disharmony between self and environment. His self-concepts are also confirmed, through the same vision of life, by the opinion of those around him. Biological and social inheritance

combine with potent fate to limit his possibilities and frustrate his efforts at self-reform. Imagery and symbolism reinforce this pessimistic outlook, providing a unified vision of life as subverting man's efforts to achieve inner security and self-improvement. (CUB)

Fernández Flórez, W. 7462. Zaetta, Robert. "Wenceslao Fernández Flórez' Comic Technique in *El sistema Pelegrín*." *RomN* 15(1973):234-37.
Toward the end of his career, Wenceslao Fernández Flórez focused his satire upon man's lack of common sense, his flightiness, and his frivolity. The basic comic technique that he employs is called by Bergson "interférence des series" and involves two series of events which come into rational conflict. Throughout the novel *El sistema Pelegrín* we are aware of Pelegrín's double role of charlatan and teacher. The comic occurs each time the roles of teacher and charlatan overlap. Fernández Flórez creates comic absurdity by making the illogical appear logical, heaping nonsense upon nonsense, and making a great to do about vanity. (RZ)

García Lorca. 7472. Baumgarten, Murray. " 'Body's Image': *Yerma, The Player Queen*, and the Upright Posture." *CompD* 8:290-99.
Both Lorca and Yeats seek to renew their respective national cultures by creating a poetic theater with its roots in legend and myth. Their plays raise fundamental questions about the human condition. In both *The Player Queen* and *Yerma* the image of the body and the theme of the upright posture expresses a philosophical anthropology. The theatrical dialectic in both plays emerges from the tension of player, role, posture, and posturing. In *The Player Queen* the ambivalence of the upright posture is transformed into the potential strength of human nature and cultural renewal. In *Yerma* the upright posture is counterpointed against the structure of human barrenness, which is revealed as the inability to choose human renewal. (MB)

7487. Jiménez-Vera, Arturo. "Violence in *La casa de Bernarda Alba*." *RLMC* 27:45-49.
In García Lorca's *La casa de Bernarda Alba*, violence first appears after the mother confines her daughters to their home for an 8-year period of mourning. The disruptive action occurs on two levels: among the sisters due to their hunger for men; and between the daughters and their mother because of their desire for freedom. (AJ-V)

7511. Young, Ann Venture. " 'La Pena' as the Protagonist of García Lorca's *Romancero gitano*." *CLAJ* 17:407-16.
Federico García Lorca often hesitated or even refused to play the role of the interpreter of his poetic creations. His comments on the meaning of the ballads which comprise the *Romancero gitano* point the way to a fuller understanding of the complex nature of these poems. Lorca suggests that the protagonist of the "romances" is not the gypsy so much as it is the "pena andaluza" which surrounds and mystifies the gypsy. Given García Lorca's affection for all the oppressed peoples of the world, it becomes fairly obvious that the "pena" to which he refers transcends racial and regional limitations and finds in the gypsy's existence a faithful reflection of the misery of the poor of all races and all times for whom suffering is an inescapable reality. (AVY)

Gironella. 7513. Dial, John E. "Gironella's Chronicles Revisited:A Panorama of Fratricide." *PLL* 10:98-110. [Rev. art.]
José María Gironella's *Condenados a vivir* might be looked upon as a review of future *episodios*. When Gironella began his project, he believed that only a massive work of fiction could express the reality of Spain's Civil War. The project has become an ongoing series of chronicles depicting every phase of Spanish life. In depicting Spain's fratricidal conflict, its prelude, and its aftermath, Gironella is dealing with emotionally charged issues, and both the right and the left have attacked him. Throughout he has maintained the posture of a novelist who is at least a reporter who tries to be fair. (JED)

7514. Ilie, Paul. "Fictive History in Gironella." *JSSTC* 2:77-94.
Gironella's *Los cipreses creen en Dios* and *Un millón de muertes*

raise the question of what degree of freedom a novelist enjoys in fictionalizing history while still retaining claim over the historical accuracy of his fiction. Gironella ignores the rational quality of historiographical presentation—its search for causality. Instead he substitutes anthropological concepts to explain the Civil War. These reactionary explanations obscure the political and economic reasons behind the War and behind the situations fictionalized in the novels. Gironella's practices lead the observer to conclude that the novels do not reflect the historical world to any significant degree. On the contrary, they create a fictive history which lacks much of the accuracy found in historical fiction because it is based upon irrational explanations instead of political or social cause-and-effect. (PI)

Goytisolo, Juan. 7520. Anderson, Reed. "*Señas de identidad*: Chronicle of Rebellion." *JSSTC* 2:3-19.
Goytisolo's *Señas de identidad* is the product of the narrator's crisis of identity. The narrator refers to himself in the past only as "you" (tú) or "he" (él or Alvaro), never as "I." His crisis can be understood by analyzing the two facets of his personality and experience suggested by these two perspectives. The contradictions between his background as heir to the values of Spain's old bourgeoisie and his efforts to align himself with radical and progressive social and political causes comprises the critical tensions in his search for a coherent sense of identity. While a final integration of the two facets of the narrator's subjective personality is suggested at the end, his final aggressive rebellion is individualistic and alienated rather than integrated on the level of collective political or social struggle. (RA)

7529. Romero, Héctor R. "Los mitos de la España sagrada en *Reivindicación del Conde don Julián*." *JSSTC* 1(1973):169-85.
The creative process followed by Goytisolo in *Reivindicación del Conde don Julián* may be described as destructive-constructive. Through an innovative and experimental use of the language, he launches a bitter attack against all the myths and fallacies that Spanish conservatism has helped to perpetuate as part of a false national image. Only by the complete annihilation of the narrative style, themes and cultural myths of the Spanish literary heritage, can Goytisolo succeed in creating a new text that may be interpreted in different ways and at different levels. This linguistic experimentation marks a new period in the narrative evolution of Juan Goytisolo, and makes this novel one of the richest and most difficult of contemporary Spain. (HRR)

Muñiz, Carlos. 7605. Donahue, Francis. "Carlos Muñiz and the Expressionist Imagination." *RomN* 15(1973):230-33.
The protagonist in Muñiz' farce *El tintero* (1961) confronts the "Bosses" in the office, who as antagonists represent authoritarianism in Spanish society of the early 1960s. The protagonist is termed a rebel, for good reason: he doesn't talk about football or women in the office, he keeps flowers on his desk, and has even been known to sing at work. The "Bosses," in attacking this menace, employ clown-like aides who, in brandishing mammoth fountain pens like sabers, chant "One must obey, one must conform, one must be silent, one must smile." Muñiz eschews psychological verisimilitude in character delineation, engages in puppet-like exaggeration, and, instead of the German expressionist's full-throated "Schrei" of social indignation, he is limited to an implied "Schrei" due to threat of censorship. (FD)

Ortega y Gasset. 7614. Orringer, Nelson R. "Esthetic Enjoyment in Ortega y Gasset and in Geiger, a Newly Discovered Source." *RLC* 48:33-56.
Geiger's theories of esthetic enjoyment had profound impact upon Ortega's major writings on art. For both thinkers, delight in beauty calls for disinterested contemplation of the enjoyed object in its fullness. Ortega, however, carves away from Geiger's ideas all references to self-consciousness and to the suspension of metaphysical judgments in contemplating art. Such omissions offer new evidence that Ortega achieves a phenomenology of human existence before all other philosophers. Ortega systematically extends Geiger's theories to the creative process in the arts. (NRO)

Sastre. 7640. Donahue, Francis. "Alfonso Sastre and Dialectical Realism." *ArQ* 29:197-213.

Alfonso Sastre heralds tragedy as an instrument to revolutionize Spanish bourgeois, neocapitalist society in the direction of humanitarian socialism. To that end, Sastre, in a series of works on dramatic theory—*Drama y sociedad* (1956), *Anatomía del realismo* (1965), and *La revolución y la crítica de la cultura* (1970)—has moved from adherence to Aristotle's "dramatic" tragedy to acceptance of Bertolt Brecht's dialectical negation of Aristotle, and on to his own dialectical negation of Brecht, culminating in Sastre's contemporary "poetics" for a revolutionary theater, Dialectical Realism, an esthetic-ideological scaffolding on which a new type of drama may be erected. This new drama, the adumbrated materialization on stage of the tenets of Dialectical Realism, is termed "Complex Tragedy." To date, two works fall under the rubic of "Complex Tragedy": Peter Weiss's *Marat/Sade* and Sastre's *La sangre y la ceniza*. In applying his dramatic theory to the writing of revolutionary theater, Sastre hopes to foster in audiences a commitment to sociopolitical activism and a growing awareness of the dialectical evolution of history toward an inevitable socialist future. (FJD)

7642. Seator, Lynette. "Alfonso Sastre's 'Homenaje a Kierkegaard':*La sangre de Dios*." *RomN* 15:546-55.

In *La sangre de Dios* Sastre did not follow the basic social orientation typical of his theater but wrote a play dealing primarily with philosophical matters. Yet an examination reveals the work to be more profoundly rooted in a reaction to Kierkegaard's humanity rather than his theology. In spite of the fact that *Sangre* is a modern day presentation of the story of Abraham and Isaac, implicit and of prime importance is Sastre's concern with man's need for human love. (LS)

Sender. 7647. Henn, David. "The Priest in Sender's *Réquiem por un campesino español*." *IFR* 1:106-11.

Sender's *Réquiem por un campesino español* is frequently regarded as a general indictment of an anachronistic and unjust social system in rural northern Spain of the 1920s and 1930s. However, more salient and thematically constant in the work is the suggestion of the deficiency of the Spanish Church, epitomized by the village priest, Mosén Millán. Sender gradually exposes and censures the priest and his Church and in so doing indicates his principal objective in the novel. (DFN)

7652. O'Brien, Mary E. "Fantasy in *El fugitivo*." *JSSTC* 2:95-108.

Ramón J. Sender's *El fugitivo* blends vital themes with fantastic reality. *El fugitivo*'s theme of man's freedom struggles in a dialectic with social and ideological commitment on one level and with fate or destiny on a more metaphysical level. The fugitive, Joaquín, enacts the thematic conflict as he flees death, then life, and finally death again. Fantasy acts as a stimulus to the imagination to perceive innumerable ramifications of the novel's theme. Primary elements of fantasy in *El fugitivo* are a pervading air of mystery, poetic incongruity stemming from nonhuman characters, and enlightening symbolism and allegory. The mysteries inherent in fantasy reflect the thematic mysteries, which Sender justifiably never fully resolves. (MEO'B)

Unamuno. 7670. Fiddian, R.W. "Unamuno-Bergson:A Reconsideration." *MLR* 69:787-95.

The theories of *intrahistoria* and *durée* of Unamuno and Bergson can fruitfully be compared and contrasted. Both thinkers postulate the existence of an autonomous cosmic force in which qualitative timelessness transcends the quantitative framework of historical time. But Bergson's dynamic and monistic view of mind and matter as homogeneous activity is at variance with Unamuno's quietist and dualistic interpretation of reality as a combination of opposites such as mobility and stasis, time and eternity. In addition, whereas the two systems accommodate the notions of humanity and God, Unamuno's admission of teleological consciousness, plenitude and transcendence in *intrahistoria* differs from Bergson's immanentist philosophy of *durée* which

denies the purposive faculty of mind, diverges from the conventional idea of God, and sees the temporal structure of the world as open-ended. (RWF)

Valle-Inclán. 7692. Boring, Phyllis Z. "More on Parody in Valle-Inclán." *RomN* 15(1973):246-47.

It is well known that Valle-Inclán utilized parody in his works. Specific episodes in his works parody scenes from Shakespeare or from Spanish literature, notably the Quijote. Two more examples which may be added to the list are the parody of *King Lear* in *Romance de lobos* and of *La Celestina* in *Divinas palabras*. Like the Shakespearian hero, Montenegro of *Romance de lobos* has divided his estate among his children and is left homeless, but Valle-Inclán's protagonist is a burlesque version of a feudal king. The parody of *La Celestina* is presented in two scenes of *Divinas palabras*: the intervention of the go-between in Act III and Pedro Gailo's attempted suicide at the end of the play. (PZB)

7696. Dougherty, Dru. "*Luces de bohemia* and Valle-Inclán's Search for Artistic Adequacy." *JSSTC* 2:61-75.

Max Estrella in Valle-Inclán's *Luces de bohemia* is examined as a fictional surrogate whose situation reflects Valle-Inclán's esthetic crisis following World War I. The writer's awareness that he had to modernize his style or suffer a complete artistic eclipse is objectified in Max's quest for an adequate form. The structure of that search, the development of Max as a character, and the issues dramatized in the first "esperpento" respond to Valle-Inclán's self-scrutiny as an artist in the context of his society. The success of *Luces de bohemia* is its transmutation of personal experience into an autonomous work of art, which, nevertheless, owes certain features to its autobiographical genesis. (DD)

7697. Garlitz, Virginia M. "Teosofismo in *Tirano Banderas*." *JSSTC* 2:21-29.

Roque Cepeda's view of man as prisoner of the infernal circle of time is the key to understanding Valle-Inclán's *Tirano Banderas*. Cepeda believes that salvation can be achieved if man assumes his moral responsibilities and he advocates revolution as one way of doing this; however, the structural and figurative elements of the novel governed by the circle and the magical numbers 3 and 7 indicate that revolution only binds men more tightly to it since man's sinful nature leads him to revolution for selfish rather than higher purposes. Only Roque Cepeda assumes his obligations and thus controls his own destiny while the others find themselves helpless pawns in the game of the stars. The Tyrant's violent death signals the beginning of yet another revolution of the infinite circle of time. (VMG)

7705. Ling, David. "Human Dignity and Passions in Valle-Inclán's *Retablo de la avaricia, la lujuria y la muerte*." *REH* 8:271-300.

Valle-Inclán's *La rosa de papel*, *La cabeza del Bautista*, *Ligazón*, and *Sacrilegio* represent an alternate view to his grim vision of the human condition in the *esperpentos*. If in the latter, he sees his little men as walking marionettes, here, he indicates the way for them to become human beings again. To do so, Valle-Inclán feels that they, who still exist in the spiritual vacuum of an *España negra*, must transcend farce to experience genuine passion. At the same time, the moralist in Valle-Inclán sees his characters' final acts of self-realization in their affirmation of their basic individual worth and human dignity in life and in death. (DL)

7712. Penuel, Arnold M. "Archetypal Patterns in Valle-Inclán's *Divinas palabras*." *REH* 8:83-93.

Valle-Inclán's stylization in *Divinas palabras* does not necessarily present a dehumanized vision of man, but rather a depersonalization of man. Through stylization Valle makes his readers perceive immediately the archetypal patterns of his characters' behavior. In *Divinas palabras*, traditional but inadequate ways of behaving in certain typical situations are replaced by more suitable attitudes and patterns of behavior. This archetypal form of behavior is conserved, but the contents of the archetype change to meet the needs of the expanding consciousness of the characters. (AMP)

PORTUGUESE AND BRAZILIAN LITERATURE†

I. PORTUGUESE LITERATURE

Camões. 7812. Batchelor, C. Malcolm. "Joaquim Nabuco e Camões." *Hispania* 57:246-53.

As ambassador and a major figure in Pan Americanism Joaquin Nabuco (1849-1910) felt compelled to inform American youth of his nation's role in the hemisphere. But more important was his wish to further appreciation and understanding of Camões' poetry. Hence Nabuco's three lectures on Camões. "The Place of Camões in Literature" (Yale, 14 May 1908) dealt primarily with *Os Lusíadas* and consisted of discussion of seven "great impressions"; "Camões, the Lyric Poet" (Vassar, 21 April 1909) stressed the part women had played in the poet's work; "The *Lusíadas* as the Epic of Love" (Cornell, 23 April 1909) analyzed three main factors in the composition of the *Lusíadas*: Camões' life-habit of love, his classical knowledge, and his national ambition. (CMB)

7827. Jones, Roger S. "The Epic Similes of *Os Lusíadas*." *Hispania* 57:239-45.

Camões' *Os Lusíadas* has as its subject the truth of Portuguese history and part of the poem's historical vision is Camões' belief that his nation is the Christian successor of Rome. Vasco da Gama's voyage is the commencement of a confrontation between Moslem barbarism and Portuguese piety and civilization. This confrontation could lead to a second "Augustan" empire of peace and order or to the corruption of Portugal by the power and wealth deriving from that empire. The nature similes of Camões' poem do little more than illustrate and enliven the immediate narrative context, those comparisons drawn from Classical mythology and history are used to measure the achievements and failures of Portugal and her heroes. Heroic figures are likened to mythic and historic heroes and the Moslems to their enemies. Barbarous events and figures are given Classical parallels. Other Classical similes are deliberately incongruous, likening ideal heroes to their barbaric "double." Finally, Jupiter's prophecy of Portuguese success is marked by a thoroughly ambiguous comparison which provides two possibilities for Portugal's future—an empire of order and peace or one of barbaric decadence. (RISJ)

7837. Moser, Gerald M. "Camões' Shipwreck." *Hispania* 57:213-19.

Luís de Camões' mention of his own shipwreck on the coast of Indochina in his epic poem *Os Lusíadas* has, it is suggested, a far-reaching symbolic significance, enhanced by its location in the poem, its conformity with the use of the shipwreck theme in Iberian Golden Age literature, and the parallel with a classical anecdote of Julius Caesar saving himself and the manuscript of his *Commentaries*. (GMM)

7842. Pierce, Frank. "Ancient History in *Os Lusíadas*." *Hispania* 57:220-30.

It has been fully recognized that Camões makes extensive use in his poem of the history of his own country, of pagan mythology, and of the *Aeneid* of Virgil. The many references, however, to ancient history in *Os Lusíadas* have not been studied in any detail. Camões sought ancient credentials for his nation and thus showed particular interest in some of the great figures from Roman history, notably those concerned with the Roman Civil War and subsequent events, as well as the earlier figures of Viriathus and Sertorius whom he regards as forerunners of his country's independence. Camões' use of ancient history takes the form of comparisons and similes. In many cases the comparison favors his own country which he sees as the successor to Rome. Thus the heroes of Portuguese national history are likened to their counterparts in the past. They are seen to be their equals, both in military prowess and heroism as well as in other personal qualities. (FP)

7843. Piper, Anson C. "The Feminine Presence in *Os Lusíadas*." *Hispania* 57:231-38.

Camões' *Os Lusíadas* exalts the two major tenets of chivalry: defense of the Christian faith and the cult of perfect womanhood. Although the poem is mainly concerned with recounting Portuguese history (particularly in the East), the spirit of Renaissance humanism which permeates its ten cantos requires the poet to raise the concept of love to the level of a supreme universal law governing gods, men, and even nature. Female deities play a central role: Venus, as the champion of the Portuguese, rewards them with the Isle of Love; sea nymphs rescue the mariners on various occasions; the episode of Inês de Castro is a lyrical apotheosis of feminine self-sacrifice; and the Twelve of England story illustrates the proper courtly attitude toward virtuous ladies. Women, in short, are portrayed as intellectuals, as seen in Tethys' scholarly discourse (x, 76-142) on the mechanics of the universe and the future greatness of Portugal throughout the world. (ACP)

Maia, Carlos S. 7913. Brown, Timothy, Jr. "Values in Five Plays of Carlos Sampaio Maia." *RomN* 15:536-40.

Carlos Sampaio Maia's *A última batalha, Nem tudo o que luz é ouro, É perigoso caçar borboletas, A flor que fugiu do ramo,* and *A solução final* are discussed. Common to all of these plays is the problem of living and functioning in a society in which accepted values are threatened. In *A última batalha,* the meaning of words has been changed to suit the political goals of nations and parties. In the remaining plays the author transfers the conflict of values to the domestic scene, where it proves more difficult to deal with. In *Nem tudo* and *A flor,* the conflict is between the value systems of different societies. In *É perigoso* and *A solução,* the characters must deal with the conflicts and the collapse of values in their own society. (TB,Jr)

Miguéis. 7921. Kerr, John A., Jr. "A Thumbnail Sketch of the Life and Works of José Rodrigues Miguéis." [F 19]:35-39.

José Rodrigues Miguéis was born in Lisbon in 1901. By the time of his graduation from the University of Lisbon, he had begun establishing himself as an illustrator, protestor of social ills, and a writer of fiction. In 1932, he received acclaim as the author of *Páscoa Feliz,* particularly for its psychological insights. In 1935, he emigrated to the United States, publishing *Onde a Noite se Acaba* in Brazil in 1946. In 1959 he was awarded the first Prémio Camilo Castelo Branco for his collection *Léah e Outras Histórias* (1958). Other major works have followed. His contributions to Portuguese literature over the years have been many and varied. In spite of his residence abroad he had always been faithful to the best in the Portuguese nation, while viewing it from a cosmopolitan perspective. (JAK,Jr)

Queirós, Eça de. 7978. Fedorchek, Robert M. "Luisa's Dream Worlds in *O primo Basílio*." *RomN* 15:532-35.

Eça de Queirós' *O primo Basílio* is the story of Luísa's and Basílio's adulterous affair. Luísa's reading of Romantic literature has engendered in her a fantasy world made up of dreams of perfect love. In time they become a substitute form of life and when Luísa is confronted by Basílio's seemingly honest declarations of passion, she succumbs to the model of procedure acted out in her novels. Both her daydreams and sleep-produced dreams are stylistic devices to reinforce her character and parallel the thematic development of the novel. Luísa's dreams are a reconstruction of her fantasy, an escape which explains both her fanciful bliss and the anguish brought on by Juliana's relentless revenge. (RMF)

Tolentino. 8020. Preto-Rodas, R[ichard] A. "The Ironic Humor of Nicolau Tolentino's Satiras." *LBR* 11,i:89-97.

Analysis of the ironic perspective in the poetry of Tolentino de Almeida reveals that the common view of the poet as a satirist is inaccurate. Although at times he specifies evils with a view to

---

† *Festschriften* and Other Analyzed Collections are listed in the first division of this volume. "F" numbers in brackets following a title refer to these items.

correction he is more inclined to assume an amoral, detached viewpoint which indicates that human existence is incongruous and somewhat ridiculous. There is no attempt to provide an ethical solution for society's foibles and posturing nor is there any possibility of reconciling theoretical principle with actual behavior. He is as disparaging regarding himself as with others, showing that a gentle mockery with illusion is the only defense against corrosive lucidity. (RAP-R)

Vicente, Gil. 8031. Mosely, William W. "'O rei do mar': Portugal, the Sea, and Gil Vicente." *LBR* 11,i:98-104.
Gil Vicente lived during the period of Portuguese maritime exploration and expansion, and among the varied themes he treats as court playwright is that of the sea. Vicente alludes frequently to maritime exploration, commerce, military feats, and to the glory from Portugal's emerging empire. He is familiar with maritime terms, even highly technical ones, both in Portuguese and in Spanish, although his knowledge of such terms in Spanish is less certain than in Portuguese, and Portuguesisms sometimes occur in his Spanish. His use of maritime terms is not always accurate, but his knowledge of such vocabulary is remarkable for one who was not a seaman. (WWM)

8032. Rangel-Guerrero, Daniel. "Gil Vicente. Comedia sobre *A divisa da cidade de Coimbra*:Una interpretación." [F 19]:40-44.
Vicente's *Coimbra* is a comic piece, a court mask. The plot is a mixture of jokes played on several members of important families of the court, incredible adventures involving knights, princes and princesses, wild men, courtly love situations, and an explanation of the meaning of the coat of arms of the city of Coimbra. (DR-G)

II. BRAZILIAN LITERATURE

Almeida, J.A. de. 8226. Tomlins, Jack E. "The Cashew Tree:Diction and Structure in *A Bagaceira*." [F 19]:56-60.
A Bagaceira (1928) has earned its place in Brazilian letters principally as the "romance-padrão" of the so-called North-eastern novel. *A Bagaceira* is an intricately dramatic novel whose motus depends ultimately on contradictions that are at once psychological, biological, sociological, and even ecological. Language serves the dramatic heart of the conflict in the creation of a baroque work where the beauty of the word belies the ugliness of the deed. Almeida's credo that nothing is as it merely seems links him with that Hispanic tradition of the past where ancient glories fall to dust. (JET)

Bandeira. 8297. Vásquez, Washington R. "A antropologia literária de Manuel Bandeira (A verdade do ser, o não-ser, o ser-ser), Parte II:O ser-ser." [F 19]:45-51.
The literary anthropology in Bandeira's poetry is centered in his placing of given individuals in his poetic world. More than two hundred names appear in his poetry. As Picasso's anthropology contains numerous individuals on canvas, so Bandeira shows a whole gallery of beings as being perfectly situated in time-space; i.e., Brazil in the 1900s. (In Portuguese) (WRV)

Suassuna. 8523. Lyday, Leon F. "The *Barcas* and the *Compadecida*:Autos Past and Present." *LBR* 11,i:84-88.
Discusses Ariano Suassuna's contemporary Brazilian play, *Auto da Compadecida*, and Gil Vicente's 16th-century *Os Autos das Barcas*. Various features found in both works but which are commonplaces in the "auto" tradition and therefore not necessarily reflective of any direct relationship between the two are pointed out. One shared feature Suassana almost certainly did adapt specifically from Gil Vicente's play is examined: the two passages which describe the bishop in the *Compadecida* constitute a paraphrasing of the passage describing the pope in the *Barcas*, these two being the church's highest representatives in their respective plays. Suassuna may have drawn some of the other shared features directly from Vicente. (LFL)

ROMANIAN LITERATURE†

I. GENERAL

General and Miscellaneous. 8558. Bălan, Ion D. "Conscience esthétique et spécifique national." *CREL* 1:64-73.
In Romanian literature, patriotic poetry holds a necessarily privileged place that finds its explanation in historical conditions. Each period in Romanian literature—from folklore to the chroniclers and the Transylvanian School down to pre-Romanticism, Romanticism, the great classics and the works created in the revolutionary period after the Liberation—has added new dimensions and nuances to patriotic literature. The Motherland is a topos of Romanian poetry, and patriotism one of its essential constants. Patriotic poetry after the Liberation is richer in nuances than in earlier periods. Patriotic poetry has been cultivated by all contemporary poets: Arghezi, Blaga, Z. Stancu, Eugen Jebeleanu, Al. Andrițoiu, Ştefan Aug. Doinaş. (IDB)

II. LITERATURE

General and Miscellaneous. 8701. Ivaşiuc, Alexandru. "L'esthétique marxiste en tant qu'esthétique appliquée." *CREL* 1:85-88.
The Marxist critic must make a complex value judgment relating to the intrinsic quality of the work and also relating it to the practical action potential, bearing in mind that, besides the individual factors that concur to produce it, there is its historical necessity that must be taken into account. The Marxist critic approaches the work with the austerity of a scientist, standing at a distance from the object in his capacity as the knowing subject. Just as any other science, Marxism disenchants, it reveals a reality that tends to disguise itself. The absence of a prescriptive Marxist esthetic thought corresponds to the premises of Marx's thinking for he systematically avoided closed systems. (AI)

8737. Piru, Alexandru. "Les débuts de la littérature roumaine actuelle." *CREL* 1:4-11.
Presents a critical outline necessary for the understanding of the period 1940-50. General and systematic references to the poetry, prose, drama, criticism, and literary history of the decade are included. At the same time the writers are classified according to age: the elderly generation, the middle-aged generation, and the young generation. These generalizations refer to the peculiarities determined by the moral, political, and social conditions obtaining during the years of war and fascism and the first years after the Liberation. The main characteristic of poetry is nonconformity; prose writers are hostile to obscurantism and herald innovations based on real values; dramatists offer few works; G. Călinescu dominates literary history and criticism. (AP)

† *Festschriften* and Other Analyzed Collections are listed in the first division of this volume. "F" numbers in brackets following a title refer to these items.

Drama and Theater. 8810. Râpeanu, Valeriu. "La nouvelle dramaturgie roumaine, image en raccourci." *CREL* 1:59-63.

In the first years following the Liberation, Romanian drama passed through a crisis. Some of the dramatists (Victor Ion Popa, George Mihail Zamfirescu, Mihail Sebastian) had died, while other "great" playwrights underwent a period of depression in which they produced works of lesser value. In 1944-48, Romanian drama passed through a period of good intentions and response to the generous ideas of the time. Young writers produced amusing plays fired with humanitarian sentiments, dramatic pamphlets committed to the commands of the moment, or plays in which social concern was coming to life. Then the problems of the world and of the new society made themselves increasingly felt, manifest in a new emphasis on history plays: an endeavor to transcend romanticism and deal with modern problems in a modern way. (VR)

Poetry. 8851. Simion, Eugen. "Où va la poésie roumaine?" *CREL* 1:12-22.
Analyzes and comments on Romanian lyrical poetry of the last three decades in an attempt to outline the interior mutations that have led to original forms in present day Romanian poetry. Romanian lyrical poetry has passed through a process of disenchantment in its very province. Forms of escapism, of non-commitment, painful isolationism, and dissimulation frequent in earlier poetry have changed, within the framework of a new civilization based on humanistic principles, into more direct forms of communication with the epoch and a closer relationship with existence. Present-day Romanian poetry is characterized by breadth and variety in themes and a corresponding range and diversity of sensitive types and lyrical formulae of expression. A special place is held by the lyrical revival of the sixties which began with a restatement of the very idea of poetry. (ES)

Prose Fiction. 8864. Balotă, Nicolae. "Mutations dans la conscience éthique et esthétique." *CREL* 1:74-84.
A study of the ethical aspect of contemporary Romanian prose-writing which offers a public examination of "consciousness." This term has a twofold aspect: first, an examination of public consciousness, a testimony of the sociohistorical and moral existence of Romanian society in the last decades and, second, an examination of the condition of the novel in itself, an examination of the conscience of the novelist relating to the condition of the Romanian novel between the two world wars. The contemporary Romanian novel is passing through a creative crisis in which a revision of its peculiar structures is being carried out. A twofold process—ethical and esthetical—is manifest especially on examining the message of representative works, such as the novels of Marin Preda, D.R. Popescu, Zaharia Stancu, Fănuş Neagu, Al. Ivasiuc, Petru Popescu, Augustin Buzura, Laurenţiu Fulga. (NB)
8877. Hobana, Ion. "Futurism and Fantasy in Romanian Science Fiction." *CREL* 2:72-84.
Science fiction in Romanian literature has its origins in the 19th century in the writings of Victor Anestin and Henri Stahl. Writers of note, such as Alexandru Macedonski, Victor Eftimiu, Gib Mihăescu, Felix Aderca, and Tudor Arghezi have dabbled in the genre, thus promoting a modern spirit in Romanian literature before World War II. (IH)
8881. Manolescu, Nicolae. "Nouvellistes et conteurs, quelques analyses." *CREL* 1:42-50.
The works of Marin Preda, Eugen Barbu, D.R. Popescu, and Fănuş Neagu illustrate the peculiarities of the short stories and tales of contemporary Romanian writers. Preda is an "analyst" because he focuses his attention on cases involving conscience, on the moral significance derived from observing mental states. What is striking in his prose is the pleasure of discovering uncommon movements of mind in common or uncommon situations. Barbu is concerned with epic events, laying special stress on dynamic, spectacular developments. He is at home in the milieu of the working class. Popescu has a special talent for the symbolic or the prose of atmosphere. He creates hallucinating situations in an uncommon imaginary vision. Neagu is a remarkable storyteller with a taste for vitalism and the picturesque which places him on a level with Panait Istrati. (NM)

Sadoveanu, M. 9467. Nicolescu, Vasile. "M. Sadoveanu, une mythologie spirituelle." *CREL* 1:23-27.
In Sadoveanu's art there is a blending of learned inspiration and technique, an overflowing of interior lava, Persian miniature ornamentals, a mythical vision, and clockwork precision. Sadoveanu's prose is euphonious and captivating, never lacking in epic spirit and legendary character. He is inclined to contemplation, enamored of open spaces, of light, and of the elements that circumscribe the movement or the very existence of his world. Poet and prose writer, Sadoveanu belongs to the great European stream of evocative prose which finds its source in the writings of Chateaubriand. An unmatched delineator of character, a writer of expressive prose, Sadoveanu is the creator of a pluri-dimensional world in which the epic element finds its natural place as a necessary component. (VN)
9468. Simms, Norman T. "From Stasis to Freedom in Mihail Sadoveanu's *The Hatchet*." *Mosaic* 7,ii:45-56.
Sadoveanu's novel *Baltagul* (*The Hatchet*) exemplifies him as a major Romanian novelist and as a European writer. The plot of the novel derives from the popular Romanian ballad "Miorit" ("The Little Ewe-Lamb") and develops situation and character by reference to implicit notions in the concept of the folk-poem. Sadoveanu focuses on his own created character, Vitoria Lipan, wife of the shepherd in "Miorita." In the fictional world of the novel many social and psychological details must be created which are not found in the sparse and static scheme of the ballad. At the same time as he limits Vitoria's consciousness to concepts available to a mid-19th century Moldavian peasant, Sadoveanu shows Vitoria approaching a freedom of action which, in Marxist terms, makes man the creator of his own destiny. Sadoveanu's technical problem is to reconcile Vitoria's range of articulation through the language and scenario of "Miorita" and the novel's presentation of a more mature and rational (Marxist) understanding of her situation. (NTS)

GERMAN LITERATURE†

II. THEMES, TYPES, SPECIAL TOPICS

Poetry. 9824. Paulin, Roger. "Six Sapphic Odes 1753-1934:A Study in Literary Reception." *Seminar* 10:181-98.
A brief historical survey of the ode genre in German, using the Sapphic ode as an example of how German poets adapted classical stanza forms for the needs of their own language. Poems by Klopstock, Platen, R.A. Schröder, and Weinheber provide illustrations, together with short interpretations. What begins as a major renewing force in German lyric poetry gradually becomes an exercise in metrical correctness, proceeding into the 20th century as a conservative survival with controversial associations.

† *Festschriften* and Other Analyzed Collections are listed in the first division of this volume. "F" numbers in brackets following a title refer to these items.

The original impulse through Klopstock and his followers does not regard classical form as an absolute, but is basically concerned with liberating poetic diction. (RCP)

Prose Fiction. 9833. Miles, David H. "The Picaro's Journey to the Confessional:The Changing Image of the Hero in the German Bildungsroman." *PMLA* 89:980-92.
From Goethe's *Wilhelm Meister* through Keller's *Grüne Heinrich* to Rilke's *Malte*, the hero of the German Bildungsroman develops from non-self-conscious adventurer in the outer world to compulsive explorer of the world within. This transformation in the hero from "picaro" to "confessor" implies a change in the concept of *Bildung*: the "self" no longer accumulates, but must be recollected. This transformation of the literary hero in the 19th

century mirrors in turn the historical rise of alienated, self- conscious man. (DHM)

III. LITERATURE BEFORE 1500

General and Miscellaneous. 9861. Baeumer, Max L. " 'Voluptas' und 'Frühbürgerliche Revolution':Neue Sichtweisen der Literatur des 15. und 16. Jahrhunderts." *Monatshefte* 65(1973): 393-415. [Rev. art.]
Previous histories of the literature of the 15th and 16th centuries were regarded by their authors only as material collections and broad outlines of a vague and obscure period. Four new historical presentations offer different fundamental conceptions for a first real and comprehensive history of literature of that age. H.O. Burger and H. Rupprich take the conservative approach of a history of intellectual and esthetic ideas ("Geistesgeschichte"). Burger follows up the leitmotif of "Voluptas" as "affective rhetoricism" and as change from the medieval "contemptus mundi" to the "voluptas mundi" in every domain of worldly pleasure. B. Könneker and an East German authors' collective emphasize the popular character of the literature of the period and the revolutionary tendency and impact of the Reformation. Könneker and the East Germans measure Renaissance and Humanism by their influence on the rising bourgeois society and its realistic, didactic, and propagandistic literature. Following remarks of Marx and Engels, the collective considers the writings of that era exclusively as literature of the early-bourgeois revolution. Future histories of literature of the 15th and 16th centuries will have to proceed from the sociological basis of the early-bourgeois society, but avoid the extreme of an exclusively socioeconomic point of view. (In German) (MLB)

9890. Knapp, Gerhard P. "Hector und Achill:Die Rezeption des Trojastoffes in deutschen Mittelalter. Personenbild und struktureller Wandel." *Utah Studies in Lit. and Ling.* 1:116ff.
The study begins with a survey of the medieval tradition of the story of Troy. It then analyzes role and function of the main characters, Hector and Achilles, in the adaptations of Herbort von Fritzlar, Konrad von Würzburg, and of the anonymous *Göttweiger Trojanerkrieg*. The many interrelations between characterization and structure of the texts are shown; the French and Latin sources are compared to the texts in those cases where there is no previous reliable research. As a result, a cogent system of knightly values emerges from Herbort's *Liet*, an obviously manneristic approach from Konrad's *Trojanerkrieg*, and a unique combination of the Story of Troy with âventiure-structures from the *Göttweiger Trojanerkrieg*. (GPK)

Hartmann von Aue. 9994. Salmon, Paul. " 'Âne Zuht': Hartmann von Aue's Criticism of Iwein." *MLR* 69:556-61.
Iwein, says Hartmann von Aue, pursued the mortally wounded Askalon *âne zuht*, and later lunged at him with his spear from behind. If *âne zuht* means "showing ill-breeding," the words constitute a serious criticism of the hero, and there is a discrepancy between the ideals of chivalry and their realization. It is possible, however, that the lunge was no more than an expedient to cover a lacuna in the source, and that the critical phrase means no more than "at full tilt." If this is the case, there remains no overt criticism of the hero and no necessary support for an interpretation of the text as a whole which credits Hartmann with an attitude of ironic detachment to courtly and chivalrous society. (PBS)

Heinrich von dem Türlin. 10000. Read, Ralph R. "Heinrich von dem Türlin's *Diu Krône* and Wolfram's *Parzival*." *MLQ* 35:129-39.
Heinrich von dem Türlin was a German poet who composed a verse epic, *Diu Krône*, about 1230. Heinrich knew Chrétien's *Perceval* and Wolfram's *Parzival*, but the poet whose artistry he most admired was Hartmann. In the course of composing *Diu Krône*, Heinrich seems to have given it a program. Heinrich wishes to outdo all his sources, and the result is confusion, grotesqueness, and prolixity. He inflates the figure of Gawein to heroic proportions and plays him off against Parzival, whom he belittles. Finally, he sets out to "defeat" Wolfram by creating an anti-*Parzival*. Parzival appears in twelve passages in the epic, usually shown in a bad light compared to Gawein. Parzival is reproached three times for not asking the "Mitleidsfrage." Gawein takes over the grail quest from Parzival and carries it out successfully. Heinrich attempts to rival Wolfram in form, too. At one point he begins to write in a series of sections of even length, but then gives it up after 350 lines. His prologue is even more formally involuted and confusing than Wolfram's, but whether it is profound is another question. (RRR)

Heinrich von Morungen. 10003. Gray, Clayton,Jr. "Platonic Light and Light-Imagery in the Verse of Heinrich von Morungen." *CLAJ* 18:101-13.
Light imagery is conspicuous in the verse of Heinrich von Morungen. In a 1951 essay (*London Mediaeval Studies*, 2, 116-24) E.J. Morrall discusses the relationship of this imagery to that in Roman and Middle Latin literature. He does not, however, mention Plato, whose influence on the High Middle Ages is usually considered to be minimal. There is, nonetheless, evidence that Platonism is quite alive in the 12th and 13th centuries. Both Plato and Heinrich von Morungen depict light as a scintillating ideal. (CG)

Hildebrandslied. 10014. Twaddell, W.F. "The *Hildebrandslied* Manuscript in the U.S.A." *JEGP* 73:157-68.
The codex containing the two sheets of the *Hildebrandslied* belongs to the Murhardsche Bibliothek in Kassel; it was stored 1943-45 in Bad Wildungen. Its disappearance from the bunker there was discovered in June 1945. An American dealer bought the codex in November 1945 and removed the first sheet. The codex was offered for sale to the Pierpont Morgan Library, which declined to buy it after examination had revealed the absence of sheet one. In 1949 the Estelle Doheny Collection in Camarillo, California, bought the codex. The purchase was reported in a bibliophilic journal; the U.S. State Department was alerted, secured the codex, and supervised its return to the owner in 1954. The location of sheet one became publicly known in 1972, when the Rosenbach Foundation Museum in Philadelphia announced its presence in the collection. After legal negotiations, sheet one and the Willehalm Codex (which was also found in the Foundation Museum) were returned in September 1972 to representatives of the Federal Republic of Germany and the director of the Murhardsche Bibliothek der Stadt Kassel und Landesbibliothek. (WFT)

Konrad von Würzburg. 10032. Wailes, Stephen L. "Konrad von Würzburg and Pseudo-Konrad:Varieties of Humour in the 'Märe'." *MLR* 69:98-114.
Authors of amusing tales in the medieval German genre *Märe* frequently interpret traditional plots so that they rub against the prejudices of their audiences. Two texts by Konrad von Würzburg (*Das Herzmære* and *Heinrich von Kempten*) and one by Pseudo-Konrad (*Die halbe Birne A*) are analyzed to show this. In the *Herzmære*, Konrad draws attention to the discrepancy between crudity of plot (the eaten heart) and refinement of theme (true love) through techniques of *ornatus facilis*. The text displays intellectual play. *Heinrich von Kempten* is a charade of courtliness, for the hero's behavior in both episodes plays havoc with the breeding valued by author and audience. Konrad amuses us at the expense of Heinrich. Pseudo-Konrad brings his hero into conflict with the same values of breeding, but to ridicule and disparage these. The key to the text is the episode with the pear, a careful parody of an episode in Konrad von Würzburg's *Engelhard*. All three stories are intelligent and subtle, supporting current opinion that the *Märe* is a fully literate genre. (SLW)

Nibelungenlied. 10042. Bekker, Hugo. "The *Nibelungenlied*: Rüdiger von Bechlaren and Dietrich von Bern." *Monatshefte* 66:239-53.

In the *Nibelungenlied*, the poet depicts its world as dedicated to joy ("fröide") for the sake of order, peace, and harmony. This explains Rüdeger's readiness to promise things to Kriemhild upon an oath. The preoccupation with "fröide" in all its ramifications lies at the root of Rüdeger's failure to warn the Burgundians that enmity is brewing. Dietrich, on the other hand, envisions joy as at best a momentary reprieve from the ever-present menace of chaos. While displaying hospitality and largesse as the customary means with which to uphold society, he does so without conviction. When it becomes evident that "fröide" cannot be retained, Dietrich finds strength within himself. Rüdeger's position, however, becomes full of pathos when his *raison d'être* is annihilated by the forces which his rash oath and his failure to give a warning have been instrumental in unleashing. (HB)

10046. Mahlendorf, Ursula R., and Frank J. Tobin. "Legality and Formality in the *Nibelungenlied*." *Monatshefte* 66:225-38.
An understanding of the *Nibelungenlied* is greatly increased if one examines it from the point of view of the law of the times and with an appreciation of the extreme formalism inherent in medieval society. Siegfried's refusal to abide by custom and law or to take formalistic attitudes seriously and his sole reliance on personal qualities contribute to his downfall. The poet's use of the word *künec* demonstrates his attitude toward formalism. Gunther's bungling of court procedure demonstrates another dimension of his ineptitude as king. Knowledge of the law also helps the reader better understand Hagen's actions relating to the murder of Siegfried and the full extent of guilt incurred by the kings here and in their subsequent treatment of Kriemhild. By their transgressing the laws they put Burgundian society outside the legal order and their ensuing destruction can be viewed as the necessary result of their criminal actions. (URM & FJT)

Oswald von Wolkenstein. 10059. Jones, George F. "The 'Signs of Old Age' in Oswald von Wolkenstein's *Ich sich und hör*." *MLN* 89:767-86.
Wolkenstein's song "Ich sich und hör" follows in the tradition of the *planctus animae damnatae*, or lament of the corpse rotting in its tomb while its soul is suffering in hell. But he makes the narrator an ancient man about to die after a misspent life who wishes to warn young men to prepare early for a good death. Wolkenstein utilized traditional signs of old age derived from Horace, Ovid, Pseudo-Cyprian, Maximianus, and others. By letting his poetic "I" recite the signs of old age in the first person, Wolkenstein achieved emotional impact and immediacy. (GFJ)

Tauler. 10086. McLaughlin, Eleanor. "The Heresy of the Free Spirit and Late Medieval Mysticism." *M&H* 4(1973):37-54.
Many historians today are still quoting medieval reports that the Free Spirits were in theory and practice antinomians and libertines, given to the most crass excesses of sensuality. A reason for the lack of unanimity on the nature of this heresy lies in the absence of a trustworthy body of sources for its history. No source material from the hands of the accused is known to exist. This paper offers a partial solution to that dilemma by presenting a new set of witnesses for the history of the heresy of the Free Spirit, an alternative to the typological accounts of inquisitor and chronicler. This new perspective is to be found in the orthodox mystics of the 14th and 15th centuries and is argued with reference to a representative sample of the evidence available: the *Mirror of Simple Souls*, an early 14th-century Beguine devotional treatise, and the sermons of Johannes Tauler. (EMcL)

Wiener Osterspiel. 10118. Blosen, Hans. "Zum Lied der Wächter im *Wiener Osterspiel*:Zugleich Bemerkungen zum Refrain in mittelhochdeutscher Lyrik." *OL* 29:183-216.
The *Wiener Osterspiel* handed down a verse which turns out as dance verse when theatrically produced. Each stanza is clearly divided into two and consists of a segment A with two lines of four beats each and a segment B with two lines of two beats each and one line of four beats. Comparison with other related metrical forms in Middle High German lyric poetry indicates that the primary issue is one of a pre- or external courtly choral dance form, which later was also taken up in courtly lyric poetry. Analogous forms which are found in the Danish "Folkeviser," the French "caroles," and the English "carols" place the verse beyond that of the play into the traditional context of a medieval chain dance, the "carole." It cannot be shown with certainty whether the verse was in addition sung and danced by a choir leader and responding group in conformity with the "carole" standard, even if the text and at least one of the two traditional melodies would have been suitable for such a delivery. (HB)

Wolfram von Eschenbach. 10124. Benkert, Renate L. "Wolfram von Eschenbach's Kyot." *WVUPP* 21:3-8.
The person "Kyot" in Wolfram's *Parzival* remains an enigma. Benkert discusses the scholarly speculation on Wolfram's intent. (RLB)

10130. Gray, Clayton,Jr. "The Symbolic Role of Wolfram's Feirefiz." *JEGP* 73:363-74.
At the end of Book I of Wolfram's *Parzival* the heathen black Moorish Queen Belakane, spouse of the white Christian knight Gahmuret Angevin, gives birth to a black and white son, Feirefiz. Wolfram makes frequent reference to this dual coloring, which functions as a reminder of the fact that his heritage is both heathen and Christian. The poet establishes Feirefiz as an exemplary knight, partially by having him measure up to the titular hero Parzival. The juxtaposition of the colors of this knight symbolizes the equality of heathenry and Christianity in the eyes of Wolfram, for although Feirefiz did not let himself be baptized out of true conviction, his devotion to his heathen gods had not been greater than his dedication to Christianity. (CG,Jr)

10134. Hofmeister, Rudolf A. "Lachmann's Role in the Transmission of *Parzival*." *Seminar* 10:87-100.
Lachmann's 1833 edition of *Parzival* is authoritative. A survey of the extant *Parzival* transmission and comparison of it to Lachmann's work shows discrepancies between Lachmann's text and the manuscript evidence. Even though Lachmann stated that he listed all of the readings in his base manuscripts *D* and *G*, there are many cases in which he failed to list important variants from his base manuscripts. Lachmann criticized other editors for disregarding extant manuscripts in their editions, yet he failed to examine five *Parzival* manuscripts which he must have known existed. Lachmann selected his readings from either *D* or *G* to fit a pattern of 30 lines per narrative unit. This selective addition or omission of verses may have resulted in the omission of genuine verses and the introduction of spurious verses in Lachmann's text. (RAH)

10135. Horgan, A.D. "The Grail in Wolfram's *Parzival*." *MS* 36:354-81.
Wolfram's Grail-stone is identified as the rock, which, according to the Jewish story cited by Paul in I Corinthians, followed the Israelites over the desert. This story of the rock harks back to the Horeb water-miracle and the rebellion of Israel. In Numbers and *Parzival* an elect community, living in the wilderness, is sustained by a wonderful rock which provides for them. This rock "mediates" between them and God and seems to be connected with the Blessed Sacrament. An eminent person transgresses against the community's sexual ethic and is hideously wounded in the genitals. Further comparisons between Numbers and French Grail-material is set forth in an appendix. Parallels are adduced between *Parzival* and St. Bernard's anagogic way. (ADH)

IV. SIXTEENTH AND SEVENTEENTH CENTURIES

General and Miscellaneous. 10194. Potter, G.R. "Zwingli and His Publisher." [F 88]:108-17.
The success of the Reformation depended very much on the printing press and upon the availability of vernacular translations of the Bible. In Zürich Zwingli had the assistance of the press newly set up by Christopher Froschauer in 1517. This enabled Zwingli's ideas to reach a large public. The press was also used for the reproduction of government decrees. The most important

publication was the complete Zürich Bible in 1529, preceding the Lutheran version. Froschauer's press was used by the government of Berne to make material available for the decisive debate of 1528. The spread of Zwinglian ideas in the south German cities was encouraged by Froschauer's active and successful salesmanship. (GRP)

Drama and Theater. 10202. Dimler, G. Richard. "A Geographic and Genetic Survey of Jesuit Drama in German-Speaking Territories 1555-1602." *Archivum Historicum Soc. Jesu* 43:133-46.
This survey encompasses the time from the first Jesuit Drama in German-speaking countries performed in Vienna in 1555, to *Cenodoxus*, performed in Augsburg in 1602. A list of German-born Jesuit dramatists who worked in this period is followed by an analysis of their educational and religious training. A statistical analysis of the typology of the dramas (morality, dialog, Schuldramen, saints-plays, and the Bible) is correlated with the geographical and linguistic aspects. In conclusion a statistical table is provided which lists the plays according to the four provinces of the German Assistency together with their typology. (GRD)
10205. Kelly, Genevieve. "The Drama of Student Life in the German Renaissance." *ETJ* 26:291-307.
The drama of student life, a lively, realistic subgenre almost buried under the mass of biblical plays in 16th-century Germany, united Reformation plays on the Prodigal Son theme with humanist student dialogs. The first playwright to make the combination was the Dutch humanist Macropedius, whose *Rebelles* (1535) and *Petriscus* (1536) were influential in Germany. Ironically, the transferral of the Prodigal Son theme into a schoolroom setting carried with it a reversal of its graciously forgiving theology into the morality of rewards and punishments characterizing the student dialogs. The strictness of this morality tightens throughout a series of related German plays by Binder, Ackermann, and Wickram. Stymmelius' *Studentes* (1545) masterfully parodies the theme to satirize its materialistic morality. Nevertheless the student-life playwrights of the last quarter of the century (Hayneccius, Knaust) return to the heavy-handed morality developed by Wickram. Elements of the Continental plays have parallels in the English plays of student life —*Disobedient Child, Nice Wanton*, Gascoigne's *Glasse of Government*, and the Parnassus trilogy. (GRK)

Faustbuch. 10236. Wentersdorf, Karl P. "A *Faustsplitter* from Rome." *Seminar* 10:101-03. [Faust in the *Annales ecclesiastici*, 1646-77.]
In the *Annales ecclesiastici* (Rome, 1646-77), a history of the Church begun by Baronius and continued by Odorico Rinaldi, the entries for the year 1507 include a hitherto unnoticed reference to the activities of the German magician Faust— Georgius Sabellicus-Faust. Rinaldi describes Faust as a blasphemous impostor and as a forerunner of Luther. This reference, supported with quotations from the denunciation of Sabellicus-Faust by Johannes Trithemius, underscores the view that the historical magician took an extremist position in the Renaissance controversy over the validity of biblical and post-biblical miracles. (KPW)

Schönborn. 10236a. Marigold, Walter G. "Deutschsprachige Huldigungsgedichte für den Kurfürsten Lothar Franz von Schönborn." *Mainzer Zeitschrift* 69:164-67.
Laudatory poems flourished particularly during the Renaissance and Baroque eras. German only gradually replaced Latin for such works, particularly in Catholic Germany. Here the importance of the ecclesiastical states and the Jesuit order kept Latin alive until well into the 18th century. A group of German poems written on the death (in 1729) of Lothar Franz von Schönborn, Elector-Archbishop of Mainz, is of considerable interest. The poems by such officials as Christian Ignaz Isserstaedt and Johann Baptist Roth compare not unfavorably with similar works contained in the *Neukirchsche Sammlung* and elsewhere. They, as well as the poems by unknown authors, are of genuine interest to scholars in the fields of literature and history, particularly the intellectual history of the Baroque period. (MWG)

Grimmelshausen. 10240. Dimler, G. Richard. "Alienation in *Don Quixote* and *Simplicius Simplicissimus*." *Thought* 49:72-80.
Cervantes' novel *Don Quixote* first intimates the modern existential crisis of alienation; Grimmelshausen's novel *Simplicius Simplicissimus* records it for the first time in German literature. Both novels provide the reader with a strikingly similar problem, man's alienation. In *Simplicissimus* man's alienation from his environment, from himself, and from God is demonstrated. Both Quixote and Simplicius find themselves in conflict with their environments. (GRD)

Gryphius, A. 10252. Stackhouse, Janifer G. "The Mysterious Regicide in Gryphius' Stuart Drama. Who Is Poleh?" *MLN* 89:797-811.
In his reference note to the first line of Poleh's monologue, Andreas Gryphius indicates that this penitent, demented regicide added to the second version (B) of *Ermordete Majestät. Oder Carolus Stuardus König von Gross Britannien* (1663) was based upon a real historical figure. The identity of the historical figure represented by Poleh has remained open to controversy. Consideration of this scene in conjunction with the sources which Gryphius used for the revised version of his drama indicates the probability of identifying Poleh as John Cook, the English lawyer and prosecuting attoney at the trial of King Charles I. (JGS)

Kuhlmann. 10260. Gogol, John M. "The Archpriest Avvakum and Quirinus Kuhlmann:A Comparative Study in the Literary Baroque." *GSlav* 2(1973):35-48.
Similarities in the lives and literary legacies of Quirinus Kuhlmann and the Archpriest Avvakum, two of the most dynamic personalities of 17th-century Europe, provide an opportunity for a comparative study in the literary Baroque of East-Central Europe. Through comparison with Kuhlmann, Avvakum may be viewed as the high point of the Russian Baroque, rather than as a queer, isolated phenomenon in the development of Russian literature. Soviet literary historians have long denied the existence of such a literary phase as an integral part of Russian literary development, but a study of Avvakum's writings reveal that he does belong to the spirit of the times in Europe and has much in common with German Baroque writers. (JMG)

Schönborn. 10286. Marigold, Walter G. "De Leone Schönbornico:Huldigungsgedichte an Johann Philipp und Lothar Franz von Schönborn." *Archiv für Mittelrheinische Kirchengeschichte* 26:203-42.
The laudatory poems (*Huldigungsgedichte*) of the German Baroque period, both in Latin and in German, celebrate the achievements and bemoan the death of Johann Philipp and Lothar Franz von Schönborn. The Latin works, most of them the work of unidentified Jesuits, are more ambitious and of greater literary value. The transition to German took place relatively late in Catholic Germany, where professional writers were few and where the Latin-educated clergy played a leading role in cultural life. (WGM)
10287. ——— "Katholische Evangelien- und Episteldichtung: Die Schriften des Kurfürsten Johann Philipp von Schönborn (1605-1673)." *Daphnis* 3:41-59.
Despite its important role in German literature, *Perikopendichtung*, particularly that of Catholic Germany, is still neglected. More than a century after the earliest Lutheran versification of the gospel readings, Johann Philipp von Schönborn, Elector-Archbishop of Mainz, wrote the first Catholic versions. *Catholische Sonn-und Feiertägliche Evangelia* appeared in 1653. Like most *Perikopenlieder*, they must be considered primarily as religious, not literary works. However, Johann Philipp's poems compare favorably with works of the same type by such writers as Opitz, Heermann or Rist, while their presence in later hymnbooks is proof of their popular success. (WGM)

Spee. 10290. Dimler, G. Richard. "On the Structure and Composition of Friedrich Spee's *Trutznachtigall*." *MLN* 89:787-96.
One can account for Spee's wide-ranging themes of hope and love

in *Trutznachtigall* (*TN*) 2-32 without constraining Spee's poetic reconstruction of Christ's life in poems 33-51. The poems of the *Güldenes Tugend Buch* (*GTB*) play a decisive role in the progression of the *TN* and the two-fold development in the 52 poems. Section I (*TN* 2-32) progresses in accord with the virtues of hope and love as Spee explains them in Books I and II of the *GTB*. Section II (*TN* 33-51) develops in accord with the principle events of Christ's life. This structural progression also explains why Spee transferred the original *GTB* poems to the positions they have in the *TN*. (GRD)

10291. Rener, Frederick M. "Friedrich Spee's 'Arcadia' Revisited." *PMLA* 89:967-79.

Spee's descriptions of nature are variations of the topos *locus amoenus* with many of its less common classical features: the park-orchard-garden varieties of landscape, typical epithets, and catalogs of trees and plants. In the *Trutznachtigall*, the section with the largest pattern of the topos are the *laudes*, commonly considered to be derivations of the Psalms, while the eclogues ("Arcadia"), a genre traditionally associated with the topos, have only a few samples of it. Rather than being a rigid formula the topos becomes an elastic pattern whose size and components are tailored to the individual poem, providing at the same time a distinct diction and a variety of formulations. (FMR)

Werder. 10295a. Dünnhaupt, Gerhard. "Diedrich von dem Werder and the 'Fruchtbringende Gesellschaft'." *MLR* 69:796-804.

The Fruchtbringende Gesellschaft actively encouraged the publications of original works and translations of foreign literature. Prince Ludwig von Anhalt-Köthen (1579-1650), the society's first president, established a printing plant where many of its publications were produced. Members were required to submit their manuscripts to Köthen in order to gain permission to publish in the name of the society, even if their books were printed elsewhere. Most active behind the scenes was the poet Diederich von dem Werder (1584-1657) who carried the bulk of the editorial duties, and without whose expert advice the Prince apparently never approved a manuscript. Werder's diplomatic training qualified him particularly for the often difficult negotiations between the conservative Prince and some of the progressive members clamoring for reforms in poetics, in grammar, and in orthography. (GD)

Zeiller. 10300. Stackhouse, Janifer G. "Early Critical Response to Milton in Germany:The *Dialogi* of Martin Zeiller." *JEGP* 73:487-96.

When Martin Zeiller included a summary of the dispute between Claudius Salmasius and John Milton in his publication *Ein Hundert Dialogi, oder Gespräch Von unterschiedlichen Sachen zu erbaulicher Nachricht auch Nutzlichem Gebrauch und Belustigung* (1653), he carried off nothing less than a journalistic scoop. His discussion is the first known commentary about Milton in the German language, preceding what has heretofore been accepted as the first German commentary by 8 years. The same year marks the date when Milton's original influence in Germany as a political theoretician could extend beyond those able to read previous criticism written in Latin about his treatise. (JGS)

V. EIGHTEENTH AND EARLY NINETEENTH CENTURIES

Brentano, C. 10369. Greenway, Geri D. " 'Schweig Herz! Kein Schrei!' by Clemens Brentano." *Monatshefte* 66:166-72.

Brentano's subjective poem "Schweig Herz! kein Schrei!" (1817) is usually treated not as a poem, but as an illustration of Brentano's frustrated love for Luise Hensel. An analysis of Brentano's use in this poem of the light-dark image complex, rigid structure through rhyme repetition and refrain, and image identity suggested through structure contradicts the common but superficial explication of an optimistic relationship between the narrator (Brentano) and his beloved (Luise Hensel). (GDG)

Chamisso. 10374. Flores, Ralph. "The Lost Shadow of Peter Schlemihl." *GQ* 47:567-84.

Chamisso's *Peter Schlemihls Wundersame Geschichte* has been critically examined but no one has accounted for the work's puzzling complexity. Thus there is a need to reconsider the work's basic elements—money, shadow, and soul—in a wider perspective. In the figure of Peter Schlemihl, each of the story's key values is portrayed as being irreconcilably antagonistic: money could be viewed as a cause of alienation or as a necessary social connective; the shadow, as a measure of personal humanity and social commitment or as something valued only out of narrow-minded prejudice. The soul itself is "saved" by being condemned to isolation from the human world. A continuous and psychologically realistic process of increasing alienation is depicted. (RF)

Goethe. 10397. Allentuck, Marcia. "Byron and Goethe:New Unpublished References by Henry Gally Knight." *PQ* 52(1973):777-79.

After commenting on the puzzling aspects of the Byron-Goethe relationship, Allentuck quotes from an unpublished letter at the Huntington Library by Henry Gally Knight, which details a visit to Goethe after Byron's death and sheds new light on Goethe's complex responses to Byron. (MEA)

10400. Becker-Cantarino, Baerbel. "The Spanish Background in Goethe's *Clavigo*." *SCB* 34:143-46.

The analysis of the Spanish background in Goethe's *Clavigo* complements existing interpretations from the sociohistorical perspective. Goethe made the social scene an integral part of the drama which mirrors the conflict of the poet who belongs emotionally to the bourgeois class, but can find recognition only among the nobility. It is this conflict which triggers Clavigo's tragic death linking the drama to the *bürgerliche Trauerspiel* of the 18th century. (BB-C)

10428. Haimberger, Nora. "Goethe's *Heidenröslein*:A Comparative Study of Poetry and Music." [F 19]:122-27.

Both Reichardt's and Schubert's musical settings of Goethe's poem "Heidenröslein" keep to the strophic form: Reichardt's version aims at simplicity of melody, harmony, and rhythm, in order to bind words and sound into an inseparable unit. Schubert did not follow formal considerations, but composed spontaneously. (NEH)

10440. Kahn, Ludwig W. "Erlebte Rede in Goethes *Wahlverwandtschaften*." *PMLA* 89:268-77.

Goethe's *Die Wahlverwandtschaften* is an early example of the sustained and systematic use of "erlebte Rede." This has remained generally unrecognized to the detriment of a correct reading. It is of paramount importance to know whether Goethe or a narrator speaks with authorial authority, or whether a narrator draws back the curtain to let us overhear the pre-formulated, groping meditations of one of the characters. By its very nature, "erlebte Rede" is ambiguous, multileveled, hovering between objective assertion and subjective consciousness. By using "erlebte Rede" the narrator does not withdraw behind his characters; he is often present as an ironic artist who manipulates and "exhibits" his characters. (LWK)

10450. Latimer, Dan. "Homunculus as Symbol:Semantic and Dramatic Functions of the Figure in Goethe's *Faust*." *MLN* 89:812-20.

The character of Homunculus in *Faust* II provokes a number of puzzling dramatic and thematic comparisons with other figures and scenes in Goethe's poem. As disembodied spirit, Homunculus recalls Faust's early ambitions of transcendence. But in his longing for a proper birth, Homunculus illustrates the philosophical shift in Part II away from transcendent to immanent prejudices. The suggestion of menace in Homunculus derives from his kinship with Mephisto and from the frustration of organic law in his alchemical nativity. (DRL)

10457. Mommsen, Katharina. "Goethes Vorstellung von einer idealen Lesergemeinde." *Seminar* 10:1-18.

In Goethe's own judgment, the success of his works was

frequently due to a misunderstanding. He did not regard his writings as suitable for the general reading public; he was actually addressing only a small congregation. He thought of this congregation as distinguished less by esthetic abilities than through special properties of character. Only such readers whose views were congruent with his own could derive ethical benefit from his works. Goethe, however, consistently declined to play the role of a prophet, wishing to act only as a poet. (MK)

10461. Ohlendorf, Harald. "The Poet and His Masks:Some Remarks on Implicit Structures in Goethe's *West-östlicher Divan*." *MLR* 69:562-74.

Goethe's comments on his *Westöstlicher Divan* suggest that the work is characterized by a sustained structural paradox of fragmentariness and completeness. This quality stems from the poet's desire to enlist the participation of the reader in the act of creation. The creative process would thereby become continuous, but the author would nevertheless maintain control. If successful he would transcend his historical limitations. Textual analysis of three groups of poems suggests that Goethe stylizes historical figures as masks for a typology serving as the basic for a poetical dialectic. In its focus, the poet is set off first against the prophet, then against the despot. All three believe in their divinely sanctioned uniqueness. Yet the prophet is prone to dogmatic rigidity, caught up in his own historicity. The despot, imposing his unrelenting will on the world, is prone to total human isolation. The poet in contrast to both knows of the malleability of language and its forms and is predominantly concerned with reaching his audience. (HHO)

10474. Riggan, William. "*Werther, Adolphe*, and *Eugene Onegin*:The Decline of the Hero of Sensibility." *RS* 41(1973): 252-67.

Goethe's *Die Leiden des jungen Werthers* (1774) established a new type of literary hero: a highly emotional and strongly subjective young man with passionate sensibilities and profound *Welt-schmerz*. The novel's epistolary form contributes to the portrayal of these traits by including only letters from Werther himself and by presenting the reader with a catalog of his feelings and reactions. Later works which take at least some of their impetus from Goethe's novel present heroes with decidedly less imme-diacy and intensity. Constant's *Adolphe* (1816) adopts a retro-spective first-person technique and a dry, factual style, sacrificing spontaneity for analysis and reducing the hero from an impassioned human figure to a case study. In Pushkin's *Eugene Onegin* (1823-30), the hero's deadened sensibilities have rendered him incapable of narrating his own story. He is ultimately overwhelmed by the complex narrator and by the strong character of the heroine, Tatyana, as the major interest in the novel bearing his name. The "new hero's" partial decline in Adolphe thus becomes total in Onegin. (WR)

10488. Stock, Irvin. "Goethe's Tragedy:A View of *Elective Affinities*." *Mosaic* 7,iii:17-27.

Goethe's *Elective Affinities* combines and reconciles his youthful romanticism and the classicism of his prime. This novel dramatizes the justice in the claims of both passion and that larger view which subordinates it to the requirements of the human community. These opposing claims can only be honored equally by certain rare people. Ottilie, who remains true to her love of Edward and the principle which demands that she renounce him, and whose double allegiance fulfils itself in a death which inspires miracles of faith is Goethe's understanding of sainthood, its beauty and blessedness, and the earthly tragedy it entails. (IS)

10496. Warde, Anton. "The Identity of Real and Ideal in Goethe's *Faust*:A Unifying Irony." *GQ* 47:544-55.

The contradiction between nature as described by the archangels in the "Prolog im Himmel" and Faust's misconceived idealiztion of it unifies the play by making Faust the victim of a lifelong irony. The nature-seeking protagonist of Goethe's *Faust* is never more innocently at one with his ideal than in the agitation of his opening soliloquy. His career is one of tortuous progress toward perception of the reality of his original ideal of spiritual unity with nature and a fitting revision of his aspirations. He attaiⁿs the spiritual serenity of his original ideal in the closing scene, as his *Unsterbliches* is extracted from terrestrial nature. (AW)

Heinse. 10521. Klinger, Uwe R. "Heinse's Birth Date:1746 or 1749?" *GN* 5:5-8.

Complementary evidence in the Langewiesen baptismal record and the student register at the Arnstadt "Gymnasium" establishes 15 February 1746 as Heinse's birth date. The alternate date of 1749 has attained widespread currency. The origin of this assumption is probably a contemporary etching of Heinse, bearing the inscription, "Wilhelm Heinse, Professor zu Mainz, geb. 1749 au Langenwiesen in Thüringen." Heinse's apparent corroboration of this date in a letter to Wieland is very likely due to a misreading of the manuscript. Beginning with Jördens' literary lexicon of 1807, most bio-bibliographical sources during the 19th century list the wrong date, whereas Koberstein and Hettner in their respective literary histories correctly chose 1746 as the year of Heinse's birth. (URK)

Hölderlin. 10531. Blunden, Allan. "A Question of Time:Notes on Hölderlin's 'Sonnenuntergang' and Lessing's *Laokoon*." *MLR* 69:821-28.

Lessing's *Laokoon* and Hölderlin's "Sonnenuntergang" are mutually illuminating, because the poem exemplifies Lessing's thesis that poetry should deal with events in time rather than objects in space. In the *Laokoon* Lessing associates poetry with music and sees music as essentially transient. In "Sonnen-untergang," which describes the sunset as a musical phenomenon, form and content are matched; the poem is about music and is, in its linguistic forms, a model of the transience it portrays. All the verbs reflect a continuous passing of time, the present becoming past: correspondingly, the references to Apollo record the movement from presence to absence. The poem explores the double meanings of present/presence and of its own title and illustrates Hölderlin's extreme sensitivity to the possibilities of language. The validity of Lessing's esthetic in general is confirmed by contrasting the merits of Klopstock (whom he admired) and Hölderlin with the work of Brockes and Haller. (AGB)

10537. Gaskill, P.H. "Hölderlin's Contact with Pietism." *MLR* 69:805-20.

Gathers and evaluates evidence of Hölderlin's first-hand contact with pietism: Hölderlin certainly knew at least one work by the 18th-century Swabian pietist, Johann Albrecht Bengel. He grew up in an atmosphere tempered by moderate pietism. It is unlikely that he encountered pietism at the University of Tübingen, although he did make contact with well-known pietists such as Lavater and Schubart. His renewed interest in Christ and Christianity after 1798 is likely to have involved his reading pietist commentaries on the Book of Revelation, and this most probably influenced the hymn "Patmos." (PHG)

Hoffmann. 10563. Peters, Diana S. "E.T.A. Hoffmann:The Conciliatory Satirist." *Monatshefte* 66:55-73.

Hoffmann's views concerning the nature of the creative process and the function of art lie at the center of his work. The fundamental presupposition for Hoffmann's extensive use of irony and humor as literary devices for satirical criticism is his belief in the existence of a dualistic world and in the necessity of constructing a creative dynamism between the everyday world of the philistine and the "Other Realm" of the artist. The essentially conciliatory nature of Hoffmann's satire is expressed most succinctly through the metaphor that the ladder to heavenly heights must be grounded on earth. Exploring possible channels for synthesis, Hoffmann examines critically both the philistine and the overly enthusiastic artist, housewives and courtesans (the anti-muse figure), and ethereal, spiritual Woman (the muse). (DSP)

Jung-Stilling. 10587. Panthel, H.W. "Jung-Stillings Welt-endzeit und Zar Alexander I von Russland:Einige unbekannte Briefpassagen." *GSlav* 2(1973):61-66.

Traditional research on Stilling's millennarian views and his relationship with Czar Alexander I of Russia deals with epistolary material different from the author's newly collected documen-tation presented here. This limited number of letters by Stilling affords insight into the role which he assigned to the leading

European monarchs of his time in arresting the tide of rationalistic and enlightened thinking. Considering the imminence of the "new age," Stilling not only speculates about it in general philosophical terms, but at times resorts to mathematical proof. The majority of the letters are addressed to J. G. Siebel, then mayor of Freudenberg. (HWP)

Kleist. 10605. Frank, Luanne T. " 'The Strangest Love Scene in World Literature' (The Dismemberment of Achilles in Kleist's *Penthesilea*) Reassessed." [F 19]:236-41.
The events in the dismemberment scenes of Kleist's *Penthesilea* resemble events familiar from Attic tragedy. What remains unrecognized is the significance of these resemblances for an understanding of the dismemberment scenes and the drama proper. A reading of the scenes in their most characteristic mode, however, that of myth in Jung's sense, reveals them to be an integral part of the work and indispensable to an understanding of it, and to be positive and constructive rather than negative and destructive in their cultural import. (LTF)
10620. St. Leon, R. "The Question of Guilt in Kleist's *Penthesilea*." *Seminar* 10:19-37.
That Kleist's *Penthesilea*'s dramatic impetus derives from tensions between flesh and spirit emerges from close examination of its language and imagery. Penthesilea's sense of mission, centered on Achilles, is a religious ideal which she fails to reconcile with her intense, half-understood sexuality. Themes are expressed largely in sharp shifts of language: from delicate lyricism to heavy sensuality. (RPFS)

Kotzebue. 10632. Zipes, Jack. "Dunlap, Kotzebue, and the Shaping of American Theater: A Reevaluation from a Marxist Perspective." *EAL* 8:272-84.
William Dunlap and August von Kotzbue played a vital role in the historical development of American theater; yet, scholars generally dismiss their works as *kitsch* (trivial art). A re-evaluation from a Marxist perspective reveals the ramifications of their relationship up to the present. First, it is important to note that Kotzbue and Dunlap shared similar views on theater as a moral institution but often compromised themselves to support the status quo and the hegemony of the ruling classes. A close study of the comedies *Der Opfertod* and *The Italian Father* (and other dramas) supports this contention. Furthermore, Kotzbue and Dunlap contributed to the growth of the well-made play in the 19th century which, in turn, gave rise to commercial theater. (JZ)

Lenz. 10638. Diffey, Norman R. "Lenz, Rousseau, and the Problem of Striving." *Seminar* 10:165-80.
J.-J. Rousseau attracted much criticism from contemporary and later German writers through his ideal of rest ("paix") as the ultimate good. J.M.R. Lenz is deeply influenced by his social and cultural criticism, but cannot reconcile his doctrine of "minimum movement" with his own dynamic view of existence as endless striving. Lenz adheres to a moral creed of constant activity ("Handeln") aimed at social reform. His failures in this sphere underline the significance of his rejection of Rousseau's ideal, which aims at balancing volition and ability. Lenz cannot accept Rousseau's passive definition of virtue as virtuous feeling without action. (NRD)
10639. Osborne, John. "Exhibitionism and Criticism: J.M.R. Lenz's *Briefe über die Moralität der* Leiden des jungen Werthers." *Seminar* 10:199-212.
In his *Briefe über die Moralität der Leiden des jungen Werthers* Lenz defends Goethe's novel in an extreme and provocative fashion. Lenz rejects the rationalist, condemnation of *Werther*, claiming that it is a moral work, since it contributes to the refinement and extension of the sensibility of the reader. The novel's emphasis on the emotions is, argues Lenz, necessitated by the restrictive society for which it was written. Lenz dissociates himself from this society by a rhetoric which ostentatiously emphasizes his isolation. (JO)

Lessing, G. 10643. Desch, Joachim. "Emilia Galotti—A Victim of Misconceived Morality." *Trivium* 9:88-99.
Lessing wrote his play as a tragic counterpart to his optimistic

comedy *Minna von Barnhelm*. In each case he criticizes a rigorous pseudo-rational code upheld either as a matter of self-evident principle or as a means of safeguarding human conduct against emotional motivation. Lessing aims his criticism not at the court, but at a self-righteous *Bürgertum* in its moralistic hubris. (JD)
10658. Loeb, Ernst. "Lessing's 'Samuel Henzi': Eine aktuelle Thematik." *Monatshefte* 65(1973):351-60.
Lessing's attempted dramatization of the abortive conspiracy against the ruling tyranny of Berne remained a fragment. So deeply had he been moved, particularly by the human qualities and ethical purpose of Samuel Henzi, the leader of this attempt, that he began to write his drama in the very same year, 1749. Loeb discusses the work not as a "republican tragedy," but rather with a view to the contrasting positions of Henzi and his principal opponent. The "enlightened" hero, committed to reason as the irresistible political argument and convinced of the proposition that the means have to be commensurate with so lofty an end as the demand of equal rights under a commonly accepted law, is confronted by the eternal "realist"—committed to the realization of his aims in all circumstances, with moral considerations relegated, at best, to the never-never land somewhere after "victory." Henzi's downfall shows the futility of his position. The fragmentary character of the work is inherent in a problem incapable of solution by "enlightened" means. Thus, Lessing's attempt would seem to pose a very timely question: one to which, as is shown, only "fragmentary" answers have ever been given. (In German) (EL)
10659. Marshall, Madeleine F. "Millwood and Marwood: Fallen Women and the Moral Interest of Sentimental Tragedy." *Mary Wollstonecraft Jour.* 2,ii:2-12.
In the morality of sentimental tragedy, as exemplified in Lillo's *The London Merchant; or, The History of George Barnwell* and Lessing's *Miss Sara Sampson*, moral evil is real and complex. Lillo's Millwood and Lessing's Marwood strongly defend themselves and bitterly criticize the evil of the "good" people of the plays. As in sentimental comedy, where a carefully reserved exemplary heroine gains her desired ends, so in sentimental tragedy, virtue is right reason and rarely attained in this world. The fallen woman, formerly the butt of ridicule, is the victim of sexual injustice. According to Millwood, the male sex has made her an evil, mercenary woman. Marwood knows that she and Sara are alike victims of Mellefont. (MFM)
10667. Schutz, H. "Eighteenth Century German Pedagogy and Lessing." *RLV* 39(1973):538-45; 40:56-65.
Ideas concerning education scattered throughout Lessing's work rank with those of his contemporaries. For Lessing "education" stands at the beginning of the tradition which stressed religious, ethical, esthetic, and humanitarian elements in its pedagogic aims. The Neo-humanist trend sought to cast its view of ideal man into a Neo-hellenic mold; the well established trend toward a "Staatserziehung" was giving way to a "Nationalerziehung" by the early 19th century. Finally, the introduction of the concept of perfectability and the dynamism of the individual helped reshape the goals of education toward the development of a humanitarian spirit. Lessing's views on education point him toward moral idealism. While Rousseau pursues an aim in political science, Lessing aims at promoting a society based on individual ethics. (HS)

Novalis. 10691. Michaud, Stéphane. "La politique de Novalis." *DHS* 6:225-34.
The standard interpretation by critics has long been to consider early German Romanticism as reactionary and anti-Enlightenment. Novalis became the symbol of counter-revolutionary thought. Novalis had nothing to do with pietist circles hostile to the Revolution; his thought combines that of Lessing, Schlegel, Kant, and Fichte, to produce an original synthesis. (SM)

Schiller. 10704. Bangerter, Lowell A. "A Leftist View of Schiller." *RS* 41(1973):118-24.
References to Friedrich Schiller in the writings of Friedrich Wolf reflect the characteristic ambivalence of the East German view of Schiller. Despite the generalizations of critics which have related

Wolf's works to those of Schiller, it becomes apparent upon closer examination that Wolf did not have a positive orientation toward the earlier dramatist. Comments in his early writings indicate that in the 1920's Wolf rejected Schiller outright as irrelevant. Although his experiences in Russia in the thirties and forties seem to have stimulated a modification in his stance, Wolf was actually aroused only to possibilities of exploiting Schiller to achieve political aims. Pertinent echoes of Schiller's works in Wolf's dramas emphasize the negative nature of his underlying attitude concerning Schiller. At most Wolf accepted a few of his ideas on the purpose of the drama. (LAB)

10730. Phelps, Reginald H. "Schiller's *Fiesco*:A Republican Tragedy?" *PMLA* 89:442-53.
Schiller's subtitle, "Ein republikanisches Trauerspiel," creates serious difficulties of interpretation. His four principal historical sources give little basis for regarding the conspirators or the conspiracy as "republican" in the sense of "antimonarchical." A study of the vocabulary shows that such politically emotional words as *Republik, Freiheit, Bürger, Volk* are infrequently used and are likely to bear a neutral or negative-ironic meaning. Schiller's two later versions, the Mannheim stage version and the Leipzig-Dresden manuscript, show no conspicuous change in his use of such terms. The play concerns *Republik* in the older sense of *res publica* rather than in the modern meaning. Not Rousseau, but Plutarch as translated by G.B. von Schirach, most strongly influenced Schiller in theme, incidents, traits of character, and perhaps political attitude. The play appears as a conflict among three strong personalities—Fiesco, Verrina, and Andrea Doria—for power within the state; and Doria, representing the essence of the state, may be the real "hero." (RHP)

Tieck. 10755. Gries, Frauke. "Two Critical Essays by Ludwig Tieck:On Literature and Its Sociological Aspects." *Monatshefte* 66:157-65.
Tieck's essays "Kritik und deutsches Bücherwesen" and "Goethe und seine Zeit" reveal his intent as a literary critic and its affinity to modern views. Tieck perceives strong reciprocal connections between a writer and his audience. He defends the merits of light popular literature since it lends itself more advantageously to the elucidation of cultural and historical constellations than does great literature. Although Tieck accuses Goethe of neglecting in his later works the political importance and consequences of art, he acknowledges enthusiastically the poetic merits of Goethe's works. Tieck stresses that all literature plays a significant role in the understanding of an era and its society; a thorough investigation by a sensitive critic will lead to historical and sociological insights. Thus he attempts and advocates an approach to, and interpretation of, literature which are basically "intrinsic" but transcend the particular composition under consideration. (FG)

VI. NINETEENTH AND EARLY TWENTIETH CENTURIES

General and Miscellaneous. 10797. Boulby, Mark. "The Matter of Consciousness:A Romantic Legacy?" *HAB* 25:122-40. [Novalis, Hesse, Kafka, Bernhard, et al.]
In the Romantic period the matter of consciousness becomes a central concern for philosophy and imaginative literature. Romantic literature is rich in descriptions of changes of consciousness and in symbols that pertain to this. Consciousness is capable of converting all to gold—or else to darkness. In modern literature Hesse and Kafka exemplify these alternatives. Much mid-20th-century writing, dealing as it does with a hopelessly isolated self-consciousness, tends toward darkness. The novels of Beckett and Thomas Bernhard's *Verstörung* show the recurrence of traditional symbols and patterns. (MB)

10821. Horwath, Peter. "Antiklerikalismus und National-itätenhader in der Literatur Deutschösterreichs (1894-1917)." *MAL* 7,i/ii:34-50.
The six Austrian *Grenzlandromane* (1894-1917) discussed reflect the national strife in the ethnically mixed border regions of Cisleithania. The purpose of these novels was to make the German minorities aware of the values inherent in their heritage, and to stiffen their resistance against attempts of Slavization by Czechs and Slovenes. The Roman clergy is represented as an active or passive agent of the de-Germanization process. The authors demand a defection from Catholicism and the subsequent acceptance of an ethnically and culturally compatible form of public or private religiosity. This religiosity is at times of a bizarre nature. (PH)

Drama and Theater. 10890. Hoegel, Rolf K. "Young German Message Plays." *Monatshefte* 65(1973):361-69.
Several of Laube's and Gutzkow's dramas are entrusted with a political message appealing to German and Austrian citizens dissatisfied with the general state of affairs in the restoration era. This dissatisfaction is prevalent among large segments of the middle and working class population. Laube's *Struensee* (1844) proclaims the ideals of the German liberal movement: democratic government, spiritual independence, emancipation of women, German national unity. The message is enhanced by the psychologically skillful way of presenting Struensee, its herald and champion. The drama was offered an invariably favorable reception all over Germany. Gutzkow's *Uriel Acosta* (1846) is concerned with the liberation of all citizens from spiritual and from political oppression. It also pleads for the emancipation of women. *Uriel Acosta*, too, was given an enthusiastic reception by theatergoers, but encountered severe criticism from the state authorities. The Young German message plays must be regarded as part of the spiritual forces that contributed to the historical development leading to the revolution of 1848. (RKH)

Prose Fiction. 10920. Plank, Robert. "Imaginary Voyages and Toy Novels." *HSL* 6:221-42. [On works by Austrian, Ital., Eng., and Danish writers.]
Some speculative fiction reveals its character best when conceptualized as both "imaginary voyage" and "toy novel." Four Austrian novels of the turn of the century (Th. Hertzka, *Eine Reise nach Freiland*; Th. Herzl, *Altneuland*; A. Kubin, *Die andere Seite*; F.V. Herzmanovsky-Orlando, *Maskenspiel der Genien*) give a realistic but perfunctory description of the real world and focus on the small imaginary country. Examples of the toy novel, notably some of Andersen's *Fairy Tales*, clarify the underlying longings and the derivation of political ideas from father figures. The imaginary voyage embodies the often unconscious fantasies, the toy novel makes them innocuous, hence acceptable. (RP)

Broch. 10949. Watt, Roderick H. "Hermann Broch's *Die unbekannte Grösse*:The Central Symbol of 'Sterne im Wasser'." *MLN* 89:840-48.
Broch wrote *Die unbekannte Grösse* to demonstrate his conviction that rational and irrational experience fulfill complementary functions in life. The novel shows that love and death must be accepted as integral and significant facets of existence. Broch shows the developing awareness of the main character to this truth by tracing his reactions to the recurring symbol of a star reflected in dark water. The value and reality of love and death stand out as self-evident, if incomprehensible, truths against the dark mystery around them. Broch tries to use the symbol to give formal unity to a novel too slight to carry the conceptual weight demanded of it. (RHW)

Büchner. 10960. Stodder, Joseph H. "Influences of *Othello* on Büchner's *Woyzeck*." *MLR* 69:115-20.
Critical interest in Shakespearean influence on Georg Büchner's dramatic work has generally centered on two plays, *Leonce und Lena* and *Dantons Tod*. Most critics have either ignored or dismissed influence on *Woyzeck*. But the plot and central character relationship of *Woyzeck*, if not the overall tone, is often reminiscent of *Othello*, and a close parallel reading of these two plays suggests striking instances of specific borrowings. These examples reflect similarities in dramatic situation, character relationship, imagery, and in psychological development of the

protagonist. Review of these specific examples affords a more rewarding appreciation of Büchner's play. (JHS)

Dauthendey, M. 10967. Szépe, Helena. "Dauthendey's 'Stummen des Schweigens'." *OL* 29:123-32.
Because of *Ultra-Violett* and the section of it entitled "Voices of Silence," Dauthendey has been viewed as a forerunner of expressionism. A comparison of diary entries, which served as a model for these different poems, however, shows that Dauthendey strictly adhered to impressionistic principles. The peculiarity of these early poems lies rather in the use of theatrical effects and in the scenic character of the landscape. (HS)

Droste-Hülshoff. 10974. Belchamber, N.P. "A Case of Identity:A New Look at *Die Judenbuche*." *ML* 55:80-82.
Most critics of Annette von Droste-Hülsoff's *Die Judenbuche* accept the official verdict that the body hanging in the Jews' beech is that of Friedrich Mergel, but can Mergel, returning from years of Turkish slavery, be identified? At times Mergel's mother could not distinguish her son from Johannes Niemand. Missing for three days, Niemand is found hanged in the Jews' beech. The squire in naming the corpse Mergel refers as proof to a scar on its neck, perhaps to protect Niemand's name. Droste-Hülshoff furthers his ambivalence by calling this a true event. Her introductory poem warns the reader not to judge, but leave the question open. (NPB)

Fontane. 10984. Bance, A.F. "Fontane's *Mathilde Möhring*." *MLR* 69:121-33.
Theodor Fontane's *Mathilde Möhring* owes its neglect largely to the beliefs that it is merely a fragment, and that the title-figure is disproportionately unpleasant. The first myth has been corrected by Gotthard Erler's new edition (1969), which prompts the reassessment. The second underestimates the subtleties of the novel, a highly individuated treatment of a familiar Fontane theme, the woman as victim of social circumstances. Fontane's interest in his theme goes beyond social criticism. He explores the problematical concept of character, role-playing, even reality itself. The theater is used to bring out his theme of reality and appearance. The interest of the book is that Mathilde remains an enigma. (AFB)

George. 11023. Furst, Lilian. "Stefan George's *Die Blumen des Bösen*:A Problem of Translation." *RLC* 48:203-17.
Stefan George's rendering of Baudelaire's *Fleurs du mal* presents a striking example of the intrusion of the translator's personality. George has enobled and purified Baudelaire by his selective choice of poems, by his changes and omissions in the text, and by his tendency to greater abstraction. Linguistically, George's imprint is ever more evident. In part these changes are due to the need to transfer alexandrines into pentameters. In the main *Die Blumen des Bösen* were for George not so much a question of translation as an exercise of considerable importance in his training as a poet. (LRF)

Gerstäcker. 11033. McClain, William H., and Lieselotte E. Kurth-Voigt,eds. *Friedrich Gerstäckers Briefe an Hermann Costenoble*. Frankfurt: Archiv für Geschichte des Buchwesens. 80 pp.
This edition of 147 previously unpublished letters which Gerstäcker wrote between 1861 and 1872 to Costenoble illuminates a relationship which was in many ways typical. While the letters deal mainly with contracts and other matters of concern to an author dependent upon his writings for his income, they also touch on matters of more general interest. In the letters Gerstäcker evaluates the work of several contemporary writers, discusses his own contribution to literature, and comments from time to time on political and social issues of the day. The introduction sketches the life and work of Gerstäcker, discusses briefly the critical reception of his works and his impact as a writer, and presents a bibliography of his collected writings. Notes clarify the numerous allusions to personalities, works, and contemporary events. (WHM & LEK-V)

Gotthelf. 11038. Thomas, L.H. "The Late Stories of Jeremias Gotthelf (1852-55)." *Hermathena* 116(1973):66-80.
Gotthelf became a writer of fiction in order to further the reforms he championed. Remote from Weimar classicism, he generally showed little interest in the writings of his contemporaries or predecessors. His linguistic medium is a blend of the dialect of the Bernese Oberland and of High German, a mixture demanding a certain effort for German-speaking readers outside of Switzerland to master. His own nature drove him to create stories and was responsible for his remarkable originality. Gotthelf's best stories of his last years include the three discussed in detail as typical of these years. "Barthli der Korber" is the longest story, "Die Frau Pfarrerin" a third shorter and "Der Besuch" much shorter and of an anecdotal character. (LHC)

Greve. 11045. Morley, Patricia. "*Over Prairie Trails*:'a poem woven of impressions'." *HAB* 25:225-31.
Over Prairie Trails (1922) illustrates the artistic maturity which Grove had achieved by his early forties in his adopted language. The work is an account of seven journeys made in 1917-18 in the wilds of Manitoba. Grove describes his technique as one of allowing impressions to ripen into words. He calls his work a mood-poem with a symphonic structure. Each of the seven chapters has a distinctive mood: "Fog" is melancholy and weird; "Snow," macabre and sinister; "Dawn and Diamonds" is a Christmas pastoral of joy and innocence. Grove's poetic prose combines an imaginative approach with scientific accuracy. (PAM)

11047. Spettigue, Douglas O., and Anthony W. Riley. "Felix Paul Greve Redivivus:Zum früheren Leben des kanadischen Schriftstellers Frederick Philip Grove." *Seminar* 9(1973):148-55.
In all German reference books listing the life and works of the novelist, poet, and translator Felix Paul Greve, the date of his death is given as 1910. In fact, Greve did not die in that year, but emigrated to North America, where in Canada he began a totally new life as Frederick Philip Grove. It was under this name that Grove established himself as one of the major Canadian twentieth-century novelists, and his literary reputation has grown over the years since his death in 1948. It is only now that careful research has revealed the identity of Grove with Greve, thus making further investigation of Grove's early career as a German writer essential for scholars interested in Canadian literature in general and in German-Canadian literary relationships in particular. (DOS & AWR)

Heine. 11160. Steinhauer, Harry. "Heine and Cecile Furtado." *MLN* 89:422-47.
A re-examination of the correspondence between Heine and his Hamburg relations on the one hand and the Furtados of Paris on the other shows that Cécile Furtado felt an adolescent "love" for the already eminent poet and that Heine exploited this infatuation for his own advantage, without involving himself erotically. His own later claim, "I was the lover of his [Carl's] wife" is examined in context and explained. (HS)

11168. Veit, Philipp F. "Heine:The Marrano Pose." *Monatshefte* 66:145-56.
Heine occasionally intimated that he was of noble descent on the maternal side of his family. The ultimate implication was that his ancestors had been Marrano refugees. As Sephardic Jews the latter were the heirs to a highly sophisticated heritage and considered themselves an élite group. Heine's genealogical conjecture coalesced with a tendency among his German-Jewish contemporaries to reorient themselves toward the Hispano-Jewish tradition. He affected the pose of a latter-day Marrano and, by its infusion into his writings, it not only assumed technical and thematic significance, but also permitted him to speak with several voices about his relations to Judaism. (PFV)

Hesse. 11178. Brink, A.W. "Hermann Hesse and the Oedipal Quest." *L&P* 24:66-79.
Examines Hesse's attraction to Freudian and Jungian psychological theories in the context of his own life and art. During 1916 and 1917 Hesse had a partial Jungian analysis, but it was Freud's

theory of the Oedipal complex that shaped the basic themes of *Demian* and *Steppenwolf*. In both there appears in the main protagonists ambivalence toward women as attachment objects, suggesting Hesse's own relational preoccupation. In the later novels, *Narziss and Goldmund* and *The Glass Bead Game*, idealized male relationships predominate, dissolving the obsessional defense usual in latent homosexuality as it concerns women. Hesse's quest is thus traced to intrapsychic conflict from which he wished to be free but never quite was. (AWB)

11182. Fickert, Kurt J. "The Portrait of the Artist in Hesse's 'Klein und Wagner'." *HSL* 6:108-87.
Hesse's concern about the destiny of the artist, specifically the *Dichter*, lies at the root of his novella "Klein und Wagner." Like the story's protagonist Klein, Hesse fled a life of social obligations in the North in order to begin anew in the South. As Klein considers what made him perpetrate an embezzlement, Hesse ponders what constitutes the artist and decides it is his devotion to a calling which compels him to be individualistic and anti-social. Klein's encounter with a prostitute, Teresina, provides him with a companion in the demimonde, but it also provides Hesse with a guide to the nether reaches of his conscious, where the wellsprings of creative activity originate. But Klein fails in an attempt to accept unreservedly the amorality of the instincts, just as Hesse, at this point, cannot forgive himself for having abandoned his family and the successful author of slick fiction. Klein drowns himself (less than deliberately); his letting himself fall in the water becomes, however, the moment of triumph for the *Dichter*, his self-realization. (KJF)

11183. Field, G.W. "Hermann Hesse:Polarities and Symbols of Synthesis." *QQ* 81:87-101.
From *Siddhartha* to *Das Glasperlenspiel* Hesse's works present dualisms and conflicts and a concomitant quest for oneness. Dissensions reflect reality while synthesis belongs to the esthetic realm. Successive novels reveal a pattern of *Steigerung* and increasing emphasis on *Geist*. Demian merges in Sinclair liberating the unconscious to attain a higher stage of psychic unity. *Siddhartha* reflects East-West polarity and points to unity through *Om*, the river and the smile which conveys what words cannot. The polarities of *Narziss und Goldmund* remain unresolved. *Der Steppenwolf* suggests bridging of dissensions through humor based on ironic objectivity, development of the whole personality, but under the control of *Geist* exemplified in music and Mozart-Pable. In *Das Glasperlenspiel* music becomes the principal carrier both of polarities and their transcendent union. Knecht and the Altmusikmeister follow parallel paths to apotheosis, one in Castalia, the other in the real world, while the convergent paths of Designori and Knecht are polarities pointing to a resolution only attainable in the imagination. But the ideal goal is a beacon: moral and esthetic guide through life. (GWF)

11194. Olsen, Gary R. "To Castalia and Beyond:The Function of Time and History in the Later Works of Hermann Hesse." *ArQ* 30:343-54.
Hesse's concern after World War I was the extent of the contemporary descent into process, flux, and time. Having been nurtured on prerelativistic ideas, he could not reconcile himself to the argument of Heidegger and others that time is the very essence of Being. Consequently, in his novels, he sought escapes from time and historical relativism. Ultimately, however, he concluded that such an effort was self-defeating and naive. It is this recognition which dominates his last and most significant work, *Das Glasperlenspiel*. (GRO)

11198. Taylor, Harley U. "Friendship in the Life of Hermann Hesse." *WVUPP* 21:54-66.
Hesse's personal experiences are the basis for many of the concerns in his novels. The friendships in his own life can be best considered according to categories of association. Some lasting friendships date from schoolboy days. The most notable of these is with Otto Hartmann. Most of Hesse's important friendships were made, however, in his adult years. A mutuality of interest and similar attitudes accounted for friendships with Finckh, Mann, Rolland, Gide, Ball, Fischer, Suhrkamp, and Bodmer. J.B. Lang was both Hesse's psychiatrist and good friend. Hesse's interests in music and art led to friendships with Schlenker, Brunn, Durigo, Schoeck, Bucherer, Stürzenegger, Welti, Morgen-

thaler, and Böhmer. (HUT)

Hofmannsthal. 11238. Mistry, Freny. "Towards Buddhahood:Some Remarks on the Sigismund Figure in Hofmannsthal's *Turm* Plays." *MLR* 69:337-47.
An examination of diverse sources of Hofmannsthal's knowledge of Indian thought throws new light upon the controversial personality of Sigismund in the three versions of *Der Turm*. They are shown to exemplify the doctrine of *karma* (deed), which states that individual actions produce corresponding rewards and that freedom from *karma* is possible only through volitional effort. Hofmannsthal used the karmic notion as he found it in Lafcadio Hearn's writings on Buddhism, but extended it to include the concept of "totality," a concept foreign to Buddhism. Whereas the fragmentary notes to *Das Leben ein Traum* ((1902-10) develop *karma* as a retributive agent in Sigismund's life and environment, the subsequent "Turm" plays dramatize his attainment of spiritual freedom. His aspirations toward this freedom, thwarted by his participation in the prevailing violence (1925 version), are ultimately fulfilled by his total rejection of physical force (1927 version). In living the ideals of suffering, perseverance, and self-abnegation Sigismund becomes a powerful political force to be eliminated. His death thus provides testimony of Hofmannsthal's faith in man's spiritual prowess. (FM)

11256. Winkler, Michael. "How to Write Hofmannsthal's Life:Annals, Biography of His Work, or Poet in His Time?" *MAL* 7,i/ii:113-16.
The centenary of Hofmannsthal's birth reveals the need for a comprehensive account of his literary achievement. Since no critical biography of his life and work exists, a discussion of the major problems posed by such a task is of general interest. A look at George, Rilke, and Thomas Mann places the problem into comparative perspective and shows that different artistic and historical circumstances brought about a different approach to writing their biographies. Annals provide a synchronic perspective as they indicate diachronic continuity, a description of Hofmannsthal's artistic development should emphasize the coherence of his themes, and an analysis of the poet in his time must concentrate on his esthetic realization of historical experiences. (MW)

Kafka. 11283. Grimes, Margaret. "Kafka's Use of Cue-Names:Its Importance for an Interpretation of *The Castle*." *CentR* 18:221-30.
In *The Castle* (1926) Franz Kafka employs many of the modes of medieval literature, one of the most important of which is the use of cue-names, that is names which suggest a psychological trait, a historical event, or a well known literary work without limiting the character to a mere representation of the idea referred to. Two of the most important names in *The Castle* are those of Arthur and Jeremiah, which are meant to suggest the New and the Old Testaments respectively. *The Castle* is a multi-level parable in which one can find social criticism and sexual symbolism, but in which the dominant theme is a religious one. (MWG)

11288. Karl, Frederick R. "Enclosure, the Adversary Culture, and the Nature of the Novel." *Mosaic* 7,iii:1-15.
Kafka's presentation of burrow and castle keep in his short story "The Burrow" has profound reverberations in cultural terms, for such an enclosure represents those time considerations which have dominated our thought since the early 18th century. It represents the profane nature of our society, as apart from the sacred, which is space oriented, and the resistance to development, adventure, and exploration which are a concomitant of the need to move out and seek. Here, inward-turning becomes an adversary movement. Rejecting, turning back, burrowing in, building a castle keep—all of these indicate a culture that rejects a regularizing, moderating society which creates, establishes, "makes things possible." (FRK)

11295. Miles, David. "Kafka's Hapless Pilgrims and Grass's Scurrilous Dwarf:Notes on Representative Figures in the Anti-Bildungsroman." *Monatshefte* 65(1973):341-50.
Four of the most significant German Bildungsromane in the 20th century are Kafka's three novels and Grass's *Die Blechtrommel*. Kafka's three protagonists are engaged upon a quest for spiritual

growth and identity, but the Rousseauean Pelagianism of a *Wilhelm Meister* has given way to an uncontrollable sense of guilt. In *Das Schloss* and *Der Prozess* the anonymous "tutorial" institution has usurped the role of the normally eponymous hero. Unlike Kafka's forgetful confessors, Grass's garrulous dwarf revels in drumming up his blasphemous past; from his madhouse memoirs emerges a portrait of the young *Bildungsheld* as a juvenile delinquent. There is only the instinctual urge to regress; the principle of growth portrayed is not spiritual, but phallic. Instead of dreaming of a "theatrical mission" like Wilhelm Meister, Oscar shatters the facade of Danzig's *Stadttheater*—its "Bildungstempel." Kafka's and Grass's heroes hold up a mirror to the distorted image of twentieth-century man and also reject, by implication, the humanistic tradition from which the Bildungsroman emerged. (DHM)

Keller, G. 11315. Radant, Friedhelm. "Transitional Time in Keller's *Züricher Novellen*." *PMLA* 89:77-84.
The historical phenomenon of periods in transition, particularly the individual response to the fact and realization of transition, appear as the main theme of Keller's *Züricher Novellen*. The fictive present in each novella is a period removed from the actual high point of a given era. *Hadlaub*, e.g., takes place at the very end of the *Minnesang* period, representing a latecomer among the minnesingers, one who plays an anachronistic role; and *Ursula* treats events surrounding religious change. To underscore the idea of transition, Keller makes use of the ironic narrator who frequently voices his discriminating opinion about the characters, and who in the frame novella clearly relates the issue of "transitional time" to Keller's own age, also a period of transition, and in so doing censures those writers who are oblivious to the needs of the present and seek refuge in a glorious portrayal of the past. (FKIR)
11317. Thomas, Barry G. "The Function of the Eyes in Gottfried Keller's 'Die missbrauchten Liebesbriefe'." *Monatshefte* 66:46-54.
Keller uses eyes as a means of characterization, of clarifying interpersonal relationships, and of revealing depths of personality not easily expressed in words. In "Die missbrauchten Liebesbriefe" the eyes are the central motif. Through them Keller describes the collapse of one relationship and the growth of another and illuminates the development of the various individuals. The eyes may also become the "windows to the soul," enabling the characters to reach levels of understanding not fully attainable through words. Wilhelm and Gritli achieve a new awareness of love, time, and death. In this context the eyes may also be considered a point of contact between the individual and his experience of man's original, common source. (BGT)

Kornfeld. 11327. Pazi, Margarita. "*Smither kauft Europa*: Über eine unbekannte Komödie von Paul Kornfeld." *OL* 29:133-59.
In turning toward comedy Paul Kornfeld demonstrated to countless other dramatists of this period his estrangement from expressionism. In *Smither kauft Europa* his more positive frame of mind was again dissolved. The comedy raises anew the gloomy uncertainty of the first drama, this time distorted into grotesque proportions. Kornfeld conveyed the charge against the soulless society of the years 1914-18 to his contemporaries in postwar Europe. The picture of a world threatened by the loss of all ethical values and the dissolution of the European spirit is symbolized through the reactions of the protagonist. In the confrontation of the American multi-millionaire Smither with the characters of the comedy, human limitations are exposed. The necessity of Smither's purchases becomes paradigmatic as the final outcome of a perceptivity dislodged by utilitarian considerations is revealed, to which the "poor" multi-millionaire also falls victim. (MP)

Kraus, Karl. 11331. Bäuml, Gustav H. and Franz H. "Namenverzeichnis zu Karl Kraus' *Die Fackel*." *MAL* 7,i/ii:141-73. [See 6,iii/iv(1973):139-60, for Part I.]
Karl Kraus' *Die Fackel* appeared periodically from 1899 to 1936 and is the fundament of his entire literary production. The present index, which will appear in installments, will make the contents of

Die Fackel readily accessible for the first time. (GHB & FHB)

Mann, H. 11359. Linn, Rolf N. "Wilhelm und Wulckow: Die zwei Gesichter der Macht im *Untertan*." *Seminar* 10:104-15.
William II, as depicted by Heinrich Mann in *Der Untertan*, is a deluded weakling who acts the mighty monarch, concealing his cowardice behind hazardous histrionics. Diederich Hessling models himself after his Kaiser; for this reason one tends to overlook Baron von Wulckow, the second representative of power, who scorns theatrical patriotism and openly pursues his selfish aims. Diederich recognizes that William and Wulckow constitute the power he worships. Mann's caricatures of Kaiser, Junker, and Hessling are deft and memorable and the two incarnations of power are juxtaposed in a fine structural balance. (RNL)
11365. Siefken, Hinrich. "Emperor William II and His Loyal Subject—Montage and Historical Allusions in Heinrich Mann's Satirical Novel *Der Untertan*." *Trivium* 8(1973):69-82.
Mann creates a simplified historical background dominated by the Emperor, while the main actor on the fictional stage is his loyal subject, a man without individual identity or personality. He merely models himself on the official image of the Emperor. Apparently not talking of the Emperor, *Der Untertan* is, in fact, not talking of the loyal subject, but of Imperial Germany. Hessling is the target for satire; the real aim of the satire lies beyond this target. Such satire is achieved effectively through satirical linguistic allusion and montage. However, as a novel and as satire the work has serious flaws. Where it aims at the cheap effect, the reader is unable to take the target of satire seriously. Also, the characters are, almost without exception, the puppets of their own convictions and obsessions, they are not even humanly inhuman. As we have no sympathy for them, we do not understand their actions. In literary terms the loyal subject is too much a man of straw. (HCS)

Mann, T. 11387. Elstun, Esther N. "Two Views of the Mountain: Thomas Mann's *Zauberberg* and Konstantin Fedin's *Sanatorium Arktur*." *GSlav* 3:55-71.
Mann's *Zauberberg* and *Sanatorium Arktur* are a study in contrasts. The authors' disparate points of view led to pronounced differences in their treatment of the same themes, their characterization of the protagonists, and their use of symbolism and imagery. For Castorp the magic mountain is a refuge from the rigors of life and the site of dangerous but fascinating adventures in sickness and death. For Levshin it is a place of resolute preparation for return to a useful and rewarding life in society; death is in no wise attractive, but an insidious enemy against whom he pits all of his energies. Both novels treat the decline of Western values. (ENE)
11397. Honsa, William M.,Jr. "Parody and Narrator in Thomas Mann's *Dr. Faustus* and *The Holy Sinner*." *OL* 29:61-76.
The method of parody is analyzed as a means for Mann to explore myth and legends without attempting to look at them directly. The device of narrator is also used to elucidate realities of faith and feeling. Zeitblom is the onlooker-narrator, often used as a vehicle for Mann's irony, but also the other protagonist of the novel. The narrator in *The Holy Sinner*, Clemens, is not involved in the action, but is free to shape it and comment on it. The artist-narrator, Clemens, balances between joy and sorrow and rises beyond a mere spokesman for the unbelievable. Both parody and narrator allow Mann "to bring in his points through the back door," conciliating systematic rational belief with the realities of faith and feeling. (WMH,Jr)
11401. Krotkoff, Hertha. "Arthur Schnitzler—Thomas Mann: Briefe." *MAL* 7,i/ii:1-33.
Only a small number of the letters exchanged by Mann and Schnitzler from 1904 to 1929 survive, All of Mann's messages are in the Schnitzler Archives at the University Library at Cambridge; 2 of Schnitzler's letters are in the Mann archives at the Eidgenössische Technische Hochschule in Zürich, 2 other copies with Heinrich Schnitzler in Vienna. The letters contain conventional polite exchanges, personal and business matters, remarks on works of both authors, and reflect a relationship marked by mutual admiration and esteem. The correspondence recalls

Mann's attraction to the refined culture of the declining Hapsburg monarchy which permeated Schnitzler's personality and work. The letters after World War I shed light on both authors' cooperation with the *Dial* and the Book of the Month Club in the U.S. (HK)

11404. Latta, Alan D. "The Mystery of Life:A Theme in *Der Zauberberg.*" *Monatshefte* 66:19-32.
The appearance of Joachim Ziemssen's ghost during a séance in *The Magic Mountain* has generally embarrassed or irritated critics of Mann's novel. Its presence is thematically motivated: it is the novel's final word on the theme "Geheimnis des Lebens." Throughout the novel, Ludovico Settembrini has tried to convert a skeptical Hans Castorp to his own narrow, exclusively sociopolitical view of man and the universe. Hans Castorp, unwilling to see life thus robbed of its possible mysteries, resists, and the ghost is the counter-example which shatters Settembrini's world-view. By virtue of the way in which the ghost exists ("zeit-telephathisches Moment"), it speaks across the boundary between fiction and life directly to the readers of the novel, not to say that mysteries of this kind do exist, but that they may exist. (ADL)

11406. Magliola, Robert. "The Magic Square:Polar Unity in Thomas Mann's *Doctor Faustus.*" *HSL* 6:55-71.
The content and structure of Mann's *Dr. Faustus* are controlled by the ontology identified with Leverkühn's theory. The novel shows Zeitblom's humanism, and its devotion to the "middle way," as philosophically invalid. Leverkühn's philosophy posits a theory of "polar unity": (1) extremes are in reality one, and (2) this oneness is possessed only through the simultaneous possession of both extremes (since polar unity is the unmediated fusion of extremes). The theory, while beholden to Nietzsche's philosophy, differs from his. Sigmund Freud, interpreted according to Mann's own lights, is a decidedly important influence. Toward the end of the novel, Leverkühn's conversion to "feeling" takes place. It is his realization he has neglected the unmediated fusion of pure feeling and "mystical intellect." This realization is Leverkühn's psychological "breakthrough," and effects his musical "breakthrough" to perfect art. Perfect art is obtainable through the polar unity of love and mysticism. (RM)

11410. Meyers, Jeffrey. "Shakespeare and Mann's *Doctor Faustus.*" *MFS* 19(1973):541-45.
Shakespeare's *Love's Labour's Lost* plays a significant though minor role in Mann's *Doktor Faustus* for it is used as a comic parody of the Faustian themes of the book and is subtly related to the recurrent motifs and rich fabric of tradition which Adrian spins round himself like a cocoon. The seeds of Adrian's genius and the tragic pattern of his allegorical life are foreshadowed in his demonically inspired adaptation of Shakespeare's play, for as Zeitblom regretfully confesses, the very definition of Germanism is "implicit Satanism." (JM)

11428. Viswanathan, Jacqueline. "Point of View and Unreliability in Brontë's *Wuthering Heights*, Conrad's *Under Western Eyes*, and Mann's *Doktor Faustus.*" *OL* 29:42-60.
Point of view is used as the basis for a comparison of the three novels. Analyzes the common features of the narrators' position and the various narrative techniques which enable the reader to go beyond the narrators' comments. (JV)

11438. Zaloscer, Hilde. "Ägypten in Thomas Manns Josephsroman:Zum Problem des 'Bildzitats'." *Seminar* 10:116-30.
Thomas Mann made extensive use of the technique of montage, drawing his material from varied areas of life and art. These "visual quotations" (*Bildzitate*) are particularly characteristic of the spirit and style of Mann's work. There are three types of *Bildzitat*: in the first a work of art is absorbed into the language and transformed into a metaphor; in the second type a scene portrayed in art is turned in the novel into an event—the "momentary" art work becomes a chronological sequence; the third type consists of the transference of artistic portrayal to the external appearance of individual characters. (HZ)

Musil. 11491. Johnston, Walter E. "The Shepherdess in the City." *CL* 26:124-41.
Modern novelists often reflect the traditional ideals and conventions of pastoral poetry when they place an extremely simple,

virtuous, "natural" character in the center of a sophisticated "city" novel or story: the praises of natural virtue are directly "sung" by the narrator or are implicit in the narration. Virgil's first Eclogue is used to establish a definition of pastoral as an exile's song which suggests the limitations of the idyll through praise of its virtues. This perspective is applied in detail to Lena Grove in Faulkner's *Light in August* (1932) and Tonka in Musil's "Tonka" (1924). Their significance as pastoral emblems, and allusions by Faulkner and Musil to Romantic writers, lead to a consideration of the special emphasis that Romantic writers brought to pastoral emblems and to a contrast of the use of the dominant conventions of pastoral by Wordsworth and the modern writers. The novelists are dramatizing the failure of the mind to arrive at any new understanding or harmony through contemplation of pastoral simplicity; even the potential of the pastoral as a symbol of human values is ironically undercut. (WEJ)

11495. Reniers-Servranckx, Anne. "Musils Kunsttheorie en levensleer:De schrijver als theoreticus." *RLV* 39(1973):516-19.
Musil's theoretical and critical writings, essays and diary are as yet only partially known. Roth has systematically researched forgotten texts. Her book, based on published as well as unpublished texts, reveals Musil's wide intellectual horizons. It emphasizes the continuity of his meditations and demonstrates that the theoretical or critical stands taken by Musil always refer to the same set of convictions and goals, based on the close relationship he believes exists between ethics and esthetics. The author emphatically stresses the importance of the "Erlebnis" (total experience), which constitutes for Musil the only absolute criteria of truth and value. (AR-S)

Nietzsche. 11517. Dyck, J.W. "Aspects of Nihilism in German and Russian Literature:Nietzsche—Tolstoy." *HAB* 25:187-96.
In the 19th century Nihilism became a major theme in European literature and culminated in Nietzsche's attempt to assign the causes of Nihilism to the nature of Christian morality and to provide a systematic analysis of the various aspects of this intellectual phenomenon. Tolstoi was among the most outspoken adversaries of Nietzschean thought and advocacy. Nietzsche's "God is dead" is seen as a more honest logical conclusion to the bankruptcy of Christian morality than Tolstoi's "The Good is God." Tolstoi had misunderstood Nietzsche. Nietzsche's "Amor fati" testifies to the fact that he had remained a God-seeker to the very end of his life. (JWD)

11521. Green, Eleanor H. "Blueprints for Utopia:The Political Ideas of Nietzsche and D.H. Lawrence." *RMS* 18:141-61.
The similarity in political theory between Nietzsche and Lawrence is striking enough to suggest that Nietzsche exercised a strong influence over Lawrence's thought. Both men were "heroic vitalists" who stressed the importance in their utopian state of a strong leader, a hierarchical social structure, the total submission of the lower orders to their superiors, the subjugation of women to men, harsh discipline and military training for boys, and a powerful and spontaneous interrelationship between man and the natural forces of the universe. It is in Lawrence's "leadership" novels that Nietzschean political ideas are most fully used and developed. (EHG)

11542. Schacht, Richard. "Philosophy as Linguistic Analysis: A Nietzschean Critique." *PhS* 25:153-71.
Nietzsche is a philosopher who regards the analysis of ordinary language and specialized forms of language as important and fruitful without being committed to a conception of philosophy as linguistic analysis. The twofold purpose of this discussion is to suggest some respects in which the conception of philosophy as linguistic analysis may be open to criticism and to investigate the philosophers involved in this type of pursuit. (LLBA)

Rilke. 11584. Crowhurst, G.W. "Time and Memory in Rilke's *Die Aufzeichnungen des Malte Laurids Brigge.*" *Theoria* 41(1973): 63-78.
Rilke's *The Notebooks of Malte Laurids Brigge* (1910) revolves around time and memory. Individual existence is formed by time. This individual being, however, has to have continuity, and thus

identity, to counteract the dissolving effects of passing time. Malte is unable to control or exclude objective reality; still less is he able to co-relate occurrences and experiences. The existential experiences of "erkennen" (to recognize) and "Erinnerung" (retentive memory as opposed to "Gedächtnis," a more physical remembrance) are the keys to a possibility of life for Malte. He has to get away from mere seeing and "Gedächtnis." "Erinnerung" guarantees a continuity of identity and thereby constitutes being. Only within the medium of time can Malte's ego establish an identity. An opportunity to do this is offered by the memories connected with his childhood. If he can establish a real relationship between his present ego and his childhood ego, then he can cope with life and consequently with death. If Malte can discover and find his identity in his childhood, he will find a personal death, full of being. (GWC)

11587. Frey, Eleonore. "Literatur als Utopie:Zu einem Text Rilkes." *OL* 29:107-22.
The question about the essence of fiction is a constantly renewed concern of Rilke. In one work literature appears as a Utopia, as a speech that will arise from a destruction of all that which hitherto was called language and therefore can be of importance only through negation of itself. This breakthrough to genuine fiction is the transition from a speech which refers back to a certain opinion or meaning, to a language which opens itself up to all possibilities contained within it and thus remains by itself. The solution which the writer of fiction must achieve is revealed in the central themes of *The Notebooks of Malte Laurids Brigge*—death, decay, disintegration widen the scope of absolute fiction. (EF)

11602. Saalmann, Dieter. "R.M. Rilkes 'Erlebnis' als symbolistiches Phänomen." *OL* 29:93-106.
Attempts to interpret Rilke's "experience" under the aspect of French symbolism. Rilke's essay "Moderne Lyrik" describes the experience of "the fallen barriers" which corresponds, in its overcoming of the empirical, to the symbolistic "déformation" of those in the forefront. Through negation of them, the protagonist of the "experience" fragment succeeds in temporarily eliminating the antithesis of subject and object and reaches the state of "pure" objectivity. This elimination of the material takes place through the example of a tree, in which its material substance yields to its abstract essence. The language of "experience" is accordingly transformed into a perishable appearance of words. Rilke's prose fragment embodies therefore a distinguishing feature of the modern trend, namely the self-reflexion of the literary work of art over its creative premises. (DS)

11619. Woods, Roy. "Some Aspects of Seeing in Rilke's Poetry." *Trivium* 8(1973):95-108.
"Einsehen," the direct perception of a thing in its pristine essence, untainted by pre-conceptions, is not only central to Rilke's creative method but also occurs as subject matter in *Neue Gedichte* (1908). A number of representative poems are examined to show how Rilke implies a correlation between power of seeing and power of being and secondly how the eye is a major channel of communication between inner and outer worlds, changing as Rilke's understanding of the interplay between these "two" worlds changed. The earlier work accepts the distinction between inner and outer whereas the later work reunites the two. After *Malte Laurids Brigge* (1910) Rilke gradually moved from seeing, "Werk des Gesichts," toward feeling, "Herzwerk," a move which is reflected in the tendency away from the eye as dominant sense organ to the ear, which acts as less of a barrier between inner and outer experience. Lament in *Duinese Elegien* (1912/1922) about man's disinheritance from a unified world gives way in *Die Sonette an Orpheus* (1922) to jubilant praise of an existence reunified by feeling, of a world in which all opposites, including life and death, are reunited: the blissful realm of the angels, "weltinnerraum." (RW)

Roth, J. 11623. Derré, Françoise. "Militärerziehung und Vater-Sohnkonflikt in österreichischer Sicht." *MAL* 7,i/ii:51-67.
Roth and Werfel have treated the problem of the conflict between father and son, in the Austrian-Hungarian empire before World War I. This conflict results from an extreme reservedness and habit of blind obedience and from a denial of authority based only on tradition. The military education without maternal affection strengthens a trend to hostility which reaches to self-destruction and murder. Roth evinces skepticism, a nostalgia for the past and uses an impressionistic style where pity appears. His heroes are the willing victims of destiny. Werfel writes with passion, revolt, and a typical expressionistic richness of color, which attenuates the critical attitude of the reader and makes plausible the optimistic issue of a renovated life in the New World. (FD)

11628. Johnston, Otto W. "Joseph Roth's 'Büste des Kaisers':The Quest for an Authentic Text." *MLN* 89:448-58.
Roth's short story "Büste des Kaisers" contains the essence of his political thinking in 1934 as well as a sophisticated integration of those stylistic elements fundamental to his prose technique. His political stance at this time represents a departure from prior convictions: this story shows the key differences. Roth works his new political convictions into material which had occupied him for some time. However, there is considerable controversy in scholarly circles regarding the authenticity of the printed German text. It is maintained that the printed German version is actually a retranslation (back into German) of the French translation prepared by Blanche Gidon. (OWJ)

Schnitzler. 11639. Alexander, Theodor W. "Olga Waissnix: The Model for the Character of the Married Woman in the Early Works of Arthur Schnitzler." *MAL* 7,i/ii:99-112.
By analyzing the character of Olga Waissnix as it is revealed in Schnitzler's *Jugend in Wien: Eine Autobiographie* (1968) and Schnitzler and Waissnix's *Liebe, die starb vor der Zeit: Ein Briefwechsel* fictional equivalents of Olga Waissnix are found in Schnitzler's early works. Olga is the *Mondaine* who is envious of the *süsse Mädel*, the coquette who has a secret rendezvous with a would-be lover, and the wife who is afraid of a jealous, suspicious husband. She is the admirer of artistic accomplishments as well as the toy to be played with by a man who wants to possess her. Gabriele of *Weihnachtseinkäufe* represents the intellectual Olga; Else of *Agonie* the sensual Olga; and Beatrice of *Der Schleier der Beatrice* the complete, yet highly complex Olga. (TWA)

11640. Berlin, Jeffrey B. "Arthur Schnitzler Bibliography for 1973-74." *MAL* 7,i/ii:174-91.
The increasing amount of primary and secondary literature on Schnitzler suggests the need for an annual Schnitzler bibliography. The present bibliography includes material for the first five months of 1974 and should be used in conjunction with the two previous Schnitzler bibliographies in *Modern Austrian Literature*. Six categories comprise the present work: Primary Literature: 1973-1974; Secondary Literature: 1973-1974; Supplement: 1965-1972; Book Reviews; Descriptive Listing of Schnitzler Dissertations: 1973-1974, with Supplement; Research in Progress. Annotations are given when deemed necessary. (JBB)

11641. —— "Arthur Schnitzler's *Die Frau mit dem Dolche*: *Déjà Vu* Experience or Hypnotic Trance?" *MAL* 7:108-12.
Schnitzler's *Die Frau mit dem Dolche* concerns Pauline's relationships with her husband and with Leonhard, her lover. In a museum with Leonhard, she likens herself to a particular painting. As she observes it, the scene changes and reveals her thoughts in the form of a fantasy. Why does she identify with the painting? What is the nature of her experience as Paola in the trance scene? Why does she kill her lover in the trance? These issues are examined by investigating Pauline's psychological processes. It is shown that while the trance scene may seem to be a déjà vu experience, it is actually a self-induced hypnotic trance that permits repressed material to emerge from the unconscious and thus represents an attempt to effect abreaction. (JBB)

11642. —— "The Element of 'Hope' in Arthur Schnitzler's 'Sterben'." *Seminar* 10:38-49.
Scant critical attention has been given to Arthur Schnitzler's *Sterben* (1894), usually thought of as a "psychological case-study." To be sure, this particular narrative work is more than an exemplification of man's response to impending death. The importance of "hope" for Felix and Marie is discussed. A critical examination of the text reveals that basic to an understanding of Felix's and Marie's response to impending death is, in fact, an awareness of their concept of hope. (JBB)

Stifter. 11675. Sjögren, Christine O. "*Tuch* as a Symbol for Art in Stifter's 'Der Hochwald'." *JEGP* 73:375-87.
The *Tuch*, an incongruous symbol which applies to a lake in the primeval forest of Stifter's "Der Hochwald," images the role of art in man's existence. Presented basically as a positive value in its function as a means of concealment and beautification of the terrifying ground of existence, the *Tuch* image and other images representative of art also contain negative qualities. Beneath the charming surface story lies the author's serious endeavor to deal with philosophic problems inherent in the esthetic orientation toward existence. (COS)

Storm. 11686. Kardel, Harboe. "Der geschichtliche und örtliche Hintergrund der Novelle 'Ein Fest auf Haderslevhuus'." *SSG* 23:39-46.
Some themes of Storm's *Ein Fest auf Haderslevhuus* are taken from *Sagen des Neckartals* by F. Baader. Storm transferred the scene of the novel to Nordschleswig, to the castles Törning and Haderslevhuus at Hadersleben. Storm had several ties to Nordschleswig; his son Ernst was a court lawyer in Toftlund, Nordschleswig in the late 1880s for example. The focal point of the novel is the Schleswig noble family of Lembek, who lived in the 14th century at castle Törning. The second castle, Haderslevhuus, Storm assumed on the hill of Böghoved, in the vicinity of Hadersleben. (HK)
11692. Martini, Fritz. "Theodor Storms Lyrik:Tradition, Produktion, Rezeption." *SSG* 23:9-27.
In his lyrics Storm acknowledged only two laws, the law of intuition and the law of sentiment. Facing a multitude of writing contemporaries he retained strong immediacy and depth of emotion. His use of differentiated poetic devices and the artistic shaping of language and form are remarkable. Storm stands along with Heine at the beginning of the "Moderne." (FM)
11700. Schuster, Ingrid. "Storms 'Ein Doppelgänger' und Brechts *Der gute Mensch von Sezuan*:Eine Gegenüberstellung." *SSG* 23:33-38.
Storm's novella and Brecht's drama reveal surprising parallels; mainly the problem of dual structure of Man which is represented by means of split identity of the protagonist. In conflict with the established social order the problem in both cases is clarified and developed. Man's justifiable strivings for happiness stand in opposition to social and divine laws. Both heroes belong to the lowest social categories and a sentence is passed on both in a final court scene. At this point, however, the difference of the world-outlooks of the authors becomes obvious: for Storm society is a natural phenomenon, and thus he pleads for the individual. Brecht calls for social change, he does not plead for the individual or a mistreated minority, but for the mass of the oppressed. These philosophical differences determine the manner of representation: for Storm a description of the emotional state, for Brecht a critical parable. (IS)
11701. Struve, Reinhard. "Funktionen des Rahmens in Theodor Storms Novelle 'Aquis submersus'." *SSG* 23:28-32.
Many of Storm's *novellas* take place in the past. In most of them a detached narrator leads the reader to the content of the inner story (*Binnenerzählung*). The functions of the frame story for the inner story of *Aquis Submersus* are discussed: the relation of the detached narrator to the reader, the receptiveness of the reader, temporal and spatial approximation of the historical events, finding of the manuscript, references to persons and actions of the inner story, and evaluations of the detached narrator. (RS)
11703. Terpstra, Jan U. "Storms Novelle 'Renate' und der Würzburger Hexenprozess der Renata Singer im Jahre 1749." *SSG* 23:47-54.

Storm is fascinated by the witch-theme, and he consequently treats it in *Renate* to an extensive degree. The novella draws on materials from local history and theology from the 1700s. The name "Renate," however, does not fit into this context. Storm's knowledge of the witch-trials and his Würzburg journeys while working on the novella lead to Renata Singer who was executed in 1749 in Würzburg. The figure and situation of both Renates are compared. Themes such as the intelligence of these witches, their noble, yet isolated position in society, their aversion for the nunnery, the mysterious mice magic (*Mäusezauber*), and the contemptuous treatment of the eucharistic host reinforce the impression of the interdependency. There is further reference to the possibility of Storm having used local sources for the witch-trial as well as the peculiar ambiguity of the Last Supper-Scene, which could be connected with the historical Last Supper-Issue of Schleswig-Holstein. (JUT)

Wagner, R. 11718. Lemco, Gary. "Henry James and Richard Wagner:*The American*." *HSL* 6:147-58.
This comparative analysis of Henry James's *The American* and Richard Wagner's opera *Lohengrin* is an outgrowth of the mythic critical concepts of Northrop Frye. The approach utilizes mythic considerations in its singular investigation of the relation between literature and music, or music and ideas. Contrary to those interpretations which have denied the influence of myth in James's work, Christopher Newman of the *The American* reveals striking similarity to Wagner's legendary hero, Lohengrin. The demand for implicit and unquestioning faith permeates the sensibilities of both protagonists as each embodies the authors' conceptions of a spiritual force incarnate in a world fraught with conflict and hypocrisy. (GL)

Zweig, S. 11737. Daviau, Donald G., and Harvey I. Dunkle. "Stefan Zweig's *Schachnovelle*." *Monatshefte* 65(1973):370-84.
Schachnovelle, Zweig's masterpiece, has never been analyzed in its own terms and from the standpoint of literary quality. Rather, critics have viewed the story as showing a basic change in Zweig's literary objectives and political outlook or as reflecting the pessimistic mood that led to his suicide. Such unproven contentions are rejected here in favor of a conclusion that the story is a psychological character study and as such fits into the pattern of Zweig's works. Through the confrontation over chess of two unique monomaniacs, Dr. B., the monomaniac created artificially by brain washing, and Czentovic, the monomaniac by accident of birth, Zweig demonstrates the insidious psychological aftereffects of brain washing. Zweig's intuitive psychological description of Dr. B.'s condition and behavior has been confirmed by research in sensory deprivation. Judged as a psychological *Novelle*, *Schachnovelle* in form and structure deserves its reputation as Zweig's finest narrative work. (DGD)
11739. Mitrovich, Mirco. "Stefan Zweig:A Vision of a European." *GN* 5:8-11.
Zweig is an example *par excellence* of a man of belles-lettres with regard to his services for humanity. Zweig began looking at life by turning to the authorities for their opinions of what men live for. His book *Europäisches Erbe* is encyclopedic in its realm, dealing with the masters representing all of Europe and contributing greatly to European culture and civilization. Because of his personal concern to preserve the past on one side and his deep belief in a better future for humanity and a New Europe on the other, Zweig is an essential part of that part of humanity which is worth studying. (MMM)

VII. RECENT

General and Miscellaneous. 11768. Eifler, Margret. "Prämissen zur DDR-Literatur." *UP* 7,ii:81-90.
Socialist literature is basically a functional literature and its esthetic values can only be discussed in the context of its particular ideology. An approach to GDR literature must recognize the decisive influence of the official cultural policies and the principles established by literary theoreticians, although

in recent years restrictive literary guidelines have been increasingly liberalized. Consequently, an upsurge of artistic innovations in both content and form is expected while socialist precepts retain their importance. At the same time, Western interpretations must concentrate more on the increasing artistic originality and the portrayal of universal concerns within socialist determinants. (ME)

11779. Grimm, Reinhold. "Romanticism Today:An Outsider's View." *HAB* 25:95-107.
Many symptoms indicate a revival of Romanticism in modern life, art, and literature. One possible key to these symptoms is the idea of "transgression" (*Entgrenzung*) which can be shown to play an integral part in all romantic movements. Based mainly on examples from modern German literature, Grimm lays bare the various problems but also the inherent dialectics of a "Romanticism Today." (RG)

11790. Hirschbach, Frank D. "DDR-Literatur im Unterricht —wie, was und für wen?" *UP* 7,ii:68-81.
The study of East German literature is a relatively new field for Americans and requires an adjustment to unfamiliar terms, realities, and ideas. The East German writer is ever conscious of his political and social task. His literature is realistic, optimistic, easily intelligible, and the plot usually dominates the form. A course on GDR literature cannot ignore Marxist cultural, especially literary, theory and should include a history of the GDR. The teacher encounters certain practical problems in selecting titles to be read and procuring the texts. (FDH)

11828. Pabisch, Peter. "Distanzierung und Engagement in deutscher Nachkriegsliteratur aus Österreich." *MAL* 7,i/ii:69-78.
Great differences between modern and traditional German literature are apparent after World War II. Reasons for this phenomenon often stem from the effect of the war on many authors who were very young at the time. A distance between them and the world emanates from their works and manifests itself mainly in new forms of literary expression. Recent works also contain social and even moral engagement. What might appear to be abstraction or nonsense at first sight may represent a mask for a writer's despair about a hopeless situation. Five examples from Austrian postwar authors give evidence of literary distance as well as engagement. (PKP)

11862. Wishard, Armin. "Literature of Dissent and Party Politics in the German Democratic Republic." [F 19]:105-09.
At the 9th Party Congress in May 1973, Party leaders in the German Democratic Republic publicly attacked developments on the local cultural scene since the 7th Party Congress of 1971. They deplored excessive individualism and a lack of true socialist spirit, especially in some works by young authors. An example of such "antagonistic" literature is Rainer Kirsch's *Heinrich Schlaghands Höllenfahrt*. This Faust-play presents strong criticism of East German life and letters by attacking numerous institutions and everyday practices. Subsequent discussions appear to foreshadow a hardening of controls over artists in the DDR to bring them in line with Party ideology and prevent such individualistic departures as Kirsch's play. (AW)

Prose Fiction. 11906. Bänziger, Hans. "Der österreichische Roman des zwanzigsten Jahrhunderts." *MAL* 7,i/ii:117-31.
Austrian novels are in general less likely to become bestsellers than those from West Germany, East Germany, or even Switzerland. They seem to be too old-fashioned. Joseph Roth's works provide light reading in a certain sense and contain impressive scenes like the death of a servant in *Radetzkymarsch* and others which show his father-orientation. Doderer writes in a more challenging style. *Die Strudelhofstiege* deals with the profundity of the past; from 1925 the author looks back to 1910 like one of his protagonists, Stangeler, who looks down the steps of the Strudelhofstiege. His world is a colorful stage of action. In Bernhard's *Kalkwerk*, a negative variation of the *Heimatroman*, there is almost no action, but the sentences are full of tension. (HB)

11916. Lauckner, Nancy A. "The Surrogate Jew in the Postwar German Novel." *Monatshefte* 66:133-44.
An interesting facet of the postwar novel is the appearance of the surrogate Jew, a non-Jewish outsider who by his suffering fills the role of the "Jew." Only rarely does the surrogate Jew serve as a vehicle for masked anti-Semitism; Gerd Gaiser's *Eine Stimme hebt an* and *Schlussball* may admit of such an interpretation. Usually novelists treat the surrogate Jew as a symbolic warning against anti-Semitism and develop many situations which reflect the Nazi persecution of the Jews. Wetchy, the Hungarian Calvinist in Hermann Broch's *Der Versucher*, represents the best portrayal of such a surrogate Jew. Wolfgang Koeppen's *Tauben im Gras* and Walter Matthias Diggelmann's *Die Hinterlassenschaft* carry the theme one step further by using the scapegoat to symbolize the Jews and to demonstrate the continuation of prejudice and persecution against postwar minorities, American Negro soldiers and Communists respectively. (NAL)

11918. Lüthe, Rudolf. "Fiktionalität als konstitutives Element literarische Rezeption." *OL* 29:1-15.
Attempts a new definition of the concept of fiction in order to make it productive as a delineating criterion of literature as opposed to other types of texts. Text is understood as textual idea whose actual character is limited in particular respects. Literary textual notions are subject to the view of fictionality whose characteristic trait is indifference to truth. This starting point yields a new understanding of the fundamental difference between types of texts. Problems are also discussed which are connected with the definition of the new concept of fiction. Most important is the exact clarification of the relationships between fiction, reality, and truth. (RL)

Andersch. 11930. George, E.F. "Paths of Escape in Alfred Andersch's Works." *OL* 29:160-69.
Andersch's own moral position restrains him from affirming the right to withdraw from social responsibilities. Andersch's strength as an author, his insight into human nature, and his view of life are discussed. (EFG)

Bobrowski. 11978. Hoefert, Sigfrid. "Zur internationalen Verständigung im Werk Johannes Bobrowskis." [F 19]:110-13.
The portrayal of the relations between Germans and Non-Germans in the European East stood in the center of Johannes Bobrowski's literary activity and is reflected in his two novels: *Levins Mühle* and *Litauische Claviere*. It can also be discerned in some of his stories as well as in his lyrics. Rather than presenting the manifold evidence, the novels and the poem "Dorfstrasse" are discussed. Attention is drawn to the fact that Bobrowski also introduces to his poetic landscape the voice of the Russian philosopher P.Y. Chaadayev. (SH)

Böll. 11983. Cunliffe, W.G. "Heinrich Böll's Eccentric Rebels." *HAB* 25:298-303.
In his early novels, Böll is on the side of the individual against the claims of the state. The Böll hero is harmless and unenterprising with an admirably tough core of resistance to authority. In stories with an early post-war setting, middle-class values still provide a shield against the new prosperity. In these stories, however, obligations to the individual can no longer be overlooked. Moreover, integrity and non-conformism have become illusory in the post-war world. From *Billiard um halbzehn* on Böll creates characters who are activists, feeling responsibility for the community, yet individualists, rejecting current ideologies. In his eccentric rebels he expresses the humanitarian liberal's dilemma. (WGC)

11993. Parent, David J. "Böll's 'Wanderer, kommst du nach Spa-,' a Reply to Schiller's 'Der Spaziergang'." *ELWIU* 1:109-17.
Böll's "Traveler, if you go to Spa-" is related by more than its allusive fragmentary title to Schiller's didactic poem "The Walk." The basic structure of both works consists of their deployment of space and of external objects along a forward and upward line of motion of an observer, and inclusions of reflective subjectivity. But these parallel structures are filled with antithetical worlds. Schiller's external world consists of vast panoramic vistas of living nature; Böll's is illustrated by the technological still-life of the broken lightbulb; it is a world of artifacts produced by a perverse ideology in process of self-destruction. But the point at issue is this: Schiller's poem accepts the basic goodness of the Greek achievement in launching Western civilization, despite subsequent corruption and the possibility of a Rousseauistic return to nature, while Böll's story focuses on the negative militaristic side of Greek civilization, its propagandistic misuse in the humanistic *Gymnasium*, and its evil and ruinous culmination in Prusso-Nazism. (DJP)

11997. Reid, James H. "Böll's Names." *MLR* 69:575-83.
Böll uses proper names for their intrinsic musical quality, to link

characters by acoustic association, and to imply significance. Geographical names are usually fictitious; however, the real East European names of the war stories exercise by their exotic sounds a magical fascination on the characters. Anonymity in the war stories indicates the insignificance of the individual soldier; Christian names suggest independence from, surnames dependence on, the military bureaucracy. *Wo warst du, Adam?* (1951) links most of its characters by the sounds of their names, suggesting that even the most disparate individuals share responsibility for the war, Böll uses a similar technique in *Doktor Murkes gesammeltes Schweigen* (1955) and *Ende einer Dienstfahrt* (1966). The post-war novels frequently introduce personal names which, while realistically plausible, associatively underpoint important themes and characteristics. Finally, in *Gruppenbild mit Dame* (1971) names themselves become thematic. (JHR)

11998. Robinson, Walter L. "Heinrich Böll's Indifferent Heroes." [F 19]:133-37.
The attitude of indifference (Gleichgültigkeit) as a characterizing device in the works of Böll is recurrent in the early works. While *Gleichgültigkeit* is not a main motif in the latest novel, *Gruppenbild mit Dame*, the naiveté or *Ahnungslosigkeit* of the heroine, Leni Pfeiffer, is not unlike the indifferent attitudes of other of Böll's fictional characters. (WLR)

Brecht. 12009. Berckman, Edward M. "Comedy and Parody of Comedy in Brecht's *Puntila*." *ELWIU* 1:248-60.
Bertolt Brecht's *Herr Puntila und sein Knecht Matti* is neither tragedy nor casual entertainment but an ironic comedy serving Marxist didactic purposes. Brecht introduces traditional comic types and patterns, similar to those in commedia dell' arte and comedy of manners. The audience anticipates a happy ending of marriage between the chauffeur Matti and his employer's daughter, comradeship between Puntila and Matti, and the inclusion of the poor women of Kurgela in nuptial festivities. Brecht allows none of these expectations to be fulfilled in order to emphasize that the barrier between working and owning classes is insurmountable. The prospect of liberation is envisioned and dramatized so that the audience is moved toward realization outside the theater of that harmony with justice which fails to be achieved on stage. (EMB)

12018. Fuegi, John. "Whodunit:'Brecht's' Adaptation of Molière's *Don Juan*." *CLS* 11:159-72.
Most previous studies of "Brecht's" adaptation of Molière's *Don Juan* have assumed Brecht's authorship of the adaptation bearing his name. An examination of source materials found in the Brecht Archive in East Berlin enables us to show, however, that Brecht's own contribution to the German adaptation was but slight. Not only does the German text given in Brecht's collected works draw heavily on an extant but unacknowledged translation by Eugen Neresheimer but significant portions of the rest of the adaptation can be directly traced to Brecht's two collaborators on the play, Benno Besson and Elisabeth Hauptmann. "Brecht's" *Don Juan* should henceforward be clearly identified as a play "of the school of Brecht." (JF)

12035. Nieschmidt, H.W. "Weniger Gips:Zum Schlussakt in Brechts *Hannibal*-Fragment." *MLN* 89:849-61.
In the course of adapting Grabbe's tragedy *Hannibal*, Brecht moved further and further away from the original. Of the scenes of the fragment extant and as yet unpublished, those from the last act are of special interest, since in Brecht's essay "Weniger Gips!!!" (1926) the end of Grabbe's tragedy is mentioned and satirized as an example of an out-moded monumental style of classical German theater. In the final act of his adaptation he depicts Hannibal's unheroic end in total social isolation, doing this with dramatic means of expression which stand in contrast to Grabbe's monumental style. (HWN)

12045. Suvin, Darko. "Brecht's *Caucasian Chalk Circle* and Marxist Figuralism:Open Dramaturgy as Open History." *ClioW* 3:257-76.
Brecht's *Caucasian Chalk Circle* has a privileged position among his plays: only here (and in *The Mother*) is there a first approximation to his utopian "look backward" from classless humanity at our bloody age. The play's three "stories" (Kolkhoz, Grusha, Azdak) demonstrate that its theme is a humanized *telos*

of history, and its philosophy of history and compositional method Marxist figuralism. The prefigurational sequence Persian Weavers' revolt-Azdak's judgeship-participatory Kolkhoz socialism is a humanist salvation-history and makes the wrongly doubted Kolkhoz framework necessary for the play's look backward. Marxist figuralism develops, however, along an asymptotic curve, and even the privileged Kolkhoz is no static fulfillment but only another, relatively more advanced figure: Judgment Day is also Genesis. (DRS)

Buber. 12053. Johnston, William M. "Martin Buber's Literary Debut:'On Viennese Literature' (1897)." *GQ* 47:556-66.
Buber's essays on the Viennese authors Hermann Bahr, Hugo von Hofmannsthal, Peter Altenberg, and Arthur Schnitzler are translated from Polish for the first time. Buber shows sufficient affinity with the four Viennese Impressionists to be interpreted as one of them. He shares their fascination with flux, twilight states, and the disintegration of the ego. But he anticipates his later religious quest when he condemns them for absence of unity, for lassitude, and for superficial curiosity. As Buber's first published works, these essays display their author's lifelong traits of exuberance, erudition, and universal sympathy. (WMJ)

Canetti. 12054. Barnouw, Dagmar. "Doubting Death:On Elias Canetti's Drama *The Deadlined*." *Mosaic* 7,ii:1-23.
Elias Canetti's *Die Befristeten* is analyzed in the context of his response and reaction to the social satire of Karl Kraus and Canetti's studies of the reactions of crowds and power in the magnetic field of death (*Masse und Macht*). The drama presents the Utopian society of the deadlined, a society where one of the social problems is taken literally and thereby exposed in all its destructive potential: the definition of the individual by numerical time, his devaluation by the acceptance of death as natural law that makes death imminent from the beginning of life and corrupts all social relations at their root. Canetti's concentration on language as the key witness to social relations and his anthropological interest in the most varied documents of man's attempts at social existence reinforce the drama's argument for doubting all certainty, even that of death. (DB)

Celan. 12062. Gogol, John M. "Paul Celan and Osip Mandelstam:Poetic Language as Ontological Essence." *RLV* 40:341-54.
Much of the strength of the poetry of Paul Celan and Osip Mandelstam derives from their unique relationships to their respective native languages. Both poets experienced language, particularly poetic language, as the essence of being. The essential poetic techniques, metaphors, and imagery of both poets developed out of each poet's personal relationship to language. Both are obsessed by the word and its role in defining existence in the 20th century, and each explores the limits of language. (JG)

12066. Weimar, Karl S. "Paul Celan's 'Todesfuge':Translation and Interpretation." *PMLA* 89:85-96.
Translation is a synthetic approach to interpretation and a paradoxical awareness of the crisis of language. Some of the translator's problems, such as rhythms, grammar, lexical layers, syntax, are illustrated with reference to the five published English translations of Celan's "Todesfuge"; their resolution leads to creative apprehension. The provenience of the poem is biblical. The devices of oxymoron, surrealist metaphor, disparate rhythms and meter, inversion of time sequence, and the erotic counter-subject all function as verbal correlatives to the paradox and absurdity which are the poem's theme and represent a peculiar combination of esoteric artistry and commitment. The fugue is structured by four voices (statements with contrapuntal variations) and the echoed simultaneity of "poppy" (verbal narcotic) and "remembrance" (of unreal reality). The poem is placed in the frame of Celan's later development. (KSW)

Diggelmann. 12070. Waidson, H.M. "Childhood, Youth, and Autobiography in the Work of Walter Matthias Diggelmann." *Seminar* 10:213-25.
Walter Matthias Diggelmann's publications in book form began in 1959, and in 1960-69 he published 5 novels and 1 volume of

short stories; a further fictional volume, "a diary in stories," appeared in 1972. Diggelmann's fiction is rich in incident and in the variety of the backgrounds evoked, and the action moves with speed and clarity. The central figures of the novels may be problematic in a number of ways, though at the same time they are capable of impulsive, spontaneous action. Autobiographical, social, and political issues play a considerable part in Diggelmann's work. (HMW)

Dürrenmatt. 12090. Struc, Roman S. "Sinn und Sinnlosigkeit des Opfers:Gotthelfs *Die schwarze Spinne* und Dürrenmatts *Der Besuch der alten Dame.*" [F 19]:114-17.
The form of Gotthelf's *Die Schwarze Spinne* and Dürrenmatt's *Der Besuch der alten Dame* is essentially dramatic, the technique analytical, and both authors subject their protagonists to situations in which they have to act out the ethical maxims they profess. In Gotthelf's *Novelle*, the community and the individual pass the test, whereas in Dürrenmatt's play, the community's moral standards turn out to be meaningless. The heroic deeds of men and women in *Die Schwarze Spinne* are meaningful for them as well as for their community; in *Der Besuch*, Ill's acceptance of the judgment of his fellow citizens does not provide the catharsis still possible in Gotthelf's work. Ill's sacrifice is not meaningless, though it is highly ambivalent. This play can be seen as Dürrenmatt's plea for a new morality capable of doing justice to the complexities of our age. (RS)

Eich. 12093. Jakobsh, Frank K. "Günther Eich:Homage to Bakunin." *GSlav* 3:37-46.
Günter Eich is widely recognized as an eminent lyric poet of the "romantic" tradition. But in the light of his poetry since 1960 this assessment requires re-examination since he gradually abandoned tradition and proceeded to publish poetic texts which are anarchistic in terms of form and content. This development reaches its climax in the "Maulwürfe," where he not only rejects all traditional poetic devices, but identifies with anarchism and writes one passage in "Homage to Bakunin." An analysis of this "poem" clarifies the concerns and methods of these texts. (FKJ)

Frisch. 12113. Musgrave, Marian E. "The Evolution of the Black Character in the Works of Max Frisch." *Monatshefte* 66:117-32.
Max Frisch has included a surprising number of black characters in his dramas and novels, though the portrayals have been marked by stereotyping. Starting with a minstrel-show caricature in *Santa Cruz*, Frisch next presented the black as "natural entertainer" in *Als der Krieg zu Ende war*. During a visit to the United States in 1951, he met and talked with a number of American blacks. These meetings affected his portrayals of blacks in *Stiller* and *Homo Faber*. These blacks bear a strong resemblance to the creations of the "cabaret school" of writers during the Harlem Renaissance of the 1920s and can be classified as "exotic primitives." Frisch, in his most recent play, *Biographie: Ein Spiel*, has created, in the role of Helen the Mulatta, an artistically and humanly sound black. (MEM)
12115. Quenon, J. "Anthroponymie et caractérisation dans le théâtre de Max Frisch." *RLV* 39(1973):526-37; 40:25-39.
Examines Frisch's use of descriptive terms for purposes of direct characterization in his plays. The means he employs and gradually organizes into a system are described in relation to their dramatic effectiveness. After his fourth play, Frisch stops defining important characters by the etymological value of their names and develops the technique he had been using for early subsidiary figures. He points out the difference between important and subsidiary characters by contrasting grand names and familiar abbreviations. He uses proper names again, but at this stage emphasizing their symbolic values and their sound-effects. Later, family names and Christian names are used to give direct, or ironic, or mixed commentary on the character itself. (JQ)

Grass. 12132. Enderstein, Carl O. "Zahnsymbolik und ihre Bedeutung in Günter Grass' Werken." *Monatshefte* 66:5-18.
Grass's protagonists are frequently afflicted with toothache, grinding, and loss of teeth. This reference to an individual's tooth problem alludes to his impotence in the broadest sense of the term: artistic sterility, professional incompetence, inhibition, frustration, inability to cope with the manifold demands of life, sexual inadequacy, or even complete existential failure. The mention of strong and beautiful teeth in Grass's works can denote a person's heightened sexuality, aggressiveness, political and economic awareness. Knowledge about the significance of this tooth symbol provides insight into Grass's own creative potency and adds vital information for the understanding of such complex figures as Heini Pilenz and Eberhard Starusch, narrators of *Katz und Maus* and *Örtlich betäubt*. (COE)
12133. Ezergailis, Inta M. "Gunter Grass's 'Fearful Symmetry':Dialectic, Mock and Real, in *Katz und Maus* and *Die Blechtrommel.*" *TSLL* 16:221-35.
Grass's work is permeated with dialectical rhythms, in theme as well as in structure. In *Katz* this dialectic becomes explicit—as an obsession with "counterweights." A counterweight may be an object, usually fraught with symbolism, which serves to balance another. It can also describe parallel and simultaneous actions that counterbalance each other in space, time, or symbolic import. At its highest level, the counterweight can explain the imbalance in the narrative process itself, the discrediting of the character-narrator which asks the reader to provide a balance. In *The Tin Drum* the counterweight appears in similar ways and on the same levels. (IE)

Ingrisch. 12175. Lederer, Herbert. "Die Dramen Lotte Ingrischs." *MAL* 7,i/ii:132-40.
Life and death, reality and illusion, dreaming and waking dominate the work of Lotte Ingrisch. In her plays, which deal with the hopeless effort to preserve one's illusions, "fairies and spirits break into the era of science and technology." Black humor strikes her as the only means for making a senseless existence bearable. Absolute reality does not exist for Ingrisch. Man as co-creator of an existence which he provides with meaning is a conflict of the Baroque and simultaneously a paradox of our own time. (HL)

Jahnn. 12176. Detsch, Richard R. "The Themes of the Black Race in the Works of Hans Henny Jahnn." *Mosaic* 7,ii:165-87.
In Jahnn's *Medea* (1925) and *Street Corner: A Place, an Action* (1931) he deals with the disastrous results of the exclusion of blacks from the dominant white community. His Medea, a black woman endowed with tremendous vitality and capacity for love, mercilessly avenges her rejection by the Greeks of Corinth. In contrast to Medea, the hero of *Street Corner* is a submissive black in a large American city. Nevertheless, the play ends with a dire warning to the whites to desist from their persecution of blacks. Elsewhere, Jahnn proposes miscegenation as a means of insuring the survival of the human race. The second part of Jahnn's novel trilogy *River without Shores* (1949-50) deals, in part, with the sufferings of blacks in Africa at the hands of colonial governments. (RRD)

Johnson. 12184. Boulby, Mark. "Surmises on Love and Family Life in the Work of Uwe Johnson." *Seminar* 10:131-41.
Johnson criticism has generally concentrated on stylistic or topical political and social matters. *Jahrestage*, however, encourages a study of "Familienroman" elements in all his novels and suggests the presence in them of a tissue of classical or archetypal erotic conflicts and an important level of autochthonous human encounter. (MB)
12186. Cock, Mary E. "Uwe Johnson:An Interpretation of Two Novels." *MLR* 69:348-58.
Although Uwe Johnson's novels *Mutmassungen über Jakob* (1959) and *Das dritte Buch über Achim* (1961) have been deemed obscure, close examination of their complex structures reveals that both are carefully designed to assert the value of the individual in face of political systems or modes of life which foster uniformity or lead to emotional and intellectual isolation. The earlier novel's intermingling of methods of narration emphasizes the complexity of individual existence, employing almost cinematic techniques for vividness, and also how inadequate a grasp most individuals have of the totality of experience, confined within their own

problems. In the later novel the question and answer form reveals a reluctance in the narrator to talk freely; this derives from his inability to come to terms with his subject. The novel's technique emphasizes the disturbing fact that Communism has its own view of truth, but also that the West has its prejudices too which distort experience. (MEC)

12187. Fletcher, John. "The Themes of Alienation and Mutual Incomprehension in the Novels of Uwe Johnson." *IFR* 1:81-87.
Since the defeat of the Third Reich in 1945, German literature has occupied a difficult position in trying to re-establish cultural links with other literatures. Of all the novelists engaged in this activity, Johnson is the most accomplished. *The Third Book about Achim* is discussed and Fletcher demonstrates why the internal frontier separating East and West Germany is a metaphor for all forms of alienation and mutual incomprehension in modern society. The novel persuades us that all fictional attempts to render reality faithfully are doomed to failure. Johnson demonstrates that reality is ultimately impossible to grasp because from our own viewpoint we misinterpret. Fiction is reduced to doubt its own premises and validity and ultimately to the sterility of turning in circles around itself. (JF)

12188. Miller, Leslie L. "Uwe Johnson's *Jahrestage*:The Choice of Alternatives." *Seminar* 10:50-70.
An important thematic unity links Johnson's *Jahrestage* with each of his earlier works, despite differences in geographical and historical setting. In *Jahrestage* as in the earlier novels, situations characteristic either of a totalitarian society, or one in which profound social and political injustices prevail, confront each of the central figures with a difficult, sometimes irresolvable, choice of alternatives. In this work as in his others, Johnson is concerned with the nature of these alternatives and the factors which motivate their choice. (LM)

Kramp. 12201. Hadley, Michael L. "Ideology and Fiction:A Case for Christian Realism in Germany and Russia in the Thought of Willy Kramp." *GSlav* 2(1973):5-18.
Set against the background of literary secularization, and seen in the light of literary problems confronting the Christian writer in modern Germany, Hadley examines how an author's theological views are transformed into fiction without becoming ideological. The answer is found in "Christian Realism," a term formulated by the German novelist and essayist Willy Kramp (1909-) to characterize not only his own aspirations and particularly his major novel *Brüder und Knechte* (1965), but the works of such diverse writers as Leskov and Solzhenitsyn. Hitherto unpublished material highlights Kramp's concern for a kind of Christian literature which focuses on the inner dynamics of human struggle and suffering rather than on demonstrations of canons of faith which, he feels, can elicit no positive response from secular society. (MLH)

Kroetz. 12202. Herzfeld-Sander, Margaret. "Kroetz' *Heimarbeit*:The Stratification of Language." *NTLTL* 14,i:34-41.
Modern literary texts require a knowledge of various levels of language. The use of language in literary texts can be studied in order to recognize levels of language and understand their social implications. Contemporary German writers are interested in exposing the human condition by revealing the inability of characters to communicate. In the play *Heimarbeit* by Franz Xaver Kroetz, the restricted manner in which characters use language has a direct bearing on their inability to understand their own lives, their actions, and the world around them. Kroetz demonstrates the link between inarticulate behavior and human aggression. (MMH-S)

Lebert. 12208. Caputo-Mayr, Maria L. "Hans Leberts Romane:Realismus und Dämonie, Zeitkritik und Gerichtstag." *MAL* 7,i/ii:79-98.
Lebert's *Die Wolfshaut* and *Der Feuerkreis* deepen his early preoccupation with the themes of good and evil, guilt, repentance, and judgment. His convictions belong to the Western Judeo-Christian tradition, which he tests for validity in our time and against whose values he measures the postwar European man. He presents average citizens who live in forgetfulness and inertia until a hidden God takes them to task. Lebert contrasts with the average crowd several exemplary figures who represent the struggle between good and evil, enact God's judgment, and have to come to terms with God and the mystery of life. Their struggles are proof of God's existence and plans, and they emphasize modern man's personal responsibility for the continuity of human and religious values. (MLC-M)

Lenz. 12210. Elstren, Esther N. "How It Seems and How It Is:Marriage in Three Stories by Siegfried Lenz." *OL* 29:170-79.
Discusses Lenz's treatment of disintegrating marital relationships in "Ein Haus aus lauter Liebe," "Der langere Arm," and "Der sechste Geburtstag." In all three stories the central theme is seen to be the devastating discrepancy between appearance and reality. The structure of all three stories is an integral part of Lenz's treatment of the central theme, with the external action depicting the realm of appearances and functioning simultaneously as a frame for Lenz's portrayal of the inner reality. This effective juxtaposition of the two realms intensifies the reader's awareness of the discrepancy between them. The motif of failure, a variation of the theme of guilt, is discussed as another element the stories have in common. (ENE)

12211. Hanson, William P. "Siegfried Lenz's Short Story 'Die Festung'." *ML* 55:26-32.
A brief outline is given of Lenz's career and his reputation in Germany, together with an attempt to characterize his writing and attitudes in general terms. The short story "Die Festung" is analyzed to encourage discussion concerning tension, atmosphere, characterization, linguistic control, and the possible meaning of the story. Stress is laid on the open-ended quality of many of Lenz's stories. (WPH)

Nossack. 12224. Goessl, Ingeborg M. "Der handlungslose Raum bei Hans Erich Nossack." *Monatshefte* 66:33-45.
Most of Nossack's major characters are aware of a place which is void of all empirical reality and exists outside of time and action. They are drawn to it and consider it the only place where they can escape the catastrophe that hangs over mankind. It brings truth instead of peace, the ability to view this life as absurd or unreal. Starting with *Nekyia* (1949), a story told from the beyond and continuing through the recent *Der Fall d'Arthez* (1968), the awareness of the existence of this other reality gives the characters the strength to endure their present situation until they can cross over. This visionary place has its origin in the depths of the self and, therefore, each person can only enter it alone. (IMG)

Remarque. 12233. Szépe, Helena. "Der deklassierte Kleinbürger in den Romanen Erich Maria Remarques." *Monatshefte* 65(1973):385-92.
Erich Maria Remarque is generally regarded as a politically progressive writer. A close examination of the ideas which he propagated in his novels shows that this image needs revision. Excepting his pacifist and antifascistic notions, Remarque expounded a rather reactionary set of ideas which includes the elevation of mediocrity to a general virtue, the rejection of culture as mere "bourgeois habits," the equation of material and social success with immorality, an anarchical view of law and society, contempt for politics as a dirty game, and the glorification of war-time friendships as models for peace-time relationships. During the years of the Weimar Republic, these concepts appealed especially to members of the German petty-bourgeoisie whose social and economic status had been significantly reduced. In his novels, Remarque reinforced the feelings of isolation and frustration within this group and unwittingly helped strengthen the already existing anti-democratic attitudes among his middle-class readers. (HS)

Stern, K. 12256. Maloney, Stephen R. "The Works and Days of Karl Stern." *GaR* 28:245-56.
Karl Stern's *The Pillar of Fire* (1951) is a neglected, but highly significant, work of art. This autobiography anticipates some of Stern's later works, such as *The Third Revolution* (on psychology and religion) and *The Flight from Woman* (literature, psychology,

and religion). In *The Pillar of Fire* Stern describes his childhood in pre-Hitler Germany and shows his growing dissatisfaction with secular humanism. Unable to live a fragmented, "modern" life, Stern sought to fuse three main threads of his life: art, psychoanalysis, and religion. (SRM)

VIII. AMERICANA GERMANICA

Bibliography. 12304. Fink, Albert B. "A Bibliography of German-Language and Related Items in the Rare Book Collection of the Beeghly Library, Heidelberg College, Tiffin, Ohio." *GAS* 7:50-67.
The Rare Book Collection of Heidelberg College contains 115 German-language and related items whose publication dates span 5 centuries. A major portion of the holdings seems to have come into the library's possession as donations from early members of the college faculty, most notably from professors in the Theological Seminary who served the Ohio Synod of the Reformed Church. The collection is of a predominantly theological nature. Included are numerous bibles dating from 1655 to 1874, church histories, catechisms, collections of sermons and hymnals along with a smaller number of secular works dealing with history, languages, natural science, and practical medicine. (ABF)

General and Miscellaneous. 12308. Haberland, Paul M. "The Reception of German Literature in Baltimore's Literary Magazines, 1800-1875." *GAS* 7:69-92.
Scholarship concerning the reception of German literature in America during the 19th century concentrates on the major Northern cities, Boston, New York, and Philadelphia. It neglects the appraisal of German literature in Baltimore, gateway to the South. A systematic search through 19th-century Baltimore's literary magazines reveals a fascinating chronological development of opinion regarding German authors and their works. Early in this period Baltimoreans consider German literature morally pernicious and tasteless. The Civil War introduces a hiatus of concern, but a renewed interest follows the War's conclusion. (PMH)

12315. Wiley, Raymond A. "The German American Verse of Dr. Franz Lahmeyer." *GAS* 7:14-29.
This MS German poem, written in Baltimore, Maryland, consists of 49 six-line verses of basically iambic tetrameter rhythm, generally in an *ababcc* rhyme scheme. The German script is by an author about whom nothing is known save that he debarked at Baltimore on 1 Jan. 1833. Content of the poem, whose original MS is owned by a New York City resident, consists of a rather one-sided contrast of the evils of European—and in particular German—governmental systems with that of the yound American states. Addressed to friends in Hannover, all oppressed Germans are urged to migrate to the land of freedom from petty taxes and harassments for a better future. (RAW)

NETHERLANDIC LITERATURE†

I. GENERAL

General and Miscellaneous. 12343. Fajn, Max. "Marc-Michel Rey:Boekhandelaar op de Bloemmarkt (Amsterdam)." *PAPS* 118:260-68.
The career of the publisher Marc-Michel Rey illustrates the inter-relationship between private and societal factors at the level of the enterprise and the processes by which publishers contributed to the determination of the scope of the Enlightenment. (MF)

III. NETHERLANDIC LITERATURE TO 1500

General and Miscellaneous. 12392. Braswell, Laurel. "The Middle Dutch Prose Legendary in the McMaster University Library, Hamilton, Canada." *MS* 36:134-43.
McMaster University Library MS. 41, acquired in 1968 as part of the Barry Brown Collection, contains in 163 paper folios 11 whole and fragmentary saints' legends written ca. 1380-1450 probably in the area of Liège. The legendary is not a Middle Dutch version of the highly popular *Legenda aurea*, but represents an independent and earlier tradition as reflected by the use of pseudo-Theotimus' life of Saint Margaret and a 10th-century life of Saint Pantaleon. Textual evidence indicates an agglomerate work which evolved as several series for the *Somer Stuc* (summer feasts) were collated. The manuscript now contains the lives of Saints Margaret, ff. 1-30ᵛ; Pantaleon, ff. 31-54ᵛ; Boniface, ff. 55-57; Odulphus, ff. 57-58ᵛ; Marcus and Marcellianus, ff. 59-61; Martin (translation and miracle), ff. 61-62ᵛ; Tiburtius, ff. 63-63ᵛ; Barbara, ff. 64-138ᵛ; Dorothea, ff. 138ᵛ-50ᵛ; Barbara (*exemplum* at Gorinchem, 1448), ff. 151-56ᵛ; Fides, Spes, Caritas, and Sophia, ff. 157-63. (LAB)

IV. SIXTEENTH AND SEVENTEENTH CENTURIES

Erasmus. 12479. Bietenholz, P.G. "Ambiguity and Consistency in the Work of Erasmus of Rotterdam." *WascanaR* 9:134-42.
An analysis of the occurrence and significance of ambiguity in the literary work of Erasmus. Chiefly Erasmus' correspondence from 1517 to 1520 was examined to determine his ambiguity and his consistency against the background of biographical fact, in particular his involvement in the controversies involving Reuchlin and Luther. (PGB)

12493. Fisher, Alan S. "An End to the Renaissance:Erasmus, Hobbes, and *A Tale of a Tub*." *HLQ* 38:1-20.
In *A Tale of a Tub* Swift asserts a curious personal presence which one senses in the brilliant irrelevance of his analogy-making. The analogies are at their best when Swift is describing something wicked or dangerous, and they add an atmosphere of having fun, just at those points in the *Tale* where Swift's contemplation seems bleakest. The effect is paradoxical, as if a free intellect were attesting a world where determinism and mindlessness are the only realities. Paradoxes remind one of Erasmus, but if Erasmus obliterated meaningless distinctions in the light of a higher truth, Swift obliterates distinctions which are not meaningless—the very distinctions on which civilization depends. Swift senses that we can, alas, no longer see the truths Erasmus saw. Between Swift and Erasmus lies Hobbes, whose reduction of human qualities to mechanism Swift found strangely unanswerable. But if Swift cannot answer Hobbes, he can subvert his system. The Digression on Madness purports to support Hobbist premises and argues them with buffoonish enthusiasm into paradox, just the kind of discourse Hobbes found most wrong. (ASF)

12494. Fleischauer, John F. "A New Sixteenth-Century

† *Festschriften* and Other Analyzed Collections are listed in the first division of this volume. "F" numbers in brackets following a title refer to these items.

Translation of Erasmus." *PBSA* 68:164-66.

An unlisted copy of Erasmus' *De Civilitate Morum Puerilium* at the University of Pennsylvania library is identified as printed by John Walley, ca. 1550. The Pennsylvania copy, lacking both title page and colophon, contains both a Latin text and, curiously, an English text which is half the work of an anonymous translator and half that of Robert Whittinton. The anonymous translation is more fluent but less artful than Whittinton's earlier version. The Pennsylvania copy has been misplaced, so closer examination must wait; meanwhile, Fleischauer's copies of a portion of the text (duplicates of which are in the Houghton Library) are all that remain. (JFF)

12511. Logan, George M. "Erasmus' Intellectual Development." *HAB* 25:232-43. [Rev. art.]

Rabil's *Erasmus and the New Testament* and Thompson's *Under Pretext of Praise* prompt a reassessment of Erasmus' intellectual development. Rabil views this development as a dialectical process in which Erasmus articulates a series of resolutions of a conflict between childhood religion and adolescent humanism. The difficulty in this thesis is that Erasmus before his first visit to England in 1499-1500 exhibits no more than conventional interest in religion and seems content with the conventional reconciliations of literary study with religion. In fact, Erasmus' stay in England produced not only (as Rabil and others think) a resolution of the tension between religion and humanism but also the tension itself. After *The Praise of Folly* (1509), Erasmus' development continues in an essentially linear rather than dialectical fashion. His constant focus on morality, together with his growing skepticism of reason, leads him close to the pragmatic view that, on many of the subtler points of doctrine, one may as well believe whatever is most conducive to morality. (GML)

12518. McLean, Andrew. "Another English Translation of Erasmus' *Coniugium*:Snawsel's *Looking Glasse for Maried Folkes* (1610)." *Moreana* 43-44:55-64.

Snawsel's *A Looking Glasse for Maried Folkes* (1610) combines a translation of Erasmus' *Coniugium* with a catechistical dialogue on the duty of husbands and wives. Little is known about the translator, a Yorkshire gentleman whose sons attended Cambridge. Examples from the Latin original and Snawsel's translation concern an anecdote paralleling More's courtship of Jane Colt and illustrate how the translator uses picturesque and proverbial sayings to maintain a colloquial idiom. Snawsel's changes in translation affect expression rather than meaning. (AMM)

12529. Rebhorn, Wayne A. "The Metamorphoses of Moria: Structure and Meaning in *The Praise of Folly*." *PMLA* 89:463-76.

Following Moria's metamorphoses, Erasmus' *Praise* falls into three sections whose interrelationships generate its total meaning. Moving from section to section, Folly leads her auditors through a dialectic of conversion. At first ironic, Folly is the goddess of metamorphosis, a variant of Circe, offering men her gift of pleasurable illusion. She wants them to accept life as a comic play and attacks the "Stoic" for attempting self-divinization while rejecting the play of life. But in the satirical middle section, Folly betrays them by showing them the real tragedy of their lot. While revealing that one cannot separate life-preserving, pleasurable folly from destructive madness, by her transformation into a "Stoic" truth-teller, Folly prevents men from placing their faith in her benevolence. Thus, in the final section, she turns with them to Christian folly, the faith that leads men out of Plato's cave to God's unchanging, benevolent reality. Folly's final, ecstatic vision gives her followers a transcendent perspective redefining and including the comitragic visions of the first two sections. (WAR)

SCANDINAVIAN LITERATURES†

II. THE SCANDINAVIAN LITERATURES TO 1500

Sagas. 12962. Harris, Joseph. "Christian Form and Christian Meaning in *Halldórs Þáttr I*." [F 1]:249-64.

The first of the *Þættir* comprises three interesting narrative structures of a type common to the genre and a fourth innermost structure, included as a retrospective "entertainment," which provides the motivation for resolving the conflicts of the other three. The retrospective narrative is patterned typologically on Christian myth, and a number of biblical texts and details of the *Þáttr* support this argument. Structural replications in the story are linked intimately with its message, justifying the thesis that Christian meaning here creates Christian form, showing how intricately a "standard" generic form may be varied, and carrying implications for the familiar saga esthetic of symmetry. (JH)

12965. Hieatt, Constance B. "*Karlamagnús saga* and the *Pseudo-Turpin Chronicle*." *SS* 46:140-50.

The Old Norse saga "King Agulandus," which is Part iv of the *Karlamagnús Saga*, is based on two sources. One of these is the Pseudo-Turpin Chronicle (PT). The version of PT on which the saga was originally based belongs to the "C" group of "longer" PT MSS. The theory that the saga derives from such a "C" text is attractive because of the special connection of that group with England, whence most parts of the saga derive; but there is no trace in the saga of the earmarks of later English PT versions. Detailed comparison of the saga text(s) with the identifiable characteristics of the "C" group make this belief look very dubious, so it must derive from a hybrid version of PT remarkably close to that of Codex Calixtinus. No more precise identification of the source is possible. (CBH)

12967. Hume, Kathryn. "The Thematic Design of *Grettis saga*." *JEGP* 73:469-86.

Grettis saga is a mixture of wonder-tale, history, and romance, and Grettir's character an odd blend of irascibility and forbearance. The contrasts suggest that the author wrote to explore a thematic problem: the viability of a heroic ideal within society. The author's insertion of lordly figures and folktale monsters indicate that he pictured Grettir as suited to the *fornöld*. Grettir has much in common with the stylized heroes of *fornaldarsaga* fantasy, but within real society he becomes a menace. The heroic ideal he represents is ultimately rejected by the author, but the alternative social ideal represented by the farmers is no compensation for the loss of Grettir's virtues. (KH)

12968. Johnston, George,tr. "The Faroe Islanders' Saga." *HAB* 24(1973):32-38.

Excerpt from a translation of *Faereyinga Saga* from Old Icelandic with a comment by the translator. (GBJ)

12980. Scheps, Walter. "Historicity and Oral Narrative in *Njáls saga*." *SS* 46:120-33.

Njáls Saga is "historical" for a medieval auditor or reader in the same sense that the work of Gregory of Tours or Geoffrey of Monmouth is historical, i.e., morally true; it is "oral" in the same sense that Scott's unacknowledged revision of popular ballads is oral, i.e., a brilliant imitation or extension by a literary author of material taken from oral tradition. (WS)

III. DANISH (AND FAROESE) LITERATURE

Nineteenth Century

† *Festschriften* and Other Analyzed Collections are listed in the first division of this volume. "F" numbers in brackets following a title refer to these items.

Goldschmidt. 13100. Ober, Kenneth H. "Meïr Goldschmidt as a Writer of English." *OL* 29:231-44.

Goldschmidt's published English writings have traditionally been either ignored or belittled, and his manuscript notes for an English novel have been scoffed at. A close examination of his published correspondence traces his progressive mastery of the English language, and a careful study of his publications in English journals, as well as his notes for the novel, demonstrates that this aspect of his literary activity deserves to be taken seriously. Argument over whether Goldschmidt could or would have become a great novelist in English, if he had not returned to Denmark, is pointless. His English writings, published and unpublished, must be taken into account, however, in determining Goldschmidt's place in the history of literature. (KO)

Kierkegaard. 13147. Fauteck, Heinrich. "Kierkegaards Antigone." *Skandinavistik* 4:81-100.
Kierkegaard's outline of a modern *Antigone* in his *Either-Or*, aims at a renewal of the tragic from Greek antiquity. The conception of guilt is defined as "hereditary guilt." Antigone "participates" in the guilt of her father. She does not perish by a collision of her love with the idea of state, represented by Kreon. The tragedy of his Antigone arises from an inner conflict depending on her solidarity with her father. A special and essential aspect of this outline is the close connection with the historical situation. In Kierkegaard's mind, the renewal of the tragic could be a remedy for this malady of his time. (HF)

Twentieth Century

Blixen. 13244. Whissen, Thomas R. "The Bow of the Lord:Isak Dinesen's 'Portrait of the Artist'." *SS* 46:47-58.
According to Dinesen, the artist is the chosen receiver of the myths of creation. As God's "mouthpiece," he is privileged to know the symbols of the "immortal story" but not to know their meaning. Just as God has struck a receptive chord in him, so must the artist transmit the myth so as to strike an equally receptive chord in the souls of men farther removed from the divine source. The artist deals with his audience as God dealt with Job, wagering with Satan for their souls and arguing for their acceptance of the myth at the expense of their understanding of it. God imagines the myths; the artist articulates the experience of them. For the privilege of perceiving the "masks of God," the artist is denied certain human benefits. "If he is without potency, he has been given a small bit of omnipotence." (TRW)

V. NORWEGIAN LITERATURE

Nineteenth Century

Ibsen. 13385. Durbach, E[rrol]. "Sacrifice and Absurdity in *The Wild Duck*." *Mosaic* 7,iv:99-107.
In several of Ibsen's plays the Abrahamic myth is invoked, only to be inverted. Ibsen's anti-heroes, by making Gods of their own fallible ideals and neurotic wills, fail to set in operation the redemptive effects of the ritual. A child dies—but instead of a sacramental sacrifice, a *Kindermord* is dramatized. Brand allows his son to die, believing that he is suffering an Abrahamic testing—but his God is ultimately indistinguishable from his own defective personality. In *The Wild Duck*, there is an implicit rejection of Kierkegaard's acquiescence in a suspension of human ethics in favor of a higher teleological imperative. Gregers Werle precipitates Hedvig's "sacrifice"—but its consequence is not an affirmation of Absurdity as extraordinary faith. It merely confirms a sense of the Absurd as redefined by the agnostic existentialists: meaninglessness and man's failure to merit redemption. (ED)
13402. Marker, Lise-Lone and Frederick J. "William Bloch and Naturalism in the Scandinavian Theatre." *ThS* 15,ii:85-104.
Stage naturalism made its first appearance in Scandinavia unaccompanied by the fanfare or enthusiastic manifestoes which heralded its arrival in many countries. The methods and techniques of the new style were introduced at the Danish Royal Theater by William Bloch. Of particular interest are Bloch's productions of Ibsen, the earliest and most characteristic of which is his staging of *An Enemy of the People* in 1883. The remarkably detailed manuscript records of this production, preserved in the Royal Theater Library and analyzed and illustrated for the first time in this article, make it possible to reconstruct in detail one of naturalistic theater's most typical and significant achievements. (L-LM & FJM)
13409. Rogers, Katharine M. "A Woman Appreciates Ibsen." *CentR* 18:91-108.
Criticism of *A Doll's House* and *Ghosts*, Ibsen's two plays which focus on society's oppression of women, reveals a variety of attempts to devalue Ibsen's message. Some critics depreciate these plays relative to his "more characteristic" work; some denigrate the two heroines, making Nora a flightly self-indulgent creature and Mrs. Alving a repressed puritan who destroyed her husband's masculinity. They ignore the social forces at work in the plays. Those who feel compelled to react seriously to Nora and *A Doll's House* reconcile their admiration with their reluctance to think about women's rights by claiming that the play is about human rights in general: its significant concern is "the tyranny of one human being over another" and it "would be just as valid were Torvald the wife and Nora the husband." (KMR)
13419. Volz, Ruprecht. "Ein unveröffentlichter Brief Henrik Ibsens an Gunnar Heiberg." *Skandinavistik* 4:101-04.
On 18 April 1888 Ibsen wrote a letter to Gunnar Heiberg, in which he rejected a recommendation in favor of Heiberg. This hitherto unknown letter is edited and discussed in view of the relation between the two dramatists. (RV)

Twentieth Century

Borgen. 13464. Birn, Randi. "Dream and Reality in Johan Borgen's Short Stories." *SS* 46:59-72.
In Borgen's short stories a crisis of consciousness jolts the protagonist out of his diurnal constancy and he realizes his insignificance within the universal order. Far from provoking fear, awareness of death instills in the character an irresistible longing to reunite with the cosmos. The only emotion sufficiently authentic to challenge this "boundless longing" is love, which Borgen represents as a positive, life-affirming force. While love offers flashes of happiness, it does not offer a permanent solution for the protagonist, whose most profound impulse is usually the death-oriented quest for the source of the self. (RB)

Hamsun. 13482. Knutsen, Nils M. "Eine nordnorwegische Feudalgesellschaft:Eine Analyse der sozialen Machtstruktur in Knut Hamsuns *Benoni* und *Rosa*." *Skandinavistik* 4:25-36.
An analysis of the power relations in *Benoni* and *Rosa* show that these works present an important introduction to Hamsun's social works. Because of his wealth Benoni holds a position between the merchant Mack and the general public; however, he cannot cope with this social role which causes a number of conflicts between Benoni and Mack on the one hand, and Benoni and the townspeople on the other. These conflicts reveal the power structures in the commercial town and their powerful results. Mack's power system has a number of points in common with the power structures of feudal society in medieval Europe. (NMK)

VI. SWEDISH LITERATURE

Nineteenth Century

Almqvist. 13558. Romberg, Bertil. "Über C.J.L. Almqvists Romankunst." *OL* 29:16-33.
The structure and narrative technique of four novels by Almqvist are examined with particular attention to characteristic epic and

dramatic features. At the same time a review of Almqvist's narrative technique from *Murnis* (1819) to *Det gar an* (1839) is furnished, illuminating his literary development from romanticism to realism. (BR)

Strindberg. 13587. Hamilton, Mary G. "Strindberg's Alchemical Way of the Cross." *Mosaic* 7,iv:139-53.
In *To Damascus* gold plays a vital role as a complex symbol of both worldly and spiritual existence: the alchemist's quest is a search not only for material benefits, but also for spiritual and psychological perfection. Although all three parts of the play are concerned with alchemy, each expresses a different mode of life. Part I is the private road of passive, "feminine" faith; Part II the public road of active, "masculine" science; and Part III the "androgynous" synthesis of the first two in the path of intellect. Only in Part III is the alchemical process truly completed. (MGH)

Twentieth Century

General and Miscellaneous. 13612. Kuhn, Hans. "*Grönköpings Veckoblad.*" *Skandinavistik* 4:105-20.
Grönköpings Veckoblad is unique among humorous periodicals in having survived for seven decades with an almost unchanged fictional framework. The common stylistic denominator is unintentional incongruousness with comic effect. Life in a self-contented, self-satisfied late 19th-century provincial town is preserved in spirit and presentation, while the specific subject matter is largely topical-satirical. While originally a criticism of backward and conceited provincialism from the point of view of the radical enlightened city-dweller, the paper has gradually assumed a distinctly nostalgic quality and is now mostly critical of the progressive establishment. Ekelöf shows the serious poetic use of which the Grönköping medium is capable. (HK)

Lagerkvist. 13691. Bloch, Adèle. "The Mythical Female in the Fictional Works of Pär Lagerkvist." *IFR* 1,i:48-53.
Lagerkvist's heroes unconsciously pattern their lives after mythological archetypes. Some come to understand the forces shaping their destinies, while others do not. All place themselves under the aegis of the Magna Mater upon which they project their fears, desires, and guilt. This anima image may assume many guises according to the age or situation of the hero. This myth projection has little to do with the real nature of women who fall victims to the task of role enactment which their partners thrust upon them. (AB)

Martinsson. 13719. Oberholzer, Otto. "Zur Gliederung von Harry Martinssons *Aniara.*" *Skandinavistik* 4:37-48.
Aniara is divided into 103 cantos. Interesting and hitherto scarcely noticed is the inner structure which is determined by time elements. The structure of the contents is reflected in the time structure of "Aniara." From the takeoff of the space ship, until the expiration of all life, 24 years rush by, which split into phases of six-year intervals. Each phase corresponds to certain manners of behavior exhibited by the Aniara characters. (OO)

MODERN GREEK LITERATURE†

I. GENERAL AND MISCELLANEOUS

Bibliography. 13750. Clark, Richard C. "Modern Greek Literature:Bibliographical Spectrum and Review Article." *RNL* 5,ii:137-59.
Although two books have recently appeared in English titled *A History of Modern Greek Literature*, one by Dimaras and the other by Politis, they are more adequately described as encyclopedic handbooks, rather than histories. For English-speaking readers, the introductions in Friar's *Modern Greek Poetry: From Cavafis to Elytis* and Keeley and Bien's *Modern Greek Writers* are of greater value. Of still greater value are two chapters of *Modern Greece* by Campbell and Sherrard: "The Idea of the Greek Nation" and "Modern Greek Literature." (RCC)

General and Miscellaneous. 13787. Paolucci, Anne. "Introduction:Inescapable Greece." *RNL* 5,ii:9-12. [Introd. to spec. no., "Greece:The Modern Voice."]
Hellenism is as inescapable a legacy of the modern world as Hebraism. The tradition has come down from the great epic, lyric, and dramatic poets of the Hellenic age; through the professional scholars of Hellenistic Pergamum and Alexandria; through Christianized and orientalized Byzantium, to the rebirth of secularized literature in all the Western European lands that experienced a renaissance of classical antiquity at the same time that they struggled for national identity. Since the days of Byron, a future-looking longing for Greek national identity and a revived sense of continuity with the classical past have converged to inspire an impressive, highly individualized, literary output. (AP)

Poetry. 13808. Levitt, Morton P. "Modern Greek Poetry: 'Waiting for the Barbarians'." *Mosaic* 7,iv:171-78. [Rev. art., on K. Friar's anthology (1973).]
A viable and worthy literary tradition flourishes in modern Greece which is particularly evident in Greek verse translated and collected by Kimon Friar in *Modern Greek Poetry*. Poets such as Caváfis, Seféris, Kazantzákis, Elýtis, Rítsos, Gátsos, Engonópoulos, Papatsónis, and Sikelianós are part of an artistic flowering that is unique in this century. The central themes of this verse are the vital demotic language of modern Greece, its harsh but magnificent landscape, and its tragic history in the 20th century. Together they form a new mythology that is as creative and epical as the old. (MPL)

III. MEDIEVAL LITERATURE IN THE VERNACULAR

Drama and Theater. 13841. Sticca, Sandro. "The *Christos Paschon* and the Byzantine Theater." [F 6]:13-44.
A critical reading of *Christos Paschon*, the only authentic dramatic expression of the Byzantine religious theater, is undertaken in terms of the play's imaginative range, intellectual and liturgical content, and against the background of the origins and development of the theater. After an analysis of its meager documentary evidence, the focus centers on the *Christos Paschon*, the redaction of the play attributed to Gregory Nazianzenus. The *Christos Paschon* constitutes an intermediate link between Classical Antiquity and the Byzantine Middle Ages. Structurally, the play is a dramatic trilogy comprising three successive episodes which abide by the norms of biblical and classical tradition. Theologically, the play propounds the anti-Apollinarian thesis by emphasizing Christ's Incarnation and Mary's role in it as the *theotokos*, Mother of God. (SS)

---

† *Festschriften* and Other Analyzed Collections are listed in the first division of this volume. "F" numbers in brackets following a title refer to these items.

VI. LITERATURE 1831–1880

Prose Fiction. 13858. Vitti, Mario. "Rural Greekness in Greek Prose Fiction." *RNL* 5,ii:27-40.
The short story and the novel were literary genres new to Greece in the first half of the 19th century. It was feared that foreign novels exerted a baneful influence on genuine Greek manners and the Greek ethos. Thus there arose the demand for a "national novel" (1869). It was the rural population that attracted almost all the attention of writers after 1880. This prose fiction presented a "Greekness" which was idyllic and idealized. Thanks to ideas of realism and socialism, however, some writers, concerned to expose the conditions of backwardness and injustice in which the rural population lived, gave a different picture of the countryside and thus created a new concept of "Greekness." (MV)

VII. LITERATURE 1881–1922

Kavafis. 13878. Keeley, Edmund. "Cavafy's Hellenism." *RNL* 5,ii:66-89.
The Hellenism represented in Cavafy's mature poetry is a blend of idiosyncratic and traditional elements. The idiosyncrasy is manifest in the hedonistic bias of the life depicted in his mythical Alexandria. A more traditional element is the passionate commitment of his ancient Alexandrians to the Greek language, an element which also gave coherence to the broader Hellenic world that completed the poet's myth. Cavafy's later poetry turned toward the world of Hellenism beyond Alexandria and demonstrated that the special life of a Cavafian Hellene who worships the gods eros and art will remain available through the centuries. (EK)

Palamas. 13890. Robinson, Christopher. "Greece in the Poetry of Costis Palamas." *RNL* 5,ii:41-65.
In his prose writings, particularly *My Poetic*, Palamas suggests that it is only the public aspect of his poetry which is essentially Greek. Further examination reveals that his own definition of how he writes about his private persona and about metaphysical problems implies the necessary use of Greek themes to express these too. The early collections of poetry show him moving from a tentative exploration of separate areas to an integrated view of what Greece should mean to modern man. Initially he applies this new view to himself, then expands it to embrace a full concept of national renaissance. (CR)

VIII. MODERN LITERATURE AFTER 1922

Poetry. 13912. Anghelaki-Rooke, Katerina. "The Greek Poetic Landscape:Recent Trends in Greek Poetry." *RNL* 5,ii:13-26.
The poetic landscape of Greece is defined in a special way by the physical setting. This dependence is reinforced by a strong sense of national identity, which gives modern Greek poetry a substantial core. The elegaic poetry of George Seferis is infused with a feeling of loss rooted in a strong historical sensitivity. Dionysios Solomos metamorphosed the natural landscape of harmonious dialogue between man and the environment into an ethical expression of man's instinct striving toward goodness. The influence of these two major poets is traced briefly. (KA-R)

Kazantzakis. 13940. Bien, Peter. "The Mellowed Nationalism of Kazantzakis' *Zorba the Greek*." *RNL* 5,ii:113-36.
Kazantzakis' *Zorba the Greek* deserves a political interpretation. Zorba, representing the new nationalism, enters the Boss's life as a replacement for Stavridaki, who represents the pre-1922 Dragoumian ideology. The Boss moves from Buddhistic with-drawal to a "Zorbiatic" political as well as artistic appreciation of the earth's simple joys. Zorba rejects both the goals of the Dragoumian Great Idea and the means: warfare. To be Greek, the novel says, is to endure: to suffer with dignity by virtue of a resilience and good humor based on allegiance to life's small joys. (PB)

Sikelianos. 13991. Sherrard, Philip. "Anghelos Sikelianos and His Vision of Greece." *RNL* 5,ii:90-112.
Anghelos Sikelianos aspired to be a religious, metaphysical poet in the full sense of the term. As a Greek poet, he sought to identify and align himself with the Greek tradition which most adequately represented those spiritual values his poetry was to communicate. This led him to the religious life of the ancient, pre-Socratic world—to Orphism and the cult of Dionysos, Pythagoras, and the mystic and mantic centers of Eleusis and Delphi, in which he saw enshrined the spiritual essence of "Greekness." (PS)

ORIENTAL LITERATURES†

IV. NEAR- AND MIDDLE-EASTERN LITERATURE

General and Miscellaneous. 14038. Bijlefeld, Willem A. "Some Recent Contributions to Qur'ānic Studies:Selected Publications in English, French, and German, 1964-73." *MW* 64:79-102,172-79,259-74.
Four very different introductions to the Qur'ān constitute the subject matter of the second installment. The third installment surveys 14 publications on a wide variety of Qur'anic topics, arranged in four sections: (1) on Revelation, God and Man, Predestination; (2) on Abraham and Jesus; (3) on Death and Eternal Life; (4) on Ethico-Religious Concepts and Fasting.
The number of monographs in Western languages devoted to the study of the Qur'ān and published since 1964 reflects an increased interest in this field of study. The more than 20 titles included in this survey show a definite moving away from a primary focus on the question of Jewish and Christian "sources" of the Qur'ān. The first installment discusses three Qur'ān translations with notes and commentary. (WAB) (WAB)

14041. Boullata, Issa J. "Modern Qur'ān Exegesis:A Study of Bint al-Shāṭi"s Method." *MW* 64:103-13.
In her exegesis of the Qur'ān, Bint al-Shāṭī presents a modern and refreshing view of the Holy Book of Islam. She collects all verses on a specific topic and comes to an understanding of the text by a careful and objective study of the Arabic words and usages. She avoids all sectarian interpretations as well as all extra-qur'ānic explanations and rejects many of the opinions of past and modern exegetes. Though her concern is mainly stylistic and literary, her exegesis has theological overtones. (IJB)

14047. Civil, Miguel. "The Anzu-Bird and Scribal Whimsies." *JAOS* 92(1972):271.
A reading "anzu (d)" for the logogram an.im.mi/dugud was first proposed by Landsberger in 1961 and has been slowly gaining acceptance, although it has encountered some skepticism, and understandably so, since Landsberger's arguments although very persuasive hardly can be considered a definitive proof. (MC)

Iran. 14090. Brockway, Duncan. "The Macdonald Collection

† *Festschriften* and Other Analyzed Collections are listed in the first division of this volume. "F" numbers in brackets following a title refer to these items.

of Arabian Nights." *MW* 63(1973):185-205; 64:16-32. [Pt. I appeared in *MW* 61(1971):256-66; see Bibliog. for 1971, Vol. I, Item 1489; Vol. II, Item 11729.]
A bibliography of the Arabic texts of the Arabian Nights, of the translations into languages other than English, and of works about the Arabian Nights held by Case Memorial Library, Hartford Seminary Foundation, in its Macdonald Collection. (DB)

Israel. 14168. Bronner, Leah. "Trends in Contemporary Israeli Writing." *Theoria* 42:19-28.
Bronner describes the changes since the 1960s in Israeli literature. Earlier Hebrew letters were strongly national, overtly didactic in tone, and mainly influenced by the European literary schools. Contemporary Israeli writing is far more introspective, drawing its inspiration generally from Anglo-Saxon countries. It no longer mirrors the social "we," but the more personal "I," and the realities of life are conveyed through the prism of individual experience. Modern Israeli literature treats the themes of alienation, loneliness, anxiety, and the "identity crisis" in the impersonal age of technology. (LB)

14174. Cutter, William. "Setting as a Feature of Ambiguity in S.Y. Agnon's *Sippur Pashut*." *Crit* 15,iii:66-80.
The broad outlines of the novel are indeed simple, though Agnon utilizes a wide range of literary devices to complicate both plot and theme. A 17-year-old boy is trapped between the values of his bourgeois parents and his own spiritual needs at a time of severe

change within the Jewish world. The novel treats the conflict and resolutions which grow out of this situation, since the society in which the protagonist is ensconced dictates that he must marry an "appropriate" partner instead of the more sensual girl he loves. The character's mental breakdown and ultimate rehabilitation are delineated through intricate treatments of the various settings to which he cannot become adjusted but which are actually a part of him. (WC)

14212. Haephrati, Joseph. "A Study of Bialik's 'Who Am I and What Am I'." *Hasifrut* 5:1-7. [In Hebr.; sum. in Eng.]
The basic situation presented in the poem is that of a man, despairing of God's blessing, involuntarily finding himself faced with manifestations of grace shown him by the grass, the breeze, and the sunbeam that he meets on his way, all of which he rejects because they do not correspond to his inner condition. A parallel situation is known from other poems by Bialik which treat the "I-you (pl.)" theme. (JH)

Turkey. 14403. Paolucci, Anne. "Introduction:Ottoman Cosmopolitanism and Turkish Universality." *RNL* 4,i(1973):8-12. [Introd. to spec. no., "Turkey:From Empire to Nation."]
Modern Turkey, quite deliberately freed of its old imperial cosmopolitanism by the political labors of Mustafa Kemal and the philosophical-critical labors of Ziya Gökalp, is now producing a genuinely national literature with great potential for universality. (AP)

VI. SOUTH ASIAN LITERATURE

Burma. 14456. Goswami, Praphulladatta. "Burmese Law Tales." *FolkloreC* 16:274-75,277.
Discusses a tale that has some amount of legal validity and which can be used by an advocate at a court of law. The tale narrates how the three claimants for a husband were judged in favor of one who protected him and how this decision was accepted by all. (PG)

India. 14474. Bocaz, Sergio H. "Pantheistic Tendencies in Rabindranath Tagore and Pablo Neruda:Two Mystics in Search of Identity in Nature." [F 19]:246-51.
Rabindranath Tagore and Pablo Neruda have many similarities, the most striking being their mysticism. This mystical goal is achieved through the use of simple elements of Nature in their poems and in the authors' longing to become one with such elements. This mystical effort materializes in a clearly pantheistic tendency toward an identification with water, air, metals, and

dust. Another important pantheistic link in their mystical ideals is stressed through the love for their wives as an important part in their mystical fulfillment through the pantheistic tendencies which permeate their poetry as a whole. (SHB)

14509. Parameswaran, Uma. "On the Theme of Paternal Love in the Novels of R.K. Narayan." *IFR* 1:146-48. [In *The Financial Expert* and *The Sweet-Vendor*.]
Narayan insinuates that a man who has no paternal love in himself is fit for treasons, stratagems, and spoils. Except for Vasu the Man-Eater of Malgudi, there is no character in Narayan's work who is so vile as not to respond warmly to children. This theme of paternal love is the central element in *The Financial Expert* and *The Sweet-Vendor*. Margayya and Jagan each have two overwhelming passions in life, one of these for each is his son. Whereas Margayya never finds himself as father, Jagan ascends to a higher level of perception through his discovery of the limits of a father's responsibilities. (UP)

VII. SOUTHEAST ASIAN LITERATURE

Oceania. 14543. Boore, W.H. "Papua New Guinea Writers." *AWR* 24,liii:143-45. [On Okut Matak, Jack Lahui, Aloysius Aita, Peter Kilala.]
Words and antics respectively evoke the gods behind Wales and Papua New Guinea; eloquence and pageantry make gaudy faiths in both. Both peoples come new to the English language in which they write. The Welsh have a long literary tradition in their own ancient tongue. Papua New Guinea, however, was divided by a babel of languages without any written word. Both are initiating their own style in English—the Welsh discovering new emphases upon an age-old scene, the Papua New Guinean finding a new wholeness in what was utterly fragmented. (WHB)

14544. Brash, Elton T. "Creative Writing, Literature and Self-Expression in Papua New Guinea." *ALS* 6(1973):167-76.
Papua New Guinea has already produced creative writers who effectively use the language and literary modes of English. While their efforts can be attributed to discernible influences and have so far followed predictable courses, they have manifested the kinds of sensitivity and insight that have been lacking in the considerable body of expatriate fiction about Papua New Guinea that has so far appeared. The emergent literature of Papua New Guinea is concerned with anti-colonial themes and with the revelation of individual and social consciousness. A number of works draw on the rich tradition of oral literature. (ETB)

VIII. EAST ASIAN LITERATURE

China. 14600. Chin, Tsung. "Can the Presentation of Particle *le* Be Simpler?" [F 19]:143-47.
There are two *le*'s in Mandarin Chinese which are represented by the same character in writing. Le_2 occurs before the object and Le_1 after it, both following the verb. Successful presentation of this particle (character *le*) hinges upon the functional differ-

entiation of the two linguistic forms. Le_1 used in the absence of le_2 denotes occurredness of the verb action, that is something took place. Though there is the meaning of "past" in le_1 it is not the same as saying le_1 signals the past tense in English. The function of le_2 is to provide current relevance for the verb, with or without the modification of le_1, in much the same way as *have-en* signals the perfect aspect in English. (TC)

14603. Crump, J.I. "The Ch'u and Its Critics." *LE&W* 16(1972):961-79.

Critics modern and ancient have insisted that the literary "song" or *ch'ü* popular in 14th-century China required a large mixture of vernacular expressions. Three samples of the genre are translated and examined, ranging from very short to very long. The strong colloquial flavor of the longer *ch'ü* was the result of its being a performed genre. (JIC)

14613. Frankel, Hans H. "The Chinese Ballad 'Southeast Fly the Peacocks'." *HJAS* 34:248-71.

This anonymous *yüeh-fu* (ballad) tells in 355 lines the story of a young couple driven to double suicide by their elders. It must have been composed around the mid-third century A.D. The mode of presentation is divided between dialogue and objective narration. At three points the objective narrative briefly shifts to monologue. Such shifts occur when the ballad singer gives up his detached stance and impersonates the protagonist. This is one of the marks of the orally transmitted *yüeh-fu* genre. Other marks are formulaic language, stock characters, and typical uses of sounds and symbols from the natural environment. (HHF)

14622. Hanan, Patrick. "The Technique of Lu Hsün's Fiction." *HJAS* 34:53-96.

Lu Hsün, pioneer of modern Chinese fiction, was influenced, in terms of the governing technique of his short stories, mainly by Sienkiewicz, Gogol, and Andreev in the initial stages. He went on to develop a short story in which the use of a persona and the use of irony are characteristic elements: the irony of the uninvolved narrator, character irony, and juxtapositional irony, among other types. (PH)

14625. Hayden, George A. "The Courtroom Plays of the Yüan and Early Ming Periods." *HJAS* 34:192-220.

A discussion of the "courtroom" category in Chinese northern drama from the late 13th to the early 15th century. 26 plays, identified as courtroom plays, share three ingredients: a crime (usually murder); the crime's solution and punishment in a courtroom scene; and a judge or court clerk who solves the crime. The crime and its solution and punishment are presented on stage, and the detective is a significant character in the plot. The crime is the central element of the plot, and its successful detection concludes the play. The theme centers on justice, rather than mystery. (GAH)

14660. Liu, James J.Y. "Prolegomena to a Study of Traditional Chinese Theories of Literature." *LE&W* 16(1972):935-49.

Traditional Chinese theories of literature are seldom systematically expounded but generally lie latent in scattered writings. This, together with the fact that critics often use the same terms to denote different concepts and vice versa, necessitates analysis and interpretation. Liu has devised an analytical scheme based on the four elements involved in the artistic process—universe, writer, work, and reader. Applying these to Chinese critical writings, six kinds of theories are discerned: metaphysical, deterministic, expressive, technical, esthetic, and pragmatic. (JJYL)

14664. Lynn, Richard J. "Some Attitudes of Yuan Critics Toward The San-ch'u." *LE&W* 16(1972):950-60.

A study of what contemporary critics thought of the popular song-verse of the Yüan Dynasty (1234-1368). The critics involved, Teng Tzu-chin and Kuan Yün-shih, were typical of the critics of the time in that they regarded the *san-chu'ü* as the latest stage in a long tradition of popular lyric poetry. People of the Yüan called the *san-chu'ü* by the same term as people of the T'ang-Sung eras (8th-13th centuries) called the popular song-verse of their day—the *tz'u* (which literally means "words for singing"). They apparently felt no need to distinguish their own popular tunes from the earlier *tz'u*. (RJL)

14665. Magner, Thomas F. "The Latin Alphabet and the Languages of China." *JGE* 26:205-18.

The People's Republic of China is attempting to make the traditional Chinese orthography more accessible to its huge population by simplifying the characters while at the same time experimenting with a new orthography based on the Latin alphabet. The character script has immense prestige and contributes to a feeling of national unity as the characters have the same meaning in all dialect areas. The alphabetic script is more efficient in terms of learning and usage, but since it can also be used for the various Chinese dialects it might create in time distinctively different Chinese languages. (TFM)

14667. Meserve, Walter J. and Ruth I. "Lao Sheh:From People's Artist to 'An Enemy of the People'." *CompD* 8:143-56.

Traces the career of Lao Shê (1898-1966). From his designation in 1950 as a People's Artist to his purging in 1966. His plays are discussed in terms of their critical reception in China and as they reveal his seeming enthusiasm for the new Chinese government prior to his retreat from contemporary to historical and fanciful themes. Finally, the purging of Lao Shê is explained through the subtle satire of aspects of the People's Republic of China apparent in his plays during the 1950s. (WJM)

14670. Miao, Ronald. "Literary Criticism at the End of the Eastern Han." *LE&W* 16(1972):1013-34.

Offers translations of three documents composed during the formative phase of Chinese literary criticism during the 3rd century A.D. The texts in question are Ts'ao P'ei's (187-226) "Lun wen," a chapter from his *Tien lun*; Ts'ao P'ei's "Letter to Wu Chih"; and Ts'ao Chih's (192-232) "Letter to Yang Te-tsu." Miao relates Ts'ao P'ei's critical thought to certain innovate lines of inquiry contained in the writings of earlier critics. (RM)

14681. Owen, Stephen. "Hsieh Hui-lien's 'Snow Fu':A Structural Study." *JAOS* 94:14-23.

The complex structure of Hsieh Hui-lien's "Snow Fu" shows the potential of the *fu* genre to use formal variations as part of its cognitive meaning and to go beyond its descriptive limitations to arrive at a more complete definition of its topic. The *fu* consists of three styles—epideictic *fu*, Western Han song, and *ssu-yen shih*—and four speakers—Ssu-ma Hsiang-ju, Tsou Yang, Mei Ch'eng, and the persona of the snow itself—set within a narrative context. The range of styles, points of view, and levels of distance from the reader are used to exhaust the possibilities of ways to perceive the topic. In this way the more concentrated Nan-pei-ch'ao *fu* can achieve a completeness comparable to that of the older epideictic *fu*. (SO)

14683. Palandri, Angela J. "The Dream-Elegies of Yüan Chen." [F 19]:160-67.

Yüan Chen's *Hui chen chi* gave the impression that he was unscrupulous. His critics considered his marriage a political one, made for purposes of advancement. Examination of the elegies written after his wife's death shows his undying devotion to her. The six dream-elegies allow us a glimpse of the various states of mind he experienced during the times of composition. (AJP)

14695. Schafer, Edward H. "Two Late T'ang Poems on Music." *LE&W* 16(1972):980-96.

A study of two late T'ang dynasty poems (9th century) whose subject is the power of a virtuoso musical performance over the cosmos. The study of the poems is prefaced by remarks on topic vs. tone in poetry. Remarks on the Chinese tradition of the intimate relations between music and the natural world are made. (EHS)

14702. Smith, Barbara J. "Reference Tools for the Study of Modern China." *JGE* 26:262-66.

Lists and briefly discusses reference tools in English useful in beginning research concerning the People's Republic of China, which should be readily available in academic libraries in the United States. Emphasis is on recent reference works. (BJS)

14717. Wang, John C. "M.H. Abrams' Four Artistic Co-ordinates and Fiction Criticism in Traditional China." *LE&W* 16(1972):997-1012.

Because of the ignoble position fiction occupied in traditional China, critics who chose to write seriously about it were usually sympathetic toward its cause and wanted to elevate it to the realm of orthodox literature. It is not until the turn of the 20th century when political conditions in China were such that a dramatic shift in attitude among the intellectuals took place. Fiction is now considered not only serious literature, but also the most eminent of all literary forms. (JCW)

14719. Wilkinson, J. Norman. "The White-Haired Girl:From *Yangko* to Revolutionary Modern Ballet." *ETJ* 26:164-74.

In the late 1930s the Chinese Communists found the *yangko* or "planting song" of the peasants of Shansi and Shensi to have great potential as a propaganda tool. Communist cultural cadres have worked to make the *yangko* an effective means of popularizing the policies of the New Democracy. *The White-Haired Girl* is the most successful dramatic production to emerge from a *yangko* source, and it has become a landmark in Chinese Communist theater history. From its initial production in 1945 as a five-act play, it has undergone numerous and constant changes to evolve into the revolutionary modern ballet of 1965. (JNW)

14724. Yip, Wai-Lim. "Classical Chinese and Modern Anglo-American Poetry:Convergence of Languages and Poetry." *CLS* 11:21-47.
The sparseness of syntactical demands of the classical Chinese poetic medium promotes a unique mode of presentation. The Chinese poets are able to authenticate the fluctuation of concrete events with a most immediate cinematic visuality. The objects form an ambience in which the reader may move and directly take part in completing the esthetic experience. Using montage or mobile points of view in the perceiving act, the Chinese poets highlight the acting-out of these visual objects and events, letting the spatial tensions reflect conditions and situations rather than coercing them into some preconceived artificial orders by sheer human interpretive elaboration. This language, as a medium for poetry, is supported by an age-old esthetic horizon in which the self easily dissolves into the undifferentiated mode of existence. There is an inseparability between medium and poetics, between language and worldview. The rejection of abstract systems for concrete existence, and the attempt to negate or underplay the garrulous self in modern Anglo-American poetics have brought about an adjustment of the English language to the degree of violating the normal syntactical structures, achieving certain significant parallels to the esthetic ideal of the Chinese. (WY)

Japan. 14775. Etiemble, [René]. "Sur une bibliographie du *haiku* dans les langues européenes." *CLS* 11:1-20.
G.L. Brower and D.W. Foster have been courageous enough to try to fill a vacuum and to publish a critical bibliography of Japanese "Haiku in Western Languages." Unfortunately, their book does not fill the vacuum: first of all, because English, French, German, Portuguese, and Spanish are not the only "western languages" on which the impact of haiku is to be felt. Moreover, because, even in the few languages here taken into consideration, the items are selected at random, with many factual errors and without a critical approach. (RE)

14776. Falke, Wayne. "Japanese Tradition in Kenzaburo Oe's *A Personal Matter*." *Crit* 15,iii:43-52.
The similarity of Kenzaburo Oe's *A Personal Matter* to a number of Western novels has led to misinterpretation by Western critics.

In contrast to the Western value of fighting against the odds as a way of escaping the tedium of ordinary bourgeois life, Oe's central figure, Bird, chooses to accept as inevitable his aging, his imperfect child, his unexciting marriage, and his dreary job. In choosing to accept he gains a measure of satisfaction. The novel affirms traditional Japanese values in contrast to the Western, romantic values of Bird's friend, Himiko. Too many critics have failed to see that the novel ends somewhat bleakly, that no one is going to live happily ever after. (WF)

14797. Hijiya, Yukihito. "A Religion of Humanity:A Study of Osamu Dazai's *No Longer Human*." *Crit* 15,iii:34-41.
No Longer Human is Dazai's manifesto of his faith in humanity. Dazai sees post-war Japan as a "no-longer-human" wasteland governed by a wretched cycle of exchange of deceptions. Yozo Oba, the protagonist of the novel, faces despair because his humane values clash with the values cherished by the people around him. His attempts to be a part of the society that seems to ignore human worth are always threatened with defeat because that society fails to appreciate the qualities that make Oba most human. Oba's sensitivity to and willingness to cling to the goodness of humanity is what Dazai believes to be the way to redeem the moral wasteland. (YH)

14822. Jones, Rhys S. "Symbolism and Zen:Two Views of Reality." *Trivium* 9:144-50.
Poetry is an attempt to describe "reality." East and West differ profoundly in this, but one finds a resemblance between the cosmogony of the *Upanishads* and Valéry's. Describing the origins of consciousness and language—and therefore of poetry—both reach the impasse of putting the ineffable into words. As Mallarmé realized, one can only "suggest." But how best to do so? The Symbolists used words as symbols of reality; whereas Zen-Buddhist poetry effectively suggests reality without being symbolic. Zenists concluded long ago that conceptual dichotomies like seer and seen, abstract and concrete, natural and supernatural, were profoundly misleading. (RSJ)

14845. Kitahara, Michio. "A Theme of Japanese Culture." *FolkloreC* 16:283-88,299.
Many diverse aspects of Japanese culture often seem to be unrelated to each other in terms of a consistent theme. Several phenomena of Japanese culture which are superficially unrelated to sophisticated culture can be consistently seen in terms of a theme of manipulation. This theme appears to be especially useful in understanding Japanese ideas on man, suicide, hedonism, religion, the universe, science and technology, capitalism, achievement, perfection, art, and interpersonal relations. (KM)

AFRICAN LITERATURES†

I. GENERAL AND MISCELLANEOUS

15077. Gowda, H.H. Anniah. "The Association for Commonwealth Language and Literature Studies Conference in Kampala." *RAL* 5:219-22.
Provides a brief account of the fourth conference of the Association for Commonwealth Literature and Language Studies which was held at the University of Makerere in Kampala, Uganda in December 1973-January 1974. The theme of the conference was "The Problem and Challenges of Language." Scholars from Africa, Asia, Europe, and the United States participated by reading papers. (AHHG)

15079. Heywood, Christopher. "African Literature at the ACLALS Conference in Liège." *RAL* 5:223-26.
The annual conference of the European branch of the Association of Commonwealth Language and Literature Studies, held at Liège, included 9 papers on writers using English in most parts of Africa. The writers most frequently referred to were Soyinka, Achebe, La Guma, and others from southern Africa. (CH)

15085. Jones, Norma R. "Africa, as Imaged by Cullen & Co." *NALF* 8:263-67.
Not until the 1920s produced a new race-consciousness and racial pride did Africa become a positive symbol in black literature. The emphasis on Africa meant that a displaced people were finally discovering roots. Black writers of the Harlem Awakening had varying motivation and points of view when the theme of Africa came into their works. The idea of noble and ancient lineage in Cullen's "Heritage" also appears in works of Hughes and Toomer. Also pervasive is the stress on the primitive, also found in Cullen, Hughes, and Toomer. Although Fisher and McKay pointed out the danger of a degraded view of primitivism infusing the images of Africa, the leading figures presented the savage and the sensual, the fear and danger of Africa, in their images. Although the idea of Africa as ancestral homeland aided American blacks of the 1920s in developing a favorable self-concept, the image of Africa in many works negated the positive results achieved by the new sense of racial roots. (HH)

† *Festschriften* and Other Analyzed Collections are listed in the first division of this volume. "F" numbers in brackets following a title refer to these items.

II. BIBLIOGRAPHY

15154. Schmidt, Nancy J. "A Bibliography of African Dissertations and Theses on African Literature." *RAL* 5:89-92. A list of 21 completed theses and dissertations and 10 theses in progress which was compiled from responses to a letter of inquiry sent to African university libraries in July 1972. Entries cover author, title, university, date, length, and supervisor. A list of universities where no theses or dissertations on African literature have been prepared is also included. (NJS)

III. FOLKLORE

Myths and Legends. 15330. Trieber, J. Marshall. "Creation: An African Yoruba Myth." *CLAJ* 18:114-18.
Presented is an adaptation of the Yoruba creation myth into narrative form as the traditional tribal drummer and story-teller might recount it. After a conventionalized historical praise of the early Yoruba rulers and those who came before them back to the Nok, Trieber relates how Olodumare, chief of the Yoruba deities, ordered his lieutenant, Orisha-Nla, to scatter earth over the watery waste that then existed in the world and thus provide a place for man to dwell. (JMT)

Rhymes and Verses. 15395. Ọlajubu, Oludare. "Iwī Egúngún Chants—An Introduction." *RAL* 5:31-51.
Iwì Egúngún is a genre of the oral poetry of the Oyo Yoruba. It is chanted exclusively by members of the Egúngún (masquerade) cult during Egúngún performances. The Egúngún cult, an essentially male cult, is concerned with ancestor worship. The ancestors are believed to visit the people every year in the form of masqueraders to bless and entertain. Iwì is chanted by special types of masqueraders and by talented members of the cult in a special tone of voice. Iwì resembles Ìjálá and Rárà, two other genres of Oyo Yoruba poetry, because they draw from a common source of oral tradition for their composition. Iwì is, however, distinct from the two. Ìjálá sings the praise of Ogun (the god of iron) and its devotees—farmers, hunters, blacksmiths. It also sings of animal and plant life and the exploits of hunters in the bush. Rárà sings the praise of individual persons with the sole aim of attracting gifts. Iwì does not sing of any particular god, nor is it concerned with animal and plant life. It is not directed at single individuals with the sole aim of attracting gifts. It is in praise of man in general, man living and dead, man in society. (OOOO)

IV. LITERATURE

General and Miscellaneous. 15448. Emenyonu, Ernest. "African Literature Revisited: A Search for Critical Standards." *RLC* 48:387-97.
Many modern African works are written in English or in French, but the settlers' language is but a tool of communication made necessary by the diversity of African communities. The critic's task in this case will be to appreciate the alterations brought by the writer into the initial language and to determine to what stylistic and artistic use this linguistic tool has been put. Written literature is based on an important oral tradition which is the traditional medium of communication among African peoples. The relationship with these original patterns should be examined (for instance, the circular structure of African novels stems from a typical folklore pattern). The critic wishing to establish profiles will need to be possessed of a sound African culture, since African literature cannot be gauged by mere European standards. (EE)

15465. Harris, Rodney E. "Le rôle du dramaturge dans le théâtre négro-africain moderne." *RLC* 48:590-95.
An increasing number of creations proves the vitality of the modern black African theater. Césaire tries to show Africans that they have to take their own fate in hand. Charles Nokan thinks that the African artist must fight cultural imperialism and neo-colonialism. Other playwrights, such as Guillaume Oyônô-Mbia, have for their main object not to moralize but to entertain. By making his countrymen laugh, he tries to make them think. Bernard B. Dadié also uses satire to criticize African society corrupted by money. Thanks to the use of dance, of music, of a multilevel language, Soyinka succeeds in being more deeply African than the French-speaking authors. (REH)

15484. Kane, Mohamadou. "Sur les 'formes traditionelles' du roman africain." *RLC* 48:536-68.
African novelists today address themselves to their own countrymen. But the novel is an imported genre in a continent where the notion of separate genres has no basis in tradition. A few novels are analyzed here as representative of the frequent recurrence of a three-phase time structure and of themes like the dream world, the voyage as initiation. Autobiography is much favored, which shows a concern not to be fully dependent on home tradition; but it is happily balanced, in the diary-novel, by the author's presence in the background, reminding us of the voice of the village teller of tales who freely comments, in knowledgeable or ironic mood, on the characters in his story. (MK)

15494. Killam, G.D. "African Literature and Canada: A Progress Report and One or Two Analogies." *DR* 53(1973-74):672-87.
The production of African literature in English is comparatively recent in origin, more recent and less abundant than Canadian literature. Yet African universities and schools have been much quicker and more forceful in making the study of African literature the center of their concern than have schools and universities in Canada in regard to the study of Canadian literature. A shift in the emphasis which currently exists in Canada is suggested. The intrinsic worth and the development of a Canadian tradition can be focused and enriched by adding to our syllabuses examples of the literature in English from countries other than those in which we dwell—from Africa, the Caribbean, India, Australia, and New Zealand—literatures with which we have more in common than might at first be supposed. (GDK)

15516. Mercier, Roger. "La littérature négro-africaine et son public." *RLC* 48:398-408.
The readers of black African literature were first exclusively Europeans, and sought exoticism's charm, but always criticized contents and form of the works according to traditional criteria. The extension of this literature nowadays requires the understanding of its conditions. Oral literature patterns exercise a profound influence on black writers; therefore it is impossible to file them into the usual categories of literary typology. The tokens of this influence are the absence of strict distinction between genres and a share of the audience in the creation, which often gives them a theatrical structure. The struggles against colonialism simultaneously aroused the development of a militant literature, which, owing to limited alphabetization, addressed itself less to the African peoples themselves than to their colonizers. The future of black African literature now depends both on the rise of a real African public and on the adaptation of the writers to the feelings and taste of this public. (RM)

15536. Nwoga, D. Ibe. "The Limitations of Universal Critical Criteria." *DR* 53(1973-74):608-30. ["The Case for an Aesthetics of African Literature."]
Enough literature written by Africans is now available for a valid attempt to be made to establish intrinsic criteria for its criticism. These criteria, without being exclusive to this literature, must characterize it adequately for full appreciation of its thematic intentions and stylistic achievements. The successful critic, African or non-African, must acknowledge that "universal critical criteria" have been culturally determined by European literature. These criteria have to be adjusted or new ones developed, derived from an intimate awareness of certain factors. One is the

sociohistorical context of the literature and the particularity of the traditional mode of esthetic perception. The critic's role is that of explorer and explainer, of midwife between artist and audience, of guide to both within the limitations imposed by the tentative nature of the criteria. (DIN)

15545. Oke, Olusola. "Essai sur la spécificité de la littérature africaine actuelle." *FaN* 8,iii(1973):5-13.
The name "African literature" attributed to creative writing by Africans in foreign languages fails to resolve the crisis of identity surrounding this literature. This crisis, having been provoked by a search for an African literary identity and specificity, is far from being a literary problem exclusively. It is bound to bring into literature non-literary considerations. Characterized by an affinity with foreign literatures while constituting the most valid product of the psychological awakening experienced by African intellectuals, writing by Africans in foreign languages reflects a deep commitment to modern sociopolitical issues while maintaining a thematic and stylistic relationship with traditional African literary expression. (OO)

15553. Palmer, Eustace. "The Criticism of African Fiction:Its Nature and Function." *IFR* 1:112-19.
While the weakest African novels lack certain qualities of Western ones, the best possess them. There are differences in language and viewpoint but this does not suggest the use of different criteria. Furthermore, the African novel did not derive from indigenous sources (e.g., oral tradition), and consequently this could not be used as an argument for non-Western standards. Irele stresses that allowances must be made for the African writer's special language problems; he pleads not just for a literary, but for a sociological approach. This is not entirely acceptable since sociological criticism should reinforce not replace evaluative criticism. (EJTP)

15564. Robertson, R.T. "Interpreters All:The Commonwealth Context of African Literature in English." *RAL* 5:52-59.
Kerr's checklist of African literature courses indicates that African literature is taught in the context of Commonwealth literature courses; it is also taught in several other kinds of courses, e.g., World Literature; all these courses use texts prepared by Africanists. But both the cultural assumptions and the aims of these courses may differ from those in African literary studies: what may appear to be African concerns are universal matters. The theme of culture conflict and the different roles of male and female characters in this conflict are found in African and Commonwealth stories, forming a monomyth of the New World hero "no longer at ease" in his changing culture. This is found in Canadian literature as a search for personal and cultural identity, but the old African cultural identity lies in the past, the new Canadian in the future. Both African and Canadian writers are therefore "interpreters" of another identity to their own societies and themselves participants in the New World monomyth which incorporates the struggle for both personal and cultural identity. (RTR)

15570. Stegeman, Beatrice. "The Divorce Dilemma:The New Woman in Contemporary African Novels." *Crit* 15,iii:81-93.
The new woman and the old divorce trial are used as literary devices by several modern African authors to represent contrasting theories of value on four different levels: the locus, the determination, the standard, and the responsibility of value. Easman's *The Burnt-Out Marriage* and Aluko's *One Man, One Wife* contrast traditional tribal communalism with modern industrial individualism through the new woman who represents a theory of personhood where the individual exists as an independent entity rather than a group member, where she is defined by her experiences rather than her kinship relations, where she has a responsibility to realize her potential for happiness rather than accept her role, and where she must reason about her own values rather than submit to a stereotyped tradition. (BS)

French. 15630. Gérard, Albert S. "La francophonie dans les lettres africaines." *RLC* 48:371-86.
A comparative appraisal of the place and function of francophone literature in the spectrum and history of the written art in Africa. Created in Paris immediately after World War II, this production, through its strident anticolonialism and its advocacy of negritude, provided the impetus and set the model for the rapid growth of written literature throughout British and Portuguese Africa in the early 1960s. Beginning with Nigeria, however, anglophone writing soon shed French influence and acquired a personality of its own. At the same time, the decade following the granting of independence to the French colonies witnessed a swift decline of francophone writing. Some of the factors accounting for this are briefly discussed. The late sixties saw some portents of renewal: attempts were made to free African writing for the tutelage of Paris publishing firms, and a few writers emerged whose works illustrate a determination to escape the commonplaces of negritude and anticolonialism and to bend the French language and western narrative techniques to the needs of African experience. (AG)

15658. Pageard, Robert. "La vie traditionelle dans la littérature de l'Afrique Noire d'expression française." *RLC* 48:420-54.
Having defined tradition both in its evolution and permanency, Pageard tries to find out what importance these elements retain in modern African literature. This first part is completed by the study of the mentions, made in literary works, of the alteration of the original ways of life under the influence of European ways and foreign religions. The second part is devoted to the study of the controversy about the merits of tradition and the role it could play in tomorrow's society. The controversy is still very much alive and open but the most progressive writers are remarkable for always finding a way of expressing their regard for some aspects of the traditional African way of life. The works quoted were published between 1935 and 1972 (see the bibliography at the end of this article). (RP)

Negritude. 15669. Benamou, Michel. "The Testament of Negritude:'Dit d'errance' by Aimé Césaire." *NTLTL* 14,i:1-11.
A cultural preparation through language should precede any contact with a foreign poem or story; for Caribbean literature in French this is particularly necessary. Aimé Césaire's poetry requires knowledge of the history of colonization. The semantic preparation incorporates such knowledge through fill-in exercises. A "mimetic reading" demonstrates the African beat of lines resisting standard French scanning. Finally the poem is divided into speech units ("énonciation") which 4 groups of the class read aloud, each group asking the others questions about their units. Thus active participation replaces the ordinary explication de texte. (MB)

15671. Condé, Maryse. "Négritude césairienne, négritude senghorienne." *RLC* 48:409-19.
Examines the notion of negro as illustrated by Aimé Césaire's *Cahier d'un retour au pays natal* and by several of Léopold Senghor's works. Césaire begins by taking in charge the humiliations common to all negroes and, reversing his attitude, he claims the sufferings of all colored people to be positive values. Senghor demands that African values be acknowledged on the same level as those which form part of the civilization of the colonist. In both cases the reasons are the same and are based on an acceptance of ideas forged by the white man for his own benefit. There is no specifically negro quality or negro poverty, but only a condition characteristic of all those who are exploited. The only rebellion which is not simply sentimental mystification is that which is based on awareness of this exploitation, whether it be due to the traditional social structures of black countries or to capitalist imperialism. (MC)

Algeria. 15708. Sellin, Eric. "The Algerian Novel of French Expression." *IFR* 1,i:38-47.
In Algeria, the history of Francophone literature has evolved according to the writers' approach to French models; writers first adopted epistolary and other episodic forms existing in French literature to satisfy their inner compulsions but have moved more and more toward a direct expression of their own being, even to the extent of deliberately brutalizing the French language. The degree to which writers have adopted the French literary heritage along with the language differs for the Arab and the Kabyle. (ES)

Ghana. 15756. Ridden, Geoffrey M. "Language and Social Status in Ama Ata Aidoo." *Style* 8:452-61.

English has the capacity not only to convey information but also to indicate the social relationship between addresser and addressee. In Ama Ata Aidoo's short story "For Whom Things Did Not Change" (1970), the servant Zirigu is unsure of his relationship with his fellow-Ghanaian visitor, Kobbina, a doctor, and Zirigu's English reflects this insecurity. Although he is capable of speaking "standard English," he adopts a substandard variety in his early conversations with Kobbina, which he abandons only when he is convinced by Kobbina's egalitarianism. It is clear from a comparison of the grammar of Zirigu's two varieties of English that the one is no more complex than the other, but merely more consistent in the application of syntactic rules. (GMR)

Ivory Coast. 15768. Langlois, Emile. "*Les soleils des indépendances*, roman de la stérilité?" *PFr* 8:95-102.
Les Soleils des indépendances is a novel by the Ivory Coast writer Ahmadou Kourouma. One of its most important themes is sterility. The heroine, Salimata, appears sterile at the beginning of the book, but one gradually discovers that although she may be sterile, it is her husband, Fama, who is actually impotent. His whole life has been one of sterility and failure—his ancestors' land has become poverty-stricken, he has failed as a tradesman and a politician. Only when he decides to grant his wife her freedom does he reach real tragic greatness. His subsequent death is a return to the glorious past of his ancestors. (EAL)

15770. MacGaffey, Wyatt. "The Black Loincloth and the Son of Nzambi Mpungu." *RAL* 5:23-30. [Comp. analysis of Dadié's story and a Kongo dilemma tale.]
Two stories, one a recent literary work from the Ivory Coast and one a Kongo folktale of the turn of the century, are seen to have a common structure. They presume similar cosmologies, and their symbolic contents lend themselves in large measure to a common and consistent interpretation derived from Kongo rules. The comparison enhances the interest of both stories. (WM)

15773. Tidjani-Serpos, Nouréini. "L'image de la femme africaine dans le théâtre ivoirien:Le cas de Bernard Dadié et de Charles Nokan." *RLC* 48:455-61.
While Dadié's *Béatrice du Congo* shows the central character following the traditional way of life, in Nokan's play a modern African woman becomes conscious of her own alienation and takes up the long-despised culture. Three tenets of tradition are here called upon in an attempt to assess woman's position and role in a fast changing African society: feminine silence, motherhood as a duty, woman's occult power. There is no ideal portrait of the African woman in either play. The message of both authors is simply that if the present is to take shape, it can only build on the past. Women, too, must learn to put on a new face. (NT-S)

Lesotho. 15791. Kunene, Daniel P. "Towards as Aesthetic of Sesotho Prose." *DR* 53(1973-74):701-19.
The Mosotho writer, like his oral narrator counterpart, assumes the role of guardian of a system of ethics which he expects everyone to uphold. Unlike the oral narrator, however, he speaks of values that are to varying degrees foreign to his audience, values he has to persuade them to accept before they can concur in his judgments. His didacticism is both disintegrative and reintegrative, whereas that of the oral narrator is integrative. He has an affection/disaffection relationship with his characters. He is deeply involved with character, event, and situation; his attitude to his characters is either communicated directly to his audience during a digression that interrupts the continuity of the story or it is carried in manipulations of the language so that the comment is implied and flows with the story. The non-digressive style includes anastrophe, filial-relationship, special use of the adjective, judicious choice of emotive words, etc. The works of Thomas Mofolo (1876-1948), the gifted Mosotho story teller, best illustrate these story features. (DPK)

Mali. 15800. Lubin, Maurice A. "Interview avec Mamadou El-Béchir Gologo—Ecrivain malien:Propos recueillis par Maurice A. Lubin." *PFr* 8:38-52.
Mamadou Gologo, author of the autobiographical novel *Le Rescapé de l'Ethylos*, knows that his country, an integral part of the French colonial empire, can rely on its learning and moral characteristics to rid itself of foreign domination and work for the improvement of the standard of living of the Mali people. *Le Rescapé de l'Ethylos* is not really a novel, a product of the imagination, but an exhortation to young consciences to bring about the mental decolonization without which their country can only know a cultural bondage. The Malian case is not so different from the situation which prevails in all of Africa. The problems are common: perversion of customs, numerous military putsches. The improvement of the quality of life in Africa is only possible through a capturing of revolutionary consciousness and action in the way of progress. (MAL)

Nigeria. 15834. Champion, Ernest A. "The Story of a Man and His People:Chinua Achebe's *Things Fall Apart*." *NALF* 8:272-77.
In *Things Fall Apart* Achebe uses literary tools to examine the worth and dignity of a culture before and immediately after its collision course with an alien culture. *Things Fall Apart* transcends the narrow confines of a group of villages and reflects the trauma of nations that seek to expand their horizons without sacrificing cultural values that are traditional and indigenous. The novel moves on two levels: that of Okonkwo, the intense individual with a passionate belief in all the values and traditions of his people, and that of Umuofia, a clan of nine villages. Okonkwo's inflexibility runs counter to the flexibility of a society in which the seeds of change are inherent. The ironic end signifies the conflict of a man who stood inflexible, believing he was defending a heritage. (HH)

15856. Gérard, Albert S. "Biographies of Eleven Nigerian Writers." *RAL* 5:206-12.
Biographies of Abdullahi dan Fodio, Alhaji Muhammadu Bello, Muhammadu Bello, Alhaji Muhammadu Gwarzo, 'Femi Jeboda, E. Latunde Odeku, Joseph Akinyele Omoyajowo, A. Mohammed Sada, Shu'aibu Makarfi, Alhadji Mudi Sipikin, Usumanu dan Fodio—Nigerians writing in Arabic, Hausa, Yoruba, and English. (ASG)

15872. Lindfors, Bernth. "Achebe's Followers." *RLC* 48:569-89.
Of the 16 Nigerians who wrote novels in English between 1952 and 1968, 8 were profoundly influenced by the writing of Chinua Achebe. All 8 were Igbo, and all but one had been educated in Nigerian universities. Nzekwu, the only veteran novelist among them, was a late convert to the "School of Achebe," but he, like the others, proved himself a faithful follower in the mid-60s. The Nigerians who had written in the 50s had received their inspiration from oral tradition and from the literatures of England and America. But those who wrote in the next decade, particularly the Igbo novelists, looked primarily to Achebe, and occasionally to Ekwensi, for guidance. (BL)

15886. Moore, Gerald. "Reintegration with the Lost Self:A Theme in Contemporary African Literature." *RLC* 48:488-503. [Also pub. *Afras*(Sussex) 1,iv(1973):7-12.]
Studies the poetry of Christopher Okigbo and compares it to the works of another poet and novelist, Kofi Awoonor from Ghana. In both there is a common theme—the quest of the lost self—projected in different ways: either in a desperate attempt to recreate the vision of one's own childhood or to create the vision of the other self, the feminine counterpart, through the fantastic fabric of dreams. (GM)

15890. Noss, Philip A. "The Cruel City." *RLC* 48:462-73.
Comparison between Ekwensi's *The People of the City* and Mongo Beti's *Ville Cruelle* is followed by two bibliographical lists of some 15 titles each on the same theme, Nigerian and Camerounian novels respectively. In both novels, descriptions of the heart of the city offer an opportunity of satirizing—in an ironical rather than cruel mood—the white settlers of the fashionable districts. Nigerians and Camerounians alike draw on the fascination exerted by the "cruel" city, with its powers of corruption and destruction of soul and body. (ANP)

15904. Ponnuthurai, Charles S. "The Pessimism of Chinua Achebe." *Crit* 15,iii:95-109.
Chinua Achebe is essentially a pessimistic writer. Traditional

society, though it had an inadequate mastery of the environment and harsh laws governing social conduct, was integrated and dignified. In contrast, modern society has neither cohesion nor the strength to live up to its own norms. Traditional society called forth a simple, masculine heroism; the contemporary protagonist, caught in a transitional phase where the old way of life has been destroyed by the white man's imperialism and religion, faces a more complex and difficult challenge. The pessimistic awareness of Achebe is that of a heroic age destroyed by external forces and a debilitated present; his excellence lies in his ability to vividly evoke traditional society and to portray wider historical movements through the life of the individual. (CSP)

15914. Skinner, Neil, Tom Allen, and Charles N. Davis. "*Wakar Bushiya*:A Hausa Satirical Poem by Isa Hashim." *RAL* 5:180-93.

This is a poem of frustration written by Isa Hashim, relieving his feelings against a senior in the hierarchy. Skinner gives Hausa text, English translation and notes, while Allen and Davis describe the tune as sung by the poet himself. The melody is borrowed by him from a popular song of love and longing and given words in a classical Arabic meter, traditional for Hausa learned poetry. These include a mixture of violent abuse of the object of the poet's wrath with threats of hellfire, reinforced by references to the Koran and traditions. Skinner's commentary sets the whole in the framework of other Hausa poetry. (NS)

15930. Weales, Gerald. "Wole Soyinka:Yoruba Plays for All Tribes." *HC* 11,v:1-13.

Although Wole Soyinka's work is plainly marked with the Yoruba culture and traditions from which he derives, his is a highly sophisticated use of English language and literary history, and his concerns are the universal ones that preoccupy most major contemporary writers. This can be seen most impressively in his plays in which recurrent themes—the ritual cleansing of the community, the obligation of tyranny and tradition, the search for the essences of life, death, the individual—and theatrical techniques can be traced from the short plays of the late 1950s to the more impressive works that began in the late 1960s. (GW)

Rhodesia. 15937. Joyner, Nancy. "The Underside of the Butterfly:Lessing's Debt to Woolf." *JNT* 4:204-11.

To the Lighthouse and *The Golden Notebook* bear strong resemblances in style and theme. While Woolf splices the events of two days together by the casual mention that ten years have passed, Lessing ranges over a long period of years but in the middle includes a minute account of the events of a single day. Rather than focusing on one person through a number of characters' minds, as Woolf does, Lessing uses a variety of attitudes of a single person through the device of the notebooks. Thematically, both novels center upon the difficulties of a creative woman, and in both there is an explicit hostility toward men. Even the device of using the repetitive "I" to indicate men's excessive egotism appears in both books. The conclusions of the two novels sharply diverge, however, for Lily Briscoe discovers with relief that the achievement of her art means more to her than a conventional life, while Anna Wulf presumably gives up her art because of her inability to live independently. (NJ)

15942. Markow, Alice B. "The Pathology of Feminine Failure in the Fiction of Doris Lessing." *Crit* 16,i:88-100.

Examination of the etiology of feminine "failure" in Lessing's fiction suggests that it is rooted in a diseased male/female relationship, which is symptomatic of a larger neurosis. Both Lessing's "free" and traditional feminine characters betray neurotic-psychotic symptoms, in part, because they are caught in transition between two conflicting ideologies. Though they demonstrate cognitive awareness of the constricting effects of adherence to the old mythology of domesticity, Lessing's feminine characters illustrate her own ambivalence about roles in the form of nostalgia. A permanent lassitude characterizes these traditionalists, yet Lessing's "free" women are equally devitalized, primarily because they are self-destructively committed to romantic love. (ABM)

15945. Porter, Dennis. "Realism and Failure in *The Golden Notebook*." *MLQ* 35:56-65.

Doris Lessing's *Golden Notebook* appears at first sight somewhat disappointing on account of the conventional character of its realism. The work's developing complexity soon makes it clear that Lessing is challenging the fictional techniques in which she seemed to put her initial trust. Further, the acknowledgment of the inadequacy of its own techniques is thematically linked to a more generalized sense of failure, which is both personal and sociohistorical. It follows, therefore, that the structural cumbersomeness and the untidy realism of *The Golden Notebook* are willed. The apparent failure of the literary imagination to control its material is symptomatic of a general malaise. If *The Golden Notebook* does not display the elegant mastery of Gide's *Counterfeiters*—the classic example of the novel probing the limits of its power to represent reality—it is because Lessing's strengths are of a dourer, non-esthetic kind. She chooses to employ the techniques of conventional realism to suggest the formlessness and grainy texture of our collective living, while at the same time she questions the appropriateness of such techniques. (DDP)

Senegal. 15962. El Nouty, Hassan. "La polysémie de *L'aventure ambiguë*." *RLC* 48:475-87.

The semantic keyboard of Kane's *L'Aventure ambiguë* can be compared to a set of widening concentric circles. The theme of alienation is encompassed by the theme of social palingenesis, as illustrated by the same Samba Diallo who, in many respects, is vested with an exemplarity that refers us to the collective destiny of his people, the Diallobé. In this latter perspective, the characters are raised to a first level of allegorical signification. The metaphysical dimension of the novel and the way it is structured indicate that Kane's work constitutes above all a piece of Moslem apologetics. This is reflected in the theme of the chess game which represents a second level of allegorical signification. A political reading unveils the real import of the novel. A careful examination reveals a class consciousness that has shaped its whole composition. (ENH)

15983. Savage, Nadine D. "Entretien avec Léopold Sédar Senghor." *FR* 47:1065-71.

This interview focuses on Léopold Senghor, his early association with Léon Damas and Aimé Césaire in Paris, and their definition of the Movement of Negritude in the 1930s. Senghor comments on his interpretation of Negritude and the unique contribution of African writers to world literature. He evokes his background, his childhood, the influence of his family, his admiration for the "griots" (professional singers and poets of Africa) and for the popular poetess Marone N'Diaye. He explains the traditional techniques of poetry writing in West Africa, the use of metaphors, the emphasis on the expression of emotion which is a unique attribute of African art. Senghor also explains the religious experience which the writing of poetry represents for him. He describes in philosophical terms his relationship with the universe. (NDS)

South Africa. 15991. Beeton, D.R. "Pauline Smith and South African Literature in English." *UES* 11(Mar 1973):35-50.

Pauline Smith's contribution to South African English literature is considerable; she has strong affinities with other South African writers in English. She had a deep understanding of a specific setting and of a community, and brought considerable insight to her delineation of people. She, like Olive Schreiner, was given her impetus as an artist by the somewhat bleak Karoo area of South Africa: Olive Schreiner wrote of the desolate Great Karoo; Pauline Smith wrote of the Little Karoo with its simple Afrikaner communities. Pauline Smith was born in Oudtshoorn in the Karoo and spent her first twelve years there. She was then sent to a boarding school in England and was only to visit South Africa periodically for the remainder of her life. Yet the memory of her childhood, recalled principally during these visits, permitted the production of her most considerable work: the short stories entitled *The Little Karoo* and the novel *The Beadle*. She also owed much of her success as a writer to the encouragement of Arnold Bennett who became a life-long friend and a sympathetic literary adviser. (DRB)

16019. Jahn, Janheinz, Ulla Schild, and Almut Nordmann. "Two African Writers:Nathaniel Nakasa and Issa Traoré." *RAL* 5:67-69.

To continue the work begun in the authors' *Who's Who in African Literature* (Tübingen, 1972), two biographies of African writers are presented: of the South African Nathaniel Nakasa, founder-editor of *The Classic* and columnist for *Drum* and *Golden City Post*, and of the Malian writer Issa Traoré, a former principal of schools and now research worker at the Institute des Sciences Humaines in Bamako, and author of two novels and a collection of traditional stories. (JJ, US, & AN)

16035. McCartney, Barney C. "Dramaturgical Movement in Lewis Nkosi's *The Rhythm of Violence*." *NALF* 8:268-70.
By looking at Nkosi's *The Rhythm of Violence* as drama rather than literature, we can discover patterns and devices that reveal a somewhat more complex artistic unity than an ordinary reading of the play will indicate. Its expressionistic method works in much the same way as a musical composition that requires a performance and more than one listening. There are several kinds of dramatic movement in *The Rhythm of Violence* and they interact quite successfully to create an artistic expression of the human condition in South Africa: an expression of violence and suffering, but of celebration as well. Nkosi's message is not simply a denunciation of apartheid; it is the art of the blues—expressing the tragedy and pathos, but also the courage, of those who suffer injustice. (HH)

Togo. 16072. Ricard, Alain. "The Concert Party as a Genre:The Happy Stars of Lomé." *RAL* 5:165-79.
Every Saturday afternoon Pascal and the Happy Star parade through Lomé advertising the evening show: five hours of dancing, singing, and drama to the sounds of high-life. Improvising on stories drawn from folktales and adapted to an urban setting, the Happy Star concert band invents theater. This article, with pictures and sketches of the performances, attempts to analyze the theatrical elements (setting, time, players, stories) of the shows. (AR)

Tunisia. 16078. Fontaine, Jean. "Aspects de la littérature tunisienne contemporaine:Tahar Guiga." *IBLA* 27:163-77.
Born 30 December 1922 at Takrouna, Tahar Guiga received his diploma in Arabic and French. He holds a cultural administrative position in Tunisia. He is the author of an account of a journey to China and of collections of stories. His first short stories discuss the problems created by Tunisia's independence. The following texts concern the animal world. The present translation is from the book *Aigles et grenouilles* which combines poetry and political symbolism. (JF)

16087. Yetiv, Isaac. "Albert Memmi:The Syndrome of Self-exile." *IFR* 1:125-34.
Albert Memmi's work is an introspective search into the inner self; it is a vain attempt to understand himself and his society. His investigation follows a systematic and rigorous pattern and evolves from his ego (*La Statue de Sel*, 1953) through the couple and the problem of mixed marriage (*Agar*, 1955) to the ethnic groups (*Colonized*, 1957; *Jew*, 1962). It finally covers all mankind (*L'Homme dominé*, 1968). Unfortunately Memmi fails to resolve his own "alienation" and will live with his "impossibilities" in perpetual self-exile. (IY)

EAST EUROPEAN LITERATURES†

I. GENERAL

Russia. 16227. Keenan, Edward L.,Jr. "The Trouble with Muscovy:Some Observations upon Problems of the Comparative Study of Form and Genre in Historical Writing." *M&H* 5:103-26.
Russian historians have had some difficulty deciding upon a periodization for what they call "Russian" history; no conceptually helpful definition of "the Russian Middle Ages" has been put forward. In view of the fact that Slavic cultural history is a part of the general development of Christian European culture, it might well be a matter of some consternation to the comparativist, as well as to the historian of Russia, that repeated attempts to "align" Muscovite institutions with those of the West or to bring her development into "phase" with Western cultural history have been at best brilliant and appealing hypotheses and more commonly hindrances to the progress of historical understanding. This article considers the historiography of Muscovy and the mentality of those who shaped the historical consciousness of Muscovy at a time when she began to play a prominent role in Eastern Europe. (ELK,Jr)

Yugoslavia. 16260. Clark, Richard C. "Review Article:Is There a Yugoslav Literature?" *RNL* 5,i:141-46.
Sveta Lukic's *Contemporary Yugoslav Literature: A Sociopolitical Approach* identifies the forces that have prevented the development of a single Yugoslav national literature: the felt unity of diverse national groups, the trend toward technocracy or Americanization, and the strong arm ideology of the Stalinist bureaucratic-dogmatic school. Even as late as 1972 the concept of Yugoslavia still could not mediate among the various national literatures, the chief obstacle being the sterilizing all-persuading influence of the Marxist-Leninist bureaucratic ideology. Lukic concludes that before "Yugoslav" literature can achieve world-wide recognition it must first become relevant to a national Yugoslav consciousness. (RCC)

16261. Coote, Mary P. "Yugoslavia:Bibliographical Spectrum." *RNL* 5,i:127-40.

Since the early 19th century, Yugoslavia has been a popular field for anthropological and folklore study. Most of the research done in Europe on Yugoslav literature has come from German, Italian, and Hungarian scholars, although English, French, and Russian scholars have also contributed. Much work in English is due to Yugoslavs. While translation of Yugoslav works into European languages was once limited to folk poetry and a few classics, contemporary literature is now well represented by anthologies, often with critical introductions, and individual works. (MPC)

16265. Nejgebauer, Aleksander. "Trends in Modern Yugoslav Poetry." *RNL* 5,i:13-17.
There is a body of essential Yugoslav poetry, transcending linguistic and national differences. The variety is great among the Serbians since the 1930s, from Matić, Vučo, and Popa to Lalić, Hristić, and Melvinger; no pat generalities can characterize the poetic output of the Croatians Gotovac, Slamnig, Parun, and Mihalić. Slovenian poetry has been various to the point of being eclectic in its response to past and contemporary foreign influences, though there is a valuable identity in the works of Zajc and Strnisz. The emergence of Macedonian as a literary language in the post-war era has been a spectacular development. (AN)

16266. Paolucci, Anne and Henry. "Yugoslav Dialogues." *RNL* 5,i:37-85.
In each of the sub-capitals of the Yugoslav union—Belgrade and Zagreb—there is a strong sense of cultural distinctiveness. Local intelligentsias stress the mixture of Mediterranean, Middle European, and Slavic, as well as Moslem, influences. The labors of the great cultural unifiers of the South Slavs have left a substantial, highly valued structure. The great modern authors have been major stars in a constellation made up of scholars, grammarians, lexicographers, and critics, as well as creative artists ranged in a network that links all the cultural capitals. These and related matters are pursued in informal discussions with representative writers, scholars, and government officials. (AP & HP)

† *Festschriften* and Other Analyzed Collections are listed in the first division of this volume. "F" numbers in brackets following a title refer to these items.

II. BALTIC (AND BALTO-SLAVIC) LITERATURE

LATVIAN

General and Miscellaneous

16278. Birznieks, Ilmars. "Notes on German Influence in the Emergence of Latvian Written Literature." *GN* 5:2-5.
The German influx into the Baltic area began in the 12th century. The German church assumed the responsibility for Latvian literary development. At the beginning of the 16th century the first Latvian translations of spiritual songs and the Ten Commandments appeared. After this initial start, both the Protestant and Catholic churches were competitively interested in rendering more Latvian translations. At the end of the 16th century, the emergence period of Latvian written literature came to an end. Although it was almost totally religious in character, it did, however, set an example for Latvian secular literature to follow. (IB)

Twentieth Century Literature

General and Miscellaneous. 16355. Lazdiņa, Terēze. "Skaņu izvēle modernās latviešu dzejas alliterācijās." *JGa* 100:114-17; 101:50-52. [Sum. in Eng.]
More words in Latvian begin with the consonants *s* and *p* than any other sounds. Detailed tabulation and analysis of alliteration and consonant frequencies in the work of seven contemporary poets indicate that *s* and *p* are also the sounds most frequently alliterated; their occurrence is thus proportional to their frequency in the language. Other sounds favored by individual poets vary greatly. The choices seem not only related to each author's sense of euphony, but can also reflect his psychological outlook. (IŠ-L)

16357. Melngaile, Valda. "Spēle un nopietnība:Piezīmes par jauniem meklējumiem mūsu trimdas dzejā." *JGa* 100:11-14; 101:12-14. [Sum. in Eng.]
The idiom and style of some Latvian exile poetry of the 1970s distinguishes it from poetry written earlier. Sound has become more important than meaning—rather, meaning grows out of sound. Words are used as in a game or a magic formula for expressing the inexpressible. Images are rarely used; the human narrator is absent or passive, landscape and life are missing. Behind the word-games, one can often glimpse a sense of emptiness, helplessness, or dehumanization. The cold, experimental quality of such poetry may sometimes repel; nevertheless, it demands great mastery and control of the language. (IŠ-L)

16362. Nollendorfs, Valters. "Riga in the Lyric Poetry of the Postwar Latvian Generation." *JBalS* 5,ii:100-11.
Latvia's capital Riga plays an important cultural and political role for Latvians. It is a poetic object for Latvian poets of the postwar generation both in exile and in Latvia. In exile, temporal distance dominates even for poets who have recently visited there. In Latvia, the living present predominates even in poems talking of absence from Riga. But for both groups Riga is a positive symbol; metropolitan problems tend to be relegated to the anonymous "city." For both, Riga as a poetic symbol is based primarily on personal experience that sometimes culminates in a mystic union with the city. (VN)

Bels. 16407. Silenieks, Juris. "Alberts Bels:In Search of

Man." *JBalS* 5,i:34-39.
Alberts Bels probes for the universal human dimensions behind the games of gregarious living. His non-hero is a forsaken creature condemned to a Sisyphean toil by a system solicitous of his physical well-being but indifferent to his aspirations. In his second novel, *Būris* (*The Cage*), the narrative focuses on a socially respectable architect, assaulted by auto thieves, encaged, and forsaken in a thicket. The novel is an ironic morality tale that changes from detective story, to satire debunking the ideals of consumer society, to a myth of universal dimensions in search of man's authentic identity. (JS)

Čaks. 16419. Saliņš, Gunars. "Bezgala spoguļi:Piezīmes par Aleksandru Čaku un viņa poēmu *Matīss, kausu bajārs*." *JGa* 98:3-20. [Sum. in Eng.]
Čaks's poetry was always permeated by loneliness, suffering, unrequited emotions, and longing for something great and unattainable. Personal emotional crises are often reflected in his work. In the unfinished verse play, *Matiss, Prince of Drunkards*, two characters function, to some extent, as Čaks's personae: the old puppetmaster of the prologue whose dolls come to life even as he, driven by his creative demon, finds salvation in death; and Matiss himself, a drunkard of life who abandons dissipation to search for some mysterious, idealized reality. The manuscript ends with Matiss broken and disillusioned; the last act, which was presumably to portray his redemption, remained unwritten. Thus Matiss' fate may foreshadow Čaks's own untimely death. (IŠ-L)

Rainis. 16515. Richards, Emma S. "English Romanticism and the Latvian Poet Jānis Rainis." *JBalS* 5,ii:126-35.
In *The Religious Philosophy of Jānis Rainis, Latvian Poet*, Ziendonis reveals the influences shaping the work of Rainis: the revolutionary spirit of his epoch, the interest in mythology and folklore, the view of nature as a part of religious experience, and the use of poetry as an instrument for achieving social change. Examples drawn from the work of Blake, Shelley, Wordsworth, and Coleridge illustrate similar influences characterizing the English Romantic period. The link between the earlier English poets and Rainis is their acquaintance with German culture. (ESR)

Ruņģis. 16525. Nollendorfs, Valters. "The Lonesome Patriot in the Prose of Latvian Writer Aivars Ruņģis." *Lituanus* 20,iii:12-27.
All three books of prose fiction by exile Latvian writer Aivars Ruņģis grapple with problems of individual and national identity. For Ruņģis both are interrelated—only the individual with a strong bond to his ethnic heritage can maintain his own identity—and both are threatened by forces of conformism. Just as the conflicts of mass ideologies have left the Latvian nation on the verge of extinction, destructive ideological forces within the nation threaten the integrity of the individual and thus the source of national survival. True patriotism is not conformistic but individualistic. (VN)

III. EAST SLAVIC LITERATURES

RUSSIAN

Miscellaneous

General and Miscellaneous. 16802. Duncan, Phillip A. "Echoes of Zola's Experimental Novel in Russia." *SEEJ* 18:11-19.
Emile Zola's early writing earned him great prestige in Russia, particularly among anti-Czarist groups and in 1875, he began a collaboration on the *Vestnik Evropy* which continued until 1880.

Zola first formulated his theory of the experimental novel in the September 1879 issue of the *Vestnik Evropy*. This concept disappointed Russian activitists who insisted on tendentious belles-lettres. In the repressive period of the eighties, however, Zola's "objective" novel seemed inevitable and a bland and sterile Russian naturalism appeared. In 1891 there was renewed interest in the early 19th-century critic, Valerian Majkov, and in "scientific esthetics." Many radicals hailed Zola's critical theory as a contemporary expression of Majkov's ideas. Dmitrij Ovsjaniko-Kulikovskij, who at this same time developed his theory of literature based on Zola's concept of experimental writing, was the last and most authoritative Russian champion of Zola's "scientific" novel. (PAD)

16807. Glowacki-Prus, Xenia. "A Brief Survey of Memoirs Written in Russian from Peter the Great to S.T. Aksakov." *NZSJ* 12(Sum 1973):10-26.
Discusses the memoirs written in Russian from the 17th century up to the time of S.T. Aksakov (1789-1859). Included are memoirs from the Petrine period, trends in 18th- and early 19th-century memoir literature, military and political memoirs, memoirs by famous writers, "the gossip-columnists," and memoirs about everyday life. (XXG-P)

16809. Goodliffe, John D. "The Image of New Zealand in Russia." *NZSJ* 12(Sum 1973):142-52.
Judging by a reference in A.P. Chekhov's story "Drama na okhote" (1884), at that time the name "New Zealand" was synonymous with barbarous and uncivilized behavior. Two works which helped foster this image were F.F. Bellinsgauzen's account of his 1819-21 South Pacific voyage published in St. Petersburg in 1831 and the memoirs of Jacques Arago, published in Paris in 1839, translated from the French and published in St. Petersburg in 1845. Here New Zealanders were depicted as untamed savages. More balanced and sympathetic views were presented in Richard Taylor's "Te Ika a Maui," published in London in 1855 and reviewed in "Russkii Vestnik" in February 1856, and in a lecture given by Professor T.N. Granovskii in 1852 which was printed in the same journal the previous month. (JDG)

16829. Rannit, Aleksis. "Iran in Russian Poetry." *SEEJ* 17:265-72.
The poetic vision called "Iran" has haunted the minds of Russian poets for some 150 years. The man who seems to have discovered the exquisiteness of Persian verse for Russian letters was Vasilij Zhukovski. In original Russian verse, Iran and Iranians first appear in the works of Pushkin and Lermontov. Among the poets of the second half of the 19th century whose work reflects the Persian influence, Afanasij Fet is outstanding. In the 20th century, specifically in the period between 1900 and 1917, the "Persian era" of Russian poetry is of considerable importance. It was characterized in part by the involuted arabesque delicacy of musical design in poetic structure, as well as in metaphorical, iconic ideas which remind one vividly of both Persian illuminated manuscripts and Persian poetry. (AR)

16830. Rubenstein, Roberta. "Genius of Translation." *ColQ* 22:359-68. [On Constance Garnett.]
Constance Garnett learned Russian in a casual manner from Russian friends in England and went on to become the primary translator of Russian literature into English. During her lifetime she translated over seventy volumes of works by Russian authors. Her enormous contribution to literature is even more remarkable in view of the fact that she was partially blind during more than half of her career. Her son, David Garnett, notes that she received little remuneration or recognition for her efforts, not even receiving royalties until late in her career. A Russian linguist, Augusta Tovey, undertook a comparative study of the Garnett and other translations from Russian into English, and concluded that Garnett's were superior in style, rhythm, and nuance to other translations, including more recent ones. Tovey attributed Garnett's excellence as a translator to her sense of rhythm and her musical ear. (RR)

16835. Thompson, Ewa M. "The Archetype of the Fool in Russian Literature." *CSP* 15(1973):245-73.
Russian letters have been dominated by the archetype of the single-minded seeker of truth and justice, "the godly fool." He emerged because of certain characteristics of Russian social life and because of the philosophical preferences of Russian writers. The social types called "the fool for Christ's sake" (*jurodivyj Xrista radi*) and the wanderer (*strannik*) had thrived in Russian social life from the Kievan times until the October revolution. Due to the features they had in common, they merged into one archetype and are represented in literature by such characters as Prince Myshkin, Semën Jakovlevich, Pierre Bezuxov, Doctor Zhivago, and in the folktale, Ivan the Fool. Apart from the commonly recognized admixture of Christian elements, the gnostic idea of the chosen and the enlightened ones is a strong ingredient in the spiritual makeup of such characters. In contrast, a different fool archetype has developed in Western Europe. He is represented there by Till Eulenspiegel, Simplicius Simplicissimus, and the courtly buffoons. (EMT)

Literature before 1700

General and Miscellaneous. 16859. McLean, Hugh. "Window into the World of Old Russia." *SlavR* 32(1973):129-33.
A new edition (1970) of Dmitrii Likhachev's *Chelovek v literature drevnei Rusi (Man in the Literature of Old Russia)* offers an occasion for a brief survey of his work. His earlier books and articles were considerably marred by the strident nationalism and xenophobia obligatory in the late Stalinist period, but in his post-"thaw" works Likhachev has largely surmounted these faults. Although he draws his illustrative materials almost exclusively from his own period of specialization, Russian literature of the eleventh to seventeenth centuries, Likhachev's books, including also *Tekstologiia* (*Textology,* 1962) and *Poetika drevne-russkoi literatury* (*The Poetics of Old Russian Literature,* 1967), in fact contain important contributions to the general theory of literature. Likhachev has also pioneered, at least in Russia, in exploring connections between literature and the visual arts. (HMcL)

Eighteenth Century Literature

Derzhavin. 16881. Hart, Pierre R. "Aspects of the *Anacreontea* in Deržavin's Verse." *SEEJ* 17:375-89.
Derzhavin began to give attention to shorter lyric genres in the early 1790s. Of such forms the anacreontic assumed particular importance, as evidenced by the separate volume, *Anacreontic Songs,* which he published in 1804. Thematically, the collection was quite diverse including works which combined panegyric devices from the ode with the recall of private experience, as well as original compositions inspired by the *Anacreontea* which were among Derzhavin's finest lyric statements. Several factors contributed to this poetic shift. Although Derzhavin viewed his responsibilities as a civic spokesman seriously, the genres appropriate to such statements restricted his expression of more personal experiences. In his best solemn odes he included a number of lyric moments but he remained aware of the genre's integrity. (PRH)

Nineteenth Century Literature

General and Miscellaneous. 16914. Hollingsworth, Barry. "The Friendly Literary Society." *NZSJ* 1:23-41.
The Druzheskoe Literaturnoe Obshchestvo (Friendly Literary Society) existed from January to June 1801 and had eight founder-members: Andrey and Alexander Turgenev; the three Kaysarov brothers, Pyotr, Mikhail, and Andrey. V.A. Zhukovski, A.F. Merzlyakov and A.F. Voyeikov. It was patterned to a large extent on the Friendly Scientific Society and the circles of Moscow University and the University Boarding School for Nobles. In spite of its cult of friendship the society was not a united group and imposed no one set of values, ethical or esthetic, on its members. The society played an important role in the popularization of German literature in Russia, but the problem of serfdom in Russia did not loom large in their discussions or correspondence. (BH)

Aksakov, S. 16935. Glowacki-Prus, Xenia. "Sergey Aksakov as a Biographer of Childhood." *NZSJ* N.S. 2:19-37.
Aksakov's biographical writings are descriptive of events, customs, traditions, and people in Russia and in Siberia at the beginning of the 19th century. The lack of an intentional fictional element, the extreme truthfulness of the author, and his sense of the beauty of nature as perceived many years earlier by the child render his work quite unique. The role of the narrator, i.e., of the child, is interesting for there is an inner dialogue between the

child and the old man writing down his reminiscences. The theory that this is "life seen through the eyes of a child" is therefore disclaimed. (XG-P)

Chekhov. 16968. Glad, John. "Chekhov Adapted." *CSP* 16:99-103. [Sum. in Fr.]
"Poka ne prišel paroxod" ("Until the Boat Arrives") by Valentin Tublin is a reworking of Chekov's religious story "The Student," where a young man overhears a moving conversation centering around the Bible. The impressionistic presentation of the material in both works is identical. Juxtaposition of individual passages shows amazing similarities. The protagonists walk through virtually identical scenes, come upon the same sort of country folk, and engage in conversations that amount to moralistic stories. Evident here is not just the influence of Chekov's style on a modern Soviet writer, but a distinct case of imitation of a specific work. (JG)

16980. Maxwell, David. "A System of Symbolic Gesture in Čexov's *Step*." *SEEJ* 17:146-54.
A system of symbolic gesture gives Chekhov's "The Steppe" a greater unity than is generally attributed to it. The dominant theme is one of solitude, aimlessness, futility, and despair. This theme is presented within three major structural categories of the story: the setting, the characters, and the plot. All three categories are united by symbolic gesture involving the verb *maxat'/maxnut* and its prefixed forms. The verb signals a passage presenting the dominant theme, and in this way acts as a narrative thread consolidating the presentation of the theme. Descriptions of the steppe, with many elements of setting, thematic implications, and devices similar to those of "The Steppe," appeared in several of Chekhov's stories during the 1800's. The incorporation of these motifs, themes, and devices into a considerably larger work with an intensified focus on the steppe itself, as well as Chekhov's increasing awareness as an artist, created new challenges to the author's imagination. (DEM)

16984. Newcombe, Josephine M. "Was Čexov a Tolstoyan?" *SEEJ* 18:143-52.
It is maintained that Chekhov attempted to expound Tolstoian moral teachings in a few stories written in the late 1880s and in *Ward No. 6* and *My Life* he demonstrated his rejection of Tolstoi. However, the only evidence of Chekhov's Tolstoian phase is contained in a letter to Suvorin in 1894. His remarks were interpreted too literally; a re-examination of the earlier stories reveals no attempt to propound Tolstoian doctrines. Chekhov's later stories are concerned not with challenging Tolstoi but with attacking the intelligentsia's lack of social responsibility and use of abstract ideas to justify selfish behavior. (JMN)

16991. Rubenstein, Roberta. "Virginia Woolf, Chekhov, and *The Rape of the Lock*." *DR* 54:429-35.
Woolf's admiration of Russian writers appears in several of her major essays and in a curious unpublished MS review of a new edition of Pope's *Rape of the Lock*. The unlikely juxtaposition of Russian literature and Pope can be explained by Woolf's literary preference for the complexities of the soul over the frivolities of the dressing table. The contrast developed between the two reveals Woolf's characteristic critical method of viewing one work against another and the opportunity to trace her own "stream of consciousness" associations as she moves from the "Russian mist" to the large virtues of Russian hearts, to the contrasting smallness of Pope's imagined world, to the pettiness of Pope's personality. Adjusting her focus, she attempts to identify the virtues of *The Rape of the Lock*, but her lack of sympathy toward Pope and his "diseased soul" (an attitude repeated in *Orlando*) and her susceptibility to the Russian mood interferes with critical objectivity. The review concludes with Woolf's ambivalent recognition of the English tendency to distort the judgment of their literature by exalting and exaggerating the virtues of Russian writers and their works. (RR)

Dal. 16998. Perelmuter, Joanna. "Russian Substandard Usage and the Attitude of Soviet Lexicography." *CSP* 16:436-47. [Sum. in Fr.]
With the coming of the Revolution, interest in the development of research of the substandard aspects of Russian language became

less apparent as stress shifted to another branch of lexicographic scholarship—normative dictionaries. Strict normativeness in Russian lexicography was enforced in the 1930s and lasted until de-Stalinization took place 25 years later. If Soviet lexicography in the field of Russian substandard usage is presently more in the process of development than it has ever been in the post-revolutionary period, this development has only affected one category of substandard: Russian dialects. Other non-dialect substandard usage phenomena remain taboo in the Soviet Union. (JEP)

Dostoevski. 17001. Adams, Barbara B. "Sisters under Their Skins: The Women in the Lives of Raskolnikov and Razumov." *Conradiana* 6:113-24.
Conrad patterned many elements of *Under Western Eyes* after Dostoevski's *Crime and Punishment*. This similarity can be traced in the relationships between the male protagonists and the women in their lives. Women form the primary motive for action in these men who cannot act without their sexual-saintly stimulus. They are feared and loved, untouched and untouchable. Both Raskolnikov and Razumov are obsessed with real mothers and an unobtainable symbolic Mother Russia. Raskolnikov's mother moves him to a destructive act, just as Victor Haldin's mother moves Razumov, his murderous proxy, to a self-destructive act of confession. Lesser female characters relate to these men in similar ways. In a reversal of the usual roles, the women in these novels act; the men, Razumov and Raskolnikov, re-act. (BBA)

17007. Chances, Ellen. "*Pochvennichestvo*: Ideology in Dostoevsky's Magazines." *Mosaic* 7,ii:71-88.
In 1861, Dostoevski and his brother Mixail founded a political and literary "think journal" *Vremja* (*Time*) (1861-63), which later reopened as *Èpokha* (*Epoch*) (1864-65). The editors espoused the ideology of "pochvennichestvo," or "concept of the soil." The aim was to synthesize Westernism and Slavophilism. According to the "pochvenniki," the problem with Russia was that the educated class had become torn away from the simple people. In order to remedy the situation, the "pochvenniki" advanced concrete suggestions. Educational reform was important, as was encouragement of a free press. An examination of these arguments reveals that although the "pochvenniki" later found their solutions to society's problems in the world of metaphysics, they at first advocated specific proposals. (EBC)

17019. Hollander, Robert. "The Apocalyptic Framework of Dostoevsky's *Idiot*." *Mosaic* 7,ii:123-39.
Dostoevski changed the main referential system of *The Idiot* from the Gospels to the Apocalypse. In February 1868 Dostoevski formed a new design for his continuation of *The Idiot*, one that reflected his rekindled interest in the Book of Revelation. Starting with the second chapter of Part Two, the Apocalypse begins to be felt as a major shaping force in the novel. The characters Lebedyev and Ippolit are two major foci of Dostoevski's new plan. A series of references to the new Russian railway and to several recent murders in Russia underlines the new theme of Russia's "time of tribulation." (RH)

17035. Leatherbarrow, W.J. "Dostoevsky's Treatment of the Theme of Romantic Dreaming in *Khozyayka* and *Belyye Nochi*." *MLR* 69:584-95.
The theme of romantic dreaming occupies a position of fundamental importance in Dostoevski's work, since it connects Dostoevski's early heroes with the Underground Man and other characters from his mature fiction. The dreamer-heroes of *Khozyayka* and *Belyye nochi* (1847 and 1848 respectively) summarize the qualities of Dostoevski's earlier characters and anticipate those of the Underground Man. Even within the context of *Khozyayka* and *Belyye nochi* the figure of the dreamer and the artistic treatment of the theme of romantic dreaming undergo a development which highlights the close relationship between hero and form in Dostoevski's work. The narrative techniques used in the two tales show that, although Dostoevski frequently borrows thematic material from Gogol, his use of this material is modeled on the works of Pushkin. (WJL)

17037. Marchant, Peter. "The Mystery of Lizaveta." *MLS* 4,ii:5-13.
Although Raskolnikov's murder of Lizaveta should be more

disturbing than that of her half-sister, the old pawnbroker, it is forgotten by Raskolnikov and the critics. However, *Crime and Punishment* has an inner logic, introduced by Raskolnikov's nightmare of the beating of the overburdened mare, which explains this and reveals the real motivation for the murders. Raskolnikov killed the wrong women. Only his mother's death in the Epilogue releases Raskolnikov from his conflict between love and hate, aggression and guilt. Since Lizaveta's death is not part of his matricidal fantasies, it is of no consequence. (PM)

17052. Roseberry, Robert L. "Schillerean Elements in the Works of Dostoevskij, *A review of recent criticism.*" *GSlav* 3:17-35. With the sole exception of Čiževskij, the critics restrict their analyses to the more superficial aspects (plot, characters, etc.) shared by the works of Schiller and Dostoevski. Works of Dostoevski's later period—especially *Besy* and *Idiot*—are ignored entirely. A Dostoevskian sympathy for Schillerean idealistic philosophy becomes more strongly apparent, however, in Dostoevski's post-Siberian period, and the way in which this philosophy is incorporated into Dostoevski's works is misunderstood or ignored by nearly all the critics. (RLR)

17053. Rosenshield, Gary. "First- versus Third-Person Narration in *Crime and Punishment.*" *SEEJ* 17:399-407. The effects and merits of the third-person narration of the final version of Dostoevski's *Crime and Punishment* are illuminated by comparing a passage of the final version with a representative, but almost identical, passage from the first-person diary plan for the novel. The emphasis in the diary is clearly on the narrating and not on the experiencing self, for the diary is, in effect, a dramatization of the narrator's attempt to understand the significance of past events for his present situation. The emphasis in the final version, on the other hand, is on the experiencing self. Third-person narration permitted Dostoevski to present Raskolnikov's consciousness as he is experiencing the events, thereby achieving a psychological immediacy and suspense which directly involves the reader in Raskolnikov's fate and dramatically demonstrates the implications and consequences of his crime. (GR)

17055. Rubinstein, S. Leonard. "Dostoyevsky:The Identity of Crime and Punishment." *JGE* 26:139-46. Raskolnikov commits a crime to punish the wicked, to demonstrate his superiority, and to rescue the innocent. He is punished—as are all criminals in *Crime and Punishment*—by the futility of his crime. The crime is the result of assuming the right to judge other men. When Raskolnikov recognizes that all men are in the same condition, he refuses to judge. Discovering love, he is delivered from his crime. (SLR)

17061. Shaw, J. Thomas. "Raskol'nikov's Dreams." *SEEJ* 17:131-45. Raskolnikov's dreams are the most vivid passages in Dostoevski's *Crime and Punishment*. Raskolnikov lives out his own theory of crime and sickness; his four dreams within the novel proper are punishment: before the murder, for conceiving of it, and, after the murder, for committing it. The novel proper presents the punishment of sickness, of which these dreams are part, as impelling Raskolnikov to confess that he killed the old woman, though that confession is not of guilt for the deed or for the theory justifying it. Raskolnikov's final dream in the Epilogue is punishing, but is also curative because it suggests the solution to the problem of guilt, and hence makes regeneration possible. The focus of the novel is on the crime and the punishment that lead to the confession to the police. The final dream, unlike the others, is given in Raskolnikov's generalized, past-tense consciousness, appropriate for the generalizing function of an epilogue, but without the experimental vividness of his other dreams. (JTS)

17062. Shein, Louis J. "An Examination of the Kantian Antinomies in *The Brothers Karamazov.*" *GSlav* 2(1973):49-60. Ya. E. Golosovker's argument that Dostoevski structured *The Brothers Karamazov* on the four Kantian antinomies is examined. Golosovker's claims are found to be in keeping with Dostoevski's views on the basic problems dealt with in the antinomies, namely, the existence of God, immortality of the soul, and human freedom. These arguments are probed in terms of the actual novel as well as in terms of Dostoevski's own views on these problems. Dostoevski was setting forth his own views through his main

characters, thus trying to refute the individualism and rationalism peculiar to German idealism and more especially Kant's view of morality in its relation to religious belief. While Dostoevski did not consciously structure his novel on the Kantian antinomies as claimed by Golosovker, the problems dealt with in the novel are the same as those expressed by the Kantian antinomies. Dostoevski advocated the arguments of the Kantian thesis in order to set forth his Christian Weltanschauung in literary form. (LJS)

17065. Traschen, Isadore. "Existential Ambiguities in *Notes from Underground.*" *SAQ* 73:[363]-76. The hero of Dostoevski's *Notes from the Underground* is usually seen as an existential figure. Supporting this view is his polemic against positivism, scientism, and rationalism. He is comic in his excessively refined sensitivity, a parody of Hamlet. Further, he is a romantic idealist, but his love of freedom, the sublime, and the beautiful becomes a tyrannical depravity in practice. His idealist doctrines fall apart when confronted with an actual person. Though he theorizes about freedom as an intellectual, he is enslaved by the conventional language and emotions of books. He is incapable of an existential encounter for he has no authentic self. This low estimate of this anti-hero is in keeping with the Dostoevskian hierarchy of values which puts the religious spirit first, passion second, and intellect last. (IT)

17067. Vivas, Eliseo. "Dostoyevsky, 'Poet' in Spite of Himself." *SoR* 10:307-28. Dostoevski's critics assume that "the poet" accomplished in his fiction what the man planned to write: to attack the socialism that led to his imprisonment and to defend his post-Siberian conservatism, his radical rejection of the West, and his profession of Christianity by an act of will. In Ivan Karamazov's poem, "The Grand Inquisitor," the inquisitor's reproaches to Jesus are preceded by Ivan's account of outrageous crimes committed against children. The Inquisitor maintains that men want bread and happiness and gladly accept slavery through miracle, mystery, and authority. Jesus offers men freedom, but freedom entails the crimes that outrage Ivan. Dostoevski the idealogue rightly feared that he had not "answered" Ivan. He did not. The conflict is in the poet's fiction. This is still the conflict of the century following Dostoevski's death in 1881 and gives his work its value for us. But the Inquisitor enslaved men with a heavy heart because fraud was profoundly distasteful to him. Not so to his dystopian successors. (EV)

17068. Wasiolek, Edward. "Raskolnikov's Motives:Love and Murder." *AI* 31:252-69. Raskolnikov kills the pawnbroker in a futile attempt to cut out of his own psyche the hateful and repugnant mother he had fantasized and later repressed. The murder is an attempt to remake himself by killing the ugly Raskolnikov within him. He reaches for the freedom he feels lacking within and imagines a beautiful Raskolnikov who helps family and humanity as a compensation for the ugly Raskolnikov he fears himself to be. He cannot kill part of himself and he is led to reconciliation with the hateful mother by Sonia, who is not only a religious redemptrice but also a sexual redemptrice. (EW)

Gogol. 17088. Mills, Judith O. "Gogol's 'Overcoat':The Pathetic Passages Reconsidered." *PMLA* 89:1106-12. The influence of the narrator on the structure and the pathetic passages of Gogol's "The Overcoat" is essential to reconciling the juxtaposition of humor and pathos. The narrator constructs a plot based on a moral principle: excessive self-confidence receives retribution. The narrator is as guilty of this same self-confidence as his characters. Fearing similar retribution, he rejects responsiblity for his satiric creation by limiting his omniscient point of view and placing the blame for negative portrayals on his objective depiction of reality. His own attitude, expressed in plot, point of view, and his own pathetic passage, is superimposed on his characters. (JOM)

17091. Shepard, Elizabeth C. "Pavlov's 'Demon' and Gogol's 'Overcoat'." *SlavR* 33:288-301. Pavlov's "The Demon" (1839) may be one source for Gogol's "The Overcoat" (1842). Gogol probably heard about "The Demon" in July 1839, when he drafted "The Overcoat." Two months later Gogol returned to Russia and read and re-read Pavlov's story. There are striking structural and thematic similarities, as well as textual congruences, between the two works. A close comparison suggests that "The Overcoat" may reflect his negative response to Pavlov's skeptical and Westernizer-oriented view of the little Russian Everyman, the "poor petty clerk," the typically philanthropic and neosentimental portrayal of whom Pavlov deliberately undermines in "The Demon." (ECS)

Korolenko. 17112. Babenko, Victoria. "Nature Descriptions and Their Function in Korolenko's Stories." *CSP* 16:424-35. [Sum. in Fr.]
The artistic devices apparent in Korolenko's nature pictures are in keeping with his widely acclaimed humanity. They reflect the changing moods of his protagonists and the deep forces buried below the surface that make them capable of violent, unexpected actions, extreme cruelty, and moving tenderness. They range from factual observations to symbolic, metaphysical ones, that encompass the cosmic harmony and unity. His characters, drawn from a variety of social classes and geographical regions of Russia, are often dehumanized by adversity but regain their human dignity against the backdrop of nature, with its potential for reconciliation. (VAB)

Merezhkovski. 17147. Rosenthal, Bernice G. "Nietzsche in Russia: The Case of Merezhkovsky." *SlavR* 33:429-52.
In the 1890s Merezhkovski was one of the chief popularizers of Nietzsche in Russia. In his interpretation, Nietzscheanism was esthetic individualism and art itself was a religion. Viewed in the context of the European-wide *fin de siècle* and of a specifically Russian crisis of values, Merezhkovski's Nietzscheanism was an ideology of revolt against all restraints on the individual. Though he soon abandoned pure Nietzscheanism for a new form of Christianity based on the Apocalypse, the Nietzscheanism he had popularized served as a battering ram to break down old orthodoxies and was a major factor in the period of esthetic creativity and philosophic ferment known as the "silver age." (BGR)

Pushkin. 17193. Briggs, Anthony. "The Hidden Forces of Unification in *Boris Godunov*." *NZSJ* 1:43-54.
The construction of Pushkin's *Boris Godunov* is that of a five-act tragedy. The 23 unnumbered scenes divide into 5 groups separated from each other by longer time lapses than occur within them. The movement into a new direction is particularly noticeable between Acts I and II. Pushkin may have disguised this construction from a desire to appear independent of Shakespeare. A system of interrelated references binds together otherwise disparate scenes. These are references in different scenes to the same event outside the action of the play, predictions of future events, and ordinary allusions forward and backward to other incidents within the play. (ADB)
17194. Briggs, Anthony, tr. and introd. " 'The Robber Brothers' by A.S. Pushkin." *NZSJ* 12(Sum 1973):101-13.
Pushkin's poem "Brat'ya-razboyniki" ("The Robber Brothers") was written in 1821-22 as the introduction to a longer narrative poem which was never finished. The story is complete in itself, telling how the narrator and his brother were arrested, imprisoned and then seen to escape, only for the brother to die shortly afterwards, tormented by sickness, delirium, and visions of the violent crimes in which they had been involved. This metrical translation, which follows the meter and rhyme-scheme of the original, is the first into English. (ADB)
17252. Prizel, Yuri. "Evolution of a Tale: From Literary to Folk." *SFQ* 38:211-22.
When a tale written by a professional writer is "adopted" by oral tradition, its structure and general make-up should change. One such transformation of a tale written by Pushkin is studied, and it is shown how it conformed to the rules of oral tradition. (YP)

Rozanov. 17283a. Stammler, Heinrich A. "Apocalypse: V.V. Rozanov and D.H. Lawrence." *CSP* 16:221-44. [Sum. in Fr.]
Compares the work and thought-worlds of D.H. Lawrence and V.V. Rozanov and discusses Rozanov's influence on Lawrence. (HAS)

Sologub. 17291. Brodsky, Patricia P. "Fertile Fields and Poisoned Gardens: Sologub's Debt to Hoffmann, Pushkin, and Hawthorne." *ELWIU* 1:96-108.
The Russian symbolists, including Fedor Sologub, are usually considered to have been influenced primarily by French Symbolism. Yet Sologub based his story "Otravlenny sad" ("The Poisoned Garden") on earlier, non-French traditions, represented by E.T.A. Hoffmann's story "Datura Fastuosa," Alexander Pushkin's poem "Ančar," and Nathaniel Hawthorne's tale "Rappaccini's Daughter." The four works share the basic image of poisonous flowers as a symbol of evil. In each of the three stories a conflict is set up, expressed in Hoffmann as good vs. evil, in Hawthorne as body vs. spirit, and in Sologub as real vs. ideal worlds. To Pushkin's plot Sologub adds motifs of revenge and class struggle. Hoffmann's influence is in the image of a garden of temptation and in symbolic language. From Hawthorne Sologub takes directly the general structure and certain descriptions. His characters are sympathetically portrayed. His concern is not, like Hoffmann's, with balance, or, like Hawthorne's, with salvation, but with liberation and transcendence. (PPB)

Turgenev, I. 17328. Blair, Joel. "The Architecture of Turgenev's *Fathers and Sons*." *MFS* 19(1973):555-63.
Critics contrast Turgenev's creation of strong characters with defects in his architecture. Concentration on Bazarov in *Fathers and Sons* results in a narrow reading of it as a social or political document. If one instead notices the composition of the novel—basically a grouping and regrouping of characters—then emphasis moves from Bazarov and his ideas to his failure to establish human relationships, as opposed to the seemingly weaker characters. The life of Bazarov's apparent opponent, Pavel, is the model for Bazarov's; Pavel's previous affair with the Princess and its deadening effect on him is re-enacted in the middle section of the novel as Bazarov tries but fails to make Odinstov love him. Bazarov and Pavel attempt to prove themselves alive by an attachment to Fenichka, Nikolai's mistress, which results in their duel. From this point, Bazarov moves toward his physical death while Arkady and Katya, the "weaker" couple, fall in love. While the novel laments the loss of a daring soul, Bazarov, it celebrates the father and son who accede to the elemental process of love, marriage, and procreation. (JB)

Turgenev, I. 17330a. Delany, Paul, and Dorothy E. Young. "Turgenev and the Genesis of 'A Painful Case'." *MFS* 20:217-21.
James Joyce was reluctant to acknowledge any indebtedness to Turgenev. In part, he criticized Turgenev just to annoy Stanislaus Joyce, who considered him a better writer than Tolstoi. In "A Painful Case," known to be a satire on Stanislaus, Joyce made the joke more appropriate by borrowing heavily from the plot and characterization of Turgenev's "Clara Militch." The hero of both stories is a withdrawn intellectual who, through pusillanimity, causes the death of a woman who seeks his love. Joyce also was indebted to "Clara Militch" for its handling of one of the major themes in *Dubliners*, the connection between the living and the dead. (DP & DEY)
17331. Eliason, Lynn R. "A Nineteenth-Century Solution to the Problem of the Generations—Turgenev and Theodor Fontane." *GSlav* 2(1973):29-34.
The literary connection between two 19th-century realists, the Russian Turgenev (1818-83) and the German Theodor Fontane (1819-98), has been a subject of controversy since their deaths. Investigations over the past two decades convincingly show, however, that Fontane did in fact regard the Russian writer, in his own words, as his "master and model." The problem of the generations which underlies their fiction reveals similar relationships: the old stands in opposition to the new, the conflict presupposes political tendentiousness and lack of resolution. One finds, nevertheless, warmness, restraint, and ultimately a solution. For Turgenev and Fontane, both generations have their strengths and weaknesses. Neither can claim an absolute moral victory, so they must learn to live together. (LRE)
17333. Loewen, Harry. "Human Involvement in Turgenev's and Kafka's Country Doctors." *GSlav* 3:47-54.
The striking similarities between Kafka's *Ein Landarzt* and Turgenev's *The Country Doctor* not only raise the question of

"influence" but, more importantly, also seem to throw light on the essential meaning of Kafka's tale. In both stories the doctors are called upon to help their patients. While in Turgenev's story the doctor becomes professionally and personally involved and falls in love with his beautiful female patient, in Kafka's tale the doctor fails to involve himself with his patient and other human beings. Turgenev's patient dies with the knowledge that she is loved by her doctor; Kafka's patient, who suffers from an incurable wound, dies deceived and betrayed by his doctor. (HL)

17336. Waddington, Patrick. "Turgenev and Trollope:Brief Crossings of Paths." *AUMLA* 42:199-201.
Turgenev and Trollope first met at George Eliot's London home in 1871, when Turgenev and his friends the Viardots were refugees from the Franco-Prussian conflict. The two may not have read each other's works, but Trollope liked Turgenev well enough to invite him to the Athenaeum Club. They met again in London ten years later, when Turgenev was the guest of honor at a dinner given by Ralston and attended by several English novelists and journalists. Here again Turgenev and Trollope had little impact on one another; but their deaths gave rise to obituaries in which they were compared. One such notice defined Trollope's art as "informative" and Turgenev's as "suggestive"; but most British commentators were as ignorant of the latter's works as Trollope had probably been. (PW)

17337. —— "Turgenev's Last Will and Testament." *NZSJ* N.S. 2:39-64.
On Turgenev's death at Bougival in 1883 most of his personal and movable property was left to Pauline Viardot. The succession was immediately contested in France by Turgenev's son-in-law and in Russia by some very distant relatives. A few items of literary and historical interest did find their way back to Russia, as well as a considerable sum of money, but all the furniture, paintings, manuscripts, letters, and other documents found in Turgenev's rooms in Paris and at Bougival remained in the possession of the Viardot family. It can now be seen that Turgenev in fact made several different wills, and that if some of his requests were not faithfully carried out this was generally due to some discrepancy. (PW)

Zhukovski. 17346. Ober, Kenneth and Warren U. "Zukovskij and Southey's Ballads:The Translator as Rival." *WC* 5:76-88.
Zhukovski's genius is clearly illustrated in his 1831 translations of five ballads by Robert Southey. Occasionally sacrificing the advantage Southey derives from monotone and understatement, Zhukovski strengthens the ballads by providing concrete and vivid images, editorial comments, and supplementary details which bring the ballads into sharper focus. A personal and immediate involvement with his themes and characters and a real talent for choosing the right setting, the precise image, and the effective additional detail enable Zhukovski to successfully translate Southey's ballads. (WVO & KHO)

Twentieth Century Literature

General and Miscellaneous. 17378. Davis, Roderick. "Under Eastern Eyes:Conrad and Russian Reviewers." *Conradiana* 6:126-30.
The remarkable success of *Under Western Eyes* in Russia is discussed in contrast to the indifference accorded it in England. Four reviews have been located in Russian journals, two from 1912, when the first translation appeared, and two from 1925, when the work was translated anew. These reviews are summarized and analyzed to illustrate the divergent responses of the critics to Conrad's knowledge of Russia, his imaginative abilities, his political and psychological perceptivity, and his general artistry as a novelist. A concluding comparison is made between pre- and post-revolutionary viewpoints that seem implicit in these reviews and that indicate the novel's endurance beyond its immediate historical context. (RD)

17411. Hosking, Geoffrey A. "The Russian Peasant Rediscovered:'Village Prose' of the 1960s." *SlavR* 32:705-24.
The attempted agrarian reforms of Khrushchev provoked a relatively frank discussion of rural life, which went further than Khrushchev intended. Studying the life of the peasant gave Soviet fiction writers abundant material with which to explore man's nature in extreme situations. In the works of writers such as Fedor Abramov, Boris Mozhaev, and Vasilii Belov, people are seen as creatures of the soil and the seasons, of their families and communities; but this identity is constantly under threat from urbanization and the bureaucratization of modern life. These are partly in the tradition of Socialist Realism (*narodnost'*, realism, the positive hero) but abandon certain features of it (*partiinost'*, *ideinost'* and social optimism). Literary critics have used "village prose" as the basis for discussion of progress and change in Soviet society and the relevance to it of moral values rooted in the past. (GAH)

17430. Kosin, Igor. "The 'War Theme' in Soviet Literature." *RS* 41(1973):282-95. [Rev. art.]
For Soviet journalists and literati World War II remains a vibrantly live subject. In newspapers and other mass circulation media it appears as news stories and articles, timed to coincide with the commemoration of major military events on the Soviet front between 1941 and 1945. The war theme is recurrent in novels, short stories, plays, memoirs, and poems. This reflects the regime's determination to keep the memory of the war alive in the national consciousness of the Soviet people, to maintain the link of emotional comradeship between the contemporary Soviet citizen and war-time counterparts. The direction of this journalistic and literary effort has changed with time: the urgency of the war years to repel the German invaders was later replaced by the call for national reconstruction. More recently the objective has been to teach the people to regard the war not so much as the time of mass suffering but as the time when the nation demonstrated its determination to survive and to develop as the home of an evolving communist society. This new direction has been aimed particularly at the post-war Soviet youth, for whom the war could become a historical abstraction. (ILK)

17509. Wilson, A.C. "Lenin's Ideas on Art and Discussion of Them." *NZSJ* 12(Sum 1973):130-41.
Although Lenin was not a systematic philosopher of art and wrote little on the subject, his ideas exert a great influence on Soviet esthetics. They have also been subject to different interpretations by critics. The hard-line approach insists that Lenin wanted to make all art subject to political control and had little respect for the integrity of the esthetic as such. The moderate line insists that Lenin was not a totalitarian in the artistic sphere and that he was sensitive toward "esthetic integrity." Wilson suggests that Lenin wanted neither to politicize all art nor to examine the necessary and sufficient conditions of great art. (ACW)

Blok. 17562. Banjanin, Milica. "The Problem of Evil in the City Poetry of Aleksandr Blok." *ELWIU* 1:236-47.
Discusses the problem of evil in Aleksandr Blok's city poetry, which is contained in the cycles of poems "Gorod" ("The City") and "Strašnyj mir" ("The Terrible World"). In his visual and musical perception of Petersburg, Blok gives a personal "impression" rather than a realistic study. Blok's city poetry involves a search for an ideal beauty amidst the "flowers of evil"—the creatures of the city. His poetic inspiration oscillates between the ideal beauty of his earlier poetry and the new type of evil beauty found in the city. The evil seen and experienced, then, becomes an inspiration for poetry, a source of beauty. The dichotomy between good and evil as well as the duality of the artist become the essential elements of the poem's "suggestive magic." (MB)

Bulgakov. 17582. Bagby, Lewis. "Eternal Themes in Mixail Bulgakov's *The Master and Margarita*." *IFR* 1,i:27-31.
Examination of dominant stylistic and character-oriented organizing principles as they relate to eternal themes in Bulgakov's *The Master and Margarita*. A system of parallel views of all the relationships between the central dramatis personae is established by the coalescence of the three story-line styles and by the use of "frustrated anticipation" to reverse our common expectations. This produces a sometimes grotesque, sometimes moving comedy wherein the devil becomes an agent of good, the mythic Jerusalem real, and the real Moscow mythic. Bulgakov suggests that in a larger, eternal context there can be good in evil and that social and political evil can and must be overcome. (LB)

17585. Kejna-Sharratt, Barbara. "Narrative Techniques in *The Master and Margarita*." *CSP* 16:1-13. [Sum. in Fr.]
The structure of Bulgakov's *The Master and Margarita* can be

explained in terms of the narrative modes employed. There are essentially three narrative modes in this novel: humorous *skaz* with an omniscient, "hidden" narrator, the objective third person narrator who tells Pilate's story, and the rhetorical-literary narrator who features prominently in the Margarita chapter (xix) and alternates with the *skaz* narrator in the second part of the novel. The three modes of narration reflect the novel's division into three planes of action and reflect Bulgakov's changing attitude to his characters. The use of the objective mode in the Pilate story makes it a separate entity, different from the rest of the novel. The story is presented as an objective account of real events, thus giving testimony to the historical existence of Jesus. (BIK-S)

Esenin. 17610. Fisher, Lynn V. "Esenin's Literary Reworking of the Riddle." *SEEJ* 18:20-30.
Folklore and the riddle play an important role in Sergei Esenin's poetry. His poetry has so far been studied in regard to actual use of folklore material, but the poet does not merely borrow from already existing material. He transforms the metaphor of riddle into simile and builds on his own imagery, changing the original riddle into an integral part of his lyric poetry. The majority of Esenin's images based on riddles deal with natural phenomena and a large number of them are concerned with the sun and moon. (LVF)

Il'f and Petrov. 17658. Wright, John L. "Ostap Bender as a Picaroon." [F 19]:265-68.
The hero of Il'f and Petrov's novels *The Twleve Chairs* (1928) and *The Golden Calf* (1931), Ostap Bender, is in many respects a picaroon, the delinquent hero of the picaresque novel. Although Ostap Bender enters the plot of *Twelve Chairs* only in the fifth chapter, he becomes the dominating element of the novel soon after his entrance there. Like earlier picaroons Bender plays a large number of roles in both novels, but only in the last part of *The Golden Calf* are his disguises assumed for reasons other than immediate material gain, and there they resemble the traditional picaroon's role-playing for survival. Before parting with their hero, Il'f and Petrov attempt to convert him to socialism. However, Bender is not converted, and his character remains fixed throughout. (JLW)

Olesha. 17744. Wilson, Wayne P. "The Objective of Jurij Oleša's *Envy*." *SEEJ* 18:31-40.
The mode of visual perception of each of Olesha's characters in *Envy* is connected with that character's point of view. The frenzied use of various optical devices by the narrator of Part One, Kavalerov, to protect himself from a threatening world reflects both his awareness of an objective external world and of his own alienation from it. He ultimately seeks solace in a street mirror, but the mirror also forces him to undergo careful self-examination. The shift from first- to third-person narration at this point assists in this reappraisal by developing other characters more fully. Kavalerov realizes his situation in two epiphany-like scenes—the latter a virtual enlargement of the former—in which Valja is the central, illuminating figure. (WPW)

Pasternak. 17749. Dyck, J.W. "Boris Pasternak:The Caprice of Beauty." *CSP* 16:612-26. [Sum. in Fr.]
Pasternak recognizes beauty as a potent force in man's process of becoming. For him there is beauty as manifested in the genius and in woman with both traveling the road of suffering. The force of suffering beauty is the leitmotif of his work where distinctions are drawn between beauty and good, beauty and duty. In showing its link with love and immortality, beauty becomes the source and object of creativity. Pasternak doesn't see the distinction between physical and inward beauty. Nevertheless they confront each other in woman, especially in *The Last Summer, Second Birth*, and *Dr. Zhivago*. (JWD)
17750. Fortin, René E. "Home and the Uses of Creative Nostalgia in *Doctor Zhivago*." *MFS* 20:203-09.
The symbolic action of homecoming seems to be one of the organizing centers of Boris Pasternak's *Doctor Zhivago*, binding together the historical, religious, and esthetic concerns of the novel. The historical theme opposes the frantic home-destroying motion of the Revolution to the values embodied in the home symbol: serenity, order, and loyalty to the past. On the religious level, the home symbol expresses the Christian view of man "at home in history" and at home even in death in a cosmic process paternally ordered by God. Finally the novel is centrally concerned with the implications of Zhivago's view of art as "homecoming"; the poet Zhivago elaborates an esthetic theory paralleling that which Heidegger developed in his essays on Hölderlin: art is a homecoming in that it is a return to the primordial archetypes, restoring one's contact with the intimations of the sacred experienced in childhood. (REF)
17757. Scherr, Barry P. "The Structure of *Doctor Zhivago*." [F 19]:274-79.
Boris Pasternak's *Doctor Zhivago* relies on repetitions, parallels, and frames to unify the narration. These devices divide the novel into five sections while the epilogue and the poems at the end stand apart from the main action of the novel and present Pasternak's ideas from a new standpoint. The poems reveal a structure similar to that of the novel as a whole. The basic five sections form two main divisions: the first two are largely introductory in nature; the next three contain a symmetrical presentation of Zhivago's quest for understanding that serves as the core of the novel. (BPS)

Pilniak. 17769. Mills, Judith M. "Narrative Technique in Pil'nyak's *Mother Earth*." *JRS* 28:13-21.
Pilniak's "Mother Earth" is structured around two narrative techniques: plotted and non-plotted, which are thematically motivated and integrated by the imagery. In the non-plotted narration the peasant, symbol of irrational primitive energies and natural revolutionary instincts, thrives, and the Communist hero, symbol of Bolshevik rationality, experiences frustration and fragmentation. Although the hero is more comfortable in the more predictable context of the plotted narration, he is undone when the heroine proves to be an incarnation of the peasants' Earth Goddess. Though the heroine seems an instinctive revolutionary, she too has been perverted by her contact with Petersburg's rationality. (JMM)

Serafimovich. 17787. Lafferty, Vera. "A.S. Serafimovich's Forgotten Novel, *City in the Steppe* (1912)." *CSP* 16:202-20. [Sum. in Fr.]
Much of Serafimovich's pre-revolutionary work has been eclipsed by the fame and popularity in the Soviet Union of his "proletarian classic" *The Iron Flood*, 1924. *City in the Steppe*, one of his more talented works, is a tragic portrait of the capitalist era in Russia at the end of the 19th century. His masterly examination of the inner world of the novel's principal protagonists, Zakharka and Polynov, reflects Serafimovich's considerable psychological perception and artistic imagination. Serafimovich exposes the souls of two men destined to be destroyed by the bestiality of a capitalist milieu. Secondary and episodic characters are rendered equally memorable. There are occasional weaknesses in characterization, some banalities and exaggeration, and the distinct pessimism of the author's viewpoint, yet the novel withstands the test of time on its graphic and disturbing analysis of human nature alone. Serafimovich's realistic development of events adds social and historical value to the novel. (VL)

Solzhenitsyn. 17839. Kern, Gary. "Solzhenitsyn's Portrait of Stalin." *SlavR* 33:1-22.
In Solzhenitsyn's portrait of Stalin in *The First Circle* he prepares the reader for the portrait by introducing characters in their order of rank within the Soviet prison system. In the portrait itself, Solzhenitsyn employs four perspectives: (1) omniscient author, (2) Stalin's interior monologue, (3) ironic author, (4) direct quotation. The interplay of these voices unmasks Stalin's depravity. Historical record accuses him. Allusions to Dante's *Inferno* compare him to Satan. References to Lenin oppose the purity of Leninism to the decadence of Stalinism. Contrast of Stalin with several convicts reveals their moral superiority. They emerge as moral paragons, expressing the author's lesson: do not participate in evil, remian true to your innate ideal of perfection. (GK)

17873. Weisberg, Richard H. "Solzhenitsyn's View of Soviet Law in *First Circle*." *U. of Chicago Law Rev.* 41:417-38.
An understanding of the meaning of *First Circle* is difficult without some comprehension of the precise legal system under which all of its major characters have been prosecuted. Within the larger framework of the Stalinist criminal law, Article 58 of the Code of 1926 plays a role in the personal histories of Lev Rubin, Gleb Nerzhin, and most of the minor characters in the novel. Its analysis and research into the way the article was employed by Soviet authorities at the time of the fictional events in *First Circle*, helps place the work in its proper social perspective. The relationship between the restrictive criminal code and the developing party line on esthetic matters draws the two major themes in the work together. (RHW)

Tvardovski. 17883. Knowles, A.V. "Some Aspects of the Poetry of Alexander Tvardovsky." *NZSJ* 12(Sum 1973):80-89.
Tvardovski's early poems are concerned with collectivization; later World War II is discussed both from the soldier's and the civilian's viewpoint. His long poems discuss a journey and a search but never the arrival or the finding; the central heroes are both individual and generalized. The pre-war long poems are descriptive, realistic, and optimistic; the post-war ones are more reflective, explanatory, almost guilt-ridden. The material used is factual but colored by some obvious omissions; the subject matter is historical. Tvardovski is concerned with human problems and suggests that most of the Soviet Union's serious problems have been caused by forgetting human values. (AVK)

Voznesenski. 17898. Bailey, James. "The Verse of Andrej Voznesenskij as an Example of Present-Day Russian Versification." *SEEJ* 17:155-73.
During the past fifteen years, there has been a revival of "modernism" in Russian poetry; Andrei Voznesenski is one of the better known poets involved in this trend. Study of his verse may provide some indication of what new contributions contemporary poets are making to the evolution of Russian versification. Investigation of Voznesenski's poetry is difficult because he uses

the harsh aftermath of the Revolution, he was taken to task and eventually hounded into exile in 1931. Since then he has been ignored in the Soviet Union. The critical reception abroad has taken exactly the opposite direction: at first he was totally unknown, but as his work grew so did his reputation. Today, he is accepted as an important writer in world literature. (VDM)
several graphic devices to disrupt the "integrity" of the line and because he often employs classical meters loosely. Analysis reveals eight verse forms: binary meters, binary meters with strong caesura, ternary meters, various "free" meters, the *dol'nik*, accentual verse, polymetrical verse, and free verse. However, Voznesenski resorts largely to classical meters and the *dol'nik*. He has intensified regressive accentual dissimilation as much if not more than most previous poets and he has spread this feature to some ternary meters. Although many critics have stated that he continues the rhythmical tradition of Majakovski, for the most part Voznesenski utilizes a very different typology of meters. Similarities are more evident in the usage of graphic devices, types of rhymes, and themes. (JOB)

Zamiatin. 17905. Beauchamp, Gorman. "Future Words: Language and the Dystopian Novel." *Style* 8:462-76. [Considers Orwell's *1984* and Zamiatin's *We.*]
Although dystopias are ideologically opposite utopias, writers of both face the same artistic problems. One concerns creating a "language" that reflects the political and technological realities of their fictive futures. Most utopian/dystopian writers fail to solve this problem successfully; exceptions are Orwell's *1984* and Zamiatin's *We.* Orwell demonstrates the stultification of language in a totalitarian regime where heretical ideas cease to exist because the words to express them are systematically eliminated. Zamiatin develops a technologese perfectly in accord with its mechanized anthill society. (GB)
17910. Mihailovich, Vasa D. "Critics on Evgeny Zamyatin." *PLL* 10:317-34. [Rev. art.]
During and shortly after the Revolution Evgeny Zamiatin was favorably received by critics, but as soon as he began to criticize

UKRAINIAN

Twentieth Century Literature

Čubaj. 18865a. Chernenko, Alexandra. "The Birth of a New Spiritual Awareness." *CSP* 16:73-98. [Sum. in Fr.]
"The Search for the Accomplice" is the work of contemporary Ukrainian poet Hryhorii Čubai. English translation by Danylo Struk appeared in *CSP*, 14,ii (1972). Chernenko advances a new interpretation of the poem, based on the findings of C.G. Jung and particularly on the mystical philosophy of the 18th-century

Ukrainian thinker, Hryhorii Skovoroda. "The Search for the Accomplice" abounds in archetypal symbols which belong to the sphere of the collective rather than to that of the personal unconscious. The poem reflects the psyche's process of individuation: after a hard struggle with the dark forces of the unconscious, the mind reaches self-knowledge through an encounter with the resurrected Christ. While possessing a universal significance for mankind in our times, Čubai's poem also testifies to the spiritual rebirth taking place in the Ukraine. (AC)

IV. WEST SLAVIC LITERATURES

CZECH

Twentieth Century Literature

Hostovský. 19855. Liehm, Antonin. "Egon Hostovský:The Last Conversation." *CSP* 16:539-68. [Sum. in Fr.]
Egon Hostovský spent the war years in the U.S. and returned there in the late 1940s after a short stay in Czechoslovakia. Just before his death he discussed life as a writer who had experienced several emigrations. Letters from Czechoslovakian friends reveal how, in 1968, Hostovský planned a trip to his country which never occurred because of the Soviet occupation. During several conversations Hostovský summarizes life as a writer who was forced to leave his country but who continued writing in his mother tongue. Literature, Judaism, emigration, European and American literature are other subjects of this literary testament. (AJL)

Kundera. 19864. Porter, Robert. "Milan Kundera and His Novel *The Joke*." *Trivium* 8(1973):1-10.
A detailed review of *Žert* based primarily on the Czech text and reviews in Czech publications is presented. The article deals with the hero's character, his self-deception in human relationships, his three love affairs, and his inappropriate desire for revenge. His resultant skepticism is not the real key to his character, for he returns to traditional values to find a future *modus vivendi*. *The Joke*'s criticism of Stalinism goes further than simple social protest. Kundera sees excessive zeal in the revolutionary era as the cause of cultural distortions and consequently distortions in people's values and behavior. The passages on folk music and jazz provide one concrete example of this. Finally, the article examines the question of the generation gap. Youth is doomed to play-act and the young people in *The Joke* are subtly mocked. *The Joke*,

though highly relevant to all nations, possesses a peculiarly Czech quality—the transformation of a historical tragedy into a literary comedy. (RP)

POLISH

Twentieth Century Literature

Irzykowski. 20212. Sen, Colleen T. "Karol Irzykowski's *Pałuba:* A Guidebook to the Future." *SEEJ* 17:288-300.
Irzykowski's *Pałuba* is one of the earliest psychological novels, the bulk of the work consisting of the author's dissection of his characters' inner lives. To Irzykowski man is a fundamentally inauthentic creature whose "character" consists only of the roles he plays. Man derives these roles and his artificial constructions of reality from literature. Thus on one level *Pałuba* is an attack on the artificiality of the novel of the day. One of Irzykowski's goals was "to discredit the mysteries of creation, at least my own." To do this, he inserts entire literary essays explaining his methods and esthetic views into the text of the novel. He also appends a set of footnotes ("Remarks"), two explanatory essays and a short story, "Dreams of Maria Dunin," written in an obscure poetic style characteristic of contemporary Polish fiction. (CTS)

Kosinski. 20249. Richter, David H. "The Three Denouements of Jerzy Kosinski's *The Painted Bird*." *ConL* 15:370-85.
Kosinski's *The Painted Bird*, first published in 1965, was revised in 1966 and again in 1970. In all three editions its protagonist is driven to accept one ideology after another in order to make sense of the atrocities of which he is witness and victim; in all three he withdraws into hysterical muteness, taking refuge from humanity.

All versions end with the boy rejecting his ideologies, achieving autonomy, and finding his place in society, but Kosinski's revisions are designed to alter our response to the boy's resocialization. The 1965 edition concludes with an epilogue describing the inevitable conflicts between the independent youth and his newly-collectivized state; the 1966 edition omits the epilogue entirely, and the tension between socialization and autonomy survives only in a few phrases; in the 1970 edition even these are excised or palliated. Each revision makes less ambiguous our relief at the Painted Bird's return to his flock, but the price of Kosinski's happy ending is a weakening of his savagely ironic portrayal of an inhuman humankind. (DHR)

Mrożek. 20284. Kejan-Sharratt, Barbara. "Sławomir Mrożek and the Polish Tradition of the Absurd." *NZSJ* 1:75-86.
The current interest in the Theater of the Absurd in Poland originated from two sources—from the development of this mode in Western Europe and from the Polish tradition of the absurd represented by such writers as Witkacy (1885-1939), Schulz (1892-1942), Gombrowicz (1904-74), and the poet Gałczyński (1905-53). The dramas of Sławomir Mrożek reflect various literary influences. Mrożek created his own brand of the grotesque which has been labeled "logical" since it exploits the possibilities of the language to produce absurd situations. (BIK-S)

V. SOUTH SLAVIC LITERATURES

BULGARIAN

Twentieth Century Literature

Bagrjana. 20563. Knudsen, Erika. "The Counter-Points of Elisaveta Bagrjana." *CSP* 16:353-70. [Sum. in Fr.]
Elisaveta Bagrjana's latest collection of poems *Kontrapunkti* requires a new view of her. She was once considered the interpreter of woman's free love, but after thorough examination this conception is too narrow. In this poetry life teaches the incompatibility of love and freedom and that the lyrical self cannot reach the Faustian loftiness she aimed at. The tension between her expectations and reality forms the fundamental theme as reflected in her favorite themes and within the structure of every poem. A characteristic feature of Bagrjana's verse is tonality which never becomes sentimental. (EK)

MACEDONIAN

20575. Koneski, Blaže. "The Macedonian Dictionary." *RNL* 5,i:25-36.
The separate and distinct identity of Macedonian as a national language dates from efforts to standardize the usage of folk-speech during the 19th century. A major advance was made with the publishing of a Macedonian orthography in 1945. Institutional support for Macedonian linguistic studies came with the establishment in 1946 of the Department of South Slavic

Languages at Skopje University's Faculty of the Arts. The Commission for a Macedonian Dictionary was established in 1951. The lexicographers labored to draw words from all the Macedonian dialects while fashioning a literary language with a secure folklore base. The Institute of the Macedonian Language published Volume I of the *Dictionary* in 1961. Volumes II and III followed in 1963 and 1965, to complete a three-volume edition containing 64,522 lexical entries on 1711 pages. (BK)

SERBIAN

Nineteenth Century Literature

Karadžić. 20646. Lord, Albert B. "The Nineteenth-Century Revival of National Literatures: Karadžić, Njegoš, Radičević, the Illyrians, and Preseren." *RNL* 5,i:101-11.
Serbia, Montenegro, Croatia, and Slovenia all produced some truly heroic literary figures in the mid-19th century. The Serbian Vuk Karadžić labored to perfect a Serbian literary language. The Slovenian Jernej Kopitar inspired much labor of the same kind among the South Slavs as did the Croatian Ljudevit Gaj. In the category of original writings, the greatest name is that of the Montenegrin Prince-Bishop Njegoš, author of *The Mountain Wreath*. Coupled with him are the Croatians of the Illyrian

movement, the Serbian Branko Radičević, and France Prešeren, whose poems formed the literary language of Slovenia. (ABL)

Twentieth Century Literature

Andrić. 20697. Loud, John. "Between Two Worlds: Andrić the Storyteller." *RNL* 5,i:112-26.
Upon receiving the Nobel Prize in 1961, Ivo Andrić described himself as a storyteller above all else. His storytelling is rooted in historical Bosnia, on the borderland "between the two worlds" of Islam and the West, with Orthodox Serb, Sephardic Jew, Roman Catholic, and "Turk" living cheek to jowl. His great short-story figures are the Franciscan monk Fra Marko, the professional

warrior Mustafa Madžar, and the monstrously ambiguous Mephistopholean jailer, Karadoz. The condition of a prison-house, at once material and spiritual, is the central theme, veined throughout with ambiguous intimations of a transcendent order. (JL)

CROATIAN

Literature before 1700

General and Miscellaneous. 20917. Torbarina, Josip. "The Slav Petrarchists of Renaissance Dalmatia." *RNL* 5,i:86-100. Renaissance Dalmatia made a distinctive contribution to European Petrarchism through the poetry of Domenico Ragnina (Dinko Ranjina), Georgio Bizanti, and Lodovico Paschale (Paskalič). Though they wrote much, if not exclusively, in Italian, all three were Slav poets, belonging to the same nation and to the same school of poetry. Directly or indirectly, these Dalmatian Petrarchists appear to have had some influence on French and English writers of sonnets, including Shakespeare. One may justly conclude that the Dalmatian poets too could "expand" a little when they chose and make a contribution to the Petrarchism of Europe. (JT)

VI. NON-INDO-EUROPEAN LITERATURE

ESTONIAN

Miscellaneous

General and Miscellaneous. 21054. Puhvel, Jaan. "The Mythical Element in Estonian Poetry." *JBalS* 5,ii:87-99. Poetic applications of mythic material extend from the mythic, through the codificatory function of formal epic application, to deliberate exploitation of myth as a formal system of artistic reference, to the literary creation of mythical content and values as a form of poetic self-expression. In Estonian literature these developments occurred in just over one century. This provides a laboratory for studying the symptoms and results of accelerated interactions of myth and poetry, from the living folk poetry of the 19th century to the emergence of a literature nurtured by native heritage and international tradition. (JP)

Twentieth Century Literature

Rannit. 21087. Terras, Victor. "The Poetics of Aleksis Rannit:Observations on the Condition of the Émigré Poet." *JBalS* 5,ii:112-16. An examination of the poetry of the Estonian Aleksis Rannit reveals that it is ideally suited to flourish under conditions of exile. Its emphasis on sound (as against phraseology), on lyrical moods (as against epic or dramatic), and on deep elementary imagery over empirical surface imagery make it independent of a particular environment. (VT)

HUNGARIAN

Twentieth Century Literature

General and Miscellaneous. 21359. Barta, János. "The English 'New Agriculture' in Contemporary Hungarian Agricultural Literature." *HSE* 8:77-88. In the second half of the 18th century the development of Hungarian agriculture was hindered much more by home feudal circumstances than by an insufficient knowledge of the new English methods. These were continuously incorporated in Hungarian agricultural works, if not directly from the original English books then using a German or French translation or revision. Between the 1770s and 1790s, Hungarian authors kept pace with the best writers on the Continent. A literature advocating new agricultural methods in Hungary was not called for by actual needs but by the enlightened policy of the Hapsburg state or by the authors' personal convictions and optimism. (JB)

Ady. 21394. Congdon, Lee. "Endre Ady's Summons to National Regeneration in Hungary, 1900-1919." *SlavR* 33:302-22. In *fin de siècle* Hungary, Endre Ady was the central figure in a cultural renascence and the leading advocate of his country's national rebirth. He declared war on Hungary's social life and challenged his countrymen to create a society governed by moral principles rather than by class privilege. A victim of syphilis, he came to identify his personal tragedy with that of his country and to seek salvation in the struggle for a new Hungary. Thus he sang of a semi-mythological "Ady"—the symbol of Hungary regenerated. This "Ady" was pagan, Magyar, internationalist, and socialist. Despite his paganism, Ady was captivated by the figure of Christ. With Hungary near defeat in World War I and his disease terminal, his messianic identification was complete. In 1918-19, both the democratic and Soviet republics claimed his legacy. (LC)

Konrád. 21503. Varnai, Paul. "György Konrád's Novel *A látogató." IFR* 1,i:57-59. In Konrád's *A látogató* the reader is introduced into a substratum of the physically and mentally disabled. The narrator heads an office assigning guardians to children, regards the problems of his clients as incurable, and has little faith in institutional interference. When no individual or institution will take care of the abandoned child, the narrator moves into the flat and realizes that he is just as ineffective as the parents were. The fantasy stops when he is ordered back to the office. The assumption that genuine problems seldom adhere to regulations is confirmed. *A látogató* resembles works by Dostoevski, Gogol, Chekhov, as well as the French *nouveau roman* and suggests little faith in progress. (PV)

Lukács. 21515. Kiralyfalvi, Bela. "Lukács:A Marxist Theory of Aesthetic Effect." *ETJ* 26:506-12. Lukács finds the ultimate effect of art to be ethical in nature. He does not mean, however, that art is didactic, that it intends to interfere with the practical lives of men (artists are not "engineers of the soul" as Stalin put it). The ethical effect occurs only during the after-stage of the direct-emotional esthetic experience. Even at this stage, it is a possible consequence rather than a necessary result. The core of the esthetic experience proper is the catharsis, which consists not of empathic response or "intoxication," but of a sense of joy aroused by the perception of the beautiful portrayal of man's intensive totality, the perception of new and freshly seen contents. These perceptions overflow into ethical categories only in the after-stage of the direct artistic experience, bringing about a readiness for the morally good in the individual receiver. (BK)

21516. Lukács, György. "About the Principles of Dramatic Form." *ETJ* 26:512-20. [Tr. Bela Kiralyfalvi.] Drama's aim, to affect the masses, necessitates sensuousness, while the limitations of its magnitude necessitate universality. That the masses respond better to symbols and pictures than to abstractions further justifies universality. Typical characters in typical actions make the dramatic universality concrete in substance. Manifested through struggle in a social context, the will symbolizes the whole man and his destiny. The drama is built from social struggle and a world view which is the chief element of its forming. The struggle arises in ages of class decline. Drama is born at times of sharp struggle between the old and the new. (BK)

VII. FOLKLORE

Indo-European

Latvian. 21673. Vīķis-Freibergs, Vaira, and Stephen Reynolds. "A Recent Study in Latvian Mythology." *JBalS* 5,iii:226-36. [Rev. art. on Haralds Biezais' *Die himmlische Götterfamilie der alten Letten.*]
Die himmlische Götterfamilie der alten Letten by Haralds Biezais discusses the sky-gods of Latvian folklore with Latvian folksongs or dainas as source material. Mythological personifications of the Morning Star, Thunder, the Moon, the Sun, Sun's daughters, and God's sons are members of an extended family of gods. The characteristics and activities of these deities are described and are essentially those of individuals in a peasant society. The criteria for Godhead are nowhere unambiguously defined and some defining characteristics fail to carry conviction. Consequently the attribution of divine status to some of the mythological figures can be questioned. (VVF)

Russian. 21739. Smith, G.S. "Modern Russian Underground Song:An Introductory Survey." *JRS* 28:3-12.
The underground song is currently one of the most vital and genuinely popular genres of Russian poetry. The incursion of the private tape recorder has meant that during the last 15 years underground songs have been preserved and circulated in the author's performance. The repertoire consists of narrative ballads of everyday life and personal lyrics; there are thematic and stylistic influences from gypsy song, criminal song, and some Western European traditions like the German cabaret song. The genre is dominated by Bulat Okudzhava, Vladimir Vysotsky, and Alexander Galich. (GSS)

Non-Indo-European

Estonian. 21862. Oinas, Felix J. "The Position of the Setus in Estonian Folklore." *JBalS* 5,i:18-25.
The folklore of the Setus, Orthodox inhabitants of southeastern Estonia (Setumaa), is similar to the folklore of the Ingrians and the Votes near Leningrad. The similarities appear in numerous epic and other songs and have been attributed to the relic status of Setu folklore, parallel development, etc. The reason for the close tradition between these groups is the direct connection that was maintained formerly by Lake Peipus and by land. Religious pilgrimages to Petseri monastery in Setumaa also contributed to the exchange of folklore. (FJO)

Subject Index

1974 MLA ABSTRACTS
of Articles in
Scholarly Journals

Volume III

Linguistics

Compiled by

WALTER S. ACHTERT AND EILEEN M. MACKESY
*with the assistance of those whose
names appear in the staff list*

Published by

THE MODERN LANGUAGE ASSOCIATION OF AMERICA

1976

This is Volume III of three volumes of the 1974 *MLA Abstracts*. The three volumes are collected in a cumulative edition for libraries.

The *MLA Abstracts* is partially supported by a grant from the National Endowment for the Humanities.

ISBN 0-87352-236-2

1974 MLA ABSTRACTS

MLA Abstracts is a three volume annual following the arrangement of the *MLA International Bibliography*. This is Volume Three of the set, and includes items on linguistics. Volume One includes sections on General, English, American, Medieval and Neo-Latin, Celtic literatures, and Folklore; and Volume Two contains sections on European, Asian, African, and Latin-American literatures. All three volumes are available separately to MLA members, or together in a bound "Library Edition."

The 1974 *MLA Abstracts* provides a classified, indexed collection of abstracts of journal articles on the modern languages and literatures to be used in conjunction with the 1974 *MLA International Bibliography*. All items for which abstracts appear in this volume are indicated by an asterisk preceding the item number in the appropriate volume of the 1974 *Bibliography*. Journals from which abstracts appear in this volume are preceded by an asterisk in the Master List of Journal Acronyms in the *Bibliography*.

The *MLA Abstracts* is intended to supplement the author, title listings in the annual *Bibliography* and thus provide for the scholar and student additional access to current scholarship. It is thought that a scholar beginning research on an author or topic will turn first to the appropriate sections of the *Bibliography* to obtain lists of all the items of possible relevance. Then the researcher may turn to the abstracts collections to learn more about the articles included there. The *MLA Abstracts* includes a subject index in which articles are indexed according to approaches, themes, genres, and special techniques. The index is intended primarily as a means of manual access into the collections. These terms will later be used in automatic retrieval of the abstracts data.

The abstracts have been set from tapes and will eventually be available for indexing and automatic retrieval. Spellings have been regularized within the body of the abstracts, but not in the titles of the articles.

Entry form follows that used by the *MLA International Bibliography*. Arabic numbers have replaced roman to denote the volume number of a journal. Undated items are understood to have been published in 1974. When an issue number of a journal is required for a given entry, it appears in lower case roman immediately after the arabic volume number. An arabic number preceded by F in square brackets following an entry title refers to an item listed in the *Festschriften* and Other Analyzed Collections division which begins this volume.

In the main, these abstracts have been prepared by the authors of the original articles, whose initials appear at the end of the abstract. Where an abstract has been prepared by another person, the abstractor's initials appear at the end of the abstract. Through a special arrangement, the MLA exchanges abstracts with *Language and Language Behavior Abstracts*. Abstracts ending with the initials LLBA have been supplied by *LLBA*. These collections could not have appeared without the generous assistance of the editors of the journals listed in the Table of Journal Acronyms and the thousands of authors who have prepared abstracts of their articles.

Staff for the 1974 *MLA Abstracts*

TABLE OF CONTENTS
VOLUME III

TABLE OF JOURNAL ACRONYMS

ELT	English Literature in Transition (1880–1920)
ELWIU	Essays in Literature (Western Ill. U.)
Emily Dickinson Bulletin	
EngR	English Record
ESA	English Studies in Africa (Johannesburg)
ESQ	Emerson Society Quarterly
ETC: A Review of General Semantics (LLBA)	
ETJ	Educational Theatre Journal
EWN	Evelyn Waugh Newsletter
Expl	Explicator
FaN	Le Français au Nigeria
FHA	Fitzgerald/Hemingway Annual
FI	Forum Italicum
FLang	Foundations of Language (Dordrecht, Neth.) (LLBA)
FM	Le Français Moderne (LLBA)
FMonde	Le Français dans le Monde (LLBA)
FN	Filologičeskie Nauki (LLBA)
Focus on Robert Graves	
FoLi	Folia Linguistica (LLBA)
FolkloreC	Folklore (Calcutta)
ForumH	Forum (Houston)
FR	French Review
FsD	Fonetică şi Dialectologie
FUF	Finnisch-ugrische Forschungen: Zeitschrift für Finnisch-ugrische Sprach- und Volkskunde
GaR	Georgia Review
GAS	German-American Studies
GL	General Linguistics
Glossa: The Journal of Linguistics	
GN	Germanic Notes
GQ	German Quarterly
GR	Germanic Review
GRM	Germanisch-romanische Monatsschrift, Neue Folge
GSlav	Germano-Slavica
GSLI	Giornale Storico della Letteratura Italíana
HAB	Humanities Association Bulletin (Canada)
Hasifrut: Quarterly for the Study of Literature	
HC	Hollins Critic (Hollins Coll., Va.)
HCompL	Hebrew Computational Linguistics
Hermathena: A Dublin University Review	
Hispania (U. of Mass.)	
Historiographia Linguistica	
HJAS	Harvard Journal of Asiatic Studies
HJb	Hebbel-Jahrbuch
HLQ	Huntington Library Quarterly
HR	Hispanic Review
HSE	Hungarian Studies in English (L. Kossuth U., Debrecen)
HSL	Hartford Studies in Literature
HUSL	Hebrew University Studies in Literature
IAN	Isvestija Akademii Nauk S.S.S.R., Serija Literatury i Jazyka (Moscow) (LLBA)
IBLA	Institut des Belles-Lettres Arabes Revue
IEY	Iowa English Bulletin: Yearbook
IF	Indogermanische Forschungen (LLBA)
IFR	International Fiction Review
IIJ	Indo-Iranian Journal (LLBA)
IJAL	International Journal of American Linguistics (LLBA)
IJAS	Indian Journal of American Studies
IncL	Incorporated Linguist (London) (LLBA)
Independent Shavian	
IR	Iliff Review (Denver)
ItalAm	Italian Americana
Italica	
ITL: Review of Applied Linguistics	

JAmS	Journal of American Studies
JAOS	Journal of the American Oriental Society
JArabL	Journal of Arabic Literature
JAS	Journal of the Acoustical Society (LLBA)
JBalS	Journal of Baltic Studies
JDSG	Jahrbuch der Deutschen Schiller-Gesellschaft
JEGP	Journal of English and Germanic Philology
JEngL	Journal of English Linguistics
JGa	Juană Gaita (Hamilton, Ont.)
JGE	Journal of General Education
JHI	Journal of the History of Ideas
JIES	Journal of Indo-European Studies
JISHS	Journal of the Illinois State Historical Society
JML	Journal of Modern Literature
JNES	Journal of Near Eastern Studies (Chicago)
JNT	Journal of Narrative Technique
Journal of Ethnic Studies	
Journal of the International Phonetic Association	
JPS	Journal of the Polynesian Society (Auckland) (LLBA)
JQ	Journalism Quarterly
JRS	Journal of Russian Studies [Formerly *ATRJ*]
JSHD	Journal of Speech and Hearing Disorders (LLBA)
JSHR	Journal of Speech and Hearing Research (LLBA)
JSSTC	Journal of Spanish Studies: Twentieth Century
JWGV	Jahrbuch des Wiener Goethe-Vereins
KanQ	Kansas Quarterly [Formerly *KM*]
KFQ	Keystone Folklore Quarterly
Kivung: Journal of the Ling. Soc. of the U. of Papua and New Guinea (LLBA)	
KSJ	Keats-Shelley Journal
L&S	Language and Speech
Langages (Paris) (LLBA)	
Lang&S	Language and Style
LangS	Language Sciences
Language	
LanM	Les Langues Modernes
LATR	Latin American Theater Review
LB	Leuvense Bijdragen (LLBA)
LBib	Linguistica Biblica: Interdisziplinäre Zeitschrift für Theologie und Linguistik
LBR	Luso-Brazilian Review
LC	Library Chronicle (U. of Penn.)
LCUT	Library Chronicle of the University of Texas
LE&W	Literature East and West
LeS	Lingua e Stile (Bologna)
LHR	Lock Haven Review (Lock Haven State Coll., Pa.)
LimR	Limbă Română (Bucureşti) (LLBA)
Lingua (Amsterdam) (LLBA)	
Linguistics	
Linguistique (Paris) (LLBA)	
Lithanus: Lithuanian Quarterly (Chicago)	
LL	Language Learning
LLBA	Language and Language-Behavior Abstracts
LOS	Literary Onomastics Studies
LP	Lingua Posnaniensis (LLBA)
LSoc	Language in Society
LURev	Lakehead University Review
LY	Lessing Yearbook
LyC	Lenguaje y Ciencias (Univ. Nacional de Trujillo) (LLBA)
MagN	Magyar Nyelvör (LLBA)
MAL	Modern Austrian Literature: Journal of the Intl. Arthur Schnitzler Research Assn. [Supersedes *JIASRA*]
M&C	Memory & Cognition

M&H	Medievalia et Humanistica (North Texas State U.)
ManR	Manchester Review
Manuscripta	
MarkhamR	Markham Review
Mary Wollstonecraft Journal	
MDAC	Mystery and Detection Annual (Beverly Hills, Calif.)
MelbSS	Melbourne Slavonic Studies
Menckeniana	
MFS	Modern Fiction Studies
MichA	Michigan Academician [Supersedes *PMASAL*]
MiltonQ	Milton Quarterly [Formerly *MiltonN*]
MiltonS	Milton Studies
MinnR	Minnesota Review
MissQ	Mississippi Quarterly
ML	Modern Languages (London)
MLN	Modern Language Notes
MLQ	Modern Language Quarterly
MLR	Modern Language Review
MLS	Modern Language Studies
MNy	Magyar Nyelv (LLBA)
Monatschefte	
Moreana (Angers)	
Mosaic: A Journal for the Comparative Study of Literature and Ideas	
Mov	Movoznavstvo (Kiev) (LLBA)
MQ	Midwest Quarterly (Pittsburg, Kan.)
MQR	Michigan Quarterly Review
MS	Mediaeval Studies (Toronto)
MTJ	Mark Twain Journal
MW	Muslim World (Hartford, Conn.)
NALF	Negro American Literature Forum
Names	
NC	Nuova Corrente (LLBA)
NCarF	North Carolina Folklore
NCF	Nineteenth-Century Fiction
NCFS	Nineteenth-Century French Studies
NDQ	North Dakota Quarterly
NewL	New Letters [Formerly *University Review*]
NHJ	Nathaniel Hawthorne Journal
NK	Nyelvtudományi Közlemények (LLBA)
NLauR	New Laurel Review (The Pennington School, Pennington, N.J.)
NLH	New Literary History (U. of Va.)
NS	Die Neueren Sprachen (LLBA)
NsM	Neusprachliche Mitteilungen aus Wissenschaft und Praxis
NTLTL	Teaching Language Through Literature
NWZam	New Writing from Zambia
NYH	New York History
NZSJ	New Zealand Slavonic Journal
Oceania	
OcL	Oceanic Linguistics
OhR	Ohio Review
OL	Orbis Litterarum
OntarioR	Ontario Review: A North American Journal of the Arts
Orbis (Louvain) (LLBA)	
PAAS	Proceedings of the American Antiquarian Society
PADS	Publication of the American Dialect Society
PAPS	Proceedings of the American Philosophical Society
Paunch (Buffalo, N.Y.)	
PBML	Prague Bulletin of Mathematical Linguistics (Charles U., Praha) (LLBA)
PBSA	Papers of the Bibliographical Society of America
PCP	Pacific Coast Philology
PFr	Présence Francophone
PIL	Papers in Linguistics

PLL	Papers on Language and Literature
PMLA: Publications of the Modern Language Association of America	
PoeS	Poe Studies
PolP	Polish Perspectives
PPR	Philosophy and Phenomenological Research (LLBA)
PQ	Philological Quarterly (Iowa City)
Proceedings of the Comparative Literature Symposium	
Proceedings of the Pacific Northwest Conference on Foreign Languages	
Proof: Yearbook of American Bibliographical and Textual Studies	
QJLC	Quarterly Journal of the Library of Congress
QJS	Quarterly Journal of Speech
QQ	Queen's Quarterly
RAL	Research African Literatures
RALS	Resources for American Literary Studies
RdSO	Revista degli Studi Orientali (Roma)
RECTR	Restoration and 18th Century Theatre Research
REH	Revista de Estudios Hispánicos (U. of Ala.)
RELC	RELC Journal (Singapore)
Renascence	
RenD	Renaissance Drama (Northwestern U.)
RES	Review of English Studies
RevR	Revue Romane (LLBA)
RJŠ	Russkij Jazyk v Škole (LLBA)
RLC	Revue de Littérature Comparée
RLI	Rassegna della Letteratura Italiana
RLM	La Revue des Lettres Modernes
RLMC	Revista di Letterature Moderne e Comparate (Firenze)
RLV	Revue des Langues Vivantes (Bruxelles)
RNL	Review of National Literatures
RomN	Romance Notes (U. of N.C.)
RORD	Research Opportunities in Renaissance Drama
RPL	Revue Philosophique de Louvain (LLBA)
RQ	Riverside Quarterly (U. of Saskatchewan)
RS	Research Studies (Wash. State U.)
RUS	Rice University Studies
SAF	Studies in American Fiction
S&W	South & West
SAQ	South Atlantic Quarterly
SB	Studies in Bibliography: Papers of the Bibliographical Society of the University of Virginia
SBHT	Studies in Burke and His Time [Formerly *The Burke Newsletter*]
Scan	Scandinavica
SCB	South Central Bulletin
SCN	Seventeenth-Century News
Scottish Literary News	
SCR	South Carolina Review
SDR	South Dakota Review
SE	Slovenski Ethnograf (LLBA)
Sean O'Casey Review	
SeAQ	Southeast Asia Quarterly
SEEJ	Slavic and East European Journal
SEL	Studies in English Literature, 1500–1900
Seminar: A Journal of Germanic Studies (Victoria Coll., Toronto; and Newcastle U., New South Wales)	
Serif	The Serif (Kent, Ohio)
SFQ	Southern Folklore Quarterly
SFS	Science-Fiction Studies
SFUS	Sovetskoe Finno-Ugrovedenie/Soviet Fenno-Ugric Studies
SH	Studia Hibernica (Dublin)
ShakS	Shakespeare Studies (U. of Cincinnati)
ShawR	Shaw Review
SHR	Southern Humanities Review
ShS	Shakespeare Survey

SIL	Studies in Linguistics
SIR	Studies in Romanticism (Boston U.)
Skandinavistik	
SL	Studia Linguistica (Lund) (LLBA)
SlavR	Slavic Review (Seattle)
SLitI	Studies in the Literary Imagination (Ga. State Coll.)
SLJ	Southern Literary Journal
SlReč	Slovenská Reč (Bratislava) (LLBA)
SM	Speech Monographs
SML	Statistical Methods in Linguistics (Stockholm) (LLBA)
SNNTS	Studies in the Novel (North Texas State U.)
SoQ	Southern Quarterly (U. of So. Miss.)
SoR	Southern Review (Louisiana State U.)
Soundings: A Journal of Interdisciplinary Studies [Formerly *ChS*]	
SP	Studies in Philology
Speculum	
Spirit: A Magazine of Poetry	
SQ	Shakespeare Quarterly
SRC	Studies in Religion. A Canadian Journal
SRen	Studies in the Renaissance
SS	Scandinavian Studies
SSG	Schriften der Theodor-Storm-Gesellschaft
StCL	Studii si Cercetări Lingvistice (LLBA)
Studi Italiani di Linguistica Teorica Applicata	
Studies in 18th Century Culture	
STS	Scottish Text Society (LLBA)
Style (U. of Arkansas)	
Sub-stance: A Review of Theory and Literary Criticism	
SwAL	Southwestern American Literature
SWR	Southwest Review
Synthese (Dordrecht, Holland) (LLBA)	
TCL	Twentieth Century Literature
TD	Theatre Documentation
TDR	The Drama Review [Formerly *Tulane Drama Review*]
TESOLQ	Teachers of English to Speakers of Other Languages Quarterly
Theoria: A Journal of Studies in the Arts, Humanities, and Social Sciences	
Thesaurus: Boletín del Instituto Caro y Cuervo (LLBA)	
Thoth (Dept. of English, Syracuse U.)	
Thought	
ThR	Theatre Research/Recherche Theatrales
ThS	Theatre Survey (Amer. Soc. for Theatre Research)
Tlalocan (Mexico)	
TLL	Travaux de Linguistique et de Littérature Publiés par le Centre de Philologie et de Littératures Romanes de l'Université de Strasbourg (LLBA)

TN	Theatre Notebook
TNTL	Tijdschrift voor Nederlandse Taal- en Letterkunde (Leiden)
TPS	Transactions of the Philological Society (London)
Transactions of the Samuel Johnson Society of the Northwest	
Trivium (St. David's Coll., Lampeter, Cardiganshire, Wales)	
TSB	Thoreau Society Bulletin
TSE	Tulane Studies in English
T. S. Eliot Newsletter	
TSL	Tennessee Studies in Literature
TSLL	Texas Studies in Literature and Language
UCTSE	University of Cape Town Studies in English
UDQ	University of Denver Quarterly
UDR	University of Dayton Review
UES	Unisa English Studies
UP	Unterrichtspraxis
Vir	Virittäjä: Revue de Kotikielen Seura (Société pour l'Etude de la Langue Maternelle) (LLBA)
VJa	Voprosy Jazykoznanija (Moscow) (LLBA)
VLang	Visible Language
VMHB	Virginia Magazine of History and Biography
VMU	Vestnik Moskovskogo U. Ser VII. Filologija, Žurnalistika (LLBA)
VN	Victorian Newsletter
VP	Victorian Poetry (W. Va. U.)
VPN	Victorian Periodicals Newsletter
VR	Vox Romanica (LLBA)
VS	Victorian Studies (Indiana U.)
WascanaR	Wascana Review (Regina, Sask.)
WC	Wordsworth Circle
WF	Western Folklore
WHR	Western Humanities Review
WMQ	William and Mary Quarterly
WPL	Working Papers in Linguistics (Ohio State U.)
WPLUH	Working Papers in Linguistics (U. of Hawaii)
WVUPP	West Virginia University Philological Papers
WW	Wirkendes Wort (LLBA)
WWR	Walt Whitman Review
WZUG	Wissenschaftliche Zeitschrift der Ernst Moritz Arndt-Universität Griefswald (LLBA)
YCGL	Yearbook of Comparative and General Literature
YFS	Yale French Studies
Zambezia (Salisbury, Rhodesia)	
ZMF	Zeitschrift für Mundartforschung (LLBA)
ZPSK	Zeitschrift für Phonetik, Sprachwissenschaft und Kommunikationsforschung (LLBA)
ZRP	Zeitschrift für Romanische Philologie (Halle) (LLBA)

Linguistics

Linguistics. 51. Kraft, Walter C.,ed. *Proceedings:Pacific Northwest Conference on Foreign Languages.* Twenty-fifth Annual Meeting, April 19-20, 1974, Eastern Washington State College. Vol. xxv, *Part 1: Literature and Linguistics.* Corvallis: Ore. State U. 296 pp.

Articles from this *Festschrift* are abstracted separately below.

GENERAL LINGUISTICS†

I. GENERALITIES

Bibliography

123. Koerner, E.F.K. "An Annotated Chronological Bibliography of Western Histories of Linguistic Thought, 1822-1972. Part I:1822-1915." *HL* 1:81-94.
This is the first part of a comprehensive annotated bibliography of Western histories of linguistic thought of the last 150 years. The majority of titles listed cover the period 1822-1915 and are written in German. Only book-length studies or individual publications are included, though on certain occasions a significant article or contribution to a collective volume is listed as well. Monographs devoted to a single author, a highly specialized aspect of linguistics, or a limited period of time are not included. (LLBA)

125. Kulmala, Vuokko. "Veröffentlichungen von Matti Liimola 1933-1972." *FUF* 40(1973):340-44.
A bibliography of Matti Liimola's published production, 1933-72. (VK)

History of Linguistics

General and Miscellaneous. 144. Chevalier, Jean-Claude. "Idéologie grammaticale et changement linguistique." *Langages* 32(1973):115-21.
A demonstration, based on examples from the 17th century and contemporary times, that grammatical theories, being inseparable from pragmatics, must be placed in relation to the discourse of the epoch and through this discourse in relation to the ideologies of which they are instances. (LLBA)

163. Henderson, Michael M.T. "A Sixteenth-Century Exercise in Applied Linguistics." *LangS* 33:1-4.
Matthias Ringmann (1482-1511) devised a card game for teaching the elements of Latin grammar as desribed by Donatus in his *Ars Minor*. Parts of speech are represented by characters such as kings, monks, and fools; and grammatical categories are represented both by pictures that show their meaning and pictures of objects arranged to resemble graphemic representations of their form. The game is noteworthy for its humor and its insights into the structure of Latin, and for the implication that language teaching was considered a useful occupation so long ago. (MH)

165. Hickson, Mark,III. "Dewey's Reflex Arc and Reflective Thought:A Comparison with Korzybski." *ETC* 30(1973):127-30.
Two of Dewey's concepts may be combined to form a theory comparable to general semantics: the reflex arc and reflective thinking. The reflex arc comprises a more comprehensive, organic unity, while criticizing the stimulus-response system for its omission of sensory motor coordinations that are prerequisite for any type of response. This adds to Korzybski's principle that life is an ongoing process with various electrons continually in motion. Dewey suggested that the reason for unique responses was that, in each case, a new situation evolves. Although there are similarities between Dewey and Korzybski, one distinction is found in the type of communication intended following their respective investigative methods. Dewey was more concerned with intrapersonal communication—with man's finding the "truth" for himself—while Korzybski was concerned with interpersonal communication for the betterment of relationships with others. Whether or not this assumption is true, the philosophy of one could be incorporated with that of the other. Both were attempting to find methods for arriving at the "truth" as a pragmatic element. (LLBA)

189. Robins, R.H. "Theory-Orientation versus Data-Orientation:A Recurrent Theme in Linguistics." *HL* 1:11-26.
Two contrasting attitudes toward the scientific study of language have been apparent from the earliest period of linguistic studies in Europe. In Greece the debate was between the claim of grammar to be a science and the opinion that it was no more than practical knowledge. In the Middle Ages the scholastic speculative grammarians maintained that their theory of grammar embodied a superior level of adequacy over the mere accurate record of observed fact provided by Priscian and the didactic grammarians. A similar opposition was seen in the 17th and 18th centuries between rationalist linguists, with their emphasis on universals and on the importance of "general grammar," and the empiricists, who paid most attention to the individual differences of each language. These continuing attitudes are still a matter of controversy today, and each has an essential place in the progress of linguistic science. (RHR)

191. Salmon, Paul B. "The Beginnings of Morphology: Linguistic Botanizing in the 18th Century." *HL* 3:313-39.
By providing an assured basis in morphology for subsequent phonological comparison Sir William Jones's celebrated remarks about the resemblance and relationship between Sanskrit, Greek, and Latin marked a turning point in the study of language. Some scholars anticipated his conclusions, but their findings appear to have remained largely unknown. The present study compares some of the lines of thought common to comparative linguistics and comparative anatomy and suggests that in the biological sciences, too, resemblance implied common origin sooner and more generally than is sometimes held. (PBS)

Scholars. 219. Cherubim, Dieter. "Hermann Paul und die moderne linguistik." *ZDL* 40(1973):310-22.
The position of Hermann Paul and his work in the history of linguistics, as well as his significance for contemporary linguistics, is examined. Paul's position was a turning point in the history of linguistics. Though bound up with the historical-empirical linguistics of Jacob Grimm, he nevertheless went beyond it in specific ways. (LLBA)

220. Christophersen, Paul. "Otto Jespersen:A Retrospect." *TPS* (for 1972 [1973]):1-19.
From having been a rebel against traditional grammar and ways of teaching languages, Jespersen came later in life to feel a lack of sympathy with Saussurean and Bloomfieldian structuralism. Although some of Jespersen's views once more attract attention, TG grammar would have appeared as uncongenial to his down-to-earth temperament as the school that it succeeded. In his youth Jespersen was interested in language teaching reform and particularly the use of phonetics. Despite this practical aim his contribution to the development of theoretical phonetics was considerable. Another concern was sound-changes and their causes. Volume I of his *Modern English Grammar* is a "History of English Sound-Changes," including the Great Vowel Shift, to

---

† *Festschriften* and Other Analyzed Collections are listed in the first division of this volume. "F" numbers in brackets following a title refer to these items.

which Jespersen gave its present name. After about 1910 Jespersen concentrated mostly on syntax and developed his theories of Rank and of Junction and Nexus, which formed a framework on which he arranged the syntactic material in his *Grammar*. His nexus theory has recently attracted some attention and been responsible for the claim that he was trying to "explicate linguistic competence." (PC)

221. Constantinescu, Ilinca. "John Wallis (1616-1703): A Reappraisal of His Contributions to the Study of English." *HL* 3:297-311.
Three centuries after its publication, John Wallis' *Grammatica Linguae Anglicanae* (1653) is still worth the attention of readers interested in the study of English. Considered within the context of its day, it appears as a significant contribution to the field, and indeed a work which constitutes a landmark in the history of the study of English. Wallis succeeded in handling facts of the English language (both phonetics and grammar) better than any of his predecessors. His work, which illustrates the empirical approach, is important through the degree of independence attained in it from the Latin model which, at that time, still exerted a strong influence on attempts at describing the European vernaculars. (IC)

226. Fellman, Jack. "The First Historical Linguist." *Linguistics* 137:31-33.
The beginnings of historical linguistics can be traced back over a century before Sir William Jones's well-known Third Anniversary Discourse of 1786. The first historical linguist was the Dutch classical scholar Marcus Zuerius Boxhorn (1612-53) who, in his unpublished *The Scythian Origins of the Peoples and the Languages of Europe*, posited Scythian as the common proto-language source for Greek, Latin, German, and Persian. (JF)

226a. Fleisch, Henri. "Note sur Al-Astarābādhī." *HL* 1:165-68.
Little is known about Muḥammed Raḍī al-Dīn Ibn Ḥasan al-Astarābādhī, the famous Arab grammarian who died about 1289, and even this date depends on whether the colophons of his two major works, the *Sharḥ al-Shāfiya* and the *Sharḥ al-Kāfiya*, offer reliable information. Indeed, for long one did not even know his name; he has generally been referred to as the "Star of the Imams" in view of the authority ascribed to his treatises of Arabic. Although al-Astarābādhī followed in many respects the analysis advanced in the *Kitāb* by Sībawayhi (8th century), his works contain a number of important observations of his own. He was the first to explain the phenomenon of rhotacism in Arabic and he analyzed the function of particular cases and demonstrative pronouns which had hitherto been unsolved in Arabic linguistic scholarship. (HF)

251. Miner, Kenneth L. "John Eliot of Massachusetts and the Beginnings of American Linguistics." *HL* 1:169-83.
The Indian Grammar Begun (1666) of John Eliot of Massachusetts (1604-90) constitutes the first published account of an "exotic" language that can rightfully be called scientific. The first portion of the argument treats Eliot's English-based orthography and the problems it poses in the description of a language completely different from English. Eliot's use of a "morphophonemic" transcription is presented. Eliot's *The Logick Primer* (1672) is suggested as a source of particular insight into the Puritan understanding and use of logic. Having speculated about the impact that Jesus College, Cambridge, may have had on Eliot's linguistic accomplishments in his analysis of an Amerindian language, the author concludes that Eliot deserves to be called the true founder of American linguistics, in particular since he anticipated modern use of levels of representation by more than a century. (KLM)

256. Peeters, Christian. "Saussure néogrammairien et l'antinomie synchronie/diachronie." *Linguistics* 133:53-62.
In Saussure's *Cours de linguistique générale* it is above all the chapters on synchronic linguistics that have been investigated, although the chapters on diachrony are quantitatively more important. In the field of diachrony Saussure was an orthodox neogrammarian. He considered language change as entirely dominated by the blind action of sound laws tempered by analogy. It is the neogrammarian conception of diachrony that led to a very sharp distinction between synchrony and diachrony. The sharp distinction between synchrony and diachrony made by

Saussure has been misunderstood. (CLP)

259. Rasmussen, Karen. "Inconsistency in Campbell's *Rhetoric*: Explanation and Implications." *QJS* 60:190-200.
Campbell's *Philosophy of Rhetoric* is an overlay of 18th-century philosophical and psychological thought on classical rhetorical canons; hence, his approach was highly integrative and substantially influenced by the thought of his contemporaries. Campbell's synthesis, however, resulted in a methodological-epistemological inconsistency: he followed Hume and other skeptical-empiricists in advocating reliance on observation to yield theoretical formulations but at the same time adhered to the dicta of the Common Sense school of philosophy which relied on intuitive proof. The conceptual implications of this inconsistency for contemporary theorizing are twofold: critical to theoretical efforts is the examination of the consistency of the premises underlying a theoretical system; conceptual narrowness or the failure to entertain multiple alternatives can result in limited formulations having minimal theoretical utility. However, entertaining multiple alternatives may produce points of view incompatible with each other. Thus, a sound theoretical approach should work for consistency within the systems and for openness to divergent approaches. (KLR)

260. Ricken, Ulrich. "La critique sensualiste à l'encontre du 'Discours sur l'universalité de la langue française' d'Antoine de Rivarol." *HL* 1:67-80.
Urbain Domergue's (1745-1810) opposition to Antoine Rivarol's (1753-1801) explanation of the *Clarté française* on the basis of the rationalist doctrine of "natural" word order was not primarily motivated by Rivarol's negative attitude toward the Revolution. On the contrary, it is demonstrated that immediately after the appearance of Rivarol's *Discours* (1784) Domergue opposed Rivarol's theory of the "natural" word order of French (advocating instead a sensualist position established by Condillac), and that Domergue's arguments put forward in 1799 were essentially those of 1785, though now with additions furnished by predominantly philosophical and political experiences made during the period of the Revolution. (UR)

269. Slagle, Uhlan V. "The Kantian Influence on Humboldt's Linguistic Thought." *HL* 3:341-50.
Humboldt's theory of language reflects Kant's influence to a far greater extent than is generally realized. In fact, Kantian cognitive and perceptual universals play a crucial role in the later formulations of Humboldt's linguistic thinking. Not only did Humboldt derive the universals of grammatical case from the Kantian categories of relation in his mature work, but he also applied Kant's schema concept in a systematic way to the fundamental problems of language during his last period of scholarly activity. It can be shown that the Kantian aspects of his theory do not conflict with his widely quoted and misinterpreted formulations concerning the nature of linguistic diversity. One can plausibly argue that Humboldt was correct in assuming that Kant, not Descartes, provided linguistics with the key for dealing adequately with the central problems of language and mind. (UVS)

270. Sorokoletov, F.P. "Akademik Jakov Karlovič Grot." *RJR* 1:68-72.
Academician Ja.K. Grot was a major figure in research on the language and style of Russian 18th- and 19th-century writers. He did significant work on Scandinavian folklore and mythology as well. His *Filologič eskie razyskanija* reflects his varied interests —grammar, lexicology, stress. He was responsible for numerous editions of Russian classics of Lomonosov, Fonvizin, Derzhavin, Karamzin, etc. He is most famous for his work on Russian orthography, *Spornye voprosy russkogo pravopisanija ot Petra Velikogo donyne*, which gives a systematic description of Russian orthography from the beginning of the 18th century through the 1880s. The latter part of Grot's life was primarily devoted to work on dictionaries. His dictionary of the Russian language is characterized by exactness of definitions and by stylistic characterization. One of Grot's most important late works is the *Slovar' k stixhotvorenijam Deržavina* (1883). (FPS)

281. Washabaugh, William. "Saussure, Durkheim, and Sociolinguistic Theory." *ArL* 5:25-34.
The dynamic paradigm in contemporary linguistics demands that

grammars be dynamic, variable, and social and claims that none of these characteristics can be found in grammars based on the Saussurean paradigm. A study of Saussure's work, beyond his Course in General Linguistics, shows, however, that he did outline concepts for writing dynamic grammars. Moreover, Saussure's approach to dynamics differs from that of many proponents of the dynamic paradigm, just as it differed from Durkheim's approach, by stressing the individual aspect of the language system. Thus, a careful review of Saussure will provide needed refinements in the dynamic paradigm. (WW)

286. Wunderli, Peter. "Zur Saussure-Rezeption bei Gustave Guillaume und in seiner Nachfolge." *HL* 1:27-66.
The main aspects of Gustave Guillaume's linguistic theory are discussed. Central portions of his system are quite distinct from Saussure's position. Apart from a number of other differences between the two, there are two important components that receive special treatment, namely, Guillaume's attempt at introducing the dynamic aspect into the (synchronic) system of language, and the renunciation of the bilateral concept of the sign (*signifié/ signifiant*) within *langue*. In an effort to avoid the essentially static conceptions of certain structuralist trends, Guillaume regards the content of individual signs as such as not actually existing. In his understanding, on this linguistic level, only a given series of programs is entitled to be taken as an entity within which individual moneme-signifiers represent merely virtual positions. It is only on the threshold between *langue* and *discours* that these signifiers are related to the contents generated within the framework of a given *temps opératif*, in order to form a sentence, the basic unit of *discours*. Taking Saussure's theory as a starting-point, Guillaume's linguistic argument is critically analyzed. It is shown that Guillaume misunderstood Saussure frequently. (PW)

Linguistic Theory

297. Atherton, Margaret, and Robert Schwartz. "Linguistic Innateness and Its Evidence." *JP* 71:155-68.
Every new instance of animal communication, especially those seeming to involve natural language, has been heralded as important evidence disproving the nativist thesis that there are innate factors critically responsible for man's linguistic competence. As an alternative mode of thinking about language, the process whereby humans come to possess language might be thought of as a variation of the imprinting process that is especially associated with birds, making use of important inputs from the environment. Mental structures introduced to solve this inductive problem will bring about the resolution of whether or not animals are capable of fluent English. (LLBA)

345. Frentz, Thomas S. "Toward a Resolution of the Generative Semantics/Classical Theory Controversy:A Psycholinguistic Analysis of Metaphor." *QJS* 60:125-33.
An important issue in contemporary grammatical theory concerns whether the meaning of a sentence is a function of the meanings of the explicit lexical items in the sentence (classical theory) or a function of the meanings of implicit lexical items underlying the sentence (generative semantics). The semantic interpretation of metaphorical sentences provides behavioral data relevant to this linguistic controversy. Three models of metaphor were developed and empirically tested. The results indicated that all models verified the psychological relevance of implicit constituent meanings to metaphorical interpretation, that the procedures used in Models II and III to operationalize implicit lexical items were adequate, but that Models II and III did not clarify the interrelationships among implicit constituent meanings. (TSF)

348. Gamkrelidze, Thomas V. "The Problem of 'l'arbitraire du signé'." *Language* 50:102-10.
In defining a sign of a semiotic system, we must consider not only the vertical relationship between the two components of a sign taken in isolation, but also the twofold horizontal relations existing between the respective components of the interrelated signs. The Saussurean thesis of the arbitrariness of the sign is partial and incomplete in that it specifies only the vertical relations, disregarding the nature of the horizontal ones. If the verbal sign is conceived of as a unity of the vertical and horizontal

relations, the opposed propositions concerning the nature of the relations between the signans and signatum present themselves not as contradictory, but as complementary to each other. (TVG)

354. Gray, Bennison. "Toward a Semi-Revolution in Grammar." *LangS* 29:1-12.
Transformational grammar's complete dependence on the concept of immediate constituent analysis—hierarchical and formal—of its inductivist predecessors precludes its incorporating the basic grammatical principles of parallel structure and restrictive-nonrestrictive modification and therefore of attaining its aim of generating all and only the sentences of the language. Semantic grammar, in *The Grammatical Foundations of Rhetoric* (forthcoming), maps the assertion—its classification, modification, structure, and integration into sentences and larger units of composition—for the purpose of enabling users of the language to increase their skill in generating meaningful discourse. (BG)

355. Gumpel, L. "The Essence of 'Reality' As a Construct of Language." *FLang* 11:167-85.
A detailed analysis of the reality solely contained in linguistic meaning, whose minimal irreducible component becomes posited as the word. Since the word fundamentally resides in the linguistic corpus of semantic differentiation, this sphere becomes separated from that of semantic integration pertaining to (syntactic) expression. Upon closer scrutiny, the word is said to harbor a "wordsound" or semantic threshold aligning sound (or written sign) to sense, a "name" qualifying as a semiotic pointer, and a "linguistic concept" bearing a signitive complex of relevance. The linguistic concept is then differentiated from the concept proper. Further empirical substantiation of the difference is offered by delving into language acquisition of young children. (LLBA)

382. Kohrt, Manfred. " 'Command' and Rightward Movement Rules." *LingB* 30:26-32.
Ross proposed the following putative universal for rightward movement rules in a transformational grammar: In all rules whose structural index is the form ". . . A Y" and whose structural change specifies that A is to be adjoined to the right of Y, A must command Y. The view that this constraint holds for all natural languages is challenged. The discussion of two rightward movement rules in the grammar of German and their respective ordering in the sequence of transformations reveals that at least the German rule of extraposition does not always obey the constraints in question. (LLBA)

387. Krupa, Victor. "O niektorých problémoch skúmania jazyka." *Jazykovedný časopis* 24(1973):124-30.
Marxist linguistics stresses the dialectic unity of content and form as well as the need to investigate both. Form is comprised of substance (i.e., elements) and structure (i.e., relations). Substance consists of distinctive and meaningful elements. The latter are either associative or relational. The word as a nominative unit represents both types of meaning, at least in the inflective languages. The sentence, unlike the word, has communicative value. Speech (i.e., the set of all imaginable sentences) reflects the infinite number of relations between phenomena of objective reality. (LLBA)

393. Lee, Patricia. "Perlocution and Illocution." *WPLUH* 6,iii:115-23.
Certain types of illocutionary acts crucially involve some intended perlocutionary effect. For such acts (among which are commands, suggestions, and requests) it is necessary to distinguish between those perlocutionary effects which are essential to the illocutionary force and those which are accidental. Three main types of tests may distinguish illocutionary from purely perlocutionary effect. The first involves the sort of response appropriate to illocutionary suggestions and requests as opposed to perlocutionary ones. The second is a co-occurence test: certain tags such as *please* and *why don't you* are restricted in their occurrence according to which type of act is involved. Lastly, there is a difference between the way in which the two kinds of acts can be accurately reported. (PL)

404. Lizanec, P.N. "A nyelvföldrajzi aspektus a nyelvek közötti kapcsolatok vizsgálatában." *NK* 75(1973):103-23.
Linguistic geography has its origin in the search for more precise and universal methods for the study of language, particularly dialects. The authenticity of a linguistic atlas depends on three

basic conditions: (1) the compiling of high-quality questionnaires; (2) the methods of collecting and recording data; and (3) the establishment of clear-cut principles of cartography, i.e., the correct plotting of data on the map. The questions compiled in the present questionnaire-list are thematically grouped. The method of data collection for the "Atlas leksicheskikh mad'yarizmov..." was both active and passive. The data collected is plotted on the map with the aid of a three-figured system, corresponding to etymological (genetic) principles. (LLBA)

407. Macura, Vladimír. "Hierarchie hodnocení jazyků u Jungmanna a jeho doby." *SaS* 34(1973):280-87.
An attempt to reveal, on the basis of individual statements about the qualities of different languages in the second generation of the Czech Revival, regularities of the obligatory norm of evaluation. Three hierarchical levels in the Jungmannian model are shown: (1) On the top are the Slavic languages, Old Greek, Latin, and Sanskrit; (2) On the next level are the different Slavic languages—"dialects," individually; and (3) At the bottom are the modern non-Slavic languages. Languages of a lower level are never evaluated as "better" than any language of a higher one. The hierarchy is interpreted from the point of view of its function in the system of culture. (LLBA)

413. Meisel, Jürgen M. "On the Possibility of Non-Cartesian Linguistics." *Linguistics* 122:25-38.
Philosophical considerations and the problem of writing a history of linguistic theories are of crucial importance for linguistics. Chomsky ("Cartesian linguistics") deals with related questions, but rather unsatisfactorily. There is no necessity to call modern linguistics "rationalist." The choice is not so much between rationalism and empiricism as between idealism and materialism. The unfortunate term "innate ideas" seems to indicate that Transformational Grammar is in the line of idealist thought. An epistemology based on dialectic materialism would be much more adequate. The labels "Cartesian" and "rationalist" not only do not provide any significant insights; they furthermore restrict our attention to one aspect of language: its formal conditions as determined by the organization of the human mind. (JMM)

426. Olshshewsky, Thomas M. "On Competence and Performance." *Linguistics* 122:47-62.
The distinction made by Chomsky between competence and performance is discussed in terms of the conceptual difficulties inherent in the employment of such a distinction. One impetus for the employment of the competence/performance categories for psycholinguistics is the possibility of developing a hypothetico-deductive model for linguistics and psycholinguistics. If the theory of language serves as a competence model for the performance of speaking then it will be a device for understanding the nature of the speaking process and a basis for inferring possible speech acts that can be verified through psychological observation. This makes a competence model theoretically much more powerful than other approaches to psycholinguistics. (LLBA)

429. Peng, Fred C.C. "On the Separability of Semantics and Syntax." *LangS* 29:13-19.
The separability of semantics and syntax has been the focus of linguistic discussion for many centuries. Two seemingly opposite stances may be cited: separable and not separable. The latter is further complicated by two diverse opinions: one holds that semantics is subsumed by syntax, whereas, more recently, the other holds that semantics subsumes syntax. Given a set of linguistic utterances, well-formed grammatically, there is more than one way to deal with the semantic and syntactic problems involved. Typical, among others, are compounds such as "paper towel," "butter knife," and "iron curtain," each differing from the others in some significant way, although they are all endocentric constructions. The proponent of any of the above-mentioned viewpoints could well handle the problems involved, semantically and syntactically, but no single approach can claim that it solves those problems to the exclusion of the other approaches. (FCCP)

452. Sologub, A.I. "Lingvogeograficheskie dannye kak istochnik dlya izucheniya istorii yazykovykh yavlenii." *VJa* 23,vi:92-100.
The recent trend to relate dialectology to geography provides valuable new insights into some nagging problems of the history of Russian. Application of linguistic geography helps elucidate several such problems. For this reason, the publication of the new linguo-geographic atlas, now in preparation, is eagerly awaited. (LLBA)

459. Terts, István. "Ferenc Kovács:Linguistic Structures and Linguistic Laws." *ALASH* 22(1972):206-10.
Ferenc Kovács' study is an epistemological-historical survey of the last hundred years of linguistics focusing on the special development of the discipline in Hungary. The main themes are: (1) the autonomy of linguistics; (2) language as a system (structure of the linguistic sign); (3) the nature and structure of meaning; (4) the relation between content (meaning) and linguistic form; (5) essential features of linguistic laws. The survey is undoubtedly an important contribution to the discipline of the "theory and history of science" because of its wide horizons and its Marxist methodology. Its purpose is also to make clear the status of linguistics in Hungary. The author is more objective and just in dealing with the past than in dealing with the present. (LLBA)

474. Wilks, Yorick. "One Small Head—Models and Theories in Linguistics." *FLang* 11:77-95.
The notion of model is used in linguistics in such a way that there is no single clear answer to the question "what is a linguistic theory a theory of?" A number of obvious answers to the question are examined, demonstrating that none of them is wholly satisfactory. The reason in each case is that in order to be a model, *something* must be modeled, in the sense of admitting of a point-by-point correspondence between items of the model and of the entity modeled. The only entities which will serve in the required position are algorithms for the production and analysis of natural language. One consequence of accepting this would be to admit computational linguistics to a place nearer to the center of linguistics than it presently occupies. (LLBA)

479. Zwicky, Arnold M. "Homing In:On Arguing for Remote Representations." *JL* 10:55-69.
In linguistic "homing in," facts are seen as a kind of puzzle, and the analyst is to determine remote entities by solving for an answer in some way. Some argumentation is examined, using "homing in" from Chomsky and Halle's *The Sound Pattern of English* (the analysis of surface diphthong [ɔj]), and it is concluded that its structure is impeccable, even though it results in an indefensible analysis. This case is contrasted with a structurally similar one from Sanskrit. (LLBA)

480. —— "Taking a False Step." *Language* 50:215-24.
A special abstractness problem in generative grammar—that of intermediate derivational stages containing elements or sequences that are not well-formed as surface representations—is examined. Suspicious analyses employing such false steps are cited from the phonological and syntactic literature. False steps cannot be ruled out in general, because there is support for many false-step analyses, in both syntax and phonology; a Welsh morphophonemic case is treated in some detail. (AMZ)

Professional Topics

General and Miscellaneous. 499. Englefield, Ronald. "Linguistics:Science or Pseudo-science?" *Trivium* 9:1-18.
The popularity of Chomsky's theories is largely due to two erroneous assumptions: that since language obviously did not evolve, its fundamentals must be innate and not invented; and that such a theory is the only rational alternative to behaviorism. Chomsky makes an absolute distinction between human language and any form of animal communication. He thereby exaggerates the importance of language in human thinking and at the same time underestimates the capacity of the higher mammals to think effectively without words. Such premises have led to detailed studies of the minutiae of grammar and speech forms which amount to little more than expressing insignificant facts in forbidding terminology. (CL)

513. Hartmann, Peter. "Bedingungen sprachlicher Kommunikation im Fremdsprachenunterricht." *NsM* 27:144-63.
The communication base, viz. the elementary role of language, gives a permanent substratum for all other modes of using

language (cognitive, volitive, actional, informative) and is regularly internationalized by learning of the primary language. The conditions of communicative values should be explored in a reliable heuristic manner because the teaching of a second language is based upon it. Rank of the language learned, differences in type and (un-)restricted value, and the way of teaching are relevant points of view. (PH)

529. Lévery, F. "Les problèmes poses par le vocabulaire documentaire et l'organisation des dictionnaires et thésaurus." *TAI* 1(1972):1-8.
The creation of documentary card files assumes that the information contained in a text can be characterized using a certain number of signs. The body of signs used or available for use constitutes a documentary vocabulary with two purposes: (1) the characterization of texts (analysis of contents); and (2) the expression of documentary research. These two functions require a documentary vocabulary which is extensive and structured. Structured documentary dictionaries or thesauri seem the indispensible liaison between the authors and questioners. Practical methods for producing such thesauri are described. (LLBA)

540. Ondruš, Šimon. "Stav a úlohy slovanskej a indoeurópskej historickoporovnávacej jazykovedy v ČSSR." *SaS* 34(1973):298-301.
Soviet linguistic-political discussion in 1950 brought about a regeneration of historical-comparative linguistics, not only in the Soviet Union but also in Czechoslovakia. The following are important for the enrichment of Marxist-historical linguistic research: (1) more intensive concentration on the linguistics of socialist countries; (2) preparation of a scientific conference on the origin of the Czech and Slovak languages from the point of view of historical materialism; (3) study and review of etymological research on the Slavic vocabulary from the point of view of the newer Indo-European theory and the relationship of Slavic vocabulary to that of neighboring peoples; and (4) preparation for the development of synchronic comparative dictionaries and grammars of the Czech and Slovak languages in comparison to the other Slavic and non-Slavic languages. (LLBA)

569. Walsh, Gordon. "Another Note on RP Notation." *IPAJ* 4:31-36.
Transcriptions of RP used for TEFL purposes should represent both qualitative and quantitative distinctions. The simplified notations sometimes used, as well as the original system used in the *English Pronouncing Dictionary*, are misleading in suggesting that the difference between "bead" and "bid" is principally one of vowel length. Notations that rely solely on typographically different letters to distinguish the RP monophthongs are misleading in their implication that quality is the only important

distinguishing feature. It is helpful if both features are suggested, by using different letters for all monophthongs and retaining the length mark for the long vowels. This also reflects the phonetic facts. Further, such a notation is as compatible as is possible with the *EPD* system. (NGW)

Terminology. 601. Hoffmann, Dietrich. "Sprachimmanente Methodenorientierung—Sprachtranszendente 'Objektorientierung':Zum heutigen Unterschied zwischen Linguistik und Philologie." *ZDL* 40(1973):295-310.
A discussion of the distinction between philology and linguistics and the proper goals of each discipline. Modern linguistics is preoccupied with unity and purity in methodology; it considers language an autonomous phenomenon and attempts to exclude non-linguistic facts from its inquiry. Philology deals with old texts and examples of language which would be incomprehensible without consideration of the non-linguistic context; it cannot afford to be as concerned with methodological purity and must have the freedom to use any method that might further understanding. While philology may make use of modern linguistic methods in the solution of textual problems, this use will be restricted by the fact that these methods take little account of the non-linguistic aspects of the text. (LLBA)

602. Sayward, Charles. "The Received Distinction Between Pragmatics, Semantics and Syntax." *FLang* 11:97-104.
The distinction between pragmatics, semantics, and syntax has been traditionally formulated in terms of three factors: expressions, designata of expressions, and speakers. Concentrating on Carnap's *Introduction to Semantics* as an example, the distinction has various defects. Carnap's original statement only defines the conditions under which investigations are pragmatic, semantic, or syntactic. Yet the most cursory review of the literature using the distinction reveals an uncritical application of the three terms to all sorts of things besides investigations. The definition, as it applies to investigations, is also criticized. (LLBA)

605. Wuster, Eugen. "Die allgemeine Terminologielehre—Ein Grenzgebiet zwischen Sprachwissenschaft, Logik, Ontologie, Informatik und den Sachwissenschaften." *Linguistics* 119:60-106.
The science of terminology differs from linguistics devoted to common language in its particular approaches to the state and development of language. Exact correspondence between term and meaning and clear structure of concept systems have priority over the form of terms, vocabulary over grammar, and synchronic analysis over historic analysis. Linguistic development in terminology is determined by conscious shaping of the language system, by international unification, and by priority of the written form over the spoken form. These particularities are reflected in the layout of the basic technical glossaries and vocabularies. (EW)

II. MATHEMATICAL AND COMPUTATIONAL LINGUISTICS

Mathematical Models in Linguistics

608. Bánczerowski, Janusz. "A nyelvi modell és a nyelvi kommunikáció néhány kérdése." *NK* 75(1973):232-46.
The model of linguistic communication (MLC) generally presupposes the existence of a sender, a receiver, a channel, and a message. Linguistic communication (LC) is closely related to data processing. The general grammar that models the process of LC must consist of subgrammars that model the specific steps of this process. Analysis of the data row (DR) (the message) from the point of view of the quantity and quality of data can lead to a more complete understanding of the functioning of a natural language. The linguistic message forms an integral part of the system of linguistic communication; it must be analyzed strictly within the bounds of this system. (LLBA)

613. Brodda, Benny. "Some Classes of Solvable Categorial Expressions." *SML* 9(1973):5-41.
It is well known that all context-free (CF) languages are decidable. Given a grammar G and an arbitrary string, it is usually impossible to "see" immediately whether the string belongs to the language L(G) defined by the grammar. The grammar usually has to be "run" backwards to its initial symbol

S. A very restricted family of CF languages—closely related to the languages defined by so-called Categorial Grammars—is examined. It is possible to establish general criteria to determine the grammaticalness of a string according to the given grammar, these criteria not being of the type "run the grammar backwards." (LLBA)

614. Chumbley, Robert. "On Model Building On Model Building On Model Building." *Diacritics* 4,iii:15-19. [Rev. art.]
Anthony Wilden's *System and Structure* provides a point of departure for a discussion of model-building in the context of semiotics. In order to erect a proper model, there must be homology between structures, not just similarity between elements or relations of structures. Such a distinction is essential when the doors are opened to transdisciplinary work such as that of Wilden. If careful mapping by homology is not followed, the path of analogy can lead to confusion or even incongruity. In order to avoid these pitfalls, C.S. Peirce's semiotic model which affords the possibility of reference is preferred to Saussurian signification. The general problem of the nature and use of signs subtends an analysis of Wilden's efforts to integrate concepts from various disciplines. (REC)

616. Čulík, K. "Basic Problems in the Mathematical Theory

of Languages." *Linguistics* 118(1973):5-42.

A comparative study of natural languages and artificial programming languages leads to the initial question: What must be stated in order to determine a language fully? A programming language theory and its models are introduced by which a rather simplified description is given of the relations between "machine independent" programming languages and their applications to particular computers. The subject is discussed in three sections: (1) determination of a language; (2) language theories and models; and (3) schemes and grammars. (LLBA)

628. Heller, Bruno. "Formale Sprachen:Ein Thema zwischen Mathematik und Linguistik." *LuD* 4(1973):303-12.

An overview of the relationships of formal languages to the algorithmic concept and computer science is presented. The discussion proceeds from the aspect of calculability. In the process, algorithms are considered as formulas for the alternation of symbol chains. The calculations which thereby arise establish the field of formal languages, which are analyzed according to their development. This leads to Chomsky's structural grammar; these formulas are used in examples of natural as well as algebraic language. (LLBA)

635. Lowe, Ivan. "An Algebraic Theory of Pronominal Reference." *Semiotica* 10:43-74, 233-54.

A continuation of a group-theoretical treatment of English pronominal reference for a limited case. This theory is extended to give an algebraic description of the derivation of plurals from singulars by regrouping processes which take place during the course of events in a discourse. A canonical form for the group index of an interaction between two participant sets, one of which has more than one participant, is reached. This complex group index contains information in condensed form on the derivational history of the plural and on the cast permutation involved and allows the enumeration of plurals exhaustively and systematically. Three types of pluralization are distinguished: object pluralization, subject pluralization, and reciprocalization.

In the third part of this study, attention is concentrated on two different types of situation where the unexpected often arises, interpositions and detours. An interposition is a speech act immediately following another in which a bystander of the first speech becomes the speaker of the second speech act and addresses out of turn the first speaker. A detour is a speech act in which a participant chooses a long way around in a conversation. To arrive at a meaningful account of these conversations, social and contextual factors are considered; these situations are analyzed using concepts previously developed. (LLBA)

642. Panevová, Jarmila. "Ještě k užltí teorie grafù v lingvistice." *SaS* 34(1973):335-38.

A survey of the use of dependency graphs in linguistics. Some works attempting to use the mathematical theory of graphs in solutions of linguistic problems are commented upon. The works of the Prague group of algebraic linguists on functional generative description are analyzed in this context, one of the main features of this approach being the use of rooted tree diagrams in the description of sentence structure. (LLBA)

658. Znojil, Jiří. "On Some Properties of Trees with Ordered Vertices." *PBML* 20(1973):59-70.

A study of a rooted tree, the vertex set of which is ordered. Concepts which can be defined are defined only on a set which has both binary operations of taking the maximal and taking the minimal element on the arc connecting two vertices and similar concepts derived from them. Some properties of these concepts are derived, and the properties relevant to them are found. (LLBA)

Statistical Studies of Language

General and Miscellaneous. 661. Cedergren, Henrietta J., and David Sankoff. "Variable Rules:Performance as a Statistical Reflection of Competence." *Language* 50:333-55.

Speech performances are considered as statistical samples drawn from a probabilistic language competence. This competence is modeled in conventional generative terms, except that optional rules are assigned application probabilities as functions of the structure of the input strings, possibly depending on the extralinguistic environment as well. We develop the mathematical background for these variable rules and apply the theory and methodology to examples from Spanish, French, and English. The data consist of relative frequencies of rule application for different types of input string, and they provide a check on the frequencies predicted by variable rules. The various features in rule structural descriptions tend to act independently, in the statistical sense, on rule probabilities. (HJC & DS)

668. Szanser, Adam J. "A Study of the Paragraph Structure." *SML* 9(1973):79-90.

The results of an investigation carried out at the National Physical Laboratory in 1972-73 on the linguistic structure of the paragraph in scientific English. The goal of the investigation was to discover any regularities in the construction of paragraphs in the language register mentioned above. The average number of semantic units was established for a paragraph, and an attempt was made to determine its possible relationship to the number of "levels" in the human span of short-term memory. Experiments were conducted on the automatic division of a continuous text into paragraphs based on the formalizations obtained. Results confirm the relationship between the average number of semantic units and levels in human short-term memory; they indicate that a continuous scientific text can be automatically subdivided into paragraphs with acceptable results. (LLBA)

669. Van der Biest, A. "Essai de synthèse mathématique de certains textes littéraires." *RLV* 39(1973):284-63.

A report of both the methods and results of an original attempt to induce students specializing in mathematics to translate literary texts, the analysis of which had already been made with the teacher into a symbol system that they were familiar with. The texts included poems as well as prose. In addition to the pupil's ability to create and adapt symbols, the experiment proved that the great concepts of poststructural linguistics and "text theory" can be assimilated and rediscovered by young students very easily. (LLBA)

Mechanolinguistics

Automated Analysis. 717. Haroche, C., and M. Pêcheux. "Manuel pour l'utilisation de la méthode d'analyse automatique du discours (A.A.D.)." *TAI* 1(1972):13-55.

Describes a procedure of text analysis intended to avoid both the stumbling blocks of frequency treatments and the arbitrary interpretations of "qualitative" analyses. The basic hypothesis rests on the idea that semantics cannot be confined exclusively to the domain of linguistics, but that it is essentially discursive and historical. The result is that all recourse to a system of key words, an a priori dictionary, etc., is done away with; the object instead is to produce (using an algorithm presently realized on computer) the families of paraphrases inherent to a collection of texts submitted to analysis. (LLBA)

III. INFORMATION AND COMMUNICATION THEORY

784. Hopster, Norbert. "Sachtext—Text—Kommunikation." *LuD* 4(1973):249-64.

The traditionally applied concepts of "description," "discussion," "report," etc., are linguistically based on the concept of "special text." In the trivial introduction of subject and object as

alternatives, the origins are pointed out of the basic error in German didactics of assigning "technical" relevance to specific text types and not to others ("poetic"), which are seen as a possibility for the construction of their own "reality." (LLBA)

817. Slagle, Uhlan V. "The Relationship of the Structure of

Meaning to the Structure of Experienced Reality." *Linguistics* 138:81-95.

The brilliant experimental work of the Gestalt psychologists may well provide the key to understanding the nature of thought and its relationship to the structure of experienced reality. By examining their experimental findings in the light of certain relevant Kantian insights, one can show that concepts are "rules"

of categorization and that these "rules" are based on the functioning of similarity and contiguity as principles underlying spontaneous unification in sensory fields. Certainly, the linguistic evidence which led to the localist theory of case provides powerful support for such a theory. Moreover, one can easily show that recent split-brain research does not invalidate this approach. (UVS)

IV. STYLISTICS

General

832. Bailey, Richard W., et al. "Annual Bibliography for 1972." *Style* 8,supp.:155-207.
A listing of more than 400 books and articles concerned with stylistics, each item provided with a brief, amplifying annotation. The material is arranged topically under seven headings. (RWB)

836. Blankenship, Jane. "The Influence of Mode, Sub-Mode, and Speaker Predilection on Style." *SM* 41:85-118.
With four basic assumptions about the nature of style as orientation, Blankenship focuses on six subjects across two general modes and six sub-modes of discourse. After discussing "style markers," a "stylistic profile" of the subjects is sketched including not only these style markers but editing behaviors as well. Although subjects appear to have been influenced by modal and sub-modal dimensions of style, individual predilections appear also to have been heavily influenced by factors relating to "epistemic stance." (JB)

838. Brockriede, Wayne. "Rhetorical Criticism as Argument." *QJS* 60:165-74.
Rhetorical criticism is more useful when critics argue than when they do not. The critic must state the criteria he has used in arriving at his judgment with the philosophical or theoretical foundations on which they rest. Analytic criticism fails to argue unless the critic accounts for how some aspect of the rhetorical experience worked by relating it to a concept more general than itself. The critic who argues invites confrontation that tests the intersubjective reliability of the argument and hence contributes toward a better understanding of rhetorical experiences or of rhetoric. (WB)

840. Carson, Julie. "Proper Stylistics." *Style* 8:290-304.
Linguistic Stylistics in America developed primarily out of the research of three men: Archibald Hill, Samuel Levin, and Richard Ohmann. Though the three worked within different schools of linguistics, structuralism and generative theory, they shared a general procedural framework for the linguistic analysis of literature: the description and analysis of linguistic structures, identification of a pattern those structures effect, and suggestion of the significance of that pattern for critical interpretation. Their work was not altogether successful; that is to say, at times either their linguistics or their criticism was misguided. But they did provide guidelines for further research in the field, and did emphasize the need for other linguist-analysts to pay close attention to consistency, objectivity, and accuracy when applying linguistic analysis to literary texts. (JC)

843. D'Angelo, Frank D. "Style as Structure." *Style* 8:322-63.
Style is more than a string of isolated stylistic features that can be easily identified and classified on the sentence level. Style is the totality of an extended discourse. The complex interrelationships that exist between style and structure can best be demonstrated by a holistic approach to the study of style, using a methodology that is unified and contextual, one that derives from studies in linguistics and rhetorical analysis. (FJD'A)

844. de Pater, Wim A. "Erschliessungssituationen und religiöse Sprache." *LBib* 33:64-88.
Discusses the relation between disclosure situations and religious language. Religious language is situated in cosmic situations or disclosures. The disclosure gives to religious language its objectivity and its reference, the speaking in models makes it possible to give articulation to the experience which was revealed in the disclosure. (WAdP)

846. Delany, Sheila. "Political Style/Political Stylistics." *Style*

8:437-51.
The relation between politics and style is not necessarily a predictable one. Style is amenable to political analysis, political discourse is amenable to stylistic analysis. One can analyze the style of many communist writers as an expression of their commitment to dialectical process, to revolutionary change, and to the unity of theory and practice. (SD)

849. Gregory, Michael. "A Theory for Stylistics—Exemplified: Donne's 'Holy Sonnet XIV'." *Lang&S* 7:108-18.
Stylistics can be seen as an activity we pursue when we focus attention on the language of a text in terms of its internal and external patterns. This needs a model of linguistics which not only accounts for patterning at the levels of grammar, lexis, phonology/graphology, but also has a contextual level to handle the situational aspect of language events. With such a model, stylistics becomes fully interpretive. Donne's "Holy Sonnet 14" is analyzed by means of this model. (MJG)

856. Kintgen, Eugene R. "Is Transformational Stylistics Useful?" *CE* 35:799-824.
One can question the usefulness of transformational grammar in stylistic studies on both practical and theoretical grounds. The practical difficulties are: (1) the theory will be misapplied in a number of ways; (2) changes in the theory itself will to some extent invalidate the conclusions based on earlier formations. On theoretical grounds transformational grammar can only be useful when the object of study is not merely the text itself, but the competence of the author or the reader. Future advances in semantic theory and psycholinguistics might make transformational grammar a useful tool for stylistic analysis, but until then, the twin dangers that its descriptions will reveal more about theory than the text, and that the unwary will accept even those descriptions as explanations, overshadow whatever utility it might have. (ERK)

861. Michiels, Archibald. "A propos du concept d'ambigu-ïté." *RLV* 40:633-49.
Calls attention to recent studies of "inference" and "isotopie," insofar as these attempt to account for essential mechanisms by which information is built up in texts, highlight the relevance of cultural assumptions in the semantic description of discourse, and thus help to bridge the gap between two ways of looking at ambiguity. The first is illustrated in the main trends of present-day linguistics in which ambiguity is made use of as an adequacy test in the recognition of different levels of grammatical analysis. The second is to be found in literary theory, which looks at ambiguity as a privileged device of fantastic literature and studies its mechanisms at text-level, but in a much looser frame than that of linguistics. (AM)

863. Nevo, Ruth. "'Esso Keeps Your World Happening': A Test Case for Metaphor." *HUSL* 2:1-29.
Theories of metaphor tend to stress either the object-comparison theories or the verbal-opposition theories and have encountered difficulties in their explanations of the difference between noun and verb metaphors, the relationship between metaphor and simile on the one hand, and between metaphor and metonymy on the other, and the puzzling co-presence of the concrete and the abstract in metaphor. Metaphor is a special process of analysis and synthesis requiring two coordinates—an axis of classification violation and an axis of cross-comparison—in order to forge the new identity we call a metaphor. Four elements whereby a metaphor is rendered intelligible are distinguished. (RN)

871. Sastri, M.I. "Deviance and Poetic Style." *LangS* 31:11-12.

Poetry is effectively distinguished from casual language in terms of its deviation from the norm. Linguistic deviance in poetry is but a function of the thought process that goes into the poem. The clue to poetic style therefore resides in the poet's unusual way of looking at things. The notion of deviance in thought might help bridge the gap between linguistic stylistics and literary criticism in their approaches to the explication of poetry. (MIS)

872. Saukkonen, Pauli. "Stylistics, Grammar, Vocabulary." *Linguistics* 108(1973):68-77.
In the descriptive representation of a language, phenomena must be defined qualitatively, quantitatively, and combinatorily. Each of the three properties has been dealt with in linguistic research, but the operational field has become fragmented so that grammar and vocabulary account for the qualitative and combinatory characteristics, and peripheral stylistics for the quantitative properties. If we move the aggregate or quantitative properties into grammar and vocabulary, a separate stylistics is rendered quite unnecessary. Grammars and vocabularies must then be contextually defined. Micro-languages are shaped by a communication context, which depends on four factors: sender, receiver, channel, and message. Linguistic competence involves a knowledge of quantitative properties, usually frequency probabilities. When competence is transferred into a concrete grammar and vocabulary, the approximate quantitative probability value (P) of a qualitative category (K) is the empirical relative frequency calculated from a representative sample. The formula for a grammar (G) or vocabulary (V) corresponding to a certain context (c) is: $G_c/V_c = \{P(K_1), P(K_2), P(K_3), \ldots P(K_i)\}$. G_c and V_c can be considered a micro-grammar and a micro-vocabulary. (PS)

874. Seaman, John. "The Style of Political Discourse: An Annotated Bibliography." *Style* 8:477-528.
A selective bibliography devoted to the style of discourse with political intentions or implications. Organized in six categories: (1) language and culture, (2) literary and non-literary documents, (3) rhetoric and public address, (4) semiotics and metaphor, (5) semantics and content analysis, and (6) miscellaneous. (JS)

876. Shopen, Tim. "Some Contributions from Grammar to the Theory of Style." *CE* 35:775-98. [Incl. bibliog.]
Claims about the grammatical structure of language are significant for style because they say what grammmatical structures are available to speakers and writers for putting their ideas into linguistic form. Elliptical utterances such as "The airport!" and "Don't forget!" provide examples. The grammatical choices involved are typically just the ones for the words pronounced. The mind is free to move along parameters of structure other than language for the rest of the concept being transmitted. The choice to ellipse or not to ellipse is not just a matter of surface grammatical form, but also an important stylistic decision affecting the extent to which thought submits to being channeled into the conventional categories of language. (TAS)

Linguistics-&-Literature

885. Antoine, Gérald. "La nouvelle critique: How Far Has It Got?" *Style* 8:18-33.
After a brief history of the French "Nouvelle Critique" school, the problematics of criticism are examined under four major questions: (1) critical method and objectivity; (2) criticism, the science of literature vs. a "literature about literature"; (3) thematic criticism vs. stylistic criticism; and (4) stylistic criticism vs. poetic criticism. Tentative classification of the movement is suggested and proposals are offered. (LLBA)

887. Bamberg, Michael "Generativismus-Logischer Empirismus-Strukturalismus." *LBib* 33:34-63.
"Generative Poetics" suffers from the problems of logical empirism constituent in the linguistic concept of generative-transformational grammar made explicit by Chomsky. This linguistic concept is the fundament also of "Generative Poetics" which has never made explicit its theoretical rules. "Generative Poetics" implies therefore some theoretical conflicts which can be solved only by means of the principles of "Dialectical Materialism." (MB)

891. Bivens, William P., III. "Noun Phrase Case Schemes in the Deep Structure of Poems." *Style* 8:305-21.
Using an analytical model based on Charles Fillmore's case grammar—an analysis of the deep structure of English sentences in terms of the roles noun phrases play in the action or state denoted by the verb—deep structure schemes may be made available for examination and shown to subtly re-enforce both the meaning and the artistic features in poems. (WPB,III)

909. Guttgemanns, Erhardt. "Die synoptische Frage im Licht der modernen Sprach- und Literaturwissenschaft." *LBib* 29/30(1973):2-40.
Analysis of the contributions of leading authorities to the four traditional solutions of the synoptic problem. All four solutions involve specific linguistic aspects which serve as hints for a modern linguistic solution. The solutions of Schleiermacher and Wilke are full of text grammatical details and theoretical reflections which are omitted in the isagogic tradition. A modern linguistic solution of the synoptic problem can only be a generative transformational text grammar which integrates a grammar of narratives. (LLBA)

914. Hamon, Philippe. "Narrative Semiotics in France." *Style* 8:34-45.
The situation of narrative semiotics in France is described and a bibliography as complete and as detailed as possible is set up. Narrative semiotics developed in the 1960s against the conceptual domination and the loose concepts of literary history and traditional critics, first under the influence of structural linguistics, then under the influence of semiotics liberated from the linguistic model. The main theoretical efforts in this field are those of Greimas, Barthes, Brémond, Todorov, Genette, Coquet, and Rastier. (LLBA)

924. Kress-Rosen, Nicole. "The Analysis of the Speech Event in Stylistic Study." *Style* 8:46-55.
The theory of the speech event uses some concepts that are by certain of their aspects integrated into transformational linguistics. Its applications heretofore have been practically limited to the fields of historical and political texts, toward making evident an implicit discourse, which may be the ideological one. From this point of view, the field of literary texts has been neglected, leading to the need to study how stylistics may be interested in applying this new linguistic theory. It appears that some literary texts, especially those in the first person, which have been studied by the concepts of classical psychology, may be analyzed with success from the original point of view of the speech event. (LLBA)

930. Levenston, E.A. "A Scheme for the Inter-Relation of Linguistic Analysis and Poetry Criticism." *Linguistics* 129:29-47.
Critics of poetry interested in applying the insights of linguistic analysis to the study of literature should be eclectic in their exploitation of linguistic theory and descriptive techniques. The traditional tripartite view of language—phonology plus grammar plus semantics—is too vague to provide an overall framework for the study of poetry. Any statement about the language of a poem belongs in one of nine cells in a grid, three by three, containing the phonological (grammatical, semantic) aspects of the phonology (grammar, semantics). In addition to providing straightforward descriptive statements at each level, such an approach stimulates the critic into seeking interrelationships between the levels which might otherwise go unnoticed. (EAL)

945. Pryse, Marjorie. " 'The Stonecarver's Poem'—A Linguistic Interpretation." *Lang&S* 7:62-71.
Denise Levertov's "The Stonecarver's Poem" is ambiguous at the level of surface structure. Charles Fillmore's model of case grammar provides a theoretical basis for analyzing two possible reconstructions of the surface structure and choosing one as the only grammatically possible reconstruction. The transformational history includes John R. Ross's transformation "Gapping," which reveals a syntactic basis for an interpretive metaphoric ration between parallel elements in the poem. There are two instances where a fully grammatical surface structure would require anaphoric *the*-deictic modifiers. Analyzing their omission indicates that the first line of the poem, "Hand of man," without *the*-deictics, may be interpreted as either "hand of Man" (universal man) or "(the) hand of (the) man" (the stonecarver's hand). Fillmore's case theory again provides the framework for

revealing the process of creation as the interpretive semantic root of the two verbs implicit in the title, "carve" and "write," thus adding a third set of elements to the metaphoric ratio which models the interpretation of the poem—poet : poem :: stone-carver : stone violet :: god : Adam. (MP)

948. Ross, Robert N. "Conceptual Network Analysis." *Semiotica* 10:1-18.
A method for systematically investigating part-whole relations in literature is described which would permit the framing of verifiable hypotheses about literary phenomena. This method differs from methods of content analysis in two important respects: (1) It is based on new ideas of structure developed by linguists; and (2) It is designed specifically for the analysis of complex texts. One important feature is that it permits the analysis of how the elements of content are connected within a text. The proposed method is illustrated with an analysis of a poem. (LLBA)

958. Tsur, Reuven. "Poem, Prayer and Meditation:An Exercise in Literary Semantics." *Style* 8:404-24.
The three possible uses of one message may be related to it via Jakobson's model of linguistic functions. In a poem, the poetic (message-oriented) function is dominant; in a prayer, the conative (addressee-oriented) function; in a meditation, the emotive (addresser-oriented) function (in each of them, several functions serve in a hierarchy). The three uses relate to one another like three deep structures of one surface structure. The different hierarchies have significant logical and psychological corollaries. (RT)

963. Wright, George T. "The Lyric Present:Simple Present Verbs in English Poems." *PMLA* 89:563-79.
Poets writing in English frequently use the simple present form of action verbs where the progressive form would be more natural in speech. They do so in order to take advantage of overtones resident in the simple form, overtones that permit a physical action to seem timeless yet permanent, pastlike yet edging toward the future, repeatable yet provisional, urgent yet distant, ceremonious and archaic. The action verb cast in the lyric present serves every epoch of English literary history differently but is always expressive of the poets' deepest perceptions and fears. (GTW)

V. PSYCHOLINGUISTICS

General

968. Anderson, Norman H., and Lola L. Lopes. "Some Psycholinguistic Aspects of Person Perception." *M&C* 2:67-74.
A study of adjective-noun combinations in person perception analyzed from an integration-theoretical view, with special reference to judgments of likableness, occupational proficiency, and social value. Different theoretical considerations apply to these three judgment dimensions, but all can be conceptualized in terms of the valuation and integration operations of integration theory. Experimental support for this conceptual analysis is given for likableness and occupational proficiency. Advantages of the integration-theoretical analysis over congruity formulations are pointed out. (LLBA)

989. Bruter, C.P. "Quelques aspects de la percepto-linguistique." *TAI* 2(1972):16-19.
An analogy is drawn between the biological phenomena of growth and development and those of mental growth, specifically in terms of language and perception. The basic rule is that the evolutionary stages of an individual's language recapitulate the evolutionary stages of his lineage. Each biological individual has an embryology, as does each mental individual. Language evolves and becomes more refined in the same way as an embryo differentiates. A justification is given for the use of the term "perceptuo." Since our evolution leads us to perceive our environment with greater refinement, it is natural that language should follow the same evolution. (LLBA)

999. Cordonnier-Vermes, Geneviève. "Evolution des théories de traitement du comportement de langage:Niveau(x) et unité(s) d'analyse." *L'Année psychologique* 73(1973):587-610.
Presents a frame of reference of the extent of research concerning language in psychology. An extremely economical explicative schema is discovered on the basis of the behaviorist principle of the prevalence of experience—one single process can account for the mechanism of predication and reference. The rule is based on the recognition of a single unit, the lexical unit, and of a single level of organization. Predication is reduced to a transition of significations, these being understood as exclusively referential. This definition of discourse as a sequence of association and of speech as the product of single habits has been sophisticated by a cut between mode of learning and mode of functioning. Learning of lexical transitions is basic to the secondary determination of functionally characterized equivalence classes; these categories are new units corresponding to another level of analysis and functioning, syntagmatic grammar. (LLBA)

1000. Criado de Val, Manual. "Transcripciones coloquiales." *Yelmo* 15:5-11.
A report of the first in a series of conversations recorded and transcribed by teams of students from the School of Linguistics Research of OFINES. Two degrees of "authenticity" are distinguished: (1) those conversations in which the participants are unaware of being recorded and converse freely among themselves; and (2) those in which the participants, while still unaware of being recorded, are provoked into discussing certain themes by an investigator. The settings for the conversations included public places, sports arenas, student residences, private homes, public vehicles, and places of business. Telephone conversations were also used. The transcriptions were of two types: (1) those suitable for detailed phonetic study; and (2) those oriented more toward lexical, morphological, or syntactic problems. (LLBA)

1006. Ervin-Tripp, Susan M. "Is Second Language Learning Like the First." *TESOLQ* 8:111-27.
Evidence has been collected about the order and process of mother tongue acquisition. This study compares these findings to second language acquisition in a natural milieu in which communication is the learner's focus of attention, and where the language is heard most of the day. In many respects the development of comprehension of syntax and of morphological features follows the order in the mother tongue studied. Older children learned much faster than younger children for the sample in the range of 4-9. (SME)

1021. Grieve, Robert. "Definiteness in Discourse." *L&S* 16(1973):365-72.
A recent study attempted to relate definiteness to topicalization. In an utterance with two nominals, there is a tendency to distinguish the nominals in the topic from the nominal in the comment by marking the former with *the* and the latter with *a*, for in discourse the speaker must presuppose of his listener knowledge of topic (the + noun), and ignorance of comment (a + noun). However, since this clearly assumes that use of *the* is related to knowledge, and *a* to lack of knowledge, the present study attempts to test these assumptions. The results of two experiments support the hypotheses. (RG)

1033. Ingarden, Roman. "Psychologism and Psychology in Literary Scholarship." *NLH* 5:213-23. [Tr. John Fizer.]
A critique of the use of psychology and psychologism in literary scholarship is made. A distinction is made between the science of psychology and psychologism, where this science transcends its own field. Psychologism is a point of view where epistemological, critical, and esthetic investigations are psychologically oriented. In literary scholarship, the following can be investigated from a psychological point of view: (1) the relationship between literary creation process and psychology; (2) relations between the author's psychology and the literary work; (3) reader reactions; and (4) a work's content. A totally psychological approach is limiting and often misleading. (LLBA)

1046. Leone, Shirley. "Associational-Metaphorical Activity: Another View of Language and Mind." *AA* 75(1973):1276-81.
An analysis and extension of Sapir's idea that language embodies intertwined and isolable patterns of two distinct orders—patterns

of reference (communication) and patterns of expression (associational-metaphorical activity). From the standpoint that language is a continuum of usages ranging from schizophrenic usage, at one extreme, to objective, representational usage at the other, associational-metaphorical activity is seen as variously operative throughout. Illustrations of how this dimension is woven into normal communication are presented. There is speculation on the source of associational-metaphorical activity and the light it throws on human mentality as projected in language. (LLBA)

1068. Panasyuk, Aleksei T. "K voprosu ob ekspressii kak lingvisticheskoi kategorii." *VMU* 28,vi(1973):29-38.
The term "expression" on the linguistic level is characterized by: (1) the indistinctness of expressive means in speech and language; and (2) the identification of stylistic and expressive meaning. Linguistic expression should be considered a semantic phenomenon. The object of analysis is the expressive component in the semantic structure of words whose subject is the spontaneous, emotional, and volitional impulses of humanity. The problem is complicated by the fact that these impulses can be expressed not only through linguistic means, but also through non-linguistic ones. (LLBA)

1073. Průcha, Jan. "Pokroky v sovětské psycholingvistice." *Jazykovedný časopis* 24(1973):189-95.
A review of the most important results of Soviet psycholinguistics from 1971 to 1972. Most important for contemporary Soviet psycholinguistics are: (1) a new orientation that leads to a joining of the theory of speech activity with sociolinguistics and social psychology (psychosociology of speech); and (2) a growing interest in applied investigations, especially in the areas of foreign language teaching and mass communications. (LLBA)

1082. Rosa, Alfred F. "The Psycholinguistics of Updike's 'Museums and Women'." *MFS* 20:107-11.
In "Museums and Women" John Updike uses an interesting technical device, sound or phonetic symbolism, as the basis for the theme of his story. Updike suggests that "museums" and "women" as words are naturally paired because the letters "m" and "w" are related in various ways; they are physically reflective of each other, parts of a greater whole as are *m*an and *w*oman, and are resonant consonants making the words in which they appear "hum." By pointing out the relationship between the words, he has also emotionally surcharged them for his readers. Updike sees the relationship of the words and what they symbolize as providential. This is a perceptual mode that is American, derived from his reading of Barth, and a part of his family heritage. (AFR)

1085. Schwenk, Mary Ann, and Joseph H. Danks. "A Developmental Study of the Pragmatic Communication Rule for Prenominal Adjective Ordering." *M&C* 2:149-52.
First-, fourth-, and eighth-grade children and college undergraduates indicated preference for either normal or inverted orders of prenominal adjectives to describe a pictorial referent. Preference for the normal order of adjectives first appeared with the fourth graders. When communication context was varied by presenting a nonreferent that required a color adjective for discrimination from the referent, college students increased their preference for the inverted order. (LLBA)

1092. Steer, Angela B. "Sex Differences, Extraversion and Neuroticism in Relation to Speech Rate During the Expression of Emotion." *L&S* 17:80-86.
Examines the relation between extraversion, neuroticism, and sex of subject and speech rate changes when subjects express anger and pleasure while counting aloud. 48 male and female subjects completed the Eysenck Personality Inventory and then performed the counting task after practice. Analysis indicated that although there were no significant effects for extraversion and neuroticism, male subjects showed a significantly lower rate of change than did females when expressing anger. (ABS)

1095. Sullivan, Laraine. "The Acceptability of Linguistic Connectives as a Function of the Relationship Between the Referent Events." *L&S* 17:278-95.
An investigation of the effects of experiential and linguistic variables on the preference for within sentence connectives. 8 items were constructed, each consisting of 2 clauses describing sequential events which varied in the perceived frequency of

relationship and perceived temporal order (determined by subject ratings). Subjects in each condition ($n = 13$) ranked connectives in order of preference for each item. Results showed that frequency of relationship between described events was most likely to be a determining factor in connective preference when the clauses were in the perceived temporal order or when they were in the Past Tense. (LS)

Intellection

General and Miscellaneous. 1122. Cooper, Roger M. "The Control of Eye Fixation by the Meaning of Spoken Language: A New Methodology for the Real-Time Investigation of Speech Perception, Memory, and Language Processing." *CPsy* 6:84-107.
Approximately 55% of all appropriately directed fixation responses elicited by the informative words of a prose passage were initiated even while these words were being pronounced and nearly 40% of post-word responses occurred within the first fifth of a second following word termination. The linguistic sensitivity of this response system together with its associated small latencies suggests its use as a practical new research tool for the real-time investigation of perceptual and cognitive processes and for the detailed study of speech perception, memory, and language processing. (LLBA)

Cognition. 1154. Chafe, Wallace L. "Language and Consciousness." *Language* 50:111-33.
The notion of consciousness is important to the linguistic distinction between given and new information. Given information is that which the speaker assumes to be already present in the addressee's consciousness at the time of an utterance. Attention is given to contrastiveness, a separate phenomenon which is apt to be confused with new information. The question of why a speaker treats certain information as given is discussed as well as the converse question of why a speaker may stop treating something as given. In certain definable instances, speakers exhibit a mild degree of egocentrism in their assumptions regarding the addressee's consciousness. (WLC)

1155. Danks, Joseph H., and Mary Ann Schwenk. "Comprehension of Prenominal Adjective Orders." *M&C* 2:34-38.
In two experiments phrases describing a referent object contained two prenominal adjectives in either normal or inverted order. The time to identify the position of the referent in a display was a function of both the adjective order and the nonreferent context. If the referent appeared with a nonreferent differing from it only in size or number, the normal order of adjectives facilitated responding. However, if the referent appeared with a nonreferent differing from it only in color, the inverted order of adjectives resulted in faster identification times. These results support a pragmatic communication rule that, when the more discriminating adjectives are ordered earlier in a series, comprehension is facilitated. (LLBA)

1169. Graham, Norman C. "Response Strategies in the Partial Comprehension of Sentences." *L&S* 17:205-21.
In a sentence comprehension task subjects had to select a correct picture from an array of 4 presented immediately after hearing a relevant sentence. Sentences were representative of 12 different grammatical structures and were 8 words in length. In each array 3 incorrect pictures (distractors) were representations of lexical variants of the presented sentence. Three groups of subjects from Nursery Schools, Primary Schools, and Special Schools for the Educationally Subnormal were tested. Gross differences in overall error rate between groups were observed though patterns of choices among distractors were the same for all groups. Failure to comprehend was associated with loss of information about specific lexical items. (NCG)

1183. Just, Marcel Adam. "Comprehending Quantified Sentences: The Relation Between Sentence-Picture and Semantic Memory Verification." *CPsy* 6:216-36.
Subjects were timed as they decided whether quantified sentences like *All (some) of the round figures are red* were true or false of an accompanying picture. Response latency was a function of the quantifier and the relation between the sets mentioned in the subject and predicate of the sentence. The pattern of latencies was

similar to the pattern found for sentences that refer to concepts in semantic memory. This result suggests that the same process may be operating in both domains. Two alternative models of the process are considered. (LLBA)

1193. Largen, Robert G. "Self-embedded Sentences and the Syllogistic Form: An Investigation of Their Interaction." *Jour. of Gen. Psychology* 90:17-23.

Three hypotheses derived from an explanation sketch of the ability of some individuals to understand self-embedded (SE) sentences with two embeddings involving syllogistic reasoning ability were tested with positive results. The data indicate that: (1) those who can understand SE sentences with two embeddings will be better able to reason with the use of the syllogistic form than those who cannot; (2) those who can reason with the use of the syllogistic form will be able to understand SE sentences with two embeddings; and (3) those who cannot reason with the use of the syllogistic form will not be able to understand SE sentences with two embeddings. (LLBA)

1220. Seitz, Michael R., and Bruce A. Weber. "Effects of Response Requirements on the Location of Clicks Superimposed on Sentences." *M&C* 2:43-46.

A study comparing two methods of identifying the location of clicks superimposed on sentences. When Ss first wrote out the entire sentence and then marked the location of the clicks, the perceived clicks tended to migrate toward the major constituent breaks of the sentences. This trend was not observed when Ss responded by marking the position of clicks on prepared scripts of the stimulus sentence. In addition, both response procedures resulted in a significant trend for the perceived clicks to be located before the actual click locations. The findings of this study resolve the conflicting results obtained from previous investigations in this area. (LLBA)

Memory and Recall. 1260. Brewer, William F., and Edward H. Lichtenstein. "Memory for Marked Semantic Features Versus Memory for Meaning." *JVLVB* 13:172-80.

Memory-for-marked-semantic-features theory was juxtaposed to a memory-for-meaning theory. In Exp. 1, Ss recalled sentences containing one member of a marked-unmarked antonym pair or their negations (*short, tall, not short, not tall*). Antonym shifts occurring in recall tended to go from marked to unmarked forms only in sentences with morphologically transparent marking (*unfair* to *not fair*) and tended to conserve meaning. Exp. 2 replicated Exp. 1 with all affirmative sentences. Without *nots*, antonym shifting could not conserve meaning and was virtually eliminated. The results are interpreted as supporting a global memory-for-meaning theory as opposed to a theory of memory for marked semantic features. (LLBA)

1326. Leonard, Laurence B. "The Role of Intonation in the Recall of Various Linguistic Stimuli." *L&S* 16(1973):327-35.

The effects of intonation on the recall of normal sentences, anomalous (grammatical but unmeaningful) sentences, anagram (ungrammatical but meaningful) strings, and word lists were examined. Intonation facilitated recall only in the anomalous sentence condition, suggesting that, in such learning situations, intonation may function as an additional component of grammar, rather than as an independent linguistic variable. (LBL)

1358. Perfetti, Charles A., and Robert Lindsey. "Polysemy and Memory." *JPsyR* 3:75-89.

The degree of ambiguity of words with multiple meanings was estimated by the semantic uncertainty of a word as measured by word association and sentence generation tasks. Ambiguous words defined in this way were as well remembered in a recognition memory test as control words. When words were first presented in sentences that would determine their encoded sense, it was found that successive encodings of an ambiguous word converged more when the word appeared in its primary sense than when it appeared in its secondary sense. (LLBA)

1383. Segui, J., and Geneviève Oléron. "La rétention de noms et de membres nominaux non-adjectif." *L'Année psychologique* 73(1973):507-20.

The retention of nouns (N) and noun phrases (NP) of the form noun-adjective in three experiments on short-term memory was studied. Noun phrases were either strongly associated (NP+) or weakly associated (NP-). Results indicate that nouns are always better recalled than noun phrases. Among noun phrases, the NP+ are better recalled than the NP-, and this increases as the inter-item interval is reduced. The fact that the NP+ are less well recalled than the N is interpreted in terms of a "memory load," whereas the difference between the two types of NP is attributed to different degrees of internal structure. (LLBA)

Linguistics in Neurology and Psychopathology

General and Miscellaneous. 1427. Black, John W., Elizabeth Hooker, Judith Long, and Karen Wilkens. "The Teaching of Constructed Responses in Language Therapy." *L&S* 17:17-26.

Equal numbers of aphasic adults, deaf children aged 9-10, and deaf adolescents aged 13-17 were required to complete stems of sentences. The incomplete sentences were typed automatically in the presence of the individual subject who constructed the final word of each sentence, monitored and corrected letter by letter. The responses were 55 words, 11 of which were predicted on each of five test days, which were repeated four times daily for four days, making 20 experiences (days) for each participant. The response words varied in numbers of letters and in numbers of phonemes. Results showed that the deaf adolescents made the fewest errors and the aphasic adults, the most. (JWB, EH, JL, & KW)

1474. Mulac, Anthony, and A. Robert Sherman. "Behavioral Assessment of Speech Anxiety." *QJS* 60:134-43.

Seeks to develop and evaluate an instrument for the behavioral assessment of speech anxiety. The BASA was tested on videotape-recorded classroom speeches of male college students and proved highly reliable. Encouraging evidence for the concurrent and construct validity of data generated by the instrument was provided by several sources. The four orthological BASA factors resulting from varimax rotation, rigidity, inhibition, disfluency, and agitation support a multi-dimensional conceptualization of the speech anxiety phenomenon. (AM & ARS)

1478. Papçun, George, et al. "Is the Left Hemisphere Specialized for Speech, Language and/or Something Else?" *JAS* 55:319-27.

Morse code signals were presented dichotically to Morse code operators and to Ss who did not know Morse code. Morse code operators demonstrated right ear superiority, indicating left hemisphere dominance, for the perception of dichotically presented Morse code letters. Naive Ss also showed right ear superiority, indicating left hemisphere dominance, when presented with a set of dot-dash patterns which was restricted to pairs including seven or fewer elements, counting dots and dashes each as elements. It is speculated that the left hemisphere is specialized for processing the sequential parts of which a stimulus is composed. Consideration of these findings suggests that language is lateralized to the left hemisphere because of its dependence on segmental subparts and that this dependence characterizes language perception as distinct from most other human perception. (LLBA)

1485. Salus, Peter H. and Mary W. "Developmental Neurophysiology and Phonological Acquisition Order." *Language* 50:151-60.

Neurophysiological evidence seems to indicate that the differentiation of [+ strident] consonants is a function of degree of myelination of the auditory nerve and the cortical bodies with which it is connected. Evidence from pathological cases supports the hypothesis that differentiation of high frequencies is impaired in cases of demyelinating disease. It is concluded that the fricative consonants are acquired last because they are auditorily discriminated last by the developing child. (PHS & MWS)

1492. Shands, Harley C. "Schizophrenia and the Once-Objective Universe." *LangS* 32:1-6.

Modern physical scientists have abandoned materialism in favor of theories emphasizing relations and the language of probabilities while mental scientists continue to use obsolete materialistic conceptual models in theory construction. The use in psychiatry of contemporary physical models derived from relativity and quantum theory is discussed in combination with ideas borrowed from structural linguistics with special reference to schizophrenia. Psychic or mental deviance is seen as relativistic since it occurs only in specifically human universes in which norms are established not by natural but by consensual process, an assumption necessitating wholesale revision of outmoded paradigms to resolve anomalies apparent in the use of obsolete conceptual models enshrined in common sense. (HCS)

1497. Studdert-Kennedy, Michael, and Kerstin Hadding. "Auditory and Linguistic Processes in the Perception of Intonation Contours." *L&S* 16:(1973):293-313.
The fundamental frequency contour of a 700-msc utterance, "November," was systematically varied to produce 72 contours, different in f_o at the stress and over the terminal glide. The contours were recorded carried on the speech wave and as modulated sine waves. Swedish and American subjects classified both speech and sine-wave contours as either terminally rising or terminally falling (psychophysical judgments) and speech contours as questions or statements (linguistic judgments). For both groups, two factors acted in complementary relation to govern linguistic judgments: perceived glide and f_o at the stress. Listeners tended to classify contours with an apparent terminal rise and/or high stress as questions, contours with an apparent terminal fall and/or low stress as statements. For both speech and sine waves psychophysical judgments of terminal glide were influenced by earlier sections of the contour, but the effects were reduced for sine-wave contours and there were several instances in which speech psychophysical judgments followed the linguistic more closely than the sine wave judgments. (MS-K & KH)

1505. West, Jacqueline J., and Jack L. Weber. "A Linguistic Analysis of the Morphemic and Syntactic Structures of a Hard-of-Hearing Child." *L&S* 17:68-79.
Presents a detailed study of the expressive language of one hearing-impaired 4-year-old girl using concepts of both descriptive and generative linguistics as the means of analysis. Morpheme boundaries, word boundaries, and syntactic functions were derived out of the systematic verbal behavior of the subject. The results showed a large number of single-morpheme words identical in structure to adult English. However, in various other words she exhibited a level of morphemic combinative control which did not reproduce standard English forms. Other words which in standard English illustrate morphemic combinations were not beyond the monomorphemic structure level. Her only productive affix that is also a standard form was the diminutive "-y" as in "doggy." Syntactically six word-clsses were derived using the syntactic slot technique. Seven main rules combined these words in two- and three-word syntactic structures. By applying grammatical terms to the above syntactic combinations, five types of syntactic relations emerge. (JJW & JLW)

Aphasia. 1540. Schnitzer, Marc L. "Aphasiological Evidence for Five Linguistic Hypotheses." *Language* 50:300-15.
Aphasiological evidence is presented in support of various linguistic hypotheses. The transmodal performances of an aphasic subject provide clear evidence in favor of performative analysis, discourse rules, a copula-creation rule for English, the partial independence of syntax and semantics, and, the function of pronouns as pure variables. The possible contribution of neurolinguistics to linguistic theory is evaluated. (MLS)

Psychopathology. 1570. Hofmann, Joanne, and John M. Panagos. "Mothers' and Non-Mothers' Semantic Adaptation to Deviant Speech." *L&S* 16(1973):396-404.
This study examined whether a group of mothers of children with deviant speech, and a group of non-mothers, could adapt their comprehension strategies to decode command sentences spoken by a child known to generate patterned deviant utterances. While subjects made significant improvement in their comprehension performance (adaptation), no significant difference between groups was observed. Perceptual adaptation to variant linguistic codes may be so basic to decoding performance that maternal experience with child speech would not provide mothers with a decoding advantage over native speakers engaged in everyday adaptive communication. (JH & JMP)

Genesis of Language

1588. Hill, Jane H. "Possible Continuity Theories of Language." *Language* 50:134-50.
Some of the difficulties with existing continuity theories of the relationship between human language and systems of communication in other animals seem to be inherent in the assumption that continuity theories must be theories of comparative intellect. These difficulties can be avoided by theories which place their major emphasis on the adaptive functions of communication systems in their ecological context. Recent work on the ontogeny of bird song provides a basis for such a theory, within which a new evaluation may be made of the significance of recent experiments on language abilities in chimpanzees. (JHH)

Child Language

General and Miscellaneous. 1601. Braine, Martin D.S. "Length Constraints, Reduction Rules, and Holophrastic Processes in Children's Word Combinations." *JVLVB* 13:448-56.
Evidence is presented that questions the presumption, implicit in the length-constraint claim, that a constituent is less likely to be expanded (without deletion) when there are cooccurring constituents. The special character of both early word combinations and holophrases is explained by a lexical-insertion process in which a word representing a salient feature of the communication is inserted into an inappropriately high node, because the child lacks complete control of rules to realize the communication more fully. (LLBA)

1604. Cambon, J., and H. Sinclair. "Relations Between Syntax and Semantics: Are They 'Easy to See'?" *BJP* 65:133-40.
Recent findings in developmental psycholinguistics demonstrate that below the age of eight, children have difficulty in understanding English sentences that do not conform to the normal SVO pattern. Experiments with French-speaking children are reported which duplicate and extend this research. Results for English and French are compared. A hypothesis based on Piaget's developmental psychology is formulated to link these findings to the more general trends of cognitive development. (LLBA)

1622. Genshaft, Judy L., and Michael Hirt. "Language Differences between Black Children and White Children." *DP* 10:451-56.
Black children and white children, matched for social class and nonverbal intelligence, were examined in a free recall situation on vocabulary words and sentences presented in black dialect and standard English. The results indicate that on standard English sentences, both groups performed equally well. On sentences in black dialect, the white Ss performed significantly worse. These findings are interpreted as support for bilingual language development in black ghetto children. (LLBA)

1638. Lawson, Everdina A., and M.R. Murray. "Unidentifiable Utterances in Children's Speech." *L&S* 17:296-304.
Junior school children were found to produce unidentifiable utterances in dichotic as well as monotic shadowing. The phenomenon was investigated by providing practice at increased presentation rates of the input and exploring right ear advantages for verbal material. The poor articulation increased with higher input rates and could not be explained by lack of lateralization. An explanation in terms of inadequate monitoring of speech production appeared most appropriate. (EAL & MRM)

Development of Language. 1703. Braine, Martin D.S. "On What Might Constitute Learnable Phonology." *Language* 50:270-99.
The main learning process in pronunciation consists of discovering and gaining control over the articulatory features required to make sounds heard. The lexical representation differs from the phonetic output at all stages because actual pronunciations are constrained by primitive or acquired articulatory processes that have the effect of imposing a phonotactic filter on the speech output. Rules and representations depict "competence" and have "psychological reality" by describing the articulatory analysis made by the learner, together with the constraints imposed by the filter. (MDSB)

1707. Chambers, John Kenneth. "Remarks on Topicalization in Child Language." *FLang* 9(1973):442-46.
Two points are raised relevant to the hypothesis of Jeffrey S. Gruber that topic-comment constructions typical of child language are precursors of subject-pred icate constructions of adult language. First, his analysis of the data is roughly equivalent to earlier analyses (like Braine's pivot-open class analysis) when the notational differences are neutralized. Secondly, his projection from the data to a developmental hypothesis can be enriched by incorporating a notion of focus into the grammatical apparatus. In this view, topic-comment constructions provide a primitive device for realizing focus, which in adult grammars is realized with considerable subtlety by a variety of syntactic devices, including passivization, clefting, contrastive stressing, and so on. (LLBA)

1708. Chipman, Harold H., and Catherine de Dardel. "Developmental Study of the Comprehension and Production of the Pronoun 'It'." *JPsyR* 3:91-99.
Forty-two English-speaking children aged 3.3 to 7 were asked to act out instructions of the type "There is clay on the table, give it to me," where the pronoun "it" occurs in object position and refers to a collective noun, or to a count noun, or to a noun ("chocolate") which can be either. A hierarchical pattern of behavior emerged and unexpected errors were noted. The results do not appear to be interpretable from the purely linguistic point of view; it is argued that analogous observations have been made in problem-solving tasks and that, therefore, cognitive development in general must play an important part. (LLBA)

1709. Clark, Eve V. "Non-Linguistic Strategies and the Acquisition of Word Meanings." *Cognition* 2(1973):161-82.
Children aged 1;6 to 5;0 were given instructions requiring comprehension of the locative terms *in*, *on*, and *under*. Results indicate that children go through three stages: (1) They consistently use certain non-linguistic strategies that can be characterized by two ordered rules; (2) They apply these rules to only one or two of the locative instructions; and (3) They exhibit full semantic knowledge of the three word meanings. Use of these non-linguistic strategies, it is argued, determines the order of acquisition of the three locative terms. (LLBA)

1712. Clark, Ruth, Sandy Hutcheson, and Paul Van Buren. "Comprehension and Production in Language Acquisition." *JL* 10:39-53.
In a study of a boy in his third year learning the contrast between down and up, it was found that though he responded appropriately to *up* in other people's speech before he began to produce it himself, he responded far less readily than he did to the word *down*, which he himself could already produce. Furthermore, at this stage he was producing *down* in the meaning of both down and up, and his understanding of the word *down* when it was produced by others was as erroneous as his own usage. The hypothesis is advanced that syntactic progress may come about through the child's contemplation of his own speech, rather than his analysis of the speech he hears. (LLBA)

1717. Curtiss, Susan, et al. "The Linguistic Development of Genie." *Language* 50:528-54.
Discusses the linguistic development of Genie, an adolescent girl who for most of her life underwent a degree of social isolation and experiential deprivation unparalleled in the reports of scientific investigation. The relationship between cognition and language, the interdependence or autonomy of linguistic competence and performance, the mental abilities underlying language, proposed universal stages in language learning, the critical age for language acquisition, and the biological foundations of language are discussed. (SC, VF, SK, DR & MR)

1718. Dannequin, Claudine. "Syntaxe et sémantique dans l'acquisition du langage." *ELA* 11(1973):77-83.
The acquisition of a certain part of the child's vocabulary is not independent of the acquisition of the syntactic structures in which the vocabulary elements are employed. Reference is made to a series of research reports which have uncovered the difficulties of lexical-syntactic order which face the child during acquisition of the passive, negation, or of certain grammatical structures. It is concluded that: (1) Vocabulary acquisition cannot be reduced to a simple question of memory; (2) The process of acquisition

extends for a considerable period of time; and (3) Teachers, particularly in the early grades, must take these difficulties into account and should question the validity of traditional vocabulary lessons. (LLBA)

1722. Dreher, Barbara B. "Children's Informal Learning of a Second Language." *LangS* 31:13-16.
A series of studies was made to determine how much language learning occurs through social contact. 30 Spanish and English speakers at an international camp for 11-year-olds were tested for phonology. Campers scored significantly higher than a matched control group. Results on alternate forms of the Ammons and Ammons Picture Vocabulary Test in English showed significant increases in word recognition for both Spanish and English speakers. Subsequently, 12 English speakers (age 12-14) who lived with German families for a month were tested for recognition of German vocabulary. Their scores were no better than those of a matched control group. Analysis of errors showed that the experimental group depended on semantic recall in performing the task. (BBD)

1758. Maratsos, Michael P. "Children Who Get Worse at Understanding the Passive: A Replication of Bever." *JPsyR* 3:65-74.
A report of children three and four years old tested for their competence in understanding three full passives as a pretest for another experimental task. The proportion of those failing two or more of three passives rose significantly in the age periods three, 8.3, and 11. The present results are discussed in light of earlier findings of Bever; his outline of the general sequence of language acquisition in the child is also considered. (LLBA)

1766. Moerk, Ernst L. "A Design for Multivariate Analysis of Language Behaviour and Language Development." *L&S* 17:240-54.
By means of a short survey of studies of language development the complexity of this area is demonstrated. The use of multivariate designs and the concentration upon the performance aspects of verbal behavior is advocated. The pragmatic and semantic aspects are analyzed as the two main dimensions affecting the verbal statement. The pragmatic dimension is subdivided into person variables and variables of the behavior setting. Further subdivisions of the person variables are made, and possibilities to subdivide the other dimensions are suggested. The theoretical argument is supported by illustrative examples of the verbal behavior of two young children. It is concluded that the search for language competence has to be a search for a multitude of psychological variables. (ELM)

1767. —— "Changes in Verbal Child-Mother Interactions with Increasing Language Skills of the Child." *JPsyR* 3:101-16.
Protocols of language interactions between mothers and children are analyzed. The children ranged in age from 2.2 to 5 years. Systematic changes in the interactions were found with the increasing level of language skills of the child. Mothers generally proved to be sensitive measuring instruments of the language capacities of their children, and they adapted their verbal utterances to these capacities. The syntactic forms as well as the communicated contents of the message changed with increasing language skill. (LLBA)

1771. Nelson, Katherine. "Concept, Word, and Sentence: Interrelations in Acquisition and Development." *PsychologR* 81:267-85.
A conceptual model is proposed to account for the child's initial translation of meanings into words. The model is discussed in terms of the characteristics of word acquisition and of the relation between first words and first sentences. While concept formation theory, semantic feature theory, and Piagetian theory are each alone inadequate to account for this process, each makes a contribution to a solution. The resulting model rests upon the assumption that the young child translates the dynamic functional relations of objects into conceptual "core" meanings to which identificational features of concept instances are attached. (LLBA)

1785. Sheldon, Amy. "The Role of Parallel Function in the Acquisition of Relative Clauses in English." *JVLVB* 13:272-81.
Study of the acquisition of subject and object relative clauses by English speaking children between the ages of 3¾ and 5½. The

children were tested for their comprehension of four types of relative sentence in order to determine the role of the following factors in comprehension: (1) position of the embedded clause; (2) word order in the embedded clause; and (3) grammatical functions of the identical noun phrases. The results indicate that if the identical noun phrases have the same function in their respective clauses the sentence is significantly easier to understand. (LLBA)

1796. Suppes, Patrick. "The Semantics of Children's Language." *AmP* 29:103-14.

Discusses the relevance of the logical tradition in semantics that begins with Frege and has been stimulated by the important work of Tarski and his students on the analysis of children's language. Application of model-theoretic semantics or logical semantics to context-free grammars, to the semantics of the definite article in English, and to the semantics of adjectives and quantifiers is given. Early expression of propositional attitudes in children's speech is discussed and a sketch of how recent work in the semantics of modal logic can be applied to the analysis of such speech. (LLBA)

Psychoacoustics

1834. Lehiste, Ilse, and David Meltzer. "Vowel and Speaker Identification in Natural and Synthetic Speech." *L&S* 16(1973): 356-64.

In a listening test, subjects were required to identify both the vowel and the sex of the speaker. Ten monophthongal American English vowels were selected and were produced by a male speaker, a female speaker, and a child. Formant values were read from spectrograms made of these vowels and used for synthesizing the same 30 vowels on a Glace-Holmes synthesizer. A third set of vowels was generated synthetically using formant and fundamental frequency values reported by Peterson and Barney (1952). In this set, the fundamental frequency characteristic of male, female, and children's voices was combined with male, female, and children's formants. The set of 150 stimuli was presented to 60 listeners. Speaker identification scores were higher than vowel identification scores for both normal speakers and vowels synthesized from measurements; for the Peterson-Barney set, the scores were approximately the same. The highest correct score was 88.3%, obtained for the normal male speaker; and the lowest correct score was 31.0%, obtained for children's vowels synthesized from measurements. (IL & DM)

VI. SOCIO- AND ETHNOLINGUISTICS

General

1855. Baubkus, Lutz, and Wolfgang Viereck. "Recent American Studies in Sociolinguistics." *ArL* 4(1973):103-11. [Rev. art.] The Detroit survey is the latest of several large-scale urban language projects carried out recently in the United States. It turns out, however, that the procedures followed in this survey and adopted in derivative studies suffer from such serious shortcomings that the conclusions arrived at are only of rather restricted value. (LB & WV)

1866. Khubchandani, Lachman M. "Language in a Behavioral Framework:An Overview on Sociolinguistics." *RELC* 5:16-26.

A number of aspects of language use fall within sociolinguistics. The way speech behavior is structured both spatially and temporally has social dimensions. The entire speech matrix in a community may be an amalgam or a conglomeration of different speech varieties with diverse and heterogeneous structures. The notion of uniformity and homogeneity even in the speech behavior of an individual is only a myth. We need to distinguish between speech as an integral activity in society and language as an ideal norm. In identifying language people perceive their own speech and that of others in categorical terms as discrete language A or B as if it were uniform and homogeneous. (LMK)

1867. Lakoff, Robin. "Language and Woman's Place." *LSoc* 2(1973):45-80.

Our use of language embodies attitudes as well as referential meanings. "Woman's language" has as foundation the attitude that women are marginal to the serious concerns of life. This marginality and powerlessness is reflected in both the ways women are expected to speak and the ways in which women are spoken of. In appropriate women's speech, strong expression of feeling is avoided, expression of uncertainty is favored, and means of expression in regard to subject-matter deemed "trivial" to the "real" world are elaborated. Speech about women implies an object whose sexual nature requires euphemism and whose social roles are derivative and dependent. These aspects of English are explored with regard to lexicon and syntax as concerns speech by women. Speech about women is analyzed with regard to *lady : woman, master : mistress, widow : widower,* and *Mr : Mrs., Miss,* with notice of differential use of role terms not explicitly marked for sex (e.g., *professional*) as well. (RL)

Sociolinguistics

General and Miscellaneous. 1887. Barton, Stephen N., and

John B. O'Leary. "The Rhetoric of Rural Physician Procurement Campaigns:An Application of Tavistock." *QJS* 60:144-54.

Six rural Minnesota communities participated in joint recruitment of physicians. An intergroup consisting of delegates from each of the six communities requested the assistance of the authors. The primary role of the authors was to focus the intergroup on the task of understanding its own behavior and to grasp responsibility rather than abdicate it. Rhetorical themes of the large groups (communities) conformed with the themes of small physician procurement groups. The intergroup formulated a new rhetoric with themes that satisfied fantasies of potential physicians. (SNB & JBO'L)

1892. Brent, Edmund. "Accounting for Synchronic Variation." *FoLi* 6(1972):263-72.

Examines proposals by Labov, Weinreich, and Hard dealing with intralinguistic variation and its application to German, Canadian, and French data. Labov and Weinreich proposed a linguistic variable composed of an intralinguistic variable and an extralinguistic variable, abandoning the concept of a linguistic homogeneous speech community. Hard pointed out the importance of situational conditions in determining intralocal and intraspeaker variants in a number of German dialects. Synchronic intralinguistic variation is the unpredictability of language or the choice among "free variants." That the speaker "controls" a set of varieties of the same language and, often, a set of languages, dialects, and varieties is stressed by this study of Canadian, French, and German data, but this does not preclude that much linguistic behavior is socially shared by the community. (LLBA)

1893. Bricker, V.R. "Some Cognitive Implications of Informant Variability in Zinacanteco Speech Classification." *LSoc* 3:69-82.

Some cases of inter- and intra-informant variability cannot be explained in terms of social and contextual factors and do not seem to require probabilistic models to account for them. Analysis of several Zinacanteco speech taxonomies suggests that what are called variant responses are often only incomplete responses and that if the cognitive system is represented as a taxonomy, then it is a taxonomy which is made up of a number of partial taxonomies, each of which is produced by a different informant or group of informants or by the same informant on different occasions. (VRB)

1903. Duncan, Starkey,Jr. "On the Structure of Speaker-Auditor Interaction During Speaking Turns." *LSoc* 3:161-80. The structure of speaker-auditor interaction during speaking turns was explored, using detailed transcriptions of language, paralanguage, and body-motion behaviors displayed by both participants in dyadic, face-to-face conversations. On the basis of observed regularities in these behaviors, three signals were hypothesized: (a) a speaker within-turn signal, (b) an auditor back-channel signal, and (c) a speaker continuation signal. These signals were composed of various behaviors in language and in body motion. The display of appropriate ordered sequences of these signals by both participants served to mark "units of interaction" during speaking turns. (SD,Jr)

1905. Eskey, David E. "The Case for the Standard Language." *CE* 35:769-74.
The primary function of standard English is to provide the basic means by which the educated members of English-speaking society can communicate, as easily as possible, with each other. Standard English is essentially a complex set of rules and abandoning the rules or stretching them too far can result in a total breakdown. That the rules of standard English are an arbitrary set intrinsically no better than those of nonstandard dialects in no way detracts from their immeasurable value as the agreed upon rules. (DEE)

1935. Jefferson, Gail. "Error Correction as an Interactional Resource." *LSoc* 3:181-99.
Some small errors which occur in natural talk may be treated as matters of competence, both in the production of coherent speech and the conduct of meaningful interaction. Focusing on a rule-governed occurrence of the interjection "uh," a format is described by which one can display that one is correcting an error one almost produced. There are systematic ways in which someone who hears such talk can find that an error was almost made and what that error would have been. For interactional errors, the error correction format can be used to invoke alternatives to some current formulation of self and other(s), situation and relationship, and thereby serve as a resource for negotiating and perhaps reformulating a current set of identities. (GJ)

1941. Khubchandani, Lachman M. "Sociolinguistics:An Overview." *LangS* 31:7-10.
Highlights some of the issues considered "deviant" or "trivial" in synchronic and diachronic studies in linguistics: spacial characteristics of language, the paradox of performance and perception in speech behavior, conceptual fluidity regarding mother tongue. An overall ecological perspective for understanding India as a language area is provided and attention is drawn to the studies in language demography as a tool for scientific inquiry and its utility in the sphere of social planning. (LMK)

1956. Macaulay, Ronald. "Double Standards." *AA* 75(1973): 1324-37.
One of the unsatisfactory characteristics of recent work in sociolinguistics is the indiscriminate use of the labels "standard" and "nonstandard," particularly in dealing with varieties of language such as black English. The danger is to identify standard English with an upper class accent instead of considering the two notions as separate, though related, phenomena. The definition of the term "standard language" is examined with reference to the status of Schwyzertütsch, Scottish English, and black English. (LLBA)

1965. Morse, J. Mitchell. "Race, Class, and Metaphor." *CE* 35:545-54,563-65.
Sometimes literal terms are taken metaphorically, as in the cases of "petrified" (scared), "clothes horse" (well-dressed woman), and "bastard" (disagreeable person), because literal meanings are not known. This is a rather rare disorder of the vocabulary and does little harm. Much more frequently, and with much worse effects, metaphorical terms are taken literally. The social and political effects of using metaphors as if they were statements of fact are extremely harmful. (LLBA)

1977. Poole, Millicent E. "Comparison of the Factorial Structure of Oral Coding Patterns for a Middle-Class and a Working-Class Group." *L&S* 17:222-39.
Comparison of the factorial structure of oral coding patterns for a middle-class and a working-class group in terms of a Bernstein derived thesis of greater differentiation and specificity for middle-class subjects because of their ability to manipulate more of the semantic and structural resources of language. 28 indices of oral coding elaboration were obtained from 40 middle-class amd 40 working-class tertiary students. Pearson Product-Moment correlations were obtained and, by using principal components factor analysis, the middle-class matrix yielded nine factors, the working-class matrix eight. The thesis of greater differentiation and specificity in middle-class code elaboration was sustained. (MEP)

1989. Sacks, Harvey, Emanuel A. Schegloff, and Gail Jefferson. "A Simplest Systematics for the Organization of Turn-Taking for Conversation." *Language* 50:696-735.
The organization of taking turns to talk is fundamental to conversation. A model for the turn-taking organization for conversation is proposed and is examined for its compatibility with a list of observable facts about conversation. The results of the examination suggest that a model for turn-taking in conversation will be characterized as locally managed, party-administered, interactionally controlled, and sensitive to recipient design. Several general consequences of the model are explicated and contrasts are sketched with turn-taking organizations for other speech-exchange systems. (HS, EAS, & GJ)

2005. Wildgen, Wolfgang. "Eine Antwort auf Oevermanns Bemerkungen zur 'Kode-Theorie'." *LingB* 27(1973):50-51.
A reply to a previous article wherein the sociolinguistic position of Bernstein is defended against recent criticism: (1) The theory of Bernstein leads to misunderstandings as basic terms remain obscure; (2) the authors do not succeed in refuting the reproach of "naive ideologization"; (3) Opposed to Oevermann, it is argued that Speech Act Theory can be relevant to sociolinguistic theory and vice versa; and (4) The scope of a theory of linguistic competence depends on its goals. As sociolinguistic theories have a narrow scope, they must subdivide these "competences." The analysis of language variation must separate differences of competence from variation on the background of a common competence. (LLBA)

Social Dialects. 2020. Levy, Betty B., and Harold Cook. "Dialect Proficiency and Auditory Comprehension in Standard and Black Nonstandard English." *JSHR* 16(1973):642 -49.
A dialect proficiency task and an auditory comprehension task were administered to 32 black second graders. Half of the Ss received the auditory comprehension task in black nonstandard English; the other half received the task in standard English. Subjects were asked to identify the race of the speakers and how well they liked the stories and speakers. Performance was significantly better on the questions in the standard treatment. The results are discussed in terms of a "difference" vs. a "bicultural" model of dialect proficiency and achievment. (LLBA)

2026. Ramer, Andrya L.H., and Norma S. Rees. "Selected Aspects of the Development of English Morphology in Black American Children of Low Socioeconomic Background." *JSHR* 16(1973):569-77.
A modification of Berko's test was used to explore the use of six morphological rules, as a function of age, by black children living in New York City. For each of the six morphological rules tested, black English and standard American English take different forms. The results indicate that, in the presence of the one white examiner, the occurrence of basilect (black English forms) responses decreased while the occurrence of standard English responses increased as the age of the children increased. (LLBA)

2027. Rémillard, Louis, G. Richard Tucker, and Margaret Bruck. "The Role of Phonology and Lexicon in Eliciting Reactions to Dialect Variation." *AnL* 15(1973):383-97.
An examination of students' reactions to the written and oral presentation of Canadian French (CF) and European French (EF) lexical items and phrases in five selected social settings. Information obtained by questionnaires was supplemented by informal conversations with Ss. Results suggest an acceptance of both EF and CF style speech in informal settings, but a preference for EF style speech in formal settings. The relatively more adverse reactions to CF phrases than to the CF lexical items suggest that syntax may play an important role in eliciting reactions to speech variation. (LLBA)

2051. Ramos, Alcida R. "How the Sanumá Acquire Their Names." *Ethnology* 13:171-85.
Sanumá name-giving is examined, exposing key features in the social structure. Personal names are described in terms of the domains from which they are derived and of the social aspects entailed in the practice 'of name-giving. In order to insure a coherent presentation of the data, the names under consideration have been divided into two groups: (1) names selected through a ritualized series of social actions that follow the birth of a new member, involving the killing of an animal in a ritual hunt and (2) names given by a number of alternative naming techniques that involve no special observances—these represent the majority of personal names on record. (LLBA)

Language Policy

2076. Fishman, Joshua A. "Language Planning and Language Planning Research:The State of the Art." *Linguistics* 119:15-34. Reviews recent research and theory in the field of language planning with particular attention to conceptual dimensions, policy decision making processes, codification and elaboration processes, implementation and evaluation processes. These are examined in conjunction with the creation and revision of writing systems, the formulation and change of language models, the expansion and modernization of lexicons, and the pursuit of intertranslatability and stylistic diversity. (JAF)

VII. LANGUAGE INTERACTION

Language Contact

General and Miscellaneous. 2117. Nash, Rose. "Spanglish: Language Contact in Puerto Rico." *AS* 45(1970; pub. 1974):223-33.
Puerto Rican *Spanglish* has at least one characteristic of an autonomous language: a large number of native speakers. Examples of Spanglish can be divided into three main types: Type 1 is characterized by extensive use of English lexical items occurring in their original form in otherwise Spanish utterances. In Type 2 Spanglish, English spelling and/or pronunciation are changed—they lose their non-Spanish identity and assume the morphological characteristics of Spanish words. Some Type 3 Spanglish reveals English syntactic influence, some involves literal translation of English loan phrases, and some involves not only a merging of Spanish and English but also a reflection of the unique Puerto Rican way of life. (LLBA)

2121. Peacock, F.W. "Languages in Contact in Labrador." *RLS* 5:1-3.
Introducing words from foreign groups to express concepts not native to the Eskimo people was necessary. The wider their contact with the groups, the more foreign words were introduced to the exclusion of Eskimo words and phrases. For example, Eskimos use Latin words to identify certain church festivals. The simpler, German system of counting replaced the Eskimo system, and the Germans also left their mark on religious vocabulary. English missionaries and storekeepers have played their part in introducing new words into the Labrador Eskimo dialect. Swear words have also been introduced, and the Eskimoization of commonly used Christian names is apparent. The list of borrowed words in Eskimo speech is quite considerable and increases year by year. (LLBA)

2122. Peciar, Štefan. "O jazykových kontaktach." *SlReč* 38(1973):257-64.
Discusses linguistic contacts, bilingualism, and linguistic interference in terms of Marxist-Leninist theory with emphasis on the relationship between literary Czech and Slovak in Czechoslovakia today. (LLBA)

Bi- or Multilingualism

General and Miscellaneous. 2130. Baldwin, Barry. "Bi-culturalism and Bi-lingualism in the Roman Empire." [F 51]:65-68.
Rome's military conquest of Greece was redressed by Hellenism's cultural conquest of Rome. Within these basic parameters, various attitudes clash and co-exist on occasion. Some Romans distrusted Greeks and their culture as importing foreign permissiveness and subverting the old-time religion. Others welcomed it in the name of trendiness, inspired by neophilia. The basic situation has interest for modern debates over American cultural imperialism as a rival in Canada to the former British variety. (BB)

2131. Brennan, Eileen M., and Ellen B. Ryan. "Reported Language Usage and Verbal Fluency of Bilingual Mexican American Adolescents." *AnL* 15(1973):398-405.
A discussion of language usage and verbal fluency of bilingual Mexican adolescents in two conversational situations. A language usage questionnaire was designed to study language choice of conversational components in school and at home. The completed questionnaire was administered to 36 male students of a private high school in East Los Angeles. The Ss reported themselves to be native born, to have Spanish as their native language, and to be of Mexican origin. Results of testing indicate that neither home nor school fluency was significantly related to differences between the usage ratings for the two domains. (LLBA)

2132a. Cassano, Paul V. "The Substrate Theory in Relation to the Bilingualism of Paraguay:Problems and Findings." *AnL* 15(1973):406-26.
A representative sampling of opinions concerning the role of the indigenous languages of Spanish America in relation to Spanish. Includes a survey of pertinent thinking on the subject with critical illumination of the paradoxical position taken by substratum students. The second section summarizes the first substratum claims advanced with reference to American Spanish. Also included are substratum hypotheses concerning the Spanish of Paraguay. (LLBA)

Translation

2185. Goldman-Eisler, Frieda, and Michele Cohen. "An Experimental Study of Interference Between Receptive and Productive Processes Relating to Simultaneous Translation." *L&S* 17:1-10.
The question of the interference between the reception and production of speech is basic to an understanding of the processes involved in simultaneous translation. An experiment designed to throw light on this problem by controlling the level of interference between decoding and encoding speech using hesitancy as an indicator of interference is discussed. This proved effective in spotting the levels at which interference takes place. Encoding without processing did not interfere with the monitoring of even highly complex intellectual material, but encoding involving complex processing did so in proportion to the hesitancy of the input. Such encoding was facilitated at the end of the monitored sentences and inhibited while they were being monitored. (FG-E & MC)

2188. House, Juliane. "On the Limits of Translatability." *Babel* 19(1973):166-67.
Certain limits to translatability do exist, if the following phenomena are taken into account: (1) connotations (too elusive to be rendered correctly in translation); (2) absence of knowledge of cultural and situational context of a linguistic unit on the part of the translator; (3) cases in which language adopts a different function over and above its "normal" communicative function (i.e., in poetry, metalanguage, and "plays on words"); and (4) intralinguistic variation, i.e., that linguistic usage reflects sociological, geographical, and situational factors. (LLBA)

2189. Ivir, Vladimir. "Linguistic and Extra-Linguistic Considerations in Translation." *SRAZ* 33-36(1972-73):615-26.

There are two causes for the failure of linguistics to deal adequately with the phenomenon of translation. Linguistics is still not developed enough to make a contribution that practicing translators might recognize as useful. It possesses an inherent inability to deal with certain aspects of translation. Therefore a comprehensive theory of translation cannot be purely linguistic in nature, but must be approached from a multidisciplinary angle. A satisfactory theory of translation must: (1) trace and explain the intuitive processes of the translator while he is engaged in the act of translating; and (2) describe the results produced by these processes. (LLBA)

2191. Jamieson, Kathleen M. "The Quagmire of Translation." *SM* 41:357-63.

Humanae Vitae, the 1968 papal proscription of artificial methods of birth regulation, addressed the modern world in Latin. This article assesses Latin's ability to communicate papal ideas and examines the adequacy of the Spanish, French, and English translations of the Encyclical. Three arguments are advanced: (1) The English, Spanish, and French translations alter in small but significant respects the meaning carried in the Latin document; (2) Choice of certain Latin vocabulary reinforced critical papal assumptions; (3) The Latin employed by the document embodies a world view of the document's audience. (KMJ)

2192. Jáuregui S., Beto. "La terminologia cientifica en la traducción." *LyC* 13:82-87.

A common problem for all languages where scientific terminology is not well developed is the creation of new terms when translating scientific literature. This creation should be regulated by fixed principles. This study establishes a six-step procedure for selecting a denomination and a list of 11 principles ruling the selection procedure. (LLBA)

2201. Newmark, Peter. "An Approach to Translation." *Babel* 19(1973):3-19.

An attempt to clarify certain theoretical issues in translation where they are related to linguistics. Artistic and scientific aspects of translation are distinguished, using Frege's terms as a basis. The translator, however, cannot sharply separate *Vorstellung* and *Sinn*, either in the mind of the source language author or in his own, except insofar as he takes a stand on the "rightness" of some words and word-groups in his translation, and allows for alternatives of words, word-groups, and syntactic structures in other cases; usually, *Vorstellung* and *Sinn* shade off into each other. Ideally, *Sinn* excludes *Vorstellung* for the translator. However, what is entirely *Sinn* to the translator is partly *Sinn* and partly the translator's *Vorstellung* to the second reader, and even more to the third reader, the critic. Whatever the piece, however, a certain elegance, neatness, conciseness, discrimination, *Spürsinn* for appropriateness and essentials distinguishes the best translators. (LLBA)

2203. Popovic, Anton. "Zum Status der Übersetzungskritik." *Babel* 19(1973):161-65.

In the existing literature on literary translation, a basic work to deal with the communication status of literary translation criticism is missing. The communication model of literary translation criticism is a reliable way to distinguish its specific signs. In the criticism of translation, a specific metalinguistic activity is understood, the object of which is the process of translation. The criticism of translation differs from the criticism of original literature in two respects: (1) Its object is a "doubled communication string"; and (2) Its object is not only a present-day work as seen in criticism of original literature, but may also be a translated work from an older literary period. (LLBA)

2204. Quesada, Francisco Miro. "Algunas reflexiones sobre el concepto de traducibilidad." *LyC* 13(1973):129-63.

The concept of translatability cannot be defined without the concept of meaning, for translating a phrase from language L into another phrase of a language L^l means finding two phrases from two different languages both having the same meaning. In using the concept of denotation to define meaning and limiting the concept to the field of propositional expressions, the concepts of structure and model must be used. In using Cartesian products, a strict definition of interpretation is obtained. Through this procedure, a definition of the meaning of a proposition in a formal language L is given. This formulation permits a definition of the concept of translatability by using the open statement $T(L, L^l)$, thus read: "Language L is translatable into language L^l." (LLBA)

2205. Rey, Alain. "Lexicologie et traduction." *Babel* 19(1973):19-24.

The act of translation is doubly creative: it proposes an interpretation of messages through the production of equivalent messages in another code. It is a reading (creative transfer of meaning) and a writing (production of significant forms), an analysis and a synthesis, and, finally, a technique and an art. In regard to linguistic theories, the translator finds himself in a situation analogous to that of the lexicographer. The translator is dependent upon the linguist to know how and why his work is irreducible to a matter of linguistics. The relationship of translation to lexicology is formally discussed in three parts: (1) the lexicon in language; (2) the operation of translation; and (3) the lexicon in translation. (LLBA)

2213. Tabernig de Pucciarelli, Elsa. "La traducción:Enfoque lingüístico." *Babel* 19(1973):117-26.

Linguists feel that the main difficulty of translation lies in its semantic aspect derived from syntax. The problematics of translation are evaded by empirical study and are relegated to scientific investigation. Through science, new approaches to language teaching and essential principles for a theory of translation must be sought. Thoughts on translational processes are discussed from philosophical, linguistic, and phonetic viewpoints. (LLBA)

2215. Tello, René Medina. "El rol de la traducción en la enseñanza de idiomas extranjeros." *LyC* 13(1973):120-28.

Translation can aid in language teaching, especially when other didactic resources are ambiguous. The instructor's use of translation must observe certain principles in order to be useful in language teaching. The translation of the instructor must be preferred over that of the students, and it must be made at the enunciation level according to context, never at the word or phrase level. There are many cases in which the use of translation is not necessary. (RMT)

2218. Vanriest, Jean B. "La traduction impossible." *LyC* 13(1973):176-83.

Regardless of the text, whether written or spoken, it should be interpreted in its entirety. Therefore, in a written text the short sentence is understood by the facts and sentiments that surround and explain it. But, context in writing is quite different from context in speaking. If experts teach that the style of a text is the man who has produced it, then this would be truer for the orator than for the writer. It is illusive to hope for an adequate translation of the oral: it will be but a substitute, a transposition of an aspect or a piece of activity; the orator himself is untranslatable. (LLBA)

2221. Wilss, W. "Probleme und Perspektiven der Ubersetzungskritik." *IRAL* 12:23-41.

The translation critic is concerned with conceptual explication, his task being to establish the extent to which two functionally related texts are qualitatively congruent. Endeavors to achieve greater objectivity in translation criticism appear to be concentrated in the area of the utility norm, because source and target language display pre-existing linguistic expression schemata, well-established modes of linguistic behavior and restrictive rules, all of which it must be possible to correlate. A linguistic approach can provide a basis on which factors relevant in translating which relate to language as such and to the context of situation can be critically differentiated, systematized, and evaluated. From this point of view, translation criticism takes on the character of an applied science. (LLBA)

2226. Zierer, Ernesto. "Ensayo de una teoría formalizada de la traducción." *LyC* 13(1973):75-81.

A general description of the process of translation is given employing the concepts of text, source language, target language, transmitter, recodifier, and interpretation. The process of translation is defined from the point of view of bilingual communication, establishing functional relations between the terms of communicative meaning, semantic information, communicative effect, expressive potentiality of languages, and the region of the language of the speaker, the translator, and the reader of the translation. In recodification direct equivalences are obtained by means of a simple substitution and indirect equivalences across the metastructure. (LLBA)

Pidgins and Creoles

2230. Bickerton, Derek. "Creolization, Linguistic Universals, Natural Semantax and the Brain." *WPLUH* 6,iii:125-41.
Hitherto, the only explanation for the grammatical similarities that exist among creole languages has been that of monogenesis, i.e., the theory that all European-based creoles descend from a single ancestor. However, there is no evidence that such a proto-pidgin could have been transported to Hawaii. Indeed, surviving pidgin speakers in Hawaii show few features of the grammatical systems shared by other creoles. On the other hand, the verbal system of creole speakers in Hawaii who have not undergone decreolization is virtually identical with the verbal systems of those languages. Comparison of the outputs of first-generation (pidgin) and second-generation (creole) speakers in Hawaii leads to the conclusion that the former is inadequate to provide a natural language and that creole speakers had recourse to natural universals to produce an adequate system. (DB)

2241. Harewood, Hyacinth. "An Enigmatic Paragraph in Linguistics." *Cahiers linguistiques d'Ottawa* 7,iii(1973):43-47. [With ref. to R.A. Hall,Jr., *Pidgin and Creole Languages*.]
A key paragraph from Robert A. Hall, Jr.'s *Pidgin and Creole Languages* is used to demonstrate a lack of clarity in linguistic literature. The discussion defines what Hall was saying about the true character of pidgin languages. Two conditions must be met for a true pidgin: (1) The grammatical structure and its vocabulary must be sharply reduced; and (2) The resultant language must be native to none of the people who use it. (LLBA)

2248. Schumann, John H. "The Implications of Interlanguage Pidginization and Creolization for the Study of Adult Second Language Acquisition." *TESOLQ* 8:145-52.
Describes several recent views of second language learning, all of which see learner speech as systematic attempts to perform in the target language. The social functions of pidgin and creole languages are presented as a basis for a model of the development of the learner language. Within this model, the learner language is seen to simplify and reduce when it is restricted to a strictly communicative function; it is seen to complicate and expand when it is extended to integrative and expressive functions. (JHS)

2256. Wittmann, Henri. "Le joual, c'est-tu un créole?" *Linguistique* 9,ii(1973):83-93.
The distinction between creole languages and hybrid languages leads to the supposition that Joual is genetically different from creolization. A lexico-statistical comparison of the Joual of Montreal with Gaspesian, Parisian, and two French Creoles confirms the results of traditional genetic classification based on the criterion of spatio-temporal discontinuities. On the other hand, hybrid and creole languages in general and Québécois and French creoles in particular share a number of analogies of a typological and sociolinguistic order. (LLBA)

VIII. DIALECTOLOGY

2270. O'Cain, Raymond K. "Pathology versus Dialectology: A Review of the Lincolnland Conferences on Dialectology." *JEngL* 8:57-65.
The three Lincolnland Conferences consisted of 16 invited papers and extensive informal discussions. Most of the papers are by speech pathologists, who neither address dialectology directly nor in a fashion characteristic of linguists. Only three papers were by practicing dialectologists. The intent of the conferences was to explore the role of speech pathologists in changing the speech of disadvantaged—but normal—persons. From the papers and the discussions it is obvious they have a great deal to learn about the significance of variation in normal speech. (RKO'C)

2276. Trudgill, Peter. "Linguistic Change & Diffusion: Description and Explanation in Sociolinguistic Dialect Geography." *LSoc* 3:215-46.
Linguistic geography has remained relatively unaffected by recent developments in sociolinguistic theory and method and theoretical geography. Insights and techniques from both these disciplines will be of value in improving descriptions of geographical variation in language, and these improvements will in turn lead to more adequate explanations for certain social and spatial characteristics of linguistic change. Evidence in favor of a sociolinguistic methodology and new cartographic techniques in dialect geography is drawn from empirical studies in urban dialectology, in East Anglia, England, and rural dialectology, in Norway. (PT)

THEORETICAL AND DESCRIPTIVE LINGUISTICS†

I. PHONOLOGY

General

2320. Anderson, John, and Charles Jones. "Three Theses Concerning Phonological Representations." *JL* 10:1-26.
Phonological representations are per se more highly structured than usually proposed by generative phonologists. Morpheme structure conditions are reducible to constraints on the structure of syllables, provided that the bracketing into syllables may be non-proper. Dependency trees provide an appropriate means of representing syllable structures (with syllabic segment as head), morpheme structures (with stressed segment as head), and also the internal structure of segments. Some segments incorporate subparts which can otherwise constitute an entire segment. (LLBA)

2327. Dinnsen, Daniel A. "Constraints on Global Rules in Phonology." *Language* 50:29-51.

† *Festschriften* and Other Analyzed Collections are listed in the first division of this volume. "F" numbers in brackets following a title refer to these items.

Evidence has been advanced recently in favor of incorporating a generalized version of derivational history (or global rules) into phonological theory. However, any theory that incorporates a generalized version of derivational history characterizes a wider range of relationships than need be ascribed to natural language. All empirically defensible cases of derivational history are characteristically restricted to deletion phenomena. The restricted nature of this evidence demands a highly constrained version of derivational history. Thus the "Null Segment Hypothesis" is here proposed as a possible and appropriate constraint. The hypothesis and its related constraints narrowly define the set of all and only those processes in the necessary empirically defensible derivational history relationship. (DAD)

2329. Dubravčić, Maja. "A View upon the Distribution of Emphasis in Speech." *SRAZ* 33-36(1972-73):727-44.
Analyzes the parts of speech that are emphasized more frequently than nouns and full verbs. The term "emphasis" can be defined phonetically, syntactically, semantically, and stylistically and, for this reason, notions about it are vague. A given sample of speech is examined in an attempt to find out which parts of an utterance

bear the distribution of emphasis. The analysis concentrates on the general effect which emphasis produces on the listener. (LLBA)

2330. Edelman, D.I. "K tipologii indoevropeiskikh gutturalnykh." *IAN* 32(1973):540-46.
Several Indo-European scholars who dispute the possibility of establishing three series of gutturals (simple, palatal, and labial) for the general system of Indo-European assert that these three series are not to be found in a single Indo-European language. One of the languages of the Northern Pamir group of West Iranian languages has precisely these three in its consonant system; other Indo-Iranian languages also possess elements of this threefold division. The operation of positional variants and other factors could lead to the obscuring of the threefold system, so that it might still have been present in proto-Indo-European. (LLBA)

2341. Jensen, John T. "A Constraint on Variables in Phonology." *Language* 50:675-86.
Two kinds of variables have been used in generative phonology: abbreviatory variables, which have only one expansion in the application of a given rule to a string; and essential variables, which have many values simultaneously. Essential variables can be dispensed with entirely if rules are allowed to apply iteratively rather than simultaneously. Abbreviatory variables can be severely constrained by the relevancy condition proposed here, which allows only irrelevant material to intervene between the focus and determinant of a rule. (JTJ)

2350. Koutsoudas, Andreas, Gerald Sanders, and Craign Noll. "The Application of Phonological Rules." *Language* 50:1-28.
Phonological evidence is presented in support of the hypothesis that all restrictions on the relative order of application of grammatical rules are determined by universal rather than language-specific principles. For a systematically representative set of synchronic and diachronic facts, previously accounted for by means of non-universal extrinsic-ordering constraints, there are alternative explanations of equal or greater generality in which the relative order of application of rules is either entirely unrestricted, or else fully predictable from the forms of the rules by a universal principle of proper inclusion precedence. (AK, GS, & CN)

2356. Leiberman, Philip, Edmund S. Crelin, and Dennis H. Klatt. "Reply to 'A Note on Phonetic Ability'." *AA* 75(1973): 1719-21.
A reply to a critique (see Nett, below) of a previous work on the evolution of phonetic ability and the related anatomy in humans, Neanderthal man, and in primates. Speech perception, synthetic speech, and the role of archeology in the study of language development are discussed. (LLBA)

2360. Nett, Elizabeth Gayle. "A Note on Phonetic Ability." *AA* 75(1973):1717-19.
A critique of "Phonetic Ability and Related Anatomy of the Newborn and Adult Human, Neanderthal Man, and the Chimpanzee" by Lieberman, Crelin, and Klatt. The problems of sound approximation, mechanical speech reproduction, and archeological techniques in the study of speech development are discussed. (LLBA)

2362. Perry, J.A.,Jr. "Phoneme and Supralect." *IPAJ* 4:13-19.
Presently, phonemes are classified with reference to whether the phoneme is to be regarded as a unit of an idiolect, dialect, multidialect, or supralect. Advocates of an idiolectal phoneme were Jones (1936) and Pike (1947); of a dialectal phoneme, Bloomfield (1935) and Bloch (1948); of a multidialectal phoneme, Swadesh (1947) and Trager and Smith (1957); and of a supralectal phoneme, Müller (1876) and Perry (1972). Major objections to the first three viewpoints are the blurred distinctions between phonetics and phonemics, the confusion between the individual language and the common language, and the logical impossibility and inutility of "taxonomic phonemics" in a transformational grammar. Only a "supralectal phonemics" does not lead to unsurmountable complications in practice. (JAP,Jr)

2364. Platt, John T. "Alphabet Soups or a Mess of Pottage?" *FLang* 11:295-97.
Some alphabetical abbreviations co-occur with the definite article, e.g., the U.S.A., while others do not, e.g., GM-General

Motors. A relation between occurrences of the with appellations and non-occurrence of the with names has been suggested. Some abbreviations occur with or without the, but the tendency seems to be toward the-exclusion because of two factors: (1) greater familiarity with the alphabetical title; and (2) lack of awareness of what the full form is. (LLBA)

2365. Reimold, Peter M. "An Alternative to Ladefoged's System of Universal Phonological Parameters." *LingB* 30:33-43.
A phonological feature system is presented using complex symbols of the form [MAIN $sub_i(x)...(z)$], where MAIN = main category, sub_i = subcategories, and x, z = numerical values of subcategories. Main categories denote physiological entities, subcategories properties of these entities, and numerical values the degree of such properties. Complex gestures (affricates, prenasalized segments) have double values. Phonemes are reinterpreted as "psychophones," the latter being defined as bundles of sensory targets. Three types of target are distinguished: tactile, auditory, and motor, with main categories falling into one of the three classes. (LLBA)

2366. Sampson, Geoffrey. "Is There a Universal Phonetic Alphabet?" *Language* 50:236-59.
Many physical phonetic variables are continuous, so physically there is an infinitely large range of possible sounds. The generative phonologists believe in a universal level of systematic phonetics where only a fixed finite number of distinct values are possible for each phonetic variable, and hence there is only a finite set of possible segments. To justify this hypothesis it would be necessary (a) to show that facts follow from it which are arbitrary on Bloomfield's theory, and (b) to explain away any counter-evidence. Hardly any true predictions have been shown to follow from the hypothesis, and evidence is offered against it. (GS)

General and Instrumental Phonetics

General and Miscellaneous. 2377. Barkai, Malachi. "An Attack on the Defense of Non-Uniqueness of Phonological Representations." *Linguistics* 126:5-9.
J.L. Malone (*Language*, 46, 1970) argued that forms in Classical Mandaic, a Semitic language, were created in apparent defiance of the principle of non-uniqueness and that therefore this principle must be seriously doubted. In rebuttal of this claim, further examples from another Semitic language, Hebrew, are cited, showing that if Malone's position is accepted, it would lead to the illogical conclusion that unique phonological representations must also be doubted, since new forms in the latter language have been created in "defiance" of these also. (MB)

2379. Brame, Michael K. "The Cycle in Phonology:Stress in Palestinian, Maltese, and Spanish." *LingI* 5:39-60.
The hypothesis that stress rules apply cyclically in natural languages is supported. A survey of phonological alternations in Palestinian, Arabic, Maltese, and Spanish leads to the postulation of an ordered set of phonological rules for each language. Constraints and rules on natural bracketings and constraints on the cycle in phonology are proposed based on these data. (LLBA)

2380. Carroll, John B., and John T. Lamendella. "Subjective Estimates of Consonant Phoneme Frequencies." *L&S* 17:47-59.
Subjective magnitude estimates of the frequencies of 24 consonant phonemes were obtained from 65 university students, by a method used for judgments of letter frequencies. Reliabilities of averaged judgments for comparably sized groups of 30 judges were estimated as in the neighborhood of .95. Averages of logarithmically transformed judgments were correlated with log frequencies from objective counts with coefficients in the range .736 to .876. Despite the high reliabilities and predictive validities, there was evidence that the judgments were strongly influenced by experienced frequencies of letters of the alphabet. (JBC & JTL)

2384. Lewis, Frederick C. "Distinctive Feature Confusions in Production and Discrimination of Selected Consonants." *L&S* 17:60-67.
Twenty-five children with defective articulation and 25 normal speaking children were matched for age and IQ score. They identified pictures representing 18 consonants. The consonant

confusions were analyzed in terms of six selected distinctive features. The subjects also listened to syllable pairs containing consonants separated by one and two of the six features. Comparison of the performance on the discrimination task with that on the articulation task revealed that children with articulation disorders had significantly greater difficulty discriminating between consonants separated by one and two features than did the normal speaking children. Children with defective articulation also had significantly greater difficulty discriminating auditorily between sounds separated by one feature than they did between consonants separated by two features. (FCL,Jr)

2386. Melikišvili, I.G. "K izučeniju ierarxičeskix otnošenij edinic fonologičeskogo urovnja." *VJa* 23,iii:94-105.
A review of research on the class of voiced phonemes from the point of view of universally-functional relations and the phonetic characteristics of sound. The results of the research are organized into groups by two functional criteria: (1) distribution of the gaps in paradigmatic systems and (2) frequency of relations of phonemes. On the basis of these criteria, the class of the voiced phoneme was examined in the Iberian-Caucasian system within a differentiated class of voiced symbols, where there exist signs of voiced, glottalic aspiration and intensity. (LLBA)

2392. Tilkov, D. "A propos du phonème indéterminé." *Linguistique* 9,ii(1973):141-44.
An attempt to specify the characteristics of the "indeterminate" phoneme, which may be defined purely phonetically. Due to its indeterminate character, it is usually found outside the classes of localization and, thus, does not participate in any opposition of this type. The vocalic systems of a number of languages contain this vowel but in most cases there is a partial system in which many oppositions are neutralized. The neutral vowel could have any of three different functional manifestations depending upon the phonological system of the language. (LLBA)

Acoustic Analysis. 2393. Nihalani, Paroo. "Lip and Jaw Movements in the Production of Stops in Sindhi." *IPAJ* 3(1973):75-80.
An investigation of the hypothesis that lip-position is conditioned by the vowel sound of the syllable in which the stop functions as the initiating component. Lip and mandible movements in the explosive phase of the production of stops in Sindhi were examined. The following dimensions were measured: (1) width of lip opening; (2) height of lip opening; (3) area of lip opening; (4) distance between outermost-points of lips; (5) protrusion of the upper lip; (6) protrusion of the lower lip; and (7) mandible movement. (LLBA)

Acoustic Phonetics. 2397. Bond, Z.S. "The Perception of Sub-Phonemic Phonetic Differences." *L&S* 16(1973):351-55.
In a preliminary study, Fry (1968) discovered that he was able to discriminate between mono-morphemic words of identical phonemic shape, such as *lax* v. *lacks*. In this study, 10 such assumedly homophonous word pairs were tested for subjects' ability to identify them. When total scores for each word pair were considered, subjects were unable to identify any of the word pairs correctly at a statistically significant level. However, in the case of some individual productions of the "homophone" pairs, subjects were consistent in how they labeled the words. The productions which were most consistently labeled were analyzed to determine what acoustic cues the subjects were employing. Apparently, subjects were able to make use of certain cues that are sometimes considered subphonemic. That these cues are not linguistically significant is indicated by the fact that besides correct identifications, the subjects also produced equally consistent mislabelings. (ZSB)

2405. Irvin, Bruce E. "The Influence of Four Factors on the Identification of Vowels from Minimal Temporal Cues." *SM* 41:139-50.
Tests the effect of four principal variables on the ability of listeners to identify the vowel contained in voiceless plosive-consonant syllables when the listener was presented only with the plosive burst plus aspiration or shortened versions of these stimuli. The four variables examined were consonant, duration,

listener, and talker. These were found to contribute significantly to the total variance. In addition, the interactions between consonant and duration, talker and duration, listener and consonant, and talker and consonant and duration were found to be significant. Possible sources for these effects are discussed. (BEI)

2411. Michaels, David. "Sound Replacements and Phonological Systems." *Linguistics* 126:69-81.
The evidence from linguistic interference in language contact can serve as empirical data with which to test the claims of linguistic theory. In learning a second language (L2), sounds of L2 are typically identified and replaced by sounds of the first language (L1). Since sound replacements are consistent they must reflect the phonological system of L1 and thus provide a source of evidence as to its structure. A framework which defines a hierarchy among phonological features can make predictions about sound replacements. The approach to describing sound replacements through markedness hierarchies not only offers an explanation for particular sound replacements in terms of a set of universal constraints on phonological systems, but also tests proposed markedness conventions. (DM)

2417. Stevens, Kenneth N., and Dennis H. Klatt. "Role of Formant Transitions in the Voiced-Voiceless Distinction for Stops." *JAS* 55:653-59.
Previous research on acoustic cues responsible for the voiced-voiceless distinction in prestressed English plosives has emphasized the importance of voicing onset time (VOT) with respect to plosive release. Voiced plosives in English normally have a short VOT and a significant formant transition following voice onset. Voiceless plosives in prestressed position, on the other hand, have relatively long VOTs and the formant transitions are essentially completed prior to voice onset. Experiments with synthetic speech compare the role of VOT and the presence or absence of a significant formant transition following voicing onset as cues for the voiced-voiceless distinction. The data indicate that there is a significant trading relationship between these two cues. (LLBA)

Articulation, Physiology of Speech. 2443. Koike, Yasuo. "Application of Some Acoustic Measures for the Evaluation of Laryngeal Dysfunction." *Studia Phonologica* 7(1973):17-23.
Perturbation of pitch period of voice was compared in patients with laryngeal diseases and normal Ss. Special attention was paid to the initial period of phonation and the data of this period were compared with those of steady periods of phonation. In the initial period, there existed marked perturbations of pitch, and they were closely related to the type of initiation. Fundamental frequency also affected pitch perturbation. A relative average perturbation was defined on the basis of a smoothed trend line of the pitch. The possibility of applying these measures to the screening and evaluation of laryngeal disorders is discussed. (LLBA)

2459. Sigurd, Bengt. "Maximum Rate and Minimal Duration of Repeated Syllables." *L&S* 16(1973):373-95.
Among the questions related to tongue-twisters is how fast syllables of different types can be repeated. A simple pilot experiment with strings of open syllables such as [tatata . . .], [stastasta . . .] was carried out. Differences in the results are interpreted as due to individual differences in motor skills and to differences in the phonetic material of the syllables. Two simple mathematical models are derived to predict the data. The last model predicts repetition rate from assumed inherent durational values of the consonants involved. A correction factor is established to compensate for the difference between observed and predicted values. This factor seems to depend on difficulties in coordinating articulatory movements. Some hypotheses and speculations concerning the connection between the results and the phonological structure of languages are advanced. (BS)

2461. Tatham, M.A.A., and Katherine Morton. "Electromyographic and Intraoral Air-Pressure Studies of Bi-labial Stops." *L&S* 16(1973):336-50.
There have been a number of electromyographic (EMG) studies of the lips and at least one involving simultaneous measurement of intraoral air-pressure behind bilabial stops. The experiment reported here was one of a series designed to throw light on the problem of deciding how much of the output of speech

production is dependent upon the phonology and how much on the phonetics. Many EMG studies of the lips have undertaken comparisons between the occurrences of certain segments in various positions within the word, under various degrees of stress, between segments labeled in the phonology as plus/minus voice/tense, and so on. In this experiment we try to examine in a more detailed way the relationship between the contraction of just one muscle (m. orbicularis oris) and the event which it is principally responsible for in bilabial stop consonants—achieving lip-closure. The lip-closure results in (or is brought about to achieve) an increase in intraoral air-pressure, so we took measurements of this variable during the experiment. (MAAT & KM)

Speech Processing and Synthesis. 2473. Claxton, Guy L. "Initial Consonant Groups Function as Units in Word Production." *L&S* 17:271-77.
Subjects were presented with single consonants, consonant-consonant pairs, and consonant-vowel pairs and asked to produce words beginning with these letters. Three presentation methods were used: visual tachistoscopic, acoustic with the letters "spelled," and acoustic with the letters pronounced as they would be in a word. Latency measures revealed that the acoustic "spelling" condition took longer than the other two and consonant-vowel took longer than consonant-consonant. These results are interpreted as supporting a conception of verbal memory in which initial consonant clusters are stored as integral units. (GC)

2476. Koike, Yasuo, and Minoru Hirano. "Glottal-Area Time Function and Subglottal-Pressure Variation." *JAS* 54(1973): 1618-27.
High-speed photography of the vibrating laryngeal structures involving one female S simultaneously with direct recording of the vibratory air-pressure variation in the trachea is described. Glottal dimensions and pressure data were obtained from this film using a semiautomated digital-reduction technique. The glottal-width function may be considered to be an approximate estimate of the glottal-area function if the vibrating structure in the larynx is unaffected by pathology. (LLBA)

Distinctive Features

2483. Anwar, Mohamed Sami. "Consonant Devoicing at Word Boundary as Assimilation." *LangS* 32:6-12.
Consonant devoicing at word boundary is a case of assimilation and strengthening. If a language has final devoicing, it also has regressive assimilation; if a language has initial and final devoicing, it typically has progressive and regressive assimilation; if a language has initial devoicing, there should be progressive assimilation. This process of assimilation explains the phenomenon of "permitted finals" since word boundary functions as a voiceless abstruent. Devoicing is also a strengthening process, understood as tensing and resistance to lenition. The hierarchy of devoiced consonants is: stops(b,d,g), spirants(sibilants, non-sibilants), nasals(ŋŋ,n,m)/liquids (r/l), and glides(w/y). (MSA)

2484. Campbell, Lyle. "Phonological Features:Problems and Proposals." *Language* 50:52-65.
Inadequacies in the *Sound Pattern of English* feature system, in the

realm of unattained natural classes and unaccommodated contrasts, are shown; and alternative solutions to these problems are considered. One involves added features; the other involves the notational innovation of the complex symbol. (LC)

2485. de Souza, Roberto, and Germaine M. Kempf. "De l'unité phonétique:Phone, Segment, Trait." *Linguistique* 9,ii(1973):59-82.
Three units of phonic substance are analyzed: phone, segment, and feature. The validity of each of these units is discussed within the framework of the three levels of phonetics and some conclusions are drawn: (1) At the articulatory and acoustic levels, the unit studied is the articulatory segment and acoustical segment, respectively; (2) At the perceptual level, the unit of study appears to be the perceptive phone; and (3) Feature, at the articulatory and acoustical levels, is the result of projection of the perceptive level at the other levels. The distinction between phone, segment, and feature is necessary both from theoretical and methodological viewpoints. In applied phonetics, the proposed distinction would allow more precise analysis and classification of phonic changes. (LLBA)

2487. Kortlandt, F.H.H. "The Identification of Phonemic Units." *Linguistique* 9,ii(1973):119-30.
A formula is provided to define the set of initial objects of phonemic analysis. The case of "joint features" is analogous to the case of different phonetic features jointly constituting a single relevant feature. The essential characteristic of joint features is that of a single relevant feature as part of a number of successive phonemic units. The existence of the phonemic units, the establishment of which should be based on the formula provided, is presupposed, and only the relative ordering of a specific relevant feature with respect to the relevant features which constitute the phonemic units is questioned. (LLBA)

Segmental Phonology

General and Miscellaneous. 2497. Smith, Riley B. "Hyperformation and Basilect Reconstruction." *JEngL* 7(1973):48-56.
Hyperforms provide indirect evidence of basilect rules because they reflect the stereotype—and inaccurate—phonological relationships between the basilect and the acrolect as perceived by the basilect speaker. Basilect rules and forms can in this sense be reconstructed from the evidence of hyperforms. Unproductive interviews may thus provide a wealth of indirect data for the analyst. Illustrative data is provided from language of east Texas blacks. (RBS)

Phonemics and Phonotactics. 2500. Sommerstein, Alan H. "On Phonotactically Motivated Rules." *JL* 10:71-97.
The grammars of natural languages contain an exhaustive set of surface phonotactic rules. If there is a surface phonotactics, certain phonological rules (P-rules) will entirely or partly duplicate phonotactic constraints. The statement of such P-rules can be simplified if they are defined to apply only when their application helps to cure a phonotactic violation or when their application does not create a phonotactic violation. One of these rules leads us to make a further distinction between P-rules motivated by a particular phonotactic constraint and those motivated by the phonotactics as a whole. (LLBA)

II. PROSODY (SUPRASEGMENTALS)

General

2506. Bowley, C.C. "Metrics and the Generative Approach." *Linguistics* 121:5-19.
In *English Stress* (1971) Morris Halle and Samuel Jay Keyser refer to a standard theory of iambic pentameter based upon standard treatises of metrics. Standard theory recognizes the line of five iambs as a norm, lines with non-iambic substitutions being deviations. However, study of such treatises shows that lines with non-iambic feet are accepted as part of the norm for iambic pentameter. Therefore a generative theory of metrics must take as

basic the premise that metered verse permits a variety of underlying metrical patterns. It is possible to account for all possible metrical patterns by four phrase-structure rules. Transformations, however, would not provide an appropriate part of the descriptive apparatus. The fact that transformations fail as a theoretical device in metrics suggests that the traditional view of variants as substitutions is unsound. (CCB)

2517. Scott, Charles T. "Towards a Formal Poetics:Metrical Patterning in 'The Windhover'." *Lang&S* 7:91-107.
After re-examining certain formal characteristics of Hopkins' "The Windhover" and pointing out the inadequacy of certain

traditional conclusions about these formal charactersitics, a reanalysis of the metrical pattern of the poem is given by utilizing the Halle-Keyser theory of the iambic line. A revised format for the poem, which is defensible in terms of linguistic and stylistic considerations, and which is also iambic in its metrical patterning, is presented. Hopkins achieved a masterful interweaving of the Old English alliterative tradition and the iambic tradition by suggesting the appearance of the one while actually adhering to the principles of the other. (CTS)

Loudness, Stress, and Amplitude

2522. Neo, George. "A Theory of Stress." *RELC* 5:50-63. In spoken English the degree of stress on an item is inversely proportional to the degree to which that item can be predicted in a sequence of items. The hypothesis brings coherence to previous observations of word stress and sentence stress, and of grammatical and attitudinal stress. It is scientific in the sense that it can be put to experimental test. Such a test is described and test findings support the hypothesis. Functional and other anomalies are discussed, and the concept of predictability further examined. (HVG & BCN)

2523. Schmerling, Susan F. "A Re-examination of 'Normal Stress'." *Language* 50:66-73.
"Normal stress" has never been adequately defined. Linguists have apparently made a tacit assumption that the stress in citations elicited from an informant is the same as the stress used by a speaker making a minimum of special assumptions; but this is shown to be false. "Normal stress," a notion inherited from structural linguistics, was required by assumptions inconsistent with those of the generative framework; this notion is not particularly useful. (SFS)

Pitch

General and Miscellaneous. 2529. Rivara, Rene. "Pour une description intégrée de l'intonation." *Linguistics* 117(1973):59-76. Up to now, intonation has not received the attention it deserves. Yet, there can be little doubt that it plays a major role in determining the total meaning of spoken sentences. The problem is to give an account of how intonation interacts with syntax and lexical meanings to produce the meaning of sentences. It seems there are three aspects to the linguistic function of intonation (cf. Halliday, *Intonation and Grammar in British English*, 1967). First, the division into tone-groups reveals, in some well-defined cases, the syntactic structure of the sentence and thereby may occasionally raise an ambiguity. Second, the placing of the

nuclear stress in a tone-group has a semantic function; in particular, it determines partly the division of the semantic content of a sentence into the explicit part and the presupposed part. Lastly, the nature of the nuclear tone determines the "modality" of the sentence (its declarative, imperative, or interrogative nature). (RR)

Intonation. 2531. Collier, René. "Intonation from a Structural Linguistic Viewpoint:A Criticism." *Linguistics* 129:5-28.
Current generative phonological approaches to intonation strongly rely on the observational data and the theoretical insights about pitch that have been accumulated during the preceding structural linguistic decades. TG phonology does not question these traditional findings but rather tries to account for them in a more explanatory and systematic way. Yet, the critical examination of the methods and results of structural linguistic intonation analysis reveals some important shortcomings. Because of these imperfections structural linguistic writings about intonation may not be an adequate basis for the construction of a generative phonological theory of pitch in speech. (RC)

2533. Hirst, D.J. "Intonation and Context." *Linguistics* 141:5-16.
We must specify the context of an utterance to predict its intonation, but T-G grammar can only generate single sentences. Chomsky has shown that certain sentences with identical deep structures have, because of their intonation, differing semantic interpretations. Sentences in utterance are reduced forms of surface structures, and that reduction, involving the suppression of part of the surface structure is a distinct operation from ellipsis, involving the deletion of part of the deep structure. We can thus predict the intonative features of a sentence as a direct result of the underlying surface structure. We can also reject polysystemic approaches to intonation. (DJH)

Tone Systems. 2536. Fromkin, Victoria A. "Tone Features and Tone Rules." *SAL* 3(1972):47-76.
Surveys various proposals regarding the representation of tone in generative phonology. Different tone feature sets are evaluated, including those which represent tone by acoustic or auditory features and a more recent set using laryngeal features. The laryngeal features proposed by Morris Halle do not represent physiological reality and are unable to account for certain tonal phenomena. The discussion of "contour" features maintains that while certain contour tones should be represented as sequences of level tones, contour features are required at least on the phonetic level of representation. (LLBA)

III. WRITING SYSTEMS

General

2546. Herrick, Earl M. "A Taxonomy of Alphabets and Scripts." *VLang* 8:5-32.
A taxonomy or system of classification is set forth to describe alphabets and to indicate the various degrees of formal similarity which they bear to one another. The principles of this taxonomy, largely borrowed from the biological sciences, are briefly stated; three taxonomic levels, corresponding to three degrees of similarity, are defined. For each level, the kinds and degrees of similarity which alphabets must have to be included within one taxon are described; these similarities are illustrated by several different taxa and some of the alphabets which belong to them. Several problems in the comparison of writing systems are considered. (LLBA)

Epigraphy and Paleography

Decipherment. 2557. Chakravorty, Banka B. "A New Thought on the Decipherment of Indus Script." *FolkloreC* 16:334-60(to be cont.).
A short history of the origin of the problem of Indus script since 1875, followed by a consideration of the theories of script interpretation is presented. The inscriptions are believed to indicate proper names and the characteristics of proper names are examined. The method of decipherment based on 4 presumptions is discussed in detail. 86 seals all bearing proper names are presented for consideration by scholars. Chakravorty presents his conclusions on the provenance, purpose, and language of the seals. (BBC)

IV. LEXIS

General

2578. Lehrer, Adrienne. "Homonymy and Polysemy:Measuring Similarity of Meaning." *LangS* 32:33-38.

Katz has challenged the traditional homonymy-polysemy dichotomy, arguing that the distinction is one of degree. Moreover, similarity of meaning can be determined by counting semantic markers. To test these hypotheses, subjects were asked to rate pairs of items on a five point scale of similarity. Experiment 1 compared responses of English and French Ss on matched words for which the semantic markers are the same in both languages. Results showed that the two groups weighed components differently. In experiment 2 English speakers rated a set of words twice—with a month between. For homonyms there was high agreement among Ss and consistency from one month to the next. On polysemous items there was variability and inconsistency. These data suggest that Katz is not correct. (AL)

2582. Sprigg, R.K. "The Lexical Item as a Phonetic Entity." *IPAJ* 4:20-30.
Words in English that have been described as identical in pronunciation, or as rhyming, are phonetically distinct, and the phonetic distinction can be related to a difference in the number of lexical items within the word, both for monosyllabic and polysyllabic words. Sharp, in "Stress and Juncture in English" (1960), ascribed similar phonetic distinctions in polysyllabic words to syllable-division; but syllable-division would not account for such distinctions in monosyllabic words, e.g., "mist," "missed." Finally, there is phonetic evidence, in sentence-initial vowel or consonant length, for supposedly elided sentence-initial words. (RKS)

Etymology

2585. Baldinger, Kurt. "A propos de l'influence de la langue sur la pensée:Etymologie populaire et changement semantique parallèle." *RLiR* 37(1973):241-73.
The relation between language and thought is discussed. Numerous cases which demonstrate how language itself can be the basis for the conceptions men develop about material and spiritual realities are examined. Special attention is given to the ways in which words acquire new meanings through popular etymology, since popular etymologies often lead to significant conceptual shifts as a result of their characteristic attempt to establish semantic parallels. (LLBA)

2586. Kiparsky, Valentin. "About Etymology." *GSlav* 3:5-16.
The modern American linguist's total neglect of vocabulary, especially etymology studies, is discussed. Emphasis is nowadays focused on the structure (i.e., syntax) of the language. Examples of the primary importance of vocabulary both for primitive and for modern man are given. The beginning of scientific etymology is discussed as are the heydays of etymological studies during the neo-grammarians' time, Meillet's disappointment and cynical statements, and the reactions of the 1950s linguists, their attempts to create a real "scientific" etymology with the help of mathematical formulae (Ross, Rudnyckyj). Kiparsky cites examples of the still open possibilities of etymological studies. (VK)

Lexicography

General and Miscellaneous. 2594a. Chapman, Robert L. "Roget's *Thesaurus* and Semantic Structure:A Proposal for Work." *LangS* 31:27-31.
A project for enlarging Roget's *Thesaurus* and perfecting its representation of the English vocabulary would be an excellent way of focusing on semantic theory by the route of empirical work which could be dispersed among scholars according to their particular interests. One useful task would be to incorporate componential analysis by semantic markers into RT so that each term would be shown with its markers and restrictions. Such work might lead to a "thessictionary" in which terms are clustered by semantic association and at the same time given dictionary definitions. (RLC)

2604a. Motley, Michael T. "Verbal Conditioning-Generalization in Encoding:A Hint at the Structure of the Lexicon." *SM* 41:151-62.
Insight into the structure of the communicator's lexicon is claimed through a major variation on the classical "semantic generalization" paradigm. Primarily, the variation consists of the investigation of verbal generalization in encoding rather than decoding, and the simultaneous consideration of three generalization types—semantic generalization, phonological general-

ization, and syntactic generalization. The results provide evidence of a lexicon organized upon a semantic-phonological-syntactic hierarchy. (MTM)

2605. Muraki, Masa. "Presupposition in Cyclic Lexical Insertion." *FLang* 11:188-214.
Presuppositions and assertions must be distinguished in the meaning of a sentence. A word like *succeed* cannot be a constituent of any semantic structure since it combines both the presuppositional and assertive meanings. It must be inserted by lexical insertion; but, if lexical insertion is cyclic, and therefore substitutes a lexical item for a subtree of the phrase structure, transformations that bring the relevant presuppositions into the appropriate part of the assertion are needed. A transformation "presupposition lowering" is proposed and predicate raising is reformulated so that a word like *succeed* may replace only a subtree that contains the required presuppositions. (LLBA)

2609. Schade, Walter. "Zur Verwendung des Kontextes bel der Auswahl von Wörterbuchäquivalenten." *Fremdsprachen* 17(1973):239-45.
The chief limitation of the bilingual dictionary is its restriction to a certain number of equivalents for words whose meanings may vary greatly according to context. But the real problem in present dictionaries of this type is not the limited number of equivalents given, but rather their prescriptive character. On the basis of the results of structural semantic investigations, dictionaries could be developed that would combine the advantages of the definition dictionary and the bilingual dictionary. (LLBA)

Onomastics

2628. González, Alfonso. "Onomastics and Creativity in *Doña Bárbara* y *Pedro Páramo*." *Names* 21:40-45.
Naming in Rómulo Gallegos' *Doña Bárbara* and in Juan Rulfo's *Pedro Páramo* serves a more profound function than the mere symbolical. Names are an integral part of each author's worldview. Onomastics in those novels present the reader with two different attitudes toward the phenomenon of "caciquismo" or political bossism. The names of persons and places in *Doña Bárbara* present the reader with a type of "caciquismo" which will vanish into oblivion as soon as progress is introduced as an alternative. The optimism of the author is reflected in the names he gives. Names in *Pedro Páramo* suggest an eternal "caciquismo" which is left unchanged by a revolution and by the death of the "cacique." The narrator communicates his pessimism through suggestions embodied in the names of characters and places. (AG)

2636. Nicolaisen, W.F.H. "Names as Verbal Icons." *Names* 22:104-10.
Names in their lexical meaninglessness lend themselves to being used as onomastic metaphors or verbal icons, both in traditional ballads and in sophisticated literature. They become more than convenient localizing devices and, even when their lexical meaning is known, operate on an onomastic rather than on a lexical level. Authors who are aware of, and utilize, the iconographic potential of names are, among others, Stephen Vincent Benét, Carl Sandburg, and Thomas Wolfe. (WFHN)

2641. Soltész, Katalin J. "Homonymie, Polysemie und Synonymie der Eigennamen." *ALASH* 22(1972):107-17.
Homonymy is composed of similar sounding, yet different descriptive proper names, such as, for example, "Paris," or informal or shortened forms of different first names within a language if they are of different origins or if their relation in different entities appears to be coincidental in spite of like etymologies. If the relation of meanings is clear, we speak of polysemy, as in the case of personal names possessed by many people, or the carryover of names. Homonymy and polysemy often cause difficulty in comprehension. Synonymous proper names denote the same thing. Typical cases of synonymy are, for example, women's and girls' names, and true names and pseudonyms. In the case of name changes we can speak of synonymy if the old and new name exist simultaneously for a period of time and, therefore, are interchangeable. (LLBA)

Slang, Idiom, Cliché

2646. Hager, Philip E. "More Linguistic Reminders of Everyone's *Doppelgänger*." *AS* 45(1970; pub. 1974):305-06.
Many everyday phrases suggest remnants of a belief in the *Doppelgänger* or second self. Most of the examples of this are phrases to describe states of mental or emotional distress "beside himself." Some indicate a split between the physical and non-physical self which is not always negative. (LLBA)

2647. Koller, Werner. "Intra- und interlinguale Aspekte idiomatischer. Redensarten." *Skandinavistik* 4:1-24.
Idiomatic expressions such as *ins Gras beissen, give someone the cold shoulder, passer un savon à quelqu'un, skära pipor i vassen* are analyzed with respect to syntactic, lexico-semantic, and stylistic features, and with respect to constraints in their usage and occurrence in various texts. The following problems are also discussed: (1) Do idiomatic expressions generally belong to a colloquial register of the spoken language? and (2) What are their semantic and stylistic functions? Examples are given from German, French, English, and Swedish in order to systematize types of equivalence and translation procedures. (WK)

2648. Rowland, Beryl. "The Oven in Popular Metaphor from Hosea to the Present Day." *AS* 45(1970; pub. 1974):215-22.
The oven is a natural metaphor for the womb; it is a figure which has its origins deep in the human psyche and in the culture of primitive communities. Many psychologists have observed that cooking is frequently equated with the process of pregnancy and birth and that the womb is the stove in which the child is baked. Whether *oven* as an isolated term for the womb has had a *sub rosa* existence is hard to determine. It certainly continued into this century in the phrase "bun in the oven." But this expression is now on its way out and the reason for its decline is not far to seek—it has not the emotional response of a taboo four-letter word. Pregnancy has become too respectable and commonplace to require metaphorical expression. (LLBA)

2649. Stanley, Julia P. "When We Say 'Out of the Closets'!" *CE* 36:385-91.
Gay slang reflects the rapid changes occurring within the gay community, in particular that portion of the community actively involved in gay liberation. Although a majority of the terms are restricted in their usage to gay men, the few terms familiar to both lesbians and gay men have developed political, rather than sexual, meanings, expanding their meanings to encompass the political activities of the gay activists. In addition, some terms, e.g., *dyke, lesbian, faggot, homosexual*, have become more specific in their reference and reflect the development of political distinctions among the members of the gay community. There are indications that those terms with political significance will survive, while those that reflect the sexist, racist, and classist attitudes of the larger society may cease to be useful among the users of gay slang. (JPS)

Word Borrowing

2652. Stanforth, A.W. "Lexical Borrowing from German Since 1933 as Reflected in the British Press." *MLR* 69:325-36.
Over a period of 3 years 151 Germanisms were collected at random from the British Press. 136 were loan-words, 15 loan-translations or semantic loans. Of the 136 loan-words 116 do not appear in the *OED* and its (1933) Supplement. The loan-words fall into 4 large classes according to the degree to which they have been accepted into the English language. Thus the first consists of nonce-loans, the second of arcane and technical terms, the third of widely recognized German loans, and the fourth of the most frequently used and most fully assimilated words. The items were largely drawn from the areas of warfare, politics, music, and food. (AWS)

V. GRAMMAR

General

2656. Bedell, George. "The Arguments about Deep Structure." *Language* 50:423-45.
The notion of deep structure has served to crystalize a number of recent controversies in syntactic theory. Several arguments which have appeared in the literature of transformational grammar are examined. These arguments are not compelling and the issue of the existence of deep structure is not an empirical one at present. (GB)

2661. Cook, V.J. "Is Explanatory Adequacy Adequate?" *Linguistics* 133:21-31.
Explanatory adequacy accounts for the descriptively adequate grammar of the language in terms of properties of the acquisition model. Chomsky and Halle's model is instantaneous not only for reasons of convenience but also because of the competence/performance distinction: it can take no account of evidence about the child's acquisition of language but is confined to the global relations between the total primary linguistic data and the final adult grammar. If a non-instantaneous model is used, the theory can evaluate grammars in terms of developing primary linguistic data, perceptual and learning processes, and grammars. (VJC)

2668. Farsi, Ali Abdullah. "Change Verbs." *LangS* 31:21-23.
In a forthcoming paper, Carlota Smith hypothesizes that certain verbs in English (change verbs), because of their meaning, can be used both transitively and intransitively. Farsi presents a list of synonyms of such verbs and demonstrates that they are transitive or intransitive, but not both. Farsi concludes that whether one and the same verb can be both transitive and intransitive is no more predictable than whether one and the same form can be used as a different part of speech. (AAF)

2675. Hetzron, Robert. "A Synthetical-Generative Approach to Language." *Linguistics* 138:29-62.
Most linguistic schools, from traditional to generative-transformational, have been analytic in that they proceed from larger units to smaller ones, breaking down units into constituents. This is not the appropriate format for a theory. Following criticism of analytic linguistics, a proposal is made for a synthetical approach in which atomic units are first given, followed by rules indicating how these are combined into larger structures. The atoms are semantic primitives, each being the member of a cognitive category. There is a finite set of such categories. Elementary predication is birhemic, i.e., one-place. All the more complex constructions are composed of birhemes. Cases are predicates and the nouns they are attached to are their subjects. (RH)

2680. Langacker, Ronald W. "Movement Rules in Functional Perspective." *Language* 50:630-64.
A survey of reasonably well-established movement transformations in English reveals certain asymmetries in the classes of such rules and in their formal properties. The special formal properties of backing rules correlate with their function, which is different from the function of raising, lowering, and fronting rules. The latter three types can be given a uniform functional characterization in terms of the notion "objective content." Raising, lowering, and fronting rules all serve the function of increasing the prominence of objective content in surface structure. This hypothesis accounts for the asymmetries noted in regard to the movement rules of English, and it also provides a motivated explanation for the fact that backing rules are upward bounded. (RWL)

2683. Lecointre, Simone, and Jean Le Galliot. "Le changement linguistique:Problématiques nouvelles." *Langages* 32(1973):7-26.
With the sudden enrichment of theories which relate linguistics to its environment, the problem of change takes on a new relevance in decidedly different types of solution. The question is raised whether from this diversity a coherent theory of change can be derived and the conditions necessary for its production. A theory of change by its own productive power purely on the level of analysis of the processes must be able to account for the

phenomenon. Related to these preliminary considerations is an analysis of the following successive models: generative, psycholinguistic, and sociolinguistic. An attempt is made to evaluate their power to explain and their ability to flesh out the bare bones of a theory of linguistic change. Paralinguistic theories represent a start at building a theory of linguistic change, even if they are still somewhat inadequate. (LLBA)

2685. Makkai, Adam. "'Take One' on *Take*:Lexo-Ecology Illustrated." *LangS* 31:1-6.
Examines Langendoen's statement that "grammar is in trouble and needs help from rhetoric." To illustrate his point Langendoen uses a number of sentences whose "derivational history" is obscure: "Mary takes life seriously but Ollie lightly" can be said to be a result of conjunction reduction or gapping. This is a pseudo-dilemma caused by the transformational-generative frame of reference that disappears as soon as one looks at the "ambiguous" sentences in context and recognizes that "take X seriously/lightly" is best described as a part of American English phraseology, a part of the language traditionally ignored in transformational-generative work. "Attractions" of the verb take are also discussed. (AM)

2693. Robert, Françoise. "Aspects sociaux du changement dans une grammaire générative." *Langages* 32(1973):88-97.
The new perspectives opened by the redefinition of the concept of *competence* by U. Weinreich, W. Labov, and M. Herzog are examined. The consequences of this redefinition for the form of grammar and its rules are considered. The different types of rule necessary for the description of heterogeneous competence are studied. The question is then raised of the extent to which it can still be claimed that such a description can constitute a generative grammar. The different and more complex problems which must be overcome in using this model in syntax are discussed. (LLBA)

Morphophonemics

2706. Oh, Choon-Kyu. "Presupposition and the Applicability of Rules." *Linguistics* 138:63-71.
The plausibility of Lakoff's claim that the principles governing the distribution of morphemes will involve presuppositional information is discussed. The applicability of transformational rules depends on the speaker's presupposition: either obligatory or blocked if the speakers share certain presuppositions concerned with a sentence in question, optional if such sharing is absent among speakers. Most so-called optional rules become obligatory once the presupposition is specified. One of the major processes in Korean syntax—the deletion of reflexive pronouns—illustrates this point. Three cases are considered: where the deletion is blocked; where the deletion is obligatory; where the deletion is optional or up to the individual. (CO)

2707. Reinheimer-Rîpeanu, Sanda. "Suffixe zéro?" *RRL* 17(1972):261-69.
The necessity of recognizing the existence of a derivative postposed to the zero morphophonemic realization tempered by the synchronic description of the derivation is established. The point of view adopted permits a classification of the roots of a language according to the combinations actualized with derivatives and flexives. (LLBA)

Morphology

2709. Georgiev, Vladimir I. "L'interdépendance de la syntaxe et de la morphologie (Structures paradigmatiques isosémantiques et isomorphiques)." *Linguistique* 9,ii(1973):51-58.
An examination of the way in which morphological laws function in the evolution of a language is made. One type of development in presenting evolutionary principles is focused upon—the retention or loss of a contrast between certain cases as marked by distinct or identical endings respectively. (LLBA)

2711. Harris, Roy. "Performative Paradigms." *TPS* (for 1972 [1973]):44-58.
English may be considered as representative of languages which have developed OP verbs ("occasional performatives") but have not provided such verbs with any uniformly distinctive morphological equipment. An OP verb is one which conforms to a pattern typified by *apologize*: whereas utterance of, e.g., the words "John apologized" functions, under appropriate circumstances, as a report or account of what John did, namely apologize, utterance of the words "I apologize," under appropriate circumstances, functions not as a report or account of my apologizing, but as my apology. An NP verb ("non-performative") is one like *walk*: there are no circumstances under which uttering a form of words using this verb constitutes or implements the performance of an act of walking. English may also have EP verbs ("exclusive performatives"), i.e., verbs reserved for use in performative utterances. If the OP-NP-EP classification is valid, the traditional assumption of the paradigmatic invariance of lexical meaning needs to be re-examined. At the same time, the semantic assumptions underlying definitions of "performative" need reconsideration. Various arguments support drawing a distinction for OP verbs between a performative meaning and a non-performative meaning, definable independently. (RH)

2712. Kiefer, Ferenc. "A Propos Derivational Morphology." *SML* 9(1973):42-59.
Since lexicalization occurs with individual words more often than with sentences, generative rules are necessary to account for the creativity in derivational processes. A discussion of five important issues follows. (LLBA)

Syntax

2730. Anderson, John. "All and Equi Ride Again." *ArL* 5:1-10.
Certain pairs of sentences, like "Every optimist expects (every optimist) to win," show that in such cases Equi-NP Deletion is optional and meaning-changing. Carden has proposed an account, involving an interpretation of quantifiers as higher predicates and a rule of Quantifier Lowering, which avoids both these conclusions. However, this account is semantically inappropriate and fails to allow for similar pairs lacking quantifiers. It is argued here that the analysis of quantified NPs (and relative constructions) as partitive structures, together with the possibility of indicating co-reference, provides a means of characterizing the semantic distinction between all such pairs while maintaining the unitary, meaning-preserving character of Equi. (JA)

2733. —— "Remarks on the Hierarchy of Quasi-predications." *RRL* 17(1972):193-202.
Quasi-predication structures containing a locative in place of the third nominative phrase characterize the predication of tense. What is universal about tense is the existence of temporal adverbs which mark various semantic distinctions correlating with time reference. In semantic representations, tense is associated with a noun in a locative phrase. The sort of representation implied by such a claim is examined more closely. There are three sets of temporal adverbs: (1) forms which refer unambiguously to past or future; (2) forms which are either past or future; and (3) proximate forms which can be past, present, or future. The fact that only a subset of temporal adverbials (the first of the three groups mentioned) appear to show the distinction crucial for the development of tense concord in the verb is illustrated. This leads to a consideration of "expletive do." It is proposed that *do* realizes the *V* in a quasi-predication which always comes immediately above a non-adjectival verb. Thus, the full verb is not absorbed directly into the tense complex, but only an auxiliary, either one of the "ordinary" ones, or, if none of these come above it, the *do*-form. The *do*-predication is a transitive ergative structure, perhaps of a type in which the ergative phrase is empty. (LLBA)

2738. Balin, B.M., and V.A. Žerebkov. "Aspektuell Relevanter Kontext in den germanischen Sprachen." *Linguistics* 117(1973):5-13.
The absence of grammatical aspectual forms in a language or language group does not indicate that they are incapable of expressing aspectual meanings in a functional-semantic way. When these forms are lacking, there is a multiplicity of functional-semantic devices which appear as a complex of lexical groups and syntactic combinations. Those aspects characteristic of the devices which exist in contemporary Germanic languages for the expression of these meanings are discussed. (LLBA)

2752. Cârstea, Mihaela. "Sulla generazione dell'infinito retto da aggettivi." *RRL* 17(1972):237-60.

The "adjectival" represents a linguistic problem of considerable importance. The more adjectives contained within a structure, the more complicated and intricate the structure seems. Wherever communication takes place in a generative sense, between verb and adjective, the diversity in which authors express this union is great. Of the many arguments advanced, the one which most fits the facts concerning the prepositional complement is that the adjective obeys the governing state and agrees with the principle of verbal complementarity. (LLBA)

2761. Danielsen, Niels. "Plädoyer gegen die generativen Tiefenoperationen:Kritik einer Scheinlehre." *Archiv* 210(1973): 241-62.

A critique of transformational grammar which uses examples from several languages to show that the transformational rules that Chomsky develops from English examples are often either inapplicable or must be modified to the extent that they no longer explain anything. An example is the rule for the transformation of adjectives, i.e., the assertion that an attributive adjective corresponds to a deep structure in which the adjective is in the predicative position. In non-Indo-European languages different positions of adjectives sometimes have widely different meanings, and thus the positing of this rule is purely arbitrary and leads into endless difficulties. Transformational grammarians when confronted with such cases simply bend the rules or create special lexical rules, making their theory "immune" to refutation. (LLBA)

2776. Hsieh, Hsin-I. "On the Psychological Reality of Resultative Clauses." *LangS* 33:15-17.

An experiment was conducted to determine whether Fillmore's resultative construction is a part of the knowledge of English speakers. The results indicated that about one-third of the subjects had full knowledge of this type of construction, while the rest lacked knowledge to different degrees. Resultative construction is psychologically real for some, but not all, speakers of English. (HH)

2777. Huddleston, R.D. "Further Remarks on the Analysis of Auxiliaries as Main Verbs." *FLang* 11:215-29.

J.R. Ross has argued against Chomsky's analysis of the English modal, tense, and aspectual auxiliaries, proposing that they should be treated as main verbs taking sentential complements. Further arguments in support of this analysis are given, including discussions of the verbs "ought," "used," and "be" and of surface structure. The question of whether the auxiliaries are intransitive, transitive, or ditransitive is also discussed. (LLBA)

2779. Hudson, R.A. "Systemic Generative Grammar." *Linguistics* 139:5-42.

"Systemic grammar" is a theory of syntax developed historically out of "Scale and Category" grammar, due to M.A.K. Halliday; however, the version outlined here is different from earlier versions. It has been influenced by transformational-generative grammar and may be used as a generative model of language, like transformational grammar. It is also different from the latter in a number of important respects. In "systemic grammar" deep relations among sentences are shown by means of abstract classificatory features, which are organized in the grammar in "system networks" and are related to the syntactic structure of the sentence by means of "realization rules." This apparatus may be used to generate sentences involving extraposition, recursion, and coordination, all of which are constructions that cannot be generated by less sophisticated models. (RAH)

2786. Kenyon, Roger A. "Rule Matrices for Syntactic Deep Structure." *Linguistics* 122:5-10.

Rule matrices can be used in transformational syntax to eliminate bracketing and formalize the "pictorial" aspect of transformations. (RAK)

2790. Knowles, John. "The Degree Adverbial." *JEngL* 7(1973):21-31.

The concept of degree adverbial is an inheritance from traditional grammar which must be shown to be useful for the more demanding generative model of today. It can be defined in terms of transformational grammar as the modifier of an adjective (or de-adjectival adverbial) of the verb. It is itself divisible into two classes: (1) those that modify the comparable adjective; and (2) those that modify the "absolute" or non-comparable adjective. It may be easily confused with both the frequentative and the measure phrase. However, there are possibilities of distinguishing them through transformational potential. (JDK)

2791. Kravif, Diane. "The Structure-Preserving Constraint and the Universal Base Hypothesis." *Linguistics* 116(1973):21-47.

One measure of the adequacy of transformational grammar theory is the weak generative power of the grammars allowed by the theory. Previous work, mainly that of Peters and Ritchie, has shown that the generative power of transformational grammars is equal to that of Turing machines, even if we require that all transformational grammars must have the same base component (the "universal base hypothesis"). These results are a consequence of the power of cyclically applied transformations. Emonds has proposed a linguistically (nonmathematically) motivated constraint on transformati ons, namely that they be either structure-preserving or root transformations or minor movement rules. It is proposed that there exists a phrase structure grammar p such that given a recursively enumerable language L over the alphabet $\{a_1 \ldots a_n\}$, there exists a set of transformations T all of whose members obey the structure-preserving constraint such that if $G = (P, T)$ and the terminal alphabet of G is $\{a_1 \ldots a_n\}$, then $L(G) = L$. (DK)

2795. Kuno, Susumu. "A Note on Subject Raising." *LingI* 5:137-44.

In generative grammar with extrinsically ordered cyclic rules, subject raising precedes passivization, which does not explain why a verb phrase must obligatorily be shifted to sentence-final position in certain instances and not in others. Two possible solutions to this problem are found in the framework of extrinsic rule ordering. One maintains that subject raising precedes passivization, but that the deep structure of passive sentences has a place holder represented by *by Passive*. The other proposes that *by Passive* does not exist in the deep structure of a passive sentence, but that passivization precedes subject raising. The merits of the possible explanations are discussed and evaluated. (LLBA)

2796. ——— "The Position of Relative Clauses and Conjunctions." *LingI* 5:117-36.

A discussion of relative clauses and conjunctions, including the position of relative clauses in SOV and VSO languages and the position of conjunctions in SOV and SVO language. In any explanation of these structures, certain syntactic patterns can cause perceptual difficulties. Whether these patterns arise or not is determined primarily by the interaction of major constituent word orders; languages will embody devices to minimize those patterns that cause perceptual difficulties. (LLBA)

2801. Larreya, Paul. "Enoncés performatifs, cause, et référence." *Degrés* 4(1973):m-m25.

An adequate definition of performatives must distinguish between the function of an utterance and its meaning. This distinction may be based on the following representation of the speech act: (intention → meani ng) → code → (meaning → interpretation) → reaction. The function consists of the reaction the speaker intends to produce in the hearer. All speech acts are performative as to their function, but only explicit performatives are performative as to their meaning. A grammar of performatives can be based on the following analysis of causatives: [*Mary ProVP the floor*] *caused the floor to become clean.* (If ProVP → 0) > *Mary cleaned the floor; (if ProVP → vacuumed the floor*) > *Mary vacuumed the floor clean.* Similarly, *I reserve this table* has as its semantic structure: [*I ProVP*] *cause this table to become reserved*, where *ProVP*, rewritten 0, is understood to refer to the speech act itself. (PL)

2802. Lee, Patricia A. "Perlocution and Illocution." *JEngL* 7(1973):32-40.

Suggestions are speech acts whereby the speaker attempts to cause the hearer to consider a proposition. The performance of these depends to some degree upon their perlocutionary effect. It is difficult to tell when a suggestion is an indirect illocutionary act and when it has the force of a suggestion by virtue of its perlocutionary effect. A variety of tests are provided to distinguish perlocutionary suggestions from indirect illocutionary suggestions. The tests are contextual and syntactic. (PAL)

2803. Lehmann, W.P. "Subjectivity." *Language* 50:622-29. Historical linguistics has primarily used phonological evidence for genealogical classification. The evidence consists of characteristic facts and details, in Meillet's terms. Syntactic evidence can now be used. Subjectivity, i.e., the subjective dominance of the principal verb in a sentence, is cited as an illustration of a characteristic fact in Proto-Indo-European and its dialects. (WPL)

2811. Lucas, Michael A. "The Surface Structure of Relative Clauses." *Linguistics* 139:83-120.
English relative clauses fall into three main classes. The intonation distinction between tight and loose relative clauses is the starting point for a ternary classification based on a classification of antecedent nominals according to their determinative constituents. Nominals may be (1) proper names; (2) personal pronouns; (3) anaphoric-link nominals; (4) cataphoric-link nominals; (5) partitive nominals; or (6) categorial nominals. Of these classes, (1) and (3) may cooccur with loose clauses, (4) and (6) with tight clauses, and (5) with either type of clause. The three classes of relative clauses are: (A) nominal-constituent clauses, which are occurence-dependent on the nominal head and dominated by the determiner; (B) determinative-constituent clauses, which together with the cataphoric definite article are mutually occurence-dependent with the nominal head; and (C) loose relative clauses, which are linked anaphorically, not structurally, with their antecedents. (MAL)

2819. McKay, K.L. "Further Remarks on the 'Historical' Present and Other Phenomena." *FLang* 11:247-51.
P. Kiparsky has propounded a theory of conjunction reduction to explain the historic present, some uses of the oblique moods, and the Homeric treatment of the augment. The Greek examples quoted to support this are examined in relation to their full contexts and are shown not to support the theory and in some cases to be misquoted. (LLBA)

2820. Mellema, Paul. "A Brief Against Case Grammar." *FLang* 11:39-76.
Charles Fillmore has suggested that the base of a transformational grammar should contain phrase-structure rules which introduce semantic roles or cases into deep structures. In support of this view, Fillmore presents a methodological argument, as well as various semantic and syntactic arguments. Fillmore's methodological argument is question-begging; semantic and syntactic evidence tends to refute rather than support the theory of case grammar. Certain unsupported and implausible psychological consequences of the deep-case hypothesis are cited, concluding that the theory of case grammar should be rejected. (LLBA)

2824. Mittwoch, Anita. "Is There an Underlying Negative Element in Comparative Clauses?" *Linguistics* 122:39-45.
Jespersen and other scholars have postulated the presence of an underlying negative in comparative clauses. Most of the discussion has dealt only with one type of such clauses, viz. those with *more* or *-er*, while ignoring those with *less* or *as ... as*. The hypothesis of an underlying negative is tested by examining the use of *need*, *ever*, and *yet*, which function as negative indicators in English, in all three types of clauses. (AM)

2828. Myhill, John. "Empirical Meaningfulness and Intuitionistic Logic." *PPR* 33(1972):186-91.
Consider a vocabulary of "observation-predicates," and let a "meaningful predicate" be one whose holding can be established by establishing a finite number of observation-predicates. Define the conjunction and disjunction of meaningful predicates in the usual way, and define the negation of a meaningful predicate P to be the presence of a finite number of observation-pre dicates, which jointly entail the absence of P. It has been proven that the algebra of predicates generated by these three operators stands in the same relation to Boolean algebra as the intuitionistic propositional calculus (without implications) stands to the classical propositional calculus. It is argued that the intuitional propositional calculus is a more appropriate language for "vague" predicates than the three-valued logic which has been suggested. (LLBA)

2832. Palmer, F.R. "Noun-Phrase and Sentence:A Problem in Semantics/Syntax." *TPS* (for 1972 [1973]):20-43.
English syntax appears to reflect the semantic distinction between "talking about" a person, creature, or object and "talking about" an event, action, or state. An investigation of this distinction in some familiar sentence structures shows that (i) in some (e.g., *Columbus is believed to have discovered America* and sentences with *seen* and *believe*) the syntax fails to accord with the semantics; (ii) in others (e.g., *I ordered the chauffeur to come at four, John began to dislike Mary, The man is tough to convince*) there is ambiguity (in both semantics and syntax) that is in principle irresolvable. A possible explanation of both sets of sentences in terms of focus proves unsatisfactory. The distinction between epistemic and non-epistemic modals appears to relate to the distinction, but the modals raise even greater complexity. No kind of "deep structure" as at present proposed appears to provide a solution to the problem. (FRP)

2837. Peterson, Thomas H. "Auxiliaries." *LangS* 30:1-12.
An examination of two generative treatments of auxiliaries in English: the traditional analysis of Chomsky (1957) where auxiliaries are generated as a finite non-recursive set, and that of Ross (1969) where auxiliaries are viewed as main verbs with sentential complements. Difficulties for the Chomskian analysis are pointed out: 1) creation of the frequently recurring group of symbols Te ({Modal, be, have}) for which there is no formal category; 2) failure to adequately treat the dialectal difference in British and American English between auxiliary and main verb have; 3) the inability to handle negative contraction; 4) the necessity for the ad hoc introduction of word boundary by the affix-hopping rule; 5) the failure to capture the similarities between "syntactic" auxiliaries and verbs of the *begin* class. The major flaw in Ross's analysis is the failure to distinguish the differences between auxiliaries and verbs of the *want* class. An alternative analysis is put forward in which all auxiliaries and verbs of the *begin* class are seen as verbs which take VP as a complement. A set of rules for English auxiliary constructions is provided. (THP)

2840. Pullum, G.K. "Lowth's Grammar:A Re-Evaluation." *Linguistics* 137:63-78.
Accusations that prescriptive grammarians such as Robert Lowth confused grammar with logic are anachronistic and simplistic. Though aiming to prescribe standards of correctness, *Short Introduction to English Grammar* (1762) represents a reliable description of the English of Lowth's time. He employs historical criteria, but suggestions that he confuses phonic and graphic substance are overstated, as are claims that his description forces English into a grammatical mold made for Latin. Like other 18th-century grammarians, he didn't follow his inherited tradition. He is not a perceptive philosophical grammarian, nor is he the structuralist's stereotype of a blinkered prescriptive tyrant. (GKP)

2853. Scott, Robert Ian. "Grammatical Acceptability as a Negative Function of Disruption." *LangS* 33:5-7.
The kernel subject-verb-object-qualifier (SVOQ) produces more sentence patterns with fewer transformations and less ambiguity than any other. Ten experiments using permuted orders of the four elements of SVOQ in both English and French sentences have shown that successive departures from SVOQ lead to progressive drops in mean judgments of grammatical acceptability and progressive increases in subjective confusion. In general, subjects find QSVO, SQVO, and SVQO acceptable to a degree depending upon the type of qualifier and the possibility of changing its meaning, and use SVOQ as a model for the production of grammatical sentences. (RIS)

2864. Streeter, Victor J. "A Look at Sentence-Type Cohesion." *Lang&S* 2(1973):109-16.
The concept of linguistic structure beyond the sentence level deserves careful definition and explication. Linguists have expressed disparate views on the existence of such structure. The nonrandom patterning of linguistic elements must be regarded as a prerequisite for higher-level structure. Two texts were examined in an attempt to discover nonrandom patterning of adjacent sentence types. Such sentence-type cohesion was found in one text, but not the other. The level of sentence-type cohesion in a text may also contribute to the characterization of the author's style. (VJS)

2866. Sussex, Roland. "The Deep Structure of Adjectives in

Noun Phrases." *JL* 10:111-31.

In transformational generative grammars, attributive adjectives are normally derived from predicative adjectives in underlying relative clauses. The standard justification for this procedure is the Katz-Postal paraphrase requirement on grammars. The sentential paraphrase does not always contain a predicative adjective. The need for paraphrases containing complex semantic representations is demonstrated by the problem of the semantic order-slots of prenominal attributives and by the difficulties of deriving, ordering, and assigning semantic readings to adjectives in this structure. (LLBA)

2871. Valesio, Paolo. "The Art of Syntax and Its History." *LeS* 9:1-30.

The "historicist" trend in linguistics seems to imply the claim that one can make linguistics only when one knows the genesis and historical development of the problem at hand. Actually, explicit methodological assumptions are necessary in order to arrive at any significant conclusion in linguistic history. Analysis of the relative complexity of syntactic structures should be conducted in a descriptive way, without jumping to evaluations. The underlying and the surface structure of the syntactic construction is involved; these points are illustrated on the basis of Romance data. (PV)

2876. Wachowicz, Krystyna A. "Against the Universality of a Single Wh-Question Movement." *FLang* 11:155-66.

In multiple questions, Polish and Russian have all the wh-constituents in clause-initial position, i.e., more than one wh-constituent is moved. On the basis of the assumption that there can be only a single wh-question movement per simple sentence, various mechanisms have been proposed to account for facts about questions. The data from Polish and Russian provide evidence against such proposals. Additional explanation of a fact previously accounted for in terms of the Q-morpheme hypothesis is provided. (LLBA)

2879. Werth, Paul. "Some Thoughts on Non-Restrictive Relatives." *Linguistics* 142:33-67.

Examples indicating the conjunction source of non-restrictive relatives (NRs) are in fact ungrammatical for different reasons: NRs must be declarative, and conjuncts need not be; NRs can appear in a quantified NP, conjuncts absolutely cannot. The counterexample, actually shows that the "Yes-No Question" rule must "follow" NR relativization. Furthermore, the ordinary and appositive conjunct equivalents of NRs do not necessarily share the same implicational possibilities: in particular, NRs often imply relationships of concession, causation, reason, etc., while conjuncts rarely do. This seems to suggest that NRs often, and conjuncts sometimes, are stylistic variants of more explicit concessional, causative, structures, while conjuncts often, and NRs sometimes, are variants of information-adding and temporal succession structures. (PNW)

Word Classes and Categories

2885. Bartsch, Werner. "Methoden grammatischer Definition." *WW* 23(1973):411-19.

An examination of the results of German sentence analysis: (1) The present tense and future I are interchangeable because they are alike in meaning; the only possible distinction between the present tense and future I is that the latter provides the additional information that a given event has not yet begun at the moment of speaking; and (2) The preterite indicates that an event is concluded at the moment of speaking while the perfect indicates that the availability for use of a concluded event is not terminated at the moment of speaking. The German verbal system is not also differentiated according to tense and mood alone, but also according to the kind of action involved. (LLBA)

2887. Buyssens, E. "La classification des adjectifs." *RLV* 39(1973):152-64.

This study, based on French, Dutch, German, and English, presents the syntactic facts which permit and justify an objective classification of adjectives. The lists of the different kinds of adjectives is comparable to the lists in most traditional grammar reference texts; the differences appear in classification, particularly those of articles and numerals. (LLBA)

Discourse Analysis

2903. Langacker, Ronald W. "The Question of Q." *FLang* 11:1-37.

Discusses the special segmental morpheme Q to mark interrogatives in deep structure in a transformational description of English questions. Examined in turn are a Q with performative sense, a non-operator Q lacking performative value, and an operator Q lacking performative value. In each case, either Q has no legitimate function at all when the full range of facts are considered, or there is no advantage to using Q rather than some other device, in particular an abstract performative predicate, to identify questions in deep structure. (LLBA)

VI. SEMANTICS

General and Miscellaneous

2919. Agar, M. "Talking About Doing:Lexicon and Event." *LSoc* 3:83-89.

Sociolinguists have not attended to participants' terminology for events. For this, the usual ethnosemantic focus on relationships of inclusion within a taxonomic structure is insufficient. Stage-process relationships and case-grammar notions of agent, object, instrument, and result account for the conceptual structure encoded in a set of addict's argot terms. The addict's argot functions as a needed, standardized terminology, not just for concealment. (MA)

2922. Baron, Jonathan. "Semantic Components and Conceptual Development." *Cognition* 2(1973):299-317.

Several phenomena in the acquisition of word meanings may be accounted for by a theory of component-by-component acquisition, a mechanism analogous to that proposed for phonological development. By defining a concept as a habitual plan and a component as a subplan, this theory may be extended to the acquisition of concepts in general. The ideas of component-by-component acquisition and of transfer of learning between concepts sharing components thus provide an alternative to developmental stage theories. (LLBA)

2944. Fourquet, J. "Le plan du signifie." *TAI* 1(1972):9-11.

The object of grammatical analysis must be to elucidate how the speaker translates what he has to say into an assemblage of *signifiés* united by connectors which are themselves significant and how he then transcodes this construct of *signifiés* into a phonic chain formed of *signifiants*. Algorithms of transcodage from the level of *signifiés* to that of *signifiants* must be constructed; rules of passage from one formation to the other must be developed. From an organized level of *signifiés*, the communicator positions *signifiants* in a phonic chain. The division of these *signifiants* into phonemes must be regarded as a secondary act. (LLBA)

2963. Kemper, Karl-Friedrich. "Religiöser Wortschatz als Gegenstand der Soziolinguistik bzw. Soziosemantik." *LBib* 25/26(1973):33-42.

In reply to Manfred Kaempfert's critique of his sociosemantic theory of "religious" language, the author makes some precisions concerning semantics, the norm, and the opposition synchrony/diachrony. "Religiousness" of language is an object of sociosemantics, not of an isolated semantics alone, i.e., "religiousness" of language is only defined in terms of the category of "communicative action-games'' which are a framework of "roles" in certain sociological contexts. (K-FK)

2967. Křížek, Pavel. "Towards a Formal Account of the Semantics of Noun Phrases." *PBML* 20(1973):43-58.

A presentation of a formal apparatus for the solution of some questions concerning the description of distributive properties of noun phrases in semantic representations of sentences, within the framework of functional generative description. A modified linguistic application of predicate calculus is employed in the analysis of sentences in natural language. The classification of expressions of language in propositions (sentences), names, functors, and operators, which is commonly used in logical research of both natural and symbolic languages, is accepted. (LLBA)

2973. Ljung, Magnus. "Some Remarks on Antonymy." *Language* 50:74-88.
Discusses the notion of "antonymous adjective." Only noun-based adjectives can be antonymous, and a useful delimitation of the term "antonymous adjective" can be achieved in terms of the inherentness of the underlying nouns: all scalar nouns taken to be inherently possessed by some entity may serve as the base for a set of antonymous adjectives. This conclusion is supported by a comparison with adjectives derived from so-called inalienable nouns: the two types of adjective are found to share many characteristics. (ML)

2986. Podraza, Bill. "General Semantics—What's it all About?" *ETC* 30(1973):59-60.
A dramatic revelation of one man's affective reactions to his encounter with the actual meaning of words, brought about through his exposure to general semantics. (LLBA)

2999. Stati, S. "Les traits sémantiques de l'adjectif." *CdL* 23(1973):51-61.
An attempt to establish the systems of semantic traits of the lexical class of adjectives. An inventory of types of semic traits is presented. Distinction is made between semic constants and variables and between paradigmatic and syntagmatic traits. Some observations are made on the hierarchy of traits. The semic formulas resulting do not completely exclude significations from the language under study, but further research should be able to isolate other semes or to increase the number of variables from the constants proposed here. (LLBA)

3009. Williams, William J. "Epistemics as an Analytical Method." *ETC.* 31:65-72.
The implementation of the new process and discipline of epistemics is discussed through a brief view of epistemics as a tool, method, and theoretical frame with emphasis on the analytic approach rather than the synthetic. Numerous examples illustrate this analytic approach. These examples bring us face to face with the happening-meanings construct: analytic-synthetic. The incidents cited are personal and impersonal. The personal one concerns corruption in government and the Attica situation, illustrating the vehicular use of the epistemic philosophical frame and method of analysis. Finally, it is shown how the early tools and techniques of general semantics are woven into this new framework. (LLBA)

Semantic Theory

3015. Antley, Kenneth. "McCawley's Theory of Selectional Restriction." *FLang* 11:257-72.
McCawley's theory of generative semantics, in which selectional restrictions are semantic in nature instead of syntactic, is discussed. Examples are given to demonstrate the importance of syntax in determining the correctness of a sentence. The importance of presuppositions in evaluating the grammaticality of a sentence is noted, as is the determination of which linguistic items denote specific objects. McCawley and generative semanticists are criticized for not examining the meaning of words and the nature of synonymy more extensively, and for not explaining more about involvement in meaning. (LLBA)

3017. Bajun, Lilia. "On Some Possibilities of Element Identification on the Plane of Content." *Linguistics* 123:5-15.
Aspects of the formal analysis method of a limited context are examined on the level of morphemes and words. An assumption is made that if a letter (letter chain) is a syntactic morpheme, then it has in a certain position frequency higher than in other positions. This frequency considerably exceeds that of the other letters found in this position. A letter/letter chain having a maximum ω-value is viewed as a hypothetical syntactic element. A few checking operations are suggested and formal rules of

segmenting words are formulated. The discrimination between the formal classes of words is done by the equivalence of objects criterion. (LLBA)

3020. Benešová, E., E. Hajičová, and Petr Sgall. "Remarks on the Topic/Comment Articulation:Part II." *PBML* 20(1973):3-42.
The second in a series of brief discussions on various issues related to several aspects of topic/comment articulation (TCA) and its semantic relevance. A basis for explaining TCA is formulated, followed by a discussion of the notion of the stock of shared knowledge and the usefulness of the study of TCA in analysis of units larger than the sentence. Attention is devoted to some specific questions concerning TCA. Some remarks are included on the distinction between pragmatic and logical presuppositions and on other phenomena closely related to TCA. (LLBA)

3024. Cole, Peter. "Indefiniteness and Anaphoricity." *Language* 50:665-74.
Grammarians working within the framework of semantically-based grammar have argued that syntactic representations are not arbitrary, but rather have their basis in semantics. Syntactic process (rules and constraints) may also have a semantic basis. Evidence is presented that the constraint against backward pronominalization with indefinite antecedents, which is found in a wide variety of languages, derives from the semantic properties of various classes of definite noun phrases. (PC)

3029. Dolgix, N.G. "Teorija semantičeskogo polja na sovremennom ètape razvitija semasiologii." *FN* 1(1973):89-98. [Semantic field.]
An evaluation of many theoretical concepts and methodological approaches involved in current work on systemic relations between words. Some scholars approach the problem from the semantic point of view, others from the linguistic one. The work of L. Weisgerber, W. Porzig, A. A. Ufimtseva, and others is reviewed. Particular attention is given to the existing definitions of semantic field and the criteria used to set the boundaries of a semantic field. Among these criteria, the following are found: structural, psychophysiological, statistical, psycholinguistic, and semantico-logical. (LLBA)

3035. Droste, F.G. "Qualifying and Relational Terms as Linguistic Universals." *Linguistics* 118(1973):43-88.
Apart from qualifying terms as a means to subcategorize the semantic aspects of linguistic entities, a set of relational terms is introduced accounting for the semantic relations between lexical entities as well as within (structured) entities. Both sets intend to cover the whole semantic field of the universal linguistic model every natural language can be described with. In consequence a set of so-called scope-operations is introduced which accounts for a correct mapping of universal semantic constructs onto language-specific patterns. Both sets of terms constitute a specific subset of an ideological model, i.e., of the general set of ideas, but, at the same time, minimal features for linguistic description. The implication of this theory is such that no less than six models should be distinguished in language functioning, viz. reality and ideology, describing the pre-linguistic world; communication, an intermediate model; conceptuality (with universal validity), a semantic level, and discourse (the latter two comparable to competence and performance). (FGD)

3037. Dürbeck, Helmut G. "Grundfragen der Funktions- und Bedeutungsbestimmung." *MSzS* 31(1973):15-51.
Erwin Koschmieder's "Beiträge zur allgemeinen Syntax" clarifies the following concepts and terms: (1) "Function" is the meaning of grammatical category; (2) If the function concept is used for a "symbol value" (Symbolwert) the term is designated by *Function (S)*; and (3)"Grammatical category" (Feldwert) is marked by the same type of use under conditions of highly different word forms. Grammatical categories as well as individual words can be ambiguous. On this, Koschmieder's distinction between sign, what is signified, and what is meant is developed. (LLBA)

3040. Elliott, Dale E. "Toward a Grammar of Exclamations." *FLang* 11:231-46.
A syntactic construction, the special purpose of which is to express particularly strong emotive responses, is proposed. In English and in several other languages, there are remarkable surface structure similarities between exclamations and questions.

How tall is she? vs. *How tall she is!* is an apt example for which the two constructions must be distinguished on both syntactic and semantic grounds. In English, exclamations cannot be negated, which is explained. (LLBA)

3041. Fónagy, Ivan. "Poids sémantique et 'poids phonique'." *Linguistique* 9,ii(1973):5-35.
The disaccentuation of the determinant within the adverbial syntagm has created in Hungarian a whole series of accentual minimal pairs. The semantic differences have been isolated through the aid of translations furnished by bilingual Hungarian Ss. On the level of the *signifiant*, an adverbial syntagm in which the principal accent affects the determinant is opposed to an adverbial syntagm in which the accent affects the determined. This simple opposition invariably contrasts with the great variety of semantic differences created by disaccentuation on the level of the *signifié*. (LLBA)

3043. Grady, Michael. "Generative Semantics, Presupposition, and Deep-Structure *be*." *Linguistics* 131:5-10.
A generative semantic interpretation of locative prepositional phrases must see them as re-nominalizations of an underlying stative-patient relationship, the stative a deep-level "existential *be*." Further, the postulation of a deep-level *be* has independent justification in that it accounts for one species of "presupposition." (MG)

3049. Hofmann, Thomas R. "Semantic Studies III:Descriptions in Natural Language." *LangS* 30:13-19.
Descriptions are central to every language act. They comprise a major portion of every sentence and are implicated in every reference. They may also be composed of many sentences as in a text. Descriptions are thus semantic units of expression. Descriptions are the only recursive part of semantics. An elementary theory of descriptions (using C-nets) is sketched, and its relations to reference, performatives, and presuppositions are discussed. (TRH)

3050. —— "Semantic Studies IV:In Support of Semantic Atoms." *LangS* 32:12-18.
5 common hypotheses about the nature of word meaning are arranged in order of increasing generality. Each of these hypotheses is rejected using various linguistic modes of evidence such as distinctive semantic differences, kinship terminology, morphological relationships, and contrasts in the meanings of selected words. A sixth hypothesis, which is consistent with the C-net theory of semantic representation is proposed. (TRH)

3052. Ikegami, Yoshihiko. "A Set of Basic Patterns for the Semantic Structure of the Verb." *Linguistics* 117(1973):15-58.
There are two types of "abstract motion," "change in possessorship" and "change in condition." The linguistic representation of these as well as of "concrete motion" (i.e., "change in locus") can be described in terms of an essentially common set of structural patterns. How these patterns are realized in English and Japanese is illustrated. Some of the implications of positing such structural patterns and also some further problems to be explored (e.g., the possibility of defining a corresponding set of patterns for the "statal" verbs, some speculations on how the patterns may have evolved, the number of "cases" that need to be set up in the deepest stratum of language, etc.) are suggested. (YI)

3054. Kahn, E. "Algebraic Semantics for Narrative." *Linguistics* 141:27-33.
Semantic properties of narrative are modeled by finite automata. These automata are thought of as producing paraphrases of the underlying plot. Plot is represented as a directed graph where the vertices are characters and the arrows binary relations between characters. Different models of a narrative can be compared by studying the relation of simulation between the corresponding automata. The traditional notion of dramatic allegory is interpreted as a condition on two automata that one simulate the other. In this context each automaton represents a level of meaning, one of which is dependent on the other. All tests of the simulation relation are conducted from the algebraic point of view. Semigroups for each automaton are constructed by computer, then simulation is reduced to an algebraic condition on the semigroups which is easy to check. (EK)

3056. Kempson, Ruth R.M. "Presupposition:A Problem for Linguistic Theory." *TPS* 1973(1974):29-54.
There are two distinct concepts labeled presupposition: one is defined in terms of the speaker's belief in uttering sentences, the other as a truth relation between two statements. Both concepts involve issues for linguistic theory and neither should be part of natural-language semantics. The first is excluded on the basis that a linguistic theory cannot be predictive if it incorporates such a concept. The second is excluded on the grounds that every type of sentence for which a presuppositional analysis has been postulated can be better explained in terms of entailment, a relation defined within the standard two-valued logic. Both of these conclusions leave certain apparent anomalies. Each of these anomalies can be naturally explained within a separate theory of pragmatics, outlined along the lines of H.P. Grice (1961, 1968, 1969). What remains open is the question of the status of pragmatics within an overall linguistic framework. (RMK)

3067. Moskalskaya, Olga I. "Problemy semanticheskogo modelirovaniya v sintaksise." *VJa* 6:33-43.
There are many difficulties with semantic modeling stemming from the fact that modeling is usually carried out on the level of surface rather than deep syntactic structures. The structural scheme of a sentence (surface structure) should not be taken as the unit of semantic modeling but rather as the structure of the meaning of the sentence, i.e., its semantic model. (LLBA)

3072. O'Donnell, W.R. "On Generative Gymnastics." *ArL* 5:53-81. [Rev. art.]
The sheer weight of publications produced by those engaged in the debate concerning generative semantics has conferred upon that debate such an importance that no conscientious student of linguistics can reasonably ignore it. Indeed, it sometimes begins to seem that this debate is linguistics. But those who have taken part in the debate have tended to be strongly committed to one side or the other, and it is important that neutral voices be heard. The present paper is an attempt by an uncommitted observer to discuss and evaluate the ideas put forward in a number of important contributions by members of what might be called the dissenting party, i.e., the generative semanticists. (WRO)

3073. Osgood, Charles E. "Probing Subjective Culture Part I:Cross-linguistic Tool-making." *JC* 24:21-35.
Subjective culture is most naturally and directly assessed through the medium of language, and in cross-cultural comparisons this means that what has been called "the language barrier" must somehow be pierced. A very brief, but necessary, description of the Semantic Differential (SD) Technique for measuring meaning, as developed through the decade of the 1950s with a strictly ethnocentric (American English) focus is presented. Then, shifting to a broader anthropocentric focus, the "tool-making" and "tool-using" phases of cross-cultural research described are traced. (LLBA)

3077. Pelletier, Francis Jeffry. "On Some Proposals for the Semantics of Mass Nouns." *JPL* 3:87-108.
Mass nouns are such terms as "water," "mud," "leaded gold," etc. Syntactically, uses or senses of such terms are indicated by the occurrence of the unstressed "some" as an indefinite article, "much" as a quantifier, etc. Semantically the uses or senses are distinguished by the properties of *collectiveness*. An account of the "logical form" of sentences containing mass nouns is attempted. There is no set of things over which to quantify, and so many modifications of theory have been proposed. (LLBA)

3083. Price, J.T. "Linguistic Competence and Metaphorical Use." *FLang* 11:253-56.
In "Concerning a 'Linguistic Theory' of Metaphor" Matthews offers several considerations which he hopes will prefigure an adequate theory of metaphor, by which is meant a theory which stays wholly within the realm of linguistic "competence" as opposed to "performance." Matthews' account of metaphor depends, however, upon the notion of human intention, which apparently is an aspect of "performance." The present issue is part of a more general problem, i.e., that many current linguistic theories address themselves to what Chomsky has called "rule-governed creativity," while metaphor, whose meaning cannot be separated from its use, is an example of "rule-changing creativity." (LLBA)

3091. Sekaninová, Ella. "Obsah 'aspektuálnosti' ako funkčno-sémantickej kategórie." *Jazykovedný časopis* 24(1973):184-88.

Aspect comprises various means for expressing the character of action indicated by verbs. Verb form appears as the morphological kernel of this category, and the modes of verbal action are shown in the surrounding components. The characteristic modes of verbal action appear above all in the verbs with prefixes. Prefixes are a fertile means for formulating modes of verbal action and thus play an important role in the entire category of aspect. The present work attempts to demonstrate the complexity and interaction of formal and semantic changes engendered by prefixing within the limits of aspect as a functional-semantic category. (LLBA)

3094. Slagle, Uhlan V. "On the Possibility of Correlating the Structure of Perception with the Structure of Thought and Meaning." *Linguistics* 117(1973):85-96.

An adequate theory of meaning is possible only within the framework of an adequate theory of mind. Although the transformationalists have made many significant contributions, their rationalism is inherently inadequate. The key to an adequate theory of mind lies in a synthesis of Kant's schema concept and the relevant insights and findings of Gestalt psychology. This synthesis provided the basis for showing that the immanent organizational factors of perception are the immanent organizational factors of thought. The suggested theoretical framework offers a viable solution to the problems of reference and semantic-cognitive universals, while also supplying plausible answers to the unavoidable problems of imageless thought and the experimental foundation of the constructs of mathematics and physics. It appears that only by correlating the structure of perception with the structure of thought and meaning can one avoid confusing the constructs of analysis with immanent psychological reality. (UVS)

3103. Vardul, I.F. "Ob izuchenii semanticheskogo aspekta yazyka." *VJa* 6:9-21.

Linguistics is generally considered to be the study of language, while logic is the study of thinking. Since language cannot be separated from thinking, such a division is most unfortunate. The most promising approach is that of information theory, but here two trends are competing. Ways are suggested to reconcile the various approaches by applying the concept of ideal referent and investigating its relation to reality. The system of these ideal referents is called "presemantics." (LLBA)

VII. PHILOSOPHY OF LANGUAGE

Philosophy of Language

3117. Abaev, V.I. "Obščegumanitarnye aspekty teoretičeskogo jazykosnanija." *IAN* 32(1973):524-29.

Linguistics must be considered one of the general ideological struggles of our times. The background of European humanism is discussed. Formalism was a major trend in Russian literary studies in the 1920s. This approach considered language as a self-contained system, rather than as the subsystem it actually is. It is hoped that linguists will continue to develop the best tradition of European humanism, rather than be led further afield by the formalism that still influences Soviet linguistics. (LLBA)

3139. Čikobava, A. "Jazyk i 'teorija jazyka' v filosofii i lingvistike." *IAN* 32(1973):519-23.

The theory of language is the cornerstone of linguistic theory: the status of language as the subject of linguistics is determinant for solving all the other principal problems of linguistic theory. To understand the essence of language in modern theoretical linguistics, a central position is occupied by: (1) problems of the function and structure of language; and (2) the interrelation of statics and dynamics, i.e., the interrelation of the history of language and the language system ("diachrony" and "synchrony"). Apart from linguistics, other branches of science which investigate language and its different aspects are discussed. (LLBA)

3161. Herman, A.L. "C.I. Lewis and the Similetic Use of Language Introduction." *PPR* 33(1973):349-65.

C.I. Lewis' doctrine of expressive language is both unique and paradoxical: unique in that it allows Lewis to solve a puzzle that has been "the problem of knowledge ever since Empedocles," but paradoxical in that in order to solve that problem of knowledge, Lewis must resort to statements which are at once both certain and empirical. Part I recalls Lewis' doctrine of expressive statements ("expressives"); Part II states the criticisms that have been set against it; Part III develops the thesis that Lewis' expressives are really similes; Part IV shows that criticisms of the sort mentioned in Part II seem to rest on a misunderstanding of expressives and expressive language. Part IV employs the language model of simile and the talk about the similetic use of language developed in Part III to meet the criticisms mentioned in Part II. (ALH)

3164. Hottois, Gilbert. "Métalangage ou praxis inavouée." *Degrés* 1(1973):n-n3.

In the semantic, logical, and scientific approaches to language one is able to see not a purely theoretical attitude but a practical one where language (in the dimension of meaning, of *signifié*) is translated, inflected, manipulated. Contemporary "linguisticism" does not leave things as they are: thought becomes language, object; creativity is mechanized. The opening or gap of language or of the work created by a combinative cybernetic conceals in fact a closure: the mechanical creativity of contemporary models is only a combinative determinism where the creative mistake does not exist. (AH)

3177. Land, Stephen K. "The Cartesian Language Test and Professor Chomsky." *Linguistics* 122:11-24.

In *Language and Mind* and *Cartesian Linguistics* Noam Chomsky cites the "creative aspect" of language use as characteristic of ordinary language which renders it incapable of explanation in terms of behaviorism. He claims a precedent for his argument in Descartes' view of language as a "test" to distinguish rational from mechanical creatures. Chomsky argues that the Cartesian language test isolates qualities of language use which show the inadequacy of stimulus-response models in linguistics, but employment of such an experimental test in an argument against behaviorism results in a paradox. Chomsky cannot apply the Cartesian language test as he does without violating the principles of experimental procedure announced in his review of B.F. Skinner's *Verbal Behavior*. (SKL)

3178. Lanigan, Richard L. "The Phenomenology of Speech and Linguistic Discontinuity." *Degrés* 2(1973):b-b7.

Discusses the linguistic concept of discontinuity as a paradigmatic or syntagmatic function of sentence use as compared to the concepts of separation and reversibility in phenomenological philosophy. Within paradigmatic relations, the linguistic notions of contrast and free variation are compared to the phenomenological concept of "imaginative free variation." The idea of syntagmatic relations in linguistics is compared to the philosophic idea of an "intentional object" as the synergistic product of speech acts and speech perception. (AH)

3199. Rey, Alain. "Langage et temporalités." *Langages* 32(1973):53-78.

A review of the concrete usages of ambiguous signs, along with the ideological consequences implied by these usages. "Time" may designate an abstract milieu, an articulation of events and ideas, a biological or physical model, an interval between two events, or a localization of events. The different conceptions of time implied by linguistic theories are able to isolate and consider the physical temporality of communication and the psychophysiological temporality of discourse. The problem is how this may be related to the evolutionary time of language. (LLBA)

3204. Schacht, Richard. "Philosophy as Linguistic Analysis: A Nietzschean Critique." *PhS* 25:153-71.

Nietzsche is a philosopher who regards the analysis of ordinary language and specialized forms of language as important and fruitful without being committed to a conception of philosophy as linguistic analysis. The twofold purpose of this discussion is to suggest some respects in which the conception of philosophy as linguistic analysis may be open to criticism and to investigate the philosophers involved in this type of pursuit. (LLBA)

3208. Serebrennikov, B.A. "O putjax razvitija jazykoznanija." *IAN* 32(1973):513-18.

A discussion of the question of whether linguistics is to be regarded as one of the humanities, as an exact science, or as a social science. Certain problems of the object of linguistics are considered. Neither the extreme structuralist viewpoint nor the approach which takes linguistics as a purely human science is justified. (LLBA)

3221. Valesio, Paolo. "On Reality and Unreality in Lan-guage." *Semiotica* 10:75-92.

In data from modern Italian and English and from various literary texts, five degrees of unreality are identified, ranging from complete unreality (equaling nonexistence) to the least unreal of unrealities (that of entities which once existed but no longer exist). Only synchronic (un-)reality and the reference of noun phrase are considered, leaving aside diachrony and the problems of whole sentences. The lexical structure of words whose meanings point to unreal referents is as complex as the lexical structure of words whose meanings point to real referents, and there is no clear boundary between reality and unreality. (LLBA)

COMPARATIVE AND HISTORICAL LINGUISTICS†

I. COMPARATIVE

Typology and Universals of Language

3254. Gak, V.G. "Sopostavitel'noe izučenie jazykov i lingvis-tičeskaja tipologija." *RJR* 3:52-58.

The comparative study of languages has become increasingly close to linguistic typology, which attempts to find those features languages have in common and on this basis derive the specifics of the given language. Practical goals of such research include the discovery of similarities and differences in features of language which are important in teaching; the study of concrete partic-ularities of a given language; the discovery of general facts common to all languages. The following aspects of analysis are major: the volume of material examined; general-particular typology; character of differences; quantitative-qualitative ty-pology; levels of analysis; structural-functional typology. Within structural typology there exist two categories: purely structural (formal) and semantic (content). Semasiological-onomasiological typology is also considered. (VGG)

3257. Hyman, Larry M., and Russell G. Schuh. "Universals of Tone Rules:Evidence from West Africa." *LingI* 5:81-115.

A theoretical distinction is made between rules which are natural from a diachronic point of view (and redundantly from a synchronic point of view as well) and rules which are natural from a synchronic point of view (but are not natural from a diachronic point of view). On the basis of numerous examples from West African Niger-Congo and Chadic languages, certain universals of diachronic and synchronic tone rules are proposed. Certain consonant types can interfere with natural tone processes by exerting a blocking effect. (LLBA)

Contrastive Analysis

3275. Filipović, Rudolf. "The Use of a Corpus in Contrastive Studies." *SRAZ* 33-36(1972-73):489-500.

The Yugoslav "Serbo-Croatian—English Contrastive Project" combines theoretical work with the empirical study of a corpus of English text and its translation into Serbo-Croatian. A corpus cannot replace theory; it should not come before theory nor instead of it. No contrastive project can be regarded as complete before its results are verified and completed by means of a corpus. Only a corpus can verify some doubtful cases of grammaticality. The frequency and distribution of some forms can be assessed only be means of a corpus. Stylistic values cannot be discussed without a corpus. Without a corpus it would be impossible to get a more or less exhaustive listing of all items that belong to a certain class, which is very important for contrastive analysis and its practical application. (LLBA)

3287. Maneca, Constant. "La fisionomia lessicale comparata del rumeno e dell'italiano." *RRL* 17(1972):203-16.

The inherited Latin stock gives the specific traits typical of the physiognomies of both Romanian and Italian. The Latin stock of Romanian, though less extensive, is possessed of a higher frequency which compensates for its numerical inferiority to the traditional Latin stock of Italian. On the basis of two standard language samples of equal length (each consisting of 5000 words) and stylistic make-up, the etymological composition of two vocabularies, Romanian and Italian, is analyzed. The selected vocabularies have the following characteristics: (1) Romanian, 6171 types; Italian, 6030; (2) average frequency 7.80 and 7.74 respectively; (3) lexical richness (calculated according to the formula of Pierre Guiraud) is 27.71 in Romanian and 27.88 in Italian. The vocabularies are classified etymologically into three groups: inherited words, borrowings from other languages, and created words. (LLBA)

3291. Potter, Simeon. "Contrastive Linguistics in Action." *IncL* 13:1-5.

After a survey of work in progress in confrontational linguistics in the universities of Europe and America, a strong plea for further studies in the distinctive features of living languages is made. The value of transformational grammar is recognized, but it is regretted that many of Chomsky's epigones spoke no foreign languages. Themes for contrastive study are suggested: de-terminers, intensifiers, downtoners, positions of adjectives, negation, interrogation, yes-no substitutes, sentence connectives, superlative genitives, and reflexive comparatives. Models of auxiliary verbs in German and English are discussed to demonstrate that every language is a system of systems. (LLBA)

II. DIACHRONICS

General

3319. Noeth, Winfried. "Perspektiven der diachronen Lin-guistik." *Lingua* 33:199-233.

The current trends and the main problems of diachronic linguistics are discussed with particular reference to: (1) progress attained in the analysis of sound change; (2) the classical field of diachronic linguistics; and (3) the results obtained in the diachronic analysis of the other levels of linguistic description. The study concentrates on research in the history of English and deals primarily with methodological and theoretical aspects of diachronic linguistics. (LLBA)

Processes of Language Change

3330. Malkiel, Yakov. "Deux frontières entre la phonologie et

---

† *Festschriften* and Other Analyzed Collections are listed in the first division of this volume. "F" numbers in brackets following a title refer to these items.

la morphologie en diachronie." *Langages* 32(1973):79-87.
In the context of phonological situations, certain processes easily lend themselves to smooth analysis once they have been replaced in the realm of morphology, where they belong. Thus once all efforts to explain through the interplay of "sound laws" the split of Latin *ipse/ipsum* "same" into Portuguese *ese* (masc.) vs. *isso* (neut.) "that" or the fission of Latin *totum* "all, whole" into Portuguese *todo* (masc.) vs. *tudo* (neut.) have proven futile, everything falls quickly into place if one appeals to hyper-characterization of the three genders in the ranks of pronouns, as opposed to nouns and adjectives. (LLBA)

3334. O'Bryan, Margie. "The Interaction of Morphological and Phonological Processes in Historical Change." *Linguistics* 137:49-61.
Generative phonologists are aware of morphology's role in grammars and are considering the interaction between morphological and phonological processes. Morphological generalizations go unnoticed because they appear characterizable as phonological exceptions. Marking items as exceptions to phonological rules describes a situation explainable from a perspective

in which morphological processes are considered. Such studies are important for the linguist's goal of gaining insights into the nature of processes operating within the system and how they interact. The interaction within the perspective of historical change is important, for linguists base conclusions concerning some aspect of language on a superficial look at synchronic structure. (MO)

3338. Traugott, Elizabeth. "Le changement linguistique et sa relation à l'acquisition de la langue maternelle." *Langages* 32(1973):39-52. [Tr. Jean-Marie Hombert and Sylviane Pratelli.]
The generative transformational model of language change developed by Kiparsky is discussed and modified to incorporate sociolinguistic and acquisitional factors. Emphasis is on the importance of acquisition of perceptual strategies and strategies of expression, as well as universal properties of language, and on the processes of restructuring and rule elaboration undergone by children in constructing hypotheses about their language. Insofar as language change is caused by processes of language acquisition, it is seen not as a matter of simplification but rather of the degree to which elaboration is achieved by each generation. (LLBA)

III. INDO-EUROPEAN STUDIES

General

3358. Kumakhov, M.A. "Teoriya monovokalizma i zapadno-kavkazskie yazyki." *VJa* 6:54-67.
Vocalism in West Caucasian languages provides material for solving certain problems of general phonology, for reconstructing phonological models of various languages, and for verifying the position on monovocalism of Indo-European origin. Positions on the subject are critically reviewed and their conclusions are tested using factual material from West Caucasian languages. As a result, monovocalic theory is vigorously rejected. (LLBA)

Proto-Indo-European

3386. Allen, W. Sidney. "χθών, 'ruki', and Related Matters: A Reappraisal." *TPS* 1973(1974):98-126.
Re-examination of the evidence, mainly from a comparison of Indo-Iranian with Greek, which has led to the postulation of a series of fricative or affricate consonants in Proto-Indo-European. Allen reviews previous approaches to the problem and pays particular attention to the Greek evidence. The problem is related to that of the Indian retroflexion and Iranian palatalization of **s* after *i, u, r*, and *k*. The proposed solution tends to support the traditional reconstruction of a fricative phoneme, but with a different phonetic interpretation (viz. a [pre-]palatal **š*, as earlier suggested by Collitz) and a historical development which is

congruent with other palatal developments in Greek. (WSA)

3396. Hock, Hans H. "On the Indo-Iranian Accusative Plural of Consonant Stems." *JAOS* 94:73-95.
The predesinential Ø-grade of the Indo-Iranian accusative plural of consonant stems has been considered by most earlier linguists as inherited from Proto-Indo-European. In more recent publications, however, the view prevails that it must be of secondary origin. The latter view is more likely to be correct and to give a more plausible morphological motivation for the secondary nature of the predesinential Ø-grade. (HHH)

3398. Klimov, G.A. "Tipologija jazykov aktivnogo stroja i rekonstrukcija protoindoevropejskogo." *IAN* 32(1973):442-47.
The hypothetical reconstruction of proto-Indo-European establishes a division between "transitive" (ergative) and "intransitive" forms, whose functioning was connected with the lexical division into non-neuter and neuter. Comparative linguists consider that the fundamental lexical and grammatical opposition in proto-Indo-European is that between "activity" and "inactivity." The corresponding linguistic structure is very close to the so-called ergative system constructed by Lyons for diachronic classification of languages of nominative construction. On the other hand, it corresponds in its principle traits to the scheme of active construction. An attempt is made to correlate these facts with an "active construction" hypothesis for proto-Indo-European. (LLBA)

INDO-EUROPEAN A: ITALIC LINGUISTICS†

I. GENERAL AND PRE-ROMANCE

General

3424. Fucilla, Joseph G. "Increasing the Offshoots of *Castrum* and *Castellum*." *Names* 22:59-74.
In *The Toponomastic Reflexes of Castellum and Castrum: A Comparative Pan-Romanic Study* Henri Diament discusses 143 form-types of the two place terms appearing in present and former Romania, that is, the two core words current in the different languages and dialects and the same terms plus suffixes. By utilizing sources Diament has not consulted, one can supply numerous new types and extend their geographical range to

Austria, Czechoslovakia, Hungary, and Turkey. This constitutes a comprehensive coverage of the form-types which designate the two toponomia. (JGF)

3441. Rosoff, Gary H. "The Phonetic Framework of the Universal Sound Correlates in Romance Vowel Diachrony." *Linguistics* 135:57-71.
The ten vowels of Classical Latin may be interpreted as a matrix of polar coordinates which consisted of three inherent oppositions and a single prosodic opposition of length. The loss of the prosodic length feature would have reduced the Classical Latin system to a five vowel Vulgar Latin inventory. In the transition from Vulgar Latin to Romance, the phonetic configuration of the vowels of Vulgar Latin was modified by the action of the articulatory and laryngeal speech centers. As the vowels changed their phonetic shape, a new series of distinctive correlates was

† *Festschriften* and Other Analyzed Collections are listed in the first division of this volume. "F" numbers in brackets following a title refer to these items.

generated which increased the number of nonredundant combinatory possibilities. These subsequently made inevitable the emergence of distinct phonological patterns in Romance. (GHR)

Latin

Etymology, Lexicography, and Lexicology. 3473. Avery, William T. "*Annos habere*:A Roman Idiom." *RomN* 15:622-24.
The Romance idiom "to have" with the number of years involved to express a person's age had its origin in classical Latin. This is demonstrated by instances of the use of *habere* with the number of years in the accusative in Cicero, Livy, Quintilian, and Petronius. (WTA)

3474. Clark, Larry V. "The Turkic and Mongol Words in William of Rubruck's *Journey* (1253-1255)." *JAOS* 93(1973):181-89.
Twenty Turkic and Mongol words, excluding onomastica, appear in the Latin text of a 13th-century travel account. Although all but a few of these words had been identified in older editions of the work, these identifications were either inaccurate or insufficiently documented in the light of modern scholarship. Here, each word is placed in its original context and provided with textual and etymological commentary. The words are for the most part technical terms randomly noted and referring to the material and spiritual culture of the Inner Asian peoples encountered by Rubrouck. The study reveals that Turkic lexica preponderate over Mongol lexica. This nonetheless does not constitute adequate evidence for inferring that Turkic was the "internati onal language" in use during the inception of the Mongol Empire. The rich descriptive detail accompanying the words in Rubrouck's account make it an important early source for the historical lexicography of the Turkic and Mongol languages. (LVC)

Morphology

Morphology. 3496. Szemerényi, Oswald J.L. "Marked-Unmarked and a Problem of Latin Diachrony." *TPS* 1973(1974):55-74.
The grammars of several Indo-European languages exhibit a rule which voices final stops or obstruents; this is particularly clear at certain stages of Latin (and Italic), Germanic, Celtic, and Indo-Iranian. The interpretation of such a rule is impossible both within the usual limits of Prague phonological theory and within the current framework of the markedness theory of transformational grammar. Adhering to the basic tenet of Trubetzkoi's neutralization theory, it becomes clear that only tenseness can enter into the problem at issue. This result is an important addition to general phonological theory. Research effort should be concentrated on establishing the existence of this rule in other languages and language-families of the world. (OJLS)

Oscan

Morphology. 3515. Untermann, Jürgen. "The Osco-Umbrian Preverbs *ā-, ad-* and *an-*." *JIES* 1(1973):387-93.
The Osco-Umbrian preverbs *a-, ad-,* and *an-* are examined. The graphic ambiguity among these preverbs may have been matched by a tendency toward homophony in the spoken language. (JU)

Umbrian

General and Miscellaneous. 3516. Nussbaum, Alan J. "*Benuso, couortuso,* and the Archetype of *Tab. Ig.* I and VI-VIIa." *JIES* 1(1973):356-69.
Two versions of basically the same ritual text in the Umbrian dialect are examined and it is suggested that both were copied from an original archetype that employed the second person form. (AJN)

II. WEST ROMANCE LANGUAGES

Catalan

Phonology. 3569. Brasington, R.W. "On the Phonological Interpretation of Catalan Sibilants." *ArL* 5:11-24.
Although a number of accounts of Catalan phonology have appeared in recent years it seems worthwhile considering some further possible interpretations of the sibilant system, aiming in particular to highlight the close phonological relationship between /tʃ/,/dʒ/and /ʒ/. The general conclusion reached is that, given the frequent complexity of phonological inter-relationships, it is unwise to expect to find one single "correct" account of a system. Rather we should be prepared to accept that each one of a set of perhaps mutually exclusive descriptions may have its own explanatory value. (RWPB)

French

General and Miscellaneous. 3599. Clifford, Paula M. "The Grammarians' View of French Word-Order in the Sixteenth Century." *PQ* 53:380-88.
The 16th-century grammars of French may be more informative and of greater general interest than is often supposed. Their treatment of word-order illustrates the diverse approaches to a theory of the vernacular language at this time. (PMC)

3609. Gorog, Ralph de. "*Comparer* et ses concurrents en français mediéval." *ZRP* 90:73-98.
After a brief survey of the words expressing the concept "to compare" and its various nuances in Classical Latin writers and in the Vulgate, the medieval French words for the concept are studied, with examples of their use from the 12th to the 17th centuries. (RPdG)

Dialectology. 3663. Bénouis, Mustapha K. "Parlez-vous sabir . . . ou pied-noir?" *FR* 47:578-82.
Sabir has been improperly defined as a mixture of French, Arabic, Spanish, and Italian, and more recently confused with *Pied-noir*. North Africans thought it was French and the French thought it was Arabic. Both *Sabir* and *Pied-noir* have been regarded as the sources of recent Arabic borrowings in French. *Sabir* contained neither French nor Arabic but was rather a Romanic pidgin (Provençl, Spanish, and Italian) with some Turkish seasoning, spoken by Mediterranean traders from the 17th to the 19th centuries. The penetration of French in the Maghreb resulted in its disappearance though the term was kept to designate a corrupt French supposedly spoken by North Africans. This modern *Sabir* used in parodies is closer to the French dialect of *Pied-noir* than to the original *Sabir*. The absence of Arabic words in *Sabir* and their minimal number in *Pied-noir* preclude their being the source of Arabic borrowings in French. (MKB)

3665. Chaudenson, R. "Pour une étude comparée des créoles et parlers français d'outre-mer:Survivance et innovation." *RLiR* 37(1973):342-71.
A comparison of the linguistic systems of the French creoles of the Antilles and Indian Ocean and the Canadian and Louisiana French dialects reveals certain common traits and convergent tendencies which cannot be seen in standard French but are present in old popular French and in the dialects of eastern and northeastern France. Such a study provides new and more reliable information on former French dialects. A comparison of Canadian French with the various creoles aids in tracing their genesis and reveals evolutionary tendencies similar to those of "advanced French." (LLBA)

Etymology, Lexicography, and Lexicology. 3696. Goldis, A. "L'importance des néologismes français dans le développement de la langue roumaine littéraire." *CdL* 23(1973):63-81.
French has been the most important source of lexical borrowings in Romanian. The historical and cultural conditions accounting for this are discussed. The influence of translations and of personal contacts is emphasized. The process of adaptation of neologisms is described in reference to the phonetic, morpho-

syntactic, and semantic aspects. French neologisms are a consequence of the growing complexity of Romanian society in the 18th century. Most had no equivalent in Romanian and hence answered a real need. (LLBA)

3699. Hanon, Suzanne. "The Study of English Loan-Words in Modern French." *CHum* 7(1973):389-98.
The validity of the synchronic approach to loan-words is tested through the employment of a computer to sort and search certain elements and sequences of elements. Such a method is described with respect to English loans in contemporary French. The computer can check the linguist's working hypothesis simultaneously while eliminating irrelevant elements; it thus offers an economy of time. However, the linguist will always need to make the final decisions. (LLBA)

3713. Lyne, A.A. "L'élaboration des listes de fréquence:A la recherche d'une solution aux problèmes d'affectation des mots-occurrences dans les classes de mots." *CdL* 23(1973):83-108.
Unlike the author of a conventional dictionary, the frequency-list compiler attempts to produce an exhaustive reproducible inventory of the lexical items in a given corpus. Any inconsistency in classifying every textual segment will result in an unreliable list as a basis for statistical analysis, especially for comparisons between different corpora. A decision-procedure is presented to be followed by a human editor, with or without computer assistance, in assigning each textual word-token to the appropriate word-class. (LLBA)

3734. Scoones, S.T.H. "Écuyer." *AUMLA* 41:64-74.
Clarifies the semantic evolution of *écuyer* (<*scutarius*) through an analysis of Latin and vernacular texts from classical times to the 13th century. (STHS)

Morphology. 3768. Rochet, Bernard. "A Morphologically-Determined Sound Change in Old French." *Linguistics* 135:43-56.
Investigation of the transition problem concerning the merger of [ẽ] and [ã] in Old French reveals that this development seems to have been triggered by a particular analogical leveling within the verb system. This hypothesis receives support from the spread of the change as revealed by the earliest literary documents: first, the replacement of *-ent* with *-ant* as a present participle ending, then the extension of the alternation [ẽ]~[ã] to the rest of the lexicon. Since the change considered has been historically instrumental in the formulation of the substantive universal that "nasal vowels tend to lower," its interpretation as a morphologically-determined development casts serious doubts on the validity of this universal. (BLR)

Phonology. 3795. Love, Nigel, and Roy Harris. "A Note on French Nasal Vowels." *Linguistics* 126:63-68.
Three types of argument (elegance, economy, and rule ordering) have been adduced to support the assumption that nasal vowels are to be derived in a generative phonology of Modern French from underlying oral vowels. In the argument from rule ordering as formulated by Schane, a sibilant voicing rule (RSV) is held to precede the nasalization rule, thus explaining /s/ and /z/ as surface exponents of underlying /s/ in *persister*, *insister*, and *résister*. But the distribution of /s/ and /z/ in the total set of forms exhibiting the morpheme *sist* does not support this. The argument for rule ordering involving a sibilant voicing rule (RSV) and the associated assumption that nasal vowels are lacking in deep phonology has no greater explanatory power than an account based on the contrary assumption. The possibility of treating nasal vowels as independent phonological units thus appears to deserve more serious consideration than it has thus far received. (NLL & RH)

3807. Walker, Douglas C. "Syllabification and French Phonology." *Cahiers linguistiques d'Ottawa* 7,iii(1973):25-41.
Recent studies have proposed the incorporation of syllable boundaries into generative phonological theory. Syllable boundaries are used in the reformulation of several phonological rules of Modern French, particularly consonant deletion and nasalization. In addition, French data are used to confront some of the proposals for theoretical modification, notably the "anywhere" nature of the rules involving syllable boundaries, problems involved in resyllabification, and the interaction between various processes affecting syllable structure. (LLBA)

Semantics. 3815. Ford, Jerome C. "The Semantics of Direct Address Pronouns in French." *FR* 47:1142-57.
Examines the semantic features of direct address pronouns in French. Relevant factors regulating usage appear to include not only personal attributes as status, sex, age but also social situations. Nine notions associated with the pronouns are identified: reverence, respect, formality, distance, disdain, camaraderie, intimacy, acceptance, and condescension. The basic power/solidarity dichotomy proves not to apply unequivocally. Furthermore, conditions of stress on the entire system, such as the events of May 1968, alter that system, initiating both temporary and permanent modifications in usage. (JCF)

Stylistics. 3827. Allen, John R. "Methods of Author Identification through Stylistic Analysis." *FR* 47:904-16.
Although principles of author identification through stylistic analysis have been known for more than a century, they have been little used in the study of French literature, perhaps because many critics feel unqualified to undertake such research. Yet often the critic is the most qualified to use these methods: the amount of further training is minimal, as the critic's background enables him to formulate questions which can be studied with computational stylistics. This method isolates traits of style which shed light on previously unsolved problems of author attribution and literary history. Some criteria which can be used toward that goal are: average word and/or sentence length, distribution of parts of speech, vocabulary choice, word length of parts of speech, vocabulary distribution, and relative entropy. Statistical tests already developed measure the significance of any traits observed. Given the proven effectiveness of computational stylistics in other fields, critics ought to examine the possibilities for applying these methods to the study of French literature. (JRA)

Syntax. 3867. Liebold, Harald. "Zur Typologie des Französischen:Wesen und Funktion der Modi." *Fremdsprachen* 17(1973):256-59.
The French *indicatif* is a semantically neutral correlative mood that does not merely express facts. The *subjonctif* used in subordinate clauses expresses a modality already expressed in the principal clause and is also a correlative mood. It is an unnecessary grammatical form that, from the standpoint of semantics, can be replaced by the indicative. From the semantic point of view, the subjunctive is an optional modality. Some remarks are presented concerning the classification of conditional forms, and some guidelines on how to teach and learn the subjunctive mood are given. (LLBA)

3872. Morin, Yves Ch. "A Computer Tested Transformational Grammar of French." *Linguistics* 116(1973):49-113.
A report of a study on the transcription of a relative formal grammar into the notation of a computer system. The original grammar was aimed only at describing the phrase structure and the transformation of a subset of French. A lexicon had to be built containing some contextual features, redundancy rules, and entries. The grammar has been modified in accomodation to the system developed for the purpose of making accurate sentences possible. The method employed exemplifies the tutorial value of the system for computational linguistics. (LLBA)

3880. Reed, J. "Ellipsis of Pronoun Subjects After Direct Speech in French." *ML* 55:116-20.
Separate sentences may be coordinated in a sequence with the subject stated only in the first. This may seem to be breaking the normal rules for sentence production in French. A specific and not uncommon example of this feature consists of a sequence made up of introductory verb with expressed subject, direct speech, and sequential verb with ellipsed subject. Various examples of this fundamental structure are analyzed and certain stylistic values are suggested. (JR)

3884. Rothe, Wolfgang. "Die Genusbildung des französischen Adjektivs auf der Ebene der Hörbarkeit." *NsM* 27:216-21.
Spoken French exhibits a complex adjectival gender formation. It

contains a great number of different gender morphemes and a lack of a single underlying form from which the other respective gender form could be derived. While gender is marked in other Indo-European languages by a vowel, the spoken French adjective is recognizable by means of a consonant. The synchronic analysis includes all surface manifestations in a comprehensive series of gender grammeme rules and refers to irregular forms and neutralizations which appear on the syntactic level. (WR)

3896. Straub, Sylvia A. "The Passive Prepositions *De* and *Par*." *FR* 47:583-93.
There is a wide range of explanations in studies of French passive sentences concerning restrictions on the occurrence of *de* and *par* before agentive complement nouns. Such studies attribute these restrictions to properties either of the complement phrase or of the verb or else to properties of both these elements. With one exception, however, the explanations are invalid because the sentences which contradict them are too numerous to be explained as exceptions. The only explanation which appears valid is the statement that *par* must occur in passive sentences with verbs denoting a non-state and that *de* may occur in passives with stative verbs. It is not always possible to substitute *par* for *de* in passive sentences with stative verbs. In fact, *par* may replace *de* in such sentences without affecting their meaning or grammaticalness only when the verb requires the agentive complement noun to be animate. (SAS)

3900. Trammell, Robert L., and Marie-Geneviève Garcia. "Structural Ambiguity in French." *FR* 48:30-39.
A wide selection of ambiguous constructions is examined within the framework of transformational generative grammar and various means of disambiguating them are suggested. Lexical and phonological ambiguities are mentioned but the emphasis is on structural ambiguities. A distinction is made between surface- and deep-structure ambiguity: the former involves different groupings of words in a sentence while the latter is based on different logical relations between elements of a sentence. Distinctions are also made between structures which are ambiguous in speech or writing only, or in both. The various constructions are divided into ambiguities of the Noun Phrase and those of the Verb Phrase. (RLT)

3905. Vanriest, Jean B. "La place de l'adjectif qualificatif épithète en français et sa correspondance en espagnol." *LyC* 13(1973):95-108.
The French adjective is often placed after the noun; the same occurs in Spanish. If the adjective is followed by a complement, it normally follows the noun in French and precedes it in Spanish if it expresses an emotive value. In both languages the adjective appears before proper nouns, with some exceptions. Short adjectives normally precede the noun. For adjectives that normally occur both in ante- and postposition, preceding the noun denotes a more subjective value. Numerous adjectives change meanings with different positions. Adjectives with adverb and complement, and those made on a past participle form always follow the noun in French and always precede it in Spanish. (LLBA)

3910. Woledge, Brian. "Noun Declension in Twelfth-Century French." *TPS* 1973(1974):75-97.
The traditional statement that Old French nouns have two cases, nominative and oblique, is unsatisfactory both because up to 40% of Old French nouns have no case-distinctions and because, where case-distinctions exist, some writers use them inconsistently. It is useful to analyze separately the syntax of writers who use case-distinctions consistently and those who do not. Chrétien de Troyes is a good example of the first type; writers who are inconsistent in using case-distinctions seem to choose one or the other form under the influence of various unconscious forces. The use of declension varied geographically: it was used consistently in the North, in Champagne, and in the Ile-de-France, but not in the West. Inconsistent use of case-distinctions has wrongly been regarded as a grammatical mistake. (BW)

Translation. 3914. Chavy, Paul. "Les premiers translateurs français." *FR* 47:557-65.
The learned men who, in the 12th or 13th centuries, concerned themselves with French translations were far from being naive. They had a fairly clear concept of what "faithfulness" should be. However, many a medieval translation appears untrue to the original. At least four sorts of reasons can be put forward to explain the "distortions" in such texts. For one, there is the didactic trend, which leads the translator to compile useful information from every source available. There is also the need for him to comply with the tastes of the less-educated public that reads only the vernacular. Conventions of literary style bring forth other factors of inaccuracy. Finally, early French translators were confronted with the intricate problem—encountered by translators of all times—of bridging the gap between widely separated cultures. In any case, they should not be judged by modern standards, but studied with respect to their own aims and means. (PC)

Portuguese

Etymology, Lexicography, and Lexicology. 3925. Azevedo, Milton M. "Sobre gírias velhas e novas." *Hispania* 57:933-35.
The value of the analysis of Brazilian Portuguese slang in Fody's "Uma nova lista de gírias" in *Hispania*, 55 (1972), 909-12 is debatable. Fody's methods of data-collecting and his informants are poorly characterized and the article suffers from the absence of a sound initial definition of slang as a linguistic phenomenon. Many of the allegedly new slang terms listed have been in use for decades, and the distinction made between old and new terms is not supported by documentation. The lexical list fails to characterize the circumstances in which colloquial and obscene expressions are employed as well as their users as a sociolinguistic group. (MMA)

Morphology. 3937. Malkiel, Yakov. "Typological Affinity of Italian *eglino, elleno* 'They' to the Portuguese Inflected Infinitive." *RomN* 14(1973):636-39.
Fundamentally, there exist two schools of thought on the rise of the "inflected infinitive" in Portuguese: some experts view it as an archaism, others as an innovation. Typological analysis enables us to liken it to the expansion of the Italian personal pronouns: *egili(no), elle (no)*, at one time used in reference to animate nouns. This affinity increases the likelihood of the inflected infinitive having been an innovation. (YM)

Phonology. 3942. Brakel, C. Arthur, Jr. "Portuguese //r≈ř//, Lusitanean and Brazilian Allophones." *SIL* 24:1-16.
Re-examines Portuguese sounds represented orthographically by *r*, phonemicizations of these sounds, and standard descriptions of their patterning. It then contrasts the above with corpora elicited from 5 native speakers concluding that the biphonemic interpretation of the 2 sets of sounds is most appropriate. (CAB)

3943. Harris, James W. "Evidence from Portuguese for the 'Elsewhere Condition' in Phonology." *LingI* 5:61-80.
In *The Sound Pattern of English*, Chomsky and Halle propose a principle whereby abbreviability of rules by means of parentheses and angled brackets imposes disjunctive ordering. Kiparsky argues that this principle is neither necessary nor sufficient and proposes an alternative one, called the "elsewhere condition," that assigns disjunctive ordering independently of abbreviatory notations. Data from Brazilian Portuguese supports the "elsewhere condition" and two of its generalizations tentatively suggested by Kiparsky; arguments are presented for two key morphophonemic rules. (LLBA)

Syntax. 3947. Azevedo, Milton M. "On the Semantics of *estar* plus Participle Sentences in Portuguese." *Linguistics* 135:25-33.
Portuguese sentences formed with the construction *estar* + participle have received different, sometimes conflicting interpretations, probably because of their semantic and syntactic similarity with passives, which are formed with the construction *ser* + participle. The specification of the relationship between the two types of sentences is not so crucial as a semantic characterization of the various kinds of sentences with *estar* + participle. The possibility of achieving such characterization on the basis of the model described in Chafe 1970 is discussed and

certain semantic features are proposed. (MMA)

Spanish

Bibliography. 4007. Teschner, Richard V. "A Critical Annotated Bibliography of Anglicisms in Spanish." *Hispania* 57:631-78. This bibliography annotates and analyzes 209 books, articles, parts of books, Ph.D. dissertations, etc., which deal with the influence of English on the Spanish of Mexico, Central America, the Caribbean, South America, and Spain. Entries are categorized geographically and topically; topical classifications include phonology, orthography, sports terminology, argot, and morphosyntaxis. The majority of studies are classified according to the region or nation they deal with: the largest number (50) bear on Puerto Rican Spanish, 28 deal with Mexican, 16 with peninsular Spanish, and smaller numbers with Argentinian, Chilean, Colombian, Venezuelan, Panamanian, Cuban, etc. (RVT)

General and Miscellaneous. 4015. Delgado, José. "Los acrónimos en el habla de Puerto Rico." *LangS* 30:19-21. The use of acronyms has intensified in Puerto Rico during the past few years. This phenomenon has mostly been the product of the application of linguistic and pyschological theories by government and commercial organizations in naming agencies or corporations which become widely known when their titles are converted into acronyms. Both the intensive use of acronyms and the marked influence English has had on Puerto Rican speech may eventually result in the development of what could be called "acronymized Spanglish." A catalog of common acronyms in use in Puerto Rico is included. (JD)

4016. Feldman, David M. "On Spanish Designations of Language." *Hispania* 57:83-89. Spanish uses the four terms *lengua, lenguaje, idioma,* and *habla* interchangeably to designate the sets of data to which the term language can be applied. Contemporary dictionaries and the authors of reference grammars and linguistic treatises do not provide a satisfactory explanation of the semantic distribution of these terms. A survey reveals that *lenguaje* is largely restricted to meanings including language as a whole, metaphorical references to non-human communication, or language-type codes. *Lengua* identifies specific languages, forms of communication within individual languages, and is used in certain predictable set phrases. *Habla* covers speech, spoken language behavior, spoken regional dialects, and idiolects. *Idioma* reflects above all the idiosyncratic notion of particular languages, real or invented. (DMF)

4029. Turner, Ronald C. "An Automated Procedure for Quantification of Rhythmical Patterning in Spanish." *Linguistics* 121:89-98. By means of a statistical model, the computer assigns an "index of rhythmical structuredness" to any sample of Spanish text. The index in turn serves as a significant parameter to distinguish among literary and non-literary genres. The statistical model is based on the notion of entropy as developed in information theory. "Information" is taken in an abstract sense to refer solely to the overall degree of structuredness or patterning in the rhythmic string (composed of stresses and non-stresses). The plausibility of linking rhythmic structuredness with genre is enhanced by the intuitive notion that the "ascending" scale of genres (journalistic prose, essay, novel, poetry) corresponds to a scale of rhythmic tightness; this correspondence is in fact borne out by the preliminary findings of the study. The same computer programs which have analyzed the data of this study will in turn be used to examine a larger corpus of Spanish text and should also prove useful in the solution of a variety of linguistic problems. (RCT)

Dialectology. 4051. Sacks, Norman P. "*Acá* in Santiago de Chile." *Hispania* 57:89-93. Generalizations concerning the oral use of the Spanish locative adverbs *aquí* and *acá* may be risky if based primarily upon written questionnaires administered to native informants. Field work leads to more reliable generalizations. A doctoral dissertation dealing with Spanish adverbs meaning "here" concluded, as a result of the use of written questionnaires with native informants, that whereas *acá* is used more in Chilean speech than in the speech of a number of other Spanish-speaking countries, *aquí* in Chile seems to predominate. One year's residence in Chile indicated to Sacks that Acá was the audio-lingual norm —certainly in Santiago—whereas *aquí* was the visual norm. (NPS)

4052. Sánchez-Rojas, Arturo. "Crudeza y eufemismo en el habla popular." *Hispania* 57:498-500. Two tendencies in popular language produce a "special" vocabulary and an idiomatic usage of other expressions: (1) The description of reality is exaggerated or veiled; and (2) There is a tendency to apply zoological terms to persons. The latter calls for a pejorative language, conversion of human beings into objects of animals, and exaggeration of human defects. The former is an attenuation of truth, veiling it hypocritically in order to make it more palatable. (AS-R)

4053. Tessen, Howard W. "Some Aspects of the Spanish of Asunción, Paraguay." *Hispania* 57:935-37. Paraguay is primarily a Guaraní-speaking nation. Bilingualism is found principally in urban districts. Guaraní has affected Spanish to a limited extent at some social and educational levels. Frequent contact with speakers of Argentinian Spanish has also served to affect the Spanish spoken in Asunción and other parts of Paraguay. The differentiating elements of Asunción Spanish are phonological, morphological, syntactic, and lexical in nature. (HWT)

4055. Valdés-Fallis, Guadalupe. "Spanish and the Mexican Americans." *ColQ* 22:483-93. The most important characteristics of the Spanish spoken in the American Southwest are: (1) Presence of *seseo* (pronunciation of *c* before *e* and *i* like *s*) and *yeísmo* (pronunciation of *ll* as *y*); (2) Many Americanisms, Mexicanisms, and borrowings from Indian languages; (3) Reflects the social dialect of the working classes, while retaining many archaic forms; (4) Includes many borrowings from English (the prestige language in the contact situation); (5) Can include occasional lexical items from *Pachuco* (a colloquial slang); these items serve as identity markers among young Chicanos. (GV-F)

Etymology, Lexicography, and Lexicology. 4068. Fernández-Galiano, Manuel. "Algunas consideraciones sobre etimología." *Babel* 19(1973):174-81. [See also Bibliog. for 1973, Vol. III, Item 4537.] A discussion of a set of 10 precepts for avoiding false etymologies, among which are: (1) Avoid etymologies that require phonetic changes other than the normal ones; (2) Respect the norms of suffixing and word formation; (3) Avoid derivations that require too great a semantic extension and those that go against historical or historical-linguistic presuppositions; (4) Prefer simple explanations to complicated ones; (5) Take care in distinguishing words that existed in classical or Byzantine Greek from scientific neologisms that could not have been sources for Spanish etymologies; and (6) When in doubt, abstain. (LLBA)

4073. Jurado, Arturo. "El lenguaje en evolución." *Hispania* 57:938-40. A list of examples is compiled which proves that the Spanish spoken in Mexico is somewhat different from what grammars, dictionaries, and renowned authors dictate. All who speak this Spanish or at least the vast majority of the upper, middle, and lower classes understand said lexicon, even though they may be accustomed to using it in an informal situation. (AJ)

4084. Terry, Edward D. "Spanish Lexicography and the Real Academia Española:A Sketch." *Hispania* 57:958-64. The history of Spanish lexicography really begins with the *Tesoro de la lengua castellana o española* (1611) by Sebastián de Covarrubias. After this no important Spanish lexicographical work appeared until the *Diccionario de Autoridades* (1726-39) was published in six volumes by the Real Academia Española. In 1780 it began to publish its *Diccionario de la lengua española* in one volume and had continued to do so at irregular intervals until 1970 when the 19th edition appeared. (EDT)

4085. Teschner, Richard V. "*Adicto a droga(s) drogadicto, morfinómano* or *toxicómano*?:Lexical Lag in the Fixing of a Standard Spanish Equivalent for English *Drug Addict.*" *Hispania*

57:310-12.
Seeks to determine which of the following "best" renders the English term "drug addict" in Spanish: *adicto a droga(s), drogadicto, morfinómano,* or *toxicómano*? Because current dictionary information lacks uniformity and seldom provides full satisfaction, the problem of concluding which of the several is actually preferred in Spanish will demand further attention. (RVT)

4089. Waltman, Franklin M. "Synonym Choice in the *Cantar de Mio Cid.*" *Hispania* 57:452-61.
A polemic has existed for several years as to whether there is one or more than one author responsible for the composition of the *Cantar de Mío Cid.* The viewpoints expressed by critics have been varied and numerous. The choice of particular synonyms within the poem are studied to determine if there is any great difference within the three parts of the poem. Synonyms were located by using a concordance print-out entitled *Concordance to Poema de Mío Cid.* Opinions of other critics are given first, followed by the presentation of the ideas expressed by Ramón Menéndez Pidal. Based on his beliefs, a scheme of verses is established with the study of synonym choices following. The study of synonyms, based on this scheme of verses, tends to disprove the existence of two poets. (FMW)

Morphology. 4095. Hartman, Steven L. "Alfonso el Sabio and the Varieties of Verb Grammar." *Hispania* 57:48-55.
King Alfonso x of Castile and León (1226-84) is called Alfonso el Sabio because of the scholarly activity which he fostered at his court. He is thought to have supervised closely the work of his scribes as they wrote the Alfonsine treatises on history, astronomy, science, and law, and so he has been credited with "founding," standardizing, and stabilizing Castilian prose. However, a statisical examination shows that Alfonsine prose is internally inconsistent on certain items of verb morphology, and a diachronic comparison indicates that other such items emerge as temporary fashions which pass out of use shortly after the 13th century, returning to an earlier form. In view of these signs of inconsistency and impermanence of Alfonsine verb morphology, it would be well to redefine and perhaps further specify the contribution of Alfonso x to the history of Castilian. (SLH)

4106. St. Clair, Robert, and Cynthia Park. "The Irregular Present Tense Verbs of Spanish." *Linguistics* 135:73-99.
The irregular verb system of the Spanish present tense is reanalyzed within the theoretical framework of generative phonology. It differs from the standard descriptions not only by its attempts to synchronically motivate and substantiate the verbal forms underlying the paradigms, but also by its efforts to explicitly demonstrate the nature of the idiosyncracies associated with each verbal item. (RSC & CP)

Phonology. 4118. Haden, Ernest F., and Joseph H. Matluck. "Cuban Phonology." [F 51]:20-34.
400 hours of Havana Spanish were tape-recorded in Miami by the University of Texas at Austin in 450 interviews involving 750 informants from Havana, Cuba as part of a global research project sponsored by the Inter-American Program for Linguistics and Language Teaching (PILEI). Segmental analysis shows a five-phoneme vowel system with additional morphophonemic contrasts signalling grammatical differences and the weak consonantism to be expected in the Caribbean zone. A suprasegmental analysis describes the intonation patterns encountered in the materials studied. (JHM)

4121. Lococo, Veronica G. "Irregularities of a Regular Verb." *Hispania* 57:500-02.
The influence of analogy is especially strong where one is somewhat familiar with a given speech form. The first person singular present indicative of the Spanish verb *roer* is one such example. Spanish grammars cite three forms for it: (1) a regular one, which because of the combination [oo] seems to violate the Spanish sound system; and (2) two irregular ones, one of them analogous to the *uir* verbs, and a homophone of *rollo.* Native Spanish speakers were asked to supply what they thought was the proper form. Results show that education and analogy, especially to a verb of high frequency, are important factors in the choice of

form. (VGL)

Semantics. 4136. Bernstein, J.S. "On the Semantics of Certain English Phrasal Verbs and Their Rendering into Spanish." *BR/RB* 1:59-66.
A discussion of several phrasal verbs from the standpoint of semantics. Problems of translation into Spanish can probably be solved in given cases with the sensitive use of good dictionaries, attention to etymologies and cognate verb families, and perhaps consultation with native speakers. Lists of verb + preposition combinations, together with the Spanish translations, offer examples of assorted members of phrasal verb families. (LLBA)

Syntax. 4147. Almasov, Alexey. "Special Uses of *tú* and *usted.*" *Hispania* 57:56-57.
Diego Marín's "El uso de *tú* y *usted* en el español actual" (*Hispania,* Dec. 1972) elicits the following remarks: (1) *Tú* is not always familiar address. When directed to the deity, nature, etc., or when used in church, in poetry, and in high-flown oratory, regardless of the addressee, it clearly has a solemn connotation. In the countries where the *voseo* is generally accepted, *tú* has retained only its solemn aspect and *vos* carries the familiar function. (2) There is no uniformity throughout Spanish America in the use of the familiar address versus the formal address. (AA)

4148. —— "*Vos* and *vosotros* as Formal Address in Modern Spanish." *Hispania* 57:304-10.
The formal *vos* address disappeared from everyday speech during the 17th century and is not usually considered a part of modern Spanish. It is still used, however, both on the Peninsula and in Spanish America to render archaic speech in literary works whose action is placed in periods preceding the 18th century; in contemporary Spain, in addressing persons of high authority; in addressing God, the Virgin, and the saints. In all these cases the plural counterpart of *vos* is *vosotros,* which, consequently, also may have a solemn connotation. (AA)

4152. Bishop, Ann. "Some Aspects of the Future Tense in Spanish and English." *LyC* 13(1973):88-94.
A list of some of the main expressions of futurity in Spanish and English with indication of some differences between them. 13 points concerning future tense are illustrated with 26 examples. (LLBA)

4153. Bolinger, Dwight. "One Subjunctive or Two?" *Hispania* 57:462-71.
Spanish verbs governing the subjunctive fall into several classes, two of which are the optative and the dubitative. Lozano errs in attributing the features of the main verb to the subordinate verb as well, yielding an "optative subjunctive" and a "dubitative subjunctive." The subjunctive has its own contrastive feature, "attitude," which distinguishes it from the "intelligence" of the indicative. There is a relationship of compatibility between the optative-dubitative features and the attitudinal feature, but not a relationship of determination. Various tests prove that the subjunctive is a unitary phenomenon. (DB)

4158. Devera P., Sanson. "Tipos de transposición." *LyC* 13(1973):116-19.
Transposition is the transfer of semantic value from one part of speech in the source language to another in the target language. The types of transposition are: dilution, concentration, substitution, and double transposition. Dilution occurs when one sign in the source language (SL) is translated by several in the target language (TL). Contraction is the reverse phenomenon: one sign of the TL represents several in the SL. Substitution occurs when the TL sign belongs to a category different from that of the SL sign. Double transposition can be optional or obligatory. It is obligatory when to two or more signs of the SL no equivalents in the TL exist, and is optional when signs of the SL exchange their grammatical categories when transferred into the TL. (LLBA)

4160. Foster, David W. "The Spanish Subjunctive as a Non-Semantic Category." *English Lang. Jour.* 4(1973):191-200.
The Spanish subjunctive must be considered exclusively a phenomenon of surface syntax; it cannot be identified with any one underlying category, single or complex, of the universal semantic base. The implication is that any non-indicative, dependent moods of language are to be considered surface

phenomena without any specific underlying meaning. The implications for the teaching of English to native speakers of Spanish are discussed. (LLBA)

4164. Goldin, Mark G. "A Psychological Perspective of the Spanish Subjunctive." *Hispania* 57:295-301.
A generative semantic analysis of the Spanish subjunctive shows: (1) only two or three principles affect the choice of mood in Spanish; (2) the principles are conceptual rather than grammatical. One requires subjunctive in a subordinate clause when the predicate of the main clause indicates an evaluative reaction. A second principle determines subjunctive in a subordinate clause when a speaker's presupposition about the truth of that proposition is negative or indefinite. (MGG)

4174. Roldán, Mercedes. "On the So-Called Auxiliaries *ser* and *estar*." *Hispania* 57:292-95.
A continuation of Roldán's "Towards a Semantic Characterization of *ser* and *estar*." The arguments presented here are strictly semantic in nature. The meanings of existence in the case of *ser* and presence at locus in the case of *estar* are also operative in their roles as so-called auxiliaries. These arguments tend to support Ross's claim that the "auxiliary" as a grammatical category should be stricken from the grammars of both English and Spanish and, possibly, from the inventory of universal grammar. (MR)

4175. —— "Toward a Semantic Characterization of *ser* and *estar*." *Hispania* 57:68-75.
Grammarians have failed to notice in the various constructions with *ser* and *estar* the natural extensions of the basic meanings of the two verbs. The basic meaning of *ser* is existence and some of its extensions are: (a) Assertion of identification of the subject

with its predicate, (b) statement of identification of the subject, (c) Happening, i.e., the existence of events, (d) definitions, descriptions, and statements of set membership. The semantic feature existence is presupposed by *estar*, beyond this, *estar* asserts the presence of the subject at a specific point in space or time. Its main extension is the presence of the subject in the state or condition denoted by the predicate at the time specified by the sentence. (MR)

4181. Terrel, Tracy, and Joan Hooper. "A Semantically Based Analysis of Mood in Spanish." *Hispania* 57:484-94.
There are several basic attitudes a speaker can adopt toward a proposition, and these attitudes govern both the choice of verb form and matrix. Sentences are classified into six semantic types, and it is shown that the classification is motivated both syntactically and semantically, explaining not only the use of the subjunctive but also the indicative verb forms in Spanish. Certain ambiguous sentences are examined showing that the analysis offers a straightforward explanation for their ambiguity. (TT & JH)

Translation. 4185. Walsh, Donald D. "Poets Betrayed by Poets." *Hispania* 57:140-44.
The first requirement of a translator is that he know thoroughly the language of his author. The second requirement is that he have as good a command of his own language as his author has of his language. The third requirement is that his translation express his author's concepts and style and not his own. Numerous examples of English-speaking poets translating 20th-century Hispanic poets and failing to meet one, two, or all of the above requirements are given. (DDW)

III. CENTRAL AND EAST ROMANCE LANGUAGES

Italian

General and Miscellaneous. 4212. Pietropaolo, Domenico. "Aspects of English Interference on the Italian Language in Toronto." *CMLR* 30:234-41.
The five vowel phonemes of Italo-Canadian spoken in Toronto are listed. A phenomenon related to initial doubling is the reinforcement of the first syllable by geminating the initial consonant and preceding it with a euphonic support vowel. The position of the suprasegmental stress phoneme shows that there is a general tendency to adapt Canadian-English words to Italian accentual patterns. The ascending order of the number of loans in each pattern is the following: oxytones, proparoxytones, paroxytones. Also illustrated through examples are: (1) the phenomena of extending the semantic value of a loan by using it in fixed noun phrases: (2) metynomic semantic expansion; and (3) the derivation of verbs from borrowed nouns. For many loan words, the differences among dialects of the speakers give rise to more than one variant. (LLBA)

4218. Vicentini, Giuseppina. "Cambiamenti linguistici di una communità italo-brasiliana." *RILA* 5(1973):333-50.
In the Pedrinhas community, both Italian and Portuguese are prominent languages. Some of the social changes that have occurred there because of Italian immigration are described. One result of Italian spoken in Pedrinha is the Italianization of some verbal phrases and common expressions. Results of surveys involving Italians of all ages indicate that the use of Italian is diminishing in Pedrinhas because it is largely restricted to the home. (LLBA)

Etymology, Lexicography, and Lexicology. 4261. O'Connor, D.J. "John Florio's Contribution in Italian-English Lexicography." *Italica* 49(1972):49-67.
The first Italian-English dictionary, compiled by William Thomas in 1550, contained only 8,000 words on the collections made by Francisco Alunno and Acarisio da Cento in 1543. John Florio for his *Worlde of Wordes*, however, went much further and ransacked the Italian literature of the period—both dialectal and Florentine —c onsulting 72 works for his first edition (1598) and no less than

253 for his second (1611). His dictionary thus became not only a valuable teaching aid but also a means for spreading among English students of Italian a knowledge of the colorful Italian literature of the sixteenth century. In 1659 Torriano used Florio's two editions to produce a slightly larger Italian-English, English-Italian dictionary. Altieri in 1726 and Baretti in 1760 preferred instead to use as a basis for their bilingual dictionaries the renowned Florentine *Vocabolario della Crusca*. Nonetheless their works still contain some words and definitions which can be traced back to Florio's earlier mammoth efforts. (DJO'C)

4263. Regan, Mariann S. "Petrarch's Courtly and Christian Vocabularies:Language in *Canzoniere* 61-63." *RomN* 15:527-31.
The group of *Canzoniere* 61, 62, and 63 demonstrate how specific word meanings can change with context, revealing the clash of secular and religious values. These three poems form a "repentance cycle" sequence in which the speaker shifts roles from earthly lover to Christian penitent and back to earthly lover. In 61 the speaker joyously displays a full courtly love vocabulary. In the next poem the language of the suffering courtly lover is redefined by the new religious framework. As the speaker of 63 returns to honoring his "donna," a number of words given religious emphasis in 62 now possess courtly meanings. (MR)

Semantics. 4288. Bencivegna, Ermanno. "Alcuni sviluppi nella teoria dell'uso referenziale delle descrizioni." *LeS* 9:147-58.
Donnellan's distinction between the attributive and the referential uses of descriptive expressions leads to a development of a new procedure for the evaluation of the utterances containing descriptions and clarifies the connection existing between proper names and groups of descriptions which allows the identification of the reference of these names. The basic epistemological concept is that of cognitive space: it is in this space, in fact, and not in a presumed real space that the identifications take place. (EB)

Rhaeto-Romansch

Etymology, Lexicography, and Lexicology. 4325. Keller, Hans E. "Two Toponymical Problems in Geoffrey of Monmouth and

Wace:*Estrusia* and *Siesia*." *Speculum* 49:687-98.
Certain place-names in Geoffrey of Monmouth and Wace (Layamon) still elude identification, both in the formation of name as well as in their geographical location. *Estrusia* belongs to the first category, and linguistic data from French dialectology and Germanic studies are necessary to recognize that Geoffrey's *Estruenses* means "settlers along a river." The place of the decisive battle between Arthur and the Romans was known to be somewhere in Burgundy. Medieval documents show that Geoffrey must have thought of the Val Suzon. (HEK)

Onomastics. 4331. Richardson, Peter N. "Some Notes on a Swiss Bicultural Onomasticon." *Names* 22:45-51.
Graubünden (Grischun, Grigioni), the only trilingual canton of Switzerland, is ideally suited for studies of cultural contact. Speakers of the archaic idiom of Rhaeto-Romansh have for centuries been in close contact with German speakers here, and the effects of the interference are visible in aspects of culture ranging from language to architecture. Name-giving traditions shed light on contact at the most personal level and reveal when true cultural interpenetration has taken place. Church records, tax lists, and community archives in Graubünden show that for the period 1200-1700 given names of both Germanic and Christian-Romance origin were changed according to Swiss German and Romansh language patterns. (PNR)

Romanian

General and Miscellaneous. 4378. Lobiuc, Ioan. "Interacţiuni lexicale şi fonetice ucraino-române (I)." *StCL* 24(1973):455-60.
Discusses the influence of Ukrainian on Daco-Romanian: (1) the linguistic geography and lexical-semantic aspects of Ukrainian borrowings in Daco-Romanian; (2) the etymology of many Ukrainian borrowings; and (3) the "channel" of some Romanian words currently considered to be of German, Polish, and Hungarian origins. The phonetic principle was also used when considering the etymologies of the borrowed words. The current practice of listing only the literary etymologies of words is insufficient: one must include the immediate and accurate dialectal source of the word. (LLBA)
4384. Maneca, Constant. "Statistica lexicală şi stilurile limbii." *LimR* 22(1973):529-44.
An examination of Romanian texts in which statistical methods were used to determine the characteristics of three styles: literary, scientific, and colloquial. The study determined the number and frequency of words in literary, scientific, and popular texts, the frequency of elements from different etymological sources, the frequency of usage of different genders, grammatical constructions, frequency of neologisms, etc. The result is a clear

delineation of literary and scientific styles. (LLBA)

Etymology, Lexicography, and Lexicology. 4441. Hristea, Theodor. "Pseudo-anglicisme de provenienţă franceză în limba română." *LimR* 23:61-71.
Neither lexicographers nor researchers who have studied the elements of English origin in the Romanian vocabulary have remarked that besides anglicisms of genuine origin there also exists a relatively small number of words borrowed from French (pseudoanglicisms). Most Romanian pseudoanglicisms belong to sports terminology, such as: tennisman (tennis player) and tenniswoman, recordman (record holder) and recordwoman, davis-coup-man (Davis Cup Player or member of the Davis Cup Team), etc. Although they appear to sound English, these words were created in French by combining themes and formative elements of English origin: tennis + man = tennisman, record + man = recordman, etc. The model of such formations is provided by the older genuine anglicisms, which French borrowed from English. (LLBA)

Morphology. 4461. Augerot, James E. "The Conjugation of the Rumanian Verb." *SEEJ* 18:47-55.
The Romanian verbal system resists simple classification into the traditional Latin one of four conjunctions. Such classification is almost meaningless when the verbal system is analyzed by means of a generative transformational approach. All forms of most Romanian verbs are predictable from a basic stem and a single set of underlying endings. A crucial problem remains unsolved in the present description: the form of some of the endings is dependent upon the form of the full stem, but are added to a secondary, truncated stem. This calls for a redundant classification of each stem type since the final stem vowel is not truncated in a predictable fashion in strict phonological terms. (JEA)

Syntax. 4533. Carlton, Charles M. "Defining the Romanian Past Participle." *Linguistics* 135:35-41.
While traditional grammars label a small class of high-frequency Romanian verbs "irregular," most have a participle formation identical to that for other verbs of a characteristic infinitive type: -á (I) and -í, -î (IV) assume a weak termination in voiceless dental stop /-t/; -eá (II) is replaced by /-ú-/ plus the characteristic /-t/, with possible secondary consonantal or vocalic changes in the stem. This leaves a residue of participles whose shape is not wholly predictable from the infinitive type (*fost, stiut*), plus three sub-classes of III conjugation verbs. An examination of the structural properties of the participle types, with the aim of making explicit their relationship with the infinitive, is given. (CMC)

INDO-EUROPEAN B: BALTIC AND SLAVIC LINGUISTICS†

II. BALTIC

General

Morphology. 4632. Bammesberger, Alfred. "The Formation of the East Baltic Stative Verbs *stāw-ē-* and *dēw-ē-*." *Language* 50:687-95.
The East Baltic stative verbs *stāw-ē-* and *dēw-ē-* do not derive from alleged Indo-European perfect forms in *-w-*. Their starting point must be seen in the otherwise well-known roots IE *stā- and *dhē-*. The *-w-* is ultimately due to the active perfect participle, whose strong form IE *-woōs* was abandoned in Baltic (and Slavic), but left its trace in a phonologic rule according to which vowel-initial suffixes were linked to roots ending in a long vowel by means of *-w-*. (AB)

Lithuanian

Phonology. 4754. Tanaka, Yoshio. "The Accent Types in Standard Lithuanian." *Linguistics* 127:75-116.
An attempt to develop an adequate symbolism for a completely explicit and rigorous treatment of the accent types in Standard Lithuanian. The discussion format is: (1) statement of the problem, with brief history; (2) development of the tone-stress model and associated models to provide the necessary notation; (3) assumption of intensity as the basic variable for this problem and justification; (4) tentative definitions of the accent types and justification; and (5) definitive set-notational definitions of the accent types. (YT)

† *Festschriften* and Other Analyzed Collections are listed in the first division of this volume. "F" numbers in brackets following a title refer to these items.

III. GENERAL AND EARLY SLAVIC

General and Miscellaneous

4817. Hamilton, William S.,Jr. "Deep and Surface Changes in Four Slavic Noun Systems." *Linguistics* 127:27-73.
This descriptive reference work develops a new structural technique of organizing diachronic data. The noun systems of Czech, Polish, Russian, and Serbo-Croatian sufficiently resemble the Common Slavic parent system to be described under identical structural criteria: 1) six cases, occurring both singular and plural, 2) patterns of syncretism between these cases, and 3) different sets of endings fitting the same pattern of syncretism. The deep structures of the modern languages are represented in terms of Common Slavic components such as *jers* and nasal vowels so that surface change, which can be explained by the addition of a phonological rule to the grammar, can be separated from deep change, which cannot be so explained. A chart for each modern language, showing the deep changes since Common Slavic and the results of the application of surface changes, describes what actually happened and is contrasted with a chart showing the system which would have resulted in the the absence of any deep change. (WSH)

Onomastics. 4857. Lekov, Ivan. "Nasledstveni i po-novi tendencii na slovoobrazuvane pri glavnite slavjanski edinično-lični naimenovanija za narodnostna prinadležnost." *BE* 23(1973):3-9.
In order to further the systematization and structuralization of lexical and grammatical composition of language and to reveal its derivational processes and adaptive factors, a comparative typological analysis of intra-Slavic ethnic nomenclature is presented from both diachronic and synchronic points of view. Russian, Czech, Ukrainian, Belorussian, Polish, Slovak, Bulgarian, Serbo-Croatian, and Slovene were examined. Characteristic suffixes for both masculine and feminine nouns are tabulated and analyzed in correlation with geographical distribution. (LLBA)

IV. EAST SLAVIC

Russian

General and Miscellaneous. 4910. Barxudarov, L.S. "Russko-anglijskie jazykovye paralleli:Očerk pjatyj." *RJR* 2:60-64. [Rus.-Eng. ling. parallels.]
The formal category of mood as a whole is simpler in English than in Russian. In general, Russian and English active voice correspond. While both languages have three persons and singular and plural, in English these forms are much less clearly expressed or distinguished. Russian verb forms include the infinitive, participle, and gerund. The infinitive is often used nominally. In English the distinction must be made between the gerund and the present active participle, which together can be considered as one form in "ing." The participle in English, as distinguished from Russian, cannot express gender, number, or case. (LSB)

4933. Stone, Gerald. "Language Planning and the Russian Standard Language." *TPS* (for 1972[1973]):165-83.
The prestige structure of Russian has been greatly changed as a result of the Revolution, and much that was formerly "incorrect" has now been destigmatized. At the same time, the tendency in the early years of Soviet power to identify nonstandard (especially rural) varieties with illiteracy has produced a situation in which nonstandard varieties have extremely low prestige. Certain left-overs from the pre-Revolutionary power structure are continuing to produce hypercorrect forms among norm-bearers, but the high degree of motivation to use the standard coupled with a pragmatic approach to the adjustment of the standard is likely to reduce the degree of difference between standard varieties and all other varieties. (GCS)

Etymology, Lexicography, and Lexicology. 4986. Horalik, L. "O roli omonimii v protsesse kommunikatsii." *RJR* 3(1973):84-85.
A report of a study of the frequency of homonyms in Russian. Homonyms have been viewed as hindering the process of communication in a language or as phenomena whose spreading may eventually interfere with that process. They actually function to facilitate communication in accordance with the linguistic principle of economy. Their frequency depends on the linguistic level, the absolute frequency of the given form, its syntactic function, etc. For native speakers of Russian, homonyms do not impede communication, but they may constitute a stumbling block for foreigners learning the language. (LLBA)

5016. Perelmuter, Joanna. "Russian Substandard Usage and the Attitude of Soviet Lexicography." *CSP* 16:436-47. [Sum. in Fr.]
With the coming of the Revolution, interest in the development of research of the substandard aspects of Russian language became less apparent as stress shifted to another branch of lexicographic scholarship—normative dictionaries. Strict normativeness in Russian lexicography was enforced in the 1930s and lasted until de-Stalinization took place 25 years later. If Soviet lexicography in the field of Russian substandard usage is presently more in the process of development than it has ever been in the post-revolutionary period, this development has only affected one category of substandard: Russian dialects. Other non-dialect substandard usage phenomena remain taboo in the Soviet Union. (JEP)

5031. Stoffel, Hans Peter. "Russian Sport Terminology:Some Examples of Lexico-Semantic Derivation and Their History." *NZSJ* 12(Sum 1973):90-100.
In studying the history of Russian sport terminology it is important to investigate not only established terms but also short-lived forms. One method of obtaining specialized terms is by giving existing words a new specialized meaning as sport terms. Examples drawn mainly from the skiing terminology show two groups of such terms: (1) the new terminological meaning does not push aside the previous meaning(s); (2) the former meanings, though retained, are overshadowed by the new specialized meaning. (H-PS)

Graphemics. 5050. Eustace, S.S. "A Proposed Transcription of Russian Cyrillic." *IPAJ* 4:37-48.
The proposed transcription described here is intended to be easier to read, type, and print, to convey Russian sounds more accurately, and to enable the Cyrillic original to be inferred exactly. Though it uses digraphs, the transcription occupies less space than the original and is probably more legible. (SSE)

Morphology. 5077. Hulanicki, Leo. "The Actional Perfect in Russian." *SEEJ* 17(1973):174-83.
The aspectual concurrence which manifests in a frequent use of past imperfective verb forms instead of their perfective counterparts has long puzzled Russian linguistics. The solution lies in the recognition of a "covered" semantic opposition of stative perfect versus actional perfect, which shares with the perfective-imperfective opposition the same surface forms. Since both kinds of the perfect are characterized by the semantic property of totality, another criterion is needed to distinguish between them. The semantic property of the "continuity" of effects of a past action serves this purpose. In this respect the stative perfect is a marked member which expresses the feature; the actional perfect, as an un-marked member, does not, merely connecting the past action with its present consequences. (LH)

Syntax. 5230. Mayer, Gerald L. "Common Tendencies in the Syntactic Development of 'Two,' 'Three,' and 'Four' in Slavic." *SEEJ* 17(1973):308-14.

Attempts to trace and compare the syntactic history of the numerals two, three, four in the modern literary Slavic languages. It was found that the resultant varying syntactic developments are based primarily on the fate of the dual number. Languages in which the dual was retained preserved the Common Slavic system of agreement for two, three, four. Languages in which the dual was lost developed the tendency for dual forms to spread to three, four or for plural forms to spread to two, or both tendencies. Syntactic development in Slavic languages without dual number is fairly uniform within each branch. Thus, West Slavic languages of this type show agreement in both oblique and direct case use. South Slavic languages have no oblique-direct case opposition but show contrasts in agreement and non-agreement based on gender. (GLM)

5239. Revzin, I.I. "O meste pravil pronominalizatsii v modeli porozhdeniya dlya russkogo yazyka." *Nauchno-tekhnicheskaya informatsiya* 11(1973):30-36.
Discusses whether pronominalization rules in a generative grammar of Russian are applied to the deep structure, as in the Chomsky model, or to the surface structure. Information extracted from both is needed and the generation must—in the special case of reflexivization—begin with some surface structure information, proceed to the deep structure, and then return to the surface structure. The relative order of reflexivization, pronominalization proper, and deletion of corresponding pronouns is investigated. (LLBA)

Translation. 5256. Rubenstein, Roberta. "Genius of Translation." *ColQ* 22:359-68.
Constance Garnett learned Russian in a casual manner from Russian friends in England and went on to become the primary translator of Russian literature into English. During her lifetime she translated over seventy volumes of works by Russian authors. Her enormous contribution to literature is even more remarkable in view of the fact that she was partially blind during more than half of her career. Her son, David Garnett, notes that she received little remuneration or recognition for her efforts, not even receiving royalties until late in her career. A Russian linguist, Augusta Tovey, undertook a comparative study of the Garnett and other translations from Russian into English, and concluded that Garnett's were superior in style, rhythm, and nuance to other translations, including more recent ones. Tovey attributed Garnett's excellence as a translator to her sense of rhythm and her musical ear. (RR)

V. SOUTH SLAVIC

General and Miscellaneous

5625. Butler, Thomas J. "Yugoslavia's Slavic Languages: A Brief Historical Perspective." *RNL* 5,i:18-24.
The tribal ancestors of the Southern Slavs all spoke the same basic language. Bifurcation first resulted from the fact that one part of them entered the Balkans from the West, another from the East. Conversion to Christianity gave them a unity of written communication. Centuries-long domination by Germans, Hungarians, and Turks deepened linguistic differences among the subject populations, as did the schism between Western and Eastern churches. A gradual shading of Serbo-Croatian dialects across the peninsula resulted. In the 19th century, Southern Slav nationalist fervor led to an agreement to direct Serbs and Croats toward the use of a common literary language based on the štokavian dialect. (TJB)

Syntax. 5630. Dejanova, M. "Kəm sintaktičnata sinonimija v južnoslavjanskite ezici." *BE* 23(1973):10-23.
One of the more interesting instances of syntactic synonymy is that of subject-verb-predicate adjective and subject-verb-adverbial modifier of manner. Analysis of many examples from modern Bulgarian, Polish, Russian, Slovene, Serbo-Croatian, and Czech demonstrates that these two constructions are often interchangeable, and an attempt is made to define the factors on which this interchangeability depends. It partially depends on the semantics of the verb. The semantic distinction of animate/inanimate is often the only relevant factor, and choice frequently depends on stylistic considerations. (LLBA)

Bulgarian

Morphology. 5656. Scatton, Ernest A. "The Alternative *e - a* in Modern Bulgarian." *SEEJ* 17(1973):427-32.
Alternations in Contemporary Standard Bulgarian of the type [m'ásto]—[mestá], [véren]—[v'árna] are considered. This alternation is accounted for by positing an additional abstract underlying phoneme /ǎ/. The phonological rules necessary to predict the phonetic realizations of this segment are discussed. From this discussion it is clear that the soft consonant before [á] is predictable and that the treatment of /a/ as [á] or [e] is a function of stress and the quality of the consonant which immediately follows /ǎ/. In this respect, this process is strikingly similar to phonological processes in Russian and Polish. (ES)

Syntax. 5664. Danchev, Andrei. "A Slavonic/Bulgarian View of the Aspectual Meaning of the Modern English De-Adjectival

-en Verbs." *Linguistics* 127:5-26.
The historical development and word-formation patterns of the de-adjectival *-en* verbs of the *darken* type in Modern English have been studied by a number of authors, but relatively little attention has been given to their aspectual meaning. This can be done by contrasting the *-en* verbs to the corresponding verbal forms in Bulgarian, where verbal aspect is marked morphologically. Despite certain similarities with the Slavonic perfective affixes, the English de-adjectival *-en* suffix differs from them because it has very limited distribution. (AD)

Macedonian

5677. Georgacas, Demetrius J. "Historical and Language Contacts and a Place-Name on Samos and in Macedonia (Greece): Karlóvasi." *Names* 22:1-33.
The place name Karlovasi on the Aegean island of Samos and the identical name in Central Macedonia resulted from the contact and interaction of Greek and Turkish. The bibliography includes more than 60 items. The historical background of Samos in the late Middle Ages, a description of the triple town of Karlovasi, the forms of the names and congeners are given, etymological attempts are reviewed (Slavic, Greek, Turkish); in the same manner the background and description of the Macedonian counterpart name, the story of the name, and attempts at etymology. The name is of Turkish origin, signifying "snow-covered level place." (DJG)

5679. Koneski, Blaže. "The Macedonian Dictionary." *RNL* 5,i:25-36.
The separate and distinct identity of Macedonian as a national language dates from efforts to standardize the usage of folk-speech during the 19th century. A major advance was made with the publishing of a Macedonian orthography in 1945. Institutional support for Macedonian linguistic studies came with the establishment in 1946 of the Department of South Slavic Languages at Skopje University's Faculty of the Arts. The Commission for a Macedonian Dictionary was established in 1951. The lexicographers labored to draw words from all the Macedonian dialects while fashioning a literary language with a secure folklore base. The Institute of the Macedonian Language published Volume I of the *Dictionary* in 1961. Volumes II and III followed in 1963 and 1965, to complete a three-volume edition containing 64,522 lexical entries on 1711 pages. (BK)

Serbo-Croatian

Etymology, Lexicography, and Lexicology. 5724. Velčić, Ivana.

"The English Element in the Croatian Sports Vocabulary." *SRAZ* 33-36(1972-73):757-71.
Analyzes English loan words in Croatian sports vocabulary. Phonemic analysis of English loan words shows that the English words have been adapted according to the phonological system of the borrowing language, i.e., Croatian phonemes have been substituted for English phonemes. Redistribution of Croatian phonemes is reflected in final consonant clusters. Morphological analysis reveals that English loan words are integrated into the Croatian system of inflections and that most are classified as masculine nouns. On the semantic level, many examples of extension can be found. (LLBA)
   5725. Vilke, Mirjana. "English Element in Serbo-Croatian Technical Vocabulary." *SRAZ* 33-36(1972-73):709-26.
A report of an investigation into the status of English loan words in Serbo-Croatian technical terminology. Four industries are considered: shipping, oil, high frequency technology (television), and nuclear physics. Phonological, morphological, and semantic analyses are performed on a representative corpus of English loans found in these industrial areas. In Serbo-Croatian terminology, two opposite trends can be discerned—one leading to internationalizing and the other to linguistic purification of terminology. (LLBA)

Syntax. 5773. Vlatković, Mira. "On the Use of Tenses in Scientific Papers, English and Croatian." *SRAZ* 33-36(1972-73):773-82.
The analysis of papers from scientific journals demonstrates that three English tenses correspond to only two in Croatian (present, present perfect, and preterite to present and perfect), and that in both languages they amount to over 9% of all finite verb forms. Further examination reveals that the sequence of tenses functions differently in each language, and that, through negative transfer, erroneous choice of the present passive over past passive to express a past action in English is frequently made. (LLBA)

Slovenian

Etymology, Lexicography, and Lexicology. 5802. Gjurin, Velemir. "Interesne govorice sleng, žargon, argo." *SlR* 22:65-81.
Slang, jargon, and argot are three special types of language. A discussion of the relationships between these three categories and the "social" types of language (standard, informal, regional dialect) and illustrations of the most important classes of slang are followed by a general survey of the influence of foreign languages upon Slovene slang and by an analysis of drug addicts' speech. (LLBA)

Phonology. 5831. Srebot, Tatjana. "Poskus kontrastivne analize slovenskega fonema /v/ z angleškim fonemom /v/." *JiS* 19(1973):89-93.
Slovene learners of English have difficulties with the English phoneme /v/, although a Slovene can articulate a voiced labiodental fricative because the Slovene language has a [v] sound. The difficulty is caused by the differences in the two phonological systems. In the prevocalic position, the two systems coincide; in the preconsonantal and final position this does not occur. Yet a Slovene learner has difficulties with /v/ even in the prevocalic position. In educated colloquial Slovene it is a voiced labiodental frictionless continuant [ʋ]; under the influence of widespread regional dialects it may even be a voiced bilabial continuant with or without friction [w] or [u̯]. The Slovene learner has much greater difficulty with English /v/ before consonants or finally, because in Slovene it is always realized as [u̯]. To a Slovene, [u̯] is just a kind of [v], not another phoneme as to an Englishman. (LLBA)

VI. WEST SLAVIC

Czech

General and Miscellaneous. 5852. Horálek, Karel. "Dnešní situace a úkoly naší jazykovědy." *SaS* 34(1973):288-97.
In the 1960s, Czechoslovakian linguists paid most attention to general theoretical questions. They departed from Prague School theory, trying to supplement and modify it in the spirit of the newest trends. However, a single broadly-based acceptance of these new concepts has not emerged. There are several reasons for this, the most important of which must be sought in the inadequacies of the theoretical foundations themselves and in the defects of the organization of linguistic institutions. (LLBA)

Dialectology. 5858. Jančák, Pavel. "Hodnocení vlivu příbuzného jazyka na slovní zásobu českého nářečí (Na materiále českých nářečí na Daruvarsku v Jugoslávii)." *SaS* 34(1973):302-19.
The influence of Serbo-Croatian on Czech dialects in the area of Daruvar in Yugoslavia can be observed most clearly in vocabulary. The material which was obtained for the Czech linguistic atlas through sampling was relatively extensive. The amount of influence on Czech was statistically analyzed. When areas are ordered according to the increasing degree of influence, it is demonstrated that the level of foreign influence is related to the age (order) of colonization and to the amount of contact with the foreign language. The consequence of the influence is the result of the combination of these two factors. (LLBA)

Phonology. 5874. Tarte, Robert D. "Phonetic Symbolism in Adult Native Speakers of Czech." *L&S* 17:87-94.
10 monolingual adult speakers of Czech were asked to label elliptical and triangular figures of different size with phonetic nonsense syllables to obtain evidence in support of the "phonetic symbolism" hypothesis. Subjects agreed about the relationship between vowel sounds and the size and shape of figures. The sound /a/ was preferred with large figures; /i/ with small; /u/ was chosen more often with ellipses; /i/ with triangles. (RDT)

Slovak

Dialectology. 5890. Ondrus, Pavel. "Súčasný stav slovenskej dialektológie." *SlReč* 38(1973):364-67.
A tendency has prevailed to collect the dialect facts from various linguistic levels and process them in monograph or book form. Although the demand for systematic and thorough monographic description of territorial dialects has not decreased, the Slovak Academy of Sciences has started to prepare the Atlas of the Slovak Language which will contain materials from all linguistic levels. New tasks for Slovak dialectology have emerged since the time when the boundary of the national language was surpassed, and the Slovak dialect elements are being evaluated in relation to the rest of the Slavonic dialects. (LLBA)

Etymology, Lexicography, and Lexicology. 5898. Ďuruľa, Ján. "Z histórie slov špán—kňahňa (kňahyňa)—kňaz." *SlReč* 38(1973):349-56.
Discusses the historical process by which the following succession took place: išpán and kneiža→špán and kňaz→špán and kňahňa→pn and pani. In addition to the replacement of certain forms by others, the broadening of the meanings of certain words and their use in a new meaning are considered. (LLBA)
   5903. Kuchar, Rudolf. "Slová dlh, dlžník vo vývine slovenčiny." *SlReč* 38(1973):357-63.
The word *dlh* is traced to its origins and changes in its meaning are demonstrated. Its usage in Slovak feudal provinces from the 1500s to the 1800s is analyzed. Semantic analysis indicates that it was used in these contexts: (1) to be paid for performing a duty, return in either money or natural goods, or not paid; (2) to claim something from someone; (3) natural goods, money, or other duty given to the feudal lord; (4) moral (not money or natural goods) duty; and (5) guilt. (LLBA)
   5904. Ondruš, Šimon. "Je sloveso *kukat'* nemeckého pôvodu?

Genetický vzťah medzi slovesami *kukať* a *čakať*.ʺ *SlReč* 38(1973):321-26.

It has been assumed that the Slovak word *kukať* (to look) was of German origin. Semantic and morphophonemic analysis reveals that the word is of Slavic origin derived from the same root as the words *čuť*, *čumiet'*, *skúmať*, and *čakať*. The German word *gucken*, thought to be the source of *kukať*, is a word borrowed into German from West Slavic. (LLBA)

5907. Ripka, Ivor. "O problematike nárečových slovních." *SlReč* 38(1973):97-103.

The thesis that a full dialect dictionary can be compiled only when it deals with one concrete dialect, forming a whole system, is presented. Compiling a full dialect dictionary covering an entire people appears practically unrealizable and theoretically inappropriate. A dictionary of Slovak popular dialects must have a differential character. It does not give a full analysis of the lexical and semantic structure of every word used at the present time in the Slovak dialects and treats the most characteristic popular vocabulary. (LLBA)

Phonology. 5929. Horák, Gejza. "Výslovnosť tvarov *prosieb*, *kresieb*." *SlReč* 38(1973):367-70.

A morphophonemic study of the pronunciation of the genitive plural forms of the words *prosba* (request) and *kresba* (drawing). Although these forms are commonly pronounced [krezi̯ep] and [prozi̯ep], the phonetic canons of literary Slovak do not support such a pronunciation. The pronunciations recommended are [prosi̯ep] for the written word *prosieb* and [kresi̯ep] for *kresieb*. (LLBA)

Semantics. 5933. Buzássyová, Klára. "Príspevok ku konfrontačnému výskumu sémantiky slovenských a českých slovies polohy." *SlReč* 38(1973):270-78,327-35.

The verbs of body position are divided into static (sediet'), medial (sadnúť), causative (posadiť), and reflexivized causative (posadiť sa) sets. The lexical units of these sets are contrasted from the point of view of their expression and content. The Slovak causative lexemes on the whole correspond semantically with their Czech counterparts. Considerable congruences can also be found by comparing the state sets of verbs of body position. On the other hand, there are considerable differences in the functioning of medial and reflexivized causative forms between Slovak and Czech due to the remnants of old medial forms in Slovak, while in Czech these forms have been replaced by reflexivized causative forms. (LLBA)

5936. Kačala, Ján. "Spájateľnosť substantív *favorit* a *ašpirant*." *SlReč* 38(1973):335-40.

Although the Slovak words "favorit" and "ašpirant" have a certain area of meaning in common, the former indicates a lack of activity on the part of the person so designated ("favorit"-the favored one), whereas the latter points to activity in the person it refers to ("ašpirant"-the one aspiring). (LLBA)

INDO-EUROPEAN C: GERMANIC LINGUISTICS†

I. GENERAL, EAST, AND PROTO-GERMANIC

East Germanic

Gothic. 6056. Ebbinghaus, Ernst A. "Gotica VIII." *GL* 14:35-37.

Explanation of the meaning of the word **peikabagms*. (EAE)

6057. ——— "Gotica x." *GL* 14:156-58.

Assessment of the grammatical category of **silbawiljis* on the basis of textual analysis. (EAE)

6073. Schmidt, Klaus M. "The Gothic Dual Second Person -*ts*." *Linguistics* 130:83-86.

The -*ts* in the dual 2 of Gothic verbs is not a reflex of the primary ending **-t(h)es/t(h)os*. Regardless of the tense form in which it occurs, Go. -*ts* comes from IE ** -dwo/dwi* 'two' plus -*s*. The -*ts* of the pret. ind. dual 2, for instance, reflects IE **-dwo/dwi-s*. Thus Go. -*ts* can be explained according to regular phonologic developments and need not be ascribed to spasmodic, unpredictable sound changes in which **-t(h)es/t(h)os* would somehow produce Go. -*ts*, though only in the dual 2. (KMS)

III. WEST GERMANIC (EXCLUDING ENGLISH)

Old Saxon

6406. Spalatin, Leonardo. "Saxon Genitive." *SRAZ* 33-36(1972-73):533-46.

The structure of the Saxon genitive (SG) is described, and its usage as the modifier element in the structure of a nominal group is discussed. The SG is a unit different from the word; even in cases where the SG consists of only one word, that word belongs to a rank higher than the word. Different classes of the SG are analyzed, and structural differences and problems of ambiguity are explored. (LLBA)

Old High German

Morphology. 6449. Wedel, Alfred R. "The Verbal Aspects of the Prefixed and Un-Prefixed Verbal Forms of *Stantan, Sizzan/Sessan, Lickan/Leckan* in the Old High German Benedictine Rule." *JEGP* 73:169-75.

The OHG Benedictine Rule illustrates Streitberg's definition of perfective aspect in Germanic by means of prefixation (see "Perfektive und imperfektive Aktionsart im Germanischen," *PBB*, 15, 1891, 70-177). The Rule provides evidence that Streitberg's system applies to verbs with basic durative meaning; in addition, however, the Rule provides examples of unprefixed verbs with non-durative meaning, such as the causatives *sezzan* and *leckan*, which disprove Streitberg's rationale for relying solely on prefixation to distinguish between durative and non-durative aspect. In this light, Fritjof A. Raven's arrangement of OHG verbs according to their durative or non-durative meaning (i.e., according to their Aktionsart) will prove to be correct (See "Aspekt und Aktionsart in den althochdeutschen Zeitwörtern, " *ZMF*, 26, 1958, 63). (ARW)

Onomastics. 6452. Wells, Christopher. "An Orthographic Approach to Early Frankish Personal Names." *TPS* (for 1972 [1973]):101-64.

This article characterizes Germanic onomastic material extant from Merovingian Gaul down to AD 750. The name-material in the Merovingian royal diplomas is taken as a basis: here the spelling conventions for rendering Germanic names and for the Latin text coincide to a very high degree, making phonological inferences difficult to draw. The distribution and functions of certain spellings ("graphies" <ch> and <gh>), which are held to reflect velar phonemes in Germanic names, are then examined. Graphie <ch> emerges as a clearly defined convention in the Merovingian royal chancelleries, although it is found elsewhere. The alternation of <ch> with other graphies, its replacement, and its occasional disappearance do not permit phonological

† *Festschriften* and Other Analyzed Collections are listed in the first division of this volume. "F" numbers in brackets following a title refer to these items.

interpretation. Replacement of <ch> may be the result of factors affecting the spelling of Latin at this period. The distribution of <gh> does not imply any clear phonetic phonemic interpretation. Graphie <gh> is regular only in the Merovingian royal chancelleries and is found only before the graphie <i> in pre-AD 750 material. An index to the Merovingian royal diplomas (edited by Lauer and Samaran) concludes the article. (CJW)

New High German

General and Miscellaneous. 6492. Bock, R., H. Harnisch, H. Langer, and G. Starke. "Zur deutschen Gegenwartssprache in der DDR und in der BRD." *ZPSK* 26(1973):511-32.
In grammar and in general vocabulary, the German language in the German Democratic Republic and in the Federal Republic of Germany has remained essentially the same. However, certain differences are to be noted. That part of the vocabulary which relates to ideology is the most important case, but there are also differences in frequency of borrowing from English or Russian, in fixing the rules of pronunciation, and in stylistic norms. (LLBA)

6505. Huffines, Marion L. "Sixteenth-Century Printers and Standardization of New High German." *JEGP* 73:60-72.
During the Early New High German period (ca. 1350-1650), the printing press was an influential factor in the development of a unified standard German language. Ulrich Schmidl, who spent twenty years (1534-54) exploring South America, wrote a diary of his adventures which Sigmund Feyerabend and Simon Hüter printed in 1567. Although this edition and Schmidl's manuscript have no demonstrable direct relationship to each other, one can observe general linguistic printing practices by comparing the two. Phonological differences between the manuscript and the edition are dialectal. Specific vocabulary items reflect morphological differences, but these are minimal. The essential difference lies in the extent and the consistency with which various syntactical constructions occur. The edition has a more economic presentation of the text, effected in part by synthetic constructions and the large amount of hypotaxis which contrasts sharply with analytic constructions and the extensive parataxis in the manuscript. Whole clauses of the manuscript often correspond to parts of clauses in the edition, and the edition lacks much of the repetition and many of the phrases and particles of little informational value which are common in the manuscript. (MLH)

Dialectology. 6539. Conner, Cora and Maurice. "A German Dialect Spoken in South Dakota:Swiss Volhynian." *GAS* 7:31-37.
After a hundred years in the Ukraine followed by a hundred years in this country, the German spoken by a number of Mennonites who now live near the town of Freeman, South Dakota, remains very similar to that spoken by their ancestors in the Palatinate before migrating to Volhynia in about 1770. The dialect as it is now spoken shows Slavic influences, mostly in the area of food and cooking, and English inroads, chiefly in commerce and in the naming of concepts and items unknown to the group in 1874. Encroachment upon the dialect by other German dialects spoken in the community is not discernible. (C&MC)

6552. Olsson, Lars. "Les problèmes linguistiques de l'Alsace vus par un Suédois." *MSpr* 68:45-70.
The cultural and linguistic history of Alsace is summarized. Annexed to France in the 17th century, the region remained linguistically part of Germany until 1789. In the 19th century, French made gradual inroads and was officially declared the language of instruction in 1853. From 1871 to 1918, and again during the Second World War, Alsace belonged to Germany and the German language made progress at the expense of French. In recent times, French has again become the official language; the majority of the population still speaks the Alsatian dialect, while High German plays a very limited role. (LLBA)

6555. Schuhmacher, W.W. "Apropos /pɛ##/, /pat#(#)...##/ 'Pferd' in der Niederfrankischen Ubergangsmundart von Velbert (Rheinland)." *Linguistics* 130:87-89.
The most extensive change in the phonological component of Old High German, when passing to Middle High German, is the (vowel) lengthening before *r*, which started early in Low Franconian. This lengthening is later extended in Low Franconian as exemplified in the behavior of the author's mother dialect. The derivation of the word for "horse" represents a case study. (WWS)

6556. Smith, J.B. "The Changing Sound Pattern of a German Dialect." *IPAJ* 4:4-12.
The sound system of the South Franconian dialect of Mudau, Odenwald, has changed over the last few decades. Three successive stages of development have been assumed: traditional dialect as it occurs in local dialect literature, the somewhat archaizing style of conservative dialect, and semi-dialect, the style used in everyday situations. The long vowels and diphthongs, the nasalized vowels, the short vowels and the consonants are examined in turn. It emerges that pressure from the standard language has brought about considerable distributional changes and caused several traditional phonemic oppositions to be neutralized. (JBS)

Etymology, Lexicography, and Lexicology. 6582. Johnson, Michael J. "German Equivalents of English 'Image'." *ML* 55:82-85.
The word "das Image" has existed in the technical vocabulary of German advertizing since 1954. The terms coined in German to accommodate the English/American word make obvious its inherent ambiguity. Does an "image" exist in the mind of a consumer as evoked by its presentation in advertisements, or is it something inherent in the product or service advertized? The German equivalents emphasize either the subjective (i.e., the recipient's) impression of the product or the objective (i.e., the product's) expression. No German word satisfactorily covers both factors, or components, of the English "image." (MJJ)

6589. McLintock, D.R. " 'To Forget' in Germanic." *TPS* (for 1972 [1973]):79-93.
Gothic differs from WGmc. in forming its verbs for "to remember" and "to forget" from the same root, Gmc. *mun-*. The WGmc. languages use the root *get-*, at first with competing prefixes (OE *forgitan* and *ofergitan*, OHG *irgezzan*), for the latter meaning. The link with the Gmc. structure represented by Gothic is provided by the OE use of *ofer-*, and OE *ofergitan* can be seen from a scrutiny of its derivatives to be the older verb. The interchange of prefixes is due to the coalescence of three once discrete morpho-semantic classes, "verbs of neglect," "verbs of contempt," and "verbs of pride." OHG partially conserves the old structure in its formations from the root *hug-*, though it is idiosyncratic in its choice of the prefix *uz-* in *irgezzan*. Late OHG substitutes *fer-*, thus bringing itself into line with the other WGmc. languages. The earlier disparity and the link with Gothic are obscured by these late developments. (DRM)

6591. Meyer, Hans-Günter. "Untersuchungen zum Einfluss des Englischen auf die deutsche Pressesprache, dargestellt an zwei deutschen Tageszeitungen." *Muttersprache* 84:97-134.
The semantic influence of English on two regional newspapers in the Rhein-Main area was investigated. The emphasis of the present study is on semantic rather than on syntactic or morphological influences, and above all on quantitative findings on anglicisms, how they are divided into different categories of loan words, and in which section of the newspaper they are found. The study classifies words, composition, and use into the categories of text, title, inscriptions, advertising, and classifieds. The anglicisms are presented in alphabetical order according to the English part of the word and exactly as they were found in the newspapers. (LLBA)

6597. Pfeffer, J. Alan. "Grunddeutsch und die deutschen Entlehnungen aus fremden Sprachen." *WW* 23(1973):420-26.
There are about 150,000 foreign lexemes, in the present day German vocabulary of 500,000 to 600,000 words, meaning that one word in four is a loan word. The large number of loan word dictionaries in existence does not, however, indicate what the actual frequency of use of foreign words is in German. To determine this, the vocabulary of basic German was examined. Of the 2,805 words involved, 6% or 180 words are still noticeably foreign. In everyday spoken and written German, the loan word is often preferred to the native equivalent. (LLBA)

Morphology. 6625. Folsom, Marvin H. "Two Productive Patterns." *UP* 7,ii:105-08.

Descriptions of the verbal prefixes are often general, abstract, and difficult to relate to actual situations. The pattern *das Kind hat sich Speise erbettelt* is usually included in such descriptions. The student can learn the pattern and meaning ('to acquire by') and extend it to understand verbs not glossed in most dictionaries (*der Fuhrmann hat sich viel Geld erfahren*) and perhaps even create new compounds (*12% "erstreikt"*). Similarly, the pattern *du hast dich bei dieser Aufgabe verrechnet* ('to make a mistake in') can be learned and used as the basis for extensions into new situations (*ich habe mich verwählt* 'I dialed the wrong number'). (MHF)

6627. Fullerton, G. Lee. "The Development of Obstruents in Four Germanic Endings." *Linguistics* 130:71-82.

The Gmc. 2nd and 3rd person singular and plural indicative verb endings derive from PGmc. sequences containing voiced spirants. The dialectal differences in these endings are due to a different ordering in each dialect group of three well-known rules. However, the orderings posited for West Germanic yield unattested results throughout much of the remaining morphology. All of the Gmc. dialects require a single ordering: (1) the stopping of *b, đ, g*; (2) rhotacism; (3) the unvoicing of spirants in word-final position. Among the pres. indic. ending this ordering accounts for all but the WGmc. 2nd singular and the Ingvaeonic plural *-aꝒ*. Attempts to derive the verb ending from the historical 2nd person and the noun ending from the historical nominative fail to account for the vowels. The vowels can be explained only if the alternative sources PGmc. 3pl. *-and* and A pl. *-anz* are posited. (GLF)

6642. Ross, Alan S.C. "*I-* and *U-* Adjectives in Germanic." *TPS* (for 1972 [1973]):94-100.

In Gothic, *a/ō-*, short-stemmed *ja/jō-*, long-stemmed *ja/jō-*, *i-* and *u*-adjectives are paradigmatically distinct mutually. In Scandinavian and West Germanic there are only two main classes, *a/ō-* and *ja/jō-*, though *u*-flexion exists in a few short-stemmed Anglo-Saxon adjectives. The stems of old *i-* and *u*-adjectives have to some extent been affected by the *i-* and *u-*. However, in Scandinavian, *a/ō-*flexion is not associated with *u*-umlaut in susceptible stems. In certain Finnish borrowings from Germanic *-is* could represent, not *-iz* of the *i*-stems, but *-īz* of the *ja/jō*-stems. Some of the *a/ō*-flexion arises in the nominative singular, where there has been loss and alteration. The origin of the West Germanic *ja/jō*-flexion in old *i*-adjectives is in part phonological, but cf. the Gothic position. Ultimate origins: *ja/jō*-flexion in *u*-adjectives—in the *svādvī*-flexion; *ja/jō*-flexion in *i*-adjectives —in the weak grade cases; lack of *u*-umlaut in old *u*-adjectives in Scandinavian—in cases such as Gothic genitive singular *sunaus.* (ASCR)

6643. Stormowska, Jadwiga E. "Nominale 'Halbsuffixe' im Deutschen und Polnischen." *DaF* 10(1973):207-11.

According to the present German word formation system, a process of suffix formation from free morphemes exists. In forms such as *Grünzeug, Knochenwerk, hoffnungsvoll,* and *aussichtslos,* the second immediate components of the words have lost their independent meaning and have become suffixes, although they have the same apparent form as the morphemes *Zeug, Werk, los,* and *voll.* In other constructions, such as *Seemann, Bildwerk, Schreibzeug,* and *Postwesen,* the second components approach the character of the suffix in their function, but retain their independent lexical-conceptual meanings. Free morphemes such as these are termed "half-suffixes." Such structures and their Polish equivalents are structurally analyzed. (LLBA)

Stylistics. 6704. Herzfeld-Sander, Margaret. "Kroetz' *Heimarbeit*:The Stratification of Language." *NTLTL* 14,i:34-41.

Modern literary texts require a knowledge of various levels of language. The use of language in literary texts can be studied in order to recognize levels of language and understand their social implications. Contemporary German writers are interested in exposing the human condition by revealing the inability of characters to communicate. In the play *Heimarbeit* by Franz Xaver Kroetz, the restricted manner in which characters use language has a direct bearing on their inability to understand their own lives, their actions, and the world around them. Kroetz

demonstrates the link between inarticulate behavior and human aggression. (MMH-S)

Syntax. 6741. Folsom, Marvin H. "Predicate Adjectives and Statal Passives." *UP* 7:110-11.

There will always be a need for distinguishing various classes of adjectives (attributive, adverbial, predicate), including those that can be used only in the predicate. A clearer definition of the attributive adjective and its use is a better solution than abandoning predicate adjectives. An alternative to abandoning the statal passive is: (1) treat the *sein*-passive before the *werden*-passive, (2) call the past participles in such constructions predicate adjectives or simply derived adjectives, (3) use carefully constructed drills that point out the relationships between past participles and adjectives with *sein.* (MHF)

6747. Grečko, V.K. "O sinonimii konstrukcii s *map* i passiva v naučnoj literature (Na materiale sovremennoj nemeckoj naučno-texničeskoj literatury)." *FN* 1(1973):70-78.

A sampling of various types of scientific literature and fiction was surveyed for the use of the German *man* (*one*) construction and the passive voice. Results were statistically analyzed. Both *man* construction and the passive were found more frequently in scientific literature than in fiction, and the passive was three times more frequent than *man* construction. Other findings were: (1) the use of *man* construction varied more depending on the type of scientific literature than the passive; (2) the meaning of doer in *man* construction is more restricted than with the passive; and (3) *man* construction and the passive are widely considered synonymous in scientific literature. (LLBA)

6756. Kefer, Michel. "Die Erforschung der Entwicklung des neuhochdeutschen Satzbaus anhand der quantitativen und der sprachtypologischen Methode." *RLV* 40:528-39.

W.P. Lehmann distinguishes VO and OV languages: the former are characterized by modified-modifier order (e.g., verb-object or noun-attributive adjunct) and by prepositions, the latter by modifier-modified order and postpositions. Lehmann observes the rise of OV patterns in New High German; however, the results of statistical research suggest that this tendency stopped at least 2 centuries ago and that a tendency toward VO constructions has appeared since. Moreover, in the first period of New High German syntax, sentences tend to contain more and more digressions and subclauses, whereas in the second period there is a tendency in the opposite direction. (MK)

6757. —— "Die syntaktische Funktion der Negation im deutschen Satz." *RLV* 40:66-84,167-76.

The kind of negation that Klima and other linguists call a sentence negation in fact only bears on the predicate or on the subject-predicate group (or just on the principal part of the predicate). This negation is opposed to another one, which only occurs in some types of sentences where the negation has a wider focus; this focus can include sentence adjuncts. A negation standing before a contrastive element bears on the nuclear of the sentence as a predicate negation does, although the contrastive nuclear can be very restricted or very wide. Related to the syntactic function of negation are many other problems such as the realization of the negative element as *nicht, kein,* etc., word order, stress, and context. (MK)

6765. Lederer, Herbert. "Two Resurrected Dinosaurs." *UP* 7:111-12.

The distinction between predicate and attributive adjectives is important for an understanding of German syntactic patterns. The fact that predicate adjectives are identical in form with adverbs makes it important to stress the difference in function. A similar functional analysis also reveals the difference between the German passive, using the past participle as a verb form, and the so-called "statal passive" or "apparent passive," in which the past participle functions like a predicate adjective. (HL)

6786. Streadbeck, Arval L., and Michael N. Grimshaw. "Phrase Structure Rules for German." *Linguistics* 123:33-43.

Phrase structure rules are proposed which could generate all or nearly all the sentences common in spoken standard High German. They should also account for the vast majority of sentences found in the written language. Certain idiomatic expressions and idiomatic usages require more explanation and further transformations to explain their forms. These phrase structure rules and transformations compose a fractional part of a complete grammar which would also have to include a lexicon and phonological rules. (LLBA)

Dutch

Phonology. 6896. Schroten, J. "Een inventarisatie van uitspraak—Verschillen tussen Spaans en Nederlands." *LT* 299(1973):380-86.
The inventory is based on well-known studies on Spanish and Dutch phonetics and phonemics. Its aim is to provide Dutch teachers of Spanish with a survey of the articulatory differences between the pronunciation of Spanish and of Dutch. (LLBA)

Semantics. 6903. Putseys, Y. "On Duration Measuring in Dutch and Flemish." *FLang* 11:273-80.
The validity of Klooster and Verkuyl's proposal that the following sentences: (1) *het platliggen van Lex duurde drie weken*; (2) *gedurende drie weken lag Lex plat*; and (3) *drie weken lang lag Lex plat* are derived structures which have one underlying structure in common is questioned on two grounds. It overlooks the fact that neither derived nominals nor action nominals are transformations of underlying sentences. It posits synonymy between the durational phrases *gedurende drie weken* and *drie weken lang*, which is not complete since there are constraints on the latter which do not apply to the former. (LLBA)

Syntax. 6908. Campenhout, F. van. "Zinnen met *zullen* en zinnen zonder *zullen* met futurische betekenis." *RLV* 40:650-70.
In Dutch grammars you can read that *zullen* is the auxiliary of the future tense. Sentences in the simple present, however, can also express a future by an adjunct of time, a modal adverb, both an adjunct of time and a modal adverb, the verb itself, or the context. Rhythm, sentence melody, stylistic factors such as the avoidance of the repetition of *zullen*, the character of the speaker or writer, etc., can explain why he uses *zullen* or why he doesn't. It is also possible that the speaker expresses a greater certainty by a structure without *zullen*. *Zullen* helps to express a lot of modalities, such as: possibility, probability, certainty, doubt, etc. This modal auxiliary *zullen* can refer both to the present and to the future. (FVC)

IV. ENGLISH

Old English

Etymology, Lexicography, and Lexicology. 7002. Berkhout, Carl I. "The Problem of OE *holmwudu*." *MS* 36:429-33.
Editors of *The Dream of the Rood* commonly favor the emendation *holtwudu* ("tree of the forest") over the MS *holmwudu* ("sea-wood, ship") in the passage comparing the Cross and Mary, ll. 90-94. The MS reading should be retained, however, for the poet is drawing upon an established figure of the Cross as the vessel, the *lignum maris*, by which earth-dwellers are transported across the "sea" of this present life to their eternal homeland. This theme is introduced in the *lifes weg* passage immediately preceding the *holmwudu* analogy and is developed throughout the entire latter half of the poem, making more vivid the eschatological meaning of the Crucifixion both for the dreamer and for the poet's audience. (CTB)

7007. Erickson, Jon L. " 'An' and 'na Þaet an' in Late Old English Prose:Some Theoretical Questions of Derivation." *ArL* 4(1973):75-88.
In the standard handbooks of Old English, adequate syntactic information and a theoretical framework viewing the language as a system of interrelated structures is lacking. The degree to which this is true can be illustrated by an examination of the OE cardinal *an* "one" and of the related sequence *na Þaet an*, the apparent first member of a correlative pair *na Þaet an / ac eac (swylce)*, usually glossed "not only / but also." From the descriptions in the OE grammars, one can infer that *an* patterns much like the adjectives. On the basis of concordance data, however, it can be shown that *an* lacks the strong-weak paradigm distinction, and the meaning differences which *an* displays must be accounted for by reference to syntax. (JLE)

Phonology. 7026. Dimler, G. Richard. "Notes on the Phonetic Status of the Initial Consonant Cluster /sk/ in Old English Alliterative Verse." *SIL* 24:21-29.
Authorities seem to agree that initial /sk/ was palatalized before velar vowels around 900 A.D., but did not undergo palatalization to [š] in words borrowed from Scandinavian or Latin. This study of the alliterative status of /sk/ in OE verse, through an analysis of some 65 instances of initial /sk/ alliteration in texts from the earliest period of OE, around the years 700-1050 A.D., indicates that the following conclusion can be drawn: in general, the Anglo-Saxon poet was more careful than not to use initial /sk/ in alliterative contexts before phonetically similar vowels. The poet was not overly concerned with the distinction between front and back vowels in the alliteration of /sk/ in initial position, a strong argument for an early palatalization of every initial /sk/ around 800 A.D. as a first stage in its development into [š]. (GRD)

7027. Hogg, Richard M. "Further Remarks on Breaking and Gemination." *ArL* 5:47-52.
This paper examines various proposals for a synchronic rule reflecting the Old English sound change of breaking. An analysis of relevant minimal pairs suggests that breaking must be considered to have been diphthongization of front vowels in the environment of velar or velarized consonants and that liquids in Old English contrasted in the feature [±back]. A consequence of this is that the synchronic rules of gemination and breaking are seen to be independent of one another, and that gemination need not be reordered after breaking. (RMH)

Syntax. 7036. Erdmann, Peter H. "Die Ableitung der Altenglischen Substantivparadigman." *Linguistics* 130:5-53.
Starting with underlying forms of the Old English noun paradigms reconstructed on the basis of Old English and further Germanic evidence, a set of rules derives the attested forms of the various declensional classes of Old English. The underlying nominal endings represent both the input to the rule mechanism and the result of an attempt to reanalyze the pre-Germanic units necessary for a description of the laws of the Germanic finals to be taken up later. The base paradigms allow for a regrouping of the traditional declensional classes. The rules needed to derive the attested forms are independent of the paradigms under consideration and are part of the phonology of Old English. (PE)

Modern English

General and Miscellaneous. 7087. Clark, Thomas L. *Marietta, Ohio:The Continuing Erosion of a Speech Island. PADS* 57(1972): 1-55.
Phonological and lexical data indicate that Marietta retains vestiges of Northern dialect features in what is now a South Midland dialect region. Phonology is usually considered the most effective indicator of dialect traces because sounds shift slowly and occur over a wide spectrum of vocabulary. In the oldest segment of Marietta's population, highly distinctive New England features like the "broad a" have not survived. But a number of other forms, like [I] in "haunted" are still to be found. Lexicon, on the other hand, changes relatively rapidly along with changes in farming technique, commerce, fashion, and custom. Many of the favorite dialect shibboleths have simply dropped from the vocabulary. The phonological findings, coupled with the discovery that obvious New England lexical items are diminishing, shows that New England influence on local speech is eroding. (TLC)

7088. Cooper, William E. "Primary Relations among English Sensation Referents." *Linguistics* 137:5-12.

For English a primacy relation exists characterizing the ability of referents of different sensory modalities to participate in syntactic processes. If a given syntactic process applies to referents of the modalities of hearing, feeling, taste, and/or smell, the same process applies to an equal or greater extent for corresponding referents of the vision modality. Extended analysis of sensation referents shows that the syntactic primacy relation is closely matched by order relations that involve processes of a semantic and a morphological nature. The relationship existing among these order relations is not coincidental but arises from a common behavioral basis. (WEC)

7097. Hall, William S., and Roy O. Freedle. "A Developmental Investigation of Standard and Non-Standard English among Black and White Children." *HD* 16(1973):440-64.
Data are reported and interpreted involving language imitation, comprehension, and free production in two English dialects. The major subgroupings of 360 Ss involved two races (black and white), sex, socioeconomic level (low SES and middle SES), and age (5, 8, and 10 years). Rate of improvement measures indicated that blacks improve at the same rate as whites in responding to standard English sentences. According to correlational results, the two dialect systems function behaviorally as separate cognitive systems. (LLBA)

7105. Milon, John P. "The Development of Negation in English by a Second Language Learner." *TESOLQ* 8:137-43.
The speech of a 7 year old Japanese boy recently arrived in Hawaii was examined in light of the hypothesis that non-native speakers, if they are well below the age of puberty, will acquire the grammatical structures of negation in English in the same developmental sequence as the acquisition of those structures by native speakers. Video tape recordings were made over a period of more than 6 months at regular intervals. There was a striking similarity between the developmental substages of negation in the acquisition of English as a first language and the development of negation in the speech of the subject. (JPM)

7109. Pride, J.B. "An Approach to the (Socio-)Linguistics of Commands and Requests in English." *ArL* 4(1973):51-74.
Language is a way of making others behave, yet linguists have scarcely begun to approach what people call commands, requests, and the like in English. Consideration is given, therefore, to some of the most recurrent structural variables in this field, so as to emphasize the vast range of choice open to every speaker. Such choice is not random, but is liable to be prompted by the operation of cultural, social, inter-personal, and many other factors distinguishable from linguistic structure itself. The basic argument is that these and other speech functions merit close analysis with a view to arriving at sociolinguistic descriptions of, and explanations for, everyday usage. (JBP)

7112. Todd, Loreto. " 'To Be or Not To Be'—What Would Hamlet Have Said in Cameroon Pidgin? An Analysis of Cameroon Pidgin's 'Be'-Verb." *ArL* 4(1973):1-15.
An analysis of Cameroon Pidgin's be-verb seen against a framework of the Cameroon VP. The analysis includes information on CP's ability to negate /na/, a recent development and one which seems to be unique in West African Pidgin English. All points are illustrated by sentences taken from transcripts of conversations recorded between 1968 and 1972. (LT)

Dialectology. 7115. Arthur, Bradford, Dorothee Farrar, and George Bradford. "Evaluation Reactions of College Students to Dialect Differences in the English of Mexican-Americans." *L&S* 17:255-70.
The English of Los Angeles Mexican-Americans ranges from the local standard to Chicano English, a non-standard ethnic dialect. Speech approaching Chicano English was negatively stereotyped by Anglo-American university students on scales related to success, ability, and social awareness. Forty-eight UCLA students rated 4 pairs of matched guise voices on 15 semantic differential scales. Dialect differences consistently affected their rating. Raters also attended to non-dialect voice differences, especially for more standard English voices. In rating standard English, students used a different, more complex procedure for judging personality. (BA, DF, & GB)

7120. Burgess, O.N. "Intonation Patterns in Australian English." *L&S* 16(1973):314-26.
An instrumental analysis was made of the intonation patterns used by a group of speakers of Australian English in producing a corpus of selected sentences. The results obtained were compared with those suggested for the same utterances in Received English. There is a broad similarity in intonatory habits between speakers of the two varieties of English. Australian English, however, tends to avoid, in general, variation of pitch within syllables and, in particular, the high-fall accent. The evidence presented does not readily support the contention that in "Yes/No" questions Australian intonation patterns are clearly differentiated from those of Received English. Instead there is some indication that differentiation is more marked with questions containing a specific word. (ONB)

7124. Dillard, J.L. "Lay My Isogloss Bundle Down:The Contribution of Black English to American Dialectology." *Linguistics* 119:5-14.
There is a variety of American English called black English despite the objections of those who find variation in areas set off by bundles of isoglosses. Studies refuting the concept of ethnic distributions in the U.S. have been heavily biased toward educated and middle-class informants. Research has shown extensive patterns of non-geographic distribution in the Americas. Since modern cartography is capable of developing a methodology for indicating variation with methods more sophisticated than isoglosses, it is suggested that the isogloss method be abandoned. (JLD)

7138. Lodge, K.R. "Stockport Revisited." *IPAJ* 3(1973):81-87.
A reinterpretation of the vowel phonemes of the Stockport dialect originally presented by Lodge (1966). The addition of a vowel +j combination not mentioned by Lodge is considered. A comparison with data from the *Survey of English Dialects* is also presented. The investigation centers on the phonemic and phonetic differences in the two types of material. Since Stockport is quite a large industrial town, a "local standard" pronunciation might well be expected. Several forms have disappeared except as humorous fossils, and the resultant "local standard" seems to draw on the surrounding areas for its forms. (LLBA)

7141. Odo, Carol. "English Pattern in Hawaii." *AS* 45(1970; pub. 1974):234-39.
Recorded data of 4-year-old Hawaiian children's speech exhibit a mixture of Standard English and Hawaiian Creole features. There are indications that the mixture is not random, but that the use of any one feature implies the use of another. The data support two hypotheses: (1) The use of Hawaiian Creole "get" implies the use of Hawaiian Creole "wan" in the same sentence; and (2) The use of "wan" implies the use of the Hawaiian Creole form of the progressive verb. A linguistic continuum appears to provide a useful theoretical model for the description of Hawaiian English. (LLBA)

7145. Pride, J.B. "The Deficit-Difference Controversy." *ArL* 5:35-46.
The main issue in this controversy concerns the "logical adequacy" of "standard" compared with "non-standard" English. This is discussed in the light of the use of the negative, in particular, but without implying that this is an especially important feature compared with others not yet researched. The problem of cross-cultural differences in the contents of texts, and in pedagogical styles generally, points to the fundamental importance of speech acts and speech functions to the whole question. In this light some closing comments point to the desirability of a reasonable degree of "co-ordinate bidialectalism" among black English children and calls for the disuse of "ghetto readers." (JBP)

7147. Şen, Ann Louise F. "Dialect Variation in Early American English." *JEngL* 8:41-47.
Early American English shows much dialect variation which is independent of regional and social stratification. By examining the phoneme /ɛ/ with three of its variants, /ī/, /æ/, and /e/, their sources are found in Old English and Middle English dialects as well as in early Modern British English. Yet in modern times these variants, hitherto unrestricted, have become markers of social or regional pronunciations suggesting that dialect variation

in a colonial country becomes marked geographically and socially, although less frequent in occurrence as the country develops it own language characteristics. (ALŞ)

7154. Underwood, Gary N. "Toward a Reassessment of Edward Eggleston's Literary Dialects." *BRMMLA* 28:109-20. Because Eggleston has been regarded as a respectable dialectologist, critics have assumed the authenticity of his literary dialects. A thorough critical study is overdue, and it should compare Eggleston's representations of dialects with accurate records of 19th-century English. In the absence of such a definitive study, *The Mystery of Metropolisville* provides material for a tentative reassessment. In this novel Eggleston represents characters from Vermont, Indiana, and Illinois as speaking in dialect, but he fails to distinguish Hoosier English from that of New England. This failure raises serious questions about Eggleston's skill. (GNU)

7156. Wolfram, Walt. "The Relationship of White Southern Speech to Vernacular Black English." *Language* 50:498-527. Data from rural Southern white speech are compared with vernacular black English (VBE) in order to determine the relationship of these varieties. Copula absence and invariant *be* are described from a viewpoint which admits structured variability as part of linguistic competence. Some lects of Southern white speech and VBE may use zero coupla quite similarly, but there is considerable difference in the uses of invariant *be*; the 'distributive' function of *be* appears to be unique to VBE in this setting. (WW)

Etymology, Lexicography, and Lexicology. 7160. Beaman, Ralph G. "Letter Structure of Long Words." *WWays* 7:6-13. Webster's *New International Dictionary of the English Language* (second edition, unabridged) contains 349 unhyphenated boldface words of 20 or more letters. Various statistical properties of this collection are examined, i.e., the number of different words decreases exponentially with word length; words of N letters are only half as numerous as words of N-1 letters. The commonest letter is not E, but O; nearly 12% of all letters in the collection are O. The letter W is the only one in the alphabet which occurs nowhere in the collection. The number of different letters in these words ranges from 8 to 16; a handful of words contain more than six identical letters. Eight pairs of words are transposals of each other, but only two words have the same substitution cipher. Evidence shows that the distribution of different letters in long words can be modeled by a process in which letters are drawn at random from a stockpile with the appropriate letter-frequencies. (LLBA)

7162. Block, Gertrude H. "A Year of Ripoffs." *AS* 45(1970; pub. 1974):210-14.
The use of the term *ripoff* was first noted on the University of Florida campus in the spring of 1971. As a verb it meant "to rob" or "steal from" and later "cheat." As a noun it meant "theft," "thief," or "swindle." Adults gradually began to borrow this youth-oriented term, frequently misusing it in their early attempts. Now there is considerable agreement among all users, and both verb and noun forms retain today the meanings originally assigned by youthful University of Florida users. Numerous illustrations from the usage of both youths and adults are cited. The origin of *ripoff* is unknown, but it may contain roots in the obsolete verb *rip* (to rob), cited as early as 1200. (LLBA)

7164. Bryant, Margaret M. "Names and Terms Used in the Fashion World." *AS* 45(1970; pub. 1974):168-94.
A list of 371 new English words originated by the fashion world and not included in recent dictionaries. In this list, 134 are compounds; 88 are blends of two words; 51 are words with affixes; and 8 are names of persons, places, or things. Thirteen terms are obtained by a transference or extension of the meaning of existing words; 15 are originally coined; 14 are foreign words; and 12 are formed by analogy with other words. Acronyms, expressions shortened from longer terms, and words formed by shifting the functions of words already in use are included. (LLBA)

7165. Burchfield, R.W. "The Treatment of Controversial Vocabulary in *The Oxford English Dictionary*." *TPS* 1973(1974): 1-28.

The expression "controversial vocabulary" is used to mean the vocabulary that lies on or near the admission/exclusion boundary in the *Oxford English Dictionary* and its Supplements. The inclusion of such vocabulary in the dictionary is governed partly by the division of work among the editorial staff and by the choice made by the readers of the sources selected for systematic reading, and partly by the necessity of drawing the line somewhere in large or unlimited classes of words. Numerous examples are provided of rare words and of *hapax legomena* that were included in the *OED* and that are being included in the new three-volume Supplement. The treatment of proprietary forms ("Bovril," etc.) and of racial and religious words ("Negro," "Jew," "Mormon," etc.) in historical dictionaries is considered. The main governing factor in the choice of words to be treated is the editability of a given item in the time available and with the editorial and other resources available. (RWB)

7175. Geissler, Eberhard. "Lateinisch/griechische Elemente in der englischen Terminologie des Maschinenwesens." *Fremdsprachen* 17(1973):250-56.
Indications of the significance and applicability of knowledge of Latin and Greek for the understanding of English mechanical engineering terms are discussed. The importance of lexical and morphological elements of the classical languages in English mechanical engineering terminology seems to be diminished by the fact that many terms from the metal-working crafts are present whose designations are based primarily on Anglo-Saxon vocabulary. (LLBA)

7178. Hackett, John. "Scholar's Lunch." *AS* 45(1970; pub. 1974):300-02. [On the meaning of "lunch."]
An attempt is made to account for the disputed provenance of a familiar slang term. A semantic explanation that would reconcile two recent hypotheses about origin and development is offered. A second familiar slang term that seems to have replaced the first, satisfying the same needs in the language subculture, is introduced for this purpose. The functionally equivalent terms appear linguistically unrelated, but both of them may derive from a common matrix, a third term which is a free-morpheme compound of the first and the second. If the original recorded term lost currency in natural conformance with normal slang entropy, the community in this case found its viable substitute term not by fresh coinage but by returning to the original source, by conservative recourse to the postulated matrix which had already been productive. (LLBA)

7187. Kirwin, William. "Newfoundland Usage in the 'Survey of Canadian English'." *RLS* 5:9-14.
The Survey of Canadian English was designed in an attempt to gather information about 103 items of interesting and divided usage in Canada. Certain more obvious points about spelling, idiom, and vocabulary were queried, and the shadings of pronunciation and a number of variants in morphology were presented to the informants in rhyme or multiple-choice questions. A commentary on the linguistic preferences favored in Newfoundland and on how they relate to the national usage percentages reported in the survey are presented. Examples of differences and similarities in grammar, vocabulary, and pronunciation are provided. (LLBA)

7191. Lawson, Sarah. "*Immigrant* in British and American Usage." *AS* 45(1970; pub. 1974):304-05.
The word *immigrant* in American usage refers mainly to a phenomenon of the past; in British usage, it refers specifically to present-day Commonwealth citizens from the West Indies, the Indian subcontinent, or black Africa. *Immigrant* in Britain has become a euphemistic label for a black person. The concepts "immigrant" and "black" have become confused because the British do not regard themselves as descendants of immigrants, and immigrants are therefore conceived of as alien and unassimilable. (LLBA)

7197. Quincunx, Ramona J. "A Spelling Rule." *WWays* 7:43-49.
The familiar spelling rule "i before e, except after c, or when sounded like a, as in *neighbor* or *weigh*" is examined. Although the diphthong ie is very common in English, there are only five basic words in which ei follows c—ceiling, conceive, deceive, perceive, and receive. If the ie/ei diphthong is pronounced as a long a, the

rule is completely correct; all such words contain the spelling ei. However, if the ie/ei diphthong is pronounced as a long or short e, there are many words containing ei preceded by consonants other than c, as well as numerous words containing ie preceded by c. If the ie/ei diphthong is pronounced as a long or short i, a few words containing ei preceded by consonants other than c occur, but there are no words in which it is preceded by c. (LLBA)

7203. Sinnema, John R. "The Dutch Origin of *Play Hookey*." *AS* 45(1970; pub. 1974):205-09.
The time of development of the term "play hookey" seems to have been the second half of the 19th century. Today it is most extensively used on the east coast from New England to Virginia. Most dictionaries give the origin of the term as "hook (it)" (escape, run away, make off) or "hook" (steal). It seems, however, to be more closely tied to the Dutch *hoeckje*, a game of hide and seek played around street corners (hooks), recorded as long ago as 1656. (LLBA)

7206. Story, G.M., and William Kirwin. " 'The Dictionary of Newfoundland English':Progress and Promise." *RLS* 5:15-17.
The *Dictionary of Newfoundland English*, now in its final phase of preparation, rests upon a broad body of evidence, some of it long-established. The completed dictionary will contain: words which appear to have entered the English language in Newfoundland or to have been recorded first, or solely, in books about Newfoundland; words which are characteristically Newfoundland by having continued in use there after they have died out or declined elsewhere, or by having assumed a different form or developed a different meaning, or by having a distinctly higher or more general degree of use; and words which have been created in Newfoundland. The dictionary will be an index of the experience of life in Newfoundland as reflected in language through 4 centuries. (LLBA)

7215. Zandvoort, R.W. "A Three-Letter Word:'Sod'." *ES* 54(1973):576-79.
The Oxford English Dictionary, Supplement 1933, defines *sod* sb.³ *vulgar* [short for sodomite] as "a term of abuse for a male person." Also used jocularly without any definite implication(="beggar," "chap," etc.). Its modern use is exemplified in Brian Glanville's novel *A Second Home* and in John Braine's novel *The Crying Game*. (LLBA)

Morphology. 7226. Soudek, Lev. "Semantic and Morphological Aspects of *-in* Nominalizations." *Linguistics* 131:77-90.
The particle *-in* is examined first in terms of its productivity among other nominalizing particles, such as *-up, -out, -off, -down*. A collection of 182 nominal *-in* formations is then analyzed by applying criteria of semantic irradiation and morphological structure. The material falls into two distinct types: (a) *blow-in*; (b) *marry-in, sick-in*. The nouns of type a could be derived transformationally from an underlying sentence containing a phrasal verb or a syntactic verb + adverb combination. The morpheme *-in* of type b has reached the stage of a new suffix that can be attached to verbal as well as nonverbal bases (*fat-in, sick-in*) to form new action nouns with semantic denotations distinctly different from any other occurrences of *in*. (LIS)

7228. Yábar Dextre, Pompeyo. "La estructura morfológica y semántica de algunos términos tecnológicos en inglés y sus equivalentes en castellano." *LyC* 13(1973):113-15.
The morphological description of technological terms in English indicates that in the majority of cases the determining factor precedes the determined element. In Castilian, the opposite occurs. The Castilian term can sometimes have a prepositional structure distinct from its equivalent in English. The determining element of these terms makes diverse references such as: finality (test tube); discoverer (Diesel oil); parts of the whole (thorium series); and, element employed (carbon-14 technique). (LLBA)

Onomastics. 7231. Ashley, Leonard R.N. "Uncommon Names for Common Plants:The Onomastics of Native and Wild Plants of the British Isles." *Names* 22:111-28.
Several hundred names of wild and native flora of the British Isles, including those derived from personal names, are examined. Mythology and folklore as well as real and imagined resemblances between some common plants and other common things

explain the names that common people gave to growing things that figured more or less significantly in their daily lives. (LRNA)

7249. Martin, Ged. " 'Bush':A Possible English Dialect Origin for an Australian Term." *ALS* 6:431-34.
By 1820 the term "bush" had supplanted "woods" in Australian English. Standard works derive it from the Dutch "bosch" and suggest a South African origin. It is however difficult to explain the mechanics of transfer. Since the term also existed in America, a common origin in Britain seems possible. The place-names of Essex provide examples with the element "bush," many of them consistent with subsequent Australian usage, and there are examples in adjoining countries. 18th-century Londoners, many of them country born, probably knew the term. Since one third of convicts transported before 1819 were Londoners, it is not surprising that "bush" should have established itself so quickly in Australian English. (GM)

Phonology. 7265. Bluhme, H. "Segmental Phonemes versus Distinctive Features in English." *Linguistics* 126:11-23.
Phonemics presupposes a segmentation of the speech chain into individual sounds; this act is based upon the listener's competence and prior acquisition of the alphabet; hence, a phonetic transcription is of a phonemic nature. This circular argumentation is repeated in the distinctive feature theory where features are wrongly assumed to be segmentable. Phonetic differences which can bring about a change of meaning cannot be described in auditory terms as these are based upon the listener's competence and, therefore, involve a circular argument. Words are sequences of morphemes, morphemes are sequences of phonemes, but phonemes are bundles of simultaneous phonetic features. Phonological features found to exist in British English are demonstrated. (AB)

7268. Downing, Bruce T. "Does English Have Word-Level Rules?" *GL* 14:1-14.
Chomsky and Halle's *The Sound Pattern of English* (*SPE*) proposes a model of Englsih phonology which incorporates a mechanism for delimiting the phonological word, a "readjustment rule" to make syntactic constituents of each word, a set of "word-level rules" that apply at the level of these constituents, and a Nuclear Stress Rule (NSR). These interdependent elements all prove unjustifiable. Given the *SPE* definition of the word, a simpler set of conventions will suffice for marking words formally in the grammar; however, this definition fails to provide boundaries between some lexical categories and does not allow for enclisis between nonconstituents. Several recent papers have questioned the cyclic NSR of *SPE*. Even accepting the notion of nuclear stress, a non-cyclic Nuclear Stress Rule followed by a rhythmic rule reducing some secondary stresses to tertiary assigns stress more correctly to phrases. If the phrase-level stress cycle is eliminated, the readjustment rule becomes unnecessary, and the "word-level" rules apply at the level of the phonological phrase. (BTD)

7269. Dundes, Alan. "The Henny-Penny Phenomenon:A Study of Folk Phonological Esthetics in American Speech." *SFQ* 38:1-9.
An examination of rhymed reduplicatives in English reveals definite patterning with respect to the pairs of initial consonants. Common pairs include /h/:/p/ and /h/:/d/ as in hocus pocus and humdrum. The apparent penchant for such pairs is reflected in names found in folktales and nursery rhymes. Thus Henny-Penny or Humpty-Dumpty may be said to indicate a folk esthetic judgment or phonological preference. This preference or Henny-Penny phenomenon may explain why certain idioms are borrowed (e.g., hoi polloi) or come into being in the first place (e.g., hot pants). (AD)

7273. Hill, Archibald A. "Word Stress and the Suffix *-ic*." *JEngL* 7(1973):6-20.
The suffix *-ic* assigns the major word stress to the preceding syllable, as in *linguist-linguistic*. There are a number of exceptions such as *Arabic, politic, Catholic*. All but one of the exceptions are three-syllable words in which the middle syllable has a liquid or a nasal capable of becoming syllabic under lack of stress. When this happens, the syllable to which the suffix has been added can be lost, as in such forms as early *cholryke, arsnike*. The one

unexplainable form is *arithmetic*, in which the medieval folk etymology *ars metric* is influential. (AAH)

7278. McCalla, K.I. "System Attraction and the Syntagm: Modern English Assibiliation." *Linguistique* 9,ii(1973):95-104. The motivating force behind sound changes in which a sequence of phonemes is reduced to a single phoneme filling a previously existing "hole" in the core pattern of phonemes is discussed. Does the motivating force reside in the syntagm, with the paradigmatic effect (filling of the hole) being an accident, or vice versa? Examination of the Early Modern English change [zj]>[ž], along with the related changes [sj]>[š], [tj]>[č], and [dj]>[ǧ], indicates that the driving force was syntagmatic. (LLBA)

7280. Menon, K.M.N., P.V.S. Rao, and R.B. Thosar. "Formant Transitions and Stop Consonant Perception in Syllables." *L&S* 17:27-46. Examines the acoustic characteristics of the English stop consonants /b,d,g/ in selected vowel-consonant-vowel syllables in order to obtain information about what consistent transition patterns exist in the vowel formants associated with these consonants. The steady state and terminal frequencies of the first three formants of the initial and final vowels were obtained spectrographically. The data showed that each of the stop consonants can be described in terms of the position of the second and third formant terminal frequencies relative to the formant frequencies of the vowels. Perception experiments with synthesized consonant-vowel syllables using the frequency values showed good agreement between the acoustic characteristics of the stop consonants and their perception. (KMNM, PVSR, & RBT)

7287. Stephenson, Edward A. "Linguistic Predictions and the Waning of Southern [ju] in *Tune, Duke, News*." *AS* 45(1970); pub. 1974):297-300. The pronunciation of *tune, duke*, and *news* was recorded among 44 juniors, seniors, and graduate students at the University of Georgia. Of these, there was an older group of 16 native white Southerners, averaging 40 years in age, a younger group of 20 native white Southerners averaging 21.3 years in age, and a group of 8 non-Southerners. In pronouncing the 3 words, the 8 non-Southerners used [u] 23 times and the traditional Southern [ju] only once. The 36 Southerners used [u] 39 times and [ju] 69 times. Apparently there is still a North vs. South contrast in this feature of pronunciation. (LLBA)

Semantics. 7298. Callary, R.E. "The Literalization of Idioms." *AS* 45(1970; pub. 1974):302-04. Besides providing new words for the lexicon, the field of advertizing influences English syntax. It may alter a single phoneme in a well-known phrase (*get the red out* for "Visine"), replacing the popular "lead" with "red," juxtapose brand names with the ordinary meanings of words (*Shouldn't your brand be True?* for cigarettes), or use an idiom in its literal sense, fusing the literal with the figurative meaning (*No matter how you slice it, it's still Oscar Mayer* for lunch meats). (LLBA)

7299. Clark, Eve V. "Normal States and Evaluative Viewpoints." *Language* 50:316-32. The deictic verbs "come" and "go," as well as "bring" and "send," may be used in idioms to refer to change of state rather than to motion. In such idiomatic uses the deictic center, corresponding to the goal of "come," is provided by some normal state of being. In contrast, "go" marks departure from a normal state. Besides normal-state deixis, "come" may be used in evaluative deixis to indicate approval of some end state, while evaluative "go" is used with a non-positive meaning. It is suggested that both classes of idioms are related to other forms of deixis, all of which derive from the basic deictic contrast between ego and non-ego. (EVC)

7302. Grannis, Oliver C. "Notes on 'On the Notion "Definite"'." *FLang* 11:105-10. A critical discussion of Thorne's "On the Notion 'Definite'" in which it is proposed that the definite article *the* is the unstressed form of *that*, and that both forms are derived from an underlying structure containing a deictic sentence with the locative expression *there*. This would imply, for example, that the expression *the man* would be derived from an underlying structure correspond-

ing to *man who is there*. Thorne's analysis is unable to account adequately for such expressions as *the man who is there, the man there*, or *that there man (over there)*. Evidence is presented to support his contention that *the* is used when a given referent is "unique within a given conversational situation" and is thus used in non-contrasting circumstances, whereas *that* implies contrast. (LLBA)

7304. Hook, Donald D. "Sexism in English Pronouns and Forms of Address." *GL* 14:86-96. Female liberationists have devised a number of pronouns and titles of address in an attempt to enhance woman's status. Most of the suggestions do structural or lexical violence to English and precipitate the question of the relationship of language to society's needs. Particular attention is given to the title Ms. Other forms of address and common nouns, both sexist and neutral, are also treated. Any language will resist structural alterations to a greater degree than lexical additions which, though introduced by individuals, are adopted only after society as a whole provides its stamp of approval. (DDH)

7305. Kalogjera, Damir. "The Semantic Uses of the Modal *Must* and the Related Frequency of Subjects and Verb Phrases." *SRAZ* 33-36(1972-73):627-38. Like several other modals in English, the modal *must* has two different and well distinguished semantic uses, indicating either obligation or conclusion. What used to be considered an absolute syntactic feature connected with these two usages is now viewed only as a probability. The probabilities of the occurrence of these two usages related to the occurrence of contextual elements which have a tendency to occur more frequently with one of the uses than with the other are explored. (LLBA)

7309. Landau, Sidney I. "Little Boy and Little Girl." *AS* 45(1970; pub. 1974):195-204. *Little boy* and *little girl* often refer specifically to children too old to be considered babies, but under 10 or 11 years of age. They are compounds which are not given separate definitions in English dictionaries, but which merit separate inclusion and definition, as the common meaning is not obtainable by the addition of the meanings of their component elements. The complexity of connotation of *little boy/little girl* has been omitted from all English dictionaries: (1) because all modern dictionaries emphasize technological words rather than terms that are qualitative or general; and/or (2) because dictionaries, even children's dictionaries, have largely neglected children's literature as a source of citation. (LLBA)

7317. Thorne, James Peter. "Notes on 'Notes on "On the Notion 'Definite'"'." *FLang* 11:111-14. A reply to a criticism of the theory that the definite article *the* is the unstressed form of *that*, and that both forms are to be derived from an underlying structure containing a deictic sentence with the locative expression *there*. The derivations of these structures based on several underlying concepts are discussed. (LLBA)

Stylistics. 7334. Noppen, J.P. van. "Spatial Metaphors in Contemporary British Religious Prose." *RLV* 40:7-24. A vocabulary study of British religious prose in the 1960s reveals that a topological, static, and vectorial concept of space prevails. The interesting places are the intersections between this world and the divine and the places of Man and God. The latter loci define bi-polarities like above/beneath and in/out. The vertical polarity is used in the supernatural projection of theism that extrapolates a transcendent God to an outside heaven. The value attributed to the various spatial categories reflects the theological climate. The study of the metaphorical twist in religious language may thus yield insight into theology from a new perspective. (JPvN)

Syntax. 7341. Albury, Donald H. "On Deriving Nominals from Causatives." *AS* 45(1970; pub. 1974):240-46. It has been claimed that in English there are no derived nominals associated with causative verbs, with the exception of causative verbs of Latin origin, which form derived nominals with suffixes also of Latin origin. That claim is wrong; its proponents have overlooked the existence of the native derived nominal suffix -ing, because it is homophonous with the gerundive nominal suffix

-ing. Thus they have not recognized that just as such native intransitive verbs as "grow" and "change" have the derived nominals "growth" and "change," the native causative verbs "grow" and "change" form the derived nominals "growing" and "changing." Some intransitive verbs also form derived nominals with the suffix -ing. The above disproved claim is the basis of Noam Chomsky's lexical hypothesis of the source of derived nominals in English. (LLBA)

7343. Anderson, Alison A. "Characteristics of the Syntax of the English Plural." *Linguistics* 133:5-19.
Comparison of the sets of paraphrases possible for the plurals occurring in 60 consecutive sentences of a descriptive text demonstrates that the uses of the plural fall into a collective class and a distributive class. The latter includes up to five subclasses which can also be distinguished by the paraphrases possible for them. The traditional philosophic distinction between a collective and a distributive use of the plural is thus consistent with the observed syntax of the plural in English. (AAA)

7346. Berman, Arlene. "On the VSO Hypothesis." *LingI* 5:1-37.
The hypothesis that the underlying word order in English is Verb Subject Object (VSO) is discussed. The argument that the surface Subject Verb Object (SVO) pattern in English is produced by a late rule of subject formation is refuted, and other arguments that support the VSO hypothesis are denied. The VSO hypothesis is defective because: (1) It implicitly defines a set of relations that are unnecessary in characterizing syntactic phenomena; (2) It does not adequately define those relations that are necessary; and (3) It requires severe complications in the grammar of surface SVO languages. (LLBA)

7348. Bolinger, Dwight. "*Do* Imperatives." *JEngL* 8:1-5.
The verb *do* as an auxiliary is a carrier of affirmation and negation. With perhaps an added component of emphasis, this is all that is required to explain the use of *do* in imperatives. Superficial lexical splits are to be avoided, and the distinction between command imperatives and other imperatives belongs to rhetoric, not to syntax. (DB)

7349. Carstensen, Broder. "Grammatik aus neuer Sicht." *NsM* 27:230-35. [Rev. art.]
The arrangement and contents of the *Grammar of Contemporary English* by Randolph Quirk and others is reviewed. The linguistic principles as well as the terminology used are treated at length. The assertions made in the grammar concerning the parts of speech and linguistic levels in the English language are given special attention and a number of grammatical classifications and decisions are scrutinized. A commentary is given on the range, completeness, and arrangement of the *Grammar*. In addition it is examined for its usefulness to the foreign language teacher as a reference work. (BC)

7355. Cooper, William E. "Syntactic Flexibility among English Sensation Referents." *Linguistics* 133:33-38.
Discusses syntactic differences that are found among English sensation referents. It is proposed as a general rule that referents of the vision modality are syntactically more flexible, i.e., more likely to undergo a given syntactic process, other factors being equal, than are the corresponding referents of any other sensory modality. This proposal is supported by evidence from four separate syntactic phenomena. The possible relation of the proposed rule to other linguistic and extra-linguistic phenomena is discussed. (WEC)

7366. Fodor, Janet Dean. "Like Subject Verbs and Causal Clauses in English." *JL* 10:95-110.
D.M. Perlmutter claimed that the Like Subject Constraint in English is a deep structure constraint. His analysis is based on the assignment of abstract deep structures containing causal clauses not present in surface structure, but the motivation for these clauses is weak. They were said to explain certain distributional and semantic observations, but these are better accounted for by a semantic constraint, the Control Constraint, requiring that the subject or object of the matrix verb have some control over whether the situation described by the complement will come about. (LLBA)

7377. Halitsky, David. "Deep-Structure Appositive and Complement NP's." *Language* 50:446-54.
A grammar of English should generate NP's with internal structures like [NP[Det the][Nplanets] [NP Mars and Venus]], as well as NP's with structures like [NP[NP the two moons of Mars][NP Phobos and Deimos]]. The transformation required by the analysis works in conjunction with Chomsky's Subjacency Condition to account for the semantic and syntactic properties of surface-structure forms. (DH)

7383. Hirst, D.J., and M. Ginesy. "An Approach to the Integration of Intonation into the Syntactic Description of English." *Linguistics* 121:45-55.
All intonation is "normal" or "unmarked," expressing the syntactic relationships existing between the formatives. Sentences are generated in a much more complete form than that which subsists when the sentences are spoken. The presence of the intonation-contour, however, makes much of the sentence redundant, and it is consequently reduced in speech by a transformation by ellipsis. It is therefore erroneous to speak of two intonation-contours as being in opposition. A sentence with two different intonation contours is in fact an example of two distinct sentences. The introduction of three rules is sufficient to account for the intonation of statements. (DJH & MG)

7426. Shen, Yao. "A Word on the Co-Occurrence of *do* and *be* in English." *SIL* 24:17-19.
Considers sentences like "Do be careful," "Don't be dogmatic," and quotes Emily Dickinson's "God made me, Sir, I didn't be myself," which doesn't mean "I wasn't myself." (GLT)

7427. Singh, Rajendra. "A Note on Multiple Negatives." *AS* 45(1970; pub. 1974):247-51.
Acceptability in usage of double negative constructions in American English was tested with 47 students at Brown University, using an operational test, a new technique in the descriptive approach to determining questions of usage. In the operational test, Ss were given 5 sentences containing double negatives and were asked to carry out a simple grammatical operation, unrelated to the double negative, on each one. If they made no changes other than those required by the operation, the sentence was considered operationally acceptable; otherwise, it was considered operationally unacceptable. Ss were also asked to judge the sentences' acceptability. (LLBA)

7432. Sunderman, Paula. "Dylan Thomas' 'A Refusal to Mourn': A Syntactic and Semantic Interpretation." *Lang&S* 7:20-35.
Some critics stress that Dylan Thomas' poem "A Refusal to Mourn" reflects Thomas' concern with the Christian theme of immortality, while others claim it concentrates solely upon a paganistic regeneration. The most promising approach to the meaning of the poem is through an analysis of the inter-relationship of syntax and semantics. Two models, those of Levin and Hill, were used to analyze the poem's linguistic features, the interrelationship of linguistic and extralinguistic features, and the relation of the poem to its cultural matrix. The results show, first, that an analysis of the poem's linguistic features can resolve its structural ambiguity. Second, the interrelated pattern of syntax and semantics explicitly relates the poem to its cultural milieu of classical and Judeo-Christian tradition; and, third, this pattern clearly demonstrates the poem's central theme: Thomas' Christian affirmation of immortality. (PWS)

INDO-EUROPEAN D: HELLENIC LINGUISTICS†

II. ANCIENT AND CLASSICAL GREEK

General and Miscellaneous. 7460. Palomo, Delores. "Homeric Epic, the Invention of Writing, and Literary Education." *CE* 36:413-21.
Both Lévi-Strauss and Roland Barthes link the appearence of writing in a culture to the proliferation of political authority: documentation, record keeping, and legal codification permit severe regulation of individual and social life, and endow the literate class with great power. An examination of the absence and presence of writing in the history of Homeric epic appears to uphold such contentions, yet Eric Havelock's investigation of pre-Socratic Greek education in his *Preface to Plato* indicates that cultural control does not depend upon written texts but rather upon a method of education intended to inculcate uncritical acceptance of the cultural image embodied in a revered text. (DJP)

III. KOINÉ

7557. Daly, Lloyd W. "A Greek Evangeliary Leaf with Ecphonetic Notation," 70-72 in William E. Miller and Thomas G. Waldman, eds. with Natalie D. Terrell, *Bibliographical Studies in Honor of Rudolf Hirsch. LC* 40,i. Philadelphia: U. of Pa. Lib., Friends of the Lib. 145 pp.
A stray leaf from a Greek Orthodox lectionary in the library of the University of Pennsylvania dates apparently from the 11th century. The text is accompanied by notation devised to guide the intonation of liturgical reading. The leaf came from France but more accurate information as to its association is not available. (LWD)

INDO-EUROPEAN E: INDIC LINGUISTICS†

IV. MODERN INDIC

Hindi

General and Miscellaneous. 7692. Durbin, Mridula Adenwala. "Formal Changes in Trinidad Hindi as a Result of Language Adaptation." *AA* 75(1973):1290-1304.
Changes in the structure of an Indic language in Trinidad are discussed. Explanations of the structural changes are sought in the socio-cultural changes of the East Indian community that have occurred since the East Indians' arrival in Trinidad. The socio-cultural changes in the community have influenced the range of functions of the Indic languages in Trinidad which, in turn, has determined the directions of structural changes in the language. (LLBA)
7697. Werbner, Richard P. "The Superabundance of Understanding:Kalanga Rhetoric and Domestic Divination." *AA* 75(1973):1414-40.
An analysis of the use of stylized rhetoric by the Kalanga of Botswana in domestic seances, i.e., the congregation is kin or neighbors and the divination takes place in the home. (LLBA)

Phonology. 7699. Becker, Donald A., and G.C. Narang. "Generative Phonology and the Retroflex Flaps of Hindi-Urdu." *GL* 14:129-55.
Following a review of the treatment accorded to the retroflex flaps in the taxonomic-phonemic literature on Hindi-Urdu, a generative-phonological analysis of Hindi-Urdu is proposed in which all occurrence of [ɾ] and [ɾʰ] are derived from underlying retroflex stops or dental flaps. Several apparent exceptions to the rule by which /ɖ/ and /ɖʰ/ become [ɾ] and [ɾʰ] are explained, and a difference between two dialects corresponding in large measure to Hindi and Urdu is accounted for in terms of rule reordering in the direction of greater rule efficiency and transparency. (DAB & GCN)
7701. Jones, W.E. "A Reading Transcription for Hindi." *IPAJ* 3(1973):88-97.
A reading transcription for Hindi primarily concerned with intonation and sentence-stress is presented. The approach to the description of intonation is through an examination of contours and contour-shapes. The following items are discussed: (1) the surface syntax of common Hindi sentences; (2) styles of utterance and their implications; (3) features of contours and sub-contours; and (4) a suggested system of notation to indicate the syntax-intonation relationship as part of a reading transcription for connected texts. (LLBA)
7702. Ohala, Manjari. "The Abstractness Controversy:Experimental Input from Hindi." *Language* 50:225-35.
The psycholinguistic test described here was designed to show whether or not a Hindi word such as [gʰõ:sla:] "nest," which appears only in this form on the surface, has an underlying form with an "abstract" ə, i.e., gʰõ:səla:. The results show that some speakers have the abstract underlying form, others do not. (MO)

Sindhi

General and Miscellaneous. 7714. Mitchell, T.F. "Aspects of Concord Revisited, with Special Reference to Sindhi and Cairene Arabic." *ArL* 4(1973):27-50.
Languages make greater or less use of available devices for various purposes, and it is premature to regard gender as universally expendable. The contrary case is illustrated by Sindhi. Although nouns are always involved in the concordial processes of gender, the typical view of gender as limited to nouns takes in a word-class cart but fails to notice much of the syntagmatic horse; Arabic, and in particular the colloquial Egyptian Arabic of Cairo, imposes a different view. Inappropriate preconceptions have led all linguists to date to recognize distinctions of grammatical gender in Cairene Arabic; such distinctions should be abandoned. (TFM)

---

† *Festschriften* and Other Analyzed Collections are listed in the first division of this volume. "F" numbers in brackets following a title refer to these items.

INDO-EUROPEAN F: IRANIAN LINGUISTICS†

I. GENERAL

Morphology. 7735. Hamp, Eric P. "Once Again Iranian *ādu-." *TPS* 1973(1974):137.
Iranian *ādu-, as Szemerényi says, is probably related to Latin *ador*, Gothic *atisk*. The Latin seems to be *$H_a$éd-es-, perhaps a normal transformation of *$H_a$ódu-. If the Iranian also reflects *$H_a$ódu- we have an interesting case bearing on the scope of Brugmann's Law and on the outcome of *o next to *a*-coloring laryngeal. (EPH)

Phonology. 7738. Schwarzschild, L.A. "Initial Retroflex Consonants in Middle Indo-Aryan." *JAOS* 93(1973):482-87.
Retroflex consonants are absent from the other old Indo-European languages, and early writers therefore thought of these sounds as typically Indian. Discussion has been centered mainly on the origin of the retroflex consonants: some writers believe that the retroflex consonants are the result of spontaneous phonetic developments, while others have favored the theory of Dravidian influence. It is not only the origin of the retroflex phonemes that is of interest, but also their distribution. There are two basic rules delimiting the position of retroflex consonants in Vedic and Classical Sanskrit: retroflex consonants are not usually found (1) in initial position and (2) in the immediate vicinity of a vocalic or consonantal *r*. Initial retroflex *ṇ*- does not occur in any ordinary Sanskrit word, though there are some artificially coined grammatical technical terms *ṇit* and *ṇyul*; there is also a rare term *ṇa* which is found with a vast variety of meanings in lexical works. (LAS)

II. OLD IRANIAN

General and Miscellaneous

7741. Dishington, James. "Old Iranian Sibilants:A Synchronic Analysis." *JAOS* 94:460-67.
The well-known *ruki*-rule found in several IE dialects, whereby *s* was palatalized in certain environments, is traditionally considered to have been no longer productive in Avestan and Old Persian because *s*'s from sources other than PIE **s* were not palatalized. It is shown here that this rule was indeed actively involved in morphophonemic alternation and that its synchronic ordering with respect to other rules has certain implications for the prehistoric developments and the synchronic status of the Old Iranian sibilants. Furthermore, certain of the rules produced surface forms that were in non-automatic alternation, and it is suggested that the apparent exceptions to these rules are of specific types which can be classified along the lines proposed by Kiparsky to elucidate the mechanisms of analogy involved. (JD)

III. MIDDLE IRANIAN

Khotanese

General and Miscellaneous. 7810. Emmerick, R.E. "Commodianus and Khotanese Metrics." *TPS* 1973(1974):138-52.
The disputed question of the nature of the metrical system used for Old Khotanese poetry is discussed in the light of what is known concerning the metrical system used in the late Latin poems of Commodianus, which may represent a similar transitional stage of development between a purely quantitative and a purely accentual system. The quantitative system underlying the Khotanese meters may have been an adaptation of an Indian meter known as the *dohā*. (REE)

IV. NEW IRANIAN

Western

Persian. 7840. Richter-Bernburg, Lutz. "Linguistic Shuʿūbīya and Early Neo-Persian." *JAOS* 94:55-64.
The 4th and 5th centuries AH saw the emergence of the Neo-Persian language as a literary medium within the framework of Islam. Thus the debate over "linguistic shuʿūbīya" was sustained for two more centuries. The place of Persian was most contested in the areas of *adab* and official correspondence, of scholarly writing, and of the liturgy, and books on religious subjects. The development of Persian prose in these fields, and the discussion of the respective merits of Arabic and Persian, are examined here in their mutual dependence. Neither can be fully understood without accounting for the other. (LR-B)

INDO-EUROPEAN G: CELTIC LINGUISTICS†

I. GENERAL AND EARLY CELTIC

General and Miscellaneous

Phonology. 7869. Hoenigswald, Henry M. "Indo-European *p in Celtic and the Claim for Relative Chronologies." *JIES* 1:324-29.
Relative chronologies are often less cogent than is claimed. For example, it is possible but not necessary to date the change of *p ... k^w to k^w ... k^w ahead of the loss of the remaining instances of *p in Celtic. Incidentally, this neither strengthens nor weakens the Italo-Celtic hypothesis. (HMH)

---

† *Festschriften* and Other Analyzed Collections are listed in the first division of this volume. "F" numbers in brackets following a title refer to these items.

II. GOIDELIC

General and Miscellaneous

Phonology. 7882. Greene, David. "The Growth of Palatalization in Irish." *TPS* 1973(1974):127-36.
In Old (and Modern) Irish each consonant has a phonologically opposed palatalized counterpart. Palatalization took place in three stages. The first of these, which took place before the apocope, affected a comparatively small number of words, but established the opposition neutral/palatalized for all consonants in intervocalic position. The second stage occurs with the apocope; lost syllables containing a front vowel palatalize the preceding consonant before falling, so that the opposition is extended to the whole range of the new final consonants. It appears that only the final consonant of clusters was liable to palatalization. The third stage comes with the syncope; in resulting clusters where one of the consonants was palatalized, palatalization was gradually generalized and final clusters adopted the same pattern; in Old Irish only the cluster [xt'] survives as an exception. By the Old Irish period, the inflectional system shows wide generalization of palatalized (marked) phonemes. (DG)

Modern Irish

Syntax. 7913. Quin, Ernest G. "The Irish Modal Preterite." *Hermathena* 117:43-60.
Modal uses of historic or past tenses of verbs occur in a wide range of Indo-European languages and cover such categories as conditional, subjunctive, present indicative, and future. Usage in Irish is diverse at all periods and is found both with the old-Irish preterite/perfect and with the modern Irish past tense. The main uses are conditional, graphic present, and subjunctive/future. The general usage may be linked to the partial transformation of the Indo-European sigmatic aorist into the old-Irish s-subjunctive. (EGQ)

III. BRITISH

Breton

General and Miscellaneous. 7920. Prudor, B.A. "Breton." *IncL* 11(1972):71-72.
A brief survey of the history, philology, and use of Breton. Breton belongs to the Brythonic group of Celtic languages. It is closely related to Welsh and Cornish, spreading with the British settlement from west to east. Like Welsh and German, Breton has the remarkable capacity of forming derivatives and compound words, which is a decided advantage in the expression of scientific and philosophical ideas. Breton is a smooth and beautiful language as well as a remarkable linguistic instrument and this, besides its value as a national symbol, amply justifies the struggle for its survival. (LLBA)

INDO-EUROPEAN J: ALBANIAN AND OTHERS†

II. ALBANIAN

Etymology, Lexicography, and Lexicology. 7978. Hamp, Eric P. "(For Roman, who is always) Number One." *IJSLP* 16(1973):1-6.
The entire series of Albanian numerals, with the exception of the highest members, is regarded as inherited from Indo-European. On grounds of semantic and syntactic features, one of two assumptions for the numeral "one" can be proposed in exactly opposite senses: (1) If the rest of the series is inherited, then the first member is, also; or (2) Since "one" is unique syntactically and semantically, it may be reasonably supposed to have diverged at an early date, and hence have a different fate. (LLBA)

INDO-EUROPEAN L: ANATOLIAN†

III. HITTITE (KANESIAN OR KANESHITE)

General and Miscellaneous. 8036. Güterbock, Hans G. "Appendix: Hittite Parallels." *JNES* 33:323-27.
Some lines of the Sumerian and Akkadian prayers edited and analyzed by Lambert occur also in Hittite prayers of the 14th through 13th centuries B.C. The Appendix presents the sections of Hittite prayers containing these lines. They occur in two sets of prayers. The authors of the Hittite prayers made free use of individual Babylonian motifs rather than imitating the whole prayers. (HGG)

Etymology, Lexicography, and Lexicology. 8056. Carter, Charles. "Some Unusual Hittite Expressions for the Time of Day." *JAOS* 94:130-39.
Discusses two unusual Hittite expressions found in some descriptions of festivals and designating the arrival of evening. (CC)

† *Festschriften* and Other Analyzed Collections are listed in the first division of this volume. "F" numbers in brackets following a title refer to these items.

Phonology. 8076. Puhvel, Jaan. "On Labiovelars in Hittite." *JAOS* 94:291-95.
The Indo-European labiovelars were preserved in Hittite in all positions, including the preconsonantal one, except for the delabialization of the initial media (g^w-> /g-/). A strict application of the so-called Sturtevant's Law in etymological postulations, coupled with a new sifting of the evidence, provides an inventory of the reflexes of all three Indo-European orders of labiovelars in most positions. The delabialization of g^w- is seen as the converse of the situation in other Indo-European languages, where precisely the media shows the most pronounced tendencies to full labialization. (JP)

Syntax. 8078. Hoffner, H.A.,Jr. "Studies of the Hittite Particles." *JAOS* 93(1973):520-26.
Die satazeinletitenden Partikeln in den indogermanisch en Sprachen Anatoliens by Onofrio Carruba marks a forward step in the understanding of the enclitic particles of the Indo-European languages of ancient Anatolia. Carruba has built not only upon the labors of his predecessors, but also upon his own earlier

studies. Carruba broadens his investigation to include not only the other sentence enclitics of cuneiform Hittite (Neshite), but also the "Satzpartikeln" of Luwain, Palaic, Lycian, and Lydian. By "Satzpartikeln" Carruba means those enclitic morphemes which in Hittite attach themselves in a more or less fixed sequence, usually to the first word of the sentence. The chain of enclitic particles in Hittite contains six ranks. In four of these, one may choose between two or more mutually exclusive particles. The particles which share the same rank perform the same syntactic function. In rank one, three (*nu, šu, ta*) of the five must be word-initial, while the remaining two (*-ma-, -(y)a*) may not be word-initial. Particles of this rank are conjunctive or disjunctive. Rank two may be filled by *-wa(r)-* or by zero. *-wa(r)* indicates the presence of direct discourse. (HAH,Jr)

ASIATIC LINGUISTICS†

I. URALIC

Finno-Ugric

Finnic. 8139. Larmouth, Donald W. "Differential Interference in American Finnish Cases." *Language* 50:356-66.
The Finnish language in Minnesota has undergone considerable interference through four generations of contact with English, largely because of syntagmatic congruence with English sentences. The noun cases have responded in a variety of ways to this interference, demonstrating that both the degree of boundness and syntactic congruence are critical to the explanation of interference, as case-endings in highly bound environments are much more resistant to interference than those in moderately or loosely bound environments. (DWL)

8163. Skousen, R. "On Limiting the Number of Phonological Descriptions." *Glossa* 7(1973):167-78.
The important problem for (morpho)phonology is to find empirical evidence that will indicate which of the many different solutions best represents how speakers themselves account for the morphological forms in the language. The Finnish illative is considered and several different ways of accounting for the illative are described. (LLBA)

Ugric. 8194. Kenesei, István. "Egyes névmások generálásáról." *NK* 75(1973):125-53.
Based on three groups of Hungarian pronouns (interrogative, negative, and indefinite), an attempt is made at their derivation from a deep-structural common pro-element instead of making immediate use of the lexicon. The proposal is based on their mutual non-occurrence in indicative, affirmative, negative, and interrogative sentences, respectively. Yet, wherever evidence is contradictory, it shows regularity, thus embedded structures have to be invoked. (LLBA)

8196. Kiss, Jenõ. "Zur synchronischen Suffixforschung in der Finnougristik." *SFUS* 9(1973):237-41.
A discussion of the synchronic description of suffixes, specifically with: (1) productivity; (2) the degree of productivity (productivity of specific suffix functions); (3) correlation (antonymic and synonymic suffixes with the same stem); (4) frequency (the number of derivations formed by means of the same suffix); and (5) stylistic evaluation (stylistic function of a suffix or suffixes). (LLBA)

II. ALTAIC

Mongolian

8248. Bawden, Charles R. "Some Recent Work in Mongol Dialect Studies." *TPS* 1973(1974):153-81.
Reviews work done in the last 20 years in the field of Mongol dialect studies; concentrates upon studies written in the People's Republic of Mongolia in the Mongol language. The Mongol spoken in the Republic justifies the opinion that it forms one language with a number of dialects. Monographs on the principal dialects have appeared, as well as a considerable number of articles. Linguistic work so far follows a pattern of collection and organization of material, and in practice forms part of a wider program of collection of folklore and oral and other traditions. It is generally accepted that dialect differences are yielding to the influence of Khalkha, the majority dialect. (CRB)

Turkic

General and Miscellaneous. 8266. Ivanov, Sergei Nikolaevich. "K istolkovaniyu mnogoznachnosti grammaticheskikh form (Na materiale tyurkskikh yazykov)." *VJa* 6:101-09.
A discussion of whether polysemantic grammatical forms have general meanings and how these are correlated with particular meanings. The general meaning of a polysemantic form cannot be a semantic common denominator of all the particular uses of the grammatical form. The general meaning is the system encompassing all the individual facts. Knowledge of the system of meaning helps in the construction of the concrete concept of the grammatical form, while extraction of the semantic common denominator is the way to establish its abstract representation. For a better understanding of the problem, the dialectical categories essence (general) and appearance (particular) are listed along with the categories object, property, and relation, which correspond to the grammatical concepts of form, meaning, and function. (LLBA)

Azerbaijani. 8275. Akhundova, F.E. "Sopostavitelnoe izuchenie sistemy padezhei v nemetskom i azerbaidzhanskom yazykakh." *IAN* 32(1973):65-73.
Comparison of the case systems of German and Azerbaijani provides a good means of ascertaining the general typological group to which they respectively belong. Azerbaijani oblique cases express a precise relation. German oblique cases are much more general in meaning, combining a number of such relations in a single case, with prepositions providing further specification. Azerbaijani is an agglutinative language in which case forms have resulted from affixing of elements. The inflectional-analytic character of German contrasts strongly with the synthetic forms of Azerbaijani. (LLBA)

---

† *Festschriften* and Other Analyzed Collections are listed in the first division of this volume. "F" numbers in brackets following a title refer to these items.

III. JAPANESE

Japanese

General and Miscellaneous. 8368. Neustupný, J.V. "The Modernization of the Japanese System of Communication." *LSoc* 3:33-50.
There is an evolutionary typology of languages (early modern, modern, contemporary, etc.) For modernization at least two types of processes, macro-modernization and micro-modernization, must be distinguished. The former concerns such tasks as the establishment of a modern national language and as far as Japan is concerned this process has been completed. The latter process concerns problems such as the individual's use of language. It still awaits completion. (JVN)

Etymology, Lexicography, and Lexicology. 8380. Howard, Irwin. "On 'Picture Nouns' in Japanese." *WPLUH* 6,iii:93-104.
It is commonly known that picture-nouns such as "picture of," "story about," etc., have peculiar properties in English, some of which involve reflexivization. Studies of Japanese syntax illustrate the contrast between *zibun* and *himself* by pointing out the ambiguity of the English reflexive in "Harry showed Bill a picture of himself" and the lack of ambiguity in the Japanese equivalent. The passive version of this sentence is ambiguous in Japanese (although not in English), a fact that is relevant to the controversy over the deep structure of the Japanese passive. (IH)

Phonology. 8399. Tabata, Koh-ichi, and Toshiyuki Sakai. "Multivariate Statistical Analysis of Japanese VCV Utterances." *Studia Phonologica* 7(1973):31-54.
Considering the amplitude outputs of a 20-channel $1/4$-octave filter analyzer of V_1CV_2 utterances as the components of a 20-dimensional vector, multivariate analysis was performed with four factors—V_1, C, V_2, and speaker; and the effects of each factor were compared. Five adult males were asked to utter each of the 75 possible combinations using one of vowels /a, i, u, e, o/ for V_1 and V_2, and one of the nasal consonants /m, n, ŋ/ for C. The relation of the variance ellipsoids of each factor was inspected along the principal axes; the notion of the direction as well as the amount is necessary for explaining the effects of each factor. These analyses were compared using principal-component analyses. (LLBA)

IV. SINO-TIBETAN

Chinese

General and Miscellaneous. 8429. Chin, Tsung. "Can the Presentation of Particle *le* Be Simpler?" [F 51]:143-47.
There are two *le*'s in Mandarin Chinese which are represented by the same character in writing. *Le₂* occurs before the object and *Le₁* after it, both following the verb. Successful presentation of this particle (character *le*) hinges upon the functional differentiation of the two linguistic forms. *Le₁* used in the absence of *le₂* denotes occurredness of the verb action, that is, something took place. Though there is the meaning of "past" in *le₁* it is not the same as saying *le₁* signals the past tense in English. The function of *le₂* is to provide current relevance for the verb, with or without the modification of *le₁*, in much the same way as *have-en* signals the perfect aspect in English. (TC)

8433. Cooper, Arthur. "The Chinese Method of Writing and Plans for a New Dictionary." *IncL* 11(1972):66-70.
A look at the Chinese method of writing and a revelation of plans for a new Chinese dictionary. Among the languages of the world, Chinese is unique in being written by a method that does not analyze the sounds of words, but represents them as entities of sound and meaning together. Because Chinese writing is not based primarily on analyzing speech sounds, it is both intertemporal and interlingual. Chinese has always been a monosyllabic language, without inflections, and the only changes in Chinese words have resulted from the kind of wearing down of the monosyllables that has made "know" and "no" in English lose all difference in sound. The latest comprehensive Chinese dictionary is in 40 volumes, and few people can afford to possess it; neither can such a gigantic work be easily kept up-to-date. Much smaller dictionaries do exist, but the reader can seldom get far in any wide range of reading with less than a battery of them on his desk. "A quick access dictionary of Chinese characters" is being prepared. This will be a dictionary, limited in its scope, but giving the most essential information about the basic roots of the language. (LLBA)

8446. Magner, Thomas F. "The Latin Alphabet and the Languages of China." *JGE* 26:205-18.
The People's Republic of China is attempting to make the traditional Chinese orthography more accessible to its huge population by simplifying the characters while at the same time experimenting with a new orthography based on the Latin alphabet. The character script has immense prestige and contributes to a feeling of national unity as the characters have the same meaning in all dialect areas. The alphabetic script is more efficient in terms of learning and usage, but since it can also be used for the various Chinese dialects it might create in time distinctively different Chinese languages. (TFM)

8448. Mártonfi, Ferenc. "Vannak-e szófajok a kínai nyelvben?" *NK* 75(1973):177-203.
A discussion of the nearly 150 years of controversy on whether Chinese has parts of speech. Two different notions, covered by the label "parts of speech," should be distinguished: (1) parts of speech in a grammatical (syntactic, morphological, and perhaps phonological) sense; and (2) parts of speech in a lexical sense. The former are universal; the latter are characteristic of but a group of human languages. Chinese has parts of speech only in the former sense. (LLBA)

8461. T'sou, Benjamin K. "Asymmetric Bilingualism:A Sociolinguistic Study of Cantonese Emigrants." *JCLTA* 8(1973): 134-44.
Discusses the different phases of development in bilingual individual and diglossic communities. A progression of linguistic developments in immigrants is discussed, and a correlation between these linguistic behaviors and certain a posteriori facets of cultural assimilation is proposed. An examination of group cohesion from the sociolinguistic point of view is attempted. Five distinct stages in linguistic assimilation are described: (1) linguistic importation; (2) linguistic assimilation; (3) code switching; (4) bilingualism; and (5) residual interference. (LLBA)

8463. Wang, William S-Y, Stephen W. Chan, and Benjamin K. T'sou. "Chinese Linguistics and the Computer." *Linguistics* 118(1973):89-117.
A discussion of computer aided research in the U.S. on Chinese phonology and Chinese-English contrastive grammatical studies. The former utilizes a large pool of computerized data on modern and ancient Chinese dialects. The latter uses a specific model for the automatic analysis of Chinese language data. (LLBA)

Mandarin. 8485. Lester, David. "Symbolism in the Chinese Language." *IJSym* 5,i:18-21.
A study was conducted to see whether evidence could be obtained for graphic and tonal symbolism in the Chinese language in addition to the evidence obtained in previous studies for phonetic symbolism. No evidence was found for the existence of graphic or tonal symbolism, indicating that the symbolic aspects of language may be limited to phonetic aspects. (LLBA)

8497. Wang, John C., and F.S. Hsueh. "The Lin-chⁱi Dialect and Its Relation to Mandarin." *JAOS* 93(1973):136-45.
A unique dialect of North China is chosen here for analysis in strictly structural terms, with a view to displaying how divergent dialects can be, even within such a limited concept as "Mandarin"

Chinese." The phonemic system of the dialect is set up, and it is found that its tone and vowel systems are drastically different from those of the Peking dialect, while the two dialects share practically the same set of initial consonants. A tentative list of essential characteristic s for Mandarin dialects is then suggested for the purpose of testing if a Chinese dialect can be classified as a Mandarin dialect or not, and if so, which subgroup of Mandarin dialects it belongs to. The Lin-ch'i dialect is thus determined in formal terms to be a Mandarin dialect (perhaps of the Northwestern group). Finally, a systematic comparison between this dialect and Pekingese is made, with frequent reference to Ancient Chinese and Old Mandarin. (JCW & FSH)

Tibeto-Burman

Tibetan. 8512. Coblin, W. South. "An Early Tibetan Word

for 'Horse'." *JAOS* 94:124-25.
A Tibeto-Burman (TB) root *m-rang* "horse" can be reconstructed on the basis of such clearly related forms as Written Burmese (WB) *mràng*, Kachin *kumrang*, Haka *rang*, etc. It has long been doubted whether Written Tibetan (WT) *rta* "horse" could be connected with this family of TB cognates, but during the past decade the number of statements in support of such a relationship has increased. While there seems to be ample concern for the TB pedigree of *rta*, there has not been any attempt to introduce the early WT word *rmang* "horse, steed" into discussion. This word was discovered by F.W. Thomas in two different Tun-huang documents as part of the compound *rmang-rogs*. (WSC)

V. SOUTH AND SOUTHEAST ASIA

Dravidian

Malayalam. 8526. Velayudhan, S., and John M. Howie. "Acoustical Measurements of Distinctive Vowel Quantity in Malayalam." *L&S* 17:95-103.
The physical nature of distinctive length in Malayalam vowels is investigated by means of sound spectrograms made of two informants' speech. Measurements of short and long vowels show that the duration of long vowels is always twice that of short vowels in comparable environments. The environment of the vowel also has a significant effect on its duration—both short and long vowels have shorter durations before long consonants than before short ones. Relative duration is the acoustic correlate of the long versus short distinction in Malayalam vowels. (SV & JMH)

Tamil. 8528. Karunatilake, W.S., and S. Suseendirarajah. "Phonology of Sinhalese and Srilanka Tamil—A Study in Contrast and Interference." *IndLing* 34(1973):180-90.
Vowel and consonant inventories for Sinhalese and Srilanka Tamil are presented and compared, followed by a survey of allophones, distribution, and syllable structure. The contrastive analysis is then applied to learning problems in either direction. The areas of difficulty that the speakers of these two languages have in learning the other language are described. (LLBA)

8531. Suseendirarajah, S. "Phonology of Srilanka Tamil and Indian Tamil Contrasted." *IndLing* 34(1973):171-79.
A report of an attempt to compare and contrast the phonemic systems of Srilanka Tamil and Indian Tamil. Based on field notes taken both in India and Ceylon 1962-67, the phonemic inventory of both dialects is discussed, followed by lists of single consonants, initial consonant clusters, intervocalic geminate clusters, intervocalic clusters of homorganic nasal plus stop, intervocalic heterogenous clusters, and distinctive vowel features. (LLBA)

Telugu. 8535. Wilkinson, Robert W. "A Phonetic Constraint on a Syncope Rule in Telugu." *Language* 50:478-97.
The basic formulation of a Telugu vowel syncope rule is discussed and certain pecularities of its application to /CVC/ sequences containing a retroflex obstruent are pointed out. These peculiarities can be explained within the framework provided by the theory of natural assimilation in Schachter (1969). Situations arise where the syncope rule must choose the vowel to be deleted

among several potentially deletable vowels. In certain cases of this sort, it is the output of a rule applying later than the syncope rule which provides a means of predicting which vowel is deleted. (RWW)

Vietnamese-Muong

Vietnamese. 8546. Thomas, David. "A Note on 'Yuan'." *JAOS* 94:123.
The Vietnamese are known throughout much of Southeast Asia by names like *yuan*, *yuôn*, *ñuôn*. These *yuan* forms are found in the Chamic languages, in Indonesia, and in many of the Mon-Khmer languages, but apparently not in the Tai languages. In some Cham inscriptions and in an Old Javanese poem the form *yavana* is found when referring to the Vietnamese, a form which is identical with the Sanskrit word *yavana* stranger, Greek, and the generally accepted etymology for *yuan* is that it is an adaptation of Skt. *yavana* applied to the "strangers" north of the Chams. But there are hesitations about this etymology, as the name is too widespread and too specific to have readily originated from such a vague general term. (DT)

Kam-Thai

Thai. 8549. Huffman, Franklin E. "Thai and Cambodian—A Case of Syntactic Borrowing?" *JAOS* 93(1973):488-509.
The syntactic parallelism between Thai and Cambodian is striking. Not only is the order and inventory of individual form classes almost identical, but also many semantically equivalent forms seem to share identical ranges of syntactic occurrence. Given syntactic similarity of such range and magnitude, there are three possible explanations: (1) Genetic relationship. In spite of their syntactic similarity, Thai and Cambodian are not, so far as has been demonstrated by traditional methods of comparative reconstruction, genetically related. (2) Coincidence. When one considers the number of different syntactic relations occurring in the same order in the two languages, the probability of chance convergence is infinitesimal. (3) Borrowing. The increasing evidence for the existence of a Southeast Asian linguistic area, along with the close geographic, cultural, and political contact between Thai and Cambodia over a period of seven centuries, strongly indicates that the syntactic similarity is due to borrowing. (FEH)

VI. UNAFFILIATED STOCKS OF EURASIA

Elamite. 8603. McAlpin, David W. "Toward Proto-Elamo-Dravidian." *Language* 50:89-101.
The Dravidian family of languages in South Asia is cognate with Elamite, an ancient language of West Asia. This demonstration is based on 57 Elamite words (mostly verb stems) paired with corresponding Dravidian terms. The correspondences are, on the whole, straightforward and interlocking. A beginning is made in reconstructing the phonology of Proto-Elamo-Dravidian.

(DWMcA)

Sumerian. 8619. Civil, Miguel. "The Anzu-Bird and Scribal Whimsies." *JAOS* 92(1972):271.
A reading "anzu (d)" for the logogram an.im.mi/dugud was first proposed by Landsberger in 1961 and has been slowly gaining acceptance, although it has encountered some skepticism, and understandably so, since Landsberger's arguments although very persuasive hardly can be considered a definitive proof. (MC)

AFRICAN LINGUISTICS†

I. GENERAL

8631. Knappert, Jan. "The State of Our Knowledge of African Languages." *Linguistics* 124:71-89.
An evaluation of the advance that has been made in the study of African languages and the work that remains to be done. More dictionaries and comprehensive textbook grammars of almost all African languages are needed, including tonal and dialect research. A complete and urgent codification of African oral literature which will have to provide much of the material for linguists and anthropologists is also necessary, as well as more rigid criteria for the classification of African languages. (LLBA)

VI. BANTU

General and Miscellaneous. 8672. Muthiani, Joseph. "KiSetla." *SIL* 24:31-44.
Kisetla is a form of Swahili developed in up-country Kenya and intensively used by the European settlers; it is an African-based pidgin. Various aspects of Kisetla phonology and morphology are compared with standard Swahili. (JM)

8674. Seitel, P. "Haya Metaphors for Speech." *LSoc* 3:51-67.
Metaphorical statements about speech embody indigenously named semantic dimensions. Hayas use these dimensions to conceive of and evaluate their own speech behavior. The dimensions are specified first through indigenous literal statements about speech, then through one-word metaphors applied to speech, and finally through ten proverbs about speech interactions that link metaphorically a named category of speech act with the alimentary act of expelling a flatus. (PS)

Semantics. 8683. Der-Houssikian, Haig. "The Semantic Content of Class in Bantu and Its Syntactic Significance." *Linguistics* 124:5-19.
Bantu languages have an average of six to eight classes counting the singular and plural forms of classes which have a singular/plural dichotomy once, and excluding inflectional classes such as abstracts, diminutives, augmentatives, locatives, and gerundives. An analysis of the semantic content of these classes in Swahili shows that class in Bantu has syntactic significance only to the extent that it corresponds to the semantic/syntactic features of the noun. The following four semantic features consistently relevant to specific Swahili classes have been observed: [human], [animate], [mass], and [sentient]. The feature [sentient] is used here to refer to plant life in general. It must be a subcategory of the feature [animate]. Where specific classes do display consistent but not necessarily exclusive semantic features, those same features are syntactically significant in spite of the class system. Class is syntactically significant to the extent that its semantic content is syntactically relevant. (HD-H)

Syntax. 8685. Hombert, Jean M. "Speaking Backwards in Bakwiri." *SAL* 4(1973):227-36.
A word game which consists of taking the last syllable of a word and transposing it before the first one is played by young Bakwiri speakers on the southern slopes of Mount Cameroun. The theoretical implications of this process are discussed. A definition of the level of psychological reality of such a word game is considered as a means for gaining insight into phonological systems. (LLBA)

8686. Perrin, Mona. "Direct and Indirect Speech in Mambila." *JL* 10:27-37.
A simple dichotomy in quoted speech of direct vs. indirect is not sufficient to account for the forms of pronoun reference in Mambila. Direct speech, taking its pronoun orientation from the clause in which it is immmediately embedded, and indirect speech, taking its pronoun orientation from other sources, both occur. However a third orientation combines features of both direct and indirect speech in one clause. Within direct speech, there are two policies of pronoun reference. One policy maintains first, second, and third person contrasts, the other distinguishes only between references to the speaker and references to anyone other than the speaker. Different sets of pronouns are involved in the two policies. A mixed form of reference also occurs in which pronouns from both of these policies are found in the same clause. (LLBA)

8688. Wald, Benji. "Syntactic Change in the Lake Languages of Northeast Bantu." *SAL* 4(1973):237-68.
One syntactic change can be motivated by the "need" to preserve a distinction which is threatened by another syntactic change. Using the example of the Lake languages of Northeast Bantu, two principles dealing with this phenomenon are proposed: (1) In any language there are certain semantic distinctions which require overt syntactic expression; and (2) No distinction is immune to the pressures of syntactic change, but in the event that one syntactic change threatens to eradicate a required distinction, another syntactic change must occur to maintain that distinction. (LLBA)

VII. KWA

Etymology, Lexicography, and Lexicology. 8695. Kronenfeld, David B. "Fanti Kinship:The Structure of Terminology and Behavior." *AA* 75(1973):1577-95.
A comparison of results from formal analysis of the three variant patterns in Fanti kinship terminology and their marking hierarchy with the results from a multi-dimensional scaling and linear regression analysis of the bases of Fanti ascription of behavior to kinsmen. Terminological categories are shown to be a product of patterns of behavior in the culture. (LLBA)

Phonology. 8700. Krohn, Robert. "Is There a Rule of Absolute Neutralization in Nupe?" *WPLUH* 6,iii:105-13.
Hyman's analysis (1970) of Nupe (a Kwa language spoken in Nigeria) contains a rule of absolute neutralization that merges

---

† *Festschriften* and Other Analyzed Collections are listed in the first division of this volume. "F" numbers in brackets following a title refer to these items.

underlying low vowels. This neutralization rule is eliminated in an alternative analysis which includes instead a rule that "breaks" the feature matrix of certain low vowels and redistributes the features of each vowel as a sequence of vowel-like transitions plus [a]. An important consequence of this proposal is that Nupe vowels are revealed as being relatively nonabstract. (RK)

Syntax. 8704. Frajzyngier, Zygmunt. "NP nɛ (NP) in Awutu: A Problem in Case Grammar." *LangS* 33:8-14.
The framework of case grammar is used to analyze surface structure constructions of the type NP-nɛ-NP in Awutu, a Guang language from southern Ghana. Agentive, objective, locative, and comitative cases are postulated. Surface structures are derived from deep structures containing two or more of the above cases. The phrase NP-nɛ-NP has two different sources: it may be the realization of two different cases as well as the result of reduction of conjoined sentences. (ZF)

8708. Lord, Carol. "Serial Verbs in Transition." *SAL* 4(1973):269-96.
Serial verb constructions are widespread in the Kwa languages of West Africa. In the serial construction the verb phrases necessarily refer to sub-parts or aspects of a single overall event. A locative verb in a true serial construction corresponds to an aspect of the single overall event that is the concern of the sentence. It is not as semantically important as the other verb phrase—the meaning of the sentence is clear and the location phrase does not need to be fully verbal. Accordingly, it loses status syntactically and remains as a mere function word. If serial verb constructions are more prevalent than prepositional phrase constructions in the language, new speakers may prefer using a semantically equivalent serial verb construction. Consequently, the preposition is heard infrequently and finally disappears. (LLBA)

AFRO-ASIATIC LINGUISTICS†

III. EGYPTIAN-COPTIC, BERBER, CUSHITIC,

Chad. 8725. Hoskison, James. "Prosodies and Verb Stems in Gude." *Linguistics* 141:17-26.
Discusses certain morphophonemic changes which take place in verbal stem formation in Gude, a Chadic language of Nigeria. The nature of these changes requires an underlying representation for Gude formatives that leads to assigning the classificatory features of the phonology to syllables rather than to single segments in the customary way. (JTH)
8730. Newman, Paul. "Grades, Vowel-Tone Classes and Extensions in the Hausa Verbal System." *SAL* 4(1973):297-346.
Discusses the Hausa verbal system, both synchronically and

diachronically. Weaknesses and minor inconsistencies in the grade system as proposed and developed by Parsons are analyzed and a number of modifications are offered. A model of the Hausa verbal system (the VTE, Vowel-Tone Class/Extension system) was based on the rejection of the basic grades as conceived in the grade system and replaced by semantically empty, strictly phonological classes. Basic verbs in the VTE system are analyzed as having final vowel and tone as an integral part of their underlying lexical representation. Derivative grades are analyzed as optional extensions that function as syntactic/semantic additions to the basic verbs. (LLBA)

IV. SEMITIC

General and Miscellaneous. 8754. Rapallo, Umberto. "Problemi di linguistica teorico relativi al consonantismo semitico." *AGI* 58(1973):105-36.
An evaluation of a project which investigated the evolution of the Semitic phonemic system as an introduction to a discussion of problems related to the study of Middle Hebrew and Aramaic Judaic. The difficulties encountered stem largely from the fact that these are "dead" Semitic languages. A comparison/contrast of the two is presented, discussing phonemic similarities, the consonant diasystem of the two languages and their generative representations, and the articulatory phonetics of the Semitic languages. (LLBA)
8756. Weinfeld, M. "Covenant Terminology in the Ancient Near East and Its Influence on the West." *JAOS* 93(1973):190-99.
In the wake of intensive political relations between the various powers in the Middle East of the 15th to 13th centuries B.C. a common treaty terminology had been established. The expressions for: treaty = "bond and oath" (Akkadian *riksu u māmītu*, Hittite *išḥiul, lingāi-*, Hebrew *bryt w'lh*) and "love and friendship" (Akkadian *ṭābtu/damiqt u, aḥḥūtu/ra'amūtu*, Hittite *aššul, kaneššuyar*, Hebrew *ḥsd/ṭwbh*, Aramaic *ṭbt'*); treaty making: "to cut a convenant" (Hebrew *krt bryt*, Phoenician *krt'lt* and Aramaic *gzr 'dy'*); observance of the treaty: "keep/remember" (Akk. *naṣāru/ḥa-sāsu* , Hebrew *šmr/zkr*, Aramaic *nṣr*); violation of the treaty: "break" (Akk. *parāṣu*, Hebrew *hpr*), "trespass" (Akk. *eṭequ*, Hebrew *br*) are almost identical all over the ancient Near East. More surprising is the fact that all these terms penetrated the Greek milieu and were later on adopted by the Romans. Thus the terms "cut a covenant" (*horkia temnein* in Greek), "bond and oath" (*synthēkē kai horkos* in Greek), "love and friendship" (*filia kai symmachia* in Greek, *amicitia et societas* in Latin), "break/trespass a covenant" (*parabainein/dēlēsasthai* in Greek, *rampere/ frangere* in Latin) are identical with the Near Eastern formulae. (MW)

Arabic. 8761. Beeston, A.F.L. "Embedding of the Theme-Predicate Structure in Arabic." *Language* 50:474-77.
An Arabic theme-predicate structure may incorporate, as its predicate element, an embedded structure which itself consists of theme plus predicate. Authorities have not stated how far this process can be continued by further embeddings. Usage indicates that a second embedding occurs only under certain limiting restrictions, and a third embedding not at all. (AFLB)
8763. Carter, Michael G. "An Arab Grammarian of the Eighth Century, A.D.:A Contribution to the History of Linguistics." *JAOS* 93(1973):146-57.
The first systematic work of Arabic grammar, the *Book* of Sībawaihi (died late 8th century A.D.), presents a type of structuralist analysis unknown to the West until the 20th century. Treating language as a form of social behavior, Sībawaihi adapted contemporary ethical criteria to evaluate linguistic correctness at all levels of analysis: *ḥasan* 'good' and *qabīḥ* 'bad' indicate structural correctness, while *mustaqīm* 'right' and *muḥāl* 'wrong' apply to the speaker's effectiveness in communicating within the conventions of his speech community. Utterances are analyzed into more than seventy function classes. Each function is normally realized as a binary unit containing one active "operator" (the speaker himself or an element of his utterance) and one passive component operated on (not "governed") by the active member of the unit. Because every utterance is reduced to binary units, Sībawaihi's method is remarkably similar to Immediate Constituent Analysis, with which it shares both common techniques and inadequacies. (MGC)
8782. Schreiber, Peter A., and Frank Anshen. "Arabic Topicalization:Alternative Approaches." *LangS* 29:19-21.
Two types of generative analyses of Arabic topic-comment sentences are exemplified by Anshen and Schreiber (A-S), "A Focus Transformation of Modern Standard Arabic," *Language*, 44, and Lewkewicz (L), "Topic-Comment and Relative Clause in

Arabic," *Language*, 47. In A-S base rules generate verb-first structures which may undergo an optional topicalization transformation that copies a NP at the left of its containing sentence; in L the base rules generate NP-first structures which become topic-comment sentences by virtue of a "filtering" transformation whose only function is to delete boundary symbols if a certain identity condition is met. Comparison of these proposals favors A-S over L because A-S avoids the necessity of stating certain arbitrary restrictions as conditions on transformations, since it assigns synonymous sentences the same underlying structures, and because, unlike L, it does not violate certain otherwise valid general principles governing the application of transformations. The comparison also suggests that rules (like L's) whose only function is to block derivations be disallowed. (PAS)

Aramaic. 8789. Isbell, Charles D. "Some Cryptograms in the Aramaic Incantation Bowls." *JNES* 33:405-07.
Many of the Aramaic incantation bowls from Babylonia contain words or phrases which cannot be understood as "normal" language. Most of these strange clusters of letters remain unreadable and nonsensical. Some can be understood through the application of strictly controlled rules of cryptogrammic writing widely known and used by Jewish authors from earliest times. Those cryptograms which can be so understood have been deciphered and explained in the present work. (CDI)
8798. Sabar, Yona. "Nursery Rhymes and Baby Words in the Jewish Neo-Aramaic Dialect of Zakho (Iraq)." *JAOS* 94:329-36.
Makes available further linguistic data of the Jewish Neo-Aramaic dialect from Zakho (Iraq). The 16 nursery rhymes and the baby words were collected by Sabar among his immediate relatives who now live in Jerusalem. The linguistic material is analyzed grammatically and etymologically in an appended glossary. (YS)

Hebrew. 8817. Cathcart, Kevin J. "Notes on Some Hebrew Words for Vessels and Their Cognates." *RdSO* 47:55-58.
Discusses Hebrew vessel-names ṣallaḥat, sᵉlōḥīt, qallaḥat, and qubbâat and their cognates. There are cognates for ṣallaḥat, ṣᵉlōḥīt in Aramaic, Syriac, Ethiopic, and Arabic. El-Amarna zilaḥda may be a Canaanite cognate, suggesting tentatively that Akkadian ṣilūtu might be related to Heb. ṣallaḥat, sᵉlōḥīt. Qubbâat, "goblet," has cognates in Ugaritic and Phoenician and probably also in Akkadian qapūtu. (KJC)
8823. Delekat, Lienhard. "Die Parahyba-Inschrift:neue Lesungen und Bemerkungen zu Cross' Verteidigung ihrer Unechtheit." *LBib* 33:1-13.
Rediscusses some linguistic problems of the Parahyba-inscription found in Brazil. A new deciphering and translation are given which demonstrate the inscription as an original in a Hebrew dialect with consecutive tenses and some orthographic pecularities. (LD)
8850. Morag, Shelomo. "On the Historical Validity of the Vocalization of the Hebrew Bible." *JAOS* 94:307-15.
In biblical scholarship there prevails a tendency to regard the vocalization of the Bible as superfluous and to consider the vocalization of those forms which phonologically or morphologically seem strange as corrupt. While it is true that there are forms the vocalization of which defies explanation, we should not surmise that any form which looks bizarre in its vocalization is corrupt and requires emendation. Many of these forms are genuine and reflect ancient phonological, morphonemic, and morphological features of Hebrew: some of them may be dialectal; others show peculiarities typical of certain periods in the history of biblical Hebrew. The historical validity of several forms is discussed. (SM)

AUSTRONESIAN AND INDO-PACIFIC LINGUISTICS†

I. GENERAL

Languages Intrusive and In Contact

General and Miscellaneous. 8889. Day, Richard R. *Patterns of Variation in Copula and Tense in the Hawaiian Post-Creole Continuum.* (WPLUH) Honolulu: U. of Hawaii, 1973. 165 pp. [Diss., 1972.]
Data gathered by sociolinguistic methods from persons living in the Hawaiian Islands supports an interpretatio n that the English language in Hawaii is a post-creole speech continuum composed of overlapping systems and that the lects in the continuum are in the process of decreolization. An analysis of 23 speakers shows that occurrences of the present tense Standard English copula can be arranged on a Guttman implicational scale in four syntactic environments. Except for this implicational patterning, the speakers cannot be grouped according to socioeconomic factors. The process of decreolizing cuts across the socioeconomic patterns in the community. The data support the claim that the progressive has as its underlying source a locative. A process of tense neutralization, whereby the past tense in conjunction with another past tense or a past time adverbial is neutralized to the unmarked, or present tense, corresponds to the claim that the past tense is an intransitive verb. (RRD)

II. INDO-PACIFIC (Non-Austronesian)

Australian

8906. Furby, Christine E. "The Pronominal System of Garawa." *OcL* 11(1972):1-31.
A tagmemic description of a language spoken in the Northern Territory of Australia. Personal pronouns have 9 inflected cases and follow the nominative-accusative case system. There is a strong preference for tense and aspect-mood to be shown on personal pronouns. Affixation of the personal pronouns is described. Five cases are indicated by first order suffixes; the other 4 cases by second order suffixes. Other second order suffixes indicate aspect-mood. Tense may be shown on the verb or on the subject, object, compound object-subject, and reflexive

pronouns. Possessive, demonstrative, and interrogative pronouns are described. (CEF)

Papuan

8932. Haiman, John. "Ablaut in the Hua Verb." *OcL* 11(1972):32-46.
Three ablaut rules affect verb-stem-final desinences in Hua, a Papuan language of New Guinea. These rules are described and evidence is presented that the environments in which they apply can be characterized only by means of a derivational constraint in which reference is made to syntactic history. Phonologically non-distinct personal desinences may be copied onto the verb stem by three transformational rules, and it is the syntactic provenance of these endings that condition the vocalic alternations themselves. (JMH)
8935. Lawrence, Marshall. "Structure and Function of

† *Festschriften* and Other Analyzed Collections are listed in the first division of this volume. "F" numbers in brackets following a title refer to these items.

Oksapmin Verbs." *OcL* 11(1972):47-66.
Verbs in Oksapmin are final, medial, and subordinate. Final verbs occur in independent clauses where they end sentences or in included clauses where they modify nouns. First order suffixes express aspect. Second order suffixes are portmanteau morphemes expressing both number and tense. Two sets of past tenses are used in Oksapmin narratives. One set indicates that a narrative is being told from the viewpoint of the participant who is subject of that clause. The other set marks events that are viewed by a participant other than the subject of that clause. Medial verbs occur in dependent clauses. Subordinate verbs act as verbal modifiers or verbal adjuncts. (ML)

III. AUSTRONESIAN (MALAYO-POLYNESIAN)

General

Proto-Austronesian. 8960. Blust, Robert A. "Proto-Austronesian Syntax:The First Step." *WPLUH* 5,x(1973):73-84.
A conservative approach to syntactic reconstruction is adopted which aims not at the scope, but at the probable validity of historical inferences in syntax. A phrase-type, called the ni-phrase, is posited for Proto-Austronesian, and some instantiations reconstructed on the basis of evidence from Fijian, Toba Batak, and Malay. Evidence is also noted which suggests that at least one particular ni-phrase had become idiomatic by Proto-Austronesian times. (RAB)

Western Austronesian

General and Miscellaneous. 8965. Lewitz, Saveros, and Philip N. Jenner. "Proto-Indonesian and Mon-Khmer." *WPLUH* 5,x(1973):113-36.
Suggestions are made to justify reopening the Austric hypothesis of Pater Wilhelm Schmidt, according to which Austronesian and Austroasiatic form a larger linguistic unit. Limiting the argument to Indonesian and Mon-Khmer, the striking parallelism and formal similarity of affixational processes and the applicability of the same analytical method to Austronesian as has been used successfully with Mon-Khmer are shown. This latter refers especially to the isolation of wordbases recurring (with variants) in Dempwolff's and Dyen's reconstructions and includes the collection of derivational sets manifesting such wordbases. A 60-item comparative wordlist forms the bulk of the paper. (SL & PNJ)

Central Indonesian. 8971. Blust, Robert A. "The Proto-North Sarawak Vowel Deletion Hypothesis." *WPLUH* 5,vii(1973):91-149. [Prelim. version.]
Apparent unconditioned phonemic split of Proto-Austronesian (PAN) *b, *d, *D, *j, and *Z is found in a number of languages spoken in western Borneo. In several of these languages the discrepant (less common) reflex can be characterized as phonetically complex. It is hypothesized that the latter segments reflect a series of unstable consonant clusters *bS, *dS, *jS, *gS (called *S clusters) derived from earlier C_1VC_1 sequences by the addition of a rule of syncope, called the "vowel deletion rule," in a language immediately ancestral to those languages that distinguish them from the reflexes of the homorganic plain voiced obstruents. This language is tentatively called "Proto-North Sarawak." (RAB)

8981. Dardjowidjojo, Soenjono. "The Role of Overt Markers in Some Indonesian and Javanese Passive Sentences." *WPLUH* 5,ix(1973):77-78. [Prelim. vers.]
Eleven verbs in Indonesian, and their counterparts in Javanese, were investigated to see what significance their morphological markers have as they are related to passive sentences. These verbs are derived from the bases *serah, tawar, ajar, beri,* and *kirim* plus the affixes *meN-* and either *-kan* or *-i.* They permit the presence of two objects. It was found that two possible passives (one with the direct object and the other with the indirect object as the subjects of the passive sentences) can be formed, if certain constraints are met. The choice of the passive subject is determined by the particular suffix of the verb: the suffix *-kan* permits only the direct object, while the suffix *-i* only the indirect object. The above phenomena conform to the general nature of the suffixational system in the language. (SD)

8998. Kridalaksana, Harimurti. "Second Participant in Indonesian Address." *LangS* 31:17-20.
The Indonesian terms of address consist of pronouns, proper names, kinship terms, titles, agentive nouns, nominal + *ku* forms, deictic words, zero feature, and some other terms. Viewed from the speaker's perspective, the selection of terms is determined firstly by social distance, secondly by in-groupness, and thirdly by the addressee's identity. Term switching occurs because of a shift in contact, a change in social distance, a change in the topic of discourse, a change in setting, the corrective factor, a change in the participant's intent, a change in the degree of respect and friendliness, and the presence of other participants. (HK)

Formosan. 9039. Starosta, Stanley. "Causative Verbs in Formosan Languages." *WPLUH* 5,ix(1973):89-155. [Prelim. vers.] Describes, analyzes, and compares the morphologically marked causative verbs in Amis, Bunun, Rukai, Saisiyat, Seedeq, and Tsou. By distinguishing case forms from case relations and classifying verbs according to case frames, it is possible to predict the syntactic properties of causative verbs by lexical derivation rules, thus relating causative and non-causative sentences without the use of transformations. The derivation "rules" turn out to be reconstructions of historically productive processes of word formation with only limited synchronic validity. (SS)

Philippinic. 9077. Forman, Michael L. "Philippine Languages in Contact:Honolulu Radio Station K.I.S.A." *WPLUH* 5, x(1973):137-52.
Everyday talk on the only all-Filipino radio station in the United States provides the data for a preliminary report on Austronesian/English language phenomena. These data illustrate difficulties in demarcating borrowing from code-switching and in the general description and classification of, or bounding of, Filipino language behavior in social context. The linguistic repertoires of these speakers require some linguistic model less simple than the ones in current use, for the notion of interference and the inventories of extant descriptions of the supposed contributing codes or systems will not suffice to handle the material presented. Covergence seems to be producing new linguistic norms. (MLF)

9085. Kess, Joseph. "Respectful Address in Tagalog:A Preliminary Study." *Cahiers linguistiques d'Ottawa* 7,iii(1973):17-24.
Tagalog forms of respectful address distinguish individuals as members of the same or different groups and designate members of one's own group as equal or unequal socially for various reasons. There are two ways of indicating respect: (1) the use of the respect particles *po* and *ho* or the lack of a respect particle; and (2) the use of a plural pronoun to address an individual person. Analyses list the particles and the plural pronouns as separate and distinct means of expressing respect. Both modes may be included under a general category of respect (R), and their absence under another general category viewed as the simple absence of respect forms (NR). A classificatory scheme is established which accounts for the choice between R and NR categories. (LLBA)

9111. Reid, Lawrence A. "The Igorot Subgroup of Philippine Languages." *WPLUH* 5,vii(1973):63-89. [Prelim. version.]
The first attempt at subgrouping the languages of the Central Cordilleran area of Northern Luzon, Philippines, is made, using a qualitative methodology. The languages are subgrouped on the basis of exclusively shared innovations in the pronominal and case marking systems of the languages involved, supported by a syntactic innovation, and a number of apparent lexical innovations. (LAR)

Oceanic

General and Miscellaneous. 9142. Pawley, Andrew K. "Some Problems in Proto-Oceanic Grammar." *WPLUH* 5,x(1973):1-72. Reconstructions of the Proto-Oceanic systems of case and possessive marking are presented, based on comparisons of more than 20 languages chosen to represent the major regions of Oceania and the major subgroups of Oceanic insofar as these are established. Several grammatical innovations, marking off Proto-Oceanic from earlier stages, are noted, thus providing further support for hypothesis (first formulated on phonological evidence) that all the better-known Austronesian languages of Malenesia belong to a subgroup (Oceanic) which also includes the Polynesian and Nuclear Micronesian languages while excluding all other Austronesian languages. (AKP)

Melanesian. 9147. Grace, George W. "Research on the Position of the New Caledonian Languages:A Progress Report." *WPLUH* 5,vii(1973):49-62. [Prelim. version.]
A critical problem of comparative Austronesian linguistics is that posed by various aberrant members of the family, e.g., the languages of southern New Caledonia. Comparison of vocabulary from one of these languages, Canala, with Proto-Oceanic reconstructions yields some hypotheses about the types of changes which have occurred in Canala and other languages of the group. There has been extensive phonemic loss, and the points of articulation of consonants seem more predictable than the manners. In vocabulary comparisons between Canala and the neighboring language of La Foa, points of articulation of consonants are again the most stable characteristics. However, a very large number of correspondences, both consonant and vowel, are identified in the first sorting which shows that a very large corpus of cognates would be necessary to establish the valid correspondences and their conditions. (GWG)

9152. Hooley, Bruce A. "Austronesian Languages of the Morobe District, Papua New Guinea." *OcL* 10(1971):79-151.
The techniques of lexicostatistics are applied to give a preliminary survey of the Austronesian languages in the Morobe District. The lack of consistency in the use of terminology to describe various degrees of linguistic relationship is discussed, as well as the difficulty of relating cognate percentages to mutual intelligibility. Such surveys, however, are useful for preliminary classification and highlight areas where further study is needed. Three major and one minor family are posited on the basis of the percentages: the Buang, Azera, Siasi, and Hote/Yamap families respectively. The membership of these families is contrasted to Capell's classification of the same languages, and the constitution of each family is considered in detail. A later independent and improved estimate of cognates is shown not to affect the classification materially. An appendix lists the words from each language which were used in the survey including the original tentative cognate judgments. (BAH)

9153. Lincoln, Peter C. "Some Possible Implications of POC *t as /1/ in Gedaged." *WPLUH* 5,x(1973):153-64.
Geographic and bibliographic background materials are introduced, and putative changes from the Proto-Oceanic to the Gedaged sound system are summarized. Evidence is adduced to show that the regular reflexes of *t and *1 are /t/ and /1/ respectively. Data from two varieties of Gedaged and several languages to the east indicate that the words involving the reflex of *t as /1/ are spreading into Gedaged from a source to the east. Thus Gedaged evidence does not necessitate the modification of the reconstructions for the words involved. (PCL)

9158. Pawley, Andrew. "The Relationships of the Austronesian Languages of Central Papua:A Preliminary Study." *WPLUH* 6,iii:1-91.
The internal and external relationships of the 10 Austronesian languages spoken in the Central District of Papua are investigated. The proposed classification is based chiefly on shared phonological innovations, but some lexical and morphological evidence is used. The Central District languages appear to form a closed subgroup, whose immediate relatives are to be found among the languages of the Milne Bay District. Glottochronological evidence suggests that the Central District group diverged from the Milne Bay languages between 3,000 and 4,000 years ago. Both sets of languages in turn belong to the larger subgroup known as Oceanic. The Central District subgroup divides into three first-order subgroups: an eastern group, a western group, and Motu, with Motu having at one time been an intermediate dialect between the eastern and western divisions. Culture historical implications of the classification are critically examined. (AP)

Micronesian. 9171. Harrison, Sheldon P. "Reduplication in Micronesian Languages." *WPLUH* 5,viii(1973):57-92. [Prelim. version.]
Analysis of the reduplication patterns of Mokilese, a Micronesian language of the Caroline Islands, reveals two basic reduplication types—left-copying and right-copying. Comparison with other Micronesian languages allows us to postulate #CV- and -CVCV# reduplication in Proto-Micronesian. A consideration of relevant features of verb morphology and syntax concludes that the postulation of a class of verbs used only atypically without an object and termed "telic" is of value in predicting the incidence of reduplicated intransitive verbs. It seems possible to characterize the functions of reduplication as either distributive or durative. (SPH)

9173. Nathan, Geoffrey S. "Nauruan in the Austronesian Language Family." *WPLUH* 5,viii(1973):125-45. [Prelim. version.]
Nauruan is an Austronesian language spoken on the island of Nauru. Comparison of cognates with Grace's Proto-Oceanic word list allows the tracing of the development of Nauruan from Proto-Oceanic. Some unusual vowel changes and most consonant changes are similar to those in other Micronesian languages. Additional comparison of the possessive system indicates that Nauruan is probably a member of the Micronesian subgroup, although more intensive comparative study with other Micronesian languages is still necessary. (GSN)

9175. Sohn, Ho-min. "Relative Clause Formation in Micronesian Languages." *WPLUH* 5,viii(1973):93-124. [Prelim. version.]
A synchronic comparison of the patterns of relative clause formation of Woleaian, Trukese, Mokilese, Marshallese, Kusaiean, and Gilbertese is made. Their common syntactic characteristics are explored. These include the processes of relativization, the equational type of relative clause, the relation between a relative clause and the antecedent, the nature of the relative marker, the function of demonstratives, and the pattern of coreference. Then 16 items of syntactic divergence among these languages are presented. They include the use of a relative marker, the function of "relative" demonstratives, the order among the antecedent, relative clause, and the relative marker. The syntactic features are used to hypothesize a subgrouping of the languages concerned. (HS)

Polynesian. 9181. Chapin, Paul G. "*Über die Hawaiische Sprache*, by Adelbert von Chamisso." *OcL* 10(1971):152-57. [Rev. art.; delayed issue.]
Chamisso's grammar, the first systematic grammatical description of the Hawaiian language, published in 1837, was republished in facsimile in 1969. Although Chamisso visited Hawaii as a young man with the Kotzebue expedition, this grammar was written twenty years later, and the data on which it was based were drawn entirely from the materials published by the Hawaiian Mission (ABCFM). The deficient missionary orthography, which treated many non-homophonous forms homographically, led Chamisso to a good deal of confusion, which was compounded by his own penchant for reductionist analysis. (PGC)

9194. Pawley, Andrew K., and Roger [C.] Green. "Dating the Dispersal of the Polynesian Languages." *WPLUH* 5,vii(1973):1-48. [Prelim. version.]
Linguistic and archaeological facts strongly suggest that the first settlers of the islands of remote Oceania were all speakers of Austronesian languages. With some exceptions on the western fringe of Micronesia, the more than 400 Austronesian languages of Oceania all belong to the Oceanic subgroup. Proto-Oceanic must have broken up no later than the date at which people began

to disperse over remote Oceania. According to present archaeological indications this was not later than about 3,000 B.C. By 1,000 B.C. all the main island groups as far east as Tonga were settled. Certain principles for correlating archaeological sequences with linguistic subgroupings are proposed, and some conclusions are drawn about the locations of certain lower-order proto-languages and the dates at which these languages broke up. (AP & RG)

AMERICAN INDIAN LINGUISTICS†

II. AMERICAN ARCTIC-PALEOSIBERIAN

Eskimo-Aleut. 9205. Hutchings, David B. "Labrador Eskimo:A Bibliography." *RLS* 5:4-8.
An attempt is made to bring together most of the published and unpublished material written in or on the Eskimo language as spoken in Labrador. As many relevant linguistic works as could be found are included, provided they deal at least partially with Labrador Eskimo. Many entries are biblical texts which have been translated into Eskimo by Moravian missionaries and others. Some items produced by Memorial University of Newfoundland's Eskimo language project have also been incorporated. (LLBA)

III. NA-DENE

General and Miscellaneous. 9223. Witherspoon, Gary. "The Central Concepts of Navajo World View (I)." *Linguistics* 119:41-59.
The Navajo world view is examined using the "ethnoscience" approach. It involves a rigorous attempt to describe the world as it is seen by the native, based on a semantic analysis of the lexicon of the native. Although the account of the Navajo world view presented focuses mainly on the analysis of a set of linguistic symbols, the linguistic symbols and their meanings are analyzed in the context of both linguistic and non-linguistic symbolism. Meanings derived from the analysis of ritual and other non-linguistic symbolism are included to complement and supplement the view of the world contained in the linguistic symbolism. (LLBA)

Athabascan. 9229. James, John R. "An Analysis of Vowel Quality in Navaho." *Linguistics* 132:33-42.
The Navajo vowel system consists of 14 phonemes: 4 vowel phonemes, 4 diphthongs, 4 tonemes, and 2 suprasegmental phonemes. Such a system fails to capture the physical facts. The difference between the long and short pairs is much more one of quality than one of quantity. An examination of the formant spread for each vowel segment demonstrates the qualitative difference between the members of a pair. As a result of distinctive feature analysis, instead of 4 vowel phonemes and length, we have 8 vowel phonemes. This accounts for the distinction of vowel segments and takes into account their acoustic properties. (JRJ)

IV. MACRO-ALGONQUIAN

Algonquian. 9246. Wolfart, H. Cristoph. "Boundary Maintenance in Algonquian:A Linguistic Study of Island Lake, Manitoba." *AA* 75(1973):1305-23.
A "mixed language" involving Cree and Ojibwa has been reported for certain isolated populations of northeastern Manitoba. Ethnohistorical and demographic studies corroborate such a view by pointing to a high degree of population mixture. Linguistic survey yields some preliminary conclusions while indicating areas for further study. (LLBA)

VII. PENUTIAN

Mayan. 9277. Salovesh, Michael. "Componential Analysis of a Tzetzil Maya Kinship System." *SIL* 24:65-91.
A presentation of kinship terms used by Tzotzil-speaking Maya Indians of San Bartolomé de los Llanos (Venustiano Carranza), Chiapas, Mexico; a componential analysis of the terminological system; and a discussion of certain theoretical problems in the componential analysis of kinship terms in the light of these empirical data. (MS)

VIII. AZTEC-TANOAN

General and Miscellaneous. 9287. Speirs, Anna. "Classificatory Verb Stems in Tewa." *SIL* 24:45-64.
Tewa, a Tanoan language of New Mexico has, for the meanings "to be in a place" (also "to have"), and "to put or set down," different verb stems for use with different classes of nouns (animate, inanimate aggregate, inanimate distributive). The examination of which of these nouns go with the different verb stems results in 16 classes of nouns which can be reduced to 5 major classes. (GLT)

IX. MACRO-OTOMANGUEAN

Mixtecan. 9299. Grimes, Joseph E. "Dialects as Optimal Communication Networks." *Language* 50:260-69.
Intelligibility tests between dialects give results with three characteristics that need to be taken into account in their interpretation: asymmetry, sensitivity to changes in threshold, and incompleteness. If we interpret dialects as networks of communication arrived at by optimization, we make adequate use of these properties. (JEG)

† *Festschriften* and Other Analyzed Collections are listed in the first division of this volume. "F" numbers in brackets following a title refer to these items.

X. MACRO-CHIBCHAN

9310. Borgman, Donald M. "Deep and Surface Case in Sanuma." *Linguistics* 132:5-18.
A study of only surface case is inadequate to describe the clause structure and the verb in Sanuma. Surface cases in Sanuma are Nominative, Dative, Ergative, and Comitative. In studying the surface structure, the necessity of describing underlying roles soon becomes apparent, for in many instances one surface case marker has a great variety of meanings. Clarification of this variety comes through positing deep case categories which include underlying role relationships. (DMB)

XI. GE-PANO-CARIB

Macro-Ge. 9318. McLeod, Ruth. "Paragraph, Aspect, and Participant in Xacante." *Linguistics* 132:51-74.
Paragraphs in Xavante are introduced by *tavamhã* 'time / location.' Xavante is a member of the Gê language family of Brazil. Pronoun / aspect markers which occur on the main event line of Xavante narrative indicate completed action without consideration of the time involved in the action, continuing action, and logical result, relating events within the paragraph. Durative and logical aspects occur together when both time and consequence are in focus. A different set of pronoun / aspect markers is used on the main event line in transitive clauses to indicate progressive action within a restricted period of time. Pronoun / aspect markers in sentences which provide background for the narrative indicate explanation, scene setting, the permanent condition of people or things, or purpose frustrated by lack of some essential factor. The use of the future aspect in Xavante makes the imperative stronger. Participants in Xavante narrative are given maximum highlighting by the use of their nominal form plus *hã*.

(RAM)

Macro-Panoan. 9319. Scot, Eugene, and Donald G. Frantz. "Sharanahua Questions and Proposed Constraints on Question Movement." *Linguistics* 132:75-86.
Yes/no questions found in Sharanahua, a Pano language of Peru, are marked by a mood-marker suffixed to the verb. Content questions have the same marker on the verb as well as sentence-initial interrogative words. Questions embedded as complements to verbs such as "know," "see," "tell" are identical in form to their non-embedded counterparts. The fact that the interrogative word of content questions, embedded or not, occurs in sentence-initial position falsifies constraints on question-word movement proposed by C.L. Baker and Emmon Bach. The question-marking particle of Sharanahua is suffixed to the verb, which itself is in last position since Sharanahua is an SOV language. The interrogative word is fronted in content questions. (DGF)

XII. ANDEAN-EQUATORIAL

Quechumaran. 9331. Yábar-Dextre, Pompeyo. "Reglas generativas para la formación de palabras de parentesco en el quechua ancashino." *LyC* 13(1973):59-66.
The kinship names used by the Ancashine Quechua of Peru present an original system of interrelations which sharply differentiates them from those of the Indo-European languages. The terms are varied so as to designate the position of the first speaker in relation to that of the second person. To clearly establish the meaning of a term, the element of "self" must be taken into account as well as the elements of generation and sex. The most representative cases of this are found between close relatives. (LLBA)

XIII. UNCLASSIFIED

Salishan. 9341. Newman, Stanley. "Linguistic Retention and Diffusion in Bella Coola." *LSoc* 3:201-14.
The ecological vocabulary of the Bella Coola, who speak a Salish language, shows a larger proportion of loanwords than of forms retained from the parent language. Over a period of centuries the Bella Coola were in contact with many non-Salish tribes, but the direction of their borrowing was highly selective. Although their most intimate contacts were with speakers of Athapaskan and Wakashan, the overwhelming proportion of their ecological loans are Wakashan. This selectivity is explained by cultural affinity rather than intimacy of contact. (SN)

COMPOSITE AND DERIVATIVE LANGUAGES; OTHER COMMUNICATIVE BEHAVIOR†

I. COMPOSITE AND DERIVATIVE LANGUAGES

General and Miscellaneous

9351. Hart, Ronald J., and Bruce L. Brown. "Interpersonal Information Conveyed by the Content and Vocal Aspects of Speech." *SM* 41:371-80.
Two experiments were conducted to identify kinds of interpersonal information conveyed by vocal and content aspects of speech. Speech samples conveying (1) vocal, (2) content, and (3) both vocal and content information were evaluated. Transmitted information was measured by agreement among subjects on adjective rating scales. Most of the information about "benevolence" was conveyed by content, while most of the information about "social attractiveness" was conveyed by the vocal aspect of speech. Information about "competence" was conveyed by both the vocal and content aspects with male subjects, but with female subjects most of this information was conveyed by the vocal aspect. (RJH & BLB)

Semiotica

9374. Dombrovszky, József. "Znak i smysl." *VJa* 6:22-32.
Language may be separated into two dialectically related units: actual language and inactual language. This dichotomy is the division between the living reality of the object and that of the

† *Festschriften* and Other Analyzed Collections are listed in the first division of this volume. "F" numbers in brackets following a title refer to these items.

subject. It is a reflection of the basic ontological model of changing empirical reality. The actual factor, distinguished by movement from subject to object, is properly regarded as an end to be attained. The inactual factor, which is immanent and essentially passive, is the means to the attainment of that end. (LLBA)

9388. Ivanov, Vjačeslav. "On Antisymmetrical and Asymmetrical Relations in Natural Languages and Other Semiotic Systems." *Linguistics* 119:35-40.
Application of the theory of symmetry, especially of antisymmetrical and asymmetrical relations, has been largely neglected in the field of linguistics in general and in the field of semiotics in particular. The most important application of its concepts lies in the sphere of paradigmatic structure, which is discussed, along with other applications in the fields of archaic mythology, the study of ritualistic systems, diachronic linguistics, and the study of natural languages and other semiotic systems. (LLBA)

9389. Ivanov, V.V., and V.N. Toporov. "Towards the Description of Ket Semiotic Systems." *Semiotica* 9(1973):318-46.
An analysis and description of semiotic systems in Ket, an Altaic language. The magico-religious systems (RS) of Ket are described by the introduction of six levels of different units, which appear as individual signs. Each of the levels is described and also discussed are: (1) the general structure of the RS system; (2) Ket divination; (3) the structure of Ket riddles; (4) structural schemes of epics and fairy tales; (5) properties of Ket drawings; and (6) the "magic number seven" in the Ket model of the universe. (LLBA)

9395. Magass, Walter. "Eine Semiotik des apostolischen Markt-verhaltens." *LBib* 33:14-33.
Develops the semiotics of the apostolic behavior on the market place. The market place is the place of cheating, of saying the truth, and of mockery. These items are semantic markers of the meaning of the apostolic behavior; they are to be found in the Pauline Letters as allusions to aspects of classical rhetoric. (WM)

9397. Marcus, Aaron. "An Introduction to the Visual Syntax of Concrete Poetry." *VLang* 8:333-60.
Many different forms of concrete poetry have emerged in the past 20 years. One way to appreciate, describe, and compare these works is to examine them in terms of their visual syntax. This includes emphasis on figure-field relationships, implied depth, spatial structure, and movement. Examples are presented which illustrate basic types of visual organization and are analyzed to relate their visual syntax to their total meaning. This initial classification could be elaborated and supplemented to provide a

basis for a semiotic of concrete poetry. (AM)

9419. Prince, Gerald. "Narrative Signs and Tangents." *Diacritics* 4,iii:2-8. [Rev. art.]
The achievements of narratology—as exemplified in *Sémiotique narrative et textuelle*, edited by Claude Chabrol—are undeniable. Yet the problems it faces are also undeniable and many of its results are denounced as trivial and/or pseudo-scientific. Fortunately, narratologists are aware of the state of their art and a fundamental program for narratology, designed to solve its most vexing problems, can be abstracted from their work. The domain of narratology must include all possible narratives without discrimination on the basis of literariness or medium of expression. A model of narrative must account only for those elements and rules which characterize narrativity. A successful semantics of narrative must be developed as well as rigorous procedures mediating between narrative structures and the symbolic systems in which they are realized. Finally, the place of pragmatics in narratology must be re-examined and, perhaps, redefined. (GP)

9423. Scotto Di Carlo, Nicole. "Analyse sémiologique des gestes et mimiques des chanteurs d'opéra." *Semiotica* 9(1973):289-317.
A descriptive inventory of the gestures and facial expressions used by operatic singers. The gestures used by modern singers are divided into two categories: those without communicative intention (gestures serving as indices) and gestures with communicative intention (gestures serving as signals). Facial expressions differ from gestures in that there must be a compromise between the requirements of expression and the requirements of vocalization in music. The existence of a double articulation as a consequence of a gestural language is denied. At the same time, gestures in opera partake of a communicative function of a linear, non-reciprocal type. (LLBA)

9425. Seem, Mark D. "The Dictatorship of the Signifier: Interview with Félix Guattari." *Diacritics* 4,iii:38-41.
Guattari states that signs are not from the realm of ideas, but are positions of desire and produced by the very productive process of desire itself. The thrust is radical in nature and directed at analyzing the workings of desire as a real material productive process. He sets out the need to analyze those semiological events that are not signifying, but productive, not reactive, but active, not dependent on the norms of organized society, but from a nomadic realm, incapable of being coded or territorialized. He concludes that structuralism betrays signs in order to tame their subversive potential and ignore their desiring economy. (MDS)

II. NONVERBAL COMMUNICATION

General and Miscellaneous

9444a. Beebe, Steven A. "Eye Contact:A Nonverbal Determinant of Speaker Credibility." *Speech Teacher* 23:21-25.
Because it is hypothesized that eye contact contributes to a speaker's perceived credibility, and because there is a dearth of studies examining the effects of eye contact in a live public-speaking situation, the effects of eye contact on speaker credibility in a live public-speaking situation are examined. Results indicate that an increase in the amount of eye contact generated by a speaker significantly increases the speaker's credibility in terms of qualification and honesty factors. (LLBA)

Paralinguistics and Kinesics

9491. Duke, Charles R. "Nonverbal Behavior and the Communication Process." *CCC* 25:397-404.
Scientists have demonstrated through research studies that kinesics, or nonverbal behavior, can be recorded and analyzed; they have also discovered that certain nonverbal behavior patterns offer clues to a speaker's or listener's attitude and meaning. Man's territorial instinct, architectural design, and the uses of gesture and eye contact are some of the nonverbal elements that affect communication. The educator who is aware of the importance of nonverbal behavior in the communication process can help promote better communication in the classroom.

(CRD)

9517. Sherzer, Joel. "Verbal and Nonverbal Deixis:The Pointed Lip Gesture among the San Blas Cuna." *LSoc* 2(1973):117-31.
The pointed lip gesture is a facial gesture in use among the Cuna Indians of San Blas, Panama. It occurs in various contexts with meanings which at first appear to be unrelated. An analysis of the contexts reveals, however, that the meaning "pointing" is always present and that further meanings are derived from the discourse structures in which the pointed lip gesture is found. (JS)

Proxemics

9546. Peng, Fred C.C. "Communicative Distance." *LangS* 31:32-38.
Communicative distance registers, indicates, adjusts, and readjusts man's verbal behavior. Pronouns, kinship terms, personal names, honorifics, and many others serve as devices to show and reflect the psychological implementation of communication distance in an actual human verbal interaction. Communicative distance exists in a one-way or a two-way communication. In the former, it is established by one and the same person, who is always the speaker. In the latter it is set up by one person, but can be modified by the other. To each communicative distance established in this fashion is assigned a socially determined cultural value that is a stereotyped connotation of what the distance is supposed to mean in a social context. (FCCP)

Subject Index